HARPER COLLINS

FRENCH-
ENGLISH

♦

ENGLISH-
FRENCH

FRENCH DICTIONARY

HarperPaperbacks
A Division of HarperCollinsPublishers

HarperPaperbacks   *A Division of* HarperCollins*Publishers*
10 East 53rd Street, New York, N.Y. 10022

This book was published in Great Britain in 1989 by William Collins Sons & Co. Inc.

First HarperPaperbacks printing: August 1991

Printed in the United States of America

HarperPaperbacks and colophon are trademarks of HarperCollins*Publishers*

20 19 18 17 16 15 14 13 12 11

INTRODUCTION

This dictionary of French and English is designed to provide the user with wide-ranging and up-to-date coverage of the two languages, and is ideal for both school and reference use.

A special feature of HarperCollins dictionaries is the comprehensive "signposting" of meanings on both sides of the dictionary, guiding the user to the most appropriate translation for a given context. We hope you will find this dictionary easy and pleasant to consult for all your study and reference needs.

ABRÉVIATIONS		ABBREVIATIONS
adjectif, locution adjective	a	adjective, adjectival phrase
abréviation	ab(b)r	abbreviation
adverbe, locution adverbiale	ad	adverb, adverbial phrase
administration	ADMIN	administration
agriculture	AGR	agriculture
anatomie	ANAT	anatomy
architecture	ARCHIT	architecture
l'automobile	AUT(O)	the motor car and motoring
aviation, voyages aériens	AVIAT	flying, air travel
biologie	BIO(L)	biology
botanique	BOT	botany
anglais de Grande-Bretagne	Brit	British English
conjonction	cj	conjunction
langue familière (! emploi vulgaire)	col (!)	colloquial usage (! particularly offensive)
commerce, finance, banque	COMM	commerce, finance, banking
informatique	COMPUT	computing
construction	CONSTR	building
nom utilisé comme adjectif, ne peut s'employer ni comme attribut, ni après le nom qualifié	cpd	compound element: noun used as an adjective and which cannot follow the noun it qualifies
cuisine, art culinaire	CULIN	cookery
déterminant: article, adjectif démonstratif ou indéfini etc	dét	determiner: article, demonstrative etc.
économie	ECON	economics
électricité, électronique	ELEC	electricity, electronics
exclamation, interjection	excl	exclamation, interjection
féminin	f	feminine
langue familière (! emploi vulgaire)	fam (!)	colloquial usage (! particularly offensive)
emploi figuré	fig	figurative use
(verbe anglais) dont la particule est inséparable du verbe	fus	(phrasal verb) where the particle cannot be separated from main verb
dans la plupart des sens; généralement	gén, gen	in most or all senses; generally
géographie, géologie	GEO	geography, geology
géométrie	GEOM	geometry
informatique	INFORM	computing
invariable	inv	invariable
irrégulier	irg	irregular
domaine juridique	JUR	law
grammaire, linguistique	LING	grammar, linguistics
masculin	m	masculine
mathématiques, algèbre	MATH	mathematics, calculus
médecine	MED	medical term, medicine
masculin ou féminin, suivant le sexe	m/f	either masculine or feminine depending on sex
domaine militaire, armée	MIL	military matters
musique	MUS	music
nom	n	noun

ABRÉVIATIONS

ABBREVIATIONS

navigation, nautisme	**NAVIG, NAUT**	sailing, navigation
adjectif ou nom numérique	**num**	numeral adjective or noun
	o.s.	oneself
péjoratif	**péj, pej**	derogatory, pejorative
photographie	**PHOT(O)**	photography
physiologie	**PHYSIOL**	physiology
pluriel	**pl**	plural
politique	**POL**	politics
participe passé	**pp**	past participle
préposition	**prép, prep**	preposition
psychologie, psychiatrie	**PSYCH**	psychology, psychiatry
temps du passé	**pt**	past tense
nom non comptable: ne peut s'utiliser au pluriel	**q**	collective (uncountable) noun: is not used in the plural
quelque chose	**qch**	
quelqu'un	**qn**	
religions, domaine ecclésiastique	**REL**	religions, church service
	sb	somebody
enseignement, système scolaire et universitaire	**SCOL**	schooling, schools and universities
singulier	**sg**	singular
	sth	something
subjonctif	**sub**	subjunctive
sujet (grammatical)	**su(b)j**	(grammatical) subject
techniques, technologie	**TECH**	technical term, technology
télécommunications	**TEL**	telecommunications
télévision	**TV**	television
typographie	**TYP(O)**	typography, printing
anglais des USA	**US**	American English
verbe	**vb**	verb
verbe ou groupe verbal à fonction intransitive	**vi**	verb or phrasal verb used intransitively
verbe ou groupe verbal à fonction transitive	**vt**	verb or phrasal verb used transitively
zoologie	**ZOOL**	zoology
marque déposée	**®**	registered trademark
indique une équivalence culturelle	**≈**	introduces a cultural equivalent

TRANSCRIPTION PHONÉTIQUE

CONSONNES

CONSONANTS

NB. **p, b, t, d, k, g** sont suivis d'une aspiration en anglais.

NB. **p, b, t, d, k, g** are not aspirated in French.

poupée	p	*puppy*
bombe	b	*baby*
tente thermal	t	*tent*
dinde	d	*daddy*
coq qui képi	k	*cork kiss chord*
gag bague	g	*gag guess*
sale ce nation	s	*so rice kiss*
zéro rose	z	*cousin buzz*
tache chat	ʃ	*sheep sugar*
gilet juge	ʒ	*pleasure beige*
	tʃ	*church*
	dʒ	*judge general*
fer phare	f	*farm raffle*
valve	v	*very rev*
	θ	*thin maths*
	ð	*that other*
lent salle	l	*little ball*
rare rentrer	ʀ	
	r	*rat rare*
maman femme	m	*mummy comb*
non nonne	n	*no ran*
agneau vigne	ɲ	
	ŋ	*singing bank*
hop!	h	*hat reheat*
yeux paille pied	j	*yet*
nouer oui	w	*wall bewail*
huile lui	ɥ	
	x	*loch*

DIVERS

MISCELLANEOUS

pour l'anglais: précède la syllabe accentuée ˈ in French wordlist and transcription: no liaison

pour l'anglais: le r final se prononce en liaison devant une voyelle *

PHONETIC TRANSCRIPTION

VOYELLES

VOWELS

NB. La mise en équivalence de certains sons n'indique qu'une ressemblance approximative.

NB. The pairing of some vowel sounds only indicates approximate equivalence.

ici vie lyre	i i:	heel bead
	ɪ	hit pity
jouer *été*	e	
lait jou*et* m*e*rci	ɛ	set tent
pl*a*t *a*mour	a æ	bat apple
b*a*s p*â*te	ɑ ɑ:	after car calm
	ʌ	fun cousin
l*e* pr*e*mier	ə	over above
b*eu*rre p*eu*r	œ	
p*eu* d*eu*x	ø ə:	urn fern work
*o*r h*o*mme	ɔ	wash pot
m*o*t *eau* g*au*che	o ɔ:	born cork
g*e*n*ou* r*ou*e	u	full soot
	u:	boon lewd
r*ue* *u*rne	y	

DIPHTONGUES

DIPHTHONGS

	ɪə	beer tier
	ɛə	tear fair there
	eɪ	date plaice day
	aɪ	life buy cry
	au	owl foul now
	əu	low no
	ɔɪ	boil boy oily
	uə	poor tour

NASALES

NASAL VOWELS

mati*n* plei*n*	ɛ̃	
bru*n*	œ̃	
sa*n*g *an* d*an*s	ɑ̃	
non po*nt*	õ	

Blanca Berger

FRANÇAIS - ANGLAIS
FRENCH - ENGLISH

A

A *abr de* **autoroute**.

a *vb voir* **avoir**.

à (*à* + *le* = **au**, *à* + *les* = **aux**) [a, o] *prép* **1** (*endroit, situation*) at, in; **être à Paris/au Portugal** to be in Paris/ Portugal; **être à la maison/à l'école** to be at home/at school; **à la campagne** in the country; **c'est à 10 km/à 20 minutes (d'ici)** it's 10 km/20 minutes away
2 (*direction*) to; **aller à Paris/au Portugal** to go to Paris/Portugal; **aller à la maison/à l'école** to go home/to school; **à la campagne** to the country
3 (*temps*): **à 3 heures/minuit** at 3 o'clock/midnight; **au printemps/mois de juin** in the spring/the month of June
4 (*attribution, appartenance*) to; **le livre est à Paul/à lui/à nous** this book is Paul's/his/ours; **donner qch à qn** to give sth to sb
5 (*moyen*) with; **se chauffer au gaz** to have gas heating; **à bicyclette** on *ou* by bicycle; **à la main/machine** by hand/ machine
6 (*provenance*) from; **boire à la bouteille** to drink from the bottle
7 (*caractérisation, manière*): **l'homme aux yeux bleus** the man with the blue eyes; **à la russe** the Russian way
8 (*but, destination*): **tasse à café** coffee cup; **maison à vendre** house for sale
9 (*rapport, évaluation, distribution*): **100 km/unités à l'heure** 100 km/units per *ou* an hour; **payé à l'heure** paid by the hour; **cinq à six** five to six.

abaisser [abese] *vt* to lower, bring down; (*manette*) to pull down; (*fig*) to debase; to humiliate; **s'~** *vi* to go down; (*fig*) to demean o.s.

abandon [abãdɔ̃] *nm* abandoning; giving up; withdrawal; **être à l'~** to be in a state of neglect.

abandonner [abãdɔne] *vt* (*personne*) to abandon; (*projet, activité*) to abandon, give up; (*SPORT*) to retire *ou* withdraw from; (*céder*) to surrender; **s'~** *vi* to let o.s. go; **s'~ à** (*paresse, plaisirs*) to give o.s. up to.

abasourdir [abazuʀdiʀ] *vt* to stun, stagger.

abat-jour [abaʒuʀ] *nm inv* lampshade.

abats [aba] *nmpl* (*de bœuf, porc*) offal *sg*; (*de volaille*) giblets.

abattement [abatmã] *nm* (*déduction*) reduction; **~ fiscal** ≈ tax allowance.

abattis [abati] *nmpl* giblets.

abattoir [abatwaʀ] *nm* slaughterhouse.

abattre [abatʀ(ə)] *vt* (*arbre*) to cut down, fell; (*mur, maison*) to pull down; (*avion, personne*) to shoot down; (*animal*) to shoot, kill; (*fig*) to wear out, tire out; to demoralize; **s'~** *vi* to crash down; **s'~ sur** to beat down on; to rain down on.

abbaye [abei] *nf* abbey.

abbé [abe] *nm* priest; (*d'une abbaye*) abbot.

abcès [apsɛ] *nm* abscess.

abdiquer [abdike] *vi* to abdicate // *vt* to renounce, give up.

abeille [abɛj] *nf* bee.

aberrant, e [abɛʀã, -ãt] *a* absurd.

abêtir [abetiʀ] *vt* to make morons of (*ou* a moron of).

abîme [abim] *nm* abyss, gulf.

abîmer [abime] *vt* to spoil, damage; **s'~** *vi* to get spoilt *ou* damaged.

ablation [ablasjɔ̃] *nf* removal.

aboiement [abwamã] *nm* bark, barking *q*.

abois [abwa] *nmpl*: **aux ~** at bay.

abolir [abɔliʀ] *vt* to abolish.

abondance [abɔ̃dãs] *nf* abundance; (*richesse*) affluence.

abondant, e [abɔ̃dã, -ãt] *a* plentiful, abundant, copious.

abonder [abɔ̃de] *vi* to abound, be plentiful; **~ dans le sens de qn** to concur with sb.

abonné, e [abɔne] *nm/f* subscriber; season ticket holder.

abonnement [abɔnmã] *nm* subscription; (*transports, concerts*) season ticket.

abonner [abɔne] *vt*: **s'~ à** to subscribe to, take out a subscription to.

abord [abɔʀ] *nm*: **être d'un ~ facile** to be approachable; **~s** *nmpl* surroundings; **au premier ~** at first sight, initially; **d'~** *ad* first.

abordable [abɔʀdabl(ə)] *a* approachable; reasonably priced.

aborder [abɔʀde] *vi* to land // *vt* (*sujet, difficulté*) to tackle; (*personne*) to approach; (*rivage etc*) to reach; (*NAVIG: attaquer*) to board.

aboutir [abutiʀ] *vi* (*négociations etc*) to succeed; **~ à/dans/sur** to end up at/in/on.

aboyer [abwaje] *vi* to bark.

abrégé [abʀeʒe] *nm* summary.

abréger [abʀeʒe] *vt* to shorten.

abreuver [abʀœve] *vt* (*fig*): **~ qn de** to

shower *ou* swamp sb with; **s'~** *vi* to drink; **abreuvoir** *nm* watering place.

abréviation [abrevjɑsjɔ̃] *nf* abbreviation.

abri [abri] *nm* shelter; **à l'~** under cover; **à l'~ de** sheltered from; *(fig)* safe from.

abricot [abriko] *nm* apricot; **abricotier** *nm* apricot tree.

abriter [abrite] *vt* to shelter; *(loger)* to accommodate; **s'~** to shelter, take cover.

abroger [abrɔʒe] *vt* to repeal.

abrupt, e [abrypt] *a* sheer, steep; *(ton)* abrupt.

abrutir [abrytir] *vt* to daze; to exhaust; to stupefy.

absence [apsɑ̃s] *nf* absence; *(MÉD)* blackout; mental blank.

absent, e [apsɑ̃, -ɑ̃t] *a* absent; *(distrait: air)* vacant, faraway // *nm/f* absentee; **s'absenter** *vi* to take time off work; *(sortir)* to leave, go out.

absolu, e [apsɔly] *a* absolute; *(caractère)* rigid, uncompromising; **~ment** *ad* absolutely.

absolve *etc vb voir* **absoudre.**

absorber [apsɔrbe] *vt* to absorb; *(gén MÉD: manger, boire)* to take.

absoudre [apsudr(ə)] *vt* to absolve.

abstenir [apstənir]: **s'~** *vi* *(POL)* to abstain; **s'~ de qch/de faire** to refrain from sth/from doing.

abstraction [apstraksjɔ̃] *nf* abstraction; **faire ~ de** to set *ou* leave aside.

abstrait, e [apstrɛ, -ɛt] *a* abstract.

absurde [apsyrd(ə)] *a* absurd.

abus [aby] *nm* abuse; **~ de confiance** breach of trust.

abuser [abyze] *vi* to go too far, overstep the mark // *vt* to deceive, mislead; **~ de** *vt* to misuse; *(violer, duper)* to take advantage of; **s'~** *vi* to be mistaken; **abusif, ive** *a* exorbitant; excessive; improper.

acabit [akabi] *nm*: **de cet ~** of that type.

académie [akademi] *nf* academy; *(ART: nu)* nude; *(SCOL: circonscription)* ≈ regional education authority.

acajou [akaʒu] *nm* mahogany.

acariâtre [akarjɑtr(ə)] *a* cantankerous.

accablement [akɑbləmɑ̃] *nm* despondency.

accabler [akɑble] *vt* to overwhelm, overcome; *(suj: témoignage)* to condemn, damn; **~ qn d'injures** to heap *ou* shower abuse on sb.

accalmie [akalmi] *nf* lull.

accaparer [akapare] *vt* to monopolize; *(suj: travail etc)* to take up (all) the time *ou* attention of.

accéder [aksede]: **~ à** *vt* *(lieu)* to reach; *(fig)* to accede to, attain; *(accorder: requête)* to grant, accede to.

accélérateur [akseleratœr] *nm* accel-

erator.

accélération [akselerɑsjɔ̃] *nf* acceleration.

accélérer [akselere] *vt* to speed up // *vi* to accelerate.

accent [aksɑ̃] *nm* accent; *(inflexions expressives)* tone (of voice); *(PHONÉTIQUE, fig)* stress; **mettre l'~ sur** *(fig)* to stress; **~ aigu/grave** acute/grave accent.

accentuer [aksɑ̃tɥe] *vt* *(LING)* to accent; *(fig)* to accentuate, emphasize; **s'~** *vi* to become more marked *ou* pronounced.

acceptation [aksɛptɑsjɔ̃] *nf* acceptance.

accepter [aksɛpte] *vt* to accept; *(tolérer)*: **~ que qn fasse** to agree to sb doing; **~ de faire** to agree to do.

acception [aksɛpsjɔ̃] *nf* meaning, sense.

accès [aksɛ] *nm* *(à un lieu)* access; *(MÉD)* attack; fit, bout; outbreak // *nmpl* *(routes etc)* means of access, approaches; **d'~ facile** easily accessible; **~ de colère** fit of anger.

accessible [aksesibl(ə)] *a* accessible; *(livre, sujet)*: **~ à qn** within the reach of sb; *(sensible)*: **~ à** open to.

accessoire [akseswar] *a* secondary; incidental // *nm* accessory; *(THÉÂTRE)* prop.

accident [aksidɑ̃] *nm* accident; **par ~** by chance; **~ de la route** road accident; **~ du travail** industrial injury *ou* accident; **accidenté, e** *a* damaged; injured; *(relief, terrain)* uneven; hilly.

acclamer [aklame] *vt* to cheer, acclaim.

accointances [akwɛ̃tɑ̃s] *nfpl*: **avoir des ~** avec to have contacts with.

accolade [akɔlad] *nf* *(amicale)* embrace; *(signe)* brace.

accoler [akɔle] *vt* to place side by side.

accommodant, e [akɔmɔdɑ̃, -ɑ̃t] *a* accommodating; easy-going.

accommoder [akɔmɔde] *vt* *(CULIN)* to prepare; *(points de vue)* to reconcile; **s'~ de** to put up with; to make do with.

accompagnateur, trice [akɔ̃paɲatœr, -tris] *nm/f* *(MUS)* accompanist; *(de voyage: guide)* guide; *(: d'enfants)* accompanying adult; *(de voyage organisé)* courier.

accompagner [akɔ̃paɲe] *vt* to accompany, be *ou* go *ou* come with; *(MUS)* to accompany.

accompli, e [akɔ̃pli] *a* accomplished.

accomplir [akɔ̃plir] *vt* *(tâche, projet)* to carry out; *(souhait)* to fulfil; **s'~** *vi* to be fulfilled.

accord [akɔr] *nm* agreement; *(entre des styles, tons etc)* harmony; *(MUS)* chord; **d'~!** OK!; **se mettre d'~** to come to an agreement; **être d'~** to agree.

accordéon [akɔrdeɔ̃] *nm* *(MUS)* accordion.

accorder [akɔrde] *vt* *(faveur, délai)* to grant; *(harmoniser)* to match; *(MUS)* to tune; s'~ to get on together; to agree.

accoster [akɔste] (*NAVIG*) *vt* to draw alongside // *vi* to berth.

accotement [akɔtmã] *nm* verge (*Brit*), shoulder.

accouchement [akuʃmã] *nm* delivery, (child)birth; labour.

accoucher [akuʃe] *vi* to give birth, have a baby; (*être en travail*) to be in labour // *vt* to deliver; ~ **d'un garçon** to give birth to a boy.

accouder [akude]: s'~ *vi*: s'~ à/contre to rest one's elbows on/against; **accoudoir** *nm* armrest.

accoupler [akuple] *vt* to couple; (*pour la reproduction*) to mate; s'~ to mate.

accourir [akuʀiʀ] *vi* to rush ou run up.

accoutrement [akutʀəmã] *nm* (*péj*: *tenue*) outfit.

accoutumance [akutymãs] *nf* (*gén*) adaptation; (*MÉD*) addiction.

accoutumé, e [akutyme] *a* (*habituel*) customary, usual.

accoutumer [akutyme] *vt*: s'~ à to get accustomed ou used to.

accréditer [akʀedite] *vt* (*nouvelle*) to substantiate.

accroc [akʀo] *nm* (*déchirure*) tear; (*fig*) hitch, snag.

accrochage [akʀɔʃaʒ] *nm* (*AUTO*) collision.

accrocher [akʀɔʃe] *vt* (*suspendre*): ~ qch à to hang sth (up) on; (*attacher: remorque*): ~ qch à to hitch sth (up) to; (*heurter*) to catch; to catch on; to hit; (*déchirer*): ~ qch (à) to catch sth (on); (*MIL*) to engage; (*fig*) to catch, attract; s'~ (*se disputer*) to have a clash ou brush; s'~ à (*rester pris à*) to catch on; (*agripper, fig*) to hang on ou cling to.

accroître [akʀwatʀ(ə)] *vt* to increase; s'~ *vi* to increase.

accroupir [akʀupiʀ]: s'~ *vi* to squat, crouch (down).

accru, e [akʀy] *pp de* **accroître**.

accueil [akœj] *nm* welcome; comité d'~ reception committee.

accueillir [akœjiʀ] *vt* to welcome; (*loger*) to accommodate.

acculer [akyle] *vt*: ~ qn à ou contre to drive sb back against.

accumuler [akymyle] *vt* to accumulate, amass; s'~ *vi* to accumulate; to pile up.

accusation [akyzasjõ] *nf* (*gén*) accusation; (*JUR*) charge; (*partie*): l'~ the prosecution; mettre en ~ to indict.

accusé, e [akyze] *nm/f* accused; defendant; ~ de réception acknowledgement of receipt.

accuser [akyze] *vt* to accuse; (*fig*) to emphasize, bring out; to show; ~ qn de to accuse sb of; (*JUR*) to charge sb with; ~ qch de (*rendre responsable*) to blame sth for; ~ réception de to acknowledge receipt of.

acerbe [asɛʀb(ə)] *a* caustic, acid.

acéré, e [aseʀe] *a* sharp.

achalandé, e [aʃalãde] *a*: bien ~ well-stocked; well-patronized.

acharné, e [aʃaʀne] *a* (*lutte, adversaire*) fierce, bitter; (*travail*) relentless, unremitting.

acharner [aʃaʀne]: s'~ *vi*: s'~ sur to go at fiercely; s'~ contre to set o.s. against; to dog; s'~ à faire to try doggedly to do; to persist in doing.

achat [aʃa] *nm* buying *q*; purchase; faire des ~s to do some shopping.

acheminer [aʃmine] *vt* (*courrier*) to forward, dispatch; (*troupes*) to convey, transport; (*train*) to route; s'~ vers to head for.

acheter [aʃte] *vt* to buy, purchase; (*soudoyer*) to buy; ~ qch à (*marchand*) to buy ou purchase sth from; (*ami etc*: *offrir*) to buy sth for; **acheteur, euse** *nm/f* buyer; shopper; (*COMM*) buyer.

achever [aʃve] *vt* to complete, finish; (*blessé*) to finish off; s'~ *vi* to end.

achoppement [aʃɔpmã] *nm*: pierre d'~ stumbling block.

acide [asid] *a* sour, sharp; (*CHIMIE*) acid(ic) // *nm* (*CHIMIE*) acid.

acier [asje] *nm* steel; **aciérie** *nf* steelworks *sg*.

acné [akne] *nf* acne.

acolyte [akɔlit] *nm* (*péj*) associate.

acompte [akõt] *nm* deposit; (*versement régulier*) instalment; (*sur somme due*) payment on account.

à-côté [akote] *nm* side-issue; (*argent*) extra.

à-coup [aku] *nm* (*du moteur*) (hic)cough; (*fig*) jolt; par ~s by fits and starts.

acoustique [akustik] *nf* (*d'une salle*) acoustics *pl*.

acquéreur [akeʀœʀ] *nm* buyer, purchaser.

acquérir [akeʀiʀ] *vt* to acquire.

acquis, e [aki, -iz] *pp de* **acquérir** // *nm* (accumulated) experience; être ~ à (*plan, idée*) to fully agree with; son aide nous est ~e we can count on her help.

acquit [aki] *vb voir* **acquérir** // *nm* (*quittance*) receipt; par ~ de conscience to set one's mind at rest.

acquitter [akite] *vt* (*JUR*) to acquit; (*facture*) to pay, settle; s'~ de to discharge, fulfil.

âcre [akʀ(ə)] *a* acrid, pungent.

acrobate [akʀɔbat] *nm/f* acrobat.

acte [akt(ə)] *nm* act, action; (*THÉÂTRE*) act; ~s *nmpl* (*compte-rendu*) proceedings; prendre ~ de to note, take note of; faire ~ de candidature to apply; faire ~ de présence to put in an appearance; ~ de naissance birth certificate.

acteur [aktœʀ] *nm* actor.

actif, ive [aktif, -iv] *a* active // *nm*

(COMM) assets pl; (fig): **avoir à son ~** to have to one's credit; **population active** working population.

action [aksjɔ̃] nf (gén) action; (COMM) share; **une bonne ~** a good deed; **actionnaire** nm/f shareholder; **actionner** vt to work; to activate; to operate.

activer [aktive] vt to speed up; **s'~** vi to bustle about; to hurry up.

activité [aktivite] nf activity.

actrice [aktʀis] nf actress.

actualiser [aktɥalize] vt to actualize; to bring up to date.

actualité [aktɥalite] nf (d'un problème) topicality; (événements): **l'~** current events; **les ~s** (CINÉMA, TV) the news.

actuel, le [aktɥɛl] a (présent) present; (d'actualité) topical; **~lement** ad at present; at the present time.

acuité [akɥite] nf acuteness.

adaptateur [adaptatœʀ] nm (ÉLEC) adapter.

adapter [adapte] vt to adapt; **~ qch à** (approprier) to adapt sth to (fit); **~ qch sur/dans/à** (fixer) to fit sth on/into/to; **s'~ (à)** (suj: personne) to adapt (to).

addition [adisjɔ̃] nf addition; (au café) bill.

additionner [adisjɔne] vt to add (up).

adepte [adɛpt(ə)] nm/f follower.

adéquat, e [adekwa, -at] a appropriate, suitable.

adhérent, e [adeʀɑ̃, -ɑ̃t] nm/f (de club) member.

adhérer [adeʀe] **~ à** vi (coller) to adhere ou stick to; (se rallier à) to join; to support; **adhésif, ive** a adhesive, sticky // nm adhesive; **adhésion** nf joining; membership; support.

adieu, x [adjø] excl goodbye // nm farewell; **dire ~ à qn** to say goodbye ou farewell to sb.

adjectif [adʒɛktif] nm adjective.

adjoindre [adʒwɛ̃dʀ(ə)] vt: **~ qch à** to attach sth to; **~ à** to add sth to; **s'~** (collaborateur etc) to take on, appoint; **adjoint, e** nm/f assistant; **adjoint au maire** deputy mayor; **directeur adjoint** assistant manager.

adjudant [adʒydɑ̃] nm (MIL) warrant officer.

adjudication [adʒydikasjɔ̃] nf sale by auction; (pour travaux) invitation to tender (Brit) ou bid (US).

adjuger [adʒyʒe] vt (prix, récompense) to award; (lors d'une vente) to auction (off); **s'~** vt to take for o.s.

adjurer [adʒyʀe] vt: **~ qn de faire** to implore ou beg sb to do.

admettre [admɛtʀ(ə)] vt (laisser entrer) to admit; (candidat: SCOL) to pass; (tolérer) to allow, accept; (reconnaître) to admit, acknowledge.

administrateur, trice [administʀatœʀ, -tʀis] nm/f (COMM) director; (ADMIN) administrator; **~ judiciaire** receiver; **~ délégué** managing director.

administration [administʀasjɔ̃] nf administration; **l'A~** ≈ the Civil Service.

administrer [administʀe] vt (firme) to manage, run; (biens, remède, sacrement etc) to administer.

admirable [admiʀabl(ə)] a admirable, wonderful.

admirateur, trice [admiʀatœʀ, -tʀis] nm/f admirer.

admiration [admiʀasjɔ̃] nf admiration.

admirer [admiʀe] vt to admire.

admis, e pp de **admettre**.

admissible [admisibl(ə)] a (candidat) eligible; (comportement) admissible, acceptable.

admission [admisjɔ̃] nf admission; acknowledgement; **demande d'~** application for membership.

adolescence [adɔlesɑ̃s] nf adolescence.

adolescent, e [adɔlesɑ̃, -ɑ̃t] nm/f adolescent, teenager.

adonner [adɔne]: **s'~ à** vt (sport) to devote o.s. to; (boisson) to give o.s. over to.

adopter [adɔpte] vt to adopt; (projet de loi etc) to pass; **adoptif, ive** a (parents) adoptive; (fils, patrie) adopted.

adorer [adɔʀe] vt to adore; (REL) to worship.

adosser [adose] vt: **~ qch à ou contre** to stand sth against; **s'~ à ou contre** to lean with one's back against.

adoucir [adusiʀ] vt (goût, température) to make milder; (avec du sucre) to sweeten; (peau, voix) to soften; (caractère) to mellow.

adresse [adʀɛs] nf (voir adroit) skill, dexterity; (domicile) address; **à l'~ de** (pour) for the benefit of.

adresser [adʀese] vt (lettre: expédier) to send; (: écrire l'adresse sur) to address; (injure, compliments) to address; **~ la parole à** to speak to, address; **s'~ à** (parler à) to speak to, address; (s'informer auprès de) to go and see; (: bureau) to enquire at; (suj: livre, conseil) to be aimed at.

adroit, e [adʀwa, -wat] a skilful, skilled.

adulte [adylt(ə)] nm/f adult, grown-up // a (chien, arbre) fully-grown; mature; (attitude) adult, grown-up.

adultère [adyltɛʀ] nm (acte) adultery.

advenir [advəniʀ] vt to happen.

adverbe [advɛʀb(ə)] nm adverb.

adversaire [advɛʀsɛʀ] nm/f (SPORT, gén) opponent, adversary; (MIL) adversary, enemy.

adverse [advɛʀs(ə)] a opposing.

aération [aeʀasjɔ̃] nf airing; ventilation.

aérer [aeʀe] vt to air; (fig) to lighten; **s'~** vi to get some (fresh) air.

aérien, ne [aeʀjɛ̃ -jɛn] a (AVIAT) air

cpd, aerial; (*câble, métro*) overhead; (*fig*) light.

aéro... [aeʀɔ] *préfixe:* ~**bic** *nm* aerobics *sg;* ~**gare** *nf* airport (buildings); (*en ville*) air terminal; ~**glisseur** *nm* hovercraft; ~**naval, e** *a* air and sea *cpd;* ~**port** *nm* airport; ~**porté, e** *a* airborne, airlifted; ~**sol** *nm* aerosol.

affaiblir [afeblir] *vt,* **s'**~ *vi* to weaken.

affaire [afɛʀ] *nf* (*problème, question*) matter; (*criminelle, judiciaire*) case; (*scandaleuse etc*) affair; (*entreprise*) business; (*marché, transaction*) deal; business *q;* (*occasion intéressante*) bargain; ~**s** *nfpl* affairs; (*activité commerciale*) business *sg;* (*effets personnels*) things, belongings; **ce sont mes** ~**s** (*cela me concerne*) that's my business; **ceci fera l'**~ this will do (nicely); **avoir** ~ **à** to be faced with; to be dealing with; **les A**~**s étrangères** Foreign Affairs; **s'affairer** *vi* to busy o.s., bustle about.

affaisser [afese]: **s'**~ *vi* (*terrain, immeuble*) to subside, sink; (*personne*) to collapse.

affaler [afale]: **s'**~ *vi:* **s'**~ **dans/sur** to collapse *ou* slump into/onto.

affamé, e [afame] *a* starving.

affecter [afɛkte] *vt* to affect; (*telle ou telle forme etc*) to take on; ~ **qch à** to allocate *ou* allot sth to; ~ **qn à** to appoint sb to; (*diplomate*) to post sb to.

affectif, ive [afɛktif, -iv] *a* emotional.

affection [afɛksjɔ̃] *nf* affection; (*mal*) ailment; **affectionner** *vt* to be fond of.

affectueux, euse [afɛktɥø, -øz] *a* affectionate.

afférent, e [aferɑ̃, -ɑ̃t] *a:* ~ **à** pertaining *ou* relating to.

affermir [afɛʀmiʀ] *vt* to consolidate, strengthen.

affichage [afiʃaʒ] *nm* billposting; (*électronique*) display.

affiche [afiʃ] *nf* poster; (*officielle*) notice; (*THÉÂTRE*) bill; **tenir l'**~ to run.

afficher [afiʃe] *vt* (*affiche*) to put up; (*réunion*) to put up a notice about; (*électroniquement*) to display; (*fig*) to exhibit, display.

affilée [afile]: **d'**~ *ad* at a stretch.

affiler [afile] *vt* to sharpen.

affiner [afine] *vt* to refine.

affirmatif, ive [afiʀmatif, -iv] *a* affirmative.

affirmation [afiʀmasjɔ̃] *nf* assertion.

affirmer [afiʀme] *vt* (*prétendre*) to maintain, assert; (*autorité etc*) to assert.

affligé, e [afliʒe] *a* distressed, grieved; ~ **de** (*maladie, tare*) afflicted with.

affliger [afliʒe] *vt* (*peiner*) to distress, grieve.

affluence [aflyɑ̃s] *nf* crowds *pl;* **heures d'**~ rush hours; **jours d'**~ busiest days.

affluent [aflyɑ̃] *nm* tributary.

affluer [aflye] *vi* (*secours, biens*) to flood in, pour in; (*sang*) to rush, flow.

affolement [afɔlmɑ̃] *nm* panic.

affoler [afɔle] *vt* to throw into a panic; **s'**~ *vi* to panic.

affranchir [afʀɑ̃ʃiʀ] *vt* to put a stamp *ou* stamps on; (*à la machine*) to frank (*Brit*), meter (*US*); (*fig*) to free, liberate; **affranchissement** *nm* postage.

affréter [afʀete] *vt* to charter.

affreux, euse [afʀø, -øz] *a* dreadful, awful.

affrontement [afʀɔ̃tmɑ̃] *nm* clash, confrontation.

affronter [afʀɔ̃te] *vt* to confront, face.

affubler [afyble] *vt* (*péj*): ~ **qn de** to rig *ou* deck sb out in; (*surnom*) to attach to sb.

affût [afy] *nm:* **à l'**~ **(de)** (*gibier*) lying in wait (for); (*fig*) on the look-out (for).

affûter [afyte] *vt* to sharpen, grind.

afin [afɛ̃]: ~ **que** *cj* so that, in order that; ~ **de faire** in order to do, so as to do.

africain, e [afʀikɛ̃, -ɛn] *a, nm/f* African.

Afrique [afʀik] *nf:* **l'**~ Africa; **l'**~ **du Sud** South Africa.

agacer [agase] *vt* to pester, tease; (*involontairement*) to irritate.

âge [aʒ] *nm* age; **quel** ~ **as-tu?** how old are you?; **prendre de l'**~ to be getting on (in years); **l'**~ **ingrat** the awkward age; **l'**~ **mûr** maturity; **âgé, e** *a* old, elderly; **âgé de 10 ans** 10 years old.

agence [aʒɑ̃s] *nf* agency, office; (*succursale*) branch; ~ **immobilière** estate (*Brit*) *ou* real estate (*US*) agent's (office); ~ **matrimoniale** marriage bureau; ~ **de voyages** travel agency.

agencer [aʒɑ̃se] *vt* to put together; to arrange, lay out.

agenda [aʒɛ̃da] *nm* diary.

agenouiller [aʒnuje]: **s'**~ *vi* to kneel (down).

agent [aʒɑ̃] *nm* (*aussi:* ~ **de police**) policeman; (*ADMIN*) official, officer; (*fig:* élément, facteur) agent; ~ **d'assurances** insurance broker; ~ **de change** stockbroker; ~ **(secret)** (secret) agent.

agglomération [aglɔmeʀɑsjɔ̃] *nf* town; built-up area; **l'**~ **parisienne** the urban area of Paris.

aggloméré [aglɔmeʀe] *nm* (*bois*) chipboard; (*pierre*) conglomerate.

agglomérer [aglɔmeʀe] *vt* to pile up; (*TECH: bois, pierre*) to compress.

aggraver [agʀave] *vt* to worsen, aggravate; (*JUR: peine*) to increase; **s'**~ *vi* to worsen.

agile [aʒil] *a* agile, nimble.

agir [aʒiʀ] *vi* to act; **il s'agit de** it's a matter *ou* question of; it is about; (*il importe que*): **il s'agit de faire** we (*ou* you *etc*) must do.

agitation [aʒitɑsjɔ̃] nf (hustle and) bustle; agitation, excitement; (politique) unrest, agitation.

agité, e [aʒite] a fidgety, restless; agitated, perturbed; (mer) rough.

agiter [aʒite] vt (bouteille, chiffon) to shake; (bras, mains) to wave; (préoccuper, exciter) to perturb.

agneau, x [aɲo] nm lamb.

agonie [agoni] nf mortal agony, death pangs pl; (fig) death throes pl.

agrafe [agraf] nf (de vêtement) hook, fastener; (de bureau) staple; **agrafer** vt to fasten; to staple; **agrafeuse** nf stapler.

agraire [agrɛr] a land cpd.

agrandir [agrɑ̃dir] vt to enlarge; (magasin, domaine) to extend, enlarge; s'~ vi to be extended; to be enlarged; **agrandissement** nm (PHOTO) enlargement.

agréable [agreabl(ə)] a pleasant, nice.

agréé, e [agree] a: concessionnaire ~ registered dealer.

agréer [agree] vt (requête) to accept; ~ à vt to please, suit; veuillez ~ ... (formule épistolaire) yours faithfully.

agrégation [agregɑsjɔ̃] nf highest teaching diploma in France; **agrégé, e** nm/f holder of the agrégation.

agrément [agremɑ̃] nm (accord) consent, approval; (attraits) charm, attractiveness; (plaisir) pleasure.

agrémenter [agremɑ̃te] vt to embellish, adorn.

agresser [agrese] vt to attack.

agresseur [agresœr] nm aggressor, attacker; (POL, MIL) aggressor.

agressif, ive [agresif, -iv] a aggressive.

agricole [agrikɔl] a agricultural.

agriculteur [agrikyltœr] nm farmer.

agriculture [agrikyltyr] nf agriculture; farming.

agripper [agripe] vt to grab, clutch; (pour arracher) to snatch, grab; s'~ à to cling (on) to, clutch, grip.

agrumes [agrym] nmpl citrus fruit(s).

aguerrir [agerir] vt to harden.

aguets [age]: aux ~ ad: être aux ~ to be on the look-out.

aguicher [agiʃe] vt to entice.

ahuri, e [ayri] a (stupéfait) flabbergasted; (idiot) dim-witted.

ai vb voir **avoir**.

aide [ɛd] nm/f assistant // nf assistance, help; (secours financier) aid; à l'~ de (avec) with the help ou aid of; **appeler** (qn) à l'~ to call for help (from sb); ~ **judiciaire** nf legal aid; ~ **sociale** nf (assistance) state aid; ~ **soignant, e** nm/f auxiliary nurse; ~~**mémoire** nm inv memoranda pages pl; (key facts) handbook.

aider [ɛde] vt to help; ~ à qch (faciliter) to help (towards) sth; s'~ de (se servir

de) to use, make use of.

aie etc vb voir **avoir**.

aïe [aj] excl ouch.

aïeul, e [ajœl] nm/f grandparent, grandfather/grandmother; forebear.

aïeux [ajø] nmpl grandparents; forebears, forefathers.

aigle [ɛgl(ə)] nm eagle.

aigre [ɛgr(ə)] a sour, sharp; (fig) sharp, cutting; **aigreur** nf sourness; sharpness; aigreurs d'estomac heartburn sg; **aigrir** vt (personne) to embitter; (caractère) to sour.

aigu, ë [egy] a (objet, arête, douleur, intelligence) sharp; (son, voix) high-pitched, shrill; (note) high(-pitched).

aiguille [egɥij] nf needle; (de montre) hand; ~ à tricoter knitting needle.

aiguiller [egɥije] vt (orienter) to direct.

aiguillon [egɥijɔ̃] nm (d'abeille) sting; **aiguillonner** vt to spur ou goad on.

aiguiser [egize] vt to sharpen; (fig) to stimulate; to excite.

ail [aj] nm garlic.

aile [ɛl] nf wing; **aileron** nm (de requin) fin; **ailier** nm winger.

aille etc vb voir **aller**.

ailleurs [ajœr] ad elsewhere, somewhere else; partout/nulle part ~ everywhere/ nowhere else; d'~ ad (du reste) moreover, besides; par ~ ad (d'autre part) moreover, furthermore.

ailloli [ajɔli] nm garlic mayonnaise.

aimable [ɛmabl(ə)] a kind, nice.

aimant [ɛmɑ̃] nm magnet.

aimer [ɛme] vt to love; (d'amitié, affection, par goût) to like; (souhait): j'aimerais... I would like...; bien ~ qn/ qch to like sb/sth; j'aime mieux ou autant vous dire que I may as well tell you that; j'aimerais autant y aller maintenant I'd rather go now; j'aimerais mieux faire I'd much rather do.

aine [ɛn] nf groin.

aîné, e [ene] a elder, older; (le plus âgé) eldest, oldest // nm/f oldest child ou one, oldest boy ou son/girl ou daughter; **aînesse** nf: droit d'aînesse birthright.

ainsi [ɛ̃si] ad (de cette façon) like this, in this way, thus; (ce faisant) thus // cj thus, so; ~ que (comme) (just) as; (et aussi) as well as; pour ~ dire so to speak; et ~ de suite and so on.

air [ɛr] nm air; (mélodie) tune; (expression) look, air; prendre l'~ to get some (fresh) air; (avion) to take off; avoir l'~ (sembler) to look, appear; avoir l'~ de to look like; avoir l'~ de faire to look as though one is doing, appear to be doing.

aire [ɛr] nf (zone, fig, MATH) area.

aisance [ɛzɑ̃s] nf ease; (richesse) affluence.

aise [ɛz] nf comfort // a: être bien ~ que to be delighted that; être à l'~ ou à son ~ to be comfortable; (pas embarrassé) to be at ease; *(financièrement)* to be comfortably off; **se mettre à l'~** to make o.s. comfortable; **être mal à l'~** *ou* **à son ~** to be uncomfortable; to be ill at ease; **en faire à son ~** to do as one likes; **aisé, e** *a* easy; *(assez riche)* well-to-do, well-off.

aisselle [ɛsɛl] *nf* armpit.

ait *vb voir* **avoir.**

ajonc [aʒɔ̃] *nm* gorse *q*.

ajourner [aʒuʀne] *vt (réunion)* to adjourn; *(décision)* to defer, postpone.

ajouter [aʒute] *vt* to add; **~ foi à** to lend *ou* give credence to.

ajusté, e [aʒyste] *a*: **bien ~** *(robe etc)* close-fitting.

ajuster [aʒyste] *vt (régler)* to adjust; *(vêtement)* to alter; *(coup de fusil)* to aim; *(cible)* to aim at; *(TECH, gén: adapter)*: **~ qch à** to fit sth to.

alambic [alɑ̃bik] *nm* still.

alarme [alaʀm(ə)] *nf* alarm; **donner l'~** to give *ou* raise the alarm; **alarmer** *vt* to alarm; **s'alarmer** *vi* to become alarmed.

album [albɔm] *nm* album.

albumine [albymin] *nf* albumin; **avoir** *ou* **faire de l'~** to suffer from albuminuria.

alcool [alkɔl] *nm*: **l'~** alcohol; **un ~** a spirit, a brandy; **~ à brûler** methylated spirits *(Brit)*, wood alcohol *(US)*; **~ à 90°** surgical spirit; **~ique** *a, nm/f* alcoholic; **~isé, e** *a* alcoholic; **~isme** *nm* alcoholism; **alco(o)test** ℝ *nm* Breathalyser ℝ; *(test)* breath-test.

aléas [alea] *nmpl* hazards; **aléatoire** *a* uncertain; *(INFORM)* random.

alentour [alɑ̃tuʀ] *ad* around (about); **~s** *nmpl* surroundings; **aux ~s de** in the vicinity *ou* neighbourhood of, around about; *(temps)* around about.

alerte [alɛʀt(ə)] *a* agile, nimble; brisk, lively // *nf* alert; warning; **alerter** *vt* to alert.

algèbre [alʒɛbʀ(ə)] *nf* algebra.

Alger [alʒe] *n* Algiers.

Algérie [alʒeʀi] *nf*: **l'~** Algeria; **algérien, ne** *a, nm/f* Algerian.

algue [alg(ə)] *nf (gén)* seaweed *q*; *(BOT)* alga *(pl* algae).

alibi [alibi] *nm* alibi.

aliéné, e [aljene] *nm/f* insane person, lunatic *(péj)*.

aligner [aliɲe] *vt* to align, line up; *(idées, chiffres)* to string together; *(adapter)*: **~ qch sur** to bring sth into alignment with; **s'~** *(soldats etc)* to line up; **s'~ sur** *(POL)* to align o.s. on.

aliment [alimɑ̃] *nm* food.

alimentation [alimɑ̃tɑsjɔ̃] *nf* feeding; supplying; *(commerce)* food trade; *(produits)* groceries *pl*; *(régime)* diet; *(INFORM)* feed.

alimenter [alimɑ̃te] *vt* to feed; *(TECH)*:

~ (en) to supply (with); to feed (with); *(fig)* to sustain, keep going.

alinéa [alinea] *nm* paragraph.

aliter [alite]: **s'~** *vi* to take to one's bed.

allaiter [alete] *vt* to (breast-)feed, nurse; *(suj: animal)* to suckle.

allant [alɑ̃] *nm* drive, go.

allécher [aleʃe] *vt*: **~ qn** to make sb's mouth water; to tempt *ou* entice sb.

allée [ale] *nf (de jardin)* path; *(en ville)* avenue, drive; **~s et venues** *nfpl* comings and goings.

alléger [aleʒe] *vt (voiture)* to make lighter; *(chargement)* to lighten; *(souffrance)* to alleviate, soothe.

allègre [alɛgʀ(ə)] *a* lively, cheerful.

alléguer [alege] *vt* to put forward (as proof *ou* an excuse).

Allemagne [aləmaɲ] *nf*: **l'~** Germany; **l'~ de l'Est/Ouest** East/West Germany; **allemand, e** *a, nm, nf* German.

aller [ale] *nm (trajet)* outward journey; *(billet: aussi:* **~ simple)** single *(Brit) ou* one-way *(US)* ticket // *vi (gén)* to go; **~ à** *(convenir)* to suit; *(suj: forme, pointure etc)* to fit; **~ avec** *(couleurs, style etc)* to go (well) with; **je vais y aller/me faire à** I'm going to go/to get angry; **~ voir** to go and see, go to see; **allez!** come on!; **allons!** come now!; **comment allez-vous?** how are you?; **comment ça va?** how are you?; *(affaires etc)* how are things?; **il va bien/mal** he's well/not well, he's fine/ill; **ça va bien/mal** *(affaires etc)* it's going well/not going well; **~ mieux** to be better; **cela va sans dire** that goes without saying; **il y va de leur vie** their lives are at stake; **s'en ~** *vi (partir)* to be off, go, leave; *(disparaître)* to go away; **~ (et) retour** *nm (trajet)* return journey *(Brit)*, round trip; *(billet)* return (ticket) *(Brit)*, round trip ticket *(US)*.

allergique [alɛʀʒik] *a*: **~ à** allergic to.

alliage [aljaʒ] *nm* alloy.

alliance [aljɑ̃s] *nf (MIL, POL)* alliance; *(mariage)* marriage; *(bague)* wedding ring.

allier [alje] *vt (métaux)* to alloy; *(POL, gén)* to ally; *(fig)* to combine; **s'~** to become allies; to combine.

allô [alo] *excl* hullo, hallo.

allocation [alɔkɑsjɔ̃] *nf* allowance; **~ (de) chômage** unemployment benefit; **~ (de) logement** rent allowance; **~s familiales** ≈ child benefit.

allocution [alɔkysjɔ̃] *nf* short speech.

allonger [alɔ̃ʒe] *vt* to lengthen, make longer; *(étendre: bras, jambe)* to stretch (out); **s'~** *vi* to get longer; *(se coucher)* to lie down, stretch out; **~ le pas** to hasten one's step(s).

allouer [alwe] *vt* to allocate, allot.

allumage [alymaʒ] *nm (AUTO)* ignition.

allume... [alym] *préfixe*: **~-cigare** *nm*

inv cigar lighter; **~-gaz** *nm inv* gas lighter.

allumer [alyme] *vt* (*lampe, phare, radio*) to put *ou* switch on; (*pièce*) to put *ou* switch the light(s) on in; (*feu*) to light; **s'~** *vi* (*lumière, lampe*) to come *ou* go on.

allumette [alymɛt] *nf* match.

allure [alyʀ] *nf* (*vitesse*) speed, pace; (*démarche*) walk; (*maintien*) bearing; (*aspect, air*) look; avoir de l'~ to have style; à toute ~ at top speed.

allusion [alyzjɔ̃] *nf* allusion; (*sous-entendu*) hint; faire ~ à to allude *ou* refer to; to hint at.

aloi [alwa] *nm*: de bon ~ of genuine worth *ou* quality.

alors [alɔʀ] *ad* **1** (*à ce moment-là*) then, at that time; il habitait ~ à Paris he lived in Paris at that time
2 (*par conséquent*) then; tu as fini? ~ je m'en vais have you finished? I'm going then; et ~? so what?
alors que *cj* **1** (*au moment où*) when, as; il est arrivé ~ que je partais he arrived as I was leaving
2 (*pendant que*) while, when; ~ qu'il était à Paris, il a visité ... while *ou* when he was in Paris, he visited ...
3 (*tandis que*) whereas, while; ~ que son frère travaillait dur, lui se reposait whereas *ou* while his brother was working hard, HE would rest.

alouette [alwɛt] *nf* (sky)lark.

alourdir [aluʀdiʀ] *vt* to weigh down, make heavy.

aloyau [alwajo] *nm* sirloin.

alpage [alpaʒ] *nm* pasture.

Alpes [alp(ə)] *nfpl*: les ~ the Alps.

alphabet [alfabe] *nm* alphabet; (*livre*) ABC (book); **alphabétiser** *vt* to teach to read and write; to eliminate illiteracy in.

alpinisme [alpinism(ə)] *nm* mountaineering, climbing; **alpiniste** *nm/f* mountaineer, climber.

Alsace [alzas] *nf* Alsace; **alsacien, ne** *a, nm/f* Alsatian.

altérer [alteʀe] *vt* to falsify; to distort; to debase; to corrupt.

alternateur [altɛʀnatœʀ] *nm* alternator.

alternatif, ive [altɛʀnatif, -iv] *a* alternating // *nf* (*choix*) alternative; **alternativement** *ad* alternately.

Altesse [altɛs] *nf* Highness.

altitude [altityd] *nf* altitude, height.

alto [alto] *nm* (*instrument*) viola.

altruisme [altʀɥism(ə)] *nm* altruism.

aluminium [alyminjɔm] *nm* aluminium (*Brit*), aluminum (*US*).

alunir [alyniʀ] *vi* to land on the moon.

amabilité [amabilite] *nf* kindness, amiability.

amadouer [amadwe] *vt* to coax, cajole; to mollify, soothe.

amaigrir [amegʀiʀ] *vt* to make thin(ner).

amande [amɑ̃d] *nf* (*de l'amandier*) almond; (*de noyau de fruit*) kernel; **amandier** *nm* almond (tree).

amant [amɑ̃] *nm* lover.

amarrer [amaʀe] *vt* (*NAVIG*) to moor; (*gén*) to make fast.

amas [amɑ] *nm* heap, pile.

amasser [amɑse] *vt* to amass.

amateur [amatœʀ] *nm* amateur; en ~ (*péj*) amateurishly; ~ de musique/sport *etc* music/sport *etc* lover.

amazone [amazon] *nf*: en ~ sidesaddle.

ambages [ɑ̃baʒ]: sans ~ *ad* plainly.

ambassade [ɑ̃basad] *nf* embassy; (*mission*): en ~ on a mission; **ambassadeur, drice** *nm/f* ambassador/ambassadress.

ambiance [ɑ̃bjɑ̃s] *nf* atmosphere.

ambiant, e [ɑ̃bjɑ̃, -ɑ̃t] *a* (*air, milieu*) surrounding; (*température*) ambient.

ambigu, ë [ɑ̃bigy] *a* ambiguous.

ambitieux, euse [ɑ̃bisjø, -øz] *a* ambitious.

ambition [ɑ̃bisjɔ̃] *nf* ambition.

ambulance [ɑ̃bylɑ̃s] *nf* ambulance; **ambulancier, ière** *nm/f* ambulance man/woman (*Brit*), paramedic (*US*).

ambulant, e [ɑ̃bylɑ̃, -ɑ̃t] *a* travelling, itinerant.

âme [ɑm] *nf* soul; ~ sœur kindred spirit.

améliorer [ameljɔʀe] *vt* to improve; **s'~** *vi* to improve, get better.

aménagements [amenaʒmɑ̃] *nmpl* developments; ~ fiscaux tax adjustments.

aménager [amenaʒe] *vt* (*agencer, transformer*) to fit out; to lay out; (: *quartier, territoire*) to develop; (*installer*) to fix up, put in; ferme aménagée converted farmhouse.

amende [amɑ̃d] *nf* fine; mettre à l'~ to penalize; faire ~ honorable to make amends.

amender [amɑ̃de] *vt* (*loi*) to amend; **s'~** *vi* to mend one's ways.

amène [amɛn] *a* affable; peu ~ unkind.

amener [amne] *vt* to bring; (*causer*) to bring about; (*baisser: drapeau, voiles*) to strike; **s'~** *vi* (*fam*) to show up, turn up.

amenuiser [amənɥize]: **s'~** *vi* to grow slimmer, lessen; to dwindle.

amer, amère [ameʀ] *a* bitter.

américain, e [ameʀikɛ̃, -ɛn] *a, nm/f* American.

Amérique [ameʀik] *nf* America; l'~ centrale/latine Central/Latin America; l'~ du Nord/du Sud North/South America.

amerrir [ameʀiʀ] *vi* to land on the sea).

amertume [ameʀtym] *nf* bitterness.

ameublement [amœbləmɑ̃] *nm* furnishing; (*meubles*) furniture.

ameuter [amøte] *vt* (*badauds*) to draw a crowd of; (*peuple*) to rouse.

ami, e [ami] *nm/f* friend; *(amant/ maîtresse)* boyfriend/girlfriend // *a: pays/groupe* ~ friendly country/group; **être ~ de l'ordre** to be a lover of order; **un ~ des arts** a patron of the arts.

amiable [amjabl(ə)]: **à l'~** *ad* *(JUR)* out of court; *(gén)* amicably.

amiante [amjãt] *nm* asbestos.

amical, e, aux [amikal, -o] *a* friendly // *nf (club)* association; **amicalement** *ad* in a friendly way; *(formule épistolaire)* regards.

amidon [amidɔ̃] *nm* starch.

amincir [amɛ̃siʀ] *vt (objet)* to thin (down); ~ **qn** to make sb thinner *ou* slimmer; **s'~** *vi* to get thinner *ou* slimmer.

amiral, aux [amiʀal, -o] *nm* admiral.

amitié [amitje] *nf* friendship; **prendre en ~ to** befriend; **faire** *ou* **présenter ses ~s à qn** to send sb one's best wishes.

ammoniac [amɔnjak] *nm*: **(gaz) ~** ammonia.

ammoniaque [amɔnjak] *nf* ammonia (water).

amoindrir [amwɛ̃dʀiʀ] *vt* to reduce.

amollir [amɔliʀ] *vt* to soften.

amonceler [amɔ̃sle] *vt*, **s'~** *vi* to pile *ou* heap up; *(fig)* to accumulate.

amont [amɔ̃]: **en ~** *ad* upstream; *(sur une pente)* uphill.

amorce [amɔʀs(ə)] *nf (sur un hameçon)* bait; *(explosif)* cap; primer; priming; *(fig: début)* beginning(s), start.

amorphe [amɔʀf(ə)] *a* passive, lifeless.

amortir [amɔʀtiʀ] *vt (atténuer: choc)* to absorb, cushion; *(bruit, douleur)* to deaden; *(COMM: dette)* to pay off; *(: mise de fonds, matériel)* to write off; ~ **un abonnement** to make a season ticket pay (for itself); **amortisseur** *nm* shock absorber.

amour [amuʀ] *nm* love; *(liaison)* love affair, love; **faire l'~** to make love; **s'~acher de** *(péj)* to become infatuated with; **~eux, euse** *a (regard, tempérament)* amorous; *(vie, problèmes)* love *cpd*; *(personne)*: **~eux (de qn)** in love (with sb) // *nmpl* courting couple(s); **~-propre** *nm* self-esteem, pride.

amovible [amɔvibl(ə)] *a* removable, detachable.

ampère [ãpɛʀ] *nm* amp(ere).

amphithéâtre [ãfiteatʀ(ə)] *nm* amphitheatre; *(d'université)* lecture hall *ou* theatre.

ample [ãpl(ə)] *a (vêtement)* roomy, ample; *(gestes, mouvement)* broad; *(ressources)* ample; **ampleur** *nf (importance)* scale, size; extent.

amplificateur [ãplifikatœʀ] *nm* amplifier.

amplifier [ãplifje] *vt (son, oscillation)* to amplify; *(fig)* to expand, increase.

ampoule [ãpul] *nf (électrique)* bulb; *(de médicament)* phial; *(aux mains, pieds)* blister.

ampoulé, e [ãpule] *a (péj)* pompous, bombastic.

amputer [ãpyte] *vt (MÉD)* to amputate; *(fig)* to cut *ou* reduce drastically.

amusant, e [amyzã, -ãt] *a (divertissant, spirituel)* entertaining, amusing; *(comique)* funny, amusing.

amuse-gueule [amyzɡœl] *nm inv* appetizer, snack.

amusement [amyzmã] *nm* amusement; *(jeu etc)* pastime, diversion.

amuser [amyze] *vt (divertir)* to entertain, amuse; *(égayer, faire rire)* to amuse; *(détourner l'attention de)* to distract; **s'~** *vi (jouer)* to amuse o.s., play; *(se divertir)* to enjoy o.s., have fun; *(fig)* to mess around.

amygdale [amidal] *nf* tonsil.

amygdalite [amidalit] *nf* tonsilitis.

an [ã] *nm* year; **le jour de l'~, le premier de l'~, le nouvel ~** New Year's Day.

analogique [analɔʒik] *a* analogical; *(IN-FORM, montre)* analog.

analogue [analɔɡ] *a*: ~ **(à)** analogous (to), similar (to).

analphabète [analfabɛt] *nm/f* illiterate.

analyse [analiz] *nf* analysis; *(MÉD)* test; **analyser** *vt* to analyse; to test.

ananas [anana] *nm* pineapple.

anarchie [anaʀʃi] *nf* anarchy.

anathème [anatɛm] *nm*: **jeter l'~ sur** to curse.

anatomie [anatɔmi] *nf* anatomy.

ancêtre [ãsɛtʀ(ə)] *nm/f* ancestor.

anchois [ãʃwa] *nm* anchovy.

ancien, ne [ãsjɛ̃, -jɛn] *a* old; *(de jadis, de l'antiquité)* ancient; *(précédent, ex-)* former, old // *nm/f (dans une tribu)* elder; **anciennement** *ad* formerly; **ancienneté** *nf* oldness; antiquity; *(AD-MIN)* (length of) service; seniority.

ancre [ãkʀ(ə)] *nf* anchor; **jeter/lever l'~** to cast/weigh anchor; **à l'~** at anchor.

ancrer [ãkʀe] *vt (CONSTR: câble etc)* to anchor; *(fig)* to fix firmly; **s'~** *vi (NA-VIG)* to (cast) anchor.

Andorre [ãdɔʀ] *nf* Andorra.

andouille [ãduj] *nf (CULIN)* sausage made of chitterlings; *(fam)* clot, nit.

âne [ɑn] *nm* donkey, ass; *(péj)* dunce.

anéantir [aneãtiʀ] *vt* to annihilate, wipe out; *(fig)* to obliterate, destroy; to overwhelm.

anémie [anemi] *nf* anaemia; **anémique** *a* anaemic.

ânerie [ɑnʀi] *nf* stupidity; stupid *ou* idiotic comment *etc*.

anesthésie [anɛstezi] *nf* anaesthesia; **faire une ~ locale/générale à qn** to give sb a local/general anaesthetic.

ange [ãʒ] *nm* angel; **être aux ~s** to be over the moon.

angélus [ãʒelys] *nm* angelus; evening

bells *pl*.

angine [ɑ̃ʒin] *nf* throat infection; ~ de poitrine angina.

anglais, e [ɑ̃glɛ, -ɛz] *a* English // *nm/f*: A~, e Englishman/woman // *nm* (*LING*) English; les A~ the English; filer à l'~e to take French leave.

angle [ɑ̃gl(ə)] *nm* angle; (*coin*) corner; ~ droit right angle.

Angleterre [ɑ̃glətɛr] *nf*: l'~ England.

anglo... [ɑ̃glɔ] *préfixe* Anglo-, anglo(-); ~**phone** *a* English-speaking.

angoissé, e [ɑ̃gwase] *a* (*personne*) full of anxieties *ou* hang-ups (*fam*).

angoisser [ɑ̃gwase] *vt* to harrow, cause anguish to // *vi* to worry, fret.

anguille [ɑ̃gij] *nf* eel.

anicroche [anikrɔʃ] *nf* hitch, snag.

animal, e, aux [animal, -o] *a*, *nm* animal.

animateur, trice [animatœr, -tris] *nm/f* (*de télévision*) host; (*de groupe*) leader, organizer.

animation [animɑsjɔ̃] *nf* (*voir animé*) busyness; liveliness; (*CINÉMA: technique*) animation.

animé, e [anime] *a* (*lieu*) busy, lively; (*conversation, réunion*) lively, animated; (*opposé à inanimé*) animate.

animer [anime] *vt* (*ville, soirée*) to liven up; (*mettre en mouvement*) to drive.

anis [ani] *nm* (*CULIN*) aniseed; (*BOT*) anise.

ankyloser [ɑ̃kiloze]: s'~ *vi* to get stiff.

anneau, x [ano] *nm* (*de rideau, bague*) ring; (*de chaîne*) link.

année [ane] *nf* year.

annexe [anɛks(ə)] *a* (*problème*) related; (*document*) appended; (*salle*) adjoining // *nf* (*bâtiment*) annex(e); (*de document, ouvrage*) annex, appendix; (*jointe à une lettre*) enclosure.

anniversaire [anivɛrsɛr] *nm* birthday; (*d'un événement, bâtiment*) anniversary.

annonce [anɔ̃s] *nf* announcement; (*signe, indice*) sign; (*aussi*: ~ publicitaire) advertisement; les petites ~s the classified advertisements, the small ads.

annoncer [anɔ̃se] *vt* to announce; (*être le signe de*) to herald; s'~ bien/difficile to look promising/difficult; **annonceur, euse** *nm/f* (*TV, RADIO: speaker*) announcer; (*publicitaire*) advertiser.

annuaire [anɥɛr] *nm* yearbook, annual; ~ téléphonique (telephone) directory, phone book.

annuel, le [anɥɛl] *a* annual, yearly.

annuité [anɥite] *nf* annual instalment.

annulaire [anɥlɛr] *nm* third finger.

annuler [anɥle] *vt* (*rendez-vous, voyage*) to cancel, call off; (*mariage*) to annul; (*jugement*) to quash (*Brit*), repeal (*US*); (*résultats*) to declare void; (*MATH, PHYSIQUE*) to cancel out.

anodin, e [anɔdɛ̃, -in] *a* harmless; in-

significant, trivial.

anonyme [anɔnim] *a* anonymous; (*fig*) impersonal.

anorak [anɔrak] *nm* anorak.

ANPE *sigle f* (= Agence nationale pour l'emploi) national employment agency.

anse [ɑ̃s] *nf* (*de panier, tasse*) handle; (*GÉO*) cove.

antan [ɑ̃tɑ̃]: d'~ *a* of long ago.

antarctique [ɑ̃tarktik] *a* Antarctic // *nm*: l'A~ the Antarctic.

antécédents [ɑ̃tesedɑ̃] *nmpl* (*MÉD etc*) past history *sg*.

antenne [ɑ̃tɛn] *nf* (*de radio*) aerial; (*d'insecte*) antenna (*pl* ae), feeler; (*poste avancé*) outpost; (*petite succursale*) sub-branch; passer à l'~ to go on the air; prendre l'~ to tune in; 2 heures d'~ 2 hours' broadcasting time.

antérieur, e [ɑ̃terjœr] *a* (*d'avant*) previous, earlier; (*de devant*) front.

anti... [ɑ̃ti] *préfixe* anti..; ~**aérien, ne** *a* anti-aircraft; **abri** ~aérien air-raid shelter; ~**alcoolique** *a* anti-alcohol; ~**atomique** *a*: abri ~atomique fallout shelter; ~**biotique** *nm* antibiotic; ~**brouillard** *a*: phare ~brouillard fog lamp.

anticipation [ɑ̃tisipɑsjɔ̃] *nf*: livre/film d'~ science fiction book/film.

anticipé, e [ɑ̃tisipe] *a*: avec mes remerciements ~s thanking you in advance *ou* anticipation.

anticiper [ɑ̃tisipe] *vt* (*événement, coup*) to anticipate, foresee.

anticonceptionnel, le [ɑ̃tikɔ̃sɛpsjɔnɛl] *a* contraceptive.

antidote [ɑ̃tidɔt] *nm* antidote.

antienne [ɑ̃tjɛn] *nf* (*fig*) chant, refrain.

antigel [ɑ̃tiʒɛl] *nm* antifreeze.

antihistaminique [ɑ̃tiistaminik] *nm* antihistamine.

Antilles [ɑ̃tij] *nfpl*: les ~ the West Indies.

antilope [ɑ̃tilɔp] *nf* antelope.

antimite(s) [ɑ̃timit] *a*, *nm*: (produit) ~ mothproofer; moth repellent.

antiparasite [ɑ̃tiparazit] *a* (*RADIO, TV*): dispositif ~ suppressor.

antipathique [ɑ̃tipatik] *a* unpleasant, disagreeable.

antiphrase [ɑ̃tifraz] *nf*: par ~ ironically.

antipodes [ɑ̃tipɔd] *nmpl* (*GÉO*): les ~ the antipodes; (*fig*): être aux ~ de to be the opposite extreme of.

antiquaire [ɑ̃tikɛr] *nm/f* antique dealer.

antique [ɑ̃tik] *a* antique; (*très vieux*) ancient, antiquated.

antiquité [ɑ̃tikite] *nf* (*objet*) antique; l'A~ Antiquity; magasin d'~s antique shop.

antirabique [ɑ̃tirabik] *a* rabies *cpd*.

antirouille [ɑ̃tiruj] *a inv* anti-rust *cpd*; traitement ~ rustproofing.

antisémite [ãtisemit] *a* anti-semitic.

antiseptique [ãtisɛptik] *a, nm* antiseptic.

antivol [ãtivɔl] *a, nm:* (dispositif) ~ anti-theft device.

antre [ãtʀ(ə)] *nm* den, lair.

anxieux, euse [ãksjø, -øz] *a* anxious, worried.

AOC *sigle f* (= appellation d'origine contrôlée) *label guaranteeing the quality of wine.*

août [u] *nm* August.

apaiser [apeze] *vt* (colère, douleur) to soothe; (faim) to appease; (personne) to calm (down), pacify; s'~ *vi* (tempête, bruit) to die down, subside.

apanage [apanaʒ] *nm:* être l'~ de to be the privilege *ou* prerogative of.

aparté [apaʀte] *nm* (THÉÂTRE) aside; (entretien) private conversation.

apatride [apatʀid] *nm/f* stateless person.

apercevoir [apɛʀsəvwaʀ] *vt* to see; s'~ de *vt* to notice; s'~ que to notice that.

aperçu [apɛʀsy] *nm* (vue d'ensemble) general survey; (intuition) insight.

apéritif [apeʀitif] *nm* (boisson) aperitif; (réunion) drinks *pl.*

à-peu-près [apøpʀɛ] *nm inv* (péj) vague approximation.

apeuré, e [apœʀe] *a* frightened, scared.

aphone [afɔn] *a* voiceless.

aphte [aft(ə)] *nm* mouth ulcer.

aphteuse [aftøz] *af:* fièvre ~ foot-and-mouth disease.

apiculture [apikyltyʀ] *nf* beekeeping, apiculture.

apitoyer [apitwaje] *vt* to move to pity; s'~ (sur) to feel pity (for).

aplanir [aplaniʀ] *vt* to level; (fig) to smooth away, iron out.

aplatir [aplatiʀ] *vt* to flatten; s'~ *vi* to become flatter; to be flattened; (fig) to lie flat on the ground.

aplomb [aplɔ̃] *nm* (équilibre) balance, equilibrium; (fig) self-assurance; nerve; d'~ *ad* steady; (CONSTR) plumb.

apogée [apɔʒe] *nm* (fig) peak, apogee.

apologie [apɔlɔʒi] *nf* vindication, praise.

apostolat [apɔstɔla] *nm* (REL) apostolate; (gén) evangelism.

apostrophe [apɔstʀɔf] *nf* (signe) apostrophe.

apostropher [apɔstʀɔfe] *vt* (interpeller) to shout at, address sharply.

apothéose [apɔteoz] *nf* pinnacle (of achievement); (MUS) grand finale.

apôtre [apotʀ(ə)] *nm* apostle.

apparaître [apaʀɛtʀ(ə)] *vi* to appear // *vb avec attribut* to appear, seem.

apparat [apaʀa] *nm:* tenue/dîner d'~ ceremonial dress/dinner.

appareil [apaʀɛj] *nm* (outil, machine) piece of apparatus, device; appliance; (politique, syndical) machinery; (avion) (aero)plane, aircraft *inv*; (téléphonique)

phone; (dentier) brace (Brit), braces (US); qui est à l'~? who's speaking?; dans le plus simple ~ in one's birthday suit; ~ photographique, ~(-photo) *nm* camera; ~ 24 x 36 *ou* petit format 35mm camera.

appareiller [apaʀeje] *vi* (NAVIG) to cast off, get under way // *vt* (assortir) to match up.

apparemment [apaʀamã] *ad* apparently.

apparence [apaʀãs] *nf* appearance.

apparent, e [apaʀã, -ãt] *a* visible; obvious; (superficiel) apparent.

apparenté, e [apaʀãte] *a:* ~ à related to; (fig) similar to.

appariteur [apaʀitœʀ] *nm* attendant, porter (in French universities).

apparition [apaʀisjɔ̃] *nf* appearance; (surnaturelle) apparition.

appartement [apaʀtəmã] *nm* flat (Brit), apartment (US).

appartenir [apaʀtəniʀ]: ~ à *vt* to belong to; il lui appartient de it is up to him to, it is his duty to.

apparu, e *pp de* apparaître.

appât [apɑ] *nm* (PÊCHE) bait; (fig) lure, bait.

appauvrir [apovʀiʀ] *vt* to impoverish.

appel [apɛl] *nm* call; (nominal) roll call; (: SCOL) register; (MIL: recrutement) call-up; faire ~ à (invoquer) to appeal to; (avoir recours à) to call on; (nécessiter) to call for, require; faire ~ (JUR) to appeal; faire l'~ to call the roll; to call the register; sans ~ (fig) final, irrevocable; ~ d'offres (COMM) invitation to tender; faire un ~ de phares to flash one's headlights; ~ (téléphonique) (tele)phone call.

appelé [aple] *nm* (MIL) conscript.

appeler [aple] *vt* to call; (faire venir: médecin etc) to call, send for; (fig: nécessiter) to call for, demand; être appelé à (fig) to be destined to; ~ qn à comparaître (JUR) to summon sb to appear; en ~ à to appeal to; s'~: elle s'appelle Gabrielle her name is Gabrielle, she's called Gabrielle; comment ça s'appelle? what is it called?

appendice [apɛ̃dis] *nm* appendix; **appendicite** *nf* appendicitis.

appentis [apãti] *nm* lean-to.

appesantir [apzãtiʀ]: s'~ *vi* to grow heavier; s'~ sur (fig) to dwell on.

appétissant, e [apetisã, -ãt] *a* appetizing, mouth-watering.

appétit [apeti] *nm* appetite; bon ~! enjoy your meal!

applaudir [aplodiʀ] *vt* to applaud // *vi* to applaud, clap; **applaudissements** *nmpl* applause *sg*, clapping *sg*.

application [aplikasjɔ̃] *nf* application.

applique [aplik] *nf* wall lamp.

appliquer [aplike] *vt* to apply; (loi) to

enforce; **s'~** *vi* (*élève etc*) to apply o.s.

appoint [apwɛ̃] *nm* (extra) contribution *ou* help; **avoir/faire l'~** (*en payant*) to have/give the right change *ou* money; **chauffage d'~** extra heating.

appointements [apwɛtmɑ̃] *nmpl* salary *sg*.

appontement [apɔ̃tmɑ̃] *nm* landing stage, wharf.

apport [apɔr] *nm* supply; contribution.

apporter [apɔrte] *vt* to bring.

apposer [apoze] *vt* to append; to affix.

apprécier [apresje] *vt* to appreciate; (*évaluer*) to estimate, assess.

appréhender [apreɑ̃de] *vt* (*craindre*) to dread; (*arrêter*) to apprehend.

apprendre [aprɑ̃dr(ə)] *vt* to learn; (*événement, résultats*) to learn of, hear of; **~ qch à qn** (*informer*) to tell sb (of) sth; (*enseigner*) to teach sb sth; **~ à faire qch** to learn to do sth; **~ à qn à faire qch** to teach sb to do sth; **appren-ti, e** *nm/f* apprentice; (*fig*) novice, beginner; **apprentissage** *nm* learning; (*COMM, SCOL: période*) apprenticeship.

apprêté, e [aprete] *a* (*fig*) affected.

apprêter [aprete] *vt* to dress, finish.

appris, e *pp de* **apprendre**.

apprivoiser [aprivwaze] *vt* to tame.

approbation [aprɔbasjɔ̃] *nf* approval.

approche [aprɔʃ] *nf* approaching; approach.

approcher [aprɔʃe] *vi* to approach, come near // *vt* to approach; (*rapprocher*): **~ qch** (**de qch**) to bring *ou* put sth near (to sth); **~ de** *vt* to draw near to; (*quantité, moment*) to approach; **s'~ de** *vt* to approach, go *ou* come near to.

approfondir [aprɔfɔ̃dir] *vt* to deepen; (*question*) to go further into.

approprié, e [aprɔprije] *a*: **~** (**à**) appropriate (to), suited to.

approprier [aprɔprije]: **s'~** *vt* to appropriate, take over.

approuver [apruve] *vt* to agree with; (*autoriser: loi, projet*) to approve, pass; (*trouver louable*) to approve of.

approvisionner [aprɔvizjɔne] *vt* to supply; (*compte bancaire*) to pay funds into; **s'~** en to stock up with.

approximatif, ive [aprɔksimatif, -iv] *a* approximate, rough; vague.

appt *abr de* **appartement**.

appui [apɥi] *nm* support; **prendre ~ sur** to lean on; to rest on; **l'~ de la fenêtre** the windowsill, the window ledge; **appui-tête, appuie-tête** *nm inv* headrest.

appuyer [apɥije] *vt* (*poser*): **~ qch sur/ contre** to lean *ou* rest sth on/against; (*soutenir: personne, demande*) to support, back (up) // *vi*: **~ sur** (*bouton,*

frein) to press, push; (*mot, détail*) to stress, emphasize; (*suj: chose: peser sur*) to rest (heavily) on, press against; **s'~ sur** *vt* to lean on; to rely on; **~ à droite** to bear (to the) right.

âpre [ɑpr(ə)] *a* acrid, pungent; (*fig*) harsh; bitter; **~ au gain** grasping.

après [aprɛ] *prép* after // *ad* afterwards; **2 heures ~** 2 hours later; **~ qu'il est** *ou* **soit parti/avoir fait** after he left/having done; **d'~** *prép* (*selon*) according to; **~ coup** *ad* after the event, afterwards; **~ tout** *ad* (*au fond*) after all; **et** (**puis**) **~?** so what?; **~-demain** *ad* the day after tomorrow; **~-guerre** *nm* post-war years *pl*; **~-midi** *nm ou nf inv* afternoon.

à-propos [aprɔpo] *nm* (*d'une remarque*) aptness; **faire preuve d'~** to show presence of mind.

apte [apt(ə)] *a* capable; (*MIL*) fit.

aquarelle [akwarɛl] *nf* (*tableau*) watercolour; (*genre*) watercolours *pl*.

aquarium [akwarjɔm] *nm* aquarium.

arabe [arab] *a* Arabic; (*désert, cheval*) Arabian; (*nation, peuple*) Arab // *nm/f*: **A~** Arab // *nm* (*LING*) Arabic.

Arabie [arabi] *nf*: **l'~** (**Saoudite**) Saudi Arabia.

arachide [araʃid] *nf* (*plante*) groundnut (plant); (*graine*) peanut, groundnut.

araignée [arɛɲe] *nf* spider.

arbitraire [arbitrɛr] *a* arbitrary.

arbitre [arbitr(ə)] *nm* (*SPORT*) referee; (: *TENNIS, CRICKET*) umpire; (*fig*) arbiter, judge; (*JUR*) arbitrator; **arbitrer** *vt* to referee; to umpire; to arbitrate.

arborer [arbɔre] *vt* to bear, display.

arbre [arbr(ə)] *nm* tree; (*TECH*) shaft; **~ généalogique** family tree; **~ de transmission** (*AUTO*) driveshaft.

arbuste [arbyst(ə)] *nm* small shrub.

arc [ark] *nm* (*arme*) bow; (*GÉOM*) arc; (*ARCHIT*) arch; **en ~ de cercle** *a* semicircular.

arcade [arkad] *nf* arch(way); **~s** arcade *sg*, arches.

arcanes [arkan] *nmpl* mysteries.

arc-boutant [arkbutɑ̃] *nm* flying buttress.

arc-bouter [arkbute]: **s'~** *vi*: **s'~ contre** to lean *ou* press against.

arceau, x [arso] *nm* (*métallique etc*) hoop.

arc-en-ciel [arkɑ̃sjɛl] *nm* rainbow.

arche [arʃ(ə)] *nf* arch; **~ de Noé** Noah's Ark.

archéologie [arkeɔlɔʒi] *nf* archeology; **archéologue** *nm/f* archeologist.

archet [arʃɛ] *nm* bow.

archevêque [arʃəvɛk] *nm* archbishop.

archipel [arʃipɛl] *nm* archipelago.

architecte [arʃitɛkt(ə)] *nm* architect.

architecture [arʃitɛktyr] *nf* architecture.

archive [aʀʃiv] nf file; ~s nfpl archives.

arctique [aʀktik] a Arctic // nm: **l'A~** the Arctic.

ardemment [aʀdamɑ̃] ad ardently, fervently.

ardent, e [aʀdɑ̃, -ɑ̃t] a (soleil) blazing; (fièvre) raging; (amour) ardent, passionate; (prière) fervent.

ardoise [aʀdwaz] nf slate.

ardt abr de **arrondissement**.

arène [aʀɛn] nf arena; ~s nfpl bull-ring sg.

arête [aʀɛt] nf (de poisson) bone; (d'une montagne) ridge; (GÉOM etc) edge.

argent [aʀʒɑ̃] nm (métal) silver; (monnaie) money; ~ liquide ready money, (ready) cash; ~ de poche pocket money; **argenterie** nf silverware; silver plate.

argentin, e [aʀʒɑ̃tɛ̃, -in] a (son) silvery; (d'Argentine) Argentinian, Argentine.

Argentine [aʀʒɑ̃tin] nf: **l'~** Argentina, the Argentine.

argile [aʀʒil] nf clay.

argot [aʀɡo] nm slang; **argotique** a slang cpd; slangy.

arguer [aʀɡɥe]: ~ **de** vt to put forward as a pretext ou reason.

argument [aʀɡymɑ̃] nm argument.

argumentaire [aʀɡymɑ̃tɛʀ] nm sales leaflet.

argumenter [aʀɡymɑ̃te] vi to argue.

argus [aʀɡys] nm guide to second-hand car etc prices.

arguties [aʀɡysi] nfpl quibbles.

aristocratique [aʀistɔkʀatik] a aristocratic.

arithmétique [aʀitmetik] a arithmetic(al) // nf arithmetic.

armateur [aʀmatœʀ] nm shipowner.

armature [aʀmatyʀ] nf framework; (de tente etc) frame.

arme [aʀm(ə)] nf weapon; (section de l'armée) arm; ~s nfpl weapons, arms; (blason) (coat of) arms; ~ à feu firearm.

armée [aʀme] nf army; ~ **de l'air** Air Force; **l'~ du Salut** the Salvation Army; ~ **de terre** Army.

armement [aʀməmɑ̃] nm (matériel) arms pl, weapons pl; (: d'un pays) arms pl, armament.

armer [aʀme] vt to arm; (arme à feu) to cock; (appareil-photo) to wind on; ~ **qch de** to fit sth with; to reinforce sth with.

armistice [aʀmistis] nm armistice; **l'A~** ≈ Remembrance (Brit) ou Veterans (US) Day.

armoire [aʀmwaʀ] nf (tall) cupboard; (penderie) wardrobe (Brit), closet (US).

armoiries [aʀmwaʀi] nfpl coat sg of arms.

armure [aʀmyʀ] nf armour q, suit of armour.

armurier [aʀmyʀje] nm gunsmith;

armourer.

arnaquer [aʀnake] vt to swindle.

aromates [aʀɔmat] nmpl seasoning sg, herbs (and spices).

aromatisé, e [aʀɔmatize] a flavoured.

arôme [aʀom] nm aroma; fragrance.

arpenter [aʀpɑ̃te] vt (salle, couloir) to pace up and down.

arpenteur [aʀpɑ̃tœʀ] nm surveyor.

arqué, e [aʀke] a bandy; arched.

arrache-pied [aʀaʃpje]: **d'~** ad relentlessly.

arracher [aʀaʃe] vt to pull out; (page etc) to tear off, tear out; (légumes, herbe) to pull up; (bras etc) to tear off; ~ **qch à qn** to snatch sth from sb; (fig) to wring sth out of sb; **s'~** vt (article recherché) to fight over.

arraisonner [aʀɛzɔne] vt (bateau) to board and search.

arrangeant, e [aʀɑ̃ʒɑ̃, -ɑ̃t] a accommodating, obliging.

arranger [aʀɑ̃ʒe] vt (gén) to arrange; (réparer) to fix, put right; (régler) to settle, sort out; (convenir à) to suit, be convenient for; **s'~** (se mettre d'accord) to come to an agreement; **je vais m'~** I'll manage; **ça va s'~** it'll sort itself out.

arrestation [aʀɛstɑsjɔ̃] nf arrest.

arrêt [aʀɛ] nm stopping; (de bus etc) stop; (JUR) judgment, decision; **rester** ou **tomber en ~ devant** to stop short in front of; **sans ~** non-stop; continually; ~ **de mort** capital sentence; ~ **de travail** stoppage (of work).

arrêté [aʀete] nm order, decree.

arrêter [aʀete] vt to stop; (chauffage etc) to turn off, switch off; (fixer: date etc) to appoint, decide on; (criminel, suspect) to arrest; ~ **de faire** to stop doing; **s'~** vi to stop.

arrhes [aʀ] nfpl deposit sg.

arrière [aʀjɛʀ] nm back; (SPORT) fullback // a inv: **siège/roue** ~ back ou rear seat/wheel; **à l'~** ad behind, at the back; **en ~** ad behind; (regarder) back, behind; (tomber, aller) backwards; **arriéré, e** a (péj) backward // (d'argent) arrears pl; **~-goût** nm aftertaste; **~-grand-mère** nf great-grandmother; **~-grand-père** nm great-grandfather; **~-pays** nm inv hinterland; **~-pensée** nf ulterior motive; mental reservation; **~-plan** nm background; **~-saison** nf late autumn; **~-train** nm hindquarters pl.

arrimer [aʀime] vt to stow; to secure.

arrivage [aʀivaʒ] nm arrival.

arrivée [aʀive] nf arrival; (ligne d'arrivée) finish; ~ **d'air/de gaz** air/gas inlet.

arriver [aʀive] vi to arrive; (survenir) to happen, occur; **il arrive à Paris à 8h** he gets to ou arrives in Paris at 8; ~ **à** (at-

teindre) to reach; ~ à faire qch to succeed in doing sth; il arrive que it happens that; il lui arrive de faire he sometimes does; **arriviste** *nm/f* go-getter.

arrogant, e [aʀɔgɑ̃, -ɑ̃t] *a* arrogant.

arroger [aʀɔʒe]: s'~ *vt* to assume (without right).

arrondir [aʀɔ̃diʀ] *vt* (*forme, objet*) to round; (*somme*) to round off; s'~ *vi* to become round(ed).

arrondissement [aʀɔ̃dismɑ̃] *nm* (*ADMIN*) ≈ district.

arroser [aʀoze] *vt* to water; (*victoire*) to celebrate (over a drink); (*CULIN*) to baste; **arrosoir** *nm* watering can.

arsenal, aux [aʀsənal, -o] *nm* (*NAVIG*) naval dockyard; (*MIL*) arsenal; (*fig*) gear, paraphernalia.

art [aʀ] *nm* art; ~s ménagers home economics *sg*.

artère [aʀtɛʀ] *nf* (*ANAT*) artery; (*rue*) main road.

arthrite [aʀtʀit] *nf* arthritis.

artichaut [aʀtiʃo] *nm* artichoke.

article [aʀtikl(ə)] *nm* article; (*COMM*) item, article; à l'~ de la mort at the point of death; ~ de fond (*PRESSE*) feature article.

articulation [aʀtikylɑsjɔ̃] *nf* articulation; (*ANAT*) joint.

articuler [aʀtikyle] *vt* to articulate.

artifice [aʀtifis] *nm* device, trick.

artificiel, le [aʀtifisjɛl] *a* artificial.

artificieux, euse [aʀtifisjø, -øz] *a* guileful, deceitful.

artisan [aʀtizɑ̃] *nm* artisan, (self-employed) craftsman; **artisanal, e, aux** *a* of *ou* made by craftsmen; (*péj*) cottage industry *cpd*, unsophisticated; **artisanat** *nm* arts and crafts *pl*.

artiste [aʀtist(ə)] *nm/f* artist; (*de variétés*) entertainer; performer; **artistique** *a* artistic.

as [ɑ] *vb voir* **avoir** // *nm* [ɑs] ace.

ascendance [asɑ̃dɑ̃s] *nf* (*origine*) ancestry.

ascendant, e [asɑ̃dɑ̃, -ɑ̃t] *a* upward // *nm* influence.

ascenseur [asɑ̃sœʀ] *nm* lift (*Brit*), elevator (*US*).

ascension [asɑ̃sjɔ̃] *nf* ascent; climb; l'A~ (*REL*) the Ascension.

aseptiser [asɛptize] *vt* to sterilize; to disinfect.

asiatique [azjatik] *a, nm/f* Asiatic, Asian.

Asie [azi] *nf*: l'~ Asia.

asile [azil] *nm* (*refuge*) refuge, sanctuary; (*POL*): droit d'~ (political) asylum; (*pour malades etc*) home.

aspect [aspɛ] *nm* appearance, look; (*fig*) aspect, side; à l'~ de at the sight of.

asperge [aspɛʀʒ(ə)] *nf* asparagus *q*.

asperger [aspɛʀʒe] *vt* to spray, sprinkle.

aspérité [aspeʀite] *nf* excrescence, protruding bit (of rock *etc*).

asphalte [asfalt(ə)] *nm* asphalt.

asphyxier [asfiksje] *vt* to suffocate, asphyxiate; (*fig*) to stifle.

aspirateur [aspiʀatœʀ] *nm* vacuum cleaner.

aspirer [aspiʀe] *vt* (*air*) to inhale; (*liquide*) to suck (up); (*suj: appareil*) to suck up; ~ à *vt* to aspire to.

aspirine [aspiʀin] *nf* aspirin.

assagir [asaʒiʀ] *vt*, **s'~** *vi* to quieten down, sober down.

assaillir [asajiʀ] *vt* to assail, attack.

assainir [aseniʀ] *vt* to clean up; to purify.

assaisonner [asɛzɔne] *vt* to season.

assassin [asasɛ̃] *nm* murderer; assassin.

assassiner [asasine] *vt* to murder; (*esp POL*) to assassinate.

assaut [aso] *nm* assault, attack; **prendre d'~** to storm, assault; **donner l'~** to attack; **faire ~ de** (*rivaliser*) to vie with each other in.

assécher [aseʃe] *vt* to drain.

assemblée [asɑ̃ble] *nf* (*réunion*) meeting; (*public, assistance*) gathering; (*assembled people*); (*POL*) assembly.

assembler [asɑ̃ble] *vt* (*joindre, monter*) to assemble, put together; (*amasser*) to gather (together), collect (together); s'~ *vi* to gather.

assener, asséner [asene] *vt*: ~ un coup à qn to deal sb a blow.

assentiment [asɑ̃timɑ̃] *nm* assent, consent; approval.

asseoir [aswaʀ] *vt* (*malade, bébé*) to sit up; to sit down; (*autorité, réputation*) to establish; s'~ *vi* to sit (o.s.) down.

assermenté, e [asɛʀmɑ̃te] *a* sworn, on oath.

asservir [asɛʀviʀ] *vt* to subjugate, enslave.

asseye *etc vb voir* **asseoir**.

assez [ase] *ad* (*suffisamment*) enough, sufficiently; (*passablement*) rather, quite, fairly; ~ de pain/livres enough *ou* sufficient bread/books; vous en avez ~? have you got enough?

assidu, e [asidy] *a* assiduous, painstaking; regular; **assiduités** *nfpl* assiduous attentions.

assied *etc vb voir* **asseoir**.

assiéger [asjeʒe] *vt* to besiege.

assiérai *etc vb voir* **asseoir**.

assiette [asjɛt] *nf* plate; (*contenu*) plate(ful); ~ anglaise assorted cold meats; ~ creuse (soup) dish, soup plate; ~ à dessert dessert plate; ~ de l'impôt basis of (tax) assessment; ~ plate (dinner) plate.

assigner [asine] *vt*: ~ qch à (*poste, part, travail*) to assign sth to; (*limites*) to set sth to; (*cause, effet*) to ascribe sth to; ~ qn à to assign sb to.

assimiler [asimile] *vt* to assimilate, absorb; (*comparer*): ~ **qch/qn à** to liken *ou* compare sth/sb to; **s'~** *vi* (*s'intégrer*) to be assimilated *ou* absorbed.

assis, e [asi, -iz] *pp de* **asseoir** // *a* sitting (down), seated // *nf* (*fig*) basis (*pl* bases), foundation; ~**es** *nfpl* (*JUR*) assizes; (*congrès*) (annual) conference.

assistance [asistɑ̃s] *nf* (*public*) audience; (*aide*) assistance.

assistant, e [asistɑ̃, -ɑ̃t] *nm/f* assistant; (*d'université*) probationary lecturer; **les** ~**s** *nmpl* (*auditeurs etc*) those present; ~**e sociale** social worker.

assisté, e [asiste] *a* (*AUTO*) power assisted.

assister [asiste] *vt* to assist; ~ **à** *vt* (*scène, événement*) to witness; (*conférence, séminaire*) to attend, be at; (*spectacle, match*) to be at, see.

association [asɔsjasjɔ̃] *nf* association.

associé, e [asɔsje] *nm/f* associate; partner.

associer [asɔsje] *vt* to associate; ~ **qn à** (*profits*) to give sb a share of; (*affaire*) to make sb a partner in; (*joie, triomphe*) to include sb in; ~ **qch à** (*joindre, allier*) to combine sth with; **s'~** (*suj pl*) to join together; (*COMM*) to form a partnership: **s'~ à** *vt* (*collaborateur*) to take on (as a partner); **s'~ à qn pour faire** to join (forces) with sb to do; **s'~ à** to be combined with; (*opinions, joie de qn*) to share in.

assoiffé, e [aswafe] *a* thirsty.

assombrir [asɔ̃bʀiʀ] *vt* to darken; (*fig*) to fill with gloom.

assommer [asɔme] *vt* to batter to death; (*étourdir, abrutir*) to knock out; to stun.

Assomption [asɔ̃psjɔ̃] *nf*: **l'~** the Assumption.

assorti, e [asɔʀti] *a* matched, matching; (*varié*) assorted; ~ **à** matching.

assortiment [asɔʀtimɑ̃] *nm* assortment, selection.

assortir [asɔʀtiʀ] *vt* to match; ~ **qch à** to match sth with; ~ **qch de** to accompany sth with; **s'~ de** to be accompanied by.

assoupi, e [asupi] *a* dozing, sleeping; (*fig*) (be)numbed; dulled; stilled.

assouplir [asupliʀ] *vt* to make supple; (*fig*) to relax.

assourdir [asuʀdiʀ] *vt* (*bruit*) to deaden, muffle; (*suj: bruit*) to deafen.

assouvir [asuviʀ] *vt* to satisfy, appease.

assujettir [asyʒetiʀ] *vt* to subject.

assumer [asyme] *vt* (*fonction, emploi*) to assume, take on.

assurance [asyʀɑ̃s] *nf* (*certitude*) assurance; (*confiance en soi*) (self-)confidence; (*contrat*) insurance (policy); (*secteur commercial*) insurance; ~ **maladie** health insurance; ~ **tous risques** (*AUTO*) comprehensive insurance; ~**s**

sociales ≈ National Insurance (*Brit*), ≈ Social Security (*US*); ~**-vie** *nf* life assurance *ou* insurance.

assuré, e [asyʀe] *a* (*certain*): ~ **de** confident of // *nm/f* insured (person); ~**ment** *ad* assuredly, most certainly.

assurer [asyʀe] *vt* to insure; (*stabiliser*) to steady; to stabilize; (*victoire etc*) to ensure; (*frontières, pouvoir*) to make secure; (*service, garde*) to provide; to operate; ~ **qch à qn** (*garantir*) to secure sth for sb; (*certifier*) to assure sb of sth; ~ **à qn que** to assure sb that; ~ **qn de** to assure sb of; **s'~** (**contre**) (*COMM*) to insure o.s. (against); **s'~ de/que** (*vérifier*) to make sure of/that; **s'~** (**de**) (*aide de qn*) to secure.

asthme [asm(ə)] *nm* asthma.

asticot [astiko] *nm* maggot.

astiquer [astike] *vt* to polish, shine.

astre [astʀ(ə)] *nm* star.

astreignant, e [astʀɛɲɑ̃, -ɑ̃t] *a* demanding.

astreindre [astʀɛ̃dʀ(ə)] *vt*: ~ **qn à qch** to force sth upon sb; ~ **qn à faire** to compel *ou* force sb to do.

astrologie [astʀɔlɔʒi] *nf* astrology.

astronaute [astʀɔnot] *nm/f* astronaut.

astronomie [astʀɔnɔmi] *nf* astronomy.

astuce [astys] *nf* shrewdness, astuteness; (*truc*) trick, clever way; (*plaisanterie*) wisecrack; **astucieux, euse** *a* clever.

atelier [atəlje] *nm* workshop; (*de peintre*) studio.

athée [ate] *a* atheistic // *nm/f* atheist.

Athènes [atɛn] *n* Athens.

athlète [atlɛt] *nm/f* (*SPORT*) athlete; **athlétisme** *nm* athletics *sg*.

atlantique [atlɑ̃tik] *a* Atlantic // *nm*: **l'(océan) A~** the Atlantic (Ocean).

atlas [atlɑs] *nm* atlas.

atmosphère [atmɔsfɛʀ] *nf* atmosphere.

atome [atom] *nm* atom; **atomique** *a* atomic, nuclear; (*nombre, masse*) atomic.

atomiseur [atɔmizœʀ] *nm* atomizer.

atone [atɔn] *a* lifeless.

atours [atuʀ] *nmpl* attire *sg*, finery *sg*.

atout [atu] *nm* trump; (*fig*) asset; trump card.

âtre [ɑtʀ(ə)] *nm* hearth.

atroce [atʀɔs] *a* atrocious.

attabler [atable]: **s'~** *vi* to sit down at (the) table.

attachant, e [ataʃɑ̃, -ɑ̃t] *a* engaging, lovable, likeable.

attache [ataʃ] *nf* clip, fastener; (*fig*) tie.

attacher [ataʃe] *vt* to tie up; (*étiquette*) to attach, tie on; (*souliers*) to do up // *vi* (*poêle, riz*) to stick; **s'~ à** (*par affection*) to become attached to; **s'~ à faire** to endeavour to do; ~ **qch à** to tie *ou* attach sth to.

attaque [atak] *nf* attack; (*cérébrale*) stroke; (*d'épilepsie*) fit.

attaquer [atake] *vt* to attack; (*en justice*) to bring an action against, sue; (*travail*) to tackle, set about // *vi* to attack.

attardé, e [ataʀde] *a* (*passants*) late; (*enfant*) backward; (*conceptions*) old-fashioned.

attarder [ataʀde]: **s'~** *vi* to linger; to stay on.

atteindre [atɛ̃dʀ(ə)] *vt* to reach; (*blesser*) to hit; (*émouvoir*) to affect.

atteint, e [atɛ̃, -ɛ̃t] *a* (*MÉD*): **être ~ de** to be suffering from // *nf* attack; **hors d'~e** out of reach; **porter ~e à** to strike a blow at; to undermine.

atteler [atle] *vt* (*cheval, bœufs*) to hitch up; (*wagons*) to couple; **s'~ à** (*travail*) to buckle down to.

attelle [atɛl] *nf* splint.

attenant, e [atnɑ̃, -ɑ̃t] *a*: **~ (à)** adjoining.

attendre [atɑ̃dʀ(ə)] *vt* (*gén*) to wait for; (*être destiné ou réservé à*) to await, be in store for // *vi* to wait; **s'~ à** (*ce que*) to expect (that); **~ un enfant** to be expecting a baby; **~ de faire/d'être** to wait until one does/is; **~ que** to wait until; **~ qch de** to expect sth of; **en attendant** *ad* meanwhile, in the meantime; be that as it may.

attendrir [atɑ̃dʀiʀ] *vt* to move (to pity); (*viande*) to tenderize.

attendu, e [atɑ̃dy] *a* (*visiteur*) expected; **~ que** *cj* considering that, since.

attentat [atɑ̃ta] *nm* assassination attempt; **~ à la bombe** bomb attack; **~ à la pudeur** indecent exposure *q*; indecent assault *q*.

attente [atɑ̃t] *nf* wait; (*espérance*) expectation.

attenter [atɑ̃te]: **~ à** *vt* (*liberté*) to violate; **~ à la vie de qn** to make an attempt on sb's life.

attentif, ive [atɑ̃tif, -iv] *a* (*auditeur*) attentive; (*travail*) scrupulous; careful; **~ à** mindful of; careful to.

attention [atɑ̃sjɔ̃] *nf* attention; (*prévenance*) attention, thoughtfulness *q*; **à l'~ de** for the attention of; **faire ~ (à)** to be careful (of); **faire ~ (à ce) que** to be *ou* make sure that; **~!** careful!, watch out!; **attentionné, e** *a* thoughtful, considerate.

atténuer [atenɥe] *vt* to alleviate, ease; to lessen.

atterrer [atere] *vt* to dismay, appal.

atterrir [ateʀiʀ] *vi* to land; **atterrissage** *nm* landing.

attestation [atɛstasjɔ̃] *nf* certificate.

attester [atɛste] *vt* to testify to.

attirail [atiʀaj] *nm* gear; (*péj*) paraphernalia.

attirant, e [atiʀɑ̃, -ɑ̃t] *a* attractive, appealing.

attirer [atiʀe] *vt* to attract; (*appâter*) to lure, entice; **~ qn dans un coin/vers soi** to draw sb into a corner/towards one; **~ l'attention de qn (sur)** to attract sb's attention (to); to draw sb's attention (to); **s'~ des ennuis** to bring trouble upon o.s., get into trouble.

attiser [atize] *vt* (*feu*) to poke (up).

attitré, e [atitʀe] *a* qualified; accredited; appointed.

attitude [atityd] *nf* attitude; (*position du corps*) bearing.

attouchements [atuʃmɑ̃] *nmpl* touching *sg*; (*sexuels*) fondling *sg*.

attraction [atʀaksjɔ̃] *nf* (*gén*) attraction; (*de cabaret, cirque*) number.

attrait [atʀɛ] *nm* appeal, attraction; lure.

attrape-nigaud [atʀapnigo] *nm* con.

attraper [atʀape] *vt* (*gén*) to catch; (*habitude, amende*) to get, pick up; (*fam: duper*) to con.

attrayant, e [atʀɛjɑ̃, -ɑ̃t] *a* attractive.

attribuer [atʀibɥe] *vt* (*prix*) to award; (*rôle, tâche*) to allocate, assign; (*imputer*): **~ qch à** to attribute sth to; **s'~** *vt* (*s'approprier*) to claim for o.s.

attribut [atʀiby] *nm* attribute; (*LING*) complement.

attrister [atʀiste] *vt* to sadden.

attroupement [atʀupmɑ̃] *nm* crowd, mob.

attrouper [atʀupe]: **s'~** *vi* to gather.

au [o] *prép* + *dét voir* **à**.

aubade [obad] *nf* dawn serenade.

aubaine [obɛn] *nf* godsend; (*financière*) windfall.

aube [ob] *nf* dawn, daybreak; **à l'~** at dawn *ou* daybreak.

aubépine [obepin] *nf* hawthorn.

auberge [obɛʀʒ(ə)] *nf* inn; **~ de jeunesse** youth hostel.

aubergine [obɛʀʒin] *nf* aubergine.

aubergiste [obɛʀʒist(ə)] *nm/f* innkeeper, hotel-keeper.

aucun, e [okœ̃, -yn] *dét* no, *tournure négative* + any; (*positif*) any // *pronom* none, *tournure négative* + any; any(one); *sans* **~ doute** without any doubt; **plus qu'~ autre** more than any other; **~ des deux** neither of the two; **~ d'entre eux** none of them; **d'~s** (*certains*) some; **aucunement** *ad* in no way, not in the least.

audace [odas] *nf* daring, boldness; (*péj*) audacity; **audacieux, euse** *a* daring, bold.

au-delà [odla] *ad* beyond // *nm*: **l'~** the hereafter; **~ de** *prép* beyond.

au-dessous [odsu] *ad* underneath; below; **~ de** *prép* under(neath), below; (*limite, somme etc*) below, under; (*dignité, condition*) below.

au-dessus [odsy] *ad* above; **~ de** *prép* above.

au-devant [odvɑ̃]: **~ de** *prép*: **aller ~**

de (*personne, danger*) to go (out) and meet; (*souhaits de qn*) to anticipate.
audience [odjãs] *nf* audience; (*JUR: séance*) hearing.
audio-visuel, le [odjɔvizɥɛl] *a* audiovisual.
auditeur, trice [oditœʀ, -tʀis] *nm/f* listener.
audition [odisjɔ̃] *nf* (*ouïe, écoute*) hearing; (*JUR: de témoins*) examination; (*MUS, THÉÂTRE: épreuve*) audition.
auditoire [oditwaʀ] *nm* audience.
auge [oʒ] *nf* trough.
augmentation [ɔgmãtɑsjɔ̃] *nf*: ~ (**de salaire**) rise (in salary) (*Brit*), (pay) raise (*US*).
augmenter [ɔgmãte] *vt* (*gén*) to increase; (*salaire, prix*) to increase, raise, put up; (*employé*) to increase the salary of // *vi* to increase.
augure [ɔgyʀ] *nm* soothsayer, oracle; **de bon/mauvais ~** of good/ill omen.
augurer [ɔgyʀe] *vt*: ~ **bien de** to augur well for.
aujourd'hui [oʒuʀdɥi] *ad* today.
aumône [omon] *nf* alms *sg* (*pl inv*); **faire l'~** (**à qn**) to give alms (to sb).
aumônier [omonje] *nm* chaplain.
auparavant [oparavã] *ad* before(hand).
auprès [opʀɛ]: ~ **de** *prép* next to, close to; (*recourir, s'adresser*) to; (*en comparaison de*) compared with.
auquel [okɛl] *prép* + *pronom voir* **lequel.**
aurai *etc vb voir* **avoir.**
auréole [ɔʀeɔl] *nf* halo; (*tache*) ring.
auriculaire [ɔʀikylɛʀ] *nm* little finger.
aurons *etc vb voir* **avoir.**
aurore [ɔʀɔʀ] *nf* dawn, daybreak.
ausculter [ɔskylte] *vt* to sound.
aussi [osi] *ad* (*également*) also, too; (*de comparaison*) as // *cj* therefore, consequently; ~ **fort que** as strong as; **moi** ~ me too; ~ **bien que** (*de même que*) as well as.
aussitôt [osito] *ad* straight away, immediately; ~ **que** as soon as.
austère [ostɛʀ] *a* austere; stern.
austral, e [ɔstʀal] *a* southern.
Australie [ɔstʀali] *nf*: **l'~** Australia; **australien, ne** *a, nm/f* Australian.
autant [otã] *ad* so much; (*comparatif*): ~ (**que**) as much (as); (*nombre*) as many (as); ~ (**de**) so much (*ou* many); as much (*ou* many); ~ **partir** we (*ou* you *etc*) may as well leave; ~ **dire que...** one might as well say that...; **pour** ~ for all that; **pour ~ que** *cj* assuming, as long as; **d'~ plus/mieux (que)** all the more/the better (since).
autel [ɔtɛl] *nm* altar.
auteur [otœʀ] *nm* author.
authentique [ɔtãtik] *a* authentic, genuine.
auto [oto] *nf* car.

auto... [oto] *préfixe* auto..., self-; ~**biographie** *nf* autobiography.
autobus [ɔtɔbys] *nm* bus.
autocar [ɔtɔkaʀ] *nm* coach.
autochtone [ɔtɔktɔn] *nm/f* native.
auto-collant, e [ɔtɔkɔlã, -ãt] *a* self-adhesive; (*enveloppe*) self-seal // *nm* sticker.
auto-couchettes [ɔtɔkuʃɛt] *a*: **train ~** car sleeper train.
autocuiseur [ɔtɔkɥizœʀ] *nm* pressure cooker.
autodéfense [ɔtɔdefãs] *nf* self-defence; **groupe d'~** vigilante committee.
autodidacte [ɔtɔdidakt(ə)] *nm/f* self-taught person.
auto-école [ɔtɔekɔl] *nf* driving school.
autogestion [ɔtɔʒɛstjɔ̃] *nf* self-management.
autographe [ɔtɔgʀaf] *nm* autograph.
auto- mate [ɔtɔmat] *nm* (*machine*) (automatic) machine.
automatique [ɔtɔmatik] *a* automatic // *nm*: **l'~** direct dialling; ~**ment** *ad* automatically; **automatiser** *vt* to automate.
automne [ɔtɔn] *nm* autumn (*Brit*), fall (*US*).
automobile [ɔtɔmɔbil] *a* motor *cpd* // *nf* (motor) car; **l'~** motoring; the car industry; **automobiliste** *nm/f* motorist.
autonome [ɔtɔnɔm] *a* autonomous; **autonomie** *nf* autonomy; (*POL*) self-government, autonomy.
autopsie [ɔtɔpsi] *nf* post-mortem (examination), autopsy.
autoradio [ɔtɔradjo] *nm* car radio.
autorisation [ɔtɔʀizɑsjɔ̃] *nf* permission, authorization; (*papiers*) permit.
autorisé, e [ɔtɔʀize] *a* (*opinion, sources*) authoritative.
autoriser [ɔtɔʀize] *vt* to give permission for, authorize; (*fig*) to allow (of), sanction.
autoritaire [ɔtɔʀitɛʀ] *a* authoritarian.
autorité [ɔtɔʀite] *nf* authority; **faire ~** to be authoritative.
autoroute [ɔtɔʀut] *nf* motorway (*Brit*), highway (*US*).
auto-stop [ɔtɔstɔp] *nm*: **faire de l'~** to hitch-hike; ~**peur, euse** *nm/f* hitch-hiker.
autour [otuʀ] *ad* around; ~ **de** *prép* around; **tout** ~ *ad* all around.
autre [otʀ(ə)] ♦ *a* **1** (*différent*) other, different; **je préférerais un ~ verre** I'd prefer another *ou* a different glass
2 (*supplémentaire*) other; **je voudrais un ~ verre d'eau** I'd like another glass of water
3: ~ **chose** something else; ~ **part** *ad* somewhere else; **d'~ part** *ad* on the other hand
♦ *pronom*: **un ~** another (one); **nous/vous ~s** us/you; **d'~s** others; **l'~** the

other (one); les ~s the others; (*autrui*)
others; l'un et l'~ both of them; se
détester l'un l'~/les uns les ~s to hate
each other *ou* one another; d'une
semaine à l'~ from one week to the
next; (*incessamment*) any week now;
entre ~s among other things.

autrefois [otʀəfwa] *ad* in the past.

autrement [otʀəmɑ̃] *ad* differently; in
another way; (*sinon*) otherwise; ~ dit in
other words.

Autriche [otʀiʃ] *nf*: l'~ Austria; **au-
trichien, ne** *a, nm/f* Austrian.

autruche [otʀyʃ] *nf* ostrich.

autrui [otʀɥi] *pronom* others.

auvent [ovɑ̃] *nm* canopy.

aux [o] *prép* + *dét voir* **à**.

auxiliaire [ɔksiljɛʀ] *a, nm/f* auxiliary.

auxquels, auxquelles [okɛl] *prép* +
pronom voir **lequel**.

av. *abr de* **avenue**.

avachi, e [avaʃi] *a* limp, flabby.

aval [aval] *nm* (*accord*) endorsement,
backing; (*GÉO*): en ~ downstream,
downriver; (*sur une pente*) downhill.

avalanche [avalɑ̃ʃ] *nf* avalanche.

avaler [avale] *vt* to swallow.

avance [avɑ̃s] *nf* (*de troupes etc*) advance; progress; (*d'argent*) advance;
(*opposé à retard*) lead; being ahead of
schedule; ~s *nfpl* overtures; (*amou-
reuses*) advances; (être) en ~ (to be)
early; (*sur un programme*) (to be)
ahead of schedule; à l'~, d'~ in advance.

avancé, e [avɑ̃se] *a* advanced; well on
ou under way.

avancement [avɑ̃smɑ̃] *nm* (*profession-
nel*) promotion.

avancer [avɑ̃se] *vi* to move forward, advance; (*projet, travail*) to make progress; (*être en saillie*) to overhang; to
jut out; (*montre, réveil*) to be fast; to
gain // *vt* to move forward, advance; (*argent*) to advance; (*montre, pendule*) to
put forward; s'~ *vi* to move forward, advance; (*fig*) to commit o.s.; to overhang;
to jut out.

avant [avɑ̃] *prép* before // *ad*: **trop/plus** ~
too far/further forward // *a inv*: **siège/
roue** ~ front seat/wheel // *nm* (*d'un
véhicule, bâtiment*) front; (*SPORT:
joueur*) forward; ~ **qu'il parte/de faire**
before he leaves/doing; ~ **tout** (*surtout*)
above all; à l'~ (*dans un véhicule*) in
(the) front; en ~ *ad* forward(s); en ~ **de**
prép in front of.

avantage [avɑ̃taʒ] *nm* advantage; ~s
sociaux fringe benefits; **avantager** *vt*
(*favoriser*) to favour; (*embellir*) to flatter; **avantageux, euse** *a* attractive; at-
tractively priced.

avant-bras [avɑ̃bʀa] *nm inv* forearm.

avant-dernier, ère [avɑ̃dɛʀnje, -ɛʀ] *a,
nm/f* next to last, last but one.

avant-goût [avɑ̃gu] *nm* foretaste.

avant-hier [avɑ̃tjɛʀ] *ad* the day before
yesterday.

avant-première [avɑ̃pʀəmjɛʀ] *nf* (*de
film*) preview.

avant-projet [avɑ̃pʀɔʒɛ] *nm* (preliminary) draft.

avant-propos [avɑ̃pʀɔpo] *nm* foreword.

avant-veille [avɑ̃vɛj] *nf*: l'~ two days
before.

avare [avaʀ] *a* miserly, avaricious // *nm/f*
miser; ~ **de** (*compliments etc*) sparing
of.

avarié, e [avaʀje] *a* rotting.

avaries [avaʀi] *nfpl* (*NAVIG*) damage
sg.

avatar [avataʀ] *nm* misadventure.

avec [avɛk] *prép* with; (*à l'égard de*)
to(wards), with.

avenant, e [avnɑ̃, -ɑ̃t] *a* pleasant; à l'~
ad in keeping.

avènement [avɛnmɑ̃] *nm* (*d'un roi*) ac-
cession, succession; (*d'un changement*)
advent, coming.

avenir [avniʀ] *nm* future; à l'~ in future; **politicien d'~** politician with
prospects *ou* a future.

Avent [avɑ̃] *nm*: l'~ Advent.

aventure [avɑ̃tyʀ] *nf* adventure;
(*amoureuse*) affair; **s'aventurer** *vi* to
venture; **aventureux, euse** *a* adventur-
ous, venturesome; (*projet*) risky,
chancy.

avenue [avny] *nf* avenue.

avérer [aveʀe]: s'~ *vb avec attribut* to
prove (to be).

averse [avɛʀs(ə)] *nf* shower.

averti, e [avɛʀti] *a* (well-)informed.

avertir [avɛʀtiʀ] *vt*: ~ **qn** (de qch/que)
to warn sb (of sth/that); (*renseigner*) to
inform sb (of sth/that); **avertissement**
nm warning; **avertisseur** *nm* horn, siren.

aveu, x [avø] *nm* confession.

aveugle [avœgl(ə)] *a* blind; **aveuglément** *ad* blindly; **aveugler** *vt* to
blind.

aviateur, trice [avjatœʀ, -tʀis] *nm/f*
aviator, pilot.

aviation [avjasjɔ̃] *nf* aviation; (*sport*)
flying; (*MIL*) air force.

avide [avid] *a* eager; (*péj*) greedy,
grasping.

avilir [aviliʀ] *vt* to debase.

avion [avjɔ̃] *nm* (aero)plane (*Brit*),
(air)plane (*US*); **aller (quelque part) en**
~ to go (somewhere) by plane, fly
(somewhere); **par** ~ by airmail; ~ **à
réaction** jet (plane).

aviron [aviʀɔ̃] *nm* oar; (*sport*): l'~ rowing.

avis [avi] *nm* opinion; (*notification*) notice; **changer d'**~ to change one's mind;
jusqu'à nouvel ~ until further notice.

avisé, e [avize] *a* sensible, wise.

aviser [avize] vt (voir) to notice, catch sight of; (informer): ~ **qn de/que** to advise ou inform sb of/that // vi to think about things, assess the situation; **s'~ de qch/que** to become suddenly aware of sth/that; **s'~ de faire** to take it into one's head to do.

avocat, e [avɔka, -at] nm/f (JUR) barrister (Brit), lawyer // nm (CULIN) avocado (pear); ~ **général** assistant public prosecutor.

avoine [avwan] nf oats pl.

avoir [avwaʀ] ♦ nm assets pl, resources pl; (COMM) credit
♦ vt **1** (posséder) to have; **elle a 2 enfants/une belle maison** she has (got) 2 children/a lovely house; **il a les yeux bleus** he has (got) blue eyes
2 (âge, dimensions) to be; **il a 3 ans** he is 3 (years old); **le mur a 3 mètres de haut** the wall is 3 metres high; voir **faim, peur** etc
3 (fam: duper) to do, have; **on vous a eu!** you've been done ou had!
4: **en ~ contre qn** to have a grudge against sb; **en ~ assez** to be fed up; **j'en ai pour une demi-heure** it'll take me half an hour
♦ vb auxiliaire **1** to have; ~ **mangé/ dormi** to have eaten/slept
2 (avoir + à + inf): ~ **à faire qch** to have to do sth; **vous n'avez qu'à lui demander** you only have to ask him
♦ vb impersonnel **1**: **il y a** (+ sing) there is; (+ pl) there are; **qu'y-a-t-il?, qu'est-ce qu'il y a?** what's the matter?, what is it?; **il doit y ~ une explication** there must be an explanation; **il n'y a qu'à ...** we (ou you etc) will just have to ...
2 (temporel): **il y a 10 ans** 10 years ago; **il y a 10 ans/longtemps que je le sais** I've known it for 10 years/a long time; **il y a 10 ans qu'il est arrivé** it's 10 years since he arrived.

avoisiner [avwazine] vt to be near ou close to; (fig) to border ou verge on.

avortement [avɔrtəmã] nm abortion.

avorter [avɔrte] vi (MÉD) to have an abortion; (fig) to fail.

avoué, e [avwe] a avowed // nm (JUR) ≈ solicitor.

avouer [avwe] vt (crime, défaut) to confess (to); ~ **avoir fait/que** to admit ou confess to having done/that.

avril [avril] nm April.

axe [aks(ə)] nm axis (pl axes); (de roue etc) axle; (fig) main line; ~ **routier** trunk road, main road; **axer** vt: **axer qch sur** to centre sth on.

ayons etc vb voir **avoir**.

azote [azɔt] nm nitrogen.

B

babines [babin] nfpl chops.

babiole [babjɔl] nf (bibelot) trinket; (vétille) trifle.

bâbord [babɔr] nm: **à** ou **par ~** to port, on the port side.

baby-foot [babifut] nm table football.

bac [bak] abr m de baccalauréat // nm (bateau) ferry; (récipient) tub; tray; tank.

baccalauréat [bakalɔrea] nm high school diploma.

bachelier, ière [baʃəlje, -jɛr] nm/f holder of the baccalauréat.

bâcher [baʃe] vt to cover (with a canvas sheet ou a tarpaulin).

bachot [baʃo] abr m de baccalauréat.

bachoter [baʃɔte] vi (fam) to cram (for an exam).

bâcler [bakle] vt to botch (up).

badaud, e [bado, -od] nm/f idle onlooker, stroller.

badigeonner [badiʒɔne] vt to distemper; to colourwash; (barbouiller) to daub.

badin, e [badɛ̃, -in] a playful.

badiner [badine] vi: ~ **avec qch** to treat sth lightly.

badminton [badmintɔn] nm badminton.

baffe [baf] nf (fam) slap, clout.

bafouer [bafwe] vt to deride, ridicule.

bafouiller [bafuje] vi, vt to stammer.

bagage [bagaʒ] nm: ~**s** luggage sg; ~**s à main** hand-luggage.

bagarre [bagar] nf fight, brawl; **se bagarrer** vi to have a fight ou scuffle, fight.

bagatelle [bagatɛl] nf trifle.

bagne [baɲ] nm penal colony.

bagnole [baɲɔl] nf (fam) car.

bagout [bagu] nm: **avoir du ~** to have the gift of the gab.

bague [bag] nf ring; ~ **de fiançailles** engagement ring; ~ **de serrage** clip.

baguette [bagɛt] nf stick; (cuisine chinoise) chopstick; (de chef d'orchestre) baton; (pain) stick of (French) bread; ~ **magique** magic wand.

bahut [bay] nm chest.

baie [bɛ] nf (GÉO) bay; (fruit) berry; ~ (vitrée) picture window.

baignade [bɛɲad] nf bathing.

baigner [bɛɲe] vt (bébé) to bath; **se ~** vi to have a swim, go swimming ou bathing; **baignoire** nf bath(tub).

bail, baux [baj, bo] nm lease.

bâiller [baje] vi to yawn; (être ouvert) to gape.

bailleur [bajœr] nm: ~ **de fonds** sponsor, backer.

bâillon [bajɔ̃] nm gag; **bâillonner** vt to gag.

bain [bɛ̃] nm bath; **prendre un ~** to have a bath; **se mettre dans le ~** (fig) to get into it ou things; **~ de foule** walkabout; **prendre un ~ de soleil** to sunbathe; **~s de mer** sea bathing sg; **faire chauffer au ~-marie** (boîte etc) to immerse in boiling water.

baiser [beze] nm kiss // vt (main, front) to kiss; (fam!) to screw (!).

baisse [bɛs] nf fall, drop; '**~ sur la viande**' 'meat prices down'.

baisser [bese] vt lower; (radio, chauffage) to turn down; (AUTO: phares) to dip (Brit), to lower (US) // vi to fall, drop, go down; **se ~** vi to bend down.

bal [bal] nm dance; (grande soirée) ball; **~ costumé** fancy-dress ball.

balader [balade] vt (traîner) to trail round; **se ~** vi to go for a walk ou stroll; to go for a drive.

balafre [balafʀ(ə)] nf gash, slash; (cicatrice) scar.

balai [balɛ] nm broom, brush; **~-brosse** nm (long-handled) scrubbing brush.

balance [balɑ̃s] nf scales pl; (de précision) balance; (signe): **la B~** Libra.

balancer [balɑ̃se] vt to swing (lancer) to fling, chuck; (renvoyer, jeter) to chuck out // vi to swing; **se ~** vi to swing; to rock; to sway; **se ~ de** (fam) not to care about; **balancier** nm (de pendule) pendulum; (perche) (balancing) pole; **balançoire** nf swing; (sur pivot) seesaw.

balayer [baleje] vt (feuilles etc) to sweep up, brush up; (pièce) to sweep; (chasser) to sweep away; to sweep aside; (suj: radar) to scan; **balayeur, euse** nm/f, nf roadsweeper.

balbutier [balbysje] vi, vt to stammer.

balcon [balkɔ̃] nm balcony; (THÉÂTRE) dress circle.

baleine [balɛn] nf whale; (de parapluie, corset) rib; **baleinière** nf whaleboat.

balise [baliz] nf (NAVIG) beacon; (marker) buoy; (AVIAT) runway light, beacon; (AUTO, SKI) sign, marker; **baliser** vt to mark out (with lights etc).

balivernes [balivɛʀn(ə)] nfpl nonsense sg.

ballant, e [balɑ̃, -ɑ̃t] a dangling.

balle [bal] nf (de fusil) bullet; (de sport) ball; (paquet) bale; (fam: franc) franc; **~ perdue** stray bullet.

ballerine [balʀin] nf ballet dancer.

ballet [balɛ] nm ballet.

ballon [balɔ̃] nm (de sport) ball; (jouet, AVIAT) balloon; (de vin) glass; **~ de football** football.

ballot [balo] nm bundle; (péj) nitwit.

ballottage [balɔtaʒ] nm (POL) second ballot.

ballotter [balɔte] vi to roll around; to toss // vt to shake about; to toss.

balnéaire [balneɛʀ] a seaside cpd.

balourd, e [baluʀ, -uʀd(ə)] a clumsy // nm/f clodhopper.

balustrade [balystʀad] nf railings pl, handrail.

bambin [bɑ̃bɛ̃] nm little child.

ban [bɑ̃] nm round of applause, cheer; **~s** nmpl (de mariage) banns; **mettre au ~ de** to outlaw from.

banal, e [banal] a banal, commonplace; (péj) trite.

banane [banan] nf banana.

banc [bɑ̃] nm seat, bench; (de poissons) shoal; **~ d'essai** (fig) testing ground; **~ de sable** sandbank.

bancaire [bɑ̃kɛʀ] a banking, bank cpd.

bancal, e [bɑ̃kal] a wobbly; bow-legged.

bandage [bɑ̃daʒ] nm bandage.

bande [bɑ̃d] nf (de tissu etc) strip; (MÉD) bandage; (motif) stripe; (magnétique etc) tape; (groupe) band; (: péj) bunch; **par la ~** in a roundabout way; **donner de la ~** to list; **faire ~ à part** to keep to o.s.; **~ dessinée** comic strip; **~ sonore** sound track.

bandeau, x [bɑ̃do] nm headband; (sur les yeux) blindfold; (MÉD) head bandage.

bander [bɑ̃de] vt (blessure) to bandage; (muscle) to tense; **~ les yeux à qn** to blindfold sb.

banderole [bɑ̃dʀɔl] nf banner, streamer.

bandit [bɑ̃di] nm bandit; **banditisme** nm violent crime, armed robberies pl.

bandoulière [bɑ̃duljɛʀ] nf: **en ~** (slung ou worn) across the shoulder.

banlieue [bɑ̃ljø] nf suburbs pl; **lignes/quartiers de ~** suburban lines/areas; **trains de ~** commuter trains.

bannière [banjɛʀ] nf banner.

bannir [baniʀ] vt to banish.

banque [bɑ̃k] nf bank; (activités) banking; **~ d'affaires** merchant bank.

banqueroute [bɑ̃kʀut] nf bankruptcy.

banquet [bɑ̃kɛ] nm dinner; (d'apparat) banquet.

banquette [bɑ̃kɛt] nf seat.

banquier [bɑ̃kje] nm banker.

banquise [bɑ̃kiz] nf ice field.

baptême [batɛm] nm christening; baptism; **~ de l'air** first flight.

baquet [bakɛ] nm tub, bucket.

bar [baʀ] nm bar.

baraque [baʀak] nf shed; (fam) house; **~ foraine** fairground stand.

baraqué, e [baʀake] a well-built, hefty.

baraquements [baʀakmɑ̃] nmpl huts (for refugees, workers etc).

baratin [baʀatɛ̃] nm (fam) smooth talk, patter; **baratiner** vt to chat up.

barbare [baʀbaʀ] a barbaric.

barbe [baʀb(ə)] nf beard; **quelle ~!** (fam) what a drag ou bore!; **à la ~ de qn** under sb's nose; **~ à papa** candy-floss (Brit), cotton candy (US).

barbelé [baʀbəle] nm barbed wire q.
barboter [baʀbɔte] vi to paddle, dabble.
barboteuse [baʀbɔtøz] nf rompers pl.
barbouiller [baʀbuje] vt to daub; **avoir l'estomac barbouillé** to feel queasy.
barbu, e [baʀby] a bearded.
barda [baʀda] nm (fam) kit, gear.
barde [baʀd(ə)] nf piece of fat bacon.
barder [baʀde] vi (fam): **ça va ~** sparks will fly, things are going to get hot.
barème [baʀɛm] nm scale; table.
baril [baʀil] nm barrel; keg.
baromètre [baʀɔmɛtʀ(ə)] nm barometer.
baron [baʀɔ̃] nm baron; **baronne** nf baroness.
baroque [baʀɔk] a (ART) baroque; (fig) weird.
barque [baʀk(ə)] nf small boat.
barrage [baʀaʒ] nm dam; (sur route) roadblock, barricade.
barre [baʀ] nf bar; (NAVIG) helm; (écrite) line, stroke.
barreau, x [baʀo] nm bar; (JUR): **le ~** the Bar.
barrer [baʀe] vt (route etc) to block; (mot) to cross out; (chèque) to cross (Brit); (NAVIG) to steer; **se ~** vi (fam) to clear off.
barrette [baʀɛt] nf (pour cheveux) (hair) slide (Brit) ou barrette (US).
barricader [baʀikade] vt to barricade.
barrière [baʀjɛʀ] nf fence; (obstacle) barrier; (porte) gate.
barrique [baʀik] nf barrel, cask.
bas, basse [bɑ, bɑs] a low // nm bottom, lower part; (vêtement) stocking // nf (MUS) bass // ad low; (parler) softly; **avoir la vue basse** to be short-sighted; **au ~ mot** at the lowest estimate; **en ~** down below; at (ou to) the bottom; (dans une maison) downstairs; **en ~ de** at the bottom of; **mettre ~** vi to give birth; **à ~ ...!** 'down with ...!'; **~ morceaux** nmpl (viande) cheap cuts.
basané, e [bazane] a tanned, bronzed.
bas-côté [bakote] nm (de route) verge (Brit), shoulder (US).
bascule [baskyl] nf: (jeu de) **~** seesaw; (balance à) **~** scales pl; **fauteuil à ~** rocking chair.
basculer [baskyle] vi to fall over, topple (over); (benne) to tip up // vt to topple over; to tip out, tip up.
base [bɑz] nf base; (POL) rank and file; (fondement, principe) basis (pl bases); **de ~** basic; **à ~ de café** etc coffee etc -based; **~ de données** database; **baser** vt to base; **se baser sur** (preuves) to base one's argument on.
bas-fond [bafɔ̃] nm (NAVIG) shallow; **~s** (fig) dregs.
basilic [bazilik] nm (CULIN) basil.
basket [baskɛt] nm trainer (Brit), sneaker (US); (aussi: **~-ball**) basket-

ball.
basque [bask(ə)] a, nm/f Basque.
basse [bɑs] a, nf voir bas; **~-cour** nf farmyard.
bassin [basɛ̃] nm (cuvette) bowl; (pièce d'eau) pond, pool; (de fontaine, GÉO) basin; (ANAT) pelvis; (portuaire) dock.
basson [basɔ̃] nm bassoon.
bastingage [bastɛ̃gaʒ] nm (ship's) rail.
bas-ventre [bavɑ̃tʀ(ə)] nm (lower part of the) stomach.
bat vb voir **battre**.
bât [bɑ] nm packsaddle.
bataille [bataj] nf battle; fight.
bâtard, e [bɑtaʀ, -aʀd(ə)] nm/f illegitimate child, bastard (péj).
bateau, x [bato] nm boat, ship; **~-mouche** nm (passenger) pleasure boat (on the Seine).
bateleur, euse [batlœʀ, -øz] nm/f street performer.
batelier, ière [batəlje, -jɛʀ] nm/f (de bac) ferryman/woman.
bâti, e [bati] a: **bien ~** well-built.
batifoler [batifɔle] vi to frolic about.
bâtiment [bɑtimɑ̃] nm building; (NAVIG) ship, vessel; (industrie) building trade.
bâtir [bɑtiʀ] vt to build.
bâtisse [bɑtis] nf building.
bâton [bɑtɔ̃] nm stick; **à ~s rompus** informally.
bâtonnier [bɑtɔnje] nm ≈ president of the Bar.
bats vb voir **battre**.
battage [bataʒ] nm (publicité) (hard) plugging.
battant [batɑ̃] nm (de cloche) clapper; (de volets) shutter, flap; (de porte) side; (fig: personne) fighter; **porte à double ~** double door.
battement [batmɑ̃] nm (de cœur) beat; (intervalle) interval (between classes, trains etc); **~ de paupières** blinking q (of eyelids); **10 minutes de ~** 10 minutes to spare.
batterie [batʀi] nf (MIL, ÉLEC) battery; (MUS) drums pl, drum kit; **~ de cuisine** pots and pans pl; kitchen utensils pl.
batteur [batœʀ] nm (MUS) drummer; (appareil) whisk.
battre [batʀ(ə)] vt to beat; (suj: pluie, vagues) to beat ou lash against; (blé) to thresh; (passer au peigne fin) to scour // vi (cœur) to beat; (volets etc) to bang, rattle; **se ~** vi to fight; **~ la mesure** to beat time; **~ en brèche** to demolish; **~ son plein** to be at its height, be going full swing; **~ des mains** to clap one's hands.
battue [baty] nf (chasse) beat; (policière etc) search, hunt.
baume [bom] nm balm.
bavard, e [bavaʀ, -aʀd(ə)] a (very) talkative; gossipy; **bavarder** vi to chatter; (indiscrètement) to gossip; to blab.

bave [bav] *nf* dribble; (*de chien etc*) slobber; (*d'escargot*) slime; **baver** *vi* to dribble; to slobber; **en baver** (*fam*) to have a hard time (of it); **bavette** *nf* bib; **baveux, euse** *a* (*omelette*) runny.

bavure [bavyʀ] *nf* smudge; (*fig*) hitch; blunder.

bayer [baje] *vi:* ~ **aux corneilles** to stand gaping.

bazar [bazaʀ] *nm* general store; (*fam*) jumble; **bazarder** *vt* (*fam*) to chuck out.

B.C.B.G. *sigle a* (= *bon chic bon genre*) preppy, smart and trendy.

B.C.G. *sigle m* (= *bacille Calmette-Guérin*) BCG.

bd. *abr de* **boulevard.**

B.D. *sigle f de* **bande dessinée.**

béant, e [beã, -ãt] *a* gaping.

béat, e [bea, -at] *a* showing open-eyed wonder; blissful; **béatitude** *nf* bliss.

beau(bel), belle, beaux [bo, bɛl] *a* beautiful, lovely; (*homme*) handsome // *nf* (*SPORT*) decider // *ad*: **il fait** ~ the weather's fine; **un** ~ **jour one** (fine) day; **de plus belle** more than ever, even more; **on a** ~ **essayer** however hard we try; **bel et bien** well and truly; **faire le** ~ (*chien*) to sit up and beg.

beaucoup [boku] *ad* **1** a lot; **il boit** ~ he drinks a lot; **il ne boit pas** ~ he doesn't drink much *ou* a lot **2** (*suivi de plus, trop etc*) much, a lot, far; **il est** ~ **plus grand** he is much *ou* a lot taller **3**: ~ **de** (*nombre*) many, a lot of; (*quantité*) a lot of; ~ **d'étudiants/de touristes** a lot of *ou* many students/tourists; ~ **de courage** a lot of courage; **il n'a pas** ~ **d'argent** he hasn't got much *ou* a lot of money **4**: **de** ~ *ad* by far.

beau-fils [bofis] *nm* son-in-law; (*remariage*) stepson.

beau-frère [bofʀɛʀ] *nm* brother-in-law.

beau-père [bopɛʀ] *nm* father-in-law; (*remariage*) stepfather.

beauté [bote] *nf* beauty; **de toute** ~ beautiful; **en** ~ *ad* brilliantly.

beaux-arts [bozaʀ] *nmpl* fine arts.

beaux-parents [bopaʀã] *nmpl* wife's/husband's family *sg ou pl*, in-laws.

bébé [bebe] *nm* baby.

bec [bɛk] *nm* beak, bill; (*de récipient*) spout; lip; (*fam*) mouth; ~ **de gaz** (*street*) gaslamp; ~ **verseur** pouring lip.

bécane [bekan] *nf* (*fam:* vélo) bike.

bec-de-lièvre [bɛkdəljɛvʀ(ə)] *nm* harelip.

bêche [bɛʃ] *nf* spade; **bêcher** *vt* to dig.

bécoter [bekɔte]: **se** ~ *vi* to smooch.

becqueter [bɛkte] *vt* (*fam*) to eat.

bedaine [bədɛn] *nf* paunch.

bedonnant, e [bədɔnã, -ãt] *a* potbellied.

bée [be] *a:* **bouche** ~ gaping.

beffroi [befʀwa] *nm* belfry.

bégayer [begeje] *vt, vi* to stammer.

bègue [bɛg] *nm/f:* **être** ~ to have a stammer.

béguin [begɛ̃] *nm:* **avoir le** ~ **de** *ou* **pour** to have a crush on.

beige [bɛʒ] *a* beige.

beignet [bɛɲɛ] *nm* fritter.

bel [bɛl] *a voir* **beau.**

bêler [bele] *vi* to bleat.

belette [bəlɛt] *nf* weasel.

belge [bɛlʒ(ə)] *a, nm/f* Belgian.

Belgique [bɛlʒik] *nf:* **la** ~ Belgium.

bélier [belje] *nm* ram; (*signe*): **le B~** Aries.

belle [bɛl] *af, nf voir* **beau;** ~-**fille** *nf* daughter-in-law; (*remariage*) stepdaughter; ~-**mère** *nf* mother-in-law; stepmother; ~-**sœur** *nf* sister-in-law.

belliqueux, euse [belikø, -øz] *a* aggressive, warlike.

belvédère [bɛlvedɛʀ] *nm* panoramic viewpoint (*or small building there*).

bémol [bemɔl] *nm* flat.

bénédiction [benediksjɔ̃] *nf* blessing.

bénéfice [benefis] *nm* (*COMM*) profit; (*avantage*) benefit; **bénéficier de** *vt* to enjoy; to benefit by *ou* from; to get, be given; **bénéfique** *a* beneficial.

benêt [bənɛ] *nm* simpleton.

bénévole [benevɔl] *a* voluntary, unpaid.

bénin, igne [benɛ̃, -iɲ] *a* minor, mild; (*tumeur*) benign.

bénir [beniʀ] *vt* to bless; **bénit, e** *a* consecrated; **eau bénite** holy water; **bénitier** *nm* font.

benjamin, e [bɛ̃ʒamɛ̃, -in] *nm/f* youngest child.

benne [bɛn] *nf* skip; (*de téléphérique*) (*cable*) car; ~ **basculante** tipper (*Brit*), dump truck (*US*).

béotien, ne [beɔsjɛ̃, -jɛn] *nm/f* philistine.

B.E.P.C. *sigle m voir* **brevet.**

béquille [bekij] *nf* crutch; (*de bicyclette*) stand.

bercail [bɛʀkaj] *nm* fold.

berceau, x [bɛʀso] *nm* cradle, crib.

bercer [bɛʀse] *vt* to rock, cradle; (*suj: musique etc*) to lull; ~ **qn de** (*promesses etc*) to delude sb with; **berceuse** *nf* lullaby.

béret (basque) [bɛʀɛ(bask(ə))] *nm* beret.

berge [bɛʀʒ(ə)] *nf* bank.

berger, ère [bɛʀʒe, -ɛʀ] *nm/f* shepherd/shepherdess.

berlingot [bɛʀlɛ̃go] *nm* (*emballage*) carton (*pyramid shaped*).

berlue [bɛʀly] *nf:* **j'ai la** ~ I must be seeing things.

berne [bɛʀn(ə)] *nf:* **en** ~ at half-mast.

berner [bɛʀne] *vt* to fool.

besogne [bəzɔɲ] *nf* work *q*, job; **beso-**

gneux, euse a hard-working.
besoin [bəzwɛ̃] nm need; (pauvreté): le ~ need, want; **faire ses ~s** to relieve o.s.; **avoir ~ de qch/faire qch** to need sth/to do sth; **au ~** if need be.
bestiaux [bɛstjo] nmpl cattle.
bestiole [bɛstjɔl] nf (tiny) creature.
bétail [betaj] nm livestock, cattle pl.
bête [bɛt] nf animal; (bestiole) insect, creature // a stupid, silly; **il cherche la petite ~** he's being pernickety ou over-fussy; **~ noire** pet hate.
bêtise [betiz] nf stupidity; stupid thing (to say ou do).
béton [betɔ̃] nm concrete; **(en) ~** (alibi, argument) cast iron; **~ armé** reinforced concrete; **bétonnière** nf cement mixer.
betterave [bɛtrav] nf beetroot (Brit), beet (US); ~ **sucrière** sugar beet.
beugler [bøgle] vi to low; (radio etc) to blare // vt (chanson) to bawl out.
beurre [bœr] nm butter; **beurrer** vt to butter; **beurrier** nm butter dish.
beuverie [bœvri] nf drinking session.
bévue [bevy] nf blunder.
Beyrouth [berut] n Beirut.
bi... [bi] préfixe bi..., two-.
biais [bjɛ] nm (moyen) device, expedient; (aspect) angle; **en ~, de ~** (obliquement) at an angle; (fig) indirectly; **biaiser** vi (fig) to sidestep the issue.
bibelot [biblo] nm trinket, curio.
biberon [bibrɔ̃] nm (feeding) bottle; **nourrir au ~** to bottle-feed.
bible [bibl(ə)] nf bible.
biblio... [biblijo] préfixe: **~bus** nm mobile library van; **~phile** nm/f booklover; **~thécaire** nm/f librarian; **~thèque** nf library; (meuble) bookcase.
bicarbonate [bikarbɔnat] nm: ~ (de soude) bicarbonate of soda.
biceps [bisɛps] nm biceps.
biche [biʃ] nf doe.
bichonner [biʃɔne] vt to groom.
bicolore [bikɔlɔr] a two-coloured.
bicoque [bikɔk] nf (péj) shack.
bicyclette [bisiklɛt] nf bicycle.
bide [bid] nm (fam: ventre) belly; (THÉÂTRE) flop.
bidet [bidɛ] nm bidet.
bidon [bidɔ̃] nm can // a inv (fam) phoney.
bidonville [bidɔ̃vil] nm shanty town.
bidule [bidyl] nm (fam) thingumajig.
bielle [bjɛl] nf connecting rod.
bien [bjɛ̃] ♦ nm **1** (avantage, profit): faire du ~ à qn to do sb good; dire du ~ de to speak well of; **c'est pour son ~** it's for his own good
2 (possession, patrimoine) possession, property; **son ~ le plus précieux** his most treasured possession; **avoir du ~** to have property; **~s** (de consommation etc) (consumer etc) goods

3 (moral): le ~ good; **distinguer le ~ du mal** to tell good from evil
♦ ad **1** (de façon satisfaisante) well; **elle travaille/mange ~** she works/eats well; **croyant ~ faire, je/il ...** thinking I/he was doing the right thing, I/he ...; **c'est ~ fait!** it serves him (ou her etc) right!
2 (valeur intensive) quite; ~ **jeune** quite young; ~ **assez** quite enough; ~ **mieux** (very) much better; **j'espère ~ y aller** I do hope to go; **je veux ~ le faire** (concession) I'm quite willing to do it; **il faut ~ le faire** it has to be done
3: ~ **du temps/des gens** quite a time/a number of people
♦ a inv **1** (en bonne forme, à l'aise): **je me sens ~** I feel fine; **je ne me sens pas ~** I don't feel well; **on est ~ dans ce fauteuil** this chair is very comfortable
2 (joli, beau) good-looking; **tu es ~ dans cette robe** you look good in that dress
3 (satisfaisant) good; **elle est ~, cette maison/secrétaire** it's a good house/she's a good secretary
4 (moralement) right; (: personne) good, nice; (respectable) respectable; **ce n'est pas ~ de ...** it's not right to ...; **elle est ~, cette femme** she's a nice woman, she's a good sort; **des gens ~** respectable people
5 (en bons termes): **être ~ avec qn** to be on good terms with sb
♦ préfixe: **~-aimé, e** a, nm/f beloved; **~-être** nm well-being; **~faisance** nf charity; **~faisant, e** a (chose) beneficial; **~fait** nm act of generosity, benefaction; (de la science etc) benefit; **~faiteur, trice** nm/f benefactor/benefactress; **~fondé** nm soundness; **~fonds** nm property; **~heureux, euse** a happy; (REL) blessed, blest
bien que cj (al)though
bien sûr ad certainly.
bienséant, e [bjɛ̃seɑ̃, -ɑ̃t] a seemly.
bientôt [bjɛ̃to] ad soon; **à ~** see you soon.
bienveillant, e [bjɛ̃vɛjɑ̃, -ɑ̃t] a kindly.
bienvenu, e [bjɛ̃vny] a welcome // nf: **souhaiter la ~e à** to welcome; **~e à** welcome to.
bière [bjɛr] nf (boisson) beer; (cercueil) bier; ~ **blonde** lager; ~ **brune** brown ale; ~ **(à la) pression** draught beer.
biffer [bife] vt to cross out.
bifteck [biftɛk] nm steak.
bifurquer [bifyrke] vi (route) to fork; (véhicule) to turn off.
bigarré, e [bigare] a multicoloured; (disparate) motley.
bigarreau, x [bigaro] nm type of cherry.
bigorneau, x [bigɔrno] nm winkle.
bigot, e [bigo, -ɔt] a (péj) a bigoted.
bigoudi [bigudi] nm curler.
bijou, x [biʒu] nm jewel; **~terie** nf

jeweller's (shop); jewellery; **~tier, ière** *nm/f* jeweller.

bikini [bikini] *nm* bikini.

bilan [bilɑ̃] *nm* (*COMM*) balance sheet(s); end of year statement; (*fig*) (net) outcome; (: *de victimes*) toll; faire le ~ de to assess; to review; déposer son ~ to file a bankruptcy statement.

bile [bil] *nf* bile; se faire de la ~ (*fam*) to worry o.s. sick.

bilieux, euse [biljø, -jøz] *a* bilious; (*fig: colérique*) testy.

bilingue [bilɛ̃g] *a* bilingual.

billard [bijar] *nm* billiards *sg*; billiard table; c'est du ~ (*fam*) it's a cinch.

bille [bij] *nf* (*gén*) ball; (*du jeu de billes*) marble; (*de bois*) log.

billet [bijɛ] *nm* (*aussi:* ~ **de banque**) (bank)note; (*de cinéma, de bus etc*) ticket; (*courte lettre*) note; ~ **circulaire** round-trip ticket; ~ **de faveur** complimentary ticket.

billion [biljɔ̃] *nm* billion (*Brit*), trillion (*US*).

billot [bijo] *nm* block.

bimensuel, le [bimɑ̃sɥɛl] *a* bimonthly.

binette [binɛt] *nf* hoe.

binocle [binɔkl(ə)] *nm* pince-nez.

bio... [bjo] *préfixe* bio...; **~graphie** *nf* biography; **~logie** *nf* biology; **~logique** *a* biological.

Birmanie [birmani] *nf* Burma.

bis, e [bi, biz] *a* (*couleur*) greyish brown // *ad* [bis]: 12 ~ 12a ou A // *excl, nm* [bis] encore // *nf* (*baiser*) kiss; (*vent*) North wind.

bisannuel, le [bizanɥɛl] *a* biennial.

biscornu, e [biskɔrny] *a* twisted.

biscotte [biskɔt] *nf* (*breakfast*) rusk.

biscuit [biskɥi] *nm* biscuit; sponge cake.

bise [biz] *a, nf voir* **bis**.

bissextile [bisɛkstil] *a*: **année ~** leap year.

bistouri [bisturi] *nm* lancet.

bistro(t) [bistro] *nm* bistro, café.

bitume [bitym] *nm* asphalt.

bizarre [bizar] *a* strange, odd.

blafard, e [blafar, -ard(ə)] *a* wan.

blague [blag] *nf* (*propos*) joke; (*farce*) trick; sans ~! no kidding!; ~ **à tabac** tobacco pouch.

blaguer [blage] *vi* to joke // *vt* to tease.

blaireau, x [blɛro] *nm* (*ZOOL*) badger; (*brosse*) shaving brush.

blairer [blere] *vt* (*fam*): je ne peux pas le ~ I can't bear ou stand him.

blâme [blɑm] *nm* blame; (*sanction*) reprimand.

blâmer [blɑme] *vt* to blame.

blanc, blanche [blɑ̃, blɑ̃ʃ] *a* white; (*non imprimé*) blank; (*innocent*) pure // *nm/f* white, white man/woman // *nm* (*couleur*) white; (*espace non écrit*) blank; (*aussi:* ~ **d'œuf**) (egg-)white; (*aussi:* ~ **de poulet**) breast, white meat;

(*aussi:* **vin ~**) white wine // *nf* (*MUS*) minim (*Brit*), half-note (*US*); ~ **cassé** off-white; **chèque en ~** blank cheque; **à ~** *ad* (*chauffer*) white-hot; (*tirer, charger*) with blanks; **~-bec** *nm* greenhorn; **blancheur** *nf* whiteness.

blanchir [blɑ̃ʃir] *vt* (*gén*) to whiten; (*linge*) to launder; (*CULIN*) to blanch; (*fig: disculper*) to clear // *vi* to grow white; (*cheveux*) to go white; **blanchisserie** *nf* laundry.

blaser [blaze] *vt* to make blasé.

blason [blazɔ̃] *nm* coat of arms.

blatte [blat] *nf* cockroach.

blazer [blazɛr] *nm* blazer.

blé [ble] *nm* wheat.

bled [blɛd] *nm* (*péj*) hole.

blême [blɛm] *a* pale.

blessé, e [blese] *a* injured // *nm/f* injured person; casualty.

blesser [blese] *vt* to injure; (*délibérément: MIL etc*) to wound; (*suj: souliers etc, offenser*) to hurt; se ~ to injure o.s.; se ~ au pied *etc* to injure one's foot *etc*.

blessure [blesyr] *nf* injury; wound.

bleu, e [blø] *a* blue; (*bifteck*) very rare // *nm* (*couleur*) blue; (*novice*) greenhorn; (*contusion*) bruise; (*vêtement*: *aussi:* ~**s**) overalls *pl*; ~ **marine** navy blue.

bleuet [bløɛ] *nm* cornflower.

bleuté, e [bløte] *a* blue-shaded.

blinder [blɛ̃de] *vt* to armour; (*fig*) to harden.

bloc [blɔk] *nm* (*de pierre etc*) block; (*de papier à lettres*) pad; (*ensemble*) group, block; **serré à ~** tightened right down; **en ~** as a whole; wholesale; ~ **opératoire** operating *ou* theatre block; ~ **sanitaire** toilet block.

blocage [blɔkaʒ] *nm* blocking; jamming; freezing; (*PSYCH*) hang-up.

bloc-notes [blɔknɔt] *nm* note pad.

blocus [blɔkys] *nm* blockade.

blond, e [blɔ̃, -ɔ̃d] *a* fair; blond; (*sable, blés*) golden; ~ **cendré** ash blond.

bloquer [blɔke] *vt* (*passage*) to block; (*pièce mobile*) to jam; (*crédits, compte*) to freeze.

blottir [blɔtir]: se ~ *vi* to huddle up.

blouse [bluz] *nf* overall.

blouson [bluzɔ̃] *nm* blouson jacket; ~ **noir** (*fig*) ≈ rocker.

bluffer [blœfe] *vi* to bluff.

bobard [bɔbar] *nm* (*fam*) tall story.

bobine [bɔbin] *nf* reel; (*ÉLEC*) coil.

bocage [bɔkaʒ] *nm* grove.

bocal, aux [bɔkal, -o] *nm* jar.

bock [bɔk] *nm* glass of beer.

bœuf [bœf, *pl* bø] *nm* ox (*pl* oxen), steer; (*CULIN*) beef.

bof! [bɔf] *excl* (*fam*) don't care!; (: *pas terrible*) nothing special.

bohème [bɔɛm] *a* happy-go-lucky, unconventional.

bohémien, ne [bɔemjɛ̃, -jɛn] nm/f gipsy.

boire [bwaʀ] vt to drink; (s'imprégner de) to soak up; ~ un coup to have a drink.

bois [bwa] nm wood; de ~, en ~ wooden.

boisé, e [bwaze] a woody, wooded.

boisson [bwasɔ̃] nf drink; pris de ~ drunk, intoxicated.

boîte [bwat] nf box; (entreprise) place, firm; aliments en ~ canned ou tinned (Brit) foods; ~ d'allumettes box of matches; (vide) matchbox; ~ (de conserves) can ou tin (Brit) (of food); à gants glove compartment; ~ aux lettres letter box; ~ de nuit night club; ~ postale (B.P.) PO Box; ~ de vitesses gear box.

boiter [bwate] vi to limp; (fig) to wobble; to be shaky.

boîtier [bwatje] nm case.

boive etc vb voir **boire**.

bol [bɔl] nm bowl; un ~ d'air a breath of fresh air.

bolide [bɔlid] nm racing car; comme un ~ at top speed, like a rocket.

bombance [bɔ̃bɑ̃s] nf: faire ~ to have a feast, revel.

bombarder [bɔ̃baʀde] vt to bomb; ~ qn de (cailloux, lettres) to bombard sb with; **bombardier** nm bomber.

bombe [bɔ̃b] nf bomb; (atomiseur) (aerosol) spray.

bomber [bɔ̃be] vi to bulge; to camber // vt: ~ le torse to swell out one's chest.

bon, bonne [bɔ̃, bɔn] ♦ a 1 (agréable, satisfaisant) good; un ~ repas/restaurant a good meal/restaurant; être ~ en maths to be good at maths 2 (charitable): être ~ (envers) to be good (to) 3 (correct) right; le ~ numéro/moment the right number/moment 4 (souhaits): ~ anniversaire happy birthday; ~ voyage have a good trip; bonne chance good luck; bonne année happy New Year; bonne nuit good night 5 (approprié, apte): ~ à/pour fit to/for 6: ~ enfant a inv accommodating, easygoing; bonne femme nf (péj) woman; de bonne heure ad early; ~ marché a inv, ad cheap; ~ mot nm witticism; ~ sens nm common sense; ~ vivant nm jovial chap; bonnes œuvres nfpl charitable works, charities ♦ nm 1 (billet) voucher; (aussi: ~ cadeau) gift voucher; ~ d'essence petrol coupon; ~ du Trésor Treasury bond 2: avoir du ~ to have its good points; pour de ~ for good ♦ nf (domestique) maid; bonne d'enfant nanny; bonne à tout faire general help ♦ ad: il fait ~ it's ou the weather is fine;

sentir ~ to smell good; tenir ~ to stand firm ♦ excl good!; ah ~? really?

bonbon [bɔ̃bɔ̃] nm (boiled) sweet.

bonbonne [bɔ̃bɔn] nf demijohn.

bond [bɔ̃] nm leap; faire un ~ to leap in the air.

bonde [bɔ̃d] nf (d'évier etc) plug; (: trou) plughole; (de tonneau) bung; bunghole.

bondé, e [bɔ̃de] a packed (full).

bondir [bɔ̃diʀ] vi to leap.

bonheur [bɔnœʀ] nm happiness; porter ~ (à qn) to bring (sb) luck; au petit ~ haphazardly; par ~ fortunately.

bonhomie [bɔnɔmi] nf goodnaturedness.

bonhomme [bɔnɔm] nm (pl bonshommes [bɔ̃zɔm]) fellow; ~ de neige snowman.

bonification [bɔnifikasjɔ̃] nf bonus.

bonifier [bɔnifje] vt to improve.

boniment [bɔnimɑ̃] nm patter q.

bonjour [bɔ̃ʒuʀ] excl, nm hello; good morning (ou afternoon).

bonne [bɔn] a, nf voir bon; ~ment ad: tout ~ment quite simply.

bonnet [bɔnɛ] nm bonnet, hat; (de soutien-gorge) cup; ~ d'âne dunce's cap; ~ de bain bathing cap.

bonneterie [bɔnɛtʀi] nf hosiery.

bonsoir [bɔ̃swaʀ] excl good evening.

bonté [bɔ̃te] nf kindness q.

bonus [bɔnys] nm no-claims bonus.

bord [bɔʀ] nm (de table, verre, falaise) edge; (de rivière, lac) bank; (de route) side; (monter) à ~ (to go) on board; jeter par-dessus ~ to throw overboard; le commandant/les hommes du ~ the ship's master/crew; au ~ de la mer at the seaside; être au ~ des larmes to be on the verge of tears.

bordeaux [bɔʀdo] nm Bordeaux (wine) // a inv maroon.

bordel [bɔʀdɛl] nm brothel; (fam!) bloody mess (!).

border [bɔʀde] vt (être le long de) to border; to line; (garnir): ~ qch de to line sth with; to trim sth with; (qn dans son lit) to tuck up.

bordereau, x [bɔʀdəʀo] nm slip; statement.

bordure [bɔʀdyʀ] nf border; en ~ de on the edge of.

borgne [bɔʀɲ(ə)] a one-eyed.

borne [bɔʀn(ə)] nf boundary stone; (aussi: ~ kilométrique) kilometre-marker, ≈ milestone; ~s nfpl (fig) limits; dépasser les ~s to go too far.

borné, e [bɔʀne] a narrow; narrow-minded.

borner [bɔʀne] vt to limit; to confine; se ~ à faire to content o.s. with doing; to limit o.s. to doing.

bosquet [bɔskɛ] nm grove.

bosse [bɔs] *nf* (*de terrain etc*) bump; (*enflure*) lump; (*du bossu, du chameau*) hump; **avoir le ~ des maths** *etc* to have a gift for maths *etc*; **il a roulé sa ~** he's been around.

bosser [bɔse] *vi* (*fam*) to work; to slave (away).

bossu, e [bɔsy] *nm/f* hunchback.

bot [bo] *am*: **pied ~** club foot.

botanique [bɔtanik] *nf* botany // *a* botanic(al).

botte [bɔt] *nf* (*soulier*) (high) boot; (*gerbe*): **~ de paille** bundle of straw; **~ de radis** bunch of radishes; **~s de caoutchouc** wellington boots.

botter [bɔte] *vt* to put boots on; to kick; (*fam*): **ça me botte** I fancy that.

bottin [bɔtɛ̃] *nm* directory.

bottine [bɔtin] *nf* ankle boot.

bouc [buk] *nm* goat; (*barbe*) goatee; **~ émissaire** scapegoat.

boucan [bukɑ̃] *nm* din, racket.

bouche [buʃ] *nf* mouth; **le ~ à ~** the kiss of life; **~ d'égout** manhole; **~ d'incendie** fire hydrant; **~ de métro** métro entrance.

bouché, e [buʃe] *a* (*temps, ciel*) overcast; (*péj: personne*) thick.

bouchée [buʃe] *nf* mouthful; **~s à la reine** chicken vol-au-vents.

boucher, ère [buʃe, -ɛʀ] *nm/f* butcher // *vt* (*pour colmater*) to stop up; to fill up; (*obstruer*) to block (up); **se ~ le nez** to hold one's nose; **se ~** *vi* (*tuyau etc*) to block up, get blocked up.

boucherie [buʃʀi] *nf* butcher's (shop); (*fig*) slaughter.

bouche-trou [buʃtʀu] *nm* (*fig*) stopgap.

bouchon [buʃɔ̃] *nm* stopper; (*en liège*) cork; (*fig: embouteillage*) holdup; (*PÊCHE*) float; **~ doseur** measuring cap.

boucle [bukl(ə)] *nf* (*forme, figure*) loop; (*objet*) buckle; **~ (de cheveux)** curl; **~ d'oreilles** earring.

bouclé, e [bukle] *a* curly.

boucler [bukle] *vt* (*fermer: ceinture etc*) to fasten; (: *magasin*) to shut; (*terminer*) to finish off; (: *budget*) to balance; (*enfermer*) to shut away; (: *quartier*) to seal off // *vi* to curl.

bouclier [buklije] *nm* shield.

bouddhiste [budist(ə)] *nm/f* Buddhist.

bouder [bude] *vi* to sulk // *vt* to turn one's nose up at; to refuse to have anything to do with.

boudin [budɛ̃] *nm* (*CULIN*) black pudding.

boue [bu] *nf* mud.

bouée [bwe] *nf* buoy; **~ (de sauvetage)** lifebuoy.

boueux, euse [bwø, -øz] *a* muddy // *nm* refuse collector.

bouffe [buf] *nf* (*fam*) grub, food.

bouffée [bufe] *nf* puff; **~ de fièvre/de honte** flush of fever/shame.

bouffer [bufe] *vi* (*fam*) to eat.

bouffi, e [bufi] *a* swollen.

bouge [buʒ] *nm* (low) dive; hovel.

bougeoir [buʒwaʀ] *nm* candlestick.

bougeotte [buʒɔt] *nf*: **avoir la ~** to have the fidgets.

bouger [buʒe] *vi* to move; (*dent etc*) to be loose; (*changer*) to alter; (*agir*) to stir // *vt* to move.

bougie [buʒi] *nf* candle; (*AUTO*) sparking plug.

bougonner [bugɔne] *vi, vt* to grumble.

bouillabaisse [bujabɛs] *nf* type of fish soup.

bouillant, e [bujɑ̃, -ɑ̃t] *a* (*qui bout*) boiling; (*très chaud*) boiling (hot).

bouillie [buji] *nf* gruel; (*de bébé*) cereal; **en ~** (*fig*) crushed.

bouillir [bujiʀ] *vi, vt* to boil.

bouilloire [bujwaʀ] *nf* kettle.

bouillon [bujɔ̃] *nm* (*CULIN*) stock *q*.

bouillonner [bujɔne] *vi* to bubble; (*fig*) to bubble up; to foam.

bouillotte [bujɔt] *nf* hot-water bottle.

boulanger, ère [bulɑ̃ʒe, -ɛʀ] *nm/f* baker.

boulangerie [bulɑ̃ʒʀi] *nf* bakery.

boule [bul] *nf* (*gén*) ball; (*pour jouer*) bowl; (*de machine à écrire*) golf-ball; **~ de neige** snowball.

bouleau, x [bulo] *nm* (silver) birch.

boulet [bulɛ] *nm* (*aussi*: **~ de canon**) cannonball.

boulette [bulɛt] *nf* ball.

boulevard [bulvaʀ] *nm* boulevard.

bouleversement [bulvɛʀsəmɑ̃] *nm* upheaval.

bouleverser [bulvɛʀse] *vt* (*émouvoir*) to overwhelm; (*causer du chagrin*) to distress; (*pays, vie*) to disrupt; (*papiers, objets*) to turn upside down.

boulier [bulje] *nm* abacus.

boulon [bulɔ̃] *nm* bolt.

boulot [bulo] *nm* (*fam: travail*) work.

boulot, te [bulo, -ɔt] *a* plump, tubby.

boum [bum] *nm* bang // *nf* party.

bouquet [bukɛ] *nm* (*de fleurs*) bunch (of flowers), bouquet; (*de persil etc*) bunch; (*parfum*) bouquet.

bouquin [bukɛ̃] *nm* (*fam*) book; **bouquiner** *vi* to read; to browse around (in a bookshop); **bouquiniste** *nm/f* bookseller.

bourbeux, euse [buʀbø, -øz] *a* muddy.

bourbier [buʀbje] *nm* (quag)mire.

bourde [buʀd(ə)] *nf* (*erreur*) howler; (*gaffe*) blunder.

bourdon [buʀdɔ̃] *nm* bumblebee.

bourdonner [buʀdɔne] *vi* to buzz.

bourg [buʀ] *nm* small market town.

bourgeois, e [buʀʒwa, -waz] *a* (*péj*) ≈ (upper) middle class; bourgeois.

bourgeoisie [buʀʒwazi] *nf* ≈ upper

middle classes *pl*; bourgeoisie.
bourgeon [buRʒɔ̃] *nm* bud.
Bourgogne [buRgɔɲ] *nf*: la ~ Burgundy // *nm*: b~ burgundy (wine).
bourguignon, ne [buRgiɲɔ̃, -ɔn] *a* of *ou* from Burgundy, Burgundian.
bourlinguer [buRlẽge] *vi* to knock about a lot, get around a lot.
bourrade [buRad] *nf* shove, thump.
bourrage [buRaʒ] *nm*: ~ de crâne brainwashing; (*SCOL*) cramming.
bourrasque [buRask(ə)] *nf* squall.
bourreau, x [buRo] *nm* executioner; (*fig*) torturer; ~ de travail workaholic.
bourrelet [buRlɛ] *nm* draught excluder; (*de peau*) fold *ou* roll (of flesh).
bourrer [buRe] *vt* (*pipe*) to fill; (*poêle*) to pack; (*valise*) to cram (full); ~ de coups to hammer blows on, pummel.
bourrique [buRik] *nf* (*âne*) ass.
bourru, e [buRy] *a* surly, gruff.
bourse [buRs(ə)] *nf* (*subvention*) grant; (*porte-monnaie*) purse; la B~ the Stock Exchange.
boursoufler [buRsufle] *vt* to puff up, bloat.
bous *vb voir* **bouillir**.
bousculade [buskylad] *nf* rush; crush.
bousculer [buskyle] *vt* to knock over; to knock into; (*fig*) to push, rush.
bouse [buz] *nf* dung *q*.
boussole [busɔl] *nf* compass.
bout [bu] *vb voir* **bouillir** // *nm* bit; (*extrémité: d'un bâton etc*) tip; (: *d'une ficelle, table, rue, période*) end; **au** ~ **de** at the end of, after; **pousser qn à** ~ to push sb to the limit; **venir à** ~ **de** to manage to finish; **à** ~ **portant** at point-blank range; ~ **filtre** filter tip.
boutade [butad] *nf* quip, sally.
boute-en-train [butɑ̃tRɛ̃] *nm inv* live wire (*fig*).
bouteille [butɛj] *nf* bottle; (*de gaz butane*) cylinder.
boutique [butik] *nf* shop; **boutiquier, ière** *nm/f* shopkeeper.
bouton [butɔ̃] *nm* button; (*BOT*) bud; (*sur la peau*) spot; (*de porte*) knob; ~ **de manchette** cuff-link; ~ **d'or** buttercup; **boutonner** *vt* to button up; **boutonnière** *nf* buttonhole; ~-**pression** *nm* press stud.
bouture [butyR] *nf* cutting.
bovins [bɔvɛ̃] *nmpl* cattle.
bowling [boliŋ] *nm* (tenpin) bowling; (*salle*) bowling alley.
box [bɔks] *nm* lock-up (garage); (*d'écurie*) loose-box.
boxe [bɔks(ə)] *nf* boxing.
boyau, x [bwajo] *nm* (*galerie*) passage(way); (narrow) gallery // *nmpl* (*viscères*) entrails, guts.
B.P. *abr de* **boîte postale**.
bracelet [bRaslɛ] *nm* bracelet; ~-**montre** *nm* wristwatch.

braconnier [bRakɔnje] *nm* poacher.
brader [bRade] *vt* to sell off.
braderie [bRadRi] *nf* cut-price shop *ou* stall.
braguette [bRagɛt] *nf* fly *ou* flies *pl* (*Brit*), zipper (*US*).
brailler [bRaje] *vi* to bawl, yell.
braire [bRɛR] *vi* to bray.
braise [bRɛz] *nf* embers *pl*.
brancard [bRɑ̃kaR] *nm* (*civière*) stretcher; (*bras, perche*) shaft; **brancardier** *nm* stretcher-bearer.
branchages [bRɑ̃ʃaʒ] *nmpl* boughs.
branche [bRɑ̃ʃ] *nf* branch.
branché, e [bRɑ̃ʃe] *a* (*fam*) trendy.
brancher [bRɑ̃ʃe] *vt* to connect (up); (*en mettant la prise*) to plug in.
branle [bRɑ̃l] *nm*: **donner le** ~ **à**, **mettre en** ~ to set in motion.
branle-bas [bRɑ̃lba] *nm inv* commotion.
branler [bRɑ̃le] *vi* to be shaky // *vt*: ~ **la tête** to shake one's head.
braquer [bRake] *vi* (*AUTO*) to turn (the wheel) // *vt* (*revolver etc*): ~ **qch sur** to aim sth at, point sth at; (*mettre en colère*): ~ **qn** to put sb's back up.
bras [bRa] *nm* arm // *nmpl* (*fig: travailleurs*) labour *sg*, hands; **saisir qn à** ~-**le-corps** to take hold of sb (a)round the waist; **à** ~ **raccourcis** with fists flying; ~ **droit** (*fig*) right hand man.
brasier [bRazje] *nm* blaze, inferno.
brassard [bRasaR] *nm* armband.
brasse [bRas] *nf* (*nage*) breast-stroke; ~ **papillon** butterfly.
brassée [bRase] *nf* armful.
brasser [bRase] *vt* to mix; ~ **l'argent**/**les affaires** to handle a lot of money/business.
brasserie [bRasRi] *nf* (*restaurant*) café-restaurant; (*usine*) brewery.
bravache [bRavaʃ] *nm* blusterer, braggart.
brave [bRav] *a* (*courageux*) brave; (*bon, gentil*) good, kind.
braver [bRave] *vt* to defy.
bravo [bRavo] *excl* bravo // *nm* cheer.
bravoure [bRavuR] *nf* bravery.
break [bRɛk] *nm* (*AUTO*) estate car.
brebis [bRəbi] *nf* ewe; ~ **galeuse** black sheep.
brèche [bRɛʃ] *nf* breach, gap; **être sur la** ~ (*fig*) to be on the go.
bredouille [bRəduj] *a* empty-handed.
bredouiller [bRəduje] *vi, vt* to mumble, stammer.
bref, brève [bRɛf, bRɛv] *a* short, brief // *ad* in short; **d'un ton** ~ sharply, curtly; **en** ~ in short, in brief.
Brésil [bRezil] *nm* Brazil.
Bretagne [bRətaɲ] *nf* Brittany.
bretelle [bRətɛl] *nf* (*de fusil etc*) sling; (*de vêtement*) strap; (*d'autoroute*) slip road (*Brit*), entrance/exit ramp (*US*); ~**s** *nfpl* (*pour pantalon*) braces (*Brit*),

suspenders (US).

breton, ne [brətɔ̃, -ɔn] a, nm/f Breton.

breuvage [brœvaʒ] nm beverage, drink.

brève [brɛv] a, nf voir **bref.**

brevet [brəvɛ] nm diploma, certificate; ~ (d'invention) patent; ~ d'études du premier cycle (B.E.P.C.) school certificate (taken at age 16); **breveté, e** a patented; (diplômé) qualified.

bribes [brib] nfpl bits, scraps; snatches; par ~ piecemeal.

bricolage [brikɔlaʒ] nm: le ~ do-it-yourself.

bricole [brikɔl] nf trifle; small job.

bricoler [brikɔle] vi to do DIY jobs; to potter about // vt to fix up; to tinker with; **bricoleur, euse** nm/f handyman/woman, DIY enthusiast.

bride [brid] nf bridle; (d'un bonnet) string, tie; à ~ abattue flat out, hell for leather; **laisser la ~ sur le cou** à to give free rein to.

bridé, e [bride] a: yeux ~s slit eyes.

brider [bride] vt (réprimer) to keep in check; (cheval) to bridle; (CULIN: volaille) to truss.

bridge [bridʒ(ə)] nm bridge.

brièvement [brijɛvmã] ad briefly.

brigade [brigad] nf (POLICE) squad; (MIL) brigade; (gén) team.

brigadier [brigadje] nm sergeant.

brigandage [brigãdaʒ] nm robbery.

briguer [brige] vt to aspire to.

brillamment [brijamã] ad brilliantly.

brillant, e [brijã, -ãt] a brilliant; bright; (luisant) shiny, shining // nm (diamant) brilliant.

briller [brije] vi to shine.

brimer [brime] vt to harass; to bully.

brin [brɛ̃] nm (de laine, ficelle etc) strand; (fig): un ~ de a bit of; ~ d'herbe blade of grass; ~ de muguet sprig of lily of the valley.

brindille [brɛ̃dij] nf twig.

brio [brijo] nm: avec ~ with panache.

brioche [brijɔʃ] nf brioche (bun); (fam: ventre) paunch.

brique [brik] nf brick // a inv brick red.

briquer [brike] vt to polish up.

briquet [brikɛ] nm (cigarette) lighter.

brise [briz] nf breeze.

briser [brize] vt, se ~ vi to break.

britannique [britanik] a British // nm/f British person, Briton; les B~s the British.

broc [bro] nm pitcher.

brocante [brɔkãt] nf junk, second-hand goods pl.

brocanteur, euse [brɔkãtœr, -øz] nm/f junkshop owner; junk dealer.

broche [brɔʃ] nf brooch; (CULIN) spit; (MÉD) pin; à la ~ spit-roasted.

broché, e [brɔʃe] a (livre) paper-backed.

brochet [brɔʃɛ] nm pike inv.

brochette [brɔʃɛt] nf skewer.

brochure [brɔʃyr] nf pamphlet, brochure, booklet.

broder [brɔde] vt to embroider // vi to embroider the facts; **broderie** nf embroidery.

broncher [brɔ̃ʃe] vi: sans ~ without flinching; without turning a hair.

bronches [brɔ̃ʃ] nfpl bronchial tubes; **bronchite** nf bronchitis.

bronze [brɔ̃z] nm bronze.

bronzer [brɔ̃ze] vt to tan // vi to get a tan; se ~ to sunbathe.

brosse [brɔs] nf brush; **coiffé en ~** with a crewcut; ~ à cheveux hairbrush; ~ à dents toothbrush; ~ à habits clothes-brush; **brosser** vt (nettoyer) to brush; (fig: tableau etc) to paint; to draw; se brosser les dents to brush one's teeth.

brouette [bruɛt] nf wheelbarrow.

brouhaha [bruaa] nm hubbub.

brouillard [brujar] nm fog.

brouille [bruj] nf quarrel.

brouiller [bruje] vt to mix up; to confuse; (rendre trouble) to cloud; (désunir: amis) to set at odds; se ~ vi (vue) to cloud over; (détails) to become confused; (gens) to fall out.

brouillon, ne [brujɔ̃, -ɔn] a disorganised; unmethodical // nm draft.

broussailles [brusaj] nfpl undergrowth sg; **broussailleux, euse** a bushy.

brousse [brus] nf: la ~ the bush.

brouter [brute] vi to graze.

broutille [brutij] nf trifle.

broyer [brwaje] vt to crush; ~ du noir to be down in the dumps.

bru [bry] nf daughter-in-law.

bruiner [bruine] vb impersonnel: il bruine it's drizzling, there's a drizzle.

bruire [bruir] vi to murmur; to rustle.

bruit [brui] nm: un ~ a noise, a sound; (fig: rumeur) a rumour; le ~ noise; sans ~ without a sound, noiselessly; ~ de fond background noise.

bruitage [bruitaʒ] nm sound effects pl.

brûlant, e [brylã, -ãt] a burning; (liquide) boiling (hot); (regard) fiery.

brûlé, e [bryle] a (fig: démasqué) blown // nm: odeur de ~ smell of burning.

brûle-pourpoint [brylpurpwɛ̃]: à ~ ad point-blank.

brûler [bryle] vt to burn; (suj: eau bouillante) to scald; (consommer: électricité, essence) to use; (feu rouge, signal) to go through // vi to burn; (jeu) to be warm; se ~ to burn o.s.; to scald o.s.; se ~ la cervelle to blow one's brains out.

brûlure [brylyr] nf (lésion) burn; (sensation) burning (sensation); ~s d'estomac heartburn sg.

brume [brym] nf mist.

brun, e [brœ̃, -yn] a brown; (cheveux, personne) dark; **brunir** vi to get a tan.

brusque [bʀysk(ə)] a abrupt; **~ment** ad abruptly; **brusquer** vt to rush.

brut, e [bʀyt] a raw, crude, rough; (COMM) gross; (données) raw // nf brute; (pétrole) ~ crude (oil).

brutal, e, aux [bʀytal, -o] a brutal; **~iser** vt to handle roughly, manhandle.

brute [bʀyt] a, nf voir **brut**.

Bruxelles [bʀysɛl] n Brussels.

bruyamment [bʀɥijamɑ̃] ad noisily.

bruyant, e [bʀɥijɑ̃, -ɑ̃t] a noisy.

bruyère [bʀɥijɛʀ] nf heather.

bu, e pp de **boire**.

buccal, e, aux [bykal, -o] a: par voie ~e orally.

bûche [byʃ] nf log; **prendre une ~** (fig) to come a cropper; ~ **de Noël** Yule log.

bûcher [byʃe] nm pyre; bonfire // vb (fam) vi to swot (Brit), slave (away) // vt to swot up (Brit), slave away at.

bûcheron [byʃʀɔ̃] nm woodcutter.

budget [bydʒɛ] nm budget.

buée [bɥe] nf (sur une vitre) mist; (de l'haleine) steam.

buffet [byfɛ] nm (meuble) sideboard; (de réception) buffet; ~ **(de gare)** (station) buffet, snack bar.

buffle [byfl(ə)] nm buffalo.

buis [bɥi] nm box tree; (bois) box(wood).

buisson [bɥisɔ̃] nm bush.

buissonnière [bɥisɔnjɛʀ] af: faire l'école ~ to skip school.

bulbe [bylb(ə)] nm (BOT, ANAT) bulb; (coupole) onion-shaped dome.

Bulgarie [bylgaʀi] nf Bulgaria.

bulle [byl] nf bubble; (papale) bull.

bulletin [byltɛ̃] nm (communiqué, journal) bulletin; (papier) form; (SCOL) report; ~ **d'informations** news bulletin; ~ **météorologique** weather report; ~ **de salaire** pay-slip; ~ **de santé** medical bulletin; ~ **(de vote)** ballot paper.

bureau, x [byʀo] nm (meuble) desk; (pièce, service) office; ~ **de change** (foreign) exchange office ou bureau; ~ **d'embauche** employment office; ~ **de location** box office; ~ **de poste** post office; ~ **de tabac** tobacconist's (shop); ~ **de vote** polling station; **~cratie** [-kʀasi] nf bureaucracy.

burin [byʀɛ̃] nm cold chisel; (ART) burin.

burlesque [byʀlɛsk(ə)] a ridiculous; (LITTÉRATURE) burlesque.

bus vb [by] voir **boire** // nm [bys] bus.

busqué, e [byske] a (nez) hook(ed).

buste [byst(ə)] nm (ANAT) chest; bust.

but [by] vb voir **boire** // nm (cible) target; (fig) goal; aim; (FOOTBALL etc) goal; de ~ **en blanc** point-blank; avoir pour ~ **de faire** to aim to do; dans le ~ **de** with the intention of.

butane [bytan] nm butane; Calor gas ®.

buter [byte] vi: ~ **contre/sur** to bump into; to stumble against // vt to antagonize; se ~ vi to get obstinate; to dig in one's heels.

butin [bytɛ̃] nm booty, spoils pl; (d'un vol) loot.

butte [byt] nf mound, hillock; être en ~ à to be exposed to.

buvais etc vb voir **boire**.

buvard [byvaʀ] nm blotter.

buvette [byvɛt] nf bar.

buveur, euse [byvœʀ, -øz] nm/f drinker.

C

c' [s] dét voir **ce**.

CA sigle m de **chiffre d'affaires**.

ça [sa] pronom (pour désigner) this; (: plus loin) that; (comme sujet indéfini) it; ~ **va?** how are you?; how are things?; (d'accord?) OK?, all right?; ~ **alors!** well really!; ~ **fait 10 ans (que)** it's 10 years (since); c'est ~ that's right.

çà [sa] ad: ~ **et là** here and there.

cabane [kaban] nf hut, cabin.

cabaret [kabaʀɛ] nm night club.

cabas [kaba] nm shopping bag.

cabillaud [kabijo] nm cod inv.

cabine [kabin] nf (de bateau) cabin; (de plage) (beach) hut; (de piscine etc) cubicle; (de camion, train) cab; (d'avion) cockpit; ~ **d'essayage** fitting room; ~ **spatiale** space capsule; ~ **(téléphonique)** call ou (tele)phone box.

cabinet [kabinɛ] nm (petite pièce) closet; (de médecin) surgery (Brit), office (US); (de notaire etc) office; (: clientèle) practice; (POL) Cabinet; ~s nmpl (w.-c.) toilet sg; ~ **d'affaires** business consultants' (bureau), business partnership; ~ **de toilette** toilet; ~ **de travail** study.

câble [kɑbl(ə)] nm cable.

cabrer [kabʀe] se ~ vi (cheval) to rear up; (avion) to nose up; (fig) to revolt, rebel.

cabriole [kabʀijɔl] nf caper; somersault.

cacahuète [kakaɥɛt] nf peanut.

cacao [kakao] nm cocoa (powder); (boisson) cocoa.

cache [kaʃ] nm mask, card (for masking) // nf hiding place.

cache-cache [kaʃkaʃ] nm: jouer à ~ to play hide-and-seek.

cachemire [kaʃmiʀ] nm cashmere.

cache-nez [kaʃne] nm inv scarf, muffler.

cacher [kaʃe] vt to hide, conceal; ~ **qch à qn** to hide ou conceal sth from sb; se ~ vi to hide; to be hidden ou concealed; il ne s'en cache pas he makes no secret of it.

cachet [kaʃɛ] nm (comprimé) tablet; (sceau: du roi) seal; (: de la poste) postmark; (*rétribution*) fee; (*fig*) style, character; **cacheter** *vt* to seal.

cachette [kaʃɛt] *nf* hiding place; **en ~** on the sly, secretly.

cachot [kaʃo] *nm* dungeon.

cactus [kaktys] *nm* cactus.

cadavre [kadavʀ(ə)] *nm* corpse, (dead) body.

caddie [kadi] *nm* (supermarket) trolley.

cadeau, x [kado] *nm* present, gift; **faire un ~ à qn** to give sb a present *ou* gift; **faire ~ de qch à qn** to make a present of sth to sb, give sb sth as a present.

cadenas [kadna] *nm* padlock.

cadence [kadɑ̃s] *nf* (*MUS*) cadence; (*: tempo*) rhythm; (*de travail etc*) rate; **en ~** rhythmically; in time.

cadet, te [kadɛ, -ɛt] *a* younger; (*le plus jeune*) youngest // *nm/f* youngest child *ou* one, youngest boy *ou* son/girl *ou* daughter.

cadran [kadʀɑ̃] *nm* dial; **~ solaire** sundial.

cadre [kadʀ(ə)] *nm* frame; (*environnement*) surroundings *pl*; (*limites*) scope // *nm/f* (*ADMIN*) managerial employee, executive; **rayer qn des ~s** to dismiss sb; **dans le ~ de** (*fig*) within the framework *ou* context of.

cadrer [kadʀe] *vi*: **~ avec** to tally *ou* correspond with // *vt* to centre.

caduc, uque [kadyk] *a* obsolete; (*BOT*) deciduous.

cafard [kafaʀ] *nm* cockroach; **avoir le ~** to be down in the dumps.

café [kafe] *nm* coffee; (*bistro*) café // *a inv* coffee(-coloured); **~ au lait** white coffee; **~ noir** black coffee; **~ tabac** *tobacconist's or newsagent's also serving coffee and spirits*; **cafetier, ière** *nm/f* café-owner // *nf* (*pot*) coffee-pot.

cafouillage [kafujaʒ] *nm* shambles *sg*.

cage [kaʒ] *nf* cage; **~** (**des buts**) goal; **~ d'escalier** (stair)well; **~ thoracique** rib cage.

cageot [kaʒo] *nm* crate.

cagibi [kaʒibi] *nm* shed.

cagneux, euse [kaɲø, -øz] *a* knock-kneed.

cagnotte [kaɲɔt] *nf* kitty.

cagoule [kagul] *nf* cowl; hood; (*SKI etc*) cagoule.

cahier [kaje] *nm* notebook; **~ de brouillons** roughbook, jotter; **~ d'exercices** exercise book.

cahot [kao] *nm* jolt, bump.

caïd [kaid] *nm* big chief, boss.

caille [kaj] *nf* quail.

cailler [kaje] *vi* (*lait*) to curdle; (*sang*) to clot.

caillot [kajo] *nm* (blood) clot.

caillou, x [kaju] *nm* (little) stone; **~teux, euse** [-tø, -øz] *a* stony; pebbly.

Caire [kɛʀ] *nm*: **le ~** Cairo.

caisse [kɛs] *nf* box; (*où l'on met la re-*

cette) cashbox; till; (*où l'on paye*) cash desk (*Brit*), check-out; (*de banque*) cashier's desk; (*TECH*) case, casing; **~ enregistreuse** cash register; **~ d'épargne** savings bank; **~ de retraite** pension fund; **caissier, ière** *nm/f* cashier.

cajoler [kaʒɔle] *vt* to wheedle, coax; to surround with love.

cake [kɛk] *nm* fruit cake.

calandre [kalɑ̃dʀ(ə)] *nf* radiator grill.

calanque [kalɑ̃k] *nf* rocky inlet.

calcaire [kalkɛʀ] *nm* limestone // *a* (*eau*) hard; (*GÉO*) limestone *cpd*.

calciné, e [kalsine] *a* burnt to ashes.

calcul [kalkyl] *nm* calculation; **le ~** (*SCOL*) arithmetic; **~** (**biliaire**) (gall)stone; **~** (**rénal**) (kidney) stone; **~ateur** *nm*, **~atrice** *nf* calculator.

calculer [kalkyle] *vt* to calculate, work out; (*combiner*) to calculate.

calculette [kalkylɛt] *nf* pocket calculator.

cale [kal] *nf* (*de bateau*) hold; (*en bois*) wedge; **~ sèche** dry dock.

calé, e [kale] *a* (*fam*) clever, bright.

caleçon [kalsɔ̃] *nm* pair of underpants, trunks *pl*; **~ de bain** bathing trunks *pl*.

calembour [kalɑ̃buʀ] *nm* pun.

calendes [kalɑ̃d] *nfpl*: **renvoyer aux ~ grecques** to postpone indefinitely.

calendrier [kalɑ̃dʀije] *nm* calendar; (*fig*) timetable.

calepin [kalpɛ̃] *nm* notebook.

caler [kale] *vt* to wedge; **~** (**son moteur/ véhicule**) to stall (one's engine/vehicle).

calfeutrer [kalføtʀe] *vt* to (make) draughtproof; **se ~** *vi* to make o.s. snug and comfortable.

calibre [kalibʀ(ə)] *nm* (*d'un fruit*) grade; (*d'une arme*) bore, calibre; (*fig*) calibre.

californien, ne [kalifuʀn] *a* astride.

câlin, e [kalɛ̃, -in] *a* cuddly, cuddlesome; tender.

câliner [kaline] *vt* to fondle, cuddle.

calmant [kalmɑ̃] *nm* tranquillizer, sedative; (*pour la douleur*) painkiller.

calme [kalm(ə)] *a* calm, quiet // *nm* calm(ness), quietness.

calmer [kalme] *vt* to calm (down); (*douleur, inquiétude*) to ease, soothe; **se ~** *vi* to calm down.

calomnie [kalɔmni] *nf* slander; (*écrite*) libel; **calomnier** *vt* to slander; to libel.

calorie [kalɔʀi] *nf* calorie.

calorifuge [kalɔʀifyʒ] *a* (heat-)insulating, heat-retaining.

calotte [kalɔt] *nf* (*coiffure*) skullcap; (*gifle*) slap.

calquer [kalke] *vt* to trace; (*fig*) to copy exactly.

calvaire [kalvɛʀ] *nm* (*croix*) wayside cross, calvary; (*souffrances*) suffering.

calvitie [kalvisi] *nf* baldness.

camarade [kamaʀad] *nm/f* friend, pal; (*POL*) comrade; **~rie** *nf* friendship.

cambiste [kɑ̃bist(ə)] *nm* (*COMM*) foreign exchange dealer, exchange agent.

cambouis [kɑ̃bwi] *nm* dirty oil *ou* grease.

cambrer [kɑ̃bʀe] *vt* to arch.

cambriolage [kɑ̃bʀijɔlaʒ] *nm* burglary.

cambrioler [kɑ̃bʀijɔle] *vt* to burgle (*Brit*), burglarize (*US*); **cambrioleur, euse** *nm/f* burglar.

came [kam] *nf*: arbre à ~s camshaft.

camelot [kamlo] *nm* street pedlar.

camelote [kamlɔt] *nf* rubbish, trash, junk.

caméra [kameʀa] *nf* (*CINÉMA*, *TV*) camera; (*d'amateur*) cine-camera.

camion [kamjɔ̃] *nm* lorry (*Brit*), truck; (*plus petit, fermé*) van; ~ de dépannage breakdown (*Brit*) *ou* tow (*US*) truck; **~-citerne** *nm* tanker; **camionnage** *nm* haulage (*Brit*), trucking (*US*); **camionnette** *nf* (small) van; **camionneur** *nm* (*entrepreneur*) haulage contractor (*Brit*), trucker (*US*); (*chauffeur*) lorry (*Brit*) *ou* truck driver; van driver.

camisole [kamizɔl] *nf*: ~ (de force) straitjacket.

camomille [kamɔmij] *nf* camomile; (*boisson*) camomile tea.

camoufler [kamufle] *vt* to camouflage; (*fig*) to conceal, cover up.

camp [kɑ̃] *nm* camp; (*fig*) side.

campagnard, e [kɑ̃paɲaʀ, -aʀd(ə)] *a* country *cpd*.

campagne [kɑ̃paɲ] *nf* country, countryside; (*MIL, POL, COMM*) campaign; à la ~ in the country.

camper [kɑ̃pe] *vi* to camp // *vt* to sketch; se ~ devant to plant o.s. in front of; **campeur, euse** *nm/f* camper.

camphre [kɑ̃fʀ(ə)] *nm* camphor.

camping [kɑ̃piŋ] *nm* camping; (*terrain de*) ~ campsite, camping site; faire du ~ to go camping.

Canada [kanada] *nm*: le ~ Canada; **canadien, ne** *a*, *nm/f* Canadian // *nf* (*veste*) fur-lined jacket.

canaille [kanaj] *nf* (*péj*) scoundrel.

canal, aux [kanal, -o] *nm* canal; (*naturel*) channel.

canalisation [kanalizasjɔ̃] *nf* (*tuyau*) pipe.

canaliser [kanalize] *vt* to canalize; (*fig*) to channel.

canapé [kanape] *nm* settee, sofa.

canard [kanaʀ] *nm* duck.

canari [kanaʀi] *nm* canary.

cancans [kɑ̃kɑ̃] *nmpl* (malicious) gossip *sg*.

cancer [kɑ̃seʀ] *nm* cancer; (*signe*): le C~ Cancer.

cancre [kɑ̃kʀ(ə)] *nm* dunce.

candeur [kɑ̃dœʀ] *nf* ingenuousness, guilelessness.

candi [kɑ̃di] *a inv*: sucre ~ (sugar-)candy.

candidat, e [kɑ̃dida, -at] *nm/f* candidate; (*à un poste*) applicant, candidate; **candidature** *nf* candidature; application; poser sa candidature to submit an application, apply.

candide [kɑ̃did] *a* ingenuous, guileless.

cane [kan] *nf* (female) duck.

caneton [kantɔ̃] *nm* duckling.

canette [kanɛt] *nf* (*de bière*) (flip-top) bottle.

canevas [kanva] *nm* (*COUTURE*) canvas.

caniche [kaniʃ] *nm* poodle.

canicule [kanikyl] *nf* scorching heat.

canif [kanif] *nm* penknife, pocket knife.

canine [kanin] *nf* canine (tooth).

caniveau, x [kanivo] *nm* gutter.

canne [kan] *nf* (walking) stick; ~ à pêche fishing rod; ~ à sucre sugar cane.

cannelle [kanɛl] *nf* cinnamon.

canoë [kanɔe] *nm* canoe; (*sport*) canoeing.

canon [kanɔ̃] *nm* (*arme*) gun; (*HISTOIRE*) cannon; (*d'une arme: tube*) barrel; (*fig*) model; (*MUS*) canon; ~ rayé rifled barrel.

canot [kano] *nm* ding(h)y; ~ pneumatique inflatable ding(h)y; ~ de sauvetage lifeboat; **canotage** *nm* rowing.

canotier [kanɔtje] *nm* boater.

cantatrice [kɑ̃tatʀis] *nf* (opera) singer.

cantine [kɑ̃tin] *nf* canteen.

cantique [kɑ̃tik] *nm* hymn.

canton [kɑ̃tɔ̃] *nm* district consisting of several communes; (*en Suisse*) canton.

cantonade [kɑ̃tɔnad]: à la ~ *ad* to everyone in general; from the rooftops.

cantonner [kɑ̃tɔne] *vt* (*MIL*) to quarter, station; se ~ dans to confine o.s. to.

cantonnier [kɑ̃tɔnje] *nm* roadmender.

canular [kanylaʀ] *nm* hoax.

caoutchouc [kautʃu] *nm* rubber; ~ mousse foam rubber.

cap [kap] *nm* (*GÉO*) cape; headland; (*fig*) hurdle; watershed; (*NAVIG*): changer de ~ to change course; mettre le ~ sur to head *ou* steer for.

C.A.P. *sigle m* (= *Certificat d'aptitude professionnelle*) vocational training certificate taken at secondary school.

capable [kapabl(ə)] *a* able, capable; ~ de qch/faire capable of sth/doing.

capacité [kapasite] *nf* (*compétence*) ability; (*JUR, contenance*) capacity; ~ (en droit) basic legal qualification.

cape [kap] *nf* cape, cloak; rire sous ~ to laugh up one's sleeve.

C.A.P.E.S. [kapɛs] *sigle m* (= *Certificat d'aptitude pédagogique à l'enseignement secondaire*) teaching diploma.

capillaire [kapilɛʀ] *a* (*soins, lotion*) hair

cpd; (vaisseau etc) capillary.
capitaine [kapitɛn] nm captain; ~ des pompiers fire chief, firemaster.
capital, e, aux [kapital, -o] a major; of paramount importance; fundamental // nm capital; (fig) stock; asset // nf (ville) capital; (lettre) capital (letter); // nmpl (fonds) capital sg; ~ (social) authorized capital; ~**iser** vt to amass, build up; ~**isme** nm capitalism; ~**iste** a, nm/f capitalist.
capiteux, euse [kapitø, -øz] a heady.
capitonné, e [kapitɔne] a padded.
caporal, aux [kapɔral, -o] nm lance corporal.
capot [kapo] nm (AUTO) bonnet (Brit), hood (US).
capote [kapɔt] nf (de voiture) hood (Brit), top (US); (fam) condom.
capoter [kapɔte] vi to overturn.
câpre [kɑpʀ(ə)] nf caper.
caprice [kapʀis] nm whim, caprice; passing fancy; **capricieux, euse** a capricious; whimsical; temperamental.
Capricorne [kapʀikɔʀn] nm: le ~ Capricorn.
capsule [kapsyl] nf (de bouteille) cap; (BOT etc, spatiale) capsule.
capter [kapte] vt (ondes radio) to pick up; (eau) to harness; (fig) to win, capture.
captieux, euse [kapsjø, -øz] a specious.
captivité [kaptivite] nf captivity.
capturer [kaptyʀe] vt to capture.
capuche [kapyʃ] nf hood.
capuchon [kapyʃɔ̃] nm hood; (de stylo) cap, top.
capucine [kapysin] nf (BOT) nasturtium.
caquet [kakɛ] nm: rabattre le ~ à qn to bring sb down a peg or two.
caqueter [kakte] vi to cackle.
car [kaʀ] nm coach // cj because, for.
carabine [kaʀabin] nf carbine, rifle.
caractère [kaʀaktɛʀ] nm (gén) character; en ~s gras in bold type; en petits ~s in small print; ~s d'imprimerie (block) capitals; avoir bon/mauvais ~ to be good-/ill-natured; **caractériel, le** a (of) character // nm/f emotionally disturbed child.
caractérisé, e [kaʀakteʀize] a: c'est une grippe ~e it is a clear(-cut) case of flu.
caractéristique [kaʀakteʀistik] a, nf characteristic.
carafe [kaʀaf] nf decanter; carafe.
caraïbe [kaʀaib] a Caribbean // n: les C~s the Caribbean (Islands); la mer des C~s the Caribbean Sea.
carambolage [kaʀɑ̃bɔlaʒ] nm multiple crash, pileup.
caramel [kaʀamɛl] nm (bonbon) caramel, toffee; (substance) caramel.
carapace [kaʀapas] nf shell.

caravane [kaʀavan] nf caravan; **caravaning** nm caravanning; (emplacement) caravan site.
carbone [kaʀbɔn] nm carbon; (feuille) carbon, sheet of carbon paper; (double) carbon (copy).
carbonique [kaʀbɔnik] a: neige ~ dry ice.
carbonisé, e [kaʀbɔnize] a charred.
carboniser [kaʀbɔnize] vt to carbonize; to burn down, reduce to ashes.
carburant [kaʀbyʀɑ̃] nm (motor) fuel.
carburateur [kaʀbyʀatœʀ] nm carburettor.
carcan [kaʀkɑ̃] nm (fig) yoke, shackles pl.
carcasse [kaʀkas] nf carcass; (de véhicule etc) shell.
cardiaque [kaʀdjak] a cardiac, heart cpd // nm/f heart patient.
cardigan [kaʀdigɑ̃] nm cardigan.
cardiologue [kaʀdjɔlɔg] nm/f cardiologist, heart specialist.
carême [kaʀɛm] nm: le C~ Lent.
carence [kaʀɑ̃s] nf incompetence, inadequacy; (manque) deficiency.
caresse [kaʀɛs] nf caress.
caresser [kaʀese] vt to caress, fondle; (fig: projet) to toy with.
cargaison [kaʀgɛzɔ̃] nf cargo, freight.
cargo [kaʀgo] nm cargo boat, freighter.
carie [kaʀi] nf: la ~ (dentaire) tooth decay; une ~ a bad tooth.
carillon [kaʀijɔ̃] nm (d'église) bells pl; (de pendule) chimes pl; (de porte) door chime ou bell.
carlingue [kaʀlɛ̃g] nf cabin.
carnassier, ière [kaʀnasje, -jɛʀ] a carnivorous.
carnaval [kaʀnaval] nm carnival.
carnet [kaʀnɛ] nm (calepin) notebook; (de tickets, timbres etc) book; (d'école) school report; (journal intime) diary; ~ de chèques cheque book.
carotte [kaʀɔt] nf carrot.
carpette [kaʀpɛt] nf rug.
carré, e [kaʀe] a square; (fig: franc) straightforward // nm (de terrain, jardin) patch, plot; (MATH) square; mètre/kilomètre ~ square metre/kilometre.
carreau, x [kaʀo] nm (en faïence etc) (floor) tile; (wall) tile; (de fenêtre) (window) pane; (motif) check, square; (CARTES: couleur) diamonds pl; (: carte) diamond; tissu à ~x checked fabric.
carrefour [kaʀfuʀ] nm crossroads sg.
carrelage [kaʀlaʒ] nm tiling; (tiled) floor.
carrelet [kaʀlɛ] nm (poisson) plaice.
carrément [kaʀemɑ̃] ad straight out, bluntly; completely, altogether.
carrer [kaʀe]: se ~ vi: se ~ dans to settle o.s. comfortably in.
carrière [kaʀjɛʀ] nf (de roches) quarry;

(*métier*) career; **militaire de ~** professional soldier.

carriole [karjɔl] *nf* (*péj*) old cart.

carrossable [karɔsabl(ə)] *a* suitable for (motor) vehicles.

carrosse [karɔs] *nm* (horse-drawn) coach.

carrosserie [karɔsri] *nf* body, coachwork *q*; (*activité, commerce*) coach-building.

carrousel [karuzɛl] *nm* (*ÉQUITATION*) carousel; (*fig*) merry-go-round.

carrure [karyr] *nf* build; (*fig*) stature, calibre.

cartable [kartabl(ə)] *nm* (*d'écolier*) satchel, (school) bag.

carte [kart(ə)] *nf* (*de géographie*) map; (*marine, du ciel*) chart; (*de fichier, d'abonnement etc, à jouer*) card; (*au restaurant*) menu; (*aussi:* **~ postale**) (post) card; (*aussi:* **~ de visite**) (visiting) card; **à la ~** (*au restaurant*) à la carte; **~ bancaire** cash card; **~ de crédit** credit card; **la ~ grise** (*AUTO*) ≈ the (car) registration book, the logbook; **~ d'identité** identity card; **~ routière** road map; **~ de séjour** residence permit.

carter [karter] *nm* sump.

carton [kartɔ̃] *nm* (*matériau*) cardboard; (*boîte*) (cardboard) box; (*d'invitation*) invitation card; **faire un ~** (*au tir*) to have a go at the rifle range; to score a hit; **~** (à dessin) portfolio;

cartonné, e *a* (*livre*) hardback, cased; **~-pâte** *nm* pasteboard.

cartouche [kartuʃ] *nf* cartridge; (*de cigarettes*) carton.

cas [kɑ] *nm* case; **faire peu de ~/grand ~ de** to attach little/great importance to; **en aucun ~** on no account; **au ~ où** in case; **en ~ de** in case of, in the event of; **en ~ de besoin** if need be; **en tout ~** in any case, at any rate; **~ de conscience** matter of conscience.

casanier, ière [kazanje, -jɛr] *a* stay-at-home.

casaque [kazak] *nf* (*de jockey*) blouse.

cascade [kaskad] *nf* waterfall, cascade; (*fig*) stream, torrent.

cascadeur, euse [kaskadœr, -øz] *nm/f* stuntman/girl.

case [kɑz] *nf* (*hutte*) hut; (*compartiment*) compartment; (*pour le courrier*) pigeonhole; (*sur un formulaire, de mots croisés, d'échiquier*) box.

caser [kaze] *vt* (*trouver de la place pour*) to put in *ou* away; to put up; (*fig*) to find a job for; to marry off.

caserne [kazɛrn(ə)] *nf* barracks.

cash [kaʃ] *ad*: **payer ~** to pay cash down.

casier [kazje] *nm* (*à journaux etc*) rack; (*de bureau*) filing cabinet; (*: à cases*) set of pigeonholes; (*case*) compartment; pigeonhole; (*: à clef*) locker; **~**

judiciaire police record.

casino [kazino] *nm* casino.

casque [kask(ə)] *nm* helmet; (*chez le coiffeur*) (hair-)drier; (*pour audition*) (head-) phones *pl*, headset.

casquette [kaskɛt] *nf* cap.

cassant, e [kasɑ̃, -ɑ̃t] *a* brittle; (*fig*) brusque, abrupt.

cassation [kasasjɔ̃] *nf*: **cour de ~** final court of appeal.

casse [kas] *nf* (*pour voitures*): **mettre à la ~** to scrap; (*dégâts*): **il y a eu de la ~** there were a lot of breakages.

casse... [kɑs] *préfixe*: **~-cou** *a inv* daredevil, reckless; **~-croûte** *nm inv* snack; **~-noisette(s)**, **~-noix** *nm inv* nut-crackers *pl*; **~-pieds** (*fam*): **il est ~-pieds** he's a pain (in the neck).

casser [kase] *vt* to break; (*ADMIN: gradé*) to demote; (*JUR*) to quash; **se ~** *vi* to break.

casserole [kasrɔl] *nf* saucepan.

casse-tête [kastɛt] *nm inv* (*jeu*) brain teaser; (*difficultés*) headache (*fig*).

cassette [kasɛt] *nf* (*bande magnétique*) cassette; (*coffret*) casket.

casseur [kasœr] *nm* hooligan.

cassis [kasis] *nm* blackcurrant; (*de la route*) dip, bump.

cassoulet [kasulɛ] *nm* bean and sausage hot-pot.

cassure [kasyr] *nf* break, crack.

castor [kastɔr] *nm* beaver.

castrer [kastre] *vt* (*mâle*) to castrate; (*: cheval*) to geld; (*femelle*) to spay.

catalogue [katalɔg] *nm* catalogue.

cataloguer [katalɔge] *vt* to catalogue, to list; (*péj*) to put a label on.

catalyseur [katalizœr] *nm* catalyst.

cataplasme [kataplasm(ə)] *nm* poultice.

cataracte [katarakt(ə)] *nf* cataract.

catastrophe [katastrɔf] *nf* catastrophe, disaster.

catastrophé [katastrɔfe] *a* (*fam*) deeply saddened.

catch [katʃ] *nm* (all-in) wrestling; **~eur, euse** *nm/f* (all-in) wrestler.

catéchisme [kateʃism(ə)] *nm* catechism.

catégorie [kategɔri] *nf* category.

cathédrale [katedral] *nf* cathedral.

catholique [katɔlik] *a, nm/f* (Roman) Catholic; **pas très ~** a bit shady *ou* fishy.

catimini [katimini]: **en ~** *ad* on the sly.

cauchemar [koʃmar] *nm* nightmare.

cause [koz] *nf* cause; (*JUR*) lawsuit, case; **à ~ de** because of, owing to; **pour ~ de** on account of; owing to; **(et) pour ~** and for (a very) good reason; **être en ~** to be at stake; to be involved; to be in question; **mettre en ~** to implicate; to call into question; **remettre en ~** to challenge.

causer [koze] *vt* to cause // *vi* to chat,

talk.

causerie [kozʀi] *nf* talk.

caution [kosjɔ̃] *nf* guarantee, security; deposit; (*JUR*) bail (bond); (*fig*) backing, support; **payer la ~ de qn** to stand bail for sb; **libéré sous ~** released on bail.

cautionner [kosjɔne] *vt* to guarantee; (*soutenir*) to support.

cavalcade [kavalkad] *nf* (*fig*) stampede.

cavalier, ière [kavalje, -jɛʀ] *a* (*désinvolte*) offhand // *nm/f* rider; (*au bal*) partner // *nm* (*ÉCHECS*) knight; **faire ~ seul** to go it alone.

cave [kav] *nf* cellar // *a*: **yeux ~s** sunken eyes.

caveau, x [kavo] *nm* vault.

caverne [kavɛʀn(ə)] *nf* cave.

caviar [kavjaʀ] *nm* caviar(e).

C.C.P. *sigle m voir* **compte.**

CD *sigle m* = **compact disc.**

ce(c'), cet, cette, ces [sə, sɛt, se] ♦ *dét* (*proximité*) this; these *pl*; (*non-proximité*) that; those *pl*; **cette maison(-ci/-là)** this/that house; **cette nuit** (*qui vient*) tonight; (*passée*) last night ♦ *pronom*: **c'est** it's **ou** it is; **c'est un peintre** he's **ou** he is a painter; **ce sont des peintres** they're **ou** they are painters; **c'est le facteur** *etc* (*à la porte*) it's the postman; **qui est-ce?** who is it?; (*en désignant*) who is he/she?; **qu'est-ce?** what is it? **2**: **~ qui, ~ que** what; (*chose qui*): **il est bête, ~ qui me chagrine** he's stupid, which saddens me; **tout ~ qui bouge** everything that **ou** which moves; **tout ~ que je sais** all I know; **~ dont j'ai parlé** what I talked about; **~ que c'est grand!** it's so big!; *voir aussi* **-ci, est-ce que, n'est-ce pas, c'est-à-dire.**

ceci [səsi] *pronom* this.

cécité [sesite] *nf* blindness.

céder [sede] *vt* to give up // *vi* (*pont, barrage*) to give way; (*personne*) to give in; **~ à** to yield to, give in to.

CEDEX [sedɛks] *sigle m* (= *courrier d'entreprise à distribution exceptionnelle*) postal service for bulk users.

cédille [sedij] *nf* cedilla.

cèdre [sɛdʀ(ə)] *nm* cedar.

C.E.E. *sigle f* (= *Communauté économique européenne*) EEC.

ceinture [sɛ̃tyʀ] *nf* belt; (*taille*) waist; (*fig*) ring; belt; circle; **~ de sécurité** safety **ou** seat belt; **ceinturer** *vt* (*saisir*) to grasp (round the waist).

cela [səla] *pronom* that; (*comme sujet indéfini*) it; **quand/où ~?** when/where (was that)?

célèbre [selɛbʀ(ə)] *a* famous.

célébrer [selebʀe] *vt* to celebrate; (*louer*) to extol.

céleri [sɛlʀi] *nm*: **~(-rave)** celeriac; **~ (en branche)** celery.

célérité [seleʀite] *nf* speed, swiftness.

célibat [seliba] *nm* celibacy; bachelor/spinsterhood.

célibataire [selibatɛʀ] *a* single, unmarried.

celle, celles [sɛl] *pronom voir* **celui.**

cellier [selje] *nm* storeroom.

cellulaire [selylɛʀ] *a*: **voiture ou fourgon ~** prison **ou** police van.

cellule [selyl] *nf* (*gén*) cell.

cellulite [selylit] *nf* excess fat, cellulite.

celui, celle, ceux, celles [səlɥi, sɛl, sø] *pronom* **1**: **~-ci/-là, celle-ci/-là** this one/that one; **ceux-ci, celles-ci** these (ones); **ceux-là, celles-là** those (ones); **~ de mon frère** my brother's; **~ du salon/du dessous** the one in (**ou** from) the lounge/below **2**: **~ qui bouge** the one which **ou** that moves; (*personne*) the one who moves; **~ que je vois** the one (which **ou** that) I see; the one (whom) I see; **~ dont je parle** the one I'm talking about **3** (*valeur indéfinie*): **~ qui veut** whoever wants.

cendre [sɑ̃dʀ(ə)] *nf* ash; **~s** (*d'un foyer*) ash(es), cinders; (*volcaniques*) ash *sg*; (*d'un défunt*) ashes; **sous la ~** (*CULIN*) in (the) embers; **cendrier** *nm* ashtray.

cène [sɛn] *nf*: **la ~** (*Holy*) Communion.

censé, e [sɑ̃se] *a*: **être ~ faire** to be supposed to do.

censeur [sɑ̃sœʀ] *nm* (*SCOL*) deputy-head (*Brit*), vice-principal (*US*); (*CINÉMA, POL*) censor.

censure [sɑ̃syʀ] *nf* censorship.

censurer [sɑ̃syʀe] *vt* (*CINÉMA, PRESSE*) to censor; (*POL*) to censure.

cent [sɑ̃] *num* a hundred, one hundred; **centaine** *nf*: **une centaine (de)** about a hundred, a hundred or so; **plusieurs centaines (de)** several hundred; **des centaines (de)** hundreds (of); **centenaire** *a* a hundred-year-old // *nm* (*anniversaire*) centenary; **centième** *num* hundredth; **centigrade** *nm* centigrade; **centilitre** *nm* centilitre; **centime** *nm* centime; **centimètre** *nm* centimetre; (*ruban*) tape measure, measuring tape.

central, e, aux [sɑ̃tʀal, -o] *a* central // *nm*: **~ (téléphonique)** (telephone) exchange // *nf* power station.

centre [sɑ̃tʀ(ə)] *nm* centre; **~ d'apprentissage** training college; **~ commercial** shopping centre; **le ~-ville** the town centre, downtown (area) (*US*).

centuple [sɑ̃typl(ə)] *nm*: **le ~ de qch** a hundred times sth; **au ~** a hundredfold.

cep [sɛp] *nm* (*vine*) stock.

cèpe [sɛp] *nm* (*edible*) boletus.

cependant [səpɑ̃dɑ̃] *ad* however.

céramique [seʀamik] *nf* ceramics *sg*.

cercle [sɛʀkl(ə)] *nm* circle; (*objet*) band, hoop; **~ vicieux** vicious circle.

cercueil [sɛʀkœj] *nm* coffin.

céréale [sereal] *nf* cereal.
cérémonie [seremɔni] *nf* ceremony; ~s (*péj*) fuss *sg*, to-do *sg*.
cerf [sɛʀ] *nm* stag.
cerfeuil [sɛʀfœj] *nm* chervil.
cerf-volant [sɛʀvɔlɑ̃] *nm* kite.
cerise [sɔʀiz] *nf* cherry; **cerisier** *nm* cherry (tree).
cerné, e [sɛʀne] *a*: les yeux ~s with dark rings *ou* shadows under the eyes.
cerner [sɛʀne] *vt* (*MIL etc*) to surround; (*fig: problème*) to delimit, define.
certain, e [sɛʀtɛ̃, -ɛn] *a* certain // *dét* certain; d'un ~ âge past one's prime, not so young; un ~ temps (quite) some time; ~s *pronom* some; **certainement** *ad* (*probablement*) most probably *ou* likely; (*bien sûr*) certainly, of course.
certes [sɛʀt] *ad* admittedly; of course; indeed (yes).
certificat [sɛʀtifika] *nm* certificate.
certitude [sɛʀtityd] *nf* certainty.
cerveau, x [sɛʀvo] *nm* brain.
cervelas [sɛʀvəla] *nm* saveloy.
cervelle [sɛʀvɛl] *nf* (*ANAT*) brain.
ces [se] *dét voir* **ce**.
C.E.S. *sigle m* (= *Collège d'Enseignement Secondaire*) ≈ (junior) secondary school (*Brit*), ≈ junior high school (*US*).
cesse [sɛs]: **sans ~** *ad* continually, constantly; continuously; **il n'avait de ~ que** he would not rest until.
cesser [sese] *vt* to stop // *vi* to stop, cease; ~ **de faire** to stop doing.
cessez-le-feu [sesefø] *nm inv* ceasefire.
c'est-à-dire [sɛtadiʀ] *ad* that is (to say).
cet [sɛt] *dét voir* **ce**.
cette [sɛt] *dét voir* **ce**.
ceux [sø] *pronom voir* **celui**.
C.F.D.T. *sigle f* = *Confédération française et démocratique du travail*.
C.G.C. *sigle f* = *Confédération générale des cadres*.
C.G.T. *sigle f* = *Confédération générale du travail*.
chacun, e [ʃakœ̃, -yn] *pronom* each; (*indéfini*) everyone, everybody.
chagrin [ʃagʀɛ̃] *nm* grief, sorrow; **chagriner** *vt* to grieve; to bother.
chahut [ʃay] *nm* uproar; **chahuter** *vt* to rag, bait // *vi* to make an uproar.
chai [ʃɛ] *nm* wine store.
chaîne [ʃɛn] *nf* chain; (*RADIO, TV*: *stations*) channel; **travail à la ~** production line work; ~ (**haute-fidélité** *ou* **hi-fi**) hi-fi system; ~ (**de montage** *ou* **de fabrication**) production *ou* assembly line; ~ (**de montagnes**) (mountain) range; ~ (**stéréo**) stereo (system).
chair [ʃɛʀ] *nf* flesh // *a*: (**couleur**) ~ flesh-coloured; **avoir la ~ de poule** to have goosepimples *ou* gooseflesh; **bien en ~** plump, well-padded; **en ~ et en os** in the flesh.

chaire [ʃɛʀ] *nf* (*d'église*) pulpit; (*d'université*) chair.
chaise [ʃɛz] *nf* chair; ~ **longue** deckchair.
chaland [ʃalɑ̃] *nm* (*bateau*) barge.
châle [ʃal] *nm* shawl.
chaleur [ʃalœʀ] *nf* heat; (*fig*) warmth; fire, fervour; heat.
chaleureux, euse [ʃalœʀø, -øz] *a* warm.
chaloupe [ʃalup] *nf* launch; (*de sauvetage*) lifeboat.
chalumeau, x [ʃalymo] *nm* blowlamp, blowtorch.
chalutier [ʃalytje] *nm* trawler.
chamailler [ʃamaje]: **se ~** *vi* to squabble, bicker.
chambard [ʃɑ̃baʀ] *nm* rumpus.
chambouler [ʃɑ̃bule] *vt* to disrupt, turn upside down.
chambranle [ʃɑ̃bʀɑ̃l] *nm* (door) frame.
chambre [ʃɑ̃bʀ(ə)] *nf* bedroom; (*TECH*) chamber; (*POL*) chamber, house; (*JUR*) court; (*COMM*) chamber; federation; **faire ~ à part** to sleep in separate rooms; ~ **à un lit/deux lits** (*à l'hôtel*) single-/twin-bedded room; ~ **à air** (*de pneu*) (inner) tube; ~ **d'amis** spare *ou* guest room; ~ **à coucher** bedroom; ~ **noire** (*PHOTO*) dark room.
chambrer [ʃɑ̃bʀe] *vt* (*vin*) to bring to room temperature.
chameau, x [ʃamo] *nm* camel.
champ [ʃɑ̃] *nm* field; **prendre du ~** to draw back; ~ **de bataille** battlefield; ~ **de courses** racecourse; ~ **de tir** rifle range.
champagne [ʃɑ̃paɲ] *nm* champagne.
champêtre [ʃɑ̃pɛtʀ(ə)] *a* country *cpd*, rural.
champignon [ʃɑ̃piɲɔ̃] *nm* mushroom; (*terme générique*) fungus (*pl* i); ~ **de Paris** button mushroom.
champion, ne [ʃɑ̃pjɔ̃, -jɔn] *a, nm/f* champion; **championnat** *nm* championship.
chance [ʃɑ̃s] *nf*: **la ~** luck; **une ~** a stroke *ou* piece of luck *ou* good fortune; (*occasion*) a lucky break; ~s *nfpl* (*probabilités*) chances; **avoir de la ~** to be lucky.
chanceler [ʃɑ̃sle] *vi* to totter.
chancelier [ʃɑ̃səlje] *nm* (*allemand*) chancellor.
chanceux, euse [ʃɑ̃sø, -øz] *a* lucky.
chandail [ʃɑ̃daj] *nm* (thick) sweater.
chandelier [ʃɑ̃dəlje] *nm* candlestick.
chandelle [ʃɑ̃dɛl] *nf* (tallow) candle; **dîner aux ~s** candlelight dinner.
change [ʃɑ̃ʒ] *nm* (*COMM*) exchange.
changement [ʃɑ̃ʒmɑ̃] *nm* change; ~ **de vitesses** gears; gear change.
changer [ʃɑ̃ʒe] *vt* (*modifier*) to change, alter; (*remplacer, COMM, rhabiller*) to change // *vi* to change, alter; **se ~** *vi* to

change (o.s.); ~ de (remplacer: adresse, nom, voiture etc) to change one's; (échanger, alterner: côté, place, train etc) to change ~ npl; ~ de couleur/direction to change colour/direction; ~ d'idée to change one's mind; ~ de vitesse to change gear.

chanson [ʃɑ̃sɔ̃] nf song.

chant [ʃɑ̃] nm song; (art vocal) singing; (d'église) hymn.

chantage [ʃɑ̃taʒ] nm blackmail; faire du ~ to use blackmail.

chanter [ʃɑ̃te] vt, vi to sing; si cela lui chante (fam) if he feels like it.

chanteur, euse [ʃɑ̃tœʀ, -øz] nm/f singer.

chantier [ʃɑ̃tje] nm (building) site; (sur une route) roadworks pl; mettre en ~ to put in hand; ~ naval shipyard.

chantilly [ʃɑ̃tiji] nf voir crème.

chantonner [ʃɑ̃tɔne] vi, to sing to oneself, hum.

chanvre [ʃɑ̃vʀ(ə)] nm hemp.

chaparder [ʃapaʀde] vt to pinch.

chapeau, x [ʃapo] nm hat; ~ mou trilby.

chapelet [ʃaplɛ] nm (REL) rosary.

chapelle [ʃapɛl] nf chapel; ~ ardente chapel of rest.

chapelure [ʃaplyʀ] nf (dried) breadcrumbs pl.

chapiteau, x [ʃapito] nm (de cirque) marquee, big top.

chapitre [ʃapitʀ(ə)] nm chapter; (fig) subject, matter.

chapitrer [ʃapitʀe] vt to lecture.

chaque [ʃak] dét each, every; (indéfini) every.

char [ʃaʀ] nm (à foin etc) (fardeau) cart, waggon; (de carnaval) float; ~ (d'assaut) tank.

charabia [ʃaʀabja] nm (péj) gibberish.

charade [ʃaʀad] nf riddle; (mimée) charade.

charbon [ʃaʀbɔ̃] nm coal; ~ de bois charcoal.

charcuterie [ʃaʀkytʀi] nf (magasin) pork butcher's shop and delicatessen; (produits) cooked pork meats pl; **charcutier, ère** nm/f pork butcher.

chardon [ʃaʀdɔ̃] nm thistle.

charge [ʃaʀʒ(ə)] nf (fardeau) load, burden; (explosif, ÉLEC, MIL, JUR) charge; (rôle, mission) responsibility; ~s nfpl (du loyer) service charges; à la ~ de (dépendant de) dependent upon; (aux frais de) chargeable to; j'accepte, à ~ de revanche I accept, provided I can do the same for you one day; prendre en ~ to take charge of; (suj: véhicule) to take on; (dépenses) to take care of; ~s sociales social security contributions.

chargement [ʃaʀʒəmɑ̃] nm (objets) load.

charger [ʃaʀʒe] vt (voiture, fusil, caméra) to load; (batterie) to charge // vi

(MIL etc) to charge; se ~ de vt to see to; ~ qn de (faire) qch to put sb in charge of (doing) sth.

chariot [ʃaʀjo] nm trolley; (charrette) waggon; (de machine à écrire) carriage.

charité [ʃaʀite] nf charity; faire la ~ à to give (something) to.

charmant, e [ʃaʀmɑ̃, -ɑ̃t] a charming.

charme [ʃaʀm(ə)] nm charm; **charmer** vt to charm.

charnel, le [ʃaʀnɛl] a carnal.

charnière [ʃaʀnjɛʀ] nf hinge; (fig) turning-point.

charnu, e [ʃaʀny] a fleshy.

charpente [ʃaʀpɑ̃t] nf frame(work); **charpentier** nm carpenter.

charpie [ʃaʀpi] nf: en ~ (fig) in shreds ou ribbons.

charrette [ʃaʀɛt] nf cart.

charrier [ʃaʀje] vt to carry (along); to cart, carry.

charrue [ʃaʀy] nf plough (Brit), plow (US).

chasse [ʃas] nf hunting; (au fusil) shooting; (poursuite) chase; (aussi: ~ d'eau) flush; la ~ est ouverte the hunting season is open; ~ gardée private hunting grounds pl; prendre en ~ to give chase to; tirer la ~ (d'eau) to flush the toilet, pull the chain; ~ à courre hunting.

chassé-croisé [ʃasekʀwaze] nm (fig) mix-up where people miss each other in turn.

chasse-neige [ʃasnɛʒ] nm inv snowplough.

chasser [ʃase] vt to hunt; (expulser) to chase away ou out, drive away ou out; **chasseur, euse** nm/f hunter // nm (avion) fighter.

châssis [ʃɑsi] nm (AUTO) chassis; (cadre) frame; (de jardin) cold frame.

chat [ʃa] nm cat; ~ sauvage wildcat.

châtaigne [ʃatɛɲ] nf chestnut; **châtaignier** nm chestnut (tree).

châtain [ʃatɛ̃] a inv chestnut (brown); chestnut-haired.

château, x [ʃɑto] nm castle; ~ d'eau water tower; ~ fort stronghold, fortified castle.

châtier [ʃatje] vt to punish; (fig: style) to polish; **châtiment** nm punishment.

chaton [ʃatɔ̃] nm (ZOOL) kitten.

chatouiller [ʃatuje] vt to tickle; (l'odorat, le palais) to titillate; **chatouilleux, euse** a ticklish; (fig) touchy, over-sensitive.

chatoyer [ʃatwaje] vi to shimmer.

châtrer [ʃɑtʀe] vt (mâle) to castrate; (: cheval) to geld; (femelle) to spay.

chatte [ʃat] nf (she-)cat.

chaud, e [ʃo, -od] a (gén) warm; (très chaud) hot; (fig) hearty; heated; il fait ~ it's warm; it's hot; avoir ~ to be warm; to be hot; ça me tient ~ it keeps

me warm; **rester au ~** to stay in the warm.
chaudière [ʃodjɛʀ] nf boiler.
chaudron [ʃodʀɔ̃] nm cauldron.
chauffage [ʃofaʒ] nm heating; **~ central** central heating.
chauffard [ʃofaʀ] nm (péj) reckless driver; hit-and-run driver.
chauffe-eau [ʃofo] nm inv water-heater.
chauffer [ʃofe] vt to heat // vi to heat up, warm up; (trop chauffer: moteur) to overheat; **se ~** vi (se mettre en train) to warm up; (au soleil) to warm o.s.
chauffeur [ʃofœʀ] nm driver; (privé) chauffeur.
chaume [ʃom] nm (du toit) thatch.
chaumière [ʃomjɛʀ] nf (thatched) cottage.
chaussée [ʃose] nf road(way).
chausse-pied [ʃospje] nm shoe-horn.
chausser [ʃose] vt (bottes, skis) to put on; (enfant) to put shoes on; **~ du 38/42** to take size 38/42.
chaussette [ʃosɛt] nf sock.
chausson [ʃosɔ̃] nm slipper; (de bébé) bootee; **~ (aux pommes)** (apple) turnover.
chaussure [ʃosyʀ] nf shoe; **~s basses** flat shoes; **~s de ski** ski boots.
chauve [ʃov] a bald.
chauve-souris [ʃovsuʀi] nf bat.
chauvin, e [ʃovɛ̃, -in] a chauvinistic.
chaux [ʃo] nf lime; **blanchi à la ~** whitewashed.
chavirer [ʃaviʀe] vi to capsize.
chef [ʃɛf] nm head, leader; (de cuisine) chef; **en ~** (MIL etc) in chief; **~ d'accusation** charge; **~ d'entreprise** company head; **~ d'état** head of state; **~ de file** (de parti etc) leader; **~ de gare** station master; **~ d'orchestre** conductor.
chef-d'œuvre [ʃɛdœvʀ(ə)] nm masterpiece.
chef-lieu [ʃɛfljø] nm county town.
chemin [ʃəmɛ̃] nm path; (itinéraire, direction, trajet) way; **en ~** on the way; **~ de fer** railway (Brit), railroad (US); **par ~ de fer** by rail.
cheminée [ʃəmine] nf chimney; (à l'intérieur) chimney piece, fireplace; (de bateau) funnel.
cheminement [ʃəminmɑ̃] nm progress; course.
cheminer [ʃəmine] vi to walk (along).
cheminot [ʃəmino] nm railwayman.
chemise [ʃəmiz] nf shirt; (dossier)-folder; **~ de nuit** nightdress.
chemisier [ʃəmizje] nm blouse.
chenal, aux [ʃənal, -o] nm channel.
chêne [ʃɛn] nm oak (tree); (bois) oak.
chenil [ʃənil] nm kennels pl.
chenille [ʃənij] nf (ZOOL) caterpillar; (AUTO) caterpillar track.
chèque [ʃɛk] nm cheque (Brit), check

(US); **~ sans provision** bad cheque; **~ de voyage** traveller's cheque; **chéquier** nm cheque book.
cher, ère [ʃɛʀ] a (aimé) dear; (coûteux) expensive, dear // ad: **cela coûte ~** it's expensive // nf: **la bonne chère** good food.
chercher [ʃɛʀʃe] vt to look for; (gloire etc) to seek; **aller ~** to go for, go and fetch; **~ à faire** to try to do.
chercheur, euse [ʃɛʀʃœʀ, -øz] nm/f researcher, research worker.
chère [ʃɛʀ] a, nf voir **cher**.
chéri, e [ʃeʀi] a beloved, dear; **(mon) ~** darling.
chérir [ʃeʀiʀ] vt to cherish.
cherté [ʃɛʀte] nf: **la ~ de la vie** the high cost of living.
chétif, ive [ʃetif, -iv] a puny, stunted.
cheval, aux [ʃəval, -o] nm horse; (AUTO): **~ (vapeur)** (C.V.) horsepower q; **faire du ~** to ride; **à ~** on horseback; **à ~ sur** astride; (fig) overlapping; **~ de course** race horse.
chevalet [ʃəvalɛ] nm easel.
chevalier [ʃəvalje] nm knight.
chevalière [ʃəvaljɛʀ] nf signet ring.
chevalin, e [ʃəvalɛ̃, -in] a: **boucherie ~e** horse-meat butcher's.
chevaucher [ʃəvoʃe] vi (aussi: se ~) to overlap (each other) // vt to be astride, straddle.
chevaux [ʃəvo] nmpl voir **cheval**.
chevelu, e [ʃəvly] a with a good head of hair, hairy (péj).
chevelure [ʃəvlyʀ] nf hair q.
chevet [ʃəvɛ] nm: **au ~ de qn** at sb's bedside; **lampe de ~** bedside lamp.
cheveu, x [ʃəvø] nm hair // nmpl (chevelure) hair sg; **avoir les ~x courts** to have short hair.
cheville [ʃəvij] nf (ANAT) ankle; (de bois) peg; (pour une vis) plug.
chèvre [ʃɛvʀ(ə)] nf (she-)goat.
chevreau, x [ʃəvʀo] nm kid.
chèvrefeuille [ʃɛvʀəfœj] nm honeysuckle.
chevreuil [ʃəvʀœj] nm roe deer inv; (CULIN) venison.
chevronné, e [ʃəvʀɔne] a seasoned.
chevrotant, e [ʃəvʀɔtɑ̃, -ɑ̃t] a quavering.
chez [ʃe] prép **1** (à la demeure de) at; (: direction) to; **~ qn** at/to sb's house ou place; **~ moi** at home; (direction) home **2** (+ profession) at; (: direction) to; **~ le boulanger/dentiste** at the baker's/dentist's; to the baker's/dentist's **3** (dans le caractère, l'œuvre de) in; **~ les renards/Racine** in foxes/Racine.
chez-soi [ʃeswa] nm inv home.
chic [ʃik] a inv chic, smart; (généreux) nice, decent // nm stylishness; **avoir le ~ de** to have the knack of; **~!** great!
chicane [ʃikan] nf (obstacle) zigzag;

(*querelle*) squabble.

chiche [ʃiʃ] *a* niggardly, mean // *excl* (*à un défi*) you're on!

chichi [ʃiʃi] *nm* (*fam*) fuss.

chicorée [ʃikɔʀe] *nf* (*café*) chicory; (*salade*) endive.

chien [ʃjɛ̃] *nm* dog; en ~ de fusil curled up; ~ de garde guard dog.

chiendent [ʃjɛ̃dɑ̃] *nm* couch grass.

chienne [ʃjɛn] *nf* dog, bitch.

chier [ʃje] *vi* (*fam!*) to crap (!).

chiffon [ʃifɔ̃] *nm* (*piece of*) rag.

chiffonner [ʃifɔne] *vt* to crumple; (*tracasser*) to concern.

chiffonnier [ʃifɔnje] *nm* rag-and-bone man.

chiffre [ʃifʀ(ə)] *nm* (*représentant un nombre*) figure; numeral; (*montant, total*) total, sum; en ~s ronds in round figures; ~ d'affaires turnover; **chiffrer** *vt* (*dépense*) to put a figure to, assess; (*message*) to (en)code, cipher.

chignon [ʃiɲɔ̃] *nm* chignon, bun.

Chili [ʃili] *nm*: le ~ Chile.

chimie [ʃimi] *nf* chemistry; **chimique** *a* chemical; **produits chimiques** chemicals.

Chine [ʃin] *nf*: la ~ China.

chinois, e [ʃinwa, -waz] *a* Chinese // *nm/f* Chinese.

chiot [ʃjo] *nm* pup(py).

chips [ʃips] *nfpl* crisps.

chiquenaude [ʃiknod] *nf* flick, flip.

chiromancien, ne [kiʀɔmɑ̃sjɛ̃, -ɛn] *nm/f* palmist.

chirurgical, e, aux [ʃiʀyʀʒikal, -o] *a* surgical.

chirurgie [ʃiʀyʀʒi] *nf* surgery; ~ esthétique plastic surgery; **chirurgien, ne** *nm/f* surgeon.

choc [ʃɔk] *nm* impact; shock; crash; (*moral*) shock; (*affrontement*) clash.

chocolat [ʃɔkɔla] *nm* chocolate; (*boisson*) (hot) chocolate; ~ au lait milk chocolate.

chœur [kœʀ] *nm* (*chorale*) choir; (*OPÉRA, THÉÂTRE*) chorus; en ~ in chorus.

choisir [ʃwaziʀ] *vt* to choose, select.

choix [ʃwa] *nm* choice, selection; avoir le ~ to have the choice; **premier** ~ (*COMM*) class one; de ~ choice, selected; au ~ as you wish.

chômage [ʃomaʒ] *nm* unemployment; mettre au ~ to make redundant, put out of work; être au ~ to be unemployed *ou* out of work; **chômeur, euse** *nm/f* unemployed person.

chope [ʃɔp] *nf* tankard.

choquer [ʃɔke] *vt* (*offenser*) to shock; (*commotionner*) to shake (up).

choriste [kɔʀist(ə)] *nm/f* choir member; (*OPÉRA*) chorus member.

chorus [kɔʀys] *nm*: faire ~ (avec) to voice one's agreement (with).

chose [ʃoz] *nf* thing; c'est peu de ~ it's

nothing (really); it's not much.

chou, x [ʃu] *nm* cabbage; **mon petit** ~ (my) sweetheart; ~ à la crème cream bun (*made of choux pastry*).

chouchou, te [ʃuʃu, -ut] *nm/f* (*SCOL*) teacher's pet.

choucroute [ʃukʀut] *nf* sauerkraut.

chouette [ʃwɛt] *nf* owl // *a* (*fam*) great, smashing.

chou-fleur [ʃuflœʀ] *nm* cauliflower.

choyer [ʃwaje] *vt* to cherish; to pamper.

chrétien, ne [kʀetjɛ̃, -ɛn] *a, nm/f* Christian.

Christ [kʀist] *nm*: le ~ Christ; **christianisme** *nm* Christianity.

chrome [kʀom] *nm* chromium; **chromé, e** *a* chromium-plated.

chronique [kʀɔnik] *a* chronic // *nf* (*de journal*) column, page; (*historique*) chronicle; (*RADIO, TV*): la ~ sportive/théâtrale the sports/theatre review; la ~ locale local news and gossip.

chronologique [kʀɔnɔlɔʒik] *a* chronological.

chronomètre [kʀɔnɔmɛtʀ(ə)] *nm* stopwatch; **chronométrer** *vt* to time.

chrysanthème [kʀizɑ̃tɛm] *nm* chrysanthemum.

C.H.U. *sigle m* (= *centre hospitalier universitaire*) ≈ (teaching) hospital.

chuchoter [ʃyʃɔte] *vt, vi* to whisper.

chuinter [ʃɥɛ̃te] *vi* to hiss.

chut [ʃyt] *excl* sh!

chute [ʃyt] *nf* fall; (*de bois, papier: déchet*) scrap; la ~ des cheveux hair loss; faire une ~ (de 10 m) to fall (10 m); ~s de pluie/neige rain/snowfalls; (*d'eau*) waterfall; ~ libre free fall.

Chypre [ʃipʀ] Cyprus.

-ci, ci- [si] *ad voir* par, ci-contre, ci-joint *etc* // *dét*: ce garçon-ci/-là this/that boy; ces femmes-ci/-là these/those women.

ci-après [siapʀɛ] *ad* hereafter.

cible [sibl(ə)] *nf* target.

ciboulette [sibulɛt] *nf* (smaller) chive.

cicatrice [sikatʀis] *nf* scar.

cicatriser [sikatʀize] *vt* to heal.

ci-contre [sikɔ̃tʀ(ə)] *ad* opposite.

ci-dessous [sidəsu] *ad* below.

ci-dessus [sidəsy] *ad* above.

cidre [sidʀ(ə)] *nm* cider.

Cie *abr* (= *compagnie*) Co.

ciel [sjɛl] *nm* sky; (*REL*) heaven; **cieux** *nmpl* sky sg, skies; à ~ ouvert open-air; (*mine*) opencast.

cierge [sjɛʀʒ(ə)] *nm* candle.

cieux [sjø] *nmpl voir* ciel.

cigale [sigal] *nf* cicada.

cigare [sigaʀ] *nm* cigar.

cigarette [sigaʀɛt] *nf* cigarette.

ci-gît [siʒi] *ad* + *vb* here lies.

cigogne [sigɔɲ] *nf* stork.

ci-inclus, e [siɛ̃kly, -yz] *a, ad* enclosed.

ci-joint, e [siʒwɛ̃, -ɛ̃t] *a, ad* enclosed.

cil [sil] *nm* (eye)lash.

ciller [sije] *vi* to blink.

cime [sim] *nf* top; (*montagne*) peak.

ciment [simɑ̃] *nm* cement; ~ armé reinforced concrete.

cimetière [simtjɛʀ] *nm* cemetery; (*d'église*) churchyard.

cinéaste [sineast(ə)] *nm/f* film-maker.

cinéma [sinema] *nm* cinema; ~tographique *a* film *cpd*, cinema *cpd*.

cinéphile [sinefil] *nm/f* cinema-goer.

cinglant, e [sɛ̃glɑ̃, -ɑ̃t] *a* (*échec*) crushing.

cinglé, e [sɛ̃gle] *a* (*fam*) crazy.

cingler [sɛ̃gle] *vt* to lash; (*fig*) to sting.

cinq [sɛ̃k] *num* five.

cinquantaine [sɛ̃kɑ̃tɛn] *nf*: une ~ (de) about fifty; avoir la ~ (*âge*) to be around fifty.

cinquante [sɛ̃kɑ̃t] *num* fifty; ~naire *a, nm/f* fifty-year-old.

cinquième [sɛ̃kjɛm] *num* fifth.

cintre [sɛ̃tʀ(ə)] *nm* coat-hanger.

cintré, e [sɛ̃tʀe] *a* (*chemise*) fitted.

cirage [siʀaʒ] *nm* (shoe) polish.

circonflexe [siʀkɔ̃flɛks(ə)] *a*: accent ~ circumflex accent.

circonscription [siʀkɔ̃skʀipsjɔ̃] *nf* district; ~ électorale (*d'un député*) constituency.

circonscrire [siʀkɔ̃skʀiʀ] *vt* to define, delimit; (*incendie*) to contain.

circonstance [siʀkɔ̃stɑ̃s] *nf* circumstance; (*occasion*) occasion.

circonstancié, e [siʀkɔ̃stɑ̃sje] *a* detailed.

circonvenir [siʀkɔ̃vniʀ] *vt* to circumvent.

circuit [siʀkɥi] *nm* (*trajet*) tour, (round) trip; (*ÉLEC, TECH*) circuit.

circulaire [siʀkylɛʀ] *a, nf* circular.

circulation [siʀkylasjɔ̃] *nf* circulation; (*AUTO*): la ~ (the) traffic.

circuler [siʀkyle] *vi* to drive (along); to walk along; (*train etc*) to run; (*sang, devises*) to circulate; faire ~ (*nouvelle*) to spread (about), circulate; (*badauds*) to move on.

cire [siʀ] *nf* wax.

ciré [siʀe] *nm* oilskin.

cirer [siʀe] *vt* to wax, polish.

cirque [siʀk(ə)] *nm* circus; (*GÉO*) cirque; (*fig*) chaos, bedlam; carry-on.

cisaille(s) [sizaj] *nf(pl)* (gardening) shears *pl*.

ciseau, x [sizo] *nm*: ~ (à bois) chisel // *nmpl* (pair of) scissors.

ciseler [sizle] *vt* to chisel, carve.

citadin, e [sitadɛ̃, -in] *nm/f* city dweller.

citation [sitasjɔ̃] *nf* (*d'auteur*) quotation; (*JUR*) summons *sg*.

cité [site] *nf* town; (*plus grande*) city; ~ universitaire students' residences *pl*.

citer [site] *vt* (*un auteur*) to quote (from); (*nommer*) to name; (*JUR*) to summon.

citerne [sitɛʀn(ə)] *nf* tank.

citoyen, ne [sitwajɛ̃, -ɛn] *nm/f* citizen.

citron [sitʀɔ̃] *nm* lemon; ~ vert lime; **citronnade** *nf* lemonade; **citronnier** *nm* lemon tree.

citrouille [sitʀuj] *nf* pumpkin.

civet [sive] *nm* stew.

civière [sivjɛʀ] *nf* stretcher.

civil, e [sivil] *a* (*JUR, ADMIN, poli*) civil; (*non militaire*) civilian; en ~ in civilian clothes; dans le ~ in civilian life.

civilisation [sivilizasjɔ̃] *nf* civilization.

civisme [sivism(ə)] *nm* public-spiritedness.

clair, e [klɛʀ] *a* light; (*chambre*) light, bright; (*eau, son, fig*) clear // *ad*: voir ~ to see clearly; tirer qch au ~ to clear sth up, clarify sth; mettre au ~ (*notes etc*) to tidy up; le plus ~ de son temps the better part of his time; ~ de lune moonlight; ~ement *ad* clearly.

clairière [klɛʀjɛʀ] *nf* clearing.

clairon [klɛʀɔ̃] *nm* bugle.

clairsemé, e [klɛʀsəme] *a* sparse.

clairvoyant, e [klɛʀvwajɑ̃, -ɑ̃t] *a* perceptive, clear-sighted.

clandestin, e [klɑ̃dɛstɛ̃, -in] *a* clandestine, covert; passager ~ stowaway.

clapier [klapje] *nm* (rabbit) hutch.

clapoter [klapɔte] *vi* to lap.

claque [klak] *nf* (*gifle*) slap.

claquer [klake] *vi* (*drapeau*) to flap; (*porte*) to bang, slam; (*coup de feu*) to ring out // *vt* (*porte*) to slam, bang; (*doigts*) to snap; se ~ un muscle to pull *ou* strain a muscle.

claquettes [klakɛt] *nfpl* tap-dancing *sg*.

clarinette [klaʀinɛt] *nf* clarinet.

clarté [klaʀte] *nf* lightness; brightness; (*d'un son, de l'eau*) clearness; (*d'une explication*) clarity.

classe [klɑs] *nf* class; (*SCOL: local*) class(room); (: *leçon, élèves*) class; faire la ~ (*SCOL*) to be a *ou* the teacher; to teach.

classement [klɑsmɑ̃] *nm* (*rang: SCOL*) place; (: *SPORT*) placing; (*liste: SCOL*) class list (in order of merit); (: *SPORT*) placings *pl*.

classer [klɑse] *vt* (*idées, livres*) to classify; (*papiers*) to file; (*candidat, concurrent*) to grade; (*JUR: affaire*) to close; se ~ premier/dernier to come first/last; (*SPORT*) to finish first/last.

classeur [klɑsœʀ] *nm* (*cahier*) file; (*meuble*) filing cabinet.

classique [klɑsik] *a* classical; (*sobre: coupe etc*) classic(al); (*habituel*) standard, classic.

claudication [klodikasjɔ̃] *nf* limp.

clause [kloz] *nf* clause.

claustrer [klostʀe] *vt* to confine.

clavecin [klavsɛ̃] *nm* harpsichord.

clavicule [klavikyl] *nf* collarbone.

clavier [klavje] *nm* keyboard.

clé *ou* **clef** [kle] *nf* key; (*MUS*) clef; (*de mécanicien*) spanner (*Brit*), wrench (*US*); **prix ~s en main** (*d'une voiture*) on-the-road price; **~ anglaise** (monkey) wrench; **~ de contact** ignition key.

clément, e [klemã, -ãt] *a* (*temps*) mild; (*indulgent*) lenient.

clerc [klɛR] *nm*: **~ de notaire** solicitor's clerk.

clergé [klɛRʒe] *nm* clergy.

cliché [kliʃe] *nm* (*PHOTO*) negative; print; (*LING*) cliché.

client, e [klijã, -ãt] *nm/f* (*acheteur*) customer, client; (*d'hôtel*) guest, patron; (*du docteur*) patient; (*de l'avocat*) client; **clientèle** *nf* (*du magasin*) customers *pl*, clientèle; (*du docteur, de l'avocat*) practice.

cligner [kliɲe] *vi*: **~ des yeux** to blink (one's eyes); **~ de l'œil** to wink.

clignotant [kliɲɔtã] *nm* (*AUTO*) indicator.

clignoter [kliɲɔte] *vi* (*étoiles etc*) to twinkle; (*lumière*) to flash; (*: vaciller*) to flicker.

climat [klima] *nm* climate.

climatisation [klimatizasjɔ̃] *nf* air conditioning; **climatisé, e** *a* air-conditioned.

clin d'œil [klɛ̃dœj] *nm* wink; **en un ~** in a flash.

clinique [klinik] *nf* nursing home.

clinquant, e [klɛ̃kã, -ãt] *a* flashy.

cliqueter [klikte] *vi* to clash; to jangle, jingle; to chink.

clochard, e [klɔʃaR, -aRd(ə)] *nm/f* tramp.

cloche [klɔʃ] *nf* (*d'église*) bell; (*fam*) clot; **~ à fromage** cheese-cover.

cloche-pied [klɔʃpje]: **à ~** *ad* on one leg, hopping (along).

clocher [klɔʃe] *nm* church tower; (*en pointe*) steeple // *vi* (*fam*) to be *ou* go wrong; **de ~** (*péj*) parochial.

cloison [klwazɔ̃] *nf* partition (wall).

cloître [klwatR(ə)] *nm* cloister.

cloîtrer [klwatRe] *vt*: **se ~** to shut o.s. up *ou* away.

cloque [klɔk] *nf* blister.

clore [klɔR] *vt* to close; **clos, e** *a voir* maison, huis // *nm* (enclosed) field.

clôture [klotyR] *nf* closure; (*barrière*) enclosure; **clôturer** *vt* (*terrain*) to enclose; (*débats*) to close.

clou [klu] *nm* nail; (*MÉD*) boil; **~s** *nmpl* = passage clouté; **pneus à ~s** studded tyres; **le ~ du spectacle** the highlight of the show; **~ de girofle** clove; **~er** *vt* to nail down *ou* up.

clown [klun] *nm* clown.

club [klœb] *nm* club.

C.N.R.S. *sigle m* = centre national de la recherche scientifique.

coasser [kɔase] *vi* to croak.

cobaye [kɔbaj] *nm* guinea-pig.

coca [kɔka] *nm* Coke ®.

cocagne [kɔkaɲ] *nf*: **pays de ~** land of plenty.

cocaïne [kɔkain] *nf* cocaine.

cocasse [kɔkas] *a* comical, funny.

coccinelle [kɔksinɛl] *nf* ladybird (*Brit*), ladybug (*US*).

cocher [kɔʃe] *nm* coachman // *vt* to tick off; (*entailler*) to notch.

cochère [kɔʃɛR] *af*: **porte ~** carriage entrance.

cochon, ne [kɔʃɔ̃, -ɔn] *nm* pig // *a* (*fam*) dirty, smutty; **cochonnerie** *nf* (*fam*) filth; rubbish, trash.

cocktail [kɔktɛl] *nm* cocktail; (*réception*) cocktail party.

coco [kɔko] *nm voir* noix; (*fam*) bloke.

cocorico [kɔkɔriko] *excl, nm* cock-a-doodle-do.

cocotier [kɔkɔtje] *nm* coconut palm.

cocotte [kɔkɔt] *nf* (*en fonte*) casserole; **~ (minute)** pressure cooker; **ma ~** (*fam*) sweetie (pie).

cocu [kɔky] *nm* cuckold.

code [kɔd] *nm* code // *a*: **phares ~s** dipped headlights; **se mettre en ~(s)** to dip one's (head)lights; **~ à barres** bar code; **~ civil** Common Law; **~ pénal** penal code; **~ postal** (*numéro*) post (*Brit*) *ou* zip (*US*) code; **~ de la route** highway code.

cœur [kœR] *nm* heart; (*CARTES: couleur*) hearts *pl*; (*: carte*) heart; **avoir bon ~** to be kind-hearted; **avoir mal au ~** to feel sick; **en avoir le ~ net** to be clear in one's own mind (about it); **par ~** by heart; **de bon ~** willingly; **cela lui tient à ~** that's (very) close to his heart.

coffre [kɔfR(ə)] *nm* (*meuble*) chest; (*d'auto*) boot (*Brit*), trunk (*US*); **~(-fort)** *nm* safe.

coffret [kɔfRɛ] *nm* casket.

cognac [kɔɲak] *nm* brandy, cognac.

cogner [kɔɲe] *vi* to knock.

cohérent, e [kɔeRã, -ãt] *a* coherent, consistent.

cohorte [kɔɔRt(ə)] *nf* troop.

cohue [kɔy] *nf* crowd.

coi, coite [kwa, kwat] *a*: **rester ~** to remain silent.

coiffe [kwaf] *nf* headdress.

coiffé, e [kwafe] *a*: **bien/mal ~** with tidy/untidy hair; **~ en arrière** with one's hair brushed *ou* combed back.

coiffer [kwafe] *vt* (*fig*) to cover, top; **~ qn** to do sb's hair; **se ~** *vi* to do one's hair; to put on one's hat.

coiffeur, euse [kwafœR, -øz] *nm/f* hairdresser // *nf* (*table*) dressing table.

coiffure [kwafyR] *nf* (*cheveux*) hairstyle, hairdo; (*chapeau*) hat, headgear *q*; (*art*): **la ~** hairdressing.

coin [kwɛ̃] *nm* corner; (*pour coincer*) wedge; **l'épicerie du ~** the local grocer; **dans le ~** (*aux alentours*) in the area, around about; **au ~ du feu** by the fireside; **regard en ~** sideways glance.

coincer [kwɛ̃se] *vt* to jam.

coïncidence [kɔɛ̃sidɑ̃s] *nf* coincidence.

coïncider [kɔɛ̃side] *vi* to coincide.

coïte [kwat] *af voir* **coi.**

col [kɔl] *nm* (*de chemise*) collar; (*encolure, cou*) neck; (*de montagne*) pass; **~ roulé** polo-neck; **~ de l'utérus** cervix.

colère [kɔlɛr] *nf* anger; **une ~ a** fit of anger; (**se mettre**) **en ~** (to get) angry; **coléreux, euse** *a*, **colérique** *a* quick-tempered, irascible.

colifichet [kɔlifiʃe] *nm* trinket.

colimaçon [kɔlimasɔ̃] *nm*: **escalier en ~** spiral staircase.

colin [kɔlɛ̃] *nm* hake.

colique [kɔlik] *nf* diarrhoea; colic (pains).

colis [kɔli] *nm* parcel.

collaborateur, trice [kɔlabɔratœr, -tris] *nm/f* (*aussi POL*) collaborator; (*d'une revue*) contributor.

collaborer [kɔlabɔre] *vi* to collaborate; **~ à** to collaborate on; (*revue*) to contribute to.

collant, e [kɔlɑ̃, -ɑ̃t] *a* sticky; (*robe etc*) clinging, skintight; (*péj*) clinging // *nm* (*bas*) tights *pl*.

collation [kɔlasjɔ̃] *nf* light meal.

colle [kɔl] *nf* glue; (*à papiers peints*) (wallpaper) paste; (*devinette*) teaser, riddle; (*SCOL fam*) detention.

collecte [kɔlɛkt(ə)] *nf* collection.

collectif, ive [kɔlɛktif, -iv] *a* collective; (*visite, billet*) group *cpd.*

collection [kɔlɛksjɔ̃] *nf* collection; (*ÉDITION*) series; **collectionner** *vt* (*tableaux, timbres*) to collect; **collectionneur, euse** *nm/f* collector.

collectivité [kɔlɛktivite] *nf* group.

collège [kɔlɛʒ] *nm* (*école*) (secondary) school; (*assemblée*) body; **collégien, ne** *nm/f* schoolboy/girl.

collègue [kɔlɛg] *nm/f* colleague.

coller [kɔle] *vt* (*papier, timbre*) to stick (on); (*affiche*) to stick up; (*enveloppe*) to stick down; (*morceaux*) to stick *ou* glue together; (*fam: mettre, fourrer*) to stick, shove; (*SCOL fam*) to keep in // *vi* (*être collant*) to be sticky; (*adhérer*) to stick; **~ à** to stick to.

collet [kɔle] *nm* (*piège*) snare, noose; (*cou*): **prendre qn au ~** to grab sb by the throat; **~ monté** *a inv* straight-laced.

collier [kɔlje] *nm* (*bijou*) necklace; (*de chien, TECH*) collar; **~ (de barbe)** narrow beard along the line of the jaw.

collimateur [kɔlimatœr] *nm*: **avoir qn/ qch dans le ~** (*fig*) to have sb/sth in one's sights.

colline [kɔlin] *nf* hill.

collision [kɔlizjɔ̃] *nf* collision, crash; en-

trer en ~ (avec) to collide (with).

colmater [kɔlmate] *vt* (*fuite*) to seal off; (*brèche*) to plug, fill in.

colombe [kɔlɔ̃b] *nf* dove.

colon [kɔlɔ̃] *nm* settler.

colonel [kɔlɔnɛl] *nm* colonel.

colonie [kɔlɔni] *nf* colony; **~ (de vacances)** holiday camp (*for children*).

colonne [kɔlɔn] *nf* column; **se mettre en ~ par deux** to get into twos; **~ de secours** rescue party; **~ (vertébrale)** spine, spinal column.

colorant [kɔlɔrɑ̃] *nm* colouring.

colorer [kɔlɔre] *vt* to colour.

colorier [kɔlɔrje] *vt* to colour (in).

coloris [kɔlɔri] *nm* colour, shade.

colporter [kɔlpɔrte] *vt* to hawk, peddle.

colza [kɔlza] *nm* rape.

coma [kɔma] *nm* coma.

combat [kɔ̃ba] *nm* fight; fighting *q*; **~ de boxe** boxing match.

combattant [kɔ̃batɑ̃] *nm*: **ancien ~** war veteran.

combattre [kɔ̃batr(ə)] *vt* to fight; (*épidémie, ignorance*) to combat, fight against.

combien [kɔ̃bjɛ̃] *ad* (*quantité*) how much; (*nombre*) how many; (*exclamatif*) how; **~ de** how much; how many; **~ de temps** how long; **~ coûte/pèse ceci?** how much does this cost/weigh?

combinaison [kɔ̃binɛzɔ̃] *nf* combination; (*astuce*) device, scheme; (*de femme*) slip; (*d'aviateur*) flying suit; (*d'homme-grenouille*) wetsuit; (*bleu de travail*) boiler suit (*Brit*), coveralls *pl* (*US*).

combine [kɔ̃bin] *nf* trick; (*péj*) scheme, fiddle (*Brit*).

combiné [kɔ̃bine] *nm* (*aussi*: **~ télépho- nique**) receiver.

combiner [kɔ̃bine] *vt* to combine; (*plan, horaire*) to work out, devise.

comble [kɔ̃bl(ə)] *a* (*salle*) packed (full) // *nm* (*du bonheur, plaisir*) height; **~s** *nmpl* (*CONSTR*) attic *sg*, loft *sg*; **c'est le ~!** that beats everything!

combler [kɔ̃ble] *vt* (*trou*) to fill in; (*besoin, lacune*) to fill; (*déficit*) to make good; (*satisfaire*) to fulfil.

combustible [kɔ̃bystibl(ə)] *nm* fuel.

comédie [kɔmedi] *nf* comedy; (*fig*) playacting *q*; **~ musicale** musical; **comédien, ne** *nm/f* actor/actress.

comestible [kɔmɛstibl(ə)] *a* edible.

comique [kɔmik] *a* (*drôle*) comical; (*THÉÂTRE*) comic // *nm* (*artiste*) comic, comedian.

comité [kɔmite] *nm* committee; **~ d'entreprise** works council.

commandant [kɔmɑ̃dɑ̃] *nm* (*gén*) commander, commandant; (*NAVIG, AVIAT*) captain.

commande [kɔmɑ̃d] *nf* (*COMM*) order; **~s** *nfpl* (*AVIAT etc*) controls; **sur ~** to

order; ~ **à distance** remote control.
commandement [kɔmɑ̃dmɑ̃] *nm* command; (REL) commandment.
commander [kɔmɑ̃de] *vt* (COMM) to order; (*diriger, ordonner*) to command; ~ **à qn de faire** to command *ou* order sb to do.
commando [kɔmɑ̃do] *nm* commando (squad).
comme [kɔm] ♦ *prép* **1** (*comparaison*) like; **tout ~ son père** just like his father; **fort ~ un bœuf** as strong as an ox; **joli ~ tout** ever so pretty
2 (*manière*) like; **faites-le ~ ça** do it like this, do it this way; **~ ci, ~, ça** so-so, middling
3 (*en tant que*) as a; **donner ~ prix** to give as a prize; **travailler ~ secrétaire** to work as a secretary
♦ *cj* **1** (*ainsi que*) as; **elle écrit ~ elle parle** she writes as she talks; **~ si** as if
2 (*au moment où, alors que*) as; **il est parti ~ j'arrivais** he left as I arrived
3 (*parce que, puisque*) as; **~ il était en retard, il ...** as he was late, he ...
♦ *ad*: **~ il est fort/c'est bon!** he's so strong/it's so good!
commémorer [kɔmemɔre] *vt* to commemorate.
commencement [kɔmɑ̃smɑ̃] *nm* beginning, start, commencement.
commencer [kɔmɑ̃se] *vt, vi* to begin, start, commence; **~ à** *ou* **de faire** to begin *ou* start doing.
comment [kɔmɑ̃] *ad* how; **~?** (*que dites-vous*) pardon? // *nm*: **le ~ et le pourquoi** the whys and wherefores.
commentaire [kɔmɑ̃tɛʀ] *nm* comment; remark.
commenter [kɔmɑ̃te] *vt* (*jugement, événement*) to comment (up)on; (RADIO, TV: *match, manifestation*) to cover.
commérages [kɔmeʀaʒ] *nmpl* gossip *sg*.
commerçant, e [kɔmɛʀsɑ̃, -ɑ̃t] *nm/f* shopkeeper, trader.
commerce [kɔmɛʀs(ə)] *nm* (*activité*) trade, commerce; (*boutique*) business; **vendu dans le ~** sold in the shops; **commercial, e, aux** *a* commercial, trading; (*péj*) commercial; **commercialiser** *vt* to market.
commère [kɔmɛʀ] *nf* gossip.
commettre [kɔmɛtʀ(ə)] *vt* to commit.
commis [kɔmi] *nm* (*de magasin*) (shop) assistant; (*de banque*) clerk; **~ voyageur** commercial traveller.
commissaire [kɔmisɛʀ] *nm* (*de police*) ≈ (police) superintendent; **~-priseur** *nm* auctioneer.
commissariat [kɔmisaʀja] *nm* police station.
commission [kɔmisjɔ̃] *nf* (*comité, pourcentage*) commission; (*message*) message; (*course*) errand; **~s** *nfpl* (*achats*)

shopping *sg*.
commissure [kɔmisyʀ] *nf*: **les ~s des lèvres** the corners of the mouth.
commode [kɔmɔd] *a* (*pratique*) convenient, handy; (*facile*) easy; (*air, personne*) easy-going; (*personne*): **pas ~** awkward (to deal with) // *nf* chest of drawers; **commodité** *nf* convenience.
commotion [kɔmosjɔ̃] *nf*: **~ (cérébrale)** concussion; **commotionné, e** *a* shocked, shaken.
commun, e [kɔmœ̃, -yn] *a* common; (*pièce*) communal, shared; (*réunion, effort*) joint // *nf* (ADMIN) commune, district; (: *urbaine*) ≈ borough; **~s** *nmpl* (*bâtiments*) outbuildings; **cela sort de l'ordinaire** it's out of the ordinary; **le ~ des mortels** the common run of people; **en ~** (*faire*) jointly; **mettre en ~** to pool, share.
communauté [kɔmynote] *nf* community; (JUR): **régime de la ~** communal estate settlement.
communication [kɔmynikasjɔ̃] *nf* communication; **~ (téléphonique)** (telephone) call; **~ interurbaine** long distance call.
communier [kɔmynje] *vi* (REL) to receive communion; (*fig*) to be united.
communion [kɔmynjɔ̃] *nf* communion.
communiquer [kɔmynike] *vt* (*nouvelle, dossier*) to pass on, convey; (*maladie*) to pass on; (*peur etc*) to communicate; (*chaleur, mouvement*) to transmit // *vi* to communicate; **se ~ à** (*se propager*) to spread to.
communisme [kɔmynism(ə)] *nm* communism; **communiste** *a, nm/f* communist.
commutateur [kɔmytatœʀ] *nm* (ÉLEC) (change-over) switch, commutator.
compact, e [kɔpakt] *a* dense; compact.
compagne [kɔpaɲ] *nf* companion.
compagnie [kɔpaɲi] *nf* (*firme*, MIL) company; (*groupe*) gathering; **tenir ~ à qn** to keep sb company; **fausser ~ à qn** to give sb the slip, slip *ou* sneak away from sb; **~ aérienne** airline (company).
compagnon [kɔpaɲɔ̃] *nm* companion.
comparable [kɔpaʀabl(ə)] *a*: **~ (à)** comparable (to).
comparaison [kɔpaʀɛzɔ̃] *nf* comparison.
comparaître [kɔpaʀɛtʀ(ə)] *vi*: **~ (devant)** to appear (before).
comparer [kɔpaʀe] *vt* to compare; **~ qch/qn à** *ou* **et** (*pour choisir*) to compare sth/sb with *ou* and; (*pour établir une similitude*) to compare sth/sb to.
comparse [kɔpaʀs(ə)] *nm/f* (*péj*) associate, stooge.
compartiment [kɔpaʀtimɑ̃] *nm* compartment.
comparution [kɔpaʀysjɔ̃] *nf* appearance.
compas [kɔpa] *nm* (GÉOM) (pair of)

compasses pl; (NAVIG) compass.
compassé, e [kɔ̃pɑse] a starchy.
compatible [kɔ̃patibl(ə)] a compatible.
compatir [kɔ̃patir] vi: ~ (à) to sympathize (with).
compatriote [kɔ̃patrijɔt] nm/f compatriot.
compenser [kɔ̃pɑ̃se] vt to compensate for, make up for.
compère [kɔ̃pɛr] nm accomplice.
compétence [kɔ̃petɑ̃s] nf competence.
compétent, e [kɔ̃petɑ̃, -ɑ̃t] a (apte) competent, capable.
compétition [kɔ̃petisjɔ̃] nf (gén) competition; (SPORT: épreuve) event; la ~ competitive sport; la ~ automobile motor racing.
complainte [kɔ̃plɛ̃t] nf lament.
complaire [kɔ̃plɛr]: se ~ vi: se ~ dans/ parmi to take pleasure in/in being among.
complaisance [kɔ̃plɛzɑ̃s] nf kindness; pavillon de ~ flag of convenience.
complaisant, e [kɔ̃plɛzɑ̃, -ɑ̃t] a (aimable) kind, obliging.
complément [kɔ̃plemɑ̃] nm complement; remainder; ~ d'information (ADMIN) supplementary ou further information; **complémentaire** a complementary; (additionnel) supplementary.
complet, ète [kɔ̃plɛ, -ɛt] a complete; (plein: hôtel etc) full // nm (aussi: ~ veston) suit; **complètement** ad completely; **compléter** vt (porter à la quantité voulue) to complete; (augmenter) to complement, supplement; to add to.
complexe [kɔ̃plɛks(ə)] a, nm complex; **complexé, e** a mixed-up, hung-up.
complication [kɔ̃plikɑsjɔ̃] nf complexity, intricacy; (difficulté, ennui) complication.
complice [kɔ̃plis] nm accomplice.
compliment [kɔ̃plimɑ̃] nm (louange) compliment; ~s nmpl (félicitations) congratulations.
compliqué, e [kɔ̃plike] a complicated, complex; (personne) complicated.
complot [kɔ̃plo] nm plot.
comportement [kɔ̃pɔrtəmɑ̃] nm behaviour.
comporter [kɔ̃pɔrte] vt to consist of, comprise; (être équipé de) to have; (impliquer) to entail; se ~ vi to behave.
composante [kɔ̃pozɑ̃t] nf component.
composé [kɔ̃poze] nm compound.
composer [kɔ̃poze] vt (musique, texte) to compose; (mélange, équipe) to make up; (faire partie de) to make up, form // vi (transiger) to come to terms; se ~ de to be composed of, be made up of; ~ un numéro to dial a number.
compositeur, trice [kɔ̃pozitœr, -tris] nm/f (MUS) composer.
composition [kɔ̃pozisjɔ̃] nf composi-

tion; (SCOL) test; de bonne ~ (accommodant) easy to deal with.
composter [kɔ̃pɔste] vt to date stamp; to punch.
compote [kɔ̃pɔt] nf stewed fruit q; ~ de pommes stewed apples; **compotier** nm fruit dish ou bowl.
compréhensible [kɔ̃preɑ̃sibl(ə)] a comprehensible; (attitude) understandable.
compréhensif, ive [kɔ̃preɑ̃sif, -iv] a understanding.
comprendre [kɔ̃prɑ̃dr(ə)] vt to understand; (se composer de) to comprise, consist of.
compresse [kɔ̃prɛs] nf compress.
compression [kɔ̃presjɔ̃] nf compression; reduction.
comprimé [kɔ̃prime] nm tablet.
comprimer [kɔ̃prime] vt to compress; (fig: crédit etc) to reduce, cut down.
compris, e [kɔ̃pri, -iz] pp de comprendre // a (inclus) included; ~ entre (situé) contained between; la maison ~e/ non ~e, y/non ~ la maison including/ excluding the house; 100 F tout ~ 100 F all inclusive ou all-in.
compromettre [kɔ̃prɔmɛtr(ə)] vt to compromise.
compromis [kɔ̃prɔmi] nm compromise.
comptabilité [kɔ̃tabilite] nf (activité, technique) accounting, accountancy; (d'une société: comptes) accounts pl, books pl; (: service) accounts office.
comptable [kɔ̃tabl(ə)] nm/f accountant.
comptant [kɔ̃tɑ̃] ad: payer ~ to pay cash; acheter ~ to buy for cash.
compte [kɔ̃t] nm count, counting; (total, montant) count, (right) number; (bancaire, facture) account; ~s nmpl accounts, books; (fig) explanation sg; en fin de ~ (fig) all things considered; à bon ~ at a favourable price; (fig) lightly; avoir son ~ (fig: fam) to have had it; pour le ~ de on behalf of; pour son propre ~ for one's own benefit; tenir ~ de to take account of; travailler à son ~ to work for oneself; rendre ~ (à qn) de qch to give (sb) an account of sth; ~ chèques postaux (C.C.P.) Post Office account; ~ courant current account; ~ à rebours countdown; voir aussi rendre.
compte-gouttes [kɔ̃tgut] nm inv dropper.
compter [kɔ̃te] vt to count; (facturer) to charge for; (avoir à son actif, comporter) to have; (prévoir) to allow, reckon; (penser, espérer): ~ réussir to expect to succeed // vi to count; (être économe) to economize; (figurer): ~ parmi to be ou rank among; ~ sur to count (up)on; ~ avec qch/qn to reckon with ou take account of sth/sb; sans ~ que besides which.
compte rendu [kɔ̃trɑ̃dy] nm account,

report; (*de film, livre*) review.

compte-tours [kɔ̃ttuʀ] *nm inv* rev(olution) counter.

compteur [kɔ̃tœʀ] *nm* meter; ~ de vitesse speedometer.

comptine [kɔ̃tin] *nf* nursery rhyme.

comptoir [kɔ̃twaʀ] *nm* (*de magasin*) counter.

compulser [kɔ̃pylse] *vt* to consult.

comte, comtesse [kɔ̃t, kɔ̃tɛs] *nm/f* count/countess.

con, ne [kɔ̃, kɔn] *a* (*fam!*) damned *ou* bloody (*Brit*) stupid (*!*).

concéder [kɔ̃sede] *vt* to grant; (*défaite, point*) to concede.

concentrer [kɔ̃sɑ̃tʀe] *vt* to concentrate; se ~ *vi* to concentrate.

concept [kɔ̃sɛpt] *nm* concept.

conception [kɔ̃sɛpsjɔ̃] *nf* conception; (*d'une machine etc*) design.

concerner [kɔ̃sɛʀne] *vt* to concern; en ce qui me concerne as far as I am concerned.

concert [kɔ̃sɛʀ] *nm* concert; de ~ *ad* in unison; together.

concerter [kɔ̃sɛʀte] *vt* to devise; se ~ *vi* (*collaborateurs etc*) to put our *ou* their *etc* heads together.

concessionnaire [kɔ̃sesjɔnɛʀ] *nm/f* agent, dealer.

concevoir [kɔ̃svwaʀ] *vt* (*idée, projet*) to conceive (of); (*méthode, plan d'appartement, décoration etc*) to plan, design; (*enfant*) to conceive; **bien/mal conçu** well-/badly- designed.

concierge [kɔ̃sjɛʀʒ(ə)] *nm/f* caretaker; (*d'hôtel*) head porter.

concile [kɔ̃sil] *nm* council.

conciliabules [kɔ̃siljabyl] *nmpl* (private) discussions, confabulations.

concilier [kɔ̃silje] *vt* to reconcile; se ~ qn to win sb over.

concitoyen, ne [kɔ̃sitwajɛ̃, -jɛn] *nm/f* fellow citizen.

concluant, e [kɔ̃klyɑ̃, -ɑ̃t] *a* conclusive.

conclure [kɔ̃klyʀ] *vt* to conclude.

conclusion [kɔ̃klyzjɔ̃] *nf* conclusion.

conçois *etc vb voir* **concevoir**.

concombre [kɔ̃kɔ̃bʀ(ə)] *nm* cucumber.

concorder [kɔ̃kɔʀde] *vi* to tally, agree.

concourir [kɔ̃kuʀiʀ] *vi* (*SPORT*) to compete; ~ à *vt* (*effet etc*) to work towards.

concours [kɔ̃kuʀ] *nm* competition; (*SCOL*) competitive examination; (*assistance*) aid, help; ~ de circonstances combination of circumstances; ~ hippique horse show.

concret, ète [kɔ̃kʀɛ, -ɛt] *a* concrete.

concrétiser [kɔ̃kʀetize] *vt* (*plan, projet*) to put in concrete form; se ~ *vi* to materialize.

conçu, e [kɔ̃sy] *pp de* **concevoir**.

concubinage [kɔ̃kybinaʒ] *nm* (*JUR*) cohabitation.

concurrence [kɔ̃kyʀɑ̃s] *nf* competition;

jusqu'à ~ de up to.

concurrent, e [kɔ̃kyʀɑ̃, -ɑ̃t] *nm/f* (*SPORT, ÉCON etc*) competitor; (*SCOL*) candidate.

condamner [kɔ̃dɑne] *vt* (*blâmer*) to condemn; (*JUR*) to sentence; (*porte, ouverture*) to fill in, block up; (*malade*) to give up (hope for); ~ **qn à 2 ans de prison** to sentence sb to 2 years' imprisonment.

condensation [kɔ̃dɑ̃sasjɔ̃] *nf* condensation.

condenser [kɔ̃dɑ̃se] *vt*, se ~ *vi* to condense.

condisciple [kɔ̃disipl(ə)] *nm/f* school fellow, fellow student.

condition [kɔ̃disjɔ̃] *nf* condition; ~s *nfpl* (*tarif, prix*) terms; (*circonstances*) conditions; sans ~ *a* unconditional // *ad* unconditionally; à ~ de/que provided that; **conditionnel, le** *a* conditional // *nm* conditional (tense); **conditionner** *vt* (*déterminer*) to determine; (*COMM: produit*) to package; (*fig: personne*) to condition; air conditionné air conditioning.

condoléances [kɔ̃dɔleɑ̃s] *nfpl* condolences.

conducteur, trice [kɔ̃dyktœʀ, -tʀis] *nm/f* driver // *nm* (*ÉLEC etc*) conductor.

conduire [kɔ̃dɥiʀ] *vt* to drive; (*délégation, troupeau*) to lead; se ~ *vi* to behave; ~ vers/à to lead towards/to; ~ qn quelque part to take sb somewhere; to drive sb somewhere.

conduite [kɔ̃dɥit] *nf* (*comportement*) behaviour; (*d'eau, de gaz*) pipe; sous la ~ de led by; ~ à gauche left-hand drive; ~ intérieure saloon (car).

cône [kon] *nm* cone.

confection [kɔ̃fɛksjɔ̃] *nf* (*fabrication*) making; (*COUTURE*): la ~ the clothing industry; vêtement de ~ ready-to-wear *ou* off-the-peg garment.

confectionner [kɔ̃fɛksjɔne] *vt* to make.

conférence [kɔ̃feʀɑ̃s] *nf* (*exposé*) lecture; (*pourparlers*) conference; ~ de presse press conference.

confesser [kɔ̃fese] *vt* to confess; se ~ *vi* (*REL*) to go to confession.

confession [kɔ̃fɛsjɔ̃] *nf* confession; (*culte: catholique etc*) denomination.

confetti [kɔ̃feti] *nm* confetti *q*.

confiance [kɔ̃fjɑ̃s] *nf* confidence, trust; faith; avoir ~ en to have confidence *ou* faith in, trust; mettre qn en ~ to win sb's trust; ~ en soi self-confidence.

confiant, e [kɔ̃fjɑ̃, -ɑ̃t] *a* confident; trusting.

confidence [kɔ̃fidɑ̃s] *nf* confidence.

confidentiel, le [kɔ̃fidɑ̃sjɛl] *a* confidential.

confier [kɔ̃fje] *vt*: ~ à qn (*objet en dépôt, travail etc*) to entrust to sb; (*secret, pensée*) to confide to sb; se ~ à qn to confide in sb.

confiné, e [kɔ̃fine] *a* enclosed; stale.
confins [kɔ̃fɛ̃] *nmpl*: aux ~ de on the borders of.
confirmation [kɔ̃firmasjɔ̃] *nf* confirmation.
confirmer [kɔ̃firme] *vt* to confirm.
confiserie [kɔ̃fizri] *nf* (*magasin*) confectioner's *ou* sweet shop; ~s *nfpl* (*bonbons*) confectionery *sg*; **confiseur, euse** *nm/f* confectioner.
confisquer [kɔ̃fiske] *vt* to confiscate.
confit, e [kɔ̃fi, -it] *a*: fruits ~s crystallized fruits // *nm*: ~ d'oie conserve of goose.
confiture [kɔ̃fityr] *nf* jam; ~ d'oranges (orange) marmalade.
conflit [kɔ̃fli] *nm* conflict.
confondre [kɔ̃fɔ̃dr(ə)] *vt* (*jumeaux, faits*) to confuse, mix up; (*témoin, menteur*) to confound; se ~ *vi* to merge; se ~ en excuses to apologize profusely.
confondu, e [kɔ̃fɔ̃dy] *a* (*stupéfait*) speechless, overcome.
conforme [kɔ̃fɔrm(ə)] *a*: ~ à in accordance with; in keeping with; true to.
conformément [kɔ̃fɔrmemɑ̃] *ad*: ~ à in accordance with.
conformer [kɔ̃fɔrme] *vt*: se ~ à to conform to.
conformité [kɔ̃fɔrmite] *nf*: en ~ avec in accordance with, in keeping with.
confort [kɔ̃fɔr] *nm* comfort; tout ~ (*COMM*) with all modern conveniences; **confortable** *a* comfortable.
confrère [kɔ̃frɛr] *nm* colleague; fellow member; **confrérie** *nf* brotherhood.
confronter [kɔ̃frɔ̃te] *vt* to confront; (*textes*) to compare, collate.
confus, e [kɔ̃fy, -yz] *a* (*vague*) confused; (*embarrassé*) embarrassed.
confusion [kɔ̃fyzjɔ̃] *nf* (*voir confus*) confusion; embarrassement; (*voir confondre*) confusion, mixing up.
congé [kɔ̃ʒe] *nm* (*vacances*) holiday; en ~ on holiday; off (work); semaine de ~ week off; prendre ~ de qn to take one's leave of sb; donner son ~ à to give in one's notice to; ~ de maladie sick leave; ~s payés paid holiday.
congédier [kɔ̃ʒedje] *vt* to dismiss.
congélateur [kɔ̃ʒelatœr] *nm* freezer, deep freeze.
congeler [kɔ̃ʒle] *vt* to freeze.
congère [kɔ̃ʒɛr] *nf* snowdrift.
congestion [kɔ̃ʒɛstjɔ̃] *nf* congestion; ~ cérébrale stroke.
congestionner [kɔ̃ʒɛstjɔne] *vt* to congest; (*MÉD*) to flush.
congrès [kɔ̃grɛ] *nm* congress.
congru, e [kɔ̃gry] *a*: la portion ~e the smallest *ou* meanest share.
conifère [kɔnifɛr] *nm* conifer.
conjoint, e [kɔ̃ʒwɛ̃, -wɛ̃t] *a* joint // *nm/f* spouse.
conjonction [kɔ̃ʒɔ̃ksjɔ̃] *nf* (*LING*) conjunction.

conjonctivite [kɔ̃ʒɔ̃ktivit] *nf* conjunctivitis.
conjoncture [kɔ̃ʒɔ̃ktyr] *nf* circumstances *pl*; climate.
conjugaison [kɔ̃ʒygɛzɔ̃] *nf* (*LING*) conjugation.
conjuguer [kɔ̃ʒyge] *vt* (*LING*) to conjugate; (*efforts etc*) to combine.
conjuration [kɔ̃ʒyrasjɔ̃] *nf* conspiracy.
conjurer [kɔ̃ʒyre] *vt* (*sort, maladie*) to avert; (*implorer*) to beseech, entreat.
connaissance [kɔnesɑ̃s] *nf* (*savoir*) knowledge *q*; (*personne connue*) acquaintance; être sans ~ to be unconscious; perdre/reprendre ~ to lose/regain consciousness; à ma/sa ~ to (the best of) my/his knowledge; avoir ~ de to be aware of; prendre ~ de (*document etc*) to peruse; en ~ de cause with full knowledge of the facts.
connaître [kɔnɛtr(ə)] *vt* to know; (*éprouver*) to experience; (*avoir*) to have; to enjoy; ~ de nom/vue to know by name/sight; ils se sont connus à Genève they (first) met in Geneva.
connecté, e [kɔnɛkte] *a* on line.
connecter [kɔnɛkte] *vt* to connect.
connerie [kɔnri] *nf* (*fam!*) stupid thing (to do *ou* say).
connu, e [kɔny] *a* (*célèbre*) well-known.
conquérir [kɔ̃kerir] *vt* to conquer, win; **conquête** *nf* conquest.
consacrer [kɔ̃sakre] *vt* (*REL*) to consecrate; (*fig: usage etc*) to sanction, establish; (*employer*) to devote, dedicate.
conscience [kɔ̃sjɑ̃s] *nf* conscience; avoir/prendre ~ de to be/become aware of; perdre ~ to lose consciousness; avoir bonne/mauvaise ~ to have a clear/guilty conscience; **consciencieux, euse** *a* conscientious; **conscient, e** *a* conscious.
conscrit [kɔ̃skri] *nm* conscript.
consécutif, ive [kɔ̃sekytif, -iv] *a* consecutive; ~ à following upon.
conseil [kɔ̃sɛj] *nm* (*avis*) piece of advice, advice *q*; (*assemblée*) council; prendre ~ (auprès de qn) to take advice (from sb); ~ d'administration board (of directors); le ~ des ministres ≈ the Cabinet.
conseiller [kɔ̃seje] *vt* (*personne*) to advise; (*méthode, action*) to recommend, advise; ~ à qn de advise sb to.
conseiller, ère [kɔ̃seje, kɔ̃sejɛr] *nm/f* adviser.
consentement [kɔ̃sɑ̃tmɑ̃] *nm* consent.
consentir [kɔ̃sɑ̃tir] *vt* to agree, consent.
conséquence [kɔ̃sekɑ̃s] *nf* consequence; en ~ (*donc*) consequently; (*de façon appropriée*) accordingly; ne pas tirer à ~ to be unlikely to have any repercussions.
conséquent, e [kɔ̃sekɑ̃, -ɑ̃t] *a* logical, rational; (*fam: important*) substantial;

par ~ consequently.

conservateur, trice [kɔ̃sɛrvatœr, -tris] nm/f (POL) conservative; (de musée) curator.

conservatoire [kɔ̃sɛrvatwar] nm academy; (ÉCOLOGIE) conservation area.

conserve [kɔ̃sɛrv(ə)] nf (gén pl) canned ou tinned (Brit) food; **en ~** canned, tinned (Brit).

conserver [kɔ̃sɛrve] vt (faculté) to retain, keep; (amis, livres) to keep; (préserver, aussi CULIN) to preserve.

considérable [kɔ̃siderabl(ə)] a considerable, significant, extensive.

considération [kɔ̃siderasjɔ̃] nf consideration; (estime) esteem.

considérer [kɔ̃sidere] vt to consider; ~ qch comme to regard sth as.

consigne [kɔ̃siɲ] nf (de gare) left luggage (office) (Brit), checkroom (US); (ordre, instruction) instructions pl; ~ (automatique) left-luggage locker.

consigner [kɔ̃siɲe] vt (note, pensée) to record; (punir) to confine to barracks; to put in detention; (COMM) to put a deposit on.

consistant, e [kɔ̃sistɑ̃, -ɑ̃t] a thick; solid.

consister [kɔ̃siste] vi: ~ en/dans/à faire to consist of/in/in doing.

consœur [kɔ̃sœr] nf (lady) colleague; fellow member.

consoler [kɔ̃sɔle] vt to console.

consolider [kɔ̃sɔlide] vt to strengthen; (fig) to consolidate.

consommateur, trice [kɔ̃sɔmatœr, -tris] nm/f (ÉCON) consumer; (dans un café) customer.

consommation [kɔ̃sɔmasjɔ̃] nf (boisson) drink; ~ **aux 100 km** (AUTO) (fuel) consumption per 100 km.

consommer [kɔ̃sɔme] vt (suj: personne) to eat ou drink, consume; (suj: voiture, usine, poêle) to use, consume // vi (dans un café) to (have a) drink.

consonne [kɔ̃sɔn] nf consonant.

conspirer [kɔ̃spire] vi to conspire.

conspuer [kɔ̃spɥe] vt to boo, shout down.

constamment [kɔ̃stamɑ̃] ad constantly.

constant, e [kɔ̃stɑ̃, -ɑ̃t] a constant; (personne) steadfast.

constat [kɔ̃sta] nm (d'huissier) certified report; (de police) report; (affirmation) statement.

constatation [kɔ̃statasjɔ̃] nf (observation) (observed) fact, observation; (affirmation) statement.

constater [kɔ̃state] vt (remarquer) to note; (ADMIN, JUR: attester) to certify; (dire) to state.

consterner [kɔ̃stɛrne] vt to dismay.

constipé, e [kɔ̃stipe] a constipated.

constitué, e [kɔ̃stiɥe] a: ~ **de** made up ou composed of.

constituer [kɔ̃stiɥe] vt (comité, équipe) to set up; (dossier, collection) to put together; (suj: éléments: composer) to make up, constitute; (représenter, être) to constitute; **se ~ prisonnier** to give o.s. up.

constitution [kɔ̃stitysjɔ̃] nf (composition) composition, make-up; (santé, POL) constitution.

constructeur [kɔ̃stryktœr] nm manufacturer, builder.

construction [kɔ̃stryksjɔ̃] nf construction, building.

construire [kɔ̃strɥir] vt to build, construct.

consul [kɔ̃syl] nm consul; **~at** nm consulate.

consultation [kɔ̃syltasjɔ̃] nf consultation; **~s** nfpl (POL) talks; **heures de ~** (MÉD) surgery (Brit) ou office (US) hours.

consulter [kɔ̃sylte] vt to consult // vi (médecin) to hold surgery (Brit), be in (the office) (US).

consumer [kɔ̃syme] vt to consume; **se ~** vi to burn.

contact [kɔ̃takt] nm contact; **au ~ de** (air, peau) on contact with; (gens) through contact with; **mettre/couper le ~** (AUTO) to switch on/off the ignition; **entrer en** ou **prendre ~ avec** to get in touch ou contact with; **~er** vt to contact, get in touch with.

contagieux, euse [kɔ̃taʒjø, -øz] a contagious; infectious.

contaminer [kɔ̃tamine] vt to contaminate.

conte [kɔ̃t] nm tale; ~ **de fées** fairy tale.

contempler [kɔ̃tɑ̃ple] vt to contemplate, gaze at.

contemporain, e [kɔ̃tɑ̃pɔrɛ̃, -ɛn] a, nm/f contemporary.

contenance [kɔ̃tnɑ̃s] nf (d'un récipient) capacity; (attitude) bearing, attitude; **perdre ~** to lose one's composure.

conteneur [kɔ̃tnœr] nm container.

contenir [kɔ̃tnir] vt to contain; (avoir une capacité de) to hold.

content, e [kɔ̃tɑ̃, -ɑ̃t] a pleased, glad; ~ **de** pleased with; **contenter** vt to satisfy, please; **se contenter de** to content o.s. with.

contentieux [kɔ̃tɑ̃sjø] nm (COMM) litigation; litigation department.

contenu [kɔ̃tny] nm (d'un bol) contents pl; (d'un texte) content.

conter [kɔ̃te] vt to recount, relate.

contestable [kɔ̃tɛstabl(ə)] a questionable.

contestation [kɔ̃tɛstasjɔ̃] nf (POL) protest.

conteste [kɔ̃tɛst(ə)]: **sans ~** ad unquestionably, indisputably.

contester [kɔ̃tɛste] vt to question, contest // vi (POL, gén) to protest, rebel (against established authority).

contexte [kɔ̃tɛkst(ə)] nm context.

contigu, ë [kɔ̃tigy] a: ~ (à) adjacent (to).

continent [kɔ̃tinɑ̃] nm continent.

continu, e [kɔ̃tiny] a continuous; (courant) ~ direct current, DC.

continuel, le [kɔ̃tinɥɛl] a (qui se répète) constant, continual; (continu) continuous.

continuer [kɔ̃tinɥe] vt (travail, voyage etc) to continue (with), carry on (with), go on (with); (prolonger: alignement, rue) to continue // vi (pluie, vie, bruit) to continue, go on; (voyageur) to go on; ~ à ou de faire to go on ou continue doing.

contorsionner [kɔ̃tɔrsjɔne]: se ~ vi to contort o.s., writhe about.

contour [kɔ̃tur] nm outline, contour.

contourner [kɔ̃turne] vt to go round.

contraceptif, ive [kɔ̃trasɛptif, -iv] a, nm contraceptive.

contraception [kɔ̃trasɛpsjɔ̃] nf contraception.

contracté, e [kɔ̃trakte] a tense.

contracter [kɔ̃trakte] vt (muscle etc) to tense, contract; (maladie, dette, obligation) to contract; (assurance) to take out; se ~ vi (métal, muscles) to contract.

contractuel, le [kɔ̃traktɥel] nm/f (agent) traffic warden.

contradiction [kɔ̃tradiksjɔ̃] nf contradiction; **contradictoire** a contradictory, conflicting.

contraindre [kɔ̃trɛ̃dr(ə)] vt: ~ qn à faire to compel sb to do.

contraint, e [kɔ̃trɛ̃, -ɛ̃t] a (mine, air) constrained, forced // nf constraint.

contraire [kɔ̃trɛr] a, nm opposite; ~ à contrary to; au ~ ad on the contrary.

contrarier [kɔ̃trarje] vt (personne) to annoy, bother; (fig) to impede; to thwart, frustrate.

contraste [kɔ̃trast(ə)] nm contrast.

contrat [kɔ̃tra] nm contract; ~ de travail employment contract.

contravention [kɔ̃travɑ̃sjɔ̃] nf (amende) fine; (P.V. pour stationnement interdit) parking ticket.

contre [kɔ̃tr(ə)] prép against; (en échange) (in exchange) for; **par** ~ on the other hand.

contrebande [kɔ̃trəbɑ̃d] nf (trafic) contraband, smuggling; (marchandise) contraband, smuggled goods pl; faire la ~ de to smuggle.

contrebas [kɔ̃trəba]: en ~ ad (down) below.

contrebasse [kɔ̃trəbas] nf (double) bass.

contrecarrer [kɔ̃trəkare] vt to thwart.

contrecœur [kɔ̃trəkœr]: à ~ ad (be)grudgingly, reluctantly.

contrecoup [kɔ̃trəku] nm repercussions

pl; par ~ as an indirect consequence.

contredire [kɔ̃trədir] vt (personne) to contradict; (témoignage, assertion, faits) to refute.

contrée [kɔ̃tre] nf region; land.

contrefaçon [kɔ̃trəfasɔ̃] nf forgery.

contrefaire [kɔ̃trəfɛr] vt (document, signature) to forge, counterfeit; (personne, démarche) to mimic; (dénaturer: sa voix etc) to disguise.

contre-jour [kɔ̃trəʒur]: à ~ ad against the sunlight.

contremaître [kɔ̃trəmɛtr(ə)] nm foreman.

contrepartie [kɔ̃trəparti] nf compensation; en ~ in return.

contre-performance [kɔ̃trəpɛrfɔrmɑ̃s] nf below-average performance.

contre-pied [kɔ̃trəpje] nm: prendre le ~ de to take the opposing view of; to take the opposite course to.

contre-plaqué [kɔ̃trəplake] nm plywood.

contrepoids [kɔ̃trəpwa] nm counterweight, counterbalance.

contrer [kɔ̃tre] vt to counter.

contresens [kɔ̃trəsɑ̃s] nm misinterpretation; mistranslation; nonsense q; à ~ ad the wrong way.

contretemps [kɔ̃trətɑ̃] nm hitch; à ~ ad (MUS) out of time; (fig) at an inopportune moment.

contrevenir [kɔ̃trəvnir]: ~ à vt to contravene.

contribuable [kɔ̃tribɥabl(ə)] nm/f taxpayer.

contribuer [kɔ̃tribɥe]: ~ à vt to contribute towards; **contribution** nf contribution; **contributions directes/indirectes** direct/indirect taxation; **mettre à contribution** to call upon.

contrôle [kɔ̃trol] nm checking q, check; supervision; monitoring; (test) test, examination; **perdre le** ~ **de** (véhicule) to lose control of; ~ **continu** (SCOL) continuous assessment; ~ **d'identité** identity check; ~ **des naissances** birth control.

contrôler [kɔ̃trole] vt (vérifier) to check; (surveiller) to supervise; to monitor, control; (maîtriser, COMM: firme) to control; **contrôleur, euse** nm/f (de train) (ticket) inspector; (de bus) (bus) conductor/tress.

contrordre [kɔ̃trɔrdr(ə)] nm: **sauf** ~ unless otherwise directed.

controversé, e [kɔ̃trovɛrse] a (personnage, question) controversial.

contusion [kɔ̃tyzjɔ̃] nf bruise, contusion.

convaincre [kɔ̃vɛ̃kr(ə)] vt: ~ qn (de qch) to convince sb (of sth); ~ qn (de faire) to persuade sb (to do); ~ qn (de (JUR: délit) to convict sb of.

convalescence [kɔ̃valesɑ̃s] nf convalescence.

convenable [kɔ̃vnabl(ə)] *a* suitable; (*assez bon, respectable*) decent.

convenance [kɔ̃vnɑ̃s] *nf*: à ma/votre ~ to my/your liking; ~s *nfpl* proprieties.

convenir [kɔ̃vniʀ] *vi* to be suitable; ~ à to suit; il convient de it is advisable to; (*bienséant*) it is right *ou* proper to; ~ de (*bien-fondé de qch*) to admit (to), acknowledge; (*date, somme etc*) to agree upon; ~ que (*admettre*) to admit that; ~ de faire to agree to do.

convention [kɔ̃vɑ̃sjɔ̃] *nf* convention; ~s *nfpl* (*convenances*) convention *sg*; ~ collective (*ÉCON*) collective agreement; **conventionné, e** *a* (*ADMIN*) applying charges laid down by the state.

convenu, e [kɔ̃vny] *pp de* **convenir** // *a* agreed.

conversation [kɔ̃vɛʀsɑsjɔ̃] *nf* conversation.

convertir [kɔ̃vɛʀtiʀ] *vt*: ~ qn (à) to convert sb (to); ~ qch en to convert sth into; se ~ (à) to be converted (to).

conviction [kɔ̃viksjɔ̃] *nf* conviction.

convienne etc *vb voir* **convenir**.

convier [kɔ̃vje] *vt*: ~ qn à (*dîner etc*) to (cordially) invite sb to.

convive [kɔ̃viv] *nm/f* guest (*at table*).

convivial, e [kɔ̃vivjal] *a* (*INFORM*) user-friendly.

convocation [kɔ̃vɔkɑsjɔ̃] *nf* (*document*) notification to attend; summons *sg*.

convoi [kɔ̃vwa] *nm* (*de voitures, prisonniers*) convoy; (*train*) train; ~ (funèbre) funeral procession.

convoiter [kɔ̃vwate] *vt* to covet.

convoquer [kɔ̃vɔke] *vt* (*assemblée*) to convene; (*subordonné*) to summon; (*candidat*) to ask to attend; ~ qn (à) (*réunion*) to invite sb (to attend).

convoyeur [kɔ̃vwajœʀ] *nm* (*NAVIG*) escort ship; ~ de fonds security guard.

coopération [kɔɔpeʀɑsjɔ̃] *nf* co-operation; (*ADMIN*): la C~ ≈ Voluntary Service Overseas (*Brit*), ≈ Peace Corps (*US alternative to military service*).

coopérer [kɔɔpeʀe] *vi*: ~ (à) to co-operate (in).

coordonner [kɔɔʀdɔne] *vt* to coordinate.

copain, copine [kɔpɛ̃, kɔpin] *nm/f* mate, pal.

copeau, x [kɔpo] *nm* shaving.

copie [kɔpi] *nf* copy; (*SCOL*) script, paper; exercise.

copier [kɔpje] *vt, vi* to copy; ~ sur to copy from.

copieur [kɔpjœʀ] *nm* (photo)copier.

copieux, euse [kɔpjø, -øz] *a* copious.

copine [kɔpin] *nf voir* **copain.**

copropriété [kɔpʀɔpʀijete] *nf* co-ownership, joint ownership.

coq [kɔk] *nm* cock, rooster.

coq-à-l'âne [kɔkalɑn] *nm inv* abrupt change of subject.

coque [kɔk] *nf* (*de noix, mollusque*) shell; (*de bateau*) hull; à la ~ (*CULIN*) (soft-)boiled.

coquelicot [kɔkliko] *nm* poppy.

coqueluche [kɔklyʃ] *nf* whooping-cough.

coquet, te [kɔkɛ, -ɛt] *a* flirtatious; appearance-conscious; pretty.

coquetier [kɔktje] *nm* egg-cup.

coquillage [kɔkijaʒ] *nm* (*mollusque*) shellfish *inv*; (*coquille*) shell.

coquille [kɔkij] *nf* shell; (*TYPO*) misprint; ~ St Jacques scallop.

coquin, e [kɔkɛ̃, -in] *a* mischievous, roguish; (*polisson*) naughty.

cor [kɔʀ] *nm* (*MUS*) horn; (*MÉD*): ~ (au pied) corn; réclamer à ~ et à cri to clamour for.

corail, aux [kɔʀaj, -o] *nm* coral *q*.

Coran [kɔʀɑ̃] *nm*: le ~ the Koran.

corbeau, x [kɔʀbo] *nm* crow.

corbeille [kɔʀbɛj] *nf* basket; ~ à papier waste paper basket *ou* bin.

corbillard [kɔʀbijaʀ] *nm* hearse.

corde [kɔʀd(ə)] *nf* rope; (*de violon, raquette, d'arc*) string; (*ATHLÉTISME, AUTO*): la ~ the rails *pl*; ~ à linge washing *ou* clothes line; ~ raide tight-rope; à sauter skipping rope; ~s vocales vocal cords; usé jusqu'à la ~ threadbare.

cordée [kɔʀde] *nf* (*d'alpinistes*) rope, roped party.

cordialement [kɔʀdjalmɑ̃] *ad* (*formule épistolaire*) (kind) regards.

cordon [kɔʀdɔ̃] *nm* cord, string; ~ sanitaire/de police sanitary/police cordon; ~ ombilical umbilical cord.

cordonnerie [kɔʀdɔnʀi] *nf* shoe repairer's (shop).

cordonnier [kɔʀdɔnje] *nm* shoe repairer.

coriace [kɔʀjas] *a* tough.

corne [kɔʀn(ə)] *nf* horn; (*de cerf*) antler.

corneille [kɔʀnɛj] *nf* crow.

cornemuse [kɔʀnəmyz] *nf* bagpipes *pl*.

corner [kɔʀnɛʀ] *nm* (*FOOTBALL*) corner (kick).

cornet [kɔʀnɛ] *nm* (*paper*) cone; (*de glace*) cornet, cone; ~ à piston cornet.

corniaud [kɔʀnjo] *nm* (*chien*) mongrel; (*péj*) twit, clot.

corniche [kɔʀniʃ] *nf* (*de meuble, neigeuse*) cornice; (*route*) coast road.

cornichon [kɔʀniʃɔ̃] *nm* gherkin.

Cornouailles [kɔʀnwaj] *nf* Cornwall.

corporation [kɔʀpɔʀɑsjɔ̃] *nf* corporate body.

corporel, le [kɔʀpɔʀɛl] *a* bodily; (*punition*) corporal.

corps [kɔʀ] *nm* body; à son ~ défendant against one's will; à ~ perdu headlong; perdu ~ et biens lost with all hands; prendre ~ to take shape; ~ à ~ *ad* hand-to-hand // *nm* clinch; le ~ électoral the electorate; le ~ enseignant the teach-

ing profession; ~ **de garde** guardroom.
corpulent, e [kɔʀpylã, -ãt] *a* stout.
correct, e [kɔʀɛkt] *a* correct; (*passable*) adequate.
correction [kɔʀɛksjɔ̃] *nf* (*voir corriger*) correction; (*voir correct*) correctness; (*rature, surcharge*) correction, emendation; (*coups*) thrashing.
correctionnel, le [kɔʀɛksjɔnɛl] *a* (*JUR*): **tribunal** ~ ≈ criminal court.
correspondance [kɔʀɛspɔ̃dãs] *nf* correspondence; (*de train, d'avion*) connection; **cours par** ~ correspondence course; **vente par** ~ mail-order business.
correspondant, e [kɔʀɛspɔ̃dã, -ãt] *nm/f* correspondent; (*TÉL*) person phoning (*ou* being phoned).
correspondre [kɔʀɛspɔ̃dʀ(ə)] *vi* to correspond, tally; ~ **à** to correspond to; ~ **avec qn** to correspond with sb.
corrida [kɔʀida] *nf* bullfight.
corridor [kɔʀidɔʀ] *nm* corridor.
corriger [kɔʀiʒe] *vt* (*devoir*) to correct; (*punir*) to thrash; ~ **qn de** (*défaut*) to cure sb of.
corrompre [kɔʀɔ̃pʀ(ə)] *vt* to corrupt; (*acheter: témoin etc*) to bribe.
corruption [kɔʀypsjɔ̃] *nf* corruption; bribery.
corsage [kɔʀsaʒ] *nm* bodice; blouse.
corse [kɔʀs(ə)] *a, nm/f* Corsican // *nf*: **la C~** Corsica.
corsé, e [kɔʀse] *a* vigorous; (*vin, goût*) full-flavoured; (*fig*) spicy; tricky.
corset [kɔʀsɛ] *nm* corset; bodice.
cortège [kɔʀtɛʒ] *nm* procession.
corvée [kɔʀve] *nf* chore, drudgery *q*.
cosmétique [kɔsmetik] *nm* beauty care product.
cossu, e [kɔsy] *a* well-to-do.
costaud, e [kɔsto, -od] *a* strong, sturdy.
costume [kɔstym] *nm* (*d'homme*) suit; (*de théâtre*) costume; **costumé, e** *a* dressed up.
cote [kɔt] *nf* (*en Bourse etc*) quotation; quoted value; (*d'un cheval*): **la** ~ **de** the odds *pl* on; (*d'un candidat etc*) rating; (*sur un croquis*) dimension; ~ **d'alerte** danger *ou* flood level.
côte [kɔt] *nf* (*rivage*) coast(line); (*pente*) slope; (*: sur une route*) hill; (*ANAT*) rib; (*d'un tricot, tissu*) rib, ribbing *q*; ~ **à** ~ *ad* side by side; **la C~ (d'Azur)** the (French) Riviera.
côté [kote] *nm* (*gén*) side; (*direction*) way, direction; **de chaque** ~ **(de)** on each side (of); **de tous les** ~**s** from all directions; **de quel** ~ **est-il parti?** which way did he go?; **de ce/de l'autre** ~ this/the other way; **du** ~ **de** (*provenance*) from; (*direction*) towards; (*proximité*) near; **de** ~ *ad* sideways; on one side; to one side; aside; **laisser/mettre de** ~ **to** leave/put to one side; **à** ~ *ad* (right)

nearby; beside; next door; (*d'autre part*) besides; **à** ~ **de** beside; next to; **être aux** ~**s de** to be by the side of.
coteau, x [kɔto] *nm* hill.
côtelette [kotlɛt] *nf* chop.
coter [kɔte] *vt* (*en Bourse*) to quote.
côtier, ière [kotje, -jɛʀ] *a* coastal.
cotisation [kɔtizasjɔ̃] *nf* subscription, dues *pl*; (*pour une pension*) contributions *pl*.
cotiser [kɔtize] *vi*: ~ **(à)** to pay contributions (to); **se** ~ *vi* to club together.
coton [kɔtɔ̃] *nm* cotton; ~ **hydrophile** cotton wool (*Brit*), absorbent cotton (*US*).
côtoyer [kotwaje] *vt* to be close to; to rub shoulders with; to run alongside.
cou [ku] *nm* neck.
couchant [kuʃã] *a*: **soleil** ~ setting sun.
couche [kuʃ] *nf* (*strate: gén, GÉO*) layer; (*de peinture, vernis*) coat; (*de bébé*) nappy (*Brit*), diaper (*US*); ~**s** *nfpl* (*MÉD*) confinement *sg*; ~**s sociales** social levels *ou* strata; ~**-culotte** *nf* disposable nappy (*Brit*) *ou* diaper (*US*) and waterproof pants in one.
couché, e [kuʃe] *a* lying down; (*au lit*) in bed.
coucher [kuʃe] *nm* (*du soleil*) setting // *vt* (*personne*) to put to bed; (*: loger*) to put up; (*objet*) to lay on its side // *vi* to sleep; **se** ~ *vi* (*pour dormir*) to go to bed; (*pour se reposer*) to lie down; (*soleil*) to set; ~ **de soleil** sunset.
couchette [kuʃɛt] *nf* couchette; (*de marin*) bunk.
coucou [kuku] *nm* cuckoo.
coude [kud] *nm* (*ANAT*) elbow; (*de tuyau, de la route*) bend; ~ **à** ~ *ad* shoulder to shoulder, side by side.
coudre [kudʀ(ə)] *vt* (*bouton*) to sew on; (*robe*) to sew (up) // *vi* to sew.
couenne [kwan] *nf* (*de lard*) rind.
couette [kwɛt] *nfpl* duvet, quilt.
couffin [kufɛ̃] *nm* Moses basket.
couiner [kwine] *vi* to squeal.
couler [kule] *vi* to flow, run; (*fuir: stylo, récipient*) to leak; (*sombrer: bateau*) to sink // *vt* (*cloche, sculpture*) to cast; (*bateau*) to sink; (*fig*) to ruin, bring down.
couleur [kulœʀ] *nf* colour; (*CARTES*) suit; **film/télévision en** ~**s** colour film/television.
couleuvre [kulœvʀ(ə)] *nf* grass snake.
coulisse [kulis] *nf*: ~**s** *nfpl* (*THÉÂTRE*) wings; (*fig*): **dans les** ~**s** behind the scenes; **coulisser** *vi* to slide, run.
couloir [kulwaʀ] *nm* corridor, passage; (*de bus*) gangway; (*sur la route*) bus lane; (*SPORT: de piste*) lane; (*GÉO*) gully; ~ **aérien/de navigation** air/shipping lane.
coup [ku] *nm* (*heurt, choc*) knock; (*affectif*) blow, shock; (*agressif*) blow;

(avec arme à feu) shot; (de l'horloge) chime; stroke; (SPORT) stroke; shot; blow; (fam: fois) time; ~ **de coude** nudge (with the elbow); ~ **de tonnerre** clap of thunder; ~ **de sonnette** ring of the bell; ~ **de crayon** stroke of the pencil; **donner un** ~ **de balai** to give the floor a sweep; **avoir le** ~ (fig) to have the knack; **boire un** ~ to have a drink; **être dans le** ~ to be in on it; **du** ~... **so** (you see)...; **d'un seul** ~ (subitement) suddenly; (à la fois) at one go; in one blow; **du premier** ~ first time; **du même** ~ at the same time; **à** ~ **sûr** definitely, without fail; ~ **sur** ~ in quick succession; **sur le** ~ outright; **sous le** ~ **de** (surprise etc) under the influence of; ~ **de chance** stroke of luck; ~ **de couteau** stab (of a knife); ~ **d'envoi** kick-off; ~ **d'essai** first attempt; ~ **de feu** shot; ~ **de filet** (POLICE) haul; ~ **franc** free kick; ~ **de frein** (sharp) braking q; ~ **de main**: **donner un** ~ **de main à qn** to give sb a (helping) hand; ~ **d'œil** glance; ~ **de pied** kick; ~ **de poing** punch; ~ **de soleil** sunburn q; ~ **de téléphone** phone call; ~ **de tête** (fig) (sudden) impulse; ~ **de théâtre** (fig) dramatic turn of events; ~ **de vent** gust of wind; **en** ~ **de vent** in a tearing hurry.

coupable [kupabl(ə)] a guilty // nm/f (gén) culprit; (JUR) guilty party.

coupe [kup] nf (verre) goblet; (à fruits) dish; (SPORT) cup; (de cheveux, de vêtement) cut; (graphique, plan) (cross) section; **être sous la** ~ **de** to be under the control of.

coupe-papier [kuppapje] nm inv paper knife.

couper [kupe] vt to cut; (retrancher) to cut (out); (route, courant) to cut off; (appétit) to take away; (vin, cidre) to blend; (: à table) to dilute // vi to cut; (prendre un raccourci) to take a shortcut; **se** ~ vi (se blesser) to cut o.s.; ~ **la parole à qn** to cut sb short.

couperosé, e [kuproze] a blotchy.

couple [kupl(ə)] nm couple.

couplet [kuplɛ] nm verse.

coupole [kupol] nf dome; cupola.

coupon [kupɔ̃] nm (ticket) coupon; (de tissu) remnant; roll; ~**-réponse** nm reply coupon.

coupure [kupyr] nf cut; (billet de banque) note; (de journal) cutting; ~ **de courant** power cut.

cour [kur] nf (de ferme, jardin) (court)yard; (d'immeuble) back yard; (JUR, royale) court; **faire la** ~ **à qn** to court sb; ~ **d'assises** court of assizes; ~ **martiale** court-martial.

courage [kuraʒ] nm courage, bravery; **courageux, euse** a brave, courageous.

couramment [kuramã] ad commonly; (parler) fluently.

courant, e [kurã, -ãt] a (fréquent) common; (COMM, gén: normal) standard; (en cours) current // nm current; (fig) movement; trend; **être au** ~ (de) (fait, nouvelle) to know (about); **mettre qn au** ~ (de) (fait, nouvelle) to tell sb (about); (nouveau travail etc) to teach sb the basics (of); **se tenir au** ~ (de) (techniques etc) to keep o.s. up-to-date (on); **dans le** ~ **de** (pendant) in the course of; **le 10** ~ (COMM) the 10th inst; ~ **d'air** draught; ~ **électrique** (electric) current, power.

courbature [kurbatyr] nf ache.

courbe [kurb(ə)] a curved // nf curve.

courber [kurbe] vt to bend.

coureur, euse [kurœr, -øz] nm/f (SPORT) runner (ou driver); (péj) womanizer/manhunter; ~ **automobile** racing driver.

courge [kurʒ(ə)] nf (CULIN) marrow.

courgette [kurʒɛt] nf courgette (Brit), zucchini (US).

courir [kurir] vi to run // vt (SPORT: épreuve) to compete in; (risque) to run; (danger) to face; ~ **les magasins** to go round the shops; **le bruit court que** the rumour is going round that.

couronne [kurɔn] nf crown; (de fleurs) wreath, circlet.

courons etc vb voir **courir**.

courrier [kurje] nm mail, post; (lettres à écrire) letters pl; **long/moyen** ~ a (AVIAT) long-/medium-haul.

courroie [kurwa] nf strap; (TECH) belt.

courrons etc vb voir **courir**.

cours [kur] nm (leçon) lesson; class; (série de leçons) course; (cheminement) course; (écoulement) flow; (COMM) rate; price; **donner libre** ~ **à** to give free expression to; **avoir** ~ (monnaie) to be legal tender; (fig) to be current; (SCOL) to have a class ou lecture; **en** ~ (année) current; (travaux) in progress; **en** ~ **de route** on the way; **au** ~ **de** in the course of, during; ~ **d'eau** waterway; ~ **du soir** night school.

course [kurs(ə)] nf running; (SPORT: épreuve) race; (d'un taxi, autocar) journey, trip; (petite mission) errand; ~**s** nfpl (achats) shopping sg; **faire des** ~**s** to do some shopping.

court, e [kur, kurt(ə)] a short // ad short // nm: ~ **de** (de tennis) (tennis) court; **tourner** ~ to come to a sudden end; **ça fait** ~ that's not very long; **à** ~ **de** short of; **prendre qn de** ~ to catch sb unawares; **tirer à la** ~**e paille** to draw lots; ~**-circuit** nm short-circuit.

courtier, ère [kurtje, -jɛr] nm/f broker.

courtiser [kurtize] vt to court, woo.

courtois, e [kurtwa, -waz] a courteous.

couru, e pp de **courir** // a: **c'est** ~ it's a safe bet.

cousais etc vb voir **coudre**.

couscous [kuskus] nm couscous.
cousin, e [kuzɛ̃, -in] nm/f cousin.
coussin [kusɛ̃] nm cushion.
cousu, e [kuzy] pp de **coudre**.
coût [ku] nm cost; **le ~ de la vie** the cost of living.
coûtant [kutɑ̃] am: **au prix ~** at cost price.
couteau, x [kuto] nm knife; **~ à cran d'arrêt** flick-knife.
coûter [kute] vt, vi to cost; **combien ça coûte?** how much is it?, what does it cost?; **coûte que coûte** at all costs; **coûteux, euse** a costly, expensive.
coutume [kutym] nf custom.
couture [kutyʀ] nf sewing; dressmaking; (points) seam.
couturier [kutyʀje] nm fashion designer.
couturière [kutyʀjɛʀ] nf dressmaker.
couvée [kuve] nf brood, clutch.
couvent [kuvɑ̃] nm (de sœurs) convent; (de frères) monastery.
couver [kuve] vt to hatch; (maladie) to be sickening for // vi (feu) to smoulder; (révolte) to be brewing.
couvercle [kuvɛʀkl(ə)] nm lid; (de bombe aérosol etc, qui se visse) cap, top.
couvert, e [kuvɛʀ, -ɛʀt(ə)] pp de **couvrir** // a (ciel) overcast // nm place setting; (place à table) place; (au restaurant) cover charge; **~s** nmpl cutlery sg; **~ de** covered with ou in; **mettre le ~** to lay the table.
couverture [kuvɛʀtyʀ] nf blanket; (de bâtiment) roofing; (de livre, assurance, fig) cover; (presse) coverage; **~ chauffante** electric blanket.
couveuse [kuvøz] nf (de maternité) incubator.
couvre... [kuvʀ(ə)] préfixe: **~-chef** nm hat; **~-feu** nm curfew; **~-lit** nm bedspread.
couvrir [kuvʀiʀ] vt to cover; **se ~** vi (ciel) to cloud over; (s'habiller) to cover up; (se coiffer) to put on one's hat.
crabe [kʀab] nm crab.
cracher [kʀaʃe] vi, vt to spit.
crachin [kʀaʃɛ̃] nm drizzle.
craie [kʀɛ] nf chalk.
craindre [kʀɛ̃dʀ(ə)] vt to fear, be afraid of; (être sensible à: chaleur, froid) to be easily damaged by.
crainte [kʀɛ̃t] nf fear; **de ~ de/que** for fear of/that; **craintif, ive** a timid.
cramoisi, e [kʀamwazi] a crimson.
crampe [kʀɑ̃p] nf cramp.
cramponner [kʀɑ̃pɔne]: **se ~** vi: **se ~ (à)** to hang ou cling on (to).
cran [kʀɑ̃] nm (entaille) notch; (de courroie) hole; (courage) guts pl; **~ d'arrêt** safety catch.
crâne [kʀɑn] nm skull.
crâner [kʀɑne] vi (fam) to show off.
crapaud [kʀapo] nm toad.

crapule [kʀapyl] nf villain.
craquement [kʀakmɑ̃] nm crack, snap; (du plancher) creak, creaking q.
craquer [kʀake] vi (bois, plancher) to creak; (fil, branche) to snap; (couture) to come apart; (fig) to break down // vt (allumette) to strike.
crasse [kʀas] nf grime, filth.
cravache [kʀavaʃ] nf (riding) crop.
cravate [kʀavat] nf tie.
crawl [kʀol] nm crawl; **dos crawlé** backstroke.
crayeux, euse [kʀɛjø, -øz] a chalky.
crayon [kʀɛjɔ̃] nm pencil; **~ à bille** ballpoint pen; **~ de couleur** crayon, colouring pencil; **~ optique** light pen.
créancier, ière [kʀeɑ̃sje, -jɛʀ] nm/f creditor.
création [kʀeasjɔ̃] nf creation.
créature [kʀeatyʀ] nf creature.
crécelle [kʀesɛl] nf rattle.
crèche [kʀɛʃ] nf (de Noël) crib; (garderie) crèche, day nursery.
crédit [kʀedi] nm (gén) credit; **~s** nmpl funds; **payer/acheter à ~** to pay/buy on credit ou on easy terms; **faire ~ à qn** to give sb credit; **créditer** vt: **créditer un compte (de)** to credit an account (with).
crédule [kʀedyl] a credulous, gullible.
créer [kʀee] vt to create; (THÉÂTRE) to produce (for the first time).
crémaillère [kʀemajɛʀ] nf (RAIL) rack; **pendre la ~** to have a house-warming party.
crématoire [kʀematwaʀ] a: **four ~** crematorium.
crème [kʀɛm] nf cream; (entremets) cream dessert // a inv cream(-coloured); **un (café) ~** ≈ a white coffee; **~ chantilly, ~ fouettée** whipped cream; **~ à raser** shaving cream; **crémerie** nf dairy; **crémeux, euse** a creamy.
créneau, x [kʀeno] nm (de fortification) crenel(le); (fig) gap, slot; (AUTO): **faire un ~** to reverse into a parking space (between cars alongside the kerb).
crêpe [kʀɛp] nf (galette) pancake // nm (tissu) crêpe; **crêpé, e** a (cheveux) backcombed; **~rie** nf pancake shop ou restaurant.
crépir [kʀepiʀ] vt to roughcast.
crépiter [kʀepite] vi to sputter, splutter; to crackle.
crépon [kʀepɔ̃] nm seersucker.
crépu, e [kʀepy] a frizzy, fuzzy.
crépuscule [kʀepyskyl] nm twilight, dusk.
cresson [kʀesɔ̃] nm watercress.
crête [kʀɛt] nf (de coq) comb; (de vague, montagne) crest.
creuser [kʀøze] vt (trou, tunnel) to dig; (sol) to dig a hole in; (bois) to hollow out; (fig) to go (deeply) into; **ça creuse** that gives you a real appetite; **se ~ (la cervelle)** to rack one's brains.

creux, euse [krø, -øz] a hollow // nm hollow; (fig: sur graphique etc) trough; **heures creuses** slack periods; off-peak periods.

crevaison [krəvɛzɔ̃] nf puncture.

crevasse [krəvas] nf (dans le sol) crack, fissure; (de glacier) crevasse.

crevé, e [krəve] a (fatigué) all in, exhausted.

crever [krəve] vt (papier) to tear, break; (tambour, ballon) to burst // vi (pneu) to burst; (automobiliste) to have a puncture (Brit) ou a flat (tire) (US); (fam) to die; **cela lui a crevé un œil** it blinded him in one eye.

crevette [krəvɛt] nf: ~ **(rose)** prawn; ~ **grise** shrimp.

cri [kri] nm cry, shout; (d'animal: spécifique) cry, call; **c'est le dernier** ~ (fig) it's the latest fashion.

criant, e [krijã, -ãt] a (injustice) glaring.

criard, e [krijar, -ard(ə)] a (couleur) garish, loud; yelling.

crible [kribl(ə)] nm riddle; **passer qch au** ~ (fig) to go over sth with a fine-tooth comb.

cric [krik] nm (AUTO) jack.

crier [krije] vi (pour appeler) to shout, cry (out); (de peur, de douleur etc) to scream, yell // vt (ordre, injure) to shout (out), yell (out).

crime [krim] nm crime; (meurtre) murder; **criminel, le** nm/f criminal; murderer.

crin [krɛ̃] nm hair q; (fibre) horsehair.

crinière [krinjɛr] nf mane.

crique [krik] nf creek, inlet.

criquet [krikɛ] nm locust; grasshopper.

crise [kriz] nf crisis (pl crises); (MÉD) attack; fit; ~ **cardiaque** heart attack; ~ **de foie** bilious attack; ~ **de nerfs** attack of nerves.

crisper [krispe] vt to tense; (poings) to clench; **se** ~ vi to tense; to clench; (personne) to get tense.

crisser [krise] vi (neige) to crunch; (pneu) to screech.

cristal, aux [kristal, -o] nm crystal.

cristallin, e [kristalɛ̃, -in] a crystal-clear.

critère [kritɛr] nm criterion (pl ia).

critiquable [kritikabl(ə)] a open to criticism.

critique [kritik] a critical // nm/f (de théâtre, musique) critic // nf criticism; (THÉÂTRE etc: article) review.

critiquer [kritike] vt (dénigrer) to criticize; (évaluer, juger) to assess, examine (critically).

croasser [krɔase] vi to caw.

croc [kro] nm (dent) fang; (de boucher) hook.

croc-en-jambe [krɔkɑ̃ʒɑ̃b] nm: **faire un** ~ **à qn** to trip sb up.

croche [krɔʃ] nf (MUS) quaver (Brit), eighth note (US).

croche-pied [krɔʃpje] nm = **croc-en-jambe**.

crochet [krɔʃɛ] nm hook; (détour) detour; (TRICOT: aiguille) crochet hook; (: technique) crochet; ~**s** nmpl (TYPO) square brackets; **vivre aux** ~**s de qn** to live ou sponge off sb; **crocheter** vt (serrure) to pick.

crochu, e [krɔʃy] a hooked; claw-like.

crocodile [krɔkɔdil] nm crocodile.

crocus [krɔkys] nm crocus.

croire [krwar] vt to believe; **se** ~ **fort** to think one is strong; ~ **que** to believe ou think that; ~ **à**, ~ **en** to believe in.

crois vb voir **croître**.

croisade [krwazad] nf crusade.

croisé, e [krwaze] a (veston) double-breasted.

croisement [krwazmɑ̃] nm (carrefour) crossroads sg; (BIO) crossing; cross-breed.

croiser [krwaze] vt (personne, voiture) to pass; (route) to cross, cut across; (BIO) to cross // vi (NAVIG) to cruise; ~ **les jambes/bras** to cross one's legs/fold one's arms; **se** ~ vi (personnes, véhicules) to pass each other; (routes, lettres) to cross; (regards) to meet.

croiseur [krwazœr] nm cruiser (warship).

croisière [krwazjɛr] nf cruise; **vitesse de** ~ (AUTO etc) cruising speed.

croisillon [krwazijɔ̃] nm lattice.

croissance [krwasɑ̃s] nf growth.

croissant [krwasɑ̃] nm (à manger) croissant; (motif) crescent.

croître [krwatr(ə)] vi to grow.

croix [krwa] nf cross; **en** ~, **ad** in the form of a cross; **la C~ Rouge** the Red Cross.

croque... [krɔk] préfixe: ~**-monsieur** nm inv toasted ham and cheese sandwich.

croquer [krɔke] vt (manger) to crunch; to munch; (dessiner) to sketch // vi to be crisp ou crunchy; **chocolat à** ~ plain dessert chocolate.

croquis [krɔki] nm sketch.

crosse [krɔs] nf (de fusil) butt; (de revolver) grip.

crotte [krɔt] nf droppings pl.

crotté, e [krɔte] a muddy, mucky.

crottin [krɔtɛ̃] nm dung, manure.

crouler [krule] vi (s'effondrer) to collapse; (être délabré) to be crumbling.

croupe [krup] nf rump; **en** ~ pillion.

croupir [krupir] vi to stagnate.

croustillant, e [krustijɑ̃, -ãt] a crisp; (fig) spicy.

croûte [krut] nf crust; (du fromage) rind; (MÉD) scab; **en** ~ (CULIN) in pastry.

croûton [krutɔ̃] nm (CULIN) crouton;

(*bout du pain*) crust, heel.
croyable [krwajabl(ə)] *a* credible.
croyant, e [krwajã, -ãt] *nm/f* believer.
C.R.S. *sigle fpl* (= *Compagnies républicaines de sécurité*) *a* state security police force // *sigle m* member of the C.R.S.
cru [kry] *pp de* croire // *a* (*non cuit*) raw; (*lumière, couleur*) harsh; (*paroles, description*) crude // *nm* (*vignoble*) vineyard; (*vin*) wine.
crû *pp de* croître.
cruauté [kryote] *nf* cruelty.
cruche [kryʃ] *nf* pitcher, jug.
crucifix [krysifi] *nm* crucifix.
crucifixion [krysifiksjõ] *nf* crucifixion.
crudités [krydite] *nfpl* (*CULIN*) salads.
crue [kry] *nf voir* cru.
cruel, le [kryɛl] *a* cruel.
crus *etc* **crûs** *etc, vb voir* croire, croître.
crustacés [krystase] *nmpl* shellfish.
Cuba [kyba] *nf* Cuba.
cube [kyb] *nm* cube; (*jouet*) brick; mètre ~ cubic metre; 2 au ~ 2 cubed.
cueillir [kœjir] *vt* (*fruits, fleurs*) to pick, gather; (*fig*) to catch.
cuiller *ou* **cuillère** [kɥijɛr] *nf* spoon; ~ à café coffee spoon; (*CULIN*) ≈ teaspoonful; ~ à soupe soup-spoon; (*CULIN*) ≈ tablespoonful; **cuillerée** *nf* spoonful.
cuir [kɥir] *nm* leather; ~ chevelu scalp.
cuirassé [kɥirase] *nm* (*NAVIG*) battleship.
cuire [kɥir] *vt* (*aliments*) to cook; (*au four*) to bake; (*poterie*) to fire // *vi* to cook; **bien cuit** (*viande*) well done; **trop cuit** overdone.
cuisant, e [kɥizã, -ãt] *a* (*douleur*) stinging; (*fig: souvenir, échec*) bitter.
cuisine [kɥizin] *nf* (*pièce*) kitchen; (*art culinaire*) cookery, cooking; (*nourriture*) cooking, food; **faire la ~** to cook; **cuisiner** *vt* to cook; (*fam*) to grill // *vi* to cook; **cuisinier, ière** *nm/f* cook // *nf* (*poêle*) cooker.
cuisse [kɥis] *nf* thigh; (*CULIN*) leg.
cuisson [kɥisõ] *nf* cooking; firing.
cuit, e *pp de* cuire.
cuivre [kɥivr(ə)] *nm* copper; **les ~s** (*MUS*) the brass.
cul [ky] *nm* (*fam!*) arse (!).
culasse [kylas] *nf* (*AUTO*) cylinder-head; (*de fusil*) breech.
culbute [kylbyt] *nf* somersault; (*accidentelle*) tumble, fall.
culminant, e [kylminã, -ãt] *a*: **point ~** highest point.
culminer [kylmine] *vi* to reach its highest point; to tower.
culot [kylo] *nm* (*effronterie*) cheek.
culotte [kylɔt] *nf* (*pantalon*) trousers *pl* (*Brit*), pants *pl* (*US*); (*de femme*) knickers *pl* (*Brit*), panties *pl*; ~ de cheval riding breeches *pl*.

culpabilité [kylpabilite] *nf* guilt.
culte [kylt(ə)] *nm* (*religion*) religion; (*hommage, vénération*) worship; (*protestant*) service.
cultivateur, trice [kyltivatœr, -tris] *nm/f* farmer.
cultivé, e [kyltive] *a* (*personne*) cultured, cultivated.
cultiver [kyltive] *vt* to cultivate; (*légumes*) to grow, cultivate.
culture [kyltyr] *nf* cultivation; growing; (*connaissances etc*) culture; ~ physique physical training; **culturisme** *nm* bodybuilding.
cumin [kymẽ] *nm* (*CULIN*) caraway seeds *pl*; cumin.
cumuler [kymyle] *vt* (*emplois, honneurs*) to hold concurrently; (*salaires*) to draw concurrently; (*JUR: droits*) to accumulate.
cupide [kypid] *a* greedy, grasping.
cure [kyr] *nf* (*MÉD*) course of treatment; **n'avoir ~ de** to pay no attention to.
curé [kyre] *nm* parish priest.
cure-dent [kyrdã] *nm* toothpick.
cure-pipe [kyrpip] *nm* pipe cleaner.
curer [kyre] *vt* to clean out.
curieux, euse [kyrjø, -øz] *a* (*étrange*) strange, curious; (*indiscret*) curious, inquisitive // *nmpl* (*badauds*) onlookers; **curiosité** *nf* curiosity; (*site*) unusual feature.
curriculum vitae [kyrikylɔmvite] *nm inv* (*abr* C.V.) curriculum vitae (C.V.).
curseur [kyrsœr] *nm* (*INFORM*) cursor.
cuti-réaction [kytireaksjõ] *nf* (*MÉD*) skin-test.
cuve [kyv] *nf* vat; (*à mazout etc*) tank.
cuvée [kyve] *nf* vintage.
cuvette [kyvet] *nf* (*récipient*) bowl, basin; (*GÉO*) basin.
C.V. *sigle m* (*AUTO*) *voir* cheval; (*COMM*) = curriculum vitae.
cyanure [sjanyr] *nm* cyanide.
cyclable [siklabl(ə)] *a*: **piste ~** cycle track.
cycle [sikl(ə)] *nm* cycle.
cyclisme [siklism(ə)] *nm* cycling.
cycliste [siklist(ə)] *nm/f* cyclist // *a* cycle *cpd*; **coureur ~** racing cyclist.
cyclomoteur [siklɔmɔtœr] *nm* moped.
cyclone [siklon] *nm* hurricane.
cygne [siɲ] *nm* swan.
cylindre [silẽdr(ə)] *nm* cylinder; **cylindrée** *nf* (*AUTO*) (cubic) capacity.
cymbale [sẽbal] *nf* cymbal.
cynique [sinik] *a* cynical.
cystite [sistit] *nf* cystitis.

D

d' *prép de* de.
dactylo [daktilo] *nf* (*aussi*: ~graphe) typist; (*aussi*: ~graphie) typing;

~**graphier** *vt* to type (out).

dada [dada] *nm* hobby-horse.

daigner [deɲe] *vt* to deign.

daim [dɛ̃] *nm* (fallow) deer *inv*; (*peau*) buckskin; (*imitation*) suede.

dalle [dal] *nf* paving stone; slab.

daltonien, ne [daltɔnjɛ̃, -jɛn] *a* colour-blind.

dam [dam] *nm*: **au grand ~ de** much to the detriment (*ou* annoyance) of.

dame [dam] *nf* lady; (CARTES, ÉCHECS) queen; ~**s** *nfpl* (*jeu*) draughts *sg* (*Brit*), checkers (*US*).

damner [dɑne] *vt* to damn.

dancing [dɑ̃siŋ] *nm* dance hall.

Danemark [danmark] *nm* Denmark.

danger [dɑ̃ʒe] *nm* danger; **dangereux, euse** *a* dangerous.

danois, e [danwa, -waz] *a* Danish // *nm/f*: D~, e Dane // *nm* (LING) Danish.

dans [dɑ̃] *prép* **1** (*position*) in; (*à l'intérieur de*) inside; c'est ~ **le tiroir/le salon** it's in the drawer/lounge; ~ **la boîte** in *ou* inside the box; **marcher ~ la ville** to walk about the town **2** (*direction*) into; **elle a couru ~ le salon** she ran into the lounge **3** (*provenance*) out of, from; **je l'ai pris ~ le tiroir/salon** I took it out of *ou* from the drawer/lounge; **boire ~ un verre** to drink out of *ou* from a glass **4** (*temps*) in; ~ **2 mois** in 2 months, in 2 months' time **5** (*approximation*) about; ~ **les 20 F** about 20 F.

danse [dɑ̃s] *nf*: **la ~** dancing; **une ~** a dance; **danser** *vi, vt* to dance; **danseur, euse** *nm/f* ballet dancer/ballerina; (*au bal etc*) dancer; partner.

dard [dar] *nm* sting (*organ*).

date [dat] *nf* date; **de longue ~** a long-standing; ~ **de naissance** date of birth; **dater** *vt, vi* to date; **dater de** to date from; **à dater de** (as) from.

datte [dat] *nf* date; **dattier** *nm* date palm.

dauphin [dofɛ̃] *nm* (ZOOL) dolphin.

davantage [davɑ̃taʒ] *ad* more; (*plus longtemps*) longer; ~ **de** more.

de (*de + le = du, de + les = des*) [də, dy, de] ♦ *prép* **1** (*appartenance*) of; **le toit de la maison** the roof of the house; **la voiture d'Élisabeth/de mes parents** Elizabeth's/my parents' car **2** (*provenance*) from; **il vient de Londres** he comes from London; **elle est sortie du cinéma** she came out of the cinema **3** (*caractérisation, mesure*): **un mur de brique/bureau d'acajou** a brick wall/ mahogany desk; **un billet de 50 F** a 50 franc note; **une pièce de 2m de large** *ou* **large de 2m** a room 2m wide, a 2m-wide room; **un bébé de 10 mois** a 10-month-old

baby; **12 mois de crédit/travail** 12 months' credit/work; **augmenter de 10 F** to increase by 10 F; **de 14 à 18** from 14 to 18

♦ *dét* **1** (*phrases affirmatives*) some (*souvent omis*); **du vin, de l'eau, des pommes** (some) wine, (some) water, (some) apples; **des enfants sont venus** some children came; **pendant des mois** for months **2** (*phrases interrogatives et négatives*) any; **a-t-il du vin?** has he got any wine? **il n'a pas de pommes/d'enfants** he hasn't (got) any apples/children, he has no apples/children.

dé [de] *nm* (à jouer) die *ou* dice (*pl* dice); (*aussi*: ~ **à coudre**) thimble.

déambuler [deɑ̃byle] *vi* to stroll about.

débâcle [debɑkl(ə)] *nf* rout.

déballer [debale] *vt* to unpack.

débandade [debɑ̃dad] *nf* rout; scattering.

débarbouiller [debarbuje] *vt* to wash; **se ~** *vi* to wash (one's face).

débarcadère [debarkadɛr] *nm* wharf.

débardeur [debardœr] *nm* docker, stevedore; (*maillot*) tank top.

débarquer [debarke] *vt* to unload, land // *vi* to disembark; (*fig*) to turn up.

débarras [debara] *nm* lumber room; junk cupboard; **bon ~!** good riddance!

débarrasser [debarase] *vt* to clear; ~ **qn de** (*vêtements, paquets*) to relieve sb of; **se ~ de** *vt* to get rid of.

débat [deba] *nm* discussion, debate.

débattre [debatr(ə)] *vt* to discuss, debate; **se ~** *vi* to struggle.

débaucher [deboʃe] *vt* (*licencier*) to lay off, dismiss; (*entraîner*) to lead astray, debauch.

débile [debil] *a* weak, feeble; (*fam: idiot*) dim-witted; ~ **mental, e** *nm/f* mental defective.

débit [debi] *nm* (*d'un liquide, fleuve*) flow; (*d'un magasin*) turnover (of goods); (*élocution*) delivery; (*bancaire*) debit; ~ **de boissons** drinking establishment; ~ **de tabac** tobacconist's; **débiter** *vt* (*compte*) to debit; (*liquide, gaz*) to give out; (*couper: bois, viande*) to cut up; (*péj: paroles etc*) to churn out; **débiteur, trice** *nm/f* debtor // *a* in debit; (*compte*) debit *cpd*.

déblayer [debleje] *vt* to clear.

débloquer [debloke] *vt* (*frein*) to release; (*prix, crédits*) to free.

déboires [debwar] *nmpl* setbacks.

déboiser [debwaze] *vt* to deforest.

déboîter [debwate] *vt* (AUTO) to pull out; **se ~ le genou** *etc* to dislocate one's knee *etc*.

débonnaire [debonɛr] *a* easy-going, good-natured.

débordé, e [deborde] *a*: **être ~ (de)** (*travail, demandes*) to be snowed under (with).

déborder [debɔʀde] vi to overflow; (lait etc) to boil over; ~ (de) qch (dépasser) to extend beyond sth.

débouché [debuʃe] nm (pour vendre) outlet; (perspective d'emploi) opening.

déboucher [debuʃe] vt (évier, tuyau etc) to unblock; (bouteille) to uncork // vi: ~ de to emerge from; ~ sur to come out onto; to open out onto.

débourser [debuʀse] vt to pay out.

debout [dəbu] ad: être ~ (personne) to be standing, stand; (: levé, éveillé) to be up; (chose) to be upright; être encore ~ (fig: en état) to be still going; se mettre ~ to stand up; se tenir ~ to stand; ~! stand up!; (du lit) get up!; cette histoire ne tient pas ~ this story doesn't hold water.

déboutonner [debutɔne] vt to undo, un-button.

débraillé, e [debʀaje] a slovenly, unti-dy.

débrancher [debʀɑ̃ʃe] vt to disconnect; (appareil électrique) to unplug.

débrayage [debʀejaʒ] nm (AUTO) clutch.

débrayer [debʀeje] vi (AUTO) to de-clutch; (cesser le travail) to stop work.

débris [debʀi] nm (fragment) fragment // nmpl rubbish sg; debris sg.

débrouillard, e [debʀujaʀ, -aʀd(ə)] a smart, resourceful.

débrouiller [debʀuje] vt to disentangle, untangle; se ~ vi to manage.

débusquer [debyske] vt to drive out (from cover).

début [deby] nm beginning, start; ~s beginnings; début sg.

débutant, e [debytɑ̃, -ɑ̃t] nm/f beginner, novice.

débuter [debyte] vi to begin, start; (faire ses débuts) to start out.

deçà [dəsa]: en ~ de prép this side of.

décacheter [dekaʃte] vt to unseal.

décadence [dekadɑ̃s] nf decadence; decline.

décaféiné, e [dekafeine] a decaf-feinated.

décalage [dekalaʒ] nm gap; dis-crepancy; ~ horaire time difference (be-tween time zones); time-lag.

décaler [dekale] vt (dans le temps: avancer) to bring forward; (: retarder) to put back; (changer de position) to shift forward ou back.

décalquer [dekalke] vt to trace; (par pression) to transfer.

décamper [dekɑ̃pe] vi to clear out ou off.

décanter [dekɑ̃te] vt to allow to settle (and decant).

décaper [dekape] vt to strip; (avec abrasif) to scour; (avec papier de verre) to sand.

décapiter [dekapite] vt to behead; (par accident) to decapitate.

décapotable [dekapɔtabl(ə)] a convert-ible.

décapsuler [dekapsyle] vt to take the cap ou top off; **décapsuleur** nm bottle-opener.

décédé, e [desede] a deceased.

décéder [desede] vi to die.

déceler [desle] vt to discover, detect; to indicate, reveal.

décembre [desɑ̃bʀ(ə)] nm December.

décemment [desamɑ̃] ad decently.

décennie [desni] nf decade.

décent, e [desɑ̃, -ɑ̃t] a decent.

déception [desɛpsjɔ̃] nf disappointment.

décerner [desɛʀne] vt to award.

décès [desɛ] nm death, decease.

décevoir [desvwaʀ] vt to disappoint.

déchaîner [deʃene] vt to unleash, arouse; se ~ to be unleashed.

déchanter [deʃɑ̃te] vi to become disillu-sioned.

décharge [deʃaʀʒ(ə)] nf (dépôt d'ordures) rubbish tip ou dump; (électri-que) electrical discharge; à la ~ de in defence of.

décharger [deʃaʀʒe] vt (marchandise, véhicule) to unload; (ÉLEC, faire feu) to discharge; ~ qn de (responsabilité) to release sb from.

décharné, e [deʃaʀne] a emaciated.

déchausser [deʃose] vt (skis) to take off; se ~ vi to take off one's shoes; (dent) to come ou work loose.

déchéance [deʃeɑ̃s] nf degeneration; decay, decline; fall.

déchet [deʃɛ] nm (de bois, tissu etc) scrap; (perte: gén COMM) wastage, waste; ~s nmpl (ordures) refuse sg, rub-bish sg.

déchiffrer [deʃifʀe] vt to decipher.

déchiqueter [deʃikte] vt to tear ou pull to pieces.

déchirement [deʃiʀmɑ̃] nm (chagrin) wrench, heartbreak; (gén pl: conflit) rift, split.

déchirer [deʃiʀe] vt to tear; (en mor-ceaux) to tear up; (pour ouvrir) to tear off; (arracher) to tear out; (fig) to rack; to tear (apart); se ~ vi to tear, rip; se ~ un muscle to tear a muscle.

déchirure [deʃiʀyʀ] nf (accroc) tear, rip; ~ musculaire torn muscle.

déchoir [deʃwaʀ] vi (personne) to lower o.s., demean o.s.

déchu, e [deʃy] a fallen; deposed.

décidé, e [deside] a (personne, air) de-termined; c'est ~ it's decided.

décidément [desidemɑ̃] ad undoubt-edly; really.

décider [deside] vt: ~ qch to decide on sth; ~ de faire/que to decide to do/that; ~ qn (à faire qch) to persuade sb (to do sth); ~ de qch to decide upon sth; (suj:

chose) to determine sth; se ~ (à faire) to decide (to do), make up one's mind (to do); se ~ pour to decide on *ou* in favour of.

décilitre [desilitʀ(ə)] *nm* decilitre.

décimal, e, aux [desimal, -o] *a, nf* decimal.

décimètre [desimɛtʀ(ə)] *nm* decimetre; **double ~** (20 cm) ruler.

décisif, ive [desizif, -iv] *a* decisive.

décision [desizjɔ̃] *nf* decision; (*fermeté*) decisiveness, decision.

déclaration [deklaʀasjɔ̃] *nf* declaration; registration; (*discours: POL etc*) statement; ~ (d'impôts) ≈ tax return; ~ (de sinistre) (insurance) claim.

déclarer [deklaʀe] *vt* to declare; (*décès, naissance*) to register; se ~ *vi* (*feu, maladie*) to break out.

déclasser [deklase] *vt* to relegate; to downgrade; to lower in status.

déclencher [deklɑ̃ʃe] *vt* (*mécanisme etc*) to release; (*sonnerie*) to set off, activate; (*attaque, grève*) to launch; (*provoquer*) to trigger off; se ~ *vi* to release itself; to go off.

déclic [deklik] *nm* trigger mechanism; (*bruit*) click.

décliner [dekline] *vi* to decline // *vt* (*invitation*) to decline; (*responsabilité*) to refuse to accept; (*nom, adresse*) to state.

déclivité [deklivite] *nf* slope, incline.

décocher [dekɔʃe] *vt* to throw; to shoot.

décoiffer [dekwafe] *vt*: ~ qn to mess up sb's hair; to take sb's hat off; se ~ *vi* to take off one's hat.

déçois *etc vb voir* **décevoir**.

décollage [dekɔlaʒ] *nm* (*AVIAT*) takeoff.

décoller [dekɔle] *vt* to unstick // *vi* (*avion*) to take off; se ~ *vi* to come unstuck.

décolleté, e [dekɔlte] *a* low-cut; wearing a low-cut dress // *nm* low neck(line); (*bare*) neck and shoulders; (*plongeant*) cleavage.

décolorer [dekɔlɔʀe] *vt* (*tissu*) to fade; (*cheveux*) to bleach, lighten; se ~ *vi* to fade.

décombres [dekɔ̃bʀ(ə)] *nmpl* rubble *sg*, debris *sg*.

décommander [dekɔmɑ̃de] *vt* to cancel; (*invités*) to put off; se ~ *vi* to cancel one's appointment *etc*, cry off.

décomposé, e [dekɔ̃poze] *a* (*pourri*) decomposed; (*visage*) haggard, distorted.

décompte [dekɔ̃t] *nm* deduction; (*facture*) detailed account.

déconcerter [dekɔ̃sɛʀte] *vt* to disconcert, confound.

déconfit, e [dekɔ̃fi, -it] *a* crestfallen.

déconfiture [dekɔ̃fityʀ] *nf* failure, defeat; collapse, ruin.

décongeler [dekɔ̃ʒle] *vt* to thaw.

déconner [dekɔne] *vi* (*fam*) to talk rubbish.

déconseiller [dekɔ̃seje] *vt*: ~ qch (à qn) to advise (sb) against sth.

déconsidérer [dekɔ̃sideʀe] *vt* to discredit.

décontracter [dekɔ̃tʀakte] *vt, se ~ vi* to relax.

déconvenue [dekɔ̃vny] *nf* disappointment.

décor [dekɔʀ] *nm* décor; (*paysage*) scenery; ~s *nmpl* (*THÉÂTRE*) scenery *sg*, décor *sg*; (*CINÉMA*) set *sg*.

décorateur [dekɔʀatœʀ] *nm* (interior) decorator; (*CINÉMA*) set designer.

décoration [dekɔʀasjɔ̃] *nf* decoration.

décorer [dekɔʀe] *vt* to decorate.

décortiquer [dekɔʀtike] *vt* to shell; (*riz*) to hull; (*fig*) to dissect.

découcher [dekuʃe] *vi* to spend the night away from home.

découdre [dekudʀ(ə)] *vt* to unpick; se ~ *vi* to come unstitched; en ~ (*fig*) to fight, do battle.

découler [dekule] *vi*: ~ de to ensue *ou* follow from.

découper [dekupe] *vt* (*papier, tissu etc*) to cut up; (*volaille, viande*) to carve; (*détacher: manche, article*) to cut out; se ~ sur (*ciel, fond*) to stand out against.

décourager [dekuʀaʒe] *vt* to discourage; se ~ *vi* to lose heart, become discouraged.

décousu, e [dekuzy] *a* unstitched; (*fig*) disjointed, disconnected.

découvert, e [dekuvɛʀ, -ɛʀt(ə)] *a* (*tête*) bare, uncovered; (*lieu*) open, exposed // *nm* (*bancaire*) overdraft // *nf* discovery.

découvrir [dekuvʀiʀ] *vt* to discover; (*apercevoir*) to see; (*enlever ce qui couvre ou protège*) to uncover; (*montrer, dévoiler*) to reveal; se ~ *vi* to take off one's hat; to take something off; (*au lit*) to uncover o.s.; (*ciel*) to clear.

décret [dekʀɛ] *nm* decree; **décréter** *vt* to decree; to order; to declare.

décrié, e [dekʀije] *a* disparaged.

décrire [dekʀiʀ] *vt* to describe.

décrocher [dekʀɔʃe] *vt* (*dépendre*) to take down; (*téléphone*) to take off the hook; (: *pour répondre*): ~ (le téléphone) to lift the receiver; (*fig: contrat etc*) to get, land // *vi* to drop out; to switch off.

décroître [dekʀwatʀ(ə)] *vi* to decrease, decline.

décrypter [dekʀipte] *vt* to decipher.

déçu, e [desy] *pp de* **décevoir**.

décupler [dekyple] *vt, vi* to increase tenfold.

dédaigner [dedεɲe] *vt* to despise, scorn; (*négliger*) to disregard, spurn.

dédain [dedɛ̃] *nm* scorn, disdain.

dédale [dedal] *nm* maze.

dedans [dədɑ̃] *ad* inside; (*pas en plein air*) indoors, inside // *nm* inside; au ~ on the inside; inside; en ~ (*vers l'intérieur*) inwards; *voir aussi* là.

dédicacer [dedikase] *vt*: ~ (à qn) to sign (for sb), autograph (for sb).

dédier [dedje] *vt* to dedicate.

dédire [dedir]: se ~ *vi* to go back on one's word; to retract, recant.

dédommager [dedɔmaʒe] *vt*: ~ qn (de) to compensate sb (for); (*fig*) to repay sb (for).

dédouaner [dedwane] *vt* to clear through customs.

dédoubler [deduble] *vt* (*classe, effectifs*) to split (into two); ~ les trains to run additional trains.

déduire [deduir] *vt*: ~ qch (de) (*ôter*) to deduct sth (from); (*conclure*) to deduce *ou* infer sth (from).

déesse [deɛs] *nf* goddess.

défaillance [defajɑ̃s] *nf* (*syncope*) blackout; (*fatigue*) (sudden) weakness q; (*technique*) fault, failure; (*morale etc*) weakness; ~ cardiaque heart failure.

défaillir [defajir] *vi* to faint; to feel faint; (*mémoire etc*) to fail.

défaire [defɛr] *vt* (*installation*) to take down, dismantle; (*paquet etc, nœud, vêtement*) to undo; se ~ *vi* to come undone; se ~ de *vt* (*se débarrasser de*) to get rid of; (*se séparer de*) to part with.

défait, e [defɛ, -ɛt] *a* (*visage*) haggard, ravaged // *nf* defeat.

défalquer [defalke] *vt* to deduct.

défaut [defo] *nm* (*moral*) fault, failing, defect; (*d'étoffe, métal*) fault, flaw, defect; (*manque, carence*): ~ de lack of; shortage of; en ~ at fault; in the wrong; faire ~ (*manquer*) to be lacking; à ~ *ad* failing that; à ~ de for lack *ou* want of; par ~ (*JUR*) in his (*ou* her *etc*) absence.

défavoriser [defavɔrize] *vt* to put at a disadvantage.

défection [defɛksjɔ̃] *nf* defection, failure to give support *ou* assistance; failure to appear; faire ~ (*d'un parti etc*) to withdraw one's support, leave.

défectueux, euse [defɛktɥø, -øz] *a* faulty, defective.

défendre [defɑ̃dr(ə)] *vt* to defend; (*interdire*) to forbid; ~ qch à qn/de faire to forbid sb sth/to do; se ~ *vi* to defend o.s.; il se défend (*fig*) he can hold his own; se ~ de/contre (*se protéger*) to protect o.s. from/against; se ~ de (*se garder de*) to refrain from; (*nier*): se ~ de vouloir to deny wanting.

défense [defɑ̃s] *nf* defence; (*d'éléphant etc*) tusk; '~ de fumer/cracher' 'no smoking/spitting'.

déférer [defere] *vt* (*JUR*) to refer; ~ à *vt* (*requête, décision*) to defer to.

déferler [defɛrle] *vi* (*vagues*) to break;

(*fig*) to surge.

défi [defi] *nm* (*provocation*) challenge; (*bravade*) defiance.

défiance [defjɑ̃s] *nf* mistrust, distrust.

déficit [defisit] *nm* (*COMM*) deficit.

défier [defje] *vt* (*provoquer*) to challenge; (*fig*) to defy, brave; se ~ de *vi* (*se méfier de*) to distrust.

défigurer [defigyre] *vt* to disfigure.

défilé [defile] *nm* (*GÉO*) (narrow) gorge *ou* pass; (*soldats*) parade; (*manifestants*) procession, march.

défiler [defile] *vi* (*troupes*) to march past; (*sportifs*) to parade; (*manifestants*) to march; (*visiteurs*) to pour, stream; se ~ *vi* (*se dérober*) to slip away, sneak off.

définir [definir] *vt* to define.

définitif, ive [definitif, -iv] *a* (*final*) final, definitive; (*pour longtemps*) permanent, definitive; (*sans appel*) final, definite // *nf*: en définitive eventually; (*somme toute*) when all is said and done.

définitivement [definitivmɑ̃] *ad* definitively; permanently; definitely.

déflagration [deflagrasjɔ̃] *nf* explosion.

défoncer [defɔ̃se] *vt* (*caisse*) to stave in; (*porte*) to smash in *ou* down; (*lit, fauteuil*) to burst (the springs of); (*terrain, route*) to rip *ou* plough up.

déformation [defɔrmasjɔ̃] *nf*: ~ professionnelle conditioning by one's job.

déformer [defɔrme] *vt* to put out of shape; (*corps*) to deform; (*pensée, fait*) to distort; se ~ *vi* to lose its shape.

défouler [defule]: se ~ *vi* to unwind, let off steam.

défraîchir [defreʃir]: se ~ *vi* to fade; to become worn.

défrayer [defreje] *vt*: ~ qn to pay sb's expenses; ~ la chronique to be in the news.

défricher [defriʃe] *vt* to clear (for cultivation).

défroquer [defrɔke] *vi* (*aussi*: se ~) to give up the cloth.

défunt, e [defœ̃, -œ̃t] *a*: son ~ père his late father // *nm/f* deceased.

dégagé, e [degaʒe] *a* clear; (*ton, air*) casual, jaunty.

dégagement [degaʒmɑ̃] *nm*: voie de ~ slip road; itinéraire de ~ alternative route (*to relieve traffic congestion*).

dégager [degaʒe] *vt* (*exhaler*) to give off; (*délivrer*) to free, extricate; (*désencombrer*) to clear; (*isoler: idée, aspect*) to bring out; se ~ *vi* (*odeur*) to be given off; (*passage, ciel*) to clear.

dégainer [degene] *vt* to draw.

dégarnir [degarnir] *vt* (*vider*) to empty, clear; se ~ *vi* (*tempes, crâne*) to go bald.

dégâts [dega] *nmpl* damage *sg*.

dégel [deʒɛl] *nm* thaw.

dégeler [deʒle] vt to thaw (out); (fig) to unfreeze // vi to thaw (out).

dégénérer [deʒenere] vi to degenerate; (empirer) to go from bad to worse.

dégingandé, e [deʒɛ̃gɑ̃de] a gangling.

dégivrer [deʒivre] vt (frigo) to defrost; (vitres) to de-ice.

déglutir [deglytir] vt, vi to swallow.

dégonflé, e [degɔ̃fle] a (pneu) flat.

dégonfler [degɔ̃fle] vt (pneu, ballon) to let down, deflate; se ~ vi (fam) to chicken out.

dégouliner [deguline] vi to trickle, drip.

dégourdi, e [degurdi] a smart, resourceful.

dégourdir [degurdir] vt: se ~ (les jambes) to stretch one's legs (fig).

dégoût [degu] nm disgust, distaste.

dégoûtant, e [degutɑ̃, -ɑ̃t] a disgusting.

dégoûté, e [degute] a disgusted; ~ de sick of.

dégoûter [degute] vt to disgust; ~ qn de qch to put sb off sth.

dégoutter [degute] vi to drip.

dégradé [degrade] nm (PEINTURE) gradation.

dégrader [degrade] vt (MIL: officier) to degrade; (abîmer) to damage, deface; se ~ vi (relations, situation) to deteriorate.

dégrafer [degrafe] vt to unclip, unhook.

degré [dəgre] nm degree; (d'escalier) step; alcool à 90 ~s surgical spirit.

dégressif, ive [degresif, -iv] a on a decreasing scale.

dégrèvement [degrɛvmɑ̃] nm tax relief.

dégringoler [degrɛ̃gɔle] vi to tumble (down).

dégrossir [degrosir] vt (fig) to work out roughly; to knock the rough edges off.

déguenillé, e [degnije] a ragged, tattered.

déguerpir [degerpir] vi to clear off.

dégueulasse [degœlas] a (fam) disgusting.

déguisement [degizmɑ̃] nm disguise.

déguiser [degize] vt to disguise; se ~ vi (se costumer) to dress up; (pour tromper) to disguise o.s.

déguster [degyste] vt (vins) to taste; (fromages etc) to sample; (savourer) to enjoy, savour.

dehors [dəɔr] ad outside; (en plein air) outdoors // nm outside // nmpl (apparences) appearances; mettre ou jeter ~ (expulser) to throw out; au ~ outside; outwardly; au ~ de outside; en ~ (vers l'extérieur) outside; outwards; en ~ de (hormis) apart from.

déjà [deʒa] ad already; (auparavant) before, already.

déjeuner [deʒœne] vi to (have) lunch; (le matin) to have breakfast // nm lunch; breakfast.

déjouer [deʒwe] vt to elude; to foil.

delà [dəla] ad: par ~, en ~ (de), au ~ (de) beyond.

délabrer [delabre]: se ~ vi to fall into decay, become dilapidated.

délacer [delase] vt to unlace.

délai [delɛ] nm (attente) waiting period; (sursis) extension (of time); (temps accordé) time limit; à bref ~ shortly, very soon; at short notice; dans les ~s within the time limit.

délaisser [delese] vt to abandon, desert.

délasser [delase] vt (reposer) to relax; (divertir) to divert, entertain; se ~ vi to relax.

délateur, trice [delatœr, -tris] nm/f informer.

délavé, e [delave] a faded.

délayer [deleje] vt (CULIN) to mix (with water etc); (peinture) to thin down.

delco [dɛlko] nm (AUTO) distributor.

délecter [delɛkte]: se ~ vi: se ~ de to revel ou delight in.

délégué, e [delege] nm/f delegate; representative.

déléguer [delege] vt to delegate.

délibéré, e [delibere] a (conscient) deliberate; (déterminé) determined.

délibérer [delibere] vi to deliberate.

délicat, e [delika, -at] a delicate; (plein de tact) tactful; (attentionné) thoughtful; (exigeant) fussy, particular; procédés peu ~s unscrupulous methods; **délicatement** ad delicately; (avec douceur) gently.

délice [delis] nm delight.

délicieux, euse [delisjø, -jøz] a (au goût) delicious; (sensation, impression) delightful.

délier [delje] vt to untie; ~ qn de (serment etc) to release sb from.

délimiter [delimite] vt to delimit, demarcate; to determine; to define.

délinquance [delɛ̃kɑ̃s] nf criminality.

délinquant, e [delɛ̃kɑ̃, -ɑ̃t] a, nm/f delinquent.

délirer [delire] vi to be delirious; (fig) to be raving, be going wild.

délit [deli] nm (criminal) offence.

délivrer [delivre] vt (prisonnier) to (set) free, release; (passeport, certificat) to issue; ~ qn de (ennemis) to deliver ou free sb from; (fig) to relieve sb of; to rid sb of.

déloger [delɔʒe] vt (locataire) to turn out; (objet coincé, ennemi) to dislodge.

deltaplane [dɛltaplan] nm hang-glider.

déluge [delyʒ] nm (biblique) Flood.

déluré, e [delyre] a smart, resourceful; (péj) forward, pert.

demain [dəmɛ̃] ad tomorrow.

demande [dəmɑ̃d] nf (requête) request; (revendication) demand; (ADMIN, formulaire) application; (ÉCON): la ~ de-

mand; '~s d'emploi' 'situations wanted';
~ en mariage (marriage) proposal; ~ de
poste job application.

demandé, e [dəmɑ̃de] *a* (*article etc*):
très ~ (very) much in demand.

demander [dəmɑ̃de] *vt* to ask for;
(*date, heure etc*) to ask; (*nécessiter*) to
require, demand; ~ qch à qn to ask sb
for sth; to ask sb sth; ~ à qn de faire to
ask sb to do; se ~ si/pourquoi *etc* to wonder if/why *etc*; (*sens purement réfléchi*)
to ask o.s. if/why *etc*; on vous demande
au téléphone you're wanted on the
phone.

demandeur, euse [dəmɑ̃dœr, -øz]
nm/f: ~ d'emploi job-seeker; (job) applicant.

démangeaison [demɑ̃ʒɛzɔ̃] *nf* itching.

démanger [demɑ̃ʒe] *vi* to itch.

démanteler [demɑ̃tle] *vt* to break up;
to demolish.

démaquillant [demakijɑ̃] *nm* make-up
remover.

démaquiller [demakije] *vt*: se ~ to remove one's make-up.

démarche [demarʃ(ə)] *nf* (*allure*) gait,
walk; (*intervention*) step; approach;
(*fig: intellectuelle*) thought processes *pl*;
approach; faire des ~s auprès de qn to
approach sb.

démarcheur, euse [demarʃœr, -øz]
nm/f (*COMM*) door-to-door salesman/
woman.

démarquer [demarke] *vt* (*prix*) to
mark down; (*joueur*) to stop marking.

démarrage [demaraʒ] *nm* start.

démarrer [demare] *vi* (*conducteur*) to
start (up); (*véhicule*) to move off; (*travaux*) to get moving; **démarreur** *nm*
(*AUTO*) starter.

démêler [demele] *vt* to untangle.

démêlés [demele] *nmpl* problems.

déménagement [demenaʒmɑ̃] *nm*
move, removal; camion de ~ removal
van.

déménager [demenaʒe] *vt* (*meubles*) to
(re)move // *vi* to move (house);
déménageur *nm* removal man; (*entrepreneur*) furniture remover.

démener [demne]: se ~ *vi* to thrash
about; (*fig*) to exert o.s.

dément, e [demɑ̃, -ɑ̃t] *a* (*fou*) mad,
crazy; (*fam*) brilliant, fantastic.

démentiel, le [demɑ̃sjɛl] *a* insane.

démentir [demɑ̃tir] *vt* to refute; ~ que
to deny that.

démerder [demɛrde] (*fam*): se ~ *vi* to
sort things out for o.s.

démesuré, e [demzyre] *a* immoder-
ate.

démettre [demɛtr(ə)] *vt*: ~ qn de
(*fonction, poste*) to dismiss sb from; se
~ (de ses fonctions) to resign (from)
one's duties; se ~ l'épaule *etc* to dislocate one's shoulder *etc*.

demeurant [dəmœrɑ̃]: au ~ *ad* for all
that.

demeure [dəmœr] *nf* residence; mettre
qn en ~ de faire to enjoin *ou* order sb to
do; à ~ *ad* permanently.

demeurer [dəmœre] *vi* (*habiter*) to
live; (*séjourner*) to stay; (*rester*) to remain.

demi, e [dəmi] *a*: et ~: trois heures/
bouteilles et ~es three and a half hours/
bottles, three hours/bottles and a half; il
est 2 heures/midi et ~e it's half past 2/12
// *nm* (*bière*) ≈ half-pint (*.25 litre*); à ~
ad half-; à la ~e (*heure*) on the half-
hour.

demi... [dəmi] *préfixe* half-, semi...,
demi-; ~cercle *nm* semicircle; en ~
cercle *a* semicircular // *ad* in a half circle; ~douzaine *nf* half-dozen, half a
dozen; ~finale *nf* semifinal; ~frère
nm half-brother; ~heure *nf* half-hour,
half an hour; ~jour *nm* half-light; ~
journée *nf* half-day, half a day; ~litre
nm half-litre, half a litre; ~livre *nf*
half-pound, half a pound; ~mot: à ~
mot *ad* without having to spell things
out; ~pension *nf* (*à l'hôtel*) half-
board; ~place *nf* half-fare.

démis, e [demi, -iz] *a* (*épaule etc*) dislocated.

demi-saison [dəmisɛzɔ̃] *nf*: vêtements
de ~ spring *ou* autumn clothing.

demi-sel [dəmisɛl] *a inv* (*beurre, fromage*) slightly salted.

demi-sœur [dəmisœr] *nf* half-sister.

démission [demisjɔ̃] *nf* resignation;
donner sa ~ to give *ou* hand in one's notice; **démissionner** *vi* (*de son poste*) to
resign.

demi-tarif [dəmitarif] *nm* half-price;
(*TRANSPORTS*) half-fare.

demi-tour [dəmitur] *nm* about-turn;
faire ~ to turn (and go) back; (*AUTO*) to
do a U-turn.

démocratie [demɔkrasi] *nf* democracy.

démocratique [demɔkratik] *a* democratic.

démodé, e [demɔde] *a* old-fashioned.

démographique [demɔgrafik] *a* demo-
graphic, population *cpd*.

demoiselle [dəmwazɛl] *nf* (*jeune fille*)
young lady; (*célibataire*) single lady,
maiden lady; ~ d'honneur bridesmaid.

démolir [demɔlir] *vt* to demolish.

démon [demɔ̃] *nm* (*enfant turbulent*)
devil, demon; le D~ the Devil.

démonstration [demɔ̃strasjɔ̃] *nf* demonstration; (*aérienne, navale*) display.

démonté, e [demɔ̃te] *a* (*fig*) raging,
wild.

démonter [demɔ̃te] *vt* (*machine etc*) to
take down, dismantle; se ~ *vi* (*personne*) to lose countenance.

démontrer [demɔ̃tre] *vt* to demonstrate.

démordre [demɔʀdʀ(ə)] vi: ne pas ~ de to refuse to give up, stick to.

démouler [demule] vt (gâteau) to turn out.

démuni, e [demyni] a (sans argent) impoverished.

démunir [demyniʀ] vt: ~ qn de to deprive sb of; se ~ de to part with, give up.

dénatalité [denatalite] nf fall in the birth rate.

dénaturer [denatyʀe] vt (goût) to alter; (pensée, fait) to distort.

dénégations [denegasjɔ̃] nfpl denials.

déniaiser [denjeze] vt: ~ qn to teach sb about life.

dénicher [denife] vt to unearth; to track ou hunt down.

dénier [denje] vt to deny.

dénigrer [denigʀe] vt to denigrate, run down.

dénivellation [denivelasjɔ̃] nf, **dénivellement** [denivelmɑ̃] nm ramp; dip; difference in level.

dénombrer [denɔ̃bʀe] vt (compter) to count; (énumérer) to enumerate, list.

dénomination [denɔminasjɔ̃] nf designation, appellation.

dénommer [denɔme] vt to name.

dénoncer [denɔ̃se] vt to denounce; se ~ vi to give o.s. up, come forward.

dénouement [denumɑ̃] nm outcome.

dénouer [denwe] vt to unknot, undo.

dénoyauter [denwajote] vt to stone.

denrée [dɑ̃ʀe] nf: ~s (alimentaires) foodstuffs.

dense [dɑ̃s] a dense.

densité [dɑ̃site] nf density.

dent [dɑ̃] nf tooth (pl teeth); en ~s de scie serrated; jagged; ~ de lait/sagesse milk/wisdom tooth; **dentaire** a dental.

dentelé, e [dɑ̃tle] a jagged, indented.

dentelle [dɑ̃tɛl] nf lace q.

dentier [dɑ̃tje] nm denture.

dentifrice [dɑ̃tifʀis] nm toothpaste.

dentiste [dɑ̃tist(ə)] nm/f dentist.

dénuder [denyde] vt to bare.

dénué, e [denye] a: ~ de devoid of; lacking in.

dénuement [denymɑ̃] nm destitution.

déodorant [deɔdɔʀɑ̃] nm deodorant.

dépannage [depanaʒ] nm: service de ~ (AUTO) breakdown service.

dépanner [depane] vt (voiture, télévision) to fix, repair; (fig) to bail out, help out; **dépanneuse** nf breakdown lorry (Brit), tow truck (US).

dépareillé, e [depaʀɛje] a (collection, service) incomplete; (objet) odd.

déparer [depaʀe] vt to spoil, mar.

départ [depaʀ] nm leaving q, departure; (SPORT) start; (sur un horaire) departure; au ~ at the start; à son ~ when he left.

départager [depaʀtaʒe] vt to decide between.

département [depaʀtəmɑ̃] nm department.

départir [depaʀtiʀ]: se ~ de vt to abandon, depart from.

dépassé, e [depase] a superseded, outmoded; (affolé) panic-stricken.

dépasser [depase] vt (véhicule, concurrent) to overtake; (endroit) to pass, go past; (somme, limite) to exceed; (fig: en beauté etc) to surpass, outshine; (être en saillie sur) to jut out above (ou in front of) // vi (jupon) to show.

dépaysé, e [depeize] a disoriented.

dépecer [depɔse] vt to joint, cut up.

dépêche [depɛʃ] nf dispatch.

dépêcher [depeʃe] vt to dispatch; se ~ vi to hurry.

dépeindre [depɛ̃dʀ(ə)] vt to depict.

dépendre [depɑ̃dʀ(ə)]: ~ de vt to depend on; (financièrement etc) to be dependent on.

dépens [depɑ̃] nmpl: aux ~ de at the expense of.

dépense [depɑ̃s] nf spending q, expense, expenditure q; (fig) consumption; expenditure.

dépenser [depɑ̃se] vt to spend; (gaz, eau) to use; (fig) to expend, use up; se ~ vi (se fatiguer) to exert o.s.

dépensier, ière [depɑ̃sje, -jɛʀ] a: il est ~ he's a spendthrift.

déperdition [depɛʀdisjɔ̃] nf loss.

dépérir [depeʀiʀ] vi to waste away; to wither.

dépêtrer [depetʀe] vt: se ~ de to extricate o.s. from.

dépeupler [depœple] vt to depopulate; se ~ vi to be depopulated.

déphasé, e [defaze] a (fig) out of touch.

dépilatoire [depilatwaʀ] a depilatory, hair removing.

dépister [depiste] vt to detect; (voleur) to track down; (poursuivants) to throw off the scent.

dépit [depi] nm vexation, frustration; en ~ de prép in spite of; en ~ du bon sens contrary to all good sense; **dépité, e** a vexed, frustrated.

déplacé, e [deplase] a (propos) out of place, uncalled-for.

déplacement [deplasmɑ̃] nm (voyage) trip, travelling q.

déplacer [deplase] vt (table, voiture) to move, shift; (employé) to transfer, move; se ~ vi to move; (voyager) to travel // vt (vertèbre etc) to displace.

déplaire [deplɛʀ] vi: ceci me déplaît I don't like this, I dislike this; **déplaisant, e** a disagreeable.

dépliant [deplijɑ̃] nm leaflet.

déplier [deplije] vt to unfold.

déployer [deplwaje] vt to open out, spread; to deploy; to display, exhibit.

dépoli, e [depɔli] *a*: **verre ~** frosted glass.

déporter [depɔrte] *vt* (*POL*) to deport; (*dévier*) to carry off course.

déposer [depoze] *vt* (*gén: mettre, poser*) to lay *ou* put down; (*à la banque, à la consigne*) to deposit; (*passager*) to drop (off), set down; (*roi*) to depose; (*ADMIN*): **faire enregistrer**) to file; to register; (*JUR*): **~ (contre)** to testify *ou* give evidence (against); **se ~** *vi* to settle; **dépositaire** *nm/f* (*COMM*) agent.

dépôt [depo] *nm* (*à la banque, sédiment*) deposit; (*entrepôt, réserve*) warehouse, store; (*gare*) depot; (*prison*) cells *pl*.

dépotoir [depɔtwar] *nm* dumping ground, rubbish dump.

dépouille [depuj] *nf* (*d'animal*) skin, hide; (*humaine*): **~ (mortelle)** mortal remains *pl*.

dépouillé, e [depuje] *a* (*fig*) bare, bald.

dépouiller [depuje] *vt* (*animal*) to skin; (*spolier*) to deprive of one's possessions; (*documents*) to go through, peruse; **~ qn/qch de** to strip sb/sth of; **~ le scrutin** to count the votes.

dépourvu, e [depurvy] *a*: **~ de** lacking in, without; **au ~** *ad* unprepared.

déprécier [depresje] *vt*, **se ~** *vi* to depreciate.

déprédations [depredasjɔ̃] *nfpl* damage *sg*.

dépression [depresjɔ̃] *nf* depression; **~ (nerveuse)** (nervous) breakdown.

déprimer [deprime] *vt* to depress.

depuis [depɥi] ♦ *prép* **1** (*point de départ dans le temps*) since; **il habite Paris ~ 1983/l'an dernier** he has been living in Paris since 1983/last year; **~ quand le connaissez-vous?** how long have you known him?
2 (*temps écoulé*) for; **il habite Paris ~ 5 ans** he has been living in Paris for 5 years; **je le connais ~ 3 ans** I've known him for 3 years
3 (*lieu*): **il a plu ~ Metz** it's been raining since Metz; **elle a téléphoné ~ Valence** she rang from Valence
4 (*quantité, rang*) from; **~ les plus petits jusqu'aux plus grands** from the youngest to the oldest
♦ *ad* (*temps*) since (then); **je ne lui ai pas parlé ~** I haven't spoken to him since (then)
depuis que *cj* (ever) since; **~ qu'il m'a dit ça** (ever) since he said that to me.

député, e [depyte] *nm/f* (*POL*) ≈ Member of Parliament (*Brit*), ≈ Member of Congress (*US*).

députer [depyte] *vt* to delegate.

déraciner [derasine] *vt* to uproot.

dérailler [deraje] *vi* (*train*) to be derailed; **faire ~** to derail.

déraisonner [derezɔne] *vi* to talk non-

sense, rave.

dérangement [derãʒmã] *nm* (*gêne*) trouble; (*gastrique etc*) disorder; (*mécanique*) breakdown; **en ~** (*téléphone*) out of order.

déranger [derãʒe] *vt* (*personne*) to trouble, bother; to disturb; (*projets*) to disrupt, upset; (*objets, vêtements*) to disarrange; **se ~** *vi* to put o.s. out; to (take the trouble to) come *ou* go out; **est-ce que cela vous dérange si...?** do you mind if...?

déraper [derape] *vi* (*voiture*) to skid; (*personne, semelles, couteau*) to slip.

déréglé, e [deregle] *a* (*mœurs*) dissolute.

dérégler [deregle] *vt* (*mécanisme*) to put out of order; (*estomac*) to upset.

dérider [deride] *vt*, **se ~** *vi* to brighten up.

dérision [derizjɔ̃] *nf*: **tourner en ~ to** deride.

dérivatif [derivatif] *nm* distraction.

dérive [deriv] *nf* (*de dériveur*) centreboard; **aller à la ~** (*NAVIG, fig*) to drift.

dérivé, e [derive] *a* (*TECH*) byproduct // *nf* (*MATH*) derivative.

dériver [derive] *vt* (*MATH*) to derive; (*cours d'eau etc*) to divert // *vi* (*bateau*) to drift; **~ de** to derive from.

dermatologue [dermatɔlɔg] *nm/f* dermatologist.

dernier, ière [dernje, -jer] *a* last; (*le plus récent*) latest, last; **lundi/le mois ~** last Monday/month; **du ~ chic** extremely smart; **les ~s honneurs** the last tribute; **en ~** *ad* last; **ce ~** the latter; **dernièrement** *ad* recently.

dérobé, e [derobe] *a* (*porte*) secret, hidden; **à la ~e** surreptitiously.

dérober [derɔbe] *vt* to steal; **~ qch à (la vue de) qn** to conceal *ou* hide sth from sb('s view); **se ~** *vi* (*s'esquiver*) to slip away; to shy away; **se ~ sous** (*s'effondrer*) to give way beneath; **se ~ à** (*justice, regards*) to hide from; (*obligation*) to shirk.

dérogation [derɔgasjɔ̃] *nf* (special) dispensation.

déroger [derɔʒe]: **~ à** *vt* to go against, depart from.

dérouiller [deruje] *vt*: **se ~ les jambes** to stretch one's legs (*fig*).

déroulement [derulmã] *nm* (*d'une opération etc*) progress.

dérouler [derule] *vt* (*ficelle*) to unwind; (*papier*) to unroll; **se ~** *vi* (*avoir lieu*) to take place; (*se passer*) to go on; to go (off); to unfold.

déroute [derut] *nf* rout; total collapse.

dérouter [derute] *vt* (*avion, train*) to reroute, divert; (*étonner*) to disconcert, throw (out).

derrière [derjer] *ad, prép* behind // *nm* (*d'une maison*) back; (*postérieur*) be-

hind, bottom; **les pattes de** ~ the back
ou hind legs; **par** ~ from behind; *(fig)*
behind one's back.

des [de] *dét, prép* + *dét voir* **de**.

dès [dɛ] *prép* from; ~ **que** *cj* as soon as;
~ **son retour** as soon as he was (*ou* is)
back; ~ **lors** *ad* from then on; ~ **lors que**
cj from the moment (that).

désabusé, e [dezabyze] *a* disillusioned.

désaccord [dezakɔr] *nm* disagreement.

désaccordé, e [dezakɔrde] *a* (*MUS*) out
of tune.

désaffecté, e [dezafɛkte] *a* disused.

désaffection [dezafɛksjɔ̃] *nf*: ~ **pour**
estrangement from.

désagréable [dezagreable(ə)] *a* unpleasant.

désagréger [dezagreʒe]: **se** ~ *vi* to disintegrate, break up.

désagrément [dezagremã] *nm* annoyance, trouble *q*.

désaltérer [dezaltere] *vt*: **se** ~ to
quench one's thirst.

désamorcer [dezamɔrse] *vt* to defuse;
to forestall.

désapprouver [dezapruve] *vt* to disapprove of.

désarçonner [dezarsɔne] *vt* to unseat,
throw; *(fig)* to throw, puzzle.

désarroi [dezarwa] *nm* disarray.

désarticulé, e [dezartikyle] *a* (*pantin,
corps*) dislocated.

désastre [dezastr(ə)] *nm* disaster.

désavantage [dezavãtaʒ] *nm* disadvantage; (*inconvénient*) drawback, disadvantage; **désavantager** *vt* to put at a
disadvantage.

désavouer [dezavwe] *vt* to disown.

désaxé, e [dezakse] *a (fig)* unbalanced.

descendre [desãdr(ə)] *vt* (*escalier,
montagne*) to go (*ou* come) down;
(*valise, paquet*) to get *ou* take down;
(*étagère etc*) to lower; (*fam: abattre*) to
shoot down // *vi* to go (*ou* come) down;
(*passager: s'arrêter*) to get out, alight;
~ **à pied/en voiture** to walk/drive down;
~ **de** (*famille*) to be descended from; ~
du train to get out of *ou* get off the train;
~ **d'un arbre** to climb down from a tree;
~ **de cheval** to dismount; ~ **à l'hôtel** to
stay at a hotel.

descente [desãt] *nf* descent, going
down; (*chemin*) way down; (*SKI*) downhill (race); ~ **de lit** bedside rug; ~ (**de
police**) (police) raid.

description [dɛskripsjɔ̃] *nf* description.

désemparé, e [dezãpare] *a* bewildered,
distraught.

désemparer [dezãpare] *vi*: **sans** ~
without stopping.

désemplir [dezãplir] *vi*: **ne pas** ~ to be
always full.

déséquilibre [dezekilibr(ə)] *nm (position)*: **en** ~ unsteady; *(fig: des forces,*

du budget) imbalance.

déséquilibré, e [dezekilibre] *nm/f*
(*PSYCH*) unbalanced person.

déséquilibrer [dezekilibre] *vt* to throw
off balance.

désert, e [dezɛr, -ɛrt(ə)] *a* deserted //
nm desert.

déserter [dezɛrte] *vi, vt* to desert.

désertique [dezɛrtik] *a* desert *cpd*; barren, empty.

désespéré, e [dezɛspere] *a* desperate.

désespérer [dezɛspere] *vt* to drive to
despair // *vi*: ~ **de** to despair of.

désespoir [dezɛspwar] *nm* despair; **en**
~ **de cause** in desperation.

déshabillé [dezabije] *nm* négligée.

déshabiller [dezabije] *vt* to undress; **se**
~ *vi* to undress (o.s.).

désherbant [dezɛrbã] *nm* weed-killer.

déshériter [dezerite] *vt* to disinherit.

déshérités [dezerite] *nmpl*: **les** ~ the
underprivileged.

déshonneur [dezɔnœr] *nm* dishonour.

déshydraté, e [dezidrate] *a* dehydrated.

desiderata [deziderata] *nmpl* requirements.

désigner [dezijne] *vt* (*montrer*) to point
out, indicate; (*dénommer*) to denote;
(*candidat etc*) to name.

désinfectant, e [dezɛ̃fɛktã, -ãt] *a, nm*
disinfectant.

désinfecter [dezɛ̃fɛkte] *vt* to disinfect.

désintégrer [dezɛ̃tegre] *vt*, **se** ~ *vi* to
disintegrate.

désintéressé, e [dezɛ̃terese] *a* disinterested, unselfish.

désintéresser [dezɛ̃terese] *vt*: **se** ~
(**de**) to lose interest (in).

désintoxication [dezɛ̃tɔksikasjɔ̃] *nf*:
faire une cure de ~ to undergo treatment
for alcoholism (*ou* drug addiction).

désinvolte [dezɛ̃vɔlt(ə)] *a* casual, offhand; **désinvolture** *nf* casualness.

désir [dezir] *nm* wish; *(fort, sensuel)* desire.

désirer [dezire] *vt* to want, wish for;
(sexuellement) to desire; **je désire ...**
(formule de politesse) I would like ...

désister [deziste]: **se** ~ *vi* to stand
down, withdraw.

désobéir [dezɔbeir] *vi*: ~ (**à qn/qch**) to
disobey (sb/sth); **désobéissant, e** *a* disobedient.

désobligeant, e [dezɔbliʒã, -ãt] *a* disagreeable.

désodorisant [dezɔdɔrizã] *nm* air
freshener, deodorizer.

désœuvré, e [dezœvre] *a* idle.

désolé, e [dezɔle] *a (paysage)* desolate;
je suis ~ I'm sorry.

désoler [dezɔle] *vt* to distress, grieve.

désolidariser [desɔlidarize] *vt*: **se** ~ **de**
ou **d'avec** to dissociate o.s. from.

désopilant, e [dezɔpilã, -ãt] *a* hi-

larious.
désordonné, e [dezɔrdɔne] *a* untidy.
désordre [dezɔrdr(ə)] *nm* disorder(liness), untidiness; (*anarchie*) disorder; **~s** *nmpl* (POL) disturbances, disorder *sg*; **en ~** in a mess, untidy.
désorienté, e [dezɔrjɑ̃te] *a* disorientated.
désormais [dezɔrmɛ] *ad* from now on.
désosser [dezose] *vt* to bone.
desquels, desquelles [dekɛl] *prép + pronom voir* **lequel.**
dessaisir [desezir]: **se ~ de** *vt* to give up, part with.
dessaler [desale] *vt* (*eau de mer*) to desalinate; (CULIN) to soak.
desséché, e [deseʃe] *a* dried up.
dessécher [deseʃe] *vt* to dry out, parch; **se ~** *vi* to dry out.
dessein [desɛ̃] *nm* design; **à ~** intentionally, deliberately.
desserrer [desere] *vt* to loosen; (*frein*) to release.
dessert [deser] *nm* dessert, pudding.
desserte [desert(ə)] *nf* (*table*) side table; (*transport*): **la ~ du village est assurée par autocar** there is a coach service to the village.
desservir [deservir] *vt* (*ville, quartier*) to serve; (*nuire à*) to go against, put at a disadvantage; (*débarrasser*): **~ (la table)** to clear the table.
dessin [desɛ̃] *nm* (*œuvre, art*) drawing; (*motif*) pattern, design; (*contour*) (out)line; **~ animé** cartoon (film); **~ humoristique** cartoon.
dessinateur, trice [desinatœr, -tris] *nm/f* drawer; (*de bandes dessinées*) cartoonist; (*industriel*) draughtsman (*Brit*), draftsman (US).
dessiner [desine] *vt* to draw; (*concevoir*) to design.
dessoûler [desule] *vt, vi* to sober up.
dessous [dəsu] *ad* underneath, beneath // *nm* underside // *nmpl* (*sous-vêtements*) underwear *sg*; **en ~, par ~** underneath; below; **au-~ (de)** below; (*peu digne de*) beneath; **avoir le ~** to get the worst of it; **~-de-plat** *nm inv* tablemat.
dessus [dəsy] *ad* on top; (*collé, écrit*) on it // *nm* top; **en ~** above; **par ~** *ad* over it // *prép* over; **au-~ (de)** above; **avoir le ~** to get the upper hand; **~-de-lit** *nm inv* bedspread.
destin [dɛstɛ̃] *nm* fate; (*avenir*) destiny.
destinataire [dɛstinatɛr] *nm/f* (POSTES) addressee; (*d'un colis*) consignee.
destination [dɛstinasjɔ̃] *nf* (*lieu*) destination; (*usage*) purpose; **à ~ de** bound for, travelling to.
destinée [dɛstine] *nf* fate; (*existence, avenir*) destiny.
destiner [dɛstine] *vt*: **~ qn à** (*poste, sort*) to destine sb for; **~ qn/qch à** (*pré-*

destiner) to destine sb/sth to + *verbe*; **~ qch à qn** (*envisager de donner*) to intend sb to have sth; (*adresser*) to intend sth for sb; to aim sth at sb; **être destiné à** (*sort*) to be destined to + *verbe*; (*usage*) to be meant for; (*suj: sort*) to be in store for.
destituer [dɛstitɥe] *vt* to depose.
désuet, ète [desɥɛ, -ɛt] *a* outdated, outmoded; **désuétude** *nf*: **tomber en désuétude** to fall into disuse.
détachant [detaʃɑ̃] *nm* stain remover.
détacher [detaʃe] *vt* (*enlever*) to detach, remove; (*délier*) to untie; (ADMIN): **~ qn (auprès de/à)** to post sb (to); **se ~** *vi* (*tomber*) to come off; to come out; (*se défaire*) to come undone; **se ~ sur** to stand out against; **se ~ de** (*se désintéresser*) to grow away from.
détail [detaj] *nm* detail; (COMM): **le ~** retail; **au ~** *ad* (COMM) retail; separately; **en ~** in detail.
détaillant [detajɑ̃] *nm* retailer.
détailler [detaje] *vt* (*expliquer*) to explain in detail; to detail; (*examiner*) to look over, examine.
détartrant [detartrɑ̃] *nm* scale remover.
détecter [detɛkte] *vt* to detect.
détective [detɛktiv] *nm* (*Brit: policier*) detective; **~ (privé)** private detective.
déteindre [detɛ̃dr(ə)] *vi* (*tissu*) to fade; (*fig*): **~ sur** to rub off on.
dételer [detle] *vt* to unharness.
détendre [detɑ̃dr(ə)] *vt*: **se ~** to lose its tension; to relax.
détenir [detnir] *vt* (*fortune, objet, secret*) to be in possession of; (*prisonnier*) to detain, hold; (*record, pouvoir*) to hold.
détente [detɑ̃t] *nf* relaxation; (*d'une arme*) trigger.
détention [detɑ̃sjɔ̃] *nf* possession; detention; holding; **~ préventive** (pre-trial) custody.
détenu, e [detny] *nm/f* prisoner.
détergent [detɛrʒɑ̃] *nm* detergent.
détériorer [deterjɔre] *vt* to damage; **se ~** *vi* to deteriorate.
déterminé, e [detɛrmine] *a* (*résolu*) determined; (*précis*) specific, definite.
déterminer [detɛrmine] *vt* (*fixer*) to determine; (*décider*): **~ qn à faire qch** to cide sb to do.
déterrer [detere] *vt* to dig up.
détersif [detɛrsif] *nm* detergent.
détestable [detɛstabl(ə)] *a* foul, ghastly; detestable, odious.
détester [detɛste] *vt* to hate, detest.
détonation [detɔnasjɔ̃] *nf* detonation, bang, report (of a gun).
détonner [detɔne] *vi* (MUS) to go out of tune; (*fig*) to clash.
détour [detur] *nm* detour; (*tournant*) bend, curve; **sans ~** (*fig*) plainly.
détourné, e [deturne] *a* (*moyen*)

roundabout.
détournement [deturnəmɑ̃] *nm*: ~ d'avion hijacking; ~ **de mineur** corruption of a minor.
détourner [deturne] *vt* to divert; (*par la force*) to hijack; (*yeux, tête*) to turn away; (*de l'argent*) to embezzle; se ~ *vi* to turn away.
détracteur, trice [detraktœr, -tris] *nm/f* disparager, critic.
détraquer [detrake] *vt* to put out of order; (*estomac*) to upset; se ~ *vi* to go wrong.
détrempé, e [detrɑ̃pe] *a* (*sol*) sodden, waterlogged.
détresse [detres] *nf* distress.
détriment [detrimɑ̃] *nm*: au ~ de to the detriment of.
détritus [detritys] *nmpl* rubbish *sg*, refuse *sg*.
détroit [detrwa] *nm* strait.
détromper [detrɔ̃pe] *vt* to disabuse.
détrôner [detrone] *vt* to dethrone.
détrousser [detruse] *vt* to rob.
détruire [detruir] *vt* to destroy.
dette [det] *nf* debt.
D.E.U.G. [døg] *sigle m* = *diplôme d'études universitaires générales.*
deuil [dœj] *nm* (*perte*) bereavement; (*période*) mourning; (*chagrin*) grief; être en ~ to be in mourning.
deux [dø] *num* two; les ~ both; ses ~ mains both his hands, his two hands; ~ points colon *sg*; **deuxième** *num* second; **deuxièmement** *ad* secondly, in the second place; ~-**pièces** *nm inv* (*tailleur*) two-piece suit; (*de bain*) two-piece (swimsuit); (*appartement*) two-roomed flat (*Brit*) *ou* apartment (*US*); ~-**roues** *nm inv* two-wheeled vehicle.
devais *etc vb voir* **devoir.**
dévaler [devale] *vt* to hurtle down.
dévaliser [devalize] *vt* to rob, burgle.
dévaloriser [devalɔrize] *vt*, se ~ *vi* to depreciate.
dévaluation [devaluasjɔ̃] *nf* depreciation; (*ÉCON: mesure*) devaluation.
devancer [dəvɑ̃se] *vt* to be ahead of; to get ahead of; to arrive before; (*prévenir*) to anticipate.
devant [dəvɑ̃] *ad* in front; (*à distance: en avant*) ahead // *prép* in front of; ahead of; (*avec mouvement: passer*) past; (*fig*) before, in front of; faced with; in view of // *nm* front; prendre les ~s to make the first move; les pattes de ~ the front legs, the forelegs; par ~ (*boutonner*) at the front; (*entrer*) the front way; aller au-~ de qn to go out to meet sb; aller au-~ de (*désirs de qn*) to anticipate.
devanture [dəvɑ̃tyr] *nf* (*façade*) (shop) front; (*étalage*) display; (shop) window.
déveine [deven] *nf* rotten luck *q*.
développement [devlɔpmɑ̃] *nm* de-

velopment.
développer [devlɔpe] *vt* to develop; se ~ *vi* to develop.
devenir [dəvnir] *vb avec attribut* to become; ~ **instituteur** to become a teacher; que sont-ils devenus? what has become of them?
dévergondé, e [devergɔ̃de] *a* wild, shameless.
déverser [deverse] *vt* (*liquide*) to pour (out); (*ordures*) to tip (out); se ~ dans (*fleuve, mer*) to flow into.
dévêtir [devetir] *vt*, se ~ to undress.
devez *etc vb voir* **devoir.**
déviation [devjasjɔ̃] *nf* deviation; (*AUTO*) diversion (*Brit*), detour (*US*).
dévider [devide] *vt* to unwind.
devienne *etc vb voir* **devenir.**
dévier [devje] *vt* (*fleuve, circulation*) to divert; (*coup*) to deflect // *vi* to veer (off course).
devin [dəvɛ̃] *nm* soothsayer, seer.
deviner [dəvine] *vt* to guess; (*prévoir*) to foresee; (*apercevoir*) to distinguish.
devinette [dəvinet] *nf* riddle.
devins *etc vb voir* **devenir.**
devis [dəvi] *nm* estimate, quotation.
dévisager [devizaʒe] *vt* to stare at.
devise [dəviz] *nf* (*formule*) motto, watchword; (*ÉCON: monnaie*) currency; ~s *nfpl* (*argent*) currency *sg*.
deviser [dəvize] *vi* to converse.
dévisser [devise] *vt* to unscrew, undo; se ~ *vi* to come unscrewed.
dévoiler [devwale] *vt* to unveil.
devoir [dəvwar] *nm* duty; (*SCOL*) homework *q*; (: *en classe*) exercise // *vt* (*argent, respect*): ~ **qch** (à qn) to owe (sb) sth; (*suivi de l'infinitif: obligation*): il doit le faire he has to do it, he must do it; (: *intention*): il doit partir demain he is (due) to leave tomorrow; (: *probabilité*): il doit être tard it must be late.
dévolu, e [devɔly] *a*: ~ à allotted to // *nm*: jeter son ~ sur to fix one's choice on.
dévorer [devɔre] *vt* to devour; (*suj: feu, soucis*) to consume.
dévot, e [devo, -ɔt] *a* devout, pious.
dévotion [devosjɔ̃] *nf* devoutness; être à la ~ de qn to be totally devoted to sb.
dévoué, e [devwe] *a* devoted.
dévouer [devwe]: se ~ *vi* (*se sacrifier*): se ~ (pour) to sacrifice o.s. (for); (*se consacrer*): se ~ à to devote *ou* dedicate o.s. to.
dévoyé, e [devwaje] *a* delinquent.
devrai *etc vb voir* **devoir.**
diabète [djabɛt] *nm* diabetes *sg*; **diabétique** *nm/f* diabetic.
diable [djabl(ə)] *nm* devil.
diacre [djakr(ə)] *nm* deacon.
diagnostic [djagnɔstik] *nm* diagnosis *sg*.
diagonal, e, aux [djagɔnal, -o] *a*, *nf* diagonal; en ~e diagonally; lire en ~e to

skim through.
diagramme [djagʀam] *nm* chart, graph.
dialecte [djalɛkt(ə)] *nm* dialect.
dialogue [djalɔg] *nm* dialogue.
diamant [djamã] *nm* diamond; **diamantaire** *nm* diamond dealer.
diamètre [djamɛtʀ(ə)] *nm* diameter.
diapason [djapazõ] *nm* tuning fork.
diaphragme [djafʀagm] *nm* diaphragm.
diaporama [djapɔʀama] *nm* slide show.
diapositive [djapozitiv] *nf* transparency, slide.
diarrhée [djaʀe] *nf* diarrhoea.
dictateur [diktatœʀ] *nm* dictator; **dictature** *nf* dictatorship.
dictée [dikte] *nf* dictation.
dicter [dikte] *vt* to dictate.
dictionnaire [diksjɔnɛʀ] *nm* dictionary.
dicton [diktõ] *nm* saying, dictum.
dièse [djɛz] *nm* sharp.
diesel [djezɛl] *nm, a inv* diesel.
diète [djɛt] *nf* (*jeûne*) starvation diet; (*régime*) diet.
diététique [djetetik] *a*: **magasin ~** health food shop.
dieu, x [djø] *nm* god; **D~** God; **mon D~!** good heavens!
diffamation [difamɑsjõ] *nf* slander; (*écrite*) libel.
différé [difeʀe] *nm* (*TV*): **en ~** (pre-)recorded.
différence [difeʀɑ̃s] *nf* difference; **à la ~ de** unlike.
différencier [difeʀɑ̃sje] *vt* to differentiate.
différend [difeʀɑ̃] *nm* difference (of opinion), disagreement.
différent, e [difeʀɑ̃, -ɑ̃t] *a*: **~ (de)** different (from); **~s objets** different *ou* various objects.
différer [difeʀe] *vt* to postpone, put off // *vi*: **~ (de)** to differ (from).
difficile [difisil] *a* difficult; (*exigeant*) hard to please; **~ment** *ad* with difficulty.
difficulté [difikylte] *nf* difficulty; **en ~** (*bateau, alpiniste*) in difficulties.
difforme [difɔʀm(ə)] *a* deformed, misshapen.
diffuser [difyze] *vt* (*chaleur, bruit*) to diffuse; (*émission, musique*) to broadcast; (*nouvelle, idée*) to circulate; (*COMM*) to distribute.
digérer [diʒeʀe] *vt* to digest; (*fig: accepter*) to stomach, put up with; **digestif** *nm* (after-dinner) liqueur.
digne [diɲ] *a* dignified; **~ de** worthy of; **~ de foi** trustworthy.
dignité [diɲite] *nf* dignity.
digression [digʀesjõ] *nf* digression.
digue [dig] *nf* dike, dyke.
dilapider [dilapide] *vt* to squander.
dilemme [dilɛm] *nm* dilemma.
diligence [diliʒɑ̃s] *nf* stagecoach; (*empressement*) despatch.

diluer [dilɥe] *vt* to dilute.
diluvien, ne [dilyvjɛ̃, -jɛn] *a*: **pluie ~ne** torrential rain.
dimanche [dimɑ̃ʃ] *nm* Sunday.
dimension [dimɑ̃sjõ] *nf* (*grandeur*) size; (*cote, de l'espace*) dimension.
diminuer [diminɥe] *vt* to reduce, decrease; (*ardeur etc*) to lessen; (*personne: physiquement*) to undermine; (*dénigrer*) to belittle // *vi* to decrease, diminish; **diminutif** *nm* (*surnom*) pet name; **diminution** *nf* decreasing, diminishing.
dinde [dɛ̃d] *nf* turkey.
dindon [dɛ̃dõ] *nm* turkey.
dîner [dine] *nm* dinner // *vi* to have dinner.
dingue [dɛ̃g] *a* (*fam*) crazy.
diplomate [diplɔmat] *a* diplomatic // *nm* diplomat; (*fig*) diplomatist.
diplomatie [diplɔmasi] *nf* diplomacy.
diplôme [diplom] *nm* diploma; **diplômé, e** *a* qualified.
dire [diʀ] *nm*: **au ~ de** according to; **leur ~s** what they say // *vt* to say; (*secret, mensonge*) to tell; **~ l'heure/la vérité** to tell the time/the truth; **~ qch à qn** to tell sb sth; **~ à qn qu'il fasse ou de faire** to tell sb to do; **on dit que** they say that; **ceci dit** that being said; (*à ces mots*) whereupon; **si cela lui dit** (*plaire*) if he fancies it; **que dites-vous de** (*penser*) what do you think of; **on dirait que** it looks (*ou* sounds *etc*) as if; **dis/dites** (*donc*) I say; (*à propos*) by the way.
direct, e [diʀɛkt] *a* direct // *nm* (*TV*): **en ~** live; **~ement** *ad* directly.
directeur, trice [diʀɛktœʀ, -tʀis] *nm/f* (*d'entreprise*) director; (*de service*) manager/eress; (*d'école*) head(teacher) (*Brit*), principal (*US*).
direction [diʀɛksjõ] *nf* management; conducting; supervision; (*AUTO*) steering; (*sens*) direction; 'toutes **~s**' 'all routes'.
dirent *vb voir* **dire**.
dirigeant, e [diʀiʒɑ̃, -ɑ̃t] *a* managerial; ruling // *nm/f* (*d'un parti etc*) leader; (*d'entreprise*) manager.
diriger [diʀiʒe] *vt* (*entreprise*) to manage, run; (*véhicule*) to steer; (*orchestre*) to conduct; (*recherches, travaux*) to supervise; (*braquer: regard, arme*): **~ sur** to point *ou* level at; **se ~** (*s'orienter*) to find one's way; **se ~ vers** *ou* **sur** to make *ou* head for.
dirigisme [diʀiʒism(ə)] *nm* (*ÉCON*) state intervention, interventionism.
dis *etc vb voir* **dire**.
discerner [disɛʀne] *vt* to discern, make out.
discipline [disiplin] *nf* discipline; **discipliner** *vt* to discipline; to control.
discontinu, e [diskõtiny] *a* intermittent.
discontinuer [diskõtinɥe] *vi*: **sans ~**

without stopping, without a break.
disconvenir [diskɔ̃vniʀ] *vi*: ne pas ~ de qch/que not to deny sth/that.
discordant, e [diskɔʀdɑ̃, -ɑ̃t] *a* discordant; conflicting.
discothèque [diskɔtɛk] *nf* (*disques*) record collection; (: *dans une bibliothèque*) record library; (*boîte de nuit*) disco(thèque).
discourir [diskuʀiʀ] *vi* to discourse, hold forth.
discours [diskuʀ] *nm* speech.
discret, ète [diskʀɛ, -ɛt] *a* discreet; (*fig*) unobtrusive; quiet.
discrétion [diskʀesjɔ̃] *nf* discretion; être à la ~ de qn to be in sb's hands; à ~ unlimited; as much as one wants.
discrimination [diskʀiminasjɔ̃] *nf* discrimination; sans ~ indiscriminately.
disculper [diskylpe] *vt* to exonerate.
discussion [diskysjɔ̃] *nf* discussion.
discutable [diskytabl(ə)] *a* debatable.
discuté, e [diskyte] *a* controversial.
discuter [diskyte] *vt* (*contester*) to question, dispute; (*débattre: prix*) to discuss // *vi* to talk; (*ergoter*) to argue; ~ de to discuss.
dise *etc vb voir* **dire**.
disette [dizɛt] *nf* food shortage.
diseuse [dizøz] *nf*: ~ de bonne aventure fortuneteller.
disgracieux, euse [disgʀasjø, -jøz] *a* ungainly, awkward.
disjoindre [disʒwɛ̃dʀ(ə)] *vt* to take apart; se ~ *vi* to come apart.
disjoncteur [disʒɔ̃ktœʀ] *nm* (*ÉLEC*) circuit breaker.
disloquer [dislɔke] *vt* (*chaise*) to dismantle; se ~ *vi* (*parti, empire*) to break up; se ~ l'épaule to dislocate one's shoulder.
disons *vb voir* **dire**.
disparaître [dispaʀɛtʀ(ə)] *vi* to disappear; (*à la vue*) to vanish, disappear; to be hidden *ou* concealed; (*se perdre: traditions etc*) to die out; faire ~ to remove; to get rid of.
disparition [dispaʀisjɔ̃] *nf* disappearance.
disparu, e [dispaʀy] *nm/f* missing person; (*défunt*) departed.
dispensaire [dispɑ̃sɛʀ] *nm* community clinic.
dispenser [dispɑ̃se] *vt* (*donner*) to lavish, bestow; (*exempter*): ~ qn de to exempt sb from; se ~ de *vt* to avoid; to get out of.
disperser [dispɛʀse] *vt* to scatter; (*fig: son attention*) to dissipate.
disponibilité [disponibilite] *nf* (*ADMIN*): être en ~ to be on leave of absence.
disponible [disponibl(ə)] *a* available.
dispos [dispo] *am*: (frais et) ~ fresh (as a daisy).
disposé, e [dispoze] *a*: bien/mal ~ (hu-

meur) in a good/bad mood; ~ à (*prêt à*) willing *ou* prepared to.
disposer [dispoze] *vt* (*arranger, placer*) to arrange // *vi*: vous pouvez ~ you may leave; ~ de *vt* to have (at one's disposal); to use; se ~ à faire to prepare to do, be about to do.
dispositif [dispozitif] *nm* device; (*fig*) system, plan of action; set-up.
disposition [dispozisjɔ̃] *nf* (*arrangement*) arrangement, layout; (*humeur*) mood; (*tendance*) tendency; ~s *nfpl* (*mesures*) steps, measures; (*préparatifs*) arrangements; (*loi, testament*) provisions; (*aptitudes*) bent *sg*, aptitude *sg*; à la ~ de qn at sb's disposal.
disproportionné, e [dispʀɔpɔʀsjɔne] *a* disproportionate, out of all proportion.
dispute [dispyt] *nf* quarrel, argument.
disputer [dispyte] *vt* (*match*) to play; (*combat*) to fight; (*course*) to run, fight; se ~ *vi* to quarrel; ~ qch à qn to fight with sb over sth.
disquaire [diskɛʀ] *nm/f* record dealer.
disqualifier [diskalifje] *vt* to disqualify.
disque [disk(ə)] *nm* (*MUS*) record; (*forme, pièce*) disc; (*SPORT*) discus; ~ compact compact disc; ~ d'embrayage (*AUTO*) clutch plate.
disquette [diskɛt] *nf* floppy disk, diskette.
disséminer [disemine] *vt* to scatter.
disséquer [diseke] *vt* to dissect.
dissertation [disɛʀtasjɔ̃] *nf* (*SCOL*) essay.
disserter [disɛʀte] *vi*: ~ sur to discourse upon.
dissimuler [disimyle] *vt* to conceal.
dissiper [disipe] *vt* to dissipate; (*fortune*) to squander; se ~ *vi* (*brouillard*) to clear, disperse; (*doutes*) to melt away; (*élève*) to become unruly.
dissolu, e [disɔly] *a* dissolute.
dissolvant, e [disɔlvɑ̃, -ɑ̃t] *nm* solvent; ~ (gras) nail polish remover.
dissonant, e [disɔnɑ̃, -ɑ̃t] *a* discordant.
dissoudre [disudʀ(ə)] *vt* to dissolve; se ~ *vi* to dissolve.
dissuader [disɥade] *vt*: ~ qn de faire/de qch to dissuade sb from doing/from sth.
dissuasion [disɥazjɔ̃] *nf*: force de ~ deterrent power.
distance [distɑ̃s] *nf* distance; (*fig: écart*) gap; à ~ at *ou* from a distance; **distancer** *vt* to outdistance.
distant, e [distɑ̃, -ɑ̃t] *a* (*réservé*) distant; ~ de (*lieu*) far away from.
distendre [distɑ̃dʀ(ə)] *vt*, se ~ *vi* to distend.
distiller [distile] *vt* to distil; **distillerie** *nf* distillery.
distinct, e [distɛ̃(kt), distɛkt(ə)] *a* distinct; **distinctif, ive** *a* distinctive.
distingué, e [distɛ̃ge] *a* distinguished.

distinguer [distɛ̃ge] *vt* to distinguish.
distraction [distraksjɔ̃] *nf* (*manque d'attention*) absent-mindedness; (*oubli*) lapse (in concentration); (*détente*) diversion, recreation; (*passe-temps*) distraction, entertainment.
distraire [distrɛr] *vt* (*déranger*) to distract; (*divertir*) to entertain, divert; se ~ *vi* to amuse *ou* enjoy o.s.
distrait, e [distrɛ, -ɛt] *a* absent-minded.
distribuer [distribɥe] *vt* to distribute; to hand out; (*CARTES*) to deal (out); (*courrier*) to deliver; **distributeur** *nm* (*COMM*) distributor; (*automatique*) (vending) machine; (: *de billets*) (cash) dispenser; **distribution** *nf* distribution; (*postale*) delivery; (*choix d'acteurs*) casting, cast.
dit, e [di, dit] *pp de* **dire** // *a* (*fixé*): le jour ~ the arranged day; (*surnommé*): X, ~ Pierrot X, known as Pierrot.
dites *vb voir* **dire**.
divaguer [divage] *vi* to ramble; to rave.
divan [divã] *nm* divan.
divers, e [divɛr, -ɛrs(ə)] *a* (*varié*) diverse, varied; (*différent*) different, various // *dét* (*plusieurs*) various, several; (*frais*) // sundries, miscellaneous (expenses).
divertir [divɛrtir] *vt* to amuse, entertain; se ~ *vi* to amuse *ou* enjoy o.s.
divin, e [divɛ̃, -in] *a* divine.
diviser [divize] *vt* (*gén*, *MATH*) to divide; (*morceler*, *subdiviser*) to divide (up), split (up); **division** *nf* division.
divorce [divɔrs(ə)] *nm* divorce; **divorcé, e** *nm/f* divorcee; **divorcer** *vi* to get a divorce, get divorced; **divorcer de** *ou* **d'avec qn** to divorce sb.
divulguer [divylge] *vt* to divulge, disclose.
dix [dis] *num* ten; **dixième** *num* tenth.
dizaine [dizɛn] *nf* (*10*) ten; (*environ 10*): une ~ (de) about ten, ten or so.
do [do] *nm* (*note*) C; (*en chantant la gamme*) do(h).
dock [dɔk] *nm* dock.
docker [dɔkɛr] *nm* docker.
docte [dɔkt(ə)] *a* learned.
docteur [dɔktœr] *nm* doctor.
doctorat [dɔktɔra] *nm*: ~ (d'Université) doctorate; ~ d'état ≈ Ph.D.
doctrine [dɔktrin] *nf* doctrine.
document [dɔkymã] *nm* document.
documentaire [dɔkymãtɛr] *a*, *nm* documentary.
documentaliste [dɔkymãtalist(ə)] *nm/f* archivist; researcher.
documentation [dɔkymãtasjɔ̃] *nf* documentation, literature; (*PRESSE*, *TV*: *service*) research.
documenter [dɔkymãte] *vt*: se ~ (sur) to gather information (on).
dodeliner [dɔdline] *vi*: ~ de la tête to

nod one's head gently.
dodo [dodo] *nm*: aller faire ~ to go to beddy-byes.
dodu, e [dody] *a* plump.
dogue [dɔg] *nm* mastiff.
doigt [dwa] *nm* finger; à deux ~s de within an inch of; un ~ de lait a drop of milk; ~ de pied toe.
doigté [dwate] *nm* (*MUS*) fingering; (*fig*: *habileté*) diplomacy, tact.
doit *etc vb voir* **devoir**.
doléances [dɔleãs] *nfpl* complaints; grievances.
dolent, e [dɔlã, -ãt] *a* doleful.
dollar [dɔlar] *nm* dollar.
D.O.M. [deɔɛm, dɔm] *sigle m ou mpl* = *département(s) d'outre-mer*.
domaine [dɔmɛn] *nm* estate, property; (*fig*) domain, field.
domanial, e, aux [dɔmanjal, -o] *a* (*forêt*, *biens*) national, state *cpd*.
domestique [dɔmɛstik] *a* domestic // *nm/f* servant, domestic.
domicile [dɔmisil] *nm* home, place of residence; à ~ at home; **domicilié, e** *a*: être domicilié à to have one's home in *ou* at.
dominant, e [dɔminã, -ãt] *a* dominant; predominant.
dominateur, trice [dɔminatœr, -tris] *a* dominating; domineering.
dominer [dɔmine] *vt* to dominate; (*passions etc*) to control, master; (*surpasser*) to outclass, surpass // *vi* to be in the dominant position; se ~ *vi* to control o.s.
domino [dɔmino] *nm* domino.
dommage [dɔmaʒ] *nm* (*préjudice*) harm, injury; (*dégâts*, *pertes*) damage *q*; c'est ~ de faire/que it's a shame *ou* pity to do/that; ~s-intérêts *nmpl* damages.
dompter [dɔ̃te] *vt* to tame; **dompteur, euse** *nm/f* trainer; liontamer.
don [dɔ̃] *nm* (*cadeau*) gift; (*charité*) donation; (*aptitude*) gift, talent; avoir des ~s pour to have a gift *ou* talent for.
donc [dɔ̃k] *cj* therefore, so; (*après une digression*) so, then.
donjon [dɔ̃ʒɔ̃] *nm* keep.
donné, e [dɔne] *a* (*convenu*) given; (*pas cher*): c'est ~ it's a gift // *nf* (*MATH*, *gén*) datum (*pl* data); étant ~ ... given .....
donner [dɔne] *vt* to give; (*vieux habits etc*) to give away; (*spectacle*) to put on; (*film*) to show; ~ qch à qn to give sb sth, give sth to sb; ~ sur (*suj*: *fenêtre*, *chambre*) to look (out) onto; ~ dans (*piège etc*) to fall into; se ~ à fond to give one's all; s'en ~ à cœur joie (*fam*) to have a great time.
dont [dɔ̃] *pronom relatif* **1** (*appartenance*: *objets*) whose, of which; (: *êtres animés*) whose; la maison ~ le toit est

rouge the house the roof of which is red, the house whose roof is red; **l'homme ~ je connais la sœur** the man whose sister I know

2 (*parmi lesquel(le)s*): **2 livres, ~ l'un est ... 2** books, one of which is ...; **il y avait plusieurs personnes, ~ Gabrielle** there were several people, among them Gabrielle; **10 blessés, ~ 2 grièvement** 10 injured, 2 of them seriously

3 (*complément d'adjectif, de verbe*): **le fils ~ il est si fier** the son he's so proud of; **ce ~ je parle** what I'm talking about; *voir adjectifs et verbes à complément prépositionnel:* **responsable de, souffrir de** etc.

doré, e [dɔʀe] *a* golden; (*avec dorure*) gilt, gilded.

dorénavant [dɔʀenavɑ̃] *ad* henceforth.

dorer [dɔʀe] *vt* (*cadre*) to gild; (*faire*) ~ (*CULIN*) to brown.

dorloter [dɔʀlɔte] *vt* to pamper.

dormir [dɔʀmiʀ] *vi* to sleep; (*être endormi*) to be asleep.

dortoir [dɔʀtwaʀ] *nm* dormitory.

dorure [dɔʀyʀ] *nf* gilding.

dos [do] *nm* back; (*de livre*) spine; 'voir au ~' 'see over'; **de ~** from the back.

dosage [dozaʒ] *nm* mixture.

dose [doz] *nf* dose.

doser [doze] *vt* to measure out; to mix in the correct proportions; (*fig*) to expend in the right amounts; to strike a balance between.

dossard [dosaʀ] *nm* number (*worn by competitor*).

dossier [dosje] *nm* (*renseignements, fichier*) file; (*de chaise*) back; (*PRESSE*) feature.

dot [dɔt] *nf* dowry.

doter [dɔte] *vt* to equip.

douane [dwan] *nf* (*poste, bureau*) customs *pl*; (*taxes*) (customs) duty; **douanier, ière** *a* customs *cpd* // *nm* customs officer.

double [dubl(ə)] *a, ad* double // *nm* (*2 fois plus*): **le ~ (de)** twice as much (*ou* many) (as); (*autre exemplaire*) duplicate, copy; (*sosie*) double; (*TENNIS*) doubles *sg*; **en ~** (*exemplaire*) in duplicate; **faire ~ emploi** to be redundant.

doubler [duble] *vt* (*multiplier par 2*) to double; (*vêtement*) to line; (*dépasser*) to overtake, pass; (*film*) to dub; (*acteur*) to stand in for // *vi* to double.

doublure [dublyʀ] *nf* lining; (*CINÉMA*) stand-in.

douce [dus] *a voir* **doux**; **~âtre** *a* sickly sweet; **~ment** *ad* gently; slowly; **~reux, euse** *a* (*péj*) sugary; **douceur** *nf* softness; sweetness; mildness; gentleness; **douceurs** *nfpl* (*friandises*) sweets.

douche [duʃ] *nf* shower; **~s** *nfpl* (*salle*) shower room *sg*; **se doucher** *vi* to have

ou take a shower.

doué, e [dwe] *a* gifted, talented; **~ de** endowed with.

douille [duj] *nf* (*ÉLEC*) socket; (*de projectile*) case.

douillet, te [dujɛ, -ɛt] *a* cosy; (*péj*) soft.

douleur [dulœʀ] *nf* pain; (*chagrin*) grief, distress; **douloureux, euse** *a* painful.

doute [dut] *nm* doubt; **sans ~** *ad* no doubt; (*probablement*) probably.

douter [dute] *vt* to doubt; **~ de** *vt* (*allié*) to doubt, have (one's) doubts about; (*résultat*) to be doubtful of; **se ~ de qch/que** to suspect sth/that; **je m'en doutais** I suspected as much.

douteux, euse [dutø, -øz] *a* (*incertain*) doubtful; (*discutable*) dubious, questionable; (*péj*) dubious-looking.

Douvres [duvʀ(ə)] *n* Dover.

doux, douce [du, dus] *a* (*gén*) soft; (*sucré, agréable*) sweet; (*peu fort: moutarde, clément: climat*) mild; (*pas brusque*) gentle.

douzaine [duzɛn] *nf* (*12*) dozen; (*environ 12*): **une ~ (de)** a dozen or so, twelve or so.

douze [duz] *num* twelve; **douzième** *num* twelfth.

doyen, ne [dwajɛ̃, -ɛn] *nm/f* (*en âge, ancienneté*) most senior member; (*de faculté*) dean.

dragée [dʀaʒe] *nf* sugared almond; (*MÉD*) (sugar-coated) pill.

dragon [dʀagɔ̃] *nm* dragon.

draguer [dʀage] *vt* (*rivière*) to dredge; to drag; (*fam*) to try to pick up.

dramatique [dʀamatik] *a* dramatic; (*tragique*) tragic // *nf* (*TV*) (television) drama.

dramaturge [dʀamatyʀʒ(ə)] *nm* dramatist, playwright.

drame [dʀam] *nm* (*THÉÂTRE*) drama.

drap [dʀa] *nm* (*de lit*) sheet; (*tissu*) woollen fabric.

drapeau, x [dʀapo] *nm* flag; **sous les ~x** with the colours, in the army.

dresser [dʀese] *vt* (*mettre vertical, monter*) to put up, erect; (*fig: liste, bilan, contrat*) to draw up; (*animal*) to train; **se ~** *vi* (*falaise, obstacle*) to stand; to tower (up); (*personne*) to draw o.s. up; **~ qn contre qn** to set sb against sb; **~ l'oreille** to prick up one's ears.

drogue [dʀɔg] *nf* drug; **la ~** drugs *pl*.

drogué, e [dʀɔge] *nm/f* drug addict.

droguer [dʀɔge] *vt* (*victime*) to drug; (*malade*) to give drugs to; **se ~** *vi* (*aux stupéfiants*) to take drugs; (*péj: de médicaments*) to dose o.s. up.

droguerie [dʀɔgʀi] *nf* hardware shop.

droguiste [dʀɔgist(ə)] *nm* keeper (*ou* owner) of a hardware shop.

droit, e [dʀwa, dʀwat] *a* (*non courbe*)

straight; (*vertical*) upright, straight; (*fig: loyal*) upright, straight(forward); (*opposé à gauche*) right, right-hand // *ad* straight // *nm* (*prérogative*) right; (*taxe*) duty, tax; (: *d'inscription*) fee; (*JUR*): le ~ law // *nf* (*POL*): la ~e the right (wing); avoir le ~ de to be allowed to; avoir ~ à to be entitled to; être en ~ de to have a *ou* the right to; être dans son ~ to be within one's rights; à ~e on the right; (*direction*) (to the) right; ~s d'auteur royalties.

droitier, ière [drwatje, -jɛr] *nm/f* right-handed person.

droiture [drwatyr] *nf* uprightness, straightness.

drôle [drol] *a* funny; ~**ment** *ad* (*très*) terribly, awfully; une ~ d'idée a funny idea.

dromadaire [drɔmadɛr] *nm* dromedary.

dru, e [dry] *a* (*cheveux*) thick, bushy; (*pluie*) heavy.

du [dy] *prép* + *dét, dét voir* **de**.

dû, due [dy] *vb voir* **devoir** // *a* (*somme*) owing, owed; (: *venant à échéance*) due; (*causé par*): ~ à due to // *nm* due; (*somme*) dues *pl*.

dubitatif, ive [dybitatif, -iv] *a* doubtful, dubious.

duc [dyk] *nm* duke; **duchesse** *nf* duchess.

dûment [dymã] *ad* duly.

Dunkerque [dœkɛrk] *n* Dunkirk.

duo [dyo] *nm* (*MUS*) duet.

dupe [dyp] *nf* dupe // *a*: (ne pas) être ~ de (not) to be taken in by.

duplex [dyplɛks] *nm* (*appartement*) split-level apartment, duplex.

duplicata [dyplikata] *nm* duplicate.

duquel [dykɛl] *prép* + *pronom voir* **lequel**.

dur, e [dyr] *a* (*pierre, siège, travail, problème*) hard; (*lumière, voix, climat*) harsh; (*sévère*) hard, harsh; (*cruel*) hard(-hearted); (*porte, col*) stiff; (*viande*) tough // *ad* hard; ~ d'oreille hard of hearing.

durant [dyrã] *prép* (*au cours de*) during; (*pendant*) for; des mois ~ for months.

durcir [dyrsir] *vt, vi, se ~ vi* to harden.

durée [dyre] *nf* length; (*d'une pile etc*) life; (*déroulement: des opérations etc*) duration.

durement [dyrmã] *ad* harshly.

durer [dyre] *vi* to last.

dureté [dyrte] *nf* hardness; harshness; stiffness; toughness.

durit [dyrit] *nf* ® (car radiator) hose.

dus *etc vb voir* **devoir**.

duvet [dyvɛ] *nm* down; (*sac de couchage*) down-filled sleeping bag.

dynamique [dinamik] *a* dynamic.

dynamite [dinamit] *nf* dynamite.

dynamiter [dinamite] *vt* to (blow up with) dynamite.

dynamo [dinamo] *nf* dynamo.

dysenterie [disãtri] *nf* dysentery.

dyslexie [dislɛksi] *nf* dyslexia, word-blindness.

E

eau, x [o] *nf* water // *nfpl* waters; prendre l'~ to leak, let in water; tomber à l'~ (*fig*) to fall through; ~ de Cologne Eau de Cologne; ~ courante running water; ~ douce fresh water; ~ de Javel bleach; ~ minérale mineral water; ~ plate still water; ~ salée salt water; ~ de toilette toilet water; ~**-de-vie** *nf* brandy; ~**-forte** *nf* etching.

ébahi, e [ebai] *a* dumbfounded.

ébattre [ebatr(ə)]: s'~ *vi* to frolic.

ébaucher [eboʃe] *vt* to sketch out, outline; s'~ *vi* to take shape.

ébène [ebɛn] *nf* ebony.

ébéniste [ebenist(ə)] *nm* cabinetmaker.

éberlué, e [ebɛrlɥe] *a* astounded.

éblouir [ebluir] *vt* to dazzle.

éblouissement [ebluismã] *nm* (*faiblesse*) dizzy turn.

éborgner [ebɔrɲe] *vt*: ~ qn to blind sb in one eye.

éboueur [ebwœr] *nm* dustman (*Brit*), garbageman (*US*).

ébouillanter [ebujãte] *vt* to scald; (*CULIN*) to blanch.

éboulement [ebulmã] *nm* rock fall.

ébouler [ebule]: s'~ *vi* to crumble, collapse.

éboulis [ebuli] *nmpl* fallen rocks.

ébouriffé, e [eburife] *a* tousled.

ébranler [ebrãle] *vt* to shake; (*rendre instable: mur*) to weaken; s'~ *vi* (*partir*) to move off.

ébrécher [ebreʃe] *vt* to chip.

ébriété [ebrijete] *nf*: en état d'~ in a state of intoxication.

ébrouer [ebrue]: s'~ *vi* to shake o.s.; (*souffler*) to snort.

ébruiter [ebrɥite] *vt* to spread, disclose.

ébullition [ebylisjɔ̃] *nf* boiling point; en ~ boiling; (*fig*) in an uproar.

écaille [ekaj] *nf* (*de poisson*) scale; (*de coquillage*) shell; (*matière*) tortoiseshell.

écailler [ekaje] *vt* (*poisson*) to scale; (*huître*) to open; s'~ *vi* to flake *ou* peel (off).

écarlate [ekarlat] *a* scarlet.

écarquiller [ekarkije] *vt*: ~ les yeux to stare wide-eyed.

écart [ekar] *nm* gap; (*embardée*) swerve; sideways leap; (*fig*) departure, deviation; à l'~ *ad* out of the way; à l'~ de *prép* away from.

écarté, e [ekarte] *a* (*lieu*) out-of-the-

way, remote; (*ouvert*): les jambes ~es
legs apart; les bras ~s arms outstretched.

écarteler [ekartəle] *vt* to quarter; (*fig*)
to tear.

écarter [ekarte] *vt* (*séparer*) to move
apart, separate; (*éloigner*) to push back,
move away; (*ouvrir: bras, jambes*) to
spread, open; (: *rideau*) to draw (back);
(*éliminer: candidat, possibilité*) to dismiss; s'~ *vi* to part; to move away; s'~
de to wander from.

écervelé, e [esɛrvəle] *a* scatterbrained,
featherbrained.

échafaud [eʃafo] *nm* scaffold.

échafaudage [eʃafodaʒ] *nm* scaffolding.

échafauder [eʃafode] *vt* (*plan*) to construct.

échalote [eʃalɔt] *nf* shallot.

échancrure [eʃɑ̃kryr] *nf* (*de robe*)
scoop neckline; (*de côte, arête rocheuse*)
indentation.

échange [eʃɑ̃ʒ] *nm* exchange; en ~ de
in exchange *ou* return for.

échanger [eʃɑ̃ʒe] *vt*: ~ qch (contre) to
exchange sth (for); **échangeur** *nm*
(*AUTO*) interchange.

échantillon [eʃɑ̃tijɔ̃] *nm* sample.

échappée [eʃape] *nf* (*vue*) vista.

échappement [eʃapmɑ̃] *nm* (*AUTO*) exhaust.

échapper [eʃape]: ~ à *vt* (*gardien*) to
escape (from); (*punition, péril*) to escape; ~ à qn (*détail, sens*) to escape sb;
(*objet qu'on tient*) to slip out of sb's
hands; s'~ *vi* to escape; laisser ~ (*cri
etc*) to let out; l'~ **belle** to have a narrow escape.

écharde [eʃard(ə)] *nf* splinter (of
wood).

écharpe [eʃarp(ə)] *nf* scarf (*pl*
scarves); (*de maire*) sash; (*MÉD*) sling.

échasse [eʃas] *nf* stilt.

échauffer [eʃofe] *vt* (*métal, moteur*) to
overheat; (*fig: exciter*) to fire, excite;
s'~ *vi* (*SPORT*) to warm up; (*dans la discussion*) to become heated.

échauffourée [eʃofure] *nf* clash, brawl.

échéance [eʃeɑ̃s] *nf* (*d'un paiement:
date*) settlement date; (: *somme due*)
financial commitment(s); (*fig*) deadline;
à brève/longue ~ *a* short-/long-term // *ad*
in the short/long run.

échéant [eʃeɑ̃]: le cas ~ *ad* if the case
arises.

échec [eʃɛk] *nm* failure; (*ÉCHECS*): ~ et
mat/au roi checkmate/check; ~s *nmpl*
(*jeu*) chess *sg*; tenir en ~ to hold in
check; faire ~ à to thwart.

échelle [eʃɛl] *nf* ladder; (*fig, d'une
carte*) scale.

échelon [eʃlɔ̃] *nm* (*d'échelle*) rung; (*AD-
MIN*) grade.

échelonner [eʃlɔne] *vt* to space out.

échevelé, e [eʃəvle] *a* tousled, di-

shevelled; wild, frenzied.

échine [eʃin] *nf* backbone, spine.

échiquier [eʃikje] *nm* chessboard.

écho [eko] *nm* echo; ~s *nmpl* (*potins*)
gossip *sg*, rumours.

échoir [eʃwar] *vi* (*dette*) to fall due;
(*délais*) to expire; ~ à *vt* to fall to.

échoppe [eʃɔp] *nf* stall, booth.

échouer [eʃwe] *vi* to fail; s'~ *vi* to run
aground.

échu, e [eʃy] *pp* de **échoir**.

éclabousser [eklabuse] *vt* to splash.

éclair [eklɛr] *nm* (*d'orage*) flash of lightning, lightning *q*; (*gâteau*) éclair.

éclairage [eklɛraʒ] *nm* lighting.

éclaircie [eklɛrsi] *nf* bright interval.

éclaircir [eklɛrsir] *vt* to lighten; (*fig*) to
clear up; to clarify; (*CULIN*) to thin
(down); s'~ (*ciel*) to clear; s'~ **la voix**
to clear one's throat; **éclaircissement**
nm clearing up; clarification.

éclairer [eklɛre] *vt* (*lieu*) to light (up);
(*personne: avec une lampe etc*) to light
the way for; (*fig*) to enlighten; to shed
light on // *vi*: ~ mal/bien to give a poor/
good light; s'~ à l'électricité to have
electric lighting.

éclaireur, euse [eklɛrœr, -øz] *nm/f*
(*scout*) (boy) scout/(girl) guide // *nm*
(*MIL*) scout.

éclat [ekla] *nm* (*de bombe, de verre*)
fragment; (*du soleil, d'une couleur etc*)
brightness, brilliance; (*d'une cérémonie*)
splendour; (*scandale*): faire un ~ to
cause a commotion; ~s de voix shouts.

éclatant, e [eklatɑ̃, -ɑ̃t] *a* brilliant.

éclater [eklate] *vi* (*pneu*) to burst;
(*bombe*) to explode; (*guerre, épidémie*)
to break out; (*groupe, parti*) to break
up; ~ en sanglots/de rire to burst out
sobbing/laughing.

éclipse [eklips(ə)] *nf* eclipse.

éclipser [eklipse]: s'~ *vi* to slip away.

éclopé, e [eklɔpe] *a* lame.

éclore [eklɔr] *vi* (*œuf*) to hatch; (*fleur*)
to open (out).

écluse [eklyz] *nf* lock.

écœurant, e [ekœrɑ̃, -ɑ̃t] *a* (*gâteau
etc*) sickly.

écœurer [ekœre] *vt*: ~ qn to make sb
feel sick.

école [ekɔl] *nf* school; aller à l'~ to go
to school; ~ **normale** teachers' training
college; **écolier, ière** *nm/f* schoolboy/
girl.

écologie [ekɔlɔʒi] *nf* ecology; envi-
ronmental studies *pl*.

éconduire [ekɔ̃dɥir] *vt* to dismiss.

économe [ekɔnɔm] *a* thrifty // *nm/f* (*de
lycée etc*) bursar (*Brit*), treasurer (*US*).

économie [ekɔnɔmi] *nf* economy;
(*gain: d'argent, de temps etc*) saving;
(*science*) economics *sg*; ~s *nfpl* (*pécule*)
savings; **économique** *a* (*avantageux*)
economical; (*ÉCON*) economic.

économiser [ekɔnɔmize] *vt, vi* to save.

écoper [ekɔpe] *vi* to bale out; (*fig*) to cop it; ~ (**de**) *vt* to get.

écorce [ekɔʀs(ə)] *nf* bark; (*de fruit*) peel.

écorcher [ekɔʀʃe] *vt* (*animal*) to skin; (*égratigner*) to graze; **écorchure** *nf* graze.

écossais, e [ekɔsɛ, -ɛz] *a* Scottish // *nm/f*: **É~, e** Scot.

Écosse [ekɔs] *nf*: l'~ Scotland.

écosser [ekɔse] *vt* to shell.

écouler [ekule] *vt* to sell; to dispose of; **s'~** *vi* (*eau*) to flow (out); (*jours, temps*) to pass (by).

écourter [ekuʀte] *vt* to curtail, cut short.

écoute [ekut] *nf* (*RADIO, TV*): temps/ heure d'~ (listening *ou* viewing) time/ hour; **prendre l'~** to tune in; **rester à l'~** (**de**) to stay tuned in (to); ~s téléphoniques phone tapping *sg*.

écouter [ekute] *vt* to listen to; **écouteur** *nm* (*TÉL*) receiver; (*RADIO*) headphones *pl*, headset.

écoutille [ekutij] *nf* hatch.

écran [ekʀɑ̃] *nm* screen.

écrasant, e [ekʀɑzɑ̃, -ɑ̃t] *a* overwhelming.

écraser [ekʀɑze] *vt* to crush; (*piéton*) to run over; **s'~** *vi* (*fam*) to pipe down; **s'~** (**au sol**) to crash; **s'~ contre** to crash into.

écrémer [ekʀeme] *vt* to skim.

écrevisse [ekʀəvis] *nf* crayfish *inv*.

écrier [ekʀije]: **s'~** *vi* to exclaim.

écrin [ekʀɛ̃] *nm* case, box.

écrire [ekʀiʀ] *vt* to write; **s'~** to write to each other; **ça s'écrit comment?** how is it spelt?; **écrit** *nm* document; (*examen*) written paper; **par écrit** in writing.

écriteau, x [ekʀito] *nm* notice, sign.

écriture [ekʀityʀ] *nf* writing; (*COMM*) entry; ~s *nfpl* (*COMM*) accounts, books; l'É~, les É~s the Scriptures.

écrivain [ekʀivɛ̃] *nm* writer.

écrou [ekʀu] *nm* nut.

écrouer [ekʀue] *vt* to imprison; to remand in custody.

écrouler [ekʀule]: **s'~** *vi* to collapse.

écru, e [ekʀy] *a* (*toile*) raw, unbleached; (*couleur*) off-white, écru.

écueil [ekœj] *nm* reef; (*fig*) pitfall; stumbling block.

écuelle [ekɥɛl] *nf* bowl.

éculé, e [ekyle] *a* (*chaussure*) down-at-heel; (*fig: péj*) hackneyed.

écume [ekym] *nf* foam; (*CULIN*) scum; **écumer** *vt* (*CULIN*) to skim; (*fig*) to plunder.

écureuil [ekyʀœj] *nm* squirrel.

écurie [ekyʀi] *nf* stable.

écusson [ekysɔ̃] *nm* badge.

écuyer, ère [ekɥije, -ɛʀ] *nm/f* rider.

eczéma [ɛgzema] *nm* eczema.

édenté, e [edɑ̃te] *a* toothless.

E.D.F. *sigle f* (= Électricité de France) national electricity company.

édifier [edifje] *vt* to build, erect; (*fig*) to edify.

édiles [edil] *nmpl* city fathers.

édit [edi] *nm* edict.

éditer [edite] *vt* (*publier*) to publish; (: *disque*) to produce; **éditeur, trice** *nm/f* editor; publisher; **édition** *nf* editing *q*; edition; (*industrie du livre*) publishing.

édredon [edʀədɔ̃] *nm* eiderdown.

éducatif, ive [edykatif, -iv] *a* educational.

éducation [edykasjɔ̃] *nf* education; (*familiale*) upbringing; (*manières*) (good) manners *pl*; ~ **physique** physical education.

édulcorer [edylkɔʀe] *vt* to sweeten; (*fig*) to tone down.

éduquer [edyke] *vt* to educate; (*élever*) to bring up; (*faculté*) to train.

effacé, e [efase] *a* unassuming.

effacer [efase] *vt* to erase, rub out; **s'~** *vi* (*inscription etc*) to wear off; (*pour laisser passer*) to step aside.

effarer [efaʀe] *vt* to alarm.

effaroucher [efaʀuʃe] *vt* to frighten *ou* scare away; to alarm.

effectif, ive [efɛktif, -iv] *a* real; effective // *nm* (*MIL*) strength; (*SCOL*) (pupil) numbers *pl*; **effectivement** *ad* effectively; (*réellement*) actually, really; (*en effet*) indeed.

effectuer [efɛktɥe] *vt* (*opération*) to carry out; (*déplacement, trajet*) to make; (*mouvement*) to execute.

efféminé, e [efemine] *a* effeminate.

effervescent, e [efɛʀvesɑ̃, -ɑ̃t] *a* effervescent; (*fig*) agitated.

effet [efɛ] *nm* (*résultat, artifice*) effect; (*impression*) impression; ~s *nmpl* (*vêtements etc*) things; **faire de l'~** (*médicament, menace*) to have an effect; **en ~** *ad* indeed.

efficace [efikas] *a* (*personne*) efficient; (*action, médicament*) effective.

effilé, e [efile] *a* slender; sharp; streamlined.

effiler [efile] *vt* (*tissu*) to fray.

effilocher [efilɔʃe]: **s'~** *vi* to fray.

efflanqué, e [eflɑ̃ke] *a* emaciated.

effleurer [eflœʀe] *vt* to brush (against); (*sujet*) to touch upon; (*suj: idée, pensée*): ~ **qn** to cross sb's mind.

effluves [eflyv] *nmpl* exhalation(s).

effondrer [efɔ̃dʀe]: **s'~** *vi* to collapse.

efforcer [efɔʀse]: **s'~ de** *vt*: **s'~ de faire** to try hard to do, try hard to.

effort [efɔʀ] *nm* effort.

effraction [efʀaksjɔ̃] *nf*: **s'introduire par** ~ **dans** to break into.

effrayant, e [efʀɛjɑ̃, -ɑ̃t] *a* frightening.

effrayer [efʀeje] *vt* to frighten, scare.

effréné, e [efʀene] *a* wild.

effriter [efʀite]: s'~ vi to crumble.

effroi [efʀwa] nm terror, dread q.

effronté, e [efʀɔ̃te] a insolent, brazen.

effroyable [efʀwajabl(ə)] a horrifying, appalling.

effusion [efyzjɔ̃] nf effusion; sans ~ de sang without bloodshed.

égal, e, aux [egal, -o] a equal; (plan: surface) even, level; (constant: vitesse) steady; (équitable) even // nm/f equal; être ~ à (prix, nombre) to be equal to; ça lui est ~ it's all the same to him; he doesn't mind; sans ~ matchless, unequalled; à l'~ de (comme) just like; d'~ à ~ as equals; ~ement ad equally; evenly; steadily; (aussi) too, as well; ~er vt to equal; ~iser vt (sol, salaires) to level (out); (chances) to equalize // vi (SPORT) to equalize; ~ité nf equality; evenness, steadiness; (MATH) identity; être à ~ité (de points) to be level.

égard [egaʀ] nm: ~s nmpl consideration sg; à cet ~ in this respect; eu ~ à in view of; par ~ pour out of consideration for; sans ~ pour without regard for; à l'~ de prép towards; concerning.

égarement [egaʀmɑ̃] nm distraction; aberration.

égarer [egaʀe] vt to mislay; (moralement) to lead astray; s'~ vi to get lost, lose one's way; (objet) to go astray; (dans une discussion) to wander.

égayer [egeje] vt (personne) to amuse; to cheer up; (récit, endroit) to brighten up, liven up.

églantine [eglɑ̃tin] nf wild ou dog rose.

églefin [egləfɛ̃] nm haddock.

église [egliz] nf church; aller à l'~ to go to church.

égoïsme [egɔism(ə)] nm selfishness; **égoïste** a selfish.

égorger [egɔʀʒe] vt to cut the throat of.

égosiller [egozije]: s'~ vi to shout o.s. hoarse.

égout [egu] nm sewer.

égoutter [egute] vt (linge) to wring out; (vaisselle) to drain // vi, s'~ vi to drip; **égouttoir** nm draining board; (mobile) draining rack.

égratigner [egʀatiɲe] vt to scratch; **égratignure** nf scratch.

égrillard, e [egʀijaʀ, -aʀd(ə)] a ribald.

Egypte [eʒipt(ə)] nf: l'~ Egypt; **égyptien, ne** a, nm/f Egyptian.

eh [e] excl hey!; ~ bien well.

éhonté, e [eɔ̃te] a shameless, brazen.

éjecter [eʒɛkte] vt (TECH) to eject; (fam) to kick ou chuck out.

élaborer [elabɔʀe] vt to elaborate; (projet, stratégie) to work out; (rapport) to draft.

élaguer [elage] vt to prune.

élan [elɑ̃] nm (ZOOL) elk, moose; (SPORT: avant le saut) run up; (d'objet en mouvement) momentum; (fig: de ten-

dresse etc) surge; prendre de l'~ to gather speed.

élancé, e [elɑ̃se] a slender.

élancement [elɑ̃smɑ̃] nm shooting pain.

élancer [elɑ̃se]: s'~ vi to dash, hurl o.s.; (fig: arbre, clocher) to soar (upwards).

élargir [elaʀʒiʀ] vt to widen; (vêtement) to let out; (JUR) to release; s'~ vi to widen; (vêtement) to stretch.

élastique [elastik] a elastic // nm (de bureau) rubber band; (pour la couture) elastic q.

électeur, trice [elɛktœʀ, -tʀis] nm/f elector, voter.

élection [elɛksjɔ̃] nf election.

électorat [elɛktɔʀa] nm electorate.

électricien, ne [elɛktʀisjɛ̃, -jɛn] nm/f electrician.

électricité [elɛktʀisite] nf electricity; allumer/éteindre l'~ to put on/off the light.

électrique [elɛktʀik] a electric(al).

électro... [elɛktʀɔ] préfixe: ~choc nm electric shock treatment; ~ménager a, nm: appareils ~ménagers, l'~ménager domestic (electrical) appliances.

électronique [elɛktʀɔnik] a electronic // nf electronics sg.

électrophone [elɛktʀɔfɔn] nm record player.

élégant, e [elegɑ̃, -ɑ̃t] a elegant; (solution) neat, elegant; (attitude, procédé) courteous, civilized.

élément [elemɑ̃] nm element; (pièce) component, part; **élémentaire** a elementary.

éléphant [elefɑ̃] nm elephant.

élevage [elvaʒ] nm breeding; (de bovins) cattle rearing.

élévation [elevasjɔ̃] nf (gén) elevation; (voir élever) raising; (voir s'elever) rise.

élevé, e [elve] a (prix, sommet) high; (fig: noble) elevated; bien/mal ~ well-/ill-mannered.

élève [elɛv] nm/f pupil.

élever [elve] vt (enfant) to bring up, raise; (bétail, volaille) to breed; (abeilles) to keep; (hausser: taux, niveau) to raise; (fig: âme, esprit) to elevate; (édifier: monument) to put up, erect; s'~ vi (avion, alpiniste) to go up; (niveau, température, aussi: cri etc) to rise; (survenir: difficultés) to arise; s'~ à (suj: frais, dégâts) to amount to, add up to; s'~ contre qch to rise up against sth; ~ la voix to raise one's voice; **éleveur, euse** nm/f breeder.

élimé, e [elime] a threadbare.

éliminatoire [eliminatwaʀ] nf (SPORT) heat.

éliminer [elimine] vt to eliminate.

élire [eliʀ] vt to elect.

elle [ɛl] pronom (sujet) she; (: chose) it; (complément) her; it; ~s they; them;

~-même herself; itself; ~s-mêmes themselves; *voir* il.

élocution [elɔkysjɔ̃] *nf* delivery; **défaut d'~** speech impediment.

éloge [elɔʒ] *nm* praise (*gén q*); **élogieux, euse** *a* laudatory, full of praise.

éloigné, e [elwaɲe] *a* distant, far-off.

éloignement [elwaɲmɑ̃] *nm* removal; putting off; estrangement; (*fig*) distance.

éloigner [elwaɲe] *vt* (*objet*): ~ **qch (de)** to move *ou* take sth away (from); (*personne*): ~ **qn (de)** to take sb away *ou* remove sb (from); (*échéance*) to put off, postpone; (*soupçons, danger*) to ward off; **s'~ (de)** (*personne*) to go away (from); (*véhicule*) to move away (from); (*affectivement*) to become estranged (from).

élongation [elɔ̃gasjɔ̃] *nf* strained muscle.

éloquent, e [elɔkɑ̃, -ɑ̃t] *a* eloquent.

élu, e [ely] *pp de* élire // *nm/f* (*POL*) elected representative.

élucubrations [elykybrasjɔ̃] *nfpl* wild imaginings.

éluder [elyde] *vt* to evade.

émacié, e [emasje] *a* emaciated.

émail, aux [emaj, -o] *nm* enamel.

émaillé, e [emaje] *a* (*fig*): ~ **de** dotted with.

émanciper [emɑ̃sipe] *vt* to emancipate; **s'~** *vi* (*fig*) to become emancipated *ou* liberated.

émaner [emane]: ~ **de** *vt* to come from; (*ADMIN*) to proceed from.

emballage [ɑ̃balaʒ] *nm* wrapping; packaging.

emballer [ɑ̃bale] *vt* to wrap (up); (*dans un carton*) to pack (up); (*fig: fam*) to thrill (to bits); **s'~** *vi* (*moteur*) to race; (*cheval*) to bolt; (*fig: personne*) to get carried away.

embarcadère [ɑ̃baʀkadɛʀ] *nm* wharf, pier.

embarcation [ɑ̃baʀkasjɔ̃] *nf* (small) boat, (small) craft *inv*.

embardée [ɑ̃baʀde] *nf*: **faire une ~** to swerve.

embarquement [ɑ̃baʀkəmɑ̃] *nm* embarkation; loading; boarding.

embarquer [ɑ̃baʀke] *vt* (*personne*) to embark; (*marchandise*) to load; (*fam*) to cart off; to nick // *vi* (*passager*) to board; **s'~** *vi* to board; **s'~ dans** (*affaire, aventure*) to embark upon.

embarras [ɑ̃baʀa] *nm* (*obstacle*) hindrance; (*confusion*) embarrassment.

embarrassant, e [ɑ̃baʀasɑ̃, -ɑ̃t] *a* embarrassing.

embarrasser [ɑ̃baʀase] *vt* (*encombrer*) to clutter (up); (*gêner*) to hinder, hamper; (*fig*) to cause embarrassment to; to put in an awkward position.

embauche [ɑ̃boʃ] *nf* hiring; **bureau d'~** labour office.

embaucher [ɑ̃boʃe] *vt* to take on, hire.

embaumer [ɑ̃bome] *vt* to embalm; to fill with its fragrance; ~ **la lavande** to be fragrant with (the scent of) lavender.

embellie [ɑ̃beli] *nf* brighter period.

embellir [ɑ̃beliʀ] *vt* to make more attractive; (*une histoire*) to embellish // *vi* to grow lovelier *ou* more attractive.

embêtements [ɑ̃bɛtmɑ̃] *nmpl* trouble *sg*.

embêter [ɑ̃bɛte] *vt* to bother; **s'~** *vi* (*s'ennuyer*) to be bored.

emblée [ɑ̃ble]: **d'~** *ad* straightaway.

emboîter [ɑ̃bwate] *vt* to fit together; **s'~ (dans)** to fit (into); ~ **le pas à qn** to follow in sb's footsteps.

embonpoint [ɑ̃bɔ̃pwɛ̃] *nm* stoutness.

embouchure [ɑ̃buʃyʀ] *nf* (*GÉO*) mouth.

embourber [ɑ̃buʀbe]: **s'~** *vi* to get stuck in the mud.

embourgeoiser [ɑ̃buʀʒwaze]: **s'~** *vi* to adopt a middle-class outlook.

embouteillage [ɑ̃buteja3] *nm* traffic jam.

emboutir [ɑ̃butiʀ] *vt* (*heurter*) to crash into, ram.

embranchement [ɑ̃bʀɑ̃ʃmɑ̃] *nm* (*routier*) junction; (*classification*) branch.

embraser [ɑ̃bʀaze]: **s'~** *vi* to flare up.

embrasser [ɑ̃bʀase] *vt* to kiss; (*sujet, période*) to embrace, encompass; (*carrière, métier*) to enter upon.

embrasure [ɑ̃bʀazyʀ] *nf*: **dans l'~ de la porte** in the door(way).

embrayage [ɑ̃bʀeja3] *nm* clutch.

embrayer [ɑ̃bʀeje] *vi* (*AUTO*) to let in the clutch.

embrigader [ɑ̃bʀigade] *vt* to recruit.

embrocher [ɑ̃bʀɔʃe] *vt* to put on a spit.

embrouiller [ɑ̃bʀuje] *vt* (*fils*) to tangle (up); (*fiches, idées, personne*) to muddle up; **s'~** *vi* (*personne*) to get in a muddle.

embruns [ɑ̃bʀœ̃] *nmpl* sea spray *sg*.

embûches [ɑ̃byʃ] *nfpl* pitfalls, traps.

embué, e [ɑ̃bɥe] *a* misted up.

embuscade [ɑ̃byskad] *nf* ambush.

éméché, e [emeʃe] *a* tipsy, merry.

émeraude [emʀod] *nf* emerald.

émerger [emɛʀʒe] *vi* to emerge; (*faire saillie, aussi fig*) to stand out.

émeri [emʀi] *nm*: **toile** *ou* **papier ~** emery paper.

émérite [emeʀit] *a* highly skilled.

émerveiller [emɛʀveje] *vt* to fill with wonder; **s'~ de** to marvel at.

émetteur, trice [emetœʀ, -tʀis] *a* transmitting; (*poste*) ~ transmitter.

émettre [emɛtʀ(ə)] *vt* (*son, lumière*) to give out, emit; (*message etc: RADIO*) to transmit; (*billet, timbre, emprunt*) to issue; (*hypothèse, avis*) to voice, put forward // *vi* to broadcast.

émeus *etc vb voir* **émouvoir**.

émeute [emøt] *nf* riot.

émietter [emjete] *vt* to crumble.

émigrer [emigʀe] *vi* to emigrate.
eminence [eminɑ̃s] *nf* distinction; (*colline*) knoll, hill; **Son É~** his (*ou* her) Eminence.
éminent, e [eminɑ̃, -ɑ̃t] *a* distinguished.
émission [emisjɔ̃] *nf* emission; transmission; issue; (*RADIO, TV*) programme, broadcast.
emmagasiner [ɑ̃magazine] *vt* to (put into) store; (*fig*) to store up.
emmailloter [ɑ̃majɔte] *vt* to wrap up.
emmanchure [ɑ̃mɑ̃ʃyʀ] *nf* armhole.
emmêler [ɑ̃mele] *vt* to tangle (up); (*fig*) to muddle up; **s'~** *vi* to get into a tangle.
emménager [ɑ̃menaʒe] *vi* to move in; **~ dans** to move into.
emmener [ɑ̃mne] *vt* to take (with one); (*comme otage, capture*) to take away; **~ qn au cinéma** to take sb to the cinema.
emmerder [ɑ̃mɛʀde] (*fam!*) *vt* to bug, bother; **s'~** *vi* to be bored stiff.
emmitoufler [ɑ̃mitufle] *vt* to wrap up (warmly).
émoi [emwa] *nm* commotion; (*trouble*) agitation.
émoluments [emɔlymɑ̃] *nmpl* remuneration *sg*, fee *sg*.
émonder [emɔ̃de] *vt* to prune.
émotif, ive [emɔtif, -iv] *a* emotional.
émotion [emosjɔ̃] *nf* emotion.
émousser [emuse] *vt* to blunt; (*fig*) to dull.
émouvoir [emuvwaʀ] *vt* (*troubler*) to stir, affect; (*toucher, attendrir*) to move; (*indigner*) to rouse; **s'~** *vi* to be affected; to be moved; to be roused.
empailler [ɑ̃paje] *vt* to stuff.
empaler [ɑ̃pale] *vt* to impale.
emparer [ɑ̃paʀe]: **s'~ de** *vt* (*objet*) to seize, grab; (*comme otage, MIL*) to seize; (*suj: peur etc*) to take hold of.
empâter [ɑ̃pɑte]: **s'~** *vi* to thicken out.
empêchement [ɑ̃pɛʃmɑ̃] *nm* (unexpected) obstacle, hitch.
empêcher [ɑ̃peʃe] *vt* to prevent; **~ qn de faire** to prevent *ou* stop sb (from) doing; **il n'empêche que** nevertheless; **il n'a pas pu s'~ de rire** he couldn't help laughing.
empereur [ɑ̃pʀœʀ] *nm* emperor.
empeser [ɑ̃pəze] *vt* to starch.
empester [ɑ̃pɛste] *vi* to stink, reek.
empêtrer [ɑ̃petʀe] *vt*: **s'~ dans** (*fils etc*) to get tangled up in.
emphase [ɑ̃faz] *nf* pomposity, bombast.
empiéter [ɑ̃pjete] *vi*: **~ sur** to encroach upon.
empiffrer [ɑ̃pifʀe]: **s'~** *vi* (*péj*) to stuff o.s.
empiler [ɑ̃pile] *vt* to pile (up).
empire [ɑ̃piʀ] *nm* empire; (*fig*) influence.
empirer [ɑ̃piʀe] *vi* to worsen, deteriorate.
emplacement [ɑ̃plasmɑ̃] *nm* site.

emplettes [ɑ̃plɛt] *nfpl* shopping *sg*.
emplir [ɑ̃pliʀ] *vt* to fill; **s'~ (de)** to fill (with).
emploi [ɑ̃plwa] *nm* use; (*COMM, ÉCON*) employment; (*poste*) job, situation; **~ du temps** timetable, schedule.
employé, e [ɑ̃plwaje] *nm/f* employee; **~ de bureau** office employee *ou* clerk.
employer [ɑ̃plwaje] *vt* (*outil, moyen, méthode, mot*) to use; (*ouvrier, main-d'œuvre*) to employ; **s'~ à faire** to apply *ou* devote o.s. to doing; **employeur, euse** *nm/f* employer.
empocher [ɑ̃pɔʃe] *vt* to pocket.
empoignade [ɑ̃pwaɲad] *nf* row, set-to.
empoigner [ɑ̃pwaɲe] *vt* to grab.
empoisonner [ɑ̃pwazɔne] *vt* to poison; (*empester: air, pièce*) to stink out; (*fam*): **~ qn** to drive sb mad.
emporter [ɑ̃pɔʀte] *vt* to take (with one); (*en dérobant ou enlevant, emmener: blessés, voyageurs*) to take away; (*entraîner*) to carry away; (*arracher*) to tear off; (*avantage, approbation*) to win; **s'~** *vi* (*de colère*) to lose one's temper; **l'~ (sur)** to get the upper hand (of); (*méthode etc*) to prevail (over); **boissons à ~** take-away drinks.
empreint, e [ɑ̃pʀɛ̃, -ɛ̃t] *a*: **~ de** marked with; tinged with // *nf* (*de pied, main*) print; (*fig*) stamp, mark; **~e (digitale)** fingerprint.
empressé, e [ɑ̃pʀese] *a* attentive.
empressement [ɑ̃pʀɛsmɑ̃] *nm* (*hâte*) eagerness.
empresser [ɑ̃pʀese]: **s'~** *vi*: **s'~ auprès de qn** to surround sb with attentions; **s'~ de faire** (*se hâter*) to hasten to do.
emprise [ɑ̃pʀiz] *nf* hold, ascendancy.
emprisonner [ɑ̃pʀizɔne] *vt* to imprison.
emprunt [ɑ̃pʀœ̃] *nm* borrowing *q*, loan.
emprunté, e [ɑ̃pʀœ̃te] *a* (*fig*) ill-at-ease, awkward.
emprunter [ɑ̃pʀœ̃te] *vt* to borrow; (*itinéraire*) to take, follow; (*style, manière*) to adopt, assume.
ému, e [emy] *pp* de **émouvoir** // *a* excited; touched; moved.
émulsion [emylsjɔ̃] *nf* (*cosmetic*) (water-based) lotion.
en [ɑ̃] ♦ *prép* 1 (*endroit, pays*) in; (*direction*) to; **habiter ~ France/ville** to live in France/town; **aller ~ France/ville** to go to France/town
2 (*moment, temps*) in; **~ été/juin** in summer/June
3 (*moyen*) by; **~ avion/taxi** by plane/taxi
4 (*composition*) made of; **c'est ~ verre** it's (made of) glass; **un collier ~ argent** a silver necklace
5 (*description, état*): **une femme (habillée) ~ rouge** a woman (dressed) in red; **peindre qch ~ rouge** to paint sth red; **~ T/étoile** T-/star-shaped; **~**

chemise/chaussettes in one's shirt-sleeves/socks; ~ soldat as a soldier; cassé ~ plusieurs morceaux broken into several pieces; ~ réparation being repaired, under repair; ~ vacances on holiday; ~ deuil in mourning; le même ~ plus grand the same but *ou* only bigger

6 (*avec gérondif*) while; on; by; ~ dormant while sleeping, as one sleeps; ~ sortant on going out, as he *etc* went out; sortir ~ courant to run out

♦ *pronom* **1** (*indéfini*): j'~ ai/veux I have/want some; ~ as-tu? have you got any?; je n'~ veux pas I don't want any; j'~ ai 2 I've got 2; combien y ~ a-t-il? how many (of them) are there?; j'~ ai assez I've got enough (of it *ou* them); (j'en ai marre) I've had enough

2 (*provenance*) from there; j'~ viens I've come from there

3 (*cause*): il ~ est malade/perd le sommeil he is ill/can't sleep because of it

4 (*complément de nom, d'adjectif, de verbe*): j'~ connais les dangers I know its *ou* the dangers; j'~ suis fier/ai besoin I am proud of it/need it; *voir le verbe ou l'adjectif lorsque 'en' correspond à 'de' introduisant un complément prépositionnel.*

E.N.A. [ena] *sigle f* (= *École Nationale d'Administration*) one of the *Grandes Écoles.*

encadrer [ākɑdʀe] *vt* (*tableau, image*) to frame; (*fig: entourer*) to surround; (*personnel, soldats etc*) to train.

encaisse [ākɛs] *nf* cash in hand; ~ or/métallique gold/gold and silver reserves.

encaissé, e [ākese] *a* steep-sided; with steep banks.

encaisser [ākese] *vt* (*chèque*) to cash; (*argent*) to collect; (*fig: coup, défaite*) to take.

encan [ākā] *nm*: à l'~ *ad* by auction.

encart [ākaʀ] *nm* insert.

encastrer [ākastʀe] *vt*: ~ qch dans (*mur*) to embed sth in(to); (*boîtier*) to fit sth into.

encaustique [ākɔstik] *nf* polish, wax.

enceinte [āsɛ̃t] *af*: ~ (de 6 mois) (6 months) pregnant // *nf* (*mur*) wall; (*espace*) enclosure.

encens [āsā] *nm* incense.

encercler [āsɛʀkle] *vt* to surround.

enchaîner [āʃene] *vt* to chain up; (*mouvements, séquences*) to link (together) // *vi* to carry on.

enchanté, e [āʃāte] *a* delighted; enchanted; ~ (de faire votre connaissance) pleased to meet you.

enchantement [āʃātmā] *nm* delight; (*magie*) enchantment.

enchâsser [āʃase] *vt* to set.

enchère [āʃɛʀ] *nf* bid; mettre/vendre aux ~s to put up for (sale by)/sell by

auction.

enchevêtrer [āʃvetʀe] *vt* to tangle (up).

enclencher [āklāʃe] *vt* (*mécanisme*) to engage; s'~ *vi* to engage.

enclin, e [āklɛ̃, -in] *a*: ~ à inclined *ou* prone to.

enclos [āklo] *nm* enclosure.

enclume [āklym] *nf* anvil.

encoche [ākɔʃ] *nf* notch.

encoignure [ākɔɲyʀ] *nf* corner.

encolure [ākɔlyʀ] *nf* (*tour de cou*) collar size; (*col, cou*) neck.

encombrant, e [ākɔ̃bʀā, -āt] *a* cumbersome, bulky.

encombre [ākɔ̃bʀ(ə)]: sans ~ *ad* without mishap *ou* incident.

encombrer [ākɔ̃bʀe] *vt* to clutter (up); (*gêner*) to hamper; s'~ de (*bagages etc*) to load *ou* burden o.s. with.

encontre [ākɔ̃tʀ(ə)]: à l'~ de *prép* against, counter to.

encore [ākɔʀ] *ad* **1** (*continuation*) still; il y travaille ~ he's still working on it; pas ~ not yet

2 (*de nouveau*) again; j'irai ~ demain I'll go again tomorrow; ~ une fois (once) again; ~ deux jours two more days

3 (*intensif*) even, still; ~ plus fort/mieux even louder/better, louder/better still

4 (*restriction*) even so *ou* then, only; ~ pourrais-je le faire si ... even so, I might be able to do it if ...; si ~ if only

encore que *cj* although.

encourager [ākuʀaʒe] *vt* to encourage.

encourir [ākuʀiʀ] *vt* to incur.

encre [ākʀ(ə)] *nf* ink; ~ de Chine Indian ink; encrier *nm* inkwell.

encroûter [ākʀute]: s'~ *vi* (*fig*) to get into a rut, get set in one's ways.

encyclopédie [āsiklɔpedi] *nf* encyclopaedia.

endetter [ādete] *vt*, s'~ *vi* to get into debt.

endiablé, e [ādjable] *a* furious; boisterous.

endiguer [ādige] *vt* to dyke (up); (*fig*) to check, hold back.

endimancher [ādimāʃe] *vt*: s'~ to put on one's Sunday best.

endive [ādiv] *nf* chicory *q*.

endoctriner [ādɔktʀine] *vt* to indoctrinate.

endommager [ādɔmaʒe] *vt* to damage.

endormi, e [ādɔʀmi] *a* asleep.

endormir [ādɔʀmiʀ] *vt* to put to sleep; (*suj: chaleur etc*) to send to sleep; (*MÉD: dent, nerf*) to anaesthetize; (*fig: soupçons*) to allay; s'~ *vi* to fall asleep, go to sleep.

endosser [ādose] *vt* (*responsabilité*) to take, shoulder; (*chèque*) to endorse; (*uniforme, tenue*) to put on, don.

endroit [ādʀwa] *nm* place; (*opposé à*

l'envers) right side; **à l'~** the right way
out; the right way up; **à l'~ de** *prép* regarding.
enduire [ɑ̃dɥiʀ] *vt* to coat.
endurant, e [ɑ̃dyʀɑ̃, -ɑ̃t] *a* tough,
hardy.
endurcir [ɑ̃dyʀsiʀ] *vt* (*physiquement*) to
toughen; (*moralement*) to harden; **s'~** *vi*
to become tougher; to become hardened.
endurer [ɑ̃dyʀe] *vt* to endure, bear.
énergie [enɛʀʒi] *nf* (*PHYSIQUE*) energy;
(*TECH*) power; (*morale*) vigour, spirit;
énergique *a* energetic; vigorous; (*mesures*) drastic, stringent.
énergumène [enɛʀɡymɛn] *nm* rowdy
character *ou* customer.
énerver [enɛʀve] *vt* to irritate, annoy;
s'~ *vi* to get excited, get worked up.
enfance [ɑ̃fɑ̃s] *nf* (*âge*) childhood; (*fig*)
infancy; (*enfants*) children *pl*.
enfant [ɑ̃fɑ̃] *nm/f* child (*pl* children); **~
de chœur** *nm* (*REL*) altar boy; **enfanter**
vi to give birth // *vt* to give birth to;
enfantillage *nm* (*péj*) childish behaviour *q*; **enfantin, e** *a* childlike; child
cpd.
enfer [ɑ̃fɛʀ] *nm* hell.
enfermer [ɑ̃fɛʀme] *vt* to shut up; (*à
clef, interner*) to lock up.
enfiévré, e [ɑ̃fjevʀe] *a* (*fig*) feverish.
enfiler [ɑ̃file] *vt* (*vêtement*) to slip on,
slip into; (*insérer*) : **~ qch dans** to stick
sth into; (*rue, couloir*) to take; (*perles*)
to string; (*aiguille*) to thread.
enfin [ɑ̃fɛ̃] *ad* at last; (*en énumérant*)
lastly; (*de restriction, résignation*) still;
well; (*pour conclure*) in a word.
enflammer [ɑ̃flame] *vt* to set fire to;
(*MÉD*) to inflame; **s'~** *vi* to catch fire; to
become inflamed.
enflé, e [ɑ̃fle] *a* swollen.
enfler [ɑ̃fle] *vi* to swell (up).
enfoncer [ɑ̃fɔ̃se] *vt* (*clou*) to drive in;
(*faire pénétrer*): **~ qch dans** to push (*ou*
drive) sth into; (*forcer: porte*) to break
open; (: *plancher*) to cause to cave in //
vi (*dans la vase etc*) to sink in; (*sol, surface*) to give way; **s'~** *vi* to sink; **s'~
dans** to sink into; (*forêt, ville*) to disappear into.
enfouir [ɑ̃fwiʀ] *vt* (*dans le sol*) to bury;
(*dans un tiroir etc*) to tuck away.
enfourcher [ɑ̃fuʀʃe] *vt* to mount.
enfourner [ɑ̃fuʀne] *vt* to put in the
oven.
enfreindre [ɑ̃fʀɛ̃dʀ(ə)] *vt* to infringe,
break.
enfuir [ɑ̃fɥiʀ]: **s'~** *vi* to run away *ou* off.
enfumer [ɑ̃fyme] *vt* to smoke out.
engageant, e [ɑ̃ɡaʒɑ̃, -ɑ̃t] *a* attractive,
appealing.
engagement [ɑ̃ɡaʒmɑ̃] *nm* (*promesse,
contrat, POL*) commitment; (*MIL: combat*) engagement.
engager [ɑ̃ɡaʒe] *vt* (*embaucher*) to take

on, engage; (*commencer*) to start; (*lier*)
to bind, commit; (*impliquer, entraîner*)
to involve; (*investir*) to invest, lay out;
(*faire intervenir*) to engage; (*inciter*) to
urge; (*faire pénétrer*) to insert; **s'~** *vi* to
hire o.s., get taken on; (*MIL*) to enlist;
(*promettre, politiquement*) to commit
o.s.; (*débuter*) to start (up); **s'~ à faire**
to undertake to do; **s'~ dans** (*rue, passage*) to turn into; (*s'emboîter*) to engage into; (*fig: affaire, discussion*) to enter into, embark on.
engelures [ɑ̃ʒlyʀ] *nfpl* chilblains.
engendrer [ɑ̃ʒɑ̃dʀe] *vt* to father.
engin [ɑ̃ʒɛ̃] *nm* machine; instrument;
vehicle; (*AVIAT*) aircraft *inv*; missile.
englober [ɑ̃ɡlɔbe] *vt* to include.
engloutir [ɑ̃ɡlutiʀ] *vt* to swallow up.
engoncé, e [ɑ̃ɡɔ̃se] *a*: **~ dans** cramped
in.
engorger [ɑ̃ɡɔʀʒe] *vt* to obstruct, block.
engouement [ɑ̃ɡumɑ̃] *nm* (sudden)
passion.
engouffrer [ɑ̃ɡufʀe] *vt* to swallow up,
devour; **s'~ dans** to rush into.
engourdir [ɑ̃ɡuʀdiʀ] *vt* to numb; (*fig*)
to dull, blunt; **s'~** *vi* to go numb.
engrais [ɑ̃ɡʀɛ] *nm* manure; **~**
(*chimique*) (chemical) fertilizer.
engraisser [ɑ̃ɡʀese] *vt* to fatten (up).
engrenage [ɑ̃ɡʀənaʒ] *nm* gears *pl*,
gearing; (*fig*) chain.
engueuler [ɑ̃ɡœle] *vt* (*fam*) to bawl at.
enhardir [ɑ̃aʀdiʀ]: **s'~** *vi* to grow
bolder.
énigme [enigm(ə)] *nf* riddle.
enivrer [ɑ̃nivʀe] *vt*: **s'~** to get drunk;
s'~ de (*fig*) to become intoxicated with.
enjambée [ɑ̃ʒɑ̃be] *nf* stride.
enjamber [ɑ̃ʒɑ̃be] *vt* to stride over;
(*suj: pont etc*) to span, straddle.
enjeu, x [ɑ̃ʒø] *nm* stakes *pl*.
enjoindre [ɑ̃ʒwɛ̃dʀ(ə)] *vt* to enjoin, order.
enjôler [ɑ̃ʒole] *vt* to coax, wheedle.
enjoliver [ɑ̃ʒɔlive] *vt* to embellish;
enjoliveur *nm* (*AUTO*) hub cap.
enjoué, e [ɑ̃ʒwe] *a* playful.
enlacer [ɑ̃lase] *vt* (*étreindre*) to embrace, hug.
enlaidir [ɑ̃lediʀ] *vt* to make ugly // *vi* to
become ugly.
enlèvement [ɑ̃lɛvmɑ̃] *nm* (*rapt*) abduction, kidnapping.
enlever [ɑ̃lve] *vt* (*ôter: gén*) to remove;
(: *vêtement, lunettes*) to take off;
(*emporter: ordures etc*) to take away;
(*prendre*): **~ qch à qn** to take sth
(away) from sb; (*kidnapper*) to abduct,
kidnap; (*obtenir: prix, contrat*) to win.
enliser [ɑ̃lize]: **s'~** *vi* to sink, get stuck.
enluminure [ɑ̃lyminyʀ] *nf* illumination.
enneigé, e [ɑ̃neʒe] *a* snowy; snowed-up.
ennemi, e [ɛnmi] *a* hostile; (*MIL*) enemy *cpd* // *nm/f* enemy.

ennui [ɑ̃nɥi] *nm (lassitude)* boredom; *(difficulté)* trouble *q*; **avoir des ~s** to have problems; **ennuyer** *vt* to bother; *(lasser)* to bore; **s'ennuyer** *vi* to be bored; **s'ennuyer de** *(regretter)* to miss; **ennuyeux, euse** *a* boring, tedious; annoying.

énoncé [enɔ̃se] *nm* terms *pl*; wording.

énoncer [enɔ̃se] *vt* to say, express; *(conditions)* to set out, state.

enorgueillir [ɑ̃nɔrgœjir]: **s'~ de** *vt* to pride o.s. on; to boast.

énorme [enɔrm(ə)] *a* enormous, huge; **énormément** *ad* enormously; **énormément de neige/gens** an enormous amount of snow/number of people.

enquérir [ɑ̃kerir]: **s'~ de** *vt* to inquire about.

enquête [ɑ̃kɛt] *nf (de journaliste, de police)* investigation; *(judiciaire, administrative)* inquiry; *(sondage d'opinion)* survey; **enquêter** *vi* to investigate; to hold an inquiry; to conduct a survey.

enquiers *etc vb voir* **enquérir**.

enraciné, e [ɑ̃rasine] *a* deep-rooted.

enragé, e [ɑ̃raʒe] *a (MÉD)* rabid, with rabies; *(fig)* fanatical.

enrageant, e [ɑ̃raʒɑ̃, -ɑ̃t] *a* infuriating.

enrager [ɑ̃raʒe] *vi* to be in a rage.

enrayer [ɑ̃reje] *vt* to check, stop; **s'~** *vi (arme à feu)* to jam.

enregistrement [ɑ̃rʒistrəmɑ̃] *nm* recording; *(ADMIN)* registration; **~ des bagages** *(à l'aéroport)* baggage check-in.

enregistrer [ɑ̃rʒistre] *vt (MUS etc, remarquer, noter)* to record; *(fig: mémoriser)* to make a mental note of; *(ADMIN)* to register; *(bagages: par train)* to register; *(: à l'aéroport)* to check in.

enrhumer [ɑ̃ryme]: **s'~** *vi* to catch a cold.

enrichir [ɑ̃riʃir] *vt* to make rich(er); *(fig)* to enrich; **s'~** *vi* to get rich(er).

enrober [ɑ̃rɔbe] *vt*: **~ qch de** to coat sth with; *(fig)* to wrap sth up in.

enrôler [ɑ̃role] *vt* to enlist; **s'~ (dans)** to enlist (in).

enrouer [ɑ̃rwe]: **s'~** *vi* to go hoarse.

enrouler [ɑ̃rule] *vt (fil, corde)* to wind (up); **~ qch autour de** to wind sth (a)round; **s'~** *vi* to coil up; to wind.

ensanglanté, e [ɑ̃sɑ̃glɑ̃te] *a* covered with blood.

enseignant, e [ɑ̃sɛɲɑ̃, -ɑ̃t] *nm/f* teacher.

enseigne [ɑ̃sɛɲ] *nf* sign; **à telle ~ que** so much so that; **~ lumineuse** neon sign.

enseignement [ɑ̃sɛɲmɑ̃] *nm* teaching; *(ADMIN)* education.

enseigner [ɑ̃seɲe] *vt, vi* to teach; **~ qch à qn/à qn que** to teach sb sth/sb that.

ensemble [ɑ̃sɑ̃bl(ə)] *ad* together // *nm (assemblage, MATH)* set; *(totalité)*: **l'~ du/de la** the whole *ou* entire; *(unité, harmonie)* unity; **impression/idée d'~** overall *ou* general impression/idea; **dans l'~** *(en gros)* on the whole.

ensemencer [ɑ̃səmɑ̃se] *vt* to sow.

ensevelir [ɑ̃səvlir] *vt* to bury.

ensoleillé, e [ɑ̃sɔleje] *a* sunny.

ensommeillé, e [ɑ̃sɔmeje] *a* drowsy.

ensorceler [ɑ̃sɔrsəle] *vt* to enchant, bewitch.

ensuite [ɑ̃sɥit] *ad* then, next; *(plus tard)* afterwards, later; **~ de quoi** after which.

ensuivre [ɑ̃sɥivr(ə)]: **s'~** *vi* to follow, ensue.

entailler [ɑ̃taje] *vt* to notch; to cut.

entamer [ɑ̃tame] *vt (pain, bouteille)* to start; *(hostilités, pourparlers)* to open; *(fig: altérer)* to make a dent in; to shake; to damage.

entasser [ɑ̃tase] *vt (empiler)* to pile up, heap up; *(tenir à l'étroit)* to cram together; **s'~** *vi* to pile up; to cram.

entendre [ɑ̃tɑ̃dr(ə)] *vt* to hear; *(comprendre)* to understand; *(vouloir dire)* to mean; *(vouloir)*: **~ être obéi/que** to mean to be obeyed/that; **j'ai entendu dire que** I've heard (it said) that; **s'~** *vi (sympathiser)* to get on; *(se mettre d'accord)* to agree; **s'~ à qch/à faire** *(être compétent)* to be good at sth/doing.

entendu, e [ɑ̃tɑ̃dy] *a (réglé)* agreed; *(au courant: air)* knowing; **(c'est) ~** all right, agreed; **c'est ~** *(concession)* all right, granted; **bien ~** of course.

entente [ɑ̃tɑ̃t] *nf* understanding; *(accord, traité)* agreement; **à double ~** *(sens)* with a double meaning.

entériner [ɑ̃terine] *vt* to ratify, confirm.

enterrement [ɑ̃tɛrmɑ̃] *nm (cérémonie)* funeral, burial.

enterrer [ɑ̃tere] *vt* to bury.

entêtant, e [ɑ̃tɛtɑ̃, -ɑ̃t] *a* heady.

entêté, e [ɑ̃tete] *a* stubborn.

en-tête [ɑ̃tɛt] *nm* heading; **papier à ~** headed notepaper.

entêter [ɑ̃tete]: **s'~** *vi*: **s'~ (à faire)** to persist (in doing).

enthousiasme [ɑ̃tuzjasm(ə)] *nm* enthusiasm; **enthousiasmer** *vt* to fill with enthusiasm; **s'enthousiasmer (pour qch)** to get enthusiastic (about sth).

enticher [ɑ̃tiʃe]: **s'~ de** *vt* to become infatuated with.

entier, ère [ɑ̃tje, -jɛr] *a (non entamé, en totalité)* whole; *(total, complet)* complete; *(fig: caractère)* unbending // *nm (MATH)* whole; **en ~** totally; in its entirety; **lait ~** full-cream milk; **entièrement** *ad* entirely, wholly.

entonner [ɑ̃tɔne] *vt (chanson)* to strike up.

entonnoir [ɑ̃tɔnwar] *nm* funnel.

entorse [ɑ̃tɔrs(ə)] *nf (MÉD)* sprain; *(fig)*: **~ au reglement** infringement of the rule.

entortiller [ɑ̃tɔrtije] *vt (envelopper)* to wrap; *(enrouler)* to twist; wind; *(duper)* to deceive.

entourage [ɑ̃turaʒ] *nm* circle; family (circle); entourage; *(ce qui enclôt)* surround.

entourer [ɑ̃ture] *vt* to surround; *(apporter son soutien à)* to rally round; ~ **de** to surround with; *(trait)* to encircle with.

entourloupettes [ɑ̃turlupɛt] *nfpl* mean tricks.

entracte [ɑ̃trakt(ə)] *nm* interval.

entraide [ɑ̃trɛd] *nf* mutual aid; **s'entraider** *vi* to help each other.

entrain [ɑ̃trɛ̃] *nm* spirit; **avec/sans** ~ spiritedly/half-heartedly.

entraînement [ɑ̃trɛnmɑ̃] *nm* training; *(TECH)* drive.

entraîner [ɑ̃trene] *vt (tirer: wagons)* to pull; *(charrier)* to carry *ou* drag along; *(TECH)* to drive; *(emmener: personne)* to take (off); *(mener à l'assaut, influencer)* to lead; *(SPORT)* to train; *(impliquer)* to entail; *(causer)* to lead to, bring about; ~ **qn à faire** *(inciter)* to lead sb to do; **s'**~ *vi (SPORT)* to train; **s'**~ **à qch/à faire** to train o.s. for sth/to do; **entraîneur, euse** *nm/f (SPORT)* coach, trainer // *nm (HIPPISME)* trainer // *nf (de bar)* hostess.

entraver [ɑ̃trave] *vt (circulation)* to hold up; *(action, progrès)* to hinder.

entre [ɑ̃tr(ə)] *prép* between; *(parmi)* among(st); **l'un d'**~ **eux/nous** one of them/us; ~ **eux** among(st) themselves.

entrebâillé, e [ɑ̃trəbaje] *a* half-open, ajar.

entrechoquer [ɑ̃trəʃɔke]: **s'**~ *vi* to knock *ou* bang together.

entrecôte [ɑ̃trəkot] *nf* entrecôte *ou* rib steak.

entrecouper [ɑ̃trəkupe] *vt:* ~ **qch de** to intersperse sth with.

entrecroiser [ɑ̃trəkrwaze]: **s'**~ *vi* intertwine.

entrée [ɑ̃tre] *nf* entrance; *(accès: au cinéma etc)* admission; *(billet)* (admission) ticket; *(CULIN)* first course; **d'**~ *ad* from the outset; ~ **en matière** introduction.

entrefaites [ɑ̃trəfɛt]: **sur ces** ~ *ad* at this juncture.

entrefilet [ɑ̃trəfilɛ] *nm* paragraph *(short article)*.

entrejambes [ɑ̃trəʒɑ̃b] *nm* crotch.

entrelacer [ɑ̃trəlase] *vt* to intertwine.

entrelarder [ɑ̃trəlarde] *vt* to lard.

entremêler [ɑ̃trəmele] *vt:* ~ **qch de** to (inter)mingle sth with.

entremets [ɑ̃trəmɛ] *nm* (cream) dessert.

entremetteur, euse [ɑ̃trəmɛtœr, -øz] *nm/f* go-between.

entremise [ɑ̃trəmiz] *nf* intervention; **par l'**~ **de** through.

entreposer [ɑ̃trəpoze] *vt* to store, put

into storage.

entrepôt [ɑ̃trəpo] *nm* warehouse.

entreprenant, e [ɑ̃trəprənɑ̃, -ɑ̃t] *a (actif)* enterprising; *(trop galant)* forward.

entreprendre [ɑ̃trəprɑ̃dr(ə)] *vt (se lancer dans)* to undertake; *(commencer)* to begin *ou* start (upon); *(personne)* to buttonhole; to tackle.

entrepreneur [ɑ̃trəprənœr] *nm:* ~ **(en bâtiment)** (building) contractor.

entreprise [ɑ̃trəpriz] *nf (société)* firm, concern; *(action)* undertaking, venture.

entrer [ɑ̃tre] *vi* to go *(ou* come) in, enter // *vt (INFORM)* to enter, input; *(faire)* ~ **qch dans** to get sth into; ~ **dans** *(gén)* to enter; *(pièce)* to go *(ou* come) into, enter; *(club)* to join; *(heurter)* to run into; *(être une composante de)* to go into; to form part of; ~ **à l'hôpital** to go into hospital; **faire** ~ *(visiteur)* to show in.

entresol [ɑ̃trəsɔl] *nm* mezzanine.

entre-temps [ɑ̃trətɑ̃] *ad* meanwhile.

entretenir [ɑ̃trətnir] *vt* to maintain; *(famille, maîtresse)* to support, keep; ~ **qn (de)** to speak to sb (about); **s'**~ **(de)** to converse (about).

entretien [ɑ̃trətjɛ̃] *nm* maintenance; *(discussion)* discussion, talk; *(audience)* interview.

entrevoir [ɑ̃trəvwar] *vt (à peine)* to make out; *(brièvement)* to catch a glimpse of.

entrevue [ɑ̃trəvy] *nf* meeting; *(audience)* interview.

entrouvert, e [ɑ̃truver, -ɛrt(ə)] *a* half-open.

énumérer [enymere] *vt* to list, enumerate.

envahir [ɑ̃vair] *vt* to invade; *(suj: inquiétude, peur)* to come over; **envahissant, e** *a (péj: personne)* interfering, intrusive.

enveloppe [ɑ̃vlɔp] *nf (de lettre)* envelope; *(TECH)* casing; outer layer.

envelopper [ɑ̃vlɔpe] *vt* to wrap; *(fig)* to envelop, shroud.

envenimer [ɑ̃vnime] *vt* to aggravate.

envergure [ɑ̃vɛrgyr] *nf (fig)* scope; calibre.

enverrai *etc vb voir* **envoyer**.

envers [ɑ̃vɛr] *prép* towards, to // *nm* other side; *(d'une étoffe)* wrong side; **à l'**~ upside down; back to front; *(vêtement)* inside out.

envie [ɑ̃vi] *nf (sentiment)* envy; *(souhait)* desire, wish; **avoir** ~ **de (faire)** to feel like (doing); *(plus fort)* to want (to do); **avoir** ~ **que** to wish that; **ça lui fait** ~ he would like that; **envier** *vt* to envy; **envieux, euse** *a* envious.

environ [ɑ̃virɔ̃] *ad:* ~ **3 h/2 km** (around) about 3 o'clock/2 km; ~**s** *nmpl* surroundings.

environnement [ɑ̃virɔnmɑ̃] *nm* envi-

ronment.
environner [ãvirɔne] *vt* to surround.
envisager [ãvizaʒe] *vt* (*examiner, con-sidérer*) to view, contemplate; (*avoir en vue*) to envisage.
envoi [ãvwa] *nm* (*paquet*) parcel, con-signment.
envoler [ãvɔle]: **s'~** *vi* (*oiseau*) to fly away *ou* off; (*avion*) to take off; (*papier, feuille*) to blow away; (*fig*) to vanish (into thin air).
envoûter [ãvute] *vt* to bewitch.
envoyé, e [ãvwaje] *nm/f* (*POL*) envoy; (*PRESSE*) correspondent.
envoyer [ãvwaje] *vt* to send; (*lancer*) to hurl, throw; **~ chercher** to send for.
épagneul, e [epaɲœl] *nm/f* spaniel.
épais, se [epɛ, -ɛs] *a* thick; **épaisseur** *nf* thickness.
épancher [epãʃe]: **s'~** *vi* to open one's heart.
épanouir [epanwiʀ]: **s'~** *vi* (*fleur*) to bloom, open out; (*visage*) to light up; (*fig*) to blossom; to open up.
épargne [eparɲ(ə)] *nf* saving.
épargner [eparɲe] *vt* to save; (*ne pas tuer ou endommager*) to spare // *vi* to save; **~ qch à qn** to spare sb sth.
éparpiller [eparpije] *vt* to scatter; (*pour répartir*) to disperse; **s'~** *vi* to scatter; (*fig*) to dissipate one's efforts.
épars, e [epar, -ars(ə)] *a* scattered.
épatant, e [epatã, -ãt] *a* (*fam*) super.
épater [epate] *vt* to amaze; to impress.
épaule [epol] *nf* shoulder.
épauler [epole] *vt* (*aider*) to back up, support; (*arme*) to raise (to one's shoul-der) // *vi* to (take) aim.
épave [epav] *nf* wreck.
épée [epe] *nf* sword.
épeler [eple] *vt* to spell.
éperdu, e [eperdy] *a* distraught, over-come; passionate; frantic.
éperon [eprɔ̃] *nm* spur.
épi [epi] *nm* (*de blé, d'orge*) ear.
épice [epis] *nf* spice.
épicer [epise] *vt* to spice.
épicerie [episri] *nf* grocer's shop; (*den-rées*) groceries *pl*; **~ fine** delicatessen.
épicier, ière *nm/f* grocer.
épidémie [epidemi] *nf* epidemic.
épier [epje] *vt* to spy on, watch closely; (*occasion*) to look out for.
épilepsie [epilepsi] *nf* epilepsy.
épiler [epile] *vt* (*jambes*) to remove the hair from; (*sourcils*) to pluck.
épilogue [epilɔg] *nm* (*fig*) conclusion, dénouement.
épiloguer [epilɔge] *vi*: **~ sur** to hold forth on.
épinards [epinar] *nmpl* spinach *sg*.
épine [epin] *nf* thorn, prickle; (*d'oursin etc*) spine; **~ dorsale** backbone.
épingle [epɛ̃gl(ə)] *nf* pin; **~ de nourrice** *ou* **de sûreté** *ou* **double** safety pin.

épingler [epɛ̃gle] *vt* (*badge, décora-tion*): **~ qch sur** to pin sth on(to); (*fam*) to catch, nick.
épique [epik] *a* epic.
épisode [epizɔd] *nm* episode; **film/roman à ~s** serial; **épisodique** *a* occa-sional.
épître [epitʀ(ə)] *nf* epistle.
éploré, e [eplɔre] *a* tearful.
épluche-légumes [eplyʃlegym] *nm inv* (potato) peeler.
éplucher [eplyʃe] *vt* (*fruit, légumes*) to peel; (*fig*) to go over with a fine-tooth comb; **épluchures** *nfpl* peelings.
épointer [epwɛ̃te] *vt* to blunt.
éponge [epɔ̃ʒ] *nf* sponge; **éponger** *vt* (*liquide*) to mop up; (*surface*) to sponge; (*fig: déficit*) to soak up; **s'éponger le front** to mop one's brow.
épopée [epɔpe] *nf* epic.
époque [epɔk] *nf* (*de l'histoire*) age, era; (*de l'année, la vie*) time; **d'~** *a* (*meuble*) period *cpd*.
époumoner [epumɔne]: **s'~** *vi* to shout o.s. hoarse.
épouse [epuz] *nf* wife (*pl* wives).
épouser [epuze] *vt* to marry; (*fig: idées*) to espouse; (*: forme*) to fit.
épousseter [epuste] *vt* to dust.
époustouflant, e [epustuflã, -ãt] *a* staggering, mind-boggling.
épouvantable [epuvãtabl(ə)] *a* appal-ling, dreadful.
épouvantail [epuvãtaj] *nm* (*à moi-neaux*) scarecrow.
épouvante [epuvãt] *nf* terror; **film d'~** horror film; **épouvanter** *vt* to terrify.
époux [epu] *nm* husband // *nmpl* (*mar-ried*) couple.
éprendre [eprãdʀ(ə)]: **s'~ de** *vt* to fall in love with.
épreuve [eprœv] *nf* (*d'examen*) test; (*malheur, difficulté*) trial, ordeal; (*PHOTO*) print; (*TYPO*) proof; (*SPORT*) event; **à l'~ des balles** bulletproof; **à toute ~** unfailing; **mettre à l'~** to put to the test.
épris, e [epri, -iz] *vb voir* **éprendre**.
éprouver [epruve] *vt* (*tester*) to test; (*marquer, faire souffrir*) to afflict, dis-tress; (*ressentir*) to experience.
éprouvette [epruvɛt] *nf* test tube.
épuisé, e [epɥize] *a* exhausted; (*livre*) out of print.
épuisement [epɥizmã] *nm* exhaustion.
épuiser [epɥize] *vt* (*fatiguer*) to exhaust, wear *ou* tire out; (*stock, sujet*) to ex-haust; **s'~** *vi* to wear *ou* tire o.s. out, ex-haust o.s.; (*stock*) to run out.
épurer [epyre] *vt* (*liquide*) to purify; (*parti etc*) to purge; (*langue, texte*) to refine.
équateur [ekwatœr] *nm* equator; (**la république de) l'É~** Ecuador.
équation [ekwasjɔ̃] *nf* equation.

équerre [ekɛʀ] nf (à dessin) (set) square; (pour fixer) brace; **en ~** at right angles; **à l'~, d'~** straight.

équilibre [ekilibʀ(ə)] nm balance; (d'une balance) equilibrium; **garder/ perdre l'~** to keep/lose one's balance; **être en ~** to be balanced; **équilibré, e** a (fig) well-balanced, stable; **équilibrer** vt to balance; **s'équilibrer** vi (poids) to balance; (fig: défauts etc) to balance each other out.

équipage [ekipaʒ] nm crew.

équipe [ekip] nf team; (bande: parfois péj) bunch.

équipé, e [ekipe] a: **bien/mal ~** well-/ poorly-equipped.

équipée [ekipe] nf escapade.

équipement [ekipmɑ̃] nm equipment; **~s** nmpl amenities, facilities; installations.

équiper [ekipe] vt to equip; (voiture, cuisine) to equip, fit out; **~ qn/qch de** to equip sb/sth with.

équitable [ekitabl(ə)] a fair.

équitation [ekitasjɔ̃] nf (horse-)riding.

équivalent, e [ekivalɑ̃, -ɑ̃t] a, nm equivalent.

équivaloir [ekivalwaʀ]: **~ à** vt to be equivalent to.

équivoque [ekivɔk] a equivocal, ambiguous; (louche) dubious.

érable [eʀabl(ə)] nm maple.

érafler [eʀafle] vt to scratch; **éraflure** nf scratch.

éraillé, e [eʀaje] a (voix) rasping.

ère [ɛʀ] nf era; **en l'an 1050 de notre ~** in the year 1050 A.D.

érection [eʀɛksjɔ̃] nf erection.

éreinter [eʀɛ̃te] vt to exhaust, wear out.

ériger [eʀiʒe] vt (monument) to erect.

ermite [ɛʀmit] nm hermit.

éroder [eʀɔde] vt to erode.

érotique [eʀɔtik] a erotic.

errer [eʀe] vi to wander.

erreur [eʀœʀ] nf mistake, error; (morale) error; **faire ~** to be mistaken; **par ~** by mistake; **~ judiciaire** miscarriage of justice.

érudit, e [eʀydi, -it] nm/f scholar.

éruption [eʀypsjɔ̃] nf eruption; (MÉD) rash.

es vb voir **être**.

ès [ɛs] prép: **licencié ~ lettres/sciences** ≈ Bachelor of Arts/Science.

escabeau, x [ɛskabo] nm (tabouret) stool; (échelle) stepladder.

escadre [ɛskadʀ(ə)] nf (NAVIG) squadron; (AVIAT) wing.

escadrille [ɛskadʀij] nf (AVIAT) flight.

escadron [ɛskadʀɔ̃] nm squadron.

escalade [ɛskalad] nf climbing q; (POL etc) escalation.

escalader [ɛskalade] vt to climb.

escale [ɛskal] nf (NAVIG) call; port of call; (AVIAT) stop(over); **faire ~ à** to

put in at; to stop over at.

escalier [ɛskalje] nm stairs pl; **dans l'~ ou les ~s** on the stairs; **~ roulant** escalator.

escamoter [ɛskamɔte] vt (esquiver) to get round, evade; (faire disparaître) to conjure away.

escapade [ɛskapad] nf: **faire une ~** to go on a jaunt; to run away ou off.

escargot [ɛskaʀgo] nm snail.

escarmouche [ɛskaʀmuʃ] nf skirmish.

escarpé, e [ɛskaʀpe] a steep.

escient [ɛsjɑ̃] nm: **à bon ~** advisedly.

esclaffer [ɛsklafe]: **s'~** vi to guffaw.

esclandre [ɛsklɑ̃dʀ(ə)] nm scene, fracas.

esclavage [ɛsklavaʒ] nm slavery.

esclave [ɛsklav] nm/f slave.

escompter [ɛskɔ̃te] vt (COMM) to discount; (espérer) to expect, reckon upon.

escorte [ɛskɔʀt(ə)] nf escort.

escouade [ɛskwad] nf squad.

escrime [ɛskʀim] nf fencing.

escrimer [ɛskʀime]: **s'~** vi: **s'~ à faire** to wear o.s. out doing.

escroc [ɛskʀo] nm swindler, conman.

escroquer [ɛskʀɔke] vt: **~ qn (de qch)/ qch (à qn)** to swindle sb (out of sth)/sth (out of sb); **escroquerie** nf swindle.

espace [ɛspas] nm space.

espacer [ɛspase] vt to space out; **s'~** vi (visites etc) to become less frequent.

espadon [ɛspadɔ̃] nm swordfish inv.

espadrille [ɛspadʀij] nf rope-soled sandal.

Espagne [ɛspaɲ(ə)] nf: **l'~** Spain; **espagnol, e** a Spanish // nm/f: **Espagnol, e** Spaniard // nm (LING) Spanish.

espagnolette [ɛspaɲɔlɛt] nf (window) catch; **fermé à l'~** resting on the catch.

espèce [ɛspɛs] nf (BIO, BOT, ZOOL) species inv; (gén: sorte) sort, kind, type; (péj): **~ de maladroit!** you clumsy oaf!; **en ~** in cash; **~s** nfpl (COMM) cash sg; **en l'~** ad in the case in point.

espérance [ɛspeʀɑ̃s] nf hope; **~ de vie** life expectancy.

espérer [ɛspeʀe] vt to hope for; **j'espère (bien)** I hope so; **~ que/faire** to hope that/to do; **~ en** to trust in.

espiègle [ɛspjɛgl(ə)] a mischievous.

espion, ne [ɛspjɔ̃, -ɔn] nm/f spy.

espionnage [ɛspjɔnaʒ] nm espionage, spying.

espionner [ɛspjɔne] vt to spy (up)on.

esplanade [ɛsplanad] nf esplanade.

espoir [ɛspwaʀ] nm hope.

esprit [ɛspʀi] nm (pensée, intellect) mind; (humour, ironie) wit; (mentalité, d'une loi etc, fantôme etc) spirit; **faire de l'~** to try to be witty; **reprendre ses ~s** to come to; **perdre l'~** to lose one's mind.

esquimau, de, x [ɛskimo, -od] a, nm/f Eskimo // nm ice lolly (Brit), popsicle

(US).

esquinter [ɛskɛ̃te] vt (fam) to mess up.

esquisse [ɛskis] nf sketch.

esquisser [ɛskise] vt to sketch; s'~ vi (amélioration) to begin to be detectable; ~ un sourire to give a vague smile.

esquiver [ɛskive] vt to dodge; s'~ vi to slip away.

essai [ɛsɛ] nm trying; testing; (tentative) attempt, try; (RUGBY) try; (LITTÉRATURE) essay; ~s (AUTO) trials; ~ gratuit (COMM) free trial; à l'~ on a trial basis.

essaim [ɛsɛ̃] nm swarm.

essayer [ɛseje] vt (gén) to try; (vêtement, chaussures) to try (on); (restaurant, méthode, voiture) to try (out) // vi to try; ~ de faire to try ou attempt to do.

essence [ɛsɑ̃s] nf (de voiture) petrol (Brit), gas(oline) (US); (extrait de plante, PHILOSOPHIE) essence; (espèce: d'arbre) species inv.

essentiel, le [ɛsɑ̃sjɛl] a essential; c'est l'~ (ce qui importe) that's the main thing; l'~ de the main part of.

essieu, x [ɛsjø] nm axle.

essor [ɛsɔʀ] nm (de l'économie etc) rapid expansion.

essorer [ɛsɔʀe] vt (en tordant) to wring (out); (par la force centrifuge) to spin-dry; **essoreuse** nf mangle, wringer; spin-dryer.

essouffler [ɛsufle] vt to make breathless; s'~ vi to get out of breath; (fig) to run out of steam.

essuie-glace [ɛsɥiglas] nm inv windscreen (Brit) ou windshield (US) wiper.

essuie-main [ɛsɥimɛ̃] nm hand towel.

essuyer [ɛsɥije] vt to wipe; (fig: subir) to suffer; s'~ vi (après le bain) to dry o.s.; ~ la vaisselle to dry up the dishes.

est [ɛst] vb [ɛ] voir être // nm east // a inv east; (région) east(ern); à l'~ in the east; (direction) to the east, east(wards); à l'~ de (to the) east of.

estafette [ɛstafɛt] nf (MIL) dispatch rider.

estaminet [ɛstaminɛ] nm tavern.

estampe [ɛstɑ̃p] nf print, engraving.

estampille [ɛstɑ̃pij] nf stamp.

est-ce que [ɛskə] ad: ~ c'est cher/c'était bon? is it expensive/was it good?; quand est-ce qu'il part? when does he leave?, when is he leaving?; voir aussi que.

esthéticienne [ɛstetisjɛn] nf beautician.

esthétique [ɛstetik] a attractive; aesthetically pleasing.

estimation [ɛstimasjɔ̃] nf valuation; assessment.

estime [ɛstim] nf esteem, regard.

estimer [ɛstime] vt (respecter) to es-

teem; (expertiser) to value; (évaluer) to assess, estimate; (penser): ~ que/être to consider that/o.s. to be.

estival, e, aux [ɛstival, -o] a summer cpd.

estivant, e [ɛstivɑ̃, -ɑ̃t] nm/f (summer) holiday-maker.

estomac [ɛstɔma] nm stomach.

estomaqué, e [ɛstɔmake] a flabbergasted.

estomper [ɛstɔ̃pe] vt (fig) to blur, dim; s'~ vi to soften; to become blurred.

estrade [ɛstʀad] nf platform, rostrum.

estragon [ɛstʀagɔ̃] nm tarragon.

estropier [ɛstʀɔpje] vt to cripple, maim; (fig) to twist, distort.

et [e] cj and; ~ lui? what about him?; ~ alors! so what!

étable [etabl(ə)] nf cowshed.

établi [etabli] nm (work)bench.

établir [etablir] vt (papiers d'identité, facture) to make out; (liste, programme) to draw up; (entreprise, camp, gouvernement, artisan) to set up; (réputation, usage, fait, culpabilité) to establish; s'~ vi (se faire: entente etc) to be established; s'~ (à son compte) to set up in business; s'~ à/près de to settle in/near.

établissement [etablismɑ̃] nm making out; drawing up; setting up, establishing; (entreprise, institution) establishment; ~ scolaire school, educational establishment.

étage [etaʒ] nm (d'immeuble) storey, floor; (de fusée) stage; (GÉO: de culture, végétation) level; à l'~ upstairs; au 2ème ~ on the 2nd (Brit) ou 3rd (US) floor; de bas ~ a low.

étagère [etaʒɛʀ] nf (rayon) shelf; (meuble) shelves pl.

étai [etɛ] nm stay, prop.

étain [etɛ̃] nm tin; (ORFÈVRERIE) pewter q.

étais etc vb voir **être**.

étal [etal] nm stall.

étalage [etalaʒ] nm display; display window; faire ~ de to show off, parade.

étaler [etale] vt (carte, nappe) to spread (out); (peinture, liquide) to spread; (échelonner: paiements, vacances) to spread, stagger; (marchandises) to display; (richesses, connaissances) to parade; s'~ vi (liquide) to spread out; (fam) to fall flat on one's face; s'~ sur (suj: paiements etc) to be spread out over.

étalon [etalɔ̃] nm (mesure) standard; (cheval) stallion.

étamer [etame] vt (casserole) to tin(plate); (glace) to silver.

étanche [etɑ̃ʃ] a (récipient) watertight; (montre, vêtement) waterproof.

étancher [etɑ̃ʃe] vt: ~ sa soif to quench

one's thirst.

étang [etɑ̃] nm pond.

étant [etɑ̃] vb voir **être, donné**.

étape [etap] nf stage; (lieu d'arrivée) stopping place; (: CYCLISME) staging point; faire ~ à to stop off at.

état [eta] nm (POL, condition) state; (liste) inventory, statement; en mauvais ~ in poor condition; en ~ (de marche) in (working) order; remettre en ~ to repair; hors d'~ out of order; être en ~/ hors d'~ de faire to be in a/in no fit state to do; en tout ~ de cause in any event; être dans tous ses ~s to be in a state; faire ~ de (alléguer) to put forward; en ~ d'arrestation under arrest; ~ civil civil status; ~ des lieux inventory of fixtures; ~s d'âme moods; **étatiser** vt to bring under state control.

état-major [etamaʒɔʀ] nm (MIL) staff.

Etats-Unis [etazyni] nmpl: les ~ the United States.

étau, x [eto] nm vice (Brit), vise (US).

étayer [eteje] vt to prop ou shore up.

et c(a)etera [etsetera], **etc.** ad et cetera, and so on, etc.

été [ete] pp de **être** // nm summer.

éteignoir [etɛɲwaʀ] nm (candle) extinguisher; (péj) killjoy, wet blanket.

éteindre [etɛ̃dʀ(ə)] vt (lampe, lumière, radio) to turn ou switch off; (cigarette, incendie, bougie) to put out, extinguish; (JUR: dette) to extinguish; s'~ vi to go out; to go off; (mourir) to pass away; **éteint, e** a (fig) lacklustre, dull; (volcan) extinct.

étendard [etɑ̃daʀ] nm standard.

étendre [etɑ̃dʀ(ə)] vt (pâte, liquide) to spread; (carte etc) to spread out; (linge) to hang up; (bras, jambes, par terre: blessé) to stretch out; (diluer) to dilute, thin; (fig: agrandir) to extend; s'~ vi (augmenter, se propager) to spread; (terrain, forêt etc) to stretch; (s'allonger) to stretch out; (se coucher) to lie down; (fig: expliquer) to elaborate.

étendu, e [etɑ̃dy] a extensive // nf (d'eau, de sable) stretch, expanse; (importance) extent.

éternel, le [etɛʀnɛl] a eternal.

éterniser [etɛʀnize]: s'~ vi to last for ages; to stay for ages.

éternité [etɛʀnite] nf eternity.

éternuer [etɛʀnɥe] vi to sneeze.

êtes vb voir **être**.

éthique [etik] a ethical.

ethnie [etni] nf ethnic group.

éthylisme [etilism(ə)] nm alcoholism.

étiez vb voir **être**.

étinceler [etɛ̃sle] vi to sparkle.

étincelle [etɛ̃sɛl] nf spark.

étioler [etjɔle]: s'~ vi to wilt.

étiqueter [etikte] vt to label.

étiquette [etikɛt] nf label; (protocole): l'~ etiquette.

étirer [etire] vt to stretch; s'~ vi (personne) to stretch; (convoi, route): s'~ sur to stretch out over.

étoffe [etɔf] nf material, fabric.

étoffer [etɔfe] vt, s'~ vi to fill out.

étoile [etwal] nf star; à la belle ~ in the open; ~ filante shooting star; ~ de mer starfish; **étoilé, e** a starry.

étole [etɔl] nf stole.

étonnant, e [etɔnɑ̃, -ɑ̃t] a amazing.

étonner [etɔne] vt to surprise, amaze; s'~ que/de to be amazed that/at; cela m'étonnerait (que) (j'en doute) I'd be very surprised (if).

étouffée [etufe]: à l'~ ad (CULIN) steamed; braised.

étouffer [etufe] vt to suffocate; (bruit) to muffle; (scandale) to hush up // vi to suffocate; s'~ vi (en mangeant etc) to choke.

étourderie [eturdəri] nf heedlessness q; thoughtless blunder.

étourdi, e [eturdi] a (distrait) scatterbrained, heedless.

étourdir [eturdir] vt (assommer) to stun, daze; (griser) to make dizzy ou giddy; **étourdissement** nm dizzy spell.

étourneau, x [eturno] nm starling.

étrange [etrɑ̃ʒ] a strange.

étranger, ère [etrɑ̃ʒe, -ɛr] a foreign; (pas de la famille, non familier) strange // nm/f foreigner; stranger // nm: à l'~ abroad; de l'~ from abroad; ~ à (fig) unfamiliar to; irrelevant to.

étranglement [etrɑ̃gləmɑ̃] nm (d'une vallée etc) constriction.

étrangler [etrɑ̃gle] vt to strangle; s'~ vi (en mangeant etc) to choke.

étrave [etrav] nf stem.

être [etr(ə)] ♦ nm being; ~ humain human being

♦ vb avec attribut **1** (état, description) to be; il est instituteur he is ou he's a teacher; **vous êtes grand/intelligent/ fatigué** you are ou you're tall/clever/tired **2** (+ à: appartenir) to be; le livre est à Paul the book is Paul's ou belongs to Paul; **c'est à moi/eux** it is ou it's mine/ theirs

3 (+ de: provenance) to be; il est de Paris he is from Paris; (: appartenance): il est des nôtres he is one of us **4** (date): nous sommes le 10 janvier it's the 10th of January (today)

♦ vi to be; je ne serai pas ici demain I won't be here tomorrow

♦ vb auxiliaire **1** to have; to be; être arrivé/allé to have arrived/gone; il est parti he has left, he is gone **2** (forme passive) to be; être fait par to be made by; il a été promu he has been promoted **3** (+ à: obligation): c'est à réparer it needs repairing; c'est à essayer it should be tried

♦ *vb impersonnel* 1: **il est** + *adjectif* it is + *adjective*; **il est impossible de le faire** it's impossible to do it 2 *(heure, date)*: **il est 10 heures, c'est 10 heures** it is *ou* it's 10 o'clock 3 *(emphatique)*: **c'est moi** it's me; **c'est à lui de le faire** it's up to him to do it.

étreindre [etRɛ̃dR(ə)] *vt* to clutch, grip; *(amoureusement, amicalement)* to embrace; **s'~** *vi* to embrace.

étrenner [etRene] *vt* to use *(ou* wear) for the first time.

étrennes [etRen] *nfpl* Christmas box *sg*.

étrier [etRije] *nm* stirrup.

étriller [etRije] *vt (cheval)* to curry; *(fam: battre)* to slaughter *(fig)*.

étriqué, e [etRike] *a* skimpy.

étroit, e [etRwa, -wat] *a* narrow; *(vêtement)* tight; *(fig: serré)* close, tight; **à l'~** cramped; **d'esprit** narrow-minded.

étude [etyd] *nf* studying; *(ouvrage, rapport)* study; *(de notaire: bureau)* office; *(: charge)* practice; *(SCOL: salle de travail)* study room; **~s** *(SCOL)* studies; **être à l'~** *(projet etc)* to be under consideration; **faire des ~s** *(de droit/ médecine)* to study (law/medicine).

étudiant, e [etydjɑ̃, -ɑ̃t] *nm/f* student.

étudié, e [etydje] *a (démarche)* studied; *(système)* carefully designed; *(prix)* keen.

étudier [etydje] *vt, vi* to study.

étui [etɥi] *nm* case.

étuve [etyv] *nf* steamroom.

étuvée [etyve]: **à l'~** *ad* braised.

eu, eue [y] *pp de* **avoir**.

euh [ø] *excl* er.

Europe [øRɔp] *nf*: **l'~** Europe; **européen, ne** *a, nm/f* European.

eus *etc vb voir* **avoir**.

eux [ø] *pronom (sujet)* they; *(objet)* them.

évacuer [evakɥe] *vt* to evacuate.

évader [evade]: **s'~** *vi* to escape.

évangile [evɑ̃ʒil] *nm* gospel.

évanouir [evanwiR]: **s'~** *vi* to faint; *(disparaître)* to vanish, disappear.

évanouissement [evanwismɑ̃] *nm (syncope)* fainting fit; *(dans un accident)* loss of consciousness.

évaporer [evapɔRe]: **s'~** *vi* to evaporate.

évaser [evaze] *vt (tuyau)* to widen, open out; *(jupe, pantalon)* to flare.

évasif, ive [evazif, -iv] *a* evasive.

évasion [evazjɔ̃] *nf* escape.

évêché [eveʃe] *nm* bishopric; bishop's palace.

éveil [evɛj] *nm* awakening; **être en ~** to be alert.

éveillé, e [eveje] *a* awake; *(vif)* alert, sharp.

éveiller [eveje] *vt* to (a)waken; **s'~** *vi* to (a)waken; *(fig)* to be aroused.

événement [evɛnmɑ̃] *nm* event.

éventail [evɑ̃taj] *nm* fan; *(choix)* range.

éventaire [evɑ̃tɛR] *nm* stall, stand.

éventer [evɑ̃te] *vt (secret)* to uncover; **s'~** *vi (parfum)* to go stale.

éventrer [evɑ̃tRe] *vt* to disembowel; *(fig)* to tear *ou* rip open.

éventualité [evɑ̃tɥalite] *nf* eventuality; possibility; **dans l'~ de** in the event of.

éventuel, le [evɑ̃tɥɛl] *a* possible; **~lement** *ad* possibly.

évêque [evɛk] *nm* bishop.

évertuer [evɛRtɥe]: **s'~** *vi*: **s'~ à faire** to try very hard to do.

éviction [eviksjɔ̃] *nf* ousting; *(de locataire)* eviction.

évidemment [evidamɑ̃] *ad* obviously.

évidence [evidɑ̃s] *nf* obviousness; obvious fact; **de toute ~** quite obviously *ou* evidently; **en ~** conspicuous; **mettre en ~** to highlight; to bring to the fore.

évident, e [evidɑ̃, -ɑ̃t] *a* obvious, evident.

évider [evide] *vt* to scoop out.

évier [evje] *nm* (kitchen) sink.

évincer [evɛ̃se] *vt* to oust.

éviter [evite] *vt* to avoid; **~ de faire/ qch ne se passe** to avoid doing/sth happening; **~ qch à qn** to spare sb sth.

évolué, e [evɔlɥe] *a* advanced.

évoluer [evɔlɥe] *vi (enfant, maladie)* to develop; *(situation, moralement)* to evolve, develop; *(aller et venir: danseur etc)* to move about, circle; **évolution** *nf* development; evolution; **évolutions** *nfpl* movements.

évoquer [evɔke] *vt* to call to mind, evoke; *(mentionner)* to mention.

ex... [ɛks] *préfixe* ex-.

exact, e [ɛgzakt] *a (précis)* exact, accurate, precise; *(correct)* correct; *(ponctuel)* punctual; **l'heure ~e** the right *ou* exact time; **~ement** *ad* exactly, accurately, precisely; correctly; *(c'est cela même)* exactly.

ex aequo [ɛgzeko] *a* equally placed.

exagéré, e [ɛgzaʒeRe] *a (prix etc)* excessive.

exagérer [ɛgzaʒeRe] *vt* to exaggerate // *vi (abuser)* to go too far; to overstep the mark; *(déformer les faits)* to exaggerate.

exalter [ɛgzalte] *vt (enthousiasmer)* to excite, elate; *(glorifier)* to exalt.

examen [ɛgzamɛ̃] *nm* examination; *(SCOL)* exam, examination; **à l'~** under consideration; *(COMM)* on approval.

examiner [ɛgzamine] *vt* to examine.

exaspérant, e [ɛgzaspeRɑ̃, -ɑ̃t] *a* exasperating.

exaspérer [ɛgzaspeRe] *vt* to exasperate; to exacerbate.

exaucer [ɛgzose] *vt (vœu)* to grant.

excédent [ɛksedɑ̃] *nm* surplus; **en ~** surplus; **~ de bagages** excess luggage.

excéder [ɛksede] *vt (dépasser)* to ex-

ceed; (agacer) to exasperate.
excellence [ɛksɛlɑ̃s] nf (titre) Excellency.
excellent, e [ɛksɛlɑ̃, -ɑ̃t] a excellent.
excentrique [ɛksɑ̃trik] a eccentric; (quartier) outlying.
excepté, e [ɛksɛpte] a, prép: les élèves ~s, ~ les élèves except for the pupils; ~ si except if.
exception [ɛksɛpsjɔ̃] nf exception; à l'~ de except for, with the exception of; d'~ (mesure, loi) special, exceptional; **exceptionnel, le** a exceptional.
excès [ɛksɛ] nm surplus // nmpl excesses; à l'~ to excess; ~ de vitesse speeding q; **excessif, ive** a excessive.
excitant, e [ɛksitɑ̃, -ɑ̃t] a exciting // nm stimulant.
excitation [ɛksitasjɔ̃] nf (état) excitement.
exciter [ɛksite] vt to excite; (suj: café etc) to stimulate; s'~ vi to get excited.
exclamation [ɛksklamasjɔ̃] nf exclamation.
exclamer [ɛksklame]: s'~ vi to exclaim.
exclure [ɛksklyr] vt (faire sortir) to expel; (ne pas compter) to exclude, leave out; (rendre impossible) to exclude, rule out; ce n'est pas exclu it's not impossible, I don't rule that out; **exclusif, ive** a exclusive; **exclusion** nf expulsion; à l'exclusion de with the exclusion ou exception of; **exclusivité** nf (COMM) exclusive rights pl; film passant en exclusivité a film showing only at.
excursion [ɛkskyrsjɔ̃] nf (en autocar) excursion, trip; (à pied) walk, hike.
excuse [ɛkskyz] nf excuse; ~s nfpl apology sg, apologies.
excuser [ɛkskyze] vt to excuse; s'~ (de) to apologize (for); 'excusez-moi' 'I'm sorry'; (pour attirer l'attention) 'excuse me'.
exécrable [ɛgzekrabl(ə)] a atrocious.
exécrer [ɛgzekre] vt to loathe, abhor.
exécuter [ɛgzekyte] vt (prisonnier) to execute; (tâche etc) to execute, carry out; (MUS: jouer) to perform, execute; (INFORM) to run; s'~ vi to comply; **exécutif, ive** a, nm (POL) executive; **exécution** nf execution; carrying out; mettre à exécution to carry out.
exemplaire [ɛgzɑ̃plɛr] nm copy.
exemple [ɛgzɑ̃pl(ə)] nm example; par ~ for instance, for example; donner l'~ to set an example; prendre ~ sur to take as a model; à l'~ de just like.
exempt, e [ɛgzɑ̃, -ɑ̃t] a: ~ de (dispensé de) exempt from; (sans) free from.
exercer [ɛgzɛrse] vt (pratiquer) to exercise, practise; (prérogative) to exercise; (influence, contrôle) to exert; (former) to exercise, train; s'~ vi (sportif, musicien) to practise; (se faire sentir: pression etc) to be exerted.

exercice [ɛgzɛrsis] nm (tâche, travail) exercise; l'~ exercise; (MIL) drill; en ~ (juge) in office; (médecin) practising.
exhaustif, ive [ɛgzostif, -iv] a exhaustive.
exhiber [ɛgzibe] vt (montrer: papiers, certificat) to present, produce; (péj) to display, flaunt; s'~ vi to parade; (suj: exhibitionniste) to expose o.s.
exhorter [ɛgzɔrte] vt to urge.
exigeant, e [ɛgziʒɑ̃, -ɑ̃t] a demanding; (péj) hard to please.
exigence [ɛgziʒɑ̃s] nf demand, requirement.
exiger [ɛgziʒe] vt to demand, require.
exigu, ë [ɛgzigy] a (lieu) cramped, tiny.
exil [ɛgzil] nm exile; ~er vt to exile; s'~er vi to go into exile.
existence [ɛgzistɑ̃s] nf existence.
exister [ɛgziste] vi to exist; il existe un/ des there is a/are (some).
exonérer [ɛgzɔnere] vt: ~ de to exempt from.
exorbité, e [ɛgzɔrbite] a: yeux ~s bulging eyes.
exotique [ɛgzɔtik] a exotic.
expatrier [ɛkspatrije] vt: s'~ to leave one's country.
expectative [ɛkspɛktativ] nf: être dans l'~ to be still waiting.
expédient [ɛkspedjɑ̃] nm (péj) expedient; vivre d'~s to live by one's wits.
expédier [ɛkspedje] vt (lettre, paquet) to send; (troupes) to dispatch; (péj: travail etc) to dispose of, dispatch; **expéditeur, trice** nm/f sender.
expédition [ɛkspedisjɔ̃] nf sending; (scientifique, sportive, MIL) expedition.
expérience [ɛksperjɑ̃s] nf (de la vie) experience; (scientifique) experiment.
expérimenté, e [ɛksperimɑ̃te] a experienced.
expérimenter [ɛksperimɑ̃te] vt to test out, experiment with.
expert, e [ɛkspɛr, -ɛrt(ə)] a, nm expert; ~ en assurances insurance valuer; **~-comptable** nm ≈ chartered accountant (Brit), ≈ certified public accountant (US).
expertise [ɛkspɛrtiz] nf valuation; assessment; valuer's (ou assessor's) report; (JUR) forensic examination.
expertiser [ɛkspɛrtize] vt (objet de valeur) to value; (voiture accidentée etc) to assess damage to.
expier [ɛkspje] vt to expiate, atone for.
expirer [ɛkspire] vi (prendre fin, mourir) to expire; (respirer) to breathe out.
explicatif, ive [ɛksplikatif, -iv] a explanatory.
explication [ɛksplikasjɔ̃] nf explanation; (discussion) discussion; argument; ~ de texte (SCOL) critical analysis.
explicite [ɛksplisit] a explicit.

expliquer [ɛksplike] vt to explain; s'~ to explain (o.s.); (discuter) to discuss things; to have it out; **son erreur s'explique** one can understand his mistake.

exploit [ɛksplwa] nm exploit, feat.

exploitation [ɛksplwatasjɔ̃] nf exploitation; running; ~ **agricole** farming concern.

exploiter [ɛksplwate] vt (mine) to exploit, work; (entreprise, ferme) to run, operate; (clients, ouvriers, erreur, don) to exploit.

explorer [ɛksplɔre] vt to explore.

exploser [ɛksploze] vi to explode, blow up; (engin explosif) to go off; (fig: joie, colère) to burst out, explode; **explosif, ive** a, nm explosive; **explosion** nf explosion.

exportateur, trice [ɛkspɔrtatœr, -tris] a export cpd, exporting // nm exporter.

exportation [ɛkspɔrtasjɔ̃] nf exportation; export.

exporter [ɛkspɔrte] vt to export.

exposant [ɛkspozɑ̃] nm exhibitor.

exposé, e [ɛkspoze] nm talk // a: ~ **au sud** facing south; **bien** ~ well situated.

exposer [ɛkspoze] vt (marchandise) to display; (peinture) to exhibit, show; (parler de) to explain, set out; (mettre en danger, orienter, PHOTO) to expose; **exposition** nf (manifestation) exhibition; (PHOTO) exposure.

exprès [ɛksprɛ] ad (délibérément) on purpose; (spécialement) specially.

exprès, esse [ɛksprɛs] a (ordre, défense) express, formal // a inv, ad (PTT) express.

express [ɛksprɛs] a, nm: (café) ~ espresso (coffee); (train) ~ fast train.

expressément [ɛkspresemɑ̃] ad expressly; specifically.

expression [ɛkspresjɔ̃] nf expression.

exprimer [ɛksprime] vt (sentiment, idée) to express; (jus, liquide) to press out; s'~ vi (personne) to express o.s.

exproprier [ɛksprɔprije] vt to buy up by compulsory purchase, expropriate.

expulser [ɛkspylse] vt to expel; (locataire) to evict; (SPORT) to send off.

exquis, e [ɛkski, -iz] a exquisite; delightful.

exsangue [ɛksɑ̃g] a bloodless, drained of blood.

extase [ɛkstaz] nf ecstasy; **s'extasier sur** to go into raptures over.

extension [ɛkstɑ̃sjɔ̃] nf (d'un muscle, ressort) stretching; (fig) extension; expansion.

exténuer [ɛkstenɥe] vt to exhaust.

extérieur, e [ɛksterjœr] a (porte, mur etc) outer, outside; (au dehors: escalier, w.-c.) outside; (commerce) foreign; (influences) external; (apparent: calme, gaieté etc) surface cpd // nm (d'une

maison, d'un récipient etc) outside, exterior; (apparence) exterior; (d'un groupe social): l'~ the outside world; à l'~ outside; (à l'étranger) abroad; ~**ement** ad on the outside; (en apparence) on the surface.

exterminer [ɛkstɛrmine] vt to exterminate, wipe out.

externat [ɛkstɛrna] nm day school.

externe [ɛkstɛrn(ə)] a external, outer // nm/f (MÉD) non-resident medical student (Brit), extern (US); (SCOL) day pupil.

extincteur [ɛkstɛ̃ktœr] nm (fire) extinguisher.

extinction [ɛkstɛ̃ksjɔ̃] nf: ~ **de voix** loss of voice.

extorquer [ɛkstɔrke] vt to extort.

extra [ɛkstra] a inv first-rate; top-quality // nm inv extra help.

extrader [ɛkstrade] vt to extradite.

extraire [ɛkstrɛr] vt to extract; **extrait** nm extract.

extraordinaire [ɛkstraɔrdinɛr] a extraordinary; (POL: mesures etc) special.

extravagant, e [ɛkstravagɑ̃, -ɑ̃t] a extravagant; wild.

extraverti, e [ɛkstraverti] a extrovert.

extrême [ɛkstrɛm] a, nm extreme; ~**ment** ad extremely; ~**-onction** nf last rites pl; **E**~**-Orient** nm Far East.

extrémité [ɛkstremite] nf end; (situation) straits pl, plight; (geste désespéré) extreme action; ~s nfpl (pieds et mains) extremities; **à la dernière** ~ on the point of death.

exutoire [ɛgzytwar] nm outlet, release.

F

F abr de **franc**.

fa [fa] nm inv (MUS) F; (en chantant la gamme) fa.

fable [fabl(ə)] nf fable.

fabricant [fabrikɑ̃] nm manufacturer.

fabrication [fabrikasjɔ̃] nf manufacture.

fabrique [fabrik] nf factory.

fabriquer [fabrike] vt to make; (industriellement) to manufacture; (fig): **qu'est-ce qu'il fabrique?** what is he doing?

fabulation [fabylasjɔ̃] nf fantasizing.

fac [fak] abr f (fam: SCOL) de **faculté**.

façade [fasad] nf front, façade.

face [fas] nf face; (fig: aspect) side // a: **le côté** ~ heads; **perdre la** ~ to lose face; **en** ~ **de** prép opposite; (fig) in front of; **de** ~ ad from the front; face on; ~ **à** prép facing; (fig) faced with, in the face of; **faire** ~ **à** to face; ~ **à** ~ ad facing each other // nm inv encounter.

facétieux, euse [fasesjø, -øz] a mischievous.

fâché, e [fɑʃe] a angry; (désolé) sorry.

fâcher [faʃe] vt to anger; se ~ vi to get angry; se ~ avec (se brouiller) to fall out with.

fâcheux, euse [faʃø, -øz] a unfortunate, regrettable.

facile [fasil] a easy; (accommodant) easy-going; ~**ment** ad easily; **facilité** nf easiness; (disposition, don) aptitude; **facilités** nfpl facilities; facilités de paiement easy terms; **faciliter** vt to make easier.

façon [fasɔ̃] nf (manière) way; (d'une robe etc) making-up; cut; ~s nfpl (péj) fuss sg; de quelle ~? (in) what way?; de ~ à/à ce que so as to/that; de toute ~ anyway, in any case.

façonner [fasɔne] vt (fabriquer) to manufacture; (travailler: matière) to shape, fashion; (fig) to mould, shape.

facteur, trice [faktœr, -tris] nm/f postman/woman (Brit), mailman/woman (US) // nm (MATH, fig: élément) factor; ~ d'orgues organ builder; ~ de pianos piano maker.

factice [faktis] a artificial.

faction [faksjɔ̃] nf faction; (MIL) guard ou sentry (duty); watch.

facture [faktyʀ] nf (à payer: gén) bill; (: COMM) invoice; (d'un artisan, artiste) technique, workmanship; **facturer** vt to invoice.

facultatif, ive [fakyltatif, -iv] a optional; (arrêt de bus) request cpd.

faculté [fakylte] nf (intellectuelle, d'université) faculty; (pouvoir, possibilité) power.

fade [fad] a insipid.

fagot [fago] nm bundle of sticks.

faible [fɛbl(ə)] a weak; (voix, lumière, vent) faint; (rendement, intensité, revenu etc) low // nm weak point; (pour quelqu'un) weakness, soft spot; ~ d'esprit feeble-minded; **faiblesse** nf weakness; **faiblir** vi to weaken; (lumière) to dim; (vent) to drop.

faïence [fajɑ̃s] nf earthenware q; piece of earthenware.

faignant, e [fɛɲɑ̃, -ɑ̃t] nm/f = **fainéant, e.**

faille [faj] vb voir **falloir** // nf (GÉO) fault; (fig) flaw, weakness.

faillir [fajiʀ] vi: j'ai failli tomber I almost ou very nearly fell.

faillite [fajit] nf bankruptcy.

faim [fɛ̃] nf hunger; avoir ~ to be hungry; rester sur sa ~ (aussi fig) to be left wanting more.

fainéant, e [fɛneɑ̃, -ɑ̃t] nm/f idler, loafer.

faire [fɛʀ] ♦ vt 1 (fabriquer, être l'auteur de) to make; ~ du vin/un offre/un film to make wine/an offer/a film; ~ du bruit to make a noise

2 (effectuer: travail, opération) to do; que faites-vous? (quel métier etc) what do you do?; (quelle activité: au moment de la question) what are you doing?; ~ la lessive to do the washing

3 (études) to do; (sport, musique) to play; ~ du droit/du français to do law/French; ~ du rugby/piano to play rugby/the piano

4 (simuler): ~ le malade/l'ignorant to act the invalid/the fool

5 (transformer, avoir un effet sur): ~ de qn un frustré/avocat to make sb frustrated/a lawyer; ça ne me fait rien (m'est égal) I don't care ou mind; (me laisse froid) it has no effect on me; ça ne fait rien it doesn't matter; ~ que (impliquer) to mean that

6 (calculs, prix, mesures): 2 et 2 font 4 2 and 2 are ou make 4; ça fait 10 m/15 F it's 10 m/15 F; je vous le fais 10 F I'll let you have it for 10 F

7: qu'a-t-il fait de sa valise? what has he done with his case?

8: ne ~ que: il ne fait que critiquer (sans cesse) all he (ever) does is criticize; (seulement) he's only criticizing

9 (dire) to say; 'vraiment?' fit-il 'really?' he said

10 (maladie) to have; ~ du diabète to have diabetes sg

♦ vi 1 (agir, s'y prendre) to act, do; il faut ~ vite we (ou you etc) must act quickly; comment a-t-il fait pour? how did he manage to?; faites comme chez vous make yourself at home

2 (paraître) to look; ~ vieux/démodé to look old/old-fashioned; ça fait bien it looks good

♦ vb substitut to do; ne le casse pas comme je l'ai fait don't break it as I did; je peux le voir? - faites! can I see it? - please do!

♦ vb impersonnel 1: il fait beau etc the weather is fine etc; voir jour, froid etc

2 (temps écoulé, durée): ça fait 2 ans qu'il est parti it's 2 years since he left; ça fait 2 ans qu'il y est he's been there for 2 years

♦ vb semi-auxiliaire: ~ + infinitif 1 (action directe) to make; ~ tomber/bouger qch to make sth fall/move; ~ démarrer un moteur/chauffer de l'eau to start up an engine/heat some water; cela fait dormir it makes you sleep; ~ travailler les enfants to make the children work ou get the children to work

2 (indirectement, par un intermédiaire): ~ réparer qch to get ou have sth repaired; ~ punir les enfants to have the children punished

se faire vi 1 (vin, fromage) to mature

2: cela se fait beaucoup/ne se fait pas it's done a lot/not done

3: se ~ + nom ou pronom: se ~ une jupe to make o.s. a skirt; se ~ des amis to make friends; se ~ du souci to worry;

il ne s'en fait pas he doesn't worry

4: se ~ + *adjectif* (*devenir*): se ~ vieux to be getting old; (*délibérément*): se ~ beau to do o.s. up

5: se ~ à (*s'habituer*) to get used to; je n'arrive pas à me ~ à la nourriture/au climat I can't get used to the food/climate

6: se ~ + *infinitif*: se ~ examiner la vue/opérer to have one's eyes tested/have an operation; se ~ couper les cheveux to get one's hair cut; il va se ~ tuer/punir he's going to get himself killed/get (himself) punished; il s'est fait aider he got somebody to help him; il s'est fait aider par Simon he got Simon to help him; se ~ faire un vêtement to get a garment made for o.s.

7 (*impersonnel*): comment se fait-il/faisait-il que? how is it/was it that?

faire-part [fɛrpar] *nm inv* announcement (*of birth, marriage etc*).

faisable [fəzabl(ə)] *a* feasible.

faisan, e [fəzɑ̃, -an] *nm/f* pheasant.

faisandé, e [fəzɑ̃de] *a* high (*bad*).

faisceau, x [fɛso] *nm* (*de lumière etc*) beam; (*de branches etc*) bundle.

faisons *vb voir* **faire**.

fait [fɛ] *nm* (*événement*) event, occurrence; (*réalité, donnée*) fact; **être le ~ de** (*causé par*) to be the work of; **être au ~ (de)** to be informed (of); **au ~** (*à propos*) by the way; **en venir au ~** to get to the point; **de ~** *a* (*opposé à: de droit*) de facto // *ad* in fact; **du ~ de ceci/qu'il a menti** because of *ou* on account of this/his having lied; **de ce ~** for this reason; **en ~** in fact; **en ~ de repas** by way of a meal; **prendre ~ et cause pour qn** to support sb, side with sb; **prendre qn sur le ~** to catch sb in the act; **~ divers** news item; **les ~s et gestes de qn** sb's actions *ou* doings.

fait, e [fɛ, fɛt] *a* (*mûr: fromage, melon*) ripe; **c'en est ~ de** that's the end of.

faîte [fɛt] *nm* top; (*fig*) pinnacle, height.

faites *vb voir* **faire**.

fait-tout *nm inv*, **faitout** *nm* [fɛtu] stewpot.

falaise [falɛz] *nf* cliff.

fallacieux, euse [falasjø, -øz] *a* fallacious; deceptive; illusory.

falloir [falwar] *vb impersonnel*: **il va ~ 100 F** we'll need 100 F; **il doit ~ du temps** that must take time; **il me faudrait 100 F** I would need 100 F; **il vous faut tourner à gauche après l'église** you have to turn left past the church; **nous avons ce qu'il (nous) faut** we have what we need; **il faut qu'il parte/a fallu qu'il parte** (*obligation*) he has to *ou* must leave/had to leave; **il a fallu le faire** it had to be done // **s'en ~**: **il s'en est fallu de 100 F/5 minutes** we (*ou* they) were 100 F short/5 minutes late (*ou* ear-

ly); **il s'en faut de beaucoup qu'il soit** he is far from being; **il s'en est fallu de peu que cela n'arrive** it very nearly happened; **ou peu s'en faut** or as good as.

falot, e [falo, -ɔt] *a* dreary, colourless.

falsifier [falsifje] *vt* to falsify; to doctor.

famé, e [fame] *a*: **mal ~** disreputable, of ill repute.

famélique [famelik] *a* half-starved.

fameux, euse [famø, -øz] *a* (*illustre*) famous; (*bon: repas, plat etc*) first-rate, first-class; (*valeur intensive*) real, downright.

familial, e, aux [familjal, -o] *a* family *cpd* // *nf* (*AUTO*) estate car (*Brit*), station wagon (*US*).

familiarité [familjarite] *nf* informality; familiarity; **~s** *nfpl* familiarities.

familier, ère [familje, -ɛr] *a* (*connu, impertinent*) familiar; (*dénotant une certaine intimité*) informal, friendly; (*LING*) informal, colloquial // *nm* regular (visitor).

famille [famij] *nf* family; **il a de la ~ à Paris** he has relatives in Paris.

famine [famin] *nf* famine.

fanal, aux [fanal, -o] *nm* beacon; lantern.

fanatique [fanatik] *a* fanatical // *nm/f* fanatic; **fanatisme** *nm* fanaticism.

faner [fane]: **se ~** *vi* to fade.

fanfare [fɑ̃far] *nf* (*orchestre*) brass band; (*musique*) fanfare.

fanfaron, ne [fɑ̃farɔ̃, -ɔn] *nm/f* braggart.

fange [fɑ̃ʒ] *nf* mire.

fanion [fanjɔ̃] *nm* pennant.

fantaisie [fɑ̃tezi] *nf* (*spontanéité*) fancy, imagination; (*caprice*) whim; extravagance // *a*: **bijou/pain (de)** ~ costume jewellery/fancy bread; **fantaisiste** *a* (*péj*) unorthodox, eccentric // *nm/f* (*de music-hall*) variety artist *ou* entertainer.

fantasme [fɑ̃tasm(ə)] *nm* fantasy.

fantasque [fɑ̃task(ə)] *a* whimsical, capricious; fantastic.

fantastique [fɑ̃tastik] *a* fantastic.

fantôme [fɑ̃tom] *nm* ghost, phantom.

faon [fɑ̃] *nm* fawn.

farce [fars(ə)] *nf* (*viande*) stuffing; (*blague*) (practical) joke; (*THÉÂTRE*) farce; **farcir** *vt* (*viande*) to stuff.

fard [far] *nm* make-up.

fardeau, x [fardo] *nm* burden.

farder [farde] *vt* to make up.

farfelu, e [farfely] *a* hare-brained.

farine [farin] *nf* flour; **farineux, euse** *a* (*sauce, pomme*) floury // *nmpl* (*aliments*) starchy foods.

farouche [faruʃ] *a* shy, timid; savage, wild; fierce.

fart [far(t)] *nm* (ski) wax.

fascicule [fasikyl] *nm* volume.

fasciner [fasine] *vt* to fascinate.

fascisme [faʃism(ə)] *nm* fascism.

fasse etc vb voir **faire**.

faste [fast(ə)] nm splendour // a: c'est un jour ~ it's his (ou our) lucky day.

fastidieux, euse [fastidjø, -øz] a tedious, tiresome.

fastueux, euse [fastɥø, -øz] a sumptuous, luxurious.

fat [fa] am conceited, smug.

fatal, e [fatal] a fatal; (inévitable) inevitable; ~ité nf fate; fateful coincidence; inevitability.

fatidique [fatidik] a fateful.

fatigant, e [fatigɑ̃, -ɑ̃t] a tiring; (agaçant) tiresome.

fatigue [fatig] nf tiredness, fatigue.

fatigué, e [fatige] a tired.

fatiguer [fatige] vt to tire, make tired; (TECH) to put a strain on, strain; (fig: importuner) to wear out // vi (moteur) to labour, strain; se ~ to get tired; to tire o.s. (out).

fatras [fatra] nm jumble, hotchpotch.

fatuité [fatɥite] nf conceitedness, smugness.

faubourg [fobur] nm suburb.

fauché, e [foʃe] a (fam) broke.

faucher [foʃe] vt (herbe) to cut; (champs, blés) to reap; (fig) to cut down; to mow down.

faucille [fosij] nf sickle.

faucon [fokɔ̃] nm falcon, hawk.

faudra vb voir **falloir**.

faufiler [fofile] vt to tack, baste; se ~ vi: se ~ dans to edge one's way into; se ~ parmi/entre to thread one's way among/between.

faune [fon] nf (ZOOL) wildlife, fauna.

faussaire [foser] nm forger.

fausse [fos] a voir **faux**.

faussement [fosmɑ̃] ad (accuser) wrongly, wrongfully; (croire) falsely.

fausser [fose] vt (objet) to bend, buckle; (fig) to distort.

fausseté [foste] nf wrongness; falseness.

faut vb voir **falloir**.

faute [fot] nf (erreur) mistake, error; (péché, manquement) misdemeanour; (FOOTBALL etc) offence; (TENNIS) fault; c'est de sa/ma ~ it's his/my fault; être en ~ to be in the wrong; ~ de (temps, argent) for ou through lack of; sans ~ ad without fail; ~ de frappe typing error; ~ professionnelle professional misconduct q.

fauteuil [fotœj] nm armchair; ~ d'orchestre seat in the front stalls; ~ roulant wheelchair.

fauteur [fotœr] nm: ~ de troubles trouble-maker.

fautif, ive [fotif, -iv] a (incorrect) incorrect, inaccurate; (responsable) at fault, in the wrong; guilty.

fauve [fov] nm wildcat // a (couleur) fawn.

faux [fo] nf scythe.

faux, fausse [fo, fos] a (inexact) wrong; (piano, voix) out of tune; (falsifié) fake; forged; (sournois, postiche) false // ad (MUS) out of tune // nm (copie) fake, forgery; (opposé au vrai): le ~ falsehood; faire ~ bond à qn to stand sb up; ~ frais nmpl extras, incidental expenses; ~ pas tripping q; (fig) faux pas; ~ témoignage (délit) perjury; fausse alerte false alarm; fausse couche miscarriage; ~-filet nm sirloin; ~-fuyant nm equivocation; ~-monnayeur nm counterfeiter, forger.

faveur [favœr] nf favour; traitement de ~ preferential treatment; à la ~ de under cover of; thanks to; en ~ de in favour of.

favorable [favɔrabl(ə)] a favourable.

favori, te [favɔri, -it] a, nm/f favourite; ~s nmpl (barbe) sideboards (Brit), sideburns.

favoriser [favɔrize] vt to favour.

fébrile [febril] a feverish, febrile.

fécond, e [fekɔ̃, -ɔ̃d] a fertile; **féconder** vt to fertilize; **fécondité** nf fertility.

fécule [fekyl] nf potato flour.

fédéral, e, aux [federal, -o] a federal.

fée [fe] nf fairy; ~rie nf enchantment; ~rique a magical, fairytale cpd.

feignant, e [fɛɲɑ̃, -ɑ̃t] nm/f = **fainéant, e**.

feindre [fɛ̃dr(ə)] vt to feign // vi to dissemble; ~ de faire to pretend to do.

feinte [fɛ̃t] nf (SPORT) dummy.

fêler [fele] vt to crack.

félicitations [felisitasjɔ̃] nfpl congratulations.

féliciter [felisite] vt: ~ qn (de) to congratulate sb (on); se ~ (de) to congratulate o.s. (on).

félin, e [felɛ̃, -in] a feline // nm (big) cat.

fêlure [felyr] nf crack.

femelle [fəmɛl] a, nf female.

féminin, e [feminɛ̃, -in] a feminine; (sexe) female; (équipe, vêtements etc) women's // nm feminine; **féministe** a feminist.

femme [fam] nf woman; (épouse) wife (pl wives); ~ de chambre; ~ de ménage cleaning lady.

fémur [femyr] nm femur, thighbone.

fendre [fɑ̃dr(ə)] vt (couper en deux) to split; (fissurer) to crack; (fig: traverser) to cut through; to cleave through; se ~ vi to crack.

fenêtre [fənɛtr(ə)] nf window.

fenouil [fənuj] nm fennel.

fente [fɑ̃t] nf (fissure) crack; (de boîte à lettres etc) slit.

féodal, e, aux [feɔdal, -o] a feudal.

fer [fɛr] nm iron; (de cheval) shoe; ~ à cheval horseshoe; ~ forgé wrought iron; ~ (à repasser) iron.

ferai etc vb voir **faire**.

fer-blanc [fɛrblɑ̃] nm tin(plate).

férié, e [ferje] a: **jour** ~ public holiday.

ferions etc vb voir **faire**.

férir [ferir]: **sans coup** ~ ad without meeting any opposition.

ferme [fɛrm(ə)] a firm // ad (travailler etc) hard // nf (exploitation) farm; (maison) farmhouse.

fermé, e [fɛrme] a closed, shut; (gaz, eau etc) off; (fig: personne) uncommunicative; (: milieu) exclusive.

fermenter [fɛrmɑ̃te] vi to ferment.

fermer [fɛrme] vt to close, shut; (cesser l'exploitation de) to close down, shut down; (eau, lumière, électricité, robinet) to put off, turn off; (aéroport, route) to close // vi to close, shut; to close down, shut down; **se** ~ vi (yeux) to close, shut; (fleur, blessure) to close up.

fermeté [fɛrməte] nf firmness.

fermeture [fɛrmətyr] nf closing; shutting; closing ou shutting down; putting ou turning off; (dispositif) catch; fastening, fastener; ~ **éclair** ® ou **à glissière** zip (fastener) (Brit), zipper (US).

fermier, ière [fɛrmje, -jɛr] nm farmer // nf woman farmer; farmer's wife.

fermoir [fɛrmwar] nm clasp.

féroce [ferɔs] a ferocious, fierce.

ferons vb voir **faire**.

ferraille [fɛrɑj] nf scrap iron; **mettre à la** ~ to scrap.

ferré, e [fɛre] a hobnailed; steel-tipped; (fam): ~ **en** well up on, hot at.

ferrer [fɛre] vt (cheval) to shoe.

ferronnerie [fɛrɔnri] nf ironwork.

ferroviaire [fɛrɔvjɛr] a rail(way) cpd (Brit), rail(road) cpd (US).

ferry(-boat) [fɛre(bɔt)] nm ferry.

fertile [fɛrtil] a fertile; ~ **en incidents** eventful, packed with incidents.

féru, e [fery] a: ~ **de** with a keen interest in.

férule [feryl] nf: **être sous la** ~ **de qn** to be under sb's (iron) rule.

fervent, e [fɛrvɑ̃, -ɑ̃t] a fervent.

fesse [fɛs] nf buttock; **fessée** nf spanking.

festin [fɛstɛ̃] nm feast.

festival [fɛstival] nm festival.

festoyer [fɛstwaje] vi to feast.

fêtard [fɛtar] nm (péj) high liver, merry-maker.

fête [fɛt] nf (religieuse) feast; (publique) holiday; (en famille etc) celebration; (kermesse) fête, fair, festival; (du nom) feast day, name day; **faire la** ~ to live it up; **faire** ~ **à qn** to give sb a warm welcome; **les** ~**s** (de fin d'année) the festive season; **la salle/le comité des** ~**s** the village hall/festival committee; ~ **foraine** (fun) fair; **la F**~ **Nationale** the national holiday; **fêter** vt to celebrate; (personne) to have a celebration for.

fétu [fety] nm: ~ **de paille** wisp of straw.

feu [fø] a inv: ~ **son père** his late father.

feu, x [fø] nm (gén) fire; (signal lumineux) light; (de cuisinière) ring; (sensation de brûlure) burning (sensation); ~**x** nmpl (éclat, lumière) fire sg; (AUTO) (traffic) lights; **au** ~! (incendie) fire!; **à** ~ **doux/vif** over a slow/brisk heat; **à petit** ~ (CULIN) over a gentle heat; (fig) slowly; **faire** ~ to fire; **prendre** ~ to catch fire; **mettre le** ~ **à** to set fire to; **faire du** ~ to make a fire; **avez-vous du** ~? (pour cigarette) have you (got) a light?; ~ **rouge/vert/orange** red/green/amber (Brit) ou yellow (US) light; ~ **arrière** rear light; ~ **d'artifice** firework; (spectacle) fireworks pl; ~ **de joie** bonfire; ~**x de brouillard** fog-lamps; ~**x de croisement** dipped (Brit) ou dimmed (US) headlights; ~**x de position** sidelights; ~**x de route** headlights.

feuillage [fœjaʒ] nm foliage, leaves pl.

feuille [fœj] nf (d'arbre) leaf (pl leaves); (de papier) sheet; ~ **d'impôts** tax form; ~ **de maladie** medical expenses claim form; ~ **de paie** pay slip; ~ **de vigne** (BOT) vine leaf; (sur statue) fig leaf; ~ **volante** loose sheet.

feuillet [fœjɛ] nm leaf (pl leaves).

feuilleté, e [fœjte] a (CULIN) flaky; (verre) laminated.

feuilleter [fœjte] vt (livre) to leaf through.

feuilleton [fœjtɔ̃] nm serial.

feuillu, e [fœjy] a leafy // nm broad-leaved tree.

feutre [føtr(ə)] nm felt; (chapeau) felt hat; (aussi: stylo-~) felt-tip pen; **feutré, e** a feltlike; (pas, voix) muffled.

fève [fɛv] nf broad bean.

février [fevrije] nm February.

fi [fi] excl: **faire** ~ **de** to snap one's fingers at.

fiable [fjabl(ə)] a reliable.

fiacre [fjakr(ə)] nm (hackney) cab ou carriage.

fiançailles [fjɑ̃sɑj] nfpl engagement sg.

fiancé, e [fjɑ̃se] nm/f fiancé/fiancée // a: **être** ~ (à) to be engaged (to).

fiancer [fjɑ̃se]: **se** ~ vi to become engaged.

fibre [fibr(ə)] nf fibre; ~ **de verre** fibreglass, glass fibre.

ficeler [fisle] vt to tie up.

ficelle [fisɛl] nf string q; piece ou length of string.

fiche [fiʃ] nf (pour fichier) (index) card; (formulaire) form; (ÉLEC) plug.

ficher [fiʃe] vt (dans un fichier) to file; (POLICE) to put on file; (planter) to stick, drive; (fam) to do; to give; to stick ou shove; **fiche(-moi) le camp** (fam) clear off; **fiche-moi la paix** (fam) leave me alone; **se** ~ **de** (fam) to make fun of; not to care about.

fichier [fiʃje] *nm* file; card index.

fichu, e [fiʃy] *pp de* **ficher** (*fam*) // *a* (*fam: fini, inutilisable*) bust, done for; (*: intensif*) wretched, darned // *nm* (*foulard*) (head)scarf (*pl* scarves); **mal ~** (*fam*) feeling lousy; useless.

fictif, ive [fiktif, -iv] *a* fictitious.

fiction [fiksjɔ̃] *nf* fiction; (*fait imaginé*) invention.

fidèle [fidɛl] *a* faithful // *nm/f* (*REL*): les **~s** the faithful; (*à l'église*) the congregation.

fief [fjɛf] *nm* fief; (*fig*) preserve; stronghold.

fier [fje] : **se ~ à** *vt* to trust.

fier, fière [fjɛʀ] *a* proud; **~té** *nf* pride.

fièvre [fjɛvʀ(ə)] *nf* fever; **avoir de la ~/ 39 de ~** to have a high temperature/a temperature of 39°C; **fiévreux, euse** *a* feverish.

fifre [fifʀ(ə)] *nm* fife; fife-player.

figer [fiʒe] *vt* to congeal; (*fig: personne*) to freeze, root to the spot; **se ~** *vi* to congeal; to freeze; (*institutions etc*) to become set, stop evolving.

figue [fig] *nf* fig; **figuier** *nm* fig tree.

figurant, e [figyʀɑ̃, -ɑ̃t] *nm/f* (*THÉÂTRE*) walk-on; (*CINÉMA*) extra.

figure [figyʀ] *nf* (*visage*) face; (*image, tracé, forme, personnage*) figure; (*illustration*) picture, diagram; **faire ~ de** to look like.

figuré, e [figyʀe] *a* (*sens*) figurative.

figurer [figyʀe] *vi* to appear // *vt* to represent; **se ~ que** to imagine that.

fil [fil] *nm* (*brin, fig: d'une histoire*) thread; (*du téléphone*) cable, wire; (*textile de lin*) linen; (*d'un couteau*) edge; **au ~ des années** with the passing of the years; **au ~ de l'eau** with the stream *ou* current; **coup de ~** phone call; **~ à coudre** (sewing) thread; **~ électrique** electric wire; **~ de fer** wire; **~ de fer barbelé** barbed wire; **~ à pêche** fishing line; **~ à plomb** plumbline.

filament [filamɑ̃] *nm* (*ÉLEC*) filament; (*de liquide*) trickle, thread.

filandreux, euse [filɑ̃dʀø, -øz] *a* stringy.

filasse [filas] *a inv* white blond.

filature [filatyʀ] *nf* (*fabrique*) mill; (*policière*) shadowing *q*, tailing *q*.

file [fil] *nf* line; (*AUTO*) lane; **~ (d'attente)** queue (*Brit*), line (*US*); **en ~ indienne** in single file; **à la ~ ou d'affilée** in succession.

filer [file] *vt* (*tissu, toile*) to spin; (*prendre en filature*) to shadow, tail; (*fam: donner*): **~ qch à qn** to slip sb sth // *vi* (*bas, liquide, pâte*) to run; (*aller vite*) to fly past; (*fam: partir*) to make off; **~ doux** to toe the line.

filet [filɛ] *nm* net; (*CULIN*) fillet; (*d'eau, de sang*) trickle; **~ (à provisions)** string bag.

filiale [filjal] *nf* (*COMM*) subsidiary.

filière [filjɛʀ] *nf*: **passer par la ~** to go through the (administrative) channels; **suivre la ~** (*dans sa carrière*) to work one's way up (through the hierarchy).

filiforme [filifɔʀm(ə)] *a* spindly; thread-like.

filigrane [filigʀan] *nm* (*d'un billet, timbre*) watermark; **en ~** (*fig*) showing just beneath the surface.

fille [fij] *nf* girl; (*opposé à fils*) daughter; **vieille ~** old maid; **~-mere** *nf* (*péj*) unmarried mother; **fillette** *nf* (little) girl.

filleul, e [fijœl] *nm/f* godchild, godson/daughter.

film [film] *nm* (*pour photo*) (roll of) film; (*œuvre*) film, picture, movie; (*couche*) film; **~ muet/parlant** silent/talking picture *ou* movie; **~ d'animation** animated film; **~ policier** thriller.

filon [filɔ̃] *nm* vein, lode; (*fig*) lucrative line, money spinner.

fils [fis] *nm* son; **~ de famille** moneyed young man; **~ à papa** daddy's boy.

filtre [filtʀ(ə)] *nm* filter; **~ à air** (*AUTO*) air filter; **filtrer** *vt* to filter; (*fig: candidats, visiteurs*) to screen // *vi* to filter (through).

fin [fɛ̃] *nf* end; **~s** *nfpl* (*but*) ends; **prendre ~** to come to an end; **mettre ~ à** to put an end to; **à la ~ ad** in the end, eventually; **sans ~** *a* endless // *ad* endlessly.

fin, e [fɛ̃, fin] *a* (*papier, couche, fil*) thin; (*cheveux, poudre, pointe, visage*) fine; (*taille*) neat, slim; (*esprit, remarque*) subtle; shrewd // *ad* (*moudre, couper*) finely // *nf* (*alcool*) liqueur brandy; **~ prêt** quite ready; **un ~ tireur** a crack shot; **avoir la vue/l'ouïe ~e** to have sharp *ou* keen eyes/ears; **vin ~** fine wine; **~ gourmet** gourmet; **une ~e mouche** (*fig*) a sharp customer; **~es herbes** mixed herbs.

final, e [final] *a, nf* final // *nm* (*MUS*) finale; **quarts de ~e** quarter finals; **8èmes/16èmes de ~e** 2nd/1st round (*in 5 round knock-out competition*); **~ement** *ad* finally, in the end; (*après tout*) after all.

finance [finɑ̃s] *nf* finance; **~s** *nfpl* (*situation*) finances; (*activités*) finance *sg*; **moyennant ~** for a fee; **financer** *vt* to finance; **financier, ière** *a* financial.

finaud, e [fino, -od] *a* wily.

finesse [finɛs] *nf* thinness; fineness; neatness, slimness; subtlety; shrewdness.

fini, e [fini] *a* finished; (*MATH*) finite; (*intensif*): **un menteur ~** a liar through and through // *nm* (*d'un objet manufacturé*) finish.

finir [finiʀ] *vt* to finish // *vi* to finish, end; **~ quelque part/par faire** to end *ou* finish up somewhere/doing; ~ **de faire** to finish doing; (*cesser*) to stop doing; **il finit par m'agacer** he's beginning to get on my nerves; ~ **en pointe/tragédie** to end in a point/in tragedy; **en ~ avec** to be ou have done with; **il va mal ~** he will come to a bad end.

finition [finisjɔ̃] *nf* finishing; finish.

finlandais, e [fɛ̃lɑ̃dɛ, -ɛz] *a* Finnish // *nm/f*: F~, e Finn.

Finlande [fɛ̃lɑ̃d] *nf*: **la ~** Finland.

fiole [fjɔl] *nf* phial.

fioriture [fjɔrityr] *nf* embellishment, flourish.

firme [firm(ə)] *nf* firm.

fis *vb voir* **faire**.

fisc [fisk] *nm* tax authorities *pl*; ~**al, e, aux** *a* tax *cpd*, fiscal; ~**alité** *nf* tax system; (*charges*) taxation.

fissure [fisyr] *nf* crack.

fissurer [fisyre] *vt*, **se** ~ *vi* to crack.

fiston [fistɔ̃] *nm* (*fam*) son, lad.

fit *vb voir* **faire**.

fixation [fiksasjɔ̃] *nf* fixing; fastening; setting; (*de ski*) binding; (*PSYCH*) fixation.

fixe [fiks(ə)] *a* fixed; (*emploi*) steady, regular // *nm* (*salaire*) basic salary; **à heure ~** at a set time; **menu à prix ~** set menu.

fixé, e [fikse] *a*: **être ~** (*sur*) (*savoir à quoi s'en tenir*) to have made up one's mind (about); to know for certain (about).

fixer [fikse] *vt* (*attacher*): ~ **qch (à/sur)** to fix ou fasten sth (to/onto); (*déterminer*) to fix, set; (*CHIMIE, PHOTO*) to fix; (*regarder*) to stare at; **se** ~ *vi* (*s'établir*) to settle down; **se** ~ **sur** (*suj: attention*) to focus on.

flacon [flakɔ̃] *nm* bottle.

flageller [flaʒele] *vt* to flog, scourge.

flageoler [flaʒɔle] *vi* (*jambes*) to sag.

flageolet [flaʒɔle] *nm* (*MUS*) flageolet; (*CULIN*) dwarf kidney bean.

flagrant, e [flagrɑ̃, -ɑ̃t] *a* flagrant, blatant; **en ~ délit** in the act.

flair [flɛr] *nm* sense of smell; (*fig*) intuition; **flairer** *vt* (*humer*) to sniff (at); (*détecter*) to scent.

flamand, e [flamɑ̃, -ɑ̃d] *a, nm* (*LING*) Flemish // *nm/f*: F~, e Fleming; **les F~s** the Flemish.

flamant [flamɑ̃] *nm* flamingo.

flambant [flɑ̃bɑ̃] *ad*: ~ **neuf** brand new.

flambé, e [flɑ̃be] *a* (*CULIN*) flambé // *nf* blaze; (*fig*) flaring-up, explosion.

flambeau, x [flɑ̃bo] *nm* (flaming) torch.

flamber [flɑ̃be] *vi* to blaze (up).

flamboyer [flɑ̃bwaje] *vi* to blaze (up); to flame.

flamme [flam] *nf* flame; (*fig*) fire, fervour; **en ~s** on fire, ablaze.

flan [flɑ̃] *nm* (*CULIN*) custard tart ou pie.

flanc [flɑ̃] *nm* side; (*MIL*) flank; **prêter le ~ à** (*fig*) to lay o.s. open to.

flancher [flɑ̃ʃe] *vi* to fail, pack up; to quit.

flanelle [flanɛl] *nf* flannel.

flâner [flane] *vi* to stroll; **flânerie** *nf* stroll.

flanquer [flɑ̃ke] *vt* to flank; (*fam: mettre*) to chuck, shove; (: *jeter*): ~ **par terre/à la porte** to fling to the ground/chuck out.

flaque [flak] *nf* (*d'eau*) puddle; (*d'huile, de sang etc*) pool.

flash, pl flashes [flaʃ] *nm* (*PHOTO*) flash; ~ (**d'information**) newsflash.

flasque [flask(ə)] *a* flabby.

flatter [flate] *vt* to flatter; **se** ~ **de qch** to pride o.s. on sth; **flatterie** *nf* flattery *q*; **flatteur, euse** *a* flattering // *nm/f* flatterer.

fléau, x [fleo] *nm* scourge.

flèche [flɛʃ] *nf* arrow; (*de clocher*) spire; (*de grue*) jib; **monter en ~** (*fig*) to soar, rocket; **partir en ~** to be off like a shot; **fléchette** *nf* dart; **fléchettes** *nfpl* (*jeu*) darts *sg*.

fléchir [fleʃir] *vt* (*corps, genou*) to bend; (*fig*) to sway, weaken // *vi* (*poutre*) to sag, bend; (*fig*) to weaken, flag; to yield.

flemmard, e [flemar, -ard(ə)] *nm/f* lazybones *sg*, loafer.

flétrir [fletrir] *vt*, **se** ~ *vi* to wither.

fleur [flœr] *nf* flower; (*d'un arbre*) blossom; **en ~** (*arbre*) in blossom; **à ~ de terre** just above the ground.

fleurer [flœre] *vt*: ~ **la lavande** to have the scent of lavender.

fleuri, e [flœri] *a* in flower ou bloom; surrounded by flowers; (*fig*) flowery; florid.

fleurir [flœrir] *vi* (*rose*) to flower; (*arbre*) to blossom; (*fig*) to flourish // *vt* (*tombe*) to put flowers on; (*chambre*) to decorate with flowers.

fleuriste [flœrist(ə)] *nm/f* florist.

fleuron [flœrɔ̃] *nm* jewel (*fig*).

fleuve [flœv] *nm* river.

flexible [flɛksibl(ə)] *a* flexible.

flexion [flɛksjɔ̃] *nf* flexing, bending.

flic [flik] *nm* (*fam: péj*) cop.

flipper [flipœr] *nm* pinball (machine).

flirter [flœrte] *vi* to flirt.

flocon [flɔkɔ̃] *nm* flake.

floraison [flɔrezɔ̃] *nf* flowering; blossoming; flourishing.

flore [flɔr] *nf* flora.

florissant, e [flɔrisɑ̃, -ɑ̃t] *vb voir* **fleurir**.

flot [flo] *nm* flood, stream; ~**s** *nmpl* (*de la mer*) waves; **être à ~** (*NAVIG*) to be afloat; (*fig*) to be on an even keel; **entrer à ~s** to stream ou pour in.

flotte [flɔt] *nf* (*NAVIG*) fleet; (*fam*) water; rain.

flottement [flɔtmã] nm (fig) wavering, hesitation.

flotter [flɔte] vi to float; (nuage, odeur) to drift; (drapeau) to fly; (vêtements) to hang loose; (monnaie) to float // vt to float; **faire ~** to float; **flotteur** nm float.

flou, e [flu] a fuzzy, blurred; (fig) woolly, vague.

flouer [flue] vt to swindle.

fluctuation [flyktɥasjɔ̃] nf fluctuation.

fluet, te [flyɛ, -ɛt] a thin, slight.

fluide [flɥid] a fluid; (circulation etc) flowing freely // nm fluid; (force) (mysterious) power.

fluor [flyɔʀ] nm fluorine.

fluorescent, e [flyɔʀesã, -ãt] a fluorescent.

flûte [flyt] nf flute; (verre) flute glass; (pain) long loaf (pl loaves); ~! drat it!; ~ **à bec** recorder.

flux [fly] nm incoming tide; (écoulement) flow; **le ~ et le reflux** the ebb and flow.

FM sigle f (= fréquence modulée) FM.

foc [fɔk] nm jib.

foi [fwa] nf faith; **sous la ~ du serment** under ou on oath; **ajouter ~ à** to lend credence to; **digne de ~** reliable; **sur la ~ de** on the word ou strength of; **être de bonne/mauvaise ~** to be sincere/insincere; **ma ~...** well....

foie [fwa] nm liver.

foin [fwɛ̃] nm hay; **faire du ~** (fig: fam) to kick up a fuss.

foire [fwaʀ] nf fair; (fête foraine) (fun) fair; **faire la ~** (fig: fam) to whoop it up; ~ **(exposition)** trade fair.

fois [fwa] nf time; **une/deux ~** once/twice; **2 ~ 2** 2 times 2; **quatre ~ plus grand (que)** four times as big (as); **une ~ (passé)** once; (futur) sometime; **une ~ pour toutes** once and for all; **une ~ que** once; **des ~ (parfois)** sometimes; **à la ~ (ensemble)** at once.

foison [fwazɔ̃] nf: **une ~ de** an abundance of; **à ~** ad in plenty.

foisonner [fwazɔne] vi to abound.

fol [fɔl] a voir **fou**.

folâtrer [fɔlɑtʀe] vi to frolic (about).

folie [fɔli] nf (d'une décision, d'un acte) madness, folly; (état) madness, insanity; (acte) folly; **la ~ des grandeurs** delusions of grandeur; **faire des ~s (en dépenses)** to be extravagant.

folklorique [fɔlklɔʀik] a folk cpd; (fam) weird.

folle [fɔl] a, nf voir **fou**; **~ment** ad (très) madly, wildly.

foncé, e [fɔ̃se] a dark.

foncer [fɔ̃se] vi to go darker; (fam: aller vite) to tear ou belt along; ~ **sur** to charge at.

foncier, ère [fɔ̃sje, -ɛʀ] a (honnêteté etc) basic, fundamental; (malhonnêteté) deep-rooted; (COMM) real estate cpd.

fonction [fɔ̃ksjɔ̃] nf (rôle, MATH, LING) function; (emploi, poste) post, position; ~**s** (professionnelles) duties; **entrer en ~s** to take up one's post ou duties; to take up office; **voiture de ~** company car; **être ~ de** (dépendre de) to depend on; **en ~ de** (par rapport à) according to; **faire ~ de** to serve as; **la ~ publique** the state ou civil (Brit) service.

fonctionnaire [fɔ̃ksjɔnɛʀ] nm/f state employee, local authority employee; (dans l'administration) ≈ civil servant.

fonctionner [fɔ̃ksjɔne] vi to work, function; (entreprise) to operate, function.

fond [fɔ̃] nm voir aussi **fonds**; (d'un récipient, trou) bottom; (d'une salle, scène) back; (d'un tableau, décor) background; (opposé à la forme) content; (SPORT): **le ~** long distance (running); **sans ~** bottomless; **au ~ de** at the bottom of; at the back of; **à ~** ad (connaître, soutenir) thoroughly; (appuyer, visser) right down ou home; **à ~ (de train)** ad (fam) full tilt; **dans le ~, au ~** ad (en somme) basically, really; **de ~ en comble** ad from top to bottom; ~ **sonore** background noise; background music; ~ **de teint** (make-up) foundation.

fondamental, e, aux [fɔ̃damãtal, -o] a fundamental.

fondant, e [fɔ̃dã, -ãt] a (neige) melting; (poire) that melts in the mouth.

fondateur, trice [fɔ̃datœʀ, -tʀis] nm/f founder.

fondation [fɔ̃dɑsjɔ̃] nf founding; (établissement) foundation; ~**s** nfpl (d'une maison) foundations.

fondé, e [fɔ̃de] a (accusation etc) well-founded; **être ~ à** to have grounds for ou good reason to // nm: ~ **de pouvoir** authorized representative.

fondement [fɔ̃dmã] nm (derrière) behind; ~**s** nmpl foundations; **sans ~** a (rumeur etc) groundless, unfounded.

fonder [fɔ̃de] vt to found; (fig) to base; **se ~ sur** (suj: personne) to base o.s. on.

fonderie [fɔ̃dʀi] nf smelting works sg.

fondre [fɔ̃dʀ(ə)] vt (aussi: **faire ~**) to melt; (dans l'eau) to dissolve; (fig: mélanger) to merge, blend // vi to melt; to dissolve; (fig) to melt away; (se précipiter): ~ **sur** to swoop down on; ~ **en larmes** to burst into tears.

fonds [fɔ̃] nm (de bibliothèque) collection; (COMM): ~ **(de commerce)** business // nmpl (argent) funds; **à ~ perdus** ad with little or no hope of getting the money back.

fondu, e [fɔ̃dy] a (beurre, neige) melted; (métal) molten // nf (CULIN) fondue.

font vb voir **faire**.

fontaine [fɔ̃tɛn] nf fountain; (source) spring.

fonte [fɔ̃t] nf melting; (métal) cast iron; **la ~ des neiges** the (spring) thaw.

fonts baptismaux [fɔ̃batismo] *nmpl* (baptismal) font *sg*.

foot [fut] *nm* (*fam*) football.

football [futbol] *nm* football, soccer; **~eur** *nm* footballer.

footing [futiaj] *nm* jogging; faire du ~ to go jogging.

for [fɔr] *nm*: dans son ~ intérieur in one's heart of hearts.

forain, e [fɔrɛ̃, -ɛn] *a* fairground *cpd* // *nm* stallholder; fairground entertainer.

forçat [fɔrsa] *nm* convict.

force [fɔrs(ə)] *nf* strength; (*puissance: surnaturelle etc*) power; (PHYSIQUE, MÉCANIQUE) force; **~s** *nfpl* (*physiques*) strength *sg*; (MIL) forces; à ~ d'insister by dint of insisting; as he (ou I *etc*) kept on insisting; de ~ *ad* forcibly, by force; être de ~ à faire to be up to doing; de première ~ first class; ~ d'âme fortitude; les **~s** de l'ordre the police.

forcé, e [fɔrse] *a* forced; unintended; inevitable.

forcément [fɔrsemɑ̃] *ad* necessarily; inevitably; (*bien sûr*) of course.

forcené, e [fɔrsəne] *nm/f* maniac.

forcer [fɔrse] *vt* (*porte, serrure, plante*) to force; (*moteur, voix*) to strain // *vi* (SPORT) to overtax o.s.; ~ la dose/l'allure to overdo it/increase the pace; se ~ (pour faire) to force o.s. (to do).

forcir [fɔrsir] *vi* (*grossir*) to broaden out; (*vent*) to freshen.

forer [fɔre] *vt* to drill, bore.

forestier, ère [fɔrɛstje, -ɛr] *a* forest *cpd*.

forêt [fɔrɛ] *nf* forest.

foreuse [fɔrøz] *nf* (electric) drill.

forfait [fɔrfɛ] *nm* (COMM) fixed *ou* set price; all-in deal *ou* price; (*crime*) infamy; déclarer ~ to withdraw; travailler à ~ to work for a lump sum; **forfaitaire** *a* inclusive; set.

forfanterie [fɔrfɑ̃tri] *nf* boastfulness *q*.

forge [fɔrʒ(ə)] *nf* forge, smithy.

forger [fɔrʒe] *vt* to forge; (*fig: personnalité*) to form; (: *prétexte*) to contrive, make up.

forgeron [fɔrʒərɔ̃] *nm* (black)smith.

formaliser [fɔrmalize]: se ~ *vi*: se ~ (de) to take offence (at).

format [fɔrma] *nm* size.

formater [fɔrmate] *vt* (*disque*) to format.

formation [fɔrmasjɔ̃] *nf* forming; training; (MUS) group; (MIL, AVIAT, GÉO) formation; ~ permanente continuing education; ~ professionnelle vocational training.

forme [fɔrm(ə)] *nf* (*gén*) form; (*d'un objet*) shape, form; **~s** *nfpl* (*bonnes manières*) proprieties; (*d'une femme*) figure *sg*; en ~ de poire pear-shaped; être en ~ (SPORT *etc*) to be on form; en

bonne et due ~ in due form.

formel, le [fɔrmɛl] *a* (*preuve, décision*) definite, positive; (*logique*) formal; **~lement** *ad* (*absolument*) positively.

former [fɔrme] *vt* to form; (*éduquer*) to train; se ~ *vi* to form.

formidable [fɔrmidabl(ə)] *a* tremendous.

formulaire [fɔrmylɛr] *nm* form.

formule [fɔrmyl] *nf* (*gén*) formula; (*formulaire*) form; ~ de politesse polite phrase; letter ending.

formuler [fɔrmyle] *vt* (*émettre: réponse, vœux*) to formulate; (*expliciter: sa pensée o.s.*) to express.

fort, e [fɔr, fɔrt(ə)] *a* strong; (*intensité, rendement*) high, great; (*corpulent*) stout; (*doué*) good, able // *ad* (*serrer, frapper*) hard; (*sonner*) loud(ly); (*beaucoup*) greatly, very much; (*très*) very // *nm* (*édifice*) fort; (*point fort*) strong point, forte; se faire ~ de ... to claim one can ...; au plus ~ de (*au milieu de*) in the thick of; at the height of; **~e tête** rebel.

fortifiant [fɔrtifjɑ̃] *nm* tonic.

fortifier [fɔrtifje] *vt* to strengthen, fortify; (MIL) to fortify.

fortiori [fɔrtjɔri]: à ~ *ad* all the more so.

fortuit, e [fɔrtɥi, -it] *a* fortuitous, chance *cpd*.

fortune [fɔrtyn] *nf* fortune; faire ~ to make one's fortune; de ~ *a* makeshift; chance *cpd*.

fortuné, e [fɔrtyne] *a* wealthy.

fosse [fos] *nf* (*grand trou*) pit; (*tombe*) grave; ~ (**d'orchestre**) (orchestra) pit *pl*; ~ **septique** septic tank.

fossé [fose] *nm* ditch; (*fig*) gulf, gap.

fossette [fosɛt] *nf* dimple.

fossile [fosil] *nm* fossil.

fossoyeur [foswajœr] *nm* gravedigger.

fou(fol), folle [fu, fɔl] *a* mad; (*déréglé etc*) wild, erratic; (*fam: extrême, très grand*) terrific, tremendous // *nm/f* madman/woman // *nm* (*du roi*) jester; être ~ de to be mad *ou* crazy about; faire le ~ to act the fool; avoir le ~ rire to have the giggles.

foudre [fudr(ə)] *nf*: la ~ lightning; **~s** *nfpl* (*colère*) wrath *sg*.

foudroyant, e [fudrwajɑ̃, -ɑ̃t] *a* lightning *cpd*, stunning; (*maladie, poison*) violent.

foudroyer [fudrwaje] *vt* to strike down; être foudroyé(e) to be struck by lightning; ~ qn du regard to glare at sb.

fouet [fwe] *nm* whip; (CULIN) whisk; de plein ~ *ad* (*se heurter*) head on; **~ter** *vt* to whip; to whisk.

fougère [fuʒɛr] *nf* fern.

fougue [fug] *nf* ardour, spirit.

fouille [fuj] *nf* search; **~s** *nfpl* (*archéologiques*) excavations.

fouiller [fuje] *vt* to search; (*creuser*) to dig // *vi* to rummage.

fouillis [fuji] *nm* jumble, muddle.

fouiner [fwine] *vi* (*péj*): ~ **dans** to nose around *ou* about in.

foulard [fular] *nm* scarf (*pl* scarves).

foule [ful] *nf* crowd; **la** ~ crowds *pl*; **les** ~**s** the masses; **une** ~ **de** masses of.

foulée [fule] *nf* stride.

fouler [fule] *vt* to press; (*sol*) to tread upon; **se** ~ *vi* (*fam*) to overexert o.s.; **se** ~ **la cheville** to sprain one's ankle; ~ **aux pieds** to trample underfoot.

foulure [fulyr] *nf* sprain.

four [fur] *nm* oven; (*de potier*) kiln; (*THÉÂTRE*: *échec*) flop.

fourbe [furb(ə)] *a* deceitful.

fourbu, e [furby] *a* exhausted.

fourche [furʃ(ə)] *nf* pitchfork; (*de bicyclette*) fork.

fourchette [furʃɛt] *nf* fork; (*STATISTIQUE*) bracket, margin.

fourgon [furgɔ̃] *nm* van; (*RAIL*) wag(g)on.

fourmi [furmi] *nf* ant; ~**s** *nfpl* (*fig*) pins and needles; ~**lière** *nf* ant-hill.

fourmiller [furmije] *vi* to swarm.

fournaise [furnɛz] *nf* blaze; (*fig*) furnace, oven.

fourneau, x [furno] *nm* stove.

fournée [furne] *nf* batch.

fourni, e [furni] *a* (*barbe, cheveux*) thick; (*magasin*): **bien** ~ (**en**) well stocked (with).

fournir [furnir] *vt* to supply; (*preuve, exemple*) to provide, supply; (*effort*) to put in; **fournisseur, euse** *nm/f* supplier.

fourniture [furnityr] *nf* supply(ing); ~**s** *nfpl* supplies.

fourrage [furaʒ] *nm* fodder.

fourrager, ère [furaʒe, -ɛr] *a* fodder *cpd*.

fourré, e [fure] *a* (*bonbon etc*) filled; (*manteau etc*) fur-lined // *nm* thicket.

fourreau, x [furo] *nm* sheath.

fourrer [fure] *vt* (*fam*) to stick, shove; **se** ~ **dans/sous** to get into/under.

fourre-tout [furtu] *nm inv* (*sac*) hold-all; (*péj*) junk room (*ou* cupboard); (*fig*) rag-bag.

fourrière [furjɛr] *nf* pound.

fourrure [furyr] *nf* fur; (*sur l'animal*) coat.

fourvoyer [furvwaje]: **se** ~ *vi* to go astray, stray.

foutre [futr(ə)] *vt* (*fam!*) = **ficher** (*fam*); **foutu, e** *a* (*fam!*) = **fichu, e** *a*.

foyer [fwaje] *nm* (*de cheminée*) hearth; (*famille*) family; (*maison*) home; (*de jeunes etc*) (social) club; hostel; (*salon*) foyer; (*OPTIQUE, PHOTO*) focus *sg*; **lunettes à double** ~ bi-focal glasses.

fracas [fraka] *nm* din; crash; roar.

fracasser [frakase] *vt* to smash.

fraction [fraksjɔ̃] *nf* fraction;

fractionner *vt* to divide (up), split (up).

fracture [fraktyr] *nf* fracture; ~ **du crâne** fractured skull; ~ **de la jambe** broken leg.

fracturer [fraktyre] *vt* (*coffre, serrure*) to break open; (*os, membre*) to fracture.

fragile [fraʒil] *a* fragile, delicate; (*fig*) frail; **fragilité** *nf* fragility.

fragment [fragmɑ̃] *nm* (*d'un objet*) fragment, piece; (*d'un texte*) passage, extract.

fraîche [frɛʃ] *a voir* **frais**; **fraîcheur** *nf* coolness; freshness; **fraîchir** *vi* to get cooler; (*vent*) to freshen.

frais, fraîche [frɛ, frɛʃ] *a* fresh; (*froid*) cool // *ad* (*récemment*) newly, fresh(ly); **il fait** ~ it's cool; **servir** ~ serve chilled // *nm*: **mettre au** ~ to put in a cool place; **prendre le** ~ to take a breath of cool air // *nmpl* (*débours*) expenses; (*COMM*) costs; charges; **faire des** ~ to spend; to go to a lot of expense; **faire les** ~ **de** to bear the brunt of; ~ **généraux** overheads; ~ **de scolarité** school fees (*Brit*), tuition (*US*).

fraise [frɛz] *nf* strawberry; (*TECH*) countersink (bit); (*de dentiste*) drill; ~ **des bois** wild strawberry.

framboise [frɑ̃bwaz] *nf* raspberry.

franc, franche [frɑ̃, frɑ̃ʃ] *a* (*personne*) frank, straightforward; (*visage*) open; (*net: refus, couleur*) clear; (*: coupure*) clean; (*intensif*) downright; (*exempt*): ~ **de port** postage paid // *ad*: **parler** ~ to be frank *ou* candid // *nm* franc.

français, e [frɑ̃sɛ, -ɛz] *a* French // *nm/f*: **F~, e** Frenchman/woman // *nm* (*LING*) French; **les F~** the French.

France [frɑ̃s] *nf*: **la** ~ France.

franche [frɑ̃ʃ] *a voir* **franc**; ~**ment** *ad* frankly; clearly; (*tout à fait*) downright.

franchir [frɑ̃ʃir] *vt* (*obstacle*) to clear, get over; (*seuil, ligne, rivière*) to cross; (*distance*) to cover.

franchise [frɑ̃ʃiz] *nf* frankness; (*douanière, d'impôt*) exemption; (*ASSURANCES*) excess.

franciser [frɑ̃size] *vt* to gallicize, Frenchify.

franc-maçon [frɑ̃masɔ̃] *nm* freemason.

franco [frɑ̃ko] *ad* (*COMM*): ~ (**de port**) postage paid.

francophone [frɑ̃kɔfɔn] *a* French-speaking; ~**phonie** *nf* French-speaking communities.

franc-parler [frɑ̃parle] *nm inv* outspokenness.

franc-tireur [frɑ̃tirœr] *nm* (*MIL*) irregular; (*fig*) freelance.

frange [frɑ̃ʒ] *nf* fringe.

frangipane [frɑ̃ʒipan] *nf* almond paste.

franquette [frɑ̃kɛt]: **à la bonne** ~ *ad* without any fuss.

frappe [frap] *nf* (*d'une dactylo, pianiste, machine à écrire*) touch; (*BOXE*) punch.

frappé, e [fʀape] a iced.

frapper [fʀape] vt to hit, strike; (étonner) to strike; (monnaie) to strike, stamp; se ~ vi (s'inquiéter) to get worked up; ~ dans ses mains to clap one's hands; ~ du poing sur to bang one's fist on; **frappé de stupeur** dumbfounded.

frasques [fʀask(ə)] nfpl escapades.

fraternel, le [fʀatɛʀnɛl] a brotherly, fraternal.

fraternité [fʀatɛʀnite] nf brotherhood.

fraude [fʀod] nf fraud; (SCOL) cheating; **passer qch en ~** to smuggle sth in (ou out); ~ **fiscale** tax evasion; **frauder** vi, vt to cheat; **frauduleux, euse** a fraudulent.

frayer [fʀeje] vt to open up, clear // vi to spawn; (fréquenter): ~ **avec** to mix with.

frayeur [fʀejœʀ] nf fright.

fredonner [fʀədɔne] vt to hum.

freezer [fʀizœʀ] nm freezing compartment.

frein [fʀɛ̃] nm brake; ~ **à main** handbrake; ~s **à disques/tambour** disc/drum brakes.

freiner [fʀene] vi to brake // vt (progrès etc) to check.

frelaté, e [fʀəlate] a adulterated; (fig) tainted.

frêle [fʀɛl] a frail, fragile.

frelon [fʀəlɔ̃] nm hornet.

frémir [fʀemiʀ] vi to tremble, shudder; to shiver; to quiver.

frêne [fʀɛn] nm ash.

frénétique [fʀenetik] a frenzied, frenetic.

fréquemment [fʀekamɑ̃] ad frequently.

fréquent, e [fʀekɑ̃, -ɑ̃t] a frequent.

fréquentation [fʀekɑ̃tasjɔ̃] nf frequenting; seeing; ~s nfpl company sg.

fréquenté, e [fʀekɑ̃te] a: **très ~** (very) busy; **mal ~** patronized by disreputable elements.

fréquenter [fʀekɑ̃te] vt (lieu) to frequent; (personne) to see; se ~ to see each other.

frère [fʀɛʀ] nm brother.

fresque [fʀɛsk(ə)] nf (ART) fresco.

fret [fʀɛ] nm freight.

fréter [fʀete] vt to charter.

frétiller [fʀetije] vi to wriggle; to quiver; (chien) to wag its tail.

fretin [fʀətɛ̃] nm: **menu ~** small fry.

friable [fʀijablə] a crumbly.

friand, e [fʀijɑ̃, -ɑ̃d] a: ~ **de** very fond of.

friandise [fʀijɑ̃diz] nf sweet.

fric [fʀik] nm (fam) cash, bread.

friche [fʀiʃ] nf: **en ~ a, ad** (lying) fallow.

friction [fʀiksjɔ̃] nf (massage) rub, rubdown; (TECH, fig) friction; **frictionner** vt to rub (down); to massage.

frigidaire [fʀiʒidɛʀ] nm ® refrigerator.

frigide [fʀiʒid] a frigid.

frigo [fʀigo] nm fridge.

frigorifier [fʀigɔʀifje] vt to refrigerate; **frigorifique** a refrigerating.

frileux, euse [fʀilø, -øz] a sensitive to (the) cold.

frimer [fʀime] vi to put on an act.

frimousse [fʀimus] nf (sweet) little face.

fringale [fʀɛ̃gal] nf: **avoir la ~** to be ravenous.

fringant, e [fʀɛ̃gɑ̃, -ɑ̃t] a dashing.

fripé, e [fʀipe] a crumpled.

fripon, ne [fʀipɔ̃, -ɔn] a roguish, mischievous // nm/f rascal, rogue.

fripouille [fʀipuj] nf scoundrel.

frire [fʀiʀ] vt, vi: **faire ~** to fry.

frisé, e [fʀize] a curly; curly-haired.

frisson [fʀisɔ̃] nm shudder, shiver; quiver; **frissonner** vi to shudder, shiver; to quiver.

frit, e [fʀi, fʀit] pp de **frire** // nf: (**pommes**) ~es **chips** (Brit), French fries; **friteuse** nf chip pan; **friture** nf (huile) (deep) fat; (plat): **friture (de poissons)** fried fish; (RADIO) crackle.

frivole [fʀivɔl] a frivolous.

froid, e [fʀwa, fʀwad] a, nm cold; **il fait ~** it's cold; **avoir/prendre ~** to be/catch cold; **être en ~ avec** to be on bad terms with; **froidement** ad (accueillir) coldly; (décider) coolly.

froisser [fʀwase] vt to crumple (up), crease; (fig) to hurt, offend; se ~ vi to crumple, crease; to take offence; se ~ **un muscle** to strain a muscle.

frôler [fʀole] vt to brush against; (suj: projectile) to skim past; (fig) to come very close to.

fromage [fʀɔmaʒ] nm cheese; ~ **blanc** soft white cheese; **fromager, ère** nm/f cheese merchant.

froment [fʀɔmɑ̃] nm wheat.

froncer [fʀɔ̃se] vt to gather; ~ **les sourcils** to frown.

frondaisons [fʀɔ̃dɛzɔ̃] nfpl foliage sg.

fronde [fʀɔ̃d] nf sling; (fig) rebellion, rebelliousness.

front [fʀɔ̃] nm forehead, brow; (MIL) front; **de ~** ad (se heurter) head-on; (rouler) together (i.e. 2 or 3 abreast); (simultanément) at once; **faire ~ à** to face up to; ~ **de mer** (sea) front.

frontalier, ère [fʀɔ̃talje, -ɛʀ] a border cpd, frontier cpd // nm/f: (**travailleurs**) ~s commuters from across the border.

frontière [fʀɔ̃tjɛʀ] nf frontier, border; (fig) frontier, boundary.

fronton [fʀɔ̃tɔ̃] nm pediment.

frotter [fʀote] vi to rub, scrape // vt to rub; (pour nettoyer) to rub (up); to scrub; ~ **une allumette** to strike a match.

fructifier [fʀyktifje] vi to yield a profit; **faire ~** to turn to good account.

fructueux, euse [fʀyktɥø, -øz] a fruit-ful; profitable.

fruit [fʀɥi] nm fruit gén q; ~s de mer seafood(s); ~s secs dried fruit sg; **fruité, e** a fruity; **fruitier, ère** a: arbre fruitier fruit tree // nm/f fruiterer (Brit), fruit merchant (US).

fruste [fʀyst(ə)] a unpolished, unculti-vated.

frustrer [fʀystʀe] vt to frustrate.

fuel(-oil) [fjul(ɔjl)] nm fuel oil; heating oil.

fugace [fygas] a fleeting.

fugitif, ive [fyʒitif, -iv] a (lueur, amour) fleeting; (prisonnier etc) fugitive, run-away // nm/f fugitive.

fugue [fyg] nf: faire une ~ to run away, abscond.

fuir [fɥiʀ] vt to flee from; (éviter) to shun // vi to run away; (gaz, robinet) to leak.

fuite [fɥit] nf flight; (écoulement, divul-gation) leak; être en ~ to be on the run; mettre en ~ to put to flight.

fulgurant, e [fylgyʀɑ̃, -ɑ̃t] a lightning cpd, dazzling.

fulminer [fylmine] vi to thunder forth.

fumé, e [fyme] a (CULIN) smoked; (verre) tinted // nf smoke.

fume-cigarette [fymsigaʀɛt] nm inv cigarette holder.

fumer [fyme] vi to smoke; (soupe) to steam // vt to smoke; (terre, champ) to manure.

fûmes etc vb voir **être**.

fumet [fyme] nm aroma.

fumeur, euse [fymœʀ, -øz] nm/f smoker.

fumeux, euse [fymø, -øz] a (péj) woolly, hazy.

fumier [fymje] nm manure.

fumiste [fymist(ə)] nm/f (péj) shirker; phoney.

fumisterie [fymistəʀi] nf (péj) fraud, con.

funambule [fynɑ̃byl] nm tightrope walk-er.

funèbre [fynɛbʀ(ə)] a funeral cpd; (fig) doleful; funereal.

funérailles [fyneʀɑj] nfpl funeral sg.

funeste [fynɛst(ə)] a disastrous; death-ly.

fur [fyʀ]: au ~ et à mesure ad as one goes along; au ~ et à mesure que as.

furet [fyʀɛ] nm ferret.

fureter [fyʀte] vi (péj) to nose about.

fureur [fyʀœʀ] nf fury; (passion): ~ de passion for; faire ~ to be all the rage.

furibond, e [fyʀibɔ̃, -ɔ̃d] a furious.

furie [fyʀi] nf fury; (femme) shrew, vix-en; en ~ (mer) raging; **furieux, euse** a furious.

furoncle [fyʀɔ̃kl(ə)] nm boil.

furtif, ive [fyʀtif, -iv] a furtive.

fus vb voir **être**.

fusain [fyzɛ̃] nm (ART) charcoal.

fuseau, x [fyzo] nm (pour filer) spindle; (pantalon) (ski) pants; ~ horaire time zone.

fusée [fyze] nf rocket; ~ éclairante flare.

fuselé, e [fyzle] a slender; tapering.

fuser [fyze] vi (rires etc) to burst forth.

fusible [fyzibl(ə)] nm (ÉLEC: fil) fuse wire; (: fiche) fuse.

fusil [fyzi] nm (de guerre, à canon rayé) rifle, gun; (de chasse, à canon lisse) shotgun, gun; **fusillade** [-jad] nf gunfire q, shooting q; shooting battle; **fusiller** vt to shoot; ~-mitrailleur nm machine gun.

fusionner [fyzjɔne] vi to merge.

fustiger [fystiʒe] vt to denounce.

fut vb voir **être**.

fût [fy] vb voir **être** // nm (tonneau) bar-rel, cask.

futaie [fytɛ] nf forest, plantation.

futile [fytil] a futile; frivolous.

futur, e [fytyʀ] a, nm future.

fuyant, e [fɥijɑ̃, -ɑ̃t] vb voir **fuir** // a (regard etc) evasive; (lignes etc) reced-ing; (perspective) vanishing.

fuyard, e [fɥijaʀ, -aʀd(ə)] nm/f run-away.

G

gabarit [gabaʀi] nm (fig) size; calibre.

gâcher [gɑʃe] vt (gâter) to spoil, ruin; (gaspiller) to waste.

gâchette [gɑʃɛt] nf trigger.

gâchis [gɑʃi] nm waste q.

gadoue [gadu] nf sludge.

gaffe [gaf] nf (instrument) boat hook; (erreur) blunder; faire ~ (fam) to be careful.

gage [gaʒ] nm (dans un jeu) forfeit; (fig: de fidélité) token; ~s nmpl (sa-laire) wages; (garantie) guarantee sg; mettre en ~ to pawn.

gager [gaʒe] vt to bet, wager.

gageure [gaʒyʀ] nf: c'est une ~ it's at-tempting the impossible.

gagnant, e [gaɲɑ̃, -ɑ̃t] nm/f winner.

gagne-pain [gaɲpɛ̃] nm inv job.

gagner [gaɲe] vt to win; (somme d'argent, revenu) to earn; (aller vers, atteindre) to reach; (envahir) to over-come; to spread to // vi to win; (fig) to gain; ~ du temps/de la place to gain time/save space; ~ sa vie to earn one's living.

gai, e [ge] a gay, cheerful; (un peu ivre) merry.

gaieté [gete] nf cheerfulness; ~s nfpl (souvent ironique) delights; de ~ de cœur with a light heart.

gaillard, e [gajaʀ, -aʀd(ə)] a (grivois) bawdy, ribald // nm (strapping) fellow.

gain [gɛ̃] nm (revenu) earnings pl;

(bénéfice: gén pl) profits *pl;* *(au jeu: gén pl)* winnings *pl;* *(fig: de temps, place)* saving; **avoir ~ de cause** to win the case; *(fig)* to be proved right.

gaine [gɛn] *nf (corset)* girdle; *(fourreau)* sheath.

galant, e [galɑ̃, -ɑ̃t] *a (courtois)* courteous, gentlemanly; *(entreprenant)* flirtatious, gallant; *(aventure, poésie)* amorous.

galbe [galb(ə)] *nm* curve(s); shapeliness.

galère [galɛʀ] *nf* galley.

galérer [galeʀe] *vi (fam)* to slog away, work hard.

galerie [galʀi] *nf* gallery; *(THÉÂTRE)* circle; *(de voiture)* roof rack; *(fig: spectateurs)* audience; **~ marchande** shopping arcade; **~ de peinture** (private) art gallery.

galet [galɛ] *nm* pebble; *(TECH)* wheel.

galette [galɛt] *nf* flat cake.

Galles [gal]: **le pays de ~** Wales.

gallois, e [galwa, -waz] *a, nm (langue)* Welsh // *nm/f:* **G~, e** Welshman/woman.

galon [galɔ̃] *nm (MIL)* stripe; *(décoratif)* piece of braid.

galop [galo] *nm* gallop.

galoper [galɔpe] *vi* to gallop.

galopin [galɔpɛ̃] *nm* urchin, ragamuffin.

galvauder [galvode] *vt* to debase.

gambader [gɑ̃bade] *vi (animal, enfant)* to leap about.

gamelle [gamɛl] *nf* mess tin; billy can.

gamin, e [gamɛ̃, -in] *nm/f* kid // *a* mischievous, playful.

gamme [gam] *nf (MUS)* scale; *(fig)* range.

gammé, e [game] *a*: **croix ~e** swastika.

gant [gɑ̃] *nm* glove; **~ de toilette** (face) flannel *(Brit)*, face cloth.

garage [gaʀaʒ] *nm* garage; **garagiste** *nm/f* garage owner; garage mechanic.

garant, e [gaʀɑ̃, -ɑ̃t] *nm/f* guarantor // *nm* guarantee; **se porter ~ de** to vouch for; to be answerable for.

garantie [gaʀɑ̃ti] *nf* guarantee; *(gage)* security, surety; **(bon de) ~** guarantee *ou* warranty slip.

garantir [gaʀɑ̃tiʀ] *vt* to guarantee; *(protéger)*: **~ de** to protect from.

garçon [gaʀsɔ̃] *nm* boy; *(célibataire)* bachelor; *(serveur)*: **~ (de café)** waiter; **~ de courses** messenger; **garçonnet** *nm* small boy; **garçonnière** *nf* bachelor flat.

garde [gaʀd(ə)] *nm (de prisonnier)* guard; *(de domaine etc)* warden // *nf (soldat, sentinelle)* guardsman // *nf* guarding; looking after; *(soldats, BOXE, ESCRIME)* guard; *(faction)* watch; *(TYPO)*: **(page de) ~** endpaper; flyleaf; **de ~** *a, ad* on duty; **monter la ~** to stand guard; **mettre en ~** to warn; **prendre ~ (à)** to be careful (of); **~ champêtre** *nm* rural policeman; **~ du corps** *nm* body-

guard; **~ des enfants** *nf (après divorce)* custody of the children; **~ des Sceaux** *nm ≈* Lord Chancellor *(Brit)*, *≈* Attorney General *(US)*; **~ à vue** *nf (JUR) ≈* police custody; **être/se mettre au ~-à-vous** to be at/stand to attention.

garde... [gaʀd(ə)] *préfixe:* **~-barrière** *nm/f* level-crossing keeper; **~-boue** *nm inv* mudguard; **~-chasse** *nm* gamekeeper; **~-fou** *nm* railing, parapet; **~-malade** *nf* home nurse; **~-manger** *nm inv* meat safe; pantry, larder.

garder [gaʀde] *vt (conserver)* to keep; *(surveiller: enfants)* to look after; *(: immeuble, lieu, prisonnier)* to guard; **~ le lit/la chambre** to stay in bed/indoors; **se ~** *vi (aliment: se conserver)* to keep; **se ~ de faire** to be careful not to do; **pêche/chasse gardée** private fishing/hunting (ground).

garderie [gaʀdəʀi] *nf* day nursery, crèche.

garde-robe [gaʀdəʀɔb] *nf* wardrobe.

gardien, ne [gaʀdjɛ̃, -jɛn] *nm/f (garde)* guard; *(de prison)* warder; *(de domaine, réserve)* warden; *(de musée etc)* attendant; *(de phare, cimetière)* keeper; *(d'immeuble)* caretaker; *(fig)* guardian; **~ de but** goalkeeper; **~ de nuit** night watchman; **~ de la paix** policeman.

gare [gaʀ] *nf (railway)* station, train station *(US)* // *excl* watch out!; **~ routière** bus station.

garer [gaʀe] *vt* to park; **se ~** *vi* to park; *(pour laisser passer)* to draw into the side.

gargariser [gaʀgaʀize]: **se ~** *vi* to gargle; **gargarisme** *nm* gargling *q;* gargle.

gargote [gaʀgɔt] *nf* cheap restaurant.

gargouille [gaʀguj] *nf* gargoyle.

gargouiller [gaʀguje] *vi* to gurgle.

garnement [gaʀnəmɑ̃] *nm* rascal, scallywag.

garni, e [gaʀni] *a (plat)* served with vegetables *(and chips or pasta or rice)* // *nm* furnished accommodation *q.*

garnir [gaʀniʀ] *vt (orner)* to decorate; to trim; *(approvisionner)* to fill, stock; *(protéger)* to fit.

garnison [gaʀnizɔ̃] *nf* garrison.

garniture [gaʀnityʀ] *nf (CULIN)* vegetables *pl;* filling; *(décoration)* trimming; *(protection)* fittings *pl;* **~ de frein** brake lining.

garrot [gaʀo] *nm (MÉD)* tourniquet.

gars [gɑ] *nm* lad; guy.

Gascogne [gaskɔɲ] *nf* Gascony; **le golfe de ~** the Bay of Biscay.

gas-oil [gazɔjl] *nm* diesel (oil).

gaspiller [gaspije] *vt* to waste.

gastronomique [gastʀɔnɔmik] *a* gastronomic.

gâteau, x [gɑto] *nm* cake; **~ sec** biscuit.

gâter [gɑte] *vt* to spoil; **se ~** *vi (dent, fruit)* to go bad; *(temps, situation)* to change for the worse.

gâterie [gɑtʀi] *nf* little treat.

gâteux, euse [gɑtø, -øz] *a* senile.

gauche [goʃ] *a* left, left-hand; *(maladroit)* awkward, clumsy // *nf (POL)* left (wing); à ~ on the left; *(direction)* (to the) left; **gaucher, ère** *a* left-handed; **gauchiste** *nm/f* leftist.

gaufre [gofʀ(ə)] *nf* waffle.

gaufrette [gofʀɛt] *nf* wafer.

gaulois, e [golwa, -waz] *a* Gallic; *(grivois)* bawdy // *nm/f*: G~, e Gaul.

gausser [gose]: se ~ de *vt* to deride.

gaver [gave] *vt* to force-feed; *(fig)*: ~ de to cram with, fill up with.

gaz [gɑz] *nm inv* gas.

gaze [gɑz] *nf* gauze.

gazéifié, e [gazeifje] *a* aerated.

gazette [gazɛt] *nf* news sheet.

gazeux, euse [gazø, -øz] *a* gaseous; *(boisson)* fizzy; *(eau)* sparkling.

gazoduc [gazodyk] *nm* gas pipeline.

gazon [gazɔ̃] *nm (herbe)* turf; grass; *(pelouse)* lawn.

gazouiller [gazuje] *vi* to chirp; *(enfant)* to babble.

geai [ʒɛ] *nm* jay.

géant, e [ʒeɑ̃, -ɑ̃t] *a* gigantic, giant; *(COMM)* giant-size // *nm/f* giant.

geindre [ʒɛ̃dʀ(ə)] *vi* to groan, moan.

gel [ʒɛl] *nm* frost; freezing.

gélatine [ʒelatin] *nf* gelatine.

gelée [ʒəle] *nf* jelly; *(gel)* frost.

geler [ʒəle] *vt*, *vi* to freeze; **il gèle** it's freezing; **gelures** *nfpl* frostbite *sg*.

gélule [ʒelyl] *nf (MÉD)* capsule.

Gémeaux [ʒemo] *nmpl*: **les** ~ Gemini.

gémir [ʒemiʀ] *vi* to groan, moan.

gemme [ʒɛm] *nf* gem(stone).

gênant, e [ʒɛnɑ̃, -ɑ̃t] *a* annoying; embarrassing.

gencive [ʒɑ̃siv] *nf* gum.

gendarme [ʒɑ̃daʀm(ə)] *nm* gendarme; **~rie** *nf* military police force in countryside and small towns; their police station or barracks.

gendre [ʒɑ̃dʀ(ə)] *nm* son-in-law.

gêne [ʒɛn] *nf (à respirer, bouger)* discomfort, difficulty; *(dérangement)* bother, trouble; *(manque d'argent)* financial difficulties *pl ou* straits *pl*; *(confusion)* embarrassment.

gêné, e [ʒene] *a* embarrassed.

gêner [ʒene] *vt (incommoder)* to bother; *(encombrer)* to hamper; to be in the way; *(embarrasser)*: ~ qn to make sb feel ill-at-ease; se ~ *vi* to put o.s. out.

général, e, aux [ʒeneʀal, -o] *a*, *nm* general // *nf*: *(répétition)* ~e final dress rehearsal; **en** ~ usually, in general; **~ement** *ad* generally.

généraliser [ʒeneʀalize] *vt*, *vi* to generalize; se ~ *vi* to become widespread.

généraliste [ʒeneʀalist(ə)] *nm/f* general practitioner, G.P.

générateur, trice [ʒeneʀatœʀ, -tʀis] *a*: ~ de which causes // *nf* generator.

génération [ʒeneʀasjɔ̃] *nf* generation.

généreux, euse [ʒeneʀø, -øz] *a* generous.

générique [ʒeneʀik] *nm (CINÉMA)* credits *pl*, credit titles *pl*.

générosité [ʒeneʀozite] *nf* generosity.

genêt [ʒənɛ] *nm* broom *q (shrub)*.

génétique [ʒenetik] *a* genetic.

Genève [ʒənɛv] *n* Geneva.

génial, e, aux [ʒenjal, -o] *a* of genius; *(fam: formidable)* fantastic, brilliant.

génie [ʒeni] *nm* genius; *(MIL)*: **le** ~ the Engineers *pl*; ~ civil civil engineering.

genièvre [ʒənjɛvʀ(ə)] *nm* juniper.

génisse [ʒenis] *nf* heifer.

genou, x [ʒnu] *nm* knee; à ~x on one's knees; se mettre à ~x to kneel down.

genre [ʒɑ̃ʀ] *nm* kind, type, sort; *(allure)* manner; *(LING)* gender.

gens [ʒɑ̃] *nmpl (f in some phrases)* people *pl*.

gentil, le [ʒɑ̃ti, -ij] *a* kind; *(enfant: sage)* good; *(endroit etc)* nice; **gentillesse** *nf* kindness; **gentiment** *ad* kindly.

géographie [ʒeogʀafi] *nf* geography.

geôlier [ʒolje] *nm* jailer.

géologie [ʒeɔlɔʒi] *nf* geology.

géomètre [ʒeomɛtʀ(ə)] *nm/f*: *(arpenteur-)~* (land) surveyor.

géométrie [ʒeometʀi] *nf* geometry; **géométrique** *a* geometric.

gérance [ʒeʀɑ̃s] *nf* management; mettre en ~ to appoint a manager for.

géranium [ʒeʀanjɔm] *nm* geranium.

gérant, e [ʒeʀɑ̃, -ɑ̃t] *nm/f* manager/manageress.

gerbe [ʒɛʀb(ə)] *nf (de fleurs)* spray; *(de blé)* sheaf *(pl* sheaves); *(fig)* shower, burst.

gercé, e [ʒɛʀse] *a* chapped.

gerçure [ʒɛʀsyʀ] *nf* crack.

gérer [ʒeʀe] *vt* to manage.

germain, e [ʒɛʀmɛ̃, -ɛn] *a*: **cousin** ~ first cousin.

germe [ʒɛʀm(ə)] *nm* germ.

germer [ʒɛʀme] *vi* to sprout; to germinate.

gésir [ʒeziʀ] *vi* to be lying (down); *voir aussi* ci-gît.

geste [ʒɛst(ə)] *nm* gesture; move; motion.

gestion [ʒɛstjɔ̃] *nf* management.

gibecière [ʒibsjɛʀ] *nf* gamebag.

gibet [ʒibɛ] *nm* gallows *pl*.

gibier [ʒibje] *nm (animaux)* game; *(fig)* prey.

giboulée [ʒibule] *nf* sudden shower.

gicler [ʒikle] *vi* to spurt, squirt.

gifle [ʒifl(ə)] *nf* slap (in the face); **gifler** *vt* to slap (in the face).

gigantesque [ʒigɑ̃tɛsk(ə)] *a* gigantic.

gigogne [ʒigɔɲ] *a*: **lits** ~s truckle *(Brit)*

ou trundle beds.

gigot [ʒigo] *nm* leg (of mutton *ou* lamb).

gigoter [ʒigɔte] *vi* to wriggle (about).

gilet [ʒile] *nm* waistcoat; (*pull*) cardigan; (*de corps*) vest; ~ pare-balles bulletproof jacket; ~ de sauvetage life jacket.

gingembre [ʒɛ̃ʒɑ̃bʀ(ə)] *nm* ginger.

girafe [ʒiʀaf] *nf* giraffe.

giratoire [ʒiʀatwaʀ] *a*: sens ~ roundabout.

girouette [ʒiʀwɛt] *nf* weather vane *ou* cock.

gisait *etc vb voir* **gésir.**

gisement [ʒizmɑ̃] *nm* deposit.

gît *vb voir* **gésir.**

gitan, e [ʒitɑ̃, -an] *nm/f* gipsy.

gîte [ʒit] *nm* home; shelter; ~ (rural) holiday cottage *ou* apartment.

givre [ʒivʀ(ə)] *nm* (hoar) frost.

glabre [glabʀ(ə)] *a* hairless; cleanshaven.

glace [glas] *nf* ice; (*crème glacée*) ice cream; (*verre*) sheet of glass; (*miroir*) mirror; (*de voiture*) window.

glacé, e [glase] *a* icy; (*boisson*) iced.

glacer [glase] *vt* to freeze; (*boisson*) to chill, ice; (*gâteau*) to ice; (*papier, tissu*) to glaze; (*fig*): ~ qn to chill sb; to make sb's blood run cold.

glacial, e [glasjal] *a* icy.

glacier [glasje] *nm* (*GÉO*) glacier; (*marchand*) ice-cream maker.

glacière [glasjɛʀ] *nf* icebox.

glaçon [glasɔ̃] *nm* icicle; (*pour boisson*) ice cube.

glaise [glɛz] *nf* clay.

gland [glɑ̃] *nm* acorn; (*décoration*) tassel.

glande [glɑ̃d] *nf* gland.

glaner [glane] *vt, vi* to glean.

glapir [glapiʀ] *vi* to yelp.

glas [glɑ] *nm* knell, toll.

glauque [glok] *a* dull blue-green.

glissant, e [glisɑ̃, -ɑ̃t] *a* slippery.

glissement [glismɑ̃] *nm*: ~ de terrain landslide.

glisser [glise] *vi* (*avancer*) to glide *ou* slide along; (*coulisser, tomber*) to slide; (*déraper*) to slip; (*être glissant*) to be slippery // *vt* to slip; se ~ dans to slip into.

global, e, aux [glɔbal, -o] *a* overall.

globe [glɔb] *nm* globe.

globule [glɔbyl] *nm* (*du sang*) corpuscle.

globuleux, euse [glɔbylø, -øz] *a*: yeux ~ protruding eyes.

gloire [glwaʀ] *nf* glory; (*mérite*) distinction, credit; (*personne*) celebrity; **glorieux, euse** *a* glorious.

glousser [gluse] *vi* to cluck; (*rire*) to chuckle.

glouton, ne [glutɔ̃, -ɔn] *a* gluttonous.

gluant, e [glyɑ̃, -ɑ̃t] *a* sticky, gummy.

glycine [glisin] *nf* wisteria.

go [go]: tout de ~ *ad* straight out.

G.O. *sigle* = grandes ondes.

gobelet [gɔblɛ] *nm* tumbler; beaker; (à dés) cup.

gober [gɔbe] *vt* to swallow.

godasse [gɔdas] *nf* (*fam*) shoe.

godet [gɔdɛ] *nm* pot.

goéland [gɔelɑ̃] *nm* (sea)gull.

goélette [gɔelɛt] *nf* schooner.

goémon [gɔemɔ̃] *nm* wrack.

gogo [gɔgo]: à ~ *ad* galore.

goguenard, e [gɔgnaʀ, -aʀd(ə)] *a* mocking.

goinfre [gwɛ̃fʀ(ə)] *nm* glutton.

golf [gɔlf] *nm* golf; golf course.

golfe [gɔlf(ə)] *nm* gulf; bay.

gomme [gɔm] *nf* (à effacer) rubber (*Brit*), eraser; **gommer** *vt* to rub out (*Brit*), erase.

gond [gɔ̃] *nm* hinge; sortir de ses ~s (*fig*) to fly off the handle.

gondoler [gɔ̃dɔle]: se ~ *vi* to warp; to buckle.

gonflé, e [gɔ̃fle] *a* swollen; bloated.

gonfler [gɔ̃fle] *vt* (*pneu, ballon*) to inflate, blow up; (*nombre, importance*) to inflate // *vi* to swell (up); (*CULIN: pâte*) to rise.

gonzesse [gɔ̃zɛs] *nf* (*fam*) chick, bird (*Brit*).

goret [gɔʀɛ] *nm* piglet.

gorge [gɔʀʒ(ə)] *nf* (*ANAT*) throat; (*poitrine*) breast.

gorgé, e [gɔʀʒe] *a*: ~ de filled with; (*eau*) saturated with // *nf* mouthful; sip; gulp.

gorille [gɔʀij] *nm* gorilla; (*fam*) bodyguard.

gosier [gozje] *nm* throat.

gosse [gɔs] *nm/f* kid.

goudron [gudʀɔ̃] *nm* tar; **goudronner** *vt* to tar(mac) (*Brit*), asphalt (*US*).

gouffre [gufʀ(ə)] *nm* abyss, gulf.

goujat [guʒa] *nm* boor.

goujon [guʒɔ̃] *nm* club, bludgeon.

goulot [gulo] *nm* neck; boire au ~ to drink from the bottle.

goulu, e [guly] *a* greedy.

gourd, e [guʀ, guʀd(ə)] *a* numb (with cold).

gourde [guʀd(ə)] *nf* (*récipient*) flask; (*fam*) (clumsy) clot *ou* oaf // *a* oafish.

gourdin [guʀdɛ̃] *nm* club, bludgeon.

gourmand, e [guʀmɑ̃, -ɑ̃d] *a* greedy; **gourmandise** *nf* greed; (*bonbon*) sweet.

gousse [gus] *nf*: ~ d'ail clove of garlic.

goût [gu] *nm* taste; de bon ~ tasteful; de mauvais ~ tasteless; prendre ~ à to develop a taste *ou* a liking for.

goûter [gute] *vt* (*essayer*) to taste; (*apprécier*) to enjoy // *vi* to have (afternoon) tea // *nm* (afternoon) tea.

goutte [gut] *nf* drop; (*MÉD*) gout; (*alcool*) brandy.

goutte-à-goutte [gutagut] *nm* (*MÉD*) drip; tomber ~ to drip.

gouttière [gutjɛʀ] nf gutter.
gouvernail [guvɛʀnaj] nm rudder; (barre) helm, tiller.
gouvernante [guvɛʀnɑ̃t] nf governess.
gouverne [guvɛʀn(ə)] nf: pour sa ~ for his guidance.
gouvernement [guvɛʀnəmɑ̃] nm government; **gouvernemental, e, aux** a government cpd; pro-government.
gouverner [guvɛʀne] vt to govern.
grâce [gʀɑs] nf grace; favour; (JUR) pardon; ~s nfpl (REL) grâce sg; faire ~ à qn de qch to spare sb sth; rendre ~(s) à to give thanks to; demander ~ to beg for mercy; ~ à prép thanks to; **gracier** vt to pardon; **gracieux, euse** a graceful.
grade [gʀad] nm rank; monter en ~ to be promoted.
gradé [gʀade] nm officer.
gradin [gʀadɛ̃] nm tier; step; ~s nmpl (de stade) terracing sg.
graduel, le [gʀaduɛl] a gradual; progressive.
graduer [gʀadue] vt (effort etc) to increase gradually; (règle, verre) to graduate.
grain [gʀɛ̃] nm (gén) grain; (NAVIG) squall; ~ de beauté beauty spot; ~ de café coffee bean; ~ de poivre peppercorn; ~ de poussière speck of dust; ~ de raisin grape.
graine [gʀɛn] nf seed.
graissage [gʀɛsaʒ] nm lubrication, greasing.
graisse [gʀɛs] nf fat; (lubrifiant) grease; **graisser** vt to lubricate, grease; (tacher) to make greasy.
grammaire [gʀamɛʀ] nf grammar; **grammatical, e, aux** a grammatical.
gramme [gʀam] nm gramme.
grand, e [gʀɑ̃, gʀɑ̃d] a (haut) tall; (gros, vaste, long) big, large; (long) long; (sens abstraits) great // ad: ~ ouvert wide open; au ~ air in the open (air); les ~s blessés the severely injured; ~ ensemble housing scheme; ~ magasin department store; ~e personne grown-up; ~e surface hypermarket; ~es écoles prestige schools of university level; ~es lignes (RAIL) main lines; ~es vacances summer holidays; **grand-chose** nm/f inv: pas grand-chose not much; **Grande-Bretagne** nf (Great) Britain; **grandeur** nf (dimension) size; magnitude; (fig) greatness; **grandeur nature** life-size; **grandir** vi to grow // vt: **grandir qn** (suj: vêtement, chaussure) to make sb look taller; ~-**mère** nf grandmother; ~-**messe** nf high mass; ~-**peine**: à ~-**peine** ad with difficulty; ~-**père** nm grandfather; ~-**route** nf main road; ~-**rue** nf high street; ~-**s-parents** nmpl grandparents.
grange [gʀɑ̃ʒ] nf barn.

granit(e) [gʀanit] nm granite.
graphique [gʀafik] a graphic // nm graph.
grappe [gʀap] nf cluster; ~ de raisin bunch of grapes.
grappiller [gʀapije] vt to glean.
grappin [gʀapɛ̃] nm grapnel; mettre le ~ sur (fig) to get one's claws on.
gras, se [gʀɑ, gʀɑs] a (viande, soupe) fatty; (personne) fat; (surface, main) greasy; (plaisanterie) coarse; (TYPO) bold // nm (CULIN) fat; faire la ~se matinée to have a lie-in (Brit), sleep late (US); ~**sement** ad: ~sement payé handsomely paid; ~**souillet, te** a podgy, plump.
gratifier [gʀatifje] vt: ~ qn de to favour sb with; to reward sb with.
gratiné, e [gʀatine] a (CULIN) au gratin.
gratis [gʀatis] ad free.
gratitude [gʀatityd] nf gratitude.
gratte-ciel [gʀatsjɛl] nm inv skyscraper.
gratte-papier [gʀatpapje] nm inv (péj) penpusher.
gratter [gʀate] vt (frotter) to scrape; (enlever) to scrape off; (bras, bouton) to scratch.
gratuit, e [gʀatui, -uit] a (entrée, billet) free; (fig) gratuitous.
gravats [gʀava] nmpl rubble sg.
grave [gʀav] a (maladie, accident) serious, bad; (sujet, problème) serious, grave; (air) grave, solemn; (voix, son) deep, low-pitched; ~**ment** ad seriously; gravely.
graver [gʀave] vt to engrave.
gravier [gʀavje] nm gravel q; **gravillons** nmpl loose gravel sg.
gravir [gʀaviʀ] vt to climb (up).
gravité [gʀavite] nf seriousness; gravity.
graviter [gʀavite] vi to revolve.
gravure [gʀavyʀ] nf engraving; (reproduction) print; plate.
gré [gʀe] nm: à son ~ to his liking; as he pleases; au ~ de according to, following; contre le ~ de qn against sb's will; de son (plein) ~ of one's own free will; bon ~ mal ~ like it or not; de ~ ou de force whether one likes it or not; savoir ~ à qn de qch to be grateful to sb for sth.
grec, grecque [gʀɛk] a Greek; (classique: vase etc) Grecian // nm/f Greek.
Grèce [gʀɛs] nf: la ~ Greece.
gréement [gʀemɑ̃] nm rigging.
greffer [gʀefe] vt (BOT, MÉD: tissu) to graft; (MÉD: organe) to transplant.
greffier [gʀefje] nm clerk of the court.
grêle [gʀɛl] a (very) thin // nf hail.
grêlé, e [gʀɛle] a pockmarked.
grêler [gʀɛle] vb impersonnel: il grêle it's hailing.
grêlon [gʀelɔ̃] nm hailstone.

grelot [grəlo] nm little bell.
grelotter [grəlɔte] vi to shiver.
grenade [grənad] nf (explosive) grenade; (BOT) pomegranate.
grenat [grəna] a inv dark red.
grenier [grənje] nm attic; (de ferme) loft.
grenouille [grənuj] nf frog.
grès [gre] nm sandstone; (poterie) stoneware.
grésiller [grezije] vi to sizzle; (RADIO) to crackle.
grève [grev] nf (d'ouvriers) strike; (plage) shore; se mettre en/faire ~ to go on/be on strike; ~ de la faim hunger strike; ~ du zèle work-to-rule (Brit), slowdown (US).
grever [grəve] vt to put a strain on.
gréviste [grevist(ə)] nm/f striker.
gribouiller [gribuje] vt to scribble, scrawl.
grief [grijef] nm grievance; faire ~ à qn de to reproach sb for.
grièvement [grijevmɑ̃] ad seriously.
griffe [grif] nf claw; (fig) signature.
griffer [grife] vt to scratch.
griffonner [grifɔne] vt to scribble.
grignoter [grinɔte] vt to nibble ou gnaw at.
gril [gril] nm steak ou grill pan.
grillade [grijad] nf grill.
grillage [grija3] nm (treillis) wire netting; wire fencing.
grille [grij] nf (clôture) railings; (portail) (metal) gate; (d'égout) (metal) grate; (fig) grid.
grille-pain [grijpɛ̃] nm inv toaster.
griller [grije] vt (aussi: faire ~: pain) to toast; (: viande) to grill; (fig: ampoule etc) to burn out, blow.
grillon [grijɔ̃] nm cricket.
grimace [grimas] nf grimace; (pour faire rire): faire des ~s to pull ou make faces.
grimer [grime] vt to make up.
grimper [grɛ̃pe] vi, vt to climb.
grincer [grɛ̃se] vi (porte, roue) to grate; (plancher) to creak; ~ des dents to grind one's teeth.
grincheux, euse [grɛ̃ʃø, -øz] a grumpy.
grippe [grip] nf flu, influenza; **grippé, e** a: être grippé to have flu.
gris, e [gri, griz] a grey; (ivre) tipsy; faire ~e mine to pull a miserable ou wry face.
grisaille [grizaj] nf greyness, dullness.
griser [grize] vt to intoxicate.
grisonner [grizɔne] vi to be going grey.
grisou [grizu] nm firedamp.
grive [griv] nf thrush.
grivois, e [grivwa, -waz] a saucy.
Groenland [grɔenlɑ̃d] nm Greenland.
grogner [grɔɲe] vi to growl; (fig) to grumble.

groin [grwɛ̃] nm snout.
grommeler [grɔmle] vi to mutter to o.s.
gronder [grɔ̃de] vi to rumble; (fig: révolte) to be brewing // vt to scold.
gros, se [gro, gros] a big, large; (obèse) fat; (travaux, dégâts) extensive; (large: trait, fil) thick, heavy // ad: risquer/ gagner ~ to risk/win a lot // nm (COMM): le ~ the wholesale business; prix de ~ wholesale price; par ~ temps/ ~se mer in rough weather/heavy seas; le ~ de the main body of; the bulk of; en ~ roughly; (COMM) wholesale; ~ lot jackpot; ~ mot coarse word; ~ plan (PHOTO) close-up; ~ sel cooking salt; ~se caisse big drum.
groseille [grozɛj] nf: ~ (rouge)/ (blanche) red/white currant; ~ à maquereau gooseberry.
grosse [gros] a voir gros.
grossesse [groses] nf pregnancy.
grosseur [grosœr] nf size; fatness; (tumeur) lump.
grossier, ière [grosje, -jer] a coarse; (travail) rough; crude; (évident: erreur) gross.
grossir [grosir] vi (personne) to put on weight; (fig) to grow, get bigger; (rivière) to swell // vt to increase; to exaggerate; (au microscope) to magnify; (suj: vêtement): ~ qn to make sb look fatter.
grossiste [grosist(ə)] nm/f wholesaler.
grosso modo [grosɔmɔdo] ad roughly.
grotte [grɔt] nf cave.
grouiller [gruje] vi to mill about; to swarm about; ~ de to be swarming with.
groupe [grup] nm group.
groupement [grupmɑ̃] nm grouping; group.
grouper [grupe] vt to group; se ~ vi to get together.
grue [gry] nf crane.
grumeaux [grymo] nmpl lumps.
gué [ge] nm ford; passer à ~ to ford.
guenilles [gənij] nfpl rags.
guenon [gənɔ̃] nf female monkey.
guépard [gepar] nm cheetah.
guêpe [gep] nf wasp.
guêpier [gepje] nm (fig) trap.
guère [ger] ad (avec adjectif, adverbe): ne ... ~ hardly; (avec verbe): ne ... ~ tournure négative + much; hardly ever; ~ tournure négative + (very) long; il n'y a ~ que/de there's hardly anybody (ou anything) but/hardly any.
guéridon [geridɔ̃] nm pedestal table.
guérilla [gerija] nf guerrilla warfare.
guérir [gerir] vt (personne, maladie) to cure; (membre, plaie) to heal // vi to recover, be cured; to heal; **guérison** nf curing; healing; recovery.
guérite [gerit] nf sentry box.
guerre [ger] nf war; (méthode): ~ atomique atomic warfare q; en ~ at

war; faire la ~ à to wage war against; de ~ lasse finally; ~ d'usure war of attrition; **guerrier, ière** a warlike // nm/f warrior.

guet [gɛ] nm: faire le ~ to be on the watch ou look-out.

guet-apens [gɛtapɑ̃] nm ambush.

guetter [gete] vt (épier) to watch (intently); (attendre) to watch (out) for; to be lying in wait for.

gueule [gœl] nf mouth; (fam) face; mouth; ta ~! (fam) shut up!; ~ de bois (fam) hangover.

gueuler [gœle] vi (fam) to bawl.

gui [gi] nm mistletoe.

guichet [giʃɛ] nm (de bureau, banque) counter, window; (d'une porte) wicket, hatch; les ~s (à la gare, au théâtre) the ticket office.

guide [gid] nm guide.

guider [gide] vt to guide.

guidon [gidɔ̃] nm handlebars pl.

guignol [giɲɔl] nm ≈ Punch and Judy show; (fig) clown.

guillemets [gijmɛ] nmpl: entre ~ in inverted commas.

guillotiner [gijɔtine] vt to guillotine.

guindé, e [gɛ̃de] a stiff, starchy.

guirlande [girlɑ̃d] nf garland; (de papier) paper chain.

guise [giz] nf: à votre ~ as you wish ou please; en ~ de by way of.

guitare [gitar] nf guitar.

gymnase [ʒimnɑz] nm gym(nasium).

gymnastique [ʒimnastik] nf gymnastics sg; (au réveil etc) keep-fit exercises pl.

gynécologie [ʒinekɔlɔʒi] nf gynaecology; **gynécologue** nm/f gynaecologist.

H

habile [abil] a skilful; (malin) clever; ~té nf skill, skilfulness; cleverness.

habilité, e [abilite] a: ~ à faire entitled to do, empowered to do.

habillé, e [abije] a dressed; (chic) dressy; (TECH): ~ de covered with; encased in.

habillement [abijmɑ̃] nm clothes pl.

habiller [abije] vt to dress; (fournir en vêtements) to clothe; s'~ vi to dress (o.s.); (se déguiser, mettre des vêtements chic) to dress up.

habit [abi] nm outfit; ~s nmpl (vêtements) clothes; ~ (de soirée) tails pl; evening dress.

habitant, e [abitɑ̃, -ɑ̃t] nm/f inhabitant; (d'une maison) occupant.

habitation [abitasjɔ̃] nf living; residence, home; house; ~s à loyer modéré (HLM) low-rent housing sg.

habiter [abite] vt to live in; (suj: sentiment) to dwell in // vi: ~ à/dans to live in ou at/in.

habitude [abityd] nf habit; avoir l'~ de faire to be in the habit of doing; (expérience) to be used to doing; d'~ usually; comme d'~ as usual.

habitué, e [abitye] nm/f regular visitor; regular (customer).

habituel, le [abityɛl] a usual.

habituer [abitye] vt: ~ qn à to get sb used to; s'~ à to get used to.

'hache ['aʃ] nf axe.

'hacher ['aʃe] vt (viande) to mince; (persil) to chop.

'hachis ['aʃi] nm mince q.

'hachoir ['aʃwar] nm chopper; (meat) mincer; chopping board.

'hagard, e ['agar, -ard(ə)] a wild, distraught.

'haie ['ɛ] nf hedge; (SPORT) hurdle; (fig: rang) line, row.

'haillons ['ajɔ̃] nmpl rags.

'haine ['ɛn] nf hatred.

'haïr ['air] vt to detest, hate.

'hâlé, e ['ale] a (sun)tanned, sunburnt.

haleine [alɛn] nf breath; hors d'~ out of breath; tenir en ~ to hold spellbound; to keep in suspense; de longue ~ a long-term.

'haler ['ale] vt to haul in; to tow.

'haleter ['alte] vt to pant.

'hall ['ol] nm hall.

'halle ['al] nf (covered) market; ~s nfpl central food market sg.

hallucinant, e [alysinɑ̃, -ɑ̃t] a staggering.

hallucination [alysinasjɔ̃] nf hallucination.

'halte ['alt(ə)] nf stop, break; stopping place; (RAIL) halt // excl stop!; faire ~ to stop.

haltère [altɛr] nm dumbbell, barbell; (poids et) ~s nmpl (activité) weight lifting sg.

'hamac ['amak] nm hammock.

'hameau, x ['amo] nm hamlet.

hameçon [amsɔ̃] nm (fish) hook.

'hanche ['ɑ̃ʃ] nf hip.

'handicapé, e ['ɑ̃dikape] nm/f physically (ou mentally) handicapped person; ~ moteur spastic.

'hangar ['ɑ̃gar] nm shed; (AVIAT) hangar.

'hanneton ['antɔ̃] nm cockchafer.

'hanter ['ɑ̃te] vt to haunt.

'hantise ['ɑ̃tiz] nf obsessive fear.

'happer ['ape] vt to snatch; (suj: train etc) to hit.

'haras ['ara] nm stud farm.

'harassant, e ['arasɑ̃, -ɑ̃t] a exhausting.

'harceler ['arsəle] vt (MIL, CHASSE) to harass, harry; (importuner) to plague.

'hardi, e ['ardi] a bold, daring.

'hareng ['arɑ̃] nm herring.

'hargne ['arɲ(ə)] nf aggressiveness.

'haricot ['ariko] nm bean; ~ blanc hari-

cot bean; ~ **vert** green bean.
harmonica [aʀmɔnika] *nm* mouth organ.
harmonie [aʀmɔni] *nf* harmony.
'harnacher ['aʀnaʃe] *vt* to harness.
'harnais ['aʀnɛ] *nm* harness.
'harpe ['aʀp(ə)] *nf* harp.
'harponner ['aʀpɔne] *vt* to harpoon; (*fam*) to collar.
'hasard ['azaʀ] *nm*: le ~ chance, fate; un ~ a coincidence; a stroke of luck; au ~ aimlessly; at random; haphazardly; par ~ by chance; à tout ~ just in case; on the off chance (*Brit*).
'hasarder ['azaʀde] *vt* (*mot*) to venture; (*fortune*) to risk.
'hâte ['ɑt] *nf* haste; à la ~ hurriedly, hastily; en ~ posthaste, with all possible speed; avoir ~ to be eager *ou* anxious to; **'hâter** *vt* to hasten; se **hâter** *vi* to hurry.
'hâtif, ive ['ɑtif, -iv] *a* hurried; hasty; (*légume*) early.
'hausse ['os] *nf* rise, increase.
'hausser ['ose] *vt* to raise; ~ les épaules to shrug (one's shoulders).
'haut, e ['o, 'ot] *a* high; (*grand*) tall; (*son, voix*) high(-pitched) // *ad* high // *nm* top (part); de 3 m de ~ 3 m high, 3 m in height; des ~s et des bas ups and downs; en ~ lieu in high places; à ~e voix, (*tout*) ~ aloud; out loud; du ~ de from the top of; de ~ en bas from top to bottom; downwards; plus ~ higher up, further up; (*dans un texte*) above; (*parler*) louder; en ~ up above; at (*ou* to) the top; (*dans une maison*) upstairs; en ~ de at the top of.
'hautain, e ['otɛ̃, -ɛn] *a* haughty.
'hautbois ['obwa] *nm* oboe.
'haut-de-forme ['odfɔʀm(ə)] *nm* top hat.
'hauteur ['otœʀ] *nf* height; (*fig*) loftiness; haughtiness; à la ~ de (*sur la même ligne*) level with; by; (*fig*) equal to; à la ~ (*fig*) up to it.
'haut-fond ['ofɔ̃] *nm* shallow, shoal.
'haut-fourneau ['ofuʀno] *nm* blast *ou* smelting furnace.
'haut-le-cœur ['olkœʀ] *nm inv* retch, heave.
'haut-parleur ['opaʀlœʀ] *nm* (loud)speaker.
'havre ['avʀ(ə)] *nm* haven.
'Haye ['ɛ] *n*: la ~ the Hague.
'hayon ['ɛjɔ̃] *nm* tailgate.
hebdo [ɛbdo] *nm* (*fam*) weekly.
hebdomadaire [ɛbdɔmadɛʀ] *a, nm* weekly.
héberger [ebɛʀʒe] *vt* to accommodate, lodge; (*réfugiés*) to take in.
hébété, e [ebete] *a* dazed.
hébreu, x [ebʀø] *am, nm* Hebrew.
hécatombe [ekatɔ̃b] *nf* slaughter.
hectare [ɛktaʀ] *nm* hectare.

'hein ['ɛ̃] *excl* eh?
'hélas ['elas] *excl* alas! // *ad* unfortunately.
'héler ['ele] *vt* to hail.
hélice [elis] *nf* propeller.
hélicoptère [elikɔptɛʀ] *nm* helicopter.
helvétique [ɛlvetik] *a* Swiss.
hémicycle [emisikl(ə)] *nm* semicircle; (*POL*): l'~ ≈ the benches (of the Commons) (*Brit*), ≈ the floor (of the House of Representatives) (*US*).
hémorragie [emɔʀaʒi] *nf* bleeding *q*, haemorrhage.
hémorroïdes [emɔʀɔid] *nfpl* piles, haemorrhoids.
'hennir ['eniʀ] *vi* to neigh, whinny.
herbe [ɛʀb(ə)] *nf* grass; (*CULIN, MÉD*) herb; en ~ unripe; (*fig*) budding; **herbicide** *nm* weed-killer; **herboriste** *nm/f* herbalist.
'here ['ɛʀ] *nm*: pauvre ~ poor wretch.
héréditaire [eʀeditɛʀ] *a* hereditary.
'hérisser ['eʀise] *vt*: ~ qn (*fig*) to ruffle sb; se ~ *vi* to bristle, bristle up.
'hérisson ['eʀisɔ̃] *nm* hedgehog.
héritage [eʀitaʒ] *nm* inheritance; (*fig*) heritage; legacy.
hériter [eʀite] *vi*: ~ de qch (de qn) to inherit sth (from sb); **héritier, ière** *nm/f* heir/heiress.
hermétique [ɛʀmetik] *a* airtight; watertight; (*fig*) abstruse; impenetrable.
hermine [ɛʀmin] *nf* ermine.
'hernie ['ɛʀni] *nf* hernia.
héroïne [eʀɔin] *nf* heroine; (*drogue*) heroin.
'héron ['eʀɔ̃] *nm* heron.
'héros ['eʀo] *nm* hero.
hésitation [ezitasjɔ̃] *nf* hesitation.
hésiter [ezite] *vi*: ~ (à faire) to hesitate (to do).
hétéroclite [eteʀɔklit] *a* heterogeneous; (*objets*) sundry.
'hêtre ['ɛtʀ(ə)] *nm* beech.
heure [œʀ] *nf* hour; (*SCOL*) period; (*moment*) time; c'est l'~ it's time; quelle ~ est-il? what time is it?; 2 ~s (du matin) 2 o'clock (in the morning); être à l'~ to be on time; (*montre*) to be right; mettre à l'~ to set right; à toute ~ at any time; 24 ~s sur 24 round the clock, 24 hours a day; à l'~ qu'il est at this time (of day); by now; sur l'~ at once; ~s supplémentaires overtime *sg*.
heureusement [œʀøzmɑ̃] *ad* (*par bonheur*) fortunately, luckily.
heureux, euse [œʀø, -øz] *a* happy; (*chanceux*) lucky, fortunate; (*judicieux*) felicitous, fortunate.
'heurt ['œʀ] *nm* (*choc*) collision; ~s (*fig*) clashes.
'heurter ['œʀte] *vt* (*mur*) to strike, hit; (*personne*) to collide with; (*fig*) to go against, upset; se ~ à *vt* (*fig*) to come up against; **'heurtoir** *nm* door knocker.

hexagone [ɛgzagɔn] *nm* hexagon; *(la France)* France *(because of its roughly hexagonal shape)*.

hiberner [ibɛʀne] *vi* to hibernate.

'hibou, x ['ibu] *nm* owl.

'hideux, euse ['idø, -øz] *a* hideous.

hier [jɛʀ] *ad* yesterday; **toute la journée d'~** all day yesterday; **toute la matinée d'~** all yesterday morning.

'hiérarchie ['jeʀaʀʃi] *nf* hierarchy.

hilare [ilaʀ] *a* mirthful.

hippique [ipik] *a* equestrian, horse *cpd*.

hippodrome [ipɔdʀom] *nm* racecourse.

hippopotame [ipɔpɔtam] *nm* hippopotamus.

hirondelle [iʀɔ̃dɛl] *nf* swallow.

hirsute [iʀsyt] *a* hairy; shaggy; tousled.

'hisser ['ise] *vt* to hoist, haul up.

histoire [istwaʀ] *nf (science, événements)* history; *(anecdote, récit, mensonge)* story; *(affaire)* business *q;* **~s** *nfpl (chichis)* fuss *q;* *(ennuis)* trouble *sg;* **historique** *a* historical; *(important)* historic.

hiver [ivɛʀ] *nm* winter; **~nal, e, aux** *a* winter *cpd;* wintry; **~ner** *vi* to winter.

HLM *sigle m ou f voir* **habitation**.

'hobby ['ɔbi] *nm* hobby.

'hocher ['ɔʃe] *vt:* **~ la tête** to nod; *(signe négatif ou dubitatif)* to shake one's head.

'hochet ['ɔʃɛ] *nm* rattle.

'hockey ['ɔkɛ] *nm:* **~ (sur glace/gazon)** (ice/field) hockey.

'hold-up ['ɔldœp] *nm inv* hold-up.

'hollandais, e ['ɔlɑ̃dɛ, -ɛz] *a, nm (LING)* Dutch // *nm/f:* **H~, e** Dutchman/woman; **les H~** the Dutch.

'Hollande ['ɔlɑ̃d] *nf:* **la ~** Holland.

'homard ['ɔmaʀ] *nm* lobster.

homéopathique [ɔmeɔpatik] *a* homœopathic.

homicide [ɔmisid] *nm* murder; **~ involontaire** manslaughter.

hommage [ɔmaʒ] *nm* tribute; **~s** *nmpl:* **présenter ses ~s** to pay one's respects; **rendre ~ à** to pay tribute ou homage to.

homme [ɔm] *nm* man; **~ d'affaires** businessman; **~ d'État** statesman; **~ de main** hired man; **~ de paille** stooge; **~-grenouille** *nm* frogman.

homogène [ɔmɔʒɛn] *a* homogeneous.

homologue [ɔmɔlɔg] *nm/f* counterpart, opposite number.

homologué, e [ɔmɔlɔge] *a (SPORT)* officially recognized, ratified; *(tarif)* authorized.

homonyme [ɔmɔnim] *nm (LING)* homonym; *(d'une personne)* namesake.

homosexuel, le [ɔmɔsɛksɥɛl] *a* homosexual.

'Hongrie ['ɔ̃gʀi] *nf:* **la ~** Hungary; **'hongrois, e** *a, nm/f* Hungarian.

honnête [ɔnɛt] *a (intègre)* honest; *(juste, satisfaisant)* fair; **~ment** *ad* honestly; **~té** *nf* honesty.

honneur [ɔnœʀ] *nm* honour; *(mérite)* credit; **en l'~ de** in honour of; *(événement)* on the occasion of; **faire ~ à** *(engagements)* to honour; *(famille)* to be a credit to; *(fig: repas etc)* to do justice to.

honorable [ɔnɔʀabl(ə)] *a* worthy, honourable; *(suffisant)* decent.

honoraire [ɔnɔʀɛʀ] *a* honorary; **~s** *nmpl* fees *pl;* **professeur ~** professor emeritus.

honorer [ɔnɔʀe] *vt* to honour; *(estimer)* to hold in high regard; *(faire honneur à)* to do credit to; **s'~ de** to pride o.s. upon; **honorifique** *a* honorary.

'honte ['ɔ̃t] *nf* shame; **avoir ~ de** to be ashamed of; **faire ~ à qn** to make sb (feel) ashamed; **'honteux, euse** *a* ashamed; *(conduite, acte)* shameful, disgraceful.

hôpital, aux [ɔpital, -o] *nm* hospital.

'hoquet ['ɔkɛ] *nm:* **avoir le ~** to have (the) hiccoughs; **'hoqueter** ['ɔkte] *vi* to hiccough.

horaire [ɔʀɛʀ] *a* hourly // *nm* timetable, schedule; **~ souple** flexitime; **~s** *nmpl (d'employé)* hours.

horizon [ɔʀizɔ̃] *nm* horizon; *(paysage)* landscape, view.

horizontal, e, aux [ɔʀizɔ̃tal, -o] *a* horizontal.

horloge [ɔʀlɔʒ] *nf* clock; **horloger, ère** *nm/f* watchmaker; clockmaker; **~rie** *nf* watch-making; watchmaker's (shop); clockmaker's (shop).

'hormis ['ɔʀmi] *prép* save.

horoscope [ɔʀɔskɔp] *nm* horoscope.

horreur [ɔʀœʀ] *nf* horror; **avoir ~ de** to loathe ou detest; **horrible** *a* horrible.

horripiler [ɔʀipile] *vt* to exasperate.

'hors ['ɔʀ] *prép* except (for); **~ de** out of; **~ pair** outstanding; **~ de propos** inopportune; **être ~ de soi** to be beside o.s.; **~-bord** *nm inv* speedboat (with outboard motor); **~-concours** *a* ineligible to compete; **~-d'œuvre** *nm inv* hors d'œuvre; **~-jeu** *nm inv* offside; **~-la-loi** *nm inv* outlaw; **~-taxe** *a (boutique, articles)* duty-free.

hospice [ɔspis] *nm (de vieillards)* home.

hospitalier, ière [ɔspitalje, -jɛʀ] *a (accueillant)* hospitable; *(MÉD: service, centre)* hospital *cpd*.

hospitalité [ɔspitalite] *nf* hospitality.

hostie [ɔsti] *nf* host *(REL)*.

hostile [ɔstil] *a* hostile; **hostilité** *nf* hostility.

hôte [ot] *nm (maître de maison)* host; *(invité)* guest.

hôtel [otɛl] *nm* hotel; **aller à l'~** to stay in a hotel; **~ (particulier)** (private) mansion; **~ de ville** town hall; **hôtelier, ière** *a* hotel *cpd* // *nm/f* hotelier; **~lerie** *nf* hotel business; *(auberge)* inn.

hôtesse [otɛs] *nf* hostess; ~ de l'air air stewardess.

'**hotte** ['ɔt] *nf* (*panier*) basket (*carried on the back*); (*de cheminée*) hood; ~ aspirante cooker hood.

'**houblon** [h'ublɔ̃] *nm* (*BOT*) hop; (*pour la bière*) hops *pl*.

'**houille** ['uj] *nf* coal; ~ blanche hydroelectric power.

'**houle** ['ul] *nf* swell.

'**houlette** ['ulɛt] *nf*: sous la ~ de under the guidance of.

'**houleux, euse** ['ulø, -øz] *a* heavy, swelling; (*fig*) stormy, turbulent.

'**houspiller** ['uspije] *vt* to scold.

'**housse** ['us] *nf* cover; dust cover; loose *ou* stretch cover.

'**houx** ['u] *nm* holly.

'**hublot** ['yblo] *nm* porthole.

'**huche** ['yʃ] *nf*: ~ à pain bread bin.

'**huer** ['ɥe] *vt* to boo.

huile [ɥil] *nf* oil; ~ de foie de morue cod-liver oil; **huiler** *vt* to oil; **huileux, euse** *a* oily.

huis [ɥi] *nm*: à ~ clos in camera.

huissier [ɥisje] *nm* usher; (*JUR*) ≈ bailiff.

'**huit** ['ɥit] *num* eight; **samedi en ~ a** week on Saturday; **une huitaine de jours** a week or so; '**huitième** *num* eighth.

huître [ɥitʀ(ə)] *nf* oyster.

humain, e [ymɛ̃, -ɛn] *a* human; (*compatissant*) humane // *nm* human (being); **humanité** *nf* humanity.

humble [œbl(ə)] *a* humble.

humecter [ymɛkte] *vt* to dampen.

'**humer** ['yme] *vt* to smell; to inhale.

humeur [ymœʀ] *nf* mood; (*tempérament*) temper; (*irritation*) bad temper; **de bonne/mauvaise ~** in a good/bad mood.

humide [ymid] *a* damp; (*main, yeux*) moist; (*climat, chaleur*) humid; (*saison, route*) wet.

humilier [ymilje] *vt* to humiliate.

humilité [ymilite] *nf* humility, humbleness.

humoristique [ymɔristik] *a* humorous; humoristic.

humour [ymuʀ] *nm* humour; **avoir de l'~** to have a sense of humour; ~ **noir** sick humour.

'**hurlement** ['yʀləmɑ̃] *nm* howling *q*, howl, yelling *q*, yell.

'**hurler** ['yʀle] *vi* to howl, yell.

hurluberlu [yʀlybɛʀly] *nm* (*péj*) crank.

'**hutte** ['yt] *nf* hut.

hydratant, e [idʀatɑ̃, -ɑ̃t] *a* (*crème*) moisturizing.

hydrate [idʀat] *nm*: ~s de carbone carbohydrates.

hydraulique [idʀolik] *a* hydraulic.

hydravion [idʀavjɔ̃] *nm* seaplane.

hydrogène [idʀɔʒɛn] *nm* hydrogen.

hydroglisseur [idʀɔglisœʀ] *nm* hydroplane.

hygiénique [iʒjenik] *a* hygienic.

hymne [imn(ə)] *nm* hymn; ~ **national** national anthem.

hypermarché [ipɛʀmaʀʃe] *nm* hypermarket.

hypermétrope [ipɛʀmetʀɔp] *a* longsighted.

hypnotiser [ipnɔtize] *vt* to hypnotize.

hypocrite [ipɔkʀit] *a* hypocritical.

hypothèque [ipɔtɛk] *nf* mortgage.

hypothèse [ipɔtɛz] *nf* hypothesis.

hystérique [isteʀik] *a* hysterical.

I

iceberg [isbɛʀg] *nm* iceberg.

ici [isi] *ad* here; **jusqu'~** as far as this; until now; **d'~ là** by then; in the meantime; **d'~ peu** before long.

idéal, e, aux [ideal, -o] *a* ideal // *nm* ideal; ideals *pl*.

idée [ide] *nf* idea; **avoir dans l'~ que** to have an idea that; ~**s noires** black *ou* dark thoughts.

identifier [idɑ̃tifje] *vt* to identify; **s'~ à** (*héros etc*) to identify with.

identique [idɑ̃tik] *a*: ~ (à) identical (to).

identité [idɑ̃tite] *nf* identity.

idiot, e [idjo, idjɔt] *a* idiotic // *nm/f* idiot.

idole [idɔl] *nf* idol.

if [if] *nm* yew.

ignare [iɲaʀ] *a* ignorant.

ignifugé, e [iɲifyʒe] *a* fireproof(ed).

ignoble [iɲɔbl(ə)] *a* vile.

ignorant, e [iɲɔʀɑ̃, -ɑ̃t] *a* ignorant.

ignorer [iɲɔʀe] *vt* (*ne pas connaître*) not to know, be unaware *ou* ignorant of; (*être sans expérience de: plaisir, guerre etc*) not to know about, have no experience of; (*bouder: personne*) to ignore.

il [il] *pronom* he; (*animal, chose, en tournure impersonnelle*) it; ~**s** they; *voir aussi* **avoir**.

île [il] *nf* island; **les ~s anglo-normandes** the Channel Islands; **les ~s Britanniques** the British Isles.

illégal, e, aux [ilegal, -o] *a* illegal.

illégitime [ileʒitim] *a* illegitimate.

illettré, e [iletʀe] *a*, *nm/f* illiterate.

illimité, e [ilimite] *a* unlimited.

illisible [ilizibl(ə)] *a* illegible; (*roman*) unreadable.

illumination [ilyminasjɔ̃] *nf* illumination, floodlighting; (*idée*) flash of inspiration.

illuminer [ilymine] *vt* to light up; (*monument, rue: pour une fête*) to illuminate, floodlight.

illusion [ilyzjɔ̃] *nf* illusion; **se faire des ~s** to delude o.s.; **faire ~** to delude *ou* fool people; **illusionniste** *nm/f* conjuror.

illustration 106 **important**

illustration [ilystʀasjɔ̃] *nf* illustration.

illustre [ilystʀ(ə)] *a* illustrious.

illustré, e [ilystʀe] *a* illustrated // *nm* illustrated magazine; comic.

illustrer [ilystʀe] *vt* to illustrate; s'~ to become famous, win fame.

îlot [ilo] *nm* small island, islet; (*de maisons*) block.

ils [il] *pronom voir* **il**.

image [imaʒ] *nf* (*gén*) picture; (*comparaison, ressemblance, OPTIQUE*) image; ~ de marque brand image; (*fig*) public image.

imagination [imaʒinasjɔ̃] *nf* imagination; (*chimère*) fancy; avoir de l'~ to be imaginative.

imaginer [imaʒine] *vt* to imagine; (*inventer: expédient*) to devise, think up; s'~ *vt* (*se figurer: scène etc*) to imagine, picture; s'~ que to imagine that.

imbécile [ɛ̃besil] *a* idiotic // *nm/f* idiot.

imberbe [ɛ̃bɛʀb(ə)] *a* beardless.

imbiber [ɛ̃bibe] *vt* to moisten, wet; s'~ de to become saturated with.

imbu, e [ɛ̃by] *a*: ~ de full of.

imitateur, trice [imitatœʀ, -tʀis] *nm/f* (*gén*) imitator; (*MUSIC-HALL*) impersonator.

imitation [imitasjɔ̃] *nf* imitation; (*sketch*) imitation, impression; impersonation.

imiter [imite] *vt* to imitate; (*contrefaire*) to forge; (*ressembler à*) to look like.

immaculé, e [imakyle] *a* spotless; immaculate.

immatriculation [imatʀikylasjɔ̃] *nf* registration.

immatriculer [imatʀikyle] *vt* to register; faire/se faire ~ to register.

immédiat, e [imedja, -at] *a* immediate // *nm*: dans l'~ for the time being; **immédiatement** *ad* immediately.

immense [imãs] *a* immense.

immerger [imɛʀʒe] *vt* to immerse, submerge.

immeuble [imœbl(ə)] *nm* building; ~ locatif block of rented flats (*Brit*), rental building (*US*).

immigration [imigʀasjɔ̃] *nf* immigration.

immigré, e [imigʀe] *nm/f* immigrant.

imminent, e [iminã, -ãt] *a* imminent.

immiscer [imise]: s'~ *vi*: s'~ dans to interfere in *ou* with.

immobile [imɔbil] *a* still, motionless; (*fig*) unchanging.

immobilier, ière [imɔbilje, -jɛʀ] *a* property *cpd* // *nm*: l'~ the property business.

immobiliser [imɔbilize] *vt* (*gén*) to immobilize; (*circulation, véhicule, affaires*) to bring to a standstill; s'~ (*personne*) to stand still; (*machine, véhicule*) to come to a halt.

immonde [imɔ̃d] *a* foul.

immondices [imɔ̃dis] *nmpl* refuse *sg*; filth *sg*.

immoral, e, aux [imɔʀal, -o] *a* immoral.

immuable [imɥabl(ə)] *a* immutable; unchanging.

immunisé, e [imynize] *a*: ~ contre immune to.

immunité [imynite] *nf* immunity.

impact [ɛ̃pakt] *nm* impact.

impair, e [ɛ̃pɛʀ] *a* odd // *nm* faux pas, blunder.

impardonnable [ɛ̃paʀdɔnabl(ə)] *a* unpardonable, unforgivable.

imparfait, e [ɛ̃paʀfɛ, -ɛt] *a* imperfect.

impartial, e, aux [ɛ̃paʀsjal, -o] *a* impartial, unbiased.

impartir [ɛ̃paʀtiʀ] *vt* to assign; to bestow.

impasse [ɛ̃pas] *nf* dead-end, cul-de-sac; (*fig*) deadlock.

impassible [ɛ̃pasibl(ə)] *a* impassive.

impatience [ɛ̃pasjãs] *nf* impatience.

impatient, e [ɛ̃pasjã, -ãt] *a* impatient; **impatienter** *vt* to irritate, annoy; s'impatienter to get impatient.

impayable [ɛ̃pɛjabl(ə)] *a* (*drôle*) priceless.

impeccable [ɛ̃pekabl(ə)] *a* faultless, impeccable; spotlessly clean; impeccably dressed; (*fam*) smashing.

impensable [ɛ̃pãsabl(ə)] *a* unthinkable; unbelievable.

impératif, ive [ɛ̃peʀatif, -iv] *a* imperative // *nm* (*LING*) imperative; ~s *nmpl* requirements; demands.

impératrice [ɛ̃peʀatʀis] *nf* empress.

impérial, e, aux [ɛ̃peʀjal, -o] *a* imperial // *nf* top deck.

impérieux, euse [ɛ̃peʀjø, -øz] *a* (*caractère, ton*) imperious; (*obligation, besoin*) pressing, urgent.

impérissable [ɛ̃peʀisabl(ə)] *a* undying; imperishable.

imperméable [ɛ̃pɛʀmeabl(ə)] *a* waterproof; (*GÉO*) impermeable; (*fig*): ~ à impervious to // *nm* raincoat.

impertinent, e [ɛ̃pɛʀtinã, -ãt] *a* impertinent.

impétueux, euse [ɛ̃petɥø, -øz] *a* fiery.

impie [ɛ̃pi] *a* impious, ungodly.

impitoyable [ɛ̃pitwajabl(ə)] *a* pitiless, merciless.

implanter [ɛ̃plãte] *vt* (*usine, industrie, usage*) to establish; (*colons etc*) to settle; (*idée, préjugé*) to implant.

impliquer [ɛ̃plike] *vt* to imply; ~ qn (dans) to implicate sb (in).

impoli, e [ɛ̃pɔli] *a* impolite, rude.

importance [ɛ̃pɔʀtãs] *nf* importance; sans ~ unimportant.

important, e [ɛ̃pɔʀtã, -ãt] *a* important; (*en quantité*) considerable, sizeable; extensive; (*péj: airs, ton*) self-important // *nm*: l'~ the important thing.

importateur, trice [ɛ̃pɔrtatœr, -tris] *nm/f* importer.

importation [ɛ̃pɔrtasjɔ̃] *nf* importation; introduction; (*produit*) import.

importer [ɛ̃pɔrte] *vt* (*COMM*) to import; (*maladies, plantes*) to introduce // *vi* (*être important*) to matter; il importe qu'il fasse it is important that he should do; peu m'importe I don't mind; I don't care; peu importe (que) it doesn't matter (if); *voir aussi* **n'importe**.

importun, e [ɛ̃pɔrtœ̃, -yn] *a* irksome, importunate; (*arrivée, visite*) inopportune, ill-timed // *nm* intruder; **importuner** *vt* to bother.

imposant, e [ɛ̃pozɑ̃, -ɑ̃t] *a* imposing.

imposer [ɛ̃poze] *vt* (*taxer*) to tax; ~ qch à qn to impose sth on sb; s'~ (*être nécessaire*) to be imperative; (*montrer sa prominence*) to stand out, emerge; (*artiste: se faire connaître*) to win recognition; en ~ à to impress.

imposition [ɛ̃pozisjɔ̃] *nf* (*ADMIN*) taxation.

impossible [ɛ̃pɔsibl(ə)] *a* impossible; il m'est ~ de le faire it is impossible for me to do it, I can't possibly do it; faire l'~ to do one's utmost.

impôt [ɛ̃po] *nm* tax; (*taxes*) taxation; taxes *pl*; ~s *nmpl* (*contributions*) (income) tax *sg*; payer 1000 F d'~s to pay 1,000 F in tax; ~ sur le chiffre d'affaires corporation (*Brit*) *ou* corporate (*US*) tax; ~ foncier land tax; ~ sur le revenu income tax.

impotent, e [ɛ̃pɔtɑ̃, -ɑ̃t] *a* disabled.

impraticable [ɛ̃pratikabl(ə)] *a* (*projet*) impracticable, unworkable; (*piste*) impassable.

imprécis, e [ɛ̃presi, -iz] *a* imprecise.

imprégner [ɛ̃preɲe] *vt* (*tissu, tampon*) to soak, impregnate; (*lieu, air*) to fill; s'~ de (*fig*) to absorb.

imprenable [ɛ̃prənabl(ə)] *a* (*forteresse*) impregnable; vue ~ unimpeded outlook.

impression [ɛ̃presjɔ̃] *nf* impression; (*d'un ouvrage, tissu*) printing; faire bonne ~ to make a good impression.

impressionnant, e [ɛ̃presjɔnɑ̃, -ɑ̃t] *a* impressive; upsetting.

impressionner [ɛ̃presjɔne] *vt* (*frapper*) to impress; (*troubler*) to upset.

imprévisible [ɛ̃previzibl(ə)] *a* unforeseeable.

imprévoyant, e [ɛ̃prevwajɑ̃, -ɑ̃t] *a* lacking in foresight; (*en matière d'argent*) improvident.

imprévu, e [ɛ̃prevy] *a* unforeseen, unexpected // *nm* unexpected incident; en cas d'~ if anything unexpected happens.

imprimante [ɛ̃primɑ̃t] *nf* printer; ~ matricielle dot-matrix printer.

imprimé [ɛ̃prime] *nm* (*formulaire*) printed form; (*POSTES*) printed matter *q*.

imprimer [ɛ̃prime] *vt* to print; (*empreinte etc*) to imprint; (*publier*) to publish; (*communiquer: mouvement, impulsion*) to impart, transmit; **imprimerie** *nf* printing; (*établissement*) printing works *sg*; **imprimeur** *nm* printer.

impromptu, e [ɛ̃prɔ̃pty] *a* impromptu; sudden.

impropre [ɛ̃prɔpr(ə)] *a* inappropriate; ~ à unsuitable for.

improviser [ɛ̃prɔvize] *vt, vi* to improvise.

improviste [ɛ̃prɔvist(ə)]: à l'~ *ad* unexpectedly, without warning.

imprudence [ɛ̃prydɑ̃s] *nf* carelessness *q*; imprudence *q*.

imprudent, e [ɛ̃prydɑ̃, -ɑ̃t] *a* (*conducteur, geste, action*) careless; (*remarque*) unwise, imprudent; (*projet*) foolhardy.

impudent, e [ɛ̃pydɑ̃, -ɑ̃t] *a* impudent; brazen.

impudique [ɛ̃pydik] *a* shameless.

impuissant, e [ɛ̃pɥisɑ̃, -ɑ̃t] *a* helpless; (*sans effet*) ineffectual; (*sexuellement*) impotent; ~ à faire powerless to do.

impulsif, ive [ɛ̃pylsif, -iv] *a* impulsive.

impulsion [ɛ̃pylsjɔ̃] *nf* (*ÉLEC, instinct*) impulse; (*élan, influence*) impetus.

impunément [ɛ̃pynemɑ̃] *ad* with impunity.

imputer [ɛ̃pyte] *vt* (*attribuer*) to ascribe, impute; (*COMM*): ~ à *ou* sur to charge to.

inabordable [inabɔrdabl(ə)] *a* (*cher*) prohibitive.

inaccessible [inaksesibl(ə)] *a* inaccessible; unattainable; (*insensible*): ~ à impervious to.

inachevé, e [inaʃve] *a* unfinished.

inadapté, e [inadapte] *a* (*gén*): ~ à not adapted to, unsuited to; (*PSYCH*) maladjusted.

inadmissible [inadmisibl(ə)] *a* inadmissible.

inadvertance [inadvɛrtɑ̃s]: par ~ *ad* inadvertently.

inaltérable [inalterabl(ə)] *a* (*matière*) stable; (*fig*) unchanging; ~ à unaffected by.

inamovible [inamɔvibl(ə)] *a* fixed; (*JUR*) irremovable.

inanimé, e [inanime] *a* (*matière*) inanimate; (*évanoui*) unconscious; (*sans vie*) lifeless.

inanition [inanisjɔ̃] *nf*: tomber d'~ to faint with hunger (and exhaustion).

inaperçu, e [inapɛrsy] *a*: passer ~ to go unnoticed.

inappréciable [inapresjabl(ə)] *a* (*service*) invaluable.

inapte [inapt(ə)] *a*: ~ à incapable of; (*MIL*) unfit for.

inattaquable [inatakabl(ə)] *a* (*texte, preuve*) irrefutable.

inattendu, e [inatɑ̃dy] *a* unexpected.

inattentif, ive [inatɑ̃tif, -iv] *a* inattentive; **~ à** (*dangers, détails*) heedless of; **inattention** *nf*: **faute d'inattention** careless mistake.

inaugurer [inɔgyʀe] *vt* (*monument*) to unveil; (*exposition, usine*) to open; (*fig*) to inaugurate.

inavouable [inavwabl(ə)] *a* shameful; undisclosable.

inavoué, e [inavwe] *a* unavowed.

incandescence [ɛ̃kɑ̃desɑ̃s] *nf*: **porter à ~** to heat white-hot.

incapable [ɛ̃kapabl(ə)] *a* incapable; **~ de faire** incapable of doing; (*empêché*) unable to do.

incapacité [ɛ̃kapasite] *nf* incapability; (*JUR*) incapacity.

incarner [ɛ̃kaʀne] *vt* to embody, personify; (*THÉÂTRE*) to play.

incartade [ɛ̃kaʀtad] *nf* prank.

incassable [ɛ̃kɑsabl(ə)] *a* unbreakable.

incendiaire [ɛ̃sɑ̃djɛʀ] *a* incendiary; (*fig: discours*) inflammatory // *nm/f* fire-raiser, arsonist.

incendie [ɛ̃sɑ̃di] *nm* fire; **~ criminel** arson *q*; **~ de forêt** forest fire.

incendier [ɛ̃sɑ̃dje] *vt* (*mettre le feu à*) to set fire to, set alight; (*brûler complètement*) to burn down.

incertain, e [ɛ̃sɛʀtɛ̃, -ɛn] *a* uncertain; (*temps*) uncertain, unsettled; (*imprécis: contours*) indistinct, blurred; **incertitude** *nf* uncertainty.

incessamment [ɛ̃sɛsamɑ̃] *ad* very shortly.

incidemment [ɛ̃sidamɑ̃] *ad* in passing.

incident [ɛ̃sidɑ̃] *nm* incident; **~ de parcours** minor hitch *ou* setback; **~ technique** technical difficulties *pl*.

incinérer [ɛ̃sineʀe] *vt* (*ordures*) to incinerate; (*mort*) to cremate.

incisive [ɛ̃siziv] *nf* incisor.

inclinaison [ɛ̃klinɛzɔ̃] *nf* (*déclivité: d'une route etc*) incline; (: *d'un toit*) slope; (*état penché*) tilt.

inclination [ɛ̃klinasjɔ̃] *nf*: **~ de (la) tête** nod (of the head); **~ (de buste)** bow.

incliner [ɛ̃kline] *vt* (*tête, bouteille*) to tilt // *vi*: **~ à qch/à faire** to incline towards sth/doing; **s'~ (devant)** to bow (before); (*céder*) to give in *ou* yield (to); **~ la tête** *ou* **le front** to give a slight bow.

inclure [ɛ̃klyʀ] *vt* to include; (*joindre à un envoi*) to enclose; **jusqu'au 10 mars inclus** until 10th March inclusive.

incoercible [ɛ̃kɔɛʀsibl(ə)] *a* uncontrollable.

incohérent, e [ɛ̃kɔeʀɑ̃, -ɑ̃t] *a* inconsistent; incoherent.

incollable [ɛ̃kɔlabl(ə)] *a*: **il est ~** he's got all the answers.

incolore [ɛ̃kɔlɔʀ] *a* colourless.

incomber [ɛ̃kɔbe]: **~ à** *vt* (*suj: devoirs, responsabilité*) to rest upon; (: *frais, tra-*

vail) to be the responsibility of.

incommensurable [ɛ̃kɔmɑ̃syʀabl(ə)] *a* immeasurable.

incommode [ɛ̃kɔmɔd] *a* inconvenient; (*posture, siège*) uncomfortable.

incommoder [ɛ̃kɔmɔde] *vt*: **~ qn** to inconvenience sb; (*embarrasser*) to make sb feel uncomfortable.

incompétent, e [ɛ̃kɔpetɑ̃, -ɑ̃t] *a* incompetent.

incompris, e [ɛ̃kɔpʀi, -iz] *a* misunderstood.

inconcevable [ɛ̃kɔsvabl(ə)] *a* incredible.

inconciliable [ɛ̃kɔsiljabl(ə)] *a* irreconcilable.

inconditionnel, le [ɛ̃kɔdisjɔnɛl] *a* unconditional; (*partisan*) unquestioning.

inconduite [ɛ̃kɔdɥit] *nf* wild behaviour *q*.

incongru, e [ɛ̃kɔgʀy] *a* unseemly.

inconnu, e [ɛ̃kɔny] *a* unknown; new, strange // *nm/f* stranger; unknown person (*ou* artist etc) // *nm*: **l'~** the unknown // *nf* unknown.

inconsciemment [ɛ̃kɔsjamɑ̃] *ad* unconsciously.

inconscient, e [ɛ̃kɔsjɑ̃, -ɑ̃t] *a* unconscious; (*irréfléchi*) thoughtless, reckless // *nm* (*PSYCH*): **l'~** the unconscious; **~ de** unaware of.

inconsidéré, e [ɛ̃kɔsideʀe] *a* ill-considered.

inconsistant, e [ɛ̃kɔsistɑ̃, -ɑ̃t] *a* flimsy, weak; runny.

incontestable [ɛ̃kɔtestabl(ə)] *a* indisputable.

inconvenant, e [ɛ̃kɔvnɑ̃, -ɑ̃t] *a* unseemly, improper.

inconvénient [ɛ̃kɔvenjɑ̃] *nm* (*d'une situation, d'un projet*) disadvantage, drawback; (*d'un remède, changement etc*) inconvenience; **si vous n'y voyez pas d'~** if you have no objections.

incorporer [ɛ̃kɔʀpɔʀe] *vt*: **~ (à)** to mix in (with); (*paragraphe etc*): **~ (dans)** to incorporate (in); (*MIL: appeler*) to recruit, call up.

incorrect, e [ɛ̃kɔʀɛkt] *a* (*impropre, inconvenant*) improper; (*défectueux*) faulty; (*inexact*) incorrect; (*impoli*) impolite; (*déloyal*) underhand.

incrédule [ɛ̃kʀedyl] *a* incredulous; (*REL*) unbelieving.

increvable [ɛ̃kʀəvabl(ə)] *a* (*fam*) tireless.

incriminer [ɛ̃kʀimine] *vt* (*personne*) to incriminate; (*action, conduite*) to bring under attack; (*bonne foi, honnêteté*) to call into question.

incroyable [ɛ̃kʀwajabl(ə)] *a* incredible; unbelievable.

incruster [ɛ̃kʀyste] *vt* (*ART*) to inlay; **s'~** *vi* (*invité*) to take root; (*radiateur etc*) to become coated with fur *ou* scale.

incubateur [ɛ̃kybatœʀ] *nm* incubator.
inculpé, e [ɛ̃kylpe] *nm/f* accused.
inculper [ɛ̃kylpe] *vt*: ~ (de) to charge (with).
inculquer [ɛ̃kylke] *vt*: ~ qch à to inculcate sth in *ou* instil sth into.
inculte [ɛ̃kylt(ə)] *a* uncultivated; (*esprit, peuple*) uncultured; (*barbe*) unkempt.
Inde [ɛ̃d] *nf*: l'~ India.
indécis, e [ɛ̃desi, -iz] *a* indecisive; (*perplexe*) undecided.
indéfendable [ɛ̃defɑ̃dabl(ə)] *a* indefensible.
indéfini, e [ɛ̃defini] *a* (*imprécis, incertain*) undefined; (*illimité, LING*) indefinite; ~**ment** *ad* indefinitely; ~**ssable** *a* indefinable.
indélicat, e [ɛ̃delika, -at] *a* tactless; dishonest.
indemne [ɛ̃dɛmn(ə)] *a* unharmed.
indemniser [ɛ̃dɛmnize] *vt*: ~ qn (de) to compensate sb (for).
indemnité [ɛ̃dɛmnite] *nf* (*dédommagement*) compensation *q*; (*allocation*) allowance; ~ de licenciement redundancy payment.
indépendamment [ɛ̃depɑ̃damɑ̃] *ad* independently; ~ de (*abstraction faite de*) irrespective of; (*en plus de*) over and above.
indépendance [ɛ̃depɑ̃dɑ̃s] *nf* independence.
indépendant, e [ɛ̃depɑ̃dɑ̃, -ɑ̃t] *a* independent; ~ de independent of.
indescriptible [ɛ̃deskʀiptibl(ə)] *a* indescribable.
indétermination [ɛ̃detɛʀminasjɔ̃] *nf* indecision; indecisiveness.
indéterminé, e [ɛ̃detɛʀmine] *a* unspecified; indeterminate.
index [ɛ̃dɛks] *nm* (*doigt*) index finger; (*d'un livre etc*) index; mettre à l'~ to blacklist.
indexé, e [ɛ̃dɛkse] *a* (*ÉCON*): ~ (sur) index-linked (to).
indicateur [ɛ̃dikatœʀ] *nm* (*POLICE*) informer; (*livre*) guide; directory; (*TECH*) gauge; indicator; ~ des chemins de fer railway timetable.
indicatif, ive [ɛ̃dikatif, -iv] *a*: à titre ~ for (your) information // *nm* (*LING*) indicative; (*RADIO*) theme *ou* signature tune; (*TÉL*) dialling code.
indication [ɛ̃dikasjɔ̃] *nf* indication; (*renseignement*) information *q*; ~s *nfpl* (*directives*) instructions.
indice [ɛ̃dis] *nm* (*marque, signe*) indication, sign; (*POLICE: lors d'une enquête*) clue; (*JUR: présomption*) piece of evidence; (*SCIENCE, ÉCON, TECH*) index.
indicible [ɛ̃disibl(ə)] *a* inexpressible.
indien, ne [ɛ̃djɛ̃, -jɛn] *a, nm/f* Indian.
indifféremment [ɛ̃diferamɑ̃] *ad* (*sans distinction*) equally (well); indiscriminately.

indifférence [ɛ̃diferɑ̃s] *nf* indifference.
indifférent, e [ɛ̃diferɑ̃, -ɑ̃t] *a* (*peu intéressé*) indifferent.
indigence [ɛ̃diʒɑ̃s] *nf* poverty.
indigène [ɛ̃diʒɛn] *a* native, indigenous; local // *nm/f* native.
indigeste [ɛ̃diʒɛst(ə)] *a* indigestible.
indigestion [ɛ̃diʒɛstjɔ̃] *nf* indigestion *q*.
indigne [ɛ̃diɲ] *a* unworthy.
indigner [ɛ̃diɲe] *vt*: s'~ (de/contre) to be indignant (at).
indiqué, e [ɛ̃dike] *a* (*date, lieu*) given; (*adéquat, conseillé*) suitable.
indiquer [ɛ̃dike] *vt* (*désigner*): ~ qch/qn à qn to point sth/sb out to sb; (*suj: pendule, aiguille*) to show; (*suj: étiquette, plan*) to show, indicate; (*faire connaître: médecin, restaurant*): ~ qch/qn à qn to tell sb of sth/sb; (*renseigner sur*) to point out, tell; (*déterminer: date, lieu*) to give, state; (*dénoter*) to indicate, point to.
indirect, e [ɛ̃diʀɛkt] *a* indirect.
indiscipline [ɛ̃disiplin] *nf* lack of discipline; **indiscipliné, e** *a* undisciplined; (*fig*) unmanageable.
indiscret, ète [ɛ̃diskʀɛ, -ɛt] *a* indiscreet.
indiscutable [ɛ̃diskytabl(ə)] *a* indisputable.
indispensable [ɛ̃dispɑ̃sabl(ə)] *a* indispensable; essential.
indisposer [ɛ̃dispoze] *vt* (*incommoder*) to upset; (*déplaire à*) to antagonize.
indistinct, e [ɛ̃distɛ̃, -ɛ̃kt(ə)] *a* indistinct; **indistinctement** *ad* (*voir, prononcer*) indistinctly; (*sans distinction*) indiscriminately.
individu [ɛ̃dividy] *nm* individual.
individuel, le [ɛ̃dividɥɛl] *a* (*gén*) individual; (*opinion, livret, contrôle, avantages*) personal; chambre ~le single room; maison ~le detached house.
indolore [ɛ̃dɔlɔʀ] *a* painless.
indomptable [ɛ̃dɔ̃tabl(ə)] *a* untameable; (*fig*) invincible, indomitable.
Indonésie [ɛ̃donezi] *nf* Indonesia.
indu, e [ɛ̃dy] *a*: à des heures ~es at some ungodly hour.
induire [ɛ̃dɥiʀ] *vt*: ~ qn en erreur to lead sb astray, mislead sb.
indulgent, e [ɛ̃dylʒɑ̃, -ɑ̃t] *a* (*parent, regard*) indulgent; (*juge, examinateur*) lenient.
indûment [ɛ̃dymɑ̃] *ad* wrongfully; without due cause.
industrie [ɛ̃dystʀi] *nf* industry; **industriel, le** *a* industrial // *nm* industrialist; manufacturer.
inébranlable [inebʀɑ̃labl(ə)] *a* (*masse, colonne*) solid; (*personne, certitude, foi*) steadfast, unwavering.
inédit, e [inedi, -it] *a* (*correspondance etc*) hitherto unpublished; (*spectacle, moyen*) novel, original.

ineffaçable [inefasabl(ə)] *a* indelible.

inefficace [inefikas] *a* (*remède, moyen*) ineffective; (*machine, employé*) inefficient.

inégal, e, aux [inegal, -o] *a* unequal; uneven.

inégalable [inegalabl(e)] *a* matchless.

inégalé, e [inegale] *a* unmatched, unequalled.

inerte [inɛʀt(ə)] *a* lifeless; inert.

inestimable [inɛstimabl(e)] *a* priceless; (*fig: bienfait*) invaluable.

inévitable [inevitabl(ə)] *a* unavoidable; (*fatal, habituel*) inevitable.

inexact, e [inɛgzakt] *a* inaccurate, inexact; unpunctual.

in extenso [inɛkstẽso] *ad* in full.

in extremis [inɛkstremis] *ad* at the last minute // *a* last-minute.

infaillible [ẽfajibl(ə)] *a* infallible.

infâme [ẽfɑm] *a* vile.

infanticide [ẽfɑ̃tisid] *nm/f* child-murderer/eress // *nm* (*meurtre*) infanticide.

infarctus [ẽfaʀktys] *nm*: ~ (du myocarde) coronary (thrombosis).

infatigable [ẽfatigabl(ə)] *a* tireless.

infect, e [ẽfɛkt] *a* vile; foul; (*repas, vin*) revolting.

infecter [ẽfɛkte] *vt* (*atmosphère, eau*) to contaminate; (*MÉD*) to infect; **s'~** to become infected *ou* septic; **infection** [-sjɔ̃] *nf* infection.

inférieur, e [ẽferjœʀ] *a* lower; (*en qualité, intelligence*) inferior; ~ à (*somme, quantité*) less *ou* smaller than; (*moins bon que*) inferior to.

infernal, e, aux [ẽfɛʀnal, -o] *a* (*chaleur, rythme*) infernal; (*méchanceté, complot*) diabolical.

infidèle [ẽfidɛl] *a* unfaithful.

infiltrer [ẽfiltʀe]: **s'~** *vi*: **s'~ dans** to penetrate into; (*liquide*) to seep into; (*fig: noyauter*) to infiltrate.

infime [ẽfim] *a* minute, tiny; (*inférieur*) lowly.

infini, e [ẽfini] *a* infinite // *nm* infinity; à l'~ (*MATH*) to infinity; (*agrandir, varier*) infinitely; (*interminablement*) endlessly; **infinité** *nf*: **une infinité de** an infinite number of.

infinitif [ẽfinitif] *nm* infinitive.

infirme [ẽfiʀm(ə)] *a* disabled // *nm/f* disabled person; ~ **de guerre** war cripple.

infirmer [ẽfiʀme] *vt* to invalidate.

infirmerie [ẽfiʀməʀi] *nf* sick bay.

infirmier, ière [ẽfiʀmje, -jɛʀ] *nm/f* nurse; **infirmière chef** sister; **infirmière visiteuse** ≈ district nurse.

infirmité [ẽfiʀmite] *nf* disability.

inflammable [ẽflamabl(ə)] *a* (in)flammable.

inflation [ẽflasjɔ̃] *nf* inflation.

inflexion [ẽflɛksjɔ̃] *nf* inflexion; ~ **de la tête** slight nod (of the head).

infliger [ẽfliʒe] *vt*: ~ **qch** (à qn) to inflict sth (on sb); (*amende, sanction*) to impose sth (on sb).

influence [ẽflyɑ̃s] *nf* influence; (*d'un médicament*) effect; **influencer** *vt* to influence; **influent, e** *a* influential.

influer [ẽflye]: ~ **sur** *vt* to have an influence upon.

informaticien, ne [ẽfɔʀmatisjẽ, -jɛn] *nm/f* computer scientist.

information [ẽfɔʀmasjɔ̃] *nf* (*renseignement*) pièce of information; (*PRESSE, TV: nouvelle*) item of news; ~**s** (*TV*) news *sg*; (*diffusion de renseignements, INFORM*) information; (*JUR*) inquiry, investigation; **voyage d'~** fact-finding trip.

informatique [ẽfɔʀmatik] *nf* (*technique*) data processing; (*science*) computer science // *a* computer *cpd*; **informatiser** *vt* to computerize.

informe [ẽfɔʀm(ə)] *a* shapeless.

informer [ẽfɔʀme] *vt*: ~ **qn (de)** to inform sb (of); **s'~ (de/si)** to inquire *ou* find out (about/whether *ou* if).

infortune [ẽfɔʀtyn] *nf* misfortune.

infraction [ẽfʀaksjɔ̃] *nf* offence; ~ **à** violation *ou* breach of; **être en** ~ to be in breach of the law.

infranchissable [ẽfʀɑ̃fisabl(ə)] *a* impassable; (*fig*) insuperable.

infrastructure [ẽfʀastʀyktyʀ] *nf* (*AVIAT, MIL*) ground installations *pl*; (*ÉCON: touristique etc*) infrastructure.

infuser [ẽfyze] *vt, vi* (*thé*) to brew; (*tisane*) to infuse; **infusion** *nf* (*tisane*) herb tea.

ingénier [ẽʒenje]: **s'~** *vi*: **s'~ à faire** to strive to do.

ingénierie [ẽʒenjəʀi] *nf* engineering.

ingénieur [ẽʒenjœʀ] *nm* engineer; ~ **du son** sound engineer.

ingénieux, euse [ẽʒenjø, -øz] *a* ingenious, clever.

ingénu, e [ẽʒeny] *a* ingenuous, artless.

ingérer [ẽʒeʀe]: **s'~** *vi*: **s'~ dans** to interfere in.

ingrat, e [ẽgʀa, -at] *a* (*personne*) ungrateful; (*sol*) poor; (*travail, sujet*) thankless; (*visage*) unprepossessing.

ingrédient [ẽgʀedjɑ̃] *nm* ingredient.

ingurgiter [ẽgyʀʒite] *vt* to swallow.

inhabitable [inabitabl(ə)] *a* uninhabitable.

inhérent, e [ineʀɑ̃, -ɑ̃t] *a*: ~ **à** inherent in.

inhibition [inibisjɔ̃] *nf* inhibition.

inhumain, e [inymẽ, -ɛn] *a* inhuman.

inhumer [inyme] *vt* to inter, bury.

inimitié [inimitje] *nf* enmity.

initial, e, aux [inisjal, -o] *a, nf* initial.

initiateur, trice [inisjatœʀ, -tʀis] *nm/f* initiator; (*d'une mode, technique*) innovator, pioneer.

initiative [inisjativ] *nf* initiative.

initier [inisje] *vt*: ~ **qn à** to initiate sb

into; *(faire découvrir: art, jeu)* to introduce sb to.

injecté, e [ɛ̃ʒɛkte] *a*: **yeux ~s de sang** bloodshot eyes.

injecter [ɛ̃ʒɛkte] *vt* to inject; **injection** [-sjɔ̃] *nf* injection; **à injection** *a* (AUTO) fuel injection *cpd*.

injure [ɛ̃ʒyʀ] *nf* insult, abuse *q*.

injurier [ɛ̃ʒyʀje] *vt* to insult, abuse; **injurieux, euse** *a* abusive, insulting.

injuste [ɛ̃ʒyst(ə)] *a* unjust, unfair; **injustice** *nf* injustice.

inlassable [ɛ̃lɑsabl(ə)] *a* tireless.

inné, e [ine] *a* innate, inborn.

innocent, e [inɔsɑ̃, -ɑ̃t] *a* innocent; **innocenter** *vt* to clear, prove innocent.

innombrable [inɔ̃bʀabl(ə)] *a* innumerable.

innommable [inɔmabl(ə)] *a* unspeakable.

innover [inɔve] *vi* to break new ground.

inoccupé, e [inɔkype] *a* unoccupied.

inoculer [inɔkyle] *vt (volontairement)* to inoculate; *(accidentellement)* to infect.

inodore [inɔdɔʀ] *a (gaz)* odourless; *(fleur)* scentless.

inoffensif, ive [inɔfɑsif, -iv] *a* harmless, innocuous.

inondation [inɔ̃dɑsjɔ̃] *nf* flooding *q*; flood.

inonder [inɔ̃de] *vt* to flood; *(fig)* to inundate, overrun.

inopérant, e [inɔpeʀɑ̃, -ɑ̃t] *a* inoperative, ineffective.

inopiné, e [inɔpine] *a* unexpected, sudden.

inopportun, e [inɔpɔʀtɶ, -yn] *a* ill-timed, untimely; inappropriate.

inoubliable [inublijabl(ə)] *a* unforgettable.

inouï, e [inwi] *a* unheard-of, extraordinary.

inox(ydable) [inɔks(idabl(ə))] *a* stainless.

inqualifiable [ɛ̃kalifjabl(ə)] *a* unspeakable.

inquiet, ète [ɛ̃kjɛ, -ɛt] *a* anxious.

inquiétant, e [ɛ̃kjetɑ̃, -ɑ̃t] *a* worrying, disturbing.

inquiéter [ɛ̃kjete] *vt* to worry; *(harceler)* to harass; **s'~** to worry; **s'~ de** to worry about; *(s'enquérir de)* to inquire about.

inquiétude [ɛ̃kjetyd] *nf* anxiety.

insaisissable [ɛ̃sezizabl(ə)] *a* elusive.

insatisfait, e [ɛ̃satisfɛ, -ɛt] *a (non comblé)* unsatisfied; unfulfilled; *(mécontent)* dissatisfied.

inscription [ɛ̃skʀipsjɔ̃] *nf* inscription; *(voir s'inscrire)* enrolment; registration.

inscrire [ɛ̃skʀiʀ] *vt (marquer: sur son calepin etc)* to note *ou* write down; (: *sur un mur, une affiche etc)* to write; (: *dans la pierre, le métal)* to inscribe;

(mettre: sur une liste, un budget etc) to put down; **~ qn à** *(club, école etc)* to enrol sb at; **s'~** *(pour une excursion etc)* to put one's name down; **s'~** *(à) (club, parti)* to join; *(université)* to register *ou* enrol *(at)*; *(examen, concours)* to register *(for)*; **s'~ en faux contre** to challenge.

insecte [ɛ̃sɛkt(ə)] *nm* insect; **insecticide** *nm* insecticide.

insensé, e [ɛ̃sɑse] *a* mad.

insensibiliser [ɛ̃sɑsibilize] *vt* to anaesthetize.

insensible [ɛ̃sɑsibl(ə)] *a (nerf, membre)* numb; *(dur, indifférent)* insensitive; *(imperceptible)* imperceptible.

insérer [ɛ̃seʀe] *vt* to insert; **s'~ dans** to fit into; to come within.

insigne [ɛ̃siɲ] *nm (d'un parti, club)* badge // *a* distinguished; **~s** *nmpl (d'une fonction)* insignia *pl*.

insignifiant, e [ɛ̃siɲifjɑ̃, -ɑ̃t] *a* insignificant; trivial.

insinuer [ɛ̃sinɥe] *vt* to insinuate, imply; **s'~ dans** *(fig)* to creep into.

insister [ɛ̃siste] *vi* to insist; *(s'obstiner)* to keep on; **~ sur** *(détail, note)* to stress.

insolation [ɛ̃sɔlɑsjɔ̃] *nf* (MÉD) sunstroke *q*.

insolent, e [ɛ̃sɔlɑ̃, -ɑ̃t] *a* insolent.

insolite [ɛ̃sɔlit] *a* strange, unusual.

insomnie [ɛ̃sɔmni] *nf* insomnia *q*, sleeplessness *q*.

insondable [ɛ̃sɔ̃dabl(ə)] *a* unfathomable.

insonoriser [ɛ̃sɔnɔʀize] *vt* to soundproof.

insouciant, e [ɛ̃susjɑ̃, -ɑ̃t] *a* carefree; *(imprévoyant)* heedless.

insoumis, e [ɛ̃sumi, -iz] *a (caractère, enfant)* rebellious, refractory; *(contrée, tribu)* unsubdued.

insoupçonnable [ɛ̃supsɔnabl(ə)] *a* unsuspected; *(personne)* above suspicion.

insoutenable [ɛ̃sutnabl(ə)] *a (argument)* untenable; *(chaleur)* unbearable.

inspecter [ɛ̃spɛkte] *vt* to inspect.

inspecteur, trice [ɛ̃spɛktɶ, -tʀis] *nm/f* inspector; **~ d'Académie** (regional) director of education; **~ des finances** ≈ tax inspector *(Brit)*, ≈ Internal Revenue Service agent *(US)*.

inspection [ɛ̃spɛksjɔ̃] *nf* inspection.

inspirer [ɛ̃spiʀe] *vt (gén)* to inspire // *vi (aspirer)* to breathe in; **s'~ de** *(suj: artiste)* to draw one's inspiration from.

instable [ɛ̃stabl(ə)] *a (meuble, équilibre)* unsteady; *(population, temps)* unsettled; *(régime, caractère)* unstable.

installation [ɛ̃stalɑsjɔ̃] *nf* putting in ou up; fitting out; settling in; *(appareils etc)* fittings *pl*, installations *pl*; **~s** *nfpl* equipment; facilities.

installer [ɛ̃stale] *vt (loger)*: **~ qn** to get sb settled; *(placer)* to put, place; *(meuble, gaz, électricité)* to put in; *(rideau,* *étagère, tente)* to put up; *(appartement)* to fit out; s'~ *(s'établir: artisan, dentiste etc)* to set o.s. up; *(se loger)* to settle (o.s.); *(emménager)* to settle in; *(sur un siège, à un emplacement)* to settle (down); *(fig: maladie, grève)* to take a firm hold.

instamment [ɛ̃stamɑ̃] *ad* urgently.

instance [ɛ̃stɑ̃s] *nf* (ADMIN: *autorité)* authority; ~s *nfpl (prières)* entreaties; affaire en ~ matter pending; être en ~ de divorce to be awaiting a divorce.

instant [ɛ̃stɑ̃] *nm* moment, instant; dans un ~ in a moment; à l'~ this instant; à tout *ou* chaque ~ at any moment; constantly; pour l'~ for the moment, for the time being; par ~s at times; de tous les ~s perpetual.

instantané, e [ɛ̃stɑ̃tane] *a (lait, café)* instant; *(explosion, mort)* instantaneous // *nm* snapshot.

instar [ɛ̃staʀ]: à l'~ de *prép* following the example of, like.

instaurer [ɛ̃stɔʀe] *vt* to institute.

instinct [ɛ̃stɛ̃] *nm* instinct.

instituer [ɛ̃stitɥe] *vt* to set up.

institut [ɛ̃stity] *nm* institute; ~ de beauté beauty salon; I~ Universitaire de Technologie (IUT) ≈ polytechnic.

instituteur, trice [ɛ̃stitytœʀ, -tʀis] *nm/f* (primary school) teacher.

institution [ɛ̃stitysjɔ̃] *nf* institution; *(collège)* private school.

instruction [ɛ̃stʀyksjɔ̃] *nf (enseignement, savoir)* education; (JUR: preliminary) investigation and hearing; ~s *nfpl* directions, instructions; ~ civique civics *sg.*

instruire [ɛ̃stʀɥiʀ] *vt (élèves)* to teach; *(recrues)* to train; (JUR: *affaire)* to conduct the investigation for; s'~ to educate o.s.; **instruit, e** *a* educated.

instrument [ɛ̃stʀymɑ̃] *nm* instrument; ~ à cordes/vent stringed/wind instrument; ~ de mesure measuring instrument; ~ de musique musical instrument; ~ de travail (working) tool.

insu [ɛ̃sy] *nm*: à l'~ de qn without sb knowing (it).

insubmersible [ɛ̃sybmɛʀsibl(ə)] *a* unsinkable.

insubordination [ɛ̃sybɔʀdinasjɔ̃] *nf* rebelliousness; (MIL) insubordination.

insuccès [ɛ̃syksɛ] *nm* failure.

insuffisant, e [ɛ̃syfizɑ̃, -ɑ̃t] *a* insufficient; *(élève, travail)* inadequate.

insuffler [ɛ̃syfle] *vt* to blow; to inspire.

insulaire [ɛ̃sylɛʀ] *a* island *cpd; (attitude)* insular.

insuline [ɛ̃sylin] *nf* insulin.

insulte [ɛ̃sylt(ə)] *nf* insult; **insulter** *vt* to insult.

insupportable [ɛ̃sypɔʀtabl(ə)] *a* unbearable.

insurger [ɛ̃syʀʒe]: s'~ *vi*: s'~ **(contre** to rise up *ou* rebel (against).

insurmontable [ɛ̃syʀmɔ̃tabl(ə)] *a (difficulté)* insuperable; *(aversion)* unconquerable.

intact, e [ɛ̃takt] *a* intact.

intangible [ɛ̃tɑ̃ʒibl(ə)] *a* intangible; *(principe)* inviolable.

intarissable [ɛ̃taʀisabl(ə)] *a* inexhaustible.

intégral, e, aux [ɛ̃tegʀal, -o] *a* complete.

intégrant, e [ɛ̃tegʀɑ̃, -ɑ̃t] *a*: faire partie ~e de to be an integral part of.

intègre [ɛ̃tegʀ(ə)] *a* upright.

intégrer [ɛ̃tegʀe] *vt* to integrate; s'~ à/ dans to become integrated into.

intellectuel, le [ɛ̃telɛktɥel] *a* intellectual // *nm/f* intellectual; *(péj)* highbrow.

intelligence [ɛ̃teliʒɑ̃s] *nf* intelligence; *(compréhension)*: l'~ de the understanding of; *(complicité)*: regard d'~ glance of complicity; *(accord)*: vivre en bonne ~ avec qn to be on good terms with sb.

intelligent, e [ɛ̃teliʒɑ̃, -ɑ̃t] *a* intelligent.

intempéries [ɛ̃tɑ̃peʀi] *nfpl* bad weather *sg.*

intempestif, ive [ɛ̃tɑ̃pɛstif, -iv] *a* untimely.

intenable [ɛ̃tnabl(ə)] *a (chaleur)* unbearable.

intendant, e [ɛ̃tɑ̃dɑ̃, -ɑ̃t] *nm/f* (MIL) quartermaster; (SCOL) bursar; *(d'une propriété)* steward.

intense [ɛ̃tɑ̃s] *a* intense; **intensif, ive** *a* intensive.

intenter [ɛ̃tɑ̃te] *vt*: ~ un procès contre *ou* à to start proceedings against.

intention [ɛ̃tɑ̃sjɔ̃] *nf* intention; (JUR) intent; avoir l'~ de faire to intend to do; à l'~ de *prép* for; *(renseignement)* for the benefit of; *(film, ouvrage)* aimed at; à cette ~ with this aim in view; **intentionné, e** *a*: bien intentionné well-meaning *ou* -intentioned; mal intentionné ill-intentioned.

intercaler [ɛ̃teʀkale] *vt* to insert.

intercepter [ɛ̃teʀsɛpte] *vt* to intercept; *(lumière, chaleur)* to cut off.

interchangeable [ɛ̃teʀʃɑ̃ʒabl(ə)] *a* interchangeable.

interclasse [ɛ̃teʀklas] *nm* (SCOL) break (between classes).

interdiction [ɛ̃teʀdiksjɔ̃] *nf* ban.

interdire [ɛ̃teʀdiʀ] *vt* to forbid; (ADMIN) to ban, prohibit; (: *journal, livre)* to ban; ~ à qn de faire to forbid sb to do, prohibit sb from doing; *(suj: empêchement)* to prevent sb from doing.

interdit, e [ɛ̃teʀdi, -it] *a (stupéfait)* taken aback // *nm* prohibition.

intéressant, e [ɛ̃teʀesɑ̃, -ɑ̃t] *a* interesting.

intéressé, e [ɛ̃teʀese] *a (parties)* involved, concerned; *(amitié, motifs)* self-interested.

intéresser [ɛ̃tɛrese] vt (captiver) to interest; (toucher) to be of interest to; (ADMIN: concerner) to affect, concern; s'~ à to be interested in.

intérêt [ɛ̃tɛrɛ] nm (aussi COMM) interest; (égoïsme) self-interest; avoir ~ à faire to do well to do.

intérieur, e [ɛ̃tɛrjœr] a (mur, escalier, poche) inside; (commerce, politique) domestic; (cour, calme, vie) inner; (navigation) inland // nm (d'une maison, d'un récipient etc) inside; (d'un pays, aussi: décor, mobilier) interior; (POL): l'I~ the Interior; à l'~ (de) inside; (fig) within.

intérim [ɛ̃terim] nm interim period; assurer l'~ (de) to deputize (for); par ~ a interim.

intérioriser [ɛ̃terjɔrize] vt to internalize.

interlocuteur, trice [ɛ̃tɛrlɔkytœr, -tris] nm/f speaker; son ~ the person he was speaking to.

interloquer [ɛ̃tɛrlɔke] vt to take aback.

intermède [ɛ̃tɛrmɛd] nm interlude.

intermédiaire [ɛ̃tɛrmedjɛr] a intermediate; middle; half-way // nm/f intermediary; (COMM) middleman; sans ~ directly; par l'~ de through.

intermittence [ɛ̃tɛrmitɑ̃s] nf: par ~ sporadically, intermittently.

internat [ɛ̃tɛrna] nm (SCOL) boarding school.

international, e, aux [ɛ̃tɛrnasjɔnal, -o] a, nm/f international.

interne [ɛ̃tɛrn(ə)] a internal // nm/f (SCOL) boarder; (MÉD) houseman.

interner [ɛ̃tɛrne] vt (POL) to intern; (MÉD) to confine to a mental institution.

interpeller [ɛ̃tɛrpele] vt (appeler) to call out to; (apostropher) to shout at; (POLICE) to take in for questioning; (POL) to question.

interphone [ɛ̃tɛrfɔn] nm intercom.

interposer [ɛ̃tɛrpoze] vt to interpose; s'~ vi to intervene; par personnes interposées through a third party.

interprète [ɛ̃tɛrprɛt] nm/f interpreter; (porte-parole) spokesman.

interpréter [ɛ̃tɛrprete] vt to interpret.

interrogateur, trice [ɛ̃terɔgatœr, -tris] a questioning, inquiring.

interrogatif, ive [ɛ̃terɔgatif, -iv] a (LING) interrogative.

interrogation [ɛ̃terɔgasjɔ̃] nf question; (SCOL) (written ou oral) test.

interrogatoire [ɛ̃terɔgatwar] nm (POLICE) questioning q; (JUR) cross-examination.

interroger [ɛ̃terɔʒe] vt to question; (INFORM) to consult; (SCOL) to test.

interrompre [ɛ̃terɔ̃pr(ə)] vt (gén) to interrupt; (travail, voyage) to break off, interrupt; s'~ to break off.

interrupteur [ɛ̃terptœr] nm switch.

interruption [ɛ̃terypsjɔ̃] nf interruption;

(pause) break.

interstice [ɛ̃tɛrstis] nm crack; slit.

interurbain [ɛ̃tɛryrbɛ̃] nm (TÉL) long-distance call service // a (TÉL) long-distance.

intervalle [ɛ̃tɛrval] nm (espace) space; (de temps) interval; dans l'~ in the meantime.

intervenir [ɛ̃tɛrvənir] vi (gén) to intervene; (survenir) to take place; ~ auprès de qn to intervene with sb.

intervention [ɛ̃tɛrvɑ̃sjɔ̃] nf intervention; (discours) paper; ~ chirurgicale (surgical) operation.

intervertir [ɛ̃tɛrvɛrtir] vt to invert (the order of), reverse.

interview [ɛ̃tɛrvju] nf interview.

intestin, e [ɛ̃tɛstɛ̃, -in] a internal // nm intestine.

intime [ɛ̃tim] a intimate; (vie, journal) private; (conviction) inmost; (dîner, cérémonie) quiet // nm/f close friend.

intimer [ɛ̃time] vt (JUR) to notify; ~ à qn l'ordre de faire to order sb to do.

intimité [ɛ̃timite] nf: dans l'~ in private; (sans formalités) with only a few friends, quietly.

intitulé, e [ɛ̃tityle] a entitled.

intolérable [ɛ̃tɔlerabl(ə)] a intolerable.

intoxication [ɛ̃tɔksikasjɔ̃] nf: ~ alimentaire food poisoning.

intoxiquer [ɛ̃tɔksike] vt to poison; (fig) to brainwash.

intraduisible [ɛ̃traduizibl(ə)] a untranslatable; (fig) inexpressible.

intraitable [ɛ̃trɛtabl(ə)] a inflexible, uncompromising.

intransigeant, e [ɛ̃trɑ̃ziʒɑ̃, -ɑ̃t] a intransigent; (morale) uncompromising.

intransitif, ive [ɛ̃trɑ̃zitif, -iv] a (LING) intransitive.

intrépide [ɛ̃trepid] a dauntless.

intrigue [ɛ̃trig] nf (scénario) plot.

intriguer [ɛ̃trige] vi to scheme // vt to puzzle, intrigue.

intrinsèque [ɛ̃trɛ̃sɛk] a intrinsic.

introduction [ɛ̃trɔdyksjɔ̃] nf introduction.

introduire [ɛ̃trɔduir] vt to introduce; (visiteur) to show in; (aiguille, clef): ~ qch dans to insert ou introduce sth into; s'~ dans to gain entry into; to get o.s. accepted into; (eau, fumée) to get into.

introuvable [ɛ̃truvabl(ə)] a which cannot be found; (COMM) unobtainable.

introverti, e [ɛ̃trɔvɛrti] nm/f introvert.

intrus, e [ɛ̃try, -yz] nm/f intruder.

intrusion [ɛ̃tryzjɔ̃] nf intrusion; interference.

intuition [ɛ̃tɥisjɔ̃] nf intuition.

inusable [inyzabl(ə)] a hard-wearing.

inusité, e [inyzite] a rarely used.

inutile [inytil] a useless; (superflu) unnecessary; **inutilisable** a unusable.

invalide [ɛ̃valid] a disabled // nm: ~ de

guerre disabled ex-serviceman.
invasion [ɛ̃vazjɔ̃] nf invasion.
invectiver [ɛ̃vɛktive] vt to hurl abuse at.
invendable [ɛ̃vɑ̃dabl(ə)] a unsaleable; unmarketable; **invendus** nmpl unsold goods.
inventaire [ɛ̃vɑ̃tɛʀ] nm inventory; (COMM: liste) stocklist; (: opération) stocktaking q; (fig) survey.
inventer [ɛ̃vɑ̃te] vt to invent; (subterfuge) to devise, invent; (histoire, excuse) to make up, invent; **inventeur** nm inventor; **inventif, ive** a inventive; **invention** [-sjɔ̃] nf invention.
inverse [ɛ̃vɛʀs(ə)] a reverse, opposite; inverse // nm inverse, reverse; **dans l'ordre ~** in the reverse order; **en sens ~** in⁻⁻ (ou from) the opposite direction; **~ment** ad conversely; **inverser** vt to invert, reverse; (ÉLEC) to reverse.
investir [ɛ̃vɛstiʀ] vt to invest; **investissement** nm investment; **investiture** nf investiture; (à une élection) nomination.
invétéré, e [ɛ̃vetere] a (habitude) ingrained; (bavard, buveur) inveterate.
invisible [ɛ̃vizibl(ə)] a invisible.
invitation [ɛ̃vitasjɔ̃] nf invitation.
invité, e [ɛ̃vite] nm/f guest.
inviter [ɛ̃vite] vt to invite; **~ qn à faire** (suj: chose) to induce ou tempt sb to do.
involontaire [ɛ̃vɔlɔ̃tɛʀ] a (mouvement) involuntary; (insulte) unintentional; (complice) unwitting.
invoquer [ɛ̃vɔke] vt (Dieu, muse) to call upon, invoke; (prétexte) to put forward (as an excuse); (loi, texte) to refer to.
invraisemblable [ɛ̃vʀɛsɑ̃blabl(ə)] a unlikely, improbable; incredible.
iode [jɔd] nm iodine.
irai etc vb voir **aller**.
Irak [iʀak] nm Iraq.
Iran [iʀɑ̃] nm Iran.
irions etc vb voir **aller**.
irlandais, e [iʀlɑ̃dɛ, -ɛz] a Irish // nm/f: **I~, e** Irishman/woman; **les I~** the Irish.
Irlande [iʀlɑ̃d] nf Ireland; **~ du Nord** Northern Ireland.
ironie [iʀɔni] nf irony; **ironique** a ironical; **ironiser** vi to be ironical.
irons etc vb voir **aller**.
irradier [iʀadje] vi to radiate // vt (aliment) to irradiate.
irraisonné, e [iʀɛzɔne] a irrational, unreasoned.
irrationnel, le [iʀasjɔnɛl] a irrational.
irréalisable [iʀealizabl(ə)] a unrealizable; impracticable.
irrécupérable [iʀekypeʀabl(ə)] a unreclaimable, beyond repair; (personne) beyond redemption.
irrécusable [iʀekyzabl(ə)] a unimpeachable; incontestable.
irréductible [iʀedyktibl(ə)] a indomitable, implacable.

irréel, le [iʀeɛl] a unreal.
irréfléchi, e [iʀefleʃi] a thoughtless.
irrégularité [iʀegylaʀite] nf irregularity; unevenness q.
irrégulier, ière [iʀegylje, -jɛʀ] a irregular; uneven; (élève, athlète) erratic.
irrémédiable [iʀemedjabl(ə)] a irreparable.
irréprochable [iʀepʀɔʃabl(ə)] a irreproachable, beyond reproach; (tenue) impeccable.
irrésistible [iʀezistibl(ə)] a irresistible; (preuve, logique) compelling.
irrespectueux, euse [iʀɛspɛktyø, -øz] a disrespectful.
irriguer [iʀige] vt to irrigate.
irritable [iʀitabl(ə)] a irritable.
irriter [iʀite] vt to irritate.
irruption [iʀypsjɔ̃] nf irruption q; **faire ~ dans** to burst into.
islamic [islamik] a Islamic.
Islande [islɑ̃d] nf Iceland.
isolant, e [izɔlɑ̃, -ɑ̃t] a insulating; (insonorisant) soundproofing.
isolation [izɔlasjɔ̃] nf insulation.
isolé, e [izɔle] a isolated; insulated.
isoler [izɔle] vt to isolate; (prisonnier) to put in solitary confinement; (ville) to cut off, isolate; (ÉLEC) to insulate; **isoloir** nm polling booth.
Israël [isʀaɛl] nm Israel; **israélien, ne** a, nm/f Israeli; **israélite** a Jewish // nm/f Jew/Jewess.
issu, e [isy] a: **~ de** descended from; (fig) stemming from // nf (ouverture, sortie) exit; (solution) way out, solution; (dénouement) outcome; **à l'~e de** at the conclusion ou close of; **rue sans ~e** dead end.
Italie [itali] nf Italy; **italien, ne** a, nm, nf Italian.
italique [italik] nm: **en ~** in italics.
itinéraire [itineʀɛʀ] nm itinerary, route.
IUT sigle m voir **institut**.
ivoire [ivwaʀ] nm ivory.
ivre [ivʀ(ə)] a drunk; **~ de** (colère, bonheur) wild with; **ivresse** nf drunkenness; **ivrogne** nm/f drunkard.

J

jachère [ʒaʃɛʀ] nf: **(être) en ~** (to lie) fallow.
jacinthe [ʒasɛ̃t] nf hyacinth.
jack [ʒak] nm jack plug.
jadis [ʒadis] ad in times past, formerly.
jaillir [ʒajiʀ] vi (liquide) to spurt out; (fig); to burst out; to flood out.
jais [ʒɛ] nm jet; **(d'un noir) de ~** jet-black.
jalon [ʒalɔ̃] nm range pole; (fig) milestone; **jalonner** vt to mark out; (fig) to mark, punctuate.
jalousie [ʒaluzi] nf jealousy; (store) (ve-

netian) blind.

jaloux, se [ʒalu, -uz] *a* jealous.

jamais [ʒamɛ] *ad* never; (*sans négation*) ever; ne ... ~ never; à ~ for ever.

jambe [ʒɑ̃b] *nf* leg.

jambon [ʒɑ̃bɔ̃] *nm* ham.

jante [ʒɑ̃t] *nf* (*wheel*) rim.

janvier [ʒɑ̃vje] *nm* January.

Japon [ʒapɔ̃] *nm* Japan; **japonais, e** *a*, *nm*, *nf* Japanese.

japper [ʒape] *vi* to yap, yelp.

jaquette [ʒakɛt] *nf* (*de cérémonie*) morning coat; (*de dame*) jacket.

jardin [ʒardɛ̃] *nm* garden; ~ d'enfants nursery school; **jardinage** *nm* gardening; **jardinier, ière** *nm/f* gardener // *nf* (*de fenêtre*) window box.

jarre [ʒaʀ] *nf* (earthenware) jar.

jarret [ʒaʀɛ] *nm* back of knee, ham; (*CULIN*) knuckle, shin.

jarretelle [ʒaʀtɛl] *nf* suspender (*Brit*), garter (*US*).

jarretière [ʒaʀtjɛʀ] *nf* garter.

jaser [ʒaze] *vi* to chatter, prattle; (*indiscrètement*) to gossip.

jatte [ʒat] *nf* basin, bowl.

jauge [ʒoʒ] *nf* (*instrument*) gauge; **jauger** *vt* (*fig*) to size up.

jaune [ʒon] *a*, *nm* yellow // *ad* (*fam*): rire ~ to laugh on the other side of one's face; ~ d'œuf (egg) yolk; **jaunir** *vi*, *vt* to turn yellow.

jaunisse [ʒonis] *nf* jaundice.

Javel [ʒavɛl] *nf voir* **eau**.

javelot [ʒavlo] *nm* javelin.

jazz [dʒaz] *nm* jazz.

J.-C. *sigle voir* **Jésus-Christ**.

je, j' [ʒ(ə)] *pronom* I.

jean [dʒin] *nm* jeans *pl*.

Jésus-Christ [ʒezykʀi(st)] *n* Jesus Christ; **600 avant/après** ~ *ou* J.-C. 600 B.C./A.D.

jet [ʒɛ] *nm* (*lancer*) throwing *q*, throw; (*jaillissement*) jet; spurt; (*de tuyau*) nozzle; (*avion*) [dʒɛt] jet; **du premier** ~ at the first attempt *or* shot; ~ d'eau fountain; spray.

jetable [ʒətabl(ə)] *a* disposable.

jetée [ʒəte] *nf* jetty; pier.

jeter [ʒəte] *vt* (*gén*) to throw; (*se défaire de*) to throw away *ou* out; (*son, lueur etc*) to shed *ou* cast; ~ qch à qn to throw sth to sb; (*de façon agressive*) to throw sth at sb; ~ un coup d'œil (à) to take a look (at); ~ un sort à qn to cast a spell on sb; se ~ dans (*fleuve*) to flow into.

jeton [ʒətɔ̃] *nm* (*au jeu*) counter; (*de téléphone*) token.

jette *etc vb voir* **jeter**.

jeu, x [ʒø] *nm* (*divertissement*, *TECH*: d'une *pièce*) play; (*TENNIS: partie*, *FOOTBALL etc*: *façon de jouer*) game; (*THÉÂTRE etc*) acting; (*au casino*): le ~ gambling; (*fonctionnement*) working, interplay; (*série d'objets*, *jouet*) set;

(*CARTES*) hand; en ~ at stake; at work; remettre en ~ to throw in; entrer/mettre en ~ to come/bring into play; ~ de cartes pack of cards; ~ d'échecs chess set; ~ de hasard game of chance; ~ de mots pun.

jeudi [ʒødi] *nm* Thursday.

jeun [ʒœ̃]: à ~ *ad* on an empty stomach.

jeune [ʒœn] *a* young; ~ fille *nf* girl; ~ homme *nm* young man.

jeûne [ʒøn] *nm* fast.

jeunesse [ʒœnɛs] *nf* youth; (*aspect*) youthfulness; youngness.

joaillerie [ʒɔajʀi] *nf* jewel trade; jewellery; **joaillier, ière** *nm/f* jeweller.

joie [ʒwa] *nf* joy.

joindre [ʒwɛ̃dʀ(ə)] *vt* to join; (*à une lettre*): ~ qch à to enclose sth with; (*contacter*) to contact, get in touch with; ~ les mains to put one's hands together; se ~ à to join.

joint, e [ʒwɛ̃, ʒwɛ̃t] *a*: pièce ~e enclosure // *nm* joint; (*ligne*) join; ~ de culasse cylinder head gasket; ~ de robinet washer.

joli, e [ʒɔli] *a* pretty, attractive; c'est du ~! (*ironique*) that's very nice!; c'est bien ~, mais... that's all very well but...

jonc [ʒɔ̃] *nm* (bul)rush.

joncher [ʒɔ̃ʃe] *vt* (*suj: choses*) to be strewed on.

jonction [ʒɔ̃ksjɔ̃] *nf* joining; (point de) ~ junction.

jongleur, euse [ʒɔ̃glœʀ, -øz] *nm/f* juggler.

jonquille [ʒɔ̃kij] *nf* daffodil.

Jordanie [ʒɔʀdani] *nf*: la ~ Jordan.

joue [ʒu] *nf* cheek; mettre en ~ to take aim at.

jouer [ʒwe] *vt* to play; (*somme d'argent*, *réputation*) to stake, wager; (*pièce, rôle*) to perform; (*film*) to show; (*simuler: sentiment*) to affect, feign // *vi* to play; (*THÉÂTRE*, *CINÉMA*) to act, perform; (*bois, porte: se voiler*) to warp; (*clef, pièce: avoir du jeu*) to be loose; ~ sur (*miser*) to gamble on; ~ de (*MUS*) to play; ~ des coudes to use one's elbows; ~ à (*jeu, sport, roulette*) to play; ~ avec (*risquer*) to gamble with; se ~ de (*difficultés*) to make light of; to deceive; ~ un tour à qn to play a trick on sb; ~ serré to play a close game; ~ de malchance to be dogged with ill-luck.

jouet [ʒwe] *nm* toy; être le ~ de (*illusion etc*) to be the victim of.

joueur, euse [ʒwœʀ, -øz] *nm/f* player; être beau ~ to be a good loser.

joufflu, e [ʒufly] *a* chubby-cheeked.

joug [ʒu] *nm* yoke.

jouir [ʒwiʀ]: ~ de *vt* to enjoy; **jouissance** *nf* pleasure; (*JUR*) use.

joujou [ʒuʒu] *nm* (*fam*) toy.

jour [ʒuʀ] *nm* day; (*opposé à la nuit*)

day, daytime; (*clarté*) daylight; (*fig:
aspect*) light; (*ouverture*) opening; au ~
le ~ from day to day; de nos ~s these
days; il fait ~ it's daylight; au grand ~
(*fig*) in the open; mettre au ~ to disclose; mettre à ~ to update; donner le ~
à to give birth to; voir le ~ to be born.

journal, aux [ʒurnal, -o] *nm*
(news)paper; (*personnel*) journal, diary;
~ parlé/télévisé radio/television news *sg*;
~ de bord log.

journalier, ière [ʒurnalje, -jɛr] *a*
daily; (*banal*) everyday.

journalisme [ʒurnalism(ə)] *nm* journal-
ism; **journaliste** *nm/f* journalist.

journée [ʒurne] *nf* day; la ~ continue
the 9 to 5 working day.

journellement [ʒurnɛlmɑ̃] *ad* daily.

joyau, x [ʒwajo] *nm* gem, jewel.

joyeux, euse [ʒwajø, -øz] *a* joyful, merry; ~ Noël! merry Christmas!; ~
anniversaire! happy birthday!

jubiler [ʒybile] *vi* to be jubilant, exult.

jucher [ʒyʃe] *vt, vi* to perch.

judas [ʒyda] *nm* (*trou*) spy-hole.

judiciaire [ʒydisjɛr] *a* judicial.

judicieux, euse [ʒydisjø, -øz] *a* judi-
cious.

judo [ʒydo] *nm* judo.

juge [ʒyʒ] *nm* judge; ~ d'instruction ex-
amining (*Brit*) ou committing (*US*) magistrate; ~ de paix justice of the peace.

jugé [ʒyʒe]: au ~ *ad* by guesswork.

jugement [ʒyʒmɑ̃] *nm* judgment; (*JUR:
au pénal*) sentence; (: *au civil*) decision.

juger [ʒyʒe] *vt* to judge; ~ qn/qch
satisfaisant to consider sb/sth (to be)
satisfactory; ~ bon de faire to see fit to
do; ~ de *vt* to appreciate.

juif, ive [ʒɥif, -iv] *a* Jewish // *nm/f* Jew/
Jewess.

juillet [ʒɥijɛ] *nm* July.

juin [ʒɥɛ̃] *nm* June.

jumeau, elle, x [ʒymo, -ɛl] *a, nm/f*
twin; **jumelles** *nfpl* binoculars.

jumeler [ʒymle] *vt* to twin.

jumelle [ʒymɛl] *a, nf voir* **jumeau**.

jument [ʒymɑ̃] *nf* mare.

jungle [ʒɔ̃gl(ə)] *nf* jungle.

jupe [ʒyp] *nf* skirt.

jupon [ʒypɔ̃] *nm* waist slip.

juré, e [ʒyre] *nm/f* juror.

jurer [ʒyre] *vt* (*obéissance etc*) to swear,
vow // *vi* (*dire des jurons*) to swear,
curse; (*dissoner*): ~ (avec) to clash
(with); (*s'engager*): ~ de faire/que to
swear *ou* vow to do/that; (*affirmer*): ~
que to swear *ou* vouch that; ~ de qch
(*s'en porter garant*) to swear to sth.

juridique [ʒyridik] *a* legal.

juron [ʒyrɔ̃] *nm* curse, swearword.

jury [ʒyri] *nm* jury; board.

jus [ʒy] *nm* juice; (*de viande*) gravy,
(meat) juice; ~ de fruit fruit juice.

jusque [ʒysk(ə)]: **jusqu'à** *prép* (*endroit*)

as far as, (up) to; (*moment*) until, till;
(*limite*) up to; ~ **sur/dans** up to; (*y compris*) even on/in; **jusqu'à ce que** until;
jusqu'à présent until now.

juste [ʒyst(ə)] *a* (*équitable*) just, fair;
(*légitime*) just, justified; (*exact, vrai*)
right; (*étroit, insuffisant*) tight // *ad*
right; tight; (*chanter*) in tune; (*seulement*) just; ~ **assez/au-dessus** just
enough/above; **au** ~ exactly; le ~ milieu
the happy medium; **~ment** *ad* rightly;
justly; (*précisément*) just, precisely;
justesse *nf* (*précision*) accuracy;
(*d'une remarque*) aptness; (*d'une opinion*) soundness; **de justesse** just.

justice [ʒystis] *nf* (*équité*) fairness, justice; (*ADMIN*) justice; **rendre la** ~ to dispense justice; **rendre** ~ à qn to do sb
justice.

justicier, ière [ʒystisje, -jɛr] *nm/f*
judge, righter of wrongs.

justifier [ʒystifje] *vt* to justify; ~ de *vt*
to prove.

juteux, euse [ʒytø, -øz] *a* juicy.

juvénile [ʒyvenil] *a* young, youthful.

K

K [ka] *nm* (*INFORM*) K.

kaki [kaki] *a inv* khaki.

kangourou [kɑ̃guru] *nm* kangaroo.

karaté [karate] *nm* karate.

karting [kartiŋ] *nm* go-carting, karting.

kermesse [kɛrmɛs] *nf* bazaar, (charity)
fête; village fair.

kidnapper [kidnape] *vt* to kidnap.

kilogramme [kilogram] *nm*, **kilo** [kilo]
nm kilogramme.

kilométrage [kilometraʒ] *nm* number
of kilometres travelled, ≈ mileage.

kilomètre [kilomɛtr(ə)] *nm* kilometre.

kilométrique [kilometrik] *a* (*distance*)
in kilometres.

kinésithérapeute [kineziterapøt] *nm/f*
physiotherapist.

kiosque [kjɔsk(ə)] *nm* kiosk, stall.

klaxon [klaksɔn] *nm* horn; **klaxonner**
vi, vt to hoot (*Brit*), honk (*US*).

km. *abr de* **kilomètre**; **~/h** (=
kilomètres/heure) ≈ m.p.h. (= *miles per
hour*).

Ko [kao] *nm* (*INFORM*: = *kilo-octet*) K.

K.-O. [kao] *a inv* (knocked) out.

kyste [kist(ə)] *nm* cyst.

L

l' [l] *dét voir* **le**.

la [la] *dét voir* **le** // *nm* (*MUS*) A; (*en
chantant la gamme*) la.

là [la] *ad* (*voir aussi* **-ci, celui**) there;
(*ici*) here; (*dans le temps*) then; elle
n'est pas ~ she isn't here; c'est ~ que

this is where; ~ **où** where; **de** ~ *(fig)*
hence; **par** ~ *(fig)* by that; **tout est** ~
(fig) that's what it's all about; ~**-bas** *ad*
there.
label [labɛl] *nm* stamp, seal.
labeur [labœʀ] *nm* toil *q*, toiling *q*.
labo [labo] *abr m* (= *laboratoire*) lab.
laboratoire [labɔʀatwaʀ] *nm* laboratory; ~ **de langues** language laboratory.
laborieux, euse [labɔʀjø, -øz] *a*
(tâche) laborious; **classes** ~**euses** working classes.
labour [labuʀ] *nm* ploughing *q*; ~**s** *nmpl*
ploughed fields; **cheval de** ~ plough- *ou*
cart-horse; **bœuf de** ~ ox *(pl* oxen).
labourer [labuʀe] *vt* to plough; *(fig)* to
make deep gashes *ou* furrows in.
labyrinthe [labiʀɛ̃t] *nm* labyrinth, maze.
lac [lak] *nm* lake.
lacer [lase] *vt* to lace *ou* do up.
lacérer [laseʀe] *vt* to tear to shreds.
lacet [lasɛ] *nm* *(de chaussure)* lace; *(de
route)* sharp bend; *(piège)* snare.
lâche [lɑʃ] *a* *(poltron)* cowardly; *(des-
serré)* loose, slack // *nm/f* coward.
lâcher [lɑʃe] *nm* *(de ballons, oiseaux)*
release // *vt* to let go of; *(ce qui tombe,
abandonner)* to drop; *(oiseau, animal:
libérer)* to release, set free; *(fig: mot,
remarque)* to let slip, come out with;
(SPORT: distancer) to leave behind // *vi*
(fil, amarres) to break, give way;
(freins) to fail; ~ **les amarres** *(NAVIG)*
to cast off (the moorings); ~ **les chiens**
to unleash the dogs; ~ **prise** to let go.
lâcheté [lɑʃte] *nf* cowardice; lowness.
lacrymogène [lakʀimɔʒɛn] *a:* **gaz** ~
teargas.
lacté, e [lakte] *a (produit, régime)* milk
cpd.
lacune [lakyn] *nf* gap.
là-dedans [ladədɑ̃] *ad* inside (there), in
it; *(fig)* in that; **là-dessous** *ad* underneath, under there; *(fig)* behind that;
là-dessus *ad* on there; *(fig)* at that
point; about that.
ladite [ladit] *dét voir* **ledit**.
lagune [lagyn] *nf* lagoon.
là-haut [la'o] *ad* up there.
laïc [laik] *a, nm/f =* **laïque**.
laid, e [lɛ, lɛd] *a* ugly; **laideur** *nf* ugli-
ness *q*.
lainage [lɛnaʒ] *nm* woollen garment;
woollen material.
laine [lɛn] *nf* wool.
laïque [laik] *a* lay, civil; *(SCOL)* state
cpd // *nm/f* layman/woman.
laisse [lɛs] *nf* *(de chien)* lead, leash;
tenir en ~ to keep on a lead *ou* leash.
laisser [lɛse] *vt* to leave // *vb auxiliaire:*
~ **qn faire** to let sb do; **se** ~ **aller** to let
o.s. go; **laisse-toi faire** let me *(ou* him)
do it; ~**-aller** *nm* carelessness, slovenli-
ness; **laissez-passer** *nm inv* pass.
lait [lɛ] *nm* milk; **frère/sœur de** ~ foster

brother/sister; ~ **condensé/concentré**
evaporated/condensed milk; **laiterie** *nf*
dairy; **laitier, ière** *a* dairy *cpd* // *nm/f*
milkman/dairywoman.
laiton [lɛtɔ̃] *nm* brass.
laitue [lɛty] *nf* lettuce.
laïus [lajys] *nm (péj)* spiel.
lambeau, x [lɑ̃bo] *nm* scrap; **en** ~**x** in
tatters, tattered.
lambris [lɑ̃bʀi] *nm* panelling *q*.
lame [lam] *nf* blade; *(vague)* wave; *(lamelle)* strip; ~ **de fond** ground swell *q*;
~ **de rasoir** razor blade.
lamelle [lamɛl] *nf* thin strip *ou* blade.
lamentable [lamɑ̃tabl(ə)] *a* appalling;
pitiful.
lamenter [lamɑ̃te]: **se** ~ *vi:* **se** ~ *(sur)*
to moan (over).
lampadaire [lɑ̃padɛʀ] *nm (de salon)*
standard lamp; *(dans la rue)* street
lamp.
lampe [lɑ̃p(ə)] *nf* lamp; *(TECH)* valve;
~ **de poche** torch *(Brit)*, flashlight *(US)*;
~ **à souder** blowlamp.
lampion [lɑ̃pjɔ̃] *nm* Chinese lantern.
lance [lɑ̃s] *nf* spear; ~ **d'incendie** fire
hose.
lancée [lɑ̃se] *nf:* **être/continuer sur sa** ~
to be under way/keep going.
lancement [lɑ̃smɑ̃] *nm* launching.
lance-pierres [lɑ̃spjɛʀ] *nm inv* catapult.
lancer [lɑ̃se] *nm (SPORT)* throwing *q*,
throw // *vt* to throw; *(émettre, projeter)*
to throw out, send out; *(produit, fusée,
bateau, artiste)* to launch; *(injure)* to
hurl, fling; *(proclamation, mandat
d'arrêt)* to issue; ~ **qch à qn** to throw
sth to sb; *(de façon agressive)* to throw
sth at sb; **se** ~ *vi (prendre de l'élan)* to
build up speed; *(se précipiter)*: **se** ~ **sur**
ou **contre** to rush at; **se** ~ **dans** *(discussion)* to launch into; *(aventure)* to embark on; ~ **du poids** *nm* putting the shot.
lancinant, e [lɑ̃sinɑ̃, -ɑ̃t] *a (regrets etc)*
haunting; *(douleur)* shooting.
landau [lɑ̃do] *nm* pram *(Brit)*, baby carriage *(US)*.
lande [lɑ̃d] *nf* moor.
langage [lɑ̃gaʒ] *nm* language.
langer [lɑ̃ʒe] *vt* to change (the nappy
(Brit) ou diaper *(US)* of).
langouste [lɑ̃gust(ə)] *nf* crayfish *inv*;
langoustine *nf* Dublin Bay prawn.
langue [lɑ̃g] *nf (ANAT, CULIN)* tongue;
(LING) language; **tirer la** ~ **(à)** to stick
out one's tongue (at); **de** ~ **française**
French-speaking; ~ **maternelle** native
language, mother tongue; ~ **verte** slang;
~ **vivante** modern language.
langueur [lɑ̃gœʀ] *nf* languidness.
languir [lɑ̃giʀ] *vi* to languish; *(conversation)* to flag; **faire** ~ **qn** to keep sb waiting.
lanière [lanjɛʀ] *nf (de fouet)* lash; *(de
valise, bretelle)* strap.

lanterne [lɑ̃tɛrn(ə)] *nf* (*portable*) lantern; (*électrique*) light, lamp; (*de voiture*) (side)light.

laper [lape] *vt* to lap up.

lapidaire [lapidɛr] *a* stone *cpd*; (*fig*) terse.

lapin [lapɛ̃] *nm* rabbit; (*peau*) rabbitskin; (*fourrure*) cony.

Laponie [laponi] *nf* Lapland.

laps [laps] *nm*: ~ de temps space of time, time *q*.

laque [lak] *nf* lacquer; (*brute*) shellac; (*pour cheveux*) hair spray.

laquelle [lakɛl] *pronom voir* **lequel**.

larcin [larsɛ̃] *nm* theft.

lard [lar] *nm* (*graisse*) fat; (*bacon*) (streaky) bacon.

lardon [lardɔ̃] *nm*: ~s chopped bacon.

large [larʒ(ə)] *a* wide; broad; (*fig*) generous // *ad*: calculer/voir ~ to allow extra/think big // *nm* (*largeur*): 5 m de ~ 5 m wide *ou* in width; (*mer*): le ~ the open sea; au ~ de off; ~ d'esprit broadminded; ~**ment** *ad* widely; greatly; easily; generously; **largesse** *nf* generosity; **largesses** liberalities; **largeur** *nf* (*qu'on mesure*) width; (*impression visuelle*) wideness, width; breadth; broadness.

larguer [large] *vt* to drop: ~ les amarres to cast off (the moorings).

larme [larm(ə)] *nf* tear; (*fig*) drop; en ~s in tears; **larmoyer** *vi* (*yeux*) to water; (*se plaindre*) to whimper.

larvé, e [larve] *a* (*fig*) latent.

laryngite [larɛ̃ʒit] *nf* laryngitis.

las, lasse [lɑ, lɑs] *a* weary.

laser [lazɛr] *nm*: (*rayon*) ~ laser (beam); **chaîne** ~ compact disc (player); **disque** ~ compact disc.

lasse [lɑs] *af voir* **las**.

lasser [lɑse] *vt* to weary, tire; **se** ~ **de** to grow weary *ou* tired of.

latéral, e, aux [lateral, -o] *a* side *cpd*, lateral.

latin, e [latɛ̃, -in] *a, nm, nf* Latin.

latitude [latityd] *nf* latitude.

latte [lat] *nf* lath, slat; (*de plancher*) board.

lauréat, e [lɔrea, -at] *nm/f* winner.

laurier [lɔrje] *nm* (*BOT*) laurel; (*CULIN*) bay leaves *pl*; ~s *nmpl* (*fig*) laurels.

lavable [lavabl(ə)] *a* washable.

lavabo [lavabo] *nm* washbasin; ~s *nmpl* toilet *sg*.

lavage [lavaʒ] *nm* washing *q*, wash; ~ de cerveau brainwashing *q*.

lavande [lavɑ̃d] *nf* lavender.

lave [lav] *nf* lava *q*.

lave-glace [lavglas] *nm* windscreen (*Brit*) *ou* windshield (*US*) washer.

laver [lave] *vt* to wash; (*tache*) to wash off; **se** ~ *vi* to have a wash, wash; **se** ~ **les mains/dents** to wash one's hands/clean one's teeth; ~ **qn de** (*accusation*)

to clear sb of; **laverie** *nf*: laverie (automatique) launderette.

lavette [lavɛt] *nf* dish cloth; (*fam*) drip.

laveur, euse [lavœr, -øz] *nm/f* cleaner.

lave-vaisselle [lavvɛsɛl] *nm inv* dishwasher.

lavoir [lavwar] *nm* wash house.

laxatif, ive [laksatif, -iv] *a, nm* laxative.

le(l'), la, les [l(ə), la, le] ♦ *article défini*
1 the; le livre/la pomme/l'arbre the book/the apple/the tree; les étudiants the students

2 (*noms abstraits*): le courage/l'amour/la jeunesse courage/love/youth

3 (*indiquant la possession*): se casser la jambe *etc* to break one's leg *etc*; levez la main put your hand up; avoir les yeux gris/le nez rouge to have grey eyes/a red nose

4 (*temps*): le matin/soir in the morning/evening; mornings/evenings; le jeudi *etc* (*d'habitude*) on Thursdays *etc*; (*ce jeudi-là etc*) on (the) Thursday

5 (*distribution, évaluation*) a, an; 10 F le mètre/kilo 10 F a *ou* per metre/kilo; le tiers/quart a third/quarter of

♦ *pronom* **1** (*personne: mâle*) him; (: *femelle*) her; (: *pluriel*) them; je le/la/les vois I can see him/her/them

2 (*animal, chose: sing*) it; (: *pl*) them; je le (*ou* la) vois I can see it; je les vois I can see them

3 (*remplaçant une phrase*): je ne le savais pas I didn't know (about it); il était riche et ne l'est plus he was once rich but no longer is

lécher [leʃe] *vt* to lick; (*laper: lait, eau*) to lick *ou* lap up; ~ les vitrines to go window-shopping.

leçon [ləsɔ̃] *nf* lesson; faire la ~ à (*fig*) to give a lecture to; ~s de conduite driving lessons.

lecteur, trice [lɛktœr, -tris] *nm/f* reader; (*d'université*) foreign language assistant // *nm* (*TECH*): ~ de cassettes cassette player; ~ de disquette disk drive.

lecture [lɛktyr] *nf* reading.

ledit [lədi], **ladite** [ladit], *mpl* **lesdits** [ledi], *fpl* **lesdites** [ledit] *dét* the aforesaid.

légal, e, aux [legal, -o] *a* legal.

légende [leʒɑ̃d] *nf* (*mythe*) legend; (*de carte, plan*) key; (*de dessin*) caption.

léger, ère [leʒe, -ɛr] *a* light; (*bruit, retard*) slight; (*superficiel*) thoughtless; (*volage*) free and easy; flighty; à la légère *ad* (*parler, agir*) rashly, thoughtlessly; **légèrement** *ad* lightly; thoughtlessly; slightly.

législatif, ive [leʒislatif, -iv] *a* legislative; **législatives** *nfpl* general election *sg*.

législature [leʒislatyr] *nf* legislature; term (of office).

légitime [leʒitim] *a* (*JUR*) lawful, legitimate; (*fig*) rightful, legitimate; **en état de ~ défense** in self-defence.

legs [lɛg] *nm* legacy.

léguer [lege] *vt*: **~ qch à qn** (*JUR*) to bequeath sth to sb; (*fig*) to hand sth down *ou* pass sth on to sb.

légume [legym] *nm* vegetable.

lendemain [lɑ̃dmɛ̃] *nm*: **le ~** the next *ou* following day; **le ~ matin/soir** the next *ou* following morning/evening; **le ~ de** the day after; **sans ~** short-lived.

lent, e [lɑ̃, lɑ̃t] *a* slow; **lentement** *ad* slowly; **lenteur** *nf* slowness *q*.

lentille [lɑ̃tij] *nf* (*OPTIQUE*) lens *sg*; (*CULIN*) lentil.

léopard [leɔpaʀ] *nm* leopard.

lèpre [lɛpʀ(ə)] *nf* leprosy.

lequel [ləkɛl], **laquelle** [lakɛl], *mpl* **lesquels**, *fpl* **lesquelles** [lekɛl] (*avec à, de*: **auquel, duquel** etc) *pronom* (*interrogatif*) which, which one; (*relatif: personne: sujet*) who; (*: objet, après préposition*) whom; (*: chose*) which // *a*: **auquel cas** in which case.

les [le] *dét voir* **le**.

lesbienne [lɛsbjɛn] *nf* lesbian.

lesdits [ledi], **lesdites** [ledit] *dét voir* **ledit**.

léser [leze] *vt* to wrong.

lésiner [lezine] *vi*: **~ (sur)** to skimp (on).

lésion [lezjɔ̃] *nf* lesion, damage *q*.

lesquels, lesquelles [lekɛl] *pronom voir* **lequel**.

lessive [lesiv] *nf* (*poudre*) washing powder; (*linge*) washing *q*, wash.

lessiver [lesive] *vt* to wash.

lest [lɛst] *nm* ballast.

leste [lɛst(ə)] *a* sprightly, nimble.

lettre [lɛtʀ(ə)] *nf* letter; **~s** *nfpl* literature *sg*; (*SCOL*) arts (subjects); **à la ~** literally; **en toutes ~s** in full.

lettré, e [letʀe] *a* well-read.

leucémie [løsemi] *nf* leukaemia.

leur [lœʀ] ♦ *a possessif* their; **~ maison** their house; **~s amis** their friends ♦ *pronom* **1** (*objet indirect*) (to) them; **je ~ ai dit la vérité** I told them the truth; **je le ~ ai donné** I gave it to them, I gave them it **2** (*possessif*): **le(la) ~, les ~s** theirs.

leurre [lœʀ] *nm* (*appât*) lure; (*fig*) delusion; snare.

leurrer [lœʀe] *vt* to delude, deceive.

levain [ləvɛ̃] *nm* leaven.

levé, e [ləve] *a*: **être ~** to be up.

levée [ləve] *nf* (*POSTES*) collection; (*CARTES*) trick; **~ de boucliers** general outcry.

lever [ləve] *vt* (*vitre, bras etc*) to raise; (*soulever de terre, supprimer: interdiction, siège*) to lift; (*séance*) to close; (*impôts, armée*) to levy // *vi* to rise // *nm*: **au ~** on getting up; **se ~** *vi* to get up; (*soleil*) to rise; (*jour*) to

break; (*brouillard*) to lift; **~ du jour** daybreak; **~ de rideau** curtain raiser; **~ de soleil** sunrise.

levier [ləvje] *nm* lever.

lèvre [lɛvʀ(ə)] *nf* lip.

lévrier [levʀije] *nm* greyhound.

levure [ləvyʀ] *nf* yeast; **~ chimique** baking powder.

lexique [lɛksik] *nm* vocabulary; lexicon.

lézard [lezaʀ] *nm* lizard.

lézarde [lezaʀd(ə)] *nf* crack.

liaison [ljɛzɔ̃] *nf* link; (*amoureuse*) affair; (*PHONÉTIQUE*) liaison; **entrer/être en ~ avec** to get/be in contact with.

liane [ljan] *nf* creeper.

liant, e [ljɑ̃, -ɑ̃t] *a* sociable.

liasse [ljas] *nf* wad, bundle.

Liban [libɑ̃] *nm*: **le ~** (the) Lebanon; **libanais, e** *a, nm/f* Lebanese.

libeller [libele] *vt* (*chèque, mandat*): **~ (au nom de)** to make out (to); (*lettre*) to word.

libellule [libelyl] *nf* dragonfly.

libéral, e, aux [liberal, -o] *a, nm/f* liberal.

libérer [libere] *vt* (*délivrer*) to free, liberate; (*: moralement, PSYCH*) to liberate; (*relâcher, dégager: gaz*) to release; to discharge; **se ~** *vi* (*de rendez-vous*) to get out of previous engagements.

liberté [liberte] *nf* freedom; (*loisir*) free time; **~s** *nfpl* (*privautés*) liberties; **mettre/être en ~** to set/be free; **en ~ provisoire/surveillée/conditionnelle** on bail/probation/parole; **~s individuelles** personal freedom *pl*.

libraire [libʀɛʀ] *nm/f* bookseller.

librairie [libʀɛʀi] *nf* bookshop.

libre [libʀ(ə)] *a* free; (*route*) clear; (*place etc*) vacant; empty; not engaged; not taken; (*SCOL*) non-state; **de ~** (*place*) free; **~ de qch/de faire** free from sth/to do; **~ arbitre** free will; **~-échange** *nm* free trade; **~-service** *nm* self-service store.

Libye [libi] *nf*: **la ~** Libya.

licence [lisɑ̃s] *nf* (*permis*) permit; (*diplôme*) degree; (*liberté*) liberty; licence (*Brit*), license (*US*); licentiousness; **licencié, e** *nm/f* (*SCOL*): **licencié ès lettres/en droit**; ≈ Bachelor of Arts/Law; (*SPORT*) member of a sports federation.

licencier [lisɑ̃sje] *vt* (*renvoyer*) to dismiss; (*débaucher*) to make redundant; to lay off.

licite [lisit] *a* lawful.

lie [li] *nf* dregs *pl*, sediment.

lié, e [lje] *a*: **très ~ avec** very friendly with *ou* close to; **~ par** (*serment*) bound by.

liège [ljɛʒ] *nm* cork.

lien [ljɛ̃] *nm* (*corde, fig: affectif*) bond; (*rapport*) link, connection; **~ de parenté** family tie.

lier [lje] *vt* (*attacher*) to tie up; (*joindre*)

to link up; (*fig: unir, engager*) to bind; (*CULIN*) to thicken; ~ qch à to tie *ou* link sth to; ~ conversation avec to strike up a conversation with; se ~ avec to make friends with.

lierre [ljɛʀ] *nm* ivy.

liesse [ljɛs] *nf*: être en ~ to be celebrating *ou* jubilant.

lieu, x [ljø] *nm* place // *nmpl* (*habitation*) premises; (*endroit: d'un accident etc*) scene *sg*; en ~ sûr in a safe place; en premier/dernier ~ in the first place/ lastly; avoir ~ to take place; avoir ~ de faire to have grounds for doing; tenir ~ de to take the place of; to serve as; donner ~ à to give rise to; au ~ de instead of.

lieu-dit *nm* (*pl* lieux-dits) [ljødi] locality.

lieutenant [ljøtnã] *nm* lieutenant.

lièvre [ljɛvʀ(ə)] *nm* hare.

ligament [ligamã] *nm* ligament.

ligne [liɲ] *nf* (*gén*) line; (*TRANSPORTS: liaison*) service; (: *trajet*) route; (*silhouette*) figure; entrer en ~ de compte to come into it.

lignée [liɲe] *nf* line; lineage; descendants *pl*.

ligoter [ligɔte] *vt* to tie up.

ligue [lig] *nf* league; **liguer** *vt*: se liguer contre (*fig*) to combine against.

lilas [lila] *nm* lilac.

limace [limas] *nf* slug.

limaille [limaj] *nf*: ~ de fer iron filings *pl*.

limande [limãd] *nf* dab.

lime [lim] *nf* file; ~ à ongles nail file; **limer** *vt* to file.

limier [limje] *nm* bloodhound; (*détective*) sleuth.

limitation [limitasjɔ̃] *nf*: ~ de vitesse speed limit.

limite [limit] *nf* (*de terrain*) boundary; (*partie ou point extrême*) limit; vitesse/ charge ~ maximum speed/load; cas ~ borderline case; date ~ deadline.

limiter [limite] *vt* (*restreindre*) to limit, restrict; (*délimiter*) to border.

limitrophe [limitʀɔf] *a* border *cpd*.

limoger [limɔʒe] *vt* to dismiss.

limon [limɔ̃] *nm* silt.

limonade [limɔnad] *nf* lemonade.

lin [lɛ̃] *nm* flax.

linceul [lɛ̃sœl] *nm* shroud.

linge [lɛ̃ʒ] *nm* (*serviettes etc*) linen; (*pièce de tissu*) cloth; (*aussi*: ~ de corps) underwear; (*aussi*: ~ de toilette) towel; (*lessive*) washing.

lingerie [lɛ̃ʒʀi] *nf* lingerie, underwear.

lingot [lɛ̃go] *nm* ingot.

linguistique [lɛ̃gµistik] *a* linguistic // *nf* linguistics *sg*.

lion, ne [ljɔ̃, ljɔn] *nm/f* lion/lioness; (*signe*): le L~ Leo; **lionceau, x** *nm* lion cub.

liqueur [likœʀ] *nf* liqueur.

liquide [likid] *a* liquid // *nm* liquid; (*COMM*): en ~ in ready money *ou* cash.

liquider [likide] *vt* (*société, biens, témoin gênant*) to liquidate; (*compte, problème*) to settle; (*COMM: articles*) to clear, sell off.

liquidités [likidite] *nfpl* (*COMM*) liquid assets.

lire [liʀ] *nf* (*monnaie*) lira // *vt, vi* to read.

lis [lis] *nm* = lys.

lisible [lizibl(ə)] *a* legible.

lisière [lizjɛʀ] *nf* (*de forêt*) edge; (*de tissu*) selvage.

lisons *vb voir* lire.

lisse [lis] *a* smooth.

liste [list(ə)] *nf* list; faire la ~ de to list; ~ électorale electoral roll.

listing [listiŋ] *nm* (*INFORM*) printout.

lit [li] *nm* (*gén*) bed; faire son ~ to make one's bed; aller/se mettre au ~ to go to/ get into bed; ~ de camp campbed; ~ d'enfant cot (*Brit*), crib (*US*).

literie [litʀi] *nf* bedding, bedclothes *pl*.

litière [litjɛʀ] *nf* litter.

litige [litiʒ] *nm* dispute.

litre [litʀ(ə)] *nm* litre; (*récipient*) litre measure.

littéraire [liteʀɛʀ] *a* literary.

littéral, e, aux [liteʀal, -o] *a* literal.

littérature [liteʀatyʀ] *nf* literature.

littoral, aux [litɔʀal, -o] *nm* coast.

liturgie [lityʀʒi] *nf* liturgy.

livide [livid] *a* livid, pallid.

livraison [livʀɛzɔ̃] *nf* delivery.

livre [livʀ(ə)] *nm* book // *nf* (*poids, monnaie*) pound; ~ de bord logbook; ~ de poche paperback (*pocket size*).

livré, e [livʀe] *a*: ~ à soi-même left to o.s. *ou* one's own devices // *nf* livery.

livrer [livʀe] *vt* (*COMM*) to deliver; (*otage, coupable*) to hand over; (*secret, information*) to give away; se ~ à (*se confier*) to confide in; (*se rendre, s'abandonner*) to give o.s. up to; (*faire: pratiques, actes*) to indulge in; (*travail*) to engage in; (: *sport*) to practise; (: *enquête*) to carry out.

livret [livʀɛ] *nm* booklet; (*d'opéra*) libretto (*pl* s); ~ de caisse d'épargne (savings) bank-book; ~ de famille (official) family record book; ~ scolaire (school) report book.

livreur, euse [livʀœʀ, -øz] *nm/f* delivery boy *ou* man/girl *ou* woman.

local, e, aux [lɔkal, -o] *a* local // *nm* (*salle*) premises *pl* // *nmpl* premises.

localiser [lɔkalize] *vt* (*repérer*) to locate, place; (*limiter*) to confine.

localité [lɔkalite] *nf* locality.

locataire [lɔkatɛʀ] *nm/f* tenant; (*de chambre*) lodger.

location [lɔkasjɔ̃] *nf* (*par le locataire, le loueur*) renting; (*par le propriétaire*) renting out, letting; (*THÉÂTRE*) booking office; '~ de voitures' 'car rental'.

locomotive [lɔkɔmɔtiv] *nf* locomotive, engine; (*fig*) pacesetter, pacemaker.

locution [lɔkysjɔ̃] *nf* phrase.

loge [lɔʒ] *nf* (*THÉÂTRE: d'artiste*) dressing room; (: *de spectateurs*) box; (*concierge, franc-maçon*) lodge.

logement [lɔʒmã] *nm* accommodation *q*; flat (*Brit*), apartment (*US*); housing *q*.

loger [lɔʒe] *vt* to accommodate // *vi* to live; **trouver à se ~** to find accommodation; **se ~ dans** (*suj: balle, flèche*) to lodge itself in; **logeur, euse** *nm/f* landlord/landlady.

logiciel [lɔʒisjel] *nm* software.

logique [lɔʒik] *a* logical // *nf* logic.

logis [lɔʒi] *nm* home; abode, dwelling.

loi [lwa] *nf* law; **faire la ~** to lay down the law.

loin [lwɛ̃] *ad* far; (*dans le temps*) a long way off; a long time ago; **plus ~** further; **~ de** far from; **au ~** far off; **de ~ ad** from a distance; (*fig: de beaucoup*) by far; **il vient de ~** (*fig*) he's come a long way.

lointain, e [lwɛ̃tɛ̃, -ɛn] *a* faraway, distant; (*dans le futur, passé*) distant, far-off; (*cause, parent*) remote, distant // *nm*: **dans le ~** in the distance.

loir [lwar] *nm* dormouse (*pl* -mice).

loisir [lwazir] *nm*: **heures de ~** spare time; **~s** *nmpl* leisure *sg*; leisure activities; **avoir le ~ de faire** to have the time *ou* opportunity to do; **à ~** at leisure; at one's pleasure.

londonien, ne [lɔ̃dɔnjɛ̃, -jɛn] *a* London *cpd*, of London // *nm/f*: **L~, ne** Londoner.

Londres [lɔ̃dr(ə)] *n* London.

long, longue [lɔ̃, lɔ̃g] *a* long // *ad*: **en savoir ~** to know a great deal // *nm*: **de 3 m de ~** 3 m long, 3 m in length // *nf*: **à la longue** in the end; **ne pas faire ~ feu** not to last long; **(tout) le ~ de** (all) along; **tout au ~ de** (*année, vie*) throughout; **de ~ en large** (*marcher*) to and fro, up and down.

longer [lɔ̃ʒe] *vt* to go (*ou* walk *ou* drive) along(side); (*suj: mur, route*) to border.

longiligne [lɔ̃ʒilin] *a* long-limbed.

longitude [lɔ̃ʒityd] *nf* longitude.

longitudinal, e, aux [lɔ̃ʒitydinal, -o] *a* (*running*) lengthways.

longtemps [lɔ̃tã] *ad* (for) a long time, (for) long; **avant ~** before long; **depuis/pendant ~** for a long time; **mettre ~ à faire** to take a long time to do.

longue [lɔ̃g] *af voir* long; **~ment** *ad* for a long time.

longueur [lɔ̃gœr] *nf* length; **~s** *nfpl* (*fig: d'un film etc*) tedious parts; **en ~ ad** lengthwise; **tirer en ~** to drag on; **à ~ journée** all day long; **~ d'onde** wavelength.

longue-vue [lɔ̃gvy] *nf* telescope.

lopin [lɔpɛ̃] *nm*: **~ de terre** patch of land.

loque [lɔk] *nf* (*personne*) wreck; **~s** *nfpl* (*habits*) rags.

loquet [lɔke] *nm* latch.

lorgner [lɔrɲe] *vt* to eye; (*fig*) to have one's eye on.

lors [lɔr]: **~ de** *prép* at the time of; during; **~ même que** even though.

lorsque [lɔrsk(ə)] *cj* when, as.

losange [lɔzãʒ] *nm* diamond; (*GÉOM*) lozenge.

lot [lo] *nm* (*part*) share; (*de loterie*) prize; (*fig: destin*) fate, lot; (*COMM, INFORM*) batch.

loterie [lɔtri] *nf* lottery; raffle.

loti, e [lɔti] *a*: **bien/mal ~** well-/badly off.

lotion [lɔsjɔ̃] *nf* lotion.

lotir [lɔtir] *vt* (*terrain*) to divide into plots; to sell by lots; **lotissement** *nm* housing development; plot, lot.

loto [lɔto] *nm* lotto; numerical lottery.

louable [lwabl(ə)] *a* commendable.

louanges [lwãʒ] *nfpl* praise *sg*.

loubard [lubar] *nm* (*fam*) lout.

louche [luʃ] *a* shady, fishy, dubious // *nf* ladle.

loucher [luʃe] *vi* to squint.

louer [lwe] *vt* (*maison: suj: propriétaire*) to let, rent (out); (: *locataire*) to rent; (*voiture etc*) to hire out (*Brit*), rent (out); to hire, rent; (*réserver*) to book; (*faire l'éloge de*) to praise; **'à louer'** 'to let' (*Brit*), 'for rent' (*US*).

loup [lu] *nm* wolf (*pl* wolves).

loupe [lup] *nf* magnifying glass.

louper [lupe] *vt* (*manquer*) to miss.

lourd, e [lur, lurd(ə)] *a, ad* heavy; **~ de** (*conséquences, menaces*) charged with; **lourdaud, e** *a* (*péj*) clumsy.

loutre [lutr(ə)] *nf* otter.

louve [luv] *nf* she-wolf.

louveteau, x [luvto] *nm* wolf-cub; (*scout*) cub (scout).

louvoyer [luvwaje] *vi* (*NAVIG*) to tack; (*fig*) to hedge, evade the issue.

lover [lɔve]: **se ~** *vi* to coil up.

loyal, e, aux [lwajal, -o] *a* (*fidèle*) loyal, faithful; (*fair-play*) fair; **loyauté** *nf* loyalty, faithfulness; fairness.

loyer [lwaje] *nm* rent.

lu, e [ly] *pp de* lire.

lubie [lybi] *nf* whim, craze.

lubrifiant [lybrifjã] *nm* lubricant.

lubrifier [lybrifje] *vt* to lubricate.

lubrique [lybrik] *a* lecherous.

lucarne [lykarn(ə)] *nf* skylight.

lucratif, ive [lykratif, -iv] *a* lucrative; profitable; **à but non ~** non profit-making.

lueur [lɥœr] *nf* (*chatoyante*) glimmer *q*; (*métallique, mouillée*) gleam *q*; (*rougeoyante, chaude*) glow *q*; (*pâle*) (faint) light; (*fig*) glimmer; gleam.

luge [lyʒ] *nf* sledge (*Brit*), sled (*US*).

lugubre [lygybʀ(ə)] *a* gloomy; dismal.
lui [lɥi] *pronom* **1** (*objet indirect: mâle*) (to) him; (*: femelle*) (to) her; (*: chose, animal*) (to) it; **je ~ ai parlé** I have spoken to him (*ou* to her); **il ~ a offert un cadeau** he gave him (*ou* her) a present
2 (*après préposition, comparatif: personne*) him; (*: chose, animal*) it; **elle est contente de ~** she is pleased with him; **je la connais mieux que ~** I know her better than he does; I know her better than him
3 (*sujet, forme emphatique*) he; **~, il est à Paris** HE is in Paris
4: **~-même** himself; itself.
luire [lɥiʀ] *vi* to shine; to glow.
lumière [lymjɛʀ] *nf* light; **~s** *nfpl* (*d'une personne*) wisdom *sg*; **mettre en ~** (*fig*) to highlight; **~ du jour/soleil** day/sunlight.
luminaire [lyminɛʀ] *nm* lamp, light.
lumineux, euse [lyminø, -øz] *a* (*émettant de la lumière*) luminous; (*éclairé*) illuminated; (*ciel, couleur*) bright; (*relatif à la lumière: rayon etc*) of light, light *cpd*; (*fig: regard*) radiant.
lunaire [lynɛʀ] *a* lunar, moon *cpd*.
lunatique [lynatik] *a* whimsical, temperamental.
lundi [lœdi] *nm* Monday; **~ de Pâques** Easter Monday.
lune [lyn] *nf* moon; **~ de miel** honeymoon.
lunette [lynɛt] *nf*: **~s** *nfpl* glasses, spectacles; (*protectrices*) goggles; **~ arrière** (AUTO) rear window; **~s noires** dark glasses; **~s de soleil** sunglasses.
lus *etc vb voir* **lire**.
lustre [lystʀ(ə)] *nm* (*de plafond*) chandelier; (*fig: éclat*) lustre.
lustrer [lystʀe] *vt* to shine.
lut *vb voir* **lire**.
luth [lyt] *nm* lute.
lutin [lytɛ̃] *nm* imp, goblin.
lutte [lyt] *nf* (*conflit*) struggle; (*sport*) wrestling; **lutter** *vi* to fight, struggle.
luxe [lyks(ə)] *nm* luxury; **de ~** *a* luxury *cpd*.
Luxembourg [lyksɑ̃buʀ] *nm*: **le ~** Luxembourg.
luxer [lykse] *vt*: **se ~ l'épaule** to dislocate one's shoulder.
luxueux, euse [lyksɥø, -øz] *a* luxurious.
luxure [lyksyʀ] *nf* lust.
lycée [lise] *nm* secondary school; **lycéen, ne** *nm/f* secondary school pupil.
lyrique [liʀik] *a* lyrical; (OPÉRA) lyric; **artiste ~** opera singer.
lys [lis] *nm* lily.

M

M *abr de* **Monsieur**.
m' [m] *pronom voir* **me**.
ma [ma] *dét voir* **mon**.
macaron [makaʀɔ̃] *nm* (*gâteau*) macaroon; (*insigne*) (round) badge.
macaronis [makaʀɔni] *nmpl* macaroni *sg*.
macédoine [masedwan] *nf*: **~ de fruits** fruit salad.
macérer [maseʀe] *vi*, *vt* to macerate; (*dans du vinaigre*) to pickle.
mâcher [maʃe] *vt* to chew; **ne pas ~ ses mots** not to mince one's words.
machin [maʃɛ̃] *nm* (*fam*) thing (umajig).
machinal, e, aux [maʃinal, -o] *a* mechanical, automatic.
machination [maʃinasjɔ̃] *nf* scheming, frame-up.
machine [maʃin] *nf* machine; (*locomotive*) engine; (*fig: rouages*) machinery; **~ à laver/coudre** washing/sewing machine; **~ à écrire** typewriter; **~ à sous** fruit machine; **~ à vapeur** steam engine; **~rie** *nf* machinery, plant; (*d'un navire*) engine room; **machinisme** *nm* mechanization; **machiniste** *nm* (*de bus, métro*) driver.
mâchoire [maʃwaʀ] *nf* jaw; **~ de frein** brake shoe.
mâchonner [maʃɔne] *vt* to chew (at).
maçon [masɔ̃] *nm* bricklayer; builder.
maçonnerie [masɔnʀi] *nf* (*murs*) brickwork; masonry, stonework; (*activité*) bricklaying; building.
maculer [makyle] *vt* to stain.
Madame [madam], *pl* **Mesdames** [medam] *nf*: **~** X Mrs X ['mɪsɪz]; **occupez-vous de ~/Monsieur/Mademoiselle** please serve this lady/gentleman/(*young*) lady; **bonjour ~/Monsieur/Mademoiselle** good morning; (*ton déférent*) good morning Madam/Sir/Madam; (*le nom est connu*) good morning Mrs/Mr/Miss X; **~/Monsieur/Mademoiselle!** (*pour appeler*) Madam/Sir/Miss!; **~/Monsieur/Mademoiselle** (*sur lettre*) Dear Madam/Sir/Madam; **chère ~/cher Monsieur/chère Mademoiselle** Dear Mrs/Mr/Miss X; **Mesdames** Ladies.
Mademoiselle [madmwazɛl], *pl* **Mesdemoiselles** [medmwazɛl] *nf* Miss; *voir aussi* **Madame**.
madère [madɛʀ] *nm* Madeira (wine).
magasin [magazɛ̃] *nm* (*boutique*) shop; (*entrepôt*) warehouse; (*d'une arme*) magazine; **en ~** (COMM) in stock.
magazine [magazin] *nm* magazine.
magicien, ne [maʒisjɛ̃, -jɛn] *nm/f* magician.
magie [maʒi] *nf/m* magic; **magique** *a* magic; (*enchanteur*) magical.

magistral, e, aux [maʒistʀal, -o] *a*
(*œuvre, adresse*) masterly; (*ton*) authoritative; (*ex cathedra*): enseignement
~ lecturing, lectures *pl*.

magistrat [maʒistʀa] *nm* magistrate.

magnétique [maɲetik] *a* magnetic.

magnétiser [maɲetize] *vt* to magnetize;
(*fig*) to mesmerize, hypnotize.

magnétophone [maɲetɔfɔn] *nm* tape
recorder; ~ à cassettes cassette recorder.

magnétoscope [maɲetɔskɔp] *nm*
video-tape recorder.

magnifique [maɲifik] *a* magnificent.

magot [mago] *nm* (*argent*) pile (of
money); nest egg.

magouille [maguj] *nf* scheming.

mai [me] *nm* May.

maigre [mɛgʀ(ə)] *a* (very) thin, skinny;
(*viande*) lean; (*fromage*) low-fat; (*végétation*) thin, sparse; (*fig*) poor, meagre,
skimpy // *ad*: faire ~ not to eat meat;
jours ~s days of abstinence, fish days;
maigreur *nf* thinness; **maigrir** *vi* to get
thinner, lose weight.

maille [maj] *nf* stitch; ~ à l'endroit/à
l'envers plain/purl stitch; avoir ~ à
partir avec qn to have a brush with sb.

maillet [majɛ] *nm* mallet.

maillon [majɔ̃] *nm* link.

maillot [majo] *nm* (*aussi*: ~ de corps)
vest; (*de danseur*) leotard; (*de sportif*)
jersey; ~ de bain swimsuit; (*d'homme*)
bathing trunks *pl*.

main [mɛ̃] *nf* hand; à la ~ in one's hand;
se donner la ~ to hold hands; donner *ou*
tendre la ~ à qn to hold out one's hand
to sb; se serrer la ~ to shake hands;
serrer la ~ à qn to shake hands with sb;
sous la ~ to *ou* at hand; attaque à ~
armée armed attack; à ~ droite/gauche
to the right/left; à remettre en ~s propres to be delivered personally; de
première ~ (*COMM: voiture etc*) second-
hand with only one previous owner; mettre la dernière ~ à to put the finishing
touches to; se faire/perdre la ~ to get
one's hand in/lose one's touch; avoir qch
bien en ~ to have (got) the hang of
sth.

main-d'œuvre [mɛ̃dœvʀ(ə)] *nf* manpower, labour.

main-forte [mɛ̃fɔʀt(ə)] *nf*: prêter ~ à
qn to come to sb's assistance.

mainmise [mɛ̃miz] *nf* seizure; (*fig*): ~
sur complete hold on.

maint, e [mɛ̃, mɛ̃t] *a* many a; ~s
many; à ~es reprises time and (time)
again.

maintenant [mɛ̃tnɑ̃] *ad* now; (*actuellement*) nowadays.

maintenir [mɛ̃tniʀ] *vt* (*retenir, soutenir*)
to support; (*contenir: foule etc*) to hold
back; (*conserver, affirmer*) to maintain;
se ~ *vi* to hold; to keep steady; to per-

maintien [mɛ̃tjɛ̃] *nm* maintaining; (*attitude*) bearing.

maire [mɛʀ] *nm* mayor.

mairie [meʀi] *nf* (*bâtiment*) town hall;
(*administration*) town council.

mais [me] *cj* but; ~ non! of course not!;
~ enfin but after all; (*indignation*) look
here!; ~ encore? is that all?

maïs [mais] *nm* maize (*Brit*), corn (*US*).

maison [mezɔ̃] *nf* house; (*chez-soi*)
home; (*COMM*) firm // *a inv* (*CULIN*)
home-made; made by the chef; (*fig*) in-
house, own; à la ~ at home; (*direction*)
home; ~ close *ou* de passe brothel; ~ de
correction reformatory; ~ des jeunes ≈
youth club; ~ mère parent company; ~
de repos convalescent home; ~ de santé
mental home; **maisonnée** *nf* household,
family; **maisonnette** *nf* small house,
cottage.

maître, esse [mɛtʀ(ə), mɛtʀɛs] *nm/f*
master/mistress; (*SCOL*) teacher,
schoolmaster/mistress // *nm* (*peintre etc*)
master; (*titre*): M~ (Me) Maître, *term
of address gen for a barrister* // *nf*
(*amante*) mistress // *a* (*principal, essentiel*) main; être ~ de (*soi-même, situation*) to be in control of; une maîtresse
femme a managing woman; ~ chanteur
blackmailer; ~/maîtresse d'école
schoolmaster/mistress; ~ d'hôtel (*domestique*) butler; (*d'hôtel*) head waiter;
~ de maison host; ~ nageur lifeguard;
maîtresse de maison hostess; housewife
(*pl* wives).

maîtrise [metʀiz] *nf* (*aussi*: ~ de soi)
self-control, self-possession; (*habileté*)
skill, mastery; (*suprématie*) mastery,
command; (*diplôme*) ≈ master's
degree.

maîtriser [metʀize] *vt* (*cheval, incendie*)
to (bring under) control; (*sujet*) to master; (*émotion*) to control, master; se ~
to control o.s.

majestueux, euse [maʒɛstɥø, -øz] *a* a
majestic.

majeur, e [maʒœʀ] *a* (*important*) major; (*JUR*) of age; (*fig*) adult // *nm*
(*doigt*) middle finger; en ~e partie for
the most part.

majorer [maʒɔʀe] *vt* to increase.

majoritaire [maʒɔʀitɛʀ] *a* majority
cpd.

majorité [maʒɔʀite] *nf* (*gén*) majority;
(*parti*) party in power; en ~ mainly.

majuscule [maʒyskyl] *a, nf*: (lettre) ~
capital (letter).

mal, maux [mal, mo] *nm* (*opposé au
bien*) evil; (*tort, dommage*) harm;
(*douleur physique*) pain, ache; (*maladie*) illness, sickness *q* // *ad* badly // *a*
bad, wrong; être ~ avec qn to be on bad terms with
sb; être au plus ~ (*malade*) to be at

death's door; (*brouillé*) to be at daggers drawn; **il a ~ compris** he misunderstood; **dire/penser du ~ de** to speak/think ill of; **ne voir aucun ~ à** to see no harm in, see nothing wrong in; **craignant ~ faire** fearing he was doing the wrong thing; **faire du ~ à qn** to hurt sb; **to harm sb; se faire ~** to hurt o.s.; **se donner du ~ pour faire qch** to go to a lot of trouble to do sth; **ça fait ~** it hurts; **j'ai ~ au dos** my back hurts, **avoir ~ à la tête/à la gorge/aux dents** to have a headache/a sore throat/toothache; **avoir le ~ du pays** to be homesick; **prendre ~** to be taken ill, feel unwell; **~ de mer** seasickness; **~ en point** *a inv* in a bad state; **maux de ventre** stomach ache *sg*; *voir* **cœur.**

malade [malad] *a* ill, sick; (*poitrine, jambe*) bad; (*plante*) diseased // *nm/f* invalid, sick person; (*à l'hôpital etc*) patient; **tomber ~** to fall ill; **être ~ du cœur** to have heart trouble *ou* a bad heart; **~ mental** mentally sick *ou* ill person.

maladie [maladi] *nf* (*spécifique*) disease, illness; (*mauvaise santé*) illness, sickness; **maladif, ive** *a* sickly; (*curiosité, besoin*) pathological.

maladresse [maladrɛs] *nf* clumsiness *q*; (*gaffe*) blunder.

maladroit, e [maladrwa, -wat] *a* clumsy.

malaise [malɛz] *nm* (*MÉD*) feeling of faintness; feeling of discomfort; (*fig*) uneasiness, malaise.

malaisé, e [maleze] *a* difficult.

malappris, e [malapri, -iz] *nm/f* ill-mannered *ou* boorish person.

malaria [malarja] *nf* malaria.

malaxer [malakse] *vt* to knead; to mix.

malchance [malʃɑ̃s] *nf* misfortune, ill luck *q*; **par ~** unfortunately.

mâle [mal] *a* (*aussi ÉLEC, TECH*) male; (*viril: voix, traits*) manly // *nm* male.

malédiction [malediksjɔ̃] *nf* curse.

malencontreux, euse [malɑ̃kɔ̃trø, -øz] *a* unfortunate, untoward.

malentendu [malɑ̃tɑ̃dy] *nm* misunderstanding.

malfaçon [malfasɔ̃] *nf* fault.

malfaisant, e [malfəzɑ̃, -ɑ̃t] *a* evil, harmful.

malfaiteur [malfɛtœr] *nm* lawbreaker, criminal; burglar, thief (*pl* thieves).

malgache [malgaʃ] *a, nm/f* Madagascan, Malagasy // *nm* (*langue*) Malagasy.

malgré [malgre] *prép* in spite of, despite; **~ tout** *ad* all the same.

malheur [malœr] *nm* (*situation*) adversity, misfortune; (*événement*) misfortune; disaster, tragedy; **faire un ~** to be a smash hit; **malheureusement** *ad* unfortunately; **malheureux, euse** *a* (*triste*) unhappy, miserable; (*infortuné,*

regrettable) unfortunate; (*malchanceux*) unlucky; (*insignifiant*) wretched // *nm/f* poor soul; unfortunate creature; **les malheureux** the destitute.

malhonnête [malɔnɛt] *a* dishonest.

malice [malis] *nf* mischievousness; (*méchanceté*): **par ~** out of malice *ou* spite; **sans ~** guileless; **malicieux, euse** *a* mischievous.

malin, igne [malɛ̃, -iɲ] *a* (*futé: f gén: maline*) smart, shrewd; (*MÉD*) malignant.

malingre [malɛ̃gr(ə)] *a* puny.

malle [mal] *nf* trunk.

mallette [malɛt] *nf* (small) suitcase; overnight case; attaché case.

malmener [malməne] *vt* to manhandle; (*fig*) to give a rough handling to.

malodorant, e [malɔdɔrɑ̃, -ɑ̃t] *a* foul *ou* ill-smelling.

malotru [malɔtry] *nm* lout, boor.

malpropre [malprɔpr(ə)] *a* dirty.

malsain, e [malsɛ̃, -ɛn] *a* unhealthy.

malt [malt] *nm* malt.

Malte [malt(ə)] *nf* Malta.

maltraiter [maltrɛte] *vt* (*brutaliser*) to manhandle, ill-treat.

malveillance [malvɛjɑ̃s] *nf* (*animosité*) ill will; (*intention de nuire*) malevolence; (*JUR*) malicious intent *q*.

malversation [malvɛrsɑsjɔ̃] *nf* embezzlement.

maman [mamɑ̃] *nf* mum(my), mother.

mamelle [mamɛl] *nf* teat.

mamelon [mamlɔ̃] *nm* (*ANAT*) nipple; (*colline*) knoll, hillock.

mamie [mami] *nf* (*fam*) granny.

mammifère [mamifɛr] *nm* mammal.

manche [mɑ̃ʃ] *nf* (*de vêtement*) sleeve; (*d'un jeu, tournoi*) round; (*GÉO*): **la M~** the Channel // *nm* (*d'outil, casserole*) handle; (*de pelle, pioche etc*) shaft; **~ à balai** *nm* broomstick; (*AVIAT, INFORM*) joystick.

manchette [mɑ̃ʃɛt] *nf* (*de chemise*) cuff; (*coup*) forearm blow; (*titre*) headline.

manchon [mɑ̃ʃɔ̃] *nm* (*de fourrure*) muff.

manchot [mɑ̃ʃo] *nm* one-armed man; armless man; (*ZOOL*) penguin.

mandarine [mɑ̃darin] *nf* mandarin (orange), tangerine.

mandat [mɑ̃da] *nm* (*postal*) postal *ou* money order; (*d'un député etc*) mandate; (*procuration*) power of attorney, proxy; (*POLICE*) warrant; **~ d'amener** summons *sg*; **~ d'arrêt** warrant for arrest; **mandataire** *nm/f* representative; proxy.

mander [mɑ̃de] *vt* to summon.

manège [manɛʒ] *nm* riding school; (*à la foire*) roundabout, merry-go-round; (*fig*) game, ploy.

manette [manɛt] *nf* lever, tap; **~ de jeu**

joystick.

mangeable [mãʒabl(ə)] a edible, eatable.

mangeoire [mãʒwaʀ] nf trough, manger.

manger [mãʒe] vt to eat; (ronger: suj: rouille etc) to eat into ou away // vi to eat.

mangue [mãg] nf mango.

maniable [manjabl(ə)] a (outil) handy; (voiture, voilier) easy to handle.

maniaque [manjak] a finicky, fussy; suffering from a mania // nm/f maniac.

manie [mani] nf mania; (tic) odd habit.

manier [manje] vt to handle.

manière [manjɛʀ] nf (façon) way, manner; ~s nfpl (attitude) manners; (chichis) fuss sg; de ~ à so as to; de telle ~ que in such a way that; de cette ~ in this way ou manner; d'une certaine ~ in a way; d'une ~ générale generally speaking, as a general rule; de toute ~ in any case.

maniéré, e [manjeʀe] a affected.

manifestant, e [manifestã, -ãt] nm/f demonstrator.

manifestation [manifestasjɔ̃] nf (de joie, mécontentement) expression, demonstration; (symptôme) outward sign; (fête etc) event; (POL) demonstration.

manifeste [manifest(ə)] a obvious, evident // nm manifesto (pl s).

manifester [manifeste] vt (volonté, intentions) to show, indicate; (joie, peur) to express, show // vi to demonstrate; se ~ vi (émotion) to show ou express itself; (difficultés) to arise; (symptômes) to appear; (témoin etc) to come forward.

manigance [manigãs] nf scheme.

manipuler [manipyle] vt to handle; (fig) to manipulate.

manivelle [manivɛl] nf crank.

mannequin [mankɛ̃] nm (COUTURE) dummy; (MODE) model.

manœuvre [manœvʀ(ə)] nf (gén) manœuvre (Brit), maneuver (US) // nm labourer.

manœuvrer [manœvʀe] vt to manœuvre (Brit), maneuver (US); (levier, machine) to operate // vi to manœuvre.

manoir [manwaʀ] nm manor ou country house.

manque [mãk] nm (insuffisance): ~ de lack of; (vide) emptiness, gap; (MÉD) withdrawal; ~s nmpl (lacunes) faults, defects.

manqué, e [mãke] a failed; garçon ~ tomboy.

manquer [mãke] vi (faire défaut) to be lacking; (être absent) to be missing; (échouer) to fail // vt to miss // vb impersonnel: il (nous) manque encore 100 F we are still 100 F short; il manque des pages (au livre) there are some pages missing ou some pages are missing

(from the book); il/cela me manque I miss him/this; ~ à vt (règles etc) to be in breach of, fail to observe; ~ de vt to lack; il a manqué (de) se tuer he very nearly got killed.

mansarde [mãsaʀd(ə)] nf attic.

mansuétude [mãsɥetyd] nf leniency.

manteau, x [mãto] nm coat; ~ de cheminée mantelpiece.

manucure [manykyʀ] nf manicurist.

manuel, le [manɥɛl] a manual // nm (ouvrage) manual, handbook.

manufacture [manyfaktyʀ] nf factory.

manufacturé, e [manyfaktyʀe] a manufactured.

manuscrit, e [manyskʀi, -it] a handwritten // nm manuscript.

manutention [manytãsjɔ̃] nf (COMM) handling; (local) storehouse.

mappemonde [mapmɔ̃d] nf (plane) map of the world; (sphère) globe.

maquereau, x [makʀo] nm (ZOOL) mackerel inv; (fam) pimp.

maquette [makɛt] nf (d'un décor, bâtiment, véhicule) (scale) model; (d'une page illustrée) paste-up.

maquillage [makijaʒ] nm making up; faking; (crème etc) make-up.

maquiller [makije] vt (personne, visage) to make up; (truquer: passeport, statistique) to fake; (: voiture volée) to do over (respray etc); se ~ vi to make up (one's face).

maquis [maki] nm (GÉO) scrub; (MIL) maquis, underground fighting q.

maraîcher, ère [maʀɛʃe, maʀɛʃɛʀ] a: cultures maraîchères market gardening sg // nm/f market gardener.

marais [maʀɛ] nm marsh, swamp.

marasme [maʀasm(ə)] nm stagnation, slump.

marathon [maʀatɔ̃] nm marathon.

marâtre [maʀɑtʀ(ə)] nf cruel mother.

maraudeur [maʀodœʀ] nm prowler.

marbre [maʀbʀ(ə)] nm (pierre, statue) marble; (d'une table, commode) marble top; **marbrer** vt to mottle, blotch.

marc [maʀ] nm (de raisin, pommes) marc; ~ de café coffee grounds pl ou dregs pl.

marchand, e [maʀʃã, -ãd] nm/f shopkeeper, tradesman/woman; (au marché) stallholder // a: prix/valeur ~(e) market price/value; ~ de charbon/vins coal/wine merchant; ~/e de couleurs ironmonger (Brit), hardware dealer (US); ~ de fruits fruiterer (Brit), fruit seller (US); ~/e de journaux newsagent; ~/e de légumes greengrocer (Brit), produce dealer (US); ~/e de quatre saisons costermonger (Brit), street vendor (selling fresh fruit and vegetables); ~/e de tableaux art dealer.

marchander [maʀʃãde] vi to bargain, haggle.

marchandise [maʁʃɑ̃diz] nf goods pl, merchandise q.

marche [maʁʃ(ə)] nf (d'escalier) step; (activité) walking; (promenade, trajet, allure) walk; (démarche) walk, gait; (MIL etc, MUS) march; (fonctionnement) running; (progression) progress; course; **ouvrir/fermer la ~** to lead the way/bring up the rear; **dans le sens de la ~** (RAIL) facing the engine; **en ~** (monter etc) while the vehicle is moving ou in motion; **mettre en ~** to start; **se mettre en ~** (personne) to get moving; (machine) to start; **~ arrière** reverse (gear); **faire ~ arrière** to reverse; (fig) to backtrack, back-pedal; **~ à suivre** (correct) procedure; (sur notice) (step by step) instructions pl.

marché [maʁʃe] nm (lieu, COMM, ÉCON) market; (ville) trading centre; (transaction) bargain, deal; **M~ commun** Common Market; **faire du ~ noir** to buy and sell on the black market; **~ aux puces** flea market.

marchepied [maʁʃəpje] nm (RAIL) step; (fig) stepping stone.

marcher [maʁʃe] vi to walk; (MIL) to march; (aller: voiture, train, affaires) to go; (prospérer) to go well; (fonctionner) to work, run; (fam) to go along, agree; to be taken in; **~ sur** to walk on; (mettre le pied sur) to step on ou in; (MIL) to march upon; **~ dans** (herbe etc) to walk in ou on; (flaque) to step in; **faire ~ qn** to pull sb's leg; to lead sb up the garden path; **marcheur, euse** nm/f walker.

mardi [maʁdi] nm Tuesday; **M~ gras** Shrove Tuesday.

mare [maʁ] nf pond; **~ de sang** pool of blood.

marécage [maʁekaʒ] nm marsh, swamp.

maréchal, aux [maʁeʃal, -o] nm marshal.

marée [maʁe] nf tide; (poissons) fresh (sea) fish; **~ haute/basse** high/low tide; **~ montante/descendante** rising/ebb tide.

marémotrice [maʁemɔtʁis] af tidal.

margarine [maʁgaʁin] nf margarine.

marge [maʁʒ(ə)] nf margin; **en ~ de** (fig) on the fringe of; cut off from; **~ bénéficiaire** profit margin.

marguerite [maʁgəʁit] nf marguerite, (oxeye) daisy; (d'imprimante) daisy-wheel.

mari [maʁi] nm husband.

mariage [maʁjaʒ] nm (union, état, fig) marriage; (noce) wedding; **~ civil/religieux** registry office (Brit) ou civil/church wedding.

marié, e [maʁje] a married // nm/f (bride)groom/bride; **les ~s** the bride and groom; **les (jeunes) ~s** the newly-weds.

marier [maʁje] vt to marry; (fig) to blend; **se ~ (avec)** to marry.

marin, e [maʁɛ̃, -in] a sea cpd, marine // nm sailor // nf navy; **~e de guerre** navy; **~e marchande** merchant navy.

marine [maʁin] af, nf voir marin // a inv navy (blue) // nm (MIL) marine.

marionnette [maʁjɔnɛt] nf puppet.

maritime [maʁitim] a sea cpd, maritime.

mark [maʁk] nm mark.

marmelade [maʁməlad] nf stewed fruit, compote; **~ d'oranges** marmalade.

marmite [maʁmit] nf (cooking-)pot.

marmonner [maʁmɔne] vt, vi to mumble, mutter.

marmotter [maʁmɔte] vt to mumble.

Maroc [maʁɔk] nm: **le ~** Morocco; **marocain, e** a, nm/f Moroccan.

maroquinerie [maʁɔkinʁi] nf leather craft; fine leather goods pl.

marquant, e [maʁkɑ̃, -ɑ̃t] a outstanding.

marque [maʁk(ə)] nf mark; (SPORT, JEU: décompte des points) score; (COMM: de produits) brand; make; (: de disques) label; **de ~** a (COMM) brand-name cpd; proprietary; (fig) high-class; distinguished; **~ déposée** registered trademark; **~ de fabrique** trademark.

marquer [maʁke] vt to mark; (inscrire) to write down; (bétail) to brand; (SPORT: but etc) to score; (: joueur) to mark; (accentuer: taille etc) to emphasize; (manifester: refus, intérêt) to show // vi (événement, personnalité) to stand out, be outstanding; (SPORT) to score; **les points** (tenir la marque) to keep the score.

marqueterie [maʁkətʁi] nf inlaid work, marquetry.

marquis, e [maʁki, -iz] nm/f marquis ou marquess/marchioness // nf (auvent) glass canopy ou awning.

marraine [maʁɛn] nf godmother.

marrant, e [maʁɑ̃, -ɑ̃t] a (fam) funny.

marre [maʁ] ad (fam): **en avoir ~ de** to be fed up with.

marrer [maʁe]: **se ~** vi (fam) to have a (good) laugh.

marron [maʁɔ̃] nm (fruit) chestnut // a inv brown; **marronnier** nm chestnut (tree).

mars [maʁs] nm March.

marsouin [maʁswɛ̃] nm porpoise.

marteau, x [maʁto] nm hammer; (de porte) knocker; **~-piqueur** nm pneumatic drill.

marteler [maʁtəle] vt to hammer.

martien, ne [maʁsjɛ̃, -jɛn] a Martian, of ou from Mars.

martinet [maʁtinɛ] nm (fouet) small whip; (ZOOL) swift.

martyr, e [maʁtiʁ] nm/f martyr.

martyre [maʁtiʁ] nm martyrdom; (fig: sens affaibli) agony, torture.

martyriser [martirize] vt (REL) to martyr; (fig) to bully; (enfant) to batter, beat.

marxiste [marksist(ə)] a, nm/f Marxist.

masculin, e [maskylɛ̃, -in] a masculine; (sexe, population) male; (équipe, vêtements) men's; (viril) manly // nm masculine.

masque [mask(ə)] nm mask.

masquer [maske] vt (cacher: paysage, porte) to hide, conceal; (dissimuler: vérité, projet) to mask, obscure.

massacre [masakr(ə)] nm massacre, slaughter.

massacrer [masakre] vt to massacre, slaughter; (fig: texte etc) to murder.

massage [masaʒ] nm massage.

masse [mas] nf mass; (péj): la ~ the masses pl; (ÉLEC) earth; (maillet) sledgehammer; une ~ de (fam) masses ou loads of; en ~ ad (en bloc) in bulk; (en foule) en masse // a (exécutions, production) mass cpd.

masser [mase] vt (assembler) to gather; (pétrir) to massage; se ~ vi to gather; **masseur, euse** nm/f masseur/masseuse.

massif, ive [masif, -iv] a (porte) solid, massive; (visage) heavy, large; (bois, or) solid; (dose) massive; (déportations etc) mass cpd // nm (montagneux) massif; (de fleurs) clump, bank.

massue [masy] nf club, bludgeon.

mastic [mastik] nm (pour vitres) putty; (pour fentes) filler.

mastiquer [mastike] vt (aliment) to chew, masticate; (fente) to fill; (vitre) to putty.

mat, e [mat] a (couleur, métal) mat(t); (bruit, son) dull // a inv (ÉCHECS): être ~ to be checkmate.

mât [ma] nm (NAVIG) mast; (poteau) pole, post.

match [matʃ] nm match; faire ~ nul to draw; ~ aller first leg; ~ retour second leg, return match.

matelas [matla] nm mattress; ~ pneumatique air bed ou mattress.

matelassé, e [matlase] a padded; quilted.

matelot [matlo] nm sailor, seaman.

mater [mate] vt (personne) to bring to heel, subdue; (révolte) to put down.

matérialiste [materjalist(ə)] a materialistic.

matériaux [materjo] nmpl material(s).

matériel, le [materjɛl] a material // nm equipment q; (de camping etc) gear q; ~ d'exploitation (COMM) plant.

maternel, le [maternɛl] a (amour, geste) motherly, maternal; (grand-père, oncle) maternal // nf (aussi: école ~le) (state) nursery school.

maternité [maternite] nf (établissement) maternity hospital; (état de mère) motherhood, maternity; (grossesse) pregnancy.

mathématique [matematik] a mathematical; ~s nfpl (science) mathematics sg.

matière [matjɛr] nf (PHYSIQUE) matter; (COMM, TECH) material, matter q; (fig: d'un livre etc) subject matter, material; (SCOL) subject; en ~ de as regards; ~s grasses fat content sg; ~s premières raw materials.

matin [matɛ̃] nm, ad morning; du ~ au soir from morning till night; de bon ou grand ~ early in the morning; **matinal, e, aux** a (toilette, gymnastique) morning cpd; (de bonne heure) early; être matinal (personne) to be up early; to be an early riser.

matinée [matine] nf morning; (spectacle) matinée.

matou [matu] nm tom(cat).

matraque [matrak] nf club; (de policier) truncheon (Brit), billy (US).

matricule [matrikyl] nf (aussi: registre ~) roll, register // nm (aussi: numéro ~: MIL) regimental number; (: ADMIN) reference number.

matrimonial, e, aux [matrimɔnjal, -o] a marital, marriage cpd.

maudire [modir] vt to curse.

maudit, e [modi, -it] a (fam: satané) blasted, confounded.

maugréer [mogree] vi to grumble.

maussade [mosad] a sullen.

mauvais, e [mɔvɛ, -ɛz] a bad; (faux): le ~ numéro/moment the wrong number/moment; (méchant, malveillant) malicious, spiteful // ad: il fait ~ the weather is bad; la mer est ~e the sea is rough; ~ plaisant hoaxer; ~e herbe weed; ~e langue gossip, scandalmonger (Brit); ~e passe difficult situation; bad patch; ~e tête rebellious ou headstrong customer.

maux [mo] nmpl voir **mal**.

maximum [maksimɔm] a, nm maximum; au ~ ad (le plus possible) to the full; as much as one can; (tout au plus) at the (very) most ou maximum.

mayonnaise [majɔnɛz] nf mayonnaise.

mazout [mazut] nm (fuel) oil.

Me abr de **Maître**.

me, m' [m(ə)] pronom me; (réfléchi) myself.

mec [mɛk] nm (fam) bloke, guy.

mécanicien, ne [mekanisjɛ̃, -jɛn] nm/f mechanic; (RAIL) (train ou engine) driver.

mécanique [mekanik] a mechanical // nf (science) mechanics sg; (technologie) mechanical engineering; (mécanisme) mechanism; engineering; works pl; ennui ~ engine trouble q.

mécanisme [mekanism(ə)] nm mechanism.

méchamment [meʃamɑ̃] ad nastily,

maliciously, spitefully.

méchanceté [meʃɑ̃ste] *nf* nastiness, maliciousness; nasty *ou* spiteful *ou* malicious remark (*ou* action).

méchant, e [meʃɑ̃, -ɑ̃t] *a* nasty, malicious, spiteful; (*enfant: pas sage*) naughty; (*animal*) vicious; (*avant le nom: valeur péjorative*) nasty; miserable; (: *intensive*) terrific.

mèche [meʃ] *nf* (*de lampe, bougie*) wick; (*d'un explosif*) fuse; (*de vilebrequin, perceuse*) bit; (*de cheveux*) lock; **de ~ avec** in league with.

mécompte [mekɔ̃t] *nm* miscalculation; (*déception*) disappointment.

méconnaissable [mekɔnɛsabl(ə)] *a* unrecognizable.

méconnaître [mekɔnɛtR(ə)] *vt* (*ignorer*) to be unaware of; (*mésestimer*) to misjudge.

mécontent, e [mekɔ̃tɑ̃, -ɑ̃t] *a*: **~ (de)** discontented *ou* dissatisfied *ou* displeased (with); (*contrarié*) annoyed (at); **mécontentement** *nm* dissatisfaction, discontent, displeasure; annoyance.

médaille [medaj] *nf* medal.

médaillon [medajɔ̃] *nm* (*portrait*) medallion; (*bijou*) locket.

médecin [medsɛ̃] *nm* doctor; **~ légiste** forensic surgeon.

médecine [medsin] *nf* medicine; **~ légale** forensic medicine.

média [medja] *nmpl*: **les ~** the media.

médiatique [medjatik] *a* media *cpd*.

médical, e, aux [medikal, -o] *a* medical.

médicament [medikamɑ̃] *nm* medicine, drug.

médiéval, e, aux [medjeval, -o] *a* medieval.

médiocre [medjɔkR(ə)] *a* mediocre, poor.

médire [mediR] *vi*: **~ de** to speak ill of; **médisance** *nf* scandalmongering (*Brit*); piece of scandal *ou* of malicious gossip.

méditer [medite] *vt* (*approfondir*) to meditate on, ponder (over); (*combiner*) to meditate // *vi* to meditate.

Méditerranée [mediteRane] *nf*: **la (mer) ~** the Mediterranean (Sea); **méditerranéen, ne** *a, nm/f* Mediterranean.

méduse [medyz] *nf* jellyfish.

meeting [mitiŋ] *nm* (*POL, SPORT*) rally.

méfait [mefe] *nm* (*faute*) misdemeanour, wrongdoing; **~s** *nmpl* (*ravages*) ravages, damage *sg*.

méfiance [mefjɑ̃s] *nf* mistrust, distrust.

méfiant, e [mefjɑ̃, -ɑ̃t] *a* mistrustful, distrustful.

méfier [mefje]: **se ~** *vi* to be wary; to be careful; **se ~ de** to mistrust, distrust, be wary of; (*faire attention*) to be careful about.

mégarde [megaRd(ə)] *nf*: **par ~** acci-

dentally; by mistake.

mégère [meʒɛR] *nf* shrew.

mégot [mego] *nm* cigarette end.

meilleur, e [mejœR] *a, ad* better; (*valeur superlative*) best // *nm*: **le ~** (*celui qui ...*) the best (one); (*ce qui ...*) the best (one) // *nf*: **la ~e** the best (one); **le ~ des deux** the better of the two; **de ~e heure** earlier; **~ marché** cheaper.

mélancolie [melɑ̃kɔli] *nf* melancholy, gloom; **mélancolique** *a* melancholic, melancholy.

mélange [melɑ̃ʒ] *nm* mixture.

mélanger [melɑ̃ʒe] *vt* (*substances*) to mix; (*vins, couleurs*) to blend; (*mettre en désordre*) to mix up, muddle (up).

mélasse [melas] *nf* treacle, molasses *sg*.

mêlée [mele] *nf* mêlée, scramble; (*RUGBY*) scrum(mage).

mêler [mele] *vt* (*substances, odeurs, races*) to mix; (*embrouiller*) to muddle (up), mix up; **se ~ à** *vi* to mix; to mingle; **se ~ à** (*suj: personne*) to join; to mix with; (: *odeurs etc*) to mingle with; **se ~ de** (*suj: personne*) to meddle with, interfere in; **~ qn à** (*affaire*) to get sb mixed up *ou* involved in.

mélodie [melɔdi] *nf* melody.

melon [məlɔ̃] *nm* (*BOT*) (honeydew) melon; (*aussi*: **chapeau ~**) bowler (hat).

membre [mɑ̃bR(ə)] *nm* (*ANAT*) limb; (*personne, pays, élément*) member // *a* member.

mémé [meme] *nf* (*fam*) granny.

même [mɛm] ♦ *a* **1** (*avant le nom*) same; **en ~ temps** at the same time
2 (*après le nom: renforcement*): **il est la loyauté ~** he is loyalty itself; **ce sont ses paroles-là ~s** they are his very words/the very ones
♦ *pronom*: **le(la) ~** the same one
♦ *ad* **1** (*renforcement*): **il n'a ~ pas pleuré** he didn't even cry; **~ lui l'a dit** even HE said it; **ici ~** at this very place
2: **à ~**: **à ~ la bouteille** straight from the bottle; **à ~ la peau** next to the skin; **être à ~ de faire** to be in a position to do, be able to do
3: **de ~**: **faire de ~** to do likewise; **lui de ~** so does (*ou* did *ou* is) he; **de ~ que** just as; **il en va de ~ pour** the same goes for.

mémento [memɛ̃to] *nm* (*agenda*) appointments diary; (*ouvrage*) summary.

mémoire [memwaR] *nf* memory // *nm* (*ADMIN, JUR*) memorandum (*pl* **s**); (*SCOL*) dissertation, paper; **~s** *nmpl* memoirs; **à la ~ de** to the *ou* in memory of; **pour ~** *ad* for the record; **de ~** *ad* from memory; **~ morte/vive** (*INFORM*) ROM/RAM.

menace [mənas] *nf* threat.

menacer [mənase] *vt* to threaten.

ménage [menaʒ] *nm* (*travail*) housekeeping, housework; (*couple*) (married) couple; (famille, ADMIN) household; faire le ~ to do the housework.

ménagement [menaʒmɑ̃] nm care and attention; ~s nmpl (égards) consideration sg, attention sg.

ménager [menaʒe] vt (traiter) to handle with tact; to treat considerately; (utiliser) to use sparingly; to use with care; (prendre soin de) to take (great) care of, look after; (organiser) to arrange; (installer) to put in; to make; ~ qch à qn (réserver) to have sth in store for sb.

ménager, ère [menaʒe, -ɛR] a household cpd, domestic // nf housewife (pl wives).

mendiant, e [mɑ̃djɑ̃, -ɑ̃t] nm/f beggar.

mendier [mɑ̃dje] vi to beg // vt to beg (for).

menées [məne] nfpl intrigues.

mener [məne] vt to lead; (enquête) to conduct; (affaires) to manage // vi: ~ (à la marque) to lead, be in the lead; ~ à/dans (emmener) to take to/into; ~ qch à terme ou à bien to see sth through (to a successful conclusion), complete sth successfully.

meneur, euse [mənœR, -øz] nm/f leader; (péj) agitator; ~ de jeu host, quizmaster.

méningite [menɛ̃ʒit] nf meningitis q.

ménopause [menɔpoz] nf menopause.

menottes [mənɔt] nfpl handcuffs.

mensonge [mɑ̃sɔ̃ʒ] nm lie; lying q; **mensonger, ère** a false.

mensualité [mɑ̃sɥalite] nf monthly payment; monthly salary.

mensuel, le [mɑ̃sɥɛl] a monthly.

mensurations [mɑ̃syRasjɔ̃] nfpl measurements.

mentalité [mɑ̃talite] nf mentality.

menteur, euse [mɑ̃tœR, -øz] nm/f liar.

menthe [mɑ̃t] nf mint.

mention [mɑ̃sjɔ̃] nf (note) note, comment; (SCOL): ~ bien etc ≈ grade B etc (ou upper 2nd class etc) pass (Brit), ≈ pass with (high) honors (US); **mentionner** vt to mention.

mentir [mɑ̃tiR] vi to lie; to be lying.

menton [mɑ̃tɔ̃] nm chin.

menu, e [məny] a slim, slight; tiny; (frais, difficulté) minor // ad (couper, hacher) very fine // nm menu; par le ~ (raconter) in minute detail; ~e monnaie small change.

menuiserie [mənɥizRi] nf (travail) joinery, carpentry; woodwork; (local) joiner's workshop; (ouvrage) woodwork q.

menuisier [mənɥizje] nm joiner, carpenter.

méprendre [mepRɑ̃dR(ə)]: se ~ vi: se ~ sur to be mistaken (about).

mépris [mepRi] nm (dédain) contempt, scorn; (indifférence) le ~ de contempt ou disregard for; au ~ de regardless of, in defiance of.

méprisable [mepRizabl(ə)] a contemptible, despicable.

méprise [mepRiz] nf mistake, error; misunderstanding.

mépriser [mepRize] vt to scorn, despise; (gloire, danger) to scorn, spurn.

mer [mɛR] nf sea; (marée) tide; en ~ at sea; prendre la ~ to put out to sea; en haute ou pleine ~ off shore, on the open sea; la ~ du Nord/Rouge the North/Red Sea.

mercantile [mɛRkɑ̃til] a (péj) mercenary.

mercenaire [mɛRsənɛR] nm mercenary, hired soldier.

mercerie [mɛRsəRi] nf haberdashery (Brit), notions (US); haberdasher's shop (Brit), notions store (US).

merci [mɛRsi] excl thank you // nf: à la ~ de qn/qch at sb's mercy/the mercy of sth; ~ de thank you for; sans ~ merciless(ly).

mercredi [mɛRkRədi] nm Wednesday.

mercure [mɛRkyR] nm mercury.

merde [mɛRd(ə)] (fam!) nf shit (!) // excl (bloody) hell (!).

mère [mɛR] nf mother; ~ célibataire unmarried mother.

méridional, e, aux [meRidjɔnal, -o] a southern // nm/f Southerner.

meringue [məRɛ̃g] nf meringue.

mérite [meRit] nm merit; le ~ (de ceci) lui revient the credit (for this) is his.

mériter [meRite] vt to deserve.

merlan [mɛRlɑ̃] nm whiting.

merle [mɛRl(ə)] nm blackbird.

merveille [mɛRvɛj] nf marvel, wonder; faire ~ to work wonders; à ~ perfectly, wonderfully.

merveilleux, euse [mɛRvɛjø, -øz] a marvellous, wonderful.

mes [me] dét voir **mon**.

mésange [mezɑ̃ʒ] nf tit(mouse) (pl mice).

mésaventure [mezavɑ̃tyR] nf misadventure, misfortune.

Mesdames voir **Madame**.

Mesdemoiselles voir **Mademoiselle**.

mésentente [mezɑ̃tɑ̃t] nf dissension, disagreement.

mesquin, e [mɛskɛ̃, -in] a mean, petty.

message [mesaʒ] nm message; **messager, ère** nm/f messenger.

messe [mɛs] nf mass; aller à la ~ to go to mass; ~ de minuit midnight mass.

Messieurs [mesjø] nmpl voir **Monsieur**.

mesure [məzyR] nf (évaluation, dimension) measurement; (étalon, récipient, contenu) measure; (MUS: cadence) time, tempo; (: division) bar; (retenue) moderation; (disposition) measure, step; sur ~ (costume) made-to-measure; à la ~ de (fig) worthy of; on the same scale as; dans la ~ où insofar as, inasmuch as; à

~ que as; être en ~ de to be in a position to.

mesurer [məzyrε] *vt* to measure; (*juger*) to weigh up, assess; (*limiter*) to limit, ration; (*modérer*) to moderate; se ~ avec to have a confrontation with; to tackle; il mesure 1 m 80 he's 1 m 80 tall.

met *vb voir* **mettre.**

métal, aux [metal, -o] *nm* metal; ~**lique** *a* metallic.

météo [meteo] *nf* weather report; ≈ Met Office (*Brit*), ≈ National Weather Service (*US*).

météorologie [meteɔrɔlɔʒi] *nf* meteorology.

méthode [metɔd] *nf* method; (*livre, ouvrage*) manual, tutor.

métier [metje] *nm* (*profession: gén*) job; (: *manuel*) trade; (*artisanal*) craft; (*technique, expérience*) (acquired) skill *ou* technique; (*aussi:* ~ **à tisser**) (weaving) loom.

métis, se [metis] *a, nm/f* half-caste, half-breed.

métisser [metise] *vt* to cross.

métrage [metraʒ] *nm* (*de tissu*) length; ≈ yardage; (*CINÉMA*) footage, length; **long/moyen/court** ~ full-length/medium-length/short film.

mètre [mεtr(ə)] *nm* metre; (*règle*) (metre) rule; (*ruban*) tape measure; **métrique** *a* metric.

métro [metro] *nm* underground (*Brit*), subway.

métropole [metrɔpɔl] *nf* (*capitale*) metropolis; (*pays*) home country.

mets [mε] *nm* dish.

metteur [metœr] *nm:* ~ **en scène** (*THÉÂTRE*) producer; (*CINÉMA*) director; ~ **en ondes** producer.

mettre [mεtr(ə)] *vt* **1** (*placer*) to put; ~ **en bouteille/en sac** to bottle/put in bags *ou* sacks

2 (*vêtements: revêtir*) to put on; (: *porter*) to wear; **mets ton gilet** put your cardigan on; **je ne mets plus mon manteau** I no longer wear my coat

3 (*faire fonctionner: chauffage, électricité*) to put on; (: *réveil, minuteur*) to set; (*installer: gaz, eau*) to put in, lay on; ~ **en marche** to start up

4 (*consacrer*): ~ **du temps à faire qch** to take time to do sth *ou* over sth

5 (*noter, écrire*) to say, put (down); **qu'est-ce qu'il a mis sur la carte?** what did he say *ou* write on the card?; **mettez au pluriel ...** put ... into the plural

6 (*supposer*): **mettons que ...** let's suppose *ou* say that ...

7: **y** ~ **du sien** to pull one's weight

se mettre *vi* **1** (*se placer*): **vous pouvez vous** ~ **là** you can sit (*ou* stand) there; **où ça se met?** where does it go?; **se** ~ **au lit** to get into bed; **se** ~ **au piano** to sit down at the piano; **se** ~ **de l'encre**

sur les doigts to get ink on one's fingers

2 (*s'habiller*): **se** ~ **en maillot de bain** to get into *ou* put on a swimsuit; **n'avoir rien à se** ~ to have nothing to wear

3: **se** ~ **à** to begin, start; **se** ~ **à faire** to begin *ou* start doing *ou* to do; **se** ~ **au piano** to start learning the piano; **se** ~ **au travail/à l'étude** to get down to work/one's studies.

meuble [mœbl(ə)] *nm* piece of furniture; furniture *q // a* (*terre*) loose, friable; **meublé** *nm* furnished flatlet (*Brit*) *ou* room; **meubler** *vt* to furnish; (*fig*): **meubler qch (de)** to fill sth (with).

meugler [møgle] *vi* to low, moo.

meule [møl] *nf* (*à broyer*) millstone; (*à aiguiser*) grindstone; (*de foin, blé*) stack; (*de fromage*) round.

meunier, ière [mønje, -jεr] *nm* miller // *nf* miller's wife.

meure *etc vb voir* **mourir.**

meurtre [mœrtr(ə)] *nm* murder; **meurtrier, ière** *a* (*arme etc*) deadly; (*fureur, instincts*) murderous // *nm/f* murderer/eress // *nf* (*ouverture*) loophole.

meurtrir [mœrtrir] *vt* to bruise; (*fig*) to wound; **meurtrissure** *nf* bruise; (*fig*) scar.

meus *etc vb voir* **mouvoir.**

meute [møt] *nf* pack.

Mexico [mεksiko] *n* Mexico City.

Mexique [mεksik] *nm:* **le** ~ Mexico.

MF *sigle f voir* **modulation.**

Mgr *abr de* **Monseigneur.**

mi [mi] *nm* (*MUS*) E; (*en chantant la gamme*) mi.

mi... [mi] *préfixe* half(-); mid-; **à la** ~-**janvier** in mid-January; **à** ~-**jambes/-corps** (up *ou* down) to the knees/waist; **à** ~-**hauteur/-pente** halfway up *ou* down/up *ou* down the hill.

miauler [mjole] *vi* to mew.

miche [miʃ] *nf* round *ou* cob loaf.

mi-chemin [miʃmε̃]: **à** ~ *ad* halfway, midway.

mi-clos, e [miklo, -kloz] *a* half-closed.

micro [mikro] *nm* mike, microphone; (*INFORM*) micro.

microbe [mikrɔb] *nm* germ, microbe.

micro-onde [mikrɔ̃d] *nf:* **four à** ~**s** microwave oven.

micro-ordinateur [mikrɔɔrdinatœr] *nm* microcomputer.

microscope [mikrɔskɔp] *nm* microscope.

midi [midi] *nm* midday, noon; (*moment du déjeuner*) lunchtime; **à** ~ at 12 (o'clock) *ou* midday *ou* noon; (*sud*) south; **en plein** ~ (right) in the middle of the day; facing south; **le M**~ the South (of France), the Midi.

mie [mi] *nf* crumb (of the loaf).

miel [mjεl] *nm* honey.

mien, ne [mjε̃, mjεn] *pronom:* **le(la)** ~(**ne**), **les** ~**s** mine; **les** ~**s** my family.

miette [mjɛt] *nf* (*de pain, gâteau*) crumb; (*fig: de la conversation etc*) scrap; en ~s (*fig*) in pieces *ou* bits.

mieux [mjø] ♦ *ad* **1** (*d'une meilleure façon*): ~ (**que**) better (than); **elle travaille/mange** ~ she works/eats better; **elle va** ~ she is better

2 (*de la meilleure façon*) best; **ce que je sais le** ~ what I know best; **les livres les** ~ **faits** the best made books

3: de ~ **en** ~ better and better

♦ *a* **1** (*plus à l'aise, en meilleure forme*) better; **se sentir** ~ to feel better

2 (*plus satisfaisant*) better; **c'est** ~ **ainsi** it's better like this; **c'est le** ~ **des deux** it's the better of the two; **le(la)** ~, **les** ~ the best; **demandez-lui, c'est le** ~ ask him, it's the best thing

3 (*plus joli*) better-looking

4: au ~ at best; **au** ~ **avec** on the best of terms with; **pour le** ~ for the best

♦ *nm* **1** (*progrès*) improvement

2: de mon/ton ~ as best I/you can (*ou* could); **faire de son** ~ to do one's best.

mièvre [mjɛvʀ(ə)] *a* mawkish (*Brit*), sickly sentimental.

mignon, ne [miɲɔ̃, -ɔn] *a* sweet, cute.

migraine [migʀɛn] *nf* headache; migraine.

mijoter [miʒɔte] *vt* to simmer; (*préparer avec soin*) to cook lovingly; (*affaire, projet*) to plot, cook up // *vi* to simmer.

mil [mil] *num* = **mille**.

milieu, x [miljø] *nm* (*centre*) middle; (*fig*) middle course *ou* way; happy medium; (*BIO, GÉO*) environment; (*entourage social*) milieu; background; circle; (*pègre*): **le** ~ the underworld; **au** ~ **de** in the middle of; **au beau** *ou* **en plein** ~ (**de**) right in the middle (of).

militaire [militɛʀ] *a* military, army *cpd* // *nm* serviceman.

militant, e [militɑ̃, -ɑ̃t] *a, nm/f* militant.

militer [milite] *vi* to be a militant; ~ **pour/contre** (*suj: faits, raisons etc*) to militate in favour of/against.

mille [mil] *num a ou* one thousand // *nm* (*mesure*): ~ (**marin**) nautical mile; **mettre dans le** ~ to hit the bull's-eye; **être bang on target; ~feuille** *nm* cream *ou* vanilla slice; **millénaire** *nm* millennium // *a* thousand-year-old; (*fig*) ancient; ~-**pattes** *nm inv* centipede.

millésime [milezim] *nm* year; **millésimé, e** *a* vintage *cpd*.

millet [mijɛ] *nm* millet.

milliard [miljaʀ] *nm* milliard, thousand million (*Brit*), billion (*US*); **milliardaire** *nm/f* multimillionaire (*Brit*), billionaire (*US*).

millier [milje] *nm* thousand; **un** ~ (**de**) a thousand *ou* so, about a thousand; **par** ~**s** in (their) thousands, by the thousand.

milligramme [miligʀam] *nm* milli-

gramme.

millimètre [milimɛtʀ(ə)] *nm* millimetre.

million [miljɔ̃] *nm* million; **deux** ~**s** two million; **millionnaire** *nm/f* millionaire.

mime [mim] *nm/f* (*acteur*) mime(r) // *nm* (*art*) mime, miming.

mimer [mime] *vt* to mime; (*singer*) to mimic, take off.

mimique [mimik] *nf* (*funny*) face; (*signes*) gesticulations *pl*, sign language *q*.

minable [minabl(ə)] *a* shabby(-looking); pathetic.

mince [mɛ̃s] *a* thin; (*personne, taille*) slim, slender; (*fig: profit, connaissances*) slight, small, weak // *excl*: ~ **alors!** drat it!, darn it! (*US*); **minceur** *nf* thinness; slimness, slenderness.

mine [min] *nf* (*physionomie*) expression, look; (*extérieur*) exterior, appearance; (*de crayon*) lead; (*gisement, exploitation, explosif, fig*) mine; **avoir bonne** ~ (*personne*) to look well; (*ironique*) to look an utter idiot; **avoir mauvaise** ~ to look unwell *ou* poorly; **faire** ~ **de faire** to make a pretence of doing; to make as if to do; ~ **de rien** *ou* with a casual air; although you wouldn't think so.

miner [mine] *vt* (*saper*) to undermine, erode; (*MIL*) to mine.

minerai [minʀɛ] *nm* ore.

minéral, e, aux [mineʀal, -o] *a, nm* mineral.

minéralogique [mineʀalɔʒik] *a*: **numéro** ~ registration number.

minet, te [minɛ, -ɛt] *nm/f* (*chat*) pussycat; (*péj*) young trendy.

mineur, e [minœʀ] *a* minor // *nm/f* (*JUR*) minor, person under age // *nm* (*travailleur*) miner.

miniature [minjatyʀ] *a, nf* miniature.

minibus [minibys] *nm* minibus.

mini-cassette [minikasɛt] *nf* cassette (recorder).

minier, ière [minje, -jɛʀ] *a* mining.

mini-jupe [miniʒyp] *nf* mini-skirt.

minime [minim] *a* minor, minimal.

minimiser [minimize] *vt* to minimize; (*fig*) to play down.

minimum [minimɔm] *a, nm* minimum; **au** ~ (*au moins*) at the very least.

ministère [ministɛʀ] *nm* (*aussi REL*) ministry; (*cabinet*) government; ~ **public** (*JUR*) Prosecution, State Prosecutor; **ministériel, le** *a* cabinet *cpd*; ministerial.

ministre [ministʀ(ə)] *nm* (*aussi REL*) minister; ~ **d'État** senior minister.

Minitel [minitɛl] *nm* ® videotext terminal and service.

minorité [minɔʀite] *nf* minority; **être en** ~ to be in the *ou* a minority; **mettre en** ~ (*POL*) to defeat.

minoterie [minɔtʀi] *nf* flour-mill.

minuit [minɥi] *nm* midnight.

minuscule [minyskyl] *a* minute, tiny // *nf*: (lettre) ~ small letter.

minute [minyt] *nf* minute; (*JUR*: *original*) minute, draft; **à la** ~ (just) this instant; there and then; **minuter** *vt* to time; **minuterie** *nf* time switch.

minutieux, euse [minysjø, -øz] *a* meticulous; minutely detailed.

mirabelle [miʀabɛl] *nf* (cherry) plum.

miracle [miʀakl(ə)] *nm* miracle.

mirage [miʀaʒ] *nm* mirage.

mire [miʀ] *nf*: **point de** ~ target; (*fig*) focal point; **ligne de** ~ line of sight.

miroir [miʀwaʀ] *nm* mirror.

miroiter [miʀwate] *vi* to sparkle, shimmer; **faire** ~ **qch à qn** to paint sth in glowing colours for sb, dangle sth in front of sb's eyes.

mis, e [mi, miz] *pp de* mettre // *a*: **bien** ~ well dressed // *nf* (*argent*: *au jeu*) stake; (*tenue*) clothing; attire; **être de** ~e to be acceptable *ou* in season; ~e **à feu** blast-off; ~e **de fonds** capital outlay; ~e **en plis** set; ~e **au point** (*fig*) clarification (*voir aussi* point); ~e **en scène** production.

miser [mize] *vt* (*enjeu*) to stake, bet; ~ **sur** *vt* (*cheval, numéro*) to bet on; (*fig*) to bank *ou* count on.

misérable [mizeʀabl(ə)] *a* (*lamentable, malheureux*) pitiful, wretched; (*pauvre*) poverty-stricken; (*insignifiant, mesquin*) miserable // *nm/f* wretch; (*miséreux*) poor wretch.

misère [mizɛʀ] *nf* (extreme) poverty, destitution; ~s *nfpl* woes, miseries; little troubles; **salaire de** ~ starvation wage.

miséricorde [mizeʀikɔʀd(ə)] *nf* mercy, forgiveness.

missile [misil] *nm* missile.

mission [misjɔ̃] *nf* mission; **partir en** ~ (*ADMIN, POL*) to go on an assignment; **missionnaire** *nm/f* missionary.

mit *vb voir* mettre.

mité, e [mite] *a* moth-eaten.

mi-temps [mitɑ̃] *nf inv* (*SPORT*: *période*) half (*pl* halves); (: *pause*) half-time; **à** ~ *a, ad* part-time.

mitigé, e [mitiʒe] *a* lukewarm; mixed.

mitonner [mitɔne] *vt* to cook with loving care; (*fig*) to cook up quietly.

mitoyen, ne [mitwajɛ̃, -ɛn] *a* common, party *cpd*.

mitrailler [mitʀaje] *vt* to machine-gun; (*fig: photographier*) to take shot after shot of; to pelt, bombard; **mitraillette** *nf* submachine gun; **mitrailleuse** *nf* machine gun.

mi-voix [mivwa]: **à** ~ *ad* in a low *ou* hushed voice.

mixage [miksaʒ] *nm* (*CINÉMA*) (sound) mixing.

mixer [miksœʀ] *nm* (food) mixer.

mixte [mikst(ə)] *a* (*gén*) mixed; (*SCOL*) mixed, coeducational; **à usage** ~ dual-purpose.

mixture [mikstyʀ] *nf* mixture; (*fig*) concoction.

MLF *sigle m* = Mouvement de libération de la femme.

Mlle, *pl* **Mlles** *abr de* **Mademoiselle**.

MM *abr de* **Messieurs**.

Mme, *pl* **Mmes** *abr de* **Madame**.

Mo *abr de* **métro**.

mobile [mɔbil] *a* mobile; (*pièce de machine*) moving; (*élément de meuble etc*) movable // *nm* (*motif*) motive; (*œuvre d'art*) mobile.

mobilier, ière [mɔbilje, -jɛʀ] *a* (*JUR*) personal // *nm* furniture.

mobiliser [mɔbilize] *vt* (*MIL, gén*) to mobilize.

moche [mɔʃ] *a* (*fam*) ugly; rotten.

modalité [mɔdalite] *nf* form, mode; ~s *nfpl* (*d'un accord etc*) clauses, terms.

mode [mɔd] *nf* fashion // *nm* (*manière*) form, mode; **à la** ~ fashionable, in fashion; ~ **d'emploi** directions pl (for use).

modèle [mɔdɛl] *a, nm* model; (*qui pose: de peintre*) sitter; ~ **déposé** registered design; ~ **réduit** small-scale model.

modeler [mɔdle] *vt* (*ART*) to model, mould; (*suj: vêtement, érosion*) to mould, shape.

modem [mɔdɛm] *nm* modem.

modéré, e [mɔdeʀe] *a, nm/f* moderate.

modérer [mɔdeʀe] *vt* to moderate; **se** ~ *vi* to restrain o.s.

moderne [mɔdɛʀn(ə)] *a* modern // *nm* modern style; modern furniture; **moderniser** *vt* to modernize.

modeste [mɔdɛst(ə)] *a* modest; **modestie** *nf* modesty.

modifier [mɔdifje] *vt* to modify, alter; **se** ~ *vi* to alter.

modique [mɔdik] *a* modest.

modiste [mɔdist(ə)] *nf* milliner.

modulation [mɔdylasjɔ̃] *nf*: ~ **de fréquence** (**FM** *ou* **MF**) frequency modulation.

module [mɔdyl] *nm* module.

moelle [mwal] *nf* marrow.

moelleux, euse [mwalø, -øz] *a* soft; (*au goût, à l'ouïe*) mellow.

moellon [mwalɔ̃] *nm* rubble stone.

mœurs [mœʀ] *nfpl* (*conduite*) morals; (*manières*) manners; (*pratiques sociales, mode de vie*) habits.

mohair [mɔɛʀ] *nm* mohair.

moi [mwa] *pronom* me; (*emphatique*): ~, **je** ... for my part, I ...., **I** myself ....

moignon [mwaɲɔ̃] *nm* stump.

moi-même [mwamɛm] *pronom* myself; (*emphatique*) I myself.

moindre [mwɛ̃dʀ(ə)] *a* lesser; lower; **le(la)** ~, **les** ~s the least, the slightest.

moine [mwan] *nm* monk, friar.

moineau, x [mwano] *nm* sparrow.

moins [mwɛ̃] ♦ *ad* **1** (*comparatif*): ~ (que) less (than); ~ **grand** que less tall than, not as tall as; ~ **je travaille, mieux je me porte** the less I work, the better I feel

2 (*superlatif*): **le** ~ (the) least; **c'est ce que j'aime le** ~ it's what I like (the) least; **le(la)** ~ **doué(e)** the least gifted; **au** ~, **du** ~ at least; **pour le** ~ at the very least

3: ~ **de** (*quantité*) less (than); (*nombre*) fewer (than); ~ **de sable/d'eau** less sand/water; ~ **de livres/gens** fewer books/people; ~ **de 2 ans** less than 2 years; ~ **de midi** not yet midday

4: **de** ~, **en** ~: 100 F/3 **jours de** ~ 100 F/3 days less; 3 **livres en** ~ 3 books fewer; 3 books too few; **de l'argent en** ~ less money; **le soleil en** ~ but for the sun, minus the sun; **de** ~ **en** ~ less and less

5: **à** ~ **de, à** ~ **que** unless; **à** ~ **de faire** unless we do (*ou* he does *etc*); **à** ~ **que tu ne fasses** unless you do; **à** ~ **d'un accident** barring any accident

♦ *prép*: 4 ~ 2 4 minus 2; **il est** ~ 5 it's 5 to; **il fait** ~ 5 it's 5 (degrees) below (freezing), it's minus 5.

mois [mwa] *nm* month; ~ **double** (*COMM*) extra month's salary.

moisi [mwazi] *nm* mould, mildew; **odeur de** ~ musty smell.

moisir [mwaziʀ] *vi* to go mouldy; (*fig*) to rot; to hang about.

moisissure [mwazisyʀ] *nf* mould *q*.

moisson [mwasɔ̃] *nf* harvest; **moissonner** *vt* to harvest, reap; **moissonneuse** *nf* (*machine*) harvester.

moite [mwat] *a* sweaty, sticky.

moitié [mwatje] *nf* half (*pl* halves); **la** ~ half; **la** ~ **de** half (of); **la** ~ **du temps/des gens** half the time/the people; **à la** ~ **de** halfway through; **à** ~ half (*avant le verbe*); half- (*avant l'adjectif*); **de** ~ by half; ~ ~ half-and-half.

mol [mɔl] *a voir* **mou**.

molaire [mɔlɛʀ] *nf* molar.

molester [mɔlɛste] *vt* to manhandle, maul (about).

molette [mɔlɛt] *nf* toothed *ou* cutting wheel.

molle [mɔl] *af voir* **mou**; ~**ment** *ad* softly; ` (*péj*) sluggishly; (*protester*) feebly.

mollet [mɔlɛ] *nm* calf (*pl* calves) // *am*: **œuf** ~ soft-boiled egg.

molletonné, e [mɔltɔne] *a* fleece-lined.

mollir [mɔliʀ] *vi* to give way; to relent; to go soft.

môme [mom] *nm/f* (*fam: enfant*) brat; (: *fille*) chick.

moment [mɔmɑ̃] *nm* moment; **ce n'est pas le** ~ this is not the (right) time; **à un certain** ~ at some point; **à un** ~ **donné** at a certain point; **pour un bon** ~

for a good while; **pour le** ~ for the moment, for the time being; **au** ~ **de** at the time of; **au** ~ **où** as; at a time when; **à tout** ~ at any time *ou* moment; constantly, continually; **en ce** ~ at the moment; at present; **sur le** ~ at the time; **par** ~**s** now and then, at times; **du** ~ **où** *ou* **que** seeing that, since; **momentané, e** *a* temporary, momentary.

momie [mɔmi] *nf* mummy.

mon [mɔ̃], **ma** [ma], *pl* **mes** [me] *dét* my.

Monaco [mɔnako] *nm*: **le** ~ Monaco.

monarchie [mɔnaʀʃi] *nf* monarchy.

monastère [mɔnastɛʀ] *nm* monastery.

monceau, x [mɔ̃so] *nm* heap.

mondain, e [mɔ̃dɛ̃, -ɛn] *a* society *cpd*; social; fashionable // *nf*: **la M~e, la police** ~**e** ≈ the vice squad.

monde [mɔ̃d] *nm* world; (*haute société*): **le** ~ (high) society; (*milieu*): **être du même** ~ to move in the same circles; (*gens*): **il y a du** ~ (*beaucoup de gens*) there are a lot of people; (*quelques personnes*) there are some people; **beaucoup/peu de** ~ many/few people; **le meilleur** *etc* **du** ~ the best *etc* in the world *ou* on earth; **mettre au** ~ to bring into the world; **pas le moins du** ~ not in the least; **se faire un** ~ **de qch** to make a great deal of fuss about sth; **mondial, e, aux** *a* (*population*) world *cpd*; (*influence*) world-wide; **mondialement** *ad* throughout the world.

monégasque [mɔnegask(ə)] *a* Monegasque, of *ou* from Monaco.

monétaire [mɔnetɛʀ] *a* monetary.

moniteur, trice [mɔnitœʀ, -tʀis] *nm/f* (*SPORT*) instructor/instructress; (*de colonie de vacances*) supervisor // *nm* (*écran*) monitor.

monnaie [mɔnɛ] *nf* (*pièce*) coin; (*ÉCON, gén: moyen d'échange*) currency; (*petites pièces*): **avoir de la** ~ to have (some) change; **faire de la** ~ to get (some) change; **avoir/faire la** ~ **de 20 F** to have change of/get change for 20 F; **rendre à qn la** ~ (**sur 20 F**) to give sb the change (out of *ou* from 20 F); **monnayer** *vt* to convert into cash; (*talent*) to capitalize on.

monologue [mɔnɔlɔg] *nm* monologue, soliloquy; **monologuer** *vi* to soliloquize.

monopole [mɔnɔpɔl] *nm* monopoly.

monotone [mɔnɔtɔn] *a* monotonous.

monseigneur [mɔ̃sɛɲœʀ] *nm* (*archevêque, évêque*) Your (*ou* His) Grace; (*cardinal*) Your (*ou* His) Eminence.

Monsieur [məsjø], *pl* **Messieurs** [mesjø] *titre* Mr ['mistə*] // *nm* (*homme quelconque*): **un/le m**~ a/the gentleman; *voir aussi* **Madame**.

monstre [mɔ̃stʀ(ə)] *nm* monster // *a*: **un travail** ~ a fantastic amount of work; an enormous job.

mont [mɔ̃] *nm*: par ~s et par vaux up hill and down dale; le M~ Blanc Mont Blanc.

montage [mɔ̃taʒ] *nm* putting up; mounting, setting; assembly; (*PHOTO*) photomontage; (*CINÉMA*) editing.

montagnard, e [mɔ̃taɲar, -ard(ə)] *a* mountain *cpd* // *nm/f* mountain-dweller.

montagne [mɔ̃taɲ] *nf* (*cime*) mountain; (*région*): la ~ the mountains *pl*; ~s russes big dipper *sg*, switchback *sg*.

montagneux, euse [mɔ̃taɲø, -øz] *a* mountainous; hilly.

montant, e [mɔ̃tɑ̃, -ɑ̃t] *a* rising; (*robe, corsage*) high-necked // *nm* (*somme, total*) (sum) total, (total) amount; (*de fenêtre*) upright; (*de lit*) post.

mont-de-piété [mɔ̃dpjete] *nm* pawnshop.

monte-charge [mɔ̃tʃarʒ(ə)] *nm inv* goods lift, hoist.

montée [mɔ̃te] *nf* rising, rise; ascent, climb; (*chemin*) way up; (*côte*) hill; au milieu de la ~ halfway up.

monter [mɔ̃te] *vt* (*escalier, côte*) to go (*ou* come) up; (*valise, paquet*) to take (*ou* bring) up; (*cheval*) to mount; (*étagère*) to raise; (*tente, échafaudage*) to put up; (*machine*) to assemble; (*bijou*) to mount, set; (*COUTURE*) to set in; to sew on; (*CINÉMA*) to edit; (*THÉÂTRE*) to put on, stage; (*société etc*) to set up // *vi* to go (*ou* come) up; (*avion etc*) to climb, go up; (*chemin, niveau, température*) to go up, rise; (*passager*) to get on; (*à cheval*): ~ bien/mal to ride well/badly; ~ à pied to walk up, go up on foot; ~ à bicyclette/en voiture to cycle/drive up, go up by bicycle/by car; ~ dans le train/l'avion to get into the train/plane, board the train/plane; ~ sur to climb up onto; ~ à cheval to get on *ou* mount a horse; se ~ à (*frais etc*) to add up to, come to.

monticule [mɔ̃tikyl] *nm* mound.

montre [mɔ̃tr(ə)] *nf* watch; faire ~ de to show, display; contre la ~ (*SPORT*) against the clock; ~-bracelet *nf* wrist watch.

montrer [mɔ̃tre] *vt* to show; ~ qch à qn to show sb sth.

monture [mɔ̃tyr] *nf* (*bête*) mount; (*d'une bague*) setting; (*de lunettes*) frame.

monument [mɔnymɑ̃] *nm* monument; ~ aux morts war memorial.

moquer [mɔke]: se ~ de *vt* to make fun of, laugh at; (*fam: se désintéresser de*) not to care about; (*tromper*): se ~ de qn to take sb for a ride.

moquette [mɔkɛt] *nf* fitted carpet.

moqueur, euse [mɔkœr, -øz] *a* mocking.

moral, e, aux [mɔral, -o] *a* moral // *nm* morale // *nf* (*conduite*) morals *pl*; (*règles*) moral code, ethic; (*valeurs*) moral

standards *pl*, morality; (*science*) ethics *sg*, moral philosophy; (*conclusion: d'une fable etc*) moral; avoir le ~ à zéro to be really down; faire la ~e à to lecture, preach at; ~ité *nf* morality; (*conduite*) morals *pl*; (*conclusion, enseignement*) moral.

morceau, x [mɔrso] *nm* piece, bit; (*d'une œuvre*) passage, extract; (*MUS*) piece; (*CULIN: de viande*) cut; mettre en ~x to pull to pieces *ou* bits.

morceler [mɔrsəle] *vt* to break up, divide up.

mordant, e [mɔrdɑ̃, -ɑ̃t] *a* scathing, cutting; biting.

mordiller [mɔrdije] *vt* to nibble at, chew at.

mordre [mɔrdr(ə)] *vt* to bite; (*suj: lime, vis*) to bite into // *vi* (*poisson*) to bite; ~ sur (*fig*) to go over into, overlap into; ~ à l'hameçon to bite, rise to the bait.

mordu, e [mɔrdy] *nm/f*: un ~ du jazz a jazz fanatic.

morfondre [mɔrfɔ̃dr(ə)]: se ~ *vi* to mope.

morgue [mɔrg(ə)] *nf* (*arrogance*) haughtiness; (*lieu: de la police*) morgue; (: à l'hôpital) mortuary.

morne [mɔrn(ə)] *a* dismal, dreary.

mors [mɔr] *nm* bit.

morse [mɔrs(ə)] *nm* (*ZOOL*) walrus; (*TÉL*) Morse (code).

morsure [mɔrsyr] *nf* bite.

mort [mɔr] *nf* death.

mort, e [mɔr, mɔrt(ə)] *pp de* mourir // *a* dead // *nm/f* (*défunt*) dead man/woman; (*victime*): il y a eu plusieurs ~s several people were killed, there were several killed // *nm* (*CARTES*) dummy; ~ ou vif dead or alive; ~ de peur/fatigue frightened to death/dead tired.

mortalité [mɔrtalite] *nf* mortality, death rate.

mortel, le [mɔrtɛl] *a* (*poison etc*) deadly, lethal; (*accident, blessure*) fatal; (*REL*) mortal; (*fig*) deathly; deadly boring.

mortier [mɔrtje] *nm* (*gén*) mortar.

mort-né, e [mɔrne] *a* (*enfant*) stillborn.

mortuaire [mɔrtɥer] *a* funeral *cpd*.

morue [mɔry] *nf* (*ZOOL*) cod *inv*.

mosaïque [mɔzaik] *nf* (*ART*) mosaic; (*fig*) patchwork.

Moscou [mɔsku] *n* Moscow.

mosquée [mɔske] *nf* mosque.

mot [mo] *nm* word; (*message*) line, note; (*bon mot etc*) saying; sally; ~ à ~ word for word; ~s croisés crossword (puzzle) *sg*; ~ d'ordre watchword; ~ de passe password.

motard [mɔtar] *nm* biker; (*policier*) motorcycle cop.

motel [mɔtɛl] *nm* motel.

moteur, trice [mɔtœr, -tris] *a* (*ANAT*,

PHYSIOL) motor; (*TECH*) driving; (*AUTO*): **à 4 roues motrices** 4-wheel drive // *nm* engine, motor; **à ~** power-driven, motor *cpd*.

motif [mɔtif] *nm* (*cause*) motive; (*décoratif*) design, pattern, motif; (*d'un tableau*) subject, motif; **~s** *nmpl* (*JUR*) grounds *pl*; **sans ~ a** groundless.

motiver [mɔtive] *vt* (*justifier*) to justify, account for; (*ADMIN, JUR, PSYCH*) to motivate.

moto [mɔto] *nf* (motor)bike; **~cyclisme** *nm* motorcycle racing; **~cycliste** *nm/f* motorcyclist.

motorisé, e [mɔtɔrize] *a* (*troupe*) motorized; (*personne*) having transport *ou* a car.

motrice [mɔtris] *a voir* **moteur**.

motte [mɔt] *nf*: **~ de terre** lump of earth, clod (of earth); **~ de gazon** turf, sod; **~ de beurre** lump of butter.

mou(mol), molle [mu, mɔl] *a* soft; (*péj*) flabby; sluggish // *nm* (*abats*) lights, lungs *pl*; (*de la corde*): **avoir du ~** to be slack.

mouche [muʃ] *nf* fly.

moucher [muʃe] *vt* (*enfant*) to blow the nose of; (*chandelle*) to snuff (out); **se ~** *vi* to blow one's nose.

moucheron [muʃrɔ̃] *nm* midge.

moucheté, e [muʃte] *a* dappled; flecked.

mouchoir [muʃwar] *nm* handkerchief, hanky; **~ en papier** tissue, paper hanky.

moudre [mudr(ə)] *vt* to grind.

moue [mu] *nf* pout; **faire la ~** to pout; (*fig*) to pull a face.

mouette [mwɛt] *nf* (sea)gull.

moufle [mufl(ə)] *nf* (*gant*) mitt(en).

mouillé, e [muje] *a* wet.

mouiller [muje] *vt* (*humecter*) to wet, moisten; (*tremper*): **~ qn/qch** to make sb/sth wet; (*couper, diluer*) to water down; (*mine etc*) to lay // *vi* (*NAVIG*) to lie *ou* be at anchor; **se ~** to get wet; (*fam*) to commit o.s.; to get o.s. involved.

moule [mul] *nf* mussel // *nm* (*creux, CULIN*) mould; (*modèle plein*) cast; **~ à gâteaux** *nm* cake tin (*Brit*) *ou* pan (*US*).

moulent *vb voir* **moudre, mouler**.

mouler [mule] *vt* (*suj: vêtement*) to hug, fit closely round; **~ qch sur** (*fig*) to model sth on.

moulin [mulɛ̃] *nm* mill; **~ à café/à poivre** coffee/pepper mill; **~ à légumes** (vegetable) shredder; **~ à paroles** (*fig*) chatterbox; **~ à vent** windmill.

moulinet [mulinɛ] *nm* (*de treuil*) winch; (*de canne à pêche*) reel; (*mouvement*): **faire des ~s avec qch** to whirl sth around.

moulinette [mulinɛt] *nf* (vegetable) shredder.

moulu, e [muly] *pp de* **moudre**.

moulure [mulyr] *nf* (*ornement*) moulding.

mourant, e [murɑ̃, -ɑ̃t] *a* dying.

mourir [murir] *vi* to die; **~ de froid/faim** to die of exposure/hunger; **~ de faim/d'ennui** (*fig*) to be starving/be bored to death; **~ d'envie de faire** to be dying to do.

mousse [mus] *nf* (*BOT*) moss; (*écume: sur eau, bière*) froth, foam; (*: shampooing*) lather; (*CULIN*) mousse // *nm* (*NAVIG*) ship's boy; **bas ~** stretch stockings; **~ carbonique** (fire-fighting) foam; **~ à raser** shaving foam.

mousseline [muslin] *nf* muslin; chiffon.

mousser [muse] *vi* to foam; to lather.

mousseux, euse [musø, -øz] *a* frothy // *nm*: (*vin*) **~** sparkling wine.

mousson [musɔ̃] *nf* monsoon.

moustache [mustaʃ] *nf* moustache; **~s** (*du chat*) whiskers *pl*.

moustiquaire [mustikɛr] *nf* mosquito net (*ou* screen).

moustique [mustik] *nm* mosquito.

moutarde [mutard(ə)] *nf* mustard.

mouton [mutɔ̃] *nm* (*ZOOL, péj*) sheep *inv*; (*peau*) sheepskin; (*CULIN*) mutton.

mouvant, e [muvɑ̃, -ɑ̃t] *a* unsettled; changing; shifting.

mouvement [muvmɑ̃] *nm* (*gén, aussi: mécanisme*) movement; (*fig*) activity; impulse; gesture; (*MUS: rythme*) tempo (*pl* s); **en ~** in motion; on the move; **mouvementé, e** *a* (*vie, poursuite*) eventful; (*réunion*) turbulent.

mouvoir [muvwar] *vt* (*levier, membre*) to move; **se ~** *vi* to move.

moyen, ne [mwajɛ̃, -ɛn] *a* average; (*tailles, prix*) medium; (*de grandeur moyenne*) medium-sized // *nm* (*façon*) means *sg*, way // *nf* average; (*MATH*) mean; (*SCOL: à l'examen*) pass mark; (*AUTO*) average speed; **~s** (*capacités*) means; **au ~ de** by means of; **par tous les ~s** by every possible means, every possible way; **par ses propres ~s** all by oneself; **en ~ne** on (an) average; **~ de transport** means of transport; **~ âge** Middle Ages; **~ne d'âge** average age.

moyennant [mwajɛnɑ̃] *prép* (*somme*) for; (*service, conditions*) in return for; (*travail, effort*) with.

Moyen-Orient [mwajɛnɔrjɑ̃] *nm*: **le ~** the Middle East.

moyeu, x [mwajø] *nm* hub.

MST *sigle f* (= *maladie sexuellement transmissible*) sexually transmitted disease.

mû, mue [my] *pp de* **mouvoir**.

muer [mɥe] *vi* (*oiseau, mammifère*) to moult; (*serpent*) to slough; (*jeune garçon*): **il mue** his voice is breaking; **se ~ en** to transform into.

muet, te [mɥe, -ɛt] *a* dumb; (*fig*): **~**

d'admiration etc speechless with admiration etc; (joie, douleur, CINÉMA) silent; (carte) blank // nm/f mute.

mufle [myfl(ə)] nm muzzle; (goujat) boor.

mugir [myʒiʀ] vi (taureau) to bellow; (vache) to low; (fig) to howl.

muguet [mygɛ] nm lily of the valley.

mule [myl] nf (ZOOL) (she-)mule.

mulet [mylɛ] nm (ZOOL) (he-)mule.

multiple [myltipl(ə)] a multiple, numerous; (varié) many, manifold // nm (MATH) multiple.

multiplication [myltiplikɑsjɔ̃] nf multiplication.

multiplier [myltiplije] vt to multiply; se ~ vi to multiply; to increase in number.

municipal, e, aux [mynisipal, -o] a municipal; town cpd, ≈ borough cpd.

municipalité [mynisipalite] nf (corps municipal) town council, corporation.

munir [myniʀ] vt: ~ qn/qch de to equip sb/sth with.

munitions [mynisjɔ̃] nfpl ammunition sg.

mur [myʀ] nm wall; ~ du son sound barrier.

mûr, e [myʀ] a ripe; (personne) mature // nf blackberry; mulberry.

muraille [myʀɑj] nf (high) wall.

mural, e, aux [myʀal, -o] a wall cpd; mural.

murer [myʀe] vt (enclos) to wall (in); (porte, issue) to wall up; (personne) to wall up ou in.

muret [myʀɛ] nm low wall.

mûrir [myʀiʀ] vi (fruit, blé) to ripen; (abcès, furoncle) to come to a head; (fig: idée, personne) to mature // vt to ripen; to (make) mature.

murmure [myʀmyʀ] nm murmur; ~s (plaintes) murmurings, mutterings; **murmurer** vi to murmur; (se plaindre) to mutter, grumble.

muscade [myskad] nf (aussi: noix ~) nutmeg.

muscat [myska] nm muscat grape; muscatel (wine).

muscle [myskl(ə)] nm muscle; **musclé, e** a muscular; (fig) strong-arm.

museau, x [myzo] nm muzzle.

musée [myze] nm museum; art gallery.

museler [myzle] vt to muzzle; **muselière** nf muzzle.

musette [myzɛt] nf (sac) lunchbag // a inv (orchestre etc) accordion cpd.

musical, e, aux [myzikal, -o] a musical.

music-hall [myzikol] nm variety theatre; (genre) variety.

musicien, ne [myzisjɛ̃, -jɛn] a musical // nm/f musician.

musique [myzik] nf music; (fanfare) band; ~ de chambre chamber music.

musulman, e [myzylmɑ̃, -an] a, nm/f

Moslem, Muslim.

mutation [mytɑsjɔ̃] nf (ADMIN) transfer.

mutilé, e [mytile] nm/f disabled person (through loss of limbs).

mutiler [mytile] vt to mutilate, maim.

mutin, e [mytɛ̃, -in] a (air, ton) mischievous, impish // nm/f (MIL, NAVIG) mutineer.

mutinerie [mytinʀi] nf mutiny.

mutisme [mytism(ə)] nm silence.

mutuel, le [mytɥɛl] a mutual // nf mutual benefit society.

myope [mjɔp] a short-sighted.

myosotis [mjozɔtis] nm forget-me-not.

myrtille [miʀtij] nf bilberry.

mystère [mistɛʀ] nm mystery; **mystérieux, euse** a mysterious.

mystifier [mistifje] vt to fool; to mystify.

mythe [mit] nm myth.

mythologie [mitɔlɔʒi] nf mythology.

N

n' [n] ad voir ne.

nacelle [nasɛl] nf (de ballon) basket.

nacre [nakʀ(ə)] nf mother of pearl; **nacré, e** a pearly.

nage [naʒ] nf swimming; style of swimming, stroke; traverser/s'éloigner à la ~ to swim across/away; en ~ bathed in perspiration.

nageoire [naʒwaʀ] nf fin.

nager [naʒe] vi to swim; **nageur, euse** nm/f swimmer.

naguère [nagɛʀ] ad formerly.

naïf, ïve [naif, naiv] a naïve.

nain, e [nɛ̃, nɛn] nm/f dwarf.

naissance [nesɑ̃s] nf birth; donner ~ à to give birth to; (fig) to give rise to.

naître [nɛtʀ(ə)] vi to be born; (fig): ~ de to arise from, be born out of; il est né en 1960 he was born in 1960; faire ~ (fig) to give rise to, arouse.

nana [nana] nf (fam: fille) chick, bird (Brit).

nantir [nɑ̃tiʀ] vt: ~ qn de to provide sb with; les **nantis** (péj) the well-to-do.

nappe [nap] nf tablecloth; (fig) sheet; layer; ~ron nm table-mat.

naquit etc vb voir **naître**.

narguer [naʀge] vt to taunt.

narine [naʀin] nf nostril.

narquois, e [naʀkwa, -waz] a derisive, mocking.

narrer [naʀe] vt to tell the story of, recount.

naseau, x [nazo] nm nostril.

natal, e [natal] a native.

natalité [natalite] nf birth rate.

natation [natɑsjɔ̃] nf swimming.

natif, ïve [natif, -iv] a native.

nation [nɑsjɔ̃] nf nation.

national, e, aux [nɑsjɔnal, -o] a national // nf: (route) ~e ≈ A road (Brit),

≈ state highway (*US*); **~iser** *vt* to nationalize; **~ité** *nf* nationality.
natte [nat] *nf* (*tapis*) mat; (*cheveux*) plait.
naturaliser [natyralize] *vt* to naturalize.
nature [natyr] *nf* nature // *a, ad* (*CULIN*) plain, without seasoning or sweetening; (*café, thé*) black, without sugar; payer en ~ to pay in kind; ~ **morte** still-life;
naturel, le *a* (*gén, aussi: enfant*) natural // *nm* naturalness; disposition, nature; (*autochtone*) native; **naturellement** *ad* naturally; (*bien súr*) of course.
naufrage [nofraʒ] *nm* (ship)wreck; (*fig*) wreck; **faire ~** to be shipwrecked.
nauséabond, e [nozeabɔ̃, -ɔ̃d] *a* foul, nauseous.
nausée [noze] *nf* nausea.
nautique [notik] *a* nautical, water *cpd*.
nautisme [notism] *nm* water sports.
navet [navɛ] *nm* turnip.
navette [navɛt] *nf* shuttle; **faire la ~** (**entre**) to go to and fro *ou* shuttle (between).
navigable [navigabl(ə)] *a* navigable.
navigateur [navigatœr] *nm* (*NAVIG*) seafarer, sailor; (*AVIAT*) navigator.
navigation [navigasjɔ̃] *nf* navigation, sailing; shipping.
naviguer [navige] *vi* to navigate, sail.
navire [navir] *nm* ship.
navrer [navre] *vt* to upset, distress; **je suis navré** I'm so sorry.
ne, n' [n(ə)] *ad vt* (*voir pas, plus, jamais etc*) (*explétif*) *non traduit*.
né, e [ne] *pp* (*voir* **naître**): ~ **en 1960** born in 1960; **~e** Scott née Scott.
néanmoins [neɑ̃mwɛ] *ad* nevertheless.
néant [neɑ̃] *nm* nothingness; **réduire à ~** to bring to nought; (*espoir*) to dash.
nécessaire [nesesɛr] *a* necessary // *nm* necessary; (*sac*) kit; ~ **de couture** sewing kit; ~ **de toilette** toilet bag; **nécessité** *nf* necessity; **nécessiter** *vt* to require; **nécessiteux, euse** *a* needy.
nécrologique [nekrɔlɔʒik] *a*: **article ~** obituary; **rubrique ~** obituary column.
néerlandais, e [neɛrlɑ̃dɛ, -ɛz] *a* Dutch.
nef [nɛf] *nf* (*d'église*) nave.
néfaste [nefast(ə)] *a* baneful; ill-fated.
négatif, ive [negatif, iv] *a* negative // *nm* (*PHOTO*) negative.
négligé, e [negliʒe] *a* (*en désordre*) slovenly // *nm* (*tenue*) negligee.
négligent, e [negliʒɑ̃, -ɑ̃t] *a* careless, negligent.
négliger [negliʒe] *vt* (*épouse, jardin*) to neglect; (*tenue*) to be careless about; (*avis, précautions*) to disregard; ~ **de faire** to fail to do, not bother to do.
négoce [negɔs] *nm* trade.
négociant [negɔsjɑ̃] *nm* merchant.
négociation [negɔsjasjɔ̃] *nf* negotiation.
négocier [negɔsje] *vi, vt* to negotiate.

nègre [nɛgr(ə)] *nm* Negro; ghost (writer).
négresse [negrɛs] *nf* Negro woman.
neige [nɛʒ] *nf* snow; **neiger** *vi* to snow; **neigeux, euse** *a* snowy, snow-covered.
nénuphar [nenyfar] *nm* water-lily.
néon [neɔ̃] *nm* neon.
néophyte [neɔfit] *nm/f* novice.
néo-zélandais, e [neozelɑ̃dɛ, -ɛz] *a* New Zealand *cpd* //: **N~, e** *nm/f* New Zealander.
nerf [nɛr] *nm* nerve; (*fig*) spirit; stamina; **nerveux, euse** *a* nervous; (*voiture*) nippy, responsive; (*tendineux*) sinewy; **nervosité** *nf* excitability; state of agitation; nervousness.
nervure [nɛrvyr] *nf* vein.
n'est-ce pas [nɛspa] *ad* isn't it?, won't you? *etc, selon le verbe qui précède*.
net, nette [nɛt] *a* (*sans équivoque, distinct*) clear; (*évident*) definite; (*propre*) neat, clean; (*COMM*: *prix, salaire*) net // *ad* (*refuser*) flatly; **s'arrêter ~** to stop dead // *nm*: **mettre au ~** to copy out; **nettement** *ad* clearly, distinctly; **~teté** *nf* clearness.
nettoyage [netwajaʒ] *nm* cleaning; ~ **à sec** dry cleaning.
nettoyer [netwaje] *vt* to clean; (*fig*) to clean out.
neuf [nœf] *num* nine.
neuf, neuve [nœf, nœv] *a* new // *nm*: **repeindre à ~** to redecorate; **remettre à ~** to do up (as good as new), refurbish.
neutre [nøtr(ə)] *a* neutral; (*LING*) neuter // *nm* (*LING*) neuter.
neuve [nœv] *a voir* **neuf**.
neuvième [nœvjɛm] *num* ninth.
neveu, x [nəvø] *nm* nephew.
névrosé, e [nevroze] *a, nm/f* neurotic.
nez [ne] *nm* nose; ~ **à ~ avec** face to face with; **avoir du ~** to have flair.
ni [ni] *cj*: ~ **l'un ~ l'autre ne sont** neither one nor the other are; **il n'a rien dit ~ fait** he hasn't said or done anything.
niais, e [nje, -ɛz] *a* silly, thick.
niche [niʃ] *nf* (*du chien*) kennel; (*de mur*) recess, niche.
nicher [niʃe] *vi* to nest.
nid [ni] *nm* nest; ~ **de poule** pothole.
nièce [njɛs] *nf* niece.
nier [nje] *vt* to deny.
nigaud, e [nigo, -od] *nm/f* booby, fool.
Nil [nil] *nm*: **le ~** the Nile.
n'importe [nɛ̃pɔrt(ə)] *ad*: ~ **qui/quoi/où** anybody/anything/anywhere; ~ **quand** any time; ~ **quel/quelle** any; ~ **lequel/laquelle** any (one); ~ **comment** (*sans soin*) carelessly.
niveau, x [nivo] *nm* level; (*des élèves, études*) standard; **de ~** (**avec**) level (with); ~ **(à bulle)** spirit level; **le ~ de la mer** sea level; ~ **de vie** standard of living.
niveler [nivle] *vt* to level.

NN *abr* (= *nouvelle norme*) revised standard of hotel classification.

noble [nɔbl(ə)] *a* noble; **noblesse** *nf* nobility; (*d'une action etc*) nobleness.

noce [nɔs] *nf* wedding; (*gens*) wedding party (*ou* guests *pl*); **faire la ~** (*fam*) to go on a binge; **~s d'or/d'argent** golden/silver wedding.

nocif, ive [nɔsif, -iv] *a* harmful, noxious.

noctambule [nɔktɑ̃byl] *nm* night-bird.

nocturne [nɔktyʀn(ə)] *a* nocturnal // *nf* late-night opening.

Noël [nɔɛl] *nm* Christmas.

nœud [nø] *nm* (*de corde, du bois*, NA-VIG) knot; (*ruban*) bow; (*fig: liens*) bond, tie; **~ papillon** bow tie.

noir, e [nwaʀ] *a* black; (*obscur, sombre*) dark // *nm/f* black man/woman, Negro/Negro woman // *nm*: **dans le ~** in the dark; **travail au ~** moonlighting // *nf* (MUS) crotchet (*Brit*), quarter note (US); **~ceur** *nf* blackness; darkness; **~cir** *vt, vi* to blacken.

noisette [nwazɛt] *nf* hazelnut.

noix [nwa] *nf* walnut; (CULIN): **une ~ de beurre** a knob of butter; **~ de cajou** cashew nut; **~ de coco** coconut.

nom [nɔ̃] *nm* name; (LING) noun; **~ d'emprunt** assumed name; **~ de famille** surname; **~ de jeune fille** maiden name.

nombre [nɔ̃bʀ(ə)] *nm* number; **venir en ~** to come in large numbers; **depuis d'années** for many years; **ils sont au ~ de 3** there are 3 of them; **au ~ de mes amis** among my friends.

nombreux, euse [nɔ̃bʀø, -øz] *a* many, numerous; (*avec nom sg: foule etc*) large; **peu ~** few; small.

nombril [nɔ̃bʀi] *nm* navel.

nommer [nɔme] *vt* (*baptiser, mentionner*) to name; (*qualifier*) to call; (*élire*) to appoint, nominate; **se ~: il se nomme Pascal** his name's Pascal, he's called Pascal.

non [nɔ̃] *ad* (*réponse*) no; (*avec loin, sans, seulement*) not; **~ que**, **~ pas que** not that; **moi ~ plus** neither do I, I don't either.

non-alcoolisé, e [nɔnalkɔlize] *a* non-alcoholic.

non-fumeur [nɔ̃fymœʀ] *nm* non-smoker.

non-lieu [nɔ̃ljø] *nm*: **il y a eu ~** the case was dismissed.

non-sens [nɔ̃sɑ̃s] *nm* absurdity.

nord [nɔʀ] *nm* North // *a* northern; north; **au ~** (*situation*) in the north; (*direction*) to the north; **au ~ de** (to the) north of; **~-est** *nm* North-East; **~-ouest** *nm* North-West.

normal, e, aux [nɔʀmal, -o] *a* normal // *nf*: **la ~e** the norm, the average; **~ement** *ad* (*en général*) normally; **~iser** *vt* (COMM, TECH) to standardize.

normand, e [nɔʀmɑ̃, -ɑ̃d] *a* of Normandy.

Normandie [nɔʀmɑ̃di] *nf* Normandy.

norme [nɔʀm(ə)] *nf* norm; (TECH) standard.

Norvège [nɔʀvɛʒ] *nf* Norway; **norvégien, ne** *a, nm, nf* Norwegian.

nos [no] *dét voir* **notre**.

nostalgie [nɔstalʒi] *nf* nostalgia.

notable [nɔtabl(ə)] *a* notable, noteworthy; (*marqué*) noticeable, marked // *nm* prominent citizen.

notaire [nɔtɛʀ] *nm* notary; solicitor.

notamment [nɔtamɑ̃] *ad* in particular, among others.

note [nɔt] *nf* (*écrite*, MUS) note; (SCOL) mark (*Brit*), grade; (*facture*) bill; **~ de service** memorandum.

noté, e [nɔte] *a*: **être bien/mal ~** (*employé etc*) to have a good/bad record.

noter [nɔte] *vt* (*écrire*) to write down; (*remarquer*) to note, notice.

notice [nɔtis] *nf* summary, short article; (*brochure*) leaflet, instruction book.

notifier [nɔtifje] *vt*: **~ qch à qn** to notify sb of sth, notify sth to sb.

notion [nɔsjɔ̃] *nf* notion, idea.

notoire [nɔtwaʀ] *a* widely known; (*en mal*) notorious.

notre, nos [nɔtʀ(ə), no] *dét* our.

nôtre [notʀ(ə)] *pronom*: **le/la ~** ours; **les ~s** ours; (*alliés etc*) our own people; **soyez des ~s** join us // *a* ours.

nouer [nwe] *vt* to tie, knot; (*fig: alliance etc*) to strike up.

noueux, euse [nwø, -øz] *a* gnarled.

nouilles [nuj] *nfpl* noodles; pasta *sg*.

nourrice [nuʀis] *nf* wet-nurse.

nourrir [nuʀiʀ] *vt* to feed; (*fig: espoir*) to harbour, nurse; **logé nourri** with board and lodging; **nourrissant, e** *a* nourishing, nutritious.

nourrisson [nuʀisɔ̃] *nm* (unweaned) infant.

nourriture [nuʀityʀ] *nf* food.

nous [nu] *pronom* (*sujet*) we; (*objet*) us; **~-mêmes** *pronom* ourselves.

nouveau(nouvel), elle, x [nuvo, -ɛl] *a* new // *nm/f* new pupil (*ou* employee) // *nf* (*piece of*) news *sg*; (LITTÉRATURE) short story; **de ~, à ~** again; **je suis sans nouvelles de lui** I haven't heard from him; **~ venu, nouvelle venue** *nm/f* newcomer; **Nouvel An** New Year; **~-né, e** *nm/f* newborn baby; **Nouvelle-Calédonie** *nf* New Caledonia; **Nouvelle-Zélande** *nf* New Zealand; **~té** *nf* novelty; (COMM) new film (*ou* book *ou* creation *etc*).

novembre [nɔvɑ̃bʀ(ə)] *nm* November.

novice [nɔvis] *a* inexperienced.

noyade [nwajad] *nf* drowning *q*.

noyau, x [nwajo] *nm* (*de fruit*) stone; (BIO, PHYSIQUE) nucleus; (ÉLEC, GÉO, *fig: centre*) core; **~ter** *vt* (POL) to infiltrate.

noyer [nwaje] *nm* walnut (tree); (*bois*)

walnut // vt to drown; (fig) to flood; to submerge; se ~ vi to be drowned, drown; (suicide) to drown o.s.

nu, e [ny] a naked; (membres) naked, bare; (chambre, fil, plaine) bare // nm (ART) nude; ~-**pieds** a inv barefoot; ~-**tête** a inv bareheaded; **se mettre ~** to strip; **mettre à ~** to bare.

nuage [nɥaʒ] nm cloud; **nuageux, euse** a cloudy.

nuance [nɥɑ̃s] nf (de couleur, sens) shade; **il y a une ~ (entre)** there's a slight difference (between); **nuancer** vt (opinion) to bring some reservations ou qualifications to.

nucléaire [nyklɛɛʀ] a nuclear.

nudiste [nydist(ə)] nm/f nudist.

nuée [nɥe] nf: **une ~ de** a cloud ou host ou swarm of.

nues [ny] nfpl: **tomber des ~** to be taken aback; **porter qn aux ~** to praise sb to the skies.

nuire [nɥiʀ] vi to be harmful; **~ à** to harm, do damage to; **nuisible** a harmful; **animal nuisible** pest.

nuit [nɥi] nf night; **il fait ~** it's dark; **cette ~** last night; tonight; **~ blanche** sleepless night; **~ de noces** wedding night.

nul, nulle [nyl] a (aucun) no; (minime) nil, non-existent; (non valable) null; (péj) useless, hopeless // pronom none, no one; **résultat ~, match ~** draw; **~le part** nowhere; **~lement** ad by no means.

numérique [nymeʀik] a numerical.

numéro [nymeʀo] nm number; (spectacle) act, turn; **~ de téléphone** (tele)phone number; **~ter** vt to number.

nuque [nyk] nf nape of the neck.

nutritif, ive [nytʀitif, -iv] a nutritional; (aliment) nutritious.

nylon [nilɔ̃] nm nylon.

O

oasis [ɔazis] nf oasis (pl oases).

obéir [ɔbeiʀ] vi to obey; **~ à** to obey; (suj: moteur, véhicule) to respond to; **obéissant, e** a obedient.

objecter [ɔbʒɛkte] vt (prétexter) to plead, put forward as an excuse; **~ (à qn) que** to object (to sb) that.

objecteur [ɔbʒɛktœʀ] nm: **~ de conscience** conscientious objector.

objectif, ive [ɔbʒɛktif, -iv] a objective // nm (OPTIQUE, PHOTO) lens sg, objective; (MIL, fig) objective; **~ à focale variable** zoom lens.

objection [ɔbʒɛksjɔ̃] nf objection.

objet [ɔbʒɛ] nm object; (d'une discussion, recherche) subject; **être ou faire l'~ de** (discussion) to be the subject of; (soins) to be given ou shown;

sans ~ a purposeless; groundless; **~ d'art** objet d'art; **~s personnels** personal items; **~s trouvés** lost property sg (Brit), lost-and-found sg (US).

obligation [ɔbligasjɔ̃] nf obligation; (COMM) bond, debenture; **obligatoire** a compulsory, obligatory.

obligé, e [ɔbliʒe] a (redevable): **être très ~ à qn** to be most obliged to sb; **obligeant, e** a obliging; kind.

obliger [ɔbliʒe] vt (contraindre): **~ qn à faire** to force ou oblige sb to do; (JUR: engager) to bind; (rendre service à) to oblige; **je suis bien obligé** I have to.

oblique [ɔblik] a oblique; **regard ~** sidelong glance; **en ~** ad diagonally; **obliquer** vi: **obliquer vers** to turn off towards.

oblitérer [ɔblliteʀe] vt (timbre-poste) to cancel.

obscène [ɔpsɛn] a obscene.

obscur, e [ɔpskyʀ] a dark; (fig) obscure; lowly; **~cir** vt to darken; (fig) to obscure; **s'~cir** vi to grow dark; **~ité** nf darkness; **dans l'~ité** in the dark, in darkness.

obséder [ɔpsede] vt to obsess, haunt.

obsèques [ɔpsɛk] nfpl funeral sg.

observateur, trice [ɔpsɛʀvatœʀ, -tʀis] a observant, perceptive // nm/f observer.

observation [ɔpsɛʀvasjɔ̃] nf observation; (d'un règlement etc) observance; (reproche) reproof.

observatoire [ɔpsɛʀvatwaʀ] nm observatory; (lieu élevé) observation post, vantage point.

observer [ɔpsɛʀve] vt (regarder) to observe, watch; (examiner) to examine; (scientifiquement, aussi: règlement, jeûne etc) to observe; (surveiller) to watch; (remarquer) to observe, notice; **faire ~ qch à qn** (dire) to point out sth to sb.

obstacle [ɔpstakl(ə)] nm obstacle; (ÉQUITATION) jump, hurdle; **faire ~ à** (lumière) to block out; (projet) to hinder, put obstacles in the path of.

obstiné, e [ɔpstine] a obstinate.

obstiner [ɔpstine]: **s'~** vi to insist, dig one's heels in; **s'~ à faire** to persist in, stubbornly to do; **s'~ sur qch** to keep working at sth, labour away at sth.

obstruer [ɔpstʀye] vt to block, obstruct.

obtempérer [ɔptɑ̃peʀe] vi to obey.

obtenir [ɔptəniʀ] vt to obtain, get; (total, résultat) to arrive at, reach; to achieve, obtain; **~ de pouvoir faire** to obtain permission to do; **~ de qn qu'il fasse** to get sb to agree to do; **obtention** nf obtaining.

obturateur [ɔptyʀatœʀ] nm (PHOTO) shutter.

obturer [ɔptyʀe] vt to close (up); (dent) to fill.

obus [ɔby] nm shell.

occasion [ɔkazjɔ̃] *nf* (*aubaine, possibilité*) opportunity; (*circonstance*) occasion; (*COMM: article non neuf*) secondhand buy; (*: acquisition avantageuse*) bargain; **à plusieurs ~s** on several occasions; **être l'~ de** to occasion, give rise to; **à l'~** *ad* sometimes, on occasions; some time; **d'~** *a, ad* secondhand; **occasionnel, le** *a* (*fortuit*) chance *cpd*; (*non régulier*) occasional; casual.

occasionner [ɔkazjɔne] *vt* to cause, bring about; **~ qch à qn** to cause sb sth.

occident [ɔksidɑ̃] *nm*: **l'O~** the West; **occidental, e, aux** western; (*POL*) Western.

occupation [ɔkypasjɔ̃] *nf* occupation.

occupé, e [ɔkype] *a* (*MIL, POL*) occupied; (*personne: affairé, pris*) busy; (*place, sièges*) taken; (*toilettes, ligne*) engaged.

occuper [ɔkype] *vt* to occupy; (*main-d'œuvre*) to employ; **s'~ (à qch)** to occupy o.s. *ou* keep o.s. busy (with sth); **s'~ de** (*être responsable de*) to be in charge of; (*se charger de: affaire*) to take charge of, deal with; (*: clients etc*) to attend to; (*s'intéresser à, pratiquer*) to be involved in; **ça occupe trop de place** it takes up too much room.

occurrence [ɔkyrɑ̃s] *nf*: **en l'~** in this case.

océan [ɔseɑ̃] *nm* ocean; **l'~ Indien** the Indian Ocean.

octet [ɔktɛt] *nm* byte.

octobre [ɔktɔbr(ə)] *nm* October.

octroyer [ɔktrwaje] *vt*: **~ qch à qn** to grant sth to sb, grant sb sth.

oculiste [ɔkylist(ə)] *nm/f* eye specialist.

odeur [ɔdœr] *nf* smell.

odieux, euse [ɔdjø, -øz] *a* hateful.

odorant, e [ɔdɔrɑ̃, -ɑ̃t] *a* sweetsmelling, fragrant.

odorat [ɔdɔra] *nm* (sense of) smell.

œil [œj], *pl* **yeux** [jø] *nm* eye; **à l'~** (*fam*) for free; **à l'~ nu** with the naked eye; **tenir qn à l'~** to keep an eye *ou* a watch on sb; **avoir l'~ à** to keep an eye on; **fermer les yeux (sur)** (*fig*) to turn a blind eye (to).

œillade [œjad] *nf*: **lancer une ~ à qn** to wink at sb, give sb a wink; **faire des ~s à** to make eyes at.

œillères [œjɛr] *nfpl* blinkers (*Brit*), blinders (*US*).

œillet [œjɛ] *nm* (*BOT*) carnation.

œuf [œf, *pl* ø] *nm* egg; **~ dur** hard-boiled egg; **~ au plat** fried egg; **~s brouillés** scrambled eggs; **~ de Pâques** Easter egg.

œuvre [œvr(ə)] *nf* (*tâche*) task, undertaking; (*ouvrage achevé, livre, tableau etc*) work; (*ensemble de la production artistique*) works *pl*; (*organisation charitable*) charity // *nm* (*d'un artiste*) works *pl*; (*CONSTR*): **le gros ~** the shell; **être à**

l'~ to be at work; **mettre en ~** (*moyens*) to make use of; **~ d'art** work of art.

offense [ɔfɑ̃s] *nf* insult.

offenser [ɔfɑ̃se] *vt* to offend, hurt; (*principes, Dieu*) to offend against; **s'~ de** to take offence at.

offert, e [ɔfɛr, -ɛrt(ə)] *pp* de **offrir**.

office [ɔfis] *nm* (*charge*) office; (*agence*) bureau, agency; (*REL*) service // *nm ou nf* (*pièce*) pantry; **faire ~ de** to act as; to do duty as; **d'~** *ad* automatically; **~ du tourisme** tourist bureau.

officiel, le [ɔfisjɛl] *a, nm/f* official.

officier [ɔfisje] *nm* officer // *vi* to officiate; **~ de l'état-civil** registrar.

officieux, euse [ɔfisjø, -øz] *a* unofficial.

officinal, e, aux [ɔfisinal, -o] *a*: **plantes ~es** medicinal plants.

officine [ɔfisin] *nf* (*de pharmacie*) dispensary; (*bureau*) agency, office.

offrande [ɔfrɑ̃d] *nf* offering.

offre [ɔfr(ə)] *nf* offer; (*aux enchères*) bid; (*ADMIN: soumission*) tender; (*ÉCON*): **l'~** supply; **~ d'emploi** job advertised; **'~s d'emploi'** 'situations vacant'; **~ publique d'achat (O.P.A.)** takeover bid.

offrir [ɔfrir] *vt*: **~ (à qn)** to offer (to sb); (*faire cadeau de*) to give (to sb); **s'~** *vi* (*occasion, paysage*) to present itself // *vt* (*vacances, voiture*) to treat o.s. to; **~ (à qn) de faire qch** to offer to do sth (for sb); **~ à boire à qn** to offer sb a drink; **s'~ comme guide/en otage** to offer one's services as (a) guide/offer o.s. as hostage.

offusquer [ɔfyske] *vt* to offend.

ogive [ɔʒiv] *nf*: **~ nucléaire** nuclear warhead.

oie [wa] *nf* (*ZOOL*) goose (*pl* geese).

oignon [ɔɲɔ̃] *nm* (*BOT, CULIN*) onion; (*de tulipe etc: bulbe*) bulb; (*MÉD*) bunion.

oiseau, x [wazo] *nm* bird; **~ de proie** bird of prey.

oiseux, euse [wazø, -øz] *a* pointless; trivial.

oisif, ive [wazif, -iv] *a* idle // *nm/f* (*péj*) man/woman of leisure.

oléoduc [ɔleɔdyk] *nm* (oil) pipeline.

olive [ɔliv] *nf* (*BOT*) olive; **olivier** *nm* olive.

olympique [ɔlɛ̃pik] *a* Olympic.

ombrage [ɔ̃braʒ] *nm* (*ombre*) (leafy) shade; **ombragé, e** *a* shaded, shady; **ombrageux, euse** *a* (*cheval*) skittish, nervous; (*personne*) touchy, easily offended.

ombre [ɔ̃br(ə)] *nf* (*espace non ensoleillé*) shade; (*ombre portée, tache*) shadow; **à l'~** in the shade; **tu me fais de l'~** you're in my light; **ça nous donne de l'~** it gives us (some) shade; **dans l'~** (*fig*) in obscurity; in the dark; **~ à paupières** eyeshadow.

ombrelle [ɔbʀɛl] *nf* parasol, sunshade.
omelette [ɔmlɛt] *nf* omelette.
omettre [ɔmɛtʀ(ə)] *vt* to omit, leave out.
omnibus [ɔmnibys] *nm* slow *ou* stopping train.
omoplate [ɔmɔplat] *nf* shoulder blade.
on [ɔ̃] *pronom*
1 (*indéterminé*) you, one; ~ peut le faire ainsi you *ou* one can do it like this, it can be done like this
2 (*quelqu'un*): ~ les a attaqués they were attacked; ~ vous demande au téléphone there's a phone call for you, you're wanted on the phone
3 (*nous*) we; ~ va y aller demain we're going tomorrow
4 (*les gens*) they; autrefois, ~ croyait ... they used to believe ...
5: ~ ne peut plus *ad*: ~ ne peut plus stupide as stupid as can be.
oncle [ɔ̃kl(ə)] *nm* uncle.
onctueux, euse [ɔ̃ktyø, -øz] *a* creamy, smooth; (*fig*) smooth, unctuous.
onde [ɔ̃d] *nf* (*PHYSIQUE*) wave; sur les ~s on the radio; mettre en ~s to produce for the radio; sur ~s courtes (o.c.) on short wave *sg*; moyennes/longues ~s medium/long wave *sg*.
ondée [ɔ̃de] *nf* shower.
on-dit [ɔ̃di] *nm inv* rumour.
ondoyer [ɔ̃dwaje] *vi* to ripple, wave.
onduler [ɔ̃dyle] *vi* to undulate; (*cheveux*) to wave.
onéreux, euse [ɔneʀø, -øz] *a* costly; à titre ~ in return for payment.
ongle [ɔ̃gl(ə)] *nm* (*ANAT*) nail; se faire les ~ to do one's nails.
onguent [ɔ̃gɑ̃] *nm* ointment.
ont *vb voir* **avoir**.
O.N.U. [ɔny] *sigle f voir* **organisation**.
onze [ɔ̃z] *num* eleven; **onzième** *num* eleventh.
O.P.A. *sigle f voir* **offre**.
opale [ɔpal] *nf* opal.
opaque [ɔpak] *a* opaque.
opéra [ɔpeʀa] *nm* opera; (*édifice*) opera house; **~-comique** *nm* light opera.
opérateur, trice [ɔpeʀatœʀ, -tʀis] *nm/f* operator; ~ (de prise de vues) cameraman.
opération [ɔpeʀasjɔ̃] *nf* operation; (*COMM*) dealing.
opératoire [ɔpeʀatwaʀ] *a* operating; (*choc etc*) post-operative.
opérer [ɔpeʀe] *vt* (*MÉD*) to operate on; (*faire, exécuter*) to carry out, make // *vi* (*remède: faire effet*) to act, work; (*procéder*) to proceed; (*MÉD*) to operate; s'~ *vi* (*avoir lieu*) to occur, take place; se faire ~ to have an operation.
opiner [ɔpine] *vi*: ~ de la tête to nod assent.
opinion [ɔpinjɔ̃] *nf* opinion; l'~ (publique) public opinion.

opportun, e [ɔpɔʀtœ̃, -yn] *a* timely, opportune; en temps ~ at the appropriate time.
opposant, e [ɔpozɑ̃, -ɑ̃t] *a* opposing; ~s *nmpl* opponents.
opposé, e [ɔpoze] *a* (*direction, rive*) opposite; (*faction*) opposing; (*couleurs*) contrasting; (*opinions, intérêts*) conflicting; (*contre*): ~ à opposed to, against // *nm*: l'~ the other *ou* opposite side (*ou* direction); (*contraire*) the opposite; à l'~ (*fig*) on the other hand; à l'~ de on the other *ou* opposite side from; (*fig*) contrary to, unlike.
opposer [ɔpoze] *vt* (*personnes, armées, équipes*) to oppose; (*couleurs, termes, tons*) to contrast; ~ qch à (*comme obstacle, défense*) to set sth against; (*comme objection*) to put sth forward against; s'~ (*sens réciproque*) to conflict; to clash; to contrast; s'~ à (*interdire, empêcher*) to oppose; (*tenir tête à*) to rebel against.
opposition [ɔpozisjɔ̃] *nf* opposition; par ~ à as opposed to, in contrast with; entrer en ~ avec to come into conflict with; être en ~ avec (*idées, conduite*) to be at variance with; faire ~ à un chèque to stop a cheque.
oppresser [ɔpʀese] *vt* to oppress; **oppression** *nf* oppression; (*malaise*) feeling of suffocation.
opprimer [ɔpʀime] *vt* to oppress; (*liberté, opinion*) to suppress, stifle; (*suj: chaleur etc*) to suffocate, oppress.
opter [ɔpte] *vi*: ~ pour to opt for; ~ entre to choose between.
opticien, ne [ɔptisjɛ̃, -ɛn] *nm/f* optician.
optimiste [ɔptimist(ə)] *nm/f* optimist // *a* optimistic.
option [ɔpsjɔ̃] *nf* option; matière à ~ (*SCOL*) optional subject.
optique [ɔptik] *a* (*nerf*) optic; (*verres*) optical // *nf* (*PHOTO: lentilles etc*) optics *pl*; (*science, industrie*) optics *sg*; (*fig: manière de voir*) perspective.
opulent, e [ɔpylɑ̃, -ɑ̃t] *a* wealthy, opulent; (*formes, poitrine*) ample, generous.
or [ɔʀ] *nm* gold // *cj* now, but; en ~ gold *cpd*; (*fig*) golden, marvellous.
orage [ɔʀaʒ] *nm* (thunder)storm; **orageux, euse** *a* stormy.
oraison [ɔʀɛzɔ̃] *nf* orison, prayer; ~ funèbre funeral oration.
oral, e, aux [ɔʀal, -o] *a, nm* oral.
orange [ɔʀɑ̃ʒ] *nf, a, inv* orange; **oranger** *nm* orange tree.
orateur [ɔʀatœʀ] *nm* speaker; orator.
orbite [ɔʀbit] *nf* (*ANAT*) (eye-)socket; (*PHYSIQUE*) orbit.
orchestre [ɔʀkɛstʀ(ə)] *nm* orchestra; (*de jazz, danse*) band; (*places*) stalls *pl* (*Brit*), orchestra (*US*); **orchestrer** *vt* (*MUS*) to orchestrate; (*fig*) to mount, stage-manage.

orchidée [ɔʀkide] *nf* orchid.
ordinaire [ɔʀdinɛʀ] *a* ordinary; everyday; standard // *nm* ordinary; (*menus*) everyday fare // *nf* (*essence*) ≈ two-star (petrol) (*Brit*), ≈ regular (gas) (*US*); **d'~** usually, normally; **à l'~** usually, ordinarily.
ordinateur [ɔʀdinatœʀ] *nm* computer; **~ domestique** home computer; **~ individuel** personal computer.
ordonnance [ɔʀdɔnɑ̃s] *nf* organization; layout; (*MÉD*) prescription; (*JUR*) order; (*MIL*) orderly, batman (*Brit*).
ordonné, e [ɔʀdɔne] *a* tidy, orderly; (*MATH*) ordered.
ordonner [ɔʀdɔne] *vt* (*agencer*) to organize, arrange; (*donner un ordre*): **~ à qn de faire** to order sb to do; (*REL*) to ordain; (*MÉD*) to prescribe.
ordre [ɔʀdʀ(ə)] *nm* (*gén*) order; (*propreté et soin*) orderliness, tidiness; (*nature*): **d'~ pratique** of a practical nature; **~s** *nmpl* (*REL*) holy orders; **mettre en ~** to tidy (up), put in order; **à l'~ de qn** payable to sb; **être aux ~s de qn/sous les ~s de qn** to be at sb's disposal/under sb's command; **jusqu'à nouvel ~** until further notice; **dans le même ~ d'idées** in this connection; **donnez-nous un ~ de grandeur** give us some idea as regards size (*ou* the amount); **de premier ~** first-rate; **~ du jour** (*d'une réunion*) agenda; (*MIL*) order of the day; **à l'~ du jour** (*fig*) topical.
ordure [ɔʀdyʀ] *nf* filth *q*; **~s** (*balayures, déchets*) rubbish *sg*, refuse *sg*; **~s ménagères** household refuse.
oreille [ɔʀɛj] *nf* (*ANAT*) ear; (*de marmite, tasse*) handle; **avoir de l'~** to have a good ear (for music).
oreiller [ɔʀeje] *nm* pillow.
oreillons [ɔʀɛjɔ̃] *nmpl* mumps *sg*.
ores [ɔʀ]: **d'~ et déjà** *ad* already.
orfèvrerie [ɔʀfɛvʀəʀi] *nf* goldsmith's (*ou* silversmith's) trade; (*ouvrage*) gold (*ou* silver) plate.
organe [ɔʀgan] *nm* organ; (*porte-parole*) representative, mouthpiece.
organigramme [ɔʀganigʀam] *nm* organization chart; flow chart.
organique [ɔʀganik] *a* organic.
organisateur, trice [ɔʀganizatœʀ, -tʀis] *nm/f* organizer.
organisation [ɔʀganizasjɔ̃] *nf* organization; **O~ des Nations Unies (O.N.U.)** United Nations (Organization) (UN, UNO); **O~ du traité de l'Atlantique Nord (O.T.A.N.)** North Atlantic Treaty Organization (NATO).
organiser [ɔʀganize] *vt* to organize; (*mettre sur pied: service etc*) to set up; **s'~** to get organized.
organisme [ɔʀganism(ə)] *nm* (*BIO*) organism; (*corps, ADMIN*) body.
organiste [ɔʀganist(ə)] *nm/f* organist.

orgasme [ɔʀgasm(ə)] *nm* orgasm, climax.
orge [ɔʀʒ(ə)] *nf* barley.
orgie [ɔʀʒi] *nf* orgy.
orgue [ɔʀg(ə)] *nm* organ; **~s** *nfpl* organ *sg*.
orgueil [ɔʀgœj] *nm* pride; **orgueilleux, euse** *a* proud.
Orient [ɔʀjɑ̃] *nm*: **l'~** the East, the Orient.
oriental, e, aux [ɔʀjɑ̃tal, -o] *a* oriental, eastern; (*frontière*) eastern.
orientation [ɔʀjɑ̃tasjɔ̃] *nf* positioning; orientation; (*d'une maison etc*) aspect; (*d'un journal*) leanings *pl*; **avoir le sens de l'~** to have a (good) sense of direction; **~ professionnelle** careers advising; careers advisory service.
orienté, e [ɔʀjɑ̃te] *a* (*fig: article, journal*) slanted; **bien/mal ~** (*appartement*) well/badly positioned; **~ au sud** facing south *ou* with a southern aspect.
orienter [ɔʀjɑ̃te] *vt* (*placer, disposer: pièce mobile*) to adjust, position; (*tourner*) to direct, turn; (*voyageur, touriste, recherches*) to direct; (*fig: élève*) to orientate; **s'~** (*se repérer*) to find one's bearings; **s'~ vers** (*fig*) to turn towards.
originaire [ɔʀiʒinɛʀ] *a*: **être ~ de** to be a native of.
original, e, aux [ɔʀiʒinal, -o] *a* original; (*bizarre*) eccentric // *nm/f* eccentric // *nm* (*document etc, ART*) original; (*dactylographie*) top copy.
origine [ɔʀiʒin] *nf* origin; **dès l'~** at *ou* from the outset; **à l'~** originally; **originel, le** *a* original.
O.R.L. *sigle nm/f de* oto-rhino-laryngologiste.
orme [ɔʀm(ə)] *nm* elm.
ornement [ɔʀnəmɑ̃] *nm* ornament; (*fig*) embellishment, adornment.
orner [ɔʀne] *vt* to decorate, adorn.
ornière [ɔʀnjɛʀ] *nf* rut.
orphelin, e [ɔʀfəlɛ̃, -in] *a* orphan(ed) // *nm/f* orphan; **~ de père/mère** fatherless/motherless; **orphelinat** *nm* orphanage.
orteil [ɔʀtɛj] *nm* toe; **gros ~** big toe.
orthographe [ɔʀtɔgʀaf] *nf* spelling; **orthographier** *vt* to spell.
orthopédiste [ɔʀtɔpedist(ə)] *nm/f* orthopaedic specialist.
ortie [ɔʀti] *nf* (stinging) nettle.
os [ɔs, *pl* o] *nm* bone.
osciller [ɔsile] *vi* (*pendule*) to swing; (*au vent etc*) to rock; (*TECH*) to oscillate; (*fig*): **~ entre** to waver *ou* fluctuate between.
osé, e [oze] *a* daring, bold.
oseille [ozɛj] *nf* sorrel.
oser [oze] *vi, vt* to dare; **~ faire** to dare (to) do.
osier [ozje] *nm* willow; **d'~, en ~** wicker(work).

ossature [ɔsatyʀ] *nf* (*ANAT*) frame, skeletal structure; (*fig*) framework.
osseux, euse [ɔsø, -øz] *a* bony; (*tissu, maladie, greffe*) bone *cpd*.
ostensible [ɔstɑ̃sibl(ə)] *a* conspicuous.
otage [ɔtaʒ] *nm* hostage; prendre qn comme ~ to take sb hostage.
O.T.A.N. [ɔtɑ̃] *sigle f voir* **organisation**.
otarie [ɔtaʀi] *nf* sea-lion.
ôter [ote] *vt* to remove; (*soustraire*) to take away; ~ qch à qn to take sth (away) from sb; ~ qch de to remove sth from.
otite [ɔtit] *nf* ear infection.
oto-rhino(-laryngologiste) [ɔtɔʀino(laʀɛ̃gɔlɔʒist(ə)] *nm/f* ear nose and throat specialist.
ou [u] *cj* or; ~ ... ~ either ... or; ~ bien or (else).
où [u] ◆ *pronom relatif* **1** (*position, situation*) where, that (*souvent omis*); la chambre ~ il était the room (that) he was in, the room where he was; la ville ~ je l'ai rencontré the town where I met him; la pièce d'~ il est sorti the room he came out of; le village d'~ je viens the village I come from; les villes par ~ il est passé the towns he went through **2** (*temps, état*) that (*souvent omis*); le jour ~ il est parti the day (that) he left; au prix ~ c'est at the price it is ◆ *ad* **1** (*interrogation*) where; ~ est-il/va-t-il? where is he/is he going?; par ~? which way?; d'~ vient que ...? how come ...? **2** (*position*) where; je sais ~ il est I know where he is; ~ que l'on aille wherever you go.
ouate [wat] *nf* cotton wool (*Brit*), cotton (*US*); (*bourre*) padding, wadding.
oubli [ubli] *nm* (*acte*): l'~ de forgetting; (*étourderie*) forgetfulness *q*; (*négligence*) omission, oversight; (*absence de souvenirs*) oblivion.
oublier [ublije] *vt* (*gén*) to forget; (*ne pas voir: erreurs etc*) to miss; (*ne pas mettre: virgule, nom*) to leave out; (*laisser quelque part: chapeau etc*) to leave behind; s'~ to forget o.s.
oubliettes [ublijɛt] *nfpl* dungeon *sg*.
oublieux, euse [ublijø, -øz] *a* forgetful.
ouest [wɛst] *nm* west // *a inv* west; (*région*) western; à l'~ in the west; (*to the*) west, westwards; à l'~ de (*to the*) west of.
ouf [uf] *excl* phew!
oui [wi] *ad* yes.
oui-dire [widiʀ]: par ~ *ad* by hearsay.
ouïe [wi] *nf* hearing; ~s *nfpl* (*de poisson*) gills.
ouïr [wiʀ] *vt* to hear; avoir ouï dire que to have heard it said that.
ouragan [uʀagɑ̃] *nm* hurricane.
ourlet [uʀlɛ] *nm* hem.
ours [uʀs] *nm* bear; ~ brun/blanc

brown/polar bear; ~ (en peluche) teddy (bear).
oursin [uʀsɛ̃] *nm* sea urchin.
ourson [uʀsɔ̃] *nm* (bear-)cub.
ouste [ust(ə)] *excl* hop it!
outil [uti] *nm* tool.
outiller [utije] *vt* (*ouvrier, usine*) to equip.
outrage [utʀaʒ] *nm* insult; faire subir les derniers ~s à (*femme*) to ravish; ~ à la pudeur indecent conduct *q*.
outrager [utʀaʒe] *vt* to offend gravely.
outrance [utʀɑ̃s]: à ~ *ad* excessively, to excess.
outre [utʀ(ə)] *nf* goatskin, water skin // *prép* besides // *ad*: passer ~ à to disregard, take no notice of; en ~ besides, moreover; ~ que apart from the fact that; ~ mesure immoderately; unduly.
outre-Atlantique [utʀəatlɑ̃tik] *ad* across the Atlantic.
outre-Manche [utʀəmɑ̃ʃ] *ad* across the Channel.
outremer [utʀəmɛʀ] *a inv* ultramarine.
outre-mer [utʀəmɛʀ] *ad* overseas.
outrepasser [utʀəpase] *vt* to go beyond, exceed.
outrer [utʀe] *vt* to exaggerate; (*choquer*) to outrage.
ouvert, e [uvɛʀ, -ɛʀt(ə)] *pp de* **ouvrir** ◆ *a* open; (*robinet, gaz etc*) on; **ouvertement** *ad* openly.
ouverture [uvɛʀtyʀ] *nf* opening; (*MUS*) overture; (*PHOTO*) ~ (du diaphragme) aperture; ~s *nfpl* (*propositions*) overtures; ~ d'esprit open-mindedness.
ouvrable [uvʀabl(ə)] *a*: jour ~ working day, weekday.
ouvrage [uvʀaʒ] *nm* (*tâche, de tricot etc, MIL*) work *q*; (*texte, livre*) work.
ouvragé, e [uvʀaʒe] *a* finely embroidered (*ou* worked *ou* carved).
ouvre-boîte(s) [uvʀəbwat] *nm inv* tin (*Brit*) *ou* can opener.
ouvre-bouteille(s) [uvʀəbutɛj] *nm inv* bottle-opener.
ouvreuse [uvʀøz] *nf* usherette.
ouvrier, ière [uvʀje, -jɛʀ] *nm/f* worker // *a* working-class; industrial, labour *cpd*; classe ouvrière working class.
ouvrir [uvʀiʀ] *vt* (*gén*) to open; (*brèche, passage, MÉD: abcès*) to open up; (*commencer l'exploitation de, créer*) to open (up); (*eau, électricité, chauffage, robinet*) to turn on // *vi* to open; to open up; s'~ *vi* to open; s'~ à qn to open one's heart to sb; ~ l'appétit à qn to whet sb's appetite.
ovaire [ɔvɛʀ] *nm* ovary.
ovale [ɔval] *a* oval.
ovni [ɔvni] *sigle m* (= *objet volant non identifié*) UFO.
oxyder [ɔkside]: s'~ *vi* to become oxidized.
oxygène [ɔksiʒɛn] *nm* oxygen; (*fig*):

cure d'~ fresh air cure.

oxygéné, e [ɔksiʒene] a: eau ~e hydrogen peroxide.

P

pacifique [pasifik] a peaceful // nm: le P~, l'océan P~ the Pacific (Ocean).

pacte [pakt(ə)] nm pact, treaty.

pactiser [paktize] vi: ~ avec to come to terms with.

pagaie [pagɛ] nf paddle.

pagaille [pagaj] nf mess, shambles sg.

page [paʒ] nf page // nm page; à la ~ (fig) up-to-date.

paie [pɛ] nf = **paye**.

paiement [pɛmã] nm = **payement**.

païen, ne [pajɛ̃, -jɛn] a, nm/f pagan, heathen.

paillard, e [pajar, -ard(ə)] a bawdy.

paillasson [pajasɔ̃] nm doormat.

paille [paj] nf straw; (défaut) flaw.

paillettes [pajɛt] nfpl (décoratives) sequins, spangles; lessive en ~ soapflakes pl.

pain [pɛ̃] nm (substance) bread; (unité) loaf (pl loaves) (of bread); (morceau): ~ de cire etc bar of wax etc; ~ bis/complet brown/wholemeal (Brit) ou wholewheat (US) bread; ~ d'épice gingerbread; ~ grillé toast; ~ de mie sandwich loaf; ~ de sucre sugar loaf.

pair, e [pɛr] a (nombre) even // nm peer; aller de ~ to go hand in hand ou together; jeune fille au ~ au pair.

paire [pɛr] nf pair.

paisible [pɛzibl(ə)] a peaceful, quiet.

paître [pɛtr(ə)] vi to graze.

paix [pɛ] nf peace; (fig) peacefulness, peace; faire/avoir la ~ to make/have peace.

Pakistan [pakistã] nm: le ~ Pakistan.

palace [palas] nm luxury hotel.

palais [palɛ] nm palace; (ANAT) palate.

pale [pal] nf (d'hélice, de rame) blade.

pâle [pal] a pale; bleu ~ pale blue.

Palestine [palɛstin] nf: la ~ Palestine; **palestinien, ne** a, nm/f Palestinian.

palet [palɛ] nm disc; (HOCKEY) puck.

palette [palɛt] nf (de peintre) palette; (produits) range.

pâleur [palœr] nf paleness.

palier [palje] nm (d'escalier) landing; (fig) level, plateau; (TECH) bearing; par ~s in stages.

pâlir [palir] vi to turn ou go pale; (couleur) to fade.

palissade [palisad] nf fence.

palliatif [paljatif] nm palliative; (expédient) stopgap measure.

pallier [palje] vt: ~ à; vt to offset, make up for.

palmarès [palmarɛs] nm record (of achievements); (SCOL) prize list;

(SPORT) list of winners.

palme [palm(ə)] nf (symbole) palm; (de plongeur) flipper; **palmé, e** a (pattes) webbed.

palmier [palmje] nm palm tree.

palombe [palɔ̃b] nf woodpigeon.

pâlot, te [palo, -ɔt] a pale, peaky.

palourde [palurd(ə)] nf clam.

palper [palpe] vt to feel, finger.

palpitant, e [palpitã, -ãt] a thrilling.

palpiter [palpite] vi (cœur, pouls) to beat; (: plus fort) to pound, throb.

paludisme [palydism(ə)] nm malaria.

pamphlet [pãflɛ] nm lampoon, satirical tract.

pamplemousse [pãpləmus] nm grapefruit.

pan [pã] nm section, piece // excl bang!: ~ de chemise shirt tail.

panachage [panaʃaʒ] nm blend, mix.

panache [panaʃ] nm plume; (fig) spirit, panache.

panaché, e [panaʃe] a: glace ~e mixed-flavour ice cream; bière ~e shandy.

pancarte [pãkart(ə)] nf sign, notice; (dans un défilé) placard.

pancréas [pãkreas] nm pancreas.

pané, e [pane] a fried in breadcrumbs.

panier [panje] nm basket; mettre au ~ to chuck away; ~ à provisions shopping basket.

panique [panik] nf, a panic; **paniquer** vi to panic.

panne [pan] nf (d'un mécanisme, moteur) breakdown; être/tomber en ~ to have broken down/break down; être en ~ d'essence ou sèche to have run out of petrol (Brit) ou gas (US); ~ d'électricité ou de courant power ou electrical failure.

panneau, x [pano] nm (écriteau) sign, notice; (de boiserie, de tapisserie etc) panel; ~ d'affichage notice board; ~ de signalisation roadsign.

panonceau, x [panɔ̃so] nm sign.

panoplie [panɔpli] nf (jouet) outfit; (d'armes) display; (fig) array.

panorama [panɔrama] nm panorama.

panse [pãs] nf paunch.

pansement [pãsmã] nm dressing, bandage; ~ adhésif sticking plaster.

panser [pãse] vt (plaie) to dress, bandage; (bras) to put a dressing on, bandage; (cheval) to groom.

pantalon [pãtalɔ̃] nm (aussi: ~s, paire de ~s) trousers pl, pair of trousers; ~ de ski ski pants pl.

pantelant, e [pãtlã, -ãt] a gasping for breath, panting.

panthère [pãtɛr] nf panther.

pantin [pãtɛ̃] nm jumping jack; (péj) puppet.

pantois [pãtwa] am: rester ~ to be flabbergasted.

pantomime [pãtɔmim] nf mime;

(pièce) mime show.
pantoufle [pɑ̃tufl(ə)] *nf* slipper.
paon [pɑ̃] *nm* peacock.
papa [papa] *nm* dad(dy).
pape [pap] *nm* pope.
paperasse [papʀas] *nf (péj)* bumf *q*, papers *pl*; **~rie** *nf (péj)* red tape *q*; paperwork *q*.
papeterie [papetʀi] *nf (usine)* paper mill; *(magasin)* stationer's (shop).
papier [papje] *nm* paper; *(article)* article; **~s** *(aussi:* **~s d'identité)** (identity) papers; **~ (d')aluminium** aluminium *(Brit)* ou aluminum *(US)* foil, tinfoil; **~ buvard** blotting paper; **~ carbone** carbon paper; **~ hygiénique** toilet paper; **~ journal** newsprint; *(pour emballer)* newspaper; **~ à lettres** writing paper, notepaper; **~ peint** wallpaper; **~ de verre** sandpaper.
papillon [papijɔ̃] *nm* butterfly; *(fam: contravention)* (parking) ticket; *(TECH: écrou)* wing nut; **~ de nuit** moth.
papilloter [papijɔte] *vi* to blink, flicker.
paquebot [pakbo] *nm* liner.
pâquerette [pakʀɛt] *nf* daisy.
Pâques [pak] *nm, nfpl* Easter.
paquet [pakɛ] *nm* packet; *(colis)* parcel; *(fig: tas)*: **~ de** pile ou heap of; **~-cadeau** *nm* gift-wrapped parcel.
par [paʀ] *prép* by; *finir etc* **~** to end *etc* with; **~ amour** out of love; **passer ~ Lyon/la côte** to go via ou through Lyons/ along by the coast; **~ la fenêtre** *(jeter, regarder)* out of the window; **3 ~ jour/ personne** 3 a *ou* per day/head; **2 ~ 2** two at a time; in twos; **~ ici** this way; *(dans le coin)* round here; **~-ci, ~-là** here and there.
parabole [paʀabɔl] *nf (REL)* parable.
parachever [paʀaʃve] *vt* to perfect.
parachute [paʀaʃyt] *nm* parachute.
parachutiste [paʀaʃytist(ə)] *nm/f* parachutist; *(MIL)* paratrooper.
parade [paʀad] *nf (spectacle, défilé)* parade; *(ESCRIME, BOXE)* parry.
paradis [paʀadi] *nm* heaven, paradise.
paradoxe [paʀadɔks(ə)] *nm* paradox.
paraffine [paʀafin] *nf* paraffin.
parages [paʀaʒ] *nmpl*: **dans les ~ (de)** in the area ou vicinity (of).
paragraphe [paʀagʀaf] *nm* paragraph.
paraître [paʀɛtʀ(ə)] *vb avec attribut* to seem, look, appear // *vi* to appear; *(être visible)* to show; *(PRESSE, ÉDITION)* to be published, come out, appear; *(briller)* to show off // *vb impersonnel*: **il paraît que** it seems ou appears that, they say that; **il me paraît que** it seems to me that.
parallèle [paʀalɛl] *a* parallel; *(police, marché)* unofficial // *nm (comparaison)*: **faire un ~ entre** to draw a parallel between; *(GÉO)* parallel // *nf* parallel (line).

paralyser [paʀalize] *vt* to paralyze.
parapet [paʀapɛ] *nm* parapet.
parapher [paʀafe] *vt* to initial; to sign.
paraphrase [paʀafʀaz] *nf* paraphrase.
parapluie [paʀaplɥi] *nm* umbrella.
parasite [paʀazit] *nm* parasite; **~s** *(TÉL)* interference *sg*.
parasol [paʀasɔl] *nm* parasol, sunshade.
paratonnerre [paʀatɔnɛʀ] *nm* lightning conductor.
paravent [paʀavɑ̃] *nm* folding screen.
parc [paʀk] *nm* (public) park, gardens *pl*; *(de château etc)* grounds *pl*; *(pour le bétail)* pen, enclosure; *(d'enfant)* playpen; *(MIL: entrepôt)* depot; *(ensemble d'unités)* stock; *(de voitures etc)* fleet; **~ automobile** *(d'un pays)* number of cars on the roads; **~ de stationnement** car park.
parcelle [paʀsɛl] *nf* fragment, scrap; *(de terrain)* plot, parcel.
parce que [paʀsk(ə)] *cj* because.
parchemin [paʀʃəmɛ̃] *nm* parchment.
parc(o)mètre [paʀk(ɔ)mɛtʀ(ə)] *nm* parking meter.
parcourir [paʀkuʀiʀ] *vt (trajet, distance)* to cover; *(article, livre)* to skim ou glance through; *(lieu)* to go all over, travel up and down; *(suj: frisson, vibration)* to run through.
parcours [paʀkuʀ] *nm (trajet)* journey; *(itinéraire)* route; *(SPORT: terrain)* course; *(: tour)* round; run; lap.
par-dessous [paʀdəsu] *prép, ad* under(neath).
pardessus [paʀdəsy] *nm* overcoat.
par-dessus [paʀdəsy] *prép* over (the top of) // *ad* over (the top); **~ le marché** on top of all that.
par-devant [paʀdəvɑ̃] *prép* in the presence of, before // *ad* at the front; round the front.
pardon [paʀdɔ̃] *nm* forgiveness *q* // *excl* sorry!; *(pour interpeller etc)* excuse me!; **demander ~ à qn (de)** to apologize to sb (for); **je vous demande ~** I'm sorry; excuse me.
pardonner [paʀdɔne] *vt* to forgive; **~ qch à qn** to forgive sb for sth.
pare-balles [paʀbal] *a inv* bulletproof.
pare-boue [paʀbu] *nm inv* mudguard.
pare-brise [paʀbʀiz] *nm inv* windscreen *(Brit)*, windshield *(US)*.
pare-chocs [paʀʃɔk] *nm inv* bumper.
pareil, le [paʀɛj] *a (identique)* the same, alike; *(similaire)* similar; *(tel)*: **un courage/livre ~** such courage/a book, courage/a book like this; **de ~s livres** such books; **ses ~s** one's fellow men; one's peers; **ne pas avoir son(sa) ~(le)** to be second to none; **~ à** the same as; similar to; **sans ~** unparalleled, unequalled.
parent, e [paʀɑ̃, -ɑ̃t] *nm/f*: **un/une ~/e** a relative ou relation // *a*: **être ~ de** to be

related to; ~s *nmpl* (*père et mère*) parents; **parenté** *nf* (*lien*) relationship.
parenthèse [paRɑ̃tɛz] *nf* (*ponctuation*) bracket, parenthesis; (*MATH*) bracket; (*digression*) parenthesis, digression; **ouvrir/fermer la** ~ to open/close the brackets; **entre** ~s in brackets; (*fig*) incidentally.
parer [paRe] *vt* to adorn; (*CULIN*) to dress, trim; (*éviter*) to ward off.
pare-soleil [paRsɔlɛj] *nm inv* sun visor.
paresse [paRɛs] *nf* laziness; **paresseux, euse** *a* lazy; (*fig*) slow, sluggish.
parfaire [paRfɛR] *vt* to perfect.
parfait, e [paRfɛ, -ɛt] *a* perfect // *nm* (*LING*) perfect (tense); **parfaitement** *ad* perfectly // *excl* (most) certainly.
parfois [paRfwa] *ad* sometimes.
parfum [paRfœ̃] *nm* (*produit*) perfume, scent; (*odeur: de fleur*) scent, fragrance; (: *de tabac, vin*) aroma; (*goût*) flavour; **parfumé, e** *a* (*fleur, fruit*) fragrant; (*femme*) perfumed; **parfumé au café** coffee-flavoured; **parfumer** *vt* (*suj: odeur, bouquet*) to perfume; (*mouchoir*) to put scent *ou* perfume on; (*crème, gâteau*) to flavour; **parfumerie** *nf* (*commerce*) perfumery; (*produits*) perfumes *pl*; (*boutique*) perfume shop.
pari [paRi] *nm* bet, wager; (*SPORT*) bet.
paria [paRja] *nm* outcast.
parier [paRje] *vt* to bet.
Paris [paRi] *n* Paris; **parisien, ne** *a* Parisian; (*GÉO, ADMIN*) Paris *cpd* // *nm/f*: **Parisien, ne** Parisian.
paritaire [paRitɛR] *a* joint.
parjure [paRʒyR] *nm* perjury; **se parjurer** *vi* to forswear *ou* perjure o.s.
parking [paRkiŋ] *nm* (*lieu*) car park.
parlant, e [paRlɑ̃, -ɑ̃t] *a* (*fig*) graphic, vivid; eloquent; (*CINÉMA*) talking.
parlement [paRləmɑ̃] *nm* parliament; **parlementaire** *a* parliamentary // *nm/f* member of parliament.
parlementer [paRləmɑ̃te] *vi* to negotiate, parley.
parler [paRle] *vi* to speak, talk; (*avouer*) to talk; ~ (**à qn**) **de** to talk *ou* speak (to sb) about; ~ **le/en français** to speak French/in French; ~ **affaires** to talk business; ~ **en dormant** to talk in one's sleep; **sans** ~ **de** (*fig*) not to mention, to say nothing of; **tu parles!** you must be joking!
parloir [paRlwaR] *nm* (*de prison, d'hôpital*) visiting room; (*REL*) parlour.
parmi [paRmi] *prép* among(st).
paroi [paRwa] *nf* wall; (*cloison*) partition; ~ **rocheuse** rock face.
paroisse [paRwas] *nf* parish.
parole [paRɔl] *nf* (*faculté*): **la** ~ speech; (*mot, promesse*) word; ~s (*MUS*) words, lyrics; **tenir** ~ to keep one's word; **prendre la** ~ to speak; **demander la** ~ to ask for permission to speak; **je le crois sur** ~

I'll take his word for it.
parquer [paRke] *vt* (*voiture, matériel*) to park; (*bestiaux*) to pen (in *ou* up).
parquet [paRkɛ] *nm* (*parquet*) floor; (*JUR*): **le** ~ the Public Prosecutor's department.
parrain [paRɛ̃] *nm* godfather; (*d'un nouvel adhérent*) sponsor, proposer.
pars *vb voir* **partir**.
parsemer [paRsəme] *vt* (*suj: feuilles, papiers*) to be scattered over; ~ **qch de** to scatter sth with.
part [paR] *nf* (*qui revient à qn*) share; (*fraction, partie*) part; (*FINANCE*) (non-voting) share; **prendre** ~ **à** (*débat etc*) to take part in; (*soucis, douleur de qn*) to share in; **faire** ~ **de qch à qn** to announce sth to sb, inform sb of sth; **pour ma** ~ as for me, as far as I'm concerned; **à** ~ **entière** *a* full; **de la** ~ **de** (*au nom de*) on behalf of; (*donné par*) from; **de toute(s)** ~(s) from all sides *ou* quarters; **de** ~ **et d'autre** on both sides, on either side; **de** ~ **en** ~ right through; **d'une** ~ ... **d'autre** ~ on the one hand ... on the other hand; **à** ~ *ad* separately; (*de côté*) aside // *prép* apart from, except for // *a* exceptional, special; **faire la** ~ **des choses** to make allowances.
partage [paRtaʒ] *nm* dividing up; sharing (out) *q*, share-out; sharing; **recevoir qch en** ~ to receive sth as one's share (*ou* lot).
partager [paRtaʒe] *vt* to share; (*distribuer, répartir*) to share (out); (*morceler, diviser*) to divide (up); **se** ~ *vt* (*héritage etc*) to share between themselves (*ou* ourselves).
partance [paRtɑ̃s]: **en** ~ *ad* outbound, due to leave; **en** ~ **pour** (bound) for.
partant, e [paRtɑ̃] *vb voir* **partir** // *nm* (*SPORT*) starter; (*HIPPISME*) runner.
partenaire [paRtənɛR] *nm/f* partner.
parterre [paRtɛR] *nm* (*de fleurs*) (flower) bed; (*THÉÂTRE*) stalls *pl*.
parti [paRti] *nm* (*POL*) party; (*décision*) course of action; (*personne à marier*) match; **tirer** ~ **de** to take advantage of, turn to good account; **prendre le** ~ **de qn** to stand up for sb, side with sb; **prendre** ~ (**pour/contre**) to take sides *ou* a stand (for/against); **prendre son** ~ **de** to come to terms with; ~ **pris** bias.
partial, e, aux [paRsjal, -o] *a* biased, partial.
participant, e [paRtisipɑ̃, -ɑ̃t] *nm/f* participant; (*à un concours*) entrant.
participation [paRtisipasjɔ̃] *nf* participation; sharing; (*COMM*) interest; **la** ~ **aux bénéfices** profit-sharing.
participe [paRtisip] *nm* participle.
participer [paRtisipe]: ~ **à** *vt* (*course, réunion*) to take part in; (*profits etc*) to share in; (*frais etc*) to contribute to; (*chagrin, succès de qn*) to share (in).

particularité [paʀtikylaʀite] *nf* par-
ticularity; (*distinctive*) characteristic.

particule [paʀtikyl] *nf* particle.

particulier, ière [paʀtikylje, -jɛʀ] *a*
(*personnel, privé*) private; (*spécial*) special, particular; (*caractéristique*) characteristic, distinctive; (*spécifique*) particular // *nm* (*individu*: ADMIN) private
individual; ~ **à** peculiar to; **en ~** *ad*
(*surtout*) in particular, particularly; (*en
privé*) in private; **particulièrement** *ad*
particularly.

partie [paʀti] *nf* (*gén*) part; (*profession,
spécialité*) field, subject; (*JUR etc*: *prota-
gonistes*) party; (*de cartes, tennis etc*)
game; **une ~ de campagne/de pêche** an
outing in the country/a fishing party ou
trip; **en ~** *ad* partly, in part; **faire ~ de**
to belong to; (*suj: chose*) to be part of;
prendre qn à ~ to take sb to task; (*malmener*) to set on sb; **en grande ~**
largely, in the main; ~ **civile** (*JUR*)
party claiming damages in a criminal
case.

partiel, le [paʀsjɛl] *a* partial // *nm*
(*SCOL*) class exam.

partir [paʀtiʀ] *vi* (*gén*) to go; (*quitter*)
to go, leave; (*s'éloigner*) to go (ou drive
etc) away ou off; (*moteur*) to start; ~
de (*lieu*: *quitter*) to leave; (: *
commencer à*) to start from; (*date*) to
run ou start from; **à ~ de** from.

partisan, e [paʀtizã, -an] *nm/f* partisan
// *a*: **être ~ de qch/faire** to be in favour
of sth/doing.

partition [paʀtisjɔ̃] *nf* (*MUS*) score.

partout [paʀtu] *ad* everywhere; ~ **où il
allait** everywhere ou wherever he went;
trente ~ (*TENNIS*) thirty all.

paru *pp de* **paraître**.

parure [paʀyʀ] *nf* (*bijoux etc*) finery *q*;
jewellery *q*; (*assortiment*) set.

parution [paʀysjɔ̃] *nf* publication, appearance.

parvenir [paʀvəniʀ]: ~ **à** *vt* (*atteindre*)
to reach; (*réussir*): ~ **à faire** to manage
to do, succeed in doing; **faire ~ qch à qn**
to have sth sent to sb.

parvis [paʀvi] *nm* square (*in front of a
church*).

pas [pɑ] *ad voir le mot suivant* // *nm*
(*allure, mesure*) pace; (*démarche*)
tread; (*enjambée, DANSE*) step; (*bruit*)
(foot)step; (*trace*) footprint; (*TECH*: *de
vis, d'écrou*) thread; ~ **à** ~ step by step;
au ~ at walking pace; **à** ~ **de loup**
stealthily; **faire les cent** ~ to pace up
and down; **faire les premiers** ~ to make
the first move; **sur le** ~ **de la porte** on
the doorstep.

pas [pɑ] ♦ *nm voir le mot précédent* ♦
ad **1** (*en corrélation avec ne, non etc*)
not; **il ne pleure** ~ he does not ou doesn't
cry; he's not ou isn't crying; **il n'a** ~
pleuré/ne pleurera ~ he did not ou

---

didn't/will not ou won't cry; **ils n'ont** ~
de voiture/d'enfants they haven't got a
car/any children, they have no car/
children; **il m'a dit de ne** ~ **le faire** he
told me not to do it; **non** ~ **que ...** not
that ...

2 (*employé sans ne etc*): ~ **moi** not me;
not I, I don't (ou can't etc); **une pomme**
~ **mûre** an apple which isn't ripe; ~ **plus
tard qu'hier** only yesterday; ~ **du tout**
not at all

3: ~ **mal** not bad; not badly; ~ **mal de**
quite a lot of.

passage [pɑsaʒ] *nm* (*fait de passer*)
voir **passer**; (*lieu, prix de la traversée,
extrait de livre etc*) passage; (*chemin*)
way; **de** ~ (*touristes*) passing through;
(*amants etc*) casual; ~ **clouté** pedestrian
crossing; '~ **interdit**' 'no entry'; ~ **à
niveau** level crossing; '~ **protégé**' *right
of way over secondary road(s) on your
right*; ~ **souterrain** subway (*Brit*),
underpass.

passager, ère [pɑsaʒe, -ɛʀ] *a* passing //
nm/f passenger; ~ **clandestin** stowaway.

passant, e [pɑsɑ̃, -ɑ̃t] *a* (*rue, endroit*)
busy // *nm/f* passer-by; **en** ~ in passing.

passe [pɑs] *nf* (*SPORT, magnétique, NA-
VIG*) pass // *nm* (*passe-partout*) master
ou skeleton key; **être en** ~ **de faire** to be
on the way to doing.

passé, e [pɑse] *a* (*événement, temps*)
past; (*couleur, tapisserie*) faded // *prép*
after // *nm* past; (*LING*) past (tense); ~
de mode out of fashion; ~ **composé** perfect (tense); ~ **simple** past historic.

passe-droit [pɑsdʀwa] *nm* special privilege.

passementerie [pɑsmɑ̃tʀi] *nf* trim-
mings *pl*.

passe-montagne [pɑsmɔ̃taɲ] *nm* bala-
clava.

passe-partout [pɑspaʀtu] *nm inv* master ou skeleton key // *a inv* all-purpose.

passe-passe [pɑspɑs] *nm*: **tour de** ~
trick, sleight of hand *q*.

passeport [pɑspɔʀ] *nm* passport.

passer [pɑse] *vi* (*se rendre, aller*) to go;
(*voiture, piétons: défiler*) to pass (by),
go by; (*faire une halte rapide: facteur,
laitier etc*) to come, call; (: *pour rendre
visite*) to call ou drop in; (*courant, air,
lumière, franchir un obstacle etc*) to get
through; (*accusé, projet de loi*): ~
devant to come before; (*film, émission*)
to be on; (*temps, jours*) to pass, go by;
(*couleur, papier*) to fade; (*mode*) to die
out; (*douleur*) to pass, go away;
(*CARTES*) to pass; (*SCOL*) to go up (to
the next class) // *vt* (*frontière, rivière
etc*) to cross; (*douane*) to go through;
(*examen*) to sit, take; (*visite médicale
etc*) to have; (*journée, temps*) to spend;
(*donner*): ~ **qch à qn** to pass sth to sb;
to give sb sth; (*transmettre*): ~ **qch à**

qn to pass sth on to sb; (*enfiler: vêtement*) to slip on; (*faire entrer, mettre*): (faire) ~ qch dans/par to get sth into/through; (*café*) to pour the water on; (*thé, soupe*) to strain; (*film, pièce*) to show, put on; (*disque*) to play, put on; (*marché, accord*) to agree on; (*tolérer*): ~ qch à qn to let sb get away with sth; se ~ *vi* (*avoir lieu: scène, action*) to take place; (*se dérouler: entretien etc*) to go; (*arriver*): que s'est-il passé? what happened?; (*s'écouler: semaine etc*) to pass, go by; se ~ de *vt* to go *ou* do without; se ~ les mains sous l'eau/de l'eau sur le visage to put one's hands under the tap/run water over one's face; ~ par to go through; ~ sur *vt* (*faute, détail inutile*) to pass over; ~ avant qch/qn (*fig*) to come before sth/sb; laisser ~ (*air, lumière, personne*) to let through; (*occasion*) to let slip, miss; (*erreur*) to overlook; ~ à la radio/télévision to be on the radio/on television; ~ pour riche to be taken for a rich man; ~ en seconde, ~ la seconde (*AUTO*) to change into second; ~ le balai/l'aspirateur to sweep up/hoover; je vous passe M. X (*je vous mets en communication avec lui*) I'm putting you through to Mr X; (*je lui passe l'appareil*) here is Mr X, I'll hand you over to Mr X.

passerelle [pɑsʀɛl] *nf* footbridge; (*de navire, avion*) gangway.

passe-temps [pɑstɑ̃] *nm inv* pastime.

passette [pɑsɛt] *nf* (tea-)strainer.

passeur, euse [pɑsœʀ, -øz] *nm/f* smuggler.

passible [pasibl(ə)] *a*: ~ de liable to.

passif, ive [pasif, -iv] *a* passive // *nm* (*LING*) passive; (*COMM*) liabilities *pl*.

passion [pɑsjɔ̃] *nf* passion; **passionnant, e** *a* fascinating; **passionné, e** *a* passionate; impassioned; **passionner** *vt* (*personne*) to fascinate, grip; se **passionner pour** to take an avid interest in; to have a passion for.

passoire [pɑswaʀ] *nf* sieve; (*à légumes*) colander; (*à thé*) strainer.

pastèque [pastɛk] *nf* watermelon.

pasteur [pastœʀ] *nm* (*protestant*) minister, pastor.

pastille [pastij] *nf* (*à sucer*) lozenge, pastille; (*de papier etc*) (small) disc.

patate [patat] *nf*: ~ douce sweet potato.

patauger [patoʒe] *vi* (*pour s'amuser*) to splash about; (*avec effort*) to wade about.

pâte [pɑt] *nf* (*à tarte*) pastry; (*à pain*) dough; (*à frire*) batter; (*substance molle*) paste; cream; ~s *nfpl* (*macaroni etc*) pasta *sg*; ~ d'amandes almond paste; ~ brisée shortcrust pastry; ~ de fruits crystallized fruit *q*; ~ à modeler modelling clay, Plasticine ® (*Brit*).

pâté [pɑte] *nm* (*charcuterie*) pâté;

(*tache*) ink blot; (*de sable*) sandpie; ~ en croûte ≈ pork pie; ~ de maisons block (of houses).

pâtée [pɑte] *nf* mash, feed.

patente [patɑ̃t] *nf* (*COMM*) trading licence.

patère [patɛʀ] *nf* (coat-)peg.

paternel, le [patɛʀnɛl] *a* (*amour, soins*) fatherly; (*ligne, autorité*) paternal.

pâteux, euse [pɑtø, -øz] *a* thick; pasty.

pathétique [patetik] *a* moving.

patience [pasjɑ̃s] *nf* patience.

patient, e [pasjɑ̃, -ɑ̃t] *a, nm/f* patient.

patienter [pasjɑ̃te] *vi* to wait.

patin [patɛ̃] *nm* skate; (*sport*) skating; ~s (à glace) (ice) skates; ~s à roulettes roller skates.

patinage [patinaʒ] *nm* skating.

patiner [patine] *vi* to skate; (*embrayage*) to slip; (*roue, voiture*) to spin; se ~ *vi* (*meuble, cuir*) to acquire a sheen; **patineur, euse** *nm/f* skater; **patinoire** *nf* skating rink, (ice) rink.

pâtir [pɑtiʀ]: ~ de *vt* to suffer because of.

pâtisserie [pɑtisʀi] *nf* (*boutique*) cake shop; (*métier*) confectionery; (*à la maison*) pastry- *ou* cake-making, baking; ~s *nfpl* (*gâteaux*) pastries, cakes; **pâtissier, ière** *nm/f* pastrycook; confectioner.

patois [patwa] *nm* dialect, patois.

patrie [patʀi] *nf* homeland.

patrimoine [patʀimwan] *nm* inheritance, patrimony; (*culture*) héritage.

patriotique [patʀijɔtik] *a* patriotic.

patron, ne [patʀɔ̃, -ɔn] *nm/f* boss; (*REL*) patron saint // *nm* (*COUTURE*) pattern.

patronat [patʀɔna] *nm* employers *pl*.

patronner [patʀɔne] *vt* to sponsor, support.

patrouille [patʀuj] *nf* patrol.

patte [pat] *nf* (*jambe*) leg; (*pied: de chien, chat*) paw; (: *d'oiseau*) foot; (*languette*) strap.

pâturage [pɑtyʀaʒ] *nm* pasture.

pâture [pɑtyʀ] *nf* food.

paume [pom] *nf* palm.

paumé, e [pome] *nm/f* (*fam*) drop-out.

paumer [pome] *vt* (*fam*) to lose.

paupière [popjɛʀ] *nf* eyelid.

pause [poz] *nf* (*arrêt*) break; (*en parlant, MUS*) pause.

pauvre [povʀ(ə)] *a* poor; ~té *nf* (*état*) poverty.

pavaner [pavane]: se ~ *vi* to strut about.

pavé, e [pave] *a* paved; cobbled // *nm* (*bloc*) paving stone; cobblestone; (*pavage*) paving.

pavillon [pavijɔ̃] *nm* (*de banlieue*) small (detached) house; (*kiosque*) lodge; pavilion; (*drapeau*) flag.

pavoiser [pavwaze] *vi* to put out flags; (*fig*) to rejoice, exult.

pavot [pavo] *nm* poppy.

payant, e [pɛjɑ̃, -ɑ̃t] *a* (*spectateurs etc*) paying; (*fig: entreprise*) profitable; c'est ~ you have to pay, there is a charge.

paye [pɛj] *nf* pay, wages *pl*.

payement [pɛjmɑ̃] *nm* payment.

payer [peje] *vt* (*créancier, employé, loyer*) to pay; (*achat, réparations, fig: faute*) to pay for // *vi* to pay; (*métier*) to be well-paid; (*tactique etc*) to pay off; il me l'a fait ~ 10 F he charged me 10 F for it; ~ qch à qn to buy sth for sb, buy sb sth; cela ne paie pas de mine it doesn't look much.

pays [pei] *nm* country; land; region; village; du ~ a local.

paysage [peiza3] *nm* landscape.

paysan, ne [peizɑ̃, -an] *nm/f* countryman/woman; farmer; (*péj*) peasant // *a* country *cpd*, farming; farmers'.

Pays-Bas [peiba] *nmpl*: les ~ the Netherlands.

PC *nm* (*INFORM*) PC.

PDG *sigle m voir* **président**.

péage [pea3] *nm* toll; (*endroit*) tollgate; pont à ~ toll bridge.

peau, x [po] *nf* skin; gants de ~ fine leather gloves; ~ de chamois (*chiffon*) chamois leather, shammy; **P~-Rouge** *nm/f* Red Indian, redskin.

péché [peʃe] *nm* sin.

pêche [pɛʃ] *nf* (*sport, activité*) fishing; (*poissons péchés*) catch; (*fruit*) peach; ~ à la ligne (*en rivière*) angling.

pécher [peʃe] *vi* (*REL*) to sin; (*fig: personne*) to err; (: *chose*) to be flawed.

pêcher [peʃe] *nm* peach tree // *vi* to go fishing // *vt* to catch; to fish for.

pécheur, eresse [peʃœr, peʃRɛs] *nm/f* sinner.

pêcheur [pɛʃœr] *nm* fisherman; angler.

pécule [pekyl] *nm* savings *pl*, nest egg.

pécuniaire [pekynjɛr] *a* financial.

pédagogie [pedagɔ3i] *nf* educational methods *pl*, pedagogy; **pédagogique** *a* educational.

pédale [pedal] *nf* pedal.

pédalo [pedalo] *nm* pedal-boat.

pédant, e [pedɑ̃, -ɑ̃t] *a* (*péj*) pedantic.

pédestre [pedɛstR(ə)] *a*: **tourisme** ~ hiking.

pédiatre [pedjatR(ə)] *nm/f* paediatrician, child specialist.

pédicure [pedikyR] *nm/f* chiropodist.

pègre [pɛgR(ə)] *nf* underworld.

peignais *etc vb voir* **peindre, peigner**.

peigne [pɛɲ] *nm* comb.

peigner [peɲe] *vt* to comb (the hair of); se ~ *vi* to comb one's hair.

peignoir [pɛɲwaR] *nm* dressing gown; ~ de bain bathrobe.

peindre [pɛ̃dR(ə)] *vt* to paint; (*fig*) to portray, depict.

peine [pɛn] *nf* (*affliction*) sorrow, sadness *q*; (*mal, effort*) trouble *q*, effort; (*difficulté*) difficulty; (*punition, châtiment*) punishment; (*JUR*) sentence; faire de la ~ à qn to distress *ou* upset sb; prendre la ~ de faire to go to the trouble of doing; se donner de la ~ to make an effort; ce n'est pas la ~ de faire there's no point in doing, it's not worth doing; à ~ *ad* scarcely, hardly, barely; à ~ ... que hardly ... than; défense d'afficher sous ~ d'amende billposters will be fined; ~ capitale *ou* de mort capital punishment, death sentence; peiner *vi* to work hard; to struggle; (*moteur, voiture*) to labour // *vt* to grieve, sadden.

peintre [pɛ̃tR(ə)] *nm* painter; ~ en bâtiment house painter.

peinture [pɛ̃tyR] *nf* painting; (*couche de couleur, couleur*) paint; (*surfaces peintes: aussi: ~s*) paintwork; ~ mate/brillante matt/gloss paint; '~ fraîche' 'wet paint'.

péjoratif, ive [peʒɔRatif, -iv] *a* pejorative, derogatory.

pelage [pəla3] *nm* coat, fur.

pêle-mêle [pɛlmɛl] *ad* higgledy-piggledy.

peler [pəle] *vt, vi* to peel.

pèlerin [pɛlRɛ̃] *nm* pilgrim.

pelle [pɛl] *nf* shovel; (*d'enfant, de terrassier*) spade; ~ mécanique mechanical digger.

pellicule [pelikyl] *nf* film; ~s *nfpl* (*MÉD*) dandruff *sg*.

pelote [pəlɔt] *nf* (*de fil, laine*) ball; (*d'épingles*) pin cushion; ~ basque pelota.

peloton [pəlɔtɔ̃] *nm* group, squad; (*CYCLISME*) pack; ~ d'exécution firing squad.

pelotonner [pəlɔtɔne]: se ~ *vi* to curl (o.s.) up.

pelouse [pəluz] *nf* lawn.

peluche [pəlyʃ] *nf*: animal en ~ fluffy animal, soft toy.

pelure [pəlyR] *nf* peeling, peel *q*.

pénal, e, aux [penal, -o] *a* penal.

pénalité [penalite] *nf* penalty.

penaud, e [pəno, -od] *a* sheepish, contrite.

penchant [pɑ̃ʃɑ̃] *nm* tendency, propensity; liking, fondness.

pencher [pɑ̃ʃe] *vi* to tilt, lean over // *vt* to tilt; se ~ *vi* to lean over; (*se baisser*) to bend down; se ~ sur to bend over; (*fig: problème*) to look into; se ~ au dehors to lean out; ~ pour to be inclined to favour.

pendaison [pɑ̃dɛzɔ̃] *nf* hanging.

pendant [pɑ̃dɑ̃] *nm*: faire ~ à to match; to be the counterpart of // *prép* during; ~ que while.

pendentif [pɑ̃dɑ̃tif] *nm* pendant.

penderie [pɑ̃dRi] *nf* wardrobe.

pendre [pɑ̃dR(ə)] *vt, vi* to hang; se ~

(à) (*se suicider*) to hang o.s. (on); ~ à to hang (down) from; ~ qch à to hang sth (up) on.

pendule [pɑ̃dyl] *nf* clock // *nm* pendulum.

pêne [pɛn] *nm* bolt.

pénétrer [penetʀe] *vi*, *vt* to penetrate; ~ dans to enter; (*suj: projectile*) to penetrate; (: *air, eau*) to come into, get into.

pénible [penibl(ə)] *a* (*astreignant*) hard; (*affligeant*) painful; (*personne, caractère*) tiresome; ~**ment** *ad* with difficulty.

péniche [peniʃ] *nf* barge.

pénicilline [penisilin] *nf* penicillin.

péninsule [penɛ̃syl] *nf* peninsula.

pénis [penis] *nm* penis.

pénitence [penitɑ̃s] *nf* (*repentir*) penitence; (*peine*) penance.

pénitencier [penitɑ̃sje] *nm* penitentiary.

pénombre [penɔ̃bʀ(ə)] *nf* half-light; darkness.

pensée [pɑ̃se] *nf* thought; (*démarche, doctrine*) thinking *q*; (*BOT*) pansy; en ~ in one's mind.

penser [pɑ̃se] *vi* to think // *vt* to think; (*concevoir: problème, machine*) to think out; ~ à to think of; (*songer à: ami, vacances*) to think of *ou* about; (*réfléchir à: problème, offre*): ~ à qch to think about sth *ou* think sth over; faire ~ à to remind one of; ~ faire qch to be thinking of doing sth, intend to do sth.

pension [pɑ̃sjɔ̃] *nf* (*allocation*) pension; (*prix du logement*) board and lodgings, bed and board; (*maison particulière*) boarding house; (*hôtel*) guesthouse, hotel; (*école*) boarding school; prendre qn en ~ to take sb (in) as a lodger; mettre en ~ to send to boarding school; ~ alimentaire (*d'étudiant*) living allowance; (*de divorcée*) maintenance allowance; alimony; ~ complète full board; ~ de famille boarding house, guesthouse; **pensionnaire** *nm/f* boarder; guest; **pensionnat** *nm* boarding school.

pente [pɑ̃t] *nf* slope; en ~ *a* sloping.

Pentecôte [pɑ̃tkot] *nf*: la ~ Whitsun (*Brit*), Pentecost.

pénurie [penyʀi] *nf* shortage.

pépé [pepe] *nm* (*fam*) grandad.

pépin [pepɛ̃] *nm* (*BOT: graine*) pip; (*ennui*) snag, hitch.

pépinière [pepinjɛʀ] *nf* nursery.

perçant, e [pɛʀsɑ̃, -ɑ̃t] *a* sharp, keen; piercing, shrill.

percée [pɛʀse] *nf* (*trouée*) opening; (*MIL, technologique*) breakthrough; (*SPORT*) break.

perce-neige [pɛʀsənɛʒ] *nf inv* snowdrop.

percepteur [pɛʀsɛptœʀ] *nm* tax collector.

perception [pɛʀsɛpsjɔ̃] *nf* perception;

(*d'impôts etc*) collection; (*bureau*) tax office.

percer [pɛʀse] *vt* to pierce; (*ouverture etc*) to make; (*mystère, énigme*) to penetrate // *vi* to come through; to break through; ~ une dent to cut a tooth.

perceuse [pɛʀsøz] *nf* drill.

percevoir [pɛʀsəvwaʀ] *vt* (*distinguer*) to perceive, detect; (*taxe, impôt*) to collect; (*revenu, indemnité*) to receive.

perche [pɛʀʃ(ə)] *nf* (*bâton*) pole.

percher [pɛʀʃe] *vt*: ~ qch sur to perch sth on // *vi, se* ~ *vi* (*oiseau*) to perch; **perchoir** *nm* perch.

perçois *etc vb voir* **percevoir**.

percolateur [pɛʀkɔlatœʀ] *nm* percolator.

perçu, e *pp de* **percevoir**.

percussion [pɛʀkysjɔ̃] *nf* percussion.

percuter [pɛʀkyte] *vt* to strike; (*suj: véhicule*) to crash into.

perdant, e [pɛʀdɑ̃, -ɑ̃t] *nm/f* loser.

perdition [pɛʀdisjɔ̃] *nf*: en ~ (*NAVIG*) in distress; lieu de ~ den of vice.

perdre [pɛʀdʀ(ə)] *vt* to lose; (*gaspiller: temps, argent*) to waste; (*personne: moralement etc*) to ruin // *vi* to lose; (*sur une vente etc*) to lose out; se ~ *vi* (*s'égarer*) to get lost, lose one's way; (*fig*) to go to waste; to disappear, vanish.

perdrix [pɛʀdʀi] *nf* partridge.

perdu, e [pɛʀdy] *pp de* **perdre** // *a* (*isolé*) out-of-the-way; (*COMM: emballage*) non-returnable; (*malade*): il est ~ there's no hope left for him; à vos moments ~s in your spare time.

père [pɛʀ] *nm* father; ~s (*ancêtres*) forefathers; ~ de famille father; family man; le ~ Noël Father Christmas.

perfectionné, e [pɛʀfɛksjɔne] *a* sophisticated.

perfectionner [pɛʀfɛksjɔne] *vt* to improve, perfect.

perforatrice [pɛʀfɔʀatʀis] *nf* (*pour cartes*) card-punch; (*de bureau*) punch.

perforer [pɛʀfɔʀe] *vt* to perforate; to punch a hole (*ou* holes) in; (*ticket, bande, carte*) to punch.

performant, e [pɛʀfɔʀmɑ̃, -ɑ̃t] *a*: très ~ high-performance *cpd*.

perfusion [pɛʀfyzjɔ̃] *nf*: faire une ~ à qn to put sb on a drip.

péril [peʀil] *nm* peril.

périmé, e [peʀime] *a* (out)dated; (*ADMIN*) out-of-date, expired.

périmètre [peʀimɛtʀ(ə)] *nm* perimeter.

période [peʀjɔd] *nf* period; **périodique** *a* (*phases*) periodic; (*publication*) periodical // *nm* periodical.

péripéties [peʀipesi] *nfpl* events, episodes.

périphérique [peʀifeʀik] *a* (*quartiers*) outlying; (*ANAT, TECH*) peripheral; (*station de radio*) operating from outside

France // nm (AUTO) ring road; (IN-
FORM) peripheral.
périple [peʀipl(ə)] nm journey.
périr [peʀiʀ] vi to die, perish.
périssable [peʀisabl(ə)] a perishable.
perle [peʀl(ə)] nf pearl; (de plastique,
métal, sueur) bead.
perlé, e [peʀle] a: grève ~e go-slow.
perler [peʀle] vi to form in droplets.
permanence [peʀmanɑ̃s] nf permanence; (local) (duty) office; emergency
service; assurer une ~ (service public,
bureaux) to operate ou maintain a basic
service; être de ~ to be on call ou duty;
en ~ ad permanently; continuously.
permanent, e [peʀmanɑ̃, -ɑ̃t] a permanent; (spectacle) continuous // nf
perm.
perméable [peʀmeabl(ə)] a (terrain)
permeable; ~ à (fig) receptive ou open
to.
permettre [peʀmetʀ(ə)] vt to allow,
permit; ~ à qn de faire/qch to allow sb
to do/sth; se ~ de faire to take the liberty of doing; permettez! excuse me!
permis [peʀmi] nm permit, licence; ~
de chasse hunting permit; ~ (de
conduire) (driving) licence (Brit),
(driver's) license (US); ~ de construire
planning permission (Brit), building permit (US); ~ d'inhumer burial certificate; ~ de séjour residence permit; ~ de
travail work permit.
permission [peʀmisjɔ̃] nf permission;
(MIL) leave; en ~ on leave; avoir la ~
de faire to have permission to do.
permuter [peʀmyte] vt to change
around, permutate // vi to change, swap.
Pérou [peʀu] nm Peru.
perpétuel, le [peʀpetɥɛl] a perpetual;
(ADMIN etc) permanent; for life.
perpétuité [peʀpetɥite] nf: à ~ a, ad
for life; être condamné à ~ to receive a
life sentence.
perplexe [peʀplɛks(ə)] a perplexed,
puzzled.
perquisitionner [peʀkizisjɔne] vi to
carry out a search.
perron [peʀɔ̃] nm steps pl (in front of
mansion etc).
perroquet [peʀɔkɛ] nm parrot.
perruche [peʀyʃ] nf budgerigar (Brit),
budgie (Brit), parakeet (US).
perruque [peʀyk] nf wig.
persan, e [peʀsɑ̃, -an] a Persian.
persécuter [peʀsekyte] vt to persecute.
persévérer [peʀsevere] vi to persevere.
persiennes [peʀsjɛn] nfpl (metal) shut-
ters.
persiflage [peʀsiflaʒ] nm mockery q.
persil [peʀsi] nm parsley.
Persique [peʀsik] a: le golfe ~ the (Persian) Gulf.
persistant, e [peʀsistɑ̃, -ɑ̃t] a persistent; (feuilles) evergreen.

persister [peʀsiste] vi to persist; ~ à
faire qch to persist in doing sth.
personnage [peʀsɔnaʒ] nm (notable)
personality; figure; (individu) character,
individual; (THÉÂTRE) character; (PEIN-
TURE) figure.
personnalité [peʀsɔnalite] nf personality; (personnage) prominent figure.
personne [peʀsɔn] nf person // pronom
nobody, no one; (quelqu'un) anybody,
anyone; ~s people pl; il n'y a ~ there's
nobody there, there isn't anybody there;
~ âgée elderly person; **personnel, le** a
personal // nm staff, personnel;
personnellement ad personally.
perspective [peʀspɛktiv] nf (ART) perspective; (vue, coup d'œil) view; (point
de vue) viewpoint, angle; (chose
escomptée, envisagée) prospect; en ~ in
prospect.
perspicace [peʀspikas] a clear-sighted,
gifted with (ou showing) insight.
persuader [peʀsɥade] vt: ~ qn (de/de
faire) to persuade sb (of/to do).
perte [peʀt(ə)] nf loss; (de temps)
waste; (fig: morale) ruin; à ~ (COMM)
at a loss; à ~ de vue as far as the eye
can (ou could) see; ~ sèche dead loss;
~s blanches (vaginal) discharge sg.
pertinemment [peʀtinamɑ̃] ad to the
point; full well.
pertinent, e [peʀtinɑ̃, -ɑ̃t] a apt,
relevant.
perturbation [peʀtyʀbasjɔ̃] nf disrup-
tion; perturbation; ~ (atmosphérique)
atmospheric disturbance.
perturber [peʀtyʀbe] vt to disrupt;
(PSYCH) to perturb, disturb.
pervers, e [peʀvɛʀ, -ɛʀs(ə)] a per-
verted, depraved; perverse.
pervertir [peʀvɛʀtiʀ] vt to pervert.
pesant, e [pəzɑ̃, -ɑ̃t] a heavy; (fig) bur-
densome.
pesanteur [pəzɑ̃tœʀ] nf gravity.
pèse-personne [pɛzpɛʀsɔn] nm (bathroom) scales pl.
peser [pəze] vt, vb avec attribut to
weigh // vi to be heavy; (fig) to carry
weight; ~ sur (fig) to lie heavy on; to influence.
pessimiste [pesimist(ə)] a pessimistic //
nm/f pessimist.
peste [pɛst(ə)] nf plague.
pester [pɛste] vi: ~ contre to curse.
pétale [petal] nm petal.
pétanque [petɑ̃k] nf type of bowls.
pétarader [petaʀade] vi to backfire.
pétard [petaʀ] nm banger (Brit), fire-
cracker.
péter [pete] vi (fam: casser, sauter) to
burst; to bust; (fam!) to fart (!).
pétiller [petije] vi (flamme, bois) to
crackle; (mousse, champagne) to bubble; (yeux) to sparkle.
petit, e [pəti, -it] a (gén) small; (main,

objet, colline, en âge: enfant) small, little; (*voyage*) short, little; (*bruit etc*) faint, slight; (*mesquin*) mean // *nmpl* (*d'un animal*) young *pl*; **faire des ~s** to have kittens (*ou* puppies *etc*); **les tout-petits** the little ones, the tiny tots; **~ à ~** bit by bit, gradually; **~(e) ami/e** boyfriend/girlfriend; **les ~es annonces** the small ads; **~ déjeuner** breakfast; **~ pain (bread) roll; ~s pois** garden peas; **~-bourgeois, ~-bourgeoise** *a* (*péj*) middle-class; **~e-fille** *nf* granddaughter; **~-fils** *nm* grandson; **~s-enfants** *nmpl* grandchildren.

pétition [petisjɔ̃] *nf* petition.

pétrin [petrɛ̃] *nm* kneading-trough; (*fig*): **dans le ~** in a jam *ou* fix.

pétrir [petriR] *vt* to knead.

pétrole [petrɔl] *nm* oil; (*pour lampe, réchaud etc*) paraffin (oil); **pétrolier, ière** *a* oil *cpd* // *nm* oil tanker.

peu [pø] ♦ *ad* **1** (*modifiant verbe, adjectif, adverbe*): **il boit ~** he doesn't drink (very) much; **il est ~ bavard** he's not very talkative; **~ avant/après** shortly before/afterwards

2 (*modifiant nom*): **~ de:** **~ de gens/d'arbres** few *ou* not (very) many people/trees; **il a ~ d'espoir** he hasn't (got) much hope, he has little hope; **pour ~ de temps** for (only) a short while

3: **~ à ~** little by little; **à ~ près** just about, more or less; **à ~ près 10 kg/10 F** approximately 10 kg/10 F

♦ *nm* **1**: **le ~ de gens qui** the few people who; **le ~ de sable qui** what little sand, the little sand which

2: **un ~** a little; **un petit ~** a little bit; **un ~ d'espoir** a little hope

♦ *pronom*: **~ le savent** few know (it); **avant** *ou* **sous ~** shortly, before long; **de ~** (only) just.

peuple [pœpl(ə)] *nm* people.

peupler [pœple] *vt* (*pays, région*) to populate; (*étang*) to stock; (*suj: hommes, poissons*) to inhabit; (*fig: imagination, rêves*) to fill.

peuplier [pøplije] *nm* poplar (tree).

peur [pœR] *nf* fear; **avoir ~** (de/de faire/que) to be frightened *ou* afraid (of/of doing/that); **faire ~ à** to frighten; **de ~ de/que** for fear of/that; **~eux, euse** *a* fearful, timorous.

peut *vb voir* **pouvoir.**

peut-être [pøtɛtR(ə)] *ad* perhaps, maybe; **~ que** perhaps, maybe; **~ bien qu'il fera/est** he may well do/be.

peux *etc vb voir* **pouvoir.**

phare [faR] *nm* (*en mer*) lighthouse; (*de véhicule*) headlight; **mettre ses ~s** to put on one's headlights; **~s de recul** reversing lights.

pharmacie [faRmasi] *nf* (*magasin*) chemist's (*Brit*), pharmacy; (*officine*) dispensary; (*de salle de bain*) medicine

cabinet; **pharmacien, ne** *nm/f* pharmacist, chemist (*Brit*).

phase [faz] *nf* phase.

phénomène [fenɔmɛn] *nm* phenomenon (*pl* a); (*monstre*) freak.

philanthrope [filɑ̃tRɔp] *nm/f* philanthropist.

philosophe [filɔzɔf] *nm/f* philosopher // *a* philosophical.

philosophie [filɔzɔfi] *nf* philosophy; **philosophique** *a* philosophical.

phobie [fɔbi] *nf* phobia.

phonétique [fɔnetik] *nf* phonetics *sg*.

phoque [fɔk] *nm* seal; (*fourrure*) sealskin.

phosphorescent, e [fɔsfɔResɑ̃, -ɑ̃t] *a* luminous.

photo [fɔto] *nf* photo(graph); **en ~** in *ou* on a photograph; **prendre en ~** to take a photo of; **aimer la/faire de la ~** to like taking/take photos; **~ d'identité** passport photograph.

photo... [fɔto] *préfixe*: **~copie** *nf* photocopying; photocopy; **~copier** *vt* to photocopy; **~graphe** *nm/f* photographer; **~graphie** *nf* (*procédé, technique*) photography; (*cliché*) photograph; **~graphier** *vt* to photograph.

phrase [fRaz] *nf* (*LING*) sentence; (*propos, MUS*) phrase.

physicien, ne [fizisjɛ̃, -ɛn] *nm/f* physicist.

physionomie [fizjɔnɔmi] *nf* face.

physique [fizik] *a* physical // *nm* physique // *nf* physics *sg*; **au ~** physically; **~ment** *ad* physically.

piaffer [pjafe] *vi* to stamp.

piailler [pjaje] *vi* to squawk.

pianiste [pjanist(ə)] *nm/f* pianist.

piano [pjano] *nm* piano.

pianoter [pjanɔte] *vi* to tinkle away (at the piano); (*tapoter*): **~ sur** to drum one's fingers on.

pic [pik] *nm* (*instrument*) pick(axe); (*montagne*) peak; (*ZOOL*) woodpecker; **à ~** *ad* vertically; (*fig*) just at the right time.

pichet [piʃɛ] *nm* jug.

picorer [pikɔRe] *vt* to peck.

picoter [pikɔte] *vt* (*suj: oiseau*) to peck // *vi* (*irriter*) to smart, prickle.

pie [pi] *nf* magpie; (*fig*) chatterbox.

pièce [pjɛs] *nf* (*d'un logement*) room; (*THÉÂTRE*) play; (*de mécanisme, machine*) part; (*de monnaie*) coin; (*COUTURE*) patch; (*document*) document; (*de drap, fragment, de collection*) piece; **dix francs ~** ten francs each; **vendre à la ~** to sell separately; **travailler/payer à la ~** to do piecework/pay piece rate; **un maillot une ~** a one-piece swimsuit; **un deux-~s cuisine** a two-room(ed) flat (*Brit*) *ou* apartment (*US*) with kitchen; **~ à conviction** exhibit; **~ d'eau** ornamental lake *ou* pond; **~ d'identité**

avez-vous une ~ d'identité? have you got any (means of) identification?; ~ montée tiered cake; ~s détachées spares, (spare) parts; ~s justificatives supporting documents.

pied [pje] *nm* foot (*pl* feet); (*de verre*) stem; (*de table*) leg; (*de lampe*) base; (*plante*) plant; à ~ on foot; à ~ sec without getting one's feet wet; au ~ de la lettre literally; de ~ en cap from head to foot; en ~ (*portrait*) full-length; avoir ~ to be able to touch the bottom, not to be out of one's depth; avoir le ~ marin to be a good sailor; sur ~ (*debout, rétabli*) up and about; mettre sur ~ (*entreprise*) to set up; mettre à ~ to dismiss; to lay off; ~ de vigne vine.

piédestal, aux [pjedɛstal, -o] *nm* pedestal.

pied-noir [pjenwaʀ] *nm* Algerian-born Frenchman.

piège [pjɛʒ] *nm* trap; **prendre au ~** to trap; **piéger** *vt* (*avec une bombe*) to booby-trap; **lettre/voiture piégée** letter-/car-bomb.

pierraille [pjeʀaj] *nf* loose stones *pl*.

pierre [pjɛʀ] *nf* stone; ~ à briquet flint; ~ fine semiprecious stone; ~ de taille freestone *q*; ~ tombale tombstone.

pierreries [pjeʀʀi] *nfpl* gems, precious stones.

piétiner [pjetine] *vi* (*trépigner*) to stamp (one's foot); (*marquer le pas*) to stand about; (*fig*) to be at a standstill // *vt* to trample on.

piéton, ne [pjetɔ̃, -ɔn] *nm/f* pedestrian; **piétonnier, ière** *a*: **rue/zone piétonnière** pedestrian precinct.

pieu, x [pjø] *nm* post; (*pointu*) stake.

pieuvre [pjœvʀ(ə)] *nf* octopus.

pieux, euse [pjø, -øz] *a* pious.

piffer [pife] *vt* (*fam*): **je ne peux pas le ~** I can't stand him.

pigeon [piʒɔ̃] *nm* pigeon.

piger [piʒe] *vi, vt* (*fam*) to understand.

pigiste [piʒist(ə)] *nm/f* freelance(r).

pignon [piɲɔ̃] *nm* (*de mur*) gable; (*d'engrenage*) cog(wheel), gearwheel.

pile [pil] *nf* (*tas*) pile; (*ÉLEC*) battery // *ad* (*s'arrêter etc*) dead; **à deux heures ~** at two on the dot; **jouer à ~ ou face** to toss up (for it); **~ ou face?** heads or tails?

piler [pile] *vt* to crush, pound.

pileux, euse [pilø, -øz] *a*: **système ~** (body) hair.

pilier [pilje] *nm* pillar.

piller [pije] *vt* to pillage, plunder, loot.

pilon [pilɔ̃] *nm* pestle.

pilote [pilɔt] *nm* pilot; (*de char, voiture*) driver // *a* pilot *cpd*; ~ de ligne/d'essai/ de chasse airline/test/fighter pilot; ~ de course racing driver.

piloter [pilɔte] *vt* to pilot, fly; to drive.

pilule [pilyl] *nf* pill; **prendre la ~** to be

on the pill.

piment [pimɑ̃] *nm* (*BOT*) pepper, capsicum; (*fig*) spice, piquancy.

pimpant, e [pɛ̃pɑ̃, -ɑ̃t] *a* spruce.

pin [pɛ̃] *nm* pine (tree); (*bois*) pine(wood).

pinard [pinaʀ] *nm* (*fam*) (cheap) wine, plonk (*Brit*).

pince [pɛ̃s] *nf* (*outil*) pliers *pl*; (*de homard, crabe*) pincer, claw; (*COUTURE: pli*) dart; ~ à sucre/glace sugar/ice tongs *pl*; ~ à épiler tweezers *pl*; ~ à linge clothes peg (*Brit*) ou pin (*US*).

pincé, e [pɛ̃se] *a* (*air*) stiff // *nf*: **une ~e de** a pinch of.

pinceau, x [pɛ̃so] *nm* (paint)brush.

pincer [pɛ̃se] *vt* to pinch; (*MUS: cordes*) to pluck; (*fam*) to nab.

pincettes [pɛ̃sɛt] *nf/pl* (*pour le feu*) (fire) tongs.

pinède [pinɛd] *nf* pinewood, pine forest.

pingouin [pɛ̃gwɛ̃] *nm* penguin.

ping-pong [piŋpɔ̃g] *nm* table tennis.

pingre [pɛ̃gʀ(ə)] *a* niggardly.

pinson [pɛ̃sɔ̃] *nm* chaffinch.

pintade [pɛ̃tad] *nf* guinea-fowl.

pioche [pjɔʃ] *nf* pickaxe; **piocher** *vt* to dig up (with a pickaxe).

piolet [pjɔlɛ] *nm* ice axe.

pion [pjɔ̃] *nm* (*ÉCHECS*) pawn; (*DAMES*) piece.

pionnier [pjɔnje] *nm* pioneer.

pipe [pip] *nf* pipe.

pipeau, x [pipo] *nm* (reed-)pipe.

piquant, e [pikɑ̃, -ɑ̃t] *a* (*barbe, rosier etc*) prickly; (*saveur, sauce*) hot, pungent; (*fig*) racy; biting // *nm* (*épine*) thorn, prickle; (*fig*) spiciness, spice.

pique [pik] *nf* pike; (*fig*) cutting remark // *nm* (*CARTES: couleur*) spades *pl*; (: *carte*) spade.

pique-nique [piknik] *nm* picnic.

piquer [pike] *vt* (*percer*) to prick; (*planter*): ~ **qch dans** to stick sth into; (*MÉD*) to give a jab to; (: *animal blessé etc*) to put to sleep; (*suj: insecte, fumée, ortie*) to sting; (*suj: poivre*) to burn; (: *froid*) to bite; (*COUTURE*) to machine (stitch); (*intérêt etc*) to arouse; (*fam*) to pick up; (: *voler*) to pinch; (: *arrêter*) to nab // *vi* (*avion*) to go into a dive; **se ~ de faire** to pride o.s. on doing; ~ **un galop/un cent mètres** to break into a gallop/put on a sprint.

piquet [pikɛ] *nm* (*pieu*) post, stake; (*de tente*) peg; ~ de grève (strike-)picket; ~ d'incendie fire-fighting squad.

piqûre [pikyʀ] *nf* (*d'épingle*) prick; (*d'ortie*) sting; (*de moustique*) bite; (*MÉD*) injection, shot (*US*); (*COUTURE*) (straight) stitch; straight stitching; **faire une ~ à qn** to give sb an injection.

pirate [piʀat] *nm, a* pirate; ~ de l'air hijacker.

pire [piʀ] *a* worse; *(superlatif)*: le(la) ~
... the worst ... // *nm*: le ~ (de) the worst
(of).

pis [pi] *nm (de vache)* udder; *(pire)*: le
~ the worst // *a, ad* worse; **pis-aller** *nm
inv* stopgap.

piscine [pisin] *nf* (swimming) pool; ~
couverte indoor (swimming) pool.

pissenlit [pisɑ̃li] *nm* dandelion.

pistache [pistaʃ] *nf* pistachio (nut).

piste [pist(ə)] *nf (d'un animal, sentier)*
track, trail; *(indice)* lead; *(de stade, de
magnétophone)* track; *(de cirque)* ring;
(de danse) floor; *(de patinage)* rink; *(de
ski)* run; *(AVIAT)* runway; ~ **cyclable**
cycle track.

pistolet [pistɔlɛ] *nm (arme)* pistol, gun;
(à peinture) spray gun; ~ **à air
comprimé** airgun; **~-mitrailleur** *nm*
submachine gun.

piston [pistɔ̃] *nm (TECH)* piston;
pistonner *vt (candidat)* to pull strings
for.

piteux, euse [pitø, -øz] *a* pitiful, sorry
(avant le nom).

pitié [pitje] *nf* pity; **faire** ~ to inspire
pity; **avoir** ~ **de** *(compassion)* to pity,
feel sorry for; *(merci)* to have pity *ou*
mercy on.

piton [pitɔ̃] *nm (clou)* peg; ~ **rocheux**
rocky outcrop.

pitoyable [pitwajabl(ə)] *a* pitiful.

pitre [pitʀ(ə)] *nm* clown; **pitrerie** *nf*
tomfoolery *q*.

pittoresque [pitɔʀɛsk(ə)] *a* picturesque.

pivot [pivo] *nm* pivot; **pivoter** *vi* to
swivel; to revolve.

P.J. *sigle f voir* **police**.

placard [plakaʀ] *nm (armoire)* cupboard; *(affiche)* poster, notice;
placarder *vt (affiche)* to put up.

place [plas] *nf (emplacement, situation,
classement)* place; *(de ville, village)*
square; *(espace libre)* room, space; *(de
parking)* space; *(siège: de train,
cinéma, voiture)* seat; *(emploi)* job; **en**
~ *(mettre)* in its place; **sur** ~ on the
spot; **faire** ~ **à** to give way to; **faire de
la** ~ **à** to make room for; **ça prend de la**
~ it takes up a lot of room *ou* space; **à
la** ~ **de** in place of, instead of; **il y a 20
~s assises/debout** there are 20 seats/there
is standing room for 20.

placement [plasmɑ̃] *nm* placing; *(FI-
NANCE)* investment; **bureau de** ~ employment agency.

placer [plase] *vt* to place; *(convive,
spectateur)* to seat; *(capital, argent)* to
place, invest; *(dans la conversation)* to
put *ou* get in; **se** ~ **au premier rang** to
go and stand *(ou* sit) in the first row.

plafond [plafɔ̃] *nm* ceiling.

plafonner [plafɔne] *vi* to reach one's *(ou*
a) ceiling.

plage [plaʒ] *nf* beach; *(fig)* band, brack-

et; *(de disque)* track, band; ~ **arrière**
(AUTO) parcel *ou* back shelf.

plagiat [plaʒja] *nm* plagiarism.

plaider [plede] *vi (avocat)* to plead;
(plaignant) to go to court, litigate // *vt*
to plead; ~ **pour** *(fig)* to speak for;
plaidoyer *nm (JUR)* speech for the defence; *(fig)* plea.

plaie [plɛ] *nf* wound.

plaignant, e [plɛɲɑ̃, -ɑ̃t] *nm/f* plaintiff.

plaindre [plɛ̃dʀ(ə)] *vt* to pity, feel sorry
for; **se** ~ *vi (gémir)* to moan; *(protester,
rouspéter)*: **se** ~ **(à qn) (de)** to complain
(to sb) (about); *(souffrir)*: **se** ~ **de** to
complain of.

plaine [plɛn] *nf* plain.

plain-pied [plɛ̃pje]: **de** ~ **(avec)** on the
same level (as).

plainte [plɛ̃t] *nf (gémissement)* moan,
groan; *(doléance)* complaint; **porter** ~ to
lodge a complaint.

plaire [plɛʀ] *vi* to be a success, be successful; to please; ~ **à**: **cela me plaît** I
like it; **se** ~ **quelque part** to like being
somewhere *ou* like it somewhere; **s'il
vous plaît** please.

plaisance [plɛzɑ̃s] *nf (aussi: navigation
de* ~) (pleasure) sailing, yachting.

plaisant, e [plɛzɑ̃, -ɑ̃t] *a* pleasant;
(histoire, anecdote) amusing.

plaisanter [plɛzɑ̃te] *vi* to joke;
plaisanterie *nf* joke; joking *q*.

plaise *etc vb voir* **plaire**.

plaisir [plɛziʀ] *nm* pleasure; **faire** ~ **à
qn** *(délibérément)* to be nice to sb,
please sb; *(suj: cadeau, nouvelle etc)*:
ceci me fait ~ I'm delighted *ou* very
pleased with this; **pour le** *ou* **par** ~ for
pleasure.

plaît *vb voir* **plaire**.

plan, e [plɑ̃, -an] *a* flat // *nm* plan;
(GÉOM) plane; *(fig)* level, plane; *(CINÉ-
MA)* shot; **au premier/second** ~ in the
foreground/middle distance; **à l'arrière**
~ in the background; ~ **d'eau** lake;
pond.

planche [plɑ̃ʃ] *nf (pièce de bois)* plank,
(wooden) board; *(illustration)* plate; **les
~s** *(THÉÂTRE)* the stage *sg*, the boards;
~ **à repasser** ironing board; ~ **à
roulettes** skateboard; ~ **de salut** *(fig)*
sheet anchor.

plancher [plɑ̃ʃe] *nm* floor; floorboards
pl; *(fig)* minimum level // *vi* to work
hard.

planer [plane] *vi* to glide; ~ **sur** *(fig)* to
hang over; to hover above.

planète [planɛt] *nf* planet.

planeur [plance](r)] *nm* glider.

planification [planifikasjɔ̃] *nf (economic)* planning.

planifier [planifje] *vt* to plan.

planning [planiŋ] *nm* programme,
schedule; ~ **familial** family planning.

plant [plɑ̃] *nm* seedling, young plant.

plante [plãt] *nf* plant; ~ **d'appartement** house *ou* pot plant; ~ **du pied** sole (of the foot).

planter [plãte] *vt* (*plante*) to plant; (*enfoncer*) to hammer *ou* drive in; (*tente*) to put up, pitch; (*fam*) to dump; to ditch; **se** ~ (*fam: se tromper*) to get it wrong.

plantureux, euse [plãtyrø, -øz] *a* copious, lavish; (*femme*) buxom.

plaque [plak] *nf* plate; (*de verglas, d'eczéma*) patch; (*avec inscription*) plaque; ~ (**minéralogique** *ou* **d'immatriculation**) number (*Brit*) *ou* license (*US*) plate; ~ **chauffante** hotplate; ~ **de chocolat** bar of chocolate; ~ **d'identité** identity disc; ~ **tournante** (*fig*) centre.

plaqué, e [plake] *a*: ~ **or/argent** gold-/silver-plated; ~ **acajou** veneered in mahogany.

plaquer [plake] *vt* (*aplatir*): ~ **qch sur/ contre** to make sth stick *ou* cling to; (*RUGBY*) to bring down; (*fam: laisser tomber*) to drop.

plastic [plastik] *nm* plastic explosive.

plastique [plastik] *a, nm* plastic.

plastiquer [plastike] *vt* to blow up (*with a plastic bomb*).

plat, e [pla, -at] *a* flat; (*cheveux*) straight; (*personne, livre*) dull // *nm* (*récipient, CULIN*) dish; (*d'un repas*): **le premier** ~ the first course; **à** ~ **ventre** *ad* face down; **à** ~ *ad*, (*pneu, batterie*) flat; (*personne*) dead beat; ~ **cuisiné** pre-cooked meal; ~ **du jour** day's special (*menu*); ~ **de résistance** main course.

platane [platan] *nm* plane tree.

plateau, x [plato] *nm* (*support*) tray; (*GÉO*) plateau; (*de tourne-disques*) turntable; (*CINÉMA*) set; ~ **à fromages** cheeseboard.

plate-bande [platbãd] *nf* flower bed.

plate-forme [platform(ə)] *nf* platform; ~ **de forage/pétrolière** drilling/oil rig.

platine [platin] *nm* platinum // *nf* (*d'un tourne-disque*) turntable.

plâtras [platra] *nm* rubble *q*.

plâtre [platr(ə)] *nm* (*matériau*) plaster; (*statue*) plaster statue; (*MÉD*) (plaster) cast; **avoir un bras dans le** ~ to have an arm in plaster.

plein, e [plɛ̃, -ɛn] *a* full; (*porte, roue*) solid; (*chienne, jument*) big (with young) // *nm*: **faire le** ~ (**d'essence**) to fill up (with petrol); **à ~es mains** (*ramasser*) in handfuls; (*empoigner*) firmly; **à** ~ **régime** at maximum revs; (*fig*) full steam; **à** ~ **temps** full-time; **en** ~ **air** in the open air; **en** ~ **soleil** in direct sunlight; **en** ~**e nuit/rue** in the middle of the night/street; **en** ~ **jour** in broad daylight; **en** ~ **sur** right on; ~**-emploi** *nm* full employment.

plénitude [plenityd] *nf* fullness.

pleurer [plœre] *vi* to cry; (*yeux*) to wa-

ter // *vt* to mourn (for); ~ **sur** *vt* to lament (over), to bemoan.

pleurnicher [plœrnife] *vi* to snivel, whine.

pleurs [plœr] *nmpl*: **en** ~ in tears.

pleut *vb voir* **pleuvoir**.

pleuvoir [pløvwar] *vb impersonnel* to rain // *vi* (*fig*): ~ (**sur**) to shower down (upon); to be showered upon; **il pleut** it's raining.

pli [pli] *nm* fold; (*de jupe*) pleat; (*de pantalon*) crease; (*aussi*: **faux** ~) crease; (*enveloppe*) envelope; (*lettre*) letter; (*CARTES*) trick.

pliant, e [plijã, -ãt] *a* folding // *nm* folding stool, campstool.

plier [plije] *vt* to fold; (*pour ranger*) to fold up; (*table pliante*) to fold down; (*genou, bras*) to bend // *vi* to yield; (*fig*) to yield; **se** ~ **à** to submit to.

plinthe [plɛ̃t] *nf* skirting board.

plisser [plise] *vt* (*rider, chiffonner*) to crease; (*jupe*) to put pleats in.

plomb [plɔ̃] *nm* (*métal*) lead; (*d'une cartouche*) (lead) shot; (*PÊCHE*) sinker; (*sceau*) (lead) seal; (*ÉLEC*) fuse.

plombage [plɔ̃baʒ] *nm* (*de dent*) filling.

plomber [plɔ̃be] *vt* (*canne, ligne*) to weight (with lead); (*dent*) to fill.

plomberie [plɔ̃bri] *nf* plumbing.

plombier [plɔ̃bje] *nm* plumber.

plongeant, e [plɔ̃ʒã, -ãt] *a* (*vue*) from above; (*tir, décolleté*) plunging.

plongée [plɔ̃ʒe] *nf* (*SPORT*) diving *q*; (: *sans scaphandre*) skin diving.

plongeoir [plɔ̃ʒwar] *nm* diving board.

plongeon [plɔ̃ʒɔ̃] *nm* dive.

plonger [plɔ̃ʒe] *vi* to dive // *vt*: ~ **qch dans** to plunge sth into.

ployer [plwaje] *vt* to bend // *vi* to sag; to bend.

plu *pp de* **plaire, pleuvoir**.

pluie [plɥi] *nf* rain; (*fig*): ~ **de** shower of.

plume [plym] *nf* (*oiseau*) feather; (*pour écrire*) (pen) nib; (*fig*) pen.

plumer [plyme] *vt* to pluck.

plumier [plymje] *nm* pencil box.

plupart [plypar]: **la** ~ *pronom* the majority, most (of them); **la** ~ **des** most, the majority of; **la** ~ **du temps/d'entre nous** most of the time/of us; **pour la** ~ *ad* for the most part, mostly.

pluriel [plyrjɛl] *nm* plural.

plus ♦ *vb* [ply] *voir* **plaire**

♦ *ad* **1** [ply] (*forme négative*): **ne** ... ~ no more, no longer; **je n'ai** ~ **d'argent** I've got no more money *ou* no money left; **il ne travaille** ~ he's no longer working, he doesn't work any more

2 [ply, plyz + *voyelle*] (*comparatif*) more, ...+er; (*superlatif*): **le** ~ the most, the ...+est; ~ **grand/intelligent** (**que**) bigger/more intelligent (than); **le** ~

grand/intelligent the biggest/most intelligent; **tout au ~** at the very most
3 [plys] (*davantage*) more; **il travaille ~ (que)** he works more (than); **~ il travaille, ~ il est heureux** the more he works, the happier he is; **~ de pain** more bread; **~ de 10 personnes** more than 10 people, over 10 people; **3 heures de ~ que** 3 hours more than; **de ~** what's more, moreover; **3 kilos en ~** 3 kilos more; **en ~** de in addition to; **de ~ en ~** more and more; **~ ou moins** more or less; **ni ~ ni moins** no more, no less
♦ *prép* [plys]: **4 ~ 2** 4 plus 2.
plusieurs [plyzjœR] *dét, pronom* several; **ils sont ~** there are several of them.
plus-que-parfait [plyskəparfɛ] *nm* pluperfect, past perfect.
plus-value [plyvaly] *nf* appreciation; capital gain; surplus.
plut *vb voir* **plaire**.
plutôt [plyto] *ad* rather; **je ferais ~ ceci** I'd rather *ou* sooner do this; **fais ~ comme ça** try this way instead, you'd better try this way; **~ que (de) faire** rather than *ou* instead of doing.
pluvieux, euse [plyvjø, -øz] *a* rainy, wet.
PMU *sigle m* (= **pari mutuel urbain**) system of betting on horses; (*café*) betting agency.
pneu [pnø] *nm* tyre (*Brit*), tire (*US*).
pneumatique [pnømatik] *nm* tyre (*Brit*), tire (*US*).
pneumonie [pnømɔni] *nf* pneumonia.
poche [pɔʃ] *nf* pocket; (*déformation*): **faire une/des ~(s)** to bag; (*sous les yeux*) bag, pouch; **de ~** pocket *cpd*.
pocher [pɔʃe] *vt* (*CULIN*) to poach.
pochette [pɔʃɛt] *nf* (*de timbres*) wallet, envelope; (*d'aiguilles etc*) case; (*mouchoir*) breast pocket handkerchief; **~ de disque** record sleeve.
pochoir [pɔʃwaR] *nm* (*ART*) stencil.
poêle [pwal] *nm* stove // *nf*: **~ (à frire)** frying pan.
poêlon [pwalɔ̃] *nm* casserole.
poème [pɔɛm] *nm* poem.
poésie [pɔezi] *nf* (*poème*) poem; (*art*): **la ~** poetry.
poète [pɔɛt] *nm* poet.
poids [pwa] *nm* weight; (*SPORT*) shot; **vendre au ~** to sell by weight; **prendre du ~** to put on weight; **~ lourd** (*camion*) lorry (*Brit*), truck (*US*).
poignard [pwaɲaR] *nm* dagger; **poignarder** *vt* to stab, knife.
poigne [pwaɲ] *nf* grip; (*fig*): **à ~** firm-handed.
poignée [pwaɲe] *nf* (*de sel etc, fig*) handful; (*de couvercle, porte*) handle; **~ de main** handshake.
poignet [pwaɲɛ] *nm* (*ANAT*) wrist; (*de chemise*) cuff.

poil [pwal] *nm* (*ANAT*) hair; (*de pinceau, brosse*) bristle; (*de tapis*) strand; (*pelage*) coat; **à ~** *a* (*fam*) starkers; **au ~** *a* (*fam*) hunky-dory; **poilu, e** *a* hairy.
poinçon [pwɛ̃sɔ̃] *nm* awl; bodkin; (*marque*) hallmark; **poinçonner** *vt* to stamp; to hallmark; (*billet*) to punch.
poing [pwɛ̃] *nm* fist.
point [pwɛ̃] *nm* (*marque, signe*) dot; (: *de ponctuation*) full stop, period (*US*); (*moment, de score etc, fig*: *question*) point; (*endroit*) spot; (*COUTURE, TRICOT*) stitch // **ad = pas**; **faire le ~** (*NAVIG*) to take a bearing; (*fig*) to take stock (of the situation); **en tout ~** in every respect; **sur le ~ de faire** (just) about to do; **à tel ~ que** so much so that; **mettre au ~** (*mécanisme, procédé*) to develop; (*appareil-photo*) to focus; (*affaire*) to settle; **à ~** (*CULIN*) medium; just right; **à ~ (nommé)** just at the right time; **~ (de côté)** stitch (*pain*); **~ d'eau** spring; water point; **~ d'exclamation** exclamation mark; **~ faible** weak point; **~ final** full stop, period; **~ d'interrogation** question mark; **~ mort** (*AUTO*): **au ~ mort** in neutral; **~ de repère** landmark; (*dans le temps*) point of reference; **~ de vente** retail outlet; **~ de vue** viewpoint; (*fig*: *opinion*) point of view; **~s de suspension** suspension points.
pointe [pwɛ̃t] *nf* point; (*fig*): **une ~ de** a hint of; **être à la ~ de** (*fig*) to be in the forefront of; **sur la ~ des pieds** on tiptoe; **en ~** *ad* (*tailler*) into a point // *a* pointed, tapered; **de ~** *a* (*technique etc*) leading; **heures/jours de ~** peak hours/days; **~ de vitesse** burst of speed.
pointer [pwɛ̃te] *vt* (*cocher*) to tick off; (*employés etc*) to check in; (*diriger: canon, doigt*): **~ vers qch** to point at sth // *vi* (*employé*) to clock in.
pointillé [pwɛ̃tije] *nm* (*trait*) dotted line.
pointilleux, euse [pwɛ̃tijø, -øz] *a* particular, pernickety.
pointu, e [pwɛ̃ty] *a* pointed; (*clou*) sharp; (*voix*) shrill; (*analyse*) precise.
pointure [pwɛ̃tyR] *nf* size.
point-virgule [pwɛ̃virgyl] *nm* semi-colon.
poire [pwaR] *nf* pear; (*fam*: *péj*) mug.
poireau, x [pwaRo] *nm* leek.
poirier [pwaRje] *nm* pear tree.
pois [pwa] *nm* (*BOT*) pea; (*sur une étoffe*) dot, spot; **à ~** (*cravate etc*) spotted, polka-dot *cpd*.
poison [pwazɔ̃] *nm* poison.
poisse [pwas] *nf* rotten luck.
poisseux, euse [pwasø, -øz] *a* sticky.
poisson [pwasɔ̃] *nm* fish *cpd*; **les P~s** (*signe*) Pisces; **~ d'avril!** April fool!; **~ rouge** goldfish; **poissonnerie** *nf* fish-shop; **poissonnier, ière** *nm/f* fishmonger (*Brit*), fish merchant (*US*).

poitrine [pwatʀin] *nf* chest; (*seins*) bust, bosom; (*CULIN*) breast; ~ de bœuf brisket.

poivre [pwavʀ(ə)] *nm* pepper; **poivrier** *nm* (*ustensile*) pepperpot.

poivron [pwavʀɔ̃] *nm* pepper, capsicum.

pôle [pol] *nm* (*GÉO, ÉLEC*) pole.

poli, e [pɔli] *a* polite; (*lisse*) smooth; polished.

police [pɔlis] *nf* police; peine de simple ~ *sentence given by magistrates' or police court*; ~ d'assurance insurance policy; ~ judiciaire (P.J.) ≈ Criminal Investigation Department (*Brit*), ≈ Federal Bureau of Investigation (*US*); ~ des mœurs ≈ vice squad; ~ secours ≈ emergency services *pl* (*Brit*), ≈ paramedics *pl* (*US*).

policier, ière [pɔlisje, -jɛʀ] *a* police *cpd* // *nm* policeman; (*aussi*: **roman** ~) detective novel.

polio [pɔljɔ] *nf* polio.

polir [pɔliʀ] *vt* to polish.

polisson, ne [pɔlisɔ̃, -ɔn] *a* naughty.

politesse [pɔlitɛs] *nf* politeness.

politicien, ne [pɔlitisjɛ̃, -ɛn] *nm/f* politician.

politique [pɔlitik] *a* political // *nf* (*science, pratique, activité*) politics *sg*; (*mesures, méthode*) policies *pl*; **politiser** *vt* to politicize.

pollen [pɔlɛn] *nm* pollen.

pollution [pɔlysjɔ̃] *nf* pollution.

Pologne [pɔlɔɲ] *nf*: la ~ Poland; **polonais, e a**, *nm* (*LING*) Polish; **Polonais, e** *nm/f* Pole.

poltron, ne [pɔltʀɔ̃, -ɔn] *a* cowardly.

poly... [pɔli] *préfixe*: **~copier** *vt* to duplicate.

Polynésie [pɔlinezi] *nf*: la ~ Polynesia.

polyvalent, e [pɔlivalɑ̃, -ɑ̃t] *a* versatile; multi-purpose.

pommade [pɔmad] *nf* ointment, cream.

pomme [pɔm] *nf* (*BOT*) apple; tomber dans les ~ (*fam*) to pass out; ~ d'Adam Adam's apple; ~ d'arrosoir (sprinkler) rose; ~ de pin pine *ou* fir cone; ~ de terre potato.

pommeau, x [pɔmo] *nm* (*boule*) knob; (*de selle*) pommel.

pommette [pɔmɛt] *nf* cheekbone.

pommier [pɔmje] *nm* apple tree.

pompe [pɔ̃p] *nf* pump; (*faste*) pomp (and ceremony); ~ à essence petrol pump; ~s funèbres funeral parlour *sg*, undertaker's *sg*.

pomper [pɔ̃pe] *vt* to pump; (*évacuer*) to pump out; (*aspirer*) to pump up; (*absorber*) to soak up.

pompeux, euse [pɔ̃pø, -øz] *a* pompous.

pompier [pɔ̃pje] *nm* fireman.

pompiste [pɔ̃pist(ə)] *nm/f* petrol (*Brit*) *ou* gas (*US*) pump attendant.

poncer [pɔ̃se] *vt* to sand (down).

ponctuation [pɔ̃ktɥasjɔ̃] *nf* punctuation.

ponctuel, le [pɔ̃ktɥɛl] *a* (*à l'heure, aussi TECH*) punctual; (*fig: opération etc*) one-off, single; (*scrupuleux*) punctilious, meticulous.

ponctuer [pɔ̃ktɥe] *vt* to punctuate.

pondéré, e [pɔ̃deʀe] *a* level-headed, composed.

pondre [pɔ̃dʀ(ə)] *vt* to lay; (*fig*) to produce.

poney [pɔnɛ] *nm* pony.

pont [pɔ̃] *nm* bridge; (*AUTO*) axle; (*NAVIG*) deck; faire le ~ to take the extra day off; ~ de graissage ramp (*in garage*); ~ suspendu suspension bridge; P~s et Chaussées highways department.

pont-levis [pɔ̃lvi] *nm* drawbridge.

pop [pɔp] *a inv* pop.

populace [pɔpylas] *nf* (*péj*) rabble.

populaire [pɔpylɛʀ] *a* popular; (*manifestation*) mass *cpd*; (*milieux, clientèle*) working-class.

population [pɔpylasjɔ̃] *nf* population.

populeux, euse [pɔpylø, -øz] *a* densely populated.

porc [pɔʀ] *nm* (*ZOOL*) pig; (*CULIN*) pork; (*peau*) pigskin.

porcelaine [pɔʀsəlɛn] *nf* porcelain, china; piece of china(ware).

porcelet [pɔʀsəlɛ] *nm* piglet.

porc-épic [pɔʀkepik] *nm* porcupine.

porche [pɔʀʃ(ə)] *nm* porch.

porcherie [pɔʀʃəʀi] *nf* pigsty.

pore [pɔʀ] *nm* pore.

pornographique [pɔʀnɔgʀafik] *a* (abr **porno**) pornographic.

port [pɔʀ] *nm* (*NAVIG*) harbour, port; (*ville*) port; (*de l'uniforme etc*) wearing; (*pour lettre*) postage; (*pour colis, aussi: posture*) carriage; ~ d'arme (*JUR*) carrying of a firearm.

portail [pɔʀtaj] *nm* gate; (*de cathédrale*) portal.

portant, e [pɔʀtɑ̃, -ɑ̃t] *a*: bien/mal ~ in good/poor health.

portatif, ive [pɔʀtatif, -iv] *a* portable.

porte [pɔʀt(ə)] *nf* door; (*de ville, forteresse, SKI*) gate; mettre à la ~ to throw out; ~ d'entrée front door; ~ à ~ *nm* door-to-door selling.

porte... [pɔʀt(ə)] *préfixe*: **~-à-faux** *nm*: en **~-à-faux** cantilevered; (*fig*) in an awkward position; **~-avions** *nm inv* aircraft carrier; **~-bagages** *nm inv* luggage rack; **~-clefs** *nm inv* key ring; **~-documents** *nm inv* attaché *ou* document case.

portée [pɔʀte] *nf* (*d'une arme*) range; (*fig*) impact, import; scope, capability; (*de chatte etc*) litter; (*MUS*) stave, staff (*pl* staves); à/hors de ~ (de) within/out of reach (of); à ~ de (la) main within (arm's) reach; à ~ de voix within earshot; à la ~ de qn (*fig*) at sb's level, within sb's capabilities.

porte-fenêtre [pɔʀtəfnɛtʀ(ə)] *nf* French window.

portefeuille [pɔʀtəfœj] *nm* wallet; (*POL, BOURSE*) portfolio.

porte-jarretelles [pɔʀtʒaʀtɛl] *nm inv* suspender belt.

portemanteau, x [pɔʀtmãto] *nm* coat hanger; coat rack.

porte-mine [pɔʀtəmin] *nm* propelling (*Brit*) *ou* mechanical (*US*) pencil.

porte-monnaie [pɔʀtmɔnɛ] *nm inv* purse.

porte-parole [pɔʀtpaʀɔl] *nm inv* spokesman.

porter [pɔʀte] *vt* to carry; (*sur soi: vêtement, barbe, bague*) to wear; (*fig: responsabilité etc*) to bear, carry; (*inscription, marque, titre, patronyme, suj: arbre: fruits, fleurs*) to bear; (*apporter*): ~ **qch quelque part/à qn** to take sth somewhere/to sb // *vi* (*voix, regard, canon*) to carry; (*coup, argument*) to hit home; ~ **sur** (*peser*) to rest on; (*accent*) to fall on; (*conférence etc*) to concern; (*heurter*) to strike; **se** ~ *vi* (*se sentir*): **se** ~ **bien/mal** to be well/unwell; **être porté à faire** to be apt *ou* inclined to do; **se faire** ~ **malade** to report sick; ~ **la main à son chapeau** to raise one's hand to one's hat; ~ **son effort sur** to direct one's efforts towards; ~ **à croire** to lead one to believe.

porte-serviettes [pɔʀtsɛʀvjɛt] *nm inv* towel rail.

porteur [pɔʀtœʀ] *nm* (*de bagages*) porter; (*de chèque*) bearer.

porte-voix [pɔʀtəvwa] *nm inv* megaphone.

portier [pɔʀtje] *nm* doorman.

portière [pɔʀtjɛʀ] *nf* door.

portillon [pɔʀtijɔ̃] *nm* gate.

portion [pɔʀsjɔ̃] *nf* (*part*) portion, share; (*partie*) portion, section.

portique [pɔʀtik] *nm* (*RAIL*) gantry.

porto [pɔʀto] *nm* port (wine).

portrait [pɔʀtʀɛ] *nm* portrait; photograph; ~-**robot** *nm* Identikit ® *ou* photo-fit ® picture.

portuaire [pɔʀtɥɛʀ] *a* port *cpd*, harbour *cpd*.

portugais, e [pɔʀtygɛ, -ɛz] *a, nm/f* Portuguese.

Portugal [pɔʀtygal] *nm*: **le** ~ Portugal.

pose [poz] *nf* laying; hanging; (*attitude, d'un modèle*) pose; (*PHOTO*) exposure.

posé, e [poze] *a* serious.

poser [poze] *vt* (*déposer*): ~ **qch (sur)/ qn à** to put sth down (on)/drop sb at; (*placer*): ~ **qch sur/quelque part** to put sth on/somewhere; (*installer: moquette, carrelage*) to lay; (*rideaux, papier peint*) to hang; (*question*) to ask; (*principe, conditions*) to lay *ou* set down; (*problème*) to formulate; (*difficulté*) to pose // *vi* (*modèle*) to pose; **se** ~ *vi*

(*oiseau, avion*) to land; (*question*) to arise.

positif, ive [pozitif, -iv] *a* positive.

position [pozisjɔ̃] *nf* position; **prendre** ~ (*fig*) to take a stand.

posséder [pɔsede] *vt* to own, possess; (*qualité, talent*) to have, possess; (*bien connaître: métier, langue*) to have mastered, have a thorough knowledge of; (*sexuellement, aussi: suj: colère etc*) to possess; **possession** *nf* ownership *q*; possession.

possibilité [pɔsibilite] *nf* possibility; ~**s** *nfpl* (*moyens*) means; (*potentiel*) potential *sg*.

possible [pɔsibl(ə)] *a* possible; (*projet, entreprise*) feasible // *nm*: **faire son** ~ to do all one can, do one's utmost; **le plus/ moins de livres** ~ as many/few books as possible; **le plus/moins d'eau** ~ as much/little water as possible; **dès que** ~ as soon as possible.

postal, e, aux [pɔstal, -o] *a* postal.

poste [pɔst(ə)] *nf* (*service*) post, postal service; (*administration, bureau*) post office // *nm* (*fonction, MIL*) post; (*TÉL*) extension; (*de radio etc*) set; **mettre à la** ~ to post; **P**~**s, Télécommunications et Télédiffusion (P.T.T.)** *postal and telecommunications service*; ~ **d'essence** *nm* petrol *ou* filling station; ~ **d'incendie** *nm* fire point; ~ **de pilotage** *nm* cockpit; ~ **(de police)** *nm* police station; ~ **restante** *nf* poste restante (*Brit*), general delivery (*US*); ~ **de secours** *nm* first-aid post; ~ **de travail** *nm* work station.

poster *vt* [pɔste] to post // *nm* [pɔstɛʀ] poster.

postérieur, e [pɔsteʀjœʀ] *a* (*date*) later; (*partie*) back // *nm* (*fam*) behind.

posthume [pɔstym] *a* posthumous.

postiche [pɔstiʃ] *nm* hairpiece.

postuler [pɔstyle] *vt* (*emploi*) to apply for, put in for.

posture [pɔstyʀ] *nf* posture; position.

pot [po] *nm* jar, pot; (*en plastique, carton*) carton; (*en métal*) tin; **boire** *ou* **prendre un** ~ (*fam*) to have a drink; ~ **(de chambre)** (chamber)pot; ~ **d'échappement** exhaust pipe; ~ **de fleurs** plant pot, flowerpot; (*plante*) pot plant.

potable [pɔtabl(ə)] *a*: **eau (non)** ~ (not) drinking water.

potage [pɔtaʒ] *nm* soup; soup course.

potager, ère [pɔtaʒe, -ɛʀ] *a* (*plante*) edible, vegetable *cpd*; (*jardin*) ~ **kitchen** *ou* vegetable garden.

pot-au-feu [pɔtofø] *nm inv* (beef) stew.

pot-de-vin [podvɛ̃] *nm* bribe.

pote [pɔt] *nm* (*fam*) pal.

poteau, x [pɔto] *nm* post; ~ **indicateur** signpost.

potelé, e [pɔtle] *a* plump, chubby.

potence [pɔtɑ̃s] *nf* gallows *sg*.

potentiel, le [pɔtɑ̃sjɛl] *a, nm* potential.

poterie [pɔtʀi] *nf* pottery; piece of pottery.

potier [pɔtje] *nm* potter.

potins [pɔtɛ̃] *nmpl* gossip *sg*.

potiron [pɔtiʀɔ̃] *nm* pumpkin.

pou, x [pu] *nm* louse (*pl* lice).

poubelle [pubɛl] *nf* (dust)bin.

pouce [pus] *nm* thumb.

poudre [pudʀ(ə)] *nf* powder; (*fard*) (face) powder; (*explosif*) gunpowder; en ~: café en ~ instant coffee; lait en ~ dried *ou* powdered milk; **poudrier** *nm* (powder) compact.

pouffer [pufe] *vi*: ~ (de rire) to snigger; to giggle.

pouilleux, euse [pujø, -øz] *a* flea-ridden; (*fig*) grubby; seedy.

poulailler [pulaje] *nm* henhouse.

poulain [pulɛ̃] *nm* foal; (*fig*) protégé.

poule [pul] *nf* (*ZOOL*) hen; (*CULIN*) (boiling) fowl.

poulet [pulɛ] *nm* chicken; (*fam*) cop.

poulie [puli] *nf* pulley; block.

pouls [pu] *nm* pulse; prendre le ~ de qn to feel sb's pulse.

poumon [pumɔ̃] *nm* lung.

poupe [pup] *nf* stern; en ~ astern.

poupée [pupe] *nf* doll.

poupon [pupɔ̃] *nm* babe-in-arms; **pouponnière** *nf* crèche, day nursery.

pour [puʀ] *prép* for // *nm*: le ~ et le contre the pros and cons; ~ **faire** (so as) to do, in order to do; ~ **avoir fait** for having done; ~ **que** so that, in order that; ~ **100 francs d'essence** 100 francs' worth of petrol; ~ **cent** per cent; ~ **ce qui est de** as for.

pourboire [puʀbwaʀ] *nm* tip.

pourcentage [puʀsɑ̃taʒ] *nm* percentage.

pourchasser [puʀʃase] *vt* to pursue.

pourparlers [puʀpaʀle] *nmpl* talks, negotiations.

pourpre [puʀpʀ(ə)] *a* crimson.

pourquoi [puʀkwa] *ad, cj* why // *nm inv*: le ~ (de) the reason (for).

pourrai *etc vb voir* **pouvoir**.

pourri, e [puʀi] *a* rotten.

pourrir [puʀiʀ] *vi* to rot; (*fruit*) to go rotten *ou* bad // *vt* to rot; (*fig*) to spoil thoroughly; **pourriture** *nf* rot.

pourrons *etc vb voir* **pouvoir**.

poursuite [puʀsɥit] *nf* pursuit, chase; ~s (*JUR*) legal proceedings.

poursuivre [puʀsɥivʀ(ə)] *vt* to pursue, chase (after); (*relancer*) to hound, harry; (*obséder*) to haunt; (*JUR*) to bring proceedings against, prosecute; (: au civil) to sue; (*but*) to strive towards; (*voyage, études*) to carry on with, continue // *vi* to carry on, go on; se ~ *vi* to go on, continue.

pourtant [puʀtɑ̃] *ad* yet; c'est ~ facile (and) yet it's easy.

pourtour [puʀtuʀ] *nm* perimeter.

pourvoir [puʀvwaʀ] *vt*: ~ qch/qn de to equip sth/sb with // *vi*: ~ à to provide for; (*emploi*) to fill; se ~ *vi* (*JUR*): se ~ en cassation to take one's case to the Court of Appeal.

pourvoyeur [puʀvwajœʀ] *nm* supplier.

pourvu, e [puʀvy] *a*: ~ de equipped with; ~ **que** *cj* (si) provided that, so long as; (*espérons que*) let's hope (that).

pousse [pus] *nf* growth; (*bourgeon*) shoot.

poussé, e [puse] *a* exhaustive.

poussée [puse] *nf* thrust; (*coup*) push; (*MÉD*) eruption; (*fig*) upsurge.

pousser [puse] *vt* to push; (*inciter*): ~ qn à to urge *ou* press sb to + *infinitif*; (*acculer*): ~ qn à to drive sb to; (*émettre: cri etc*) to give; (*stimuler*) to urge on; to drive hard; (*poursuivre*) to carry on (further) // *vi* to push; (*croître*) to grow; se ~ *vi* to move over; **faire** ~ (*plante*) to grow.

poussette [pusɛt] *nf* (*voiture d'enfant*) push chair (*Brit*), stroller (*US*).

poussière [pusjɛʀ] *nf* dust; (*grain*) speck of dust; **poussiéreux, euse** *a* dusty.

poussin [pusɛ̃] *nm* chick.

poutre [putʀ(ə)] *nf* beam; (*en fer, ciment armé*) girder.

pouvoir [puvwaʀ] ♦ *nm* power; (*POL: dirigeants*): le ~ those in power; les ~s publics the authorities; ~ **d'achat** purchasing power

♦ *vb semi-auxiliaire* **1** (être en état de) can, be able to; je ne peux pas le réparer I can't *ou* I am not able to repair it; déçu de ne pas ~ le faire disappointed not to be able to do it

2 (avoir la permission) can, may, be allowed to; vous pouvez aller au cinéma you can *ou* may go to the pictures

3 (probabilité, hypothèse) may, might, could; il a pu avoir un accident he may *ou* might *ou* could have had an accident; il aurait pu le dire! he might *ou* could have said (so)!

♦ *vb impersonnel* may, might, could; il peut arriver que it may *ou* might *ou* could happen that

♦ *vt* can, be able to; j'ai fait tout ce que j'ai pu I did all I could; je n'en peux plus (*épuisé*) I'm exhausted; (à bout) I can't take any more

se pouvoir *vi*: il se peut que it may *ou* might be that; cela se pourrait that's quite possible.

prairie [pʀeʀi] *nf* meadow.

praline [pʀalin] *nf* sugared almond.

praticable [pʀatikabl(ə)] *a* passable, practicable.

praticien, ne [pʀatisjɛ̃, -jɛn] *nm/f* practitioner.

pratique [pʀatik] *nf* practice // *a* practical.

pratiquement [pratikmɑ̃] *ad* (*pour ainsi dire*) practically, virtually.

pratiquer [pratike] *vt* to practise; (*SPORT etc*) to go (in for); to play; (*intervention, opération*) to carry out; (*ouverture, abri*) to make.

pré [pre] *nm* meadow.

préalable [prealabl(ə)] *a* preliminary; condition ~ (de) precondition (for), prerequisite (for); au ~ beforehand.

préambule [preɑ̃byl] *nm* preamble; (*fig*) prelude; sans ~ straight away.

préavis [preavi] *nm* notice; communication avec ~ (*TÉL*) personal *ou* person to person call.

précaution [prekosjɔ̃] *nf* precaution; avec ~ cautiously; par ~ as a precaution.

précédemment [presedamɑ̃] *ad* before, previously.

précédent, e [presedɑ̃, -ɑ̃t] *a* previous // *nm* precedent; sans ~ unprecedented; le jour ~ the day before, the previous day.

précéder [presede] *vt* to precede; (*marcher ou rouler devant*) to be in front of.

précepteur, trice [preseptœr, -tris] *nm/f* (private) tutor.

prêcher [preʃe] *vt* to preach.

précieux, euse [presjø, -øz] *a* precious; invaluable; (*style, écrivain*) précieux, precious.

précipice [presipis] *nm* drop, chasm; (*fig*) abyss.

précipitamment [presipitamɑ̃] *ad* hurriedly, hastily.

précipitation [presipitasjɔ̃] *nf* (*hâte*) haste; ~s (*pluie*) rain.

précipité, e [presipite] *a* hurried, hasty.

précipiter [presipite] *vt* (*faire tomber*): ~ qn/qch du haut de to throw sb/sth off *ou* from; (*hâter: marche*) to quicken; (: *départ*) to hasten; se ~ *vi* to speed up; se ~ sur/vers to rush at/towards.

précis, e [presi, -iz] *a* precise; (*tir, mesures*) accurate, precise // *nm* handbook; **précisément** *ad* precisely; **préciser** *vt* (*expliquer*) to be more specific about, clarify; (*spécifier*) to state, specify; se **préciser** *vi* to become clear(er); **précision** *nf* precision; accuracy; **précisions** point *ou* detail (*made clear or to be clarified*).

précoce [prekɔs] *a* early; (*enfant*) precocious; (*calvitie*) premature.

préconiser [prekɔnize] *vt* to advocate.

prédécesseur [predesesœr] *nm* predecessor.

prédilection [predilɛksjɔ̃] *nf:* avoir une ~ pour to be partial to; de ~ favourite.

prédire [predir] *vt* to predict.

prédominer [predɔmine] *vi* to predominate; (*avis*) to prevail.

préface [prefas] *nf* preface.

préfecture [prefɛktyr] *nf* prefecture; ~ de police police headquarters.

préférable [preferabl(ə)] *a* preferable.

préféré, e [prefere] *a, nm/f* favourite.

préférence [preferɑ̃s] *nf* preference; de ~ preferably.

préférer [prefere] *vt:* ~ qn/qch (à) to prefer sb/sth (to), like sb/sth better (than); ~ faire to prefer to do; je préférerais du thé I would rather have tea, I'd prefer tea.

préfet [prefɛ] *nm* prefect.

préfixe [prefiks(ə)] *nm* prefix.

préhistorique [preistɔrik] *a* prehistoric.

préjudice [preʒydis] *nm* (*matériel*) loss; (*moral*) harm *q*; porter ~ à to harm, be detrimental to; au ~ de at the expense of.

préjugé [preʒyʒe] *nm* prejudice; avoir un ~ contre to be prejudiced *ou* biased against.

préjuger [preʒyʒe]: ~ de *vt* to prejudge.

prélasser [prelase]: se ~ *vi* to lounge.

prélèvement [prelɛvmɑ̃] *nm:* faire un ~ de sang to take a blood sample.

prélever [prelve] *vt* (*échantillon*) to take; (*argent*): ~ (sur) to deduct (from); (: *sur son compte*): ~ (sur) to withdraw (from).

prématuré, e [prematyre] *a* premature; (*retraite*) early // *nm* premature baby.

premier, ière [prəmje, -jɛr] *a* first; (*branche, marche*) bottom; (*fig*) basic; prime; initial // *nf* (*THÉÂTRE*) first night; (*AUTO*) first (gear); (*AVIAT, RAIL etc*) first class; (*CINÉMA*) première; (*exploit*) first; le ~ venu the first person to come along; P- Ministre Prime Minister; **premièrement** *ad* firstly.

prémonition [premɔnisjɔ̃] *nf* premonition.

prémunir [premynir]: se ~ *vi*: se ~ contre to guard against.

prénatal, e [prenatal] *a* (*MÉD*) antenatal.

prendre [prɑ̃dr(ə)] *vt* to take; (*ôter*): ~ qch à to take sth from; (*aller chercher*) to get, fetch; (*se procurer*) to get; (*malfaiteur, poisson*) to catch; (*passager*) to pick up; (*personnel, aussi: couleur, goût*) to take on; (*locataire*) to take in; (*élève etc: traiter*) to handle; (*voix, ton*) to put on; (*coincer*): se ~ les doigts dans to get one's fingers caught in // *vi* (*liquide, ciment*) to set; (*greffe, vaccin*) to take; (*feu: foyer*) to go; (: *incendie*) to start; (*allumette*) to light; (*se diriger*): ~ à gauche to turn (to the) left; à tout ~ on the whole, all in all; se ~ pour to think one is; s'en ~ à to attack; se ~ d'amitié/d'affection pour to befriend/become fond of; s'y ~ (*procéder*) to set about it.

preneur [prənœr] *nm*: être/trouver ~ to be willing to buy/find a buyer.

preniez, prenne *etc vb voir* **prendre**.

prénom [prenɔ̃] *nm* first *ou* Christian name.

prénuptial, e, aux [prenypsjal, -o] *a* premarital.

préoccupation [preɔkypasjɔ̃] *nf* (*souci*) concern; (*idée fixe*) preoccupation.

préoccuper [preɔkype] *vt* to concern; to preoccupy.

préparatifs [preparatif] *nmpl* preparations.

préparation [preparasjɔ̃] *nf* preparation; (*SCOL*) piece of homework.

préparer [prepare] *vt* to prepare; (*café*) to make; (*examen*) to prepare for; (*voyage, entreprise*) to plan; se ~ *vi* (*orage, tragédie*) to brew, be in the air; se ~ (à qch/faire) to prepare (o.s.) ou get ready (for sth/to do); ~ qch à qn (*surprise etc*) to have sth in store for sb.

prépondérant, e [prepɔ̃derɑ̃, -ɑ̃t] *a* major, dominating.

préposé, e [prepoze] *a*: ~ à in charge of // *nm/f* employee; official; attendant.

préposition [prepozisjɔ̃] *nf* preposition.

près [prɛ] *ad* near, close; ~ de *prép* near (to), close to; (*environ*) nearly, almost; de ~ *ad* closely; à 5 kg ~ to within about 5 kg; à cela ~ que apart from the fact that.

présage [prezaʒ] *nm* omen.

présager [prezaʒe] *vt* to foresee.

presbyte [prɛsbit] *a* long-sighted.

presbytère [prɛsbitɛr] *nm* presbytery.

prescription [prɛskripsjɔ̃] *nf* (*instruction*) order, instruction; (*MÉD, JUR*) prescription.

prescrire [prɛskrir] *vt* to prescribe.

préséance [preseɑ̃s] *nf* precedence *q*.

présence [prezɑ̃s] *nf* presence; (*au bureau etc*) attendance; ~ d'esprit presence of mind.

présent, e [prezɑ̃, -ɑ̃t] *a, nm* present; à ~ (que) now (that).

présentation [prezɑ̃tasjɔ̃] *nf* introduction; presentation; (*allure*) appearance.

présenter [prezɑ̃te] *vt* to present; (*sympathie, condoléances*) to offer; (*soumettre*) to submit; (*invité, conférencier*): ~ qn (à) to introduce sb (to) // *vi*: ~ mal/bien to have an unattractive/a pleasing appearance; se ~ *vi* (*sur convocation*) to report, come; (à une élection) to stand; (*occasion*) to arise; se ~ bien/mal to look good/not too good; se ~ à (*examen*) to sit.

préservatif [prezɛrvatif] *nm* sheath, condom.

préserver [prezɛrve] *vt*: ~ de to protect from; to save from.

président [prezidɑ̃] *nm* (*POL*) presi-

dent; (*d'une assemblée, COMM*) chairman; ~ directeur général (PDG) chairman and managing director.

présider [prezide] *vt* to preside over; (*dîner*) to be the guest of honour at; ~ à *vt* to direct; to govern.

présomptueux, euse [prezɔ̃ptyø, -øz] *a* presumptuous.

presque [prɛsk(ə)] *ad* almost, nearly; ~ rien hardly anything; ~ pas hardly (at all); ~ pas de hardly any.

presqu'île [prɛskil] *nf* peninsula.

pressant, e [prɛsɑ̃, -ɑ̃t] *a* urgent; se faire ~ to become insistent.

presse [prɛs] *nf* press; (*affluence*): heures de ~ busy times.

pressé, e [prɛse] *a* in a hurry; (*air*) hurried; (*besogne*) urgent; orange ~e fresh orange juice.

pressentiment [presɑ̃timɑ̃] *nm* foreboding, premonition.

pressentir [presɑ̃tir] *vt* to sense; (*prendre contact avec*) to approach.

presse-papiers [prɛspapje] *nm inv* paperweight.

presser [prɛse] *vt* (*fruit, éponge*) to squeeze; (*bouton*) to press; (*allure, affaire*) to speed up; (*inciter*): ~ qn de faire to urge *ou* press sb to do // *vi* to be urgent; rien ne presse there's no hurry; se ~ *vi* (*se hâter*) to hurry (up); se ~ contre qn to squeeze up against sb.

pressing [presiŋ] *nm* steam-pressing; (*magasin*) dry-cleaner's.

pression [presjɔ̃] *nf* pressure; faire ~ sur to put pressure on; ~ artérielle blood pressure.

pressoir [preswar] *nm* (*wine ou oil etc*) press.

pressurer [presyre] *vt* (*fig*) to squeeze.

prestance [prɛstɑ̃s] *nf* presence, imposing bearing.

prestataire [prɛstatɛr] *nm/f* supplier.

prestation [prɛstasjɔ̃] *nf* (*allocation*) benefit; (*d'une entreprise*) service provided; (*d'un artiste*) performance.

prestidigitateur, trice [prɛstidiʒitatœr, -tris] *nm/f* conjurer.

prestigieux, euse [prɛstiʒjø, -øz] *a* prestigious.

présumer [prezyme] *vt*: ~ que to presume *ou* assume that; ~ de to overrate.

présupposer [presypoze] *vt* to presuppose.

prêt, e [prɛ, prɛt] *a* ready // *nm* lending *q*; loan; **prêt-à-porter** *nm* ready-to-wear *ou* off-the-peg (Brit) clothes *pl*.

prétendant [pretɑ̃dɑ̃] *nm* pretender; (*d'une femme*) suitor.

prétendre [pretɑ̃dr(ə)] *vt* (*affirmer*): ~ que to claim that; (*avoir l'intention de*): ~ faire qch to mean *ou* intend to do sth; ~ à *vt* (*droit, titre*) to lay claim to; **prétendu, e** *a* (*supposé*) so-called.

prête-nom [prɛtnɔ̃] *nm* (*péj*) figurehead.

prétentieux, euse [pretãsjø, -øz] a pretentious.

prétention [pretãsjɔ̃] nf claim; pretentiousness.

prêter [prete] vt (livres, argent): ~ qch (à) to lend sth (to); (supposer): ~ à qn (caractère, propos) to attribute to sb // vi (aussi: se ~: tissu, cuir) to give; ~ à (commentaires etc) to be open to, give rise to; se ~ à to lend o.s. (ou itself) to; (manigances etc) to go along with; ~ assistance à to give help to; ~ attention à to pay attention to; ~ serment to take the oath; ~ l'oreille to listen.

prétexte [pretɛkst(ə)] nm pretext, excuse; sous aucun ~ on no account.

prétexter [pretɛkste] vt to give as a pretext ou an excuse.

prêtre [pretr(ə)] nm priest.

preuve [prœv] nf proof, (indice) proof, evidence q; faire ~ de to show; faire ses ~s to prove o.s. (ou itself).

prévaloir [prevalwar] vi to prevail; se ~ de vt to take advantage of; to pride o.s. on.

prévenant, e [prevnã, -ãt] a thoughtful, kind.

prévenir [prevnir] vt (avertir): ~ qn (de) to warn sb (about); (informer): ~ qn (de) to tell ou inform sb (about); (éviter) to avoid, prevent; (anticiper) to forestall; to anticipate.

prévention [prevãsjɔ̃] nf prevention; ~ routière road safety.

prévenu, e [prevny] nm/f (JUR) defendant, accused.

prévision [previzjɔ̃] nf: ~s predictions; forecast sg; en ~ de in anticipation of; ~s météorologiques weather forecast sg.

prévoir [prevwar] vt (deviner) to foresee; (s'attendre à) to expect, reckon on; (prévenir) to anticipate; (organiser) to plan; (préparer, réserver) to allow; prévu pour 10h scheduled for 10 o'clock.

prévoyance [prevwajãs] nf: caisse de ~ contingency fund.

prévoyant, e [prevwajã, -ãt] a gifted with (ou showing) foresight.

prévu, e [prevy] pp de **prévoir**.

prier [prije] vi to pray // vt (Dieu) to pray to; (implorer) to beg; (demander): ~ qn de faire to ask sb to do; se faire ~ to need coaxing ou persuading; je vous en prie (allez-y) please do; (de rien) don't mention it.

prière [prijer] nf prayer; '~ de faire ...' 'please do ...'.

primaire [primer] a primary; (péj) simple-minded; simplistic // nm (SCOL) primary education.

prime [prim] nf (bonification) bonus; (subside) premium; allowance; (COMM: cadeau) free gift; (ASSURANCES,

BOURSE) premium // a: de ~ abord at first glance.

primer [prime] vt (l'emporter sur) to prevail over; (récompenser) to award a prize to // vi to dominate; to prevail.

primeurs [primœr] nfpl early fruits and vegetables.

primevère [primver] nf primrose.

primitif, ive [primitif, -iv] a primitive; (originel) original.

prince, esse [prɛ̃s, prɛ̃sɛs] nm/f prince/princess.

principal, e, aux [prɛ̃sipal, -o] a principal, main // nm (SCOL) principal, head(master); (essentiel) main thing.

principe [prɛ̃sip] nm principle; pour le ~ on principle; de ~ a (accord, hostilité) automatic; par ~ on principle; en ~ (habituellement) as a rule; (théoriquement) in principle.

printemps [prɛ̃tã] nm spring.

priorité [prijɔrite] nf (AUTO): avoir la ~ (sur) to have right of way (over); ~ à droite right of way to vehicles coming from the right.

pris, e [pri, priz] pp de **prendre** // a (place) taken; (journée, mains) full; (billets) sold; (personne) busy; avoir le nez/la gorge ~ (e) to have a stuffy nose/a hoarse throat; être ~ de panique to be panic-stricken.

prise [priz] nf (d'une ville) capture; (PÊCHE, CHASSE) catch; (de judo ou catch, point d'appui ou pour empoigner) hold; (ÉLEC: fiche) plug; (: femelle) socket; être aux ~s avec to be grappling with; ~ de courant power point; ~ multiple adaptor; ~ de sang blood test; ~ de terre earth; ~ de vue (photo) shot.

priser [prize] vt (tabac, héroïne) to take; (estimer) to prize, value // vi to take snuff.

prison [prizɔ̃] nf prison; aller/être en ~ to go to/be in prison ou jail; faire de la ~ to serve time; **prisonnier, ière** nm/f prisoner // a captive.

prit vb voir **prendre**.

privé, e [prive] a private; en ~ in private.

priver [prive] vt: ~ qn de to deprive sb of; se ~ de to go ou do without.

privilège [privilɛʒ] nm privilege.

prix [pri] nm (valeur) price; (récompense, SCOL) prize; hors de ~ exorbitantly priced; à aucun ~ not at any price; à tout ~ at all costs; ~ d'achat/de vente/de revient purchasing/selling/cost price.

probable [prɔbabl(ə)] a likely, probable; ~ment ad probably.

probant, e [prɔbã, -ãt] a convincing.

problème [prɔblɛm] nm problem.

procédé [prɔsede] nm (méthode) process; (comportement) behaviour q.

procéder [prɔsede] vi to proceed; to be-

have; ~ à vt to carry out.
procès [prɔsɛ] nm trial; (*poursuites*) proceedings pl; **être en ~ avec** to be involved in a lawsuit with.
processus [prɔsesys] nm process.
procès-verbal, aux [prɔsɛvɛrbal, -o] nm (*constat*) statement; (*aussi:* **P.V.**): **avoir un ~** to get a parking ticket; to be booked; (*de réunion*) minutes pl.
prochain, e [prɔʃɛ̃, -ɛn] a next; (*proche*) impending; near // **la** ~ **fois/semaine** ~**e** next time/ week; **prochainement** ad soon, shortly.
proche [prɔʃ] a nearby; (*dans le temps*) imminent; (*parent, ami*) close; ~**s** nmpl close relatives; **être** ~ (**de**) to be near, be close (to); **de ~ en ~** gradually; **le P~ Orient** the Middle East.
proclamer [prɔklame] vt to proclaim.
procuration [prɔkyrasjɔ̃] nf proxy; power of attorney.
procurer [prɔkyre] vt: ~ **qch à qn** (*fournir*) to obtain sth for sb; (*causer: plaisir etc*) to bring sb sth; **se** ~ vt to get.
procureur [prɔkyrœr] nm public prosecutor.
prodige [prɔdiʒ] nm marvel, wonder; (*personne*) prodigy.
prodigue [prɔdig] a generous; extravagant; **fils** ~ prodigal son.
prodiguer [prɔdige] vt (*argent, biens*) to be lavish with; (*soins, attentions*): ~ **qch à qn** to give sb sth.
producteur, trice [prɔdyktœr, -tris] nm/f producer.
production [prɔdyksjɔ̃] nf (*gén*) production; (*rendement*) output.
produire [prɔduir] vt to produce; **se** ~ vi (*acteur*) to perform, appear; (*événement*) to happen, occur.
produit [prɔdui] nm (*gén*) product; ~**s agricoles** farm produce sg; ~ **d'entretien** cleaning product.
prof [prɔf] nm (*fam*) teacher.
profane [prɔfan] a (*REL*) secular // nm/f layman.
proférer [prɔfere] vt to utter.
professer [prɔfese] vi to teach.
professeur [prɔfesœr] nm teacher; (*titulaire d'une chaire*) professor; ~ (**de faculté**) (university) lecturer.
profession [prɔfesjɔ̃] nf profession; **sans** ~ unemployed; **professionnel, le** a, nm/f professional.
profil [prɔfil] nm profile; (*d'une voiture*) line, contour; **de** ~ in profile; ~**er** vt to streamline.
profit [prɔfi] nm (*avantage*) benefit, advantage; (*COMM, FINANCE*) profit; **au** ~ **de** in aid of; **tirer** ~ **de** to profit from.
profitable [prɔfitabl(ə)] a beneficial; profitable.
profiter [prɔfite] vi: ~ **de** to take advantage of; to make the most of; ~ **à** to

benefit; to be profitable to.
profond, e [prɔfɔ̃, -ɔ̃d] a deep; (*méditation, mépris*) profound; **profondeur** nf depth.
progéniture [prɔʒenityr] nf offspring inv.
programme [prɔgram] nm programme; (*TV, RADIO*) programmes pl; (*SCOL*) syllabus, curriculum; (*INFORM*) program; **programmer** vt (*TV, RADIO*) to put on, show; (*INFORM*) to program; **programmeur, euse** nm/f programmer.
progrès [prɔgrɛ] nm progress q; **faire des** ~ to make progress.
progresser [prɔgrese] vi to progress; (*troupes etc*) to make headway ou progress; **progressif, ive** a progressive.
prohiber [prɔibe] vt to prohibit, ban.
proie [prwa] nf prey q.
projecteur [prɔʒɛktœr] nm projector; (*de théâtre, cirque*) spotlight.
projectile [prɔʒɛktil] nm missile.
projection [prɔʒɛksjɔ̃] nf projection; showing; **conférence avec** ~**s** lecture with slides (ou a film).
projet [prɔʒɛ] nm plan; (*ébauche*) draft; ~ **de loi** bill.
projeter [prɔʒte] vt (*envisager*) to plan; (*film, photos*) to project; (*passer*) to show; (*ombre, lueur*) to throw, cast; (*jeter*) to throw up (ou off ou out).
prolixe [prɔliks(ə)] a verbose.
prolongations [prɔlɔ̃gasjɔ̃] nfpl (*FOOTBALL*) extra time sg.
prolongement [prɔlɔ̃ʒmɑ̃] nm extension; ~**s** (*fig*) repercussions, effects; **dans le** ~ **de** running on from.
prolonger [prɔlɔ̃ʒe] vt (*débat, séjour*) to prolong; (*délai, billet, rue*) to extend; (*suj: chose*) to be a continuation ou an extension of; **se** ~ vi to go on.
promenade [prɔmnad] nf walk (ou drive ou ride); **faire une** ~ to go for a walk; **une** ~ **en voiture/à vélo** a drive/ (bicycle) ride.
promener [prɔmne] vt (*chien*) to take out for a walk; (*doigts, regard*): ~ **qch sur** to run sth over; **se** ~ vi to go for (ou be out for) a walk.
promesse [prɔmɛs] nf promise.
promettre [prɔmɛtr(ə)] vt to promise // vi to be ou look promising; ~ **à qn de faire** to promise sb that one will do.
promiscuité [prɔmiskɥite] nf crowding; lack of privacy.
promontoire [prɔmɔ̃twar] nm headland.
promoteur, trice [prɔmɔtœr, -tris] nm/f (*instigateur*) instigator, promoter; ~ (**immobilier**) property developer (*Brit*), real estate promoter (*US*).
promotion [prɔmɔsjɔ̃] nf promotion.
promouvoir [prɔmuvwar] vt to promote.
prompt, e [prɔ̃, prɔ̃t] a swift, rapid.

prôner [prone] vt to advocate.

pronom [prɔnɔ̃] nm pronoun.

prononcer [prɔnɔ̃se] vt (son, mot, jugement) to pronounce; (dire) to utter; (allocution) to deliver; se ~ vi to reach a decision, give a verdict; se ~ sur to give an opinion on; se ~ contre to come down against; **prononciation** nf pronunciation.

pronostic [prɔnɔstik] nm (MÉD) prognosis (pl oses); (fig: aussi: ~s) forecast.

propagande [prɔpagɑ̃d] nf propaganda.

propager [prɔpaʒe] vt, se ~ vi to spread.

prophète [prɔfɛt] nm prophet.

prophétie [prɔfesi] nf prophecy.

propice [prɔpis] a favourable.

proportion [prɔpɔrsjɔ̃] nf proportion; toute(s) ~(s) gardée(s) making due allowance(s).

propos [prɔpo] nm (paroles) talk q, remark; (intention) intention, aim; (sujet): à quel ~? what about?; à ~ de about, regarding; à tout ~ for no reason at all; à ~ ad by the way; (opportunément) at the right moment.

proposer [prɔpoze] vt (suggérer): ~ qch (à qn)/de faire to suggest sth (to sb)/doing, propose sth (to sb)/to do; (offrir): ~ qch à qn/de faire to offer sb sth/to do; (candidat, loi, motion) to put forward; (loi, motion) to propose; se ~ to offer one's services; se ~ de faire to intend ou propose to do; **proposition** nf suggestion; proposal; offer; (LING) clause.

propre [prɔpr(ə)] a clean; (net) neat, tidy; (possessif) own; (sens) literal; (particulier): à peculiar to; (approprié): ~ à suitable for; (de nature à): ~ à faire likely to do // nm: recopier au ~ to make a fair copy of; ~ment ad cleanly; neatly, tidily; le village ~ment dit the village itself; à ~ment parler strictly speaking; ~té nf cleanliness; neatness; tidiness.

propriétaire [prɔprijetɛr] nm/f owner; (pour le locataire) landlord/lady.

propriété [prɔprijete] nf (gén) property; (droit) ownership; (objet, immeuble, terres) property gén q.

propulser [prɔpylse] vt (missile) to propel; (projeter) to hurl, fling.

proroger [prɔrɔʒe] vt to put back, defer; (prolonger) to extend.

proscrire [prɔskrir] vt (bannir) to banish; (interdire) to ban, prohibit.

prose [proz] nf prose (style).

prospecter [prɔspɛkte] vt to prospect; (COMM) to canvass.

prospectus [prɔspɛktys] nm leaflet.

prospère [prɔspɛr] a prosperous.

prosterner [prɔstɛrne]: se ~ vi to bow low, prostrate o.s.

prostituée [prɔstitɥe] nf prostitute.

protecteur, trice [prɔtɛktœr, -tris] a protective; (air, ton: péj) patronizing // nm/f protector.

protection [prɔtɛksjɔ̃] nf protection; (d'un personnage influent: aide) patronage.

protéger [prɔteʒe] vt to protect; se ~ de/contre to protect o.s. from.

protéine [prɔtein] nf protein.

protestant, e [prɔtɛstɑ̃, -ɑ̃t] a, nm/f Protestant.

protestation [prɔtɛstasjɔ̃] nf (plainte) protest.

protester [prɔtɛste] vi: ~ (contre) to protest (against ou about); ~ de (son innocence, sa loyauté) to protest.

prothèse [prɔtɛz] nf artificial limb, prosthesis; ~ dentaire denture.

protocole [prɔtɔkɔl] nm (fig) etiquette.

proue [pru] nf bow (s pl), prow.

prouesse [prues] nf feat.

prouver [pruve] vt to prove.

provenance [prɔvnɑ̃s] nf origin; (de mot, coutume) source; avion en ~ de plane (arriving) from.

provenir [prɔvnir]: ~ de vt to come from; (résulter de) to be the result of.

proverbe [prɔvɛrb(ə)] nm proverb.

province [prɔvɛ̃s] nf province.

proviseur [prɔvizœr] nm ≈ head-(teacher) (Brit), ≈ principal (US).

provision [prɔvizjɔ̃] nf (réserve) stock, supply; (avance: à un avocat, avoué) retainer, retaining fee; (COMM) funds pl (in account); reserve; ~s (vivres) provisions, food q.

provisoire [prɔvizwar] a temporary; (JUR) provisional.

provoquer [prɔvɔke] vt (inciter): ~ qn à to incite sb to; (défier) to provoke; (causer) to cause, bring about.

proxénète [prɔksenɛt] nm procurer.

proximité [prɔksimite] nf nearness, closeness; (dans le temps) imminence, closeness; à ~ near ou close by; à ~ de near (to), close to.

prude [pryd] a prudish.

prudemment [prydamɑ̃] ad carefully, cautiously; wisely, sensibly.

prudence [prydɑ̃s] nf carefulness, caution; avec ~ carefully; cautiously; par (mesure de) ~ as a precaution.

prudent, e [prydɑ̃, -ɑ̃t] a (pas téméraire) careful, cautious; (: en général) safety-conscious; (sage, conseillé) wise, sensible; (réservé) cautious.

prune [pryn] nf plum.

pruneau, x [pryno] nm prune.

prunelle [prynɛl] nf pupil; eye.

prunier [prynje] nm plum tree.

psaume [psom] nm psalm.

pseudonyme [psødɔnim] nm (gén) fictitious name; (d'écrivain) pseudonym, pen name; (de comédien) stage name.

psychanalyste [psikanalist(ə)] nm/f

psychoanalyst.

psychiatre [psikjatʀ(ə)] *nm/f* psychiatrist.

psychiatrique [psikjatʀik] *a* psychiatric.

psychique [psiʃik] *a* psychological.

psychologie [psikɔlɔʒi] *nf* psychology; **psychologique** *a* psychological; **psychologue** *nm/f* psychologist.

P.T.T. *sigle fpl voir* **poste**.

pu *pp de* **pouvoir**.

puanteur [pɥɑ̃tœʀ] *nf* stink, stench.

pub [pyb] *abr f* (*fam:* = *publicité*): la ~ advertising.

public, ique [pyblik] *a* public; (*école, instruction*) state *cpd // nm* public; (*assistance*) audience; en ~ in public.

publicitaire [pyblisitɛʀ] *a* advertising *cpd*; (*film, voiture*) publicity *cpd*.

publicité [pyblisite] *nf* (*méthode, profession*) advertising; (*annonce*) advertisement; (*révélations*) publicity.

publier [pyblije] *vt* to publish.

publique [pyblik] *af voir* **public**.

puce [pys] *nf* flea; (*INFORM*) chip; ~s *nfpl* (*marché*) flea market *sg*.

pucelle [pysɛl] *af:* être ~ to be a virgin.

pudeur [pydœʀ] *nf* modesty.

pudique [pydik] *a* (*chaste*) modest; (*discret*) discreet.

puer [pɥe] (*péj*) *vi* to stink.

puéricultrice [pɥeʀikyltʀis] *nf* p(a)ediatric nurse.

puériculture [pɥeʀikyltyʀ] *nf* p(a)ediatric nursing; infant care.

puéril, e [pɥeʀil] *a* childish.

pugilat [pyʒila] *nm* (fist) fight.

puis [pɥi] *vb voir* **pouvoir** // *ad* then.

puiser [pɥize] *vt:* ~ (**dans**) to draw (from).

puisque [pɥisk(ə)] *cj* since.

puissance [pɥisɑ̃s] *nf* power; en ~ *a* potential.

puissant, e [pɥisɑ̃, -ɑ̃t] *a* powerful.

puisse *etc vb voir* **pouvoir**.

puits [pɥi] *nm* well; ~ de mine mine shaft.

pull(-over) [pul(ɔvœʀ)] *nm* sweater.

pulluler [pylyle] *vi* to swarm.

pulpe [pylp(ə)] *nf* pulp.

pulvérisateur [pylveʀizatœʀ] *nm* spray.

pulvériser [pylveʀize] *vt* to pulverize; (*liquide*) to spray.

punaise [pynɛz] *nf* (*ZOOL*) bug; (*clou*) drawing pin (*Brit*), thumbtack (*US*).

punch [pɔ̃ʃ] *nm* (*boisson*) punch; [pœnʃ] (*BOXE, fig*) punch.

punir [pyniʀ] *vt* to punish; **punition** *nf* punishment.

pupille [pypij] *nf* (*ANAT*) pupil // *nm/f* (*enfant*) ward; ~ de l'État child in care.

pupitre [pypitʀ(ə)] *nm* (*SCOL*) desk; (*REL*) lectern; (*de chef d'orchestre*) rostrum.

pur, e [pyʀ] *a* pure; (*vin*) undiluted;

(*whisky*) neat; en ~e perte to no avail.

purée [pyʀe] *nf:* ~ (**de pommes de terre**) mashed potatoes *pl*; ~ de marrons chestnut purée.

purger [pyʀʒe] *vt* (*radiateur*) to drain; (*circuit hydraulique*) to bleed; (*MÉD, POL*) to purge; (*JUR: peine*) to serve.

purin [pyʀɛ̃] *nm* liquid manure.

pur-sang [pyʀsɑ̃] *nm inv* thoroughbred.

pusillanime [pyzilanim] *a* fainthearted.

putain [pytɛ̃] *nf* (*fam!*) whore (!).

puzzle [pœzl(ə)] *nm* jigsaw (puzzle).

P.V. *sigle m* = **procès-verbal**.

pyjama [piʒama] *nm* pyjamas *pl*.

pyramide [piʀamid] *nf* pyramid.

Pyrénées [piʀene] *nfpl:* les ~ the Pyrenees.

Q

QG [kyʒe] *voir* **quartier**.

QI [kyi] *sigle m* (= *quotient intellectuel*) IQ.

quadragénaire [kadʀaʒenɛʀ] *nm/f* man/woman in his/her forties.

quadriller [kadʀije] *vt* (*papier*) to mark out in squares; (*POLICE*) to keep under tight control.

quadruple [k(w)adʀypl(ə)] *nm:* le ~ de four times as much as; **quadruplés, ées** *nm/fpl* quadruplets, quads.

quai [ke] *nm* (*de port*) quay; (*de gare*) platform; être à ~ (*navire*) to be alongside; (*train*) to be in the station.

qualifier [kalifje] *vt*, se ~ *vi* (*SPORT*) to qualify; ~ qch/qn de to describe sth/sb as.

qualité [kalite] *nf* quality; (*titre, fonction*) position.

quand [kɑ̃] *cj, ad* when; ~ je serai riche when I'm rich; ~ même all the same; really; ~ **bien même** even though.

quant [kɑ̃]: ~ à *prép* as for, as to; regarding.

quant-à-soi [kɑ̃taswa] *nm:* rester sur son ~ to remain aloof.

quantité [kɑ̃tite] *nf* quantity, amount; (*SCIENCE*) quantity; (*grand nombre*): une *ou* des ~(s) de a great deal of.

quarantaine [kaʀɑ̃tɛn] *nf* (*MÉD*) quarantine; avoir la ~ (*âge*) to be around forty; une ~ (de) forty or so, about forty.

quarante [kaʀɑ̃t] *num* forty.

quart [kaʀ] *nm* (*fraction, partie*) quarter; (*surveillance*) watch; un ~ de beurre a quarter kilo of butter; un ~ de vin a quarter litre of wine; une livre un ~ *ou* et ~ one and a quarter pounds; le ~ de a quarter of; ~ d'heure quarter of an hour.

quartier [kaʀtje] *nm* (*de ville*) district, area; (*de bœuf*) quarter; (*de fruit, fromage*) piece; ~s *nmpl* (*MIL, BLASON*) quarters; **cinéma de ~** local cinema; **avoir ~ libre** (fig) to be free; **~ général (QG)** headquarters (HQ).

quartz [kwaʀts] nm quartz.

quasi [kazi] ad almost, nearly; **~ment** ad almost, nearly.

quatorze [katɔʀz(ə)] num fourteen.

quatre [katʀ(ə)] num four; **à ~ pattes** on all fours; **tiré à ~ épingles** dressed up to the nines; **faire les ~ cent coups** to get a bit wild; **se mettre en ~ pour qn** to go out of one's way for sb; **~ à ~** (monter, descendre) four at a time; **~-vingt-dix** num ninety; **~-vingts** num eighty; **quatrième** num fourth.

quatuor [kwatɥɔʀ] nm quartet(te).

que [kə] ♦ cj 1 (introduisant complétive) that; **il sait ~ tu es là** he knows (that) you're here; **je veux ~ tu acceptes** I want you to accept; **il a dit ~ oui** he said he would (ou it was etc)

2 (reprise d'autres conjonctions): **quand il rentrera et qu'il aura mangé** when he gets back and (when) he has eaten; **si vous y allez ou ~ vous ... ~** if you go there or if you ...

3 (en tête de phrase: hypothèse, souhait etc): **qu'il le veuille ou non** whether he likes it or not; **qu'il fasse ce qu'il voudra!** let him do as he pleases!

4 (après comparatif) than; as; voir **plus, aussi, autant** etc

5 (seulement): **ne ... ~** only; **il ne boit ~ de l'eau** he only drinks water

♦ ad (exclamation): **qu'il ou qu'est-ce qu'il est bête/court vite!** he's so silly!/he runs so fast!; **~ de livres!** what a lot of books!

♦ pronom 1 (relatif: personne) whom; (: chose) that, which; **l'homme ~ je vois** the man (whom) I see; **le livre ~ tu vois** the book (that ou which) you see; **un jour ~ j'étais ...** a day when I was ...

2 (interrogatif) what; **~ fais-tu?, qu'est-ce que tu fais?** what are you doing?; **qu'est-ce que c'est?** what is it?, what's that?; **~ faire?** what can one do?

quel, quelle [kɛl] a 1 (interrogatif: personne) who; (: chose) what; which; **~ est cet homme?** who is this man?; **~ est ce livre?** what is this book?; **~ livre/homme?** what book/man?; (parmi un certain choix) which book/man?; **~s acteurs préférez-vous?** which actors do you prefer; **dans ~s pays êtes-vous allé?** which ou what countries did you go to?

2 (exclamatif): **~le surprise!** what a surprise!

3: **~(le) que soit: ~ que soit le coupable** whoever is guilty; **~ que soit votre avis** whatever your opinion.

quelconque [kɛlkɔ̃k] a (médiocre) indifferent, poor; (sans attrait) ordinary, plain; (indéfini): **un ami/pretexte ~** some friend/pretext or other.

quelque [kɛlkə] ♦ a 1 some; a few; (tournure interrogative) any; **~ espoir** some hope; **il a ~s amis** he has a few ou some friends; **a-t-il ~s amis?** has he any friends?; **les ~s livres qui** the few books which; **20 kg et ~(s)** a bit over 20 kg

2: **~ ... que: ~ livre qu'il choisisse** whatever (ou whichever) book he chooses

3: **~ chose** something; (tournure interrogative) anything; **~ chose d'autre** something else; anything else; **~ part** somewhere; anywhere; **en ~ sorte** as it were

♦ ad 1 (environ): **~ 100 mètres** some 100 metres

2: **~ peu** rather, somewhat.

quelquefois [kɛlkəfwa] ad sometimes.

quelques-uns, -unes [kɛlkəzœ̃, -yn] pronom a few, some.

quelqu'un [kɛlkœ̃] pronom someone, somebody, (tournure interrogative + anyone ou anybody; **~ d'autre** someone ou somebody else; anybody else.

quémander [kemɑ̃de] vt to beg for.

qu'en dira-t-on [kɑ̃diʀatɔ̃] nm inv: **le ~** gossip, what people say.

querelle [kəʀɛl] nf quarrel.

quereller [kəʀele]: **se ~** vi to quarrel.

qu'est-ce que (ou qui) [kɛskə(ki)] voir **que, qui**.

question [kɛstjɔ̃] nf (gén) question; (fig) matter; issue; **il a été ~ de** we (ou they) spoke about; **de quoi est-il ~?** what is it about?; **il n'en est pas ~** there's no question of it; **hors de ~** out of the question; **remettre en ~** to question.

questionnaire [kɛstjɔnɛʀ] nm questionnaire; **questionner** vt to question.

quête [kɛt] nf collection; (recherche) quest, search; **faire la ~** (à l'église) to take the collection; (artiste) to pass the hat round; **quêter** vi (à l'église) to take the collection.

quetsche [kwɛtʃ(ə)] nf damson.

queue [kø] nf tail; (fig: du classement) bottom; (: de poêle) handle; (: de fruit, feuille) stalk; (: de train, colonne, file) rear; **faire la ~** to queue (up); **~ de cheval** ponytail; **~-de-pie** nf (habit) tails pl, tail coat.

qui [ki] pronom (personne) who, prép + whom; (chose, animal) which, that; **qu'est-ce ~ est sur la table?** what is on the table?; **~ est-ce qui?** who?; **~ est-ce que?** who?; whom?; **à ~ est ce sac?** whose bag is this?; **à ~ parlais-tu?** who were you talking to?; to whom were you talking?; **amenez ~ vous voulez** bring who you like; **~ que ce soit** whoever it may be.

quiconque [kikɔ̃k] pronom (celui qui) whoever, anyone who; (personne) anyone, anybody.

quiétude [kjetyd] nf (d'un lieu) quiet, tranquillity; **en toute ~** in complete peace.

quille [kij] *nf*: (jeu de) ~s skittles *sg* (*Brit*), bowling (*US*).

quincaillerie [kɛ̃kajʀi] *nf* (*ustensiles*) hardware; (*magasin*) hardware shop; **quincaillier, ière** *nm/f* hardware dealer.

quinine [kinin] *nf* quinine.

quinquagénaire [kɛ̃kaʒenɛʀ] *nm/f* man/woman in his/her fifties.

quintal, aux [kɛ̃tal, -o] *nm* quintal (*100 kg*).

quinte [kɛ̃t] *nf*: ~ (de toux) coughing fit.

quintuple [kɛ̃typl(ə)] *nm*: le ~ de five times as much as; **quintuplés, ées** *nm/ fpl* quintuplets, quins.

quinzaine [kɛ̃zɛn] *nf*: une ~ (de) about fifteen, fifteen or so; une ~ (de jours) a fortnight, two weeks.

quinze [kɛ̃z] *num* fifteen; demain en ~ a fortnight *ou* two weeks tomorrow; dans ~ jours in a fortnight('s time), in two weeks(' time).

quiproquo [kipʀɔko] *nm* misunderstanding.

quittance [kitɑ̃s] *nf* (*reçu*) receipt; (*facture*) bill.

quitte [kit] *a*: être ~ envers qn to be no longer in sb's debt; (*fig*) to be quits with sb; être ~ de (*obligation*) to be clear of; en être ~ à bon compte to have got off lightly; ~ à faire even if it means doing.

quitter [kite] *vt* to leave; (*espoir, illusion*) to give up; (*vêtement*) to take off; se ~ *vi* (*couples, interlocuteurs*) to part; ne quittez pas (*au téléphone*) hold the line.

qui-vive [kiviv] *nm*: être sur le ~ to be on the alert.

quoi [kwa] *pronom* (*interrogatif*) what; ~ de neuf? what's the news?; as-tu de ~ écrire? have you anything to write with?; il n'a pas de ~ se l'acheter he can't afford it; ~ qu'il arrive whatever happens; ~ qu'il en soit be that as it may; ~ que ce soit anything at all; 'il n'y a pas de ~' '(please) don't mention it'; à ~ bon? what's the use?; en ~ puis-je vous aider? how can I help you?

quoique [kwak(ə)] *cj* (al)though.

quolibet [kɔlibɛ] *nm* gibe, jeer.

quote-part [kɔtpaʀ] *nf* share.

quotidien, ne [kɔtidjɛ̃, -ɛn] *a* daily; (*banal*) everyday // *nm* (*journal*) daily (paper).

R

r. *abr de* **route, rue.**

rab [ʀab] *abr m* (*fam*) *de* **rabiot.**

rabâcher [ʀabaʃe] *vt* to keep on repeating.

rabais [ʀabɛ] *nm* reduction, discount.

rabaisser [ʀabese] *vt* (*rabattre*) to reduce; (*dénigrer*) to belittle.

rabattre [ʀabatʀ(ə)] *vt* (*couvercle,*

siège) to pull down; (*gibier*) to drive; se ~ *vi* (*bords, couvercle*) to fall shut; (*véhicule, coureur*) to cut in; **se ~ sur** *vt* to fall back on.

rabbin [ʀabɛ̃] *nm* rabbi.

rabiot [ʀabjo] *nm* (*fam*) extra, more.

râblé, e [ʀɑble] *a* stocky.

rabot [ʀabo] *nm* plane.

rabougri, e [ʀabugʀi] *a* stunted.

rabrouer [ʀabʀue] *vt* to snub.

racaille [ʀakaj] *nf* (*péj*) rabble, riffraff.

raccommoder [ʀakɔmɔde] *vt* to mend, repair; (*chaussette etc*) to darn.

raccompagner [ʀakɔ̃paɲe] *vt* to take *ou* see back.

raccord [ʀakɔʀ] *nm* link.

raccorder [ʀakɔʀde] *vt* to join (up), link up; (*suj: pont etc*) to connect, link.

raccourci [ʀakuʀsi] *nm* short cut.

raccourcir [ʀakuʀsiʀ] *vt* to shorten.

raccrocher [ʀakʀɔʃe] *vt* (*tableau*) to hang back up; (*récepteur*) to put down // *vi* (*TÉL*) to hang up, ring off; se ~ à *vt* to cling to, hang on to.

race [ʀas] *nf* race; (*d'animaux, fig*) breed; (*ascendance*) stock, race; de ~ a purebred, pedigree.

rachat [ʀaʃa] *nm* buying; buying back.

racheter [ʀaʃte] *vt* (*article perdu*) to buy another; (*davantage*): ~ du lait/3 œufs to buy more milk/another 3 eggs *ou* 3 more eggs; (*après avoir vendu*) to buy back; (*d'occasion*) to buy; (*COMM: part, firme*) to buy up; (: *pension, rente*) to redeem; se ~ *vi* (*fig*) to make amends.

racial, e, aux [ʀasjal, -o] *a* racial.

racine [ʀasin] *nf* root; ~ carrée/cubique square/cube root.

raciste [ʀasist(ə)] *a, nm/f* raci(al)ist.

racket [ʀakɛt] *nm* racketeering *q*.

racler [ʀakle] *vt* (*surface*) to scrape; (*tache, boue*) to scrape off.

racoler [ʀakɔle] *vt* (*attirer: suj: prostituée*) to solicit; (: *parti, marchand*) to tout for.

racontars [ʀakɔ̃taʀ] *nmpl* gossip *sg*.

raconter [ʀakɔ̃te] *vt*: ~ à (à qn) (*décrire*) to relate (to sb), tell (sb) about; (*dire*) to tell (sb).

racorni, e [ʀakɔʀni] *a* hard(ened).

radar [ʀadaʀ] *nm* radar.

rade [ʀad] *nf* (*natural*) harbour; rester en ~ (*fig*) to be left stranded.

radeau, x [ʀado] *nm* raft.

radiateur [ʀadjatœʀ] *nm* radiator, heater; (*AUTO*) radiator; ~ électrique/à gaz electric/gas heater *ou* fire.

radiation [ʀadjasjɔ̃] *nf* (*voir radier*) striking off *q*; (*PHYSIQUE*) radiation.

radical, e, aux [ʀadikal, -o] *a* radical.

radier [ʀadje] *vt* to strike off.

radieux, euse [ʀadjø, -øz] *a* radiant; brilliant, glorious.

radin, e [ʀadɛ̃, -in] *a* (*fam*) stingy.

radio [ʀadjo] *nf* radio; (*MÉD*) X-ray //

nm radio operator; **à la ~** on the radio.
radio... [Radjo] *préfixe:* **~actif, ive** *a* radioactive; **radiodiffuser** *vt* to broadcast; **~graphie** *nf* radiography; *(photo)* X-ray photograph; **~phonique** *a* radio *cpd;* **~télévisé, e** *a* broadcast on radio and television.
radis [Radi] *nm* radish.
radoter [Radɔte] *vi* to ramble on.
radoucir [Radusiʀ]: **se ~** *vi (se réchauffer)* to become milder; *(se calmer)* to calm down; to soften.
rafale [Rafal] *nf (vent)* gust (of wind); *(tir)* burst of gunfire.
raffermir [RafɛʀmiR] *vt,* **se ~** *vi (tissus, muscle)* to firm up; *(fig)* to strengthen.
raffiner [Rafine] *vt* to refine; **raffinerie** *nf* refinery.
raffoler [Rafɔle]: **~ de** *vt* to be very keen on.
rafle [Rafl(ə)] *nf (de police)* raid.
rafler [Rafle] *vt (fam)* to swipe, nick.
rafraîchir [RafʀeʃiR] *vt (atmosphère, température)* to cool (down); *(aussi:* **mettre à ~)** to chill; *(fig: rénover)* to brighten up; **se ~** *vi* to grow cooler; to freshen up; to refresh o.s; **rafraîchissant, e** *a* refreshing; **rafraîchissement** *nm* cooling; *(boisson)* cool drink; **rafraîchissements** *(boissons, fruits etc)* refreshments.
rage [Raʒ] *nf (MÉD):* **la ~** rabies; *(fureur)* rage, fury; **faire ~** to rage; **~ de dents** (raging) toothache.
ragot [Rago] *nm (fam)* malicious gossip *q.*
ragoût [Ragu] *nm (plat)* stew.
raide [Rɛd] *a (tendu)* taut, tight; *(escarpé)* steep; *(droit: cheveux)* straight; *(ankylosé, dur, guindé)* stiff; *(fam)* steep, stiff; flat broke // *ad (en pente)* steeply; **~ mort** stone dead; **raidir** *vt (muscles)* to stiffen; *(câble)* to pull taut; **se raidir** *vi* to stiffen; to become taut; *(personne)* to tense up; to brace o.s.
raie [Rɛ] *nf (ZOOL)* skate, ray; *(rayure)* stripe; *(des cheveux)* parting.
raifort [Refɔʀ] *nm* horseradish.
rail [Rɑj] *nm* rail; *(chemins de fer)* railways *pl;* **par ~** by rail.
railler [Raje] *vt* to scoff at, jeer at.
rainure [Renyʀ] *nf* groove; slot.
raisin [Rezɛ̃] *nm (aussi:* **~s)** grapes *pl;* **~s secs** raisins.
raison [Rezɔ̃] *nf* reason; **avoir ~** to be right; **donner ~ à qn** to agree with sb; to prove sb right; **se faire une ~** to learn to live with it; **perdre la ~** to become insane; to take leave of one's senses; **~ de plus** all the more reason; **à plus forte ~** all the more so; **en ~ de** because of; according to; in proportion to; **à ~ de** at the rate of; **~ sociale** corporate name; **raisonnable** *a* reasonable, sensible.
raisonnement [Rezɔnmɑ̃] *nm* reason-

ing; arguing; argument.
raisonner [Rezɔne] *vi (penser)* to reason; *(argumenter, discuter)* to argue // *vt (personne)* to reason with.
rajeunir [RaʒœniR] *vt (suj: coiffure, robe):* **~ qn** to make sb look younger; *(suj: cure etc)* to rejuvenate; *(fig)* to give a new look to; to inject new blood into // *vi* to become (*ou* look) younger.
rajouter [Raʒute] *vt:* **~ du sel/un œuf** to add some more salt/another egg.
rajuster [RaʒystE] *vt (vêtement)* to straighten, tidy; *(salaires)* to adjust; *(machine)* to readjust.
ralenti [Ralɑ̃ti] *nm:* **au ~** *(AUTO):* **tourner au ~** to tick over, idle; *(CINÉMA)* in slow motion; *(fig)* at a slower pace.
ralentir [RalɑtiR] *vt, vi,* **se ~** *vi* to slow down.
râler [Rale] *vi* to groan; *(fam)* to grouse, moan (and groan).
rallier [Ralje] *vt (rassembler)* to rally; *(rejoindre)* to rejoin; *(gagner à sa cause)* to win over; **se ~ à** *(avis)* to come over *ou* round to.
rallonge [Ralɔ̃ʒ] *nf (de table)* (extra) leaf *(pl* leaves); *(argent etc)* extra *q.*
rallonger [Ralɔ̃ʒe] *vt* to lengthen.
rallye [Rali] *nm* rally; *(POL)* march.
ramassage [Ramasaʒ] *nm:* **~ scolaire** school bus service.
ramassé, e [Ramase] *a (trapu)* squat.
ramasser [Ramase] *vt (objet tombé ou par terre, fam)* to pick up; *(recueillir)* to collect; *(récolter)* to gather; **se ~** *vi (sur soi-même)* to huddle up; to crouch; **ramassis** *nm (péj)* bunch; jumble.
rambarde [Rɑ̃baʀd(ə)] *nf* guardrail.
rame [Ram] *nf (aviron)* oar; *(de métro)* train; *(de papier)* ream.
rameau, x [Ramo] *nm (small)* branch; **les R~x** *(REL)* Palm Sunday *sg.*
ramener [Ramne] *vt* to bring back; *(reconduire)* to take back; *(rabattre: couverture, visière):* **~ qch sur** to pull sth back over; **~ qch à** *(réduire à, aussi MATH)* to reduce sth to.
ramer [Rame] *vi* to row.
ramollir [RamɔliR] *vt* to soften; **se ~** *vi* to go soft.
ramoner [Ramɔne] *vt* to sweep.
rampe [Rɑ̃p] *nf (d'escalier)* banister(s *pl);* *(dans un garage, d'un terrain)* ramp; *(THÉÂTRE):* **la ~** the footlights *pl;* **~ de lancement** launching pad.
ramper [Rɑ̃pe] *vi* to crawl.
rancard [RɑkaR] *nm (fam)* date; tip.
rancart [RɑkaR] *nm:* **mettre au ~** to scrap.
rance [Rɑ̃s] *a* rancid.
rancœur [RɑkœR] *nf* rancour.
rançon [Rɑ̃sɔ̃] *nf* ransom; *(fig)* price.
rancune [Rɑkyn] *nf* grudge, rancour; **garder ~ à qn (de qch)** to bear sb a

grudge (for sth); sans ~! no hard feelings!; **rancunier, ière** a vindictive, spiteful.

randonnée [Rɑ̃dɔne] nf ride; (à pied) walk, ramble; hike, hiking q.

rang [Rɑ̃] nm (rangée) row; (grade, classement) rank; ~s (MIL) ranks; se mettre en ~s/sur un ~ to get into ou form rows/a line; au premier ~ in the first row; (fig) ranking first.

rangé, e [Rɑ̃ʒe] a (sérieux) orderly, steady.

rangée [Rɑ̃ʒe] nf row.

ranger [Rɑ̃ʒe] vt (classer, grouper) to order, arrange; (mettre à sa place) to put away; (voiture dans la rue) to park; (mettre de l'ordre dans) to tidy up; (arranger) to arrange; (fig: classer): ~ qn/qch parmi to rank sb/sth among; se ~ vi (véhicule, conducteur) to pull over ou in; (piéton) to step aside; (s'assagir) to settle down; se ~ à (avis) to come round to.

ranimer [Ranime] vt (personne) to bring round; (forces, courage) to restore; (troupes etc) to kindle new life in; (douleur, souvenir) to revive; (feu) to rekindle.

rapace [Rapas] nm bird of prey.

râpe [Rɑp] nf (CULIN) grater.

râpé, e [Rɑpe] a (tissu) threadbare.

râper [Rɑpe] vt (CULIN) to grate.

rapetisser [Raptise] vt to shorten.

rapide [Rapid] a fast; (prompt) quick // nm express (train); (de cours d'eau) rapid; ~ment ad fast; quickly.

rapiécer [Rapjese] vt to patch.

rappel [Rapɛl] nm (THÉÂTRE) curtain call; (MÉD: vaccination) booster; (ADMIN: de salaire) back pay q; (d'une aventure, d'un nom) reminder.

rappeler [Raple] vt to call back; (ambassadeur, MIL) to recall; (faire se souvenir): ~ qch à qn to remind sb of sth; se ~ vt (se souvenir de) to remember, recall.

rapport [RapɔR] nm (compte rendu) report; (profit) yield, return; revenue; (lien, analogie) relationship; (MATH, TECH) ratio (pl s); ~s (entre personnes, pays) relations; avoir ~ à to have something to do with; être en ~ avec (idée de corrélation) to be related to; être/se mettre en ~ avec qn to be/get in touch with sb; par ~ à in relation to; ~s (sexuels) (sexual) intercourse sg.

rapporter [RapɔRte] vt (rendre, ramener) to bring back; (apporter davantage) to bring more; (suj: investissement) to yield; (: activité) to bring in; (relater) to report // vi (investissement) to give a good return ou yield; (: activité) to be very profitable; ~ qch à (fig: rattacher) to relate sth to; se ~ à (correspondre à) to relate to; s'en ~ à to

rely on; **rapporteur, euse** nm/f (de procès, commission) reporter; (péj) telltale // nm (GÉOM) protractor.

rapprochement [RapRɔʃmɑ̃] nm (de nations, familles) reconciliation; (analogie, rapport) parallel.

rapprocher [RapRɔʃe] vt (chaise d'une table): ~ qch (de) to bring sth closer (to); (deux objets) to bring closer together; (réunir) to bring together; (comparer) to establish a parallel between; se ~ vi to draw closer ou nearer; se ~ de to come closer to; (présenter une analogie avec) to be close to.

rapt [Rapt] nm abduction.

raquette [Rakɛt] nf (de tennis) racket; (de ping-pong) bat; (à neige) snowshoe.

rare [RaR] a rare; (main-d'œuvre, denrées) scarce; (cheveux, herbe) sparse.

rarement [RaRmɑ̃] ad rarely, seldom.

ras, e [Rɑ, Rɑz] a (tête, cheveux) close-cropped; (poil, herbe) short // ad short; en ~e campagne in open country; à ~ bords to the brim; au ~ de level with; en avoir ~ le bol (fam) to be fed up; ~ du cou a (pull, robe) crew-neck.

rasade [Razad] nf glassful.

raser [Rɑze] vt (barbe, cheveux) to shave off; (menton, personne) to shave; (fam: ennuyer) to bore; (démolir) to raze (to the ground); (frôler) to graze, skim; se ~ vi to shave; (fam) to be bored (to tears); **rasoir** nm razor.

rassasier [Rasazje] vt to satisfy.

rassemblement [Rasɑ̃bləmɑ̃] nm (groupe) gathering; (POL) union.

rassembler [Rasɑ̃ble] vt (réunir) to assemble, gather; (regrouper, amasser) to gather together, collect; se ~ vi to gather.

rassis, e [Rasi, -iz] a (pain) stale.

rassurer [RasyRe] vt to reassure; se ~ vi to be reassured; rassure-toi don't worry.

rat [Ra] nm rat.

rate [Rat] nf spleen.

raté, e [Rate] a (tentative) unsuccessful, failed // nm/f failure // nm misfiring q.

râteau, x [Rɑto] nm rake.

râtelier [Rɑtəlje] nm rack; (fam) false teeth pl.

rater [Rate] vi (affaire, projet etc) to go wrong, fail // vt (cible, train, occasion) to miss; (démonstration, plat) to spoil; (examen) to fail.

ration [Rasjɔ̃] nf ration; (fig) share.

ratisser [Ratise] vt (allée) to rake; (feuilles) to rake up; (suj: armée, police) to comb.

R.A.T.P. sigle f (= Régie autonome des transports parisiens) Paris transport authority.

rattacher [Rataʃe] vt (animal, cheveux) to tie up again; (incorporer: ADMIN etc): ~ qch à to join sth to; (fig: relier): ~ qch à to link sth with; (: lier): ~ qn à to bind *ou* tie sb to.

rattraper [ʀatʀape] *vt* (*fugitif*) to recapture; (*empêcher de tomber*) to catch (hold of); (*atteindre, rejoindre*) to catch up with; (*réparer: imprudence, erreur*) to make up for; **se ~** *vi* to make good one's losses; to make up for it; **se ~** (*à*) (*se raccrocher*) to stop o.s. falling (by catching hold of).

rature [ʀatyʀ] *nf* deletion, erasure.

rauque [ʀok] *a* raucous; hoarse.

ravages [ʀavaʒ] *nmpl*: **faire des ~** to wreak havoc.

ravaler [ʀavale] *vt* (*mur, façade*) to restore; (*déprécier*) to lower.

ravi, e [ʀavi] *a*: **être ~ de/que** to be delighted with/that.

ravin [ʀavɛ̃] *nm* gully, ravine.

ravir [ʀaviʀ] *vt* (*enchanter*) to delight; (*enlever*): **~ qch à qn** to rob sb of sth; **à ~** *ad* beautifully.

raviser [ʀavize]: **se ~** *vi* to change one's mind.

ravissant, e [ʀavisɑ̃, -ɑ̃t] *a* delightful.

ravisseur, euse [ʀavisœʀ, -øz] *nm/f* abductor, kidnapper.

ravitailler [ʀavitaje] *vt* to resupply; (*véhicule*) to refuel; **se ~** *vi* to get fresh supplies.

raviver [ʀavive] *vt* (*feu, douleur*) to revive; (*couleurs*) to brighten up.

rayé, e [ʀeje] *a* (*à rayures*) striped.

rayer [ʀeje] *vt* (*érafler*) to scratch; (*barrer*) to cross out; (*d'une liste*) to cross off.

rayon [ʀejɔ̃] *nm* (*de soleil etc*) ray; (*GÉOM*) radius; (*de roue*) spoke; (*étagère*) shelf (*pl* shelves); (*de grand magasin*) department; **dans un ~ de** within a radius of; **~ d'action** range; **~ de soleil** sunbeam; **~s X** X-rays.

rayonnement [ʀejɔnmɑ̃] *nm* radiation; (*fig*) radiance; influence.

rayonner [ʀejɔne] *vi* (*chaleur, énergie*) to radiate; (*fig*) to shine forth; to be radiant; (*touriste*) to go touring (*from one base*).

rayure [ʀejyʀ] *nf* (*motif*) stripe; (*éraflure*) scratch; (*rainure, d'un fusil*) groove.

raz-de-marée [ʀɑdmaʀe] *nm inv* tidal wave.

ré [ʀe] *nm* (*MUS*) D; (*en chantant la gamme*) re.

réacteur [ʀeaktœʀ] *nm* jet engine.

réaction [ʀeaksjɔ̃] *nf* reaction; **moteur à ~** jet engine.

réadapter [ʀeadapte] *vt* to readjust; (*MÉD*) to rehabilitate; **se ~ (à)** to readjust (to).

réagir [ʀeaʒiʀ] *vi* to react.

réalisateur, trice [ʀealizatœʀ, -tʀis] *nm/f* (*TV, CINÉMA*) director.

réalisation [ʀealizasjɔ̃] *nf* carrying out; realization; fulfilment; achievement;

production; (*œuvre*) production; creation; work.

réaliser [ʀealize] *vt* (*projet, opération*) to carry out, realize; (*rêve, souhait*) to realize, fulfil; (*exploit*) to achieve; (*achat, vente*) to make; (*film*) to produce; (*se rendre compte de, COMM: bien, capital*) to realize; **se ~** *vi* to be realized.

réaliste [ʀealist(ə)] *a* realistic.

réalité [ʀealite] *nf* reality; **en ~** in (actual) fact; **dans la ~** in reality.

réanimation [ʀeanimasjɔ̃] *nf* resuscitation; **service de ~** intensive care unit.

réarmer [ʀeaʀme] *vt* (*arme*) to reload // *vi* (*état*) to rearm.

rébarbatif, ive [ʀebaʀbatif, -iv] *a* forbidding.

rebattu, e [ʀəbaty] *a* hackneyed.

rebelle [ʀəbɛl] *nm/f* rebel // *a* (*troupes*) rebel; (*enfant*) rebellious; (*mèche etc*) unruly; **~ à** unamenable to.

rebeller [ʀəbele]: **se ~** *vi* to rebel.

rebondi, e [ʀəbɔ̃di] *a* rounded; chubby.

rebondir [ʀəbɔ̃diʀ] *vi* (*ballon: au sol*) to bounce; (: *contre un mur*) to rebound; (*fig*) to get moving again; **rebondissement** *nm* new development.

rebord [ʀəbɔʀ] *nm* edge.

rebours [ʀəbuʀ]: **à ~** *ad* the wrong way.

rebrousse-poil [ʀəbʀuspwal]: **à ~** *ad* the wrong way.

rebrousser [ʀəbʀuse] *vt*: **~ chemin** to turn back.

rebut [ʀəby] *nm*: **mettre au ~** to scrap.

rebuter [ʀəbyte] *vt* to put off.

récalcitrant, e [ʀekalsitʀɑ̃, -ɑ̃t] *a* refractory.

recaler [ʀəkale] *vt* (*SCOL*) to fail.

récapituler [ʀekapityle] *vt* to recapitulate; to sum up.

receler [ʀəsəle] *vt* (*produit d'un vol*) to receive; (*malfaiteur*) to harbour; (*fig*) to conceal; **receleur, euse** *nm/f* receiver.

récemment [ʀesamɑ̃] *ad* recently.

recenser [ʀəsɑ̃se] *vt* (*population*) to take a census of; (*inventorier*) to list.

récent, e [ʀesɑ̃, -ɑ̃t] *a* recent.

récépissé [ʀesepise] *nm* receipt.

récepteur [ʀeseptœʀ] *nm* receiver; **~ (de radio)** radio set *ou* receiver.

réception [ʀesɛpsjɔ̃] *nf* receiving *q*; (*accueil*) reception, welcome; (*bureau*) reception desk; (*réunion mondaine*) reception, party; **réceptionniste** *nm/f* receptionist.

recette [ʀəsɛt] *nf* (*CULIN*) recipe; (*fig*) formula, recipe; (*COMM*) takings *pl*; **~s** *nfpl* (*COMM: rentrées*) receipts.

receveur, euse [ʀəsvœʀ, -øz] *nm/f* (*des contributions*) tax collector; (*des postes*) postmaster/mistress; (*d'autobus*) conductor/conductress.

recevoir [ʀəsvwaʀ] *vt* to receive;

(*client, patient*) to see // *vi* to receive visitors; to give parties; to see patients *etc*; se ~ *vi* (*athlète*) to land; être reçu (*à un examen*) to pass.

rechange [rəʃɑ̃ʒ]: de ~ *a* (*pièces, roue*) spare; (*fig: solution*) alternative; des vêtements de ~ a change of clothes.

rechaper [rəʃape] *vt* to remould, retread.

réchapper [reʃape]: ~ de ou à *vt* (*accident, maladie*) to come through.

recharge [rəʃarʒ(ə)] *nf* refill.

recharger [rəʃarʒe] *vt* (*camion, fusil, appareil-photo*) to reload; (*briquet, stylo*) to refill; (*batterie*) to recharge.

réchaud [reʃo] *nm* (portable) stove; plate-warmer.

réchauffer [reʃofe] *vt* (*plat*) to reheat; (*mains, personne*) to warm; se ~ *vi* (*température*) to get warmer.

rêche [rɛʃ] *a* rough.

recherche [rəʃɛrʃ(ə)] *nf* (*action*): la ~ de the search for; (*raffinement*) affectedness, studied elegance; (*scientifique etc*): la ~ research; ~s *nfpl* (*de la police*) investigations; (*scientifiques*) research *sg*; se mettre à la ~ de to go in search of.

recherché, e [rəʃɛrʃe] *a* (*rare, demandé*) much sought-after; (*raffiné*) studied, affected.

rechercher [rəʃɛrʃe] *vt* (*objet égaré, personne*) to look for; (*causes, nouveau procédé*) to try to find; (*bonheur, amitié*) to seek.

rechute [rəʃyt] *nf* (*MÉD*) relapse.

récidiver [residive] *vi* to commit a subsequent offence; (*fig*) to do it again.

récif [resif] *nm* reef.

récipient [resipjɑ̃] *nm* container.

réciproque [resiprɔk] *a* reciprocal.

récit [resi] *nm* story.

récital [resital] *nm* recital.

réciter [resite] *vt* to recite.

réclamation [reklamasjɔ̃] *nf* complaint; ~s (*bureau*) complaints department *sg*.

réclame [reklam] *nf* ad, advert(isement); **article en ~** special offer.

réclamer [reklame] *vt* (*aide, nourriture etc*) to ask for; (*revendiquer*) to claim, demand; (*nécessiter*) to demand, require // *vi* to complain.

réclusion [reklyzjɔ̃] *nf* imprisonment.

recoin [rəkwɛ̃] *nm* nook, corner; (*fig*) hidden recess.

reçois *etc vb voir* **recevoir**.

récolte [rekɔlt(ə)] *nf* harvesting; gathering; (*produits*) harvest, crop; (*fig*) crop, collection.

récolter [rekɔlte] *vt* to harvest, gather (in); (*fig*) to collect; to get.

recommandé [rəkɔmɑ̃de] *nm* (*POSTES*): **en ~** by registered mail.

recommander [rəkɔmɑ̃de] *vt* to recommend; (*suj: qualités etc*) to commend;

(*POSTES*) to register; se ~ de qn to give sb's name as a reference.

recommencer [rəkɔmɑ̃se] *vt* (*reprendre: lutte, séance*) to resume, start again; (*refaire: travail, explications*) to start afresh, start (over) again; (*récidiver: erreur*) to make again // *vi* to start again; (*récidiver*) to do it again.

récompense [rekɔ̃pɑ̃s] *nf* reward; (*prix*) award; **récompenser** *vt*: récompenser qn (de ou pour) to reward sb (for).

réconcilier [rekɔ̃silje] *vt* to reconcile; se ~ (avec) to be reconciled (with).

reconduire [rəkɔ̃dɥir] *vt* (*raccompagner*) to take ou see back; (*JUR, POL*: renouveler) to renew.

réconfort [rekɔ̃fɔr] *nm* comfort.

réconforter [rekɔ̃fɔrte] *vt* (*consoler*) to comfort; (*revigorer*) to fortify.

reconnaissance [rəkɔnɛsɑ̃s] *nf* recognition; acknowledgement; (*gratitude*) gratitude, gratefulness; (*MIL*) reconnaissance, recce.

reconnaissant, e [rəkɔnɛsɑ̃, -ɑ̃t] *a* grateful.

reconnaître [rəkɔnɛtr(ə)] *vt* to recognize; (*MIL: lieu*) to reconnoitre; (*JUR: enfant, dette, droit*) to acknowledge; ~ que to admit ou acknowledge that; ~ qn/qch à to recognize sb/sth by.

reconstituer [rəkɔ̃stitɥe] *vt* (*monument ancien*) to recreate; (*fresque, vase brisé*) to piece together, reconstitute; (*événement, accident*) to reconstruct; (*fortune, patrimoine*) to rebuild.

reconstruire [rəkɔ̃strɥir] *vt* to rebuild.

record [rəkɔr] *nm, a* record.

recoupement [rəkupmɑ̃] *nm*: **par ~** by cross-checking.

recouper [rəkupe]: se ~ *vi* (*témoignages*) to tie ou match up.

recourbé, e [rəkurbe] *a* curved; hooked; bent.

recourir [rəkurir]: ~ à *vt* (*ami, agence*) to turn ou appeal to; (*force, ruse, emprunt*) to resort to.

recours [rəkur] *nm* (*JUR*) appeal; **avoir ~ à** = recourir à; **en dernier ~** as a last resort; **~ en grâce** plea for clemency.

recouvrer [rəkuvre] *vt* (*vue, santé etc*) to recover, regain; (*impôts*) to collect; (*créance*) to recover.

recouvrir [rəkuvrir] *vt* (*couvrir à nouveau*) to re-cover; (*couvrir entièrement, aussi fig*) to cover; (*cacher, masquer*) to conceal, hide; se ~ *vi* (*se superposer*) to overlap.

récréation [rekreasjɔ̃] *nf* recreation, entertainment; (*SCOL*) break.

récrier [rekrije]: se ~ *vi* to exclaim.

récriminations [rekriminasjɔ̃] *nfpl* remonstrations, complaints.

recroqueviller [rəkrɔkvije]: se ~ *vi* (*feuilles*) to curl ou shrivel up; (*per-*

sonne) to huddle up.

recrudescence [ʀəkʀydesɑ̃s] *nf* fresh outbreak.

recrue [ʀəkʀy] *nf* recruit.

recruter [ʀəkʀyte] *vt* to recruit.

rectangle [ʀɛktɑ̃gl(ə)] *nm* rectangle; **rectangulaire** *a* rectangular.

recteur [ʀɛktœʀ] *nm* ≈ (regional) director of education (*Brit*), ≈ state superintendent of education (*US*).

rectifier [ʀɛktifje] *vt* (*tracé, virage*) to straighten; (*calcul, adresse*) to correct; (*erreur, faute*) to rectify.

rectiligne [ʀɛktiliɲ] *a* straight; (*GÉOM*) rectilinear.

reçu, e [ʀəsy] *pp de* recevoir // *a* (*admis, consacré*) accepted // *nm* (*COMM*) receipt.

recueil [ʀəkœj] *nm* collection.

recueillir [ʀəkœjiʀ] *vt* to collect; (*voix, suffrages*) to win; (*accueillir: réfugiés, chat*) to take in; **se ~** *vi* to gather one's thoughts; to meditate.

recul [ʀəkyl] *nm* retreat; recession; decline; (*d'arme à feu*) recoil, kick; **avoir un mouvement de ~** to recoil; **prendre du ~** to stand back.

reculé, e [ʀəkyle] *a* remote.

reculer [ʀəkyle] *vi* to move back, back away; (*AUTO*) to reverse, back (up); (*fig*) (be on the) decline; to be losing ground; (*: se dérober*) to shrink back // *vt* to move back; to reverse, back (up); (*fig: possibilités, limites*) to extend; (*: date, décision*) to postpone.

reculons [ʀəkylɔ̃]: **à ~** *ad* backwards.

récupérer [ʀekypeʀe] *vt* to recover, get back; (*heures de travail*) to make up; (*déchets*) to salvage; (*délinquant etc*) to rehabilitate // *vi* to recover.

récurer [ʀekyʀe] *vt* to scour.

récuser [ʀekyze] *vt* to challenge; **se ~** *vi* to decline to give an opinion.

reçut *vb voir* recevoir.

recycler [ʀəsikle] *vt* (*SCOL*) to reorientate; (*employés*) to retrain; (*TECH*) to recycle.

rédacteur, trice [ʀedaktœʀ, -tʀis] *nm/f* (*journaliste*) writer; subeditor; (*d'ouvrage de référence*) editor, compiler; **~ en chef** chief editor; **~ publicitaire** copywriter.

rédaction [ʀedaksjɔ̃] *nf* writing; (*rédacteurs*) editorial staff; (*bureau*) editorial office(s); (*SCOL: devoir*) essay, composition.

reddition [ʀedisjɔ̃] *nf* surrender.

redemander [ʀədmɑ̃de] *vt* to ask again for; to ask for more of.

redescendre [ʀədesɑ̃dʀ(ə)] *vi* to go back down // *vt* (*pente etc*) to go down.

redevable [ʀədvabl(ə)] *a*: **être ~ de qch à qn** (*somme*) to owe sb sth; (*fig*) to be indebted to sb for sth.

redevance [ʀədvɑ̃s] *nf* (*TÉL*) rental

charge; (*TV*) licence fee.

rédiger [ʀediʒe] *vt* to write; (*contrat*) to draw up.

redire [ʀədiʀ] *vt* to repeat; **trouver à ~ à** to find fault with.

redoublé, e [ʀəduble] *a*: **à coups ~s** even harder, twice as hard.

redoubler [ʀəduble] *vi* (*tempête, violence*) to intensify; (*SCOL*) to repeat a year; **~ de** *vt* to be twice as + *adjectif*.

redoutable [ʀədutabl(ə)] *a* formidable, fearsome.

redouter [ʀədute] *vt* to fear; (*appréhender*) to dread.

redresser [ʀədʀese] *vt* (*arbre, mât*) to set upright; (*pièce tordue*) to straighten out; (*situation, économie*) to put right; **se ~** *vi* (*objet penché*) to right itself; (*personne*) to sit (*ou* stand) up (straight).

réduction [ʀedyksjɔ̃] *nf* reduction.

réduire [ʀeduiʀ] *vt* to reduce; (*prix, dépenses*) to cut, reduce; (*MÉD: fracture*) to set; **se ~ à** (*revenir à*) to boil down to; **se ~ en** (*se transformer en*) to be reduced to.

réduit [ʀedui] *nm* tiny room; recess.

rééducation [ʀeedykasjɔ̃] *nf* (*d'un membre*) re-education; (*de délinquants, d'un blessé*) rehabilitation; **~ de la parole** speech therapy.

réel, le [ʀeɛl] *a* real.

réellement [ʀeɛlmɑ̃] *ad* really.

réévaluer [ʀeevalɥe] *vt* to revalue.

réexpédier [ʀeɛkspedje] *vt* (*à l'envoyeur*) to return, send back; (*au destinataire*) to send on, forward.

refaire [ʀəfɛʀ] *vt* (*faire de nouveau, recommencer*) to do again; (*réparer, restaurer*) to do up.

réfection [ʀefɛksjɔ̃] *nf* repair.

réfectoire [ʀefɛktwaʀ] *nm* refectory.

référence [ʀefeʀɑ̃s] *nf* reference; **~s** (*recommandations*) reference *sg*.

référer [ʀefeʀe]: **se ~ à** *vt* to refer to; **en ~ à qn** to refer the matter to sb.

réfléchi, e [ʀefleʃi] *a* (*caractère*) thoughtful; (*action*) well-thought-out; (*LING*) reflexive.

réfléchir [ʀefleʃiʀ] *vt* to reflect // *vi* to think; **~ à** *ou* **sur** to think about.

reflet [ʀəflɛ] *nm* reflection; (*sur l'eau etc*) sheen *q*, glint.

refléter [ʀəflete] *vt* to reflect; **se ~** *vi* to be reflected.

réflexe [ʀeflɛks(ə)] *nm, a* reflex.

réflexion [ʀeflɛksjɔ̃] *nf* (*de la lumière etc, pensée*) reflection; (*fait de penser*) thought; (*remarque*) remark; **~ faite, à la ~** on reflection.

refluer [ʀəflɥe] *vi* to flow back; (*foule*) to surge back.

reflux [ʀəfly] *nm* (*de la mer*) ebb.

réforme [ʀefɔʀm(ə)] *nf* reform; (*REL*): **la R~** the Reformation.

réformer [ʀefɔʀme] vt to reform; (MIL) to declare unfit for service.

refouler [ʀəfule] vt (envahisseurs) to drive back; (liquide) to force back; (fig) to suppress; (PSYCH) to repress.

réfractaire [ʀefʀaktɛʀ] a: être ~ à to resist.

refrain [ʀəfʀɛ̃] nm (MUS) refrain, chorus; (air, fig) tune.

réfréner, refréner [ʀəfʀene, ʀefʀene] vt to curb, check.

réfrigérateur [ʀefʀiʒeʀatœʀ] nm refrigerator, fridge.

refroidir [ʀəfʀwadiʀ] vt to cool // vi to cool (down); se ~ vi (prendre froid) to catch a chill; (temps) to get cooler ou colder; (fig) to cool (off); **refroidissement** nm (grippe etc) chill.

refuge [ʀəfyʒ] nm refuge; (pour piétons) (traffic) island.

réfugié, e [ʀefyʒje] a, nm/f refugee.

réfugier [ʀefyʒje]: se ~ vi to take refuge.

refus [ʀəfy] nm refusal; ce n'est pas de ~ I won't say no, it's welcome.

refuser [ʀəfyze] vt to refuse; (SCOL: candidat) to fail; ~ qch à qn to refuse sb sth; ~ du monde to have to turn people away; se ~ à faire to refuse to do.

regagner [ʀəgaɲe] vt (argent, faveur) to win back; (lieu) to get back to; ~ le temps perdu to make up (for) lost time.

regain [ʀəgɛ̃] nm (renouveau): un ~ de renewed + nom.

régal [ʀegal] nm treat.

régaler [ʀegale]: se ~ vi to have a delicious meal; (fig) to enjoy o.s.

regard [ʀəgaʀ] nm (coup d'œil) look, glance; (expression) look (in one's eye); au ~ de (loi, morale) from the point of view of; en ~ (vis à vis) opposite; en ~ de in comparison with.

regardant, e [ʀəgaʀdɑ̃, -ɑ̃t] a: très/peu ~ (sur) quite fussy/very free (about); (économe) very tight-fisted/quite generous (with).

regarder [ʀəgaʀde] vt (examiner, observer, lire) to look at; (film, télévision, match) to watch; (envisager: situation, avenir) to view; (considérer: son intérêt etc) to be concerned with; (être orienté vers): ~ (vers) to face; (concerner) to concern // vi to look; ~ à vt (dépense) to be fussy ou over; ~ qn/qch comme to regard sb/sth as.

régie [ʀeʒi] nf (COMM, INDUSTRIE) state-owned company; (THÉÂTRE, CINÉMA) production; (RADIO, TV) control room.

regimber [ʀəʒɛ̃be] vi to balk, jib.

régime [ʀeʒim] nm (POL) régime; (ADMIN: carcéral, fiscal etc) system; (MÉD) diet; (TECH) (engine) speed; (fig) rate, pace; (de bananes, dattes) bunch; se mettre au/suivre un ~ to go on/be on a diet.

régiment [ʀeʒimɑ̃] nm regiment; (fig: fam): un ~ de an army of.

région [ʀeʒjɔ̃] nf region; **régional, e, aux** a regional.

régir [ʀeʒiʀ] vt to govern.

régisseur [ʀeʒisœʀ] nm (d'un domaine) steward; (CINÉMA, TV) assistant director; (THÉÂTRE) stage manager.

registre [ʀəʒistʀ(ə)] nm (livre) register; logbook; ledger; (MUS, LING) register.

réglage [ʀeglaʒ] nm adjustment; tuning.

règle [ʀɛgl(ə)] nf (instrument) ruler; (loi, prescription) rule; ~s nfpl (PHYSIOL) period sg; en ~ (papiers d'identité) in order; en ~ générale as a (general) rule; ~ à calcul slide rule.

réglé, e [ʀegle] a well-ordered; steady; (papier) ruled; (arrangé) settled.

règlement [ʀegləmɑ̃] nm (paiement) settlement; (arrêté) regulation; (règles, statuts) regulations pl, rules pl; **réglementaire** a conforming to the regulations; (tenue) regulation cpd.

réglementer [ʀegləmɑ̃te] vt to regulate.

régler [ʀegle] vt (mécanisme, machine) to regulate, adjust; (moteur) to tune; (thermostat etc) to set, adjust; (conflit, facture) to settle; (fournisseur) to settle up with.

réglisse [ʀeglis] nf liquorice.

règne [ʀɛɲ] nm (d'un roi etc, fig) reign; (BIO): le ~ végétal/animal the vegetable/animal kingdom.

régner [ʀeɲe] vi (roi) to rule, reign; (fig) to reign.

regorger [ʀəgɔʀʒe] vi: ~ de to overflow with, be bursting with.

regret [ʀəgʀɛ] nm regret; à ~ with regret; avec ~ regretfully; être au ~ de devoir faire to regret having to do.

regrettable [ʀəgʀetabl(ə)] a regrettable.

regretter [ʀəgʀete] vt to regret; (personne) to miss; je regrette I'm sorry.

regrouper [ʀəgʀupe] vt (grouper) to group together; (contenir) to include, comprise; se ~ vi to gather (together).

régulier, ière [ʀegylje, -jɛʀ] a (gén) regular; (vitesse, qualité) steady; (répartition, pression, paysage) even; (TRANSPORTS: ligne, service) scheduled, regular; (légal, réglementaire) lawful, in order; (fam: correct) straight, on the level; **régulièrement** ad regularly; steadily; evenly; normally.

rehausser [ʀoose] vt to heighten, raise.

rein [ʀɛ̃] nm kidney; ~s nmpl (dos) back sg.

reine [ʀɛn] nf queen.

reine-claude [ʀɛnklod] nf greengage.

réintégrer [ʀeɛ̃tegʀe] vt (lieu) to return to; (fonctionnaire) to reinstate.

rejaillir [ʀəʒajiʀ] vi to splash up; ~ sur to splash up onto; (fig) to rebound on; to fall upon.

rejet [ʀəʒɛ] *nm* (*action, aussi MÉD*) rejection.

rejeter [ʀəʒte] *vt* (*relancer*) to throw back; (*vomir*) to bring *ou* throw up; (*écarter*) to reject; (*déverser*) to throw out, discharge; ~ **la responsabilité de qch sur qn** to lay the responsibility for sth at sb's door.

rejoindre [ʀəʒwɛ̃dʀ(ə)] *vt* (*famille, régiment*) to rejoin, return to; (*lieu*) to get (back) to; (*suj: route*) to meet, join; (*rattraper*) to catch up (with); **se ~** *vi* to meet; **je te rejoins au café** I'll see *ou* meet you at the café.

réjouir [ʀeʒwiʀ] *vt* to delight; **se ~** *vi* to be delighted; to rejoice; **réjouissances** *nfpl* (*joie*) rejoicing *sg*; (*fête*) festivities.

relâche [ʀəlɑʃ] *nf*: **faire ~** *vi* (*CINÉMA*) to be closed; **sans ~** *ad* without respite *ou* a break.

relâché, e [ʀəlɑʃe] *a* loose, lax.

relâcher [ʀəlɑʃe] *vt* to release; (*étreinte*) to loosen; **se ~** *vi* to loosen; (*discipline*) to become slack *ou* lax; (*élève etc*) to slacken off.

relais [ʀəlɛ] *nm* (*SPORT*): **(course de) ~** relay (race); **équipe de ~** shift team; (*SPORT*) relay team; **prendre le ~ (de)** to take over (from); **~ routier** ≈ transport café (*Brit*), ≈ truck stop (*US*).

relancer [ʀəlɑ̃se] *vt* (*balle*) to throw back; (*moteur*) to restart; (*fig*) to boost, revive; (*personne*): **~ qn** to pester sb.

relater [ʀəlate] *vt* to relate, recount.

relatif, ive [ʀəlatif, -iv] *a* relative.

relation [ʀəlasjɔ̃] *nf* (*récit*) account, report; (*rapport*) relation(ship); **~s** *nfpl* (*rapports*) relations; relationship *sg*; (*connaissances*) connections; **être/entrer en ~(s) avec** to be/get in contact with.

relaxer [ʀəlakse] *vt* to relax; (*JUR*) to discharge; **se ~** *vi* to relax.

relayer [ʀəleje] *vt* (*collaborateur, coureur etc*) to relieve; **se ~** *vi* (*dans une activité*) to take it in turns.

reléguer [ʀəlege] *vt* to relegate.

relent(s) [ʀəlɑ̃] *nm(pl)* (foul) smell.

relevé, e [ʀəlve] *a* (*manches*) rolled-up; (*sauce*) highly-seasoned // *nm* (*lecture*) reading; (*liste*) statement; list; (*facture*) account; **~ de compte** bank statement.

relève [ʀəlɛv] *nf* relief; relief team (*ou* troops *pl*); **prendre la ~** to take over.

relever [ʀəlve] *vt* (*statue, meuble*) to stand up again; (*personne tombée*) to help up; (*vitre, niveau de vie*) to raise; (*col*) to turn up; (*style, conversation*) to elevate; (*plat, sauce*) to season; (*sentinelle, équipe*) to relieve; (*fautes, points*) to pick out; (*constater: traces etc*) to find, pick up; (*répliquer à: remarque*) to react to, reply to; (*: défi*) to accept, take up; (*noter: adresse etc*) to

take down, note; (*: plan*) to sketch; (*: cotes etc*) to plot; (*compteur*) to read; (*ramasser: cahiers*) to collect, take in; **~ de** *vt* (*maladie*) to be recovering from; (*être du ressort de*) to be a matter for; (*ADMIN: dépendre de*) to come under; (*fig*) to pertain to; **se ~** *vi* (*se remettre debout*) to get up; **~ qn de** (*fonctions*) to relieve sb of; **~ la tête** to look up; to hold up one's head.

relief [ʀəljɛf] *nm* relief; **~s** *nmpl* (*restes*) remains; **mettre en ~** (*fig*) to bring out, highlight.

relier [ʀəlje] *vt* to link up; (*livre*) to bind; **~ qch à** to link sth to.

religieux, euse [ʀəliʒjø, -øz] *a* religious // *nm* monk // *nf* nun; (*gâteau*) cream bun.

religion [ʀəliʒjɔ̃] *nf* religion; (*piété, dévotion*) faith.

relire [ʀəliʀ] *vt* (*à nouveau*) to reread, read again; (*vérifier*) to read over.

reliure [ʀəljyʀ] *nf* binding.

reluire [ʀəlɥiʀ] *vi* to gleam.

remanier [ʀəmanje] *vt* to reshape, recast; (*POL*) to reshuffle.

remarquable [ʀəmaʀkabl(ə)] *a* remarkable.

remarque [ʀəmaʀk(ə)] *nf* remark; (*écrite*) note.

remarquer [ʀəmaʀke] *vt* (*voir*) to notice; **se ~** *vi* to be noticeable; **faire ~ (à qn)** que to point out (to sb) that; **faire ~ qch (à qn)** to point sth out (to sb); **remarquez, ...** mind you ....

remblai [ʀɑ̃blɛ] *nm* embankment.

rembourrer [ʀɑ̃buʀe] *vt* to stuff; (*dossier, vêtement, souliers*) to pad.

remboursement [ʀɑ̃buʀsəmɑ̃] *nm* repayment; **envoi contre ~** cash on delivery.

rembourser [ʀɑ̃buʀse] *vt* to pay back, repay.

remède [ʀəmɛd] *nm* (*médicament*) medicine; (*traitement, fig*) remedy, cure.

remémorer [ʀəmemɔʀe]: **se ~** *vt* to recall, recollect.

remerciements [ʀəmɛʀsimɑ̃] *nmpl* thanks.

remercier [ʀəmɛʀsje] *vt* to thank; (*congédier*) to dismiss; **~ qn de/d'avoir fait** to thank sb for/for having done.

remettre [ʀəmɛtʀ(ə)] *vt* (*vêtement*): **~ qch** to put sth back on; (*replacer*): **~ qch quelque part** to put sth back somewhere; (*ajouter*): **~ du sel/un sucre** to add more salt/another lump of sugar; (*ajourner*): **~ qch (à)** to postpone sth (until); **~ qch à qn** (*rendre, restituer*) to give sth back to sb; (*donner, c.nfier: paquet, argent*) to hand over sth to sb, deliver sth to sb; (*: prix, décoration*) to present sb with sth; **se ~** *vi* to get better, recover; **se ~ de** to recover from;

get over; **s'en ~ à** to leave it (up) to.

remise [ʀəmiz] *nf* delivery; presentation; (*rabais*) discount; (*local*) shed; **~ en jeu** (*FOOTBALL*) throw-in; **~ de peine** reduction of sentence.

remontant [ʀəmɔ̃tɑ̃] *nm* tonic, pick-me-up.

remonte-pente [ʀəmɔ̃tpɑ̃t] *nm* skilift.

remonter [ʀəmɔ̃te] *vi* to go back up; (*jupe*) to ride up // *vt* (*pente*) to go up; (*fleuve*) to sail (*ou* swim *etc*) up; (*manches, pantalon*) to roll up; (*col*) to turn up; (*niveau, limite*) to raise; (*fig: personne*) to buck up; (*moteur, meuble*) to put back together, reassemble; (*montre, mécanisme*) to wind up; **~ le moral à qn** to raise sb's spirits; **~ à** (*dater de*) to date *ou* go back to.

remontrance [ʀəmɔ̃tʀɑ̃s] *nf* reproof, reprimand.

remontrer [ʀəmɔ̃tʀe] *vt* (*fig*): **en ~ à** to prove one's superiority over.

remords [ʀəmɔʀ] *nm* remorse *q*; **avoir des ~** to feel remorse.

remorque [ʀəmɔʀk(ə)] *nf* trailer; **être en ~** to be on tow; **remorquer** *vt* to tow; **remorqueur** *nm* tug(boat).

remous [ʀəmu] *nm* (*d'un navire*) (back)wash *q*; (*de rivière*) swirl, eddy // *nmpl* (*fig*) stir *sg*.

remparts [ʀɑ̃paʀ] *nmpl* walls, ramparts.

remplaçant, e [ʀɑ̃plasɑ̃, -ɑ̃t] *nm/f* replacement, stand-in; (*THÉÂTRE*) understudy; (*SCOL*) supply teacher.

remplacement [ʀɑ̃plasmɑ̃] *nm* replacement; (*job*) replacement work *q*.

remplacer [ʀɑ̃plase] *vt* to replace; (*tenir lieu de*) to take the place of; **~ qch/qn par** to replace sth/sb with.

rempli, e [ʀɑ̃pli] *a* (*emploi du temps*) full, busy; **~ de** full of, filled with.

remplir [ʀɑ̃pliʀ] *vt* to fill (up); (*questionnaire*) to fill out *ou* up; (*obligations, fonction, condition*) to fulfil; **se ~** *vi* to fill up.

remporter [ʀɑ̃pɔʀte] *vt* (*marchandise*) to take away; (*fig*) to win, achieve.

remuant, e [ʀəmɥɑ̃, -ɑ̃t] *a* restless.

remue-ménage [ʀəmɥmena ʒ] *nm inv* commotion.

remuer [ʀəmɥe] *vt* to move; (*café, sauce*) to stir // *vi*, **se ~** *vi* to move.

rémunérer [ʀemyneʀe] *vt* to remunerate.

renard [ʀənaʀ] *nm* fox.

renchérir [ʀɑ̃ʃeʀiʀ] *vi* (*fig*): **~ (sur)** to add something (to).

rencontre [ʀɑ̃kɔ̃tʀ(ə)] *nf* meeting; (*imprévue*) encounter; **aller à la ~ de qn** to go and meet sb.

rencontrer [ʀɑ̃kɔ̃tʀe] *vt* to meet; (*mot, expression*) to come across; (*difficultés*) to meet with; **se ~** *vi* to meet; (*véhicules*) to collide.

rendement [ʀɑ̃dmɑ̃] *nm* (*d'un*

travailleur, d'une machine) output; (*d'une culture*) yield; (*d'un investissement*) return; **à plein ~** at full capacity.

rendez-vous [ʀɑ̃devu] *nm* (*rencontre*) appointment; (*: d'amoureux*) date; (*lieu*) meeting place; **donner ~ à qn** to arrange to meet sb; **avoir/prendre ~** (**avec**) to have/make an appointment (with).

rendre [ʀɑ̃dʀ(ə)] *vt* (*livre, argent etc*) to give back, return; (*otages, visite etc*) to return; (*sang, aliments*) to bring up; (*exprimer, traduire*) to render; (*faire devenir*): **~ qn célèbre/qch possible** to make sb famous/sth possible; **se ~** *vi* (*capituler*) to surrender, give o.s. up; (*aller*): **se ~ quelque part** to go somewhere; **se ~ compte de qch** to realize sth.

rênes [ʀɛn] *nfpl* reins.

renfermé, e [ʀɑ̃fɛʀme] *a* (*fig*) withdrawn // *nm*: **sentir le ~** to smell stuffy.

renfermer [ʀɑ̃fɛʀme] *vt* to contain.

renflement [ʀɑ̃fləmɑ̃] *nm* bulge.

renflouer [ʀɑ̃flue] *vt* to refloat; (*fig*) to set back on its (*ou* his/her *etc*) feet.

renfoncement [ʀɑ̃fɔ̃smɑ̃] *nm* recess.

renforcer [ʀɑ̃fɔʀse] *vt* to reinforce.

renfort [ʀɑ̃fɔʀ]: **~s** *nmpl* reinforcements; **à grand ~ de** with a great deal of.

renfrogné, e [ʀɑ̃fʀɔɲe] *a* sullen.

rengaine [ʀɑ̃gɛn] *nf* (*péj*) old tune.

renier [ʀənje] *vt* (*parents*) to disown, repudiate; (*foi*) to renounce.

renifler [ʀənifle] *vi, vt* to sniff.

renne [ʀɛn] *nm* reindeer *inv*.

renom [ʀənɔ̃] *nm* reputation; (*célébrité*) renown; **renommé, e** *a* celebrated, renowned // *nf* fame.

renoncer [ʀənɔ̃se] *vi*: **~ à** *vt* to give up; **~ à faire** to give up the idea of doing.

renouer [ʀənwe] *vt*: **~ avec** (*tradition*) to revive; (*habitude*) to take up again; **~ avec qn** to take up with sb again.

renouveler [ʀənuvle] *vt* to renew; (*exploit, méfait*) to repeat; **se ~** *vi* (*incident*) to recur, happen again; **renouvellement** *nm* renewal; recurrence.

rénover [ʀenɔve] *vt* (*immeuble*) to renovate, do up; (*enseignement*) to reform; (*quartier*) to redevelop.

renseignement [ʀɑ̃sɛɲmɑ̃] *nm* information *q*, piece of information; (**guichet des**) **~s** information desk.

renseigner [ʀɑ̃sɛɲe] *vt*: **~ qn (sur)** to give information to sb (about); **se ~** *vi* to ask for information, make inquiries.

rentable [ʀɑ̃tabl(ə)] *a* profitable.

rente [ʀɑ̃t] *nf* income; pension; government stock *ou* bond; **rentier, ière** *nm/f* person of private means.

rentrée [ʀɑ̃tʀe] *nf*: **~ d'argent** cash *q* coming in; **la ~ (des classes)** the start of the new school year.

rentrer [ʀɑ̃tʀe] vi (entrer de nouveau) to go (ou come) back in; (entrer) to go (ou come) in; (revenir chez soi) to go (ou come) (back) home; (air, clou: pénétrer) to go in; (revenu, argent) to come in // (foins) to bring in; (véhicule) to put away; (chemise dans pantalon etc) to tuck in; (griffes) to draw in; (fig: larmes, colère etc) to hold back; ~ le ventre to pull in one's stomach; ~ dans (heurter) to crash into; ~ dans l'ordre to be back to normal; ~ dans ses frais to recover one's expenses.

renversant, e [ʀɑ̃vɛʀsɑ̃, -ɑ̃t] a astounding.

renverse [ʀɑ̃vɛʀs(ə)]: à la ~ ad backwards.

renverser [ʀɑ̃vɛʀse] vt (faire tomber: chaise, verre) to knock over, overturn; (piéton) to knock down; (liquide, contenu) to spill, upset; (retourner) to turn upside down; (: ordre des mots etc) to reverse; (fig: gouvernement etc) to overthrow; (stupéfier) to bowl over; se ~ vi to fall over; to overturn; to spill.

renvoi [ʀɑ̃vwa] nm (référence) cross-reference; (éructation) belch.

renvoyer [ʀɑ̃vwaje] vt to send back; (congédier) to dismiss; (lumière) to reflect; (son) to echo; (ajourner): ~ qch (à) to put sth off ou postpone sth (until); ~ qn à (fig) to refer sb to.

repaire [ʀəpɛʀ] nm den.

répandre [ʀepɑ̃dʀ(ə)] vt (renverser) to spill; (étaler, diffuser) to spread; (lumière) to shed; (chaleur, odeur) to give off; se ~ vi to spill; to spread; **répandu, e** a (opinion, usage) widespread.

réparation [ʀepaʀasjɔ̃] nf repair.

réparer [ʀepaʀe] vt to repair; (fig: offense) to make up for, atone for; (: oubli, erreur) to put right.

repartie [ʀəpaʀti] nf retort; avoir de la ~ to be quick at repartee.

repartir [ʀəpaʀtiʀ] vi to set off again; to leave again; (fig) to get going again; ~ à zéro to start from scratch (again).

répartir [ʀepaʀtiʀ] vt (pour attribuer) to share out; (pour disperser, disposer) to divide up; (poids, chaleur) to distribute; se ~ vt (travail, rôles) to share out between themselves; **répartition** nf sharing out; dividing up; distribution.

repas [ʀəpa] nm meal.

repasser [ʀəpase] vi to come (ou go) back // vt (vêtement, tissu) to iron; (examen) to retake, resit; (film) to show again; (leçon, rôle: revoir) to go over (again).

repêcher [ʀəpeʃe] vt (noyé) to recover the body of; (candidat) to pass (by inflating marks).

repentir [ʀəpɑ̃tiʀ] nm repentance; se ~ vi to repent; se ~ de to repent of.

répercuter [ʀepɛʀkyte] vt (information, hausse des prix) to pass on; se ~ vi (bruit) to reverberate; (fig): se ~ sur to have repercussions on.

repère [ʀəpɛʀ] nm mark; (monument etc) landmark.

repérer [ʀəpeʀe] vt (erreur, connaissance) to spot; (abri, ennemi) to locate; se ~ vi to find one's way about.

répertoire [ʀepɛʀtwaʀ] nm (liste) (alphabetical) list; (carnet) index notebook; (d'un artiste) repertoire.

répéter [ʀepete] vt to repeat; (préparer: leçon: aussi vi) to learn, go over; (THÉÂTRE) to rehearse; se ~ vi (redire) to repeat o.s.; (se reproduire) to be repeated, recur.

répétition [ʀepetisjɔ̃] nf repetition; (THÉÂTRE) rehearsal; ~ générale final dress rehearsal.

répit [ʀepi] nm respite.

replet, ète [ʀəplɛ, -ɛt] a chubby.

replier [ʀəplije] vt (rabattre) to fold down ou over; se ~ vi (troupes, armée) to withdraw, fall back.

réplique [ʀeplik] nf (repartie, fig) reply; (THÉÂTRE) line; (copie) replica.

répliquer [ʀeplike] vi to reply; (riposter) to retaliate.

répondre [ʀepɔ̃dʀ(ə)] vi to answer, reply; (freins, mécanisme) to respond; ~ à vt to reply to, answer; (avec impertinence): ~ à qn to answer sb back; (affection, salut) to return; (provocation, suj: mécanisme etc) to respond to; (correspondre à: besoin) to answer; (: conditions) to meet; (: description) to match; ~ de to answer for.

réponse [ʀepɔ̃s] nf answer, reply; en ~ à in reply to.

reportage [ʀəpɔʀtaʒ] nm (bref) report; (écrit: documentaire) story; article; (en direct) commentary; (genre, activité): le ~ reporting.

reporter nm [ʀəpɔʀtɛʀ] reporter // vt [ʀəpɔʀte] (total): ~ qch sur to carry sth forward ou over to; (ajourner): ~ qch (à) to postpone sth (until); (transférer): ~ qch sur to transfer sth to; se ~ à (époque) to think back to; (document) to refer to.

repos [ʀəpo] nm rest; (fig) peace (and quiet); peace of mind; (MIL): ~! stand at ease!; en ~ at rest; de tout ~ safe.

reposant, e [ʀəpozɑ̃, -ɑ̃t] a restful.

reposer [ʀəpoze] vt (verre, livre) to put down; (délasser) to rest; (problème) to reformulate // vi (liquide, pâte) to settle, rest; ~ sur to be built on; (fig) to rest on; se ~ vi to rest; se ~ sur qn to rely on sb.

repoussant, e [ʀəpusɑ̃, -ɑ̃t] a repulsive.

repousser [ʀəpuse] vi to grow again // vt to repel, repulse; (offre) to turn down, reject; (*tiroir, personne*) to push back; (*différer*) to put back.

reprendre [Rəprãdr(ə)] *vt* (*prisonnier, ville*) to recapture; (*objet prêté, donné*) to take back; (*chercher*): **je viendrai te ~ à 4h** I'll come and fetch you at 4; (*se resservir de*): **~ du pain/un œuf** to take (*ou eat*) more bread/another egg; (*firme, entreprise*) to take over; (*travail, promenade*) to resume; (*emprunter: argument, idée*) to take up, use; (*refaire: article etc*) to go over again; (*jupe etc*) to alter; (*émission, pièce*) to put on again; (*réprimander*) to tell off; (*corriger*) to correct // *vi* (*classes, pluie*) to start (up) again; (*activités, travaux, combats*) to resume, start (up) again; (*affaires, industrie*) to pick up; (*dire*): **reprit-il** he went on; **se ~** *vi* (*se ressaisir*) to recover; **s'y ~** to make another attempt; **~ des forces** to recover one's strength; **~ courage** to take new heart; **~ la route** to set off again; **~ haleine** *ou* **son souffle** to get one's breath back.

représailles [Rəprezɑj] *nfpl* reprisals.

représentant, e [Rəprezãtã, -ãt] *nm/f* representative.

représentation [Rəprezãtasjɔ̃] *nf* (*symbole, image*) representation; (*spectacle*) performance.

représenter [Rəprezãte] *vt* to represent; (*donner: pièce, opéra*) to perform; **se ~** *vt* (*se figurer*) to imagine; to visualize.

répression [Represjɔ̃] *nf* (*voir réprimer*) suppression; repression.

réprimer [Reprime] *vt* (*émotions*) to suppress; (*peuple etc*) to repress.

repris [Rəpri] *nm*: **~ de justice** ex-prisoner, ex-convict.

reprise [Rəpriz] *nf* (*recommencement*) resumption; recovery; (*TV*) repeat; (*CINÉMA*) rerun; (*AUTO*) acceleration *q*; (*COMM*) trade-in, part exchange; **à plusieurs ~s** on several occasions.

repriser [Rəprize] *vt* to darn; to mend.

reproche [Rəprɔʃ] *nm* (*remontrance*) reproach; **faire des ~s à qn** to reproach sb; **sans ~(s)** beyond reproach.

reprocher [Rəprɔʃe] *vt*: **~ qch à qn** to reproach *ou* blame sb for sth; **~ qch à** (*machine, théorie*) to have sth against.

reproduction [Rəprɔdyksjɔ̃] *nf* reproduction.

reproduire [Rəprɔdɥir] *vt* to reproduce; **se ~** *vi* (*BIO*) to reproduce; (*recommencer*) to recur, re-occur.

reptile [Reptil] *nm* reptile.

repu, e [Rəpy] *a* satisfied, sated.

républicain, e [Repyblikẽ, -ɛn] *a, nm/f* republican.

république [Repyblik] *nf* republic.

répugnant, e [Repyɲã, -ãt] *a* repulsive; loathsome.

répugner [Repyɲe]: **~ à qn** *vt*: **~ à qn to** repel *ou* disgust sb; **~ à faire** to be loath *ou* reluctant to do.

réputation [Repytasjɔ̃] *nf* reputation; **réputé, e** *a* renowned.

requérir [Rəkerir] *vt* (*nécessiter*) to require, call for; (*JUR: peine*) to call for, demand.

requête [Rəkɛt] *nf* request; (*JUR*) petition.

requin [Rəkẽ] *nm* shark.

requis, e [Rəki, -iz] *a* required.

R.E.R. *sigle m* (= *réseau express régional*) *Greater Paris high speed train service.*

rescapé, e [Rɛskape] *nm/f* survivor.

rescousse [Rɛskus] *nf*: **aller à la ~ de qn** to go to sb's aid *ou* rescue.

réseau, x [Rezo] *nm* network.

réservation [Rezɛrvasjɔ̃] *nf* booking, reservation.

réserve [Rezɛrv(ə)] *nf* (*retenue*) reserve; (*entrepôt*) storeroom; (*restriction, d'Indiens*) reservation; (*de pêche, chasse*) preserve; **sous ~ de** subject to; **sans ~** unreservedly; **de ~** (*provisions etc*) in reserve.

réservé, e [Rezɛrve] *a* (*discret*) reserved; (*chasse, pêche*) private.

réserver [Rezɛrve] *vt* (*gén*) to reserve; (*chambre, billet etc*) to book, reserve; (*garder*) to keep *ou* save; **~ qch pour/à** to keep *ou* save sth for; **~ qch à qn** to reserve (*ou* book) sth for sb.

réservoir [Rezɛrvwar] *nm* tank.

résidence [Rezidãs] *nf* residence; **~ secondaire** second home; **(en) surveillée** (under) house arrest; **résidentiel, le** *a* residential.

résider [Rezide] *vi*: **~ à/dans/en** to reside in; **~ dans** (*fig*) to lie in.

résidu [Rezidy] *nm* residue *q*.

résigner [Rezine] *vt*: **se ~** (*à qch/à faire*) to resign o.s. (to sth/to doing).

résilier [Rezilje] *vt* to terminate.

résistance [Rezistãs] *nf* resistance; (*de réchaud, bouilloire: fil*) element.

résistant, e [Rezistã, -ãt] *a* (*personne*) robust, tough; (*matériau*) strong, hardwearing.

résister [Reziste] *vi* to resist; **~ à** (*assaut, tentation*) to resist; (*effort, souffrance*) to withstand; (*désobéir à*) to stand up to, oppose.

résolu, e [Rezɔly] *pp de* **résoudre** // *a*: **être ~ à qch/faire** to be set upon sth/doing.

résolution [Rezɔlysjɔ̃] *nf* solving; (*fermeté, décision*) resolution.

résolve *etc vb voir* **résoudre**.

résonner [Rezɔne] *vi* (*cloche, pas*) to reverberate, resound; (*salle*) to be resonant; **~ de** to resound with.

résorber [Rezɔrbe]: **se ~** *vi* (*fig*) to be reduced; to be absorbed.

résoudre [Rezudr(ə)] *vt* to solve; **se ~ à**

faire to bring o.s. to do.
respect [Rɛspɛ] nm respect; tenir en ~ to keep at bay.
respecter [Rɛspɛkte] vt to respect.
respectueux, euse [Rɛspɛktyø, -øz] a respectful; ~ de respectful of.
respiration [Rɛspiʀasjɔ̃] nf breathing q; ~ artificielle artificial respiration.
respirer [Rɛspiʀe] vi to breathe; (fig) to get one's breath; to breathe again // vt to breathe (in), inhale; (manifester: santé, calme etc) to exude.
resplendir [Rɛsplɑ̃diʀ] vi to shine; (fig): ~ (de) to be radiant (with).
responsabilité [Rɛspɔ̃sabilite] nf responsibility; (légale) liability.
responsable [Rɛspɔ̃sabl(ə)] a responsible // nm/f (du ravitaillement etc) person in charge; (de parti, syndicat) official; ~ de responsible for; (chargé de) in charge of, responsible for.
ressaisir [Rəsɛziʀ]: se ~ vi to regain one's self-control.
ressasser [Rəsase] vt to keep going over.
ressemblance [Rəsɑ̃blɑ̃s] nf resemblance, similarity, likeness.
ressemblant, e [Rəsɑ̃blɑ̃, -ɑ̃t] a (portrait) lifelike, true to life.
ressembler [Rəsɑ̃ble]: ~ à vt to be like; to resemble; (visuellement) to look like; se ~ vi to be (ou look) alike.
ressemeler [Rəsəmle] vt to (re)sole.
ressentiment [Rəsɑ̃timɑ̃] nm resentment.
ressentir [Rəsɑ̃tiʀ] vt to feel; se ~ de to feel (ou show) the effects of.
resserrer [Rəseʀe] vt (nœud, boulon) to tighten (up); (fig: liens) to strengthen; se ~ vi (vallée) to narrow.
resservir [Rəseʀviʀ] vi to do ou serve again // vt: ~ qn (d'un plat) to give sb a second helping (of a dish).
ressort [RəsɔR] nm (pièce) spring; (force morale) spirit; (recours): en dernier ~ as a last resort; (compétence): être du ~ de to fall within the competence of.
ressortir [RəsɔRtiʀ] vi to go (ou come) out (again); (contraster) to stand out; ~ de to emerge from; faire ~ (fig: souligner) to bring out.
ressortissant, e [RəsɔRtisɑ̃, -ɑ̃t] nm/f national.
ressource [RəsuRs(ə)] nf: avoir la ~ de to have the possibility of; leur seule ~ était de the only course open to them was to; ~s nfpl resources.
ressusciter [Resysite] vt (fig) to revive, bring back // vi to rise (from the dead).
restant, e [Rɛstɑ̃, -ɑ̃t] a remaining // nm: le ~ (de) the remainder (of); un ~ de (de trop) some left-over.
restaurant [RɛstɔRɑ̃] nm restaurant.
restauration [RɛstɔRasjɔ̃] nf restoration; (hôtellerie) catering; ~ rapide fast

food.
restaurer [RɛstɔRe] vt to restore; se ~ vi to have something to eat.
reste [Rɛst(ə)] nm (restant): le ~ (de) the rest (of); (de trop): un ~ (de) some left over; (vestige): un ~ de a remnant ou last trace of; (MATH) remainder; ~s nmpl left-overs; (d'une cité etc, dépouille mortelle) remains; du ~, au ~ ad besides, moreover.
rester [Rɛste] vi to stay, remain; (subsister) to remain, be left; (durer) to last, live on // vb impersonnel: il reste du pain/2 œufs there's some bread/there are 2 eggs left (over); il me reste assez de temps I have enough time left; ce qui reste à faire what remains to be done; restons-en là let's leave it at that.
restituer [Rɛstitɥe] vt (objet, somme): ~ qch (à qn) to return sth (to sb); (TECH) to release; (: son) to reproduce.
restoroute [RɛstɔRut] nm motorway (Brit) ou highway (US) restaurant.
restreindre [Rɛstʀɛ̃dʀ(ə)] vt to restrict, limit.
restriction [Rɛstʀiksjɔ̃] nf restriction; ~s (mentales) reservations.
résultat [Rezylta] nm result; (d'élection etc) results pl.
résulter [Rezylte]: ~ de vt to result from, be the result of.
résumé [Rezyme] nm summary, résumé.
résumer [Rezyme] vt (texte) to summarize; (récapituler) to sum up; se ~ à to come down to.
résurrection [RezyRɛksjɔ̃] nf resurrection; (fig) revival.
rétablir [Retabliʀ] vt to restore, re-establish; se ~ vi (guérir) to recover; (silence, calme) to return, be restored; (SPORT) pull-up.
rétablissement nm restoring; recovery; (SPORT) pull-up.
retaper [Rətape] vt (maison, voiture etc) to do up; (fam: revigorer) to buck up; (redactylographier) to retype.
retard [Rətaʀ] nm (d'une personne attendue) lateness q; (sur l'horaire, un programme) delay; (fig: scolaire, mental etc) backwardness; en ~ (de 2 heures) (2 hours) late; avoir du ~ to be late; (sur un programme) to be behind (schedule); prendre du ~ (train, avion) to be delayed; (montre) to lose (time); sans ~ ad without delay.
retardement [RətaʀdəmɑJ]: à ~ a delayed action cpd; bombe à ~ time bomb.
retarder [Rətaʀde] vt (sur un horaire): ~ qn (d'une heure) to delay sb (an hour); (départ, date): ~ qch (de 2 jours) to put sth back (2 days), delay sth (for ou by 2 days); (horloge) to put back // vi (montre) to be slow; to lose (time).
retenir [Rətniʀ] vt (garder, retarder) to keep, detain; (maintenir: objet qui glisse, fig: colère, larmes) to hold back;

(*: objet suspendu*) to hold; (*fig: empêcher d'agir*): ~ qn (de faire) to hold sb back (from doing); (*se rappeler*) to retain; (*réserver*) to reserve; (*accepter*) to accept; (*prélever*): ~ qch (sur) to deduct sth (from); se ~ *vi* (*se raccrocher*): se ~ à to hold onto; (*se contenir*): se ~ de faire to restrain o.s. from doing; ~ son souffle to hold one's breath.

retentir [ʀətɑ̃tiʀ] *vi* to ring out; (*salle*): ~ de to ring *ou* resound with.

retentissant, e [ʀətɑ̃tisɑ̃, -ɑ̃t] *a* resounding; (*fig*) impact-making.

retentissement [ʀətɑ̃tismɑ̃] *nm* repercussion; effect, impact; stir.

retenue [ʀətny] *nf* (*prélèvement*) deduction; (*SCOL*) detention; (*modération*) (self-)restraint; (*réserve*) reserve, reticence.

réticence [ʀetisɑ̃s] *nf* hesitation, reluctance *q*.

rétine [ʀetin] *nf* retina.

retiré, e [ʀətiʀe] *a* secluded; remote.

retirer [ʀətiʀe] *vt* to withdraw; (*vêtement, lunettes*) to take off, remove; (*extraire*): ~ qch de to take sth out of, remove sth from; (*reprendre: bagages, billets*) to collect, pick up.

retombées [ʀətɔ̃be] *nfpl* (*radioactives*) fallout *sg*; (*fig*) fallout; spin-offs.

retomber [ʀətɔ̃be] *vi* (*à nouveau*) to fall again; (*atterrir: après un saut etc*) to land; (*tomber, redescendre*) to fall back; (*pendre*) to fall, hang (down); (*échoir*): ~ sur qn to fall on sb.

rétorquer [ʀetɔʀke] *vt*: ~ (à qn) que to retort (to sb) that.

retors, e [ʀətɔʀ, -ɔʀs(ə)] *a* wily.

rétorsion [ʀetɔʀsjɔ̃] *nf*: mesures de ~ reprisals.

retoucher [ʀətuʃe] *vt* (*photographie*) to touch up; (*texte, vêtement*) to alter.

retour [ʀətuʀ] *nm* return; au ~ when we (*ou they etc*) get (*ou got*) back; (*en route*) on the way back; être de ~ (de) to be back (from); par ~ du courrier by return of post.

retourner [ʀətuʀne] *vt* (*dans l'autre sens: matelas, crêpe, foin, terre*) to turn (over); (*: caisse*) to turn upside down; (*: sac, vêtement*) to turn inside out; (*émouvoir: personne*) to shake; (*renvoyer, restituer*): ~ qch à qn to return sth to sb // *vi* (*aller, revenir*): ~ quelque part/à to go back *ou* return somewhere/to; ~ à (*état, activité*) to return to, go back to; se ~ *vi* to turn over; (*tourner la tête*) to turn round; se ~ contre (*fig*) to turn against; savoir de quoi il retourne to know what it is all about.

retracer [ʀətʀase] *vt* to relate, recount.

retrait [ʀətʀɛ] *nm* (*voir retirer*) withdrawal; collection; en ~ set back; ~ du permis (de conduire) disqualification

from driving (*Brit*), revocation of driver's license (*US*).

retraite [ʀətʀɛt] *nf* (*d'une armée, REL, refuge*) retreat; (*d'un employé*) retirement; (*revenu*) pension; prendre sa ~ to retire; ~ anticipée early retirement; **retraité, e** *a* retired // *nm/f* pensioner.

retrancher [ʀətʀɑ̃ʃe] *vt* (*passage, détails*) to take out, remove; (*nombre, somme*): ~ qch de to take *ou* deduct sth from; (*couper*) to cut off; se ~ **derrière/dans** to take refuge behind/in.

retransmettre [ʀətʀɑ̃smɛtʀ(ə)] *vt* (*RADIO*) to broadcast; (*TV*) to show.

rétrécir [ʀetʀesiʀ] *vt* (*vêtement*) to take in // *vi* to shrink; se ~ *vi* to narrow.

rétribution [ʀetʀibysjɔ̃] *nf* payment.

rétro [ʀetʀo] *a inv*: la mode ~ the nostalgia vogue.

rétrograde [ʀetʀoɡʀad] *a* reactionary, backward-looking.

rétrograder [ʀetʀoɡʀade] *vi* (*économie*) to regress; (*AUTO*) to change down.

rétroprojecteur [ʀetʀopʀoʒɛktœʀ] *nm* overhead projector.

rétrospective [ʀetʀospɛktiv] *nf*; retrospective exhibition/season; ~ment *ad* in retrospect.

retrousser [ʀətʀuse] *vt* to roll up.

retrouvailles [ʀətʀuvaj] *nfpl* reunion *sg*.

retrouver [ʀətʀuve] *vt* (*fugitif, objet perdu*) to find; (*occasion*) to find again; (*calme, santé*) to regain; (*revoir*) to see again; (*rejoindre*) to meet (again), join; se ~ *vi* to meet; (*s'orienter*) to find one's way; se ~ quelque part to find o.s. somewhere; s'y ~ (*rentrer dans ses frais*) to break even.

rétroviseur [ʀetʀovizœʀ] *nm* (rear-view) mirror.

réunion [ʀeynjɔ̃] *nf* bringing together; joining; (*séance*) meeting.

réunir [ʀeyniʀ] *vt* (*convoquer*) to call together; (*rassembler*) to gather together; (*cumuler*) to combine; (*rapprocher*) to bring together (again), reunite; (*rattacher*) to join (together); se ~ *vi* to rencontrer) to meet.

réussi, e [ʀeysi] *a* successful.

réussir [ʀeysiʀ] *vi* to succeed, be successful; (*à un examen*) to pass; (*plante, culture*) to thrive, do well // *vt* to make a success of; ~ à faire to succeed in doing; ~ à qn to go right for sb; (*aliment*) to agree with sb.

réussite [ʀeysit] *nf* success; (*CARTES*) patience.

revaloir [ʀəvalwaʀ] *vt*: je vous revaudrai cela I'll repay you some day; (*en mal*) I'll pay you back for this.

revaloriser [ʀəvalɔʀize] *vt* (*monnaie*) to revalue; (*salaires*) to raise the level of.

revanche [ʀəvɑ̃ʃ] *nf* revenge; en ~ on the other hand.

rêve [rɛv] nm dream; (activité psychique): le ~ dreaming.

revêche [rəvɛʃ] a surly, sour-tempered.

réveil [revɛj] nm (d'un dormeur) waking up q; (fig) awakening; (pendule) alarm (clock); (MIL) reveille; **au ~** on waking (up).

réveille-matin [revɛjmatɛ̃] nm inv alarm clock.

réveiller [reveje] vt (personne) to wake up; (fig) to awaken, revive; **se ~** vi to wake up; (fig) to reawaken.

réveillon [revɛjɔ̃] nm Christmas Eve; (de la Saint-Sylvestre) New Year's Eve; **réveillonner** vi to celebrate Christmas Eve (ou New Year's Eve).

révélateur, trice [revelatœr, -tris] a: ~ (de qch) revealing (sth) // nm (PHOTO) developer.

révéler [revele] vt (gén) to reveal; (faire connaître au public): ~ qn/qch to make sb/sth widely known, bring sb/sth to the public's notice; **se ~** vi to be revealed, reveal itself // vb avec attribut to prove (to be).

revenant, e [rəvnɑ̃, -ɑ̃t] nm/f ghost.

revendeur, euse [rəvɑ̃dœr, -øz] nm/f (détaillant) retailer; (d'occasions) secondhand dealer.

revendication [rəvɑ̃dikasjɔ̃] nf claim, demand; **journée de ~** day of action.

revendiquer [rəvɑ̃dike] vt to claim, demand; (responsabilité) to claim.

revendre [rəvɑ̃dr(ə)] vt (d'occasion) to resell; (détailler) to sell; **à ~** ad (en abondance) to spare.

revenir [rəvnir] vi to come back; (CULIN): faire ~ to brown; (coûter): ~ cher/à 100 F (à qn) to cost (sb) a lot/100 F; ~ à (études, projet) to return to, go back to; (équivaloir à) to amount to; ~ à qn (part, honneur) to go to sb, be sb's; (souvenir, nom) to come back to sb; ~ de (fig: maladie, étonnement) to recover from; ~ sur (question, sujet) to go back over; (engagement) to go back on; ~ à la charge to return to the attack; ~ à soi to come round; **n'en pas ~**: je n'en reviens pas I can't get over it; ~ sur ses pas to retrace one's steps; cela revient à dire que/au même it amounts to saying that/the same thing.

revenu [rəvny] nm income; (de l'État) revenue; (d'un capital) yield; ~s nmpl income sg.

rêver [reve] vi, vt to dream; ~ de/à to dream of.

réverbère [reverbɛr] nm street lamp ou light.

réverbérer [reverbere] vt to reflect.

révérence [reverɑ̃s] nf (salut) bow; (: de femme) curtsey.

rêverie [revri] nf daydreaming q, daydream.

revers [rəver] nm (de feuille, main)

back; (d'étoffe) wrong side; (de pièce, médaille) back, reverse; (TENNIS, PING-PONG) backhand; (de veston) lapel; (de pantalon) turn-up; (fig: échec) setback.

revêtement [rəvɛtmɑ̃] nm (de paroi) facing; (des sols) flooring; (de chaussée) surface; (de tuyau etc: enduit) coating.

revêtir [rəvetir] vt (habit) to don, put on; (fig) to take on; ~ qn de (fig) to endow ou invest sb with; ~ qch de to cover sth with; (fig) to cloak sth in.

rêveur, euse [revœr, -øz] a a dreamy // nm/f dreamer.

revient [rəvjɛ̃] vb voir **revenir**.

revigorer [rəvigɔre] vt to invigorate, brace up; to revive, buck up.

revirement [rəvirmɑ̃] nm change of mind; (d'une situation) reversal.

réviser [revize] vt (texte, SCOL: matière) to revise; (machine, installation, moteur) to overhaul, service; (JUR: procès) to review.

révision [revizjɔ̃] nf revision; auditing q; overhaul; servicing q; review; **la ~ des 10000 km** (AUTO) the 10,000 km service.

revivre [rəvivr(ə)] vi (reprendre des forces) to come alive again; (traditions) to be revived // vt (épreuve, moment) to relive.

revoir [rəvwar] vt to see again; (réviser) to revise // nm: **au ~** goodbye.

révoltant, e [revɔltɑ̃, -ɑ̃t] a a revolting; appalling.

révolte [revɔlt(ə)] nf rebellion, revolt.

révolter [revɔlte] vt to revolt; to outrage, appal; **se ~ (contre)** to rebel (against).

révolu, e [revɔly] a past; (ADMIN): âgé de 18 ans ~s over 18 years of age; **après 3 ans ~s** when 3 full years have passed.

révolution [revɔlysjɔ̃] nf revolution; **révolutionnaire** a, nm/f revolutionary.

revolver [revɔlver] nm gun; (à barillet) revolver.

révoquer [revɔke] vt (fonctionnaire) to dismiss; (arrêt, contrat) to revoke.

revue [rəvy] nf (inventaire, examen, MIL) review; (périodique) review, magazine; (de music-hall) variety show; **passer en ~** to review; to go through.

rez-de-chaussée [redʃose] nm inv ground floor.

RF sigle = République Française.

RFA sigle f = République fédérale d'Allemagne.

Rhin [rɛ̃] nm: le ~ Rhine.

rhinocéros [rinɔserɔs] nm rhinoceros.

Rhône [ron] nm: le ~ Rhone.

rhubarbe [rybarb(ə)] nf rhubarb.

rhum [rɔm] nm rum.

rhumatisme [rymatism(ə)] nm rheumatism q.

rhume [rym] nm cold; ~ **de cerveau** head cold; **le ~ des foins** hay fever.

ri [ʀi] *pp de* **rire**.

riant, e [ʀjã, -ãt] *a* smiling, cheerful.

ricaner [ʀikane] *vi* (*avec méchanceté*) to snigger; (*bêtement*) to giggle.

riche [ʀiʃ] *a* (*gén*) rich; (*personne, pays*) rich, wealthy; ~ **en** rich in; ~ **de** full of; rich in; **richesse** *nf* wealth; (*fig*) richness; **richesses** *nfpl* wealth *sg*; treasures.

ricin [ʀisɛ̃] *nm*: **huile de** ~ castor oil.

ricocher [ʀikɔʃe] *vi*: ~ (**sur**) to rebound (off); (*sur l'eau*) to bounce (on *ou* off).

ricochet [ʀikɔʃɛ] *nm*: **faire des** ~**s** to skip stones; **par** ~ *ad* on the rebound; (*fig*) as an indirect result.

rictus [ʀiktys] *nm* grin; (*snarling*) grimace.

ride [ʀid] *nf* wrinkle; (*fig*) ripple.

rideau, x [ʀido] *nm* curtain; (*POL*): **le** ~ **de fer** the Iron Curtain.

rider [ʀide] *vt* to wrinkle; (*eau*) to ripple; **se** ~ *vi* to become wrinkled.

ridicule [ʀidikyl] *a* ridiculous // *nm*: **le** ~ ridicule; **se ridiculiser** *vi* to make a fool of o.s.

rien [ʀjɛ̃] ♦ *pronom*
1: (**ne**) ... ~ nothing, *tournure négative* + anything; **qu'est-ce que vous avez?** : ~ what have you got? - nothing; **il n'a** ~ **dit/fait** he said/did nothing; he hasn't said/done anything; **il n'a** ~ (*n'est pas blessé*) he's all right; **de** ~! not at all!
2 (*quelque chose*): **a-t-il jamais** ~ **fait pour nous?** has he ever done anything for us?
3: ~ **de**: ~ **d'intéressant** nothing interesting; ~ **d'autre** nothing else; ~ **du tout** nothing at all
4: ~ **que** just, only; nothing but; ~ **que pour lui faire plaisir** only *ou* just to please him; ~ **que la vérité** nothing but the truth; ~ **que cela** that alone
♦ *nm*: **un petit** ~ (*cadeau*) a little something; **des** ~**s** trivia *pl*; **un** ~ **de** a hint of; **en un** ~ **de temps** in no time at all.

rieur, euse [ʀjœʀ, -øz] *a* cheerful.

rigide [ʀiʒid] *a* stiff; (*fig*) rigid; strict.

rigole [ʀigɔl] *nf* (*conduit*) channel; (*filet d'eau*) rivulet.

rigoler [ʀigɔle] *vi* (*rire*) to laugh; (*s'amuser*) to have (some) fun; (*plaisanter*) to be joking *ou* kidding.

rigolo, ote [ʀigɔlo, -ɔt] *a* (*fam*) funny // *nm/f* comic; (*péj*) fraud, phoney.

rigoureux, euse [ʀiguʀø, -øz] *a* (*morale*) rigorous, strict; (*personne*) stern, strict; (*climat, châtiment*) rigorous, harsh; (*interdiction, neutralité*) strict.

rigueur [ʀigœʀ] *nf* rigour; strictness; harshness; **être de** ~ to be the rule; **à la** ~ at a pinch; possibly; **tenir** ~ **à qn de qch** to hold sth against sb.

rime [ʀim] *nf* rhyme.

rinçage [ʀɛ̃saʒ] *nm* rinsing (out); (*opération*) rinse.

rincer [ʀɛ̃se] *vt* to rinse; (*récipient*) to rinse out.

ring [ʀiŋ] *nm* (boxing) ring.

ringard, e [ʀɛ̃gaʀ, -aʀd(ə)] *a* old-fashioned.

rions *vb voir* **rire**.

riposter [ʀipɔste] *vi* to retaliate // *vt*: ~ **que** to retort that; ~ **à** *vt* to counter; to reply to.

rire [ʀiʀ] *vi* to laugh; (*se divertir*) to have fun // *nm* laugh; **le** ~ laughter; ~ **de** *vt* to laugh at; **pour** ~ (*pas sérieusement*) for a joke *ou* a laugh.

risée [ʀize] *nf*: **être la** ~ **de** to be the laughing stock of.

risible [ʀizibl(ə)] *a* laughable.

risque [ʀisk(ə)] *nm* risk; **le** ~ danger; **à ses** ~**s et périls** at his own risk.

risqué, e [ʀiske] *a* risky; (*plaisanterie*) risqué, daring.

risquer [ʀiske] *vt* to risk; (*allusion, question*) to venture, hazard; **ça ne risque rien** it's quite safe; ~ **de**: **il risque de se tuer** he could get himself killed; **ce qui risque de se produire** what might *ou* could well happen; **il ne risque pas de recommencer** there's no chance of him doing that again; **se** ~ **à faire** (*tenter*) to venture *ou* dare to do.

rissoler [ʀisɔle] *vi, vt*: (**faire**) ~ to brown.

ristourne [ʀistuʀn(ə)] *nf* rebate.

rite [ʀit] *nm* rite; (*fig*) ritual.

rivage [ʀivaʒ] *nm* shore.

rival, e, aux [ʀival, -o] *a, nm/f* rival.

rivaliser [ʀivalize] *vi*: ~ **avec** to rival, vie with; (*être comparable*) to hold its own against, compare with.

rivalité [ʀivalite] *nf* rivalry.

rive [ʀiv] *nf* shore; (*de fleuve*) bank.

river [ʀive] *vt* (*clou, pointe*) to clinch; (*plaques*) to rivet together.

riverain, e [ʀivʀɛ̃, -ɛn] *nm/f* riverside (*ou* lakeside) resident; local resident.

rivet [ʀivɛ] *nm* rivet.

rivière [ʀivjɛʀ] *nf* river.

rixe [ʀiks(ə)] *nf* brawl, scuffle.

riz [ʀi] *nm* rice.

R.N. *sigle f de* **route nationale**.

robe [ʀɔb] *nf* dress; (*de juge, d'ecclésiastique*) robe; (*de professeur*) gown; (*pelage*) coat; ~ **de soirée/de mariée** evening/wedding dress; ~ **de chambre** dressing gown; ~ **de grossesse** maternity dress.

robinet [ʀɔbinɛ] *nm* tap.

robot [ʀɔbo] *nm* robot.

robuste [ʀɔbyst(ə)] *a* robust, sturdy.

roc [ʀɔk] *nm* rock.

rocaille [ʀɔkaj] *nf* loose stones *pl*; rocky *ou* stony ground; (*jardin*) rockery, rock garden.

roche [ʀɔʃ] *nf* rock.

rocher [ʀɔʃe] *nm* rock.

rocheux, euse [ʀɔʃø, -øz] *a* rocky.

rodage [ʀɔdaʒ] *nm*: en ~ running in.

roder [ʀɔde] *vt* (AUTO) to run in.

rôder [ʀɔde] *vi* to roam about; (*de façon suspecte*) to lurk (about *ou* around); **rôdeur, euse** *nm/f* prowler.

rogne [ʀɔɲ] *nf*: être en ~ to be in a temper.

rogner [ʀɔɲe] *vt* to clip; ~ **sur** (*fig*) to cut down *ou* back on.

rognons [ʀɔɲɔ̃] *nmpl* kidneys.

roi [ʀwa] *nm* king; le jour *ou* la fête des R~s, les R~s Twelfth Night.

roitelet [ʀwatlɛ] *nm* wren.

rôle [ʀol] *nm* role; (*contribution*) part.

romain, e [ʀɔmɛ̃, -ɛn] *a*, *nm/f* Roman.

roman, e [ʀɔmɑ̃, -an] *a* (ARCHIT) Romanesque // *nm* novel; ~ **d'espionnage** spy novel *ou* story; ~ **photo** romantic picture story.

romance [ʀɔmɑ̃s] *nf* ballad.

romancer [ʀɔmɑ̃se] *vt* to make into a novel; to romanticize.

romancier, ière [ʀɔmɑ̃sje, -jɛʀ] *nm/f* novelist.

romanesque [ʀɔmanɛsk(ə)] *a* (*fantastique*) fantastic; storybook *cpd*; (*sentimental*) romantic.

roman-feuilleton [ʀɔmɑ̃fœjtɔ̃] *nm* serialized novel.

romanichel, le [ʀɔmaniʃɛl] *nm/f* gipsy.

romantique [ʀɔmɑ̃tik] *a* romantic.

romarin [ʀɔmaʀɛ̃] *nm* rosemary.

rompre [ʀɔ̃pʀ(ə)] *vt* to break; (*entretien, fiançailles*) to break off // *vi* (*fiancés*) to break it off; se ~ *vi* to break; (MÉD) to burst, rupture.

rompu, e [ʀɔ̃py] *a*: ~ à with wide experience of; inured to.

ronces [ʀɔ̃s] *nfpl* brambles.

ronchonner [ʀɔ̃ʃɔne] *vi* (*fam*) to grouse, grouch.

rond, e [ʀɔ̃, ʀɔ̃d] *a* round; (*joues, mollets*) well-rounded; (*fam: ivre*) tight // *nm* (*cercle*) ring; (*fam: sou*): je n'ai plus un ~ I haven't a penny left // *nf* (*gén: de surveillance*) rounds *pl*, patrol; (*danse*) round (dance); (MUS) semibreve (*Brit*), whole note (US); en ~ (*s'asseoir, danser*) in a ring; à la ~e (*alentour*): à 10 km à la ~e for 10 km round; **rondelet, te** *a* plump.

rondelle [ʀɔ̃dɛl] *nf* (TECH) washer; (*tranche*) slice, round.

rondement [ʀɔ̃dmɑ̃] *ad* briskly, frankly.

rondin [ʀɔ̃dɛ̃] *nm* log.

rond-point [ʀɔ̃pwɛ̃] *nm* roundabout.

ronéotyper [ʀɔneɔtipe] *vt* to duplicate.

ronfler [ʀɔ̃fle] *vi* to snore; (*moteur, poêle*) to hum; to roar.

ronger [ʀɔ̃ʒe] *vt* to gnaw (at); (*suj: vers, rouille*) to eat into; se ~ les sangs to worry o.s. sick; se ~ les ongles to bite one's nails; **rongeur** *nm* rodent.

ronronner [ʀɔ̃ʀɔne] *vi* to purr.

roquet [ʀɔkɛ] *nm* nasty little lap-dog.

roquette [ʀɔkɛt] *nf* rocket.

rosace [ʀɔzas] *nf* (*vitrail*) rose window.

rosbif [ʀɔsbif] *nm*: du ~ roasting beef; (*cuit*) roast beef; un ~ a joint of beef.

rose [ʀoz] *nf* rose // *a* pink.

rosé, e [ʀoze] *a* pinkish; (*vin*) ~ rosé.

roseau, x [ʀozo] *nm* reed.

rosée [ʀoze] *nf* dew.

roseraie [ʀozʀɛ] *nf* rose garden.

rosier [ʀozje] *nm* rosebush, rose tree.

rosse [ʀɔs] *nf* (*péj: cheval*) nag // *a* nasty, vicious.

rossignol [ʀɔsiɲɔl] *nm* (ZOOL) nightingale.

rot [ʀo] *nm* belch; (*de bébé*) burp.

rotatif, ive [ʀɔtatif, -iv] *a* rotary.

rotation [ʀɔtasjɔ̃] *nf* rotation; (*fig*) rotation, swap-around; turnover.

roter [ʀɔte] *vi* (*fam*) to burp, belch.

rôti [ʀoti] *nm*: du ~ roasting meat; (*cuit*) roast meat; un ~ de bœuf/porc a joint of beef/pork.

rotin [ʀɔtɛ̃] *nm* rattan (cane); **fauteuil en** ~ cane (arm)chair.

rôtir [ʀotiʀ] *vi*, *vt* (*aussi*: faire ~) to roast; **rôtisserie** *nf* steakhouse; roast meat counter (*ou* shop); **rôtissoire** *nf* (roasting) spit.

rotule [ʀɔtyl] *nf* kneecap, patella.

roturier, ière [ʀɔtyʀje, -jɛʀ] *nm/f* commoner.

rouage [ʀwaʒ] *nm* cog(wheel), gearwheel; (*de montre*) part; (*fig*) cog.

roucouler [ʀukule] *vi* to coo.

roue [ʀu] *nf* wheel; ~ **dentée** cogwheel; ~ **de secours** spare wheel.

roué, e [ʀwe] *a* wily.

rouer [ʀwe] *vt*: ~ qn de coups to give sb a thrashing.

rouet [ʀwɛ] *nm* spinning wheel.

rouge [ʀuʒ] *a*, *nm/f* red // *nm* red; (*fard*) rouge; (*vin*) ~ red wine; sur la liste ~ ex-directory (*Brit*), unlisted (US); passer au ~ (*signal*) to go red; (*automobiliste*) to go through a red light; ~ (à lèvres) lipstick; **~-gorge** *nm* robin (redbreast).

rougeole [ʀuʒɔl] *nf* measles *sg*.

rougeoyer [ʀuʒwaje] *vi* to glow red.

rouget [ʀuʒɛ] *nm* mullet.

rougeur [ʀuʒœʀ] *nf* redness.

rougir [ʀuʒiʀ] *vi* (*de honte, timidité*) to blush, flush; (*de plaisir, colère*) to flush; (*fraise, tomate*) to go *ou* turn red; (*ciel*) to redden.

rouille [ʀuj] *nf* rust.

rouillé, e [ʀuje] *a* rusty.

rouiller [ʀuje] *vt* to rust // *vi* to rust, go rusty; se ~ *vi* to rust.

roulant, e [ʀulɑ̃, -ɑ̃t] *a* (*meuble*) on wheels; (*surface, trottoir*) moving.

rouleau, x [ʀulo] *nm* (*de papier, tissu*,

SPORT) roll; (de machine à écrire) roller, platen; (à mise en plis, à peinture, vague) roller; ~ **compresseur** steamroller; ~ **à pâtisserie** rolling pin.

roulement [Rulmã] nm (bruit) rumbling q, rumble; (rotation) rotation; turnover; **par ~** on a rota (Brit) ou rotation (US) basis; ~ **(à billes)** ball bearings pl; ~ **de tambour** drum roll.

rouler [Rule] vt to roll; (papier, tapis) to roll up; (CULIN: pâte) to roll out; (fam) to do, con // vi (bille, boule) to roll; (voiture, train) to go, run; (automobiliste) to drive; (cycliste) to ride; (bateau) to roll; (tonnerre) to rumble, roll; **se ~ dans** (boue) to roll in; (couverture) to roll o.s. (up) in.

roulette [Rulɛt] nf (de table, fauteuil) castor; (de pâtissier) pastry wheel; (jeu): **la ~** roulette; **à ~s** on castors.

roulis [Ruli] nm roll(ing).

roulotte [Rulɔt] nf caravan.

Roumanie [Rumani] nf Rumania.

rouquin, e [Rukɛ̃, -in] nm/f (péj) redhead.

rouspéter [Ruspete] vi (fam) to moan.

rousse [Rus] a voir roux.

roussi [Rusi] nm: **ça sent le ~** there's a smell of burning; (fig) I can smell trouble.

roussir [Rusir] vt to scorch // vi (feuilles) to go ou turn brown; (CULIN): **faire ~** to brown.

route [Rut] nf road; (fig: chemin) way; (itinéraire, parcours) route; (fig: voie) road, path; **par (la) ~** by road; **il y a 3h de ~** it's a 3-hour ride ou journey; **en ~** ad on the way; **mettre en ~** to start up; **se mettre en ~** to set off; **faire ~ vers** to head towards; ~ **nationale** ≈ A road (Brit), ≈ state highway (US); **routier, ière** a road cpd // nm (camionneur) (long-distance) lorry (Brit) ou truck (US) driver; (restaurant) transport café (Brit), ≈ truck stop (US) // nf (voiture) touring car.

routine [Rutin] nf routine; **routinier, ière** a (péj) humdrum; addicted to routine.

rouvrir [Ruvrir] vt, vi, **se ~** vi to reopen, open again.

roux, rousse [Ru, Rus] a red; (personne) red-haired // nm/f redhead.

royal, e, aux [Rwajal, -o] a royal; (fig) princely.

royaume [Rwajom] nm kingdom; (fig) realm; **le R~-Uni** the United Kingdom.

royauté [Rwajote] nf (dignité) kingship; (régime) monarchy.

ruban [Rybã] nm (gén) ribbon; (d'acier) strip; ~ **adhésif** adhesive tape.

rubéole [Rybeɔl] nf German measles sg, rubella.

rubis [Rybi] nm ruby.

rubrique [Rybrik] nf (titre, catégorie)

heading; (PRESSE: article) column.

ruche [Ryʃ] nf hive.

rude [Ryd] a (barbe, toile) rough; (métier, tâche) hard, tough; (climat) severe, harsh; (bourru) harsh, rough; (fruste) rugged, tough; (fam) jolly good; **~ment** ad; (fam: très) terribly; (: beaucoup) terribly hard.

rudimentaire [Rydimãtɛr] a rudimentary, basic.

rudoyer [Rydwaje] vt to treat harshly.

rue [Ry] nf street.

ruée [Rɥe] nf rush.

ruelle [Rɥɛl] nf alley(-way).

ruer [Rɥe] vi (cheval) to kick out; **se ~** vi: **se ~ sur** to pounce on; **se ~ vers/dans/hors de** to rush ou dash towards/into/out of.

rugby [Rygbi] nm Rugby (football).

rugir [Ryʒir] vi to roar.

rugueux, euse [Rygø, -øz] a rough.

ruine [Rɥin] nf ruin; **~s** nfpl ruins.

ruiner [Rɥine] vt to ruin.

ruisseau, x [Rɥiso] nm stream, brook.

ruisseler [Rɥisle] vi to stream.

rumeur [Rymœr] nf (bruit confus) rumbling; hubbub q; murmur(ing); (nouvelle) rumour.

ruminer [Rymine] vt (herbe) to ruminate; (fig) to ruminate on ou over, chew over.

rupture [Ryptyr] nf (de câble, digue) breaking; (de tendon) rupture, tearing; (de négociations etc) breakdown; (de contrat) breach; (séparation, désunion) break-up, split.

rural, e, aux [Ryral, -o] a rural, country cpd.

ruse [Ryz] nf: **la ~** cunning, craftiness; trickery; **une ~** a trick, a ruse; **rusé, e** a cunning, crafty.

russe [Rys] a, nm, nf Russian.

Russie [Rysi] nf: **la ~** Russia.

rustique [Rystik] a rustic.

rustre [Rystr(ə)] nm boor.

rutilant, e [Rytilã, -ãt] a gleaming.

rythme [Ritm(ə)] nm rhythm; (vitesse) rate; (: de la vie) pace, tempo.

S

s' [s] pronom voir se.

sa [sa] dét voir son.

S.A. sigle voir société.

sable [sabl(ə)] nm sand; **~s mouvants** quicksand(s).

sablé [sable] nm shortbread biscuit.

sabler [sable] vt to sand; (contre le verglas) to grit; ~ **le champagne** to drink champagne.

sablier [sablije] nm hourglass; (de cuisine) egg timer.

sablonneux, euse [sablɔnø, -øz] a sandy.

saborder [sabɔʀde] vt (navire) to scuttle; (fig) to wind up, shut down.

sabot [sabo] nm clog; (de cheval, bœuf) hoof; ~ **de frein** brake shoe.

saboter [sabɔte] vt to sabotage.

sac [sak] nm bag; (à charbon etc) sack; **mettre à ~** to sack; ~ **à provisions/de voyage** shopping/travelling bag; ~ **de couchage** sleeping bag; ~ **à dos** rucksack; ~ **à main** handbag.

saccade [sakad] nf jerk.

saccager [sakaʒe] vt (piller) to sack; (dévaster) to create havoc in.

saccharine [sakaʀin] nf saccharin(e).

sacerdoce [sasɛʀdɔs] nm priesthood; (fig) calling, vocation.

sache etc vb voir **savoir**.

sachet [saʃɛ] nm (small) bag; (de lavande, poudre, shampooing) sachet; ~ **de thé** tea bag.

sacoche [sakɔʃ] nf (gén) bag; (de bicyclette) saddlebag.

sacre [sakʀ(ə)] nm coronation; consecration.

sacré, e [sakʀe] a sacred; (fam: satané) blasted; (: fameux): **un ~ ...** a heck of a ...

sacrement [sakʀəmã] nm sacrament.

sacrifice [sakʀifis] nm sacrifice.

sacrifier [sakʀifje] vt to sacrifice; ~ **à** vt to conform to.

sacristie [sakʀisti] nf sacristy; (culte protestant) vestry.

sadique [sadik] a sadistic.

sage [saʒ] a wise; (enfant) good // nm wise man; sage.

sage-femme [saʒfam] nf midwife (pl wives).

sagesse [saʒɛs] nf wisdom.

Sagittaire [saʒitɛʀ] nm: **le ~** Sagittarius.

Sahara [saaʀa] nm: **le ~** the Sahara (desert).

saignant, e [sɛɲã, -ãt] a (viande) rare.

saignée [seɲe] nf (fig) heavy losses pl.

saigner [seɲe] vi to bleed // vt to bleed; (animal) to kill (by bleeding); ~ **du nez** to have a nosebleed.

saillie [saji] nf (sur un mur etc) projection; (trait d'esprit) witticism.

saillir [sajiʀ] vi to project, stick out; (veine, muscle) to bulge.

sain, e [sɛ̃, sɛn] a healthy; (lectures) wholesome; ~ **et sauf** safe and sound, unharmed; ~ **d'esprit** sound in mind, sane.

saindoux [sɛ̃du] nm lard.

saint, e [sɛ̃, sɛ̃t] a holy; (fig) saintly // nm/f saint; **le S~ Esprit** the Holy Spirit ou Ghost; **la S~e Vierge** the Blessed Virgin; **la S~-Sylvestre** New Year's Eve; **sainteté** nf holiness.

sais etc vb voir **savoir**.

saisie [sezi] nf seizure; ~ **(de données)** (data) capture.

saisir [seziʀ] vt to take hold of, grab; (fig: occasion) to seize; (comprendre) to grasp; (entendre) to get, catch; (données) to capture; (suj: émotions) to take hold of, come over; (CULIN) to fry quickly; (JUR: biens, publication) to seize; (: juridiction): ~ **un tribunal d'une affaire** to submit ou refer a case to a court; **se ~ de** vt to seize; **saisissant, e** a startling, striking.

saison [sezɔ̃] nf season; **morte ~** slack season; **saisonnier, ière** a seasonal.

sait vb voir **savoir**.

salade [salad] nf (BOT) lettuce etc; (CULIN) (green) salad; (fam) tangle, muddle; ~ **de fruits** fruit salad; **saladier** nm (salad) bowl.

salaire [salɛʀ] nm (annuel, mensuel) salary; (hebdomadaire, journalier) pay, wages pl; (fig) reward; ~ **de base** basic salary (ou wage); ~ **minimum interprofessionnel de croissance** (SMIC) index-linked guaranteed minimum wage.

salarié, e [salaʀje] nm/f salaried employee; wage-earner.

salaud [salo] nm (fam!) sod (!), bastard (!).

sale [sal] a dirty, filthy.

salé, e [sale] a (liquide, saveur) salty; (CULIN) salted; (fig) spicy; steep.

saler [sale] vt to salt.

saleté [salte] nf (état) dirtiness; (crasse) dirt, filth; (tache etc) dirt q; (fig) dirty trick; rubbish q; filth q.

salière [saljɛʀ] nf saltcellar.

salin, e [salɛ̃, -in] a saline // nf saltworks sg; salt marsh.

salir [saliʀ] vt to (make) dirty; (fig) to soil the reputation of; **se ~** vi to get dirty; **salissant, e** a (tissu) which shows the dirt; (métier) dirty, messy.

salle [sal] nf room; (d'hôpital) ward; (de restaurant) dining room; (d'un cinéma) auditorium; (: public) audience; **faire ~ comble** to have a full house; ~ **d'attente** waiting room; ~ **de bain(s)** bathroom; ~ **de classe** classroom; ~ **commune** (d'hôpital) ward; ~ **de concert** concert hall; ~ **de consultation** consulting room; ~ **d'eau** shower-room; ~ **d'embarquement** (à l'aéroport) departure lounge; ~ **de jeux** games room; playroom; ~ **à manger** dining room; ~ **d'opération** (d'hôpital) operating theatre; ~ **de séjour** living room; ~ **de spectacle** theatre; cinema; ~ **des ventes** saleroom.

salon [salɔ̃] nm lounge, sitting room; (mobilier) lounge suite; (exposition) exhibition, show; ~ **de thé** tearoom.

salopard [salɔpaʀ] nm (fam!) bastard (!).

salope [salɔp] nf (fam!) bitch (!).

saloperie [salɔpʀi] nf (fam!) filth q; dirty trick; rubbish q.

salopette [salɔpɛt] nf dungarees pl;

(d'ouvrier) overall(s).

salsifis [salsifi] *nm* salsify.

salubre [salybʀ(ə)] *a* healthy, salubrious.

saluer [salɥe] *vt (pour dire bonjour, fig)* to greet; *(pour dire au revoir)* to take one's leave; *(MIL)* to salute.

salut [saly] *nm (sauvegarde)* safety; *(REL)* salvation; *(geste)* wave; *(parole)* greeting; *(MIL)* salute // *excl (fam)* hi (there).

salutations [salytɑsjɔ̃] *nfpl* greetings; recevez mes ~ distinguées *ou* respectueuses yours faithfully.

samedi [samdi] *nm* Saturday.

SAMU [samy] *sigle f (= service d'assistance médicale d'urgence)* ≈ ambulance (service) *(Brit)*, ≈ paramedics *pl (US)*.

sanction [sɑ̃ksjɔ̃] *nf* sanction; *(fig)* penalty; **sanctionner** *vt (loi, usage)* to sanction; *(punir)* to punish.

sandale [sɑ̃dal] *nf* sandal.

sandwich [sɑ̃dwitʃ] *nm* sandwich.

sang [sɑ̃] *nm* blood; en ~ covered in blood; se faire du mauvais ~ to fret, get in a state.

sang-froid [sɑ̃fʀwa] *nm* calm, sangfroid; de ~ in cold blood.

sanglant, e [sɑ̃glɑ̃, -ɑ̃t] *a* bloody, covered in blood; *(combat)* bloody.

sangle [sɑ̃gl(ə)] *nf* strap.

sanglier [sɑ̃glije] *nm* (wild) boar.

sanglot [sɑ̃glo] *nm* sob.

sangsue [sɑ̃sy] *nf* leech.

sanguin, e [sɑ̃gɛ̃, -in] *a* blood *cpd*; *(fig)* fiery.

sanguinaire [sɑ̃ginɛʀ] *a* bloodthirsty; bloody.

sanisette [sanizɛt] *nf* (automatic) public toilet.

sanitaire [sanitɛʀ] *a* health *cpd*; **~s** *nmpl* bathroom *sg*.

sans [sɑ̃] *prép* without; ~ qu'il s'en aperçoive without him *ou* his noticing; **~-abri** *nmpl* homeless; **~-façon** *a inv* fuss-free; free and easy; **~-gêne** *a inv* inconsiderate; **~-logis** *nmpl* homeless.

santé [sɑ̃te] *nf* health; en bonne ~ in good health; boire à la ~ de qn to drink (to) sb's health; 'à la ~ de' 'here's to'; à ta/votre ~! cheers!

saoudien, ne [saudjɛ̃, -jɛn] *a* Saudi Arabian // *nm/f:* S~(ne) Saudi Arabian.

saoul, e [su, sul] *a* = **soûl, e**.

saper [sape] *vt* to undermine, sap.

sapeur [sapœʀ] *nm* sapper; **~-pompier** *nm* fireman.

saphir [safiʀ] *nm* sapphire.

sapin [sapɛ̃] *nm* fir (tree); *(bois)* fir; ~ de Noël Christmas tree.

sarcastique [saʀkastik] *a* sarcastic.

sarcler [saʀkle] *vt* to weed.

Sardaigne [saʀdɛɲ] *nf:* la ~ Sardinia.

sardine [saʀdin] *nf* sardine.

S.A.R.L. *sigle voir* **société**.

sas [sas] *nm (de sous-marin, d'engin spatial)* airlock; *(d'écluse)* lock.

satané, e [satane] *a* confounded.

satellite [satelit] *nm* satellite.

satin [satɛ̃] *nm* satin.

satire [satiʀ] *nf* satire; **satirique** *a* satirical.

satisfaction [satisfaksjɔ̃] *nf* satisfaction.

satisfaire [satisfɛʀ] *vt* to satisfy; ~ à *vt (engagement)* to fulfil; *(revendications, conditions)* to satisfy, meet; to comply with; **satisfaisant, e** *a* satisfactory; *(qui fait plaisir)* satisfying; **satisfait, e** *a* satisfied; satisfait de happy *ou* satisfied with.

saturer [satyʀe] *vt* to saturate.

sauce [sos] *nf* sauce; *(avec un rôti)* gravy; **saucière** *nf* sauceboat.

saucisse [sosis] *nf* sausage.

saucisson [sosisɔ̃] *nm* (slicing) sausage.

sauf [sof] *prép* except; ~ si *(à moins que)* unless; ~ erreur if I'm not mistaken; ~ avis contraire unless you hear to the contrary.

sauf, sauve [sof, sov] *a* unharmed, unhurt; *(fig: honneur)* intact, saved; laisser la vie sauve à qn to spare sb's life.

sauge [soʒ] *nf* sage.

saugrenu, e [sogʀəny] *a* preposterous.

saule [sol] *nm* willow (tree).

saumon [somɔ̃] *nm* salmon *inv*.

saumure [somyʀ] *nf* brine.

sauna [sona] *nm* sauna.

saupoudrer [sopudʀe] *vt:* ~ qch de to sprinkle sth with.

saur [sɔʀ] *am:* hareng ~ smoked *ou* red herring, kipper.

saurai *etc vb voir* **savoir**.

saut [so] *nm* jump; *(discipline sportive)* jumping; faire un ~ chez qn to pop over to sb's (place); au ~ du lit on getting out of bed; ~ en hauteur/longueur high/long jump; ~ à la corde skipping; ~ à la perche pole vaulting; ~ périlleux somersault.

saute [sot] *nf* sudden change.

saute-mouton [sotmutɔ̃] *nm:* jouer à ~ to play leapfrog.

sauter [sote] *vi* to jump, leap, *(exploser)* to blow up, explode; *(: fusibles)* to blow; *(se rompre)* to snap, burst; *(se détacher)* to pop out *(ou* off) // *vt* to jump (over), leap (over); *(fig: omettre)* to skip, miss (out); faire ~ to blow up; to burst open; *(CULIN)* to sauté; ~ au cou de qn to fly into sb's arms.

sauterelle [sotʀɛl] *nf* grasshopper.

sautiller [sotije] *vi* to hop; to skip.

sautoir [sotwaʀ] *nm:* ~ (de perles) string of pearls.

sauvage [sovaʒ] *a (gén)* wild; *(peuplade)* savage; *(farouche)* unsociable;

(*barbare*) wild, savage; (*non officiel*) unauthorized, unofficial // *nm/f* savage; (*timide*) unsociable type.

sauve [sov] *af voir* **sauf**.

sauvegarde [sovgaʀd(ə)] *nf* safeguard; **sauvegarder** *vt* to safeguard; (*INFORM*: *enregistrer*) to save; (: *copier*) to back up.

sauve-qui-peut [sovkipø] *excl* run for your life!

sauver [sove] *vt* to save; (*porter secours à*) to rescue; (*récupérer*) to salvage, rescue; **se ~** *vi* (*s'enfuir*) to run away; (*fam: partir*) to be off; **sauvetage** *nm* rescue; **sauveteur** *nm* rescuer; **sauvette**: **à la sauvette** *ad* (*vendre*) without authorization; (*se marier etc*) hastily, hurriedly; **sauveur** *nm* saviour (*Brit*), savior (*US*).

savais *etc vb voir* **savoir**.

savamment [savamɑ̃] *ad* (*avec érudition*) learnedly; (*habilement*) skilfully, cleverly.

savant, e [savɑ̃, -ɑ̃t] *a* scholarly, learned; (*calé*) clever // *nm* scientist.

saveur [savœʀ] *nf* flavour; (*fig*) savour.

savoir [savwaʀ] *vt* to know; (*être capable de*): **il sait nager** he can swim // *nm* knowledge; **se ~** *vi* (*être connu*) to be known; **à ~** *ad* that is, namely; **faire ~ qch à qn** to let sb know sth; **pas que je sache** not as far as I know.

savon [savɔ̃] *nm* (*produit*) soap; (*morceau*) bar of soap; (*fam*): **passer un ~ à qn** to give sb a good dressing-down; **savonnette** *nf* bar of soap; **savonneux, euse** *a* soapy.

savons *vb voir* **savoir**.

savourer [savuʀe] *vt* to savour.

savoureux, euse [savuʀø, -øz] *a* tasty; (*fig*) spicy, juicy.

saxo(phone) [saksɔ(fɔn)] *nm* sax(o-phone).

scabreux, euse [skabʀø, -øz] *a* risky; (*indécent*) improper, shocking.

scandale [skɑ̃dal] *nm* scandal; (*tapage*): **faire du ~** to make a scene, create a disturbance; **faire ~** to scandalize people; **scandaleux, euse** *a* scandalous, outrageous.

scandinave [skɑ̃dinav] *a, nm/f* Scandinavian.

Scandinavie [skɑ̃dinavi] *nf* Scandinavia.

scaphandre [skafɑ̃dʀ(ə)] *nm* (*de plongeur*) diving suit; (*de cosmonaute*) space-suit.

scarabée [skaʀabe] *nm* beetle.

sceau, x [so] *nm* seal; (*fig*) stamp, mark.

scélérat, e [seleʀa, -at] *nm/f* villain.

sceller [sele] *vt* to seal.

scénario [senaʀjo] *nm* (*CINÉMA*) scenario; script; (*fig*) scenario.

scène [sɛn] *nf* (*gén*) scene; (*estrade, fig: théâtre*) stage; **entrer en ~** to come on

stage; **mettre en ~** (*THÉÂTRE*) to stage; (*CINÉMA*) to direct; (*fig*) to present, introduce.

sceptique [sɛptik] *a* sceptical.

schéma [ʃema] *nm* (*diagramme*) diagram, sketch; (*fig*) outline; pattern; **schématique** *a* diagrammatic(al), schematic; (*fig*) oversimplified.

sciatique [sjatik] *nf* sciatica.

scie [si] *nf* saw; **~ à découper** fretsaw; **~ à métaux** hacksaw.

sciemment [sjamɑ̃] *ad* knowingly.

science [sjɑ̃s] *nf* science; (*savoir*) knowledge; (*savoir-faire*) art, skill; **~s naturelles** (*SCOL*) natural science *sg*, biology *sg*; **scientifique** *a* scientific // *nm/f* scientist; science student.

scier [sje] *vt* to saw; (*retrancher*) to saw off; **scierie** *nf* sawmill.

scinder [sɛ̃de] *vt*, **se ~** *vi* to split (up).

scintiller [sɛ̃tije] *vi* to sparkle.

scission [sisjɔ̃] *nf* split.

sciure [sjyʀ] *nf*: **~** (**de bois**) sawdust.

sclérose [skleʀoz] *nf*: **~ en plaques** multiple sclerosis.

scolaire [skɔlɛʀ] *a* school *cpd*; (*péj*) schoolish; **scolariser** *vt* to provide with schooling (*ou* schools); **scolarité** *nf* schooling.

scooter [skutɛʀ] *nm* (motor) scooter.

score [skɔʀ] *nm* score.

scorpion [skɔʀpjɔ̃] *nm* (*signe*): **le S~** Scorpio.

Scotch [skɔtʃ] *nm* ® adhesive tape.

scout, e [skut] *a, nm* scout.

script [skʀipt] *nm* printing; (*CINÉMA*) (shooting) script; **~-girl** [-gœʀl] *nf* continuity girl.

scrupule [skʀypyl] *nm* scruple.

scruter [skʀyte] *vt* to scrutinize; (*l'obscurité*) to peer into.

scrutin [skʀytɛ̃] *nm* (*vote*) ballot; (*ensemble des opérations*) poll.

sculpter [skylte] *vt* to sculpt; (*suj: érosion*) to carve; **sculpteur** *nm* sculptor.

sculpture [skyltyʀ] *nf* sculpture; **~ sur bois** wood carving.

se, s' [s(ə)] *pronom* **1** (*emploi réfléchi*) oneself, *m* himself, *f* herself, *sujet non humain* itself; *pl* themselves; **~ voir comme l'on est** to see o.s. as one is

2 (*réciproque*) one another, each other; **ils s'aiment** they love one another *ou* each other

3 (*passif*): **cela ~ répare facilement** it is easily repaired

4 (*possessif*): **~ casser la jambe/laver les mains** to break one's leg/wash one's hands; *autres emplois pronominaux: voir le verbe en question.*

séance [seɑ̃s] *nf* (*d'assemblée, récréative*) meeting, session; (*de tribunal*) sitting, session; (*musicale, CINÉMA, THÉÂTRE*) performance; **~ tenante** forthwith.

seau, x [so] *nm* bucket, pail.

sec, sèche [sɛk, sɛʃ] *a* dry; (*raisins, figues*) dried; (*cœur, personne: insensible*) hard, cold // *nm*: **tenir au ~** to keep in a dry place // *ad* hard; **je le bois ~** I drink it straight *ou* neat; **à ~** a dried up.

sécateur [sekatœʀ] *nm* secateurs *pl* (*Brit*), shears *pl.*

sèche [sɛʃ] *af voir* **sec.**

sèche-cheveux [sɛʃʃəvø] *nm inv* hairdrier.

sécher [seʃe] *vt* to dry; (*dessécher: peau, blé*) to dry (out); (: *étang*) to dry up // *vi* to dry; to dry out; to dry up; (*fam: candidat*) to be stumped; **se ~** (*après le bain*) to dry o.s.

sécheresse [seʃʀɛs] *nf* dryness; (*absence de pluie*) drought.

séchoir [seʃwaʀ] *nm* drier.

second, e [səɡɔ̃, -ɔ̃d] *a* second // *nm* (*assistant*) second in command; (*NAVIG*) first mate // *nf* second; **voyager en ~e** to travel second-class; **de ~e main** secondhand; **secondaire** *a* secondary; **seconder** *vt* to assist.

secouer [səkwe] *vt* to shake; (*passagers*) to rock; (*traumatiser*) to shake (up).

secourir [səkuʀiʀ] *vt* (*aller sauver*) to (go and) rescue; (*prodiguer des soins à*) to help, assist; (*venir en aide à*) to assist, aid; **secourisme** *nm* first aid; life saving.

secours [səkuʀ] *nm* help, aid, assistance // *nmpl* aid *sg*; **au ~!** help!; **appeler au ~** to shout *ou* call for help; **porter ~ à qn** to give sb assistance, help sb; **les premiers ~** first aid *sg.*

secousse [səkus] *nf* jolt, bump; (*électrique*) shock; (*fig: psychologique*) jolt, shock; **~ sismique** *ou* **tellurique** earth tremor.

secret, ète [səkʀɛ, -ɛt] *a* secret; (*fig: renfermé*) reticent, reserved // *nm* secret; (*discrétion absolue*): **le ~** secrecy; **au ~** in solitary confinement.

secrétaire [səkʀetɛʀ] *nm/f* secretary // *nm* (*meuble*) writing desk; **~ de direction** private *ou* personal secretary; **~ d'État** junior minister; **secrétariat** *nm* (*profession*) secretarial work; (*bureau*) office; (: *d'organisation internationale*) secretariat.

secteur [sɛktœʀ] *nm* sector; (*ADMIN*) district; (*ÉLEC*): **branché sur le ~** plugged into the mains (supply).

section [sɛksjɔ̃] *nf* section; (*de parcours d'autobus*) fare stage; (*MIL: unité*) platoon; **sectionner** *vt* to sever.

Sécu [seky] *abr f de* **sécurité sociale.**

séculaire [sekylɛʀ] *a* secular; (*très vieux*) age-old.

sécuriser [sekyʀize] *vt* to give (a feeling of) security to.

sécurité [sekyʀite] *nf* safety; security; **système de ~** safety system; **être en ~** to be safe; **la ~ routière** road safety; **la ~ sociale** ≈ (the) Social Security (*Brit*), ≈ Welfare (*US*).

sédition [sedisjɔ̃] *nf* insurrection; sedition.

séduction [sedyksjɔ̃] *nf* seduction; (*charme, attrait*) appeal, charm.

séduire [seduiʀ] *vt* to charm; (*femme: abuser de*) to seduce; **séduisant, e** *a* (*femme*) seductive; (*homme, offre*) very attractive.

ségrégation [seɡʀeɡasjɔ̃] *nf* segregation.

seigle [sɛɡl(ə)] *nm* rye.

seigneur [sɛɲœʀ] *nm* lord.

sein [sɛ̃] *nm* breast; (*entrailles*) womb; **au ~ de** *prép* (*équipe, institution*) within; (*flots, bonheur*) in the midst of.

séisme [seism(ə)] *nm* earthquake.

seize [sɛz] *num* sixteen; **seizième** *num* sixteenth.

séjour [seʒuʀ] *nm* stay; (*pièce*) living room; **~ner** *vi* to stay.

sel [sɛl] *nm* salt; (*fig*) wit; spice; **~ de cuisine/de table** cooking/table salt.

sélection [selɛksjɔ̃] *nf* selection; **sélectionner** *vt* to select.

self-service [sɛlfsɛʀvis] *a, nm* self-service.

selle [sɛl] *nf* saddle; **~s** *nfpl* (*MÉD*) stools; **seller** *vt* to saddle.

sellette [sɛlɛt] *nf*: **être sur la ~** to be on the carpet.

selon [səlɔ̃] *prép* according to; (*en se conformant à*) in accordance with; **~ que** according to whether; **~ moi** as I see it.

semaine [səmɛn] *nf* week; **en ~** during the week, on weekdays.

semblable [sɑ̃blabl(ə)] *a* similar; (*de ce genre*): **de ~s mésaventures** such mishaps // *nm* fellow creature *ou* man; **~ à** similar to, like.

semblant [sɑ̃blɑ̃] *nm*: **un ~ de vérité** a semblance of truth; **faire ~ (de faire)** to pretend (to do).

sembler [sɑ̃ble] *vb avec attribut* to seem // *vb impersonnel*: **il semble (bien) que/inutile de** it (really) seems *ou* appears that/useless to; **il me semble que** it seems to me that; **I think (that); comme bon lui semble** as he sees fit.

semelle [səmɛl] *nf* sole; (*intérieure*) insole, inner sole.

semence [səmɑ̃s] *nf* (*graine*) seed.

semer [səme] *vt* to sow; (*fig: éparpiller*) to scatter; (: *confusion*) to spread; (: *poursuivants*) to lose, shake off; **semé de** (*difficultés*) riddled with.

semestre [səmɛstʀ(ə)] *nm* half-year; (*SCOL*) semester.

séminaire [seminɛʀ] *nm* seminar.

semi-remorque [səmiʀəmɔʀk(ə)] *nm*

articulated lorry (*Brit*), semi (trailer) (*US*).

semonce [səmɔ̃s] *nf*: un coup de ~ a shot across the bows.

semoule [səmul] *nf* semolina.

sempiternel, le [sɛ̃pitɛrnɛl] *a* eternal, never-ending.

sénat [sena] *nm* Senate; **sénateur** *nm* Senator.

sens [sɑ̃s] *nm* (PHYSIOL, *instinct*) sense; (*signification*) meaning, sense; (*direction*) direction; **à mon ~** to my mind; **reprendre ses ~** to regain consciousness; **dans le ~ des aiguilles d'une montre** clockwise; **~ commun** common sense; **~ dessus dessous** upside down; **~ interdit**, **~ unique** one-way street.

sensass [sɑ̃sas] *a* (*fam*) fantastic.

sensation [sɑ̃sasjɔ̃] *nf* sensation; **à ~** (*péj*) sensational.

sensé, e [sɑ̃se] *a* sensible.

sensibiliser [sɑ̃sibilize] *vt*: **~ qn à** to make sb sensitive to.

sensibilité [sɑ̃sibilite] *nf* sensitivity.

sensible [sɑ̃sibl(ə)] *a* sensitive; (*aux sens*) perceptible; (*appréciable: différence, progrès*) appreciable, noticeable; **~ment** *ad* (*notableement*) appreciably, noticeably; (*à peu près*): **ils ont ~ment le même poids** they weigh approximately the same; **~rie** *nf* sentimentality; squeamishness.

sensuel, le [sɑ̃sɥɛl] *a* sensual; sensuous.

sentence [sɑ̃tɑ̃s] *nf* (*jugement*) sentence; (*adage*) maxim.

sentier [sɑ̃tje] *nm* path.

sentiment [sɑ̃timɑ̃] *nm* feeling; **recevez mes ~s respectueux** yours faithfully; **sentimental, e, aux** *a* sentimental; (*vie, aventure*) love *cpd*.

sentinelle [sɑ̃tinɛl] *nf* sentry.

sentir [sɑ̃tir] *vt* (*par l'odorat*) to smell; (*par le goût*) to taste; (*au toucher, fig*) to feel; (*répandre une odeur de*) to smell of; (: *ressemblance*) to smell like; (*avoir la saveur de*) to taste of; to taste like // *vi* to smell; **~ mauvais** to smell bad; **se ~ bien** to feel good; **se ~ mal** (*être indisposé*) to feel unwell ou ill; **se ~ le courage/la force de faire** to feel brave/strong enough to do; **il ne peut pas le ~** (*fam*) he can't stand him.

séparation [separasjɔ̃] *nf* separation; (*cloison*) division, partition; **~ de corps** legal separation.

séparé, e [separe] *a* (*appartements, pouvoirs*) separate; (*époux*) separated; **~ment** *ad* separately.

séparer [separe] *vt* (*gén*) to separate; (*suj: divergences etc*) to divide; to drive apart; (: *différences, obstacles*) to stand between; (*détacher*): **~ qch de** to pull sth (off) from; (*diviser*): **~ qch par** to divide sth (up) with; **~ une pièce en deux** to divide a room into two; **se ~** *vi*

(*époux, amis, adversaires*) to separate, part; (*se diviser: route, tige etc*) to divide; (*se détacher*): **se ~ (de)** to split off (from); to come off; **se ~ de** (*époux*) to separate ou part from; (*employé, objet personnel*) to part with.

sept [sɛt] *num* seven.

septembre [sɛptɑ̃br(ə)] *nm* September.

septentrional, e, aux [sɛptɑ̃trijonal, -o] *a* northern.

septicémie [sɛptisemi] *nf* blood poisoning, septicaemia.

septième [sɛtjɛm] *num* seventh.

septique [sɛptik] *a*: **fosse ~** septic tank.

sépulture [sepyltyr] *nf* burial; burial place, grave.

séquelles [sekɛl] *nfpl* after-effects; (*fig*) aftermath *sg*; consequences.

séquestrer [sekɛstre] *vt* (*personne*) to confine illegally; (*biens*) to impound.

serai *etc vb voir* **être**.

serein, e [sərɛ̃, -ɛn] *a* serene; (*jugement*) dispassionate.

serez *vb voir* **être**.

sergent [sɛrʒɑ̃] *nm* sergeant.

série [seri] *nf* (*de questions, d'accidents*) series *inv*; (*de clés, casseroles, outils*) set; (*catégorie: SPORT*) rank; class; **en ~** in quick succession; (*COMM*) mass *cpd*; **de ~** a standard; **hors ~** (*COMM*) custom-built; (*fig*) outstanding.

sérieusement [serjøzmɑ̃] *ad* seriously; reliably; responsibly.

sérieux, euse [serjø, -øz] *a* serious; (*élève, employé*) reliable, responsible; (*client, maison*) reliable, dependable // *nm* seriousness; reliability; **garder son ~** to keep a straight face; **prendre qch/qn au ~** to take sth/sb seriously.

serin [sərɛ̃] *nm* canary.

seringue [sərɛ̃g] *nf* syringe.

serions *vb voir* **être**.

serment [sɛrmɑ̃] *nm* (*juré*) oath; (*promesse*) pledge, vow.

sermon [sɛrmɔ̃] *nm* sermon.

serpent [sɛrpɑ̃] *nm* snake; **~ à sonnettes** rattlesnake.

serpenter [sɛrpɑ̃te] *vi* to wind.

serpentin [sɛrpɑ̃tɛ̃] *nm* (*tube*) coil; (*ruban*) streamer.

serpillière [sɛrpijɛr] *nf* floorcloth.

serre [sɛr] *nf* (AGR) greenhouse; **~s** *nfpl* (*griffes*) claws, talons.

serré, e [sere] *a* (*réseau*) dense; (*écriture*) close; (*habits*) tight; (*fig: lutte, match*) tight, close-fought; (*passagers etc*) (tightly) packed.

serrer [sere] *vt* (*tenir*) to grip ou hold tight; (*comprimer, coincer*) to squeeze; (*poings, mâchoires*) to clench; (*suj: vêtement*) to be too tight for; to fit tightly; (*rapprocher*) to close up, move closer together; (*ceinture, nœud, frein, vis*) to tighten // *vi*: **~ à droite** to keep ou get over to the right; **se ~** *vi* (*se rap-*

procher) to squeeze up; se ~ **contre qn** to huddle up to sb; ~ **la main à qn** to shake sb's hand; ~ **qn dans ses bras to** hug sb, clasp sb in one's arms.

serrure [seryr] *nf* lock.

serrurier [seryrje] *nm* locksmith.

sert *etc vb voir* **servir**.

sertir [sertir] *vt* (*pierre*) to set.

servante [servɑ̃t] *nf* (maid)servant.

serveur, euse [servœr, -øz] *nm/f* waiter/waitress.

serviable [servjabl(ə)] *a* obliging, willing to help.

service [servis] *nm* (*gén*) service; (*série de repas*): **premier ~** first sitting; (*assortiment de vaisselle*) set, service; (*bureau: de la vente etc*) department, section; (*travail*): **pendant le ~** on duty; **~s** *nmpl* (*travail*, ÉCON) services; **faire le ~** to serve; **rendre ~ à** to help; **rendre un ~ à qn** to do sb a favour; **mettre en ~** to put into service *ou* operation; **hors ~** out of order; **~ après vente** after-sales service; **~ militaire** military service; **~ d'ordre** police (*ou* stewards) in charge of maintaining order; **~s secrets** secret service *sg*.

serviette [servjet] *nf* (*de table*) (table) napkin, serviette; (*de toilette*) towel; (*porte-documents*) briefcase; **~ hygiénique** sanitary towel.

servir [servir] *vt* (*gén*) to serve; (*au restaurant*) to wait on; (*au magasin*) to serve, attend to; (*fig: aider*): **~ qn** to aid sb; to serve sb's interests; (*COMM: rente*) to pay // *vi* (*TENNIS*) to serve; (*CARTES*) to deal; **vous êtes servi?** are you being served?; **se ~** *vi* (*prendre d'un plat*) to help o.s.; **se ~ de** (*plat*) to help o.s. to; (*voiture, outil, relations*) to use; **~ à qn** (*diplôme, livre*) to be of use to sb; **~ à qch/faire** (*outil etc*) to be used for sth/doing; **à quoi cela sert-il (de faire)?** what's the use (of doing)?; **cela ne sert à rien** it's no use; **~ (à qn) de** to serve as (for sb); **~ à dîner (à qn)** to serve dinner to sb).

serviteur [servitœr] *nm* servant.

servitude [servityd] *nf* servitude; (*fig*) constraint.

ses [se] *dét voir* **son**.

seuil [sœj] *nm* doorstep; (*fig*) threshold.

seul, e [sœl] *a* (*sans compagnie*) alone; (*avec nuance affective: isolé*) lonely; (*unique*): **un ~ livre** only one book, a single book; **le ~ livre** the only book; ~ **ce livre, ce livre ~** this book alone, only this book // *ad* (*vivre*) alone, on one's own; **parler tout ~** to talk to oneself; **faire qch (tout) ~** to do sth (all) on one's own *ou* (all) by oneself // *nm, nf*: **il en reste un(e) ~(e)** there's only one left; **à lui (tout) ~** single-handed, on his own.

seulement [sœlmɑ̃] *ad* only; **non ~ ... mais aussi** *ou* **encore** not only ... but

also.

sève [sev] *nf* sap.

sévère [sever] *a* severe.

sévices [sevis] *nmpl* (physical) cruelty *sg*, ill treatment *sg*.

sévir [sevir] *vi* (*punir*) to use harsh measures, crack down; (*suj: fléau*) to rage, be rampant.

sevrer [səvre] *vt* (*enfant etc*) to wean.

sexe [seks(ə)] *nm* sex; (*organe mâle*) member.

sexuel, le [seksɥel] *a* sexual.

seyant, e [sejɑ̃, -ɑ̃t] *a* becoming.

shampooing [ʃɑ̃pwɛ̃] *nm* shampoo; **se faire un ~** to shampoo one's hair.

short [ʃɔrt] *nm* (pair of) shorts *pl*.

si [si] ♦ *nm* (*MUS*) B; (*en chantant la gamme*) ti
♦ *ad* **1** (*oui*) yes
2 (*tellement*) so; ~ **gentil/rapidement** so kind/fast; (*tant et*) ~ **bien que** so much so that; ~ **rapide qu'il soit** however fast he may be
♦ *cj* if; ~ **tu veux** if you want; **je me demande** ~ I wonder if *ou* whether; ~ **seulement** if only.

Sicile [sisil] *nf*: **la ~** Sicily.

SIDA [sida] *sigle m* (= *syndrome immuno-déficitaire acquis*) AIDS *sg*.

sidéré, e [sidere] *a* staggered.

sidérurgie [sideryrʒi] *nf* steel industry.

siècle [sjɛkl(ə)] *nm* century; (*époque*) age.

siège [sjɛʒ] *nm* seat; (*d'entreprise*) head office; (*d'organisation*) headquarters *pl*; (*MIL*) siege; ~ **social** registered office.

siéger [sjeʒe] *vi* to sit.

sien, ne [sjɛ̃, sjɛn] *pronom*: **le(la) ~(ne), les ~s(~nes)** his; hers; its; **faire des ~nes** (*fam*) to be up to one's (usual) tricks; **les ~s** (*sa famille*) one's family.

sieste [sjɛst(ə)] *nf* (*afternoon*) snooze *ou* nap, siesta; **faire la ~** to have a snooze *ou* nap.

sieur [sjœr] *nm*: **le ~ Thomas** Master Thomas.

sifflement [sifləmɑ̃] *nm* whistle, whistling *q*; wheezing *q*; hissing *q*.

siffler [sifle] *vi* (*gén*) to whistle; (*en respirant*) to wheeze; (*serpent, vapeur*) to hiss // *vt* (*chanson*) to whistle; (*chien etc*) to whistle for; (*fille*) to whistle at; (*pièce, orateur*) to hiss, boo; (*faute*) to blow one's whistle at; (*fin du match, départ*) to blow one's whistle for; (*fam: verre*) to guzzle.

sifflet [sifle] *nm* whistle; **coup de ~** whistle.

siffloter [siflote] *vi*, *vt* to whistle.

sigle [sigl(ə)] *nm* acronym.

signal, aux [sinal, -o] *nm* (*signe convenu, appareil*) signal; (*indice, écriteau*) sign; **donner le ~ de** to give the signal for; ~ **d'alarme** alarm signal; **signaux (lumineux)** (*AUTO*) traffic signals.

signalement [siɲalmã] *nm* description, particulars *pl*.

signaler [siɲale] *vt* to indicate; to announce; to report; *(faire remarquer)*: ~ qch à qn/(à qn) que to point out sth to sb/to sb that; se ~ **(par)** to distinguish o.s. (by).

signaliser [siɲalize] *vt* to put up road-signs on; to put signals on.

signature [siɲatyʀ] *nf* signature *(action)*, signing.

signe [siɲ] *nm* sign; *(TYPO)* mark; **faire un ~ de la main** to give a sign with one's hand; **faire ~ à qn** *(fig)* to get in touch with sb; **faire ~ à qn d'entrer** to motion (to) sb to come in.

signer [siɲe] *vt* to sign; se ~ *vi* to cross o.s.

signet [siɲɛ] *nm* bookmark.

significatif, ive [siɲifikatif, -iv] *a* significant.

signification [siɲifikasjɔ̃] *nf* meaning.

signifier [siɲifje] *vt* *(vouloir dire)* to mean; *(faire connaître)*: ~ qch (à qn) to make sth known (to sb); *(JUR)*: ~ qch à qn to serve notice of sth on sb.

silence [silãs] *nm* silence; *(MUS)* rest; **garder le ~** to keep silent, say nothing; **passer sous ~** to pass over (in silence); **silencieux, euse** *a* quiet, silent // *nm* silencer.

silex [silɛks] *nm* flint.

silhouette [silwɛt] *nf* outline, silhouette; *(lignes, contour)* outline; *(figure)* figure.

silicium [silisjɔm] *nm* silicon; **plaquette de ~** silicon chip.

sillage [sijaʒ] *nm* wake; *(fig)* trail.

sillon [sijɔ̃] *nm* furrow; *(de disque)* groove; **sillonner** *vt* to criss-cross.

simagrées [simagʀe] *nfpl* fuss *sg*; airs and graces.

similaire [similɛʀ] *a* similar; **similicuir** *nm* imitation leather; **similitude** *nf* similarity.

simple [sɛ̃pl(ə)] *a* *(gén)* simple; *(non multiple)* single; **~s** *nmpl* *(MÉD)* medicinal plants; **~ messieurs** *nm* *(TENNIS)* men's singles *sg*; **un ~ particulier** an ordinary citizen; **~ d'esprit** *nm/f* simpleton; **~ soldat** private.

simulacre [simylakʀ(ə)] *nm* *(péj)*: **un ~ de** a pretence of.

simuler [simyle] *vt* to sham, simulate.

simultané, e [simyltane] *a* simultaneous.

sincère [sɛ̃sɛʀ] *a* sincere; genuine; **sincérité** *nf* sincerity.

sine qua non [sinekwanɔn] *a*: **condition ~** indispensable condition.

singe [sɛ̃ʒ] *nm* monkey; *(de grande taille)* ape.

singer [sɛ̃ʒe] *vt* to ape, mimic.

singeries [sɛ̃ʒʀi] *nfpl* antics; *(simagrées)* airs and graces.

singulariser [sɛ̃gylaʀize] *vt* to mark

out; se ~ *vi* to call attention to o.s.

singularité [sɛ̃gylaʀite] *nf* peculiarity.

singulier, ière [sɛ̃gyljе, -jɛʀ] *a* remarkable, singular // *nm* singular.

sinistre [sinistʀ(ə)] *a* sinister // *nm* *(incendie)* blaze; *(catastrophe)* disaster; *(ASSURANCES)* damage *(giving rise to a claim)*; **sinistré, e** *a* disaster-stricken // *nm/f* disaster victim.

sinon [sinɔ̃] *cj* *(autrement, sans quoi)* otherwise, or else; *(sauf)* except, other than; *(si ce n'est)* if not.

sinueux, euse [sinɥø, -øz] *a* winding; *(fig)* tortuous.

sinus [sinys] *nm* *(ANAT)* sinus; *(GÉOM)* sine; **sinusite** *nf* sinusitis.

siphon [sifɔ̃] *nm* *(tube, d'eau gazeuse)* siphon; *(d'évier etc)* U-bend.

sirène [siʀɛn] *nf* siren; **~ d'alarme** air-raid siren; fire alarm.

sirop [siʀo] *nm* *(à diluer: de fruit etc)* syrup; *(boisson)* fruit drink; *(pharmaceutique)* syrup, mixture.

siroter [siʀote] *vt* to sip.

sis, e [si, siz] *a* located.

sismique [sismik] *a* seismic.

site [sit] *nm* *(paysage, environnement)* setting; *(d'une ville etc: emplacement)* site; **~** *(pittoresque)* beauty spot; **~s touristiques** places of interest.

sitôt [sito] *ad*: **~ parti** as soon as he *etc* had left; **~ après** straight after; **pas de ~** not for a long time.

situation [sitɥasjɔ̃] *nf* *(gén)* situation; *(d'un édifice, d'une ville)* situation, position; location.

situé, e [sitɥe] *a*: **bien ~** well situated; **~ à** situated at.

situer [sitɥe] *vt* to site, situate; *(en pensée)* to set, place; se ~ *vi*: **se ~ à/près de** to be situated at/near.

six [sis] *num* six; **sixième** *num* sixth.

ski [ski] *nm* *(objet)* ski; *(sport)* skiing; **faire du ~** to ski; **~ de fond** cross-country skiing; **~ nautique** water-skiing; **~ de piste** downhill skiing; **~ de randonnée** cross-country skiing; **skier** *vi* to ski; **skieur, euse** *nm/f* skier.

slip [slip] *nm* *(sous-vêtement)* pants *pl*, briefs *pl*; *(de bain: d'homme)* trunks *pl*; *(: du bikini)* (bikini) briefs *pl*.

slogan [slɔgã] *nm* slogan.

S.M.I.C. [smik] *sigle m voir* **salaire**.

smoking [smɔkiaʒ] *nm* dinner *ou* evening suit.

S.N.C.F. *sigle f (= société nationale des chemins de fer français)* French railways.

snob [snɔb] *a* snobbish // *nm/f* snob.

sobre [sɔbʀ(ə)] *a* temperate, abstemious; *(élégance, style)* sober; **~ de** *(gestes, compliments)* sparing of.

sobriquet [sɔbʀikɛ] *nm* nickname.

social, e, aux [sɔsjal, -o] *a* social.

socialisme [sɔsjalism(ə)] *nm* socialism;

socialiste nm/f socialist.

société [sɔsjete] nf society; (sportive) club; (COMM) company; la ~ d'abondance/de consommation the affluent/consumer society; ~ anonyme (S.A.) ≈ limited (Brit) ou incorporated (US) company; ~ à responsabilité limitée (S.A.R.L.) type of limited liability company (with non-negotiable shares).

sociologie [sɔsjɔlɔʒi] nf sociology.

socle [sɔkl(ə)] nm (de colonne, statue) plinth, pedestal; (de lampe) base.

socquette [sɔkɛt] nf ankle sock.

sœur [sœʀ] nf sister; (religieuse) nun, sister.

soi [swa] pronom oneself; cela va de ~ that ou it goes without saying; ~-disant a inv so-called // ad supposedly.

soie [swa] nf silk; (de porc, sanglier: poil) bristle; ~rie nf (tissu) silk.

soif [swaf] nf thirst; avoir ~ to be thirsty; donner ~ à qn to make sb thirsty.

soigné, e [swaɲe] a (tenue) well-groomed, neat; (travail) careful, meticulous; (fam) whopping; stiff.

soigner [swaɲe] vt (malade, maladie: suj: docteur) to treat; (suj: infirmière, mère) to nurse, look after; (blessé) to tend; (travail, détails) to take care over; (jardin, chevelure, invités) to look after.

soigneux, euse [swaɲø, -øz] a (propre) tidy, neat; (méticuleux) painstaking, careful; ~ de careful with.

soi-même [swamɛm] pronom oneself.

soin [swɛ̃] nm (application) care; (propreté, ordre) tidiness, neatness; ~s nmpl (à un malade, blessé) treatment sg, medical attention sg; (attentions, prévenance) care and attention sg; (hygiène) care sg; prendre ~ de to take care of, look after; prendre ~ de faire to take care to do; les premiers ~s first aid sg; aux bons ~s de c/o, care of.

soir [swaʀ] nm evening; ce ~ this evening, tonight; demain ~ tomorrow evening, tomorrow night.

soirée [swaʀe] nf evening; (réception) party.

soit [swa] vb voir être // cj (à savoir) namely; (ou): ~ ... ~ either ... or // ad so be it, very well; ~ que ... ou que ou que whether ... or whether.

soixantaine [swasɑ̃tɛn] nf: une ~ (de) sixty or so, about sixty; avoir la ~ (âge) to be around sixty.

soixante [swasɑ̃t] num sixty; ~-dix seventy.

soja [sɔʒa] nm soya; (graines) soya beans pl.

sol [sɔl] nm ground; (de logement) floor; (revêtement) flooring q; (territoire, AGR, GÉO) soil; (MUS) G; (: en chantant la gamme) so(h).

solaire [sɔlɛʀ] a solar, sun cpd.

soldat [sɔlda] nm soldier.

solde [sɔld(ə)] nf pay // nm (COMM) balance; ~s nmpl ou nfpl (COMM) sale goods; sales; en ~ at sale price.

solder [sɔlde] vt (compte) to settle; (marchandise) to sell at sale price, sell off; se ~ par (fig) to end in; article soldé (à) 10 F item reduced to 10 F.

sole [sɔl] nf sole inv (fish).

soleil [sɔlɛj] nm sun; (lumière) sun(light); (temps ensoleillé) sun(shine); (BOT) sunflower; il fait du ~ it's sunny; au ~ in the sun.

solennel, le [sɔlanɛl] a solemn; ceremonial; **solennité** nf (d'une fête) solemnity.

solfège [sɔlfɛʒ] nm rudiments pl of music; (exercices) ear training q.

solidaire [sɔlidɛʀ] a (personnes) who stand together, who show solidarity; (pièces mécaniques) interdependent; être ~ de (collègues) to stand by; **solidarité** nf solidarity; interdependence; par solidarité (avec) in sympathy (with).

solide [sɔlid] a solid; (mur, maison, meuble) solid, sturdy; (connaissances, argument) sound; (personne, estomac) robust, sturdy // nm solid.

soliste [sɔlist(ə)] nm/f soloist.

solitaire [sɔlitɛʀ] a (sans compagnie) solitary, lonely; (lieu) lonely // nm/f recluse; loner.

solitude [sɔlityd] nf loneliness; (paix) solitude.

solive [sɔliv] nf joist.

sollicitations [sɔlisitɑsjɔ̃] nfpl entreaties, appeals; enticements; (TECH) stress sg.

solliciter [sɔlisite] vt (personne) to appeal to; (emploi, faveur) to seek; (suj: occupations, attractions etc): ~ qn to appeal to sb's curiosity; to entice sb; to make demands on sb's time.

sollicitude [sɔlisityd] nf concern.

soluble [sɔlybl(ə)] a soluble.

solution [sɔlysjɔ̃] nf solution; ~ de facilité easy way out.

solvable [sɔlvabl(ə)] a solvent.

sombre [sɔ̃bʀ(ə)] a dark; (fig) gloomy.

sombrer [sɔ̃bʀe] vi (bateau) to sink; ~ dans (misère, désespoir) to sink into.

sommaire [sɔmɛʀ] a (simple) basic; (expéditif) summary // nm summary.

sommation [sɔmɑsjɔ̃] nf (JUR) summons sg; (avant de faire feu) warning.

somme [sɔm] nf (MATH) sum; (fig) amount; (argent) sum, amount // nm: faire un ~ to have a (short) nap; en ~ ad all in all; ~ toute all in all.

sommeil [sɔmɛj] nm sleep; avoir ~ to be sleepy; **sommeiller** vi to doze; (fig) to lie dormant.

sommelier [sɔmǝlje] nm wine waiter.

sommer [sɔme] *vt*: ~ qn de faire to command *ou* order sb to do; (*JUR*) to summon sb to do.

sommes *vb voir* **être**.

sommet [sɔme] *nm* top; (*d'une montagne*) summit, top; (*fig: de la perfection, gloire*) height.

sommier [sɔmje] *nm* (bed) base.

sommité [sɔmite] *nf* prominent person, leading light.

somnambule [sɔmnɑ̃byl] *nm/f* sleepwalker.

somnifère [sɔmnifɛʀ] *nm* sleeping drug *q* (*ou* pill).

somnoler [sɔmnɔle] *vi* to doze.

somptueux, euse [sɔ̃ptɥø, -øz] *a* sumptuous; lavish.

son [sɔ̃], **sa** [sa], *pl* **ses** [se] *dét* (*antécédent humain mâle*) his; (: *femelle*) her; (: *valeur indéfinie*) one's, his/her; (: *non humain*) its.

son [sɔ̃] *nm* sound; (*de blé*) bran.

sondage [sɔ̃daʒ] *nm*: ~ (d'opinion) (opinion) poll.

sonde [sɔ̃d] *nf* (*NAVIG*) lead *ou* sounding line; (*MÉD*) probe; catheter; feeding tube; (*TECH*) borer, driller; (*pour fouiller etc*) probe.

sonder [sɔ̃de] *vt* (*NAVIG*) to sound; (*atmosphère, plaie, bagages etc*) to probe; (*TECH*) to bore, drill; (*fig*) to sound out; to probe.

songe [sɔ̃ʒ] *nm* dream.

songer [sɔ̃ʒe] *vi*: ~ à (*penser à*) to think of; ~ que to consider that; to think that; **songeur, euse** *a* pensive.

sonnant, e [sɔnɑ̃, -ɑ̃t] *a*: à 8 heures ~es on the stroke of 8.

sonné, e [sɔne] *a* (*fam*) cracked; il est midi ~ it's gone twelve.

sonner [sɔne] *vi* to ring // *vt* (*cloche*) to ring; (*glas, tocsin*) to sound; (*portier, infirmière*) to ring for; (*messe*) to ring the bell for; ~ **faux** (*instrument*) to sound out of tune; (*rire*) to ring false; ~ **les heures** to strike the hours.

sonnerie [sɔnʀi] *nf* (*son*) ringing; (*sonnette*) bell; (*mécanisme d'horloge*) striking mechanism; ~ **d'alarme** alarm bell.

sonnette [sɔnɛt] *nf* bell; ~ **d'alarme** alarm bell; ~ **de nuit** night-bell.

sono [sɔno] *abr f de* **sonorisation**.

sonore [sɔnɔʀ] *a* (*voix*) sonorous, ringing; (*salle, métal*) resonant; (*ondes, film, signal*) sound cpd.

sonorisation [sɔnɔʀizasjɔ̃] *nf* (*installations*) public address system, P.A. system.

sonorité [sɔnɔʀite] *nf* (*de piano, violon*) tone; (*de voix, mot*) sonority; (*d'une salle*) resonance; acoustics *pl*.

sont *vb voir* **être**.

sophistiqué, e [sɔfistike] *a* sophisticated.

sorbet [sɔʀbɛ] *nm* water ice, sorbet.

sorcellerie [sɔʀsɛlʀi] *nf* witchcraft *q*.

sorcier, ière [sɔʀsje, -jɛʀ] *nm/f* sorcerer/witch *ou* sorceress.

sordide [sɔʀdid] *a* sordid; squalid.

sornettes [sɔʀnɛt] *nfpl* twaddle *sg*.

sort [sɔʀ] *nm* (*fortune, destinée*) fate; (*condition, situation*) lot; (*magique*) curse, spell; **tirer au** ~ to draw lots.

sorte [sɔʀt(ə)] *nf* sort, kind; **de la** ~ *ad* in that way; **de (telle)** ~ **que, en** ~ **que** so that; so much so that; **faire en** ~ **que** to see to it that.

sortie [sɔʀti] *nf* (*issue*) way out, exit; (*MIL*) sortie; (*fig: verbale*) outburst; sally; (*promenade*) outing; (*le soir: au restaurant etc*) night out; (*COMM: somme*): ~s items of expenditure; outgoings *sans sg*; ~ **de bain** (*vêtement*) bathrobe; ~ **de secours** emergency exit.

sortilège [sɔʀtilɛʒ] *nm* (magic) spell.

sortir [sɔʀtiʀ] *vi* (*gén*) to come out; (*partir, se promener, aller au spectacle etc*) to go out; (*numéro gagnant*) to come up // *vt* (*gén*) to take out; (*produit, ouvrage, modèle*) to bring out; (*INFORM*) to output; (: *sur papier*) to print out; (*fam: expulser*) to throw out; ~ **de** (*gén*) to leave; (*endroit*) to go (*ou* come) out of, leave; (*rainure etc*) to come out of; (*cadre, compétence*) to be outside; **se** ~ **de** (*affaire, situation*) to get out of; **s'en** ~ (*malade*) to pull through; (*d'une difficulté etc*) to get through.

sosie [sozi] *nm* double.

sot, sotte [so, sɔt] *a* silly, foolish // *nm/f* fool; **sottise** *nf* silliness, foolishness; silly *ou* foolish thing.

sou [su] *nm*: **près de ses** ~s tight-fisted; **sans le** ~ penniless.

soubresaut [subʀəso] *nm* start; jolt.

souche [suʃ] *nf* (*d'arbre*) stump; (*de carnet*) counterfoil (*Brit*), stub; **de vieille** ~ of old stock.

souci [susi] *nm* (*inquiétude*) worry; (*préoccupation*) concern; (*BOT*) marigold; **se faire du** ~ to worry.

soucier [susje]: **se** ~ **de** *vt* to care about.

soucieux, euse [susjø, -øz] *a* concerned, worried.

soucoupe [sukup] *nf* saucer; ~ **volante** flying saucer.

soudain, e [sudɛ̃, -ɛn] *a* (*douleur, mort*) sudden // *ad* suddenly, all of a sudden.

soude [sud] *nf* soda.

souder [sude] *vt* (*avec fil à souder*) to solder; (*par soudure autogène*) to weld; (*fig*) to bind together.

soudoyer [sudwaje] *vt* (*péj*) to bribe.

soudure [sudyʀ] *nf* soldering; welding; (*joint*) soldered joint; weld.

souffert, e [sufɛʀ, -ɛʀt(ə)] *pp de* **souffrir**.

souffle [sufl(ə)] *nm* (*en expirant*) breath; (*en soufflant*) puff, blow;

(*respiration*) breathing; (*d'explosion, de ventilateur*) blast; (*du vent*) blowing; être à bout de ~ to be out of breath; un ~ d'air *ou* de vent a breath of air, a puff of wind.

soufflé, e [sufle] *a* (*fam: stupéfié*) staggered // *nm* (*CULIN*) soufflé.

souffler [sufle] *vi* (*gén*) to blow; (*haleter*) to puff (and blow) // *vt* (*feu, bougie*) to blow out; (*chasser: poussière etc*) to blow away; (*TECH: verre*) to blow; (*suj: explosion*) to destroy (with its blast); (*dire*): ~ qch à qn to whisper sth to sb; (*fam: voler*): ~ qch à qn to pinch sth from sb.

soufflet [sufle] *nm* (*instrument*) bellows *pl*; (*gifle*) slap (in the face).

souffleur [sufloœr] *nm* (*THÉÂTRE*) prompter.

souffrance [sufrãs] *nf* suffering; en ~ (*marchandise*) awaiting delivery; (*affaire*) pending.

souffrant, e [sufrã, -ãt] *a* unwell.

souffre-douleur [sufrədulœr] *nm inv* butt, underdog.

souffrir [sufrir] *vi* to suffer; to be in pain // *vt* to suffer, endure; (*supporter*) to bear, stand; (*admettre: exception etc*) to allow *ou* admit of; ~ de (*maladie, froid*) to suffer from.

soufre [sufr(ə)] *nm* sulphur.

souhait [swɛ] *nm* wish; tous nos ~s de good wishes *ou* our best wishes for; riche etc à ~ as rich etc as one could wish; à vos ~s! bless you!

souhaitable [swɛtabl(ə)] *a* desirable.

souhaiter [swete] *vt* to wish for; ~ la bonne année à qn to wish sb a happy New Year.

souiller [suje] *vt* to dirty, soil; (*fig*) to sully, tarnish.

soûl, e [su, sul] *a* drunk // *nm*: tout son ~ to one's heart's content.

soulagement [sulaʒmã] *nm* relief.

soulager [sulaʒe] *vt* to relieve.

soûler [sule] *vt*: ~ qn to get sb drunk; (*suj: boisson*) to make sb drunk; (*fig*) to make sb's head spin *ou* reel; se ~ *vi* to get drunk.

soulever [sulve] *vt* to lift; (*vagues, poussière*) to send up; (*peuple*) to stir up (to revolt); (*enthousiasme*) to arouse; (*question, débat*) to raise; se ~ *vi* (*peuple*) to rise up; (*personne couchée*) to lift o.s. up; cela me soulève le cœur it makes me feel sick.

soulier [sulje] *nm* shoe.

souligner [suliɲe] *vt* to underline; (*fig*) to emphasize; to stress.

soumettre [sumetr] *vt* (*pays*) to subject, subjugate; (*rebelle*) to put down, subdue; ~ qn/qch à to subject sb/sth to; ~ qch à qn (*projet etc*) to submit sth to sb; se ~ (à) to submit (to).

soumis, e [sumi, -iz] *a* submissive;

revenus ~ à l'impôt taxable income.

soumission [sumisjɔ̃] *nf* submission; (*docilité*) submissiveness; (*COMM*) tender.

soupape [supap] *nf* valve.

soupçon [supsɔ̃] *nm* suspicion; (*petite quantité*): un ~ de a hint *ou* touch of;

soupçonner *vt* to suspect; **soupçonneux, euse** *a* suspicious.

soupe [sup] *nf* soup; ~ au lait *a inv* quick-tempered.

souper [supe] *vi* to have supper // *nm* supper.

soupeser [supəze] *vt* to weigh in one's hand(s); (*fig*) to weigh up.

soupière [supjɛr] *nf* (soup) tureen.

soupir [supir] *nm* sigh; (*MUS*) crotchet rest.

soupirail, aux [supiraj, -o] *nm* (small) basement window.

soupirer [supire] *vi* to sigh; ~ après qch to yearn for sth.

souple [supl(ə)] *a* supple; (*fig: règlement, caractère*) flexible; (: *démarche, taille*) lithe, supple.

source [surs(ə)] *nf* (*point d'eau*) spring; (*d'un cours d'eau, fig*) source; de bonne ~ on good authority.

sourcil [sursij] *nm* (eye)brow.

sourciller [sursije] *vi*: sans ~ without turning a hair *ou* batting an eyelid.

sourcilleux, euse [sursijø, -øz] *a* pernickety.

sourd, e [sur, surd(ə)] *a* deaf; (*bruit, voix*) muffled; (*douleur*) dull; (*lutte*) silent, hidden // *nm/f* deaf person.

sourdine [surdin] *nf* (*MUS*) mute; en ~ *ad* softly, quietly.

sourd-muet, sourde-muette [surmyɛ, surdmyɛt] *a* deaf-and-dumb // *nm/f* deaf-mute.

souriant, e [surjã, -ãt] *a* cheerful.

souricière [surisjɛr] *nf* mousetrap; (*fig*) trap.

sourire [surir] *nm* smile // *vi* to smile; ~ à qn to smile at sb; (*fig*) to appeal to sb; to smile on sb; garder le ~ to keep smiling.

souris [suri] *nf* mouse (*pl* mice).

sournois, e [surnwa, -waz] *a* deceitful, underhand.

sous [su] *prép* (*gén*) under; ~ la pluie/le soleil in the rain/sunshine; ~ terre *a, ad* underground; ~ peu *ad* shortly, before long.

sous-alimenté, e [suzalimãte] *a* undernourished.

sous-bois [subwa] *nm inv* undergrowth.

souscrire [suskrir]: ~ à *vt* to subscribe to.

sous-directeur, trice [sudirɛktœr, -tris] *nm/f* assistant manager/manageress.

sous-entendre [suzãtãdr(ə)] *vt* to imply, infer; **sous-entendu, e** *a* implied;

(*LING*) understood // *nm* innuendo, insinuation.

sous-estimer [suzɛstime] *vt* to underestimate.

sous-jacent, e [suʒasɑ̃, -ɑ̃t] *a* underlying.

sous-louer [sulwe] *vt* to sublet.

sous-main [sumɛ̃] *nm inv* desk blotter; **en ~** *ad* secretly.

sous-marin, e [sumarɛ̃, -in] *a* (*flore, volcan*) submarine; (*navigation, pêche, explosif*) underwater // *nm* submarine.

sous-officier [suzɔfisje] *nm* ≈ noncommissioned officer (N.C.O.).

sous-produit [suprɔdɥi] *nm* byproduct; (*fig: péj*) pale imitation.

soussigné, e [susiɲe] *a*: **je ~** I the undersigned.

sous-sol [susɔl] *nm* basement.

sous-titre [sutitr(ə)] *nm* subtitle.

soustraction [sustraksjɔ̃] *nf* subtraction.

soustraire [sustrɛr] *vt* to subtract, take away; (*dérober*): **~ qch à qn** to remove sth from sb; **~ qn à** (*danger*) to shield sb from; **se ~ à** (*autorité etc*) to elude, escape from.

sous-traitant [sutrɛtɑ̃] *nm* subcontractor.

sous-vêtements [suvɛtmɑ̃] *nmpl* underwear *sg*.

soutane [sutan] *nf* cassock, soutane.

soute [sut] *nf* hold.

soutènement [sutɛnmɑ̃] *nm*: **mur de ~** retaining wall.

souteneur [sutnœr] *nm* procurer.

soutenir [sutnir] *vt* to support; (*assaut, choc*) to stand up to, withstand; (*intérêt, effort*) to keep up; (*assurer*): **~ que** to maintain that; **~ la comparaison avec** to bear *ou* stand comparison with; **soutenu, e** *a* (*efforts*) sustained, unflagging; (*style*) elevated.

souterrain, e [sutɛrɛ̃, -ɛn] *a* underground // *nm* underground passage.

soutien [sutjɛ̃] *nm* support; **~ de famille** breadwinner.

soutien-gorge [sutjɛ̃gɔrʒ(ə)] *nm* bra.

soutirer [sutire] *vt*: **~ qch à qn** to squeeze *ou* get sth out of sb.

souvenir [suvnir] *nm* (*réminiscence*) memory; (*objet*) souvenir // *vb*: **se ~ de** *vt* to remember; **se ~ que** to remember that; **en ~ de** in memory *ou* remembrance of.

souvent [suvɑ̃] *ad* often; **peu ~** seldom, infrequently.

souverain, e [suvrɛ̃, -ɛn] *a* sovereign; (*fig: mépris*) supreme // *nm/f* sovereign, monarch.

soviétique [sɔvjetik] *a* Soviet // *nm/f*: **S~** Soviet citizen.

soyeux, euse [swajø, øz] *a* silky.

soyons etc *vb voir* **être**.

spacieux, euse [spasjø, -øz] *a* spa-

cious; roomy.

spaghettis [spageti] *nmpl* spaghetti *sg*.

sparadrap [sparadra] *nm* sticking plaster (*Brit*), bandaid ® (*US*).

spatial, e, aux [spasjal, -o] *a* (*AVIAT*) space *cpd*.

speaker, ine [spikœr, -krin] *nm/f* announcer.

spécial, e, aux [spesjal, -o] *a* special; (*bizarre*) peculiar; **~ement** *ad* especially, particularly; (*tout exprès*) specially.

spécialiser [spesjalize]: **se ~** *vi* to specialize.

spécialiste [spesjalist(ə)] *nm/f* specialist.

spécialité [spesjalite] *nf* speciality; (*SCOL*) special field.

spécifier [spesifje] *vt* to specify, state.

spécimen [spesimɛn] *nm* specimen; (*revue etc*) specimen *ou* sample copy.

spectacle [spɛktakl(ə)] *nm* (*tableau, scène*) sight; (*représentation*) show; (*industrie*) show business; **spectaculaire** *a* spectacular.

spectateur, trice [spɛktatœr, -tris] *nm/f* (*CINÉMA etc*) member of the audience; (*SPORT*) spectator; (*d'un événement*) onlooker, witness.

spéculer [spekyle] *vi* to speculate; **~ sur** (*COMM*) to speculate in; (*réfléchir*) to speculate on.

spéléologie [speleolɔʒi] *nf* potholing.

sperme [spɛrm(ə)] *nm* semen, sperm.

sphère [sfɛr] *nf* sphere.

spirale [spiral] *nf* spiral.

spirituel, le [spirityɛl] *a* spiritual; (*fin, piquant*) witty.

spiritueux [spirityø] *nm* spirit.

splendide [splɑ̃did] *a* splendid; magnificent.

spontané, e [spɔ̃tane] *a* spontaneous.

sport [spɔr] *nm* sport // *a inv* (*vêtement*) casual; **faire du ~** to do sport; **~s d'hiver** winter sports; **sportif, ive** *a* (*journal, association, épreuve*) sports *cpd*; (*allure, démarche*) athletic; (*attitude, esprit*) sporting.

spot [spɔt] *nm* (*lampe*) spot(light); (*annonce*): **~ (publicitaire)** commercial (break).

square [skwar] *nm* public garden(s).

squelette [skəlɛt] *nm* skeleton; **squelettique** *a* scrawny; (*fig*) skimpy.

stabiliser [stabilize] *vt* to stabilize; (*terrain*) to consolidate.

stable [stabl(ə)] *a* stable, steady.

stade [stad] *nm* (*SPORT*) stadium; (*phase, niveau*) stage.

stage [staʒ] *nm* training period; training course; **stagiaire** *nm/f, a* trainee.

stalle [stal] *nf* stall, box.

stand [stɑ̃d] *nm* (*d'exposition*) stand; (*de foire*) stall; **~ de tir** (*à la foire, SPORT*) shooting range.

standard [stɑdaʀ] a inv standard // nm switchboard; **standardiste** nm/f switchboard operator.

standing [stɑdiaj] nm standing; **immeuble de grand ~** block of luxury flats (Brit), condo(minium) (US).

starter [staʀtɛʀ] nm (AUTO) choke.

station [stasjɔ̃] nf station; (de bus) stop; (de villégiature) resort; (posture): **la ~ debout** standing, an upright posture; **~ de ski** ski resort; **~ de taxis** taxi rank (Brit) ou stand (US).

stationnement [stasjɔnmɑ̃] nm parking.

stationner [stasjɔne] vi to park.

station-service [stasjɔ̃sɛʀvis] nf service station.

statistique [statistik] nf (science) statistics sg; (rapport, étude) statistic // a statistical.

statue [staty] nf statue.

statuer [statɥe] vi: **~ sur** to rule on, give a ruling on.

statut [staty] nm status; **~s** nmpl (JUR, ADMIN) statutes; **statutaire** a statutory.

Sté abr de **société.**

steak [stɛk] nm steak.

sténo... [steno] préfixe: **~(dactylo)** nf shorthand typist (Brit), stenographer (US); **~(graphie)** nf shorthand.

stéréo(phonique) [steʀeo(fɔnik)] a stereo(phonic).

stérile [steʀil] a sterile; (terre) barren; (fig) fruitless, futile.

stérilet [steʀilɛ] nm coil, loop.

stériliser [steʀilize] vt to sterilize.

stigmates [stigmat] nmpl scars, marks.

stimulant [stimylɑ̃] nm (fig) stimulus (pl i), incentive.

stimuler [stimyle] vt to stimulate.

stipuler [stipyle] vt to stipulate.

stock [stɔk] nm stock; **~ d'or** (FINANCE) gold reserves pl; **~er** vt to stock.

stop [stɔp] nm (AUTO: écriteau) stop sign; (: signal) brake-light.

stopper [stɔpe] vt to stop, halt; (COUTURE) to mend // vi to stop, halt.

store [stɔʀ] nm blind; (de magasin) shade, awning.

strabisme [stʀabism(ə)] nm squinting.

strapontin [stʀapɔ̃tɛ̃] nm jump ou foldaway seat.

stratégie [stʀateʒi] nf strategy; **stratégique** a strategic.

stressant, e [stʀesɑ̃, -ɑ̃t] a stressful.

strict, e [stʀikt(ə)] a strict; (tenue, décor) severe, plain; **son droit le plus ~** his most basic right; **le ~ nécessaire/minimum** the bare essentials/minimum.

strie [stʀi] nf streak.

strophe [stʀɔf] nf verse, stanza.

structure [stʀyktyʀ] nf structure; **~s d'accueil** reception facilities.

studieux, euse [stydjø, -øz] a studious;

devoted to study.

studio [stydjo] nm (logement) (one-roomed) flatlet (Brit) ou apartment (US); (d'artiste, TV etc) studio (pl s).

stupéfait, e [stypefɛ, -ɛt] a astonished.

stupéfiant [stypefjɑ̃] nm (MÉD) drug, narcotic.

stupéfier [stypefje] vt to stupefy; (étonner) to stun, astonish.

stupeur [stypœʀ] nf astonishment.

stupide [stypid] a stupid; **stupidité** nf stupidity; stupid thing (to do ou say).

style [stil] nm style; **meuble de ~** piece of period furniture.

stylé, e [stile] a well-trained.

stylo [stilo] nm: **~ (à encre)** (fountain) pen; **~ (à) bille** ball-point pen.

su, e [sy] pp de **savoir** // nm: **au ~ de** with the knowledge of.

suave [sɥav] a sweet; (goût) mellow.

subalterne [sybaltɛʀn(ə)] a (employé, officier) junior; (rôle) subordinate, subsidiary // nm/f subordinate.

subconscient [sypkɔ̃sjɑ̃] nm subconscious.

subir [sybiʀ] vt (affront, dégâts) to suffer; (influence, charme) to be under; (opération, châtiment) to undergo.

subit, e [sybi, -it] a sudden; **subitement** ad suddenly, all of a sudden.

subjectif, ive [sybʒɛktif, -iv] a subjective.

subjonctif [sybʒɔ̃ktif] nm subjunctive.

submerger [sybmɛʀʒe] vt to submerge; (fig) to overwhelm.

subordonné, e [sybɔʀdɔne] a, nm/f subordinate; **~ à** subordinate to; subject to, depending on.

subornation [sybɔʀnasjɔ̃] nf bribing.

subrepticement [sybʀɛptismɑ̃] ad surreptitiously.

subside [sypsid] nm grant.

subsidiaire [sypsidjɛʀ] a: **question ~** deciding question.

subsister [sybziste] vi (rester) to remain, subsist; (vivre) to live; (survivre) to live on.

substance [sypstɑ̃s] nf substance.

substituer [sypstitɥe] vt: **~ qn/qch à** to substitute sb/sth for; **se ~ à qn** (évincer) to substitute o.s. for sb.

substitut [sypstity] nm (JUR) deputy public prosecutor; (succédané) substitute.

subtil, e [syptil] a subtle.

subtiliser [syptilize] vt: **~ qch (à qn)** to spirit sth away (from sb).

subvenir [sybvəniʀ]: **~ à** vt to meet.

subvention [sybvɑ̃sjɔ̃] nf subsidy, grant; **subventionner** vt to subsidize.

suc [syk] nm (BOT) sap; (de viande, fruit) juice.

succédané [syksedane] nm substitute.

succéder [syksede]: **~ à** vt (directeur, roi etc) to succeed; (venir après: dans

une série) to follow, succeed; **se ~** *vi*
(*accidents, années*) to follow one another.

succès [syksɛ] *nm* success; **avoir du ~**
to be a success, be successful; **~ de librairie** bestseller; **~** (*féminins*) conquests; **à ~** successful.

succession [syksesjɔ̃] *nf* (*série,* POL)
succession; (JUR: *patrimoine*) estate, inheritance.

succomber [sykɔ̃be] *vi* to die, succumb;
(*fig*): **~ à** to give way to, succumb to.

succursale [sykyRsal] *nf* branch.

sucer [syse] *vt* to suck.

sucette [sysɛt] *nf* (*bonbon*) lollipop; (*de
bébé*) dummy (*Brit*), pacifier (US).

sucre [sykR(ə)] *nm* (*substance*) sugar;
(*morceau*) lump of sugar, sugar lump *ou*
cube; **~ en morceaux/cristallisé/en poudre** lump/granulated/caster sugar; **~
d'orge** barley sugar; **sucré, e** *a* (*produit
alimentaire*) sweetened; (*au goût*)
sweet; (*péj*) sugary, honeyed; **sucrer** *vt*
(*thé, café*) to sweeten, put sugar in; **sucreries** *nfpl* (*bonbons*) sweets, sweet
things; **sucrier** *nm* (*récipient*) sugar
bowl.

sud [syd] *nm*: **le ~** the south // *a inv*
south; (*côte*) south, southern; **au ~** (*situation*) in the south; (*direction*) to the
south; **au ~ de** (*to the south of*; **~
africain, e** *a, nm/f* South African; **~
américain, e** *a, nm/f* South American.

sud-est [sydɛst] *nm, a inv* south-east.

sud-ouest [sydwɛst] *nm, a inv* south-west.

Suède [sɥɛd] *nf*: **la ~** Sweden; **suédois,
e** *a* Swedish // *nm/f*: **Suédois, e** Swede //
nm (LING) Swedish.

suer [sɥe] *vi* to sweat; (*suinter*) to ooze.

sueur [sɥœR] *nf* sweat; **en ~** sweating, in
a sweat.

suffire [syfiR] *vi* (*être assez*): **~** (**à qn/
pour qch/pour faire**) to be enough *ou*
sufficient (for sb/for sth/to do); **cela suffit
pour les irriter/qu'ils se fâchent** it's
enough to annoy them/for them to get
angry; **il suffit d'une négligence/qu'on
oublie pour que ...** it only takes one act
of carelessness/one only needs to forget
for ....

suffisamment [syfizamɑ̃] *ad* sufficiently, enough; **~ de** sufficient, enough.

suffisant, e [syfizɑ̃, -ɑ̃t] *a* (*temps, ressources*) sufficient; (*résultats*) satisfactory; (*vaniteux*) self-important,
bumptious.

suffixe [syfiks(ə)] *nm* suffix.

suffoquer [syfɔke] *vt* to choke, suffocate; (*stupéfier*) to stagger, astound // *vi*
to choke, suffocate.

suffrage [syfRaʒ] *nm* (POL: *voix*) vote;
(*du public etc*) approval *q*.

suggérer [syɡʒeRe] *vt* to suggest;
suggestion *nf* suggestion.

suicide [sɥisid] *nm* suicide.

suicider [sɥiside]: **se ~** *vi* to commit suicide.

suie [sɥi] *nf* soot.

suinter [sɥɛ̃te] *vi* to ooze.

suis *vb voir* **être; suivre.**

suisse [sɥis] *a* Swiss // *nm*: **S~** Swiss *pl
inv*; (*bedeau*) ≈ verger // *nf*: **la S~** Switzerland; **la S~ romande/allemande**
French-speaking/German-speaking Switzerland; **Suissesse** *nf* Swiss (woman *ou*
girl).

suite [sɥit] *nf* (*continuation: d'énumération etc*) rest, remainder; (: *de
feuilleton*) continuation; (: *second film
etc sur le même thème*) sequel; (*série:
de maisons, succès*) series *sg*;
(*conséquence*) result; (*ordre, liaison logique*) coherence; (*appartement,* MUS)
suite; (*escorte*) retinue, suite; **~s** *nfpl*
(*d'une maladie etc*) effects; **prendre la
~ de** (*directeur etc*) to succeed, take
over from; **donner ~ à** (*requête, projet*)
to follow up; **faire ~ à** to follow;
(*faisant*) **~ à votre lettre du** further to
your letter of the; **de ~** *ad* (*d'affilée*) in
succession; (*immédiatement*) at once;
par la ~ afterwards, subsequently; **à la
~ ad** one after the other; **à la ~ de** (*derrière*) behind; (*en conséquence de*) following; **par ~ de** owing to, as a result of.

suivant, e [sɥivɑ̃, -ɑ̃t] *a* next, following;
(*ci-après*): **l'exercice ~** the following exercise // *prép* (*selon*) according to; **au ~!**
next!

suivi, e [sɥivi] *a* (*régulier*) regular; (*cohérent*) consistent; coherent; **très/peu ~**
(*cours*) well-/poorly-attended.

suivre [sɥivR(ə)] *vt* (*gén*) to follow;
(SCOL: *cours*) to attend; (: *programme*)
to keep up with; (COMM: *article*) to continue to stock // *vi* to follow; (*élève*) to
attend; to keep up; **se ~** *vi* (*accidents
etc*) to follow one after the other; (*raisonnement*) to be coherent; **faire ~**
(*lettre*) to forward; **~ son cours** (*suj:
enquête etc*) to run *ou* take its course; **'à
~'** 'to be continued'.

sujet, te [syʒɛ, -ɛt] *a*: **être ~ à** (*vertige
etc*) to be liable to *ou* subject to // *nm/f*
(*d'un souverain*) subject // *nm* subject;
au ~ de *prép* about; **~ à caution** a questionable; **~ de conversation** topic *ou* subject of conversation; **~ d'examen** (SCOL)
examination question; examination paper.

summum [sɔmɔm] *nm*: **le ~ de** the
height of.

superbe [sypɛRb(ə)] *a* magnificent, superb.

super(carburant) [sypeR(kaRbyRɑ̃)] *nm*
≈ 4-star petrol (*Brit*), ≈ high-octane
gasoline (US).

supercherie [sypeRʃɔRi] *nf* trick.

superficie [sypɛʀfisi] nf (surface) area; (fig) surface.

superficiel, le [sypɛʀfisjɛl] a superficial.

superflu, e [sypɛʀfly] a superfluous.

supérieur, e [sypeʀjœʀ] a (lèvre, étages, classes) upper; (plus élevé: température, niveau): ~ (à) higher (than); (meilleur: qualité, produit): ~ (à) superior (to); (excellent, hautain) superior // nm, nf superior; à l'étage ~ on the next floor up; **supériorité** nf superiority.

superlatif [sypɛʀlatif] nm superlative.

supermarché [sypɛʀmaʀʃe] nm supermarket.

superposer [sypɛʀpoze] vt (faire chevaucher) to superimpose; lits **superposés** bunk beds.

superproduction [sypɛʀpʀɔdyksjɔ̃] nf (film) spectacular.

superpuissance [sypɛʀpɥisɑ̃s] nf super-power.

superstitieux, euse [sypɛʀstisjø, -øz] a superstitious.

superviser [sypɛʀvize] vt to supervise.

suppléant, e [syplẽ, -ãt] a (juge, fonctionnaire) deputy cpd; (professeur) supply cpd // nm/f deputy; supply teacher.

suppléer [syplee] vt (ajouter: mot manquant etc) to supply, provide; (compenser: lacune) to fill in; (: défaut) to make up for; (remplacer) to stand in for; ~ à vt to make up for; to substitute for.

supplément [syplemɑ̃] nm supplement; (de frites etc) extra portion; **un ~ de travail** extra ou additional work; **ceci est en ~** (au menu etc) this is extra, there is an extra charge for this; **supplémentaire** a additional, further; (train, bus) relief cpd, extra.

supplications [syplikasjɔ̃] nfpl pleas, entreaties.

supplice [syplis] nm (peine corporelle) torture q; form of torture; (douleur physique, morale) torture, agony.

supplier [syplije] vt to implore, beseech.

supplique [syplik] nf petition.

support [sypɔʀ] nm support; (pour livre, outils) stand.

supportable [sypɔʀtabl(ə)] a (douleur) bearable.

supporter nm [sypɔʀtɛʀ] supporter, fan // vt [sypɔʀte] (poids, poussée) to support; (conséquences, épreuve) to bear, endure; (défauts, personne) to put up with; (suj: chose: chaleur etc) to withstand; (suj: personne: chaleur, vin) to be able to take.

supposé, e [sypoze] a (nombre) estimated; (auteur) supposed.

supposer [sypoze] vt to suppose; (impliquer) to presuppose; à ~ que supposing (that).

suppositoire [sypozitwaʀ] nm suppositoire

suppression [sypʀesjɔ̃] nf removal; deletion; cancellation; suppression.

supprimer [sypʀime] vt (cloison, cause, anxiété) to remove; (clause, mot) to delete; (congés, service d'autobus etc) to cancel; (emplois, privilèges, témoin gênant) to do away with.

supputer [sypyte] vt to calculate.

suprême [sypʀɛm] a supreme.

sur, e [syʀ] a sour.

sur [syʀ] prép 1 (position) on; (pardessus) over; (au-dessus) above; **pose-le ~ la table** put it on the table; **je n'ai pas d'argent ~ moi** I haven't any money on me

2 (direction) towards; **en allant ~ Paris** going towards Paris; ~ **votre droite** on ou to your right

3 (à propos de) on, about; **un livre/une conférence ~ Balzac** a book/lecture on ou about Balzac

4 (proportion, mesures) out of; by; **un ~ 10** one in 10; (SCOL) one out of 10; **4 m ~ 2** 4 m by 2

sur ce ad hereupon.

sûr, e [syʀ] a sure, certain; (digne de confiance) reliable; (sans danger) safe; ~ **de soi** self-confident; **le plus ~ est de** the safest thing is to; ~ **et certain** absolutely certain.

suranné, e [syʀane] a outdated, outmoded.

surbaissé, e [syʀbese] a lowered, low.

surcharge [syʀʃaʀʒ(ə)] nf (de passagers, marchandises) excess load; (correction) alteration.

surcharger [syʀʃaʀʒe] vt to overload.

surchoix [syʀʃwa] a inv top-quality.

surclasser [syʀklase] vt to outclass.

surcroît [syʀkʀwa] nm: **un ~ de** additional + nom; **par ou de ~** moreover; **en ~** in addition.

surdité [syʀdite] nf deafness.

surélever [syʀelve] vt to raise, heighten.

sûrement [syʀmɑ̃] ad reliably; safely, securely; (certainement) certainly.

surenchère [syʀɑ̃ʃɛʀ] nf (aux enchères) higher bid; (sur prix fixe) overbid; (fig) overstatement; outbidding tactics pl; **surenchérir** vi to bid higher; (fig) to try and outbid each other.

surent vb voir **savoir.**

surestimer [syʀɛstime] vt to overestimate.

sûreté [syʀte] nf (voir sûr) reliability; safety; (JUR) guaranty; surety; **mettre en ~** to put in a safe place; **pour plus de ~** as an extra precaution; **to be on the safe side.**

surf [syʀf] nm surfing.

surface [syʀfas] nf surface; (superficie) surface area; **faire ~** to surface; **en ~** ad near the surface; (fig) superficially.

surfait, e [syʀfe, -ɛt] a overrated.

surfin, e [syrfɛ̃, -in] a superfine.
surgelé, e [syrʒəle] a (deep-)frozen.
surgir [syrʒir] vi to appear suddenly; (jaillir) to shoot up; (fig: problème, conflit) to arise.
surhumain, e [syrymɛ̃, -ɛn] a superhuman.
surimpression [syrɛ̃presjɔ̃] nf (PHOTO) double exposure; en ~ superimposed.
sur-le-champ [syrləʃɑ̃] ad immediately.
surlendemain [syrlɑ̃dmɛ̃] nm: le ~ (soir) two days later (in the evening); le ~ de two days after.
surligneur [syrliɲœr] nm highlighter (pen).
surmener [syrməne] vt, se ~ vi to overwork.
surmonter [syrmɔ̃te] vt (suj: coupole etc) to top; (vaincre) to overcome.
surnager [syrnaʒe] vi to float.
surnaturel, le [syrnatyrɛl] a, nm supernatural.
surnom [syrnɔ̃] nm nickname.
surnombre [syrnɔ̃br(ə)] nm: être en ~ to be too many (ou one too many).
surpeuplé, e [syrpœple] a overpopulated.
sur-place [syrplas] nm: faire du ~ to mark time.
surplomber [syrplɔ̃be] vi to be overhanging // vt to overhang; to tower above.
surplus [syrply] nm (COMM) surplus; (reste): ~ de bois wood left over.
surprenant, e [syrprənɑ̃, -ɑ̃t] a amazing.
surprendre [syrprɑ̃dr(ə)] vt (étonner, prendre à l'improviste) to surprise; (tomber sur: intrus etc) to catch; (fig) to detect; to chance upon; to overhear.
surpris, e [syrpri, -iz] a: ~ (de/que) surprised (at/that).
surprise [syrpriz] nf surprise; faire une ~ à qn to give sb a surprise.
surprise-partie [syrprizparti] nf party.
sursaut [syrso] nm start, jump; ~ de (énergie, indignation) sudden fit ou burst of; en ~ ad with a start; **sursauter** vi to (give a) start, jump.
surseoir [syrswar]: ~ à vt to defer.
sursis [syrsi] nm (JUR: gén) suspended sentence; (à l'exécution capitale, aussi fig) reprieve; (MIL) deferment.
surtaxe [syrtaks(ə)] nf surcharge.
surtout [syrtu] ad (avant tout, d'abord) above all; (spécialement, particulièrement) especially; ~, ne dites rien! whatever you do don't say anything!; ~ pas! certainly ou definitely not!; ~ que ... especially as ...
surveillance [syrvejɑ̃s] nf watch; (POLICE, MIL) surveillance; sous ~ médicale under medical supervision.
surveillant, e [syrvejɑ̃, -ɑ̃t] nm/f (de prison) warder; (SCOL) monitor; (de

travaux) supervisor, overseer.
surveiller [syrveje] vt (enfant, élèves, bagages) to watch, keep an eye on; (malade) to watch over; (prisonnier, suspect) to keep (a) watch on; (territoire, bâtiment) to (keep) watch over; (travaux, cuisson) to supervise; (SCOL: examen) to invigilate; se ~ vi to keep a check ou watch on o.s.; ~ son langage/sa ligne to watch one's language/figure.
survenir [syrvənir] vi (incident, retards) to occur, arise; (événement) to take place; (personne) to appear, arrive.
survêt(ement) [syrvɛt(mɑ̃)] nm tracksuit.
survie [syrvi] nf survival; (REL) afterlife.
survivant, e [syrvivɑ̃, -ɑ̃t] nm/f survivor.
survivre [syrvivr(ə)] vi to survive; ~ à vt (accident etc) to survive; (personne) to outlive.
survoler [syrvɔle] vt to fly over; (fig: livre) to skim through.
survolté, e [syrvɔlte] a (fig) worked up.
sus [sy(s)]: en ~ de prép in addition to, over and above; en ~ ad in addition; ~ à excl: ~ au tyran! at the tyrant!
susceptible [syseptibl(ə)] a a touchy, sensitive; ~ d'amélioration that can be improved, open to improvement; ~ de faire able to do; liable to do.
susciter [sysite] vt (admiration) to arouse; (obstacles, ennuis): ~ (à qn) to create (for sb).
suspect, e [syspɛ(kt), -ɛkt(ə)] a suspicious; (témoignage, opinions) suspect // nm/f suspect.
suspecter [syspɛkte] vt to suspect; (honnêteté de qn) to question, have one's suspicions about.
suspendre [syspɑ̃dr(ə)] vt (accrocher: vêtement): ~ qch (à) to hang sth up (on); (fixer: lustre etc): ~ qch à to hang sth from; (interrompre, démettre) to suspend; (remettre) to defer; se ~ à to hang from.
suspendu, e [syspɑ̃dy] a (accroché): ~ à hanging on (ou from); (perché): ~ au-dessus de suspended over.
suspens [syspɑ̃]: en ~ ad (affaire) in abeyance; tenir en ~ to keep in suspense.
suspense [syspɑ̃s] nm suspense.
suspension [syspɑ̃sjɔ̃] nf suspension; ~ d'audience adjournment.
sut vb voir **savoir**.
suture [sytyr] nf: point de ~ stitch.
svelte [svɛlt(ə)] a slender, svelte.
S.V.P. sigle (= s'il vous plaît) please.
syllabe [silab] nf syllable.
sylviculture [silvikyltyr] nf forestry.
symbole [sɛ̃bɔl] nm symbol; **symbolique** a symbolic(al); (geste, of-

frande) token *cpd*; (*salaire, dommage-intérêts*) nominal; **symboliser** *vt* to symbolize.

symétrique [simetʀik] *a* symmetrical.

sympa [sɛ̃pa] *a abr de* **sympathique**.

sympathie [sɛ̃pati] *nf* (*inclination*) liking; (*affinité*) fellow feeling; (*condoléances*) sympathy; **accueillir avec ~** (*projet*) to receive favourably; **croyez à toute ma ~** you have my deepest sympathy.

sympathique [sɛ̃patik] *a* nice, friendly; likeable; pleasant.

sympathisant, e [sɛ̃patizɑ̃, -ɑ̃t] *nm/f* sympathizer.

sympathiser [sɛ̃patize] *vi* (*voisins etc*: *s'entendre*) to get on (*Brit*) *ou* along (*US*) (well).

symphonie [sɛ̃fɔni] *nf* symphony.

symptôme [sɛ̃ptom] *nm* symptom.

synagogue [sinagɔg] *nf* synagogue.

syncope [sɛ̃kɔp] *nf* (*MÉD*) blackout; **tomber en ~** to faint, pass out.

syndic [sɛ̃dik] *nm* managing agent.

syndical, e, aux [sɛ̃dikal, -o] *a* (trade-)union *cpd*; **~iste** *nm/f* trade unionist.

syndicat [sɛ̃dika] *nm* (*d'ouvriers, employés*) (trade) union; (*autre association d'intérêts*) union, association; **~ d'initiative** tourist office.

syndiqué, e [sɛ̃dike] *a* belonging to a (trade) union; **non ~** non-union.

syndiquer [sɛ̃dike]: **se ~** *vi* to form a trade union; (*adhérer*) to join a trade union.

synonyme [sinɔnim] *a* synonymous // *nm* synonym; **~ de** synonymous with.

syntaxe [sɛ̃taks(ə)] *nf* syntax.

synthèse [sɛ̃tɛz] *nf* synthesis (*pl* es).

synthétique [sɛ̃tetik] *a* synthetic.

Syrie [siʀi] *nf*: **la ~** Syria.

systématique [sistematik] *a* systematic.

système [sistɛm] *nm* system; **le ~ D** resourcefulness.

T

t' [t(ə)] *pronom voir* **te**.

ta [ta] *dét voir* **ton**.

tabac [taba] *nm* tobacco; tobacconist's (shop); **~ blond/brun** light/dark tobacco; **à priser** snuff.

table [tabl(ə)] *nf* table; **à ~!** dinner *etc* is ready!; **se mettre à ~** to sit down to eat; (*fig: fam*) to come clean; **mettre la ~** to lay the table; **faire ~ rase de** to make a clean sweep of; **~ des matières** (table of) contents *pl*; **~ de nuit** *ou* **de chevet** bedside table.

tableau, x [tablo] *nm* painting; (*reproduction, fig*) picture; (*panneau*) board; (*schéma*) table, chart; **~ d'affi-**

chage notice board; **~ de bord** dashboard; (*AVIAT*) instrument panel; **~ noir** blackboard.

tabler [table] *vi*: **~ sur** to bank on.

tablette [tablɛt] *nf* (*planche*) shelf (*pl* shelves); **~ de chocolat** bar of chocolate.

tableur [tablœʀ] *nm* spreadsheet.

tablier [tablije] *nm* apron.

tabouret [tabuʀɛ] *nm* stool.

tac [tak] *nm*: **du ~ au ~** tit for tat.

tache [taʃ] *nf* (*saleté*) stain, mark; (*ART, de couleur, lumière*) spot; splash, patch.

tâche [taʃ] *nf* task; **travailler à la ~** to do piecework.

tacher [taʃe] *vt* to stain, mark; (*fig*) to sully, stain.

tâcher [taʃe] *vi*: **~ de faire** to try *ou* endeavour to do.

tacot [tako] *nm* (*péj*) banger (*Brit*), (old) heap.

tact [takt] *nm* tact; **avoir du ~** to be tactful.

tactique [taktik] *a* tactical // *nf* (*technique*) tactics *sg*; (*plan*) tactic.

taie [tɛ] *nf*: **~ (d'oreiller)** pillowslip, pillowcase.

taille [taj] *nf* cutting; pruning; (*milieu du corps*) waist; (*hauteur*) height; (*grandeur*) size; **de ~ à faire** capable of doing; **de ~** a sizeable.

taille-crayon(s) [tajkʀɛjɔ̃] *nm* pencil sharpener.

tailler [taje] *vt* (*pierre, diamant*) to cut; (*arbre, plante*) to prune; (*vêtement*) to cut out; (*crayon*) to sharpen.

tailleur [tajœʀ] *nm* (*couturier*) tailor; (*vêtement*) suit; **en ~** (*assis*) cross-legged.

taillis [taji] *nm* copse.

taire [tɛʀ] *vt* to keep to o.s., conceal // *vi*: **faire ~ qn** to make sb be quiet; (*fig*) to silence sb; **se ~** *vi* to be silent *ou* quiet.

talc [talk] *nm* talc, talcum powder.

talent [talɑ̃] *nm* talent.

talon [talɔ̃] *nm* heel; (*de chèque, billet*) stub, counterfoil (*Brit*); **~s plats/aiguilles** flat/stiletto heels.

talonner [talɔne] *vt* to follow hard behind; (*fig*) to hound.

talus [taly] *nm* embankment.

tambour [tɑ̃buʀ] *nm* (*MUS, aussi TECH*) drum; (*musicien*) drummer; (*porte*) revolving door(s *pl*).

tamis [tami] *nm* sieve.

Tamise [tamiz] *nf*: **la ~** the Thames.

tamisé, e [tamize] *a* (*fig*) subdued, soft.

tamiser [tamize] *vt* to sieve, sift.

tampon [tɑ̃pɔ̃] *nm* (*de coton, d'ouate*) wad, pad; (*amortisseur*) buffer; (*bouchon*) plug, stopper; (*cachet, timbre*) stamp; (*mémoire*) **~** (*INFORM*) buffer; **~ (hygiénique)** tampon; **tamponner** *vt* (*timbres*) to stamp; (*heurter*) to crash *ou* ram into;

tamponneuse *a*: autos tamponneuses dodgems.

tandis [tɑ̃di]: ~ que *cj* while.

tanguer [tɑ̃ge] *vi* to pitch (and toss).

tanière [tanjɛʀ] *nf* lair, den.

tanné, e [tane] *a* weather-beaten.

tanner [tane] *vt* to tan.

tant [tɑ̃] *ad* so much; ~ de (*sable, eau*) so much; (*gens, livres*) so many; ~ que *cj* as long as; ~ que (*comparatif*) as much as; ~ mieux that's great; so much the better; ~ pis never mind; too bad.

tante [tɑ̃t] *nf* aunt.

tantôt [tɑ̃to] *ad* (*parfois*): ~ ... ~ now ... now; (*cet après-midi*) this afternoon.

tapage [tapaʒ] *nm* uproar, din.

tapageur, euse [tapaʒœʀ, -øz] *a* loud, flashy, noisy.

tape [tap] *nf* slap.

tape-à-l'œil [tapalœj] *a inv* flashy, showy.

taper [tape] *vt* (*porte*) to bang, slam; (*dactylographier*) to type (out); (*fam: emprunter*): ~ qn de 10 F to touch sb for 10 F // *vi* (*soleil*) to beat down; ~ sur qn to thump sb; (*fig*) to run sb down; ~ sur qch to hit sth; to bang on sth; ~ à (*porte etc*) to knock on; ~ dans *vt* (*se servir*) to dig into; ~ des mains/pieds to clap one's hands/stamp one's feet; ~ (à la machine) to type; se ~ un travail to land o.s. with a job.

tapi, e [tapi] *a* crouching, cowering; hidden away.

tapis [tapi] *nm* carpet; (*de table*) cloth; mettre sur le ~ (*fig*) to bring up for discussion; ~ roulant conveyor belt; ~ de sol (*de tente*) groundsheet.

tapisser [tapise] *vt* (*avec du papier peint*) to paper; (*recouvrir*): ~ qch (de) to cover sth (with).

tapisserie [tapisʀi] *nf* (*tenture, broderie*) tapestry; (*papier peint*) wallpaper.

tapissier, ière [tapisje, -jɛʀ] *nm/f*: ~(-décorateur) upholsterer (and decorator).

tapoter [tapɔte] *vt* to pat, tap.

taquiner [takine] *vt* to tease.

tarabiscoté, e [taʀabiskɔte] *a* overornate, fussy.

tard [taʀ] *ad* late; plus ~ later (on); au plus ~ at the latest; sur le ~ late in life.

tarder [taʀde] *vi* (*chose*) to be a long time coming; (*personne*): ~ à faire to delay doing; il me tarde d'être I am longing to be; sans (plus) ~ without (further) delay.

tardif, ive [taʀdif, -iv] *a* late.

targuer [taʀge]: se ~ de *vt* to boast about.

tarif [taʀif] *nm* (*liste*) price list; tariff; (*barème*) rates *pl*; fares *pl*; tariff; (*prix*) rate; fare.

tarir [taʀiʀ] *vi* to dry up, run dry.

tarte [taʀt(ə)] *nf* tart.

tartine [taʀtin] *nf* slice of bread; ~ de miel slice of bread and honey; **tartiner** *vt* to spread; fromage à tartiner cheese spread.

tartre [taʀtʀ(ə)] *nm* (*des dents*) tartar; (*de chaudière*) fur, scale.

tas [tɑ] *nm* heap, pile; (*fig*): un ~ de heaps of, lots of; en ~ in a heap *ou* pile; formé sur le ~ trained on the job.

tasse [tɑs] *nf* cup; ~ à café coffee cup.

tassé, e [tɑse] *a*: bien ~ (*café etc*) strong.

tasser [tɑse] *vt* (*terre, neige*) to pack down; (*entasser*): ~ qch dans to cram sth into; se ~ *vi* (*terrain*) to settle; (*fig*) to sort itself out, settle down.

tâter [tɑte] *vt* to feel; (*fig*) to try out; ~ de (*prison etc*) to have a taste of; se ~ (*hésiter*) to be in two minds.

tatillon, ne [tatijɔ̃, -ɔn] *a* pernickety.

tâtonnement [tɑtɔnmɑ̃] *nm*: par ~s (*fig*) by trial and error.

tâtonner [tɑtɔne] *vi* to grope one's way along.

tâtons [tɑtɔ̃]: à ~ *ad*: chercher/avancer à ~ to grope around for/grope one's way forward.

tatouer [tatwe] *vt* to tattoo.

taudis [todi] *nm* hovel, slum.

taule [tol] *nf* (*fam*) nick (*fam*), prison.

taupe [top] *nf* mole.

taureau, x [tɔʀo] *nm* bull; (*signe*): le T~ Taurus.

tauromachie [tɔʀɔmaʃi] *nf* bullfighting.

taux [to] *nm* rate; (*d'alcool*) level; ~ d'intérêt interest rate.

taxe [taks] *nf* tax; (*douanière*) duty; ~ de séjour tourist tax; ~ à la valeur ajoutée (T.V.A.) value added tax (V.A.T.).

taxer [takse] *vt* (*personne*) to tax; (*produit*) to put a tax on, tax; (*fig*): ~ qn de to call sb + *attribut*; to accuse sb of, tax sb with.

taxi [taksi] *nm* taxi.

tchao [tʃao] *excl* (*fam*) bye(-bye)!

Tchécoslovaquie [tʃekɔslɔvaki] *nf* Czechoslovakia; **tchèque** *a, nm, nf* Czech.

te, t' [t(ə)] *pronom* you; (*réfléchi*) yourself.

technicien, ne [tɛknisjɛ̃, -jɛn] *nm/f* technician.

technique [tɛknik] *a* technical // *nf* technique; ~ment *ad* technically.

technologie [tɛknɔlɔʒi] *nf* technology; **technologique** *a* technological.

teck [tɛk] *nm* teak.

teignais *etc vb voir* **teindre**.

teindre [tɛ̃dʀ(ə)] *vt* to dye.

teint, e [tɛ̃, tɛ̃t] *a* dyed // *nm* (*du visage*) complexion; colour // *nf* shade; grand ~ *a inv* colourfast.

teinté, e [tɛ̃te] *a*: ~ de (*fig*) tinged with.

teinter [tɛ̃te] *vt* to tint; (*bois*) to stain;

teinture *nf* dyeing; *(substance)* dye; *(MÉD)* tincture.

teinturerie [tɛ̃tyʀʀi] *nf* dry cleaner's.

teinturier [tɛ̃tyʀje] *nm* dry cleaner.

tel, telle [tɛl] *a (pareil)* such; *(comme)*: ~ un/des ... like a/like ...; *(indéfini)* such-and-such a, a given; *(intensif)*: un ~/de ~s ... such (a)/such ...; rien de ~ nothing like it, no such thing; ~ que *cj* like, such as; ~ quel as it is *ou* stands *(ou was etc)*.

télé [tele] *abr f (= télévision)* TV, telly *(Brit)*; *(poste)* TV (set), telly; à la ~ on TV, on telly.

télé... [tele] *préfixe*: ~benne, ~cabine *nf (benne)* cable car; ~commande *nf* remote control; ~copie *nf* fax; ~distribution *nf* cable TV; ~férique *nm* = ~phérique; ~gramme *nm* telegram.

télégraphe [telegʀaf] *nm* telegraph; **télégraphier** *vt* to telegraph (off).

téléguider [telegide] *vt* to operate by remote control, radio-control.

téléjournal [teleʒuʀnal] *nm* TV news magazine programme.

télématique [telematik] *nf* telematics *sg*.

téléobjectif [teleɔbʒɛktif] *nm* telephoto lens *sg*.

téléphérique [telefeʀik] *nm* cable-car.

téléphone [telefɔn] *nm* telephone; avoir le ~ to be on the (tele)phone; au ~ on the phone; **téléphoner** *vi* to telephone, ring; to make a phone call; **téléphoner à** to phone, call up; **téléphonique** *a* (tele)phone *cpd*.

télescope [teleskɔp] *nm* telescope.

télescoper [teleskɔpe] *vt* to smash up; se ~ *(véhicules)* to concertina.

téléscripteur [teleskʀiptœʀ] *nm* teleprinter.

télésiège [telesjɛʒ] *nm* chairlift.

téléski [teleski] *nm* ski-tow.

téléspectateur, trice [telespɛktatœʀ, -tʀis] *nm/f* (television) viewer.

téléviseur [televizœʀ] *nm* television set.

télévision [televizjɔ̃] *nf* television; à la ~ on television.

télex [telɛks] *nm* telex.

telle [tɛl] *a voir* **tel.**

tellement [telmɑ̃] *ad (tant)* so much; *(si)* so; ~ de *(sable, eau)* so much; *(gens, livres)* so many; il s'est endormi ~ il était fatigué he was so tired (that) he fell asleep; pas ~ not (all) that much; not (all) that + *adjectif*.

téméraire [temeʀɛʀ] *a* reckless, rash; **témérité** *nf* recklessness, rashness.

témoignage [temwaɲaʒ] *nm (JUR: déclaration)* testimony *n*, evidence *q*; (: *faits)* evidence *q*; *(rapport, récit)* account; *(fig: d'affection etc)* token, mark; expression.

témoigner [temwaɲe] *vt (intérêt, grati-*

tude) to show // *vi (JUR)* to testify, give evidence; ~ de *vt* to bear witness to, testify to.

témoin [temwɛ̃] *nm* witness; *(fig)* testimony // *a* control *cpd*, test *cpd*; appartement ~ show flat *(Brit)*; être ~ de to witness; ~ oculaire eyewitness.

tempe [tɑ̃p] *nf* temple.

tempérament [tɑ̃peʀamɑ̃] *nm* temperament, disposition; à ~ *(vente)* on deferred (payment) terms; *(achat)* by instalments, hire purchase *cpd*.

température [tɑ̃peʀatyʀ] *nf* temperature; avoir *ou* faire de la ~ to be running *ou* have a temperature.

tempéré, e [tɑ̃peʀe] *a* temperate.

tempête [tɑ̃pɛt] *nf* storm; ~ de sable/ neige sand/snowstorm.

temple [tɑ̃pl(ə)] *nm* temple; *(protestant)* church.

temporaire [tɑ̃pɔʀɛʀ] *a* temporary.

temps [tɑ̃] *nm (atmosphérique)* weather; *(durée)* time; *(époque)* time, times *pl*; *(LING)* tense; *(MUS)* beat; *(TECH)* stroke; il fait beau/mauvais ~ the weather is fine/bad; avoir le ~/tout le ~ to have time/plenty of time; en ~ de paix/ guerre in peacetime/wartime; en ~ utile *ou* voulu in due time *ou* course; de ~ en ~, de ~ à autre from time to time; à ~ *(partir, arriver)* in time; à ~ partiel *ad*, *a* part-time; dans le ~ at one time; de tout ~ always; ~ d'arrêt pause, halt; ~ mort *(COMM)* slack period.

tenable [tənabl(ə)] *a* bearable.

tenace [tənas] *a* tenacious, persistent.

tenailler [tənaje] *vt (fig)* to torment.

tenailles [tənaj] *nfpl* pincers.

tenais *etc vb voir* **tenir.**

tenancier, ière [tənɑ̃sje, -jɛʀ] *nm/f* manager/manageress.

tenant, e [tənɑ̃, -ɑ̃t] *nm/f (SPORT)*: ~ du titre title-holder.

tendance [tɑ̃dɑ̃s] *nf (opinions)* leanings *pl*, sympathies *pl*; *(inclination)* tendency; *(évolution)* trend; avoir ~ à to have a tendency to, tend to.

tendeur [tɑ̃dœʀ] *nm (attache)* elastic strap.

tendre [tɑ̃dʀ(ə)] *a* tender; *(bois, roche, couleur)* soft // *vt (élastique, peau)* to stretch, draw tight; *(muscle)* to tense; *(donner)*: ~ qch à qn to hold sth out to sb; to offer sb sth; *(fig: piège)* to set, lay; se ~ *vi (corde)* to tighten; *(relations)* to become strained; ~ à qch/à faire to tend towards sth/to do; ~ l'oreille to prick up one's ears; ~ la main/le bras to hold out one's hand/ stretch out one's arm; ~ment *ad* tenderly; **tendresse** *nf* tenderness.

tendu, e [tɑ̃dy] *pp de* **tendre** // *a* tight; tensed; strained.

ténèbres [tenɛbʀ(ə)] *nfpl* darkness *sg*.

teneur [tənœʀ] *nf* content; *(d'une lettre)*

terms *pl*, content.
tenir [tənir] *vt* to hold; (*magasin, hôtel*) to run; (*promesse*) to keep // *vi* to hold; (*neige, gel*) to last; **se ~** *vi* (*avoir lieu*) to be held, take place; (*être: personne*) to stand; **se ~ droit** to stand up (*ou* sit up) straight; **bien se ~** to behave well; **se ~ à qch** to hold on to sth; **s'en ~ à qch** to confine o.s. to sth; to stick to sth; **~ à** *vt* to be attached to; to care about; to depend on; to stem from; **~ à faire** to want to do; **~ de** *vt* to partake of; to take after; **ça ne tient qu'à lui** it is entirely up to him; **~ qn pour** to take sb for; **~ qch de qn** (*histoire*) to have heard *ou* learnt sth from sb; (*qualité, défaut*) to have inherited *ou* got sth from sb; **~ les comptes** to keep the books; **~ le coup** to hold out; **~ au chaud** to keep hot; **tiens/tenez, voilà le stylo** there's the pen!; **tiens, Alain!** look, here's Alain!; **tiens?** (*surprise*) really?
tennis [tenis] *nm* tennis; (*court*) tennis court // *nmpl* *ou* *fpl* (*aussi:* **chaussures de ~**) tennis *ou* gym shoes; **~ de table** table tennis; **~man** *nm* tennis player.
tension [tɑ̃sjɔ̃] *nf* tension; (*fig*) tension; strain; (*MÉD*) blood pressure; **faire** *ou* **avoir de la ~** to have high blood pressure.
tentation [tɑ̃tasjɔ̃] *nf* temptation.
tentative [tɑ̃tativ] *nf* attempt, bid.
tente [tɑ̃t] *nf* tent.
tenter [tɑ̃te] *vt* (*éprouver, attirer*) to tempt; (*essayer*): **~ qch/de faire** to attempt *ou* try sth/to do; **~ sa chance** to try one's luck.
tenture [tɑ̃tyr] *nf* hanging.
tenu, e [təny] *pp* de **tenir** // *a* (*maison, comptes*): **bien ~** well-kept; (*obligé*): **~ de faire** under an obligation to do // *nf* (*action de tenir*) running; keeping; holding; (*vêtements*) clothes *pl*, gear; (*allure*) dress *q*, appearance; (*comportement*) manners *pl*, behaviour; **en petite ~e** scantily dressed *ou* clad; **~e de route** (*AUTO*) road-holding; **~e de soirée** evening dress.
ter [ter] *a*: **16 ~ 16b** *ou* **B**.
térébenthine [terebɑ̃tin] *nf*: (**essence de**) **~** (oil of) turpentine.
terme [term(ə)] *nm* term; (*fin*) end; **à court/long ~** a short-/long-term *ou* -range // *ad* in the short/long term; **avant ~** (*MÉD*) prematurely; **mettre un ~ à** to put an end *ou* a stop to.
terminaison [terminezɔ̃] *nf* (*LING*) ending.
terminal, e, aux [terminal, -o] *a* final // *nm* terminal // *nf* (*SCOL*) ≈ sixth form *ou* year (*Brit*), ≈ twelfth grade (*US*).
terminer [termine] *vt* to end; (*travail, repas*) to finish; **se ~** *vi* to end.
terne [tern(ə)] *a* dull.
ternir [ternir] *vt* to dull; (*fig*) to sully,

tarnish; **se ~** *vi* to become dull.
terrain [terɛ̃] *nm* (*sol, fig*) ground; (*COMM*) land *q*, plot (of land); site; **sur le ~** (*fig*) on the field; **~ de football/rugby** football/rugby pitch (*Brit*) *ou* field (*US*); **~ d'aviation** airfield; **~ de camping** campsite; **~ de golf** golf course; **~ de jeu** games field; playground; **~ de sport** sports ground; **~ vague** waste ground *q*.
terrasse [teras] *nf* terrace; **à la ~** (*café*) outside.
terrassement [terasmɑ̃] *nm* earthmoving, earthworks *pl*; embankment.
terrasser [terase] *vt* (*adversaire*) to floor; (*suj: maladie etc*) to lay low.
terre [ter] *nf* (*gén, aussi ÉLEC*) earth; (*substance*) soil, earth; (*opposé à mer*) land *q*; (*contrée*) land; **~s** *nfpl* (*terrains*) lands, land *sg*; **en ~** (*pipe, poterie*) clay *cpd*; **à ~** *ou* **par ~** (*mettre, être*) on the ground (*ou* floor); (*jeter, tomber*) to the ground, down; **~ cuite** earthenware; terracotta; **la ~ ferme** dry land; **~ glaise** clay; **~ à ~** *a inv* down-to-earth.
terreau [tero] *nm* compost.
terre-plein [terplɛ̃] *nm* platform.
terrer [tere]: **se ~** *vi* to hide away; to go to ground.
terrestre [terɛstr(ə)] *a* (*surface*) earth's, of the earth; (*BOT, ZOOL, MIL*) land *cpd*; (*REL*) earthly, worldly.
terreur [terœr] *nf* terror *q*.
terrible [teribl(ə)] *a* terrible, dreadful; (*fam*) terrific.
terrien, ne [terjɛ̃, -jɛn] *a*: **propriétaire ~** landowner // *nm/f* (*non martien etc*) earthling.
terrier [terje] *nm* burrow, hole; (*chien*) terrier.
terril [teril] *nm* slag heap.
terrine [terin] *nf* (*récipient*) terrine; (*CULIN*) pâté.
territoire [teritwar] *nm* territory.
terroir [terwar] *nm* (*AGR*) soil; region.
terrorisme [terorism(ə)] *nm* terrorism; **terroriste** *nm/f* terrorist.
tertiaire [tersjer] *a* tertiary // *nm* (*ÉCON*) service industries *pl*.
tertre [tertr(ə)] *nm* hillock, mound.
tes [te] *dét* voir **ton**.
tesson [tesɔ̃] *nm*: **~ de bouteille** piece of broken bottle.
test [test] *nm* test.
testament [testamɑ̃] *nm* (*JUR*) will; (*REL*) Testament; (*fig*) legacy.
tester [teste] *vt* to test.
testicule [testikyl] *nm* testicle.
tétanos [tetanos] *nm* tetanus.
têtard [tetar] *nm* tadpole.
tête [tet] *nf* head; (*cheveux*) hair *q*; (*visage*) face; **de ~** *a* (*wagon etc*) front *cpd* // *ad* (*calculer*) in one's head, mentally; **tenir ~ à qn** to stand up to sb; **la**

~ **en bas** with one's head down; **la** ~ **la première** (tomber) headfirst; **faire une** ~ (FOOTBALL) to head the ball; **faire la** ~ (fig) to sulk; **en** ~ (SPORT) in the lead; at the front; **en** ~ **à** ~ in private, alone together; **de la** ~ **aux pieds** from head to toe; ~ **de lecture** (playback) head; ~ **de liste** (POL) chief candidate; ~ **de série** (TENNIS) seeded player, seed; ~**-à-queue** nm inv: **faire un** ~**-à-queue** to spin round.

téter [tete] vt: ~ (**sa mère**) to suck at one's mother's breast, feed.

tétine [tetin] nf teat; (sucette) dummy (Brit), pacifier (US).

têtu, e [tety] a stubborn, pigheaded.

texte [tɛkst(ə)] nm text.

textile [tɛkstil] a textile cpd // nm textile; textile industry.

texture [tɛkstyʀ] nf texture.

TGV sigle m (= train à grande vitesse) high-speed train.

thé [te] nm tea; **prendre le** ~ to have tea; **faire le** ~ to make the tea.

théâtral, e, aux [teɑtʀal, -o] a theatrical.

théâtre [teɑtʀ(ə)] nm theatre; (œuvres) plays pl, dramatic works pl; (fig: lieu): **le** ~ **de** the scene of; (péj) histrionics pl, playacting; **faire du** ~ to be on the stage; to do some acting.

théière [tejɛʀ] nf teapot.

thème [tɛm] nm theme; (SCOL: traduction) prose (composition).

théologie [teɔlɔʒi] nf theology.

théorie [teɔʀi] nf theory; **théorique** a theoretical.

thérapie [teʀapi] nf therapy.

thermal, e, aux [tɛʀmal, -o] a: **station** ~**e** spa; **cure** ~**e** water cure.

thermes [tɛʀm(ə)] nmpl thermal baths.

thermomètre [tɛʀmɔmɛtʀ(ə)] nm thermometer.

thermos ® [tɛʀmɔs] nm ou nf: (**bouteille**) ~ vacuum ou Thermos ® flask.

thermostat [tɛʀmɔsta] nm thermostat.

thèse [tɛz] nf thesis (pl theses).

thon [tɔ̃] nm tuna (fish).

thym [tɛ̃] nm thyme.

tibia [tibja] nm shinbone, tibia; shin.

tic [tik] nm tic, (nervous) twitch; (de langage etc) mannerism.

ticket [tikɛ] nm ticket; ~ **de quai** platform ticket.

tiède [tjɛd] a lukewarm; tepid; (vent, air) mild, warm; **tiédir** vi to cool; to grow warmer.

tien, tienne [tjɛ̃, tjɛn] pronom: **le** ~ (**la tienne**), **les** ~**s** (**tiennes**) yours; **à la tienne!** cheers!

tiens [tjɛ̃] vb, excl voir **tenir**.

tiercé [tjɛʀse] nm system of forecast betting giving first 3 horses.

tiers, tierce [tjɛʀ, tjɛʀs(ə)] a third //

nm (JUR) third party; (fraction) third; **le** ~ **monde** the third world.

tige [tiʒ] nf stem; (baguette) rod.

tignasse [tiɲas] nf (péj) mop of hair.

tigre [tigʀ(ə)] nm tiger.

tigré, e [tigʀe] a striped; spotted.

tilleul [tijœl] nm lime (tree), linden (tree); (boisson) lime(-blossom) tea.

timbale [tɛ̃bal] nf (metal) tumbler; ~**s** nfpl (MUS) timpani, kettledrums.

timbre [tɛ̃bʀ(ə)] nm (tampon) stamp; (aussi: ~-**poste**) (postage) stamp; (MUS: de voix, instrument) timbre, tone.

timbré, e [tɛ̃bʀe] a (fam) daft.

timbrer [tɛ̃bʀe] vt to stamp.

timide [timid] a shy; timid; (timoré) timid, timorous; ~**ment** ad shyly; timidly; **timidité** nf shyness; timidity.

tins etc vb voir **tenir**.

tintamarre [tɛ̃tamaʀ] nm din, uproar.

tinter [tɛ̃te] vi to ring, chime; (argent, clefs) to jingle.

tir [tiʀ] nm (sport) shooting; (fait ou manière de tirer) firing q; (stand) shooting gallery; ~ **à l'arc** archery; ~ **au pigeon** clay pigeon shooting.

tirage [tiʀaʒ] nm (action) printing; (PHOTO) print; (de journal) circulation; (de livre) (print-)run; edition; (de cheminée) draught; (de loterie) draw; (désaccord) friction; ~ **au sort** drawing lots.

tirailler [tiʀaje] vt to pull at, tug at // vi to fire at random.

tirant [tiʀɑ̃] nm: ~ **d'eau** draught.

tire [tiʀ] nf: **vol à la** ~ pickpocketing.

tiré, e [tiʀe] a (traits) drawn // nm (COMM) drawee; ~ **par les cheveux** farfetched.

tire-au-flanc [tiʀoflɑ̃] nm inv (péj) skiver.

tire-bouchon [tiʀbuʃɔ̃] nm corkscrew.

tirelire [tiʀliʀ] nf moneybox.

tirer [tiʀe] vt (gén) to pull; (extraire): ~ **qch de** to take ou pull sth out of; to get sth out of; to extract sth from; (tracer: ligne, trait) to draw, trace; (fermer: rideau) to draw, close; (choisir: carte, conclusion, aussi COMM: chèque) to draw; (en faisant feu: balle, coup) to fire; (: animal) to shoot; (journal, livre, photo) to print; (FOOTBALL: corner etc) to take // vi (faire feu) to fire; (faire du tir, FOOTBALL) to shoot; (cheminée) to draw; **se** ~ vi (fam) to push off; **s'en** ~ to pull through, get off; ~ **sur** to pull on ou at; (fig: avoisiner) to verge on ou border on; ~ **qn de** (embarras etc) to help ou get sb out of; ~ **à l'arc/la carabine** to shoot with a bow and arrow/with a rifle.

tiret [tiʀɛ] nm dash.

tireur, euse [tiʀœʀ, -øz] nm/f gunman; (COMM) drawer; ~ **d'élite** marksman.

tiroir [tiʀwaʀ] nm drawer; ~**-caisse** nm

till.

tisane [tizan] *nf* herb tea.

tisonnier [tizɔnje] *nm* poker.

tisser [tise] *vt* to weave; **tisserand** *nm* weaver.

tissu [tisy] *nm* fabric, material, cloth *q*; (*ANAT, BIO*) tissue.

tissu-éponge [tisyepɔ̃ʒ] *nm* (terry) towelling *q*.

titre [titʀ(ə)] *nm* (*gén*) title; (*de journal*) headline; (*diplôme*) qualification; (*COMM*) security; **en ~** (*champion*) official; **à juste ~** with just cause, rightly; **à quel ~?** on what grounds?; **à aucun ~** on no account; **au même ~** (**que**) in the same way (as); **à ~ d'information** for (your) information; **à ~ gracieux** free of charge; **à ~ d'essai** on a trial basis; **à ~ privé** in a private capacity; **~ de propriété** title deed; **~ de transport** ticket.

tituber [titybe] *vi* to stagger (along).

titulaire [titylɛʀ] (*ADMIN*) *a* appointed, with tenure // *nm* incumbent; **être ~ de** (*poste*) to hold; (*permis*) to be the holder of.

toast [tost] *nm* slice *ou* piece of toast; (*de bienvenue*) (welcoming) toast; **porter un ~ à qn** to propose *ou* drink a toast to sb.

toboggan [tɔbɔgɑ̃] *nm* toboggan; (*jeu*) slide.

tocsin [tɔksɛ̃] *nm* alarm (bell).

toge [tɔʒ] *nf* toga; (*de juge*) gown.

toi [twa] *pronom* you.

toile [twal] *nf* (*matériau*) cloth *q*; (*bâche*) piece of canvas; (*tableau*) canvas; **~ d'araignée** cobweb; **~ cirée** oilcloth; **~ de fond** (*fig*) backdrop.

toilette [twalɛt] *nf* wash; (*habits*) outfit; dress *q*; **~s** *nfpl* (*w.-c.*) toilet *sg*; **faire sa ~** to have a wash, get washed; **articles de ~** toiletries.

toi-même [twamɛm] *pronom* yourself.

toiser [twaze] *vt* to eye up and down.

toison [twazɔ̃] *nf* (*de mouton*) fleece; (*cheveux*) mane.

toit [twa] *nm* roof; **~ ouvrant** sunroof.

toiture [twatyʀ] *nf* roof.

tôle [tol] *nf* (*plaque*) steel *ou* iron sheet; **~ ondulée** corrugated iron.

tolérable [tɔleʀabl(ə)] *a* tolerable, bearable.

tolérant, e [tɔleʀɑ̃, -ɑ̃t] *a* tolerant.

tolérer [tɔleʀe] *vt* to tolerate; (*ADMIN: hors taxe etc*) to allow.

tollé [tɔle] *nm* outcry.

tomate [tɔmat] *nf* tomato.

tombe [tɔ̃b] *nf* (*sépulture*) grave; (*avec monument*) tomb.

tombeau, x [tɔ̃bo] *nm* tomb.

tombée [tɔ̃be] *nf*: **à la ~ de la nuit** at the close of day, at nightfall.

tomber [tɔ̃be] *vi* to fall; **laisser ~** to drop; **~ sur** *vt* (*rencontrer*) to come across; (*attaquer*) to set about; **~ de**

fatigue/sommeil to drop from exhaustion/be falling asleep on one's feet; **ça tombe bien** that's come at the right time; **il est bien tombé** he's been lucky.

tome [tɔm] *nm* volume.

ton, ta, *pl* **tes** [tɔ̃, ta, te] *dét* your.

ton [tɔ̃] *nm* (*gén*) tone; (*MUS*) key; (*couleur*) shade, tone; **de bon ~** in good taste.

tonalité [tɔnalite] *nf* (*au téléphone*) dialling tone; (*MUS*) key; (*fig*) tone.

tondeuse [tɔ̃døz] *nf* (*à gazon*) (lawn)mower; (*du coiffeur*) clippers *pl*; (*pour la tonte*) shears *pl*.

tondre [tɔ̃dʀ(ə)] *vt* (*pelouse, herbe*) to mow; (*haie*) to cut, clip; (*mouton, toison*) to shear; (*cheveux*) to crop.

tonifier [tɔnifje] *vt* (*peau, organisme*) to tone up.

tonique [tɔnik] *a* fortifying // *nm* tonic.

tonne [tɔn] *nf* metric ton, tonne.

tonneau, x [tɔno] *nm* (*à vin, cidre*) barrel; (*NAVIG*) ton; **faire des ~x** (*voiture, avion*) to roll over.

tonnelle [tɔnɛl] *nf* bower, arbour.

tonner [tɔne] *vi* to thunder; **il tonne** it is thundering, there's some thunder.

tonnerre [tɔnɛʀ] *nm* thunder.

tonus [tɔnys] *nm* dynamism.

top [tɔp] *nm*: **au 3ème ~** at the 3rd stroke.

topinambour [tɔpinɑ̃buʀ] *nm* Jerusalem artichoke.

toque [tɔk] *nf* (*de fourrure*) fur hat; **~ de jockey/juge** jockey's/judge's cap; **~ de cuisinier** chef's hat.

toqué, e [tɔke] *a* (*fam*) cracked.

torche [tɔʀʃ(ə)] *nf* torch.

torchon [tɔʀʃɔ̃] *nm* cloth, duster; (*à vaisselle*) tea towel *ou* cloth.

tordre [tɔʀdʀ(ə)] *vt* (*chiffon*) to wring; (*barre, fig: visage*) to twist; **se ~** *vi* (*barre*) to bend; (*roue*) to twist, buckle; (*ver, serpent*) to writhe; **se ~ le pied/bras** to twist one's foot/arm.

tordu, e [tɔʀdy] *a* (*fig*) warped, twisted.

tornade [tɔʀnad] *nf* tornado.

torpille [tɔʀpij] *nf* torpedo; **torpiller** *vt* to torpedo.

torréfier [tɔʀefje] *vt* to roast.

torrent [tɔʀɑ̃] *nm* torrent.

torse [tɔʀs(ə)] *nm* (*ANAT*) torso; chest.

torsion [tɔʀsjɔ̃] *nf* twisting; torsion.

tort [tɔʀ] *nm* (*défaut*) fault; (*préjudice*) wrong *q*; **~s** *nmpl* (*JUR*) fault *sg*; **avoir ~** to be wrong; **être dans son ~** to be in the wrong; **donner ~ à qn** to lay the blame on sb; (*fig*) to prove sb wrong; **causer du ~ à** to harm; to be harmful *ou* detrimental to; **à ~** wrongly; **à ~ et à travers** wildly.

torticolis [tɔʀtikɔli] *nm* stiff neck.

tortiller [tɔʀtije] *vt* to twist; to twiddle; **se ~** *vi* to wriggle, squirm.

tortionnaire [tɔʀsjɔnɛʀ] nm torturer.

tortue [tɔʀty] nf tortoise.

tortueux, euse [tɔʀtɥø, -øz] a (rue) twisting; (fig) tortuous.

torture [tɔʀtyʀ] nf torture; **torturer** vt to torture; (fig) to torment.

tôt [to] ad early; ~ **ou tard** sooner or later; **si** ~ so early; (déjà) so soon; **au plus** ~ at the earliest; **il eut** ~ **fait de faire** he soon did.

total, e, aux [tɔtal, -o] a, nm total; **au** ~ **in total** ou all; **faire le** ~ to work out the total, add up; ~**ement** ad totally, completely; ~**iser** vt total (up).

totalité [tɔtalite] nf: **la** ~ **de** all of, the total amount (ou number) of; the whole + sg; **en** ~ entirely.

toubib [tubib] nm (fam) doctor.

touchant, e [tuʃã, -ãt] a touching.

touche [tuʃ] nf (de piano, de machine à écrire) key; (PEINTURE etc) stroke, touch; (fig: de nostalgie) touch, hint; (FOOTBALL: aussi: **remise en** ~) throw-in; (aussi: **ligne de** ~) touch-line.

toucher [tuʃe] nm touch // vt to touch; (palper) to feel; (atteindre: d'un coup de feu etc) to hit; (concerner) to concern, affect; (contacter) to reach, contact; (recevoir: récompense) to receive, get; (: salaire) to draw, get; (: chèque) to cash; **au** ~ to the touch; **se** ~ (être en contact) to touch; ~ **à** to touch; (concerner) to have to do with, concern; **je vais lui en** ~ **un mot** I'll have a word with him about it; ~ **à sa fin** to be drawing to a close.

touffe [tuf] nf tuft.

touffu, e [tufy] a thick, dense.

toujours [tuʒuʀ] ad always; (encore) still; (constamment) forever; ~ **plus** more and more; **pour** ~ forever; ~ **est-il que** the fact remains that; **essaie** ~ (you can) try anyway.

toupet [tupɛ] nm (fam) cheek.

toupie [tupi] nf (spinning) top.

tour [tuʀ] nf tower; (immeuble) high-rise block (Brit) ou building (US); (ÉCHECS) castle, rook // nm (excursion) stroll, walk; run, ride; trip; (SPORT: aussi: ~ **de piste**) lap; (d'être servi ou de jouer etc, tournure, de vis ou clef) turn; (de roue etc) revolution; (circonférence): **de 3 m de** ~ **à 3 m round**, with a circumference ou girth of 3 m; (POL: aussi: ~ **de scrutin**) ballot; (ruse, de prestidigitation) trick; (de potier) wheel; (à bois, métaux) lathe; **faire le** ~ **de** to go round; (à pied) to walk round; **c'est au** ~ **de Renée** it's Renée's turn; **à** ~ **de rôle**, ~ **à** ~ in turn; ~ **de taille/tête** waist/head measurement; ~ **de chant** song recital; ~ **de contrôle** nf control tower; ~ **de garde** spell of duty; ~ **d'horizon** (fig) general survey.

tourbe [tuʀb(ə)] nf peat.

tourbillon [tuʀbijɔ̃] nm whirlwind; (d'eau) whirlpool; (fig) whirl, swirl; **tourbillonner** vi to whirl (round).

tourelle [tuʀɛl] nf turret.

tourisme [tuʀism(ə)] nm tourism; **agence de** ~ tourist agency; **faire du** ~ to go sightseeing; to go touring; **touriste** nm/f tourist; **touristique** a tourist cpd; (région) touristic.

tourment [tuʀmã] nm torment.

tourmenter [tuʀmãte] vt to torment; **se** ~ vi to fret, worry o.s.

tournant [tuʀnã] nm (de route) bend; (fig) turning point.

tournebroche [tuʀnəbʀɔʃ] nm roasting spit.

tourne-disque [tuʀnədisk(ə)] nm record player.

tournée [tuʀne] nf (du facteur etc) round; (d'artiste, politicien) tour; (au café) round (of drinks).

tourner [tuʀne] vt to turn; (sauce, mélange) to stir; (contourner) to get round; (CINÉMA) to shoot; to make // vi to turn; (moteur) to run; (compteur) to tick away; (lait etc) to turn (sour); **se** ~ vi to turn round; **se** ~ **vers** to turn to; **turn towards**; **bien** ~ to turn out well; ~ **autour de** to go round; (péj) to hang round; ~ **à/en** to turn into; ~ **le dos à** to turn one's back on; to have one's back to; ~ **de l'œil** to pass out.

tournesol [tuʀnəsɔl] nm sunflower.

tournevis [tuʀnəvis] nm screwdriver.

tourniquet [tuʀnikɛ] nm (pour arroser) sprinkler; (portillon) turnstile; (présentoir) revolving stand, spinner.

tournoi [tuʀnwa] nm tournament.

tournoyer [tuʀnwaje] vi to whirl round; to swirl round.

tournure [tuʀnyʀ] nf (LING) turn of phrase; form; phrasing; (évolution): **la** ~ **de qch** the way sth is developing; (aspect): **la** ~ **de** the look of; ~ **d'esprit** turn ou cast of mind; **la** ~ **des événements** the turn of events.

tourte [tuʀt(ə)] nf pie.

tous dét [tu], pronom [tus] voir **tout**.

Toussaint [tusɛ̃] nf: **la** ~ All Saints' Day.

tousser [tuse] vi to cough.

tout, e, pl tous, toutes [tu, tut, tus] ♦ a **1** (avec article sing) all; ~ **le lait** all the milk; ~**e la nuit** all night, the whole night; ~ **le livre** the whole book; ~ **un pain** a whole loaf; ~ **le temps** all the time; the whole time; **c'est** ~ **le contraire** it's quite the opposite

2 (avec article pl) every; all; **tous les livres** all the books; **toutes les nuits** every night; **toutes les fois** every time; **toutes les trois/deux semaines** every third/other ou second week, every three/two weeks; **tous les deux** both ou each of us (ou them ou you); **toutes les 3** all 3 of us (ou

them *ou* you)
3 (*sans article*): à ~ âge at any age;
pour ~e nourriture, il avait ... his only
food was ...

♦ *pronom* everything, all; **il a ~ fait** he's
done everything; **je les vois tous** I can
see them all *ou* all of them; **nous y
sommes tous allés** all of us went, we all
went; **en ~ in all;** ~ **ce qu'il sait** all he
knows

♦ *nm* whole; **le ~ all of it** (*ou* them); **le
~ est de ...** the main thing is to ...; **pas
du ~** not at all

♦ *ad* **1** (*très, complètement*) very; ~
près very near; **le ~ premier** the very
first; ~ **seul** all alone; **le livre ~ entier**
the whole book; ~ **en haut** right at the
top; ~ **droit** straight ahead
2: ~ **en** while; ~ **en travaillant** while
working, as he *etc* works
3: ~ **d'abord** first of all; ~ **à coup** suddenly; ~ **à fait** absolutely; ~ **à l'heure** a
short while ago; (*futur*) in a short while,
shortly; **à ~ à l'heure!** see you later!; ~
de même all the same; ~ **le monde**
pronom everybody; ~ **de suite** immediately, straight away; ~ **terrain, tous
terrains** *a inv* all-terrain.
toutefois [tutfwa] *ad* however.
toux [tu] *nf* cough.
toxicomane [tɔksikɔman] *nm/f* drug addict.
trac [trak] *nm* nerves *pl*.
tracasser [trakase] *vt* to worry, bother;
to harass.
trace [tras] *nf* (*empreintes*) tracks *pl*;
(*marques, aussi fig*) mark; (*restes, vestige*) trace; (*indice*) sign; ~s **de pas**
footprints.
tracé [trase] *nm* line; layout.
tracer [trase] *vt* to draw; (*mot*) to trace;
(*piste*) to open up.
tract [trakt] *nm* tract, pamphlet.
tractations [traktɑsjɔ̃] *nfpl* dealings,
bargaining *sg*.
tracteur [traktœr] *nm* tractor.
traction [traksjɔ̃] *nf*: ~ **avant/arrière**
front-wheel/rear-wheel drive.
tradition [tradisjɔ̃] *nf* tradition; **tradi-
tionnel, le** *a* traditional.
traducteur, trice [tradyktœr, -tris]
nm/f translator.
traduction [tradyksjɔ̃] *nf* translation.
traduire [traduir] *vt* to translate; (*exprimer*) to render, convey.
trafic [trafik] *nm* traffic; ~ **d'armes**
arms dealing; **trafiquant, e** *nm/f*
trafficker; dealer; **trafiquer** *vt* (*péj*) to
doctor, tamper with.
tragédie [traʒedi] *nf* tragedy.
tragique [traʒik] *a* tragic.
trahir [trair] *vt* to betray; (*fig*) to give
away, reveal; **trahison** *nf* betrayal;
(*JUR*) treason.
train [trɛ̃] *nm* (*RAIL*) train; (*allure*)

pace; (*fig: ensemble*) set; **mettre qch en
~** to get sth under way; **mettre qn en
~** to put sb in good spirits; **se mettre en
~** to get started; to warm up; **se sentir en
~** to feel in good form; ~ **d'atterrissage**
undercarriage; ~**-autos-couchettes** car-
sleeper train; ~ **électrique** (*jouet*) (electric) train set; ~ **de vie** style of living.
traîne [trɛn] *nf* (*de robe*) train; **être à la
~** to be in tow; to lag behind.
traîneau, x [trɛno] *nm* sleigh, sledge.
traînée [trɛne] *nf* streak, trail; (*péj*)
slut.
traîner [trɛne] *vt* (*remorque*) to pull;
(*enfant, chien*) to drag *ou* trail along //
vi (*être en désordre*) to lie around;
(*marcher*) to dawdle (along); (*vagabonder*) to hang about; (*agir lentement*) to
idle about; (*durer*) to drag on; **se** ~ *vi* to
drag o.s. along; ~ **les pieds** to drag one's
feet.
train-train [trɛ̃trɛ̃] *nm* humdrum routine.
traire [trɛr] *vt* to milk.
trait [trɛ] *nm* (*ligne*) line; (*de dessin*)
stroke; (*caractéristique*) feature, trait;
~s *nmpl* (*du visage*) features; **d'un ~**
(*boire*) in one gulp; **de** ~ *a* (*animal*)
draught; **avoir** ~ **à** to concern; ~
d'union hyphen; (*fig*) link.
traitant, e [trɛtɑ̃, -ɑ̃t] *a*: **votre médecin
~** your usual *ou* family doctor; **crème**
~**e** conditioning cream.
traite [trɛt] *nf* (*COMM*) draft; (*AGR*)
milking; **d'une** ~ without stopping; **la** ~
des noirs the slave trade.
traité [trɛte] *nm* treaty.
traitement [trɛtmɑ̃] *nm* treatment; processing; (*salaire*) salary; ~ **de données/
texte** data/word processing.
traiter [trɛte] *vt* (*gén*) to treat; (*TECH,
INFORM*) to process; (*affaire*) to deal
with, handle; (*qualifier*): ~ **qn d'idiot** to
call sb a fool // *vi* to deal; ~ **de** *vt* to
deal with.
traiteur [trɛtœr] *nm* caterer.
traître, esse [trɛtr(ə), -trɛs] *a* (*dangereux*) treacherous // *nm* traitor.
trajectoire [traʒɛktwar] *nf* path.
trajet [traʒɛ] *nm* journey; (*itinéraire*)
route; (*fig*) path, course.
trame [tram] *nf* (*de tissu*) weft; (*fig*)
framework; texture.
tramer [trame] *vt* to plot, hatch.
trampolino [trɑ̃pɔlino] *nm* trampoline.
tramway [tramwɛ] *nm* tram(way);
tram(car) (*Brit*); streetcar (*US*).
tranchant, e [trɑ̃ʃɑ̃, -ɑ̃t] *a* sharp; (*fig*)
peremptory // *nm* (*d'un couteau*) cutting
edge; (*de la main*) edge.
tranche [trɑ̃ʃ] *nf* (*morceau*) slice;
(*arête*) edge; (*partie*) section; (*série*)
block; issue; bracket.
tranché, e [trɑ̃ʃe] *a* (*couleurs*) distinct,
sharply contrasted; (*opinions*) clear-cut,

definite // nf trench.

trancher [tʀɑ̃ʃe] vt to cut, sever; (fig: résoudre) to settle // vi to take a decision; ~ avec to contrast sharply with.

tranquille [tʀɑ̃kil] a calm, quiet; (enfant, élève) quiet; (rassuré) easy in one's mind, with one's mind at rest; se tenir ~ (enfant) to be quiet; laisse-moi/laisse-ça ~ leave me/it alone; **tranquillité** nf quietness; peace (and quiet).

transat [tʀɑ̃zat] nm deckchair.

transborder [tʀɑ̃sbɔʀde] vt to tran(s)ship.

transférer [tʀɑ̃sfeʀe] vt to transfer; **transfert** nm transfer.

transfigurer [tʀɑ̃sfiɡyʀe] vt to transform.

transformation [tʀɑ̃sfɔʀmasjɔ̃] nf transformation; (RUGBY) conversion.

transformer [tʀɑ̃sfɔʀme] vt to transform, alter; (matière première, appartement, RUGBY) to convert; ~ en to transform into; to turn into; to convert into.

transfusion [tʀɑ̃sfyzjɔ̃] nf: ~ sanguine blood transfusion.

transgresser [tʀɑ̃sɡʀese] vt to contravene, disobey.

transi, e [tʀɑ̃zi] a numb (with cold), chilled to the bone.

transiger [tʀɑ̃ziʒe] vi to compromise.

transistor [tʀɑ̃zistɔʀ] nm transistor.

transit [tʀɑ̃zit] nm transit; **~er** vi to pass in transit.

transitif, ive [tʀɑ̃zitif, -iv] a transitive.

transition [tʀɑ̃zisjɔ̃] nf transition; **transitoire** a transitional; transient.

translucide [tʀɑ̃slysid] a translucent.

transmetteur [tʀɑ̃smetœʀ] nm transmitter.

transmettre [tʀɑ̃smetʀ(ə)] vt (passer): ~ qch à qn to pass sth on to sb; (TECH, TÉL, MÉD) to transmit; (TV, RADIO: retransmettre) to broadcast.

transmission [tʀɑ̃smisjɔ̃] nf transmission.

transparaître [tʀɑ̃spaʀetʀ(ə)] vi to show (through).

transparence [tʀɑ̃spaʀɑ̃s] nf transparence; par ~ (regarder) against the light; (voir) showing through.

transparent, e [tʀɑ̃spaʀɑ̃, -ɑ̃t] a transparent.

transpercer [tʀɑ̃speʀse] vt to go through, pierce.

transpiration [tʀɑ̃spiʀasjɔ̃] nf perspiration.

transpirer [tʀɑ̃spiʀe] vi to perspire.

transplanter [tʀɑ̃splɑ̃te] vt (MÉD, BOT) to transplant; (personne) to uproot.

transport [tʀɑ̃spɔʀ] nm transport; **~s en commun** public transport sg.

transporter [tʀɑ̃spɔʀte] vt to carry, move; (COMM) to transport, convey; **transporteur** nm haulage contractor

(Brit), trucker (US).

transversal, e, aux [tʀɑ̃svɛʀsal, -o] a transverse, cross(-); cross-country; running at right angles.

trapèze [tʀapez] nm (au cirque) trapeze.

trappe [tʀap] nf trap door.

trapu, e [tʀapy] a squat, stocky.

traquenard [tʀaknaʀ] nm trap.

traquer [tʀake] vt to track down; (harceler) to hound.

traumatiser [tʀomatize] vt to traumatize.

travail, aux [tʀavaj, -o] nm (gén) work; (tâche, métier) work q, job; (ÉCON, MÉD) labour // nmpl (de réparation, agricoles etc) work sg; (sur route) road-works pl; (de construction) building (work); être sans ~ (employé) to be out of work ou unemployed; ~ (au) noir moonlighting; **travaux des champs** farmwork sg; **travaux dirigés** (SCOL) supervised practical work sg; **travaux forcés** hard labour sg; **travaux manuels** (SCOL) handicrafts; **travaux ménagers** housework sg.

travailler [tʀavaje] vi to work; (bois) to warp // vt (bois, métal) to work; (objet d'art, discipline, fig: influencer) to work on; cela le travaille it is on his mind; ~ à to work on; (fig: contribuer à) to work towards; **travailleur, euse** a hardworking // nm/f worker; **travailliste** a ≈ Labour cpd.

travée [tʀave] nf row; (ARCHIT) bay; span.

travers [tʀaveʀ] nm fault, failing; en ~ (de) across; au ~ (de) through; de ~ a askew // ad sideways; (fig) the wrong way; à ~ through; regarder de ~ (fig) to look askance at.

traverse [tʀaveʀs(ə)] nf (de voie ferrée) sleeper; chemin de ~ shortcut.

traversée [tʀaveʀse] nf crossing.

traverser [tʀaveʀse] vt (gén) to cross; (ville, tunnel, aussi: percer, fig) to go through; (suj: ligne, trait) to run across.

traversin [tʀaveʀsɛ̃] nm bolster.

travestir [tʀavestiʀ] vt (vérité) to misrepresent; se ~ vi to dress up; to dress as a woman.

trébucher [tʀebyʃe] vi: ~ (sur) to stumble (over), trip (against).

trèfle [tʀefl(ə)] nm (BOT) clover; (CARTES: couleur) clubs pl; (: carte) club.

treille [tʀej] nf vine arbour; climbing vine.

treillis [tʀeji] nm (métallique) wire-mesh.

treize [tʀez] num thirteen; **treizième** num thirteenth.

tréma [tʀema] nm diaeresis.

tremblement [tʀɑ̃bləmɑ̃] nm: ~ de terre earthquake.

trembler [tʀɑ̃ble] vi to tremble, shake;
~ de (froid, fièvre) to shiver ou tremble
with; (peur) to shake ou tremble with; ~
pour qn to fear for sb.

trémousser [tʀemuse]: se ~ vi to jig
about, wriggle about.

trempe [tʀɑ̃p] nf (fig): de cette/sa ~ of
this/his calibre.

trempé, e [tʀɑ̃pe] a soaking (wet),
drenched; (TECH) tempered.

tremper [tʀɑ̃pe] vt to soak, drench;
(aussi: faire ~, mettre à ~) to soak;
(plonger): ~ qch dans to dip sth in(to) //
vi to soak; (fig): ~ dans to be involved
ou have a hand in; se ~ vi to have a
quick dip; **trempette** nf: faire
trempette to go paddling.

tremplin [tʀɑ̃plɛ̃] nm springboard; (SKI)
ski-jump.

trentaine [tʀɑ̃tɛn] nf: une ~ (de) thirty
or so, about thirty; avoir la ~ (âge) to
be around thirty.

trente [tʀɑ̃t] num thirty; **trentième**
num thirtieth.

trépied [tʀepje] nm tripod.

trépigner [tʀepiɲe] vi to stamp (one's
feet).

très [tʀɛ] ad very; much + pp, highly +
pp.

trésor [tʀezɔʀ] nm treasure; (ADMIN)
finances pl; funds pl; T~ (public) public
revenue.

trésorerie [tʀezɔʀʀi] nf (gestion) accounts pl; (bureaux) accounts department; **difficultés de ~** cash problems,
shortage of cash ou funds.

trésorier, ière [tʀezɔʀje, -jɛʀ] nm/f
treasurer.

tressaillir [tʀesajiʀ] vi to shiver, shudder; to quiver.

tressauter [tʀesote] vi to start, jump.

tresse [tʀɛs] nf braid, plait.

tresser [tʀese] vt (cheveux) to braid,
plait; (fil, jonc) to plait; (corbeille) to
weave; (corde) to twist.

tréteau, x [tʀeto] nm trestle.

treuil [tʀœj] nm winch.

trêve [tʀɛv] nf (MIL, POL) truce; (fig)
respite; ~ de ... enough of this ....

tri [tʀi] nm sorting out q; selection;
(POSTES) sorting; sorting office.

triangle [tʀijɑ̃gl(ə)] nm triangle.

tribord [tʀibɔʀ] nm: à ~ to starboard,
on the starboard side.

tribu [tʀiby] nf tribe.

tribunal, aux [tʀibynal, -o] nm (JUR)
court; (MIL) tribunal.

tribune [tʀibyn] nf (estrade) platform,
rostrum; (débat) forum; (d'église, de
tribunal) gallery; (de stade) stand.

tribut [tʀiby] nm tribute.

tributaire [tʀibytɛʀ] a: être ~ de to be
dependent on.

tricher [tʀiʃe] vi to cheat.

tricolore [tʀikɔlɔʀ] a three-coloured;
(français) red, white and blue.

tricot [tʀiko] nm (technique, ouvrage)
knitting q; (tissu) knitted fabric; (vêtement) jersey, sweater.

tricoter [tʀikɔte] vt to knit.

trictrac [tʀiktʀak] nm backgammon.

tricycle [tʀisikl(ə)] nm tricycle.

triennal, e, aux [tʀiɛnal, -o] a three-
yearly; three-year.

trier [tʀije] vt to sort out; (POSTES,
fruits) to sort.

trimestre [tʀimɛstʀ(ə)] nm (SCOL)
term; (COMM) quarter; **trimestriel, le**
a quarterly; (SCOL) end-of-term.

tringle [tʀɛ̃gl(ə)] nf rod.

trinquer [tʀɛ̃ke] vi to clink glasses.

triomphe [tʀijɔ̃f] nm triumph.

triompher [tʀijɔ̃fe] vi to triumph, win;
~ de to triumph over, overcome.

tripes [tʀip] nfpl (CULIN) tripe sg.

triple [tʀipl(ə)] a triple; treble // nm: le
~ (de) (comparaison) three times as
much (as); en ~ exemplaire in tripli-
cate; **triplés, ées** nm/fpl triplets; **tripler** vi, vt to triple, treble.

tripoter [tʀipɔte] vt to fiddle with.

trique [tʀik] nf cudgel.

triste [tʀist(ə)] a sad; (péj): ~
personnage/affaire sorry individual/
affair; **tristesse** nf sadness.

trivial, e, aux [tʀivjal, -o] a coarse,
crude; (commun) mundane.

troc [tʀɔk] nm barter.

trognon [tʀɔɲɔ̃] nm (de fruit) core; (de
légume) stalk.

trois [tʀwa] num three; **troisième** num
third; ~-**quarts** nmpl: les ~-quarts de
three-quarters of.

trombe [tʀɔ̃b] nf: des ~s d'eau a down-
pour; en ~ like a whirlwind.

trombone [tʀɔ̃bɔn] nm (MUS) trombone; (de bureau) paper clip.

trompe [tʀɔ̃p] nf (d'éléphant) trunk;
(MUS) trumpet, horn.

tromper [tʀɔ̃pe] vt to deceive;
(vigilance, poursuivants) to elude; se ~
vi to make a mistake, be mistaken; se ~
de voiture/jour to take the wrong car/get
the day wrong; se ~ de 3 cm/20 F to be
out by 3 cm/20 F; **tromperie** nf deception, trickery q.

trompette [tʀɔ̃pɛt] nf trumpet; en ~
(nez) turned-up.

tronc [tʀɔ̃] nm (BOT, ANAT) trunk;
(d'église) collection box.

tronçon [tʀɔ̃sɔ̃] nm section.

tronçonner [tʀɔ̃sɔne] vt to saw up.

trône [tʀon] nm throne.

trop [tʀo] ad vb +, too much, too +
adjectif, adverbe; ~ (nombreux) too
many; ~ peu (nombreux) too few; ~
(souvent) too often; ~ (longtemps) (for)
too long; ~ de (nombre) too many;
(quantité) too much; de ~, en ~: des livres en ~ a few books too many; du lait

en ~ too much milk; **3 livres/3 F de ~ 3** books too many/3 F too much.

tropical, e, aux [tʀɔpikal, -o] a tropical.

tropique [tʀɔpik] nm tropic.

trop-plein [tʀɔplɛ̃] nm (tuyau) overflow ou outlet (pipe); (liquide) overflow.

troquer [tʀɔke]: ~ qch contre to barter ou trade sth for; (fig) to swap sth for.

trot [tʀo] nm trot.

trotter [tʀɔte] vi to trot; (fig) to scamper along (ou about).

trottiner [tʀɔtine] vi (fig) to scamper along (ou about).

trottinette [tʀɔtinɛt] nf (child's) scooter.

trottoir [tʀɔtwaʀ] nm pavement; **faire le ~** (péj) to walk the streets; **~ roulant** moving walkway, travellator.

trou [tʀu] nm hole; (fig) gap; (COMM) deficit; **~ d'air** air pocket; **~ de mémoire** blank, lapse of memory; **le ~ de la serrure** the keyhole.

trouble [tʀubl(ə)] a (liquide) cloudy; (image, mémoire) indistinct, hazy; (affaire) shady, murky // nm (désarroi) agitation; (embarras) confusion; (zizanie) unrest, discord; **~s** nmpl (POL) disturbances, troubles, unrest sg; (MÉD) trouble sg, disorders.

troubler [tʀuble] vt (embarrasser) to confuse, disconcert; (émouvoir) to agitate; to disturb; (perturber: ordre etc) to disrupt; (liquide) to make cloudy; **se ~** vi (personne) to become flustered ou confused.

trouée [tʀue] nf gap; (MIL) breach.

trouer [tʀue] vt to make a hole (ou holes) in; (fig) to pierce.

trouille [tʀuj] nf (fam): **avoir la ~** to be scared to death.

troupe [tʀup] nf troop; **~ (de théâtre)** (theatrical) company.

troupeau, x [tʀupo] nm (de moutons) flock; (de vaches) herd.

trousse [tʀus] nf case, kit; (d'écolier) pencil case; (de docteur) instrument case; **aux ~s de** (fig) on the heels ou tail of; **~ à outils** toolkit; **~ de toilette** toilet bag.

trousseau, x [tʀuso] nm (de mariée) trousseau; **~ de clefs** bunch of keys.

trouvaille [tʀuvaj] nf find.

trouver [tʀuve] vt to find; (rendre visite): **aller/venir ~ qn** to go/come and see sb; **je trouve que** I find ou think that; **~ à boire/critiquer** to find something to drink/criticize; **se ~** vi (être) to be; (être soudain) to find o.s.; **il se trouve que** it happens that, it turns out that; **se ~ bien** to feel well; **se ~ mal** to pass out.

truand [tʀyɑ̃] nm villain, crook.

truander [tʀyɑ̃de] vt to cheat.

truc [tʀyk] nm (astuce) way, device; (de cinéma, prestidigitateur) trick effect; (chose) thing, thingumajig; **avoir le ~ to** have the knack.

truchement [tʀyʃmɑ̃] nm: **par le ~ de** qn through (the intervention of) sb.

truelle [tʀyɛl] nf trowel.

truffe [tʀyf] nf truffle; (nez) nose.

truffé [tʀyfe] a: **~ de** (fig) peppered with; bristling with.

truie [tʀɥi] nf sow.

truite [tʀɥit] nf trout inv.

truquer [tʀyke] vt (élections, serrure, dés) to fix; (CINÉMA) to use special effects in.

T.S.V.P. sigle (= tournez s.v.p.) P.T.O.

T.T.C. sigle = toutes taxes comprises.

tu [ty] pronom you.

tu, e [ty] pp de **taire**.

tuba [tyba] nm (MUS) tuba; (SPORT) snorkel.

tube [tyb] nm tube; pipe; (chanson, disque) hit song ou record.

tuer [tɥe] vt to kill; **se ~** vi to be killed; (suicide) to kill o.s.; **tuerie** nf slaughter q.

tue-tête [tytɛt]: **à ~** ad at the top of one's voice.

tueur [tɥœʀ] nm killer; **~ à gages** hired killer.

tuile [tɥil] nf tile; (fam) spot of bad luck, blow.

tulipe [tylip] nf tulip.

tuméfié, e [tymefje] a puffy, swollen.

tumeur [tymœʀ] nf growth, tumour.

tumulte [tymylt(ə)] nm commotion.

tumultueux, euse [tymyltɥø, -øz] a stormy, turbulent.

tunique [tynik] nf tunic.

Tunisie [tynizi] nf: **la ~** Tunisia; **tunisien, ne** a, nm/f Tunisian.

tunnel [tynɛl] nm tunnel.

turbulences [tyʀbylɑ̃s] nfpl (AVIAT) turbulence sg.

turbulent, e [tyʀbylɑ̃, -ɑ̃t] a boisterous, unruly.

turc, turque [tyʀk(ə)] a Turkish // nm/f: **T~, Turque** Turk/Turkish woman // nm (LING) Turkish.

turf [tyʀf] nm racing; **~iste** nm/f racegoer.

Turquie [tyʀki] nf: **la ~** Turkey.

turquoise [tyʀkwaz] nf, a inv turquoise.

tus etc vb voir **taire**.

tutelle [tytɛl] nf (JUR) guardianship; (POL) trusteeship; **sous la ~ de** (fig) under the supervision of.

tuteur [tytœʀ] nm (JUR) guardian; (de plante) stake, support.

tutoyer [tytwaje] vt: **~ qn** to address sb as 'tu'.

tuyau, x [tɥijo] nm pipe; (flexible) tube; (fam) tip; gen q; **~ d'arrosage** hosepipe; **~ d'échappement** exhaust pipe; **~terie** nf piping q.

T.V.A. sigle f voir **taxe**.

tympan [tɛ̃pɑ̃] nm (ANAT) eardrum.
type [tip] nm type; (fam) chap, guy // a typical, standard.
typé [tipe] a ethnic (euph).
typhoïde [tifɔid] nf typhoid.
typique [tipik] a typical.
tyran [tirɑ̃] nm tyrant.
tzigane [dzigan] a gipsy, tzigane.

U

ulcère [ylsɛʀ] nm ulcer.
ulcérer [ylsere] vt (fig) to sicken, appal.
ultérieur, e [ylterjœʀ] a later, subsequent; remis à une date ~e postponed to a later date.
ultime [yltim] a final.
ultra... [yltʀa] préfixe: ~**moderne/ -rapide** ultra-modern/-fast.
un, une [œ̃, yn] ♦ article indéfini a; (devant voyelle) an; ~ garçon/vieillard a boy/an old man; une fille a girl
♦ pronom one; l'~ des meilleurs one of the best; l'~ ..., l'autre (the) one ..., the other; les ~s ..., les autres some ..., others; l'~ et l'autre both (of them); l'~ ou l'autre either (of them); l'~ l'autre, les ~s les autres each other, one another; pas ~ seul not a single one; ~ par ~ one by one
♦ num one; une pomme seulement one apple only.
unanime [ynanim] a unanimous.
unanimité nf: à l'unanimité unanimously.
uni, e [yni] a (ton, tissu) plain; (surface) smooth, even; (famille) close(-knit); (pays) united.
unifier [ynifje] vt to unite, unify.
uniforme [ynifɔʀm(ə)] a (mouvement) regular, uniform; (surface, ton) even; (objets, maisons) uniform // nm uniform; **uniformiser** vt to make uniform; (systèmes) to standardize.
union [ynjɔ̃] nf union; ~ de consommateurs consumers' association; l'U~ soviétique the Soviet Union.
unique [ynik] a (seul) only; (le même): un prix/système ~ a single price/system; (exceptionnel) unique; fils/fille ~ only son/daughter, only child; ~**ment** ad only, solely; (juste) only, merely.
unir [yniʀ] vt (nations) to unite; (éléments, couleurs) to combine; (en mariage) to unite, join together; ~ qch à to unite sth with; to combine sth with; s'~ to unite; (en mariage) to be joined together.
unité [ynite] nf (harmonie, cohésion) unity; (COMM, MIL, de mesure, MATH) unit.
univers [ynivɛʀ] nm universe.
universel, le [ynivɛʀsɛl] a universal; (esprit) all-embracing.

universitaire [ynivɛʀsitɛʀ] a university cpd; (diplôme, études) academic, university cpd // nm/f academic.
université [ynivɛʀsite] nf university.
urbain, e [yʀbɛ̃, -ɛn] a urban, city cpd, town cpd; (poli) urbane; **urbanisme** nm town planning.
urgence [yʀʒɑ̃s] nf urgency; (MÉD etc) emergency; d'~ a emergency cpd // ad as a matter of urgency.
urgent, e [yʀʒɑ̃, -ɑ̃t] a urgent.
urine [yʀin] nf urine; **urinoir** nm (public) urinal.
urne [yʀn(ə)] nf (électorale) ballot box; (vase) urn.
URSS [fareois: yʀs] sigle f: l'~ the USSR.
urticaire [yʀtikɛʀ] nf nettle rash.
us [ys] nmpl: ~ et coutumes (habits and) customs.
USA sigle mpl: les ~ the USA.
usage [yzaʒ] nm (emploi, utilisation) use; (coutume) custom; (LING): l'~ usage; à l'~ de (pour) for (use of); en ~ in use; hors d'~ out of service; wrecked; à ~ interne to be taken; à ~ externe for external use only.
usagé, e [yzaʒe] a (usé) worn; (d'occasion) used.
usager, ère [yzaʒe, -ɛʀ] nm/f user.
usé, e [yze] a worn; (banal) hackneyed.
user [yze] vt (outil) to wear down; (vêtement) to wear out; (matière) to wear away; (consommer: charbon etc) to use; s'~ vi to wear; to wear out; (fig) to decline; ~ de vt (moyen, procédé) to use, employ; (droit) to exercise.
usine [yzin] nf factory; ~ marémotrice tidal power station.
usiner [yzine] vt (TECH) to machine.
usité, e [yzite] a common.
ustensile [ystɑ̃sil] nm implement; ~ de cuisine kitchen utensil.
usuel, le [yzɥɛl] a everyday, common.
usure [yzyʀ] nf wear; worn state.
ut [yt] nm (MUS) C.
utérus [yteʀys] nm uterus, womb.
utile [ytil] a useful.
utilisation [ytilizasjɔ̃] nf use.
utiliser [ytilize] vt to use.
utilitaire [ytilitɛʀ] a utilitarian; (objets) practical.
utilité [ytilite] nf usefulness q; use; reconnu d'~ publique state-approved.

V

va vb voir aller.
vacance [vakɑ̃s] nf (ADMIN) vacancy; ~s nfpl holiday(s pl), vacation sg; prendre des/ses ~s to take a holiday/one's holiday(s); aller en ~s to go on holiday; **vacancier, ière** nm/f holiday-maker.
vacant, e [vakɑ̃, -ɑ̃t] a vacant.

vacarme [vakaʀm(ə)] nm row, din.

vaccin [vaksɛ̃] nm vaccine; (opération) vaccination; **vaccination** nf vaccination; **vacciner** vt to vaccinate; (fig) to make immune.

vache [vaʃ] nf (ZOOL) cow; (cuir) cowhide // a (fam) rotten, mean; **vachement** ad (fam) damned, hellish.

vaciller [vasije] vi to sway, wobble; (bougie, lumière) to flicker; (fig) to be failing, falter.

va-et-vient [vaevjɛ̃] nm inv (de personnes, véhicules) comings and goings pl, to-ings and fro-ings pl.

vagabond [vagabɔ̃] nm (rôdeur) tramp, vagrant; (voyageur) wanderer.

vagabonder [vagabɔ̃de] vi to roam, wander.

vagin [vaʒɛ̃] nm vagina.

vague [vag] nf wave // a vague; (regard) faraway; (manteau, robe) loose(-fitting); (quelconque): **un ~ bureau/cousin** some office/cousin or other; **~ de fond** nf ground swell.

vaillant, e [vajɑ̃, -ɑ̃t] a (courageux) gallant; (robuste) hale and hearty.

vaille vb voir **valoir**.

vain, e [vɛ̃, vɛn] a vain; **en ~** ad in vain.

vaincre [vɛ̃kʀ(ə)] vt to defeat; (fig) to conquer, overcome; **vaincu, e** nm/f defeated party; **vainqueur** nm victor; (SPORT) winner.

vais vb voir **aller**.

vaisseau, x [veso] nm (ANAT) vessel; (NAVIG) ship, vessel; **~ spatial** spaceship.

vaisselier [vesəlje] nm dresser.

vaisselle [vesɛl] nf (service) crockery; (plats etc à laver) (dirty) dishes pl; (lavage) washing-up (Brit), dishes pl.

val, vaux ou **vals** [val, vo] nm valley.

valable [valabl(ə)] a valid; (acceptable) decent, worthwhile.

valent etc vb voir **valoir**.

valet [vale] nm valet; (CARTES) jack.

valeur [valœʀ] nf (gén) value; (mérite) worth, merit; (COMM: titre) security; **mettre en ~** (terrain, région) to develop; (fig) to highlight; to show off to advantage; **avoir de la ~** to be valuable; **sans ~** worthless; **prendre de la ~** to go up ou gain in value.

valide [valid] a (en bonne santé) fit; (valable) valid; **valider** vt to validate.

valions vb voir **valoir**.

valise [valiz] nf (suit)case.

vallée [vale] nf valley.

vallon [valɔ̃] nm small valley.

valoir [valwaʀ] vi (être valable) to hold, apply // vt (prix, valeur, effort) to be worth; (causer): **~ qch à qn** to earn sb sth; **se ~** vi to be of equal merit; (péj) to be two of a kind; **faire ~** (droits, prérogatives) to assert; **faire ~ que** to point

out that; **à ~ sur** to be deducted from; **vaille que vaille** somehow or other; **cela ne me dit rien qui vaille** I don't like the look of it at all; **ce climat ne me vaut rien** this climate doesn't suit me; **~ la peine** to be worth the trouble ou worth it; **~ mieux: il vaut mieux se taire** it's better to say nothing; **ça ne vaut rien** it's worthless; **que vaut ce candidat?** how good is this applicant?

valoriser [valɔʀize] vt (ÉCON) to develop (the economy of); (PSYCH) to increase the standing of.

valse [vals(ə)] nf waltz.

valu, e [valy] pp de **valoir**.

vandale [vɑ̃dal] nm/f vandal; **vandalisme** nm vandalism.

vanille [vanij] nf vanilla.

vanité [vanite] nf vanity; **vaniteux, euse** a vain, conceited.

vanne [van] nf gate; (fig) joke.

vannerie [vanʀi] nf basketwork.

vantail, aux [vɑ̃taj, -o] nm door, leaf (pl leaves).

vantard, e [vɑ̃taʀ, -aʀd(ə)] a boastful.

vanter [vɑ̃te] vt to speak highly of, vaunt; **se ~** vi to boast, brag; **se ~ de** to pride o.s. on; (péj) to boast of.

vapeur [vapœʀ] nf steam; (émanation) vapour, fumes pl; **~s** nfpl (bouffées) vapours; **à ~** steam-powered, steam cpd; **cuit à la ~** steamed.

vapocuiseur [vapɔkɥizœʀ] nm pressure cooker.

vaporeux, euse [vapɔʀø, -øz] a (flou) hazy, misty; (léger) filmy.

vaporisateur [vapɔʀizatœʀ] nm spray.

vaporiser [vapɔʀize] vt (parfum etc) to spray.

varappe [vaʀap] nf rock climbing.

vareuse [vaʀøz] nf (blouson) pea jacket; (d'uniforme) tunic.

variable [vaʀjabl(ə)] a variable; (temps, humeur) changeable; (divers: résultats) varied, various.

varice [vaʀis] nf varicose vein.

varicelle [vaʀisɛl] nf chickenpox.

varié, e [vaʀje] a varied; (divers) various.

varier [vaʀje] vi to vary; (temps, humeur) to change // vt to vary.

variété [vaʀjete] nf variety.

variole [vaʀjɔl] nf smallpox.

vas vb voir **aller**.

vase [vɑz] nm vase // nf silt, mud.

vaseux, euse [vɑzø, -øz] a silty, muddy; (fig: confus) woolly, hazy; (: fatigué) peaky; woozy.

vasistas [vazistas] nm fanlight.

vaste [vast(ə)] a vast, immense.

vaudrai etc vb voir **valoir**.

vaurien, ne [voʀjɛ̃, -ɛn] nm/f good-for-nothing, guttersnipe.

vaut vb voir **valoir**.

vautour [votuʀ] nm vulture.

vautrer [votʀe]: se ~ *vi*: se ~ dans/sur to wallow in/sprawl on.

vaux [vo] *pl de* **val** // *vb voir* **valoir**.

veau, x [vo] *nm* (*ZOOL*) calf (*pl* calves); (*CULIN*) veal; (*peau*) calfskin.

vécu, e [veky] *pp de* **vivre**.

vedette [vədɛt] *nf* (*artiste etc*) star; (*canot*) patrol boat; launch.

végétal, e, aux [veʒetal, -o] *a* vegetable // *nm* vegetable, plant.

végétarien, ne [veʒetaʀjɛ̃, -ɛn] *a, nm/f* vegetarian.

végétation [veʒetasjɔ̃] *nf* vegetation; ~s *nfpl* (*MÉD*) adenoids.

véhicule [veikyl] *nm* vehicle; ~ utilitaire commercial vehicle.

veille [vɛj] *nf* (*garde*) watch; (*PSYCH*) wakefulness; (*jour*): **la ~ (de)** the day before; **la ~ au soir** the previous evening; **à la ~ de** on the eve of.

veillée [veje] *nf* (*soirée*) evening; (*réunion*) evening gathering; ~ (*mortuaire*) watch.

veiller [veje] *vi* to stay up; to be awake; to be on watch // *vt* (*malade, mort*) to watch over, sit up with; ~ **à** *vt* to attend to, see to; ~ **à ce que** to make sure that; ~ **sur** *vt* to keep a watch on; **veilleur de nuit** *nm* night watchman.

veilleuse [vɛjøz] *nf* (*lampe*) night light; (*AUTO*) sidelight; (*flamme*) pilot light; **en ~** *a, ad* (*lampe*) dimmed.

veine [vɛn] *nf* (*ANAT, du bois etc*) vein; (*filon*) vein, seam; (*fam: chance*): **avoir de la ~** to be lucky.

velléités [veleite] *nfpl* vague impulses.

vélo [velo] *nm* bike, cycle; **faire du ~** to go cycling.

vélomoteur [velomotœʀ] *nm* moped.

velours [vəluʀ] *nm* velvet; ~ **côtelé** corduroy.

velouté, e [vəlute] *a* (*au toucher*) velvety; (*à la vue*) soft, mellow; (*au goût*) smooth, mellow.

velu, e [vəly] *a* hairy.

venais *etc vb voir* **venir**.

venaison [vənɛzɔ̃] *nf* venison.

vendange [vɑ̃dɑ̃ʒ] *nf* (*opération, période: aussi:* ~s) grape harvest; (*raisins*) grape crop, grapes *pl*.

vendanger [vɑ̃dɑ̃ʒe] *vi* to harvest the grapes.

vendeur, euse [vɑ̃dœʀ, -øz] *nm/f* (*de magasin*) shop assistant; (*COMM*) salesman/woman // *nm* (*JUR*) vendor, seller; ~ **de journaux** newspaper seller.

vendre [vɑ̃dʀ(ə)] *vt* to sell; ~ **qch à qn** to sell sb sth; **'à ~'** 'for sale'.

vendredi [vɑ̃dʀədi] *nm* Friday; **V~ saint** Good Friday.

vénéneux, euse [venenø, -øz] *a* poisonous.

vénérien, ne [veneʀjɛ̃, -ɛn] *a* venereal.

vengeance [vɑ̃ʒɑ̃s] *nf* vengeance *q*, revenge *q*.

venger [vɑ̃ʒe] *vt* to avenge; se ~ *vi* to avenge o.s.; se ~ **de qch** to avenge o.s. for sth; to take one's revenge for sth; se ~ **de qn** to take revenge on sb; se ~ **sur** to take revenge on; to take it out on.

venimeux, euse [vənimø, -øz] *a* poisonous, venomous; (*fig: haineux*) venomous, vicious.

venin [vənɛ̃] *nm* venom, poison.

venir [vəniʀ] *vi* to come; ~ **de** to come from; ~ **de faire**: je viens d'y aller/de le voir I've just been there/seen him; s'il vient à pleuvoir if it should rain; j'en viens à croire que I have come to believe that; **faire ~** (*docteur, plombier*) to call (out).

vent [vɑ̃] *nm* wind; il y a du ~ it's windy; c'est du ~ it's all hot air; **au ~** to windward; **sous le ~** to leeward; **avoir le ~ debout/arrière** to head into the wind/ have the wind astern; **dans le ~** (*fam*) trendy.

vente [vɑ̃t] *nf* sale; **la ~** (*activité*) selling; (*secteur*) sales *pl*; **mettre en ~** to put on sale; (*objets personnels*) to put up for sale; ~ **de charité** jumble sale; ~ **aux enchères** auction sale.

venteux, euse [vɑ̃tø, -øz] *a* windy.

ventilateur [vɑ̃tilatœʀ] *nm* fan.

ventiler [vɑ̃tile] *vt* to ventilate; (*total, statistiques*) to break down.

ventouse [vɑ̃tuz] *nf* (*de caoutchouc*) suction pad; (*ZOOL*) sucker.

ventre [vɑ̃tʀ(ə)] *nm* (*ANAT*) stomach; (*fig*) belly; **avoir mal au ~** to have stomach ache (*Brit*) *ou* a stomach ache (*US*).

ventriloque [vɑ̃tʀilɔk] *nm/f* ventriloquist.

venu, e [vəny] *pp de* **venir** // *a*: **être mal ~ à** *ou* **de faire** to have no grounds for doing, be in no position to do // *nf* coming.

ver [vɛʀ] *nm voir aussi* **vers**; worm; (*des fruits etc*) maggot; (*du bois*) woodworm *q*; ~ **luisant** glow-worm; ~ **à soie** silkworm; ~ **solitaire** tapeworm; ~ **de terre** earthworm.

verbaliser [vɛʀbalize] *vi* (*POLICE*) to book *ou* report an offender.

verbe [vɛʀb(ə)] *nm* verb.

verdeur [vɛʀdœʀ] *nf* (*vigueur*) vigour, vitality; (*crudité*) forthrightness.

verdict [vɛʀdik(t)] *nm* verdict.

verdir [vɛʀdiʀ] *vi, vt* to turn green.

verdure [vɛʀdyʀ] *nf* greenery.

véreux, euse [veʀø, -øz] *a* worm-eaten; (*malhonnête*) shady, corrupt.

verge [vɛʀʒ(ə)] *nf* (*ANAT*) penis; (*baguette*) stick, cane.

verger [vɛʀʒe] *nm* orchard.

verglacé, e [vɛʀglase] *a* icy, iced-over.

verglas [vɛʀgla] *nm* (black) ice.

vergogne [vɛʀgɔɲ]: **sans ~** *ad* shamelessly.

véridique [veʀidik] a truthful.
vérification [veʀifikasjɔ̃] nf checking q, check.
vérifier [veʀifje] vt to check; (corroborer) to confirm, bear out.
véritable [veʀitabl(ə)] a real; (ami, amour) true.
vérité [veʀite] nf truth; (d'un portrait romanesque) lifelikeness; (sincérité) truthfulness, sincerity.
vermeil, le [veʀmɛj] a ruby red.
vermine [veʀmin] nf vermin pl.
vermoulu, e [veʀmuly] a worm-eaten, with woodworm.
verni, e [veʀni] a (fam) lucky; **cuir ~** patent leather.
vernir [veʀniʀ] vt (bois, tableau, ongles) to varnish; (poterie) to glaze.
vernis [veʀni] nm (enduit) varnish; glaze; (fig) veneer; **~ à ongles** nail polish ou varnish.
vernissage [veʀnisaʒ] nm varnishing; glazing; (d'une exposition) preview.
vérole [veʀɔl] nf (variole) smallpox.
verrai etc vb voir voir.
verre [veʀ] nm glass; (de lunettes) lens sg; **boire ou prendre un ~** to have a drink; **~s de contact** contact lenses.
verrerie [veʀʀi] nf (fabrique) glassworks sg; (activité) glass-making; (objets) glassware.
verrière [veʀjɛʀ] nf (grand vitrage) window; (toit vitré) glass roof.
verrons etc vb voir voir.
verrou [veʀu] nm (targette) bolt; (fig) constriction; **mettre qn sous les ~s** to put sb behind bars; **verrouillage** nm locking; **verrouiller** vt to bolt; to lock.
verrue [veʀy] nf wart.
vers [veʀ] nm line // nmpl (poésie) verse sg // prép (en direction de) toward(s); (près de) around (about); (temporel) about, around.
versant [veʀsɑ̃] nm slopes pl, side.
versatile [veʀsatil] a fickle, changeable.
verse [veʀs(ə)]: **à ~** ad: **il pleut à ~** it's pouring (with rain).
Verseau [veʀso] nm: **le ~** Aquarius.
versement [veʀsəmɑ̃] nm payment; **en 3 ~s** in 3 instalments.
verser [veʀse] vt (liquide, grains) to pour; (larmes, sang) to shed; (argent) to pay // vi (véhicule) to overturn; (fig): **~ dans** to lapse into.
verset [veʀsɛ] nm verse.
version [veʀsjɔ̃] nf version; (SCOL) translation (into the mother tongue).
verso [veʀso] nm back; **voir au ~** see over (leaf).
vert, e [veʀ, veʀt(ə)] a green; (vin) young; (vigoureux) sprightly; (cru) forthright // nm green.
vertèbre [veʀtɛbʀ(ə)] nf vertebra (pl ae).
vertement [veʀtəmɑ̃] ad (réprimander) sharply.

vertical, e, aux [veʀtikal, -o] a, nf vertical; **à la ~e** ad vertically; **~ement** ad vertically.
vertige [veʀtiʒ] nm (peur du vide) vertigo; (étourdissement) dizzy spell; (fig) fever; **vertigineux, euse** a breathtaking.
vertu [veʀty] nf virtue; **en ~ de** prép in accordance with; **~eux, euse** a virtuous.
verve [veʀv(ə)] nf witty eloquence; **être en ~** to be in brilliant form.
verveine [veʀvɛn] nf (BOT) verbena, vervain; (infusion) verbena tea.
vésicule [vezikyl] nf vesicle; **~ biliaire** gall-bladder.
vessie [vesi] nf bladder.
veste [vɛst(ə)] nf jacket; **~ droite/croisée** single-/double-breasted jacket.
vestiaire [vɛstjɛʀ] nm (au théâtre etc) cloakroom; (de stade etc) changing-room (Brit), locker-room (US).
vestibule [vɛstibyl] nm hall.
vestige [vɛstiʒ] nm relic; (fig) vestige; **~s** nmpl remains.
veston [vɛstɔ̃] nm jacket.
vêtement [vɛtmɑ̃] nm garment, item of clothing; **~s** nmpl clothes.
vétérinaire [veteʀinɛʀ] nm/f vet, veterinary surgeon.
vêtir [vetiʀ] vt to clothe, dress.
veto [veto] nm veto; **opposer un ~ à** to veto.
vêtu, e [vɛty] pp de **vêtir**.
vétuste [vetyst(ə)] a ancient, timeworn.
veuf, veuve [vœf, vœv] a widowed // nm widower // nf widow.
veuille, veuillez etc vb voir **vouloir**.
veule [vøl] a spineless.
veux vb voir **vouloir**.
vexations [vɛksasjɔ̃] nfpl humiliations.
vexer [vɛkse] vt to hurt, upset; **se ~** vi to be hurt, get upset.
viabiliser [vjabilize] vt to provide with services (water etc).
viable [vjabl(ə)] a viable.
viager, ère [vjaʒe, -ɛʀ] a: **rente viagère** life annuity.
viande [vjɑ̃d] nf meat.
vibrer [vibʀe] vi to vibrate; (son, voix) to be vibrant; (fig) to be stirred; **faire ~** to (cause to) vibrate; to stir, thrill.
vice [vis] nm vice; (défaut) fault; **~ de forme** legal flaw ou irregularity.
vice... [vis] préfixe vice-.
vichy [viʃi] nm (toile) gingham.
vicié, e [visje] a (air) polluted, tainted; (JUR) invalidated.
vicieux, euse [visjø, -øz] a (pervers) dirty(-minded); nasty; (fautif) incorrect, wrong.
vicinal, e, aux [visinal, -o] a: **chemin ~** by-road, byway.
victime [viktim] nf victim; (d'accident)

casualty.

victoire [viktwaʀ] *nf* victory.

vidange [vidɑ̃ʒ] *nf* (*d'un fossé, réservoir*) emptying; (*AUTO*) oil change; (*de lavabo: bonde*) waste outlet; ~**s** *nfpl* (*matières*) sewage *sg*; **vidanger** *vt* to empty.

vide [vid] *a* empty // *nm* (*PHYSIQUE*) vacuum; (*espace*) (empty) space, gap; (*futilité, néant*) void; **avoir peur du** ~ to be afraid of heights; **emballé sous** ~ vacuum packed; **à** ~ *ad* (*sans occupants*) empty; (*sans charge*) unladen.

vidéo [video] *nf* video // *a*: **cassette** ~ video cassette.

vide-ordures [vidɔʀdyʀ] *nm inv* (rubbish) chute.

vide-poches [vidpɔʃ] *nm inv* tidy; (*AUTO*) glove compartment.

vider [vide] *vt* to empty; (*CULIN: volaille, poisson*) to gut, clean out; **se** ~ *vi* to empty; ~ **les lieux** to quit *ou* vacate the premises; **videur** *nm* (*de boîte de nuit*) bouncer.

vie [vi] *nf* life (*pl* **lives**); **être en** ~ to be alive; **sans** ~ lifeless; **à** ~ for life.

vieil [vjɛj] *am voir* **vieux**.

vieillard [vjɛjaʀ] *nm* old man; **les** ~**s** old people, the elderly.

vieille [vjɛj] *a, nf voir* **vieux**.

vieilleries [vjɛjʀi] *nfpl* old things.

vieillesse [vjɛjɛs] *nf* old age.

vieillir [vjɛjiʀ] *vi* (*prendre de l'âge*) to grow old; (*population, vin*) to age; (*doctrine, auteur*) to become dated // *vt* to age; **vieillissement** *nm* growing old; ageing.

Vienne [vjɛn] *nf* Vienna.

vienne, viens *etc vb voir* **venir**.

vierge [vjɛʀʒ(ə)] *a* virgin; (*page*) clean, blank // *nf* virgin; (*signe*): **la V**~ Virgo; ~ **de** (*sans*) free from, unsullied by.

Viet-Nam, Vietnam [vjɛtnam] *nm* Vietnam.

vietnamien, ne [vjɛtnamjɛ̃, -jɛn] *a, nm/f* Vietnamese.

vieux(vieil), vieille [vjø, vjɛj] *a* old // *nm/f* old man/woman // *nmpl* old people; **mon** ~/**ma vieille** (*fam*) old man/girl; **prendre un coup de** ~ to put years on; ~ **garçon** *nm* bachelor; ~ **jeu** *a inv* old-fashioned.

vif, vive [vif, viv] *a* (*animé*) lively; (*alerte, brusque, aigu*) sharp; (*lumière, couleur*) brilliant; (*air*) crisp; (*vent, émotion*) keen; (*fort: regret, déception*) great, deep; (*vivant*): **brûlé** ~ burnt alive; **de vive voix** personally; **piquer qn au** ~ to cut sb to the quick; **à** ~ (*plaie*) open; **avoir les nerfs à** ~ to be on edge.

vigie [viʒi] *nf* look-out; look-out post.

vigne [viɲ] *nf* (*plante*) vine; (*plantation*) vineyard.

vigneron [viɲʀɔ̃] *nm* wine grower.

vignette [viɲɛt] *nf* (*motif*) vignette; (*de

marque*) manufacturer's label *ou* seal; (*ADMIN*) ≈ (road) tax disc (*Brit*), ≈ license plate sticker (*US*); price label (*on medicines for reimbursement by Social Security*).

vignoble [viɲɔbl(ə)] *nm* (*plantation*) vineyard; (*vignes d'une région*) vineyards *pl*.

vigoureux, euse [viguʀø, -øz] *a* vigorous, robust.

vigueur [vigœʀ] *nf* vigour; **entrer en** ~ to come into force; **en** ~ current.

vil, e [vil] *a* vile, base; **à** ~ **prix** at a very low price.

vilain, e [vilɛ̃, -ɛn] *a* (*laid*) ugly; (*affaire, blessure*) nasty; (*pas sage: enfant*) naughty.

vilebrequin [vilbʀəkɛ̃] *nm* (*outil*) (bit-)brace.

villa [vila] *nf* (detached) house.

village [vilaʒ] *nm* village; **villageois, e** *a* village *cpd* // *nm/f* villager.

ville [vil] *nf* town; (*importante*) city; (*administration*): **la** ~ ≈ the Corporation; ≈ the (town) council.

villégiature [vileʒjatyʀ] *nf* holiday; (holiday) resort.

vin [vɛ̃] *nm* wine; **avoir le** ~ **gai** to get happy after a few drinks; ~ **d'honneur** reception (*with wine and snacks*); ~ **ordinaire** table wine; ~ **de pays** local wine.

vinaigre [vinɛgʀ(ə)] *nm* vinegar; **vinaigrette** *nf* vinaigrette, French dressing.

vindicatif, ive [vɛ̃dikatif, -iv] *a* vindictive.

vineux, euse [vinø, -øz] *a* win(e)y.

vingt [vɛ̃, vɛ̃t] *num* twenty; **vingtaine** *nf*: **une vingtaine** (**de**) about twenty, twenty or so; **vingtième** *num* twentieth.

vinicole [vinikɔl] *a* wine *cpd*, winegrowing.

vins *etc vb voir* **venir**.

vinyle [vinil] *nm* vinyl.

viol [vjɔl] *nm* (*d'une femme*) rape; (*d'un lieu sacré*) violation.

violacé, e [vjɔlase] *a* purplish, mauvish.

violemment [vjɔlamɑ̃] *ad* violently.

violence [vjɔlɑ̃s] *nf* violence.

violent, e [vjɔlɑ̃, -ɑ̃t] *a* a violent; (*remède*) drastic.

violer [vjɔle] *vt* (*femme*) to rape; (*sépulture, loi, traité*) to violate.

violet, te [vjɔlɛ, -ɛt] *a, nm* purple, mauve // *nf* (*fleur*) violet.

violon [vjɔlɔ̃] *nm* violin; (*fam: prison*) lock-up.

violoncelle [vjɔlɔ̃sɛl] *nm* cello.

violoniste [vjɔlɔnist(ə)] *nm/f* violinist.

vipère [vipɛʀ] *nf* viper, adder.

virage [viʀaʒ] *nm* (*d'un véhicule*) turn; (*d'une route, piste*) bend; (*fig: POL*) about-turn.

virée [viʀe] *nf* (*courte*) run; (: *à pied*) walk; (*longue*) trip; hike, walking tour.

virement [virmã] *nm* (*COMM*) transfer.

virent *vb voir* **aussi voir**.

virer [vire] *vt* (*COMM*): ~ **qch** (**sur**) to transfer sth (into) // *vi* to turn; (*CHIMIE*) to change colour; ~ **de bord** to tack.

virevolter [virvɔlte] *vi* to twirl around.

virgule [virgyl] *nf* comma; (*MATH*) point.

viril, e [viril] *a* (*propre à l'homme*) masculine; (*énergique, courageux*) manly, virile.

virtuel, le [virtɥɛl] *a* potential; (*théorique*) virtual.

virtuose [virtɥoz] *nm/f* (*MUS*) virtuoso; (*gén*) master.

virus [virys] *nm* virus.

vis *vb* [vi] *voir* **voir, vivre** // *nf* [vis] screw.

visa [viza] *nm* (*sceau*) stamp; (*validation de passeport*) visa.

visage [vizaʒ] *nm* face.

vis-à-vis [vizavi] *ad* face to face // *nm* person opposite; house *etc* opposite; ~ **de** *prép* opposite; (*fig*) vis-à-vis; **en** ~ facing each other.

viscéral, e, aux [viseral, -o] *a* (*fig*) deep-seated, deep-rooted.

visée [vize]: ~**s** *nfpl* (*intentions*) designs.

viser [vize] *vi* to aim // *vt* to aim at; (*concerner*) to be aimed *ou* directed at; (*apposer un visa sur*) to stamp, visa; ~ **à qch/faire** to aim at sth/at doing *ou* to do.

viseur [vizœr] *nm* (*d'arme*) sights *pl*; (*PHOTO*) viewfinder.

visibilité [vizibilite] *nf* visibility.

visible [vizibl(ə)] *a* visible; (*disponible*): **est-il** ~? can he see me?, will he see visitors?

visière [vizjɛr] *nf* (*de casquette*) peak; (*qui s'attache*) eyeshade.

vision [vizjɔ̃] *nf* vision; (*sens*) (eye)sight, vision; (*fait de voir*): **la** ~ **de** the sight of.

visite [vizit] *nf* visit; (*visiteur*) visitor; (*médicale, à domicile*) visit, call; **la** ~ (*MÉD*) medical examination; **faire une** ~ **à qn** to call on sb, pay sb a visit; **rendre** ~ **à qn** to visit sb, pay sb a visit; **être en** ~ (**chez qn**) to be visiting (sb); **heures de** ~ (*hôpital, prison*) visiting hours.

visiter [vizite] *vt* to visit; (*musée, ville*) to visit, go round; **visiteur, euse** *nm/f* visitor.

vison [vizɔ̃] *nm* mink.

visser [vise] *vt*: ~ **qch** (*fixer, serrer*) to screw sth on.

visuel, le [vizɥɛl] *a* visual.

vit *vb voir* **voir; vivre**.

vital, e, aux [vital, -o] *a* vital.

vitamine [vitamin] *nf* vitamin.

vite [vit] *ad* (*rapidement*) quickly, fast; (*sans délai*) quickly; soon; **faire** ~ to act quickly; to be quick.

vitesse [vitɛs] *nf* speed; (*AUTO*: *disposi-*

tif) gear; **prendre qn de** ~ to outstrip sb; **get ahead of sb; prendre de la** ~ to pick up *ou* gather speed; **à toute** ~ at full *ou* top speed.

viticole [vitikɔl] *a* wine *cpd*, winegrowing.

viticulteur [vitikyltœr] *nm* wine grower.

vitrage [vitraʒ] *nm* glass *q*; (*rideau*) net curtain.

vitrail, aux [vitraj, -o] *nm* stained-glass window.

vitre [vitr(ə)] *nf* (*window*) pane; (*de portière, voiture*) window.

vitré, e [vitre] *a* glass *cpd*.

vitrer [vitre] *vt* to glaze.

vitreux, euse [vitrø, -øz] *a* (*terne*) glassy.

vitrine [vitrin] *nf* (*devanture*) (shop) window; (*étalage*) display; (*petite armoire*) display cabinet; ~ **publicitaire** display case, showcase.

vitupérer [vitypere] *vi* to rant and rave.

vivace *a* [vivas] (*arbre, plante*) hardy; (*fig*) indestructible, inveterate.

vivacité [vivasite] *nf* liveliness, vivacity; sharpness; brilliance.

vivant, e [vivã, -ãt] *a* (*qui vit*) living, alive; (*animé*) lively; (*preuve, exemple*) living // *nm*: **du** ~ **de qn** in sb's lifetime.

vivats [viva] *nmpl* cheers.

vive [viv] *af voir* **vif** // *vb voir* **vivre** // *excl*: ~ **le roi!** long live the king!; ~**ment** *ad* vivaciously; sharply // *excl*: ~**ment les vacances!** roll on the holidays!

viveur [vivœr] *nm* (*péj*) high liver, pleasure-seeker.

vivier [vivje] *nm* fish tank; fishpond.

vivifiant, e [vivifjã, -ãt] *a* invigorating.

vivions *vb voir* **vivre**.

vivre [vivr(ə)] *vi, vt* to live; ~**s** *nmpl* provisions, food supplies; **il vit encore** he is still alive; **se laisser** ~ to take life as it comes; **ne plus** ~ (*être anxieux*) to live on one's nerves; **il a vécu** (*eu une vie aventureuse*) he has seen life; **être facile à** ~ to be easy to get on with; **faire** ~ **qn** (*pourvoir à sa subsistance*) to provide (a living) for sb.

vlan [vlã] *excl* wham!, bang!

vocable [vɔkabl(ə)] *nm* term.

vocabulaire [vɔkabylɛr] *nm* vocabulary.

vocation [vɔkasjɔ̃] *nf* vocation, calling.

vociférer [vɔsifere] *vi, vt* to scream.

vodka [vɔdka] *nf* vodka.

vœu, x [vø] *nm* wish; (*à Dieu*) vow; **faire** ~ **de** to take a vow of; ~**x de bonne année** best wishes for the New Year.

vogue [vɔg] *nf* fashion, vogue.

voguer [vɔge] *vi* to sail.

voici [vwasi] *prép* (*pour introduire, désigner*) here is + *sg*, here are + *pl*; **et** ~ **que** ... and now it (*ou* he) ...; *voir aussi* **voilà**.

voie [vwa] *nf* way; (*RAIL*) track, line; (*AUTO*) lane; **être en bonne ~** to be going well; **mettre qn sur la ~** to put sb on the right track; **être en ~ d'achèvement/de rénovation** to be nearing completion/in the process of renovation; **par ~ buccale** *ou* **orale** orally; **à ~ étroite** narrow-gauge; **~ d'eau** (*NAVIG*) leak; **~ ferrée** track; railway line; **~ de garage** (*RAIL*) siding.

voilà [vwala] *prép* (*en désignant*) there is + *sg*, there are + *pl*; **les ~** *ou* **voici** here *ou* there they are; **en ~** *ou* **voici un** here's one, there's one; **~** *ou* **voici deux ans** two years ago; **~** *ou* **voici deux ans que** it's two years since; **et ~!** there we are!; **~ tout** that's all; **'~** *ou* **voici'** (*en offrant etc*) 'there *ou* here you are'.

voile [vwal] *nm* veil; (*tissu léger*) net // *nf* sail; (*sport*) sailing.

voiler [vwale] *vt* to veil; (*fausser: roue*) to buckle; (*: bois*) to warp; **se ~** *vi* (*lune, regard*) to mist over; (*voix*) to become husky; (*roue, disque*) to buckle; (*planche*) to warp.

voilier [vwalje] *nm* sailing ship; (*de plaisance*) sailing boat.

voilure [vwalyʀ] *nf* (*de voilier*) sails *pl*.

voir [vwaʀ] *vi, vt* to see; **se ~** *vt*: **se ~ critiquer/transformer** to be criticized/transformed; **cela se voit** (*cela arrive*) it happens; (*c'est visible*) that's obvious, it shows; **~ venir** (*fig*) to wait and see; **faire ~ qch à qn** to show sb sth; **en faire ~ à qn** (*fig*) to give sb a hard time; **ne pas pouvoir ~ qn** (*fig*) not to be able to stand sb; **voyons!** let's see now; (*indignation etc*) come (along) now!; **avoir quelque chose à ~ avec** to have something to do with.

voire [vwaʀ] *ad* indeed; nay; or even.

voisin, e [vwazɛ̃, -in] *a* (*proche*) neighbouring; (*contigu*) next; (*ressemblant*) connected // *nm/f* neighbour; **voisinage** *nm* (*proximité*) proximity; (*environs*) vicinity; (*quartier, voisins*) neighbourhood.

voiture [vwatyʀ] *nf* car; (*wagon*) coach, carriage; **~ d'enfant** pram (*Brit*), baby carriage (*US*); **~ de sport** sports car; **~-lit** *nf* sleeper.

voix [vwa] *nf* voice; (*POL*) vote; **à haute ~** aloud; **à ~ basse** in a low voice; **à 2/4 ~** (*MUS*) in 2/4 parts; **avoir ~ au chapitre** to have a say in the matter.

vol [vɔl] *nm* (*mode de locomotion*) flying; (*trajet, voyage, groupe d'oiseaux*) flight; (*larcin*) theft; **à ~ d'oiseau** as the crow flies; **au ~: attraper qch au ~** to catch sth as it flies past; **en ~** in flight; **~ libre** hang-gliding; **~ à main armée** armed robbery; **~ à voile** gliding.

volage [vɔlaʒ] *a* fickle.

volaille [vɔlaj] *nf* (*oiseaux*) poultry *pl*; (*viande*) poultry *q*; (*oiseau*) fowl.

volant, e [vɔlɑ̃, -ɑ̃t] *a voir* feuille *etc* //

nm (*d'automobile*) (steering) wheel; (*de commande*) wheel; (*objet lancé*) shuttlecock; (*bande de tissu*) flounce.

volcan [vɔlkɑ̃] *nm* volcano.

volée [vɔle] *nf* (*TENNIS*) volley; **~ de coups/de flèches** volley of blows/arrows; **à la ~: rattraper à la ~** to catch in mid air; **à toute** ~ (*sonner les cloches*) vigorously; (*lancer un projectile*) with full force.

voler [vɔle] *vi* (*avion, oiseau, fig*) to fly; (*voleur*) to steal // *vt* (*objet*) to steal; (*personne*) to rob; **~ qch à qn** to steal sth from sb.

volet [vɔlɛ] *nm* (*de fenêtre*) shutter; (*de feuillet, document*) section.

voleter [vɔlte] *vi* to flutter (about).

voleur, euse [vɔlœʀ, -øz] *nm/f* thief (*pl* thieves) // *a* thieving.

volontaire [vɔlɔ̃tɛʀ] *a* voluntary; (*caractère, personne: décidé*) self-willed // *nm/f* volunteer.

volonté [vɔlɔ̃te] *nf* (*faculté de vouloir*) will; (*énergie, fermeté*) will(power); (*souhait, désir*) wish; **à ~** as much as one likes; **bonne ~** goodwill, willingness; **mauvaise ~** lack of goodwill, unwillingness.

volontiers [vɔlɔ̃tje] *ad* (*de bonne grâce*) willingly; (*avec plaisir*) willingly, gladly; (*habituellement, souvent*) readily, willingly.

volt [vɔlt] *nm* volt.

volte-face [vɔltəfas] *nf inv* about-turn.

voltige [vɔltiʒ] *nf* (*ÉQUITATION*) trick riding; (*au cirque*) acrobatics *sg*.

voltiger [vɔltiʒe] *vi* to flutter (about).

volume [vɔlym] *nm* volume; (*GÉOM: solide*) solid; **volumineux, euse** *a* voluminous, bulky.

volupté [vɔlypte] *nf* sensual delight *ou* pleasure.

vomir [vɔmiʀ] *vi* to vomit, be sick // *vt* to vomit, bring up; (*fig*) to belch out, spew out; (*exécrer*) to loathe, abhor.

vont [vɔ̃] *vb voir* aller.

vos [vo] *dét voir* votre.

vote [vɔt] *nm* vote; **~ par correspondance/procuration** postal/proxy vote.

voter [vɔte] *vi* to vote // *vt* (*loi, décision*) to vote for.

votre [vɔtʀ(ə)], *pl* **vos** [vo] *dét* your.

vôtre [votʀ(ə)] *pronom*: **le ~, la ~, les ~s** yours; **les ~s** (*fig*) your family *ou* folks; **à la ~** (*toast*) your (good) health!

voudrai *etc vb voir* vouloir.

voué, e [vwe] *a*: **~ à** doomed to.

vouer [vwe] *vt*: **~ qch à** (*Dieu/un saint*) to dedicate sth to; **~ sa vie à** (*étude, cause etc*) to devote one's life to; **~ une amitié éternelle à qn** to vow undying friendship to sb.

vouloir [vulwaʀ] ♦ *nm*: **le bon ~ de qn** sb's goodwill; sb's pleasure
♦ *vt* **1** (*exiger, désirer*) to want; **~**

faire/que qn fasse to want to do/sb to do; **voulez-vous du thé?** would you like ou do you want some tea?; **que me veut-il?** what does he want with me?; **sans le ~** *(involontairement)* without meaning to, unintentionally; **je voudrais ceci/faire** I would ou I'd like this/to do

2 *(consentir):* **je veux bien** *(bonne volonté)* I'll be happy to; *(concession)* fair enough, that's fine; **oui, si on veut** *(en quelque sorte)* yes, if you like; **veuillez attendre** please wait; **veuillez agréer ...** *(formule épistolaire)* yours faithfully

3: en ~ à: en ~ à qn to bear sb a grudge; **s'en ~ (de)** to be annoyed with o.s. (for); **il en veut à mon argent** he's after my money

4: ~ de: l'entreprise ne veut plus de lui the firm doesn't want him any more; **elle ne veut pas de son aide** she doesn't want his help

5: ~ dire to mean.

voulu, e [vuly] *a (requis)* required, requisite; *(délibéré)* deliberate, intentional.

vous [vu] *pronom* you; *(objet indirect)* (to) you; *(réfléchi)* yourself *(pl* yourselves); *(réciproque)* each other; **~même** yourself; **~-mêmes** yourselves.

voûte [vut] *nf* vault.

voûter [vute] *vt:* **se ~** *vi (dos, personne)* to become stooped.

vouvoyer [vuvwaje] *vt:* **~ qn** to address sb as 'vous'.

voyage [vwajaʒ] *nm* journey; trip; *(fait de voyager):* **le ~** travel(ling); **partir/être en ~** to go off/be away on a journey ou trip; **faire bon ~** to have a good journey; **~ d'agrément/d'affaires** pleasure/business trip; **~ de noces** honeymoon; **~ organisé** package tour.

voyager [vwajaʒe] *vi* to travel; **voyageur, euse** *nm/f* traveller; *(passager)* passenger.

voyant, e [vwajā, -āt] *a (couleur)* loud, gaudy // *nm (signal)* (warning) light // *nf* clairvoyant.

voyelle [vwajɛl] *nf* vowel.

voyons *etc vb voir* **voir**.

voyou [vwaju] *nm* lout, hoodlum; *(enfant)* guttersnipe.

vrac [vʀak]: **en ~** *ad* higgledy-piggledy; *(COMM)* in bulk.

vrai, e [vʀɛ] *a (véridique: récit, faits)* true; *(non factice, authentique)* real; **à ~ dire** to tell the truth.

vraiment [vʀɛmā] *ad* really.

vraisemblable [vʀɛsāblabl(ə)] *a* likely, probable.

vraisemblance [vʀɛsāblās] *nf* likelihood; *(romanesque)* verisimilitude.

vrille [vʀij] *nf (de plante)* tendril; *(outil)* gimlet; *(spirale)* spiral; *(AVIAT)* spin.

vrombir [vʀɔ̃biʀ] *vi* to hum.

vu [vy] *prép (en raison de)* in view of; **~**

que in view of the fact that.

vu, e [vy] *pp de* **voir** // *a:* **bien/mal ~** *(fig)* well/poorly thought of; good/bad form.

vue [vy] *nf (fait de voir):* **la ~ de** the sight of ; *(sens, faculté)* (eye)sight; *(panorama, image, photo)* view; **~s** *nfpl (idées)* views; *(dessein)* designs; **hors de ~** out of sight; **tirer à ~** to shoot on sight; **à ~ d'œil** at visibly; at a quick glance; **en ~** *(visible)* in sight; *(COMM)* in the public eye; **en ~ de faire** with a view to doing.

vulgaire [vylgɛʀ] *a (grossier)* vulgar, coarse; *(trivial)* commonplace, mundane; *(péj: quelconque):* **de ~s touristes** common tourists; *(BOT, ZOOL: non latin)* common; **vulgariser** *vt* to popularize.

vulnérable [vylneʀabl(ə)] *a* vulnerable.

W X Y Z

wagon [vagɔ̃] *nm (de voyageurs)* carriage; *(de marchandises)* truck, wagon; **~-citerne** *nm* tanker; **~-lit** *nm* sleeper, sleeping car; **~-restaurant** *nm* restaurant ou dining car.

wallon, ne [valɔ̃, -ɔn] *a* Walloon.

waters [watɛʀ] *nmpl* toilet *sg*.

watt [wat] *nm* watt.

w.-c. [vese] *nmpl* toilet *sg*, lavatory *sg*.

week-end [wikɛnd] *nm* weekend.

western [wɛstɛʀn] *nm* western.

whisky, *pl* **whiskies** [wiski] *nm* whisky.

xérès [gzeʀɛs] *nm* sherry.

xylophone [ksilɔfɔn] *nm* xylophone.

y [i] *ad (à cet endroit)* there; *(dessus)* on it *(ou* them); *(dedans)* in it *(ou* them) // *pronom (about ou on ou of)* it : *vérifier la syntaxe du verbe employé;* **j'~ pense** I'm thinking about it; *voir aussi* **aller,** **avoir.**

yacht [jɔt] *nm* yacht.

yaourt [jauʀt] *nm* yoghurt.

yeux [jø] *pl de* **œil**.

yoga [jɔga] *nm* yoga.

yoghourt [jɔguʀt] *nm =* **yaourt**.

yougoslave [jugɔslav] *a, nm/f* Yugoslav(ian).

Yougoslavie [jugɔslavi] *nf* Yugoslavia.

zèbre [zɛbʀ(ə)] *nm (ZOOL)* zebra.

zébré, e [zebʀe] *a* striped, streaked.

zèle [zɛl] *nm* zeal; **faire du ~** *(péj)* to be over-zealous.

zéro [zeʀo] *nm* zero, nought *(Brit)*; **audessous de ~** below zero (Centigrade) ou freezing; **partir de ~** to start from scratch; **trois (buts) à ~** 3 (goals to) nil.

zeste [zɛst(ə)] *nm* peel, zest.

zézayer [zezeje] *vi* to have a lisp.

zigzag [zigzag] *nm* zigzag.

zinc [zɛ̃g] *nm (CHIMIE)* zinc; *(comptoir)* bar, counter.

zizanie [zizani] *nf*: **semer la** ~ to stir up ill-feeling.

zodiaque [zɔdjak] *nm* zodiac.

zona [zona] *nm* shingles *sg*.

zone [zon] *nf* zone, area; *(quartiers)*: **la** ~ the slum belt; ~ **bleue** ≈ restricted parking area.

zoo [zoo] *nm* zoo.

zoologie [zɔɔlɔʒi] *nf* zoology; **zoologique** *a* zoological.

zut [zyt] *excl* dash (it)! *(Brit)*, nuts! *(US)*.

ENGLISH - FRENCH
ANGLAIS - FRANÇAIS

A

A [eɪ] *n* (*MUS*) la *m*; (*AUT*): ~ **road** route nationale.

a (*before vowel or silent h*: **an**) [æ, æn] *indefinite article* **1** un(e); ~ **book** un livre; **an apple** une pomme; **she's** ~ **doctor** elle est médecin
2 (*instead of the number 'one'*) un(e); ~ **year ago** il y a un an; ~ **hundred/ thousand** *etc* **pounds** cent/mille *etc* livres
3 (*in expressing ratios, prices etc*): **3** ~ **day/week** 3 par jour/semaine; **10 km an hour** 10 km à l'heure; **30p** ~ **kilo** 30p le kilo.

A.A. *n abbr* =*Alcoholics Anonymous*; (*Brit*: =*Automobile Association*) ≈TCF *m*.

A.A.A. *n abbr* (*US*: =*American Automobile Association*) ≈TCF *m*.

aback [ə'bæk] *ad*: **to be taken** ~ être stupéfait(e).

abandon [ə'bændən] *vt* abandonner // *n* abandon *m*; **with** ~ avec désinvolture.

abashed [ə'bæʃt] *a* confus(e), embarrassé(e).

abate [ə'beɪt] *vi* s'apaiser, se calmer.

abbey ['æbɪ] *n* abbaye *f*.

abbot ['æbət] *n* père supérieur.

abbreviation [əbri:vɪ'eɪʃən] *n* abréviation *f*.

abdicate ['æbdɪkeɪt] *vt*, *vi* abdiquer.

abdomen ['æbdəmɛn] *n* abdomen *m*.

abduct [æb'dʌkt] *vt* enlever.

aberration [æbə'reɪʃən] *n* anomalie *f*.

abet [ə'bɛt] *vt see* **aid**.

abeyance [ə'beɪəns] *n*: **in** ~ (*law*) en désuétude; (*matter*) en suspens.

abide [ə'baɪd] *vt*: **I can't** ~ **it/him** je ne peux pas le souffrir *or* supporter; **to** ~ **by** *vt fus* observer, respecter.

ability [ə'bɪlɪtɪ] *n* compétence *f*; capacité *f*; (*skill*) talent *m*.

abject ['æbdʒɛkt] *a* (*poverty*) sordide; (*apology*) plat(e).

ablaze [ə'bleɪz] *a* en feu, en flammes.

able ['eɪbl] *a* compétent(e); **to be** ~ **to do sth** pouvoir faire qch, être capable de faire qch; **ably** *ad* avec compétence *or* talent, habilement.

abnormal [æb'nɔːməl] *a* anormal(e).

aboard [ə'bɔːd] *ad* à bord // *prep* à bord de.

abode [ə'bəud] *n*: **of no fixed** ~ sans domicile fixe.

abolish [ə'bɔlɪʃ] *vt* abolir.

aborigine [æbə'rɪdʒɪnɪ] *n* aborigène *m/f*.

abort [ə'bɔːt] *vt* faire avorter; ~**ion**

[ə'bɔːʃən] *n* avortement *m*; **to have an** ~**ion** se faire avorter; ~**ive** *a* manqué(e).

abound [ə'baund] *vi* abonder; **to** ~ **in** abonder en, regorger de.

about [ə'baut] *ad* **1** (*approximately*) environ, à peu près; ~ **a hundred/ thousand** *etc* environ cent/mille *etc*, une centaine/un millier *etc*; **it takes** ~ **10 hours** ça prend environ *or* à peu près 10 heures; **at** ~ **2 o'clock** vers 2 heures; **I've just** ~ **finished** j'ai presque fini
2 (*referring to place*) çà et là, de côté et d'autre; **to run** ~ courir çà et là; **to walk** ~ se promener, aller et venir
3: **to be** ~ **to do sth** être sur le point de faire qch
♦ *prep* **1** (*relating to*) au sujet de, à propos de; **a book** ~ **London** un livre sur Londres; **what is it** ~? de quoi s'agit-il?; **we talked** ~ **it** nous en avons parlé; **what or how** ~ **doing this?** et si nous faisions ceci?
2 (*referring to place*) dans; **to walk** ~ **the town** se promener dans la ville.

about turn *n* demi-tour *m*.

above [ə'bʌv] *ad* au-dessus // *prep* au-dessus de; **mentioned** ~ mentionné ci-dessus; ~ **all** par-dessus tout, surtout; ~**board** *a* franc(franche), loyal(e); honnête.

abrasive [ə'breɪzɪv] *a* abrasif(ive); (*fig*) caustique, agressif(ive).

abreast [ə'brɛst] *ad* de front; **to keep** ~ **of** se tenir au courant de.

abridge [ə'brɪdʒ] *vt* abréger.

abroad [ə'brɔːd] *ad* à l'étranger.

abrupt [ə'brʌpt] *a* (*steep, blunt*) abrupt(e); (*sudden, gruff*) brusque.

abscess ['æbsɪs] *n* abcès *m*.

abscond [əb'skɔnd] *vi* disparaître, s'enfuir.

absence ['æbsəns] *n* absence *f*.

absent ['æbsənt] *a* absent(e); ~**ee** [-'ti:] *n* absent/e; ~-**minded** *a* distrait(e).

absolute ['æbsəlu:t] *a* absolu(e); ~**ly** [-'lu:tlɪ] *ad* absolument.

absolve [əb'zɔlv] *vt*: **to** ~ **sb (from)** (*sin etc*) absoudre qn (de); **to** ~ **sb from** (*oath*) délier qn de.

absorb [əb'zɔːb] *vt* absorber; **to be** ~**ed in a book** être plongé dans un livre; ~**ent cotton** *n* (*US*) coton *m* hydrophile.

absorption [əb'zɔːpʃən] *n* absorption *f*; amortissement *m*; intégration *f*; (*fig*) concentration f.

abstain [əb'steɪn] vi: to ~ (from) s'abstenir (de).

abstemious [əb'stiːmɪəs] a sobre, frugal(e).

abstract ['æbstrækt] a abstrait(e).

absurd [əb'sɜːd] a absurde.

abuse n [ə'bjuːs] abus m, insultes fpl, injures fpl // vt [ə'bjuːz] abuser de; **abusive** a grossier(ère), injurieux(euse).

abysmal [ə'bɪzməl] a exécrable; (ignorance etc) sans bornes.

abyss [ə'bɪs] n abîme m, gouffre m.

AC abbr (=alternating current) courant alternatif.

academic [ækə'dɛmɪk] a universitaire; (pej: issue) oiseux(euse), purement théorique // n universitaire m/f.

academy [ə'kædəmɪ] n (learned body) académie f; (school) collège m; ~ of music conservatoire m.

accelerate [æk'sɛləreɪt] vt, vi accélérer; **accelerator** n accélérateur m.

accent ['æksɛnt] n accent m.

accept [ək'sɛpt] vt accepter; **~able** a acceptable; **~ance** n acceptation f.

access ['æksɛs] n accès m; **~ible** [æk'sɛsəbl] a accessible.

accessory [æk'sɛsərɪ] n accessoire m; **toilet accessories** npl articles mpl de toilette.

accident ['æksɪdənt] n accident m; (chance) hasard m; by ~ par hasard; accidentellement; **~al** [-'dɛntl] a accidentel(le); **~ally** [-'dɛntəlɪ] ad accidentellement; **~-prone** a sujet(te) aux accidents.

acclaim [ə'kleɪm] n acclamation f.

accommodate [ə'kɔmədeɪt] vt loger, recevoir; (oblige, help) obliger.

accommodating [ə'kɔmədeɪtɪŋ] a obligeant(e), arrangeant(e).

accommodation [əkɔmə'deɪʃən] n (US: ~s) logement m.

accompany [ə'kʌmpənɪ] vt accompagner.

accomplice [ə'kʌmplɪs] n complice m/f.

accomplish [ə'kʌmplɪʃ] vt accomplir; **~ment** n accomplissement m; réussite f, résultat m; **~ments** npl talents mpl.

accord [ə'kɔːd] n accord m // vt accorder; of his own ~ de son plein gré; **~ance** n: in ~ance with conformément à; **~ing to** prep selon; **~ingly** ad en conséquence.

accordion [ə'kɔːdɪən] n accordéon m.

accost [ə'kɔst] vt aborder.

account [ə'kaʊnt] n (COMM) compte m; (report) compte rendu; récit m; **~s** npl comptabilité f, comptes; of little ~ de peu d'importance; on ~ en acompte; on no ~ en aucun cas; on ~ of à cause de; to take into ~, take ~ of tenir compte de; to ~ for vt fus expliquer, rendre compte de; **~able** a responsable.

accountancy [ə'kaʊntənsɪ] n comptabilité f.

accountant [ə'kaʊntənt] n comptable m/f.

account number n (at bank etc) numéro m de compte.

accumulate [ə'kjuːmjuleɪt] vt accumuler, amasser // vi s'accumuler, s'amasser.

accuracy ['ækjurəsɪ] n exactitude f, précision f.

accurate ['ækjurɪt] a exact(e), précis(e); **~ly** ad avec précision.

accusation [ækju'zeɪʃən] n accusation f.

accuse [ə'kjuːz] vt accuser; **~d** n accusé/e.

accustom [ə'kʌstəm] vt accoutumer, habituer; **~ed** a (usual) habituel(le); **~ed to** habitué(e) or accoutumé(e) à.

ace [eɪs] n as m.

ache [eɪk] n mal m, douleur f // vi (be sore) faire mal, être douloureux(euse); my head ~s j'ai mal à la tête.

achieve [ə'tʃiːv] vt (aim) atteindre; (victory, success) remporter, obtenir; (task) accomplir; **~ment** n exploit m, réussite f.

acid ['æsɪd] a, n acide (m); ~ rain n pluies fpl acides.

acknowledge [ək'nɔlɪdʒ] vt (letter: also: ~ receipt of) accuser réception de; (fact) reconnaître; **~ment** n accusé m de réception.

acne ['æknɪ] n acné m.

acorn ['eɪkɔːn] n gland m.

acoustic [ə'kuːstɪk] a acoustique; **~s** n, npl acoustique f.

acquaint [ə'kweɪnt] vt: to ~ sb with sth mettre qn au courant de qch; to be ~ed with (person) connaître; **~ance** n connaissance f.

acquire [ə'kwaɪə*] vt acquérir.

acquit [ə'kwɪt] vt acquitter; to ~ o.s. well bien se comporter, s'en tirer très honorablement; **~tal** n acquittement m.

acre ['eɪkə*] n acre f (= 4047 m²).

acrid ['ækrɪd] a âcre.

acrobat ['ækrəbæt] n acrobate m/f.

across [ə'krɔs] prep (on the other side) de l'autre côté de; (crosswise) en travers de // ad de l'autre côté; en travers; to run/swim ~ traverser en courant/à la nage; ~ from en face de.

acrylic [ə'krɪlɪk] a, n acrylique (m).

act [ækt] n acte m, action f; (THEATRE) acte; (in music-hall etc) numéro m; (LAW) loi f // vi agir; (THEATRE) jouer; (pretend) jouer la comédie // vt (part) jouer, tenir; to ~ as servir de; **~ing** a suppléant(e), par intérim // n (of actor) jeu m; (activity): to do some ~ing faire du théâtre (or du cinéma).

action ['ækʃən] n action f; (MIL) combat(s) m(pl); (LAW) procès m, action en justice; out of ~ hors de combat; hors d'usage; **to take ~** agir, prendre des mesures; **~ replay** n (TV) répétition f de la séquence.

activate ['æktɪveɪt] vt (mechanism) actionner, faire fonctionner; (CHEM, PHYSICS) activer.

active ['æktɪv] a actif(ive); (volcano) en activité; **~ly** ad activement.

activity [æk'tɪvɪtɪ] n activité f.

actor ['æktə*] n acteur m.

actress ['æktrɪs] n actrice f.

actual ['æktjuəl] a réel(le), véritable; **~ly** ad réellement, véritablement; en fait.

acumen ['ækjumən] n perspicacité f.

acute [ə'kju:t] a aigu(ë); (mind, observer) pénétrant(e).

ad [æd] n abbr of **advertisement**.

A.D. ad abbr (= Anno Domini) ap. J.-C.

adamant ['ædəmənt] a inflexible.

adapt [ə'dæpt] vt adapter // vi: **to ~ (to)** s'adapter (à); **~able** (a device) adaptable; (person) qui s'adapte facilement; **~er** or **~or** n (ELEC) adaptateur m.

add [æd] vt ajouter; (figures: also: to ~ up) additionner // vi: **to ~ to** (increase) ajouter à, accroître; **it doesn't ~ up** (fig) cela ne rime à rien.

adder ['ædə*] n vipère f.

addict ['ædɪkt] n intoxiqué/e; (fig) fanatique m/f; **~ed** [ə'dɪktɪd] a: **to be ~ed to** (drink etc) être adonné(e) à; (fig: football etc) être une(un) fanatique de; **~ion** [ə'dɪkʃən] n (MED) dépendance f; **~ive** a qui crée une dépendance.

addition [ə'dɪʃən] n addition f; **in ~ de** plus; de surcroît; **in ~ t·** en plus de; **~al** a supplémentaire.

additive ['ædɪtɪv] n additif m.

address [ə'drɛs] n adresse f; (talk) discours m, allocution f // vt adresser; (speak to) s'adresser à.

adept ['ædɛpt] a: **~ at** expert(e) à or en.

adequate ['ædɪkwɪt] a adéquat(e); suffisant(e); compétent(e).

adhere [əd'hɪə*] vi: **to ~ to** adhérer à; (fig: rule, decision) se tenir à.

adhesive [əd'hi:zɪv] a adhésif(ive) // n adhésif m; **~ tape** n (Brit) ruban adhésif; (US: MED) sparadrap m.

adjective ['ædʒɛktɪv] n adjectif m.

adjoining [ə'dʒɔɪnɪŋ] a voisin(e), adjacent(e), attenant(e).

adjourn [ə'dʒə:n] vt ajourner // vi suspendre la séance; lever la séance; clore la session; (go) se retirer.

adjudicate [ə'dʒu:dɪkeɪt] vi se prononcer.

adjust [ə'dʒʌst] vt ajuster, régler; rajuster // vi: **to ~ (to)** s'adapter (à); **~able** a réglable.

ad-lib [æd'lɪb] vt, vi improviser // ad: **ad lib** à volonté, à discrétion.

administer [əd'mɪnɪstə*] vt adminis-

trer; (justice) rendre.

administration [ədmɪnɪs'treɪʃən] n administration f.

administrative [əd'mɪnɪstrətɪv] a administratif(ive).

admiral ['ædmərəl] n amiral m; **A~ty** n (Brit: also: **A~ty Board**) ministère m de la Marine.

admiration [ædmə'reɪʃən] n admiration f.

admire [əd'maɪə*] vt admirer.

admission [əd'mɪʃən] n admission f; (to exhibition, night club etc) entrée f; (confession) aveu m.

admit [əd'mɪt] vt laisser entrer; admettre; (agree) reconnaître, admettre; **to ~ to** vt fus reconnaître, avouer; **~tance** n admission f, (droit m d')entrée f; **~tedly** ad il faut en convenir.

admonish [əd'mɔnɪʃ] vt donner un avertissement à; réprimander.

ad nauseam [æd'nɔ:zɪæm] ad (repeat, talk) à satiété.

ado [ə'du:] n: **without (any) more ~** sans plus de cérémonies.

adolescence [ædəu'lɛsns] n adolescence f.

adolescent [ædəu'lɛsnt] a, n adolescent(e).

adopt [ə'dɔpt] vt adopter; **~ed** a adoptif(ive), adopté(e); **~ion** [ə'dɔpʃən] n adoption f.

adore [ə'dɔ:*] vt adorer.

adorn [ə'dɔ:n] vt orner.

Adriatic (Sea) [eɪdrɪ'ætɪk('si:)] n Adriatique f.

adrift [ə'drɪft] ad à la dérive.

adult ['ædʌlt] n adulte m/f.

adultery [ə'dʌltərɪ] n adultère m.

advance [əd'vɑ:ns] n avance f // vt avancer // vi s'avancer; **in ~** en avance, d'avance; **~d** a avancé(e); (SCOL: studies) supérieur(e).

advantage [əd'vɑ:ntɪdʒ] n (also TENNIS) avantage m; **to take ~ of** profiter de.

advent ['ædvənt] n avènement m, venue f; **A~** Avent m.

adventure [əd'vɛntʃə*] n aventure f.

adverb ['ædvə:b] n adverbe m.

adverse ['ædvə:s] a contraire, adverse; **~ to** hostile à.

advert ['ædvə:t] n abbr (Brit) of **advertisement**.

advertise ['ædvətaɪz] vi (vt) faire de la publicité or de la réclame (pour); mettre une annonce (pour vendre); **to ~ for** (staff) faire paraître une annonce pour trouver.

advertisement [əd'və:tɪsmənt] n (COMM) réclame f, publicité f; (in classified ads) annonce f.

advertiser ['ædvətaɪzə*] n (in newspaper etc) annonceur m.

advertising ['ædvətaɪzɪŋ] n publicité f,

réclame f.

advice [əd'vaɪs] n conseils mpl; (notification) avis m; **piece of** ~ conseil; **to take legal** ~ consulter un avocat.

advisable [əd'vaɪzəbl] a recommandable, indiqué(e).

advise [əd'vaɪz] vt conseiller; **to** ~ **sb of sth** aviser or informer qn de qch; **to** ~ **against sth/doing sth** déconseiller qch/conseiller de ne pas faire qch; ~**dly** [-'vaɪzədlɪ] ad (deliberately) délibérément; ~**r** n conseiller/ère; **advisory** [-ərɪ] a consultatif(ive).

advocate n ['ædvəkɪt] (upholder) défenseur m, avocat/e ♦ vt ['ædvəkeɪt] recommander, prôner; **to be an** ~ **of** être partisan/e de.

aerial ['ɛərɪəl] n antenne f // a aérien(ne).

aerobics [ɛə'rəubɪks] n aérobic m.

aeroplane ['ɛərəpleɪn] n (Brit) avion m.

aerosol ['ɛərəsɒl] n aérosol m.

aesthetic [ɪs'θɛtɪk] a esthétique.

afar [ə'fɑ:ʳ] ad: **from** ~ de loin.

affair [ə'fɛəʳ] n affaire f; (also: **love** ~) liaison f; aventure f.

affect [ə'fɛkt] vt affecter.

affection [ə'fɛkʃən] n affection f; ~**ate** a affectueux(euse).

affirmation [æfə'meɪʃən] n affirmation f, assertion f.

affix [ə'fɪks] vt apposer, ajouter.

afflict [ə'flɪkt] vt affliger.

affluence ['æfluəns] n abondance f, opulence f.

affluent ['æfluənt] a abondant(e); opulent(e); (person) dans l'aisance, riche.

afford [ə'fɔ:d] vt se permettre; avoir les moyens d'acheter or d'entretenir; (provide) fournir, procurer.

afield [ə'fi:ld] ad: **far** ~ loin.

afloat [ə'fləut] a, ad à flot; **to stay** ~ surnager.

afoot [ə'fut] ad: **there is something** ~ il se prépare quelque chose.

afraid [ə'freɪd] a effrayé(e); **to be** ~ **of** or **to** avoir peur de; **I am** ~ **that** je crains que + sub.

afresh [ə'frɛʃ] ad de nouveau.

Africa ['æfrɪkə] n Afrique f; ~**n** a africain(e) // n Africain/e.

aft [ɑ:ft] ad à l'arrière, vers l'arrière.

after ['ɑ:ftəʳ] prep, ad après // cj après que, après avoir or être + pp; **what/who are you** ~? que/qui cherchez-vous?; ~ **he left/having done** après qu'il fut parti/après avoir fait; **ask** ~ **him** demandez de ses nouvelles; ~ **all** après tout; ~ **you!** après vous, Monsieur (or Madame etc); ~**-effects** npl répercussions fpl; (of illness) séquelles fpl, suites fpl; ~**life** n vie future; ~**math** n conséquences fpl; **in the** ~**math of** dans les mois or années etc qui suivirent, au lendemain de;

~**noon** n après-midi m or f; ~**s** n (col: dessert) dessert m; ~**-sales service** n (Brit: for car, washing machine etc) service m après-vente (S.A.V.); ~**shave (lotion)** n after-shave m; ~**thought** n: **I had an** ~**thought** il m'est venu une idée après coup; ~**wards** ad après.

again [ə'gɛn] ad de nouveau; **to do sth** ~ refaire qch; **not** — ~ ne — plus; ~ **and** ~ à plusieurs reprises.

against [ə'gɛnst] prep contre.

age [eɪdʒ] n âge m // vt, vi vieillir; **it's been** ~**s since** ça fait une éternité que — ne; **he is 20 years of** ~ il a 20 ans; **to come of** ~ atteindre sa majorité; ~**d 10** âgé de 10 ans; **the** ~**d** ['eɪdʒɪd] les personnes âgées; ~ **group** n tranche f d'âge; ~ **limit** n limite f d'âge.

agency ['eɪdʒənsɪ] n agence f; **through** or **by the** ~ **of** par l'entremise or l'action de.

agenda [ə'dʒɛndə] n ordre m du jour.

agent ['eɪdʒənt] n agent m.

aggregate ['ægrɪgeɪt] n ensemble m, total m.

aggressive [ə'grɛsɪv] a agressif(ive).

aggrieved [ə'gri:vd] a chagriné(e), affligé(e).

aghast [ə'gɑ:st] a consterné(e), atterré(e).

agitate ['ædʒɪteɪt] vt rendre inquiet(ète) or agité(e); agiter; **to** ~ **for** faire campagne pour.

ago [ə'gəu] ad: **2 days** ~ il y a deux jours; **not long** ~ il n'y a pas longtemps; **how long** ~? il y a combien de temps (de cela)?

agog [ə'gɒg] a en émoi.

agonizing ['ægənaɪzɪŋ] a angoissant(e); déchirant(e).

agony ['ægənɪ] n grande souffrance or angoisse.

agree [ə'gri:] vt (price) convenir de // vi: **to** ~ **(with)** (person) être d'accord (avec); (statements etc) concorder (avec); (LING) s'accorder (avec); **to** ~ **to do** accepter de or consentir à faire; **to** ~ **to sth** consentir à qch; **to** ~ **that** (admit) convenir or reconnaître que; **garlic doesn't** ~ **with me** je ne supporte pas l'ail; ~**able** a agréable; (willing) consentant(e), d'accord; ~**d** a (time, place) convenu(e); ~**ment** n accord m; **in** ~**ment** d'accord.

agricultural [ægrɪ'kʌltʃərəl] a agricole.

agriculture ['ægrɪkʌltʃəʳ] n agriculture f.

aground [ə'graund] ad: **to run** ~ s'échouer.

ahead [ə'hɛd] ad en avant; devant; ~ **of** devant; (fig: schedule etc) en avance sur; ~ **of time** en avance; **go right** or **straight** ~ allez tout droit; **they were (right)** ~ **of us** ils nous précédaient (de peu), ils étaient (juste) devant nous.

aid [eɪd] *n* aide *f* // *vt* aider; in ~ of en faveur de; to ~ and abet (*LAW*) se faire le complice de.

aide [eɪd] *n* (*person*) collaborateur/trice, assistant/e.

AIDS [eɪdz] *n abbr* (=*acquired immune deficiency syndrome*) SIDA *m*.

ailing ['eɪlɪŋ] *a* malade.

ailment ['eɪlmənt] *n* petite maladie, affection *f*.

aim [eɪm] *vt*: to ~ sth at (*such as gun, camera*) braquer *or* pointer qch sur, diriger qch contre; (*missile*) lancer qch à *or* contre *or* en direction de; (*remark, blow*) destiner *or* adresser qch à // *vi* (*also*: to take ~) viser // *n* but *m*; to ~ at viser; (*fig*) viser (à); avoir pour but *or* ambition; to ~ to do avoir l'intention de faire; ~less *a* sans but.

ain't [eɪnt] (*col*) =am not, aren't, isn't.

air [εə*] *n* air *m* // *vt* aérer; (*grievances, ideas*) exposer (librement) // *cpd* (*currents, attack etc*) aérien(ne); to throw sth into the ~ jeter qch en l'air; to be on the ~ (*RADIO, TV: programme*) être diffusé(e); (: *station*) diffuser; ~bed *n* matelas *m* pneumatique; ~borne *a* en vol; aéroporté(e); ~ conditioning *n* climatisation *f*; ~craft *n, pl inv* avion *m*; ~craft carrier *n* porte-avions *m inv*; ~field *n* terrain *m* d'aviation; A~ Force *n* Armée *f* de l'air; ~ freshener *n* désodorisant *m*; ~gun *n* fusil *m* à air comprimé; ~ hostess *n* (*Brit*) hôtesse *f* de l'air; ~ letter *n* (*Brit*) aérogramme *m*; ~lift *n* pont aérien; ~line *n* ligne aérienne, compagnie *f* d'aviation; ~liner *n* avion *m* de ligne; ~lock *n* sas *m*; ~mail *n*: by ~mail par avion; ~ mattress *n* matelas *m* pneumatique; ~plane *n* (*US*) avion *m*; ~port *n* aéroport *m*; ~ raid *n* attaque aérienne; ~sick *a*: to be ~sick avoir le mal de l'air; ~strip *n* terrain *m* d'atterrissage; ~ terminal *n* aérogare *f*; ~tight *a* hermétique; ~ traffic controller *n* aiguilleur *m* du ciel; ~y *a* bien aéré(e); (*manners*) dégagé(e).

aisle [aɪl] *n* (*of church*) allée centrale; nef latérale.

ajar [ə'dʒɑ:*] *a* entrouvert(e).

akin [ə'kɪn] *a*: ~ to (*similar*) qui tient de *or* ressemble à.

alacrity [ə'lækrɪtɪ] *n* empressement *m*.

alarm [ə'lɑ:m] *n* alarme *f* // *vt* alarmer; ~ clock *n* réveille-matin *m*, réveil *m*.

alas [ə'læs] *excl* hélas!

albeit [ɔ:l'bi:ɪt] *cj* (*although*) bien que + *sub*, encore que + *sub*.

album ['ælbəm] *n* album *m*; (*L.P.*) 33 tours *m inv*.

alcohol ['ælkəhɔl] *n* alcool *m*; ~ic [-'hɔlɪk] *a, n* alcoolique (*m/f*).

alderman ['ɔ:ldəmən] *n* conseiller

municipal (*en Angleterre*).

ale [eɪl] *n* bière *f*.

alert [ə'lə:t] *a* alerte, vif(vive); vigilant(e) // *n* alerte *f* // *vt* alerter; (*fig*) éveiller l'attention de; on the ~ sur le qui-vive; (*MIL*) en état d'alerte.

algebra ['ældʒɪbrə] *n* algèbre *m*.

Algeria [æl'dʒɪərɪə] *n* Algérie *f*.

alias ['eɪlɪəs] *ad* alias // *n* faux nom, nom d'emprunt.

alibi ['ælɪbaɪ] *n* alibi *m*.

alien ['eɪlɪən] *n* étranger/ère // *a*: ~ (to) étranger(ère) (à); ~ate *vt* aliéner; s'aliéner.

alight [ə'laɪt] *a, ad* en feu // *vi* mettre pied à terre; (*passenger*) descendre; (*bird*) se poser.

alike [ə'laɪk] *a* semblable, pareil(le) // *ad* de même; to look ~ se ressembler.

alimony ['ælɪmənɪ] *n* (*payment*) pension *f* alimentaire.

alive [ə'laɪv] *a* vivant(e); (*active*) plein(e) de vie.

all [ɔ:l] ♦ *a* (*singular*) tout(e); (*plural*) tous(toutes); ~ day toute la journée; ~ night toute la nuit; ~ men tous les hommes; ~ five tous les cinq; ~ the food toute la nourriture; ~ the books tous les livres; ~ the time tout le temps; ~ his life toute sa vie

♦ *pronoun* 1 tout; I ate it ~, I ate ~ of it j'ai tout mangé; ~ of us went nous y sommes tous allés; ~ of the boys went tous les garçons y sont allés

2 (*in phrases*): above ~ surtout, par-dessus tout; after ~ après tout; at ~: not at ~ (*in answer to question*) pas du tout; (*in answer to thanks*) je vous en prie!; I'm not at ~ tired je ne suis pas du tout fatigué(e); anything at ~ will do n'importe quoi fera l'affaire; ~ in ~ tout bien considéré, en fin de compte

♦ *ad*: ~ alone tout(e) seul(e); it's not as hard as ~ that ce n'est pas si difficile que ça; ~ the more/the better d'autant plus/mieux; ~ but presque, pratiquement; the score is 2 ~ le score est 2 partout.

allay [ə'leɪ] *vt* (*fears*) apaiser, calmer.

all clear *n* (*after attack etc, also fig*) fin *f* d'alerte.

allege [ə'lɛdʒ] *vt* alléguer, prétendre; ~dly [ə'lɛdʒɪdlɪ] *ad* à ce que l'on prétend, paraît-il.

allegiance [ə'li:dʒəns] *n* fidélité *f*, obéissance *f*.

allergic [ə'lə:dʒɪk] *a*: ~ to allergique à.

allergy ['ælədʒɪ] *n* allergie *f*.

alleviate [ə'li:vɪeɪt] *vt* soulager, adoucir.

alley ['ælɪ] *n* ruelle *f*; (*in garden*) allée *f*.

alliance [ə'laɪəns] *n* alliance *f*.

allied ['ælaɪd] *a* allié(e).

all-in ['ɔ:lɪn] *a* (*Brit: also ad: charge*) tout compris; ~ wrestling *n* catch *m*.

all-night ['ɔ:l'naɪt] *a* ouvert(e) *or* qui

dure toute la nuit.

allocate ['æləkeɪt] *vt* (*share out*) répartir, distribuer; (*duties*): to ~ sth to assigner *or* attribuer qch à; (*sum, time*): to ~ sth to allouer qch à; to ~ sth for affecter qch à.

allot [ə'lɔt] *vt* (*share out*) répartir, distribuer; (*time*): to ~ sth to allouer qch à; (*duties*): to ~ sth to assigner qch à; **~ment** *n* (*share*) part *f*; (*garden*) lopin m de terre (loué à la municipalité).

all-out ['ɔ:laut] *a* (*effort etc*) total(e) // *ad*: all out à fond.

allow [ə'lau] *vt* (*practice, behaviour*) permettre, autoriser; (*sum to spend etc*) accorder; allouer; (*sum, time estimated*) compter, prévoir; (*concede*): to ~ that convenir que; to ~ sb to do permettre à qn de faire, autoriser qn à faire; he is ~ed to — on lui permet de —; to ~ for *vt fus* tenir compte de; **~ance** *n* (*money received*) allocation *f*; subside *m*; indemnité *f*; (*TAX*) somme *f* déductible du revenu imposable, abattement *m*; to make ~ances for tenir compte de.

alloy ['ælɔɪ] *n* alliage *m*.

all right ['ɔ:l'raɪt] *ad* (*feel, work*) bien; (*as answer*) d'accord.

all-round ['ɔ:l'raund] *a* compétent(e) dans tous les domaines; (*athlete etc*) complet(ète).

all-time ['ɔ:l'taɪm] *a* (*record*) sans précédent, absolu(e).

allude [ə'lu:d] *vi*: to ~ to faire allusion à.

alluring [ə'ljuərɪŋ] *a* séduisant(e), allé-chant(e).

ally ['ælaɪ] *n* allié *m*.

almighty [ɔ:l'maɪtɪ] *a* tout-puissant.

almond ['ɑ:mənd] *n* amande *f*.

almost ['ɔ:lməust] *ad* presque.

alms [ɑ:mz] *npl* aumône(s) *f*(*pl*).

aloft [ə'lɔft] *ad* en haut, en l'air; (*NAUT*) dans la mâture.

alone [ə'ləun] *a, ad* seul(e); to leave sb ~ laisser qn tranquille; to leave sth ~ ne pas toucher à qch; let ~ — sans parler de —; encore moins —.

along [ə'lɔŋ] *prep* le long de // *ad*: is he coming ~? vient-il avec nous?; he was hopping/limping ~ il venait *or* avançait en sautillant/boitant; ~ with en compagnie de; avec, en plus de; all ~ (*all the time*) depuis le début; **~side** *prep* le long de; au côté de // *ad* bord à bord; côte à côte.

aloof [ə'lu:f] *a, ad* à distance, à l'écart.

aloud [ə'laud] *ad* à haute voix.

alphabet ['ælfəbɛt] *n* alphabet *m*; **~ical** [-'bɛtɪkəl] *a* alphabétique.

alpine ['ælpaɪn] *a* alpin(e), alpestre.

Alps [ælps] *npl*: the ~ les Alpes *fpl*.

already [ɔ:l'rɛdɪ] *ad* déjà.

alright ['ɔ:l'raɪt] *ad* (*Brit*) = **all right**.

Alsatian [æl'seɪʃən] *n* (*dog*) berger

allemand.

also ['ɔ:lsəu] *ad* aussi.

altar ['ɔltə*] *n* autel *m*.

alter ['ɔltə*] *vt, vi* changer, modifier.

alternate *a* [ɔl'tə:nɪt] alterné(e), alternant(e), alternatif(ive) // *vi* ['ɔltə:neɪt] alterner; on ~ days un jour sur deux, tous les deux jours; **alter-nating** *a* (*current*) alternatif(ive).

alternative [ɔl'tə:nətɪv] *a* (*solutions*) interchangeable, possible; (*solution*) autre, de remplacement // *n* (*choice*) alternative *f*; (*other possibility*) solution *f* de remplacement *or* de rechange, autre possibilité *f*; **~ly** *ad*: ~ly one could une autre *or* l'autre solution serait de.

alternator ['ɔltə:neɪtə*] *n* (*AUT*) alternateur *m*.

although [ɔ:l'ðəu] *cj* bien que + *sub*.

altitude ['æltɪtju:d] *n* altitude *f*.

alto ['æltəu] *n* (*female*) contralto *m*; (*male*) haute-contre *f*.

altogether [ɔ:ltə'gɛðə*] *ad* entièrement, tout à fait; (*on the whole*) tout compte fait; (*in all*) en tout.

aluminium [ælju'mɪnɪəm] , (US) **alu-minum** [ə'lu:mɪnəm] *n* aluminium *m*.

always ['ɔ:lweɪz] *ad* toujours.

am [æm] *vb see* **be**.

a.m. *ad abbr* (=*ante meridiem*) du matin.

amalgamate [ə'mælgəmeɪt] *vt, vi* fusionner.

amateur ['æmətə*] *n* amateur *m* // *a* (*SPORT*) amateur *inv*; **~ish** *a* (*pej*) d'amateur.

amaze [ə'meɪz] *vt* stupéfier; to be ~d (at) être surpris(e) *or* étonné(e) (de); **~ment** *n* stupéfaction *f*, stupeur *f*; **amazing** *a* étonnant(e); exceptionnel(le).

ambassador [æm'bæsədə*] *n* ambassadeur *m*.

amber ['æmbə*] *n* ambre *m*; at ~ (*Brit AUT*) à l'orange.

ambiguous [æm'bɪgjuəs] *a* ambigu(ë).

ambition [æm'bɪʃən] *n* ambition *f*.

ambitious [æm'bɪʃəs] *a* ambitieux(euse).

amble ['æmbl] *vi* (*also*: to ~ along) aller d'un pas tranquille.

ambulance ['æmbjuləns] *n* ambulance *f*.

ambush ['æmbuʃ] *n* embuscade *f* // *vt* tendre une embuscade à.

amenable [ə'mi:nəbl] *a*: ~ to (*advice etc*) disposé(e) à écouter *or* suivre.

amend [ə'mɛnd] *vt* (*law*) amender; (*text*) corriger; to make ~s réparer ses torts, faire amende honorable.

amenities [ə'mi:nɪtɪz] *npl* aménagements *mpl* (*prévus pour le loisir des habitants*).

America [ə'mɛrɪkə] *n* Amérique *f*; **~n** *a* américain(e) // *n* Américain/e.

amiable ['eɪmɪəbl] *a* aimable, affable.

amicable ['æmɪkəbl] *a* amical(e).

amid(st) [ə'mɪd(st)] *prep* parmi, au milieu de.

amiss [ə'mɪs] *a, ad*: **there's something ~** il y a quelque chose qui ne va pas *or* qui cloche; **to take sth ~** prendre qch mal *or* de travers.

ammonia [ə'məʊnɪə] *n* (*gas*) ammoniac *m*; (*liquid*) ammoniaque *f*.

ammunition [æmju'nɪʃən] *n* munitions *fpl*.

amok [ə'mɔk] *ad*: **to run ~** être pris(e) d'un accès de folie furieuse.

among(st) [ə'mʌŋ(st)] *prep* parmi, entre.

amorous ['æmərəs] *a* amoureux(euse).

amount [ə'maʊnt] *n* (*sum*) somme *f*, montant *m*; (*quantity*) quantité *f* // *vi*: **to ~ to** (*total*) s'élever à; (*be same as*) équivaloir à, revenir à.

amp(ère) ['æmp(eə*)] *n* ampère *m*.

ample ['æmpl] *a* ample; spacieux(euse); (*enough*): **this is ~** c'est largement suffisant; **to have ~ time/room** avoir bien assez de temps/place.

amplifier ['æmplɪfaɪə*] *n* amplificateur *m*.

amuck [ə'mʌk] *ad* **=amok**.

amuse [ə'mjuːz] *vt* amuser; **~ment** *n* amusement *m*; **~ment arcade** *n* salle *f* de jeu.

an [æn] *indefinite article see* **a**.

anaemic [ə'niːmɪk] *a* anémique.

anaesthetic [ænɪs'θetɪk] *a, n* anesthésique (*m*).

analog(ue) ['ænəlɔg] *a* (*watch, computer*) analogique.

analyse ['ænəlaɪz] *vt* (*Brit*) analyser.

analysis, *pl* **analyses** [ə'næləsɪs, -siːz] *n* analyse *f*.

analyst ['ænəlɪst] *n* (*POL etc*) spécialiste *m/f*; (*US*) psychanalyste *m/f*.

analyze ['ænəlaɪz] *vt* (*US*) **=analyse**.

anarchist ['ænəkɪst] *a, n* anarchiste (*m/f*).

anarchy ['ænəkɪ] *n* anarchie *f*.

anathema [ə'næθɪmə] *n*: **it is ~ to him** il a cela en abomination.

anatomy [ə'nætəmɪ] *n* anatomie *f*.

ancestor ['ænsɪstə*] *n* ancêtre *m*, aïeul *m*.

anchor ['æŋkə*] *n* ancre *f* // *vi* (*also*: **to drop ~**) jeter l'ancre, mouiller // *vt* mettre à l'ancre; **to weigh ~** lever l'ancre.

anchovy ['æntʃəvɪ] *n* anchois *m*.

ancient ['eɪnʃənt] *a* ancien(ne), antique; (*fig*) d'un âge vénérable, antique.

ancillary ['æn'sɪlərɪ] *a* auxiliaire.

and [ænd] *cj* et; **~ so on** et ainsi de suite; **try ~ come** tâchez de venir; **he talked ~ talked** il n'a pas arrêté de parler; **better ~ better** de mieux en mieux.

anew [ə'njuː] *ad* à nouveau.

angel ['eɪndʒəl] *n* ange *m*.

anger ['æŋgə*] *n* colère *f* // *vt* mettre en colère, irriter.

angina [æn'dʒaɪnə] *n* angine *f* de poitrine.

angle ['æŋgl] *n* angle *m*; **from their ~** de leur point de vue; **~r** *n* pêcheur/euse à la ligne.

Anglican ['æŋglɪkən] *a, n* anglican(e).

angling ['æŋglɪŋ] *n* pêche *f* à la ligne.

Anglo- ['æŋgləʊ] *prefix* anglo(-).

angry ['æŋgrɪ] *a* en colère, furieux(euse); **to be ~ with sb/at sth** être furieux contre qn/de qch; **to get ~** se fâcher, se mettre en colère; **to make sb ~** mettre qn en colère.

anguish ['æŋgwɪʃ] *n* angoisse *f*.

angular ['æŋgjʊlə*] *a* anguleux(euse).

animal ['ænɪməl] *n* animal *m* // *a* animal(e).

animate *vt* ['ænɪmeɪt] animer // *a* ['ænɪmɪt] animé(e), vivant(e); **~d** *a* animé(e).

aniseed ['ænɪsiːd] *n* anis *m*.

ankle ['æŋkl] *n* cheville *f*; **~ sock** *n* socquette *f*.

annex *n* ['æneks] (*also: Brit*: **annexe**) annexe *f* // *vt* [ə'neks] annexer.

anniversary [ænɪ'vəːsərɪ] *n* anniversaire *m*.

announce [ə'naʊns] *vt* annoncer; (*birth, death*) faire part de; **~ment** *n* annonce *f*; (*for births etc: in newspaper*) avis *m* de faire-part; (: *letter, card*) faire-part *m*; **~r** *n* (*RADIO, TV*: *between programmes*) speaker/ine; (: *in a programme*) présentateur/trice.

annoy [ə'nɔɪ] *vt* agacer, ennuyer, contrarier; **don't get ~ed!** ne vous fâchez pas!; **~ance** *n* mécontentement *m*, contrariété *f*; **~ing** *a* ennuyeux(euse), agaçant(e), contrariant(e).

annual ['ænjʊəl] *a* annuel(le) // *n* (*BOT*) plante annuelle; (*book*) album *m*.

annul [ə'nʌl] *vt* annuler; (*law*) abroger.

annum ['ænəm] *n see* **per**.

anonymous [ə'nɒnɪməs] *a* anonyme.

anorak ['ænəræk] *n* anorak *m*.

another [ə'nʌðə*] *a*: **~ book** (*one more*) un autre livre, encore un livre, un livre de plus; (*a different one*) un autre livre // *pronoun* un(e) autre, encore un(e), un(e) de plus; *see also* **one**.

answer ['ɑːnsə*] *n* réponse *f*; solution *f* // *vi* répondre // *vt* (*reply to*) répondre à; (*problem*) résoudre; (*prayer*) exaucer; **to ~ the phone** répondre (au téléphone); **in ~ to your letter** suite à *or* en réponse à votre lettre; **to ~ the bell** *or* **the door** aller *or* venir ouvrir (la porte); **to ~ back** *vi* répondre, répliquer; **to ~ for** *vt fus* répondre de, se porter garant de; être responsable de; **to ~ to** *vt fus* (*description*) répondre *or* correspondre à; **~able** *a*: **~able** (**to sb/for sth**) responsable (devant qn/de qch); **~ing**

machine n répondeur m automatique.
ant [ænt] n fourmi f.
antagonism [æn'tægənɪzəm] n antagonisme m.
antagonize [æn'tægənaɪz] vt éveiller l'hostilité de, contrarier.
Antarctic [ænt'ɑ:ktɪk] n: the ~ l'Antarctique m.
antenatal ['æntɪ'neɪtl] a prénatal(e); ~ **clinic** n service m de consultation prénatale.
anthem ['ænθəm] n motet m; **national** ~ hymne national.
anthology [æn'θɒlədʒɪ] n anthologie f.
antibiotic ['æntɪbaɪ'ɒtɪk] a, n antibiotique (m).
antibody ['æntɪbɒdɪ] n anticorps m.
anticipate [æn'tɪsɪpeɪt] vt s'attendre à; prévoir; (wishes, request) aller au devant de, devancer.
anticipation [æntɪsɪ'peɪʃən] n attente f.
anticlimax ['æntɪ'klaɪmæks] n réalisation décevante d'un événement que l'on escomptait important, intéressant etc.
anticlockwise ['æntɪ'klɒkwaɪz] a, ad dans le sens inverse des aiguilles d'une montre.
antics ['æntɪks] npl singeries fpl.
antifreeze ['æntɪfri:z] n antigel m.
antihistamine [æntɪ'hɪstəmi:n] n antihistaminique m.
antiquated ['æntɪkweɪtɪd] a vieilli(e), suranné(e), vieillot(te).
antique [æn'ti:k] n objet m d'art ancien, meuble ancien or d'époque, antiquité f // a ancien(ne); (pre-mediaeval) antique; ~ **shop** n magasin m d'antiquités.
anti-Semitism [æntɪ'semɪtɪzəm] n antisémitisme m.
antiseptic [æntɪ'septɪk] a, n antiseptique (m).
antisocial ['æntɪ'səʊʃəl] a peu liant(e), sauvage, insociable; (against society) anti-social(e).
antlers ['æntləz] npl bois mpl, ramure f.
anvil ['ænvɪl] n enclume f.
anxiety [æŋ'zaɪətɪ] n anxiété f; (keenness): ~ **to do** grand désir or impatience f de faire.
anxious ['æŋkʃəs] a anxieux(euse), (très) inquiet(ète), (keen): ~ **to do/that** qui tient beaucoup à faire/à ce que; impatient(e) de faire/que.
any ['enɪ] ♦ a **1** (in questions etc: singular) du, de l', de la; (: plural) des; **have you ~ butter/children/ink?** avez-vous du beurre/des enfants/de l'encre? **2** (with negative) de, d'; **I haven't ~ money/books** je n'ai pas d'argent/de livres **3** (no matter which one) n'importe quel(le); **choose ~ book you like** vous pouvez choisir n'importe quel livre **4** (in phrases): **in ~ case** de toute façon; ~ **day now** d'un jour à l'autre; at

~ **moment** à tout moment, d'un instant à l'autre; at ~ **rate** en tout cas
♦ pronoun **1** (in questions etc) en; **have you got ~?** est-ce que vous en avez?; **can ~ of you sing?** est-ce que parmi vous il y en a qui chantent? **2** (with negative) en; **I haven't ~** (of them) je n'en ai pas, je n'en ai aucun **3** (no matter which one(s)) n'importe lequel (or laquelle); **take ~ of those books** (you like) vous pouvez prendre n'importe lequel de ces livres
♦ ad **1** (in questions etc): **do you want ~ more soup/sandwiches?** voulez-vous encore de la soupe/des sandwichs?; **are you feeling ~ better?** est-ce que vous sentez mieux? **2** (with negative): **I can't hear him ~ more** je ne l'entends plus; **don't wait ~ longer** n'attendez pas plus longtemps.
anybody ['enɪbɒdɪ] pronoun n'importe qui; (in interrogative sentences) quelqu'un; (in negative sentences): **I don't see ~** je ne vois personne.
anyhow ['enɪhaʊ] ad (at any rate) de toute façon, quand même; (haphazard) n'importe comment.
anyone ['enɪwʌn] pronoun = **anybody.**
anything ['enɪθɪŋ] pronoun (see anybody) n'importe quoi; quelque chose; ne — rien.
anyway ['enɪweɪ] ad de toute façon.
anywhere ['enɪwɛə*] ad (see anybody) n'importe où; quelque part; **I don't see him ~** je ne le vois nulle part.
apart [ə'pɑ:t] ad (to one side) à part; de côté; à l'écart; (separately) séparément; **with one's legs ~** les jambes écartées; **10 miles ~** à 10 milles l'un de l'autre; **to take ~** démonter; ~ **from** prep à part, excepté.
apartheid [ə'pɑ:teɪt] n apartheid m.
apartment [ə'pɑ:tmənt] n (US) appartement m, logement m; ~ **building** n (US) immeuble m; maison divisée en appartements.
ape [eɪp] n (grand) singe // vt singer.
aperture ['æpətʃjʊə*] n orifice m, ouverture f; (PHOT) ouverture (du diaphragme).
apex ['eɪpeks] n sommet m.
apiece [ə'pi:s] ad (for each person) chacun(e).
apologetic [əpɒlə'dʒetɪk] a (tone, letter) d'excuse.
apologize [ə'pɒlədʒaɪz] vi: **to ~** (for sth to sb) s'excuser (de qch auprès de qn), présenter des excuses (à qn pour qch).
apology [ə'pɒlədʒɪ] n excuses fpl.
apostle [ə'pɒsl] n apôtre m.
apostrophe [ə'pɒstrəfɪ] n apostrophe f.
appalling [ə'pɔ:lɪŋ] a épouvantable; (stupidity) consternant(e).
apparatus [æpə'reɪtəs] n appareil m, dispositif m; (in gymnasium) agrès mpl.

apparel [ə'pærəl] *n* (*US*) habillement *m*.
apparent [ə'pærənt] *a* apparent(e); ~**ly** *ad* apparemment.
appeal [ə'pi:l] *vi* (*LAW*) faire *or* interjeter appel // *n* (*LAW*) appel *m*; (*request*) prière *f*; appel *m*; (*charm*) attrait *m*, charme *m*; **to ~ for** demander (instamment); implorer; **to ~ to** (*subj: person*) faire appel à; (*subj: thing*) plaire à; **it doesn't ~ to me** cela ne m'attire pas; ~**ing** *a* (*nice*) attrayant(e); (*touching*) attendrissant(e).
appear [ə'pɪə*] *vi* apparaître, se montrer; (*LAW*) comparaître; (*publication*) paraître, sortir, être publié(e); (*seem*) paraître, sembler; **it would ~ that** il semble que; **to ~ in Hamlet** jouer dans Hamlet; **to ~ on TV** passer à la télé; ~**ance** *n* apparition *f*; parution *f*; (*look, aspect*) apparence *f*; aspect *m*.
appease [ə'pi:z] *vt* apaiser, calmer.
appendicitis [əpɛndɪ'saɪtɪs] *n* appendicite *f*.
appendix, *pl* **appendices** [ə'pɛndɪks, -si:z] *n* appendice *m*.
appetite ['æpɪtaɪt] *n* appétit *m*.
appetizer ['æpɪtaɪzə*] *n* amuse-gueule *m*.
applaud [ə'plɔ:d] *vt, vi* applaudir.
applause [ə'plɔ:z] *n* applaudissements *mpl*.
apple ['æpl] *n* pomme *f*; ~ **tree** *n* pommier *m*.
appliance [ə'plaɪəns] *n* appareil *m*.
applicant ['æplɪkənt] *n*: ~ (**for**) (*post*) candidat/e (à).
application [æplɪ'keɪʃən] *n* application *f*; (*for a job, a grant etc*) demande *f*; candidature *f*; ~ **form** *n* formulaire *m* de demande.
applied [ə'plaɪd] *a* appliqué(e).
apply [ə'plaɪ] *vt* (*paint, ointment*): **to ~ (to)** appliquer (sur); (*theory, technique*): **to ~ (to)** appliquer (à) // *vi*: **to ~ to** (*ask*) s'adresser à; (*be suitable for, relevant to*) s'appliquer à; se rapporter à; être valable pour; **to ~ (for)** (*permit, grant*) faire une demande (en vue d'obtenir); (*job*) poser sa candidature (pour), faire une demande d'emploi (concernant); **to ~ the brakes** actionner les freins, freiner; **to ~ o.s. to** s'appliquer à.
appoint [ə'pɔɪnt] *vt* nommer, engager; (*date, place*) fixer, désigner; ~**ment** *n* nomination *f*; rendez-vous *m*; **to make an ~ment (with)** prendre rendez-vous (avec).
appraisal [ə'preɪzl] *n* évaluation *f*.
appreciate [ə'pri:ʃieɪt] *vt* (*like*) apprécier, faire cas de; être reconnaissant(e) de; (*assess*) évaluer; (*be aware of*) comprendre; se rendre compte de // *vi* (*FINANCE*) prendre de la valeur.
appreciation [əpri:ʃi'eɪʃən] *n* appréciation *f*; reconnaissance *f*; (*COMM*) hausse *f*, valorisation *f*.
appreciative [ə'pri:ʃiətɪv] *a* (*person*) sensible; (*comment*) élogieux(euse).
apprehensive [æprɪ'hɛnsɪv] *a* inquiet(ète), appréhensif(ive).
apprentice [ə'prɛntɪs] *n* apprenti *m*; ~**ship** *n* apprentissage *m*.
approach [ə'prəʊtʃ] *vi* approcher // *vt* (*come near*) approcher de; (*ask, apply to*) s'adresser à; (*subject, passer-by*) aborder // *n* approche *f*; accès *m*, abord *m*; démarche *f* (*auprès de qn*); démarche (*intellectuelle*); ~**able** *a* accessible.
appropriate [ə'prəʊprɪɪt] *a* opportun(e); qui convient, approprié(e) // *vt* [ə'prəʊprɪeɪt] (*take*) s'approprier.
approval [ə'pru:vəl] *n* approbation *f*; **on ~** (*COMM*) à l'examen.
approve [ə'pru:v] *vt* approuver; **to ~ of** *vt fus* approuver; ~**d school** *n* (*Brit*) centre *m* d'éducation surveillée.
approximate *a* [ə'prɔksɪmɪt] approximatif(ive); ~**ly** *ad* approximativement.
apricot ['eɪprɪkɔt] *n* abricot *m*.
April ['eɪprəl] *n* avril *m*; ~ **Fool's Day** le premier avril.
apron ['eɪprən] *n* tablier *m*.
apt [æpt] *a* (*suitable*) approprié(e); (*likely*): ~ **to do** susceptible de faire; ayant tendance à faire.
aqualung ['ækwəlʌŋ] *n* scaphandre *m* autonome.
aquarium [ə'kwɛərɪəm] *n* aquarium *m*.
Aquarius [ə'kwɛərɪəs] *n* le Verseau.
Arab ['ærəb] *n* Arabe *m/f*.
Arabian [ə'reɪbɪən] *a* arabe.
Arabic ['ærəbɪk] *a* arabe // *n* arabe *m*; ~ **numerals** chiffres *mpl* arabes.
arbitrary ['ɑ:bɪtrəri] *a* arbitraire.
arbitration [ɑ:bɪ'treɪʃən] *n* arbitrage *m*.
arcade [ɑ:'keɪd] *n* arcade *f*; (*passage with shops*) passage *m*, galerie *f*.
arch [ɑ:tʃ] *n* arche *f*; (*of foot*) cambrure *f*, voûte *f* plantaire // *vt* arquer, cambrer // *a* malicieux(euse).
archaeologist [ɑ:kɪ'ɔlədʒɪst] *n* archéologue *m/f*.
archaeology [ɑ:kɪ'ɔlədʒɪ] *n* archéologie *f*.
archbishop [ɑ:tʃ'bɪʃəp] *n* archevêque *m*.
arch-enemy ['ɑ:tʃ'ɛnəmɪ] *n* ennemi *m* de toujours *or* par excellence.
archeology *etc* [ɑ:kɪ'ɔlədʒɪ] (*US*) =**archaeology** *etc*.
archer ['ɑ:tʃə*] *n* archer *m*; ~**y** *n* tir *m* à l'arc.
architect ['ɑ:kɪtɛkt] *n* architecte *m*; ~**ure** ['ɑ:kɪtɛktʃə*] *n* architecture *f*.
archives ['ɑ:kaɪvz] *npl* archives *fpl*.
archway ['ɑ:tʃweɪ] *n* voûte *f*, porche voûté *or* cintré.

Arctic ['ɑ:ktɪk] *a* arctique // *n*: the ~ l'Arctique *m*.

ardent ['ɑ:dənt] *a* fervent(e).

are [ɑ:*] *vb see* **be**.

area ['ɛərɪə] *n* (GEOM) superficie *f*; (zone) région *f*; (: smaller) secteur *m*.

aren't [ɑ:nt] =**are not**.

Argentina [ɑ:dʒən'ti:nə] *n* Argentine *f*; **Argentinian** [-'tɪnɪən] *a* argentin(e) // *n* Argentin/e.

arguably ['ɑ:gjuəblɪ] *ad*: it is ~ — on peut soutenir que c'est —.

argue ['ɑ:gju:] *vi* (quarrel) se disputer; (reason) argumenter; to ~ that objecter or alléguer que, donner comme argument que.

argument ['ɑ:gjumənt] *n* (reasons) argument *m*; (quarrel) dispute *f*, discussion *f*; (debate) discussion *f*, controverse *f*; **~ative** [-'mɛntətɪv] *a* ergoteur(euse), raisonneur(euse).

Aries ['ɛərɪz] *n* le Bélier.

arise, *pt* **arose**, *pp* **arisen** [ə'raɪz, ə'rəuz, ə'rɪzn] *vi* survenir, se présenter; to ~ from résulter de.

aristocrat ['ærɪstəkræt] *n* aristocrate *m/f*.

arithmetic [ə'rɪθmətɪk] *n* arithmétique *f*.

ark [ɑ:k] *n*: Noah's A~ l'Arche *f* de Noé.

arm [ɑ:m] *n* bras *m* // *vt* armer; ~s *npl* (weapons, HERALDRY) armes *fpl*; ~ in ~ bras dessus bras dessous.

armaments ['ɑ:məmənts] *npl* armements *mpl*.

arm: **~chair** *n* fauteuil *m*; **~ed** *a* armé(e); **~ed robbery** *n* vol *m* à main armée.

armour, (US) **armor** ['ɑ:mə*] *n* armure *f*; (also: ~-plating) blindage *m*; (MIL: tanks) blindés *mpl*; **~ed car** *n* véhicule blindé; **~y** *n* arsenal *m*.

armpit ['ɑ:mpɪt] *n* aisselle *f*.

armrest ['ɑ:mrɛst] *n* accoudoir *m*.

army ['ɑ:mɪ] *n* armée *f*.

aroma [ə'rəumə] *n* arôme *m*.

arose [ə'rəuz] *pt of* **arise**.

around [ə'raund] *ad* (tout) autour; dans les parages // *prep* autour de; (fig: about) environ; vers.

arouse [ə'rauz] *vt* (sleeper) éveiller; (curiosity, passions) éveiller, susciter, exciter.

arrange [ə'reɪndʒ] *vt* arranger; (programme) arrêter, convenir de; to ~ to do sth prévoir de faire qch; **~ment** *n* arrangement *m*; (plans etc): **~ments** dispositions *fpl*.

array [ə'reɪ] *n*: ~ of déploiement *m* or étalage *m* de.

arrears [ə'rɪəz] *npl* arriéré *m*; to be in ~ with one's rent devoir un arriéré de loyer.

arrest [ə'rɛst] *vt* arrêter; (sb's attention) retenir, attirer // *n* arrestation *f*; under ~

en état d'arrestation.

arrival [ə'raɪvəl] *n* arrivée *f*; (COMM) arrivage *m*; (person) arrivant/e; new ~ nouveau venu, nouvelle venue.

arrive [ə'raɪv] *vi* arriver.

arrogant ['ærəgənt] *a* arrogant(e).

arrow ['ærəu] *n* flèche *f*.

arse [ɑ:s] *n* (col!) cul *m* (!).

arson ['ɑ:sn] *n* incendie criminel.

art [ɑ:t] *n* art *m*; (craft) métier *m*; **A~s** *npl* (SCOL) les lettres *fpl*.

artefact ['ɑ:tɪfækt] *n* objet fabriqué.

artery ['ɑ:tərɪ] *n* artère *f*.

art gallery *n* musée *m* d'art; (small and private) galerie *f* de peinture.

arthritis [ɑ:'θraɪtɪs] *n* arthrite *f*.

artichoke ['ɑ:tɪtʃəuk] *n* artichaut *m*; Jerusalem ~ topinambour *m*.

article ['ɑ:tɪkl] *n* article *m*; (Brit LAW: training): **~s** *npl* ~stage *m*; ~ of clothing vêtement *m*.

articulate *a* [ɑ:'tɪkjulɪt] (person) qui s'exprime clairement et aisément; (speech) bien articulé(e), prononcé(e) clairement // *vi* [ɑ:'tɪkjuleɪt] articuler, parler distinctement; **~d lorry** *n* (Brit) (camion *m*) semi-remorque *m*.

artificial [ɑ:tɪ'fɪʃəl] *a* artificiel(le).

artist ['ɑ:tɪst] *n* artiste *m/f*; **~ic** [ɑ:'tɪstɪk] *a* artistique; **~ry** *n* art *m*, talent *m*.

artless ['ɑ:tlɪs] *a* naïf(naïve), simple, ingénu(e).

art school *n* ≈école *f* des beaux-arts.

as [æz] ♦ *cj* **1** (referring to time) comme, alors que; à mesure que; he came in ~ I was leaving il est arrivé comme je partais; ~ the years went by à mesure que les années passaient; ~ from tomorrow à partir de demain

2 (in comparisons): ~ big ~ aussi grand que; twice ~ big ~ deux fois plus grand que; ~ much or many ~ autant que; ~ much money/many books ~ autant d'argent/de livres que; ~ soon ~ dès que

3 (since, because) comme, puisque; he left early, ~ he had to be home by 10 comme il or puisqu'il devait être de retour avant 10h il est parti tôt

4 (referring to manner, way) comme; do ~ you wish faites comme vous voudrez

5 (concerning): ~ for or to that quant à cela, pour ce qui est de cela

6: ~ if or though comme si; he looked ~ if he was ill il avait l'air d'être malade; see also **long, such, well**

♦ *prep*: he works ~ a driver il travaille comme chauffeur; ~ chairman of the company, he — en tant que président de la compagnie, il —; dressed up ~ a cowboy déguisé en cowboy; he gave me it ~ a present il me l'a offert, il m'en a fait cadeau.

a.s.a.p. *abbr* (=as soon as possible) dès

que possible.

ascend [ə'send] *vt* gravir.

ascent [ə'sent] *n* ascension *f*.

ascertain [æsə'teɪn] *vt* s'assurer de, vérifier; établir.

ash [æʃ] *n* (*dust*) cendre *f*; (*also:* ~ **tree**) frêne *m*.

ashamed [ə'ʃeɪmd] *a* honteux(euse), confus(e); **to be** ~ **of** avoir honte de.

ashen ['æʃn] *a* (*pale*) cendreux(euse), blême.

ashore [ə'ʃɔ:*] *ad* à terre.

ashtray ['æʃtreɪ] *n* cendrier *m*.

Ash Wednesday *n* mercredi *m* des cendres.

Asia ['eɪʃə] *n* Asie *f*; ~**n** *a* Asiatique *m/f* // *a* asiatique.

aside [ə'saɪd] *ad* de côté; à l'écart // *n* aparté *m*.

ask [ɑ:sk] *vt* demander; (*invite*) inviter; **to** ~ **sb sth/to do sth** demander à qn qch/ de faire qch; **to** ~ **sb about sth** questionner qn au sujet de qch; se renseigner auprès de qn au sujet de qch; **to** ~ (**sb**) **a question** poser une question (à qn); **to** ~ **sb out to dinner** inviter qn au restaurant; **to** ~ **after** *vt fus* demander des nouvelles de; **to** ~ **for** *vt fus* demander.

askance [ə'skɑ:ns] *ad*: **to look** ~ **at sb** regarder qn de travers *or* d'un œil désapprobateur.

askew [ə'skju:] *ad* de travers, de guinguois.

asleep [ə'sli:p] *a* endormi(e); **to be** ~ dormir, être endormi; **to fall** ~ s'endormir.

asparagus [əs'pærəgəs] *n* asperges *fpl*.

aspect ['æspekt] *n* aspect *m*; (*direction in which a building etc faces*) orientation *f*, exposition *f*.

aspersions [əs'pɔ:ʃənz] *npl*: **to cast** ~ **on** dénigrer.

aspire [əs'paɪə*] *vi*: **to** ~ **to** aspirer à.

aspirin ['æsprɪn] *n* aspirine *f*.

ass [æs] *n* âne *m*; (*col*) imbécile *m/f*; (*US col*) cul *m* (!).

assailant [ə'seɪlənt] *n* agresseur *m*; assaillant *m*.

assassinate [ə'sæsɪneɪt] *vt* assassiner; **assassination** [əsæsɪ'neɪʃən] *n* assassinat *m*.

assault [ə'sɔ:lt] *n* (MIL) assaut *m*; (*gen: attack*) agression *f* // *vt* attaquer; (*sexually*) violenter.

assemble [ə'sembl] *vt* assembler // *vi* s'assembler, se rassembler.

assembly [ə'semblɪ] *n* (*meeting*) rassemblement *m*; (*construction*) assemblage *m*; ~ **line** *n* chaîne *f* de montage.

assent [ə'sent] *n* assentiment *m*, consentement *m*.

assert [ə'sɔ:t] *vt* affirmer, déclarer; établir.

assess [ə'ses] *vt* évaluer, estimer; (*tax,*

damages) établir *or* fixer le montant de; (*property etc: for tax*) calculer la valeur imposable de; ~**ment** *n* évaluation *f*, estimation *f*; ~**or** *n* expert *m* (*en matière d'impôt et d'assurance*).

asset ['æset] *n* avantage *m*, atout *m*; ~**s** *npl* capital *m*; avoir(s) *m(pl)*; actif *m*.

assign [ə'saɪn] *vt* (*date*) fixer, arrêter; (*task*): **to** ~ **sth to** assigner qch à; (*resources*): **to** ~ **sth to** affecter qch à; (*cause, meaning*): **to** ~ **sth to** attribuer qch à; ~**ment** *n* tâche *f*, mission *f*.

assist [ə'sɪst] *vt* aider, assister; secourir; ~**ance** *n* aide *f*, assistance *f*; secours *mpl*; ~**ant** *n* assistant/e, adjoint/e; (*Brit: also:* **shop** ~**ant**) vendeur/euse.

associate *a, n* [ə'səuʃiɪt] associé(e) // *vb* [ə'səuʃieɪt] *vt* associer // *vi*: **to** ~ **with sb** fréquenter qn.

association [əsəusɪ'eɪʃən] *n* association *f*.

assorted [ə'sɔ:tɪd] *a* assorti(e).

assortment [ə'sɔ:tmənt] *n* assortiment *m*.

assume [ə'sju:m] *vt* supposer; (*responsibilities etc*) assumer; (*attitude, name*) prendre, adopter; ~**d name** *n* nom *m* d'emprunt.

assumption [ə'sʌmpʃən] *n* supposition *f*, hypothèse *f*.

assurance [ə'ʃuərəns] *n* assurance *f*.

assure [ə'ʃuə*] *vt* assurer.

astern [ə'stɔ:n] *ad* à l'arrière.

asthma ['æsmə] *n* asthme *m*.

astonish [ə'stɔnɪʃ] *vt* étonner, stupéfier; ~**ment** *n* étonnement *m*.

astound [ə'staund] *vt* stupéfier, sidérer.

astray [ə'streɪ] *ad*: **to go** ~ s'égarer; (*fig*) quitter le droit chemin.

astride [ə'straɪd] *ad* à cheval // *prep* à cheval sur.

astrology [əs'trɔlədʒɪ] *n* astrologie *f*.

astronaut ['æstrənɔ:t] *n* astronaute *m/f*.

astronomy [əs'trɔnəmɪ] *n* astronomie *f*.

astute [əs'tju:t] *a* astucieux(euse).

asylum [ə'saɪləm] *n* asile *m*.

at [æt] *prep*

1 (*referring to position, direction*) à; ~ **the top** au sommet; ~ **home/school** à la maison *or* chez soi/à l'école; ~ **the baker's** à la boulangerie, chez le boulanger; **to look** ~ **sth** regarder qch

2 (*referring to time*) à; ~ **4 o'clock** à 4 heures; ~ **Christmas** à Noël; ~ **night** la nuit; ~ **times** par moments, parfois

3 (*referring to rates, speed etc*) à; ~ **£1 a kilo** une livre le kilo; **two** ~ **a time** deux à la fois; ~ **50 km/h** à 50 km/h

4 (*referring to manner*): ~ **a stroke** d'un seul coup; ~ **peace** en paix

5 (*referring to activity*): **to be** ~ **work** être à l'œuvre, travailler; **to play** ~ **cowboys** jouer aux cowboys; **to be good** ~ **sth** être bon en qch

6 (*referring to cause*): shocked/ surprised/annoyed ~ sth choqué par/ étonné de/agacé par qch; I went ~ his suggestion j'y suis allé sur son conseil.
ate [eɪt] *pt of* eat.
atheist ['eɪθɪɪst] *n* athée *m/f*.
Athens ['æθɪnz] *n* Athènes.
athlete ['æθliːt] *n* athlète *m/f*.
athletic [æθ'lɛtɪk] *a* athlétique; ~**s** *n* athlétisme *m*.
Atlantic [ət'læntɪk] *a* atlantique // *n*: the ~ (Ocean) l'Atlantique *m*, l'océan *m* Atlantique.
atlas ['ætləs] *n* atlas *m*.
atmosphere ['ætməsfɪə*] *n* atmosphère *f*.
atom ['ætəm] *n* atome *m*; ~**ic** [ə'tɔmɪk] *a* atomique; ~**(ic) bomb** *n* bombe *f* atomique; ~**izer** ['ætəmaɪzə*] *n* atomiseur *m*.
atone [ə'təun] *vi*: to ~ for expier, racheter.
atrocious [ə'trəuʃəs] *a* (*very bad*) atroce, exécrable.
attach [ə'tætʃ] *vt* (*gen*) attacher; (*document, letter*) joindre; (*employee, troops*) affecter; to be ~**ed** to sb/sth (*to like*) être attaché à qn/qch.
attaché case [ə'tæʃeɪ-] *n* mallette *f*, attaché-case *m*.
attachment [ə'tætʃmənt] *n* (*tool*) accessoire *m*; (*love*): ~ (to) affection *f* (pour), attachement *m* (à).
attack [ə'tæk] *vt* attaquer; (*task etc*) s'attaquer à // *n* attaque *f*; (*also*: heart ~) crise *f* cardiaque.
attain [ə'teɪn] *vt* (*also*: to ~ to) parvenir à, atteindre; acquérir; ~**ments** *npl* connaissances *fpl*, résultats *mpl*.
attempt [ə'tɛmpt] *n* tentative *f* // *vt* essayer, tenter; to make an ~ on sb's life attenter à la vie de qn.
attend [ə'tɛnd] *vt* (*course*) suivre; (*meeting, talk*) assister à; (*school, church*) aller à, fréquenter; (*patient*) soigner, s'occuper de; **to ~ to** *vt fus* (*needs, affairs etc*) s'occuper de; (*customer*) s'occuper de, servir; ~**ance** *n* (*being present*) présence *f*; (*people present*) assistance *f*; ~**ant** *n* employé/ e; gardien/ne // *a* concomitant(e), qui accompagne *or* s'ensuit.
attention [ə'tɛnʃən] *n* attention *f*; ~! (*MIL*) garde-à-vous!; **for the ~ of** (*ADMIN*) à l'attention de.
attentive [ə'tɛntɪv] *a* attentif(ive); (*kind*) prévenant(e).
attic ['ætɪk] *n* grenier *m*, combles *mpl*.
attitude ['ætɪtjuːd] *n* attitude *f*, manière *f*; pose *f*, maintien *m*.
attorney [ə'tɜːnɪ] *n* (*lawyer*) avoué *m*; (*having proxy*) mandataire *m*; **A~ General** *n* (*Brit*) ≈procureur général; (*US*) ≈garde *m* des Sceaux, ministre *m* de la Justice.

attract [ə'trækt] *vt* attirer; ~**ion** [ə'trækʃən] *n* (*gen pl*: *pleasant things*) attraction *f*, attrait *m*; (*PHYSICS*) attraction *f*; (*fig*: *towards sth*) attirance *f*; ~**ive** *a* séduisant(e), attrayant(e).
attribute *n* ['ætrɪbjuːt] attribut *m* // *vt* [ə'trɪbjuːt]: to ~ sth to attribuer qch à.
attrition [ə'trɪʃən] *n*: war of ~ guerre *f* d'usure.
aubergine ['əubəʒiːn] *n* aubergine *f*.
auction ['ɔːkʃən] *n* (*also*: sale by ~) vente *f* aux enchères // *vt* (*also*: to sell by ~) vendre aux enchères; (*also*: to put up for ~) mettre aux enchères; ~**eer** [-'nɪə*] *n* commissaire-priseur *m*.
audience ['ɔːdɪəns] *n* (*people*) assistance *f*, auditoire *m*; auditeurs *mpl*; spectateurs *mpl*; (*interview*) audience *f*.
audio-visual [ɔːdɪəu'vɪzjuəl] *a* audio-visuel(le); ~ **aids** *npl* supports *or* moyens audiovisuels.
audit ['ɔːdɪt] *vt* vérifier, apurer.
audition [ɔː'dɪʃən] *n* audition *f*.
auditor ['ɔːdɪtə*] *n* vérificateur *m* des comptes.
augur ['ɔːgə*] *vi*: it ~s well c'est bon signe *or* de bon augure.
August ['ɔːgəst] *n* août *m*.
aunt [ɑːnt] *n* tante *f*; ~**ie**, ~**y** *n* diminutive of **aunt**.
au pair ['əu'pɛə*] *n* (*also*: ~ girl) jeune fille *f* au pair.
aura ['ɔːrə] *n* atmosphère *f*.
auspicious [ɔːs'pɪʃəs] *a* de bon augure, propice.
austerity [ɔ'stɛrɪtɪ] *n* austérité *f*.
Australia [ɔs'treɪlɪə] *n* Australie *f*; ~**n** *a* australien(ne) // *n* Australien/ne.
Austria ['ɔstrɪə] *n* Autriche *f*; ~**n** *a* autrichien(ne) // *n* Autrichien/ne.
authentic [ɔː'θɛntɪk] *a* authentique.
author ['ɔːθə*] *n* auteur *m*.
authoritarian [ɔːθɔrɪ'tɛərɪən] *a* autoritaire.
authoritative [ɔː'θɔrɪtətɪv] *a* (*account*) digne de foi; (*study, treatise*) qui fait autorité; (*manner*) autoritaire.
authority [ɔː'θɔrɪtɪ] *n* autorité *f*; (*permission*) autorisation (formelle); the authorities *npl* les autorités *fpl*, l'administration *f*.
authorize ['ɔːθəraɪz] *vt* autoriser.
auto ['ɔːtəu] *n* (*US*) auto *f*, voiture *f*.
autobiography [ɔːtəbaɪ'ɔgrəfɪ] *n* autobiographie *f*.
autograph ['ɔːtəgrɑːf] *n* autographe *m* // *vt* signer, dédicacer.
automatic [ɔːtə'mætɪk] *a* automatique // *n* (*gun*) automatique *m*; (*Brit AUT*) voiture *f* à transmission automatique; ~**ally** *ad* automatiquement.
automation [ɔːtə'meɪʃən] *n* automatisation *f*.
automobile ['ɔːtəməbiːl] *n* (*US*) automobile *f*.

autonomy [ɔːˈtɔnəmɪ] n autonomie f.
autumn [ˈɔːtəm] n automne m.
auxiliary [ɔːgˈzɪlɪərɪ] a, n auxiliaire (m/f).
Av. abbr of **avenue**.
avail [əˈveɪl] vt: **to ~ o.s. of** user de; profiter de // n: **to no ~** sans résultat, en vain, en pure perte.
available [əˈveɪləbl] a disponible.
avalanche [ˈævəlɑːnʃ] n avalanche f.
Ave. abbr of **avenue**.
avenge [əˈvɛndʒ] vt venger.
avenue [ˈævənjuː] n avenue f.
average [ˈævərɪdʒ] n moyenne f // a moyen(ne) // vt (a certain figure) atteindre or faire etc en moyenne; **on ~** en moyenne; **to ~ out** vi: **to ~ out at** représenter en moyenne, donner une moyenne de.
averse [əˈvɜːs] a: **to be ~ to sth/doing** éprouver une forte répugnance envers qch/à faire.
avert [əˈvɜːt] vt prévenir, écarter; (one's eyes) détourner.
aviary [ˈeɪvɪərɪ] n volière f.
avocado [ævəˈkɑːdəu] n (also: Brit ~ **pear**) avocat m.
avoid [əˈvɔɪd] vt éviter.
await [əˈweɪt] vt attendre.
awake [əˈweɪk] a éveillé(e); (fig) en éveil // vb (pt awoke, pp awoken, awaked) vt éveiller // vi s'éveiller; **to be ~** être réveillé(e); ne pas dormir; **~ning** [əˈweɪknɪŋ] n réveil m.
award [əˈwɔːd] n récompense f, prix m // vt (prize) décerner; (LAW: damages) accorder.
aware [əˈwɛə*] a: **~ of** (conscious) conscient(e) de; (informed) au courant de; **to become ~ of** avoir conscience de, prendre conscience de; se rendre compte de; **~ness** n le fait d'être conscient, au courant etc.
awash [əˈwɔʃ] a recouvert(e) (d'eau); **~ with** inondé(e) de.
away [əˈweɪ] a, ad (au) loin; absent(e); **two kilometres ~** à (une distance de) deux kilomètres, à deux kilomètres de distance; **two hours ~ by car** à deux heures de voiture or de route; **the holiday was two weeks ~** il restait deux semaines jusqu'aux vacances; **~ from** loin de; **he's ~ for a week** il est parti (pour) une semaine; **to take ~** vt emporter; **to pedal/work/laugh** etc **~** la particule indique la constance et l'énergie de l'action: il pédalait etc tant qu'il pouvait; **to fade** etc **~** la particule renforce l'idée de la disparition, l'éloignement; **~ game** n (SPORT) match m à l'extérieur.
awe [ɔː] n respect mêlé de crainte, effroi mêlé d'admiration; **~-inspiring**, **~some** a impressionnant(e).
awful [ˈɔːfəl] a affreux(euse); **~ly** ad

(very) terriblement, vraiment.
awhile [əˈwaɪl] ad un moment, quelque temps.
awkward [ˈɔːkwəd] a (clumsy) gauche, maladroit(e); (inconvenient) malaisé(e), d'emploi malaisé, peu pratique; (embarrassing) gênant(e), délicat(e).
awning [ˈɔːnɪŋ] n (of tent) auvent m; (of shop) store m; (of hotel etc) marquise f (de toile).
awoke, awoken [əˈwəuk, -kən] pt, pp of **awake**.
awry [əˈraɪ] ad, a de travers; **to go ~** mal tourner.
axe, (US) ax [æks] n hache f // vt (employee) renvoyer; (project etc) abandonner; (jobs) supprimer.
axis, pl axes [ˈæksɪs, -siːz] n axe m.
axle [ˈæksl] n (also: ~-**tree**) essieu m.
ay(e) [aɪ] excl (yes) oui.

B

B [biː] n (MUS) si m.
B.A. abbr see **bachelor**.
baby [ˈbeɪbɪ] n bébé m; **~ carriage** n (US) voiture f d'enfant; **~-sit** vi garder les enfants; **~-sitter** n baby-sitter m/f.
bachelor [ˈbætʃələ*] n célibataire m; **B~ of Arts/Science (B.A./B.Sc.)** ≈ licencié/e ès or en lettres/sciences.
back [bæk] n (of person, horse) dos m; (of hand) dos, revers m; (of house) derrière m; (of car, train) arrière m; (of chair) dossier m; (of page) verso m; (FOOTBALL) arrière m // vt (candidate: also: ~ **up**) soutenir, appuyer; (horse: at races) parier or miser sur; (car) (faire) reculer // vi reculer; (car etc) faire marche arrière // a (in compounds) de derrière, à l'arrière; **~ seats/wheels** (AUT) sièges mpl/roues fpl arrière; **~ payments/rent** arriéré m de paiements/loyer // ad (not forward) en arrière; (returned): **he's ~** il est rentré, il est de retour; **he ran ~** il est revenu en courant; (restitution): **throw the ball ~** renvoie la balle; **can I have it ~?** puis-je le ravoir?; (again): **he called ~** il a rappelé; **to ~ down** vi rabattre de ses prétentions; **to ~ out** vi (of promise) se dédire; **to ~ up** vt (candidate etc) soutenir, appuyer; (COMPUT) sauvegarder; **~bencher** n (Brit) membre du parlement sans portefeuille; **~bone** n colonne vertébrale, épine dorsale; **~-cloth** n toile f de fond; **~date** vt (letter) antidater; **~dated pay rise** augmentation f avec effet rétroactif; **~drop** n = **~-cloth**; **~fire** vi (AUT) pétarader; (plans) mal tourner; **~ground** n arrière-plan m; (of events) situation f, conjoncture f; (basic knowledge) éléments mpl de base;

(*experience*) formation *f*; **family ~ground** milieu familial; **~hand** *n* (*TENNIS: also:* **~hand stroke**) revers *m*; **~handed** *a* (*fig*) déloyal(e); équivoque; **~hander** *n* (*Brit: bribe*) pot-de-vin *m*; **~ing** *n* (*fig*) soutien *m*, appui *m*; **~lash** *n* contre-coup *m*, répercussion *f*; **~log** *n*: **~log of work** travail *m* en retard; **~ number** *n* (*of magazine etc*) vieux numéro; **~pack** *n* sac *m* à dos; **~ pay** *n* rappel *m* de salaire; **~side** *n* (*col*) derrière *m*, postérieur *m*; **~stage** *ad* derrière la scène, dans la coulisse; **~stroke** *n* dos crawlé; **~up** *a* (*train, plane*) supplémentaire, de réserve; (*COMPUT*) de sauvegarde // *n* (*support*) appui *m*, soutien *m*; (*also:* **~up file**) sauvegarde *f*; **~ward** *a* (*movement*) en arrière; (*person, country*) arriéré(e); attardé(e); **~wards** *ad* (*move, go*) en arrière; (*read a list*) à l'envers, à rebours; (*fall*) à la renverse; (*walk*) à reculons; **~water** *n* (*fig*) coin reculé; bled perdu; **~yard** *n* arrière-cour *f*.

bacon ['beɪkən] *n* bacon *m*, lard *m*.

bad [bæd] *a* mauvais(e); (*child*) vilain(e); (*meat, food*) gâté(e), avarié(e); **his ~ leg** sa jambe malade; **to go ~** (*meat, food*) se gâter; (*milk*) tourner.

bade [bæd] *pt of* **bid**.

badge [bædʒ] *n* insigne *m*; (*of policeman*) plaque *f*.

badger ['bædʒə*] *n* blaireau *m*.

badly ['bædlɪ] *ad* (*work, dress etc*) mal; **~ wounded** grièvement blessé; **he needs it ~** il en a un absolument besoin; **~ off** *a, ad* dans la gêne.

badminton ['bædmɪntən] *n* badminton *m*.

bad-tempered ['bæd'tempəd] *a* ayant mauvais caractère; de mauvaise humeur.

baffle ['bæfl] *vt* (*puzzle*) déconcerter.

bag [bæg] *n* sac *m*; (*of hunter*) gibecière *f*; chasse *f* // *vt* (*col: take*) empocher; s'approprier; **~s of** (*col: lots of*) des masses de; **~gage** *n* bagages *mpl*; **~gy** *a* avachi(e), qui fait des poches; **~pipes** *npl* cornemuse *f*.

bail [beɪl] *n* caution *f* // *vt* (*prisoner: also:* **grant ~ to**) mettre en liberté sous caution; (*boat: also:* **~ out**) écoper; **on ~** (*prisoner*) sous caution; **to ~ out** (*prisoner*) payer la caution de; *see also* **bale**.

bailiff ['beɪlɪf] *n* huissier *m*.

bait [beɪt] *n* appât *m* // *vt* appâter; (*fig*) tourmenter.

bake [beɪk] *vt* (faire) cuire au four // *vi* cuire (au four); faire de la pâtisserie; **~d beans** *npl* haricots blancs à la sauce tomate; **~r** *n* boulanger *m*; **~ry** *n* boulangerie *f*; boulangerie industrielle; **baking** *n* cuisson *f*.

balance ['bæləns] *n* équilibre *m*; (*COMM: sum*) solde *m*; (*scales*) balance *f* // *vt* mettre ou faire tenir en équilibre; (*pros and cons*) peser; (*budget*) équilibrer; (*account*) balancer; (*compensate*) compenser, contrebalancer; **~ of trade/payments** balance commerciale/des comptes *or* paiements; **~d** *a* (*personality, diet*) équilibré(e); **~ sheet** *n* bilan *m*.

balcony ['bælkənɪ] *n* balcon *m*.

bald [bɔːld] *a* chauve; (*tyre*) lisse.

bale [beɪl] *n* balle *f*, ballot *m*; **to ~ out** *vi* (*of a plane*) sauter en parachute.

baleful ['beɪlful] *a* funeste, maléfique.

ball [bɔːl] *n* boule *f*; (*football*) ballon *m*; (*for tennis, golf*) balle *f*; (*dance*) bal *m*.

ballast ['bæləst] *n* lest *m*.

ball bearings *npl* roulement *m* à billes.

ballerina [bælə'riːnə] *n* ballerine *f*.

ballet ['bæleɪ] *n* ballet *m*; (*art*) danse *f* (classique).

balloon [bə'luːn] *n* ballon *m*; (*in comic strip*) bulle *f*.

ballot ['bælət] *n* scrutin *m*.

ball-point pen ['bɔːlpɔɪnt-] *n* stylo *m* à bille.

ballroom ['bɔːlrum] *n* salle *f* de bal.

balm [bɑːm] *n* baume *m*.

ban [bæn] *n* interdiction *f* // *vt* interdire.

banana [bə'nɑːnə] *n* banane *f*.

band [bænd] *n* bande *f*; (*at a dance*) orchestre *m*; (*MIL*) musique *f*, fanfare *f*; **to ~ together** *vi* se liguer.

bandage ['bændɪdʒ] *n* bandage *m*, pansement *m*.

bandaid ['bændeɪd] *n* (*US*) pansement adhésif.

bandwagon ['bændwægən] *n*: **to jump on the ~** (*fig*) monter dans *or* prendre le train en marche.

bandy ['bændɪ] *vt* (*jokes, insults*) échanger.

bandy-legged ['bændɪ'legɪd] *a* aux jambes arquées.

bang [bæŋ] *n* détonation *f*; (*of door*) claquement *m*; (*blow*) coup (violent) // *vt* frapper (violemment); (*door*) claquer // *vi* détoner, claquer.

bangle ['bæŋgl] *n* bracelet *m*.

bangs [bæŋz] *npl* (*US: fringe*) frange *f*.

banish ['bænɪʃ] *vt* bannir.

banister(s) ['bænɪstə(z)] *n(pl)* rampe *f* (d'escalier).

bank [bæŋk] *n* banque *f*; (*of river, lake*) bord *m*, rive *f*; (*of earth*) talus *m*, remblai *m* // *vi* (*AVIAT*) virer sur l'aile; **to ~ on** *vt fus* miser *or* tabler sur; **~ account** *n* compte *m* en banque; **~ card** *n* carte *f* d'identité bancaire; **~er** *n* banquier *m*; **~er's card** *n* (*Brit*) = **~ card**; **B~ holiday** *n* (*Brit*) jour férié (*où les banques sont fermées*); **~ing** *n* opérations *fpl* bancaires; profession *f* de banquier; **~note** *n* billet *m* de banque;

~ **rate** n taux m de l'escompte.
bankrupt ['bæŋkrʌpt] a en faillite; **to go
~ faire faillite; ~cy** n faillite f.
bank statement n relevé m de compte.
banner ['bænə*] n bannière f.
baptism ['bæptizəm] n baptême m.
bar [ba:*] n barre f; (of window etc)
barreau m; (of chocolate) tablette f,
plaque f; (fig) obstacle m; (pub) bar m;
d'exclusion; (pub) bar m; (counter: in
pub) comptoir m, bar; (MUS) mesure f //
vt (road) barrer; (window) munir de
barreaux; (person) exclure; (activity)
interdire; ~ **of soap** savonnette f; **the B~**
(LAW) le barreau; **behind ~s** (prisoner)
sous les verrous; ~ **none** sans exception.
barbaric [ba:'bærik] a barbare.
barbecue ['ba:bikju:] n barbecue m.
barbed wire ['ba:bd-] n fil m de fer
barbelé.
barber ['ba:bə*] n coiffeur m (pour
hommes).
bar code n (on goods) code m à barres.
bare [bɛə*] a nu(e) // vt mettre à nu,
dénuder; (teeth) montrer; ~**back** ad à
cru, sans selle; ~**faced** a impudent(e),
effronté(e); ~**foot** a, ad nu-pieds, (les)
pieds nus; ~**ly** ad à peine.
bargain ['ba:gin] n (transaction) marché m; (good buy) affaire f, occasion f //
vi (haggle) marchander; (trade)
négocier, traiter; **into the ~** par-dessus
le marché; **to ~ for** vt fus: **he got more
than he ~ed for** il ne s'attendait pas à un
coup pareil.
barge [ba:dʒ] n péniche f; **to ~ in** vi
(walk in) faire irruption; (interrupt talk)
intervenir mal à propos; **to ~ into** vt
fus rentrer dans.
bark [ba:k] n (of tree) écorce f; (of dog)
aboiement m // vi aboyer.
barley ['ba:li] n orge f.
barmaid ['ba:meid] n serveuse f (de
bar), barmaid f.
barman ['ba:mən] n serveur m (de
bar), barman m.
barn [ba:n] n grange f.
barometer [bə'rɔmitə*] n baromètre m.
baron ['bærən] n baron m; ~**ess** n
baronne f.
barracks ['bærəks] npl caserne f.
barrage ['bæra:ʒ] n (MIL) tir m de
barrage; (dam) barrage m; (fig) pluie
f.
barrel ['bærəl] n tonneau m; (of gun)
canon m.
barren ['bærən] a stérile; (hills) aride.
barricade [bæri'keid] n barricade f.
barrier ['bæriə*] n barrière f.
barring ['ba:rin] prep sauf.
barrister ['bæristə*] n (Brit) avocat
(plaidant).
barrow ['bærəu] n (cart) charrette f à
bras.
bartender ['ba:tɛndə*] n (US) serveur

m (de bar), barman m.
barter ['ba:tə*] vt: **to ~ sth for** échanger
qch contre.
base [beis] n base f // vt: **to ~ sth on**
baser or fonder qch sur // a vil(e),
bas(se).
baseball ['beisbɔ:l] n base-ball m.
basement ['beismənt] n sous-sol m.
bases ['beisi:z] npl of **basis**; ['beisiz]
npl of **base**.
bash [bæʃ] vt (col) frapper, cogner.
bashful ['bæfful] a timide; modeste.
basic ['beisik] a fondamental(e), de
base; réduit(e) au minimum, rudimentaire; ~**ally** [-li] ad fondamentalement,
à la base; en fait, au fond.
basil ['bæzl] n basilic m.
basin ['beisn] n (vessel, also GEO)
cuvette f, bassin m; (also: **wash~**)
lavabo m.
basis, pl **bases** ['beisis, -si:z] n base f.
bask [ba:sk] vi: **to ~ in the sun** se
chauffer au soleil.
basket ['ba:skit] n corbeille f; (with
handle) panier m; ~**ball** n basket-ball
m.
bass [beis] n (MUS) basse f.
bassoon [bə'su:n] n basson m.
bastard ['ba:stəd] n enfant naturel(le),
bâtard/e; (col!) salaud m (!).
bat [bæt] n chauve-souris f; (for baseball
etc) batte f; (Brit: for table tennis)
raquette f // vt: **he didn't ~ an eyelid** il
n'a pas sourcillé or bronché.
batch [bætʃ] n (of bread) fournée f; (of
papers) liasse f.
bated ['beitid] a: **with ~ breath** en
retenant son souffle.
bath [ba:θ, pl ba:ðz] n see also **baths**;
bain m; (bathtub) baignoire f // vt baigner, donner un bain à; **to have a ~**
prendre un bain.
bathe [beið] vi se baigner // vt baigner.
bathing ['beiðiŋ] n baignade f; ~ **cap** n
bonnet m de bain; ~ **costume**, (US) ~
suit n maillot m (de bain).
bath: ~**robe** n peignoir m de bain;
~**room** n salle f de bains.
baths [ba:ðz] npl établissement m de
bains(-douches).
bath towel n serviette f de bain.
baton ['bætən] n bâton m; (MUS)
baguette f; (club) matraque f.
batter ['bætə*] vt battre // n pâte f à
frire; ~**ed** a (hat, pan) cabossé(e).
battery ['bætəri] n batterie f; (of torch)
pile f.
battle ['bætl] n bataille f, combat m // vi
se battre, lutter; ~**field** n champ m de
bataille; ~**ship** n cuirassé m.
bawdy ['bɔ:di] a paillard(e).
bawl [bɔ:l] vi hurler, brailler.
bay [bei] n (of sea) baie f; **to hold sb at
~** tenir qn à distance or en échec.
bay window n baie vitrée.

bazaar [bə'zɑ:*] n bazar m; vente f de charité.

b. & b. B. & B. abbr see **bed**.

BBC n abbr (= British Broadcasting Corporation) office de la radiodiffusion et télévision britannique.

B.C. ad abbr (= before Christ) av. J.-C.

be [bi:], pt **was, were**, pp **been** ♦ auxiliary vb **1** (with present participle: forming continuous tenses): what are you doing? que faites-vous?; they're coming tomorrow ils viennent demain; I've been waiting for you for 2 hours je t'attends depuis 2 heures

2 (with pp: forming passives) être; to ~ killed être tué(e); he was nowhere to ~ seen on ne le voyait nulle part

3 (in tag questions): it was fun, wasn't it? c'était drôle, n'est-ce pas?; she's back, is she? elle est rentrée, n'est-ce pas or alors?

4 (+ to + infinitive): the house is to ~ sold la maison doit être vendue; he's not to open it il ne doit pas l'ouvrir

♦ vb + complement **1** (gen) être; I'm English je suis anglais(e); I'm tired je suis fatigué(e); I'm hot/cold j'ai chaud/froid; he's a doctor il est médecin; **2 and 2 are 4** 2 et 2 font 4

2 (of health) aller; how are you? comment allez-vous?; I'm better now je vais mieux maintenant; he's very ill il est très malade

3 (of age) avoir; how old are you? quel âge avez-vous?; I'm sixteen (years old) j'ai seize ans

4 (cost) coûter; how much was the meal? combien a coûté le repas?; that'll ~ £5, please ça fera 5 livres, s'il vous plaît

♦ vi **1** (exist, occur etc) être, exister; the best singer that ever was le meilleur chanteur qui ait jamais existé; ~ that as it may quoi qu'il en soit; so ~ it soit

2 (referring to place) être, se trouver; I won't ~ here tomorrow je ne serai pas là demain; Edinburgh is in Scotland Édimbourg est or se trouve en Écosse

3 (referring to movement) aller; where have you been? où êtes-vous allé(s)?

♦ impersonal vb **1** (referring to time, distance) être; it's 5 o'clock il est 5 heures; it's the 28th of April c'est le 28 avril; it's 10 km to the village le village est à 10 km

2 (referring to the weather) faire; it's too hot/cold il fait trop chaud/froid; it's windy il y a du vent

3 (emphatic): it's me/the postman c'est moi/le facteur.

beach [bi:tʃ] n plage f // vt échouer.

beacon ['bi:kən] n (lighthouse) fanal m; (marker) balise f.

bead [bi:d] n perle f.

beak [bi:k] n bec m.

beaker ['bi:kə*] n gobelet m.

beam [bi:m] n poutre f; (of light) rayon m // vi rayonner.

bean [bi:n] n haricot m; (of coffee) grain m; **runner** ~ haricot m (à rames); **broad** ~ fève f; **~sprouts** npl germes mpl de soja.

bear [bɛə*] n ours m // vb (pt **bore**, pp **borne**) vt porter; (endure) supporter // vi: to ~ **right/left** obliquer à droite/gauche, se diriger vers la droite/gauche; **to ~ out** vt corroborer, confirmer; **to ~ up** vi (person) tenir le coup.

beard [bɪəd] n barbe f.

bearer ['bɛərə*] n porteur m.

bearing ['bɛərɪŋ] n maintien m, allure f; (connection) rapport m; **~s** npl (also: **ball ~s**) roulement m (à billes); to take a ~ faire le point; to find one's ~s s'orienter.

beast [bi:st] n bête f; **~ly** a infect(e).

beat [bi:t] n battement m; (MUS) temps m, mesure f; (of policeman) ronde f // vt (pt **beat**, pp **beaten**) battre; **off the ~en track** hors des chemins or sentiers battus; to ~ **time** battre la mesure; ~ **it!** (col) fiche(-moi) le camp!; **to ~ off** vt repousser; **to ~ up** vt (col: person) tabasser; (eggs) battre; **~ing** n raclée f.

beautiful ['bju:tɪful] a beau(belle); **~ly** ad admirablement.

beauty ['bju:tɪ] n beauté f; ~ **salon** n institut m de beauté; ~ **spot** n grain m de beauté; (Brit TOURISM) site naturel (d'une grande beauté).

beaver ['bi:və*] n castor m.

became [bɪ'keɪm] pt of **become**.

because [bɪ'kɔz] cj parce que; ~ **of** prep à cause de.

beck [bɛk] n: to be at sb's ~ and call être à l'entière disposition de qn.

beckon ['bɛkən] vt (also: ~ **to**) faire signe (de venir) à.

become [bɪ'kʌm] vt (irg: like **come**) devenir; to ~ **thin** maigrir.

becoming [bɪ'kʌmɪŋ] a (behaviour) convenable, bienséant(e); (clothes) seyant(e).

bed [bɛd] n lit m; (of flowers) parterre m; (of coal, clay) couche f; to go to ~ aller se coucher; **single** ~ lit à une place; **double** ~ grand lit; ~ **and breakfast (b. & b.)** n (terms) chambre et petit déjeuner; **~clothes** npl couvertures fpl et draps mpl; **~ding** n literie f.

bedlam ['bɛdləm] n chahut m, cirque m.

bedraggled [bɪ'drægld] a dépenaillé(e), les vêtements en désordre.

bed: **~ridden** a cloué(e) au lit; **~room** n chambre f (à coucher); **~side** n: at sb's **~side** au chevet de qn; **~sit(ter)** n (Brit) chambre meublée, studio m;

~**spread** n couvre-lit m, dessus-de-lit m; ~**time** n heure f du coucher.

bee [bi:] n abeille f.

beech [bi:tʃ] n hêtre m.

beef [bi:f] n bœuf m; roast ~ rosbif m; ~**burger** n hamburger m; ~**eater** n hallebardier de la Tour de Londres.

beehive ['bi:haɪv] n ruche f.

beeline ['bi:laɪn] n: to make a ~ for se diriger tout droit vers.

been [bi:n] pp of **be**.

beer [bɪə*] n bière f.

beetle ['bi:tl] n scarabée m.

beetroot ['bi:tru:t] n (Brit) betterave f.

before [bɪ'fɔ:*] prep (in time) avant; (in space) devant // cj avant que + sub; avant de // ad avant; ~ going avant de partir; ~ she goes avant qu'elle (ne) parte; the week ~ la semaine précédente or d'avant; I've seen it ~ je l'ai déjà vu; ~**hand** ad au préalable, à l'avance.

beg [bɛg] vi mendier // vt mendier; (favour) quémander, solliciter; (entreat) supplier.

began [bɪ'gæn] pt of **begin**.

beggar ['bɛgə*] n mendiant/e.

begin [bɪ'gɪn], pt **began**, pp **begun** vt, vi commencer; to ~ doing or to do sth commencer à or de faire qch; ~**ner** n débutant/e; ~**ning** n commencement m, début m.

begun [bɪ'gʌn] pp of **begin**.

behalf [bɪ'hɑ:f] n: on ~ of de la part de; au nom de; pour le compte de.

behave [bɪ'heɪv] vi se conduire, se comporter; (well: also: ~ o.s.) se conduire bien or comme il faut.

behaviour, (US) **behavior** [bɪ'heɪvjə*] n comportement m, conduite f.

behead [bɪ'hɛd] vt décapiter.

beheld [bɪ'hɛld] pt, pp of **behold**.

behind [bɪ'haɪnd] prep derrière; (time) en retard sur // ad derrière; en retard // n derrière m; to be ~ (schedule) être en retard; ~ the scenes dans les coulisses.

behold [bɪ'həʊld] vt (irg: like hold) apercevoir, voir.

beige [beɪʒ] a beige.

being ['bi:ɪŋ] n être m; to come into ~ prendre naissance.

Beirut [beɪ'ru:t] n Beyrouth.

belated [bɪ'leɪtɪd] a tardif(ive).

belch [bɛltʃ] vi avoir un renvoi, roter // vt (also: ~ out: smoke etc) vomir, cracher.

belfry ['bɛlfrɪ] n beffroi m.

Belgian ['bɛldʒən] a belge, de Belgique // n Belge m/f.

Belgium ['bɛldʒəm] n Belgique f.

belie [bɪ'laɪ] vt démentir.

belief [bɪ'li:f] n (opinion) conviction f; (trust, faith) foi f; (acceptance as true) croyance f.

believe [bɪ'li:v] vt, vi croire; to ~ in (God) croire en; (method, ghosts) croire

à; ~**r** n (in idea, activity): ~**r** in partisan/e de; (REL) croyant/e.

belittle [bɪ'lɪtl] vt déprécier, rabaisser.

bell [bɛl] n cloche f; (small) clochette f, grelot m; (on door) sonnette f; (electric) sonnerie f.

bellow ['bɛləʊ] vi mugir.

bellows ['bɛləʊz] npl soufflet m.

belly ['bɛlɪ] n ventre m.

belong [bɪ'lɒŋ] vi: to ~ to appartenir à; (club etc) faire partie de; this book ~s here ce livre va ici; ~**ings** npl affaires fpl, possessions fpl.

beloved [bɪ'lʌvɪd] a (bien-)aimé(e).

below [bɪ'ləʊ] prep sous, au-dessous de // ad en dessous; en contre-bas; see ~ voir plus bas or plus loin or ci-dessous.

belt [bɛlt] n ceinture f; (TECH) courroie f // vt (thrash) donner une raclée à; ~**way** n (US AUT) route f de ceinture; (: motorway) périphérique m.

bemused [bɪ'mju:zd] a stupéfié(e).

bench [bɛntʃ] n banc m; (in workshop) établi m; the B~ (LAW) la magistrature, la Cour.

bend [bɛnd] vb (pt, pp bent) vt courber; (leg, arm) plier // vi se courber // n (Brit: in road) virage m, tournant m; (in pipe, river) coude m; to ~ down vi se baisser; to ~ over vi se pencher.

beneath [bɪ'ni:θ] prep sous, au-dessous de; (unworthy of) indigne de // ad dessous, au-dessous, en bas.

benefactor ['bɛnɪfæktə*] n bienfaiteur m.

beneficial [bɛnɪ'fɪʃəl] a salutaire; avantageux(euse).

benefit ['bɛnɪfɪt] n avantage m, profit m; (allowance of money) allocation f // vt faire du bien à, profiter à // vi: he'll ~ from it cela lui fera du bien, il y gagnera or s'en trouvera bien.

benevolent [bɪ'nɛvələnt] a bienveillant(e).

benign [bɪ'naɪn] a (person, smile) bienveillant(e), affable; (MED) bénin(igne).

bent [bɛnt] pt, pp of **bend** // n inclination f, penchant m // a (col: dishonest) véreux(euse); to be ~ on être résolu(e) à.

bequest [bɪ'kwɛst] n legs m.

bereaved [bɪ'ri:vd] n: the ~ la famille du disparu.

beret ['bɛreɪ] n béret m.

berm [bə:m] n (US AUT) accotement m.

berry ['bɛrɪ] n baie f.

berserk [bə'sə:k] a: to go ~ être pris(e) d'une rage incontrôlable; se déchaîner.

berth [bə:θ] n (bed) couchette f; (for ship) poste m d'amarrage, mouillage m // vi (in harbour) venir à quai; (at anchor) mouiller.

beseech [bɪ'si:tʃ], pt, pp **besought** vt implorer, supplier.

beset, *pt, pp* **beset** [bɪ'sɛt] *vt* assaillir.
beside [bɪ'saɪd] *prep* à côté de; **to be ~ o.s. (with anger)** être hors de soi; **that's ~ the point** cela n'a rien à voir.
besides [bɪ'saɪdz] *ad* en outre, de plus // *prep* en plus de; excepté.
besiege [bɪ'si:dʒ] *vt (town)* assiéger; *(fig)* assaillir.
besought [bɪ'sɔ:t] *pt, pp of* **beseech**.
best [bɛst] *a* meilleur(e) // *ad* le mieux; **the ~ part of** *(quantity)* le plus clair de, la plus grande partie de; **at ~** au mieux; **to make the ~ of sth** s'accommoder de qch (du mieux que l'on peut); **to do one's ~** faire de son mieux; **to the ~ of my knowledge** pour autant que je sache; **to the ~ of my ability** du mieux que je pourrai; **~ man** *n* garçon *m* d'honneur.
bestow [bɪ'stəʊ] *vt* accorder; *(title)* conférer.
bet [bɛt] *n* pari *m* // *vt, vi (pt, pp* **bet** or **betted**) parier.
betray [bɪ'treɪ] *vt* trahir; **~al** *n* trahison *f*.
better ['bɛtə*] *a* meilleur(e) // *ad* mieux // *vt* améliorer // *n*: **to get the ~ of** triompher de, l'emporter sur; **you had ~ do it** vous feriez mieux de le faire; **he thought ~ of it** il s'est ravisé; **to get ~** aller mieux; s'améliorer; **~ off** *a* plus à l'aise financièrement; *(fig)*: **you'd be ~ off this way** vous vous en trouveriez mieux ainsi.
betting ['bɛtɪŋ] *n* paris *mpl*; **~ shop** *n (Brit)* bureau *m* de paris.
between [bɪ'twi:n] *prep* entre // *ad* au milieu; dans l'intervalle.
beverage ['bɛvərɪdʒ] *n* boisson *f (gén sans alcool)*.
bevy ['bɛvɪ] *n*: **a ~ of** un essaim *or* une volée de.
beware [bɪ'wɛə*] *vi*: **to ~ (of)** prendre garde (à).
bewildered [bɪ'wɪldəd] *a* dérouté(e), ahuri(e).
bewitching [bɪ'wɪtʃɪŋ] *a* enchanteur(teresse).
beyond [bɪ'jɔnd] *prep (in space)* au-delà de; *(exceeding)* au-dessus de // *ad* au-delà; **~ doubt** hors de doute.
bias ['baɪəs] *n (prejudice)* préjugé *m*, parti pris; *(preference)* prévention *f*; **~(s)ed** *a* partial(e), montrant un parti pris.
bib [bɪb] *n* bavoir *m*, bavette *f*.
Bible ['baɪbl] *n* Bible *f*.
bicarbonate of soda [baɪ'kɑ:bənɪt-] *n* bicarbonate *m* de soude.
bicker ['bɪkə*] *vi* se chamailler.
bicycle ['baɪsɪkl] *n* bicyclette *f*.
bid [bɪd] *n* offre *f*; *(at auction)* enchère *f*; *(attempt)* tentative *f* // *vb (pt* **bid** or **bade**, *pp* **bid** or **bidden**) *vi* faire une enchère *or* offre // *vt* faire une enchère *or* offre de; **to ~ sb good day** souhaiter le

bonjour à qn; **~der** *n*: **the highest ~der** le plus offrant; **~ding** *n* enchères *fpl*.
bide [baɪd] *vt*: **to ~ one's time** attendre son heure.
bifocals [baɪ'fəʊklz] *npl* verres *mpl* à double foyer, lunettes bifocales.
big [bɪg] *a* grand(e); gros(se).
big dipper [-'dɪpə*] *n* montagnes *fpl* russes.
bigheaded ['bɪg'hɛdɪd] *a* prétentieux(euse).
bigot ['bɪgət] *n* fanatique *m/f*, sectaire *m/f*; **~ed** *a* fanatique, sectaire; **~ry** *n* fanatisme *m*, sectarisme *m*.
big top *n* grand chapiteau.
bike [baɪk] *n* vélo *m*, bécane *f*.
bikini [bɪ'ki:nɪ] *n* bikini *m*.
bilingual [baɪ'lɪŋgwəl] *a* bilingue.
bill [bɪl] *n* note *f*, facture *f*; *(POL)* projet *m* de loi; *(US: banknote)* billet *m* (de banque); *(of bird)* bec *m*; **'post no ~s'** 'défense d'afficher'; **to fit** *or* **fill the ~** *(fig)* faire l'affaire; **~board** *n* panneau *m* d'affichage.
billet ['bɪlɪt] *n* cantonnement *m (chez l'habitant)*.
billfold ['bɪlfəʊld] *n (US)* portefeuille *m*.
billiards ['bɪljədz] *n (jeu m* de) billard *m*.
billion ['bɪljən] *n (Brit)* billion *m (million de millions)*; *(US)* milliard *m*.
bin [bɪn] *n* boîte *f*; *(also: dust~)* poubelle *f*; *(for coal)* coffre *m*.
bind [baɪnd], *pt, pp* **bound** *vt* attacher; *(book)* relier; *(oblige)* obliger, contraindre; **~ing** *n (of book)* reliure *f* // *a (contract)* constituant une obligation.
binge [bɪndʒ] *n (col)*: **to go on a ~** aller faire la bringue.
bingo ['bɪŋgəʊ] *n* sorte de jeu de loto pratiqué dans des établissements publics.
binoculars [bɪ'nɔkjʊləz] *npl* jumelles *fpl*.
bio... [baɪə'...] *prefix*: **~chemistry** *n* biochimie *f*; **~graphy** [baɪ'ɔgrəfɪ] *n* biographie *f*; **~logical** *a* biologique; **~logy** [baɪ'ɔlədʒɪ] *n* biologie *f*.
birch [bə:tʃ] *n* bouleau *m*.
bird [bə:d] *n* oiseau *m*; *(Brit col: girl)* nana *f*; **~'s-eye view** *n* vue *f* à vol d'oiseau; *(fig)* vue d'ensemble *or* générale; **~ watcher** *n* ornithologue *m/f* amateur.
Biro ['baɪərəʊ] *n* ® stylo *m* à bille.
birth [bə:θ] *n* naissance *f*; **~ certificate** *n* acte *m* de naissance; **~ control** *n* limitation *f* des naissances; méthode(s) contraceptive(s); **~day** *n* anniversaire *m*; **~ rate** *n* (taux *m* de) natalité *f*.
biscuit ['bɪskɪt] *n (Brit)* biscuit *m*.
bisect [baɪ'sɛkt] *vt* couper *or* diviser en deux.
bishop ['bɪʃəp] *n* évêque *m*.
bit [bɪt] *pt of* **bite** // *n* morceau *m*; *(of*

tool) mèche *f*; (*of horse*) mors *m*; (*COMPUT*) élément *m* binaire; a ~ of un peu de; a ~ mad un peu fou; ~ by ~ petit à petit.

bitch [bɪtʃ] *n* (*dog*) chienne *f*; (*col!*) salope *f* (!), garce *f*.

bite [baɪt] *vt, vi* (*pt* **bit**, *pp* **bitten**) mordre // *n* morsure *f*; (*insect* ~) piqûre *f*; (*mouthful*) bouchée *f*; let's have a ~ (to eat) mangeons un morceau; to ~ one's nails se ronger les ongles.

bitter ['bɪtə*] *a* amer(ère); (*wind, criticism*) cinglant(e) // *n* (*Brit: beer*) bière *f* (*à forte teneur en houblon*); ~**ness** *n* amertume *f*; goût amer.

blab [blæb] *vi* jaser, trop parler.

black [blæk] *a* noir(e) // *n* (*colour*) noir *m*; (*person*): B~ noir/e // *vt* (*shoes*) cirer; (*Brit INDUSTRY*) boycotter; to give sb a ~ eye pocher l'œil à qn, faire un œil au beurre noir à qn; ~ and blue *a* couvert(e) de bleus; to be in the ~ (*in credit*) être créditeur(trice); ~**berry** *n* mûre *f*; ~**bird** *n* merle *m*; ~**board** *n* tableau noir; ~**currant** *n* cassis *m*; ~**en** *vt* noircir; ~ **ice** *n* verglas *m*; ~**leg** *n* (*Brit*) briseur *m* de grève, jaune *m*; ~**list** *n* liste noire; ~**mail** *n* chantage *m* // *vt* faire chanter, soumettre au chantage; ~ **market** *n* marché noir; ~**out** *n* panne *f* d'électricité; (*fainting*) syncope *f*; the B~ **Sea** *n* la mer Noire; ~ **sheep** *n* brebis galeuse; ~**smith** *n* forgeron *m*; ~ **spot** *n* (*AUT*) point noir.

bladder ['blædə*] *n* vessie *f*.

blade [bleɪd] *n* lame *f*; (*of oar*) plat *m*; ~ of grass brin *m* d'herbe.

blame [bleɪm] *n* faute *f*, blâme *m* // *vt*: to ~ sb/sth for sth attribuer à qn/qch la responsabilité de qch; reprocher qch à qn/qch; who's to ~? qui est le fautif *or* coupable *or* responsable?

bland [blænd] *a* affable; (*taste*) doux(douce), fade.

blank [blæŋk] *a* blanc(blanche); (*look*) sans expression, dénué(e) d'expression // *n* espace *m* vide, blanc *m*; (*cartridge*) cartouche *f* à blanc; ~ **cheque** *n* chèque *m* en blanc.

blanket ['blæŋkɪt] *n* couverture *f*.

blare [blɛə*] *vi* beugler.

blast [blɑːst] *n* souffle *m*; explosion *f* // *vt* faire sauter *or* exploser; ~**off** *n* (*SPACE*) lancement *m*.

blatant ['bleɪtənt] *a* flagrant(e), criant(e).

blaze [bleɪz] *n* (*fire*) incendie *m*; (*fig*) flamboiement *m* // *vi* (*fire*) flamber; (*fig*) flamboyer, resplendir // *vt*: to ~ a trail (*fig*) montrer la voie.

blazer ['bleɪzə*] *n* blazer *m*.

bleach [bliːtʃ] *n* (*also*: **household** ~) eau *f* de Javel // *vt* (*linen*) blanchir; ~**ed** *a* (*hair*) oxygéné(e), décoloré(e); ~**ers** *npl* (*US SPORT*) gradins *mpl* (*en plein*

soleil).

bleak [bliːk] *a* morne, désolé(e).

bleary-eyed ['blɪərɪ'aɪd] *a* aux yeux pleins de sommeil.

bleat [bliːt] *vi* bêler.

bleed, *pt, pp* **bled** [bliːd, blɛd] *vt, vi* saigner; my nose is ~ing je saigne du nez.

bleeper ['bliːpə*] *n* (*device*) bip *m*.

blemish ['blɛmɪʃ] *n* défaut *m*.

blend [blɛnd] *n* mélange *m* // *vt* mélanger // *vi* (*colours etc*) se mélanger, se fondre, s'allier.

bless, *pt, pp* **blessed** *or* **blest** [blɛs, blɛst] *vt* bénir; ~**ing** *n* bénédiction *f*; bienfait *m*.

blew [bluː] *pt of* **blow**.

blight [blaɪt] *vt* (*hopes etc*) anéantir, briser.

blimey ['blaɪmɪ] *excl* (*Brit col*) mince alors!

blind [blaɪnd] *a* aveugle // *n* (*for window*) store *m* // *vt* aveugler; ~ **alley** *n* impasse *f*; ~ **corner** *n* (*Brit*) virage *m* sans visibilité; ~**fold** *n* bandeau *m* // *a, ad* les yeux bandés // *vt* bander les yeux à; ~**ly** *ad* aveuglément; ~**ness** *n* cécité *f*; (*fig*) aveuglement *m*; ~ **spot** *n* (*AUT etc*) angle mort.

blink [blɪŋk] *vi* cligner des yeux; (*light*) clignoter; ~**ers** *npl* œillères *fpl*.

bliss [blɪs] *n* félicité *f*, bonheur *m* sans mélange.

blister ['blɪstə*] *n* (*on skin*) ampoule *f*, cloque *f*; (*on paintwork*) boursouflure *f* // *vi* (*paint*) se boursoufler, se cloquer.

blithely ['blaɪðlɪ] *ad* joyeusement.

blitz [blɪts] *n* bombardement (aérien).

blizzard ['blɪzəd] *n* blizzard *m*, tempête *f* de neige.

bloated ['bləʊtɪd] *a* (*face*) bouffi(e); (*stomach*) gonflé(e).

blob [blɔb] *n* (*drop*) goutte *f*; (*stain, spot*) tache *f*.

block [blɔk] *n* bloc *m*; (*in pipes*) obstruction *f*; (*toy*) cube *m*; (*of buildings*) pâté *m* (de maisons) // *vt* bloquer; ~**ade** [-'keɪd] *n* blocus *m* // *vt* faire le blocus de; ~**age** *n* obstruction *f*; ~**buster** *n* (*film, book*) grand succès; ~ **of flats** *n* (*Brit*) immeuble (locatif); ~ **letters** *npl* majuscules *fpl*.

bloke [bləʊk] *n* (*Brit col*) type *m*.

blonde [blɔnd] *a, n* blond(e).

blood [blʌd] *n* sang *m*; ~ **donor** *n* donneur/euse de sang; ~ **group** *n* groupe sanguin; ~**hound** *n* limier *m*; ~ **poisoning** *n* empoisonnement *m* du sang; ~ **pressure** *n* tension *f* (artérielle); ~**shed** *n* effusion *f* de sang, carnage *m*; ~**shot** *a*: ~shot eyes yeux injectés de sang; ~**stream** *n* sang *m*, système sanguin; ~ **test** *n* prise *f* de sang; ~**thirsty** *a* sanguinaire; ~**y** *a* sanglant(e); (*Brit col!*): this ~y ... ce foutu ..., ce putain de ... (!); **~y strong/good** vachement or sacrément fort/bon; **~y-minded** a (Brit col) contrariant(e), obstiné(e).

bloom [blu:m] n fleur f; (fig) épanouissement m // vi être en fleur; (fig) s'épanouir; être florissant(e).

blossom ['blɔsəm] n fleur(s) f(pl) // vi être en fleurs; (fig) s'épanouir.

blot [blɔt] n tache f // vt tacher; **to ~out** vt (memories) effacer; (view) cacher, masquer; (nation, city) annihiler.

blotchy ['blɔtʃi] a (complexion) couvert(e) de marbrures.

blotting paper ['blɔtɪŋ-] n buvard m.

blouse [blauz] n (feminine garment) chemisier m, corsage m.

blow [bləu] n coup m // vb (pt **blew**, pp **blown** [blu:, bləun]) vi souffler // vt (fuse) faire sauter; **to ~ one's nose** se moucher; **to ~ a whistle** siffler; **to ~ away** vt chasser, faire s'envoler; **to ~ down** vt faire tomber, renverser; **to ~ off** vt emporter; **to ~ out** vi éclater, sauter; **to ~ over** vi s'apaiser; **to ~ up** vi exploser, sauter // vt faire sauter; (tyre) gonfler; (PHOT) agrandir; **~-dry** n brushing m; **~lamp** n (Brit) chalumeau m; **~-out** n (of tyre) éclatement m; **~-torch** n = **~lamp.**

blue [blu:] a bleu(e); **~ film/joke** film m/ histoire f pornographique; **to come out of the ~** (fig) être complètement inattendu; **to have the ~s** avoir le cafard; **~bottle** n mouche f à viande; **~ jeans** npl blue-jeans mpl; **~print** n (fig) projet m, plan directeur.

bluff [blʌf] vi bluffer // n bluff m; **to call sb's ~** mettre qn au défi d'exécuter ses menaces.

blunder ['blʌndə*] n gaffe f, bévue f // vi faire une gaffe or une bévue.

blunt [blʌnt] a émoussé(e), peu tranchant(e); (person) brusque, ne mâchant pas ses mots // vt émousser.

blur [blə:*] n tache or masse floue or confuse // vt brouiller, rendre flou(e).

blurb [blə:b] n notice f publicitaire; (for book) texte m de présentation.

blurt [blə:t]: **to ~ out** vt (reveal) lâcher; (say) balbutier, dire d'une voix entrecoupée.

blush [blʌʃ] vi rougir // n rougeur f.

blustery ['blʌstəri] a (weather) à bourrasques.

boar [bɔ:*] n sanglier m.

board [bɔ:d] n planche f; (on wall) panneau m; (committee) conseil m, comité m; (in firm) conseil d'administration // vt (ship) monter à bord de; (train) monter dans; (NAUT, AVIAT): **on ~** à bord; **full ~** (Brit) pension complète; **half ~** (Brit) demi-pension f; **~ and lodging** n chambre f avec pension; **which goes by the ~** (fig) qu'on

laisse tomber, qu'on abandonne; **to ~ up** vt (door) condamner (au moyen de planches, de tôle); **~er** n pensionnaire m/f; (SCOL) interne m/f, pensionnaire; **~ing card** n (AVIAT, NAUT) carte f d'embarquement; **~ing house** n pension f; **~ing school** n internat m, pensionnat m; **~ room** n salle f du conseil d'administration.

boast [bəust] vi: **to ~ (about or of)** se vanter (de) // vt s'enorgueillir de // n vantardise f; sujet m d'orgueil or de fierté.

boat [bəut] n bateau m; (small) canot m; barque f; **~er** n (hat) canotier m; **~swain** ['bəusn] n maître m d'équipage.

bob [bɔb] vi (boat, cork on water: also: **~ up and down**) danser, se balancer // n (Brit col) = shilling; **to ~ up** vi surgir or apparaître brusquement.

bobby ['bɔbi] n (Brit col) ≈ agent m (de police).

bobsleigh ['bɔbsleɪ] n bob m.

bode [bəud] vi: **to ~ well/ill (for)** être de bon/mauvais augure (pour).

bodily ['bɔdɪli] a corporel(le) // ad physiquement; dans son entier or ensemble; en personne.

body ['bɔdi] n corps m; (of car) carrosserie f; (of plane) fuselage m; (fig: society) organe m, organisme m; (fig: quantity) ensemble m, masse f; (of wine) corps; **~-building** n culturisme m; **~guard** n garde m du corps; **~work** n carrosserie f.

bog [bɔg] n tourbière f // vt: **to get ~ged down** (fig) s'enliser.

boggle ['bɔgl] vi: **the mind ~s** c'est incroyable, on en reste sidéré.

bogus ['bəugəs] a bidon inv; fantôme.

boil [bɔɪl] vt (faire) bouillir // vi bouillir // n (MED) furoncle m; **to come to the (Brit) or a (US) ~** bouillir; **to ~ down** vi (fig): **to ~ down to** se réduire or ramener à; **to ~ over** vi déborder; **~ed egg** n œuf m à la coque; **~ed potatoes** npl pommes fpl à l'anglaise or à l'eau; **~er** n chaudière f; **~er suit** n (Brit) bleu m de travail, combinaison f; **~ing point** n point m d'ébullition.

boisterous ['bɔɪstərəs] a bruyant(e), tapageur(euse).

bold [bəuld] a hardi(e), audacieux(euse); (pej) effronté(e); (outline, colour) franc(franche), tranché(e), marqué(e).

bollard ['bɔləd] n (Brit AUT) borne lumineuse or de signalisation.

bolster ['bəulstə*] n traversin m; **to ~ up** vt soutenir.

bolt [bəult] n verrou m; (with nut) boulon m // ad: **~ upright** droit(e) comme un piquet // vt verrouiller; (food) engloutir // vi se sauver, filer (comme une flèche).

bomb [bɔm] *n* bombe *f* // *vt* bombarder; ~ **disposal unit** *n* section *f* de déminage; ~**er** *n* (*AVIAT*) bombardier *m*; ~**shell** *n* (*fig*) bombe *f*.

bona fide ['bəunə'faɪdɪ] *a* de bonne foi; (*offer*) sérieux(euse).

bond [bɔnd] *n* lien *m*; (*binding promise*) engagement *m*, obligation *f*; (*COMM*) obligation; **in** ~ (*of goods*) en douane.

bondage ['bɔndɪdʒ] *n* esclavage *m*.

bone [bəun] *n* os *m*; (*of fish*) arête *f* // *vt* désosser; ôter les arêtes de; ~ **idle** *a*, ~ **lazy** *a* fainéant(e).

bonfire ['bɔnfaɪə*] *n* feu *m* (de joie); (*for rubbish*) feu.

bonnet ['bɔnɪt] *n* bonnet *m*; (*Brit: of car*) capot *m*.

bonus ['bəunəs] *n* prime *f*, gratification *f*.

bony ['bəunɪ] *a* (*arm, face, MED: tissue*) osseux(euse); (*meat*) plein(e) d'os; (*fish*) plein d'arêtes.

boo [bu:] *excl* hou!, peuh! // *vt* huer.

booby trap ['bu:bɪ-] *n* engin piégé.

book [buk] *n* livre *m*; (*of stamps etc*) carnet *m*; (*COMM*): ~**s** comptes *mpl*, comptabilité *f* // *vt* (*ticket*) prendre; (*seat, room*) réserver; (*driver*) dresser un procès-verbal à; (*football player*) prendre le nom de; ~**case** *n* bibliothèque *f* (*meuble*); ~**ing office** *n* (*Brit*) bureau *m* de location; ~**-keeping** *n* comptabilité *f*; ~**let** *n* brochure *f*; ~**maker** *n* bookmaker *m*; ~**seller** *n* libraire *m/f*; ~**shop** *n*, ~**store** *n* librairie *f*.

boom [bu:m] *n* (*noise*) grondement *m*; (*busy period*) boom *m*, vague *f* de prospérité // *vi* gronder; prospérer.

boon [bu:n] *n* bénédiction *f*, grand avantage.

boost [bu:st] *n* stimulant *m*, remontant *m* // *vt* stimuler; ~**er** *n* (*MED*) rappel *m*.

boot [bu:t] *n* botte *f*; (*for hiking*) chaussure *f* (de marche); (*for football etc*) soulier *m*; (*Brit: of car*) coffre *m* // *vt* (*COMPUT*) remettre à zéro; **to** ~ (*in addition*) par-dessus le marché, en plus.

booth [bu:ð] *n* (*at fair*) baraque (foraine); (*of cinema, telephone etc*) cabine *f*; (*also:* **voting** ~) isoloir *m*.

booty ['bu:tɪ] *n* butin *m*.

booze [bu:z] *n* (*col*) boissons *fpl* alcooliques, alcool *m*.

border ['bɔ:də*] *n* bordure *f*; bord *m*; (*of a country*) frontière *f*; **the B~s** *la région frontière entre l'Écosse et l'Angleterre*; **to** ~ **on** *vt fus* être voisin(e) de, toucher à; ~**line** *n* (*fig*) ligne *f* de démarcation; ~**line case** *n* cas *m* limite.

bore [bɔ:*] *pt of* **bear** // *vt* (*hole*) percer; (*person*) ennuyer, raser // *n* (*person*) raseur/euse; (*of gun*) calibre

born [bɔ:n] *a*: **to be** ~ naître; **I was** ~ **in** 1960 je suis né en 1960.

borne [bɔ:n] *pp of* **bear**.

borough ['bʌrə] *n* municipalité *f*.

borrow ['bɔrəu] *vt*: **to** ~ **sth** (**from sb**) emprunter qch (à qn).

bosom ['buzəm] *n* poitrine *f*; (*fig*) sein *m*.

boss [bɔs] *n* patron/ne // *vt* commander; ~**y** *a* autoritaire.

bosun ['bəusn] *n* maître *m* d'équipage.

botany ['bɔtənɪ] *n* botanique *f*.

botch [bɔtʃ] *vt* (*also:* ~ **up**) saboter, bâcler.

both [bəuθ] *a* les deux, l'un(e) et l'autre // *pronoun*: ~ (*of them*) les deux, tous(toutes) (les) deux, l'un(e) et l'autre; ~ **of us went, we** ~ **went** nous y sommes allés (tous) les deux // *ad*: **they sell** ~ **the fabric and the finished curtains** ils vendent (et) le tissu et les rideaux (finis), ils vendent à la fois le tissu et les rideaux (finis).

bother ['bɔðə*] *vt* (*worry*) tracasser; (*needle, bait*) importuner, ennuyer; (*disturb*) déranger // *vi* (*also:* ~ **o.s.**) se tracasser, se faire du souci // *n*: **it is a** ~ **to have to do** c'est vraiment ennuyeux d'avoir à faire; **it's no** ~ aucun problème; **to** ~ **doing** prendre la peine de faire.

bottle ['bɔtl] *n* bouteille *f*; (*baby's*) biberon *m* // *vt* mettre en bouteille(s); **to** ~ **up** *vt* refouler, contenir; ~**neck** *n* étranglement *m*; ~**-opener** *n* ouvre-bouteille *m*.

bottom ['bɔtəm] *n* (*of container, sea etc*) fond *m*; (*buttocks*) derrière *m*; (*of page, list*) bas *m*; (*of chair*) siège *m* // *a* du fond; du bas.

bough [bau] *n* branche *f*, rameau *m*.

bought [bɔ:t] *pt, pp of* **buy**.

boulder ['bəuldə*] *n* gros rocher.

bounce [bauns] *vi* (*ball*) rebondir; (*cheque*) être refusé (*étant sans provision*) // *vt* faire rebondir // *n* (*rebound*) rebond *m*; ~**r** *n* (*col*) videur *m*.

bound [baund] *pt, pp of* **bind** // *n* (*gen pl*) limite *f*; (*leap*) bond *m* // *vt* (*leap*) bondir; (*limit*) borner // *vi*: **to be** ~ **to do sth** (*obliged*) être obligé(e) *or* avoir obligation de faire qch; **he's** ~ **to fail** (*likely*) il est sûr d'échouer, son échec est inévitable *or* assuré; ~ **for** à destination de; **out of** ~**s** dont l'accès est interdit.

boundary ['baundrɪ] *n* frontière *f*.

bout [baut] *n* période *f*; (*of malaria etc*) accès *m*, crise *f*, attaque *f*; (*BOXING etc*) combat *m*, match *m*.

bow *n* [bəu] nœud *m*; (*weapon*) arc *m*; (*MUS*) archet *m*; [bau] (*with body*) révérence f, inclination f (du buste or corps); (NAUT: also: ~s) proue f // vi [bau] faire une révérence, s'incliner; (yield): to ~ to or before s'incliner devant, se soumettre à.

bowels [bauəlz] npl intestins mpl; (fig) entrailles fpl.

bowl [bəul] n (for eating) bol m; (for washing) cuvette f; (ball) boule f; (of pipe) fourneau m // vi (CRICKET) lancer (la balle); ~s n (jeu m de) boules fpl.

bow-legged ['bəu'lɛgɪd] a aux jambes arquées.

bowler ['bəulə*] n (CRICKET) lanceur m (de la balle); (Brit: also: ~ hat) (chapeau m) melon m.

bowling ['bəulɪŋ] n (game) jeu m de boules; jeu m de quilles; ~ alley n bowling m; ~ green n terrain m de boules (gazonné et carré).

bow tie n nœud m papillon.

box [bɔks] n boîte f; (also: cardboard ~) carton m; (THEATRE) loge f // vt mettre en boîte; (SPORT) boxer avec // vi boxer, faire de la boxe; ~er n (person) boxeur m; ~ing n (SPORT) boxe f; B~ing Day n (Brit) le lendemain de Noël; ~ing gloves npl gants mpl de boxe; ~ing ring n ring m; ~ office n bureau m de location; ~ room n débarras m; chambrette f.

boy [bɔɪ] n garçon m.

boycott ['bɔɪkɔt] n boycottage m // vt boycotter.

boyfriend ['bɔɪfrɛnd] n (petit) ami.

B.R. abbr of **British Rail**.

bra [brɑː] n soutien-gorge m.

brace [breɪs] n attache f, agrafe f; (on teeth) appareil m (dentaire); (tool) vilbrequin m // vt consolider, soutenir; ~s npl (Brit) bretelles fpl; to ~ o.s. (fig) se préparer mentalement.

bracelet ['breɪslɪt] n bracelet m.

bracing ['breɪsɪŋ] a tonifiant(e), tonique.

bracken ['brækən] n fougère f.

bracket ['brækɪt] n (TECH) tasseau m, support m; (group) classe f, tranche f; (also: brace ~) accolade f; (also: round ~) parenthèse f; (also: square ~) crochet m // vt mettre entre parenthèse(s).

brag [bræg] vi se vanter.

braid [breɪd] n (trimming) galon m; (of hair) tresse f, natte f.

brain [breɪn] n cerveau m; ~s npl cervelle f; he's got ~s il est intelligent; ~child n invention personnelle f; ~wash vt faire subir un lavage de cerveau à; ~wave n idée géniale; ~y a intelligent(e), doué(e).

brake [breɪk] n (on vehicle) frein m // vt, vi freiner; ~ fluid n liquide m de freins; ~ light n feu m de stop.

bramble ['bræmbl] n (bush) ronce f; (berry) mûre f sauvage.

bran [bræn] n son m.

branch [brɑːntʃ] n branche f; (COMM) succursale f // vi bifurquer.

brand [brænd] n marque (commerciale) // vt (cattle) marquer (au fer rouge).

brand-new ['brænd'njuː] a tout(e) neuf(neuve), flambant neuf(neuve).

brandy ['brændɪ] n cognac m, fine f.

brash [bræʃ] a effronté(e).

brass [brɑːs] n cuivre m (jaune), laiton m; the ~ (MUS) les cuivres; ~ band n fanfare f.

brassière ['bræsɪə*] n soutien-gorge m.

brat [bræt] n (pej) mioche m/f, môme m/f.

brave [breɪv] a courageux(euse), brave // n guerrier indien // vt braver, affronter; ~ry n bravoure f, courage m.

brawl [brɔːl] n rixe f, bagarre f.

brawn [brɔːn] n muscle m; (meat) fromage m de tête.

bray [breɪ] vi braire.

brazen ['breɪzn] a impudent(e), effronté(e) // vt: to ~ it out payer d'effronterie, crâner.

brazier ['breɪzɪə*] n brasero m.

Brazil [brə'zɪl] n Brésil m.

breach [briːtʃ] vt ouvrir une brèche dans // n (gap) brèche f; (breaking): ~ of contract rupture f de contract; ~ of the peace attentat m à l'ordre public.

bread [brɛd] n pain m; ~ and butter n tartines (beurrées); (fig) subsistance f; ~bin, (US) ~box n boîte f à pain; (bigger) huche f à pain; ~crumbs npl miettes fpl de pain; (CULIN) chapelure f, panure f; ~line n: to be on the ~line être sans le sou ou dans l'indigence.

breadth [brɛtθ] n largeur f.

breadwinner ['brɛdwɪnə*] n soutien m de famille.

break [breɪk] vb (pt broke, pp broken) vt casser, briser; (promise) rompre; (law) violer // vi (se) casser, se briser; (weather) tourner // n (gap) brèche f; (fracture) cassure f; (rest) interruption f, arrêt m; (: short) pause f; (: at school) récréation f; (chance) chance f, occasion f favorable; to ~ one's leg etc se casser la jambe etc; to ~ a record battre un record; to ~ the news to sb annoncer la nouvelle à qn; to ~ down vt (figures, data) décomposer, analyser // vi s'effondrer; (MED) faire une dépression (nerveuse); (AUT) tomber en panne; to ~ even vi rentrer dans ses frais; to ~ free ou loose vi se dégager, s'échapper; to ~ in vt (horse etc) dresser // vi (burglar) entrer par effraction; to ~ into vt fus (house) s'introduire ou pénétrer par effraction dans; to ~ off vi (speaker) s'interrompre; (branch) se rompre; to ~ open vt (door etc) forcer, fracturer; to ~ out vi éclater, se déclarer; to ~ out in spots se couvrir de boutons; to ~ up vi (*partnership*) cesser, prendre fin; (*friends*) se séparer // *vt* fracasser, casser; (*fight etc*) interrompre, faire cesser; **~age** *n* casse *f*; **~down** *n* (AUT) panne *f*; (*in communications*) rupture *f*; (MED: *also:* **nervous ~down**) dépression (nerveuse); **~down van** *n* (Brit) dépanneuse *f*; **~er** *n* brisant *m*.

breakfast ['brɛkfəst] *n* petit déjeuner *m*.

break: **~-in** *n* cambriolage *m*; **~ing and entering** *n* (LAW) effraction *f*; **~through** *n* percée *f*; **~water** *n* brise-lames *m inv*, digue *f*.

breast [brɛst] *n* (*of woman*) sein *m*; (*chest*) poitrine *f*; **~-feed** *vt*, *vi* (*irg: like* feed) allaiter; **~-stroke** *n* brasse *f*.

breath [brɛθ] *n* haleine *f*, souffle *m*; out of **~** à bout de souffle, essoufflé(e).

Breathalyser ['brɛθəlaɪzə*] *n* ® alcootest *m*.

breathe [bri:ð] *vt*, *vi* respirer; **to ~ in** *vt*, *vi* aspirer, inspirer; **to ~ out** *vt*, *vi* expirer; **~r** *n* moment *m* de repos *or* de répit; **breathing** *n* respiration *f*.

breathless ['brɛθlɪs] *a* essoufflé(e), haletant(e); oppressé(e).

breath-taking ['brɛθteɪkɪŋ] *a* stupéfiant(e), à vous couper le souffle.

breed [bri:d] *vb* (*pt, pp* **bred** [brɛd]) *vt* élever, faire l'élevage de // *vi* se reproduire // *n* race *f*, variété *f*; **~ing** *n* reproduction *f*; élevage *m*; (*upbringing*) éducation *f*.

breeze [bri:z] *n* brise *f*.

breezy ['bri:zɪ] *a* frais(fraîche); aéré(e); désinvolte, jovial(e).

brevity ['brɛvɪtɪ] *n* brièveté *f*.

brew [bru:] *vt* (*tea*) faire infuser; (*beer*) brasser; (*plot*) tramer, préparer // *vi* (*tea*) infuser; (*beer*) fermenter; (*fig*) se préparer, couver; **~er** *n* brasseur *m*; **~ery** *n* brasserie *f* (*fabrique*).

bribe [braɪb] *n* pot-de-vin *m* // *vt* acheter; soudoyer; **~ry** *n* corruption *f*.

brick [brɪk] *n* brique *f*; **~layer** *n* maçon *m*; **~works** *n* briqueterie *f*.

bridal ['braɪdl] *a* nuptial(e).

bride [braɪd] *n* mariée *f*, épouse *f*; **~groom** *n* marié *m*, époux *m*; **~smaid** *n* demoiselle *f* d'honneur.

bridge [brɪdʒ] *n* pont *m*; (NAUT) passerelle *f* (de commandement); (*of nose*) arête *f*; (CARDS, DENTISTRY) bridge *m* // *vt* (*river*) construire un pont sur; (*gap*) combler.

bridle ['braɪdl] *n* bride *f* // *vt* refréner, mettre la bride à; (*horse*) brider; **~ path** *n* piste *or* allée cavalière.

brief [bri:f] *a* bref(brève) // *n* (LAW) dossier *m*, cause *f* // *vt* donner des instructions à; **~s** *npl* slip *m*; **~case** *n* serviette *f*; porte-documents *m inv*; **~ing** *n* instructions *fpl*; **~ly** *ad* brièvement.

bright [braɪt] *a* brillant(e); (*room,*

(*weather*) clair(e); (*person*) intelligent(e), doué(e); (*colour*) vif(vive); **~en** (*also:* **~en up**) *vt* (*room*) éclaircir; égayer // *vi* s'éclaircir; (*person*) retrouver un peu de sa gaieté.

brilliance ['brɪljəns] *n* éclat *m*.

brilliant ['brɪljənt] *a* brillant(e).

brim [brɪm] *n* bord *m*.

brine [braɪn] *n* eau salée; (CULIN) saumure *f*.

bring [brɪŋ], *pt, pp* **brought** *vt* (*thing*) apporter; (*person*) amener; **to ~ about** *vt* provoquer, entraîner; **to ~ back** *vt* rapporter; ramener; **to ~ down** *vt* abaisser; faire s'effondrer; **to ~ forward** *vt* avancer; **to ~ off** *vt* (*task, plan*) réussir, mener à bien; **to ~ out** *vt* (*meaning*) faire ressortir, mettre en relief; **to ~ round** *or* **to** *vt* (*unconscious person*) ranimer; **to ~ up** *vt* élever; (*question*) soulever; (*food: vomit*) vomir, rendre.

brink [brɪŋk] *n* bord *m*.

brisk [brɪsk] *a* vif(vive).

bristle ['brɪsl] *n* poil *m* // *vi* se hérisser.

Britain ['brɪtən] *n* (*also:* **Great ~**) Grande-Bretagne *f*.

British ['brɪtɪʃ] *a* britannique; **the ~** *npl* les Britanniques *mpl*; **the ~ Isles** *npl* les Îles *fpl* Britanniques; **B~ Rail (B.R.)** *n* compagnie ferroviaire britannique, ≈ S.N.C.F. *f*.

Briton ['brɪtən] *n* Britannique *m/f*.

Brittany ['brɪtənɪ] *n* Bretagne *f*.

brittle ['brɪtl] *a* cassant(e), fragile.

broach [brəutʃ] *vt* (*subject*) aborder.

broad [brɔ:d] *a* large; (*distinction*) général(e); (*accent*) prononcé(e); **in ~ daylight** en plein jour; **~cast** *n* émission *f* // *vb* (*pt, pp* **broadcast**) *vt* radiodiffuser; téléviser // *vi* émettre; **~en** *vt* élargir // *vi* s'élargir; **~ly** *ad* en gros, généralement; **~-minded** *a* large d'esprit.

broccoli ['brɔkəlɪ] *n* brocoli *m*.

brochure ['brəuʃjuə*] *n* prospectus *m*, dépliant *m*.

broil [brɔɪl] *vt* griller.

broke [brəuk] *pt of* **break** // *a* (col) fauché(e).

broken ['brəukn] *pp of* **break** // *a*: **~ leg** *etc* jambe *etc* cassée; **in ~ English** dans un anglais approximatif *or* hésitant; **~-hearted** *a* (ayant) le cœur brisé.

broker ['brəukə*] *n* courtier *m*.

brolly ['brɔlɪ] *n* (Brit col) pépin *m*, parapluie *m*.

bronchitis [brɔŋ'kaɪtɪs] *n* bronchite *f*.

bronze [brɔnz] *n* bronze *m*.

brooch [brəutʃ] *n* broche *f*.

brood [bru:d] *n* couvée *f* // *vi* (*hen, storm*) couver; (*person*) méditer (sombrement), ruminer.

brook [bruk] *n* ruisseau *m*.

broom [brum] *n* balai *m*; **~stick** *n*

manche *m* à balai.

Bros. *abbr* = **Brothers**.

broth [brɔθ] *n* bouillon *m* de viande et de légumes.

brothel ['brɔθl] *n* maison close, bordel *m*.

brother ['brʌðə*] *n* frère *m*; **~-in-law** *n* beau-frère *m*.

brought [brɔːt] *pt, pp of* **bring**.

brow [brau] *n* front *m*; *(rare, gen: eye~)* sourcil *m*; *(of hill)* sommet *m*.

brown [braun] *a* brun(e), marron *inv* // *n (colour)* brun *m* // *vt* brunir; *(CULIN)* faire dorer, faire roussir; **~ bread** *n* pain *m* bis.

brownie ['brauni] *n* jeannette *f*, éclaireuse (cadette).

brown paper *n* papier *m* d'emballage.

brown sugar *n* cassonade *f*.

browse [brauz] *vi (among books)* bouquiner, feuilleter les livres.

bruise [bruːz] *n* bleu *m*, ecchymose *f*, contusion *f* // *vt* contusionner, meurtrir.

brunette [bruː'net] *n* (femme) brune.

brunt [brʌnt] *n*: the **~ of** *(attack, criticism etc)* le plus gros de.

brush [brʌʃ] *n* brosse *f*; *(quarrel)* accrochage *m*, prise *f* de bec // *vt* brosser; *(also:* **~ past**, **~ against)** effleurer, frôler; **to ~ aside** *vt* écarter, balayer; **to ~ up** *vt (knowledge)* rafraîchir, réviser; **~wood** *n* broussailles *fpl*, taillis *m*.

Brussels ['brʌslz] *n* Bruxelles; **~ sprout** *n* chou *m* de Bruxelles.

brutal ['bruːtl] *a* brutal(e).

brute [bruːt] *n* brute *f* // *a*: by **~ force** par la force.

B.Sc. *abbr see* **bachelor**.

bubble ['bʌbl] *n* bulle *f* // *vi* bouillonner, faire des bulles; *(sparkle, fig)* pétiller; **~ bath** *n* bain moussant.

buck [bʌk] *n* mâle *m* *(d'un lapin, lièvre, daim etc)*; *(US col)* dollar *m* // *vi* ruer, lancer une ruade; **to pass the ~** *(to sb)* se décharger de la responsabilité *(sur qn)*; **to ~ up** *vi (cheer up)* reprendre du poil de la bête, se remonter.

bucket ['bʌkit] *n* seau *m*.

buckle ['bʌkl] *n* boucle *f* // *vt* boucler, attacher; *(warp)* tordre, gauchir; *(: wheel)* voiler.

bud [bʌd] *n* bourgeon *m*; *(of flower)* bouton *m* // *vi* bourgeonner; *(flower)* éclore.

Buddhism ['budizəm] *n* bouddhisme *m*.

budding ['bʌdiŋ] *a (poet etc)* en herbe; *(passion etc)* naissant(e).

buddy ['bʌdi] *n (US)* copain *m*.

budge [bʌdʒ] *vt* faire bouger // *vi* bouger.

budgerigar ['bʌdʒəriga:*] *n* perruche *f*.

budget ['bʌdʒit] *n* budget *m* // *vi*: **to ~ for sth** inscrire qch au budget.

budgie ['bʌdʒi] *n* = **budgerigar**.

buff [bʌf] *a* (couleur *f*) chamois *m* // *n (enthusiast)* mordu/e.

buffalo, *pl* **~** *or* **~es** ['bʌfələu] *n* buffle *m*; *(US)* bison *m*.

buffer ['bʌfə*] *n* tampon *m*; *(COMPUT)* mémoire *f* tampon.

buffet *n* ['bufei] *(food, Brit: bar)* buffet *m* // *vt* ['bʌfit] gifler, frapper; secouer, ébranler; **~ car** *n (Brit RAIL)* voiture-buffet *f*.

bug [bʌg] *n (insect)* punaise *f*; *(: gen)* insecte *m*, bestiole *f*; *(fig: germ)* virus *m*, microbe *m*; *(: spy device)* dispositif *m* d'écoute (électronique), micro clandestin // *vt* garnir de dispositifs d'écoute.

bugle ['bjuːgl] *n* clairon *m*.

build [bild] *n (of person)* carrure *f*, charpente *f* // *vt (pt, pp* **built)** construire, bâtir; **to ~ up** *vt* accumuler, amasser; accroître; **~er** *n* entrepreneur *m*; **~ing** *n* construction *f*; bâtiment *m*, construction; *(habitation, offices)* immeuble *m*; **~ing society** *n (Brit)* société *f* de crédit immobilier.

built [bilt] *pt, pp of* **build**; **~-in** *a (cupboard)* encastré(e); *(device)* incorporé(e); intégré(e); **~-up area** *n* agglomération (urbaine); zone urbanisée.

bulb [bʌlb] *n (BOT)* bulbe *m*, oignon *m*; *(ELEC)* ampoule *f*.

bulge [bʌldʒ] *n* renflement *m*, gonflement *m* // *vi* faire saillie; présenter un renflement; **to be bulging with** être plein(e) à craquer de.

bulk [bʌlk] *n* masse *f*, volume *m*; **in ~** *(COMM)* en vrac; the **~ of** la plus grande *or* grosse partie de; **~y** *a* volumineux(euse), encombrant(e).

bull [bul] *n* taureau *m*; **~dog** *n* bouledogue *m*.

bulldozer ['buldəuzə*] *n* bulldozer *m*.

bullet ['bulit] *n* balle *f* *(de fusil etc)*.

bulletin ['bulitin] *n* bulletin *m*, communiqué *m*.

bulletproof ['bulitpruːf] *a (car)* blindé(e); *(vest etc)* pare-balles *inv*.

bullfight ['bulfait] *n* corrida *f*, course *f* de taureaux; **~er** *n* torero *m*; **~ing** *n* tauromachie *f*.

bullion ['buljən] *n or m or* argent *m* en lingots.

bullock ['bulək] *n* bœuf *m*.

bullring ['buliŋ] *n* arènes *fpl*.

bull's-eye ['bulzai] *n* centre *m* *(de la cible)*.

bully ['buli] *n* brute *f*, tyran *m* // *vt* tyranniser, rudoyer; *(frighten)* intimider.

bum [bʌm] *n (col: backside)* derrière *m*; *(tramp)* vagabond/e, traîne-savates *m/f inv*.

bumblebee ['bʌmblbiː] *n* bourdon *m*.

bump [bʌmp] *n (blow)* coup *m*, choc *m*;

(*jolt*) cahot *m*; (*on road etc, on head*) bosse *f* // *vt* heurter, cogner; **to ~ into** *vt fus* rentrer dans, tamponner; **~er** *n* pare-chocs *m inv* // *a*: **~er crop/harvest** récolte/moisson exceptionnelle.

bumptious ['bʌmpʃəs] *a* suffisant(e), prétentieux(euse).

bumpy ['bʌmpɪ] *a* cahoteux(euse).

bun [bʌn] *n* petit pain au lait; (*of hair*) chignon *m*.

bunch [bʌntʃ] *n* (*of flowers*) bouquet *m*; (*of keys*) trousseau *m*; (*of bananas*) régime *m*; (*of people*) groupe *m*; **~ of grapes** grappe *f* de raisin.

bundle ['bʌndl] *n* paquet *m* // *vt* (*also:* **~ up**) faire un paquet de; (*put*): **to ~ sth/sb into** fourrer *or* enfourner qch/qn dans.

bungalow ['bʌŋgələu] *n* bungalow *m*.

bungle ['bʌŋgl] *vt* bâcler, gâcher.

bunion ['bʌnjən] *n* oignon *m* (*au pied*).

bunk [bʌŋk] *n* couchette *f*; **~ beds** *npl* lits superposés.

bunker ['bʌŋkə*] *n* (*coal store*) soute *f* à charbon; (*MIL, GOLF*) bunker *m*.

bunny ['bʌnɪ] *n* (*also:* **~ rabbit**) Jeannot *m* lapin.

bunting ['bʌntɪŋ] *n* pavoisement *m*, drapeaux *mpl*.

buoy [bɔɪ] *n* bouée *f*; **to ~ up** *vt* faire flotter; (*fig*) soutenir, épauler; **~ant** *a* (*carefree*) gai(e), plein(e) d'entrain.

burden ['bə:dn] *n* fardeau *m*, charge *f* // *vt* charger; (*oppress*) accabler, surcharger.

bureau, *pl* **~x** [bjuə'rəu, -z] *n* (*Brit: writing desk*) bureau *m*, secrétaire *m*; (*US: chest of drawers*) commode *f*; (*office*) bureau, office *m*.

bureaucracy [bjuə'rɔkrəsɪ] *n* bureaucratie *f*.

burglar ['bə:glə*] *n* cambrioleur *m*; **~ alarm** *n* sonnerie *f* d'alarme; **~y** *n* cambriolage *m*.

Burgundy ['bə:gəndɪ] *n* Bourgogne *f*.

burial ['berɪəl] *n* enterrement *m*.

burly ['bə:lɪ] *a* de forte carrure, costaud(e).

Burma ['bə:mə] *n* Birmanie *f*.

burn [bə:n] *vt, vi* (*pt, pp* **burned** *or* **burnt**) brûler // *n* brûlure *f*; **to ~ down** *vt* incendier, détruire par le feu; **~er** *n* brûleur *m*.

burnt [bə:nt] *pt, pp of* **burn**.

burrow ['bʌrəu] *n* terrier *m* // *vt* creuser.

bursar ['bə:sə*] *n* économe *m/f*; (*Brit: student*) boursier/ère; **~y** *n* (*Brit*) bourse *f* (d'études).

burst [bə:st] *vb* (*pt, pp* **burst**) *vt* crever; faire éclater // *vi* éclater; (*tyre*) crever // *n* explosion *f*; (*also:* **~ pipe**) rupture *f*, fuite *f*; **to ~ into flames** s'enflammer soudainement; **to ~ out laughing** éclater de rire; **to ~ into tears** fondre en

larmes; **to be ~ing with** être plein (à craquer) de; regorger de; **to ~ into** *vt fus* (*room etc*) faire irruption dans; **to ~ open** *vi* s'ouvrir violemment *or* soudainement.

bury ['berɪ] *vt* enterrer.

bus, ~es [bʌs, 'bʌsɪz] *n* autobus *m*.

bush [buʃ] *n* buisson *m*; (*scrub land*) brousse *f*; **to beat about the ~** tourner autour du pot.

bushy ['buʃɪ] *a* broussailleux(euse), touffu(e).

busily ['bɪzɪlɪ] *ad* activement.

business ['bɪznɪs] *n* (*matter, firm*) affaire *f*; (*trading*) affaires *fpl*; (*job, duty*) travail *m*; **to be away on ~** être en déplacement *or* en voyage; **it's none of my ~** cela ne me regarde pas, ce ne sont pas mes affaires; **he means ~** il ne plaisante pas, il est sérieux; **~like** *a* sérieux(euse); efficace; **~man/woman** *n* homme/femme d'affaires; **~ trip** *n* voyage *m* d'affaires.

busker ['bʌskə*] *n* (*Brit*) musicien ambulant.

bus-stop ['bʌsstɔp] *n* arrêt *m* d'autobus.

bust [bʌst] *n* buste *m* // *a* (*col: broken*) fichu(e), fini(e); **to go ~** faire faillite.

bustle ['bʌsl] *n* remue-ménage *m*, affairement *m* // *vi* s'affairer, se démener.

busy ['bɪzɪ] *a* occupé(e); (*shop, street*) très fréquenté(e) // *vt*: **to ~ o.s.** s'occuper; **~body** *n* mouche *f* du coche, âme *f* charitable; **~ signal** *n* (*US TEL*) tonalité *f* occupé *inv*.

but [bʌt] ♦ *cj* mais; **I'd love to come, ~ I'm busy** j'aimerais venir mais je suis occupé ♦ *prep* (*apart from, except*) sauf, excepté; **we've had nothing ~ trouble** nous n'avons eu que des ennuis; **no-one ~ him** can do it lui seul peut le faire; **~ for you/your help** sans toi/ton aide; **anything ~ that** tout sauf *or* excepté ça, tout mais pas ça

♦ *ad* (*just, only*) ne ... que; **she's ~ a child** elle n'est qu'une enfant; **had I ~ known** si seulement j'avais su; **all ~ finished** pratiquement terminé.

butcher ['butʃə*] *n* boucher *m* // *vt* massacrer; (*cattle etc for meat*) tuer.

butler ['bʌtlə*] *n* maître *m* d'hôtel.

butt [bʌt] *n* (*cask*) gros tonneau; (*thick end*) (gros) bout; (*of gun*) crosse *f*; (*of cigarette*) mégot *m*; (*Brit fig: target*) cible *f* // *vt* donner un coup de tête à; **to ~ in** *vi* (*interrupt*) s'immiscer dans la conversation.

butter ['bʌtə*] *n* beurre *m* // *vt* beurrer; **~cup** *n* bouton *m* d'or.

butterfly ['bʌtəflaɪ] *n* papillon *m*; (*SWIMMING: also:* **~ stroke**) brasse *f* papillon *inv*.

buttocks ['bʌtəks] *npl* fesses *fpl*.

button ['bʌtn] *n* bouton *m* // *vt* (*also:* ~

up) boutonner // *vi* se boutonner.

buttress ['bʌtrɪs] *n* contrefort *m*.

buxom ['bʌksəm] *a* aux formes avantageuses *or* épanouies.

buy [baɪ] *vb* (*pt, pp* **bought**) *vt* acheter; to ~ sb sth/sth from sb acheter qch à qn; to ~ sb a drink offrir un verre *or* à boire à qn; **~er** *n* acheteur/euse.

buzz [bʌz] *n* bourdonnement *m*; (*col: phone call*) coup *m* de fil // *vi* bourdonner.

buzzer ['bʌzə*] *n* timbre *m* électrique.

buzz word *n* (*col*) mot *m* à la mode.

by [baɪ] ◆ *prep* **1** (*referring to cause, agent*) par, de; killed ~ **lightning** tué par la foudre; **surrounded** ~ **a fence** entouré d'une barrière; **a painting** ~ **Picasso** un tableau de Picasso

2 (*referring to method, manner, means*): ~ **bus/car** en autobus/voiture; ~ **train** par le *or* en train; **to pay** ~ **cheque** payer par chèque; ~ **saving hard, he ...** à force d'économiser, il ...

3 (*via, through*) par; **we came** ~ **Dover** nous sommes venus par Douvres

4 (*close to, past*) à côté de; **the house** ~ **the school** la maison à côté de l'école; **a holiday** ~ **the sea** des vacances au bord de la mer; **she sat** ~ **his bed** elle était assise à son chevet; **she went** ~ **me** elle est passée à côté de moi; **I go** ~ **the post office every day** je passe devant la poste tous les jours

5 (*with time: not later than*) avant; (: *during*): ~ **daylight** à la lumière du jour; **by night** la nuit, de nuit; ~ **4 o'clock** avant 4 heures; ~ **this time tomorrow** d'ici demain à la même heure; ~ **the time I got here it was** too late lorsque je suis arrivé c'était déjà trop tard

6 (*amount*) à; ~ **the kilo/metre** au kilo/au mètre; **paid** ~ **the hour** payé à l'heure

7 (*MATH, measure*): **to divide/multiply** ~ **3** diviser/multiplier par 3; **a room 3 metres** ~ **4** une pièce de 3 mètres sur 4; **it's broader** ~ **a metre** c'est plus large d'un mètre; **one** ~ **one** un à un; **little** ~ **little** petit à petit, peu à peu

8 (*according to*) d'après, selon; **it's 3 o'clock** ~ **my watch** il est 3 heures d'après ma montre; **it's all right** ~ **me** je n'ai rien contre

9: (**all**) ~ **oneself** *etc* tout(e) seul(e)

10: ~ **the way** au fait, à propos

◆ *ad* **1** *see* **go**, **pass** *etc*

2: ~ **and** ~ un peu plus tard, bientôt; ~ **and large** dans l'ensemble.

bye(-bye) ['baɪ('baɪ)] *excl* au revoir!, salut!

by(e)-law ['baɪlɔ:] *n* arrêté municipal.

by-election ['baɪɪlekʃən] *n* (*Brit*) élection (législative) partielle.

bygone ['baɪgɒn] *a* passé(e) // *n*: let ~s

be ~s passons l'éponge, oublions le passé.

bypass ['baɪpɑ:s] *n* (route *f* de) contournement *m*; (*MÉD*) pontage *m* // *vt* éviter.

by-product ['baɪprɒdʌkt] *n* sous-produit *m*, dérivé *m*; (*fig*) conséquence *f* secondaire, retombée *f*.

bystander ['baɪstændə*] *n* spectateur/trice, badaud/e.

byte [baɪt] *n* (*COMPUT*) octet *m*.

byway ['baɪweɪ] *n* chemin *m* (écarté).

byword ['baɪwə:d] *n*: **to be a** ~ **for** être synonyme de (*fig*).

by-your-leave ['baɪjɔ:'li:v] *n*: **without so much as a** ~ sans même demander la permission.

C

C [si:] *n* (*MUS*) do *m*.

C.A. *abbr of* **chartered accountant**.

cab [kæb] *n* taxi *m*; (*of train, truck*) cabine *f*; (*horse-drawn*) fiacre *m*.

cabaret ['kæbəreɪ] *n* attractions *fpl*, spectacle *m* de cabaret.

cabbage ['kæbɪdʒ] *n* chou *m*.

cabin ['kæbɪn] *n* cabane *f*, hutte *f*; (*on ship*) cabine *f*.

cabinet ['kæbɪnɪt] *n* (*POL*) cabinet *m*; (*furniture*) petit meuble à tiroirs et rayons; (*also: display* ~) vitrine *f*, petite armoire vitrée; **~-maker** *n* ébéniste *m*.

cable ['keɪbl] *n* câble *m* // *vt* câbler, télégraphier; **~-car** *n* téléphérique *m*; ~ **television** *n* télévision *f* par câble.

cache [kæʃ] *n* cachette *f*.

cackle ['kækl] *vi* caqueter.

cactus, *pl* **cacti** ['kæktəs, -taɪ] *n* cactus *m*.

cadet [kə'det] *n* (*MIL*) élève *m* officier.

cadge [kædʒ] *vt* se faire donner.

café ['kæfeɪ] *n* ≈ café(-restaurant) *m* (*sans alcool*).

cage [keɪdʒ] *n* cage *f*.

cagey ['keɪdʒɪ] *a* (*col*) réticent(e); méfiant(e).

cagoule [kə'gu:l] *n* K-way *m* ®.

Cairo ['kaɪərəu] *n* le Caire.

cajole [kə'dʒəul] *vt* couvrir de flatteries *or* de gentillesses.

cake [keɪk] *n* gâteau *m*; ~ **of soap** savonnette *f*; ~**d** *a*: ~**d with** raidi(e) par, couvert(e) d'une croûte de.

calculate ['kælkjuleɪt] *vt* calculer; **calculation** [-'leɪʃən] *n* calcul *m*; **calculator** *n* machine *f* à calculer, calculatrice *f*.

calendar ['kæləndə*] *n* calendrier *m*; ~ **year** *n* année civile.

calf [kɑ:f], *pl* **calves** *n* (*of cow*) veau *m*; (*of other animals*) petit *m*; (*also:* ~**skin**) veau *m*, vachette *f*; (*ANAT*) mollet *m*.

calibre, (*US*) **caliber** ['kælɪbə*] *n* calibre m.

call [kɔ:l] vt (gen, also TEL) appeler // vi
appeler; (visit: also: ~ **in**, ~ **round**): to
~ **(for)** passer (prendre) // n (shout)
appel m, cri m; (visit) visite f; (also:
telephone ~) coup m de téléphone;
communication f; she's ~ed Suzanne elle
s'appelle Suzanne; to be on ~ être de
permanence; to ~ **back** vi (return)
repasser; (TEL) rappeler; to ~ **for** vt
fus demander; to ~ **off** vt annuler; to
~ **on** vt fus (visit) rendre visite à,
passer voir; (request): to ~ **on** sb to do
inviter qn à faire; to ~ **out** vi pousser
un cri or des cris; to ~ **up** vt (MIL)
appeler, mobiliser; **~box** n (Brit)
cabine f téléphonique; **~er** n personne f
qui appelle; visiteur m; **~ girl** n call-
girl f; **~-in** n (US: phone-in) programme m à ligne ouverte; **~ing** n
vocation f; (trade, occupation) état m;
~ing card n (US) carte f de visite.

callous ['kæləs] a dur(e), insensible.

calm [ka:m] a calme // n calme m // vt
calmer, apaiser; to ~ **down** vi se
calmer, s'apaiser // vt calmer, apaiser.

Calor gas ['kælə*-] n ® butane m,
butagaz m ®.

calorie ['kælərɪ] n calorie f.

calves [ka:vz] npl of **calf**.

camber ['kæmbə*] n (of road)
bombement m.

Cambodia [kæm'bəudjə] n Cambodge
m.

came [keɪm] pt of **come**.

camel ['kæməl] n chameau m.

cameo ['kæmɪəu] n camée m.

camera ['kæmərə] n appareil-photo m;
(also: cine-~, movie ~) caméra f; in ~
à huis clos, en privé; **~man** n
caméraman m.

camouflage ['kæməfla:ʒ] n camouflage
m // vt camoufler.

camp [kæmp] n camp m // vi camper.

campaign [kæm'peɪn] n (MIL, POL etc)
campagne f // vi (also fig) faire campagne.

campbed ['kæmp'bɛd] n (Brit) lit m de
camp.

camper ['kæmpə*] n campeur/euse.

camping ['kæmpɪŋ] n camping m; to go
~ faire du camping.

campsite ['kæmpsaɪt] n campement m.

campus ['kæmpəs] n campus m.

can [kæn] auxiliary vb see next
headword // n (of milk, oil, water) bidon
m; (tin) boîte f de conserve // vt mettre
en conserve.

can [kæn] ♦ n, vt see previous headword
♦ auxiliary vb (negative cannot, can't;
conditional and pt could) **1** (be able to)
pouvoir; you ~ do it if you try vous
pouvez le faire si vous essayez; I ~'t
hear you je ne t'entends pas
2 (know how to) savoir; I ~ swim/play

tennis/drive je sais nager/jouer au
tennis/conduire; ~ **you speak French?**
parlez-vous français?
3 (may) pouvoir; ~ **I use your phone?**
puis-je me servir de votre téléphone?
4 (expressing disbelief, puzzlement etc):
it ~'t be true! ce n'est pas possible!;
what CAN **he want?** qu'est-ce qu'il peut
bien vouloir?
5 (expressing possibility, suggestion
etc): he could be in the library il est
peut-être dans la bibliothèque; she could
have been delayed il se peut qu'elle ait
été retardée.

Canada ['kænədə] n Canada m.

Canadian [kə'neɪdɪən] a canadien(ne) //
n Canadien/ne.

canal [kə'næl] n canal m.

canary [kə'nɛərɪ] n canari m, serin m.

cancel ['kænsəl] vt annuler; (train) supprimer; (party, appointment) décommander; (cross out) barrer, rayer;
(stamp) oblitérer; **~lation**
[-'leɪʃən] n annulation f; suppression f;
oblitération f; (TOURISM) réservation an-
nulée.

cancer ['kænsə*] n cancer m; C~ (sign)
le Cancer.

candid ['kændɪd] a (très) franc(franche), sincère.

candidate ['kændɪdeɪt] n candidat/e.

candle ['kændl] n bougie f; (of tallow)
chandelle f; (in church) cierge m; by
~light à la lumière d'une bougie;
(dinner) aux chandelles; **~stick** n (also:
~ holder) bougeoir m; (bigger, ornate)
chandelier m.

candour, (US) **candor** ['kændə*] n
(grande) franchise or sincérité.

candy ['kændɪ] n sucre candi; (US)
bonbon m; **~-floss** n (Brit) barbe f à
papa.

cane [keɪn] n canne f // vt (Brit SCOL)
administrer des coups de bâton à.

canister ['kænɪstə*] n boîte f.

cannabis ['kænəbɪs] n (drug) cannabis
m; (also: ~ plant) chanvre indien.

canned ['kænd] a (food) en boîte, en
conserve.

cannon, pl ~ or ~s ['kænən] n (gun)
canon m.

cannot ['kænɔt] = **can not**.

canny ['kænɪ] a madré(e), finaud(e).

canoe [kə'nu:] n pirogue f; (SPORT)
canoë m.

canon ['kænən] n (clergyman) chanoine
m; (standard) canon m.

can opener [-'əupnə*] n ouvre-boîte m.

canopy ['kænəpɪ] n baldaquin m; dais
m.

can't [kænt] = **can not**.

cantankerous [kæn'tæŋkərəs] a
querelleur(euse), acariâtre.

canteen [kæn'ti:n] n cantine f; (Brit: of
cutlery) ménagère f.

canter ['kæntə*] n petit galop.

canvas ['kænvəs] n (gen) toile f.

canvassing ['kænvəsıŋ] n (POL) prospection électorale, démarchage électoral; (COMM) démarchage, prospection.

canyon ['kænjən] n cañon m, gorge (profonde).

cap [kæp] n casquette f; (of pen) capuchon m; (of bottle) capsule f // vt capsuler; (outdo) surpasser.

capability [keıpə'bılıtı] n aptitude f, capacité f.

capable ['keıpəbl] a capable.

capacity [kə'pæsıtı] n capacité f, contenance f; aptitude f.

cape [keıp] n (garment) cape f; (GEO) cap m.

capital ['kæpıtl] n (also: ~ city) capitale f; (money) capital m; (also: ~ letter) majuscule f; **~ gains tax** n impôt m sur les plus-values; **~ism** n capitalisme m; **~ist** a, n capitaliste (m/f); **~ize: to ~ize on** vt fus profiter de; **~ punishment** n peine capitale.

Capricorn ['kæprıkɔ:n] n le Capricorne.

capsize [kæp'saız] vt faire chavirer // vi chavirer.

capsule ['kæpsju:l] n capsule f.

captain ['kæptın] n capitaine m.

caption ['kæpʃən] n légende f.

captive ['kæptıv] a, n captif(ive).

capture ['kæptʃə*] vt capturer, prendre; (attention) capter // n capture f; (data ~) saisie f de données.

car [kɑ:*] n voiture f, auto f.

carafe [kə'ræf] n carafe f.

caramel ['kærəməl] n caramel m.

caravan ['kærəvæn] n caravane f; **~ site** n (Brit) camping m pour caravanes.

carbohydrates [kɑ:bəu'haıdreıts] npl (foods) aliments mpl riches en hydrate de carbone.

carbon ['kɑ:bən] n carbone m; **~ paper** n papier m carbone.

carburettor, (US) **carburetor** [kɑ:bju'rɛtə*] n carburateur m.

card [kɑ:d] n carte f; **~board** n carton m; **~ game** n jeu m de cartes.

cardiac ['kɑ:dıæk] a cardiaque.

cardigan ['kɑ:dıgən] n cardigan m.

cardinal ['kɑ:dınl] a cardinal(e) // n cardinal m.

card index ['kɑ:dındɛks] n fichier m (alphabétique).

care [kɛə*] n soin m, attention f; (worry) souci m // vi: **to ~ about** se soucier de, s'intéresser à; **~ of** (c/o) chez, aux bons soins de; **in sb's ~** à la garde de qn, confié à qn; **to take ~ (to do)** faire attention (à faire); **to take ~ of** vt s'occuper de, prendre soin de; **to ~ for** vt fus s'occuper de; (like) aimer; I don't ~ ça m'est bien égal, peu

m'importe.

career [kə'rıə*] n carrière f // vi (also: ~ along) aller à toute allure.

carefree ['kɛəfri:] a sans souci, insouciant(e).

careful ['kɛəful] a soigneux(euse); (cautious) prudent(e); **(be) ~!** (fais) attention!; **~ly** ad avec soin, soigneusement; prudemment.

careless ['kɛəlıs] a négligent(e); (heedless) insouciant(e).

caress [kə'rɛs] n caresse f // vt caresser.

caretaker ['kɛəteıkə*] n gardien/ne, concierge m/f.

car-ferry ['kɑ:fɛrı] n (on sea) ferry(-boat) m; (on river) bac m.

cargo, pl ~es ['kɑ:gəu] n cargaison f, chargement m.

car hire n location f de voiture.

Caribbean [kærı'bi:ən] a: **the ~ (Sea)** la mer des Antilles or Caraïbes.

caring ['kɛərıŋ] a (person) bienveillant(e); (society, organization) humanitaire.

carnal ['kɑ:nl] a charnel(le).

carnation [kɑ:'neıʃən] n œillet m.

carnival ['kɑ:nıvəl] n (public celebration) carnaval m; (US: funfair) fête foraine.

carol ['kærəl] n: (Christmas) ~ chant m de Noël.

carp [kɑ:p] n (fish) carpe f; **to ~ at** vt fus critiquer.

car park ['kɑ:pɑ:k] n (Brit) parking m, parc m de stationnement.

carpenter ['kɑ:pıntə*] n charpentier m.

carpentry ['kɑ:pıntrı] n charpenterie f, métier m de charpentier; (woodwork: at school etc) menuiserie f.

carpet ['kɑ:pıt] n tapis m // vt recouvrir (d'un tapis); **~ slippers** npl pantoufles fpl; **~ sweeper** n balai m mécanique.

carriage ['kærıdʒ] n voiture f; (of goods) transport m; (: cost) port m; (of typewriter) chariot m; (bearing) maintien m, port m; **~ return** n (on typewriter etc) retour m de chariot; **~way** n (Brit: part of road) chaussée f.

carrier ['kærıə*] n transporteur m, camionneur m; (MED) porteur/euse; (NAUT) porte-avions m inv; **~ bag** n (Brit) sac m en papier or en plastique.

carrot ['kærət] n carotte f.

carry ['kærı] vt (subj: person) porter; (: vehicle) transporter; (a motion, bill) voter, adopter; (involve: responsibilities etc) comporter, impliquer // vi (sound) porter; **to be** or **get carried away** (fig) s'emballer, s'enthousiasmer; **to ~ on** vi: **to ~ on with sth/doing** continuer qch/ à faire // vt entretenir, poursuivre; **to ~ out** vt (orders) exécuter; (investigation) effectuer; **~cot** n porte-bébé m; **~-on** n (col: fuss) histoires fpl.

cart [kɑ:t] n charrette f // vt transporter.

carton ['kɑːtən] n (box) carton m; (of yogurt) pot m (en carton); (of cigarettes) cartouche f.

cartoon [kɑː'tuːn] n (PRESS) dessin m (humoristique); (satirical) caricature f; (comic strip) bande dessinée; (CINEMA) dessin animé.

cartridge ['kɑːtrɪdʒ] n (for gun, pen) cartouche f; (for camera) chargeur m; (music tape) cassette f.

carve [kɑːv] vt (meat) découper; (wood, stone) tailler, sculpter; **to ~ up** vt découper; (fig: country) morceler; **carving** n (in wood etc) sculpture f; **carving knife** n couteau m à découper.

car wash n station f de lavage (de voitures).

case [keɪs] n cas m; (LAW) affaire f, procès m; (box) caisse f, boîte f, étui m; (Brit: also: suit~) valise f; **to put forward his ~** very well ses arguments ne sont guère convaincants; **in ~ of** en cas de; **in ~ he** au cas où il; **just in ~** à tout hasard.

cash [kæʃ] n argent m; (COMM) argent liquide, numéraire m; liquidités fpl; (COMM: in payment) argent comptant, espèces fpl // vt encaisser; **to pay (in) ~** payer (en argent) comptant; **~ on delivery** (C.O.D.) (COMM) payable or paiement à la livraison; **~book** n livre m de caisse; **~ card** n carte f de retrait; **~ desk** n (Brit) caisse f; **~ dispenser** n guichet m automatique de banque.

cashew [kæ'ʃuː] n (also: ~ nut) noix f de cajou.

cashier [kæ'ʃɪə*] n caissier/ère.

cashmere ['kæʃmɪə*] n cachemire m.

cash register n caisse enregistreuse.

casing ['keɪsɪŋ] n revêtement (protecteur), enveloppe (protectrice).

casino [kə'siːnəu] n casino m.

cask [kɑːsk] n tonneau m.

casket ['kɑːskɪt] n coffret m; (US: coffin) cercueil m.

casserole ['kæsərəul] n cocotte f; (food) ragoût m (en cocotte).

cassette [kæ'set] n cassette f, musicassette f; **~ player** n lecteur m de cassettes; **~ recorder** n magnétophone m à cassettes.

cast [kɑːst] vb (pt, pp cast) vt (throw) jeter; (shed) perdre; se dépouiller de; (metal) couler, fondre; (THEATRE): **to ~ sb as Hamlet** attribuer à qn le rôle d'Hamlet // n (THEATRE) distribution f; (mould) moule m; (also: plaster ~) plâtre m; **to ~ one's vote** voter, exprimer son suffrage; **to ~ off** vi (NAUT) larguer les amarres.

castaway ['kɑːstəwəɪ] n naufragé/e.

caster sugar ['kɑːstə*-] n (Brit) sucre m semoule.

casting ['kɑːstɪŋ] a: **~ vote** (Brit) voix

prépondérante (pour départager).

cast iron n fonte f.

castle ['kɑːsl] n château-fort m; (manor) château m.

castor ['kɑːstə*] n (wheel) roulette f; **~ oil** n huile f de ricin.

castrate [kæs'treɪt] vt châtrer.

casual ['kæʒjul] a (by chance) de hasard, fait(e) au hasard, fortuit(e); (irregular: work etc) temporaire; (unconcerned) désinvolte; **~ wear** n vêtements mpl sport inv; **~ly** ad avec désinvolture, négligemment; fortuitement.

casualty ['kæʒjultɪ] n accidenté/e, blessé/e; (dead) victime f, mort/e.

cat [kæt] n chat m.

catalogue, (US) **catalog** ['kætəlɔg] n catalogue m // vt cataloguer.

catalyst ['kætəlɪst] n catalyseur m.

catapult ['kætəpʌlt] n lance-pierres m inv, fronde m; (HISTORY) catapulte f.

catarrh [kə'tɑː*] n rhume m chronique, catarrhe f.

catastrophe [kə'tæstrəfɪ] n catastrophe f.

catch [kætʃ] vb (pt, pp caught) vt (ball, train, thief, cold) attraper; (person: by surprise) prendre, surprendre; (understand) saisir; (get entangled) accrocher // vi (fire) prendre // n (fish etc caught) prise f; (thief etc caught) capture f; (trick) attrape f; (TECH) loquet m; cliquet m; **to ~ sb's attention** or **eye** attirer l'attention de qn; **to ~ fire** prendre feu; **to ~ sight of** apercevoir; **to ~ on** vi saisir; (grow popular) prendre; **to ~ up** vi se rattraper, combler son retard // vt (also: ~ up with) rattraper.

catching ['kætʃɪŋ] a (MED) contagieux(euse).

catchment area ['kætʃmənt-] n (Brit SCOL) aire f de recrutement; (GEO) bassin m hydrographique.

catch phrase n slogan m; expression toute faite.

catchy ['kætʃɪ] a (tune) facile à retenir.

category ['kætɪgərɪ] n catégorie f.

cater ['keɪtə*] vi (provide food): **to ~ (for)** préparer des repas (pour), se charger de la restauration (pour); **to ~ for** vt fus (Brit: needs) satisfaire, pourvoir à; (: readers, consumers) s'adresser à, pourvoir aux besoins de; **~er** n traiteur m; fournisseur m; **~ing** n restauration f; approvisionnement m, ravitaillement m.

caterpillar ['kætəpɪlə*] n chenille f; **~ track** n chenille f.

cathedral [kə'θiːdrəl] n cathédrale f.

catholic ['kæθəlɪk] a éclectique; universel(le); libéral(e); **C~** a, n (REL) catholique (m/f).

cat's-eye [kæts'aɪ] n (Brit AUT) (clou m à) catadioptre m.

cattle ['kætl] *npl* bétail *m*, bestiaux *mpl*.

catty ['kæti] *a* méchant(e).

caucus ['kɔːkəs] *n* (*POL: group*) comité local d'un parti politique; (: *US*) comité électoral (pour désigner des candidats).

caught [kɔːt] *pt, pp* of **catch**.

cauliflower ['kɔlɪflauə*] *n* chou-fleur *m*.

cause [kɔːz] *n* cause *f* // *vt* causer.

caution ['kɔːʃən] *n* prudence *f*; (*warning*) avertissement *m* // *vt* avertir, donner un avertissement à.

cautious ['kɔːʃəs] *a* prudent(e).

cavalry ['kævəlrɪ] *n* cavalerie *f*.

cave [keɪv] *n* caverne *f*, grotte *f*; **to ~ in** *vi* (*roof etc*) s'effondrer; **~man** *n* homme *m* des cavernes.

caviar(e) ['kævɪɑː*] *n* caviar *m*.

cavort [kə'vɔːt] *vi* cabrioler, faire des cabrioles.

CB *n abbr* (= *Citizens' Band (Radio)*) CB *f*.

CBI *n abbr* (= *Confederation of British Industries*) groupement du patronat.

cc *abbr* = carbon copy, cubic centimetres.

cease [siːs] *vt, vi* cesser; **~fire** *n* cessez-le-feu *m*; **~less** *a* incessant(e), continuel(le).

cedar ['siːdə*] *n* cèdre *m*.

ceiling ['siːlɪŋ] *n* plafond *m*.

celebrate ['sɛlɪbreɪt] *vt, vi* célébrer; **~d** *a* célèbre; **celebration** [-'breɪʃən] *n* célébration *f*.

celery ['sɛlərɪ] *n* céleri *m* (en branches).

cell [sɛl] *n* (*gen*) cellule *f*; (*ELEC*) élément *m* (*de pile*).

cellar ['sɛlə*] *n* cave *f*.

'cello ['tʃɛləu] *n* violoncelle *m*.

Celt [kɛlt, sɛlt] *n* Celte *m/f*.

Celtic ['kɛltɪk, 'sɛltɪk] *a* celte.

cement [sə'mɛnt] *n* ciment *m* // *vt* cimenter; **~ mixer** *n* bétonnière *f*.

cemetery ['sɛmɪtrɪ] *n* cimetière *m*.

censor ['sɛnsə*] *n* censeur *m* // *vt* censurer; **~ship** *n* censure *f*.

censure ['sɛnʃə*] *vt* blâmer, critiquer.

census ['sɛnsəs] *n* recensement *m*.

cent [sɛnt] *n* (*US: coin*) cent *m* (= 1:100 du dollar); *see also* per.

centenary [sɛn'tiːnərɪ] *n* centenaire *m*.

center ['sɛntə*] *n* (*US*) = centre.

centi... ['sɛntɪ] *prefix*: **~grade** *a* centigrade; **~metre**, (*US*) **~meter** *n* centimètre *m*.

centipede ['sɛntɪpiːd] *n* mille-pattes *m inv*.

central ['sɛntrəl] *a* central(e); **C~ America** *n* Amérique centrale; **~ heating** *n* chauffage central.

centre ['sɛntə*] *n* centre *m* // *vt* centrer; (*PHOT*) cadrer; **~forward** *n* (*SPORT*) avant-centre *m*; **~-half** *n* (*SPORT*) demi-centre *m*.

century ['sɛntjʊrɪ] *n* siècle *m*; **20th ~** XXe siècle.

ceramic [sɪ'ræmɪk] *a* céramique.

cereal ['siːrɪəl] *n* céréale *f*.

ceremony ['sɛrɪmənɪ] *n* cérémonie *f*; **to stand on ~** faire des façons.

certain ['sɜːtən] *a* certain(e); **to make ~ of** s'assurer de; **for ~** certainement, sûrement; **~ly** *ad* certainement; **~ty** *n* certitude *f*.

certificate [sə'tɪfɪkɪt] *n* certificat *m*.

certified ['sɜːtɪfaɪd]: **~ mail** *n* (*US*): **by ~ mail** en recommandé, avec avis de réception; **~ public accountant** *n* (*US*) expert-comptable *m*.

cervical ['sɜːvɪkl] *a*: **~ cancer** cancer *m* du col de l'utérus; **~ smear** frottis vaginal.

cervix ['sɜːvɪks] *n* col *m* de l'utérus.

cesspit ['sɛspɪt] *n* fosse *f* d'aisance.

cf. *abbr* (= *compare*) cf., voir.

ch. *abbr* (= *chapter*) chap.

chafe [tʃeɪf] *vt* irriter, frotter contre.

chaffinch ['tʃæfɪntʃ] *n* pinson *m*.

chain [tʃeɪn] *n* (*gen*) chaîne *f* // *vt* (*also: ~ up*) enchaîner, attacher (avec une chaîne); **~ reaction** *n* réaction *f* en chaîne; **to ~ smoke** *vi* fumer cigarette sur cigarette; **~ store** *n* magasin *m* à succursales multiples.

chair [tʃɛə*] *n* chaise *f*; (*armchair*) fauteuil *m*; (*of university*) chaire *f* // *vt* (*meeting*) présider; **~lift** *n* télésiège *m*; **~man** *n* président *m*.

chalice ['tʃælɪs] *n* calice *m*.

chalk [tʃɔːk] *n* craie *f*.

challenge ['tʃælɪndʒ] *n* défi *m* // *vt* défier; (*statement, right*) mettre en question, contester; **to ~ sb to do** mettre qn au défi de faire; **challenging** *a* de défi, provocateur(trice).

chamber ['tʃeɪmbə*] *n* chambre *f*; **~ of commerce** chambre de commerce; **~maid** *n* femme *f* de chambre; **~ music** *n* musique *f* de chambre.

champagne [ʃæm'peɪn] *n* champagne *m*.

champion ['tʃæmpɪən] *n* champion/ne; **~ship** *n* championnat *m*.

chance [tʃɑːns] *n* hasard *m*; (*opportunity*) occasion *f*, possibilité *f*; (*hope, likelihood*) chance *f* // *vt*: **to ~ it** risquer (le coup), essayer // *a* fortuit(e), de hasard; **to take a ~** prendre un risque; **by ~** par hasard.

chancellor ['tʃɑːnsələ*] *n* chancelier *m*; **C~ of the Exchequer** *n* (*Brit*) chancelier de l'Échiquier.

chandelier [ʃændə'lɪə*] *n* lustre *m*.

change [tʃeɪndʒ] *vt* (*alter, replace, COMM: money*) changer; (*switch, substitute: gear, hands, trains, clothes, one's name etc*) changer de; (*transform*): **to ~ sb into** changer *or* transformer qn en // *vi* (*gen*) changer; (*change clothes*) se changer; (*be transformed*): **to ~ into** se changer *or* transformer en // *n* changement *m*; (*money*) monnaie *f*; **to ~ one's mind** changer d'avis; **a ~ of clothes** des vêtements de rechange; **for a ~** pour changer; **~able** *a* (*weather*) variable; **~ machine** *n* distributeur *m* de monnaie; **~over** *n* (*to new system*) changement *m*, passage *m*.

changing ['tʃeɪndʒɪŋ] *a* changeant(e); **~ room** *n* (*Brit: in shop*) salon *m* d'essayage; (: *SPORT*) vestiaire *m*.

channel ['tʃænl] *n* (*TV*) chaîne *f*; (*waveband, groove, fig: medium*) canal *m*; (*of river, sea*) chenal *m* // *vt* canaliser; **through the usual ~s** en suivant la filière habituelle; **the (English) C~** la Manche, **the C~ Islands** les îles de la Manche, les îles anglo-normandes.

chant [tʃɑːnt] *n* chant *m*; mélopée *f*; psalmodie *f* // *vt* chanter, scander; psalmodier.

chaos ['keɪɔs] *n* chaos *m*.

chap [tʃæp] *n* (*Brit col: man*) type *m*.

chapel ['tʃæpəl] *n* chapelle *f*.

chaplain ['tʃæplɪn] *n* aumônier *m*.

chapped [tʃæpt] *a* (*skin, lips*) gercé(e).

chapter ['tʃæptə*] *n* chapitre *m*.

char [tʃɑː*] *vt* (*burn*) carboniser // *n* (*Brit*) = charlady.

character ['kærɪktə*] *n* caractère *m*; (*in novel, film*) personnage *m*; (*eccentric*) numéro *m*, phénomène *m*; **~istic** [-'rɪstɪk] *a, n* caractéristique (*f*).

charcoal ['tʃɑːkəul] *n* charbon *m* de bois.

charge [tʃɑːdʒ] *n* accusation *f*; (*LAW*) inculpation *f*; (*cost*) prix (demandé); (*of gun, battery*, *MIL*: *attack*) charge *f* // *vt* (*LAW*): **to ~ sb (with)** inculper qn (de); (*gun, battery*, *MIL*: *enemy*) charger; (*customer, sum*) faire payer // *vi* (*gen with: up, along etc*) foncer; **~s** *npl*: **bank ~s** frais *mpl* de banque; **is there a ~?** doit-on payer?; **to reverse the ~s** (*TEL*) téléphoner en PCV; **to take ~ of** se charger de; **to be in ~ of** être responsable de, s'occuper de; **to ~ an expense (up) to sb** mettre une dépense sur le compte de qn; **~ card** *n* carte *f* de client (*émise par un grand magasin*).

charity ['tʃærɪtɪ] *n* charité *f*; institution *f* charitable *or* de bienfaisance, œuvre *f* (de charité).

charlady ['tʃɑːleɪdɪ] *n* (*Brit*) femme *f* de ménage.

charm [tʃɑːm] *n* charme *m* // *vt* charmer, enchanter; **~ing** *a* charmant(e).

chart [tʃɑːt] *n* tableau *m*, diagramme *m*; graphique *m*; (*map*) carte marine *f* // *vt* dresser *or* établir la carte de.

charter ['tʃɑːtə*] *vt* (*plane*) affréter // *n* (*document*) charte *f*; **~ed accountant** *n* (*Brit*) expert-comptable *m*; **~ flight** *n* charter *m*.

chase [tʃeɪs] *vt* poursuivre, pourchasser // *n* poursuite *f*, chasse *f*.

chasm ['kæzəm] *n* gouffre *m*, abîme *m*.

chat [tʃæt] *vi* (*also*: **have a ~**) bavarder, causer // *n* conversation *f*; **~ show** *n* (*Brit*) entretien télévisé.

chatter ['tʃætə*] *vi* (*person*) bavarder // *n* bavardage *m*; **my teeth are ~ing** je claque des dents; **~box** *n* moulin *m* à paroles.

chatty ['tʃætɪ] *a* (*style*) familier(ère); (*person*) enclin(e) à bavarder.

chauffeur ['ʃəufə*] *n* chauffeur *m* (de maître).

chauvinist ['ʃəuvɪnɪst] *n* (*male ~*) phallocrate *m*; (*nationalist*) chauvin/e.

cheap [tʃiːp] *a* bon marché *inv*, pas cher(chère); (*joke*) facile, d'un goût douteux; (*poor quality*) à bon marché, de qualité médiocre // *ad* à bon marché, pour pas cher; **~en** *vt* rabaisser, déprécier; **~er** *a* moins cher(chère); **~ly** *ad* à bon marché, à bon compte.

cheat [tʃiːt] *vi* tricher // *vt* tromper, duper; (*rob*) escroquer // *n* tricheur/euse; escroc *m*; (*trick*) duperie *f*, tromperie *f*.

check [tʃɛk] *vt* vérifier; (*passport, ticket*) contrôler; (*halt*) enrayer; (*restrain*) maîtriser // *n* vérification *f*; contrôle *m*; (*curb*) frein *m*; (*bill*) addition *f*; (*pattern: gen pl*) carreaux *mpl*; (*US*) = **cheque** // *a* (*also*: **~ed:** *pattern, cloth*) à carreaux; **to ~ in** *vi* (*in hotel*) remplir sa fiche (d'hôtel); (*at airport*) se présenter à l'enregistrement // *vt* (*luggage*) (faire) enregistrer; **to ~ out** *vi* (*in hotel*) régler sa note // *vt* (*luggage*) retirer; **to ~ up** *vi*: **to ~ up (on sth)** vérifier (qch); **to ~ up on sb** se renseigner sur le compte de qn; **~ered** *a* (*US*) = **chequered**; **~ers** *n* (*US*) jeu *m* de dames; **~-in (desk)** *n* enregistrement *m*; **~ing account** *n* (*US*: *current account*) compte courant; **~mate** *n* échec et mat *m*; **~out** *n* caisse *f*; **~point** *n* contrôle *m*; **~room** *n* (*US*: *left-luggage office*) consigne *f*; **~up** *n* (*MED*) examen médical, check-up *m*.

cheek [tʃiːk] *n* joue *f*; (*impudence*) toupet *m*, culot *m*; **~bone** *n* pommette *f*; **~y** *a* effronté(e), culotté(e).

cheep [tʃiːp] *vi* piauler.

cheer [tʃɪə*] *vt* acclamer, applaudir; (*gladden*) réjouir, réconforter // *vi* applaudir // *n* (*gen pl*) acclamations *fpl*, applaudissements *mpl*; bravos *mpl*, hourras *mpl*; **~s!** (à votre) santé!; **to ~ up** *vi* se dérider, reprendre courage // *vt* remonter le moral à *or* de, dérider, égayer; **~ful** *a* gai(e), joyeux(euse).

cheerio ['tʃɪərɪ'əu] *excl* (*Brit*) salut!, au revoir!

cheese [tʃiːz] *n* fromage *m*; **~board** *n* plateau *m* à fromages.

cheetah ['tʃi:tə] n guépard m.

chef [ʃef] n chef (cuisinier).

chemical ['kemɪkəl] a chimique // n produit m chimique.

chemist ['kemɪst] n (Brit: pharmacist) pharmacien/ne; (scientist) chimiste m/f; ~ry n chimie f; ~'s (shop) n (Brit) pharmacie f.

cheque [tʃek] n (Brit) chèque m; ~book n chéquier m, carnet m de chèques; ~ card n carte f (d'identité) bancaire.

chequered ['tʃekəd] a (fig) varié(e).

cherish ['tʃerɪʃ] vt chérir; (hope etc) entretenir.

cherry ['tʃerɪ] n cerise f.

chess [tʃes] n échecs mpl; ~board n échiquier m; ~man n pièce f (de jeu d'échecs).

chest [tʃest] n poitrine f; (box) coffre m, caisse f; ~ of drawers n commode f.

chestnut ['tʃesnʌt] n châtaigne f; (also: ~ tree) châtaignier m.

chew [tʃu:] vt mâcher; ~ing gum n chewing-gum m.

chic [ʃi:k] a chic inv, élégant(e).

chick [tʃɪk] n poussin m; (US col) pépée f.

chicken ['tʃɪkɪn] n poulet m; to ~ out vi (col) se dégonfler; ~pox n varicelle f.

chicory ['tʃɪkərɪ] n (for coffee) chicorée f; (salad) endive f.

chief [tʃi:f] n chef m // a principal(e); ~ executive n directeur général; ~ly ad principalement, surtout.

chiffon ['ʃɪfɔn] n mousseline f de soie.

chilblain ['tʃɪlbleɪn] n engelure f.

child, pl ~ren [tʃaɪld, 'tʃɪldrən] n enfant m/f; ~birth n accouchement m; ~hood n enfance f; ~ish a puéril(e), enfantin(e); ~like a innocent(e), pur(e); ~ minder n (Brit) garde f d'enfants.

Chile ['tʃɪlɪ] n Chili m.

chill [tʃɪl] n froid m; (MED) refroidissement m, coup m de froid // a froid(e), glacial(e) // vt faire frissonner; refroidir; (CULIN) mettre au frais, rafraîchir.

chil(l)i ['tʃɪlɪ] n piment m (rouge).

chilly ['tʃɪlɪ] a froid(e), glacé(e); (sensitive to cold) frileux(euse); to feel ~ avoir froid.

chime [tʃaɪm] n carillon m // vi carillonner, sonner.

chimney ['tʃɪmnɪ] n cheminée f; ~ sweep n ramoneur m.

chimpanzee [tʃɪmpæn'zi:] n chimpanzé m.

chin [tʃɪn] n menton m.

China ['tʃaɪnə] n Chine f.

china ['tʃaɪnə] n porcelaine f; (vaisselle f en) porcelaine.

Chinese [tʃaɪ'ni:z] a chinois(e) // n, pl inv Chinois/e; (LING) chinois m.

chink [tʃɪŋk] n (opening) fente f, fissure f; (noise) tintement m.

chip [tʃɪp] n (gen pl: CULIN) frite f; (: US: also: potato ~) chip m; (of wood) copeau m; (of glass, stone) éclat m; (also: micro~) puce f // vt (cup, plate) ébrécher; to ~ in vi mettre son grain de sel.

chiropodist [kɪ'rɔpədɪst] n (Brit) pédicure m/f.

chirp [tʃə:p] vi pépier, gazouiller.

chisel ['tʃɪzl] n ciseau m.

chit [tʃɪt] n mot m, note f.

chitchat ['tʃɪtʃæt] n bavardage m.

chivalry ['ʃɪvəlrɪ] n chevalerie f; esprit m chevaleresque.

chives [tʃaɪvz] npl ciboulette f, civette f.

chock [tʃɔk] n cale f; ~-a-block, ~-full a plein(e) à craquer.

chocolate ['tʃɔklɪt] n chocolat m.

choice [tʃɔɪs] n choix m // a de choix.

choir ['kwaɪə*] n chœur m, chorale f; ~boy n jeune choriste m.

choke [tʃəuk] vi étouffer // vt étrangler; étouffer; (block) boucher, obstruer // n (AUT) starter m.

choose [tʃu:z], pt chose, pp chosen vt choisir; to ~ to do décider de faire, juger bon de faire.

choosy ['tʃu:zɪ] a: (to be) ~ (faire le) difficile.

chop [tʃɔp] vt (wood) couper (à la hache); (CULIN: also: ~ up) couper (fin), émincer, hacher (en morceaux) // n coup m (de hache, du tranchant de la main); (CULIN) côtelette f; ~s npl (jaws) mâchoires fpl; babines fpl.

chopper ['tʃɔpə*] n (helicopter) hélicoptère m, hélico m.

choppy ['tʃɔpɪ] a (sea) un peu agité(e).

chopsticks ['tʃɔpstɪks] npl baguettes fpl.

chord [kɔ:d] n (MUS) accord m.

chore [tʃɔ:*] n travail m de routine; household ~s travaux mpl du ménage.

chortle ['tʃɔ:tl] vi glousser.

chorus ['kɔ:rəs] n chœur m; (repeated part of song, also fig) refrain m.

chose [tʃəuz] pt of choose.

chosen ['tʃəuzn] pp of choose.

Christ [kraɪst] n Christ m.

christen ['krɪsn] vt baptiser.

Christian ['krɪstɪən] a, n chrétien(ne); ~ity [-'ænɪtɪ] n christianisme m; chrétienté f; ~ name n prénom m.

Christmas ['krɪsməs] n Noël m or f; Merry ~! joyeux Noël!; ~ card n carte f de Noël; ~ Day n le jour de Noël; ~ Eve n la veille de Noël; la nuit de Noël; ~ tree n arbre m de Noël.

chrome [krəum], **chromium** ['krəumɪəm] n chrome m.

chronic ['krɔnɪk] a chronique.

chronicle ['krɔnɪkl] n chronique f.

chronological [krɔnə'lɔdʒɪkəl] a

chronologique.

chrysanthemum [krɪˈsænθəməm] *n* chrysanthème *m*.

chubby [ˈtʃʌbɪ] *a* potelé(e), rondelet(te).

chuck [tʃʌk] *vt* lancer, jeter; **to ~ out** *vt* flanquer dehors *or* à la porte; **to ~ (up)** *vt* (*Brit*) lâcher, plaquer.

chuckle [ˈtʃʌkl] *vi* glousser.

chug [tʃʌg] *vi* faire teuf-teuf; souffler.

chum [tʃʌm] *n* copain/copine.

chunk [tʃʌŋk] *n* gros morceau; (*of bread*) quignon *m*.

church [tʃəːtʃ] *n* église *f*; **~yard** *n* cimetière *m*.

churlish [ˈtʃəːlɪʃ] *a* grossier(ère); hargneux(euse).

churn [tʃəːn] *n* (*for butter*) baratte *f*; (*for transport: also*: milk ~) (grand) bidon à lait; **to ~ out** *vt* débiter.

chute [ʃuːt] *n* glissoire *f*; (*also*: rubbish ~) vide-ordures *m inv*; (*Brit: children's slide*) toboggan *m*.

chutney [ˈtʃʌtnɪ] *n* condiment *m* à base de fruits.

CIA *n abbr* (*US*: = *Central Intelligence Agency*) CIA *f*.

CID *n abbr* (*Brit*: = *Criminal Investigation Department*) ≈ P.J. *f* (= *police judiciaire*).

cider [ˈsaɪdə*] *n* cidre *m*.

cigar [sɪˈgɑː*] *n* cigare *m*.

cigarette [sɪgəˈrɛt] *n* cigarette *f*; **~ case** *n* étui *m* à cigarettes; **~ end** *n* mégot *m*.

cinder [ˈsɪndə*] *n* cendre *f*.

Cinderella [sɪndəˈrɛlə] *n* Cendrillon.

cine [ˈsɪnɪ]: **~-camera** *n* (*Brit*) caméra *f*; **~-film** *n* (*Brit*) film *m*.

cinema [ˈsɪnəmə] *n* cinéma *m*.

cinnamon [ˈsɪnəmən] *n* cannelle *f*.

cipher [ˈsaɪfə*] *n* code secret; (*fig: faceless employee etc*) numéro *m*.

circle [ˈsəːkl] *n* cercle *m*; (*in cinema*) balcon *m* // *vi* faire *or* décrire des cercles // *vt* (*surround*) entourer, encercler; (*move round*) faire le tour de, tourner autour de.

circuit [ˈsəːkɪt] *n* circuit *m*; **~ous** [səːˈkjuːɪtəs] *a* indirect(e), qui fait un détour.

circular [ˈsəːkjulə*] *a*, *n* circulaire (*f*).

circulate [ˈsəːkjulɛɪt] *vi* circuler // *vt* faire circuler; **circulation** [-ˈleɪʃən] *n* circulation *f*; (*of newspaper*) tirage *m*.

circumflex [ˈsəːkəmflɛks] *n* (*also*: ~ accent) accent *m* circonflexe.

circumstances [ˈsəːkəmstənsɪz] *npl* circonstances *fpl*; (*financial condition*) moyens *mpl*, situation financière.

circumvent [səːkəmˈvɛnt] *vt* tourner.

circus [ˈsəːkəs] *n* cirque *m*.

cistern [ˈsɪstən] *n* réservoir *m* (d'eau); (*in toilet*) réservoir de la chasse d'eau.

citizen [ˈsɪtɪzn] *n* (*POL*) citoyen/ne; (*resident*): **the ~s of this town** les

habitants de cette ville; **~ship** *n* citoyenneté *f*.

citrus fruit [ˈsɪtrəs-] *n* agrume *m*.

city [ˈsɪtɪ] *n* ville *f*, cité *f*; **the C~** la Cité de Londres (*centre des affaires*).

civic [ˈsɪvɪk] *a* civique; **~ centre** *n* (*Brit*) centre administratif (municipal).

civil [ˈsɪvɪl] *a* civil(e); poli(e), civil; **~ engineer** *n* ingénieur civil; **~ian** [sɪˈvɪlɪən] *a*, *n* civil(e).

civilization [sɪvɪlaɪˈzeɪʃən] *n* civilisation *f*.

civilized [ˈsɪvɪlaɪzd] *a* civilisé(e); (*fig*) où règnent les bonnes manières, empreint(e) d'une courtoisie de bon ton.

civil: **~ law** *n* code civil; (*study*) droit civil; **~ servant** *n* fonctionnaire *m/f*; **C~ Service** *n* fonction publique, administration *f*; **~ war** *n* guerre civile.

clad [klæd] *a*: **~ (in)** habillé(e) (de).

claim [kleɪm] *vt* revendiquer; demander, prétendre à; déclarer, prétendre // *vi* (*for insurance*) faire une déclaration de sinistre // *n* revendication *f*; demande *f*; prétention *f*, déclaration *f*; (*right*) droit *m*, titre *m*; (*insurance*) ~ déclaration *f* d'indemnisation, déclaration *f* de sinistre; **~ant** *n* (*ADMIN*, *LAW*) requérant/e.

clairvoyant [klɛəˈvɔɪənt] *n* voyant/e, extra-lucide *m/f*.

clam [klæm] *n* palourde *f*.

clamber [ˈklæmbə*] *vi* grimper, se hisser.

clammy [ˈklæmɪ] *a* humide et froid(e) (au toucher), moite.

clamour, (*US*) **clamor** [ˈklæmə*] *vi*: **to ~ for** réclamer à grands cris.

clamp [klæmp] *n* étau *m* à main; agrafe *f*, crampon *m* // *vt* serrer; cramponner; **to ~ down on** *vt fus* sévir contre, prendre des mesures draconiennes à l'égard de.

clan [klæn] *n* clan *m*.

clang [klæŋ] *n* bruit *m* or fracas *m* métallique.

clap [klæp] *vi* applaudir; **~ping** *n* applaudissements *mpl*.

claret [ˈklærət] *n* (vin *m* de) bordeaux *m* (rouge).

clarinet [klærɪˈnɛt] *n* clarinette *f*.

clarity [ˈklærɪtɪ] *n* clarté *f*.

clash [klæʃ] *n* choc *m*; (*fig*) conflit *m* // *vi* se heurter; être *or* entrer en conflit.

clasp [klɑːsp] *n* fermoir *m* // *vt* serrer, étreindre.

class [klɑːs] *n* (*gen*) classe *f* // *vt* classer, classifier.

classic [ˈklæsɪk] *a* classique // *n* (*author, work*) classique *m*; **~al** *a* classique.

classified [ˈklæsɪfaɪd] *a* (*information*) secret(ète); **~ advertisements**, **~ ads** *npl* petites annonces.

classmate [ˈklɑːsmeɪt] *n* camarade *m/f* de classe.

classroom ['klɑ:srum] n (salle f de) classe f.

clatter ['klætə*] n cliquetis m // vi cliqueter.

clause [klɔ:z] n clause f; (LING) proposition f.

claw [klɔ:] n griffe f; (of bird of prey) serre f; (of lobster) pince f; **to ~ at** vt essayer de griffer or déchirer.

clay [kleɪ] n argile f.

clean [kli:n] a propre; (clear, smooth) net(te) // vt nettoyer; **to ~ out** vt nettoyer (à fond); **to ~ up** vt nettoyer; (fig) remettre de l'ordre dans; **~er** n (person) nettoyeur/euse, femme f de ménage; (also: dry **~er**) teinturier/ière; (product) détachant m; **~ing** n nettoyage m; **~liness** ['klɛnlɪnɪs] n propreté f.

cleanse [klɛnz] vt nettoyer; purifier; **~r** n détergent m; (for face) démaquillant m; **cleansing department** n (Brit) service m de voirie.

clean-shaven ['kli:n'ʃeɪvn] a rasé(e) de près.

clear [klɪə*] a clair(e); (road, way) libre, dégagé(e) // vt dégager, déblayer, débarrasser; faire évacuer; (COMM: goods) liquider; (cheque) compenser; (LAW: suspect) innocenter; (obstacle) franchir or sauter sans heurter // vi (weather) s'éclaircir; (fog) se dissiper // ad: **~** of à distance de, à l'écart de; **to ~ the table** débarrasser la table, desservir; **to ~ up** vi s'éclaircir, se dissiper // vt ranger, mettre en ordre; (mystery) éclaircir, résoudre; **~ance** n (removal) déblayage m; (free space) dégagement m; (permission) autorisation f; **~cut** a précis(e), nettement défini(e); **~ing** n (in forest) clairière f; **~ing bank** n (Brit) banque f qui appartient à une chambre de compensation; **~ly** ad clairement; de toute évidence; **~way** n (Brit) route f à stationnement interdit.

cleaver ['kli:və*] n fendoir m, couperet m.

clef [klɛf] n (MUS) clé f.

cleft [klɛft] n (in rock) crevasse f, fissure f.

clench [klɛntʃ] vt serrer.

clergy ['klɜ:dʒɪ] n clergé m; **~man** n ecclésiastique m.

clerical ['klɛrɪkəl] a de bureau, d'employé de bureau; (REL) clérical(e), du clergé.

clerk [klɑ:k, (US) klɜ:rk] n employé/e de bureau; (US: salesman/woman) vendeur/euse.

clever ['klɛvə*] a (mentally) intelligent(e); (deft, crafty) habile, adroit(e); (device, arrangement) ingénieux(euse), astucieux(euse).

click [klɪk] vi faire un bruit sec or un dé-

clic // vt: **to ~ one's tongue** faire claquer sa langue; **to ~ one's heels** claquer des talons.

client ['klaɪənt] n client/e.

cliff [klɪf] n falaise f.

climate ['klaɪmɪt] n climat m.

climax ['klaɪmæks] n apogée m, point culminant; (sexual) orgasme m.

climb [klaɪm] vi grimper, monter // vt gravir, escalader, monter sur // n montée f, escalade f; **~down** n reculade f, dérobade f; **~er** n (also: rock **~er**) grimpeur/euse, varappeur/euse; **~ing** n (also: rock **~ing**) escalade f, varappe f.

clinch [klɪntʃ] vt (deal) conclure, sceller.

cling [klɪŋ], pt, pp **clung** vi: **to ~ (to)** se cramponner (à), s'accrocher (à); (of clothes) coller (à).

clinic ['klɪnɪk] n centre médical.

clink [klɪŋk] vi tinter, cliqueter.

clip [klɪp] n (for hair) barrette f; (also: paper **~**) trombone m; (holding hose etc) collier m or bague f (métallique) de serrage // vt (also: **~ together**: papers) attacher; (hair, nails) couper; (hedge) tailler; **~pers** npl tondeuse f; (also: nail **~pers**) coupe-ongles m inv; **~ping** n (from newspaper) coupure f de journal.

cloak [kləuk] n grande cape // vt (fig) masquer, cacher; **~room** n (for coats etc) vestiaire m; (Brit: W.C.) toilettes fpl.

clock [klɔk] n (large) horloge f; (small) pendule f; **to ~ in** or **on** vi pointer (en arrivant); **to ~ off** or **out** vi pointer (en partant); **~wise** ad dans le sens des aiguilles d'une montre; **~work** n mouvement m (d'horlogerie); rouages mpl, mécanisme m // a mécanique.

clog [klɔg] n sabot m // vt boucher, encrasser // vi se boucher, s'encrasser.

cloister ['klɔɪstə*] n cloître m.

close a, ad and derivatives [kləus] a (near): **~ (to)** près (de), proche (de); (writing, texture) serré(e); (watch) étroit(e), strict(e); (examination) attentif(ive), minutieux(euse); (weather) lourd(e), étouffant(e) // ad près, à proximité; **~ to** prep près de; **~ by**, **~ at hand** a, ad tout(e) près; **a ~ friend** un ami intime; **to have a ~ shave** (fig) l'échapper belle // vb and derivatives [kləuz] vt fermer // vi (shop etc) fermer; (lid, door etc) se fermer; (end) se terminer, se conclure // n (end) conclusion f; **to ~ down** vt, vi fermer (définitivement); **~d** a fermé(e); **~d shop** n organisation f qui n'admet que des travailleurs syndiqués; **~-knit** a (family, community) très uni(e); **~ly** ad (examine, watch) de près.

closet ['klɔzɪt] n (cupboard) placard m, réduit m.

close-up ['kləusʌp] n gros plan.

closure ['kləuʒə*] n fermeture f.

clot [klɔt] n (gen: blood ~) caillot m; (col: person) ballot m // vi (blood) former des caillots; (: external bleeding) se coaguler.

cloth [klɔθ] n (material) tissu m, étoffe f; (also: tea~) torchon m; lavette f.

clothe [kləuð] vt habiller, vêtir; ~s npl vêtements mpl, habits mpl; ~s brush n brosse f à habits; ~s line n corde f (à linge); ~s peg, (US) ~s pin n pince f à linge.

clothing ['kləuðiŋ] n =clothes.

cloud [klaud] n nuage m; ~y a nuageux(euse), couvert(e); (liquid) trouble.

clout [klaut] vt flanquer une taloche à.

clove [kləuv] n clou m de girofle; ~ of garlic gousse f d'ail.

clover ['kləuvə*] n trèfle m.

clown [klaun] n clown m // vi (also: ~ about, ~ around) faire le clown.

cloying ['klɔiiŋ] a (taste, smell) écœurant(e).

club [klʌb] n (society) club m; (weapon) massue f, matraque f; (also: golf ~) club // vt matraquer // vi: to ~ together s'associer; ~s npl (CARDS) trèfle m; ~ car n (US RAIL) wagon-restaurant m; ~house n pavillon m.

cluck [klʌk] vi glousser.

clue [klu:] n indice m; (in crosswords) définition f; I haven't a ~ je n'en ai pas la moindre idée.

clump [klʌmp] n: ~ of trees bouquet m d'arbres.

clumsy ['klʌmzɪ] a (person) gauche, maladroit(e); (object) malcommode, peu maniable.

clung [klʌŋ] pt, pp of cling.

cluster ['klʌstə*] n (petit) groupe // vi se rassembler.

clutch [klʌtʃ] n (grip, grasp) étreinte f, prise f; (AUT) embrayage m // vt agripper, serrer fort; to ~ at se cramponner à.

clutter ['klʌtə*] vt encombrer.

CND abbr = Campaign for Nuclear Disarmament.

Co. abbr of county, company.

c/o abbr (= care of) c/o, aux bons soins de.

coach [kəutʃ] n (bus) autocar m; (horse-drawn) diligence f; (of train) voiture f, wagon m; (SPORT: trainer) entraîneur/euse // vt entraîner; ~ trip n excursion f en car.

coal [kəul] n charbon m; ~ face n front m de taille; ~field n bassin houiller.

coalition [kəuə'lɪʃən] n coalition f.

coalman, coal merchant ['kəulmən, 'kəulmə:tʃənt] n charbonnier m, marchand m de charbon.

coalmine ['kəulmaɪn] n mine f de charbon.

coarse [kɔ:s] a grossier(ère), rude.

coast [kəust] n côte f // vi (with cycle etc) descendre en roue libre; ~al a côtier(ère); ~guard n garde-côte m; ~line n côte f, littoral m.

coat [kəut] n manteau m; (of animal) pelage m, poil m; (of paint) couche f // vt couvrir, enduire; ~ of arms n blason m, armoiries fpl; ~ hanger n cintre m; ~ing n couche f, enduit m.

coax [kəuks] vt persuader par des cajoleries.

cob [kɔb] n see corn.

cobbler ['kɔblə*] n cordonnier m.

cobbles, cobblestones ['kɔblz, 'kɔblstəunz] npl pavés (ronds).

cobweb ['kɔbwɛb] n toile f d'araignée.

cocaine [kə'keɪn] n cocaïne f.

cock [kɔk] n (rooster) coq m; (male bird) mâle m // vt (gun) armer; ~erel n jeune coq m; ~-eyed a (fig) de travers; qui louche; qui ne tient pas debout (fig).

cockle ['kɔkl] n coque f.

cockney ['kɔknɪ] n cockney m/f (habitant des quartiers populaires de l'East End de Londres), ≈ faubourien/ne.

cockpit ['kɔkpɪt] n (in aircraft) poste m de pilotage, cockpit m.

cockroach ['kɔkrəutʃ] n cafard m.

cocktail ['kɔkteɪl] n cocktail m; ~ cabinet n (meuble-)bar m; ~ party n cocktail m.

cocoa ['kəukəu] n cacao m.

coconut ['kəukənʌt] n noix f de coco.

cod [kɔd] n morue (fraîche), cabillaud m.

C.O.D. abbr of cash on delivery.

code [kəud] n code m.

cod-liver oil n huile f de foie de morue.

coercion [kəu'ə:ʃən] n contrainte f.

coffee ['kɔfi] n café m; ~ bar n (Brit) café m; ~ break n pause-café f; ~pot n cafetière f; ~ table n (petite) table basse.

coffin ['kɔfɪn] n cercueil m.

cog [kɔg] n dent f d'engrenage.

cogent ['kəudʒənt] a puissant(e), convaincant(e).

coil [kɔil] n rouleau m, bobine f; (one loop) anneau m, spire f; (contraceptive) stérilet m // vt enrouler.

coin [kɔin] n pièce f de monnaie // vt (word) inventer; ~age n monnaie f, système m monétaire; ~-box n (Brit) cabine f téléphonique.

coincide [kəuin'said] vi coïncider; ~nce [kəu'insidəns] n coïncidence f.

coke [kəuk] n coke m.

colander ['kɔləndə*] n passoire f (à légumes).

cold [kəuld] a froid(e) // n froid m; (MED) rhume m; it's ~ il fait froid; to be ~ avoir froid; to catch ~ prendre or attraper froid; to catch a ~ attraper un rhume; in ~ blood de sang-froid; ~ sore n bouton m de fièvre.

coleslaw ['kəulslɔ:] n sorte de salade de chou cru.

colic ['kɔlık] n colique(s) f(pl).

collapse [kə'læps] vi s'effondrer, s'écrouler // n effondrement m, écroulement m.

collapsible [kə'læpsəbl] a pliant(e); télescopique.

collar ['kɔlə*] n (of coat, shirt) col m; ~**bone** n clavicule f.

collateral [kə'lætərl] n nantissement m.

colleague ['kɔli:g] n collègue m/f.

collect [kə'lɛkt] vt rassembler; ramasser; (as a hobby) collectionner; (Brit: call and pick up) (passer) prendre; (mail) faire la levée de, ramasser; (money owed) encaisser; (donations, subscriptions) recueillir // vi se rassembler; s'amasser; **to call ~** (US TEL) téléphoner en PCV; ~**ion** [kə'lɛkʃən] n collection f; levée f; (for money) collecte f, quête f.

collector [kə'lɛktə*] n collectionneur m; (of taxes) percepteur m.

college ['kɔlıdʒ] n collège m.

collide [kə'laɪd] vi: **to ~ (with)** entrer en collision (avec).

collie ['kɔlı] n (dog) colley m.

colliery ['kɔlıərı] n mine f de charbon, houillère f.

collision [kə'lıʒən] n collision f, heurt m.

colloquial [kə'ləukwıəl] a familier(ère).

colon ['kəulən] n (sign) deux-points mpl; (MED) côlon m.

colonel ['kɔ:nl] n colonel m.

colonial [kə'ləunıəl] a colonial(e).

colony ['kɔlənı] n colonie f.

colour, (US) **color** ['kʌlə*] n couleur f // vt colorer; peindre; (with crayons) colorier; (news) fausser, exagérer // vi (blush) rougir; ~**s** npl (of party, club) couleurs fpl; ~ **bar** n discrimination raciale (dans un établissement etc); ~**blind** a daltonien(ne); ~**ed** a coloré(e); (photo) en couleur // n: ~**eds** personnes fpl de couleur; ~ **film** n (for camera) pellicule f (en) couleur; ~**ful** a coloré(e), vif(vive); (personality) pittoresque, haut(e) en couleurs; ~**ing** n colorant m; (complexion) teint m; ~ **scheme** n combinaison f de(s) couleurs; ~ **television** n télévision f en couleur.

colt [kəult] n poulain m.

column ['kɔləm] n colonne f; ~**ist** ['kɔləmnıst] n rédacteur/trice d'une rubrique.

coma ['kəumə] n coma m.

comb [kəum] n peigne m // vt (hair) peigner; (area) ratisser, passer au peigne fin.

combat ['kɔmbæt] n combat m // vt combattre, lutter contre.

combination [kɔmbı'neıʃən] n (gen) combinaison f.

combine vb [kəm'baın] vt combiner; (one quality with another) joindre (à), allier (à) // vi s'associer; (CHEM) se combiner // n ['kɔmbaın] association f; (ECON) trust m; ~ (**harvester**) n moissonneuse-batteuse(-lieuse) f.

come [kʌm], pt **came**, pp **come** vi venir; arriver; **to ~** (decision etc) parvenir or arriver à; **to ~ undone/loose** se défaire/desserrer; **to ~ about** vi se produire, arriver; **to ~ across** vt fus rencontrer par hasard, tomber sur; **to ~ along** vi = **to come on**; **to ~ away** vi partir, s'en aller; se détacher; **to ~ back** vi revenir; **to ~ by** vt fus (acquire) obtenir, se procurer; **to ~ down** vi descendre; (prices) baisser; (buildings) s'écrouler; être démoli(e); **to ~ forward** vi s'avancer; se présenter, s'annoncer; **to ~ from** vt fus être originaire de; venir de; **to ~ in** vi entrer; **to ~ in for** vt fus (criticism etc) être l'objet de; **to ~ into** vt fus (money) hériter de; **to ~ off** vi (button) se détacher; (stain) s'enlever; (attempt) réussir; **to ~ on** vi (pupil, work, project) faire des progrès, avancer; (lights, electricity) s'allumer; (central heating) se mettre en marche; ~ **on!** viens!; allons!, allez!; **to ~ out** vi sortir; (book) paraître; (strike) cesser le travail, se mettre en grève; **to ~ round** vi (after faint, operation) revenir à soi, reprendre connaissance; **to ~ to** vi revenir à soi; **to ~ up** vi monter; **to ~ up against** vt fus (resistance, difficulties) rencontrer; **to ~ up with** vt fus: he came up with an idea il a eu une idée, il a proposé quelque chose; **to ~ upon** vt fus tomber sur; ~**back** n (THEATRE etc) rentrée f.

comedian [kə'mi:dıən] n (in music hall etc) comique m; (THEATRE) comédien m.

comedown ['kʌmdaun] n déchéance f.

comedy ['kɔmıdı] n comédie f.

comeuppance [kʌm'ʌpəns] n: **to get one's ~** recevoir ce qu'on mérite.

comfort ['kʌmfət] n confort m, bien-être m; (solace) consolation f, réconfort m // vt consoler, réconforter; ~**s** npl aises fpl; ~**able** a confortable; ~**ably** ad (sit) confortablement; (live) à l'aise; ~ **station** n (US) toilettes fpl.

comic ['kɔmık] a (also: ~**al**) comique // n comique m; (magazine) illustré m; ~ **strip** n bande dessinée.

coming ['kʌmıŋ] n arrivée f // a prochain(e), à venir; ~(**s**) **and going(s)** n(pl) va-et-vient m inv.

comma ['kɔmə] n virgule f.

command [kə'mɑ:nd] n ordre m, commandement m; (MIL: authority) commandement m; (mastery) maîtrise f // vt (troops) commander; (be able to get) (pouvoir) disposer de, avoir à sa disposition; (*deserve*) avoir droit à; **~eer** [kɔmən'dɪə*] *vt* réquisitionner (par la force); **~er** *n* chef *m*; (MIL) commandant *m*.

commando [kə'mɑːndəu] *n* commando *m*; membre *m* d'un commando.

commemorate [kə'mɛməreɪt] *vt* commémorer.

commence [kə'mɛns] *vt, vi* commencer.

commend [kə'mɛnd] *vt* louer; recommander.

commensurate [kə'mɛnʃərɪt] *a*: ~ **with** en proportion de, proportionné(e) à.

comment ['kɔmɛnt] *n* commentaire *m* // *vi*: **to ~ (on)** faire des remarques (sur); **~ary** ['kɔməntəri] *n* commentaire *m*; (SPORT) reportage *m* (en direct); **~ator** ['kɔmənt31tə*] *n* commentateur *m*; reporter *m*.

commerce [kɔmə:s] *n* commerce *m*.

commercial [kə'mə:ʃəl] *a* commercial(e) // *n* (TV: *also:* ~ **break**) annonce *f* publicitaire, spot *m* (publicitaire).

commiserate [kə'mɪzəreɪt] *vi*: **to ~ with sb** témoigner de la sympathie pour qn.

commission [kə'mɪʃən] *n* (*committee, fee*) commission *f* // *vt* (MIL) nommer (à un commandement); (*work of art*) commander, charger un artiste de l'exécution de; **out of ~** (NAUT) hors de service; **~aire** [kəmɪʃə'nɛə*] *n* (Brit: *at shop, cinema etc*) portier *m* (en uniforme); **~er** *n* membre *m* d'une commission; (POLICE) préfet *m* (de police).

commit [kə'mɪt] *vt* (*act*) commettre; (*to sb's care*) confier (à); **to ~ o.s. (to do)** s'engager (à faire); **to ~ suicide** se suicider; **~ment** *n* engagement *m*; (*obligation*) responsabilité(s) *f(pl)*.

committee [kə'mɪtɪ] *n* comité *m*.

commodity [kə'mɔdɪtɪ] *n* produit *m*, marchandise *f*, article *m*; (*food*) denrée *f*.

common ['kɔmən] *a* (*gen, also pej*) commun(e); (*usual*) courant(e) // *n* terrain communal; the **C~s** *npl* (Brit) la chambre des Communes; **in ~** en commun; **~er** *n* roturier/ière; ~ **law** *n* droit coutumier; **~ly** *ad* communément, généralement; couramment; **C~ Market** *n* Marché commun; **~place** *a* banal(e), ordinaire; **~room** *n* salle commune; (SCOL) salle des professeurs; ~ **sense** *n* bon sens; **the C~wealth** *n* le Commonwealth.

commotion [kə'məuʃən] *n* désordre *m*, tumulte *m*.

communal ['kɔmjuːnl] *a* (*life*) communautaire; (*for common use*) commun(e).

commune *n* ['kɔmjuːn] (*group*) communauté *f* // *vi* [kə'mjuːn]: **to ~ with** converser intimement avec; communier avec.

communicate [kə'mjuːnɪkeɪt] *vt, vi* communiquer.

communication [kəmjuːnɪ'keɪʃən] *n* communication *f*; ~ **cord** *n* (Brit) sonnette *f* d'alarme.

communion [kə'mjuːnɪən] *n* (*also:* Holy C~) communion *f*.

communism ['kɔmjunɪzəm] *n* communisme *m*; **communist** *a, n* communiste (*m/f*).

community [kə'mjuːnɪtɪ] *n* communauté *f*; ~ **centre** *n* foyer socio-éducatif, centre *m* de loisirs; ~ **chest** *n* (US) fonds commun.

commutation ticket [kɔmju 'teɪʃən-] *n* (US) carte *f* d'abonnement.

commute [kə'mjuːt] *vi* faire le trajet journalier (de son domicile à un lieu de travail assez éloigné) // *vt* (LAW) commuer; **~r** *n* banlieusard/e (qui ... *see vi*).

compact *a* [kəm'pækt] compact(e) // *n* ['kɔmpækt] (*also:* **powder** ~) poudrier *m*; ~ **disk** *n* disque compact.

companion [kəm'pænɪən] *n* compagnon/compagne; **~ship** *n* camaraderie *f*.

company ['kʌmpənɪ] *n* (*also* COMM, MIL, THEATRE) compagnie *f*; **to keep sb** ~ tenir compagnie à qn; ~ **secretary** *n* (COMM) secrétaire général (*d'une société*).

comparative [kəm'pærətɪv] *a* comparatif(ive); (*relative*) relatif(ive); **~ly** *ad* (*relatively*) relativement.

compare [kəm'pɛə*] *vt*: **to ~ sth/sb with/to** comparer qch/qn avec *or* et/à // *vi*: **to ~ (with)** se comparer (à); être comparable (à); **comparison** [-'pærɪsn] *n* comparaison *f*.

compartment [kəm'pɑːtmənt] *n* (*also* RAIL) compartiment *m*.

compass ['kʌmpəs] *n* boussole *f*; **~es** *npl* compas *m*.

compassion [kəm'pæʃən] *n* compassion *f*, humanité *f*.

compatible [kəm'pætɪbl] *a* compatible.

compel [kəm'pɛl] *vt* contraindre, obliger; **~ling** *a* (*fig: argument*) irrésistible.

compendium [kəm'pɛndɪəm] *n* abrégé *m*.

compensate ['kɔmpənseɪt] *vt* indemniser, dédommager // *vi*: **to ~ for** compenser; **compensation** [-'seɪʃən] *n* compensation *f*; (*money*) dédommagement *m*, indemnité *f*.

compete [kəm'piːt] *vi* (*take part*) concourir; (*vie*): **to ~ (with)** rivaliser (avec), faire concurrence (à).

competence ['kɔmpɪtəns] *n* compétence *f*, aptitude *f*.

competent ['kɔmpɪtənt] *a* compétent(e), capable.

competition [kɔmpɪ'tɪʃən] n compétition f, concours m; (ECON) concurrence f.

competitive [kəm'petɪtɪv] a (ECON) concurrentiel(le); (sport) de compétition.

competitor [kəm'petɪtə*] n concurrent/e.

complacency [kəm'pleɪsnsɪ] n contentement m de soi, vaine complaisance.

complain [kəm'pleɪn] vi: to ~ (about) se plaindre (de); (in shop etc) réclamer (au sujet de); ~t n plainte f; réclamation f; (MED) affection f.

complement ['kɔmplɪmənt] n complément m; (especially of ship's crew etc) effectif complet // ['kɔmplɪment] vt (enhance) compléter; ~ary [kɔmplɪ'mentərɪ] a complémentaire.

complete [kəm'pli:t] a complet(ète) // vt achever, parachever; (a form) remplir; ~ly ad complètement; **completion** n achèvement m.

complex ['kɔmpleks] a, n complexe (m).

complexion [kəm'plekʃən] n (of face) teint m; (of event etc) aspect m, caractère m.

compliance [kəm'plaɪəns] n (submission) docilité f; (agreement): ~ with le fait de se conformer à.

complicate ['kɔmplɪkeɪt] vt compliquer; ~d a compliqué(e); **complication** [-'keɪʃən] n complication f.

compliment n ['kɔmplɪmənt] compliment m // vt ['kɔmplɪment] complimenter; ~s npl compliments mpl, hommages mpl; vœux mpl; to pay sb a ~ faire or adresser un compliment à qn; ~ary [-'mentərɪ] a flatteur(euse); (free) à titre gracieux; ~ary ticket n billet m de faveur.

comply [kəm'plaɪ] vi: to ~ with se soumettre à, se conformer à.

component [kəm'pəunənt] n composant m, élément m.

compose [kəm'pəuz] vt composer; to ~ o.s. se calmer, se maîtriser; prendre une contenance; ~d a calme, posé(e); ~r n (MUS) compositeur m.

composition [kɔmpə'zɪʃən] n composition f.

composure [kəm'pəuʒə*] n calme m, maîtrise f de soi.

compound ['kɔmpaund] n (CHEM, LING) composé m; (enclosure) enclos m, enceinte f // a composé(e); ~ **fracture** n fracture compliquée.

comprehend [kɔmprɪ'hend] vt comprendre; **comprehension** [-'henʃən] n compréhension f.

comprehensive [kɔmprɪ'hensɪv] a (très) complet(ète); ~ **policy** n

(INSURANCE) assurance f tous risques; ~ (school) n (Brit) école secondaire non sélective avec libre circulation d'une section à l'autre, ≈ C.E.S. m.

compress vt [kəm'pres] comprimer // n ['kɔmpres] (MED) compresse f.

comprise [kəm'praɪz] vt (also: be ~d of) comprendre.

compromise ['kɔmprəmaɪz] n compromis m // vt compromettre // vi transiger, accepter un compromis.

compulsion [kəm'pʌlʃən] n contrainte f, force f.

compulsive [kəm'pʌlsɪv] a (PSYCH) compulsif(ive).

compulsory [kəm'pʌlsərɪ] a obligatoire.

computer [kəm'pju:tə*] n ordinateur m; (mechanical) calculatrice f; ~ize vt traiter or automatiser par ordinateur; ~ **programmer** n programmeur/euse; ~ **programming** n programmation f; ~ **science, computing** n informatique f.

comrade ['kɔmrɪd] n camarade m/f.

con [kɔn] vt duper; escroquer // n escroquerie f.

conceal [kən'si:l] vt cacher, dissimuler.

conceit [kən'si:t] n vanité f, suffisance f, prétention f; ~ed a vaniteux(euse), suffisant(e).

conceive [kən'si:v] vt, vi concevoir.

concentrate ['kɔnsəntreɪt] vi se concentrer // vt concentrer.

concentration [kɔnsən'treɪʃən] n concentration f; ~ **camp** n camp m de concentration.

concept ['kɔnsept] n concept m.

concern [kən'sɜ:n] n affaire f; (COMM) entreprise f, firme f; (anxiety) inquiétude f, souci m // vt concerner; to be ~ed (about) s'inquiéter (de), être inquiet (au sujet de); ~ing prep en ce qui concerne, à propos de.

concert ['kɔnsət] n concert m; ~ed [kən'sɜ:tɪd] a concerté(e); ~ **hall** n salle f de concert.

concertina [kɔnsə'ti:nə] n concertina m // vi se télescoper, se caramboler.

concerto [kən'tʃɜ:təu] n concerto m.

conclude [kən'klu:d] vt conclure; **conclusion** [-'klu:ʒən] n conclusion f; **conclusive** [-'klu:sɪv] a concluant(e), définitif(ive).

concoct [kən'kɔkt] vt confectionner, composer; ~ion [-'kɔkʃən] n mélange m.

concourse ['kɔnkɔ:s] n (hall) hall m, salle f des pas perdus.

concrete ['kɔnkri:t] n béton m // a concret(ète); en béton.

concur [kən'kɜ:*] vi être d'accord.

concurrently [kən'kʌrntlɪ] ad simultanément.

concussion [kən'kʌʃən] n (MED) commotion (cérébrale).

condemn [kən'dem] vt condamner.

condensation [kɔndɛn'seɪʃən] n condensation f.

condense [kən'dɛns] vi se condenser // vt condenser; **~d milk** n lait concentré (sucré).

condition [kən'dɪʃən] n condition f // vt déterminer, conditionner; **on ~ that** à condition que + sub, à condition de; **~al** a conditionnel(le); **~er** n (for hair) baume démêlant.

condolences [kən'dəulənsɪz] npl condoléances fpl.

condom ['kɔndəm] n préservatif m.

condominium [kɔndə'mɪnɪəm] n (US: building) immeuble m (en copropriété); (: rooms) appartement m (dans un immeuble en copropriété).

condone [kən'dəun] vt fermer les yeux sur, approuver (tacitement).

conducive [kən'dju:sɪv] a: **~ to** favorable à, qui contribue à.

conduct n ['kɔndʌkt] conduite f // vt [kən'dʌkt] conduire; (manage) mener, diriger; (MUS) diriger; **to ~ o.s.** se conduire, se comporter; **~ed tour** n voyage organisé; visite guidée; **~or** n (of orchestra) chef m d'orchestre; (on bus) receveur m; (US: on train) chef m de train; (ELEC) conducteur m; **~ress** n (on bus) receveuse f.

cone [kəun] n cône m; (for ice-cream) cornet m; (BOT) pomme f de pin, cône.

confectioner [kən'fɛkʃənə*] n (of cakes) pâtissier/ière; (of sweets) confiseur/euse; **~'s (shop)** n confiserie(-pâtisserie); **~y** n pâtisserie f; confiserie f.

confer [kən'fə:*] vt: **to ~ sth on** conférer qch à // vi conférer, s'entretenir.

conference ['kɔnfərns] n conférence f.

confess [kən'fɛs] vt confesser, avouer // vi se confesser; **~ion** [-'fɛʃən] n confession f.

confetti [kən'fɛtɪ] n confettis mpl.

confide [kən'faɪd] vi: **to ~ in** s'ouvrir à, se confier à.

confidence ['kɔnfɪdns] n confiance f; (also: self-~) assurance f, confiance en soi; (secret) confidence f; **in ~** (speak, write) en confidence, confidentiellement; **~ trick** n escroquerie f; **confident** a sûr(e), assuré(e); **confidential** [kɔnfɪ-'dɛnʃəl] a confidentiel(le).

confine [kən'faɪn] vt limiter, borner; (shut up) confiner, enfermer; **~s** ['kɔnfaɪnz] npl confins mpl, bornes fpl; **~d** a (space) restreint(e), réduit(e); **~ment** n emprisonnement m, détention f; (MIL) consigne f (au quartier); (MED) accouchement m.

confirm [kən'fə:m] vt (report, REL) confirmer; (appointment) ratifier; **~ation** [kɔnfə'meɪʃən] n confirmation f; **~ed** a invétéré(e), incorrigible.

confiscate ['kɔnfɪskeɪt] vt confisquer.

conflict n ['kɔnflɪkt] conflit m, lutte f // vi [kən'flɪkt] être or entrer en conflit; (opinions) s'opposer, se heurter; **~ing** a contradictoire.

conform [kən'fɔ:m] vi: **to ~ (to)** se conformer (à).

confound [kən'faund] vt confondre.

confront [kən'frʌnt] vt confronter, mettre en présence; (enemy, danger) affronter, faire face à; **~ation** [kɔnfrən-'teɪʃən] n confrontation f.

confuse [kən'fju:z] vt embrouiller; (one thing with another) confondre; **~d** a (person) dérouté(e), désorienté(e); **confusing** a peu clair(e), déroutant(e); **confusion** [-'fju:ʒən] n confusion f.

congeal [kən'dʒi:l] vi (blood) se coaguler.

congenial [kən'dʒi:nɪəl] a sympathique, agréable.

congested [kən'dʒɛstɪd] a (MED) congestionné(e); (fig) surpeuplé(e); congestionné, bloqué(e).

congestion [kən'dʒɛstʃən] n congestion f; (fig) encombrement m.

congratulate [kən'grætjuleɪt] vt: **to ~ sb (on)** féliciter qn (de); **congratulations** [-'leɪʃənz] npl félicitations fpl.

congregate ['kɔngrɪgeɪt] vi se rassembler, se réunir.

congregation [kɔngrɪ'geɪʃən] n assemblée f (des fidèles).

congress ['kɔngres] n congrès m; **~man** n (US) membre m du Congrès.

conjunction [kən'dʒʌŋkʃən] n conjonction f.

conjunctivitis [kəndʒʌŋktɪ'vaɪtɪs] n conjonctivite f.

conjure ['kʌndʒə*] vt faire apparaître (par la prestidigitation) // vi faire des tours de passe-passe; **to ~ up** vt (ghost, spirit) faire apparaître; (memories) évoquer; **~r** n prestidigitateur m, illusionniste m/f.

conk out [kɔŋk-] vi (col) tomber or rester en panne.

conman ['kɔnmæn] n escroc m.

connect [kə'nɛkt] vt joindre, relier; (ELEC) connecter; (fig) établir un rapport entre, faire un rapprochement entre // vi (train): **to ~ with** assurer la correspondance avec; **to be ~ed with** avoir un rapport avec; avoir des rapports avec, être en relation avec; (related) être allié(e) à, être parent(e) de; **~ion** [-ʃən] n relation f, lien m; (ELEC) connexion f; (TEL) communication f; **in ~ion with** à propos de.

connive [kə'naɪv] vi: **to ~ at** se faire le complice de.

conquer ['kɔŋkə*] vt conquérir; (feelings) vaincre, surmonter.

conquest ['kɔŋkwɛst] n conquête f.

cons [kɔnz] npl see **convenience, pro.**

conscience ['kɔnʃəns] n conscience f.

conscientious [kɔnʃɪˈɛnʃəs] *a* consciencieux(euse); *(scruple, objection)* de conscience.

conscious [ˈkɔnʃəs] *a* conscient(e); **~ness** *n* conscience *f*; *(MED)* connaissance *f*.

conscript [ˈkɔnskrɪpt] *n* conscrit *m*.

consent [kənˈsɛnt] *n* consentement *m* // *vi*: **to ~ (to)** consentir (à).

consequence [ˈkɔnsɪkwəns] *n* suites *fpl*, conséquence *f*; importance *f*.

consequently [ˈkɔnsɪkwəntlɪ] *ad* par conséquent, donc.

conservation [kɔnsəˈveɪʃən] *n* préservation *f*, protection *f*.

conservative [kənˈsəːvətɪv] *a* conservateur(trice); *(cautious)* prudent(e); **C~** *a, n* (*Brit POL*) conservateur(trice).

conservatory [kənˈsəːvətrɪ] *n* *(greenhouse)* serre *f*.

conserve [kənˈsəːv] *vt* conserver, préserver; *(supplies, energy)* économiser // *n* confiture *f*, conserve *f* (de fruits).

consider [kənˈsɪdə*] *vt* considérer, réfléchir à; *(take into account)* penser à, prendre en considération; *(regard, judge)* considérer, estimer; **to ~ doing sth** envisager de faire qch.

considerable [kənˈsɪdərəbl] *a* considérable; **considerably** *ad* nettement.

considerate [kənˈsɪdərɪt] *a* prévenant(e), plein(e) d'égards.

consideration [kənsɪdəˈreɪʃən] *n* considération *f*; *(reward)* rétribution *f*, rémunération *f*.

considering [kənˈsɪdərɪŋ] *prep* étant donné.

consign [kənˈsaɪn] *vt* expédier, livrer; **~ment** *n* arrivage *m*, envoi *m*.

consist [kənˈsɪst] *vi*: **to ~ of** consister en, se composer de.

consistency [kənˈsɪstənsɪ] *n* consistance *f*; *(fig)* cohérence *f*.

consistent [kənˈsɪstənt] *a* logique, cohérent(e); **~ with** compatible avec, en accord avec.

consolation [kɔnsəˈleɪʃən] *n* consolation *f*.

consonant [ˈkɔnsənənt] *n* consonne *f*.

conspicuous [kənˈspɪkjuəs] *a* voyant(e), qui attire la vue *or* l'attention.

conspiracy [kənˈspɪrəsɪ] *n* conspiration *f*, complot *m*.

constable [ˈkʌnstəbl] *n* (*Brit*) ≈ agent *m* de police, gendarme *m*; **chief ~** ≈ préfet *m* de police.

constabulary [kənˈstæbjulərɪ] *n* ≈ police *f*, gendarmerie *f*.

constant [ˈkɔnstənt] *a* constant(e); incessant(e); **~ly** *ad* constamment, sans cesse.

constipated [ˈkɔnstɪpeɪtɪd] *a* constipé(e).

constipation [kɔnstɪˈpeɪʃən] *n* constipation *f*.

constituency [kənˈstɪtjuənsɪ] *n* circonscription électorale.

constituent [kənˈstɪtjuənt] *n* électeur/trice; *(part)* élément constitutif, composant *m*.

constitution [kɔnstɪˈtjuːʃən] *n* constitution *f*; **~al** *a* constitutionnel(le).

constraint [kənˈstreɪnt] *n* contrainte *f*.

construct [kənˈstrʌkt] *vt* construire; **~ion** [-ʃən] *n* construction *f*; **~ive** *a* constructif(ive).

construe [kənˈstruː] *vt* analyser, expliquer.

consul [ˈkɔnsl] *n* consul *m*; **~ate** [ˈkɔnsjulɪt] *n* consulat *m*.

consult [kənˈsʌlt] *vt* consulter // *vi* consulter; se consulter; **~ant** *n* (*MED*) médecin consultant; *(other specialist)* consultant *m*, (expert-)conseil *m*; **~ing room** *n* (*Brit MED*) cabinet *m* de consultation.

consume [kənˈsjuːm] *vt* consommer; **~r** *n* consommateur/trice; **~r goods** *npl* biens *mpl* de consommation; **~r society** *n* société *f* de consommation.

consummate [ˈkɔnsʌmeɪt] *vt* consommer.

consumption [kənˈsʌmpʃən] *n* consommation *f*; *(MED)* consomption *f* (pulmonaire).

cont. *abbr* = **continued**.

contact [ˈkɔntækt] *n* contact *m*; *(person)* connaissance *f*, relation *f* // *vt* se mettre en contact *or* en rapport avec; **~ lenses** *npl* verres *mpl* de contact.

contagious [kənˈteɪdʒəs] *a* contagieux(euse).

contain [kənˈteɪn] *vt* contenir; **to ~ o.s.** se contenir, se maîtriser; **~er** *n* récipient *m*; *(for shipping etc)* container *m*.

contaminate [kənˈtæmɪneɪt] *vt* contaminer.

cont'd *abbr* = **continued**.

contemplate [ˈkɔntəmpleɪt] *vt* contempler; *(consider)* envisager.

contemporary [kənˈtɛmpərərɪ] *a* contemporain(e); *(design, wallpaper)* moderne // *n* contemporain/e.

contempt [kənˈtɛmpt] *n* mépris *m*, dédain *m*; **~ of court** (*LAW*) outrage *m* à l'autorité de la justice; **~uous** *a* dédaigneux(euse), méprisant(e).

contend [kənˈtɛnd] *vt*: **to ~ that** soutenir *or* prétendre que // *vi*: **to ~ with** rivaliser avec, lutter avec; **~er** *n* prétendant/e; adversaire *m/f*.

content [kənˈtɛnt] *a* content(e), satisfait(e) // *vt* contenter, satisfaire // *n* [ˈkɔntɛnt] contenu *m*; teneur *f*; **~s** *npl* contenu; **(table of) ~s** table *f* des matières; **~ed** *a* content(e), satisfait(e).

contention [kənˈtɛnʃən] *n* dispute *f*,

contestation f; (*argument*) assertion f, affirmation f.

contest n ['kɔntest] combat m, lutte f; (*competition*) concours m // vt [kən'test] contester, discuter; (*compete for*) disputer; **~ant** [kən'testənt] n concurrent/e; (*in fight*) adversaire m/f.

context ['kɔntekst] n contexte m.

continent ['kɔntɪnənt] n continent m; **the C~** (*Brit*) l'Europe continentale; **~al** [-'nentl] a continental(e) // n Européen/ne (continental(e)); **~al quilt** n (*Brit*) couette f.

contingency [kən'tɪndʒənsɪ] n éventualité f, événement imprévu; **~ plan** n plan m d'urgence.

continual [kən'tɪnjuəl] a continuel(le).

continuation [kəntɪnju'eɪʃən] n continuation f; (*after interruption*) reprise f; (*of story*) suite f.

continue [kən'tɪnju:] vi continuer // vt continuer; (*start again*) reprendre.

continuous [kən'tɪnjuəs] a continu(e), permanent(e); **~ stationery** n papier m en continu.

contort [kən'tɔ:t] vt tordre, crisper.

contour ['kɔntuə*] n contour m, profil m; (*also:* **~ line**) courbe f de niveau.

contraband ['kɔntrəbænd] n contrebande f.

contraceptive [kɔntrə'septɪv] a contraceptif(ive), anticonceptionnel(le) // n contraceptif m.

contract n ['kɔntrækt] contrat m // vb [kən'trækt] vi (*become smaller*) se contracter, se resserrer; (*COMM*): **to ~ to do sth** s'engager (par contrat) à faire qch; **~ion** [-ʃən] n contraction f; **~or** n entrepreneur m.

contradict [kɔntrə'dɪkt] vt contredire; (*be contrary to*) démentir, être en contradiction avec.

contraption [kən'træpʃən] n (*pej*) machin m, truc m.

contrary ['kɔntrərɪ] a contraire, opposé(e); [kən'treərɪ] (*perverse*) contrariant(e), entêté(e) // n contraire m; **on the ~** au contraire; **unless you hear to the ~** sauf avis contraire.

contrast n ['kɔntrɑ:st] contraste m // vt [kən'trɑ:st] mettre en contraste, contraster.

contribute [kən'trɪbju:t] vi contribuer // vt: **to ~ £10/an article to** donner 10 livres/un article à; **to ~ to** (*gen*) contribuer à; (*newspaper*) collaborer à; **contribution** [kɔntrɪ'bju:ʃən] n contribution f; **contributor** n (*to newspaper*) collaborateur/trice.

contrive [kən'traɪv] vt combiner, inventer // vi: **to ~ to do** s'arranger pour faire, trouver le moyen de faire.

control [kən'trəul] vt maîtriser; (*check*) contrôler // n contrôle m, autorité f; maîtrise f; **~s** npl commandes fpl; **every-**

thing is under **~** tout va bien, j'ai (*or* il a *etc*) la situation en main; **to be in ~ of** être maître de, maîtriser; être responsable de; **the car went out of ~** j'ai (*or* il a *etc*) perdu le contrôle du véhicule; **~ panel** n tableau m de commande; **~ room** n salle f des commandes; (*RADIO, TV*) régie f; **~ tower** n (*AVIAT*) tour f de contrôle.

controversial [kɔntrə'və:ʃl] a discutable, controversé(e).

controversy ['kɔntrəvə:sɪ] n controverse f, polémique f.

convalesce [kɔnvə'les] vi relever de maladie, se remettre (d'une maladie).

convene [kən'vi:n] vt convoquer, assembler // vi se réunir, s'assembler.

convenience [kən'vi:nɪəns] n commodité f; **at your ~** quand *or* comme cela vous convient; **all modern ~s, all mod cons** avec tout le confort moderne, tout confort.

convenient [kən'vi:nɪənt] a commode.

convent ['kɔnvənt] n couvent m.

convention [kən'venʃən] n convention f; **~al** a conventionnel(le).

conversant [kən'və:snt] a: **to be ~ with** s'y connaître en; être au courant de.

conversation [kɔnvə'seɪʃən] n conversation f.

converse ['kɔnvə:s] n contraire m, inverse m // vi [kən'və:s] s'entretenir; **~ly** [-'və:slɪ] ad inversement, réciproquement.

convert vt [kən'və:t] (*REL, COMM*) convertir; (*alter*) transformer, aménager // n ['kɔnvə:t] converti/e; **~ible** a convertible // n (*voiture f*) décapotable f.

convey [kən'veɪ] vt transporter; (*thanks*) transmettre; (*idea*) communiquer; **~or belt** n convoyeur m, tapis roulant.

convict vt [kən'vɪkt] déclarer (*or* reconnaître) coupable // n ['kɔnvɪkt] forçat m, convict m; **~ion** [-ʃən] n condamnation f; (*belief*) conviction f.

convince [kən'vɪns] vt convaincre, persuader; **convincing** a persuasif(ive), convaincant(e).

convoluted [kɔnvə'lu:tɪd] a (*argument*) compliqué(e).

convulse [kən'vʌls] vt ébranler; **to be ~d with laughter** se tordre de rire.

coo [ku:] vi roucouler.

cook [kuk] vt (faire) cuire // vi cuire; (*person*) faire la cuisine // n cuisinier/ière; **~book** n livre m de cuisine; **~er** n cuisinière f; **~ery** n cuisine f; **~ery book** n (*Brit*) = **~book**; **~ie** n (*US*) biscuit m, petit gâteau sec; **~ing** n cuisine f.

cool [ku:l] a frais(fraîche); (*not afraid*) calme; (*unfriendly*) froid(e); (*impertinent*) effronté(e) // vt, vi rafraîchir, refroidir.

coop [ku:p] n poulailler m // vt: **to ~ up** (fig) cloîtrer, enfermer.

cooperate [kəu'ɔpəreɪt] vi coopérer, collaborer; **cooperation** [-'reɪʃən] n coopération f, collaboration f.

cooperative [kəu'ɔpərətɪv] a coopératif(ive) // n coopérative f.

coordinate vt [kəu'ɔ:dɪneɪt] coordonner // n [kəu'ɔ:dɪnət] (MATH) coordonnée f; **~s** npl (clothes) ensemble m, coordonnés mpl.

cop [kɔp] n (col) flic m.

cope [kəup] vi se débrouiller; **to ~ with** faire face à; s'occuper de.

copper [kɔpə*] n cuivre m; (col: policeman) flic m; **~s** npl petite monnaie.

coppice ['kɔpɪs] n, **copse** [kɔps] n taillis m.

copy ['kɔpɪ] n copie f; (book etc) exemplaire m // vt copier; **~right** n droit m d'auteur, copyright m.

coral ['kɔrəl] n corail m.

cord [kɔ:d] n corde f; (fabric) velours côtelé m; whipcord m; corde f.

cordial [kɔ:dɪəl] a cordial(e), chaleureux(euse) // n sirop m; cordial m.

cordon ['kɔ:dn] n cordon m; **to ~ off** vt boucler (par cordon de police).

corduroy ['kɔ:dərɔɪ] n velours côtelé.

core [kɔ:*] n (of fruit) trognon m, cœur m; (TECH) noyau m // vt enlever le trognon or le cœur de.

cork [kɔ:k] n liège m; (of bottle) bouchon m; **~screw** n tire-bouchon m.

corn [kɔ:n] n (Brit: wheat) blé m; (US: maize) maïs m; (on foot) cor m; **~ on the cob** (CULIN) épi m de maïs au naturel.

corned beef ['kɔ:nd-] n corned-beef m.

corner ['kɔ:nə*] n coin m; (AUT) tournant m, virage m // vt acculer, mettre au pied du mur; coincer; (COMM: market) accaparer // vi prendre un virage; **~stone** n pierre f angulaire.

cornet ['kɔ:nɪt] n (MUS) cornet m à pistons; (Brit: of ice-cream) cornet (de glace).

cornflakes ['kɔ:nfleɪks] npl cornflakes mpl.

cornflour ['kɔ:nflauə*] n (Brit) farine f de maïs, maïzena f ®.

cornstarch ['kɔ:nstɑ:tʃ] n (US) = **cornflour**.

Cornwall ['kɔ:nwəl] n Cornouailles f.

corny ['kɔ:nɪ] a (col) rebattu(e), galvaudé(e).

coronary ['kɔrənərɪ] n: **~ (thrombosis)** infarctus m (du myocarde), thrombose f coronaire.

coronation [kɔrə'neɪʃən] n couronnement m.

coronet ['kɔrənɪt] n couronne f.

corporal ['kɔ:pərl] n caporal m, brigadier m // a: **~ punishment** châtiment corporel.

corporate ['kɔ:pərɪt] a en commun; constitué(e) (en corporation).

corporation [kɔ:pə'reɪʃən] n (of town) municipalité f, conseil municipal; (COMM) société f.

corps [kɔ:*], pl **corps** [kɔ:z] n corps m.

corpse [kɔ:ps] n cadavre m.

correct [kə'rekt] a (accurate) correct(e), exact(e); (proper) correct, convenable // vt corriger; **~ion** [-ʃən] n correction f.

correspond [kɔrɪs'pɔnd] vi correspondre; **~ence** n correspondance f; **~ence course** n cours m par correspondance; **~ent** n correspondant/e.

corridor ['kɔrɪdɔ:*] n couloir m, corridor m.

corrode [kə'rəud] vt corroder, ronger // vi se corroder.

corrugated ['kɔrəgeɪtɪd] a plissé(e); cannelé(e); ondulé(e); **~ iron** n tôle ondulée.

corrupt [kə'rʌpt] a corrompu(e) // vt corrompre; **~ion** [-ʃən] n corruption f.

Corsica ['kɔ:sɪkə] n Corse f.

cortège [kɔ:'teɪʒ] n cortège m (gén funèbre).

cosh [kɔʃ] n (Brit) matraque f.

cosmetic [kɔz'metɪk] n produit m de beauté, cosmétique m.

cosset ['kɔsɪt] vt choyer, dorloter.

cost [kɔst] n coût m // vb (pt, pp cost) vi coûter // vt établir or calculer le prix de revient de; **~s** npl (LAW) dépens mpl; it **~s £5/too much** cela coûte cinq livres/trop cher; **at all ~s** coûte que coûte, à tout prix.

co-star ['kəustɑ:*] n partenaire m/f.

cost-effective [kɔstɪ'fektɪv] a rentable.

costly ['kɔstlɪ] a coûteux(euse).

cost-of-living [kɔstəv'lɪvɪŋ] a: **~ allowance** indemnité f de vie chère; **~ index** indexe m du coût de la vie.

cost price n (Brit) prix coûtant or de revient.

costume ['kɔstju:m] n costume m; (lady's suit) tailleur m; (Brit: also: swimming ~) maillot m (de bain); **~ jewellery** n bijoux mpl de fantaisie.

cosy, (US) **cozy** ['kəuzɪ] a douillet(te).

cot [kɔt] n (Brit: child's) lit m d'enfant, petit lit; (US: campbed) lit de camp.

cottage ['kɔtɪdʒ] n petite maison (à la campagne), cottage m; **~ cheese** n fromage blanc (maigre); **~ industry** n industrie familiale or artisanale; **~ pie** n ≈ hachis m Parmentier.

cotton ['kɔtn] n coton m; **to ~ on to** vt fus (col) piger; **~ candy** n (US) barbe f à papa; **~ wool** n (Brit) ouate f, coton m hydrophile.

couch [kautʃ] n canapé m; divan m // vt formuler, exprimer.

couchette [ku:'ʃet] n couchette f.

cough [kɔf] *vi* tousser // *n* toux *f*; ~ **drop** *n* pastille *f* pour *or* contre la toux.

could [kud] *pt of* **can**; **~n't** = **could not**.

council ['kaunsl] *n* conseil *m*; **city** *or* **town** ~ conseil municipal; ~ **estate** *n* (*Brit*) (quartier *m or* zone *f* de) logements loués à/par la municipalité; ~ **house** *n* (*Brit*) maison *f* (à loyer modéré) louée par la municipalité; **~lor** *n* conseiller/ère.

counsel ['kaunsl] *n* avocat/e; consultation *f*, délibération *f*; **~lor** *n* conseiller/ère.

count [kaunt] *vt, vi* compter // *n* compte *m*; (*nobleman*) comte *m*; **to** ~ **on** *vt fus* compter sur; **~down** *n* compte *m* à rebours.

countenance ['kauntinəns] *n* expression *f* // *vt* approuver.

counter ['kauntə*] *n* comptoir *m*; (*in post office, bank*) guichet *m*; (*in game*) jeton *m* // *vt* aller à l'encontre de, opposer; (*blow*) parer // *ad*: ~ **to** à l'encontre de; contrairement à; **~act** *vt* neutraliser, contrebalancer; **~espionage** *n* contre-espionnage *m*.

counterfeit ['kauntəfit] *n* faux *m*, contrefaçon *f* // *vt* contrefaire // *a* faux(fausse).

counterfoil ['kauntəfɔil] *n* talon *m*, souche *f*.

countermand [kauntə'ma:nd] *vt* annuler.

counterpart ['kauntəpa:t] *n* (*of document etc*) double *m*; (*of person*) homologue *m/f*.

countess ['kauntis] *n* comtesse *f*.

countless ['kauntlis] *a* innombrable.

country ['kʌntri] *n* pays *m*; (*native land*) patrie *f*; (*as opposed to town*) campagne *f*; (*region*) région *f*, pays; ~ **dancing** *n* (*Brit*) danse *f* folklorique; ~ **house** *n* manoir *m*, (petit) château; **~man** *n* (*national*) compatriote *m*; (*rural*) habitant *m* de la campagne, campagnard *m*; **~side** *n* campagne *f*.

county ['kaunti] *n* comté *m*.

coup, **~s** [ku:, ,-z] *n* beau coup; (*also*: ~ d'état) coup d'État.

couple ['kʌpl] *n* couple *m* // *vt* (*carriages*) atteler; (*TECH*) coupler; (*ideas, names*) associer; **a** ~ **of** deux.

coupon ['ku:pɔn] *n* coupon *m*, bon-prime *m*, bon-réclame *m*; (*COMM*) coupon.

courage ['kʌridʒ] *n* courage *m*.

courgette [kuə'ʒɛt] *n* (*Brit*) courgette *f*.

courier ['kuriə*] *n* messager *m*, courrier *m*; (*for tourists*) accompagnateur/trice.

course [kɔ:s] *n* cours *m*; (*of ship*) route *f*; (*for golf*) terrain *m*; (*part of meal*) plat *m*; **first** ~ entrée *f*; **of** ~ *ad* bien sûr; ~ **of action** parti *m*, ligne *f* de conduite; ~ **of lectures** série *f* de

conférences; ~ **of treatment** (*MED*) traitement *m*.

court [kɔ:t] *n* cour *f*; (*LAW*) cour, tribunal *m*; (*TENNIS*) court *m* // *vt* (*woman*) courtiser, faire la cour à; **to take to** ~ actionner *or* poursuivre en justice.

courteous ['kə:tiəs] *a* courtois(e), poli(e).

courtesy ['kə:təsi] *n* courtoisie *f*, politesse *f*; **by** ~ **of** avec l'aimable autorisation de.

court-house ['kɔ:thaus] *n* (*US*) palais *m* de justice.

courtier ['kɔ:tiə*] *n* courtisan *m*, dame *f* de cour.

court-martial, *pl* **courts-martial** ['kɔ:t'ma:ʃəl] *n* cour martiale, conseil *m* de guerre.

courtroom ['kɔ:trum] *n* salle *f* de tribunal.

courtyard ['kɔ:tja:d] *n* cour *f*.

cousin ['kʌzn] *n* cousin/e; **first** ~ cousin/e germain(e).

cove [kəuv] *n* petite baie, anse *f*.

covenant ['kʌvənənt] *n* contrat *m*, engagement *m*.

cover ['kʌvə*] *vt* couvrir // *n* (*for bed, of book*, *COMM*) couverture *f*; (*of pan*) couvercle *m*; (*over furniture*) housse *f*; (*shelter*) abri *m*; **to take** ~ (*shelter*) se mettre à l'abri; **under** ~ à l'abri; **under** ~ **of darkness** à la faveur de la nuit; **under separate** ~ (*COMM*) sous pli séparé; **to** ~ **up for sb** couvrir qn; **~age** *n* reportage *m*; (*INSURANCE*) couverture *f*; ~ **charge** *n* couvert *m* (*supplément à payer*); **~ing** *n* couverture *f*, enveloppe *f*; **~ing letter**, (*US*) ~ **letter** *n* lettre explicative; ~ **note** *n* (*INSURANCE*) police *f* provisoire.

covert ['kʌvət] *a* (*threat*) voilé(e), caché(e); (*attack*) indirect(e); (*glance*) furtif(ive).

cover-up ['kʌvərʌp] *n* tentative *f* pour étouffer une affaire.

covet ['kʌvit] *vt* convoiter.

cow [kau] *n* vache *f* // *cpd* femelle // *vt* effrayer, intimider.

coward ['kauəd] *n* lâche *m/f*; **~ice** [-is] *n* lâcheté *f*; **~ly** *a* lâche.

cowboy ['kaubɔi] *n* cow-boy *m*.

cower ['kauə*] *vi* se recroqueviller; trembler.

coxswain ['kɔksn] *n* (*abbr*: **cox**) barreur *m*; (*of ship*) patron *m*.

coy [kɔi] *a* faussement effarouché(e) *or* timide.

cozy ['kəuzi] *a* (*US*) = **cosy.**

CPA *n abbr* (*US*) *of* **certified public accountant.**

crab [kræb] *n* crabe *m*; ~ **apple** *n* pomme *f* sauvage.

crack [kræk] *n* fente *f*, fissure *f*; fêlure *f*; lézarde *f*; (*noise*) craquement *m*, coup (sec); (joke) plaisanterie f; (col: attempt): **to have a ~ at** essayer // vt fendre, fissurer; fêler; lézarder; (whip) faire claquer; (nut) casser // a (athlete) de première classe, d'élite; **to ~ down on** vt fus mettre un frein à; **to ~ up** vi être au bout de son rouleau, flancher; **~er** n pétard m; biscuit (salé), craquelin m.

crackle ['krækl] vi crépiter, grésiller.

cradle ['kreɪdl] n berceau m.

craft [krɑ:ft] n métier (artisanal); (cunning) ruse f, astuce f; (boat) embarcation f, barque f; **~sman** n artisan m, ouvrier (qualifié); **~smanship** n métier m, habileté f; **~y** a rusé(e), malin(igne), astucieux(euse).

crag [kræg] n rocher escarpé.

cram [kræm] vt (fill): **to ~ sth with** bourrer qch de; (put): **to ~ sth into** fourrer qch dans // vi (for exams) bachoter.

cramp [kræmp] n crampe f // vt gêner, entraver; **~ed** a à l'étroit, très serré(e).

cranberry ['krænbərɪ] n canneberge f.

crane [kreɪn] n grue f.

crank [kræŋk] n manivelle f; (person) excentrique m/f; **~shaft** n vilebrequin m.

cranny ['krænɪ] n see nook.

crash [kræʃ] n fracas m; (of car, plane) collision f // vt (plane) écraser // vi (plane) s'écraser; (two cars) se percuter, s'emboutir; (fig) s'effondrer; **to ~ into** se jeter or se fracasser contre; **~ course** n cours intensif; **~ helmet** n casque (protecteur); **~ landing** n atterrissage forcé or en catastrophe.

crate [kreɪt] n cageot m.

cravat(e) [krə'væt] n foulard (noué autour du cou).

crave [kreɪv] vt, vi: **to ~ (for)** avoir une envie irrésistible de.

crawl [krɔ:l] vi ramper; (vehicle) avancer au pas // n (SWIMMING) crawl m.

crayfish ['kreɪfɪʃ] n (pl inv) (freshwater) écrevisse f; (saltwater) langoustine f.

crayon ['kreɪən] n crayon m (de couleur).

craze [kreɪz] n engouement m.

crazy ['kreɪzɪ] a fou(folle); **~ paving** n dallage irrégulier (en pierres plates).

creak [kri:k] vi grincer; craquer.

cream [kri:m] n crème f // a (colour) crème inv; **~ cake** n (petit) gâteau à la crème; **~ cheese** n fromage m à la crème, fromage blanc; **~y** a crémeux(euse).

crease [kri:s] n pli m // vt froisser, chiffonner // vi se froisser, se chiffonner.

create [kri:'eɪt] vt créer; **creation** [-ʃən] n création f; **creative** a créateur(trice).

creature ['kri:tʃə*] n créature f.

crèche, creche [kreʃ] n garderie f, crèche f.

credence ['kri:dns] n: **to lend** or **give ~ to** ajouter foi à.

credentials [krɪ'dɛnʃlz] npl (papers) références fpl.

credit ['krɛdɪt] n crédit m // vt (COMM) créditer; (believe: also: **give ~ to**) ajouter foi à, croire; **~s** npl (CINEMA) générique m; **to ~ sb with** (fig) prêter or attribuer à qn; **to be in ~** (person, bank account) être créditeur(trice); **~ card** n carte f de crédit; **~or** n créancier/ière.

creed [kri:d] n croyance f; credo m, principes mpl.

creek [kri:k] n crique f, anse f; (US) ruisseau m, petit cours d'eau.

creep [kri:p], pt, pp **crept** vi ramper; (fig) se faufiler, se glisser; (plant) grimper; **~er** n plante grimpante; **~y** a (frightening) qui fait frissonner, qui donne la chair de poule.

cremate [krɪ'meɪt] vt incinérer.

crematorium, pl **crematoria** [krɛmə-'tɔ:rɪəm, -'tɔ:rɪə] n four m crématoire.

crêpe [kreɪp] n crêpe m; **~ bandage** n (Brit) bande f Velpeau ®.

crept [krɛpt] pt, pp of **creep**.

crescent ['krɛsnt] n croissant m; rue f (en arc de cercle).

cress [krɛs] n cresson m.

crest [krɛst] n crête f; **~fallen** a déconfit(e), découragé(e).

crevice ['krɛvɪs] n fissure f, lézarde f, fente f.

crew [kru:] n équipage m; **to have a ~-cut** avoir les cheveux en brosse; **~-neck** n col ras.

crib [krɪb] n lit m d'enfant // vt (col) copier.

crick [krɪk] n crampe f.

cricket ['krɪkɪt] n (insect) grillon m, cri-cri m inv; (game) cricket m.

crime [kraɪm] n crime m; **criminal** ['krɪmɪnl] a, n criminel(le).

crimson ['krɪmzn] a cramoisi(e).

cringe [krɪndʒ] vi avoir un mouvement de recul; (fig) s'humilier, ramper.

crinkle ['krɪŋkl] vt froisser, chiffonner.

cripple ['krɪpl] n boiteux/euse, infirme m/f // vt estropier, paralyser.

crisis, pl **crises** ['kraɪsɪs, -si:z] n crise f.

crisp [krɪsp] a croquant(e); (fig) vif(vive), brusque; **~s** npl (Brit) (pommes) chips fpl.

criss-cross ['krɪskrɔs] a entrecroisé(e).

criterion, pl **criteria** [kraɪ'tɪərɪən, -'tɪərɪə] n critère m.

critic ['krɪtɪk] n critique m/f; **~al** a critique; **~ally** ad (examine) d'un œil critique; (speak etc) sévèrement; **~ally ill** gravement malade; **~ism** ['krɪtɪsɪzm] n critique f; **~ize** ['krɪtɪsaɪz] vt critiquer.

croak [krəuk] *vi* (*frog*) coasser; (*raven*) croasser.

crochet ['krəuʃei] *n* travail *m* au crochet.

crockery ['krɔkəri] *n* vaisselle *f*.

crocodile ['krɔkədail] *n* crocodile *m*.

crocus ['krəukəs] *n* crocus *m*.

croft [krɔft] *n* (*Brit*) petite ferme.

crony ['krəuni] *n* copain/copine.

crook [kruk] *n* escroc *m*; (*of shepherd*) houlette *f*; **~ed** ['krukid] *a* courbé(e), tordu(e); (*action*) malhonnête.

crop [krɔp] *n* (*produce*) culture *f*; (*amount produced*) récolte *f*; (*riding ~*) cravache *f*; **to ~ up** *vi* surgir, se présenter, survenir.

cross [krɔs] *n* croix *f*; (*BIOL*) croisement *m* // *vt* (*street etc*) traverser; (*arms*, *legs*, *BIOL*) croiser; (*cheque*) barrer // *a* en colère, fâché(e); **to ~ o.s.** se signer, faire le signe de (la) croix; **to ~ out** *vt* barrer, biffer; **to ~ over** *vi* traverser; **~bar** *n* barre transversale; **~country (race)** *n* cross(-country) *m*; **~-examine** *vt* (*LAW*) faire subir un examen contradictoire à; **~-eyed** *a* qui louche; **~fire** *n* feux croisés; **~ing** *n* croisement *m*, carrefour *m*; (*sea passage*) traversée *f*; (*also*: **pedestrian ~ing**) passage clouté; **~ing guard** *n* (*US*) contractuel/le qui fait traverser la rue aux enfants; **~ purposes** *npl*: **to be at ~ purposes** ne pas parler de la même chose; **~reference** *n* renvoi *m*, référence *f*; **~roads** *n* carrefour *m*; **~ section** *n* (*BIOL*) coupe transversale; (*in population*) échantillon *m*; **~walk** *n* (*US*) passage clouté; **~wind** *n* vent *m* de travers; **~wise** *ad* en travers; **~word** *n* mots croisés *mpl*.

crotch [krɔtʃ] *n* (*of garment*) entre-jambes *m inv*.

crotchety ['krɔtʃiti] *a* (*person*) grognon(ne), grincheux(euse).

crouch [krautʃ] *vi* s'accroupir; se tapir; se ramasser.

crow [krəu] *n* (*bird*) corneille *f*; (*of cock*) chant *m* du coq, cocorico *m* // *vi* (*cock*) chanter; (*fig*) pavoiser, chanter victoire.

crowbar ['krəuba:*] *n* levier *m*.

crowd [kraud] *n* foule *f* // *vt* bourrer, remplir // *vi* affluer, s'attrouper, s'entasser; **~ed** *a* bondé(e), plein(e); **~ed with** plein de.

crown [kraun] *n* couronne *f*; (*of head*) sommet *m* de la tête, calotte crânienne; (*of hat*) fond *m*; (*of hill*) sommet *m* // *vt* couronner; **~ jewels** *npl* joyaux *mpl* de la Couronne; **~ prince** *n* prince héritier.

crow's feet *npl* pattes *fpl* d'oie (*fig*).

crucial ['kru:ʃl] *a* crucial(e), décisif(ive).

crucifixion [kru:si'fikʃən] *n* crucifiement *m*, crucifixion *f*.

crude [kru:d] *a* (*materials*) brut(e); non raffiné(e); (*fig: basic*) rudimentaire, sommaire; (: *vulgar*) cru(e), grossier(ère); **~ (oil)** *n* (pétrole) brut *m*.

cruel ['kruəl] *a* cruel(le); **~ty** *n* cruauté *f*.

cruet ['kru:it] *n* huilier *m*; vinaigrier *m*.

cruise [kru:z] *n* croisière *f* // *vi* (*ship*) croiser; (*car*) rouler; (*aircraft*) voler; (*taxi*) être en maraude; **~r** *n* croiseur *m*.

crumb [krʌm] *n* miette *f*.

crumble ['krʌmbl] *vt* émietter // *vi* s'émietter; (*plaster etc*) s'effriter; (*land*, *earth*) s'ébouler; (*building*) s'écrouler, crouler; (*fig*) s'effondrer; **crumbly** *a* friable.

crumpet ['krʌmpit] *n* petite crêpe (épaisse).

crumple ['krʌmpl] *vt* froisser, friper.

crunch [krʌntʃ] *vt* croquer; (*underfoot*) faire craquer, écraser; faire crisser // *n* (*fig*) instant *m* or moment *m* critique, moment de vérité; **~y** *a* croquant(e), croustillant(e).

crusade [kru:'seid] *n* croisade *f*.

crush [krʌʃ] *n* foule *f*, cohue *f* // *vt* écraser; (*crumple*) froisser.

crust [krʌst] *n* croûte *f*.

crutch [krʌtʃ] *n* béquille *f*.

crux [krʌks] *n* point crucial.

cry [krai] *vi* pleurer; (*shout: also*: **~ out**) crier // *n* cri *m*; **to ~ off** *vi* se dédire; se décommander.

cryptic ['kriptik] *a* énigmatique.

crystal ['kristl] *n* cristal *m*; **~-clear** *a* clair(e) comme de l'eau de roche.

cub [kʌb] *n* petit *m* (*d'un animal*); (*also*: **~ scout**) louveteau *m*.

Cuba ['kju:bə] *n* Cuba *m*.

cubbyhole ['kʌbihəul] *n* cagibi *m*.

cube [kju:b] *n* cube *m* // *vt* (*MATH*) élever au cube; **cubic** *a* cubique; **cubic metre** *etc* mètre *m etc* cube; **cubic capacity** *n* cylindrée *f*.

cubicle ['kju:bikl] *n* box *m*, cabine *f*.

cuckoo ['kuku:] *n* coucou *m*; **~ clock** *n* (pendule *f* à) coucou *m*.

cucumber ['kju:kʌmbə*] *n* concombre *m*.

cuddle ['kʌdl] *vt* câliner, caresser // *vi* se blottir l'un contre l'autre.

cue [kju:] *n* (*snooker ~*) queue *f* de billard; (*THEATRE etc*) signal *m*.

cuff [kʌf] *n* (*Brit: of shirt, coat etc*) poignet *m*, manchette *f*; (*US: of trousers*) revers *m*; **off the ~** *ad* de chic, à l'improviste; **~link** *n* bouton *m* de manchette.

cul-de-sac ['kʌldəsæk] *n* cul-de-sac *m*, impasse *f*.

cull [kʌl] *vt* sélectionner.

culminate ['kʌlmineit] *vi*: **to ~ in** finir or se terminer par; (*end in*) mener à; **culmination** [-'neiʃən] *n* point culmi-

nant.
culottes [kju:'lɔts] *npl* jupe-culotte *f*.
culpable ['kʌlpəbl] *a* coupable.
culprit ['kʌlprɪt] *n* coupable *m/f*.
cult [kʌlt] *n* culte *m*.
cultivate ['kʌltɪveɪt] *vt* (*also fig*) cultiver; **cultivation** [-'veɪʃən] *n* culture *f*.
cultural ['kʌltʃərəl] *a* culturel(le).
culture ['kʌltʃə*] *n* (*also fig*) culture *f*; **~d** *a* cultivé(e) (*fig*).
cumbersome ['kʌmbəsəm] *a* encombrant(e), embarrassant(e).
cunning ['kʌnɪŋ] *n* ruse *f*, astuce *f* // *a* rusé(e), malin(igne).
cup [kʌp] *n* tasse *f*; (*prize, event*) coupe *f*; (*of bra*) bonnet *m*.
cupboard ['kʌbəd] *n* placard *m*.
cup-tie ['kʌptaɪ] *n* (*Brit*) match *m* de coupe.
curate ['kjuərɪt] *n* vicaire *m*.
curator [kjuə'reɪtə*] *n* conservateur *m* (*d'un musée etc*).
curb [kə:b] *vt* refréner, mettre un frein à // *n* frein *m* (*fig*); (*US*) = **kerb**.
curdle ['kə:dl] *vi* (se) cailler.
cure [kjuə*] *vt* guérir; (*CULIN*) saler; fumer; sécher // *n* remède *m*.
curfew ['kə:fju:] *n* couvre-feu *m*.
curio ['kjuərɪəu] *n* bibelot *m*, curiosité *f*.
curiosity [kjuərɪ'ɔsɪtɪ] *n* curiosité *f*.
curious ['kjuərɪəs] *a* curieux(euse).
curl [kə:l] *n* boucle *f* (de cheveux) // *vt, vi* boucler; (*tightly*) friser; **to ~ up** *vi* s'enrouler; se pelotonner; **~er** *n* bigoudi *m*, rouleau *f*.
curly ['kə:lɪ] *a* bouclé(e); frisé(e).
currant ['kʌrnt] *n* raisin *m* de Corinthe, raisin sec.
currency ['kʌrnsɪ] *n* monnaie *f*; **to gain ~** (*fig*) s'accréditer.
current ['kʌrnt] *n* courant *m* // *a* courant(e); (*in*) // **~ account** *n* (*Brit*) compte courant; **~ affairs** *npl* (questions *fpl* d')actualité *f*; **~ly** *ad* actuellement.
curriculum, *pl* **~s** *or* **curricula** [kə'rɪkjuləm, -lə] *n* programme *m* d'études; **~ vitae (CV)** *n* curriculum vitae (C.V.) *m*.
curry ['kʌrɪ] *n* curry *m* // *vt*: **to ~ favour with** chercher à gagner la faveur *or* à s'attirer les bonnes grâces de.
curse [kə:s] *vi* jurer, blasphémer // *vt* maudire // *n* malédiction *f*; fléau *m*.
cursor ['kə:sə*] *n* (*COMPUT*) curseur *m*.
cursory ['kə:sərɪ] *a* superficiel(le), hâtif(ive).
curt [kə:t] *a* brusque, sec(sèche).
curtail [kə:'teɪl] *vt* (*visit etc*) écourter; (*expenses etc*) réduire.
curtain ['kə:tn] *n* rideau *m*.
curts(e)y ['kə:tsɪ] *n* révérence *f* // *vi* faire une révérence.
curve [kə:v] *n* courbe *f*; (*in the road*) tournant *m*, virage *m* // *vi* se courber;

(*road*) faire une courbe.
cushion ['kuʃən] *n* coussin *m* // *vt* (*shock*) amortir.
custard ['kʌstəd] *n* (*for pouring*) crème anglaise.
custodian [kʌs'təudɪən] *n* gardien/ne; (*of collection etc*) conservateur/trice.
custody ['kʌstədɪ] *n* (*of child*) garde *f*; (*for offenders*) détention préventive.
custom ['kʌstəm] *n* coutume *f*, usage *m*; (*LAW*) droit coutumier, coutume; (*COMM*) clientèle *f*; **~ary** *a* habituel(le).
customer ['kʌstəmə*] *n* client/e.
customized ['kʌstəmaɪzd] *a* (*car etc*) construit(e) sur commande.
custom-made ['kʌstəm'meɪd] *a* (*clothes*) fait(e) sur mesure; (*other goods*) hors série, fait(e) sur commande.
customs ['kʌstəmz] *npl* douane *f*; **~ officer** *n* douanier *m*.
cut [kʌt] *vb* (*pt, pp* **cut**) *vt* couper; (*meat*) découper; (*shape, make*) tailler; couper; creuser; graver; (*reduce*) réduire // *vi* couper; (*intersect*) se couper // *n* (*gen*) coupure *f*; (*of clothes*) coupe *f*; (*of jewel*) taille *f*; (*in salary etc*) réduction *f*; (*of meat*) morceau *m*; **to ~ a tooth** percer une dent; **to ~ down** *vt fus* (*tree etc*) couper, abattre; (*reduce: also:* **to ~ down on**) réduire; **to ~ off** *vt* couper; (*fig*) isoler; **to ~ out** *vt* ôter; découper; tailler; **to ~ up** *vt* (*paper, meat*) couper; **~back** *n* réduction *f*.
cute [kju:t] *a* mignon(ne), adorable; (*clever*) rusé(e), astucieux(euse).
cuticle ['kju:tɪkl] *n* (*on nail*): **~ remover** *n* repousse-peaux *m inv*.
cutlery ['kʌtlərɪ] *n* couverts *mpl*.
cutlet ['kʌtlɪt] *n* côtelette *f*.
cut-: **~out** *n* coupe-circuit *m inv*; (*cardboard ~*) découpage *m*; **~-price**, (*US*) **~-rate** *a* au rabais, à prix réduit; **~throat** *n* assassin *m* // *a* acharné(e).
cutting ['kʌtɪŋ] *a* tranchant(e), coupant(e); (*fig*) cinglant(e), mordant(e) // *n* (*Brit: from newspaper*) coupure *f* (de journal).
CV *n abbr of* **curriculum vitae**.
cwt *abbr of* **hundredweight(s)**.
cyanide ['saɪənaɪd] *n* cyanure *m*.
cycle ['saɪkl] *n* cycle *m* // *vi* faire de la bicyclette.
cycling ['saɪklɪŋ] *n* cyclisme *m*.
cyclist ['saɪklɪst] *n* cycliste *m/f*.
cygnet ['sɪgnɪt] *n* jeune cygne *m*.
cylinder ['sɪlɪndə*] *n* cylindre *m*; **~-head gasket** *n* joint *m* de culasse.
cymbals ['sɪmblz] *npl* cymbales *fpl*.
cynic ['sɪnɪk] *n* cynique *m/f*; **~al** *a* cynique; **~ism** ['sɪnɪsɪzəm] *n* cynisme *m*.
Cypriot ['sɪprɪət] *a* cypriote, chypriote // *n* Cypriote *m/f*, Chypriote *m/f*.
Cyprus ['saɪprəs] *n* Chypre *f*.

cyst [sıst] *n* kyste *m*.
cystitis [sıs'taıtıs] *n* cystite *f*.
czar [zɑ:*] *n* tsar *m*.
Czech [tʃɛk] *a* tchèque // *n* Tchèque *m/f*; (LING) tchèque *m*.
Czechoslovakia [tʃɛkəslə'vækıə] *n* Tchécoslovaquie *f*; **~n** *a* tchécoslovaque // *n* Tchécoslovaque *m/f*.

D

D [di:] *n* (MUS) ré *m*.
dab [dæb] *vt* (eyes, wound) tamponner; (paint, cream) appliquer (par petites touches or rapidement).
dabble ['dæbl] *vi*: **to ~ in** faire or se mêler or s'occuper un peu de.
dad, daddy [dæd, 'dædı] *n* papa *m*.
daffodil ['dæfədıl] *n* jonquille *f*.
daft [dɑ:ft] *a* idiot(e), stupide.
dagger ['dægə*] *n* poignard *m*.
daily ['deılı] *a* quotidien(ne), journalier(ère) // *n* quotidien *m* // *ad* tous les jours.
dainty ['deıntı] *a* délicat(e), mignon(ne).
dairy ['dɛərı] *n* (shop) crémerie *f*, laiterie *f*; (on farm) laiterie // *a* laitier(ère); **~ produce** *n* produits laitiers
dais ['deııs] *n* estrade *f*.
daisy ['deızı] *n* pâquerette *f*; **~ wheel** *n* (on printer) marguerite *f*.
dale [deıl] *n* vallon *m*.
dam [dæm] *n* barrage *m* // *vt* endiguer.
damage ['dæmıdʒ] *n* dégâts *mpl*, dommages *mpl*; (fig) tort *m* // *vt* endommager, abîmer; (fig) faire du tort à; **~s** *npl* (LAW) dommages-intérêts *mpl*.
damn [dæm] *vt* condamner; (curse) maudire // *n* (col): **I don't give a ~** je m'en fous // *a* (col: also: **~ed**): **this ~ ...** ce sacré or foutu ...; **~ (it)!** zut!
damp [dæmp] *a* humide // *n* humidité *f* // *vt* (also: **~en**: cloth, rag) humecter; (enthusiasm etc) refroidir.
damson ['dæmzən] *n* prune *f* de Damas.
dance [dɑ:ns] *n* danse *f*; (ball) bal *m* // *vi* danser; **~ hall** *n* salle *f* de bal, dancing *m*; **~r** *n* danseur/euse.
dancing ['dɑ:nsıŋ] *n* danse *f*.
dandelion ['dændılaıən] *n* pissenlit *m*.
dandruff ['dændrəf] *n* pellicules *fpl*.
Dane [deın] *n* Danois/se.
danger ['deındʒə*] *n* danger *m*; **there is a ~ of fire** il y a (un) risque d'incendie; **in ~** en danger; **he was in ~ of falling** il risquait de tomber; **~ous** *a* dangereux(euse).
dangle ['dæŋgl] *vt* balancer; (fig) faire miroiter // *vi* pendre, se balancer.
Danish ['deınıʃ] *a* danois(e) // *n* (LING) danois *m*.
dapper ['dæpə*] *a* pimpant(e).
dare [dɛə*] *vt*: **to ~ sb to do** défier qn or mettre qn au défi de faire // *vi*: **to ~ (to) do sth** oser faire qch; **I ~ say** (I suppose) il est probable (que); **~devil** *n* casse-cou *m inv*; **daring** *a* hardi(e), audacieux(euse) // *n* audace *f*, hardiesse *f*.
dark [dɑ:k] *a* (night, room) obscur(e), sombre; (colour, complexion) foncé(e), sombre; (fig) sombre // *n*: **in the ~** dans le noir; **in the ~ about** (fig) ignorant tout de; **after ~** après la tombée de la nuit; **~en** *vt* obscurcir, assombrir // *vi* s'obscurcir, s'assombrir; **~ glasses** *npl* lunettes noires; **~ness** *n* obscurité *f*; **~ room** *n* chambre noire.
darling ['dɑ:lıŋ] *a, n* chéri(e).
darn [dɑ:n] *vt* repriser.
dart [dɑ:t] *n* fléchette *f* // *vi*: **to ~ towards** se précipiter or s'élancer vers; **to ~ away/along** partir/passer comme une flèche; **~s** *n* jeu *m* de fléchettes; **~board** *n* cible *f* (de jeu de fléchettes).
dash [dæʃ] *n* (sign) tiret *m*; (small quantity) goutte *f*, larme *f* // *vt* (missile) jeter or lancer violemment; (hopes) anéantir // *vi*: **to ~ towards** se précipiter or se ruer vers; **to ~ away or off** *vi* partir à toute allure.
dashboard ['dæʃbɔ:d] *n* (AUT) tableau *m* de bord.
dashing ['dæʃıŋ] *a* fringant(e).
data ['deıtə] *npl* données *fpl*; **~base** *n* base *f* de données; **~ processing** *n* traitement *m* (électronique) de l'information.
date [deıt] *n* date *f*; rendez-vous *m*; (fruit) datte *f* // *vt* dater; **~ of birth** date de naissance; **to ~** *ad* à ce jour; **out of ~** périmé(e); **up to ~** à la page; mis(e) à jour; moderne; **~d** *a* démodé(e).
daub [dɔ:b] *vt* barbouiller.
daughter ['dɔ:tə*] *n* fille *f*; **~-in-law** *n* belle-fille *f*, bru *f*.
daunting ['dɔ:ntıŋ] *a* intimidant(e), décourageant(e).
dawdle ['dɔ:dl] *vi* traîner, lambiner.
dawn [dɔ:n] *n* aube *f*, aurore *f* // *vi* (day) se lever, poindre; (fig) naître, se faire jour; **it ~ed on him that ...** il lui vint à l'esprit que ...
day [deı] *n* jour *m*; (as duration) journée *f*; (period of time, age) époque *f*, temps *m*; **the ~ before** la veille, le jour précédent; **the ~ after, the following ~** le lendemain, le jour suivant; **the ~ after tomorrow** après-demain; **the ~ before yesterday** avant-hier; **by ~** de jour; **~break** *n* point *m* du jour; **~dream** *vi* rêver (tout éveillé); **~light** *n* (lumière *f* du) jour *m*; **~ return** *n* (Brit) billet *m* d'aller-retour (valable pour la journée); **~time** *n* jour *m*, journée *f*; **~-to-~** *a* journalier(ère).
daze [deız] *vt* (subj: drug) hébéter; (: blow) étourdir // *n*: **in a ~** hébété(e);

étourdi(e).

dazzle ['dæzl] *vt* éblouir, aveugler.

DC *abbr* (= *direct current*) courant continu.

deacon ['di:kən] *n* diacre *m*.

dead [dɛd] *a* mort(e); (*numb*) engourdi(e), insensible // *ad* absolument, complètement; **he was shot ~** il a été tué d'un coup de revolver; **~ on time** à l'heure pile; **~ tired** éreinté(e), complètement fourbu(e); **to stop ~** s'arrêter pile or net; **the ~** les morts; **~en** *vt* (*blow, sound*) amortir; (*make numb*) endormir, rendre insensible; **~ end** *n* impasse *f*; **~ heat** *n* (*SPORT*): **to finish in a ~ heat** terminer ex-aequo; **~line** *n* date *f* or heure *f* limite; **~lock** *n* impasse *f* (*fig*); **~ loss** *n*: **to be a ~ loss** (*col: person*) n'être bon(bonne) à rien; (*thing*) ne rien valoir; **~ly** *a* mortel(le); (*weapon*) meurtrier(ère); **~pan** *a* impassible.

deaf [dɛf] *a* sourd(e); **~en** *vt* rendre sourd; (*fig*) assourdir; **~ness** *n* surdité *f*; **~-mute** *n* sourd/e-muet/te.

deal [di:l] *n* affaire *f*, marché *m* // *vt* (*pt, pp* **dealt** [dɛlt]) (*blow*) porter; (*cards*) donner, distribuer; **a great ~** (**of**) beaucoup (de); **to ~ in** *vt fus* faire le commerce de; **to ~ with** *vt fus* (*COMM*) traiter avec; (*handle*) s'occuper or se charger de; (*be about: book etc*) traiter de; **~er** *n* marchand *m*; **~ings** *npl* (*COMM*) transactions *fpl*; (*relations*) relations *fpl*, rapports *mpl*.

dean [di:n] *n* (*REL, Brit SCOL*) doyen *m*; (*US SCOL*) conseiller/ère (principal(e)) d'éducation.

dear [dɪə*] *a* cher(chère); (*expensive*) cher, coûteux(euse) // *n*: **my ~** mon cher/ma chère; **~ me!** mon Dieu!; **D~ Sir/Madam** (*in letter*) Monsieur/ Madame; **~ly** *ad* (*love*) tendrement; (*pay*) cher.

death [dɛθ] *n* mort *f*; (*ADMIN*) décès *m*; **~ certificate** *n* acte *m* de décès; **~ duties** *npl* (*Brit*) droits *mpl* de succession; **~ly** *a* de mort; **~ penalty** *n* peine *f* de mort; **~ rate** *n* (taux *m* de) mortalité *f*.

debar [dɪ'bɑ:*] *vt*: **to ~ sb from doing** interdire à qn de faire.

debase [dɪ'beɪs] *vt* (*currency*) déprécier, dévaloriser; (*person*) abaisser, avilir.

debate [dɪ'beɪt] *n* discussion *f*, débat *m* // *vt* discuter, débattre.

debit ['dɛbɪt] *n* débit *m* // *vt*: **to ~ a sum to sb** or **to sb's account** porter une somme au débit de qn, débiter qn d'une somme.

debt [dɛt] *n* dette *f*; **to be in ~** avoir des dettes, être endetté(e); **~or** *n* débiteur/ trice.

debunk [dɪ'bʌŋk] *vt* (*theory, claim*)

montrer le ridicule de.

decade ['dɛkeɪd] *n* décennie *f*, décade *f*.

decadence ['dɛkədəns] *n* décadence *f*.

decaffeinated [dɪ'kæfɪneɪtɪd] *a* décaféiné(e).

decanter [dɪ'kæntə*] *n* carafe *f*.

decay [dɪ'keɪ] *n* décomposition *f*, pourrissement *m*; (*fig*) déclin *m*, délabrement *m*; (*also: tooth ~*) carie *f* (dentaire) // *vi* (*rot*) se décomposer, pourrir; (*fig*) se délabrer; décliner; se détériorer.

deceased [dɪ'si:st] *n* défunt/e.

deceit [dɪ'si:t] *n* tromperie *f*, supercherie *f*; **~ful** *a* trompeur(euse).

deceive [dɪ'si:v] *vt* tromper.

December [dɪ'sɛmbə*] *n* décembre *m*.

decent ['di:sənt] *a* décent(e), convenable; **they were very ~ about it** ils se sont montrés très chics.

deception [dɪ'sɛpʃən] *n* tromperie *f*.

deceptive [dɪ'sɛptɪv] *a* trompeur(euse).

decide [dɪ'saɪd] *vt* (*person*) décider; (*question, argument*) trancher, régler // *vi* se décider, décider; **to ~ to do/that** décider de faire/que; **to ~ on** décider, se décider pour; **~d** *a* (*resolute*) résolu(e), décidé(e); (*clear, definite*) net(te), marqué(e); **~dly** [-dɪdlɪ] *ad* résolument; incontestablement, nettement.

deciduous [dɪ'sɪdjuəs] *a* à feuilles caduques.

decimal ['dɛsɪməl] *a* décimal(e) // *n* décimale *f*; **~ point** *n* ≈ virgule *f*.

decipher [dɪ'saɪfə*] *vt* déchiffrer.

decision [dɪ'sɪʒən] *n* décision *f*.

decisive [dɪ'saɪsɪv] *a* décisif(ive).

deck [dɛk] *n* (*NAUT*) pont *m*; (*of bus*): **top ~** impériale *f*; (*of cards*) jeu *m*; **~chair** *n* chaise longue.

declaration [dɛklə'reɪʃən] *n* déclaration *f*.

declare [dɪ'klɛə*] *vt* déclarer.

decline [dɪ'klaɪn] *n* (*decay*) déclin *m*; (*lessening*) baisse *f* // *vt* refuser, décliner // *vi* décliner; être en baisse, baisser.

decorate ['dɛkəreɪt] *vt* (*adorn, give a medal to*) décorer; (*paint and paper*) peindre et tapisser; **decoration** [-'reɪʃən] *n* (*medal etc, adornment*) décoration *f*; **decorator** *n* peintre *m* en bâtiment.

decoy ['di:kɔɪ] *n* piège *m*.

decrease *n* ['di:kri:s] diminution *f* // *vt, vi* [di:'kri:s] diminuer.

decree [dɪ'kri:] *n* (*POL, REL*) décret *m*; (*LAW*) arrêt *m*, jugement *m*; **~ nisi** *n* jugement *m* provisoire de divorce.

dedicate ['dɛdɪkeɪt] *vt* consacrer; (*book etc*) dédier.

dedication [dɛdɪ'keɪʃən] *n* (*devotion*) dévouement *m*.

deduce [dɪ'dju:s] *vt* déduire, conclure.

deduct [dɪ'dʌkt] *vt*: **to ~ sth (from)**

déduire qch (de), retrancher qch (de); (*from wage etc*) prélever qch (sur), retenir qch (sur); **~ion** [dı'dʌkʃən] *n* (*deducting, deducing*) déduction *f*; (*from wage etc*) prélèvement *m*, retenue *f*.

deed [di:d] *n* action *f*, acte *m*; (*LAW*) acte notarié, contrat *m*.

deep [di:p] *a* (*water, sigh, sorrow, thoughts*) profond(e); (*voice*) grave; *4 metres* ~ de 4 mètres de profondeur // *ad*: *spectators stood 20* ~ il y avait 20 rangs de spectateurs; **~en** *vt* (*hole*) approfondir // *vi* s'approfondir; (*darkness*) s'épaissir; **~-freeze** *n* congélateur *m* // *vt* surgeler; **~-fry** *vt* faire frire (en friteuse); **~ly** *ad* (*breathe*) profondément; (*interested, moved*) vivement; (*grateful*) profondément, infiniment; **~-sea diving** *n* plongée sous-marine.

deer [dıə*] *n* (*pl inv*): *the* ~ les cervidés *mpl* (*ZOOL*); (*red*) ~ cerf *m*; (*fallow*) ~ daim *m*; (*roe*) ~ chevreuil *m*.

deface [dı'feıs] *vt* dégrader; barbouiller; rendre illisible.

default [dı'fɔ:lt] *vi* (*LAW*) faire défaut; (*gen*) manquer à ses engagements // *n* (*COMPUT: also:* ~ **value**) valeur *f* par défaut; **by** ~ (*LAW*) par défaut, par contumace; (*SPORT*) par forfait.

defeat [dı'fi:t] *n* défaite *f* // *vt* ·(*team, opponents*) battre; (*fig: plans, efforts*) faire échouer.

defect *n* ['di:fɛkt] défaut *m* // *vi* [dı'fɛkt]: **to** ~ **to the enemy** passer à l'ennemi; **~ive** [dı'fɛktıv] *a* défectueux(euse).

defence [dı'fɛns] *n* défense *f*; **in** ~ **of** pour défendre; **~less** *a* sans défense.

defend [dı'fɛnd] *vt* défendre; **~ant** *n* défendeur/deresse; (*in criminal case*) accusé/e, prévenu/e; **~er** *n* défenseur *m*.

defense [dı'fɛns] *n* (*US*) = **defence**.

defer [dı'fə:*] *vt* (*postpone*) différer, ajourner // *vi*: **to** ~ **to** déférer à, s'en remettre à.

defiance [dı'faıəns] *n* défi *m*; **in** ~ **of** au mépris de.

defiant [dı'faıənt] *a* provocant(e), de défi; (*person*) rebelle, intraitable.

deficiency [dı'fıʃənsı] *n* insuffisance *f*, déficience *f*; carence *f*.

deficit ['dɛfısıt] *n* déficit *m*.

defile *vb* [dı'faıl] *vt* souiller // *vi* défiler // *n* ['di:faıl] défilé *m*.

define [dı'faın] *vt* définir.

definite ['dɛfınıt] *a* (*fixed*) défini(e), (bien) déterminé(e); (*clear, obvious*) net(te), manifeste; **he was** ~ **about it** il a été catégorique; il était sûr de son fait; **~ly** *ad* sans aucun doute.

definition [dɛfı'nıʃən] *n* définition *f*.

deflate [di:'fleıt] *vt* dégonfler.

deflect [dı'flɛkt] *vt* détourner, faire dévier.

deformed [dı'fɔ:md] *a* difforme.

defraud [dı'frɔ:d] *vt* frauder; **to** ~ **sb of sth** escroquer qch à qn.

defrost [di:'frɔst] *vt* (*fridge*) dégivrer; **~er** *n* (*US: demister*) dispositif *m* antibuée *inv*.

deft [dɛft] *a* adroit(e), preste.

defunct [dı'fʌŋkt] *a* défunt(e).

defuse [di:'fju:z] *vt* désamorcer.

defy [dı'faı] *vt* défier; (*efforts etc*) résister à.

degenerate *vi* [dı'dʒɛnəreıt] dégénérer // *a* [dı'dʒɛnərıt] dégénéré(e).

degree [dı'gri:] *n* degré *m*; grade *m* (universitaire); **a** (*first*) ~ **in maths** une licence en maths; **by** ~**s** (*gradually*) par degrés; **to some** ~ jusqu'à un certain point, dans une certaine mesure.

dehydrated [di:haı'dreıtıd] *a* déshydraté(e); (*milk, eggs*) en poudre.

de-ice [di:'aıs] *vt* (*windscreen*) dégivrer.

deign [deın] *vi*: **to** ~ **to do** daigner faire.

deity ['di:ıtı] *n* divinité *f*; dieu *m*, déesse *f*.

dejected [dı'dʒɛktıd] *a* abattu(e), déprimé(e).

delay [dı'leı] *vt* retarder // *vi* s'attarder // *n* délai *m*, retard *m*.

delectable [dı'lɛktəbl] *a* délicieux(euse).

delegate *n* ['dɛlıgıt] délégué/e // *vt* ['dɛlıgeıt] déléguer.

delete [dı'li:t] *vt* rayer, supprimer.

deliberate *a* [dı'lıbərıt] (*intentional*) délibéré(e); (*slow*) mesuré(e) // *vi* [dı'lıbəreıt] délibérer, réfléchir; **~ly** *ad* (*on purpose*) exprès, délibérément.

delicacy [dɛlıkəsı] *n* délicatesse *f*; (*food*) mets fin *or* délicat, friandise *f*.

delicate ['dɛlıkıt] *a* délicat(e).

delicatessen [dɛlıkə'tɛsn] *n* épicerie fine.

delicious [dı'lıʃəs] *a* délicieux(euse).

delight [dı'laıt] *n* (grande) joie, grand plaisir // *vt* enchanter; **~ed** *a*: **~ed** (*at or with/to do*) ravi(e) (de/de faire); **~ful** *a* adorable; merveilleux(euse); délicieux(euse).

delinquent [dı'lıŋkwənt] *a, n* délinquant(e).

delirious [dı'lırıəs] *a*: **to be** ~ délirer.

deliver [dı'lıvə*] *vt* (*mail*) distribuer; (*goods*) livrer; (*message*) remettre; (*speech*) prononcer; (*warning, ultimatum*) lancer; (*free*) délivrer; (*MED*) accoucher; **~y** *n* distribution *f*; livraison *f*; (*of speaker*) élocution *f*; (*MED*) accouchement *m*.

delude [dı'lu:d] *vt* tromper, leurrer.

delusion [dı'lu:ʒən] *n* illusion *f*.

delve [dɛlv] *vi*: **to** ~ **into** fouiller dans.

demand [dı'ma:nd] *vt* réclamer, exiger // *n* exigence *f*; (*claim*) revendication *f*; (*ECON*) demande *f*; **in** ~ demandé(e), recherché(e); **on** ~ sur demande; **~ing** *a* (*boss*) exigeant(e); (*work*) astreignant(e).

demean [dɪ'mi:n] vt: to ~ o.s. s'abaisser.

demeanour, (US) **demeanor** [dɪ'mi:-nə*] n comportement m; maintien m.

demented [dɪ'mɛntɪd] a dément(e), fou(folle).

demise [dɪ'maɪz] n décès m.

demister [di:'mɪstə*] n (AUT) dispositif m anti-buée inv.

demo ['dɛməu] n abbr (col: = demonstration) manif f.

democracy [dɪ'mɔkrəsɪ] n démocratie f.

democrat ['dɛməkræt] n démocrate m/f; ~**ic** [dɛmə'krætɪk] a démocratique.

demolish [dɪ'mɔlɪʃ] vt démolir.

demonstrate ['dɛmənstreɪt] vt démontrer, prouver // vi: to ~ (for/against) manifester (en faveur de/contre); **demonstration** [-'streɪʃən] n démonstration f, manifestation f; **demonstrator** n (POL) manifestant/e.

demote [dɪ'məut] vt rétrograder.

demure [dɪ'mjuə*] a sage, réservé(e); d'une modestie affectée.

den [dɛn] n tanière f, antre m.

denatured alcohol [di:'neɪtʃəd-] n (US) alcool m à brûler.

denial [dɪ'naɪəl] n démenti m; dénégation f.

denim ['dɛnɪm] n coton émerisé; ~**s** npl (blue-)jeans mpl.

Denmark ['dɛnmɑ:k] n Danemark m.

denomination [dɪnɔmɪ'neɪʃən] n (money) valeur f; (REL) confession f; culte m.

denounce [dɪ'nauns] vt dénoncer.

dense [dɛns] a dense; (stupid) obtus(e), dur(e) or lent(e) à la comprenette.

density [dɛns] n densité f.

dent [dɛnt] n bosse f // vt (also: make a ~ in) cabosser.

dental ['dɛntl] a dentaire; ~ **surgeon** n (chirurgien/ne) dentiste.

dentist ['dɛntɪst] n dentiste m/f; ~**ry** n art m dentaire.

denture(s) ['dɛntʃə(z)] n(pl) dentier m.

deny [dɪ'naɪ] vt nier; (refuse) refuser.

deodorant [di:'əudərənt] n désodorisant m, déodorant m.

depart [dɪ'pɑ:t] vi partir; to ~ from (fig: differ from) s'écarter de.

department [dɪ'pɑ:tmənt] n (COMM) rayon m; (SCOL) section f; (POL) ministère m, département m; ~ **store** n grand magasin.

departure [dɪ'pɑ:tʃə*] n départ m; (fig): ~ from écart m par rapport à; a new ~ une nouvelle voie; ~ **lounge** n (at airport) salle f de départ.

depend [dɪ'pɛnd] vi: to ~ on dépendre de; (rely on) compter sur; it's cela dépend; ~**ing on the result** ... selon le résultat ...; ~**able** a sûr(e), digne de confiance; ~**ant** n personne f à charge;

~**ent** a: to be ~ent (on) dépendre (de) // n = ~ant.

depict [dɪ'pɪkt] vt (in picture) représenter; (in words) (dé)peindre, décrire.

depleted [dɪ'pli:tɪd] a (considérablement) réduit(e) or diminué(e).

deploy [dɪ'plɔɪ] vt déployer.

deport [dɪ'pɔ:t] vt déporter; expulser.

deportment [dɪ'pɔ:tmənt] n maintien m, tenue f.

deposit [dɪ'pɔzɪt] n (CHEM, COMM, GEO) dépôt m; (of ore, oil) gisement m; (part payment) arrhes fpl, acompte m; (on bottle etc) consigne f; (for hired goods etc) cautionnement m, garantie f // vt déposer; mettre or laisser en dépôt; fournir or donner en acompte; laisser en garantie; ~ **account** n compte m de dépôt.

depot ['dɛpəu] n dépôt m.

depress [dɪ'prɛs] vt déprimer; (press down) appuyer sur, abaisser; ~**ed** a (person) déprimé(e), abattu(e); (area) en déclin, touché(e) par le sous-emploi; ~**ing** a déprimant(e); ~**ion** [dɪ'prɛʃən] n dépression f.

deprivation [dɛprɪ'veɪʃən] n privation f; (loss) perte f.

deprive [dɪ'praɪv] vt: to ~ sb of priver qn de; enlever à qn; ~**d** a déshérité(e).

depth [dɛpθ] n profondeur f; in the ~s of au fond de; au cœur de; au plus profond de.

deputize ['dɛpjutaɪz] vi: to ~ for assurer l'intérim de.

deputy ['dɛpjutɪ] a: ~ **head** directeur adjoint, sous-directeur m // n (replacement) suppléant/e, intérimaire m/f; (second in command) adjoint/e.

derail [dɪ'reɪl] vt: to be ~ed dérailler.

derby ['də:bɪ] n (US: bowler hat) (chapeau m) melon m.

derelict ['dɛrɪlɪkt] a abandonné(e), à l'abandon.

deride [dɪ'raɪd] vt railler.

derisory [dɪ'raɪsərɪ] a (sum) dérisoire; (smile, person) moqueur(euse).

derive [dɪ'raɪv] vt: to ~ sth from tirer qch de; trouver qch dans // vi: to ~ from provenir de, dériver de.

derogatory [dɪ'rɔgətərɪ] a désobligeant(e); péjoratif(ive).

derv [də:v] n (Brit) gas-oil m.

descend [dɪ'sɛnd] vt, vi descendre; to ~ from descendre de, être issu de.

descent [dɪ'sɛnt] n descente f; (origin) origine f.

describe [dɪs'kraɪb] vt décrire; **description** [-'krɪpʃən] n description f; (sort) sorte f, espèce f.

desecrate ['dɛsɪkreɪt] vt profaner.

desert n ['dɛzət] désert m // vb [dɪ'zə:t] vt déserter, abandonner // vi (MIL) déserter; ~**er** n déserteur m; ~ **island** n île déserte; ~**s** npl: to get one's just ~s n'avoir que ce qu'on mérite.

deserve [dɪ'zɜːv] vt mériter; **deserving** a (person) méritant(e); (action, cause) méritoire.

design [dɪ'zaɪn] n (sketch) plan m, dessin m; (layout, shape) conception f, ligne f; (pattern) dessin m, motif(s) m(pl); (COMM) esthétique industrielle; (intention) dessein m // vt dessiner; concevoir; **to have ~s on** avoir des visées sur.

designer [dɪ'zaɪnə*] n (ART, TECH) dessinateur/trice; (fashion) modéliste m/f.

desire [dɪ'zaɪə*] n désir m // vt désirer, vouloir.

desk [desk] n (in office) bureau m; (for pupil) pupitre m; (Brit: in shop, restaurant) caisse f; (in hotel, at airport) réception f.

desolate ['dɛsəlɪt] a désolé(e).

despair [dɪs'pɛə*] n désespoir m // vi: **to ~ of** désespérer de.

despatch [dɪs'pætʃ] n, vt = **dispatch**.

desperate ['dɛspərɪt] a désespéré(e); (fugitive) prêt(e) à tout; **~ly** ad désespérément; (very) terriblement, extrêmement.

desperation [dɛspə'reɪʃən] n désespoir m; **in ~** à bout de nerf; en désespoir de cause.

despicable [dɪs'pɪkəbl] a méprisable.

despise [dɪs'paɪz] vt mépriser, dédaigner.

despite [dɪs'paɪt] prep malgré, en dépit de.

despondent [dɪs'pɔndənt] a découragé(e), abattu(e).

dessert [dɪ'zɜːt] n dessert m; **~spoon** n cuiller f à dessert.

destination [dɛstɪ'neɪʃən] n destination f.

destiny ['dɛstɪnɪ] n destinée f, destin m.

destitute ['dɛstɪtjuːt] a indigent(e).

destroy [dɪs'trɔɪ] vt détruire; **~er** n (NAUT) contre-torpilleur m.

destruction [dɪs'trʌkʃən] n destruction f.

detach [dɪ'tætʃ] vt détacher; **~ed** a (attitude) détaché(e); **~ed house** n pavillon m, maison(nette) (individuelle); **~ment** n (MIL) détachement m; (fig) détachement, indifférence f.

detail ['diːteɪl] n détail m // vt raconter en détail, énumérer; **in ~** en détail; **~ed** a détaillé(e).

detain [dɪ'teɪn] vt retenir; (in captivity) détenir; (in hospital) hospitaliser.

detect [dɪ'tɛkt] vt déceler, percevoir; (MED, POLICE) dépister (MIL, RADAR, TECH) détecter; **~ion** [dɪ'tɛkʃən] n découverte f; dépistage m; détection f; **~ive** n agent m de la sûreté, policier m; **private ~ive** détective privé; **~ive story** n roman policier.

detention [dɪ'tɛnʃən] n détention f; (SCOL) retenue f, consigne f.

deter [dɪ'tɜː*] vt dissuader.

detergent [dɪ'tɜːdʒənt] n détersif m, détergent m.

deteriorate [dɪ'tɪərɪəreɪt] vi se détériorer, se dégrader.

determine [dɪ'tɜːmɪn] vt déterminer; **to ~ to do** résoudre de faire, se déterminer à faire; **~d** a (person) déterminé(e).

deterrent [dɪ'tɛrənt] n effet m de dissuasion; force f de dissuasion.

detour ['diːtuə*] n détour m; (US AUT: diversion) déviation f.

detract [dɪ'trækt] vt: **to ~ from** (quality, pleasure) diminuer; (reputation) porter atteinte à.

detriment ['dɛtrɪmənt] n: **to the ~ of** au détriment de, au préjudice de; **~al** [dɛtrɪ'mɛntl] a: **~al to** préjudiciable or nuisible à.

devaluation [dɪvælju'eɪʃən] n dévaluation f.

devastating ['dɛvəsteɪtɪŋ] a dévastateur(trice).

develop [dɪ'vɛləp] vt (gen) développer; (habit) contracter; (resources) mettre en valeur, exploiter // vi se développer; (situation, disease: evolve) évoluer; (facts, symptoms: appear) se manifester, se produire; **~ing country** pays m en voie de développement; **~ment** n développement m; (of affair, case) rebondissement m, fait(s) nouveau(x).

device [dɪ'vaɪs] n (apparatus) engin m, dispositif m.

devil ['dɛvl] n diable m; démon m.

devious ['diːvɪəs] a (means) détourné(e); (person) sournois(e), dissimulé(e).

devise [dɪ'vaɪz] vt imaginer, concevoir.

devoid [dɪ'vɔɪd] a: **~ of** dépourvu(e) de, dénué(e) de.

devolution [diːvə'luːʃən] n (POL) décentralisation f.

devote [dɪ'vəut] vt: **to ~ sth to** consacrer qch à; **~d** a dévoué(e); **to be ~d to** (book etc) être consacré(e) à; **~e** [dɛvəu'tiː] n (REL) adepte m/f; (MUS, SPORT) fervent/e.

devotion [dɪ'vəuʃən] n dévouement m, attachement m; (REL) dévotion f, piété f.

devour [dɪ'vauə*] vt dévorer.

devout [dɪ'vaut] a pieux(euse), dévot(e).

dew [djuː] n rosée f.

DHSS n abbr (Brit: = Department of Health and Social Security) ≈ ministère de la Santé et de la Sécurité Sociale.

diabetes [daɪə'biːtiːz] n diabète m; **diabetic** [-'bɛtɪk] a, n diabétique (m/f).

diabolical [daɪə'bɒlɪkl] a (col: weather) atroce; (: behaviour) infernal(e).

diagnosis, pl **diagnoses** [daɪəg'nəusɪs, -siːz] n diagnostic m.

diagonal [daɪˈægənl] *a* diagonal(e) // *n* diagonale *f*.

diagram [ˈdaɪəgræm] *n* diagramme *m*, schéma *m*; graphique *m*.

dial [ˈdaɪəl] *n* cadran *m* // *vt* (*number*) faire, composer.

dialect [ˈdaɪəlɛkt] *n* dialecte *m*.

dialling: ~ **code**, (*US*) **dial code** *n* indicatif *m* (téléphonique); ~ **tone**, (*US*) **dial tone** *n* tonalité *f*.

dialogue [ˈdaɪələg] *n* dialogue *m*.

diameter [daɪˈæmɪtə*] *n* diamètre *m*.

diamond [ˈdaɪəmənd] *n* diamant *m*; (*shape*) losange *m*; ~**s** *npl* (*CARDS*) carreau *m*.

diaper [ˈdaɪəpə*] *n* (*US*) couche *f*.

diaphragm [ˈdaɪəfræm] *n* diaphragme *m*.

diarrhoea, (*US*) **diarrhea** [daɪəˈriːə] *n* diarrhée *f*.

diary [ˈdaɪərɪ] *n* (*daily account*) journal *m*; (*book*) agenda *m*.

dice [daɪs] *n* (*pl inv*) dé *m* // *vt* (*CULIN*) couper en dés or en cubes.

dictate *vt* [dɪkˈteɪt] dicter // *n* [ˈdɪkteɪt] injonction *f*.

dictation [dɪkˈteɪʃən] *n* dictée *f*.

dictator [dɪkˈteɪtə*] *n* dictateur *m*; ~**ship** *n* dictature *f*.

dictionary [ˈdɪkʃənrɪ] *n* dictionnaire *m*.

did [dɪd] *pt of* **do**.

didn't = **did not**.

die [daɪ] *vi* mourir; **to be dying for sth** avoir une envie folle de qch; **to be dying to do sth** mourir d'envie de faire qch; **to ~ away** *vi* s'éteindre; **to ~ down** *vi* se calmer, s'apaiser; **to ~ out** *vi* disparaître, s'éteindre.

diehard [ˈdaɪhɑːd] *n* réactionnaire *m/f*, jusqu'au-boutiste *m/f*.

Diesel [ˈdiːzəl]: ~ **engine** *n* moteur *m* diesel; ~ (**oil**) *n* carburant *m* diesel.

diet [ˈdaɪət] *n* alimentation *f*; (*restricted food*) régime *m* // *vi* (*also*: **be on a ~**) suivre un régime.

differ [ˈdɪfə*] *vi*: **to ~ from sth** être différent de; différer de; **to ~ from sb over sth** ne pas être d'accord avec qn au sujet de qch; ~**ence** *n* différence *f*; (*quarrel*) différend *m*, désaccord *m*; ~**ent** *a* différent(e); ~**entiate** [-ˈrenʃɪeɪt] *vi* se différencier; **to ~entiate between** faire une différence entre.

difficult [ˈdɪfɪkəlt] *a* difficile; ~**y** *n* difficulté *f*.

diffident [ˈdɪfɪdənt] *a* qui manque de confiance or d'assurance.

dig [dɪg] *vt* (*pt, pp* **dug**) (*hole*) creuser; (*garden*) bêcher // *n* (*prod*) coup *m* de coude; (*fig*) coup de griffe or de patte; **to ~ in** *vi* (*MIL*: *also*: ~ **o.s. in**) se retrancher; ⟨*col*: *eat*⟩ attaquer (un repas *etc*); **to ~ into** (*snow, soil*) creuser; **to ~ one's nails into** enfoncer ses ongles dans; **to ~ up** *vt* déterrer.

digest *vt* [daɪˈdʒɛst] digérer // *n* [ˈdaɪdʒɛst] sommaire *m*, résumé *m*; ~**ion** [dɪˈdʒɛstʃən] *n* digestion *f*.

digit [ˈdɪdʒɪt] *n* chiffre *m* (*de 0 à 9*); (*finger*) doigt *m*; ~**al** *a* digital(e); à affichage numérique or digital.

dignified [ˈdɪgnɪfaɪd] *a* digne.

dignity [ˈdɪgnɪtɪ] *n* dignité *f*.

digress [daɪˈgrɛs] *vi*: **to ~ from** s'écarter de, s'éloigner de.

digs [dɪgz] *npl* (*Brit col*) piaule *f*, chambre meublée.

dilapidated [dɪˈlæpɪdeɪtɪd] *a* délabré(e).

dilemma [daɪˈlɛmə] *n* dilemme *m*.

diligent [ˈdɪlɪdʒənt] *a* appliqué(e), assidu(e).

dilute [daɪˈluːt] *vt* diluer.

dim [dɪm] *a* (*light, eyesight*) faible; (*memory, outline*) vague, indécis(e); (*stupid*) borné(e), obtus(e) // *vt* (*light*) réduire, baisser.

dime [daɪm] *n* (*US*) = *10 cents*.

dimension [daɪˈmɛnʃən] *n* dimension *f*.

diminish [dɪˈmɪnɪʃ] *vt, vi* diminuer.

diminutive [dɪˈmɪnjutɪv] *a* minuscule, tout(e) petit(e).

dimmers [ˈdɪməz] *npl* (*US AUT*) phares *mpl* code *inv*; feux *mpl* de position.

dimple [ˈdɪmpl] *n* fossette *f*.

din [dɪn] *n* vacarme *m*.

dine [daɪn] *vi* dîner; ~**r** *n* (*person*) dîneur/euse; (*RAIL*) = **dining car**.

dinghy [ˈdɪŋgɪ] *n* youyou *m*; (*also*: rubber ~) canot *m* pneumatique; (*also*: sailing ~) voilier *m*, dériveur *m*.

dingy [ˈdɪndʒɪ] *a* miteux(euse), minable.

dining [ˈdaɪnɪŋ] *cpd*: ~ **car** *n* (*Brit*) wagon-restaurant *m*; ~ **room** *n* salle *f* à manger.

dinner [ˈdɪnə*] *n* dîner *m*; (*public*) banquet *m*; ~**'s ready!** à table!; ~ **jacket** *n* smoking *m*; ~ **party** *n* dîner *m*; ~ **time** *n* heure *f* du dîner.

dint [dɪnt] *n*: **by ~ of (doing)** à force de (faire).

dip [dɪp] *n* déclivité *f*; (*in sea*) baignade *f*, bain *m* // *vt* tremper, plonger; (*Brit AUT*: *lights*) mettre en code, baisser // *vi* plonger.

diploma [dɪˈpləʊmə] *n* diplôme *m*.

diplomacy [dɪˈpləʊməsɪ] *n* diplomatie *f*.

diplomat [ˈdɪpləmæt] *n* diplomate *m*; ~**ic** [dɪpləˈmætɪk] *a* diplomatique.

dipstick [ˈdɪpstɪk] *n* (*AUT*) jauge *f* de niveau d'huile.

dire [daɪə*] *a* terrible, extrême, affreux(euse).

direct [daɪˈrɛkt] *a* direct(e) // *vt* diriger, orienter; **can you ~ me to ...?** pouvez-vous m'indiquer le chemin de ...?

direction [dɪˈrɛkʃən] *n* direction *f*; **sense of ~** sens *m* de l'orientation; ~**s** *npl* (*advice*) indications *fpl*; ~**s for use** mode *m* d'emploi.

directly [dɪˈrɛktlɪ] *ad* (*in straight line*)

directement, tout droit; (*at once*) tout de suite, immédiatement.

director [dɪ'rɛktə*] *n* directeur *m*; administrateur *m*; (*THEATRE*) metteur *m* en scène; (*CINEMA, TV*) réalisateur/trice.

directory [dɪ'rɛktərɪ] *n* annuaire *m*.

dirt [də:t] *n* saleté *f*; crasse *f*; **~-cheap** *a* (ne) coûtant presque rien; **~y** *a* sale // *vt* salir; **~y trick** coup tordu.

disability [dɪsə'bɪlɪtɪ] *n* invalidité *f*, infirmité *f*.

disabled [dɪs'eɪbld] *a* infirme, invalide; (*maimed*) mutilé(e); (*through illness, old age*) impotent(e).

disadvantage [dɪsəd'vɑ:ntɪdʒ] *n* désavantage *m*, inconvénient *m*.

disagree [dɪsə'gri:] *vi* (*differ*) ne pas concorder; (*be against, think otherwise*): **to ~ (with)** ne pas être d'accord (avec); **~able** *a* désagréable; **~ment** *n* désaccord *m*, différend *m*.

disappear [dɪsə'pɪə*] *vi* disparaître; **~ance** *n* disparition *f*.

disappoint [dɪsə'pɔɪnt] *vt* décevoir; **~ed** *a* déçu(e); **~ing** *a* décevant(e); **~ment** *n* déception *f*.

disapproval [dɪsə'pru:vəl] *n* désapprobation *f*.

disapprove [dɪsə'pru:v] *vi*: **to ~ of** désapprouver.

disarm [dɪs'ɑ:m] *vt* désarmer; **~ament** *n* désarmement *m*.

disarray [dɪsə'reɪ] *n*: **in ~** (*army, organization*) en déroute; (*hair, clothes*) en désordre.

disaster [dɪ'zɑ:stə*] *n* catastrophe *f*, désastre *m*.

disband [dɪs'bænd] *vt* démobiliser; disperser // *vi* se séparer; se disperser.

disbelief ['dɪsbə'li:f] *n* incrédulité *f*.

disc [dɪsk] *n* disque *m*; (*COMPUT*) = **disk**.

discard [dɪs'kɑ:d] *vt* (*old things*) se défaire de; (*fig*) écarter, renoncer à.

discern [dɪ'sə:n] *vt* discerner, distinguer; **~ing** *a* judicieux(euse), perspicace.

discharge *vt* [dɪs'tʃɑ:dʒ] (*duties*) s'acquitter de; (*waste etc*) déverser; décharger; (*ELEC, MED*) émettre; (*patient*) renvoyer (chez lui); (*employee, soldier*) congédier, licencier; (*defendant*) relaxer, élargir *n* ['dɪstʃɑ:dʒ] (*ELEC, MED*) émission *f*; (*dismissal*) renvoi *m*; licenciement *m*; élargissement *m*.

discipline ['dɪsɪplɪn] *n* discipline *f*.

disc jockey *n* disque-jockey *m*.

disclaim [dɪs'kleɪm] *vt* désavouer, dénier.

disclose [dɪs'kləʊz] *vt* révéler, divulguer; **disclosure** [-'kləʊʒə*] *n* révélation *f*, divulgation *f*.

disco ['dɪskəʊ] *n abbr of* **discothèque**.

discomfort [dɪs'kʌmfət] *n* malaise *m*,

gêne *f*; (*lack of comfort*) manque *m* de confort.

disconcert [dɪskən'sə:t] *vt* déconcerter.

disconnect [dɪskə'nɛkt] *vt* détacher; (*ELEC, RADIO*) débrancher; (*gas, water*) couper.

disconsolate [dɪs'kɒnsəlɪt] *a* inconsolable.

discontent [dɪskən'tɛnt] *n* mécontentement *m*; **~ed** *a* mécontent(e).

discontinue [dɪskən'tɪnju:] *vt* cesser, interrompre.

discord ['dɪskɔ:d] *n* discorde *f*, dissension *f*; (*MUS*) dissonance *f*.

discothèque ['dɪskəʊtɛk] *n* discothèque *f*.

discount *n* ['dɪskaʊnt] remise *f*, rabais *m* // *vt* [dɪs'kaʊnt] ne pas tenir compte de.

discourage [dɪs'kʌrɪdʒ] *vt* décourager.

discover [dɪs'kʌvə*] *vt* découvrir; **~y** *n* découverte *f*.

discredit [dɪs'krɛdɪt] *vt* mettre en doute; discréditer.

discreet [dɪ'skri:t] *a* discret(ète).

discrepancy [dɪ'skrɛpənsɪ] *n* divergence *f*, contradiction *f*.

discriminate [dɪ'skrɪmɪneɪt] *vi*: **to ~ between** établir une distinction entre, faire la différence entre; **to ~ against** pratiquer une discrimination contre; **discriminating** *a* qui a du discernement; **discrimination** [-'neɪʃən] *n* discrimination *f*; (*judgment*) discernement *m*.

discuss [dɪ'skʌs] *vt* discuter de; (*debate*) discuter; **~ion** [dɪ'skʌʃən] *n* discussion *f*.

disdain [dɪs'deɪn] *n* dédain *m*.

disease [dɪ'zi:z] *n* maladie *f*.

disembark [dɪsɪm'bɑ:k] *vt, vi* débarquer.

disengage [dɪsɪn'geɪdʒ] *vt* dégager; (*TECH*) déclencher; **to ~ the clutch** (*AUT*) débrayer.

disfigure [dɪs'fɪgə*] *vt* défigurer.

disgrace [dɪs'greɪs] *n* honte *f*; (*disfavour*) disgrâce *f* // *vt* déshonorer, couvrir de honte; **~ful** *a* scandaleux(euse), honteux(euse).

disgruntled [dɪs'grʌntld] *a* mécontent(e).

disguise [dɪs'gaɪz] *n* déguisement *m* // *vt* déguiser; **in ~** déguisé(e).

disgust [dɪs'gʌst] *n* dégoût *m*, aversion *f* // *vt* dégoûter, écœurer; **~ing** *a* dégoûtant(e); révoltant(e).

dish [dɪʃ] *n* plat *m*; **to do** *or* **wash the ~es** faire la vaisselle; **to ~ up** *vt* servir; **~cloth** *n* (*for drying*) torchon *m*; (*for washing*) lavette *f*.

dishearten [dɪs'hɑ:tn] *vt* décourager.

dishevelled [dɪ'ʃɛvəld] *a* ébouriffé(e); décoiffé(e); débraillé(e).

dishonest [dɪs'ɒnɪst] *a* malhonnête.

dishonour, (*US*) **dishonor** [dɪs'ɒnə*] *n*

déshonneur m; **~able** a déshonorant(e).
dish towel n (US) torchon m.
dishwasher ['dɪʃwɔʃə*] n lave-vaisselle m; (person) plongeur/euse.
disillusion [dɪsɪ'lu:ʒən] vt désabuser, désenchanter.
disincentive [dɪsɪn'sɛntɪv] n: to be a ~ être démotivant(e); to be a ~ to sb démotiver qn.
disinfect [dɪsɪn'fɛkt] vt désinfecter; **~ant** n désinfectant m.
disintegrate [dɪs'ɪntɪgreɪt] vi se désintégrer.
disinterested [dɪs'ɪntrəstɪd] a désintéressé(e).
disjointed [dɪs'dʒɔɪntɪd] a décousu(e), incohérent(e).
disk [dɪsk] n (COMPUT) disquette f; single-/double-sided ~ disquette une face/double face; ~ **drive** n lecteur m de disque or disquette, drive m; **~ette** n (US) = **disk**.
dislike [dɪs'laɪk] n aversion f, antipathie f // vt ne pas aimer.
dislocate ['dɪsləkeɪt] vt disloquer; déboîter; désorganiser.
dislodge [dɪs'lɔdʒ] vt déplacer, faire bouger; (enemy) déloger.
disloyal [dɪs'lɔɪəl] a déloyal(e).
dismal ['dɪzməl] a lugubre, maussade.
dismantle [dɪs'mæntl] vt démonter; (fort, warship) démanteler.
dismay [dɪs'meɪ] n consternation f.
dismiss [dɪs'mɪs] vt congédier, renvoyer; (idea) écarter; (LAW) rejeter // vi (MIL) rompre les rangs; **~al** n renvoi m.
dismount [dɪs'maunt] vi mettre pied à terre.
disobedience [dɪsə'bi:dɪəns] n désobéissance f.
disobedient [dɪsə'bi:dɪənt] a désobéissant(e).
disobey [dɪsə'beɪ] vt désobéir à.
disorder [dɪs'ɔ:də*] n désordre m; (rioting) désordres mpl; (MED) troubles mpl; **~ly** a en désordre; désordonné(e).
disorientated [dɪs'ɔ:rɪenteɪtɪd] a désorienté(e).
disown [dɪs'əun] vt renier.
disparaging [dɪs'pærɪdʒɪŋ] a désobligeant(e).
dispassionate [dɪs'pæʃənət] a calme, froid(e); impartial(e), objectif(ive).
dispatch [dɪs'pætʃ] vt expédier, envoyer // n envoi m, expédition f; (MIL, PRESS) dépêche f.
dispel [dɪs'pɛl] vt dissiper, chasser.
dispensary [dɪs'pɛnsərɪ] n pharmacie f; (in chemist's) officine f.
dispense [dɪs'pɛns] vt distribuer, administrer; to ~ **with** vt fus se passer de; **~r** n (container) distributeur m; **dispensing chemist** n (Brit) pharmacie f.

disperse [dɪs'pə:s] vt disperser; (knowledge) disséminer // vi se disperser.
dispirited [dɪs'pɪrɪtɪd] a découragé(e), déprimé(e).
displace [dɪs'pleɪs] vt déplacer.
display [dɪs'pleɪ] n étalage m; déploiement m; affichage m; (screen) écran m de visualisation, visuel m; (of feeling) manifestation f; (pej) ostentation f // vt montrer; (goods) mettre à l'étalage, exposer; (results, departure times) afficher; (pej) faire étalage de.
displease [dɪs'pli:z] vt mécontenter, contrarier; **~d with** mécontent(e) de; **displeasure** [-'plɛʒə*] n mécontentement m.
disposable [dɪs'pəuzəbl] a (pack etc) jetable; (income) disponible; **~ nappy** n couche f à jeter, couche-culotte f.
disposal [dɪs'pəuzl] n (availability, arrangement) disposition f; (of property) disposition f, cession f; (of rubbish) évacuation f, destruction f; at one's ~ à sa disposition.
dispose [dɪs'pəuz] vt disposer; to ~ **of** vt (time, money) disposer de; (unwanted goods) se débarrasser de, se défaire de; (problem) expédier; **~d** a: ~d to do disposé(e) à faire; **disposition** [-'zɪʃən] n disposition f; (temperament) naturel m.
disprove [dɪs'pru:v] vt réfuter.
dispute [dɪs'pju:t] n discussion f; (also: industrial ~) conflit m // vt contester; (matter) discuter; (victory) disputer.
disqualify [dɪs'kwɔlɪfaɪ] vt (SPORT) disqualifier; to ~ sb **for** sth/**from doing** rendre qn inapte à qch/à faire; disqualifier; to ~ sb (**from driving**) retirer à qn son permis (de conduire).
disquiet [dɪs'kwaɪət] n inquiétude f, trouble m.
disregard [dɪsrɪ'gɑ:d] vt ne pas tenir compte de.
disrepair [dɪsrɪ'peə*] n mauvais état; to fall into ~ (building) tomber en ruine.
disreputable [dɪs'rɛpjutəbl] a (person) de mauvaise réputation; (behaviour) déshonorant(e).
disrupt [dɪs'rʌpt] vt (plans) déranger; (conversation) interrompre.
dissatisfaction [dɪssætɪs'fækʃən] n mécontentement m, insatisfaction f.
dissect [dɪ'sɛkt] vt disséquer.
dissent [dɪ'sɛnt] n dissentiment m, différence f d'opinion.
dissertation [dɪsə'teɪʃən] n mémoire m.
disservice [dɪs'sə:vɪs] n: to do sb a ~ rendre un mauvais service à qn; desservir qn.
dissimilar [dɪ'sɪmɪlə*] a: ~ (to) dissemblable (à), différent(e) (de).

dissipate ['dɪsɪpeɪt] *vt* dissiper; *(energy, efforts)* disperser.

dissolute ['dɪsəluːt] *a* débauché(e), dissolu(e).

dissolve [dɪ'zɔlv] *vt* dissoudre // *vi* se dissoudre, fondre; *(fig)* disparaître.

distance ['dɪstns] *n* distance *f*; **in the ~** au loin.

distant ['dɪstnt] *a* lointain(e), éloigné(e); *(manner)* distant(e), froid(e).

distaste [dɪs'teɪst] *n* dégoût *m*; **~ful** *a* déplaisant(e), désagréable.

distended [dɪs'tɛndɪd] *a* *(stomach)* dilaté(e).

distil [dɪs'tɪl] *vt* distiller; **~lery** *n* distillerie *f*.

distinct [dɪs'tɪŋkt] *a* distinct(e); *(preference, progress)* marqué(e); **as ~ from** par opposition à; **~ion** [dɪs'tɪŋkʃən] *n* distinction *f*; *(in exam)* mention *f* très bien; **~ive** *a* distinctif(ive).

distinguish [dɪs'tɪŋgwɪʃ] *vt* distinguer; différencier; **~ed** *a* *(eminent)* distingué(e); **~ing** *a* *(feature)* distinctif(ive), caractéristique.

distort [dɪs'tɔːt] *vt* déformer.

distract [dɪs'trækt] *vt* distraire, déranger; **~ed** *a* éperdu(e), égaré(e); **~ion** [dɪs'trækʃən] *n* distraction *f*; égarement *m*.

distraught [dɪs'trɔːt] *a* éperdu(e).

distress [dɪs'trɛs] *n* détresse *f*; *(pain)* douleur *f* // *vt* affliger; **~ing** *a* douloureux(euse), pénible.

distribute [dɪs'trɪbjuːt] *vt* distribuer; **distribution** [-'bjuːʃən] *n* distribution *f*; **distributor** *n* distributeur *m*.

district ['dɪstrɪkt] *n* *(of country)* région *f*; *(of town)* quartier *m*; *(ADMIN)* district *m*; **~ attorney** *n* *(US)* ≈ procureur *m* de la République; **~ nurse** *n* *(Brit)* infirmière visiteuse.

distrust [dɪs'trʌst] *n* méfiance *f*, doute *m* // *vt* se méfier de.

disturb [dɪs'tɜːb] *vt* troubler; *(inconvenience)* déranger; **~ance** *n* dérangement *m*; *(political etc)* troubles *mpl*; *(by drunks etc)* tapage *m*; **~ed** *a* *(worried, upset)* agité(e), troublé(e); **to be emotionally ~ed** avoir des problèmes affectifs; **~ing** *a* troublant(e), inquiétant(e).

disuse [dɪs'juːs] *n*: **to fall into ~** tomber en désuétude.

disused [dɪs'juːzd] *a* désaffecté(e).

ditch [dɪtʃ] *n* fossé *m* // *vt* *(col)* abandonner.

dither ['dɪðə*] *vi* hésiter.

ditto ['dɪtəu] *ad* idem.

dive [daɪv] *n* plongeon *m*; *(of submarine)* plongée *f*; *(AVIAT)* piqué *m*; *(pej)* bouge *m* // *vi* plonger; **~r** *n* plongeur *m*.

diversion [daɪ'vɜːʃən] *n* *(Brit AUT)* déviation *f*; *(distraction, MIL)* diversion

f.

divert [daɪ'vɜːt] *vt* *(traffic)* dévier; *(river)* détourner; *(amuse)* divertir.

divide [dɪ'vaɪd] *vt* diviser; *(separate)* séparer // *vi* se diviser; **~d highway** *n* *(US)* route *f* à quatre voies.

dividend ['dɪvɪdɛnd] *n* dividende *m*.

divine [dɪ'vaɪn] *a* divin(e).

diving ['daɪvɪŋ] *n* plongée (sous-marine); **~ board** *n* plongeoir *m*.

divinity [dɪ'vɪnɪtɪ] *n* divinité *f*; théologie *f.*

division [dɪ'vɪʒən] *n* division *f*; séparation *f.*

divorce [dɪ'vɔːs] *n* divorce *m* // *vt* divorcer d'avec; **~d** *a* divorcé(e); **~e** [-'siː] *n* divorcée *f.*

D.I.Y. *n abbr (Brit)* of **do-it-yourself.**

dizzy ['dɪzɪ] *a* *(height)* vertigineux(euse); **to make sb ~** donner le vertige à qn; **to feel ~** avoir la tête qui tourne.

DJ *n abbr of* **disc jockey.**

do [duː] ♦ *n* *(col: party etc)* soirée *f*, fête *f*

♦ *vb* *(pt* **did,** *pp* **done)** **1** *(in negative constructions)* non traduit; **I don't understand** je ne comprends pas

2 *(to form questions)* non traduit; **didn't you know?** vous ne le saviez pas?; **why didn't you come?** pourquoi n'êtes-vous pas venu?

3 *(for emphasis, in polite expressions)*: **she does seem rather late** je trouve qu'elle est bien en retard; **~ sit down/help yourself** asseyez-vous/servez-vous je vous en prie

4 *(used to avoid repeating vb)*: **she swims better than I ~** elle nage mieux que moi; **~ you agree? - yes, I ~/no, I don't** vous êtes d'accord? - oui/non; **she lives in Glasgow - so ~ I** elle habite Glasgow - moi aussi; **who broke it? - I did** qui l'a cassé? - c'est moi

5 *(in question tags)*: **he laughed, didn't he?** il a ri, n'est-ce pas?; **I don't know him, ~ I?** je ne le connais pas, je crois

♦ *vt* *(gen: carry out, perform etc)* faire; **what are you doing tonight?** qu'est-ce que vous faites ce soir?; **~ the cooking/washing-up** faire la cuisine/la vaisselle; **to ~ one's teeth/hair/nails** se brosser les dents/se coiffer/se faire les ongles; **the car was ~ing 100** la voiture faisait du 100 (à l'heure)

♦ *vi* **1** *(act, behave)* faire; **~ as I ~** faites comme moi

2 *(get on, fare)* marcher; **the firm is ~ing well** l'entreprise marche bien; **how ~ you ~?** comment allez-vous?; *(on being introduced)* enchanté(e)!

3 *(suit)* aller; **will it ~?** est-ce que ça ira?

4 *(be sufficient)* suffire, aller; **will £10 ~?** est-ce que 10 livres suffiront?; **that'll**

~ ça suffit, ça ira; **that'll ~!** (*in annoyance*) ça va *or* suffit comme ça!;
to make ~ (with) se contenter (de)
to do away with *vt fus* supprimer;
to do up *vt* (*laces, dress*) attacher; (*buttons*) boutonner; (*zip*) fermer; (*renovate: room*) refaire; (*: house*) remettre à neuf
to do with *vt fus* (*need*): **I could ~ with a drink/some help** quelque chose à boire/un peu d'aide ne serait pas de refus; (*be connected*): **that has nothing to ~ with you** cela ne vous concerne pas; **I won't have anything to ~ with it** je ne veux pas m'en mêler
to do without *vi* s'en passer ♦ *vt fus* se passer de.

dock [dɔk] *n* dock *m*; (*LAW*) banc *m* des accusés // *vi* se mettre à quai; **~er** *n* docker *m*; **~yard** *n* chantier *m* de construction navale.

doctor ['dɔktə*] *n* médecin *m*, docteur *m*; (*Ph.D. etc*) docteur // *vt* (*fig*) falsifier; (*drink*) frelater; **D~ of Philosophy (Ph.D.)** *n* doctorat *m*; titulaire *m/f* d'un doctorat.

doctrine ['dɔktrɪn] *n* doctrine *f*.

document ['dɔkjumənt] *n* document *m*; **~ary** [-'mɛntərɪ] *a*, *n* documentaire (*m*).

dodge [dɔdʒ] *n* truc *m*; combine *f* // *vt* esquiver, éviter.

doe [dəu] *n* (*deer*) biche *f*; (*rabbit*) lapine *f*.

does [dʌz] *vb see* do; **doesn't** = **does not.**

dog [dɔg] *n* chien/ne *m* // *vt* suivre de près; poursuivre, harceler; **~ collar** *n* collier *m* de chien; (*fig*) faux-col *m* d'ecclésiastique; **~-eared** *a* corné(e).

dogged ['dɔgɪd] *a* obstiné(e), opiniâtre.

dogsbody ['dɔgzbɔdɪ] *n* bonne *f* à tout faire, tâcheron *m*.

doings ['duɪŋz] *npl* activités *fpl*.

do-it-yourself [du:ɪtjɔ:'sɛlf] *n* bricolage *m*.

doldrums ['dɔldrəmz] *npl*: **to be in the ~** avoir le cafard; être dans le marasme.

dole [dəul] *n* (*Brit: payment*) allocation *f* de chômage; **on the ~** au chômage; **to ~ out** *vt* donner au compte-goutte.

doleful ['dəulful] *a* triste, lugubre.

doll [dɔl] *n* poupée *f*; **to ~ o.s. up** se faire beau(belle).

dollar ['dɔlə*] *n* dollar *m*.

dolphin ['dɔlfɪn] *n* dauphin *m*.

domestic [də'mɛstɪk] *a* (*duty, happiness*) familial(e); (*policy, affairs, flights*) intérieur(e); (*animal*) domestique.

dominant ['dɔmɪnənt] *a* dominant(e).

dominate ['dɔmɪneɪt] *vt* dominer; **domineering** [-'nɪərɪŋ] *a* dominateur(trice), autoritaire.

dominion [də'mɪnɪən] *n* domination *f*; territoire *m*; dominion *m*.

domino, ~es ['dɔmɪnəu] *n* domino *m*; **~es** *n* (*game*) dominos *mpl*.

don [dɔn] *n* (*Brit*) professeur *m* d'université.

donate [də'neɪt] *vt* faire don de, donner.

done [dʌn] *pp of* do.

donkey ['dɔŋkɪ] *n* âne *m*.

donor ['dəunə*] *n* (*of blood etc*) donneur/euse; (*to charity*) donateur/trice.

don't [dəunt] *vb* = **do not.**

doodle ['du:dl] *vi* griffonner, gribouiller.

doom [du:m] *n* destin *m*; ruine *f* // *vt*: **to be ~ed** (**to failure**) être voué(e) à l'échec; **~sday** *n* le Jugement dernier.

door [dɔ:*] *n* porte *f*; **~bell** *n* sonnette *f*; **~man** *n* (*in hotel*) portier *m*; (*in block of flats*) concierge *m*; **~mat** *n* paillasson *m*; **~step** *n* pas *m* de (la) porte, seuil *m*; **~way** *n* (*embrasure f de*) porte *f*.

dope [dəup] *n* (*col*) drogue *f* // *vt* (*horse etc*) doper.

dopey ['dəupɪ] *a* (*col*) à moitié endormi(e).

dormant ['dɔ:mənt] *a* assoupi(e), en veilleuse; (*rule, law*) inappliqué(e).

dormitory ['dɔ:mɪtrɪ] *n* dortoir *m*.

dose [dəus] *n* dose *f*; (*bout*) attaque *f*.

doss house ['dɔs-] *n* (*Brit*) asile *m* de nuit.

dot [dɔt] *n* point *m* // *vt*: **~ted with** parsemé(e) de; **on the ~** à l'heure tapante.

dote [dəut]: **to ~ on** *vt fus* être fou(folle) de.

dot-matrix printer [dɔt'meɪtrɪks-] *n* imprimante matricielle.

dotted line ['dɔtɪd-] *n* ligne pointillée.

double ['dʌbl] *a* double // *ad* (*fold*) en deux; (*twice*): **to cost ~ (sth)** coûter le double (de qch) *or* deux fois plus (que qch) // *n* double *m*; (*CINEMA*) doublure *f* // *vt* doubler; (*fold*) plier en deux // *vi* doubler; **on the ~, (*Brit*) at the ~** au pas de course; **~s** *n* (*TENNIS*) double *m*; **~ bass** *n* contrebasse *f*; **~ bed** *n* grand lit; **~-breasted** *a* croisé(e); **~cross** *vt* doubler, trahir; **~-decker** *n* autobus *m* à impériale; **~ glazing** *n* (*Brit*) double vitrage *m*; **~ room** *n* chambre *f* pour deux personnes; **doubly** *ad* doublement, deux fois plus.

doubt [daut] *n* doute *m* // *vt* douter de; **to ~ that** douter que; **~ful** *a* douteux(euse); (*person*) incertain(e); **~less** *ad* sans doute, sûrement.

dough [dəu] *n* pâte *f*; **~nut** *n* beignet *m*.

douse [dauz] *vt* (*drench*) tremper, inonder; (*extinguish*) éteindre.

dove [dʌv] *n* colombe *f*.

Dover ['dəuvə*] *n* Douvres.

dovetail ['dʌvteɪl] vi (fig) concorder.
dowdy ['daudɪ] a démodé(e); mal
fagoté(e).
down [daun] n (fluff) duvet m // ad en
bas // prep en bas de // vt (col: drink)
vider; ~ **with X!** à bas X!; ~**-and-out**
n clochard/e; ~**at-heel** a éculé(e); (fig)
miteux(euse); ~**cast** a démoralisé(e);
~**fall** n chute f; ruine f; ~**hearted** a
découragé(e); ~**hill** ad: to go ~**hill** descendre; ~ **payment** n acompte m;
~**pour** n pluie torrentielle, déluge m;
~**right** a franc(franche); (refusal)
catégorique; ~**stairs** ad au rez-de-
chaussée; à l'étage inférieur; ~**stream**
ad en aval; ~**to-earth** a terre à terre
inv; ~**town** ad en ville; ~ **under** ad en
Australie (or Nouvelle Zélande); ~**ward**
['daunwəd] a, ad, ~**wards** ['daunwədz]
ad vers le bas.
dowry ['daurɪ] n dot f.
doz. abbr of **dozen**.
doze [dəuz] vi sommeiller; **to ~ off** vi
s'assoupir.
dozen ['dʌzn] n douzaine f; **a ~ books**
une douzaine de livres; ~**s of** des
centaines or des milliers de.
Dr. abbr of **doctor, drive** (n).
drab [dræb] a terne, morne.
draft [drɑːft] n brouillon m; (COMM)
traite f; (US MIL) contingent m; (: call-
up) conscription f // vt faire le brouillon
de; see also **draught**.
draftsman n (US) = **draughtsman**.
drag [dræg] vt traîner; (river) draguer //
vi traîner // n (col) raseur/euse; corvée
f; (women's clothing): **in ~** (en)
travesti; **to ~ on** vi s'éterniser.
dragon ['drægən] n dragon m.
dragonfly ['drægənflaɪ] n libellule f.
drain [dreɪn] n égout m; (on resources)
saignée f // vt (land, marshes) drainer,
assécher; (vegetables) égoutter; (reser-
voir etc) vider // vi (water) s'écouler;
~**age** n système m d'égouts; ~**ing
board**, (US) ~**board** n égouttoir m;
~**pipe** n tuyau m d'écoulement.
dram [dræm] n petit verre.
drama ['drɑːmə] n (art) théâtre m, art
m dramatique; (play) pièce f; (event)
drame m; ~**tic** [drə'mætɪk] a
dramatique; spectaculaire; ~**tist**
['dræmətɪst] n auteur m dramatique;
~**tize** vt (events) dramatiser; (adapt:
for TV/cinema) adapter pour la
télévision/pour l'écran.
drank [dræŋk] pt of **drink**.
drape [dreɪp] vt draper; ~**s** npl (US)
rideaux mpl; ~**r** n (Brit) marchand/e de
nouveautés.
drastic ['dræstɪk] a sévère; énergique.
draught, (US) **draft** [drɑːft] n courant
m d'air; (NAUT) tirant m d'eau; ~**s** n
(Brit) (jeu m de) dames fpl; **on ~**
(beer) à la pression; ~**board** n (Brit)

damier m.
draughtsman, (US) **draftsman**
['drɑːftsmən] n dessinateur/trice (indus-
triel(le)).
draw [drɔː] vb (pt drew, pp drawn) vt
tirer; (attract) attirer; (picture) dessiner; (line, circle) tracer; (money)
retirer // vi (SPORT) faire match nul // n
match nul; tirage m au sort; loterie f;
to ~ near vi s'approcher; approcher;
to ~ out vi (lengthen) s'allonger // vt
(money) retirer; **to ~ up** vi (stop)
s'arrêter // vt (document) établir,
dresser; ~**back** n inconvénient m,
désavantage m; ~**bridge** n pont-levis
m.
drawer [drɔː*] n tiroir m; ['drɔːə*] (of
cheque) tireur m.
drawing ['drɔːɪŋ] n dessin m; ~ **board**
n planche f à dessin; ~ **pin** n (Brit)
punaise f; ~ **room** n salon m.
drawl [drɔːl] n accent traînant.
drawn [drɔːn] pp of **draw**.
dread [drɛd] n épouvante f, effroi m // vt
redouter, appréhender; ~**ful** a épouvantable, affreux(euse).
dream [driːm] n rêve m // vt, vi (pt, pp
dreamed or **dreamt** [drɛmt]) rêver;
~**y** a rêveur(euse).
dreary ['drɪərɪ] a triste; monotone.
dredge [drɛdʒ] vt draguer.
dregs [drɛgz] npl lie f.
drench [drɛntʃ] vt tremper.
dress [drɛs] n robe f; (clothing)
habillement m, tenue f // vi s'habiller //
vt habiller; (wound) panser; (food)
préparer; **to get ~ed** s'habiller; **to ~
up** vi s'habiller; (in fancy dress) se
déguiser; ~ **circle** n (Brit) premier
balcon; ~**er** n (THEATRE) habilleur/
euse; (furniture) vaisselier m; ~**ing**
n (MED) pansement m; (CULIN) sauce f,
assaisonnement m; ~**ing gown** n
(Brit) robe f de chambre; ~**ing room** n
(THEATRE) loge f; (SPORT) vestiaire m;
~**ing table** n coiffeuse f; ~**maker** n
couturière f; ~ **rehearsal** n (répétition)
générale; ~**y** a (col: clothes) (qui fait)
habillé(e).
drew [druː] pt of **draw**.
dribble ['drɪbl] vi tomber goutte à
goutte; (baby) baver // vt (ball) drib-
bler.
dried [draɪd] a (fruit, beans) sec(sèche);
(eggs, milk) en poudre.
drier ['draɪə*] n = **dryer**.
drift [drɪft] n (of current etc) force f;
direction f; (of sand etc) amoncellement
m; (of snow) rafale f; coulée f; (: on
ground) congère f; (general meaning)
sens général // vi (boat) aller à la
dérive, dériver; (sand, snow) s'amonceler, s'entasser; ~**wood** n bois flotté.
drill [drɪl] n perceuse f; (bit) foret m; (of
dentist) roulette f, fraise f; (MIL)

exercice *m* // *vt* percer // *vi* (*for oil*) faire un *or* des forage(s).

drink [drɪŋk] *n* boisson *f* // *vt*, *vi* (*pt* **drank**, *pp* **drunk**) boire; **to have a ~** boire quelque chose, boire un verre; prendre l'apéritif; **a ~ of water** un verre d'eau; **~er** *n* buveur/euse; **~ing water** *n* eau *f* potable.

drip [drɪp] *n* bruit *m* d'égouttement; goutte *f*; (*MED*) goutte-à-goutte *m inv*; perfusion *f* // *vi* tomber goutte à goutte; (*washing*) s'égoutter; (*wall*) suinter; **~-dry** *a* (*shirt*) sans repassage; **~ping** *n* graisse *f* de rôti.

drive [draɪv] *n* promenade *f* *or* trajet *m* en voiture; (*also*: **~way**) allée *f*; (*energy*) dynamisme *m*, énergie *f*; (*PSYCH*) besoin *m*; pulsion *f*; (*push*) effort (concerté); campagne *f*; (*SPORT*) drive *m*; (*TECH*) entraînement *m*; traction *f*; transmission *f*; (*also*: **disk** ~) lecteur *m* de disquette // *vb* (*pt* **drove**, *pp* **driven**) *vt* conduire; (*nail*) enfoncer; (*push*) chasser, pousser; (*TECH*: *motor*) actionner; entraîner // *vi* (*AUT*: *at controls*) conduire; (: *travel*) aller en voiture; **left-/right-hand ~** conduite *f* à gauche/droite; **to ~ sb mad** rendre qn fou(folle).

drivel ['drɪvl] *n* (*col*) idioties *fpl*.

driven ['drɪvn] *pp* of **drive**.

driver ['draɪvə*] *n* conducteur/trice; (*of taxi, bus*) chauffeur *m*; **~'s license** *n* (*US*) permis *m* de conduire.

driveway ['draɪvweɪ] *n* allée *f*.

driving ['draɪvɪŋ] *n* conduite *f*; **~ instructor** *n* moniteur *m* d'auto-école; **~ lesson** *n* leçon *f* de conduite; **~ licence** *n* (*Brit*) permis *m* de conduire; **~ mirror** *n* rétroviseur *m*; **~ school** *n* auto-école *f*; **~ test** *n* examen *m* du permis de conduire.

drizzle ['drɪzl] *n* bruine *f*, crachin *m*.

droll [drəul] *a* drôle.

drone [drəun] *n* bourdonnement *m*.

drool [dru:l] *vi* baver.

droop [dru:p] *vi* s'affaisser; tomber.

drop [drɔp] *n* goutte *f*; (*fall*) baisse *f*; (*also*: **parachute ~**) saut *m*; (*of cliff*) dénivellation *f*; à-pic *m* // *vt* laisser tomber; (*voice, eyes, price*) baisser; (*set down from car*) déposer // *vi* tomber; **~s** *npl* (*MED*) gouttes; **to ~ off** *vi* (*sleep*) s'assoupir // *vt* (*passenger*) déposer; **to ~ out** *vi* (*withdraw*) se retirer; (*student etc*) abandonner, décrocher; **~-out** *n* marginal/e; (*from studies*) drop-out *m/f*; **~pings** *npl* crottes *fpl*.

drought [draut] *n* sécheresse *f*.

drove [drəuv] *pt* of **drive**.

drown [draun] *vt* noyer // *vi* se noyer.

drowsy ['drauzɪ] *a* somnolent(e).

drudgery ['drʌdʒərɪ] *n* corvée *f*.

drug [drʌg] *n* médicament *m*; (*narcotic*) drogue *f* // *vt* droguer ~ **addict** *n* toxicomane *m/f*; **~gist** *n* (*US*) pharmacien/ne-droguiste; **~store** *n* (*US*) pharmacie-droguerie *f*, drugstore *m*.

drum [drʌm] *n* tambour *m*; (*for oil, petrol*) bidon *m* // *vi* tambouriner; **~s** *npl* batterie *f*; **~mer** *n* (joueur *m* de) tambour *m*.

drunk [drʌŋk] *pp* of **drink** // *a* ivre, soûl(e) // *n* (*also*: **~ard**) soûlard/e; homme/femme soûl(e); **~en** *a* ivre, soûl(e); ivrogne, d'ivrogne.

dry [draɪ] *a* sec(sèche); (*day*) sans pluie // *vt* sécher; (*clothes*) faire sécher // *vi* sécher; **to ~ up** *vi* se tarir; **~-cleaner's** *n* teinturerie *f*; **~er** *n* séchoir *m*; (*US*: *spin-dryer*) essoreuse *f*; **~ goods store** *n* (*US*) magasin *m* de nouveautés; **~ness** *n* sécheresse *f*; **~ rot** *n* pourriture sèche (*du bois*).

dual ['djuəl] *a* double; **~ carriageway** *n* (*Brit*) route *f* à quatre voies *or* à chaussées séparées.

dubbed [dʌbd] *a* (*CINEMA*) doublé(e); (*nicknamed*) surnommé(e).

dubious ['dju:bɪəs] *a* hésitant(e), incertain(e); (*reputation, company*) douteux(euse).

duchess ['dʌtʃɪs] *n* duchesse *f*.

duck [dʌk] *n* canard *m* // *vi* se baisser vivement, baisser subitement la tête; **~ling** *n* caneton *m*.

duct [dʌkt] *n* conduite *f*, canalisation *f*; (*ANAT*) conduit *m*.

dud [dʌd] *n* (*shell*) obus non éclaté; (*object, tool*): **it's a ~** c'est de la camelote, ça ne marche pas // *a* (*Brit*: *cheque*) sans provision; (: *note, coin*) faux(fausse).

due [dju:] *a* dû(due); (*expected*) attendu(e); (*fitting*) qui convient // *n* dû *m* // *ad*: **~ north** droit vers le nord; **~s** *npl* (*for club, union*) cotisation *f*; (*in harbour*) droits *mpl* (de port); **in ~ course** en temps utile *or* voulu; finalement; **~ to** dû(due) à; causé(e) par; **he's ~ to finish tomorrow** normalement il doit finir demain.

duet [dju:'ɛt] *n* duo *m*.

duffel [dʌfl] *a*: **~ bag** sac *m* marin; **~ coat** duffel-coat *m*.

dug [dʌg] *pt*, *pp* of **dig**.

duke [dju:k] *n* duc *m*.

dull [dʌl] *a* ennuyeux(euse); terne; (*sound, pain*) sourd(e); (*weather, day*) gris(e), maussade; (*blade*) émoussé(e) // *vt* (*pain, grief*) atténuer; (*mind, senses*) engourdir.

duly ['dju:lɪ] *ad* (*on time*) en temps voulu; (*as expected*) comme il se doit.

dumb [dʌm] *a* muet(te); (*stupid*) bête; **dumbfounded** [dʌm'faundɪd] *a* sidéré(e).

dummy ['dʌmɪ] n (tailor's model) mannequin m; (SPORT) feinte f; (Brit: for baby) tétine f // a faux(fausse), factice.

dump [dʌmp] n tas m d'ordures; (place) décharge (publique); (MIL) dépôt m // vt (put down) déposer; déverser; (get rid of) se débarrasser de; **~ing** n (ECON) dumping m; (of rubbish): 'no **~ing**' 'décharge interdite'.

dumpling ['dʌmplɪŋ] n boulette f (de pâte).

dumpy ['dʌmpɪ] a courtaud(e), boulot(te).

dunce [dʌns] n âne m, cancre m.

dung [dʌŋ] n fumier m.

dungarees [dʌŋgə'ri:z] npl bleu(s) m(pl); salopette f.

dungeon ['dʌndʒən] n cachot m.

Dunkirk [dʌn'kɔ:k] n Dunkerque.

duplex ['du:plɛks] n (US) maison jumelée; (: apartment) duplex m.

duplicate ['dju:plɪkət] n double m, copie exacte // vt ['dju:plɪkeɪt] faire un double de; (on machine) polycopier.

durable ['djuərəbl] a durable; (clothes, metal) résistant(e), solide.

duration [djuə'reɪʃən] n durée f.

duress [djuə'rɛs] n: **under ~** sous la contrainte.

during ['djuərɪŋ] prep pendant, au cours de.

dusk [dʌsk] n crépuscule m.

dust [dʌst] n poussière f // vt (furniture) essuyer, épousseter; (cake etc): to **~** with saupoudrer de; **~bin** n (Brit) poubelle f; **~er** n chiffon m; **~ jacket** n jaquette f; **~man** n (Brit) boueux m, éboueur m; **~y** a poussiéreux(euse).

Dutch [dʌtʃ] a hollandais(e), néerlandais(e) // n (LING) hollandais m; the **~** npl les Hollandais; **to go ~** partager les frais; **~man/woman** n Hollandais/e.

dutiful ['dju:tɪful] a (child) respectueux(euse).

duty ['dju:tɪ] n devoir m; (tax) droit m, taxe f; **duties** npl fonctions fpl; **on ~** de service; (at night etc) de garde; **off ~** libre, pas de service or de garde; **~-free** a exempté(e) de douane, hors-taxe.

duvet ['du:veɪ] n (Brit) couette f.

dwarf [dwɔ:f] n nain/e // vt écraser.

dwell, pt, pp **dwelt** [dwel, dwelt] vi demeurer; **to ~ on** vt fus s'étendre sur; **~ing** n habitation f, demeure f.

dwindle ['dwɪndl] vi diminuer, décroître.

dye [daɪ] n teinture f // vt teindre.

dying ['daɪɪŋ] a mourant(e), agonisant(e).

dyke [daɪk] n (Brit) digue f.

dynamic [daɪ'næmɪk] a dynamique.

dynamite ['daɪnəmaɪt] n dynamite f.

dynamo ['daɪnəməʊ] n dynamo f.

dyslexia [dɪs'lɛksɪə] n dyslexie f.

E

E [i:] n (MUS) mi m.

each [i:tʃ] a chaque // pronoun chacun(e); **~ one** chacun(e); **they hate ~ other** ils se détestent (mutuellement); **you are jealous of ~ other** vous êtes jaloux l'un de l'autre; **they have 2 books ~** ils ont 2 livres chacun.

eager [i:gə*] a impatient(e); avide; ardent(e), passionné(e); **to be ~ for** désirer vivement, être avide de.

eagle ['i:gl] n aigle m.

ear [ɪə*] n oreille f; (of corn) épi m; **~ache** n douleurs fpl aux oreilles; **~drum** n tympan m.

earl [ə:l] n comte m.

earlier ['ə:lɪə*] a (date etc) plus rapproché(e); (edition etc) plus ancien(ne), antérieur(e) // ad plus tôt.

early ['ə:lɪ] ad tôt, de bonne heure; (ahead of time) en avance // a précoce; anticipé(e); qui se manifeste (or se fait) tôt or de bonne heure; **to have an ~ night** se coucher tôt or de bonne heure; **in the ~ or ~ in the spring/19th century** au début or commencement du printemps/19ème siècle; **~ retirement** n retraite anticipée.

earmark ['ɪəmɑːk] vt: **to ~ sth for** réserver or destiner qch à.

earn [ə:n] vt gagner; (COMM: yield) rapporter.

earnest ['ə:nɪst] a sérieux(euse); **in ~** ad sérieusement, pour de bon.

earnings ['ə:nɪŋz] npl salaire m; gains mpl.

earphones ['ɪəfəʊnz] npl écouteurs mpl.

earring ['ɪərɪŋ] n boucle f d'oreille.

earshot ['ɪəʃɔt] n: out of/within **~** hors de portée/à portée de la voix.

earth [ə:θ] n (gen; also ELEC: Brit) terre f; (of fox etc) terrier m // vt (Brit: ELEC) relier à la terre; **~enware** n poterie f; faïence f; **~quake** n tremblement m de terre, séisme m; **~y** a (fig) terre à terre inv; truculent(e).

ease [i:z] n facilité f, aisance f // vt (soothe) calmer; (loosen) relâcher, détendre; (help pass): **to ~ sth in/out** faire pénétrer/sortir qch délicatement or avec douceur; faciliter la pénétration/la sortie de qch; **at ~** (MIL) au repos; **to ~ off or up** vi ralentir; se détendre.

easel ['i:zl] n chevalet m.

east [i:st] n est m // a d'est // ad à l'est, vers l'est; the **E~** l'Orient m.

Easter ['i:stə*] n Pâques fpl; **~ egg** n œuf m de Pâques.

easterly ['i:stəlɪ] a d'est.

eastern ['i:stən] a de l'est, oriental(e).

East Germany n Allemagne f de l'Est.

eastward(s) ['i:stwəd(z)] ad vers l'est, à l'est.

easy ['i:zɪ] a facile; (manner) aisé(e) // ad: to take it or things ~ ne pas se fatiguer; ne pas (trop) s'en faire; ~ **chair** n fauteuil m; ~**going** a accommodant(e), facile à vivre.

eat, pt **ate**, pp **eaten** [i:t, eɪt, 'i:tn] vt, vi manger; **to ~ into, to ~ away at** vt fus ronger, attaquer.

eaves [i:vz] npl avant-toit m.

eavesdrop ['i:vzdrɔp] vi: **to ~ (on** a conversation) écouter (une conversation) de façon indiscrète.

ebb [ɛb] n reflux m // vi refluer; (fig: also: ~ **away**) décliner.

ebony ['ɛbənɪ] n ébène f.

eccentric [ɪk'sɛntrɪk] a, n excentrique (m/f).

echo, ~**es** ['ɛkəʊ] n écho m // vt répéter; faire chorus avec // vi résonner; faire écho.

eclipse [ɪ'klɪps] n éclipse f.

ecology [ɪ'kɔlədʒɪ] n écologie f.

economic [i:kə'nɔmɪk] a économique; (business etc) rentable; ~**al** a économique; (person) économe; ~**s** n économie f politique.

economize [ɪ'kɔnəmaɪz] vi économiser, faire des économies.

economy [ɪ'kɔnəmɪ] n économie f.

ecstasy ['ɛkstəsɪ] n extase f.

eczema ['ɛksɪmə] n eczéma m.

edge [ɛdʒ] n bord m; (of knife etc) tranchant m, fil m // vt border; **on ~** (fig) = edgy; **to ~ away from** s'éloigner furtivement de; ~**ways** ad latéralement; **he couldn't get a word in ~ways** il ne pouvait pas placer un mot.

edgy ['ɛdʒɪ] a crispé(e), tendu(e).

edible ['ɛdɪbl] a comestible; (meal) mangeable.

edict ['i:dɪkt] n décret m.

Edinburgh ['ɛdɪnbərə] n Édimbourg.

edit ['ɛdɪt] vt éditer; ~**ion** [ɪ'dɪʃən] n édition f; ~**or** n (in newspaper) rédacteur/trice; rédacteur/trice en chef; (of sb's work) éditeur/trice; ~**orial** [-'tɔːrɪəl] a de la rédaction, éditorial(e) // n éditorial m.

educate ['ɛdjukeɪt] vt instruire; éduquer.

education [ɛdju'keɪʃən] n éducation f; (schooling) enseignement m, instruction f; ~**al** a pédagogique; scolaire; instructif(ive).

EEC n abbr (= European Economic Community) C.E.E. f (= Communauté économique européenne).

eel [i:l] n anguille f.

eerie ['ɪərɪ] a inquiétant(e), spectral(e), surnaturel(le).

effect [ɪ'fɛkt] n effet m // vt effectuer; ~**s** npl (THEATRE) effets mpl; **to take ~**

(law) entrer en vigueur, prendre effet; (drug) agir, faire son effet; **in ~** en fait; ~**ive** a efficace; ~**ively** ad efficacement; (in reality) effectivement; ~**iveness** n efficacité f.

effeminate [ɪ'fɛmɪnɪt] a efféminé(e).

efficiency [ɪ'fɪʃənsɪ] n efficacité f; rendement m.

efficient [ɪ'fɪʃənt] a efficace.

effort ['ɛfət] n effort m.

effusive [ɪ'fju:sɪv] a expansif(ive); chaleureux(euse).

e.g. ad abbr (= exempli gratia) par exemple, p. ex.

egg [ɛg] n œuf m; **to ~ on** vt pousser; ~**cup** n coquetier m; ~**plant** n (esp US) aubergine f; ~**shell** n coquille f d'œuf.

ego ['i:gəʊ] n moi m.

egotism ['ɛgəʊtɪzəm] n égotisme m.

egotist ['ɛgəʊtɪst] n égocentrique m/f.

Egypt ['i:dʒɪpt] n Égypte f; ~**ian** [ɪ'dʒɪpʃən] a égyptien(ne) // n Égyptien/ne.

eiderdown ['aɪdədaun] n édredon m.

eight [eɪt] num huit; ~**een** num dix-huit; **eighth** a, n huitième (m); ~**y** num quatre-vingt(s).

Eire ['ɛərə] n République f d'Irlande.

either ['aɪðə*] a l'un ou l'autre; (both, each) chaque; **on ~ side** de chaque côté // pronoun: ~ **(of them)** l'un ou l'autre; **I don't like ~** je n'aime ni l'un ni l'autre // ad non plus; **no, I don't ~** moi non plus // cj: ~ **good or bad** ou bon ou mauvais, soit bon soit mauvais.

eject [ɪ'dʒɛkt] vt expulser; éjecter.

eke [i:k]: **to ~ out** vt faire durer; augmenter.

elaborate a [ɪ'læbərɪt] compliqué(e), recherché(e), minutieux(euse) // vb [ɪ'læbəreɪt] vt élaborer // vi entrer dans les détails.

elapse [ɪ'læps] vi s'écouler, passer.

elastic [ɪ'læstɪk] a, n élastique (m); ~ **band** n (Brit) élastique m.

elated [ɪ'leɪtɪd] a transporté(e) de joie.

elbow ['ɛlbəʊ] n coude m.

elder ['ɛldə*] a aîné(e) // n (tree) sureau m; **one's ~s** ses aînés; ~**ly** a âgé(e) // npl: **the ~ly** les personnes âgées.

eldest ['ɛldɪst] a, n: **the ~ (child)** l'aîné(e) (des enfants).

elect [ɪ'lɛkt] vt élire; **to ~ to do** choisir de faire // a: **the president ~** le président désigné; ~**ion** [ɪ'lɛkʃən] n élection f; ~**ioneering** [ɪlɛkʃə'nɪərɪŋ] n propagande électorale, manœuvres électorales; ~**or** n électeur/trice; ~**orate** n électorat m.

electric [ɪ'lɛktrɪk] a électrique; ~**al** a électrique; ~ **blanket** n couverture chauffante; ~ **fire** n radiateur m électrique.

electrician [ɪlɛk'trɪʃən] n électricien m.

electricity [ɪlɛk'trɪsɪtɪ] n électricité f.
electrify [ɪ'lɛktrɪfaɪ] vt (RAIL) électrifier; (audience) électriser.
electronic [ɪlɛk'trɔnɪk] a électronique; ~**s** n électronique f.
elegant ['ɛlɪgənt] a élégant(e).
element ['ɛlɪmənt] n (gen) élément m; (of heater, kettle etc) résistance f; ~**ary** [-'mɛntərɪ] a élémentaire; (school, education) primaire.
elephant ['ɛlɪfənt] n éléphant m.
elevate ['ɛlɪveɪt] vt élever.
elevator ['ɛlɪveɪtə*] n élévateur m, monte-charge m inv; (US: lift) ascenseur m.
eleven [ɪ'lɛvn] num onze; ~**ses** npl (Brit) ≈ pause-café f; ~**th** a onzième.
elicit [ɪ'lɪsɪt] vt: to ~ (from) obtenir (de), arracher (à).
eligible ['ɛlɪdʒəbl] a éligible; (for membership) admissible.
elm [ɛlm] n orme m.
elongated ['i:lɔŋgeɪtɪd] a étiré(e), allongé(e).
elope [ɪ'ləup] vi (lovers) s'enfuir (ensemble).
eloquent ['ɛləkwənt] a éloquent(e).
else [ɛls] ad d'autre; **something** ~ quelque chose d'autre, autre chose; **somewhere** ~ ailleurs, autre part; **everywhere** ~ partout ailleurs; **nobody** ~ personne d'autre; **where** ~? à quel autre endroit?; **little** ~ pas grand-chose d'autre; ~**where** ad ailleurs, autre part.
elude [ɪ'lu:d] vt échapper à; (question) éluder.
elusive [ɪ'lu:sɪv] a insaisissable.
emaciated [ɪ'meɪsɪeɪtɪd] a émacié(e), décharné(e).
emancipate [ɪ'mænsɪpeɪt] vt émanciper.
embankment [ɪm'bæŋkmənt] n (of road, railway) remblai m, talus m; (riverside) berge f, quai m; (dyke) digue f.
embark [ɪm'bɑ:k] vi: to ~ (on) (s')embarquer (à bord de or sur) // vt embarquer; to ~ on (fig) se lancer or s'embarquer dans; ~**ation** [ɛmbɑ:'keɪʃən] n embarquement m.
embarrass [ɪm'bærəs] vt embarrasser, gêner; ~**ed** a géné(e); ~**ing** a gênant(e), embarrassant(e); ~**ment** n embarras m, gêne f.
embassy ['ɛmbəsɪ] n ambassade f.
embed [ɪm'bɛd] vt enfoncer; sceller.
embers ['ɛmbəz] npl braise f.
embezzle [ɪm'bɛzl] vt détourner.
embitter [ɪm'bɪtə*] vt aigrir; envenimer.
embody [ɪm'bɔdɪ] vt (features) réunir, comprendre; (ideas) formuler, exprimer.
embossed [ɪm'bɔst] a repoussé(e); gaufré(e).

embrace [ɪm'breɪs] vt embrasser, étreindre; (include) embrasser, couvrir // vi s'étreindre, s'embrasser // n étreinte f.
embroider [ɪm'brɔɪdə*] vt broder; (fig: story) enjoliver; ~**y** n broderie f.
emerald ['ɛmərəld] n émeraude f.
emerge [ɪ'mə:dʒ] vi apparaître, surgir.
emergence [ɪ'mə:dʒəns] n apparition f.
emergency [ɪ'mə:dʒənsɪ] n urgence f; **in an** ~ en cas d'urgence; ~ **cord** n (US) sonnette f d'alarme; ~ **exit** n sortie f de secours; ~ **landing** n atterrissage forcé; **the** ~ **services** npl (fire, police, ambulance) les services mpl d'urgence.
emery board ['ɛmərɪ-] n lime f à ongles (en carton émerisé).
emigrate ['ɛmɪgreɪt] vi émigrer.
eminent ['ɛmɪnənt] a éminent(e).
emit [ɪ'mɪt] vt émettre.
emotion [ɪ'məuʃən] n émotion f; ~**al** a (person) émotif(ive), très sensible; (scene) émouvant(e); (tone, speech) qui fait appel aux sentiments.
emperor ['ɛmpərə*] n empereur m.
emphasis, pl -**ases** ['ɛmfəsɪs, -si:z] n accent m; force f, insistance f.
emphasize ['ɛmfəsaɪz] vt (syllable, word, point) appuyer or insister sur; (feature) souligner, accentuer.
emphatic [ɛm'fætɪk] a (strong) énergique, vigoureux(euse); (unambiguous, clear) catégorique; ~**ally** ad avec vigueur or énergie; catégoriquement.
empire ['ɛmpaɪə*] n empire m.
employ [ɪm'plɔɪ] vt employer; ~**ee** [-'i:] n employé/e; ~**er** n employeur/euse; ~**ment** n emploi m; ~**ment agency** n agence f or bureau m de placement.
empower [ɪm'pauə*] vt: to ~ sb to do autoriser or habiliter qn à faire.
empress ['ɛmprɪs] n impératrice f.
empty ['ɛmptɪ] a vide; (threat, promise) en l'air, vain(e) // vt vider // vi se vider; (liquid) s'écouler // n (bottle) bouteille f vide; ~-**handed** a les mains vides.
emulate ['ɛmjuleɪt] vt rivaliser avec, imiter.
emulsion [ɪ'mʌlʃən] n émulsion f; ~ (paint) n peinture mate.
enable [ɪ'neɪbl] vt: to ~ sb to do permettre à qn de faire.
enact [ɪn'ækt] vt (law) promulguer; (play) jouer, représenter.
enamel [ɪ'næməl] n émail m.
encased [ɪn'keɪst] a: ~ in enfermé(e) dans, recouvert(e) de.
enchant [ɪn'tʃɑ:nt] vt enchanter; ~**ing** a ravissant(e), enchanteur(eresse).
encl. abbr (= enclosed) annexe(s).
enclose [ɪn'kləuz] vt (land) clôturer; (letter etc): to ~ (with) joindre (à); **please find** ~d veuillez trouver ci-joint.
enclosure [ɪn'kləuʒə*] n enceinte f;

(COMM) annexe f.

encompass [ɪn'kʌmpəs] vt encercler, entourer; (include) contenir, inclure.

encore [ɔŋ'kɔ:*] excl, n bis (m).

encounter [ɪn'kauntə*] n rencontre f // vt rencontrer.

encourage [ɪn'kʌrɪdʒ] vt encourager; ~ment n encouragement m.

encroach [ɪn'krəutʃ] vi: to ~ (up)on empiéter sur.

encyclop(a)edia [ɛnsaɪkləu'pi:dɪə] n encyclopédie f.

end [ɛnd] n (gen, also: aim) fin f; (of table, street etc) bout m, extrémité f // vt terminer; (also: bring to an ~, put an ~ to) mettre fin à // vi se terminer, finir; in the ~ finalement; on ~ (object) debout, dressé(e); to stand on ~ (hair) se dresser sur la tête; for 5 hours on ~ durant 5 heures d'affilée or de suite; to ~ up vi: to ~ up in finir or se terminer par; (place) finir or aboutir à.

endanger [ɪn'deɪndʒə*] vt mettre en danger.

endearing [ɪn'dɪərɪŋ] a attachant(e).

endeavour, (US) **endeavor** [ɪn'devə*] n tentative f, effort m // vi: to ~ to do tenter or s'efforcer de faire.

ending ['ɛndɪŋ] n dénouement m, conclusion f; (LING) terminaison f.

endive ['ɛndaɪv] n chicorée f.

endless ['ɛndlɪs] a sans fin, interminable; (patience, resources) inépuisable, sans limites.

endorse [ɪn'dɔ:s] vt (cheque) endosser; (approve) appuyer, approuver, sanctionner; ~ment n (on driving licence) contravention portée au permis de conduire.

endow [ɪn'dau] vt (provide with money) faire une donation à, doter; (equip): to ~ with gratifier de, doter de.

endure [ɪn'djuə*] vt supporter, endurer // vi durer.

enemy ['ɛnəmɪ] a, n ennemi(e).

energetic [ɛnə'dʒɛtɪk] a énergique; actif(ive); qui fait se dépenser (physiquement).

energy ['ɛnədʒɪ] n énergie f.

enforce [ɪn'fɔ:s] vt (LAW) appliquer, faire respecter; ~d a forcé(e).

engage [ɪn'geɪdʒ] vt engager; (MIL) engager le combat avec // vi (TECH) s'enclencher, s'engrener; to ~ in se lancer dans; ~d a (Brit: busy, in use) occupé(e); (betrothed) fiancé(e); to get ~d se fiancer; ~d tone n (Brit TEL) tonalité f occupé or pas libre; ~ment n obligation f, engagement m; rendez-vous m inv; (to marry) fiançailles fpl; (MIL) combat m; ~ment ring n bague f de fiançailles.

engaging [ɪn'geɪdʒɪŋ] a engageant(e), attirant(e).

engender [ɪn'dʒɛndə*] vt produire, causer.

engine ['ɛndʒɪn] n (AUT) moteur m; (RAIL) locomotive f; ~ driver n mécanicien m.

engineer [ɛndʒɪ'nɪə*] n ingénieur m; (US RAIL) mécanicien m; ~ing n engineering m, ingénierie f; (of bridges, ships) génie m; (of machine) mécanique f.

England ['ɪŋglənd] n Angleterre f.

English ['ɪŋglɪʃ] a anglais(e) // n (LING) anglais m; the ~ npl les Anglais; the ~ Channel n la Manche; ~man/woman n Anglais/e.

engraving [ɪn'greɪvɪŋ] n gravure f.

engrossed [ɪn'grəust] a: ~ in absorbé(e) par, plongé(e) dans.

engulf [ɪn'gʌlf] vt engloutir.

enhance [ɪn'hɑ:ns] vt rehausser, mettre en valeur.

enjoy [ɪn'dʒɔɪ] vt aimer, prendre plaisir à; (have: health, fortune) jouir de; (: success) connaître; to ~ o.s. s'amuser; ~able a agréable; ~ment n plaisir m.

enlarge [ɪn'lɑ:dʒ] vt accroître; (PHOT) agrandir // vi: to ~ on (subject) s'étendre sur.

enlighten [ɪn'laɪtn] vt éclairer; ~ed a éclairé(e); ~ment n: the E~ment (HISTORY) ≈ le Siècle des lumières.

enlist [ɪn'lɪst] vt recruter; (support) s'assurer // vi s'engager.

enmity ['ɛnmɪtɪ] n inimitié f.

enormous [ɪ'nɔ:məs] a énorme.

enough [ɪ'nʌf] a, n: ~ time/books assez or suffisamment de temps/livres; have you got ~? (en) avez-vous assez? // ad: big ~ assez or suffisamment grand; he has not worked ~ il n'a pas assez or suffisamment travaillé; ~! assez!, ça suffit!; that's ~, thanks cela suffit or c'est assez, merci; I've had ~ of him j'en ai assez de lui; ... which, funnily ~ ... qui, chose curieuse.

enquire [ɪn'kwaɪə*] vt, vi = inquire.

enrage [ɪn'reɪdʒ] vt mettre en fureur or en rage, rendre furieux(euse).

enrol [ɪn'rəul] vt inscrire // vi s'inscrire; ~ment n inscription f.

ensign n (NAUT) ['ɛnsən] enseigne f, pavillon m; (MIL) ['ɛnsaɪn] porte-étendard m.

ensue [ɪn'sju:] vi s'ensuivre, résulter.

ensure [ɪn'ʃuə*] vt assurer; garantir; to ~ that s'assurer que.

entail [ɪn'teɪl] vt entraîner, nécessiter.

entangle [ɪn'tæŋgl] vt emmêler, embrouiller.

enter ['ɛntə*] vt (room) entrer dans, pénétrer dans; (club, army) entrer à; (competition) s'inscrire à or pour; (sb for a competition) (faire) inscrire; (write down) inscrire, noter; (COMPUT) entrer, introduire // vi entrer; to ~ for vt fus s'inscrire à, se présenter pour or à; to ~ into vt fus (explanation) se lancer dans; (*debate*) prendre part à; (*agreement*) conclure; **to ~ (up)on** *vt fus* commencer.

enterprise ['ɛntəpraɪz] *n* entreprise *f*; (esprit *m* d')initiative *f*; **free ~** libre entreprise; **private ~** entreprise privée.

enterprising ['ɛntəpraɪzɪŋ] *a* entreprenant(e), dynamique.

entertain [ɛntə'teɪn] *vt* amuser, distraire; (*invite*) recevoir (à dîner); (*idea, plan*) envisager; **~er** *n* artiste *m/f* de variétés; **~ing** *a* amusant(e), distrayant(e); **~ment** *n* (*amusement*) distraction *f*, divertissement *m*, amusement *m*; (*show*) spectacle *m*.

enthralled [ɪn'θrɔːld] *a* captivé(e).

enthusiasm [ɪn'θuːzɪæzəm] *n* enthousiasme *m*.

enthusiast [ɪn'θuːzɪæst] *n* enthousiaste *m/f*; **~ic** [-'æstɪk] *a* enthousiaste; **to be ~ic about** être enthousiasmé(e) par.

entice [ɪn'taɪs] *vt* attirer, séduire.

entire [ɪn'taɪə*] *a* (tout) entier(ère); **~ly** *ad* entièrement, complètement; **~ty** [ɪn'taɪərətɪ] *n*: **in its ~ty** dans sa totalité.

entitle [ɪn'taɪtl] *vt* (*allow*): **to ~ sb to do** donner (le) droit à qn de faire; **to ~ sb to sth** donner droit à qch à qn; **~d** *a* (*book*) intitulé(e); **to be ~d to do** avoir le droit de *or* être habilité à faire.

entrance *n* ['ɛntrns] entrée *f* // *vt* [ɪn'trɑːns] enchanter, ravir; **to gain ~ to** (*university etc*) être admis à; **~ examination** *n* examen *m* d'entrée; **~ fee** *n* droit *m* d'inscription; (*to museum etc*) prix *m* d'entrée; **~ ramp** *n* (*US AUT*) bretelle *f* d'accès.

entrant ['ɛntrnt] *n* participant/e; concurrent/e.

entreat [ɛn'triːt] *vt* supplier.

entrenched [ɛn'trɛntʃt] *a* retranché(e).

entrepreneur [ɔntrəprə'nə:*] *n* entrepreneur *m*.

entrust [ɪn'trʌst] *vt*: **to ~ sth to** confier qch à.

entry ['ɛntrɪ] *n* entrée *f*; (*in register*) inscription *f*; **no ~** défense d'entrer, entrée interdite; (*AUT*) sens interdit; **~ form** *n* feuille *f* d'inscription; **~ phone** *n* interphone *m* (à l'entrée d'un immeuble).

envelop [ɪn'vɛləp] *vt* envelopper.

envelope ['ɛnvələup] *n* enveloppe *f*.

envious ['ɛnvɪəs] *a* envieux(euse).

environment [ɪn'vaɪərnmənt] *n* milieu *m*; environnement *m*; **~al** [-'mɛntl] *a* écologique; du milieu.

envisage [ɪn'vɪzɪdʒ] *vt* envisager; prévoir.

envoy ['ɛnvɔɪ] *n* envoyé/e.

envy ['ɛnvɪ] *n* envie *f* // *vt* envier; **to ~ sb sth** envier qch à qn.

epic ['ɛpɪk] *n* épopée *f* // *a* épique.

epidemic [ɛpɪ'dɛmɪk] *n* épidémie *f*.

epilepsy ['ɛpɪlɛpsɪ] *n* épilepsie *f*.

episode ['ɛpɪsəud] *n* épisode *m*.

epistle [ɪ'pɪsl] *n* épître *f*.

epitome [ɪ'pɪtəmɪ] *n* résumé *m*; quintessence *f*, type *m*; **epitomize** *vt* résumer; illustrer, incarner.

equable ['ɛkwəbl] *a* égal(e); de tempérament égal.

equal ['iːkwl] *a* égal(e) // *n* égal/e // *vt* égaler; **~ to** (*task*) à la hauteur de; **~ity** [iː'kwɔlɪtɪ] *n* égalité *f*; **~ize** *vt, vi* égaliser; **~izer** *n* but égalisateur; **~ly** *ad* également; (*just as*) tout aussi.

equanimity [ɛkwə'nɪmɪtɪ] *n* égalité *f* d'humeur.

equate [ɪ'kweɪt] *vt*: **to ~ sth with** comparer qch à; assimiler qch à; **equation** [ɪ'kweɪʒən] *n* (*MATH*) équation *f*.

equator [ɪ'kweɪtə*] *n* équateur *m*.

equilibrium [iːkwɪ'lɪbrɪəm] *n* équilibre *m*.

equip [ɪ'kwɪp] *vt* équiper; **to be well ~ped** (*office etc*) être bien équipé(e); **he is well ~ped for the job** il a les compétences *or* les qualités requises pour ce travail; **~ment** *n* équipement *m*; (*electrical etc*) appareillage *m*, installation *f*.

equities ['ɛkwɪtɪz] *npl* (*Brit COMM*) actions cotées en Bourse.

equivalent [ɪ'kwɪvələnt] *a*: **~ (to)** équivalent(e) (à) // *n* équivalent *m*.

equivocal [ɪ'kwɪvəkl] *a* équivoque; (*open to suspicion*) douteux(euse).

era ['ɪərə] *n* ère *f*, époque *f*.

eradicate [ɪ'rædɪkeɪt] *vt* éliminer.

erase [ɪ'reɪz] *vt* effacer; **~r** *n* gomme *f*.

erect [ɪ'rɛkt] *a* droit(e) // *vt* construire; (*monument*) ériger; élever; (*tent etc*) dresser; **~ion** [ɪ'rɛkʃən] *n* érection *f*.

ermine ['ɔːmɪn] *n* hermine *f*.

erode [ɪ'rəud] *vt* éroder; (*metal*) ronger.

erotic [ɪ'rɔtɪk] *a* érotique.

err [ə:*] *vi* se tromper; (*REL*) pécher.

errand ['ɛrnd] *n* course *f*, commission *f*.

erratic [ɪ'rætɪk] *a* irrégulier(ère); inconstant(e).

error ['ɛrə*] *n* erreur *f*.

erupt [ɪ'rʌpt] *vi* entrer en éruption; (*fig*) éclater; **~ion** [ɪ'rʌpʃən] *n* éruption *f*.

escalate ['ɛskəleɪt] *vi* s'intensifier.

escalator ['ɛskəleɪtə*] *n* escalier roulant.

escapade [ɛskə'peɪd] *n* fredaine *f*; équipée *f*.

escape [ɪ'skeɪp] *n* évasion *f*; fuite *f*; (*of gas etc*) échappement *m*; fuite // *vi* s'échapper, fuir; (*from jail*) s'évader; (*fig*) s'en tirer; (*leak*) s'échapper, fuir // *vt* échapper à; **to ~ from** (*person*) échapper à; (*place*) s'échapper de; (*fig*) fuir; **escapism** *n* évasion *f* (*fig*).

escort *n* ['ɛskɔːt] escorte *f* // *vt* [ɪ'skɔːt] escorter.

Eskimo ['ɛskɪməu] *n* Esquimau/de.

especially [ɪ'speʃlɪ] *ad* particulièrement; surtout; exprès.

espionage ['espɪənɑ:ʒ] *n* espionnage *m*.

Esquire [ɪ'skwaɪə*] *n* (*abbr* Esq.): J. Brown, ~ Monsieur J. Brown.

essay ['eseɪ] *n* (*SCOL*) dissertation *f*; (*LITERATURE*) essai *m*.

essence ['esns] *n* essence *f*.

essential [ɪ'senʃl] *a* essentiel(le); (*basic*) fondamental(e) // *n*: ~s éléments essentiels; **~ly** *ad* essentiellement.

establish [ɪ'stæblɪʃ] *vt* établir; (*business*) fonder, créer; (*one's power etc*) asseoir, affermir; **~ment** *n* établissement *m*; création *f*; **the E~ment** les pouvoirs établis; l'ordre établi; les milieux dirigeants.

estate [ɪ'steɪt] *n* domaine *m*, propriété *f*; biens *mpl*, succession *f*; ~ **agent** *n* agent immobilier; ~ **car** *n* (*Brit*) break *m*.

esteem [ɪ'sti:m] *n* estime *f* // *vt* estimer; apprécier.

esthetic [ɪs'θetɪk] *a* (*US*) = **aesthetic**.

estimate *n* ['estɪmət] estimation *f*; (*COMM*) devis *m* // *vt* ['estɪmeɪt] estimer; **estimation** [-'meɪʃən] *n* opinion *f*; estime *f*.

estranged [ɪ'streɪndʒd] *a* séparé(e); dont on s'est séparé(e).

etc *abbr* (= *et cetera*) etc.

etching ['etʃɪŋ] *n* eau-forte *f*.

eternal [ɪ'tə:nl] *a* éternel(le).

eternity [ɪ'tə:nɪtɪ] *n* éternité *f*.

ethical ['eθɪkl] *a* moral(e).

ethics ['eθɪks] *n* éthique *f* // *npl* moralité *f*.

Ethiopia [i:θɪ'əʊpɪə] *n* Éthiopie *f*.

ethnic ['eθnɪk] *a* ethnique.

ethos ['i:θɒs] *n* génie *m*.

etiquette ['etɪket] *n* convenances *fpl*, étiquette *f*.

Eurocheque ['jʊərəʊtʃek] *n* eurochèque *m*.

Europe ['jʊərəp] *n* Europe *f*; **~an** [-'pi:ən] *a* européen(ne) // *n* Européen/ne.

evacuate [ɪ'vækjueɪt] *vt* évacuer.

evade [ɪ'veɪd] *vt* échapper à; (*question etc*) éluder; (*duties*) se dérober à.

evaporate [ɪ'væpəreɪt] *vi* s'évaporer // *vt* faire évaporer; **~d milk** *n* lait condensé non sucré.

evasion [ɪ'veɪʒən] *n* dérobade *f*; faux-fuyant *m*.

eve [i:v] *n*: on the ~ of à la veille de.

even ['i:vn] *a* régulier(ère), égal(e); (*number*) pair(e) // *ad* même; ~ **if** même si + *indic*; ~ **though** quand (bien) même + *cond*, alors même que + *cond*; ~ **more** encore plus; ~ **so** quand même; not ~ pas même; to get ~ **with** sb prendre sa revanche sur qn; **to ~ out** *vi* s'égaliser.

evening ['i:vnɪŋ] *n* soir *m*; (*as duration*, *event*) soirée *f*; **in the** ~ le soir; ~ **class** *n* cours *m* du soir; ~ **dress** *n* (*man's*) habit *m* de soirée, smoking *m*; (*woman's*) robe *f* de soirée.

event [ɪ'vent] *n* événement *m*; (*SPORT*) épreuve *f*; **in the** ~ **of** en cas de; **~ful** *a* mouvementé(e).

eventual [ɪ'ventʃuəl] *a* final(e); **~ity** [-'ælɪtɪ] *n* possibilité *f*, éventualité *f*; **~ly** *ad* finalement.

ever ['evə*] *ad* jamais; (*at all times*) toujours; **the best** ~ le meilleur qu'on ait jamais vu; **have you** ~ **seen it?** l'as-tu déjà vu?, as-tu eu l'occasion *or* t'est-il arrivé de le voir?; ~ **since** *ad* depuis // *cj* depuis que; **~green** *n* arbre *m* à feuilles persistantes; **~lasting** *a* éternel(le).

every ['evrɪ] *a* chaque; ~ **day** tous les jours, chaque jour; ~ **other/third day** tous les deux/trois jours; ~ **other car** une voiture sur deux; ~ **now and then** de temps en temps; **~body** *pronoun* tout le monde, tous *pl*; **~day** *a* quotidien(ne); de tous les jours; **~one** = **~body**; **~thing** *pronoun* tout; **~where** *ad* partout.

evict [ɪ'vɪkt] *vt* expulser.

evidence ['evɪdns] *n* (*proof*) preuve(s) *f(pl)*; (*of witness*) témoignage *m*; (*sign*): **to show** ~ **of** donner des signes de; **to give** ~ témoigner, déposer.

evident ['evɪdnt] *a* évident(e); **~ly** *ad* de toute évidence.

evil ['i:vl] *a* mauvais(e) // *n* mal *m*.

evoke [ɪ'vəʊk] *vt* évoquer.

evolution [i:və'lu:ʃən] *n* évolution *f*.

evolve [ɪ'vɒlv] *vt* élaborer // *vi* évoluer, se transformer.

ewe [ju:] *n* brebis *f*.

ex- [eks] *prefix* ex-.

exact [ɪg'zækt] *a* exact(e) // *vt*: **to ~ sth (from)** extorquer qch (à); exiger qch (de); **~ing** *a* exigeant(e); (*work*) fatigant(e); **~ly** *ad* exactement.

exaggerate [ɪg'zædʒəreɪt] *vt, vi* exagérer; **exaggeration** [-'reɪʃən] *n* exagération *f*.

exalted [ɪg'zɔ:ltɪd] *a* élevé(e); (*person*) haut placé(e); (*elated*) exalté(e).

exam [ɪg'zæm] *n abbr* (*SCOL*) of **examination**.

examination [ɪgzæmɪ'neɪʃən] *n* (*SCOL*, *MED*) examen *m*.

examine [ɪg'zæmɪn] *vt* (*gen*) examiner; (*SCOL, LAW*: *person*) interroger; (*at customs*: *luggage*) inspecter; **~r** *n* examinateur/trice.

example [ɪg'zɑ:mpl] *n* exemple *m*; **for** ~ par exemple.

exasperate [ɪg'zɑ:spəreɪt] *vt* exaspérer; **exasperation** [ɪgzɑ:spə'reɪʃən] *n* exaspération *f*, irritation *f*.

excavate ['ekskəveɪt] *vt* excaver; (*object*) mettre au jour.

exceed [ɪk'siːd] *vt* dépasser; *(one's powers)* outrepasser; **~ingly** *ad* excessivement.

excellent ['ɛksələnt] *a* excellent(e).

except [ɪk'sɛpt] *prep (also: ~ for, ~ing)* sauf, excepté, à l'exception de // *vt* excepter; **~ if/when** sauf si/quand; **~ that** excepté que, si ce n'est que; **~ion** [ɪk'sɛpʃən] *n* exception *f*; **to take ~ion to** s'offusquer de; **~ional** [ɪk'sɛpʃənl] *a* exceptionnel(le).

excerpt ['ɛksəːpt] *n* extrait *m*.

excess [ɪk'sɛs] *n* excès *m*; **~ baggage** *n* excédent *m* de bagages; **~ fare** *n* supplément *m*; **~ive** *a* excessif(ive).

exchange [ɪks'tʃeɪndʒ] *n* échange *m*; *(also: telephone ~)* central *m* // *vt:* **to ~ (for)** échanger (contre); **~ rate** *n* taux *m* des changes.

Exchequer [ɪks'tʃɛkə*] *n:* **the ~** *(Brit)* l'Échiquier *m*, ≈ le ministère des Finances.

excise ['ɛksaɪz] *n* taxe *f*.

excite [ɪk'saɪt] *vt* exciter; **to get ~d** s'exciter; **~ment** *n* excitation *f*; **exciting** *a* passionnant(e).

exclaim [ɪk'skleɪm] *vi* s'exclamer; **exclamation** [ɛksklə'meɪʃən] *n* exclamation *f*; **exclamation mark** *n* point *m* d'exclamation.

exclude [ɪk'skluːd] *vt* exclure.

exclusive [ɪk'skluːsɪv] *a* exclusif(ive); *(club, district)* sélect(e); *(item of news)* en exclusivité; **~ of VAT** TVA non comprise.

excruciating [ɪk'skruːʃɪeɪtɪŋ] *a* atroce, déchirant(e).

excursion [ɪk'skəːʃən] *n* excursion *f*.

excuse *n* [ɪk'skjuːs] excuse *f* // *vt* [ɪk'skjuːz] excuser; **to ~ sb from** *(activity)* dispenser qn de; **~ me!** excusez-moi!, pardon!; **now if you will ~ me, ...** maintenant, si vous (le) permettez ....

ex-directory ['ɛksdɪ'rɛktərɪ] *a (Brit)* sur la liste rouge.

execute ['ɛksɪkjuːt] *vt* exécuter.

execution [ɛksɪ'kjuːʃən] *n* exécution *f*; **~er** *n* bourreau *m*.

executive [ɪg'zɛkjutɪv] *n (COMM)* cadre *m*; *(POL)* exécutif *m* // *a* exécutif(ive).

exemplify [ɪg'zɛmplɪfaɪ] *vt* illustrer.

exempt [ɪg'zɛmpt] *a:* **~ from** exempté(e) *or* dispensé(e) de // *vt:* **to ~ sb from** exempter *or* dispenser qn de.

exercise ['ɛksəsaɪz] *n* exercice *m* // *vt* exercer; *(patience etc)* faire preuve de; *(dog)* promener // *vi* prendre de l'exercice; **~ book** *n* cahier *m*.

exert [ɪg'zəːt] *vt* exercer, employer; **to ~ o.s.** se dépenser; **~ion** [-ʃən] *n* effort *m*.

exhaust [ɪg'zɔːst] *n (also: ~ fumes)* gaz *mpl* d'échappement; *(also: ~ pipe)* tuyau *m* d'échappement // *vt* épuiser; **~ed** *a* épuisé(e); **~ion** [ɪg'zɔːstʃən] *n*

épuisement *m*; **nervous ~ion** fatigue nerveuse; surmenage mental; **~ive** *a* très complet(ète).

exhibit [ɪg'zɪbɪt] *n (ART)* pièce *f* or objet *m* exposé(e); *(LAW)* pièce à conviction // *vt* exposer; *(courage, skill)* faire preuve de; **~ion** [ɛksɪ'bɪʃən] *n* exposition *f*.

exhilarating [ɪg'zɪləreɪtɪŋ] *a* grisant(e); stimulant(e).

exile ['ɛksaɪl] *n* exil *m*; *(person)* exilé/e // *vt* exiler.

exist [ɪg'zɪst] *vi* exister; **~ence** *n* existence *f*; **to be in ~ence** exister; **~ing** *a* actuel(le).

exit ['ɛksɪt] *n* sortie *f* // *vi (COMPUT, THEATRE)* sortir; **~ ramp** *n (US AUT)* bretelle *f* d'accès.

exodus ['ɛksədəs] *n* exode *m*.

exonerate [ɪg'zɔnəreɪt] *vt:* **to ~ from** disculper de.

exotic [ɪg'zɔtɪk] *a* exotique.

expand [ɪk'spænd] *vt* agrandir; accroître, étendre // *vi (trade etc)* se développer, s'accroître; s'étendre; *(gas, metal)* se dilater.

expanse [ɪk'spæns] *n* étendue *f*.

expansion [ɪk'spænʃən] *n* développement *m*, accroissement *m*; dilatation *f*.

expect [ɪk'spɛkt] *vt (anticipate)* s'attendre à, s'attendre à ce que + *sub*; *(count on)* compter sur, escompter; *(hope for)* espérer; *(require)* demander, exiger; *(suppose)* supposer; *(await, also baby)* attendre // *vi:* **to be ~ing** être enceinte; **to ~ sb to do** s'attendre à ce que qn fasse; attendre de qn qu'il fasse; **~ancy** *n (anticipation)* attente *f*; **life ~ancy** espérance *f* de vie; **~ant mother** *n* future maman; **~ation** [ɛkspɛk'teɪʃən] *n* attente *f*, prévisions *fpl*; espérance(s) *f(pl)*.

expedience, expediency [ɪk'spiːdɪəns, ɪk'spiːdɪənsɪ] *n:* **for the sake of ~** parce que c'est plus commode.

expedient [ɪk'spiːdɪənt] *a* indiqué(e), opportun(e); commode // *n* expédient *m*.

expedition [ɛkspə'dɪʃən] *n* expédition *f*.

expel [ɪk'spɛl] *vt* chasser, expulser; *(SCOL)* renvoyer, exclure.

expend [ɪk'spɛnd] *vt* consacrer; *(use up)* dépenser; **~able** *a* remplaçable; **~iture** [ɪk'spɛndɪtʃə*] *n* dépense *f*; dépenses *fpl*.

expense [ɪk'spɛns] *n* dépense *f*; frais *mpl*; *(high cost)* coût *m*; **~s** *npl (COMM)* frais *mpl*; **at the ~ of** aux dépens de; **~ account** *n* (note *f* de) frais *mpl*.

expensive [ɪk'spɛnsɪv] *a* cher(chère), coûteux(euse); **to be ~** coûter cher.

experience [ɪk'spɪərɪəns] *n* expérience *f* // *vt* connaître; éprouver; **~d** *a* expérimenté(e).

experiment [ɪk'spɛrɪmənt] *n* expérience *f* // *vi* faire une expérience; **to ~ with**

expérimenter.

expert ['ɛkspəːt] a expert(e) // n expert m; ~**ise** [-'tiːz] n (grande) compétence.

expire [ik'spaiə*] vi expirer; **expiry** n expiration f.

explain [ik'splein] vt expliquer; **explanation** [ɛksplə'neiʃən] n explication f; **explanatory** [ik'splænətri] a explicatif(ive).

explicit [ik'splisit] a explicite; (definite) formel(le).

explode [ik'spləud] vi exploser // vt faire exploser.

exploit n ['ɛksplɔit] exploit m // vt [ik'splɔit] exploiter; ~**ation** [-'teiʃən] n exploitation f.

exploratory [ik'splɔrətri] a (fig: talks) préliminaire.

explore [ik'splɔː*] vt explorer; (possibilities) étudier, examiner; ~**r** n explorateur/trice.

explosion [ik'spləuʒən] n explosion f.

explosive [ik'spləusiv] a explosif(ive) // n explosif m.

exponent [ik'spəunənt] n (of school of thought etc) interprète m, représentant m.

export vt [ɛk'spɔːt] exporter // n ['ɛkspɔːt] exportation f // cpd d'exportation; ~**er** n exportateur m.

expose [ik'spəuz] vt exposer; (unmask) démasquer, dévoiler; ~**d** a (position) exposé(e).

exposure [ik'spəuʒə*] n exposition f; (PHOT) (temps m de) pose f; (: shot) pose; **suffering from** ~ (MED) souffrant des effets du froid et de l'épuisement; ~**meter** n posemètre m.

expound [ik'spaund] vt exposer.

express [ik'sprɛs] a (definite) formel(le), exprès(esse); (Brit: letter etc) exprès inv // n (train) rapide m // ad (send) exprès // vt exprimer; ~**ion** [ik'sprɛʃən] n expression f; ~**ly** ad expressément, formellement; ~**way** n (US: urban motorway) voie f express (à plusieurs files).

exquisite [ɛk'skwizit] a exquis(e).

extend [ik'stɛnd] vt (visit, street) prolonger; (building) agrandir; (offer) présenter, offrir // vi (land) s'étendre.

extension [ik'stɛnʃən] n prolongation f; agrandissement m; (building) annexe f; (to wire, table) rallonge f; (telephone: in offices) poste m; (: in private house) téléphone m supplémentaire.

extensive [ik'stɛnsiv] a étendu(e), vaste; (damage, alterations) considérable; (inquiries) approfondi(e); (use) largement répandu(e); **he's travelled** ~**ly** il a beaucoup voyagé.

extent [ik'stɛnt] n étendue f; **to some** ~ dans une certaine mesure; **to what** ~? dans quelle mesure?, jusqu'à quel point?; **to the** ~ **of ...** au point de ....

extenuating [ik'stɛnjueitiŋ] a: ~ **circumstances** circonstances atténuantes.

exterior [ɛk'stiəriə*] a extérieur(e), du dehors // n extérieur m; dehors m.

external [ɛk'stəːnl] a externe.

extinct [ik'stiŋkt] a éteint(e).

extinguish [ik'stiŋgwiʃ] vt éteindre; ~**er** n extincteur m.

extort [ik'stɔːt] vt: **to** ~ **sth (from)** extorquer qch (à); ~**ionate** [ik'stɔːʃnət] a exorbitant(e).

extra ['ɛkstrə] a supplémentaire, de plus // ad (in addition) en plus // n supplément m; (THEATRE) figurant/e.

extra... ['ɛkstrə] prefix extra....

extract vt [ik'strækt] extraire; (tooth) arracher; (money, promise) soutirer // n ['ɛkstrækt] extrait m.

extracurricular ['ɛkstrəkə'rikjulə*] a parascolaire.

extradite ['ɛkstrədait] vt extrader.

extramarital [ɛkstrə'mæritl] a extra-conjugal(e).

extramural [ɛkstrə'mjuərl] a hors-faculté inv.

extraordinary [ik'strɔːdnri] a extraordinaire.

extravagance [ik'strævəgəns] n prodigalités fpl; (thing bought) folie f, dépense excessive or exagérée.

extravagant [ik'strævəgənt] a extravagant(e); (in spending) prodigue, dépensier(ère); dispendieux(euse).

extreme [ik'striːm] a, n extrême (m); ~**ly** ad extrêmement.

extricate ['ɛkstrikeit] vt: **to** ~ **sth (from)** dégager qch (de).

extrovert ['ɛkstrəvəːt] n extraverti/e.

eye [ai] n œil m (pl yeux); (of needle) trou m, chas m // vt examiner; **to keep an** ~ **on** surveiller; ~**ball** n globe m oculaire; ~**bath** n œillère f (pour bains d'œil); ~**brow** n sourcil m; ~**brow pencil** n crayon m à sourcils; ~**drops** npl gouttes fpl pour les yeux; ~**lash** n cil m; ~**lid** n paupière f; ~**liner** n eye-liner m; ~**opener** n révélation f; ~**shadow** n ombre f à paupières; ~**sight** n vue f; ~**sore** n horreur f, chose f qui dépare or enlaidit; ~ **witness** n témoin m oculaire.

F

F [ɛf] n (MUS) fa m.

fable ['feibl] n fable f.

fabric ['fæbrik] n tissu m.

fabrication [fæbri'keiʃən] n invention(s) f(pl), fabulation f; fait m (or preuve f) forgé(e) de toutes pièces.

fabulous ['fæbjuləs] a fabuleux(euse); (col: super) formidable.

face [feis] n visage m, figure f; expression f; (of clock) cadran m; (of *building*) façade *f*; (*side, surface*) face *f* // *vt* faire face à; ~ **down** (*person*) à plat ventre; (*card*) face en dessous; **to make or pull a** ~ faire une grimace; **in the** ~ **of** (*difficulties etc*) face à, devant; **on the** ~ **of it** à première vue; ~ **to** ~ face à face; **to** ~ **up to** *vt fus* faire face à, affronter; ~ **cloth** *n* (*Brit*) gant *m* de toilette; ~ **cream** *n* crème *f* pour le visage; ~ **lift** *n* lifting *m*; (*of building etc*) ravalement *m*, retapage *m*.

face value *n* (*of coin*) valeur nominale; **to take sth at** ~ (*fig*) prendre qch pour argent comptant.

facilities [fə'sɪlɪtɪz] *npl* installations *fpl*, équipement *m*; **credit** ~ facilités *fpl* de paiement.

facing ['feɪsɪŋ] *prep* face à, en face de // *n* (*of wall etc*) revêtement *m*; (*SEWING*) revers *m*.

facsimile [fæk'sɪmɪlɪ] *n* (*document*) télécopie *f*; (*machine*) télécopieur *m*.

fact [fækt] *n* fait *m*; **in** ~ en fait.

factor ['fæktə*] *n* facteur *m*.

factory ['fæktərɪ] *n* usine *f*, fabrique *f*.

factual ['fæktjʊəl] *a* basé(e) sur les faits.

faculty ['fækəltɪ] *n* faculté *f*; (*US: teaching staff*) corps enseignant.

fad [fæd] *n* manie *f*; engouement *m*.

fade [feɪd] *vi* se décolorer, passer; (*light, sound, hope*) s'affaiblir, disparaître; (*flower*) se faner.

fag [fæg] *n* (*col: cigarette*) sèche *f*.

fail [feɪl] *vt* (*exam*) échouer à; (*candidate*) recaler; (*subj: courage, memory*) faire défaut à // *vi* échouer; (*supplies*) manquer; (*eyesight, health, light*) baisser, s'affaiblir; **to** ~ **to do sth** (*neglect*) négliger de faire qch; (*be unable*) ne pas arriver or parvenir à faire qch; **without** ~ à coup sûr; sans faute; ~**ing** *n* défaut *m* // *prep* faute de; ~**ure** ['feɪljə*] *n* échec *m*; (*person*) raté(e); (*mechanical etc*) défaillance *f*.

faint [feɪnt] *a* faible; (*recollection*) vague; (*mark*) à peine visible // *n* évanouissement *m* // *vi* s'évanouir; **to feel** ~ défaillir.

fair [feə*] *a* équitable, juste, impartial(e); (*hair*) blond(e); (*skin, complexion*) pâle, blanc (blanche); (*weather*) beau (belle); (*good enough*) assez bon (ne); (*sizeable*) considérable // *ad* (*play*) franc-jeu // *n* foire *f*; (*Brit: funfair*) fête (foraine); ~**ly** *ad* équitablement; (*quite*) assez; ~**ness** *n* justice *f*, équité *f*, impartialité *f*.

fairy ['feərɪ] *n* fée *f*; ~ **tale** *n* conte *m* de fées.

faith [feɪθ] *n* foi *f*; (*trust*) confiance *f*; (*sect*) culte *m*, religion *f*; ~**ful** *a* fidèle; ~**fully** *ad* fidèlement.

fake [feɪk] *n* (*painting etc*) faux *m*; (*photo*) trucage *m*; (*person*) imposteur *m* // *a* faux (fausse); simulé(e) // *vt*

simuler; (*photo*) truquer; (*story*) fabriquer.

falcon ['fɔːlkən] *n* faucon *m*.

fall [fɔːl] *n* chute *f*; (*US: autumn*) automne *m* // *vi* (*pt* fell, *pp* fallen) tomber; ~**s** *npl* (*waterfall*) chute *f* d'eau, cascade *f*; **to** ~ **flat** *vi* (*on one's face*) tomber de tout son long, s'étaler; (*joke*) tomber à plat; (*plan*) échouer; **to** ~ **back** *vi* reculer, se retirer; **to** ~ **back on** *vt fus* se rabattre sur; **to** ~ **behind** *vi* prendre du retard; **to** ~ **down** *vi* (*person*) tomber; (*building, hopes*) s'effondrer, s'écrouler; **to** ~ **for** *vt fus* (*trick*) se laisser prendre à; (*person*) tomber amoureux de; **to** ~ **in** *vi* s'effondrer; (*MIL*) se mettre en rangs; **to** ~ **off** *vi* tomber; (*diminish*) baisser, diminuer; **to** ~ **out** *vi* (*friends etc*) se brouiller; **to** ~ **through** *vi* (*plan, project*) tomber à l'eau.

fallacy ['fæləsɪ] *n* erreur *f*, illusion *f*.

fallen ['fɔːlən] *pp* of **fall**.

fallout ['fɔːlaʊt] *n* retombées (radioactives); ~ **shelter** *n* abri *m* anti-atomique.

fallow ['fæləʊ] *a* en jachère; en friche.

false [fɔːls] *a* faux (fausse); **under** ~ **pretences** sous un faux prétexte; ~ **teeth** *npl* (*Brit*) fausses dents.

falter ['fɔːltə*] *vi* chanceler, vaciller.

fame [feɪm] *n* renommée *f*, renom *m*.

familiar [fə'mɪlɪə*] *a* familier(ère); **to be** ~ **with** (*subject*) connaître; ~**ity** [fəmɪlɪ'ærɪtɪ] *n* familiarité *f*.

family ['fæmɪlɪ] *n* famille *f*.

famine ['fæmɪn] *n* famine *f*.

famished ['fæmɪʃt] *a* affamé(e).

famous ['feɪməs] *a* célèbre; ~**ly** *ad* (*get on*) fameusement, à merveille.

fan [fæn] *n* (*folding*) éventail *m*; (*ELEC*) ventilateur *m*; (*person*) fan *m*, admirateur/trice; supporter *m/f* // *vt* éventer; (*fire, quarrel*) attiser; **to** ~ **out** *vi* se déployer (en éventail).

fanatic [fə'nætɪk] *n* fanatique *m/f*.

fan belt *n* courroie *f* de ventilateur.

fanciful ['fænsɪful] *a* fantaisiste.

fancy ['fænsɪ] *n* fantaisie *f*, envie *f*; imagination *f* // *a* (de) fantaisie *inv* // *vt* (*feel like, want*) avoir envie de; (*imagine*) imaginer; **to take a** ~ **to** se prendre d'affection pour; s'enticher de; ~ **dress** *n* déguisement *m*, travesti *m*; ~**-dress ball** *n* bal masqué or costumé.

fang [fæŋ] *n* croc *m*; (*of snake*) crochet *m*.

fantastic [fæn'tæstɪk] *a* fantastique.

fantasy ['fæntəsɪ] *n* imagination *f*, fantaisie *f*; fantasme *m*; chimère *f*.

far [fɑː*] *a*: **the** ~ **side/end** l'autre côté/ bout *m* // *ad* loin; ~ **away** au loin, dans le lointain; ~ **better** beaucoup mieux; ~ **from** loin de; **by** ~ de loin, de beaucoup; **go as** ~ **as the farm** allez jusqu'à la ferme; **as ~ as I know** pour autant que je sache; **~away** *a* lointain(e).

farce [fɑ:s] *n* farce *f*.

farcical ['fɑ:sɪkəl] *a* grotesque.

fare [fɛə*] *n* (*on trains, buses*) prix *m* du billet; (*in taxi*) prix de la course; (*food*) table *f*, chère *f*; **half ~** demi-tarif; **full ~** plein tarif.

Far East *n*: **the ~** l'Extrême-Orient *m*.

farewell [fɛə'wɛl] *excl*, *n* adieu (*m*).

farm [fɑ:m] *n* ferme *f* // *vt* cultiver; **~er** *n* fermier/ère; cultivateur/trice; **~hand** *n* ouvrier/ère agricole; **~house** *n* (maison *f* de) ferme *f*; **~ing** *n* agriculture *f*; **~ worker** *n* = **~hand**; **~yard** *n* cour *f* de ferme.

far-reaching ['fɑ:'ri:tʃɪŋ] *a* d'une grande portée.

fart [fɑ:t] (*col!*) *n* pet *m* // *vi* péter.

farther ['fɑ:ðə*] *ad* plus loin // *a* plus éloigné(e), plus lointain(e).

farthest ['fɑ:ðɪst] *superlative of* **far**.

fascinate ['fæsɪneɪt] *vt* fasciner; **fascinating** *a* fascinant(e).

fascism ['fæʃɪzm] *n* fascisme *m*.

fashion ['fæʃən] *n* mode *f*; (*manner*) façon *f*, manière *f* // *vt* façonner; **in ~** à la mode; **out of ~** démodé(e); **~able** *a* à la mode; **~ show** *n* défilé *m* de mannequins *or* de mode.

fast [fɑ:st] *a* rapide; (*clock*): **to be ~** avancer; (*dye, colour*) grand *or* bon teint *inv* // *ad* vite, rapidement; (*stuck, held*) solidement // *n* jeûne *m* // *vi* jeûner; **~ asleep** profondément endormi.

fasten ['fɑ:sn] *vt* attacher, fixer; (*coat*) attacher, fermer // *vi* se fermer, s'attacher; **~er**, **~ing** *n* fermeture *f*, attache *f*.

fast food *n* fast food *m*, restauration *f* rapide.

fastidious [fæs'tɪdɪəs] *a* exigeant(e), difficile.

fat [fæt] *a* gros(se) // *n* graisse *f*; (*on meat*) gras *m*.

fatal ['feɪtl] *a* mortel(le); fatal(e); désastreux(euse); **~ity** [fə'tælɪtɪ] *n* (*road death etc*) victime *f*, décès *m*.

fate [feɪt] *n* destin *m*; (*of person*) sort *m*; **~ful** *a* fatidique.

father ['fɑ:ðə*] *n* père *m*; **~-in-law** *n* beau-père *m*; **~ly** *a* paternel(le).

fathom ['fæðəm] *n* brasse *f* (*= 1828 mm*) // *vt* (*mystery*) sonder, pénétrer.

fatigue [fə'ti:g] *n* fatigue *f*; (*MIL*) corvée *f*.

fatten ['fætn] *vt, vi* engraisser.

fatty ['fætɪ] *a* (*food*) gras(se) // *n* (*col*) gros/grosse.

fatuous ['fætjuəs] *a* stupide.

faucet ['fɔ:sɪt] *n* (*US*) robinet *m*.

fault [fɔ:lt] *n* faute *f*; (*defect*) défaut *m*; (*GEO*) faille *f* // *vt* trouver des défauts à, prendre en défaut; **it's my ~** c'est de ma faute; **to find ~ with** trouver à redire *or*

à critiquer à; **at ~** fautif(ive), coupable; **to a ~** à l'excès; **~less** *a* sans fautes; impeccable; irréprochable; **~y** *a* défectueux(euse).

fauna ['fɔ:nə] *n* faune *f*.

faux pas ['fəu'pɑ:] *n* impair *m*, bévue *f*, gaffe *f*.

favour, (*US*) **favor** ['feɪvə*] *n* faveur *f*; (*help*) service *m* // *vt* (*proposition*) être en faveur de; (*pupil etc*) favoriser; (*team, horse*) donner gagnant; **to do sb a ~** rendre un service à qn; **to find ~ with** trouver grâce aux yeux de; **in ~ of** en faveur de; **~able** *a* favorable; (*price*) avantageux(euse); **~ite** [-rɪt] *a*, *n* favori(te).

fawn [fɔ:n] *n* faon *m* // *a* (*also*: **~-coloured**) fauve // *vi*: **to ~ (up)on** flatter servilement.

fax [fæks] *n* (*document*) télécopie *f*; (*machine*) télécopieur *m*.

FBI *n abbr* (*US*: = *Federal Bureau of Investigation*) F.B.I. *m*.

fear [fɪə*] *n* crainte *f*, peur *f* // *vt* craindre; **for ~ of** de peur que + *sub or* de + *infinitive*; **~ful** *a* craintif(ive); (*sight, noise*) affreux(euse), épouvantable.

feasible ['fi:zəbl] *a* faisable, réalisable.

feast [fi:st] *n* festin *m*, banquet *m*; (*REL*: *also*: **~ day**) fête *f* // *vi* festoyer.

feat [fi:t] *n* exploit *m*, prouesse *f*.

feather ['fɛðə*] *n* plume *f*.

feature ['fi:tʃə*] *n* caractéristique *f*; (*article*) chronique *f*, rubrique *f* // *vt* (*subj: film*) avoir pour vedette(s) // *vi* figurer (en bonne place); **~s** *npl* (*of face*) traits *mpl*; **~ film** *n* film principal.

February ['fɛbruərɪ] *n* février *m*.

fed [fɛd] *pt, pp of* **feed**.

federal ['fɛdərəl] *a* fédéral(e).

fed-up [fɛd'ʌp] *a*: **to be ~** en avoir marre *or* plein le dos.

fee [fi:] *n* rémunération *f*; (*of doctor, lawyer*) honoraires *mpl*; (*of school, college etc*) frais *mpl* de scolarité; (*for examination*) droits *mpl*.

feeble ['fi:bl] *a* faible.

feed [fi:d] *n* (*of baby*) tétée *f*; (*of animal*) fourrage *m*; pâture *f*; (*on printer*) mécanisme *m* d'alimentation // *vt* (*pt, pp* **fed**) nourrir; (*Brit: baby*) allaiter; donner le biberon à; (*horse etc*) donner à manger à; (*machine*) alimenter; (*data, information*): **to ~ into** fournir à; **to ~ on** *vt fus* se nourrir de; **~back** *n* feed-back *m*; **~ing bottle** *n* (*Brit*) biberon *m*.

feel [fi:l] *n* sensation *f* // *vt* (*pt, pp* **felt**) toucher, tâter, palper; (*cold, pain*) sentir; (*grief, anger*) ressentir, éprouver; (*think, believe*): **to ~ (that)** trouver que; **to ~ hungry/cold** avoir faim/froid; **to ~ lonely/better** se sentir seul/mieux; **I don't ~ well** je ne me sens pas bien; to ~ like (want) avoir envie de; to ~ about or around vi fouiller, tâtonner; ~er n (of insect) antenne f; to put out ~ers or a ~er tâter le terrain; ~ing n sensation f, sentiment m.

feet [fi:t] npl of **foot**.

feign [feɪn] vt feindre, simuler.

fell [fɛl] pt of **fall** // vt (tree) abattre.

fellow ['fɛləu] n type m; compagnon m; (of learned society) membre m // cpd: ~**countryman** n compatriote m; ~ **men** npl semblables mpl; ~**ship** n association f; amitié f, camaraderie f; sorte de bourse universitaire.

felony ['fɛlənɪ] n crime m, forfait m.

felt [fɛlt] pt, pp of **feel** // n feutre m; ~**tip pen** n stylo-feutre m.

female ['fi:meɪl] n (ZOOL) femelle f; (pej: woman) bonne femme // a (BIOL, ELEC) femelle; (sex, character) féminin(e); (vote etc) des femmes.

feminine ['fɛmɪnɪn] a féminin(e).

feminist ['fɛmɪnɪst] n féministe m/f.

fence [fɛns] n barrière f; (col: person) receleur/euse // vt (also: ~ in) clôturer // vi faire de l'escrime; **fencing** n escrime m.

fend [fɛnd] vi: to ~ **for o.s.** se débrouiller (tout seul); to ~ **off** vt (attack etc) parer.

fender ['fɛndə*] n garde-feu m inv; (US) gardeboue m inv; pare-chocs m inv.

ferment vi [fə'mɛnt] fermenter // n ['fə:mɛnt] agitation f, effervescence f.

fern [fə:n] n fougère f.

ferocious [fə'rəuʃəs] a féroce.

ferret ['fɛrɪt] n furet m.

ferry ['fɛrɪ] n (small) bac m; (large: also: ~**boat**) ferry(-boat) m // vt transporter.

fertile ['fə:taɪl] a fertile; (BIOL) fécond(e); **fertilizer** ['fə:tɪlaɪzə*] n engrais m.

fester ['fɛstə*] vi suppurer.

festival ['fɛstɪvəl] n (REL) fête f; (ART, MUS) festival m.

festive ['fɛstɪv] a de fête; the ~ **season** (Brit: Christmas) la période des fêtes.

festivities [fɛs'tɪvɪtɪz] npl réjouissances fpl.

festoon [fɛ'stu:n] vt: to ~ **with** orner de.

fetch [fɛtʃ] vt aller chercher; (sell for) se vendre.

fetching ['fɛtʃɪŋ] a charmant(e).

fête [feɪt] n fête f, kermesse f.

feud [fju:d] n dispute f, dissension f.

feudal ['fju:dl] a féodal(e).

fever ['fi:və*] n fièvre f; ~**ish** a fiévreux(euse), fébrile.

few [fju:] a peu de; they were ~ ils étaient peu (nombreux); a ~ a quelques // pronoun quelques-uns; ~**er** a moins de; moins (nombreux).

fiancé [fɪ'ɑ̃:ŋseɪ] n fiancé m; ~**e** n

fiancée f.

fib [fɪb] n bobard m.

fibre, (US) **fiber** ['faɪbə*] n fibre f; ~**glass** n fibre de verre.

fickle ['fɪkl] a inconstant(e), volage, capricieux(euse).

fiction ['fɪkʃən] n romans mpl, littérature f romanesque; fiction f; ~**al** a fictif(ive).

fictitious [fɪk'tɪʃəs] a fictif(ive), imaginaire.

fiddle ['fɪdl] n (MUS) violon m; (cheating) combine f; escroquerie f // vt (Brit: accounts) falsifier, maquiller; to ~ **with** vt fus tripoter.

fidget ['fɪdʒɪt] vi se trémousser, remuer.

field [fi:ld] n champ m; (fig) domaine m, champ m; (SPORT: ground) terrain m; ~ **marshal** n maréchal m; ~**work** n travaux mpl pratiques (sur le terrain).

fiend [fi:nd] n démon m.

fierce [fɪəs] a (look) féroce, sauvage; (wind, attack) (très) violent(e); (fighting, enemy) acharné(e).

fiery ['faɪərɪ] a ardent(e), brûlant(e); fougueux(euse).

fifteen [fɪf'ti:n] num quinze.

fifth [fɪfθ] a, n cinquième (m).

fifty ['fɪftɪ] num cinquante; ~~ a: a ~~ chance etc une chance etc sur deux // ad moitié-moitié.

fig [fɪg] n figue f.

fight [faɪt] n bagarre f; (MIL) combat m; (against cancer etc) lutte f // vb (pt, pp **fought**) vt se battre contre; (cancer, alcoholism) combattre, lutter contre // vi se battre; ~**er** n lutteur m (fig); (plane) chasseur m; ~**ing** n combats mpl.

figment ['fɪgmənt] n: a ~ **of the imagination** une invention.

figurative ['fɪgjurətɪv] a figuré(e).

figure ['fɪgə*] n (DRAWING, GEOM) figure f; (number, cipher) chiffre m; (body, outline) silhouette f, ligne f, formes fpl // vt (US) supposer // vi (appear) figurer; (US: make sense) s'expliquer; to ~ **out** vt arriver à comprendre; calculer; ~**head** n (NAUT) figure f de proue; (pej) prête-nom m; ~ **of speech** n figure f de rhétorique.

file [faɪl] n (tool) lime f; (dossier) dossier m; (folder) dossier, chemise f; (with hinges) classeur m; (COMPUT) fichier m; (row) file f // vt (nails, wood) limer; (papers) classer; (LAW: claim) faire enregistrer; déposer // vi: to ~ **in/out** entrer/sortir l'un derrière l'autre; to ~ **past** défiler devant.

filing ['faɪlɪŋ] n (travaux mpl de) classement m; ~ **cabinet** n classeur m (meuble).

fill [fɪl] vt remplir // n: to eat one's ~ manger à sa faim; to ~ **in** vt (hole) boucher; (form) remplir; to ~ **up** vt remplir; ~ **it up, please** (*AUT*) le plein, s'il vous plaît.

fillet ['fɪlɪt] *n* filet *m*; ~ **steak** *n* filet *m* de bœuf, tournedos *m*.

filling ['fɪlɪŋ] *n* (*CULIN*) garniture *f*, farce *f*; (*for tooth*) plombage *m*; ~ **station** *n* station *f* d'essence.

film [fɪlm] *n* film *m*; (*PHOT*) pellicule *f*, film // *vt* (*scene*) filmer; ~ **star** *n* vedette *f* de cinéma; **~strip** *n* (film *m* pour) projection *f* fixe.

filter ['fɪltə*] *n* filtre *m* // *vt* filtrer; ~ **lane** *n* (*Brit AUT*) voie *f* de sortie; **~-tipped** *a* à bout filtre.

filth [fɪlθ] *n* saleté *f*; **~y** *a* sale, dégoûtant(e); (*language*) ordurier(ère).

fin [fɪn] *n* (*of fish*) nageoire *f*.

final ['faɪnl] *a* final(e), dernier(ère); définitif(ive) // *n* (*SPORT*) finale *f*; **~s** *npl* (*SCOL*) examens *mpl* de dernière année; **~e** [fɪ'nɑ:lɪ] *n* finale *m*; **~ize** *vt* mettre au point; **~ly** *ad* (*lastly*) en dernier lieu; (*eventually*) enfin, finalement.

finance [faɪ'næns] *n* finance *f*; **~s** *npl* finances *fpl* // *vt* financer.

financial [faɪ'nænʃəl] *a* financier(ère).

find [faɪnd] *vt* (*pt, pp* **found**) trouver; (*lost object*) retrouver // *n* trouvaille *f*, découverte *f*; **to ~ sb guilty** (*LAW*) déclarer qn coupable; **to ~ out** *vt* se renseigner sur; (*truth, secret*) découvrir; (*person*) démasquer; **to ~ out about** se renseigner sur; (*by chance*) apprendre; **~ings** *npl* (*LAW*) conclusions *fpl*, verdict *m*; (*of report*) constatations *fpl*.

fine [faɪn] *a* beau(belle); excellent(e); (*thin, subtle*) fin(e) // *ad* (*well*) très bien; (*small*) fin, finement // *n* (*LAW*) amende *f*; contravention *f* // *vt* (*LAW*) condamner à une amende; donner une contravention à; ~ **weather** faire beau; ~ **arts** *npl* beaux-arts *mpl*.

finery ['faɪnərɪ] *n* parure *f*.

finger ['fɪŋɡə*] *n* doigt *m* // *vt* palper, toucher; **little/index** ~ auriculaire *m*/ index *m*; **~nail** *n* ongle *m* (de la main); **~print** *n* empreinte digitale; **~tip** *n* bout *m* du doigt.

finicky ['fɪnɪkɪ] *a* tatillon(ne), méticuleux(euse); minutieux(euse).

finish ['fɪnɪʃ] *n* fin *f*; (*SPORT*) arrivée *f*; (*polish etc*) finition *f* // *vt* finir, terminer // *vi* finir, se terminer; (*session*) s'achever; **to ~ doing sth** finir de faire qch; **to ~ third** arriver *or* terminer troisième; **to ~ off** *vt* finir, terminer; (*kill*) achever; **to ~ up** *vi, vt* finir; **~ing line** *n* ligne *f* d'arrivée; **~ing school** *n* institution privée (*pour jeunes filles*).

finite ['faɪnaɪt] *a* fini(e); (*verb*) conjugué(e).

Finland ['fɪnlənd] *n* Finlande *f*.

Finn [fɪn] *n* Finnois/e; Finlandais/e;

~ish *a* finnois(e); finlandais(e) // (*LING*) finnois *m*.

fir [fə:*] *n* sapin *m*.

fire ['faɪə*] *n* feu *m*; incendie *m* // *vt* (*discharge*): **to ~ a gun** tirer un coup de feu; (*fig*) enflammer, animer; (*dismiss*) mettre à la porte, renvoyer // *vi* tirer, faire feu; **on ~** en feu; ~ **alarm** *n* avertisseur *m* d'incendie; ~ **-arm** *n* arme *f* à feu; ~ **brigade**, (*US*) ~ **department** *n* (régiment *m* de sapeurs-)pompiers *mpl*; ~ **engine** *n* pompe *f* à incendie; ~ **escape** *n* escalier *m* de secours; ~ **extinguisher** *n* extincteur *m*; **~man** *n* pompier *m*; **~place** *n* cheminée *f*; **~side** *n* foyer *m*, coin *m* du feu; ~ **station** *n* caserne *f* de pompiers; **~wood** *n* bois *m* de chauffage; **~work** *n* feu *m* d'artifice; **~works** *npl* (*display*) feu(x) d'artifice.

firing ['faɪərɪŋ] *n* (*MIL*) feu *m*, tir *m*; ~ **squad** *n* peloton *m* d'exécution.

firm [fə:m] *a* ferme // *n* compagnie *f*, firme *f*; **~ly** *ad* fermement.

first [fə:st] *a* premier(ère) // *ad* (*before others*) le premier, la première; (*before other things*) en premier, d'abord; (*when listing reasons etc*) en premier lieu, premièrement // *n* (*person: in race*) premier/ère; (*SCOL*) mention *f* très bien; (*AUT*) première *f*; **at ~** au commencement, au début; **~ of all** tout d'abord, pour commencer; ~ **aid** *n* premiers secours *or* soins; **~-aid kit** *n* trousse *f* à pharmacie; **~-class** *a* de première classe; **~-hand** *a* de première main; ~ **lady** *n* (*US*) femme *f* du président; **~ly** *ad* premièrement, en premier lieu; ~ **name** *n* prénom *m*; **~-rate** *a* excellent(e).

fish [fɪʃ] *n* (*pl inv*) poisson *m*; poissons *mpl* // *vt, vi* pêcher; **to go ~ing** aller à la pêche; **~erman** *n* pêcheur *m*; ~ **farm** *n* établissement *m* piscicole; ~ **fingers** *npl* (*Brit*) bâtonnets de poisson (congelés); **~ing boat** *n* barque *f* de pêche; **~ing line** *n* ligne *f* (de pêche); **~ing rod** *n* canne *f* à pêche; **~monger** *n* marchand *m* de poisson; **~monger's (shop)** *n* poissonnerie *f*; ~ **sticks** *npl* (*US*) = ~ **fingers**; **~y** *a* (*fig*) suspect(e), louche.

fist [fɪst] *n* poing *m*.

fit [fɪt] *a* (*MED, SPORT*) en (bonne) forme; (*proper*) convenable; approprié(e) // *vt* (*subj: clothes*) aller à; (*adjust*) ajuster; (*put in, attach*) installer, poser; adapter; (*equip*) équiper, garnir, munir // *vi* (*clothes*) aller; (*parts*) s'adapter; (*in space, gap*) entrer, s'engager // *n* (*MED*) accès *m*, crise *f*; (*of coughing*) quinte *f*; **to ~ in** état de; ~ **for** digne de; apte à; **a ~ of anger** un accès de colère; **this dress is a tight/good ~** cette robe est un peu juste/

(me) va très bien; **by** ~**s and starts** par à-coups; **to** ~ **in** vi s'accorder; s'adapter; **to** ~ **out** (Brit: also: ~ **up**) vt équiper; ~**ful** a intermittent(e); ~**ment** n meuble encastré, élément m; ~**ness** n (MED) forme f physique; (of remark) à-propos m, justesse f; ~**ted carpet** n moquette f; ~**ted kitchen** n cuisine équipée; ~**ter** n monteur m; (DRESSMAKING) essayeur/euse; ~**ting** a approprié(e) // n (of dress) essayage m; (of piece of equipment) pose f, installation f; ~**ting room** n cabine f d'essayage; ~**tings** npl installations fpl.

five [faɪv] num cinq; ~**r** n (col: Brit) billet m de cinq livres; (: US) billet de cinq dollars.

fix [fɪks] vt fixer; arranger; (mend) réparer // n: **to be in a** ~ être dans le pétrin; **to** ~ **up** vt (meeting) arranger; **to** ~ **sb up with sth** faire avoir qch à qn; ~**ation** [-'eɪʃən] n (PSYCH) fixation f; (fig) obsession f; ~**ed** [fɪkst] a (prices etc) fixe; ~**ture** ['fɪkstʃə*] n installation f (fixe); (SPORT) rencontre f (au programme).

fizz [fɪz] vi pétiller.

fizzle ['fɪzl] vi pétiller; **to** ~ **out** vi rater.

fizzy ['fɪzɪ] a pétillant(e); gazeux(euse).

flabbergasted ['flæbəgɑːstɪd] a sidéré(e), ahuri(e).

flabby ['flæbɪ] a mou(molle).

flag [flæg] n drapeau m; (also: ~**stone**) dalle f // vi faiblir; fléchir; **to** ~ **down** vt héler, faire signe (de s'arrêter) à.

flagpole ['flægpəul] n mât m.

flair [flɛə*] n flair m.

flak [flæk] n (MIL) tir antiaérien; (col: criticism) critiques fpl.

flake [fleɪk] n (of rust, paint) écaille f; (of snow, soap powder) flocon m // vi (also: ~ **off**) s'écailler.

flamboyant [flæm'bɔɪənt] a flamboyant(e), éclatant(e); (person) haut(e) en couleur.

flame [fleɪm] n flamme f.

flamingo [flə'mɪŋgəu] n flamant m (rose).

flammable ['flæməbl] a inflammable.

flan [flæn] n (Brit) tarte f.

flank [flæŋk] n flanc m // vt flanquer.

flannel ['flænl] n (Brit: also: face ~) gant m de toilette; (fabric) flanelle f; ~**s** npl pantalon m de flanelle.

flap [flæp] n (of pocket, envelope) rabat m // vt (wings) battre (de) // vi (sail, flag) claquer; (col: also: **be in a** ~) paniquer.

flare [flɛə*] n fusée éclairante; (in skirt etc) évasement m; **to** ~ **up** vi s'embraser; (fig: person) se mettre en colère, s'emporter; (: revolt) éclater.

flash [flæʃ] n éclair m; (also: news ~) flash m (d'information); (PHOT) flash //

vt (switch on) allumer (brièvement); (send: message) câbler // vi briller; jeter des éclairs; (light on ambulance etc) clignoter; **in a** ~ en un clin d'œil; **to** ~ **one's headlights** faire un appel de phares; **he** ~**ed by** or **past** il passa (devant nous) comme un éclair; ~**bulb** n ampoule f de flash; ~**cube** n cube-flash m; ~**light** n lampe f de poche.

flashy ['flæʃɪ] a (pej) tape-à-l'œil inv, tapageur(euse).

flask [flɑːsk] n flacon m, bouteille f; (also: **vacuum** ~) bouteille f thermos ®.

flat [flæt] a plat(e); (tyre) dégonflé(e), à plat; (denial) catégorique; (MUS) bémolisé(e); (: voice) faux(fausse) // n (Brit: apartment) appartement m; (AUT) crevaison f; (MUS) bémol m; **to work** ~ **out** travailler d'arrache-pied; ~**ly** ad catégoriquement; ~**ten** vt (also: ~**ten out**) aplatir.

flatter ['flætə*] vt flatter; ~**ing** a flatteur(euse); ~**y** n flatterie f.

flaunt [flɔːnt] vt faire étalage de.

flavour, (US) **flavor** ['fleɪvə*] n goût m, saveur f; (of ice cream etc) parfum m // vt parfumer; **vanilla-**~**ed** à l'arôme de vanille, vanillé(e); ~**ing** n arôme m (synthétique).

flaw [flɔː] n défaut m.

flax [flæks] n lin m; ~**en** a blond(e).

flea [fliː] n puce f.

fleck [flɛk] n tacheture f; moucheture f.

flee [fliː], pt, pp **fled** [fliː-, fled] vt fuir, s'enfuir de // vi fuir, s'enfuir.

fleece [fliːs] n toison f // vt (col) voler, filouter.

fleet [fliːt] n flotte f; (of lorries etc) parc m, convoi m.

fleeting ['fliːtɪŋ] a fugace, fugitif(ive); (visit) très bref(brève).

Flemish ['flemɪʃ] a flamand(e).

flesh [fleʃ] n chair f; ~ **wound** n blessure superficielle.

flew [fluː] pt of **fly**.

flex [flɛks] n fil m or câble m électrique (souple) // vt fléchir; (muscles) tendre; ~**ible** a flexible.

flick [flɪk] n petite tape; chiquenaude f; sursaut m; **to** ~ **through** vt fus feuilleter.

flicker ['flɪkə*] vi vaciller.

flier ['flaɪə*] n aviateur m.

flight [flaɪt] n vol m; (escape) fuite f; (also: ~ **of steps**) escalier m; ~ **attendant** n (US) steward m, hôtesse f de l'air; ~ **deck** n (AVIAT) poste m de pilotage; (NAUT) pont m d'envol.

flimsy ['flɪmzɪ] a (partition, fabric) peu solide, mince; (excuse) pauvre, mince.

flinch [flɪntʃ] vi tressaillir; **to** ~ **from** se dérober à, reculer devant.

fling [flɪŋ], pt, pp **flung** vt jeter, lancer.

flint [flɪnt] n silex m; (in lighter) pierre f (à briquet).

flip [flɪp] n chiquenaude f.

flippant ['flɪpənt] a désinvolte, irrévérencieux(euse).

flipper ['flɪpə*] n (of seal etc) nageoire f; (for swimming) palme f.

flirt [fləːt] vi flirter // n flirteuse f.

flit [flɪt] vi voleter.

float [fləut] n flotteur m; (in procession) char m; (money) réserve f // vi flotter // vt faire flotter; (loan, business) lancer.

flock [flɔk] n troupeau m; (of people) foule f.

flog [flɔg] vt fouetter.

flood [flʌd] n inondation f; (of words, tears etc) flot m, torrent m // vt inonder; ~ing n inondation f; ~light n projecteur m // vt éclairer aux projecteurs, illuminer.

floor [flɔː*] n sol m; (storey) étage m; (fig: at meeting): the ~ l'assemblée f, les membres mpl de l'assemblée // vt terrasser; on the ~ par terre; ground ~, (US) first ~ rez-de-chaussée m; first ~, (US) second ~ premier étage; ~board n planche f (du plancher); ~ show n spectacle m de variétés.

flop [flɔp] n fiasco m.

floppy [flɔpi] a lâche, flottant(e); ~ (disk) n (COMPUT) disquette f.

flora ['flɔːrə] n flore f.

florid ['flɔrɪd] a (complexion) fleuri(e); (style) plein(e) de fioritures.

florist ['flɔrɪst] n fleuriste m/f.

flounce [flauns] n volant m.

flounder ['flaundə*] vi patauger // n (ZOOL) flet m.

flour ['flauə*] n farine f.

flourish ['flʌrɪʃ] vi prospérer // n fioriture f; (of trumpets) fanfare f.

flout [flaut] vt se moquer de, faire fi de.

flow [fləu] n flot m; courant m; circulation f; (tide) flux m // vi couler; (traffic) s'écouler; (robes, hair) flotter; ~ chart n organigramme m.

flower ['flauə*] n fleur f // vi fleurir; ~ bed n plate-bande f; ~pot n pot m (à fleurs); ~y a fleuri(e).

flown [fləun] pp of **fly**.

flu [fluː] n grippe f.

fluctuate ['flʌktjueɪt] vi varier, fluctuer.

fluency ['fluːənsɪ] n facilité f.

fluent ['fluːənt] a (speech) coulant(e), aisé(e); he speaks ~ French il parle le français couramment.

fluff [flʌf] n duvet m; peluche f; ~y a duveteux(euse); pelucheux(euse).

fluid ['fluːɪd] a, n fluide (m).

fluke [fluːk] n (col: luck) coup m de veine.

flung [flʌŋ] pt, pp of **fling**.

fluoride ['fluəraɪd] n fluor m.

flurry ['flʌrɪ] n (of snow) rafale f, bourrasque f; ~ of activity/excitement affairement m/excitation f soudain(e).

flush [flʌʃ] n rougeur f; excitation f;

(fig: of youth, beauty etc) éclat m // vt nettoyer à grande eau // vi rougir // a: ~ with au ras de, de niveau avec; to ~ the toilet tirer la chasse (d'eau); to ~ out vt débusquer; ~ed a (tout(e)) rouge.

flustered ['flʌstəd] a énervé(e).

flute [fluːt] n flûte f.

flutter ['flʌtə*] n agitation f; (of wings) battement m // vi battre des ailes, voleter.

flux [flʌks] n: in a state of ~ fluctuant sans cesse.

fly [flaɪ] n (insect) mouche f; (on trousers: also: **flies**) braguette f // vb (pt flew, pp flown) vt piloter; (passengers, cargo) transporter (par avion); (distances) parcourir // vi voler; (passengers) aller en avion; (escape) s'enfuir, fuir; (flag) se déployer; to ~ away or off vi (bird, insect) s'envoler; ~ing n (activity) aviation f // a: ~ing visit visite f éclair inv; with ~ing colours haut la main; ~ing saucer n soucoupe volante; ~ing start n: to get off to a ~ing start faire un excellent départ; ~over n (Brit: bridge) saut-de-mouton m; ~sheet n (for tent) double toit m.

foal [fəul] n poulain m.

foam [fəum] n écume f; (on beer) mousse f; (also: plastic ~) mousse cellulaire or de plastique // vi écumer; (soapy water) mousser; ~ rubber n caoutchouc m mousse.

fob [fɔb] n: to ~ sb off with refiler à qn; se débarrasser de qn avec.

focus ['fəukəs] n (pl: ~es) foyer m; (of interest) centre m // vt (field glasses etc) mettre au point // vi: to ~ (on) (with camera) régler la mise au point (sur); (person) fixer son regard (sur); in ~ au point; out of ~ pas au point.

fodder ['fɔdə*] n fourrage m.

foe [fəu] n ennemi m.

fog [fɔg] n brouillard m; ~gy a: it's ~gy il y a du brouillard; ~lamp n (AUT) phare m anti-brouillard.

foil [fɔɪl] vt déjouer, contrecarrer // n feuille f de métal; (kitchen ~) papier m d'alu(minium); (FENCING) fleuret m.

fold [fəuld] n (bend, crease) pli m; (AGR) parc m à moutons; (fig) bercail m // vt plier; to ~ up vi (business) fermer boutique // vt (map etc) plier, replier; ~er n (for papers) chemise f; classeur m; (brochure) dépliant m; ~ing a (chair, bed) pliant(e).

foliage ['fəulɪɪdʒ] n feuillage m.

folk [fəuk] npl gens mpl // a folklorique; ~s npl famille f, parents mpl; ~lore ['fəuklɔ:*] n folklore m; ~ song n chanson f folklorique.

follow ['fɔləu] vt suivre // vi suivre; (result) s'ensuivre; he ~ed suit il fit de même; to ~ up vt (victory) tirer parti de; (letter, offer) donner suite à; (case) suivre; **~er** n disciple m/f, partisan/e; **~ing** a suivant(e) // n partisans mpl, disciples mpl.

folly ['fɔlɪ] n inconscience f; sottise f.

fond [fɔnd] a (memory, look) tendre, affectueux(euse); **to be ~ of** aimer beaucoup.

fondle ['fɔndl] vt caresser.

food [fu:d] n nourriture f; ~ **mixer** n mixeur m; ~ **poisoning** n intoxication f alimentaire; ~ **processor** n robot m de cuisine; **~stuffs** npl denrées fpl alimentaires.

fool [fu:l] n idiot/e; (HISTORY: of king) bouffon m, fou m; (CULIN) purée f de fruits à la crème // vt berner, duper // vi (also: ~ **around**) faire l'idiot or l'imbécile; **~hardy** a téméraire, imprudent(e); **~ish** a idiot(e), stupide; imprudent(e); écervelé(e); **~proof** a (plan etc) infaillible.

foot [fut] n (pl: feet) pied m; (measure) pied (= 304 mm; 12 inches); (of animal) patte f // vt (bill) casquer, payer; **on ~** à pied; **~age** n (CINEMA: length) ≈ métrage m; (: material) séquences fpl; **~ball** n ballon m (de football); (sport: Brit) football m; (: US) football américain; **~baller** (Brit) = **~ball player**; **~ball ground** n terrain m de football; **~ball player** n joueur m de football; **~brake** n frein m à pied; **~bridge** n passerelle f; **~hills** npl contreforts mpl; **~hold** n prise f (de pied); **~ing** n (fig) position f; **to lose one's ~ing** perdre pied; **~lights** npl rampe f; **~man** n laquais m; **~note** n note f (en bas de page); **~path** n sentier m; (in street) trottoir m; **~print** n trace f (de pied); **~step** n pas m; **~wear** n chaussure(s) f(pl).

for [fɔ:*] ♦ prep **1** (indicating destination, intention, purpose) pour; **the train ~ London** le train pour or (à destination) de Londres; **he went ~ the paper** il est allé chercher le journal; **it's time ~ lunch** c'est l'heure du déjeuner; **what's it ~?** ça sert à quoi?; **what ~?** (why) pourquoi?

2 (on behalf of, representing) pour; **the MP ~ Hove** le député de Hove; **to work ~ sb/sth** travailler pour qn/qch; **G ~ George** G comme Georges

3 (because of) pour; ~ **this reason** pour cette raison; ~ **fear of being criticized** de peur d'être critiqué

4 (with regard to) pour; **it's cold ~ July** il fait froid pour juillet; **a gift ~ languages** un don pour les langues

5 (in exchange for): **I sold it ~ £5** je l'ai vendu 5 livres; **to pay 50 pence ~ a ticket** payer 50 pence un billet

6 (in favour of) pour; **are you ~ or against us?** êtes-vous pour ou contre nous?

7 (referring to distance) pendant, sur; **there are roadworks ~ 5 km** il y a des travaux sur or pendant 5 km; **we walked ~ miles** nous avons marché pendant des kilomètres

8 (referring to time) pendant; depuis; pour; **he was away ~ 2 years** il a été absent pendant 2 ans; **she will be away ~ a month** elle sera absente (pendant) un mois; **I have known her ~ years** je la connais depuis des années; **can you do it ~ tomorrow?** est-ce que tu peux le faire pour demain?

9 (with infinitive clauses): **it is not ~ me to decide** ce n'est pas à moi de décider; **it would be best ~ you to leave** le mieux serait que vous partiez; **there is still time ~ you to do it** vous avez encore le temps de le faire; ~ **this to be possible ...** pour que cela soit possible ...

10 (in spite of): ~ **all his work/efforts** malgré tout son travail/tous ses efforts; ~ **all his complaints, he's very fond of her** il a beau se plaindre, il l'aime beaucoup

♦ cj (since, as: rather formal) car.

forage ['fɔrɪdʒ] n fourrage m.

foray ['fɔreɪ] n incursion f.

forbid, pt **forbad(e)**, pp **forbidden** [fə'bɪd, -'bæd, -'bɪdn] vt défendre, interdire; **to ~ sb to do** défendre or interdire à qn de faire; **~den** a défendu(e); **~ding** a d'aspect or d'allure sévère or sombre.

force [fɔ:s] n force f // vt forcer; **the F~s** npl (Brit) l'armée f; **in ~** en force; **to come into ~** entrer en vigueur; **to ~feed** vt nourrir de force; **~ful** a énergique, volontaire.

forcibly ['fɔ:səblɪ] ad par la force, de force; (vigorously) énergiquement.

ford [fɔ:d] n gué m.

fore [fɔ:*] n: **to the ~** en évidence.

forearm ['fɔ:rɑ:m] n avant-bras m inv.

foreboding [fɔ:'bəudɪŋ] n pressentiment m (néfaste).

forecast ['fɔ:kɑ:st] n prévision f // vt (irg: like cast) prévoir.

forecourt ['fɔ:kɔ:t] n (of garage) devant m.

forefathers ['fɔ:fɑ:ðəz] npl ancêtres mpl.

forefinger ['fɔ:fɪŋɡə*] n index m.

forefront ['fɔ:frʌnt] n: **in the ~ of** au premier rang or plan de.

forego vt = **forgo**.

foregone ['fɔ:gɔn] a: **it's a ~ conclusion** c'est à prévoir, c'est couru d'avance.

foreground ['fɔ:graund] n premier plan.

forehead ['fɔrɪd] n front m.

foreign ['fɔrɪn] a étranger(ère); (trade) extérieur(e); **~er** n étranger/ère; ~ **secretary** n (Brit) ministre m des Affaires étrangères; **F~ Office** n (Brit) ministère m des Affaires étrangères.

foreleg ['fɔːleg] *n* patte *f* de devant; jambe antérieure.

foreman ['fɔːmən] *n* contremaître *m*.

foremost ['fɔːməust] *a* le(la) plus en vue; premier(ère) // *ad*: **first and ~** avant tout, tout d'abord.

forensic [fə'rɛnsɪk] *a*: **~ medicine** médecine légale.

forerunner ['fɔːrʌnə*] *n* précurseur *m*.

foresee, *pt* **foresaw**, *pp* **foreseen** [fɔː'siː, -'sɔː, -'siːn] *vt* prévoir; **~able** *a* prévisible.

foreshadow [fɔː'ʃædəu] *vt* présager, annoncer, laisser prévoir.

foresight ['fɔːsaɪt] *n* prévoyance *f*.

forest ['fɔrɪst] *n* forêt *f*.

forestall [fɔː'stɔːl] *vt* devancer.

forestry ['fɔrɪstrɪ] *n* sylviculture *f*.

foretaste ['fɔːteɪst] *n* avant-goût *m*.

foretell, *pt*, *pp* **foretold** [fɔː'tɛl, -'təuld] *vt* prédire.

forever [fə'rɛvə*] *ad* pour toujours; (*fig*) continuellement.

foreword ['fɔːwəːd] *n* avant-propos *m inv*.

forfeit ['fɔːfɪt] *n* prix *m*, rançon *f* // *vt* perdre; (*one's life, health*) payer de.

forgave [fə'geɪv] *pt of* **forgive**.

forge [fɔːdʒ] *n* forge *f* // *vt* (*signature*) contrefaire; (*wrought iron*) forger; **to ~ documents** fabriquer de faux papiers; **to ~ money** (*Brit*) fabriquer de la fausse monnaie; **to ~ ahead** *vi* pousser de l'avant, prendre de l'avance; **~r** *n* faussaire *m*; **~ry** *n* faux *m*, contrefaçon *f*.

forget [fə'gɛt], *pt* **forgot**, *pp* **forgotten** *vt*, *vi* oublier; **~ful** *a* distrait(e), étourdi(e); **~ful of** oublieux(euse) de; **~-me-not** *n* myosotis *m*.

forgive [fə'gɪv], *pt* **forgave**, *pp* **forgiven** *vt* pardonner; **to ~ sb for sth** pardonner qch à qn; **~ness** *n* pardon *m*.

forgo [fɔː'gəu], *pt* **forwent**, *pp* **forgone** *vt* renoncer à.

forgot [fə'gɔt] *pt of* **forget**.

forgotten [fə'gɔtn] *pp of* **forget**.

fork [fɔːk] *n* (*for eating*) fourchette *f*; (*for gardening*) fourche *f*; (*of roads*) bifurcation *f*; (*of railways*) embranchement *m* // *vi* (*road*) bifurquer; **to ~ out** (*col: pay*) *vt* allonger, se fendre de // *vi* casquer; **~-lift truck** *n* chariot élévateur.

forlorn [fə'lɔːn] *a* (*person*) abandonné(e); (*place*) désert(e); (*attempt, hope*) désespéré(e).

form [fɔːm] *n* forme *f*; (*SCOL*) classe *f*; (*questionnaire*) formulaire *m* // *vt* former; **in top ~** en pleine forme.

formal ['fɔːməl] *a* (*offer, receipt*) en bonne et due forme; (*person*) cérémonieux(euse); (*dinner*) officiel(le); (*ART, PHILOSOPHY*) formel(le); **~ly** *ad* officiellement; formellement; cérémo-

nieusement.

format ['fɔːmæt] *n* format *m* // *vt* (*COMPUT*) formater.

formation [fɔː'meɪʃən] *n* formation *f*.

formative ['fɔːmətɪv] *a*: **~ years** années *fpl* d'apprentissage (*fig*) or de formation.

former ['fɔːmə*] *a* ancien(ne) (*before n*), précédent(e); **the ~ ... the latter** le premier ... le second, celui-là ... celui-ci; **~ly** *ad* autrefois.

formidable ['fɔːmɪdəbl] *a* redoutable.

formula ['fɔːmjulə] *n* formule *f*.

forsake, *pt* **forsook**, *pp* **forsaken** [fə'seɪk, -'suk, -'seɪkən] *vt* abandonner.

fort [fɔːt] *n* fort *m*.

forte ['fɔːtɪ] *n* (point) fort *m*.

forth [fɔːθ] *ad* en avant; **to go back and ~** aller et venir; **and so ~** et ainsi de suite; **~coming** *a* qui va paraître or avoir lieu prochainement; (*character*) ouvert(e), communicatif(ive); **~right** *a* franc(franche), direct(e); **~with** *ad* sur le champ.

fortify ['fɔːtɪfaɪ] *vt* fortifier; **fortified wine** *n* vin liquoreux or de liqueur.

fortnight ['fɔːtnaɪt] *n* quinzaine *f*, quinze jours *mpl*; **~ly** *a* bimensuel(le) // *ad* tous les quinze jours.

fortunate ['fɔːtʃənɪt] *a*: **it is ~ that** c'est une chance que; **~ly** *ad* heureusement.

fortune ['fɔːtʃən] *n* chance *f*; (*wealth*) fortune *f*; **~teller** *n* diseuse *f* de bonne aventure.

forty ['fɔːtɪ] *num* quarante.

forward ['fɔːwəd] *a* (*ahead of schedule*) en avance; (*movement, position*) en avant, vers l'avant; (*not shy*) ouvert(e), direct(e); effronté(e) // *n* (*SPORT*) avant *m* // *vt* (*letter*) faire suivre; (*parcel, goods*) expédier; (*fig*) promouvoir, contribuer au développement or à l'avancement de; **to move ~** avancer; **~(s)** *ad* en avant.

forwent [fɔː'wɛnt] *pt of* **forgo**.

fossil ['fɔsl] *a*, *n* fossile (*m*).

foster ['fɔstə*] *vt* encourager, favoriser; **~ child** *n* enfant adopté; **~ mother** *n* mère adoptive; mère nourricière.

fought [fɔːt] *pt*, *pp of* **fight**.

foul [faul] *a* (*weather, smell, food*) infect(e); (*language*) ordurier(ère); (*deed*) infâme // *n* (*FOOTBALL*) faute *f* // *vt* salir, encrasser; (*football player*) commettre une faute sur.

found [faund] *pt*, *pp of* **find** // *vt* (*establish*) fonder; **~ation** [-'deɪʃən] *n* (*act*) fondation *f*; (*base*) fondement *m*; (*also*: **~ation cream**) fond *m* de teint; **~ations** *npl* (*of building*) fondations *fpl*.

founder ['faundə*] *n* fondateur *m* // *vi* couler, sombrer.

foundry ['faundrɪ] *n* fonderie *f*.

fount [faunt] *n* source *f*.

fountain ['fauntɪn] *n* fontaine *f*; **~ pen** *n* stylo *m* (à encre).

four [fɔ:*] num quatre; **on all ~s** à quatre pattes; **~-poster** n (also: **~-poster bed**) lit m à baldaquin; **~some** ['fɔ:səm] n partie f à quatre; sortie f à quatre; **~teen** num quatorze; **~th** num quatrième.

fowl [faul] n volaille f.

fox [fɔks] n renard m // vt mystifier.

foyer ['fɔɪeɪ] n vestibule m; (THEATRE) foyer m.

fraction ['frækʃən] n fraction f.

fracture ['fræktʃə*] n fracture f.

fragile ['frædʒaɪl] a fragile.

fragment ['frægmənt] n fragment m.

fragrant ['freɪgrənt] a parfumé(e), odorant(e).

frail [freɪl] a fragile, délicat(e).

frame [freɪm] n charpente f; (of picture) cadre m; (of door, window) encadrement m, chambranle m; (of spectacles: also: **~s**) monture f // vt encadrer; **~ of mind** n disposition f d'esprit; **~work** n structure f.

France [frɑ:ns] n France f.

franchise ['fræntʃaɪz] n (POL) droit m de vote; (COMM) franchise f.

frank [fræŋk] a franc(franche) // vt (letter) affranchir; **~ly** ad franchement.

frantic ['fræntɪk] a frénétique.

fraternity [frə'tɜ:nɪtɪ] n (club) communauté f, confrérie f; (spirit) fraternité f.

fraud [frɔ:d] n supercherie f, fraude f, tromperie f; imposteur m.

fraught [frɔ:t] a: **~ with** chargé(e) de, plein(e) de.

fray [freɪ] n bagarre f // vi s'effilocher; tempers were **~ed** les gens commençaient à s'énerver.

freak [fri:k] n (also cpd) phénomène m, créature ou événement exceptionnel par sa rareté, son caractère d'anomalie.

freckle ['frekl] n tache f de rousseur.

free [fri:] a (gen) libre; (gratis) gratuit(e); (liberal) généreux(euse), large // vt (prisoner etc) libérer; (jammed object or person) dégager; **~ (of charge), for ~** ad gratuitement; **~dom** ['fri:dəm] n liberté f; **~-for-all** n mêlée générale; **~ gift** n prime f; **~hold** n propriété foncière libre; **~ kick** n coup franc; **~lance** a indépendant(e); **~ly** ad librement; (liberally) libéralement; **~mason** n franc-maçon m; **~post** n franchise postale; **~-range** a (hen, eggs) de ferme; **~ trade** n libre-échange m; **~way** n (US) autoroute f; **~wheel** vi descendre en roue libre; **~ will** n libre arbitre m; **of one's own ~ will** de son plein gré.

freeze [fri:z] vb (pt froze, pp frozen) vi geler // vt geler; (food) congeler; (prices, salaries) bloquer, geler m; blocage m; **~-dried** a lyophilisé(e); **~r** n congélateur m.

freezing ['fri:zɪŋ] a: **~ cold** a glacial(e);

~ point n point m de congélation; **3 degrees below ~** 3 degrés au-dessous de zéro.

freight [freɪt] n (goods) fret m, cargaison f; (money charged) fret, prix m du transport; **~ train** n (US) train m de marchandises.

French [frentʃ] a français(e) // n (LING) français m; the **~** npl les Français; **~ bean** n haricot vert; **~ fried potatoes**, (US) **~ fries** npl (pommes de terre fpl) frites fpl; **~man** n Français m; **~ window** n porte-fenêtre f; **~woman** n Française f.

frenzy ['frenzɪ] n frénésie f.

frequent a ['fri:kwənt] fréquent(e) // [frɪ'kwent] fréquenter; **~ly** ad fréquemment.

fresh [freʃ] a frais(fraîche); (new) nouveau(nouvelle); (cheeky) familier(ère), culotté(e); **~en** vi (wind, air) fraîchir; **to ~en up** vi faire un brin de toilette; **~er** n (Brit SCOL: col) bizuth m, étudiant/e de 1ère année; **~ly** ad nouvellement, récemment; **~man** n (US) = **~er**; **~ness** n fraîcheur f; **~water** a (fish) d'eau douce.

fret [fret] vi s'agiter, se tracasser.

friar ['fraɪə*] n moine m, frère m.

friction ['frɪkʃən] n friction f.

Friday ['fraɪdɪ] n vendredi m.

fridge [frɪdʒ] n (Brit) frigo m, frigidaire m ®.

fried [fraɪd] pt, pp of fry // a frit(e); **~ egg** œuf m sur le plat.

friend [frend] n ami/e; **~ly** a amical(e); gentil(le); **~ship** n amitié f.

frieze [fri:z] n frise f, bordure f.

fright [fraɪt] n peur f, effroi m; **to take ~** prendre peur, s'effrayer; **~en** vt effrayer, faire peur à; **~ened** a: **to be ~ened (of)** avoir peur (de); **~ening** a effrayant(e); **~ful** a affreux(euse).

frigid ['frɪdʒɪd] a (woman) frigide.

frill [frɪl] n (of dress) volant m; (of shirt) jabot m.

fringe [frɪndʒ] n frange f; (edge: of forest etc) bordure f; (fig): on the **~** en marge; **~ benefits** npl avantages sociaux ou en nature.

frisk [frɪsk] vt fouiller.

frisky ['frɪskɪ] a vif(vive), sémillant(e).

fritter ['frɪtə*] n beignet m; **to ~ away** vt gaspiller.

frivolous ['frɪvələs] a frivole.

frizzy ['frɪzɪ] a crépu(e).

fro [frəu] see to.

frock [frɔk] n robe f.

frog [frɔg] n grenouille f; **~man** n homme-grenouille m.

frolic ['frɔlɪk] vi folâtrer, batifoler.

from [frɔm] prep 1 (indicating starting place, origin etc) de; **where do you come ~?, where are you ~?** d'où venez-vous?; **~ London to Paris** de Londres à Paris; **a**

letter ~ my sister une lettre de ma sœur; **to drink ~ the bottle** boire à (même) la bouteille

2 (*indicating time*) (à partir) de; ~ **one o'clock to** *or* **until** *or* **till two** de une heure à deux heures; ~ **January** (**on**) à partir de janvier

3 (*indicating distance*) de; **the hotel is one kilometre ~ the beach** l'hôtel est à un kilomètre de la plage

4 (*indicating price, number etc*) de; **the interest rate was increased ~ 9% to 10%** le taux d'intérêt a augmenté de 9 à 10%

5 (*indicating difference*) de; **he can't tell red ~ green** il ne peut pas distinguer le rouge du vert

6 (*because of, on the basis of*): ~ **what** he says d'après ce qu'il dit; **weak ~ hunger** affaibli par la faim.

front [frʌnt] *n* (*of house, dress*) devant *m*; (*of coach, train*) avant *m*; (*of book*) couverture *f*; (*promenade: also:* sea ~) bord *m* de mer; (MIL, POL, METEOROL-OGY) front *m*; (*fig: appearances*) contenance *f*, façade *f* // *a* de devant; premier(ère); **in ~** (**of**) devant; ~ **door** *n* porte *f* d'entrée; (*of car*) portière *f* avant; ~**ier** ['frʌntɪə*] *n* frontière *f*; ~ **page** *n* première page; ~ **room** *n* (*Brit*) pièce *f* de devant, salon *m*; ~**wheel drive** *n* traction *f* avant.

frost [frɔst] *n* gel *m*, gelée *f*; (*also:* hoar~) givre *m*; ~**bite** *n* gelures *fpl*; ~**ed** *a* (*glass*) dépoli(e); ~**y** *a* (*window*) couvert(e) de givre; (*welcome*) glacial(e).

froth ['frɔθ] *n* mousse *f*; écume *f*.

frown [fraun] *vi* froncer les sourcils.

froze [frəuz] *pt* of **freeze**; ~**n** *pp* of **freeze** // *a* (*food*) congelé(e).

fruit [fru:t] *n* (*pl inv*) fruit *m*; ~**erer** *n* fruitier *m*, marchand/e de fruits; ~**erer's** (**shop**) *n* fruiterie *f*; ~**ful** *a* fructueux(euse); (*plant, soil*) fécond(e); ~**ion** [fru:'ɪʃən] *n*: **to come to ~ion** se réaliser; ~ **juice** *n* jus *m* de fruit; ~ **machine** *n* (*Brit*) machine *f* à sous; ~ **salad** *n* salade *f* de fruits.

frustrate [frʌs'treɪt] *vt* frustrer; (*plot, plans*) faire échouer; ~**d** *a* frustré(e).

fry [fraɪ], *pt, pp* **fried** *vt* (faire) frire; **the small** ~ le menu fretin; ~**ing pan** *n* poêle *f* (à frire).

ft. *abbr* of **foot, feet.**

fuddy-duddy ['fʌdɪdʌdɪ] *n* (*pej*) vieux schnock.

fudge [fʌdʒ] *n* (CULIN) sorte de confiserie à base de sucre, de beurre et de lait.

fuel [fjuəl] *n* (*for heating*) combustible *m*; (*for propelling*) carburant *m*; ~ **tank** *n* cuve *f* à mazout, citerne *f*; (*in vehicle*) réservoir *m* de *or* à carburant.

fugitive ['fju:dʒɪtɪv] *n* fugitif/ive.

fulfil [ful'fɪl] *vt* (*function*) remplir; (*order*) exécuter; (*wish, desire*)

satisfaire, réaliser; ~**ment** *n* (*of wishes*) réalisation *f*.

full [ful] *a* plein(e); (*details, information*) complet(ète); (*skirt*) ample, large // *ad*: **to know ~ well that** savoir fort bien que; **I'm ~** (**up**) j'ai bien mangé; ~ **employment** plein emploi; **a ~ two hours** deux bonnes heures; **at ~ speed** à toute vitesse; **in ~** (*reproduce, quote*) intégralement; (*write name etc*) en toutes lettres; **to pay in ~** tout payer; ~ **moon** *n* pleine lune; ~**-scale** *a* (*attack, war*) complet(ète), total(e); (*model*) grandeur nature *inv*; ~ **stop** *n* point *m*; ~**-time** *a, ad* (*work*) à plein temps // *n* (SPORT) fin *f* du match; ~**y** *ad* entièrement, complètement; ~**y-fledged** *a* (*teacher, barrister*) diplômé(e); (*citizen, member*) à part entière.

fulsome ['fulsəm] *a* (*pej: praise, gratitude*) excessif(ive).

fumble ['fʌmbl] *vi* fouiller, tâtonner; **to ~ with** *vt fus* tripoter.

fume [fju:m] *vi* rager; ~**s** *npl* vapeurs *fpl*, émanations *fpl*, gaz *mpl*.

fun [fʌn] *n* amusement *m*, divertissement *m*; **to have ~** s'amuser; **for ~** pour rire; **to make ~ of** *vt fus* se moquer de.

function ['fʌŋkʃən] *n* fonction *f*; cérémonie *f*, soirée officielle // *vi* fonctionner; ~**al** *a* fonctionnel(le).

fund [fʌnd] *n* caisse *f*, fonds *m*; (*source, store*) source *f*, mine *f*; (*model*) fonds *mpl*.

fundamental [fʌndə'mɛntl] *a* fondamental(e).

funeral ['fju:nərəl] *n* enterrement *m*, obsèques *fpl* (*more formal occasion*); ~ **parlour** *n* dépôt *m* mortuaire; ~ **service** *n* service *m* funèbre.

fun fair *n* (*Brit*) fête (foraine).

fungus, *pl* **fungi** ['fʌŋgəs, -gaɪ] *n* champignon *m*; (*mould*) moisissure *f*.

funnel ['fʌnl] *n* entonnoir *m*; (*of ship*) cheminée *f*.

funny ['fʌnɪ] *a* amusant(e), drôle; (*strange*) curieux(euse), bizarre.

fur [fə:*] *n* fourrure *f*; (*Brit: in kettle etc*) (dépôt *m* de) tartre *m*; ~ **coat** *n* manteau *m* de fourrure.

furious ['fjuərɪəs] *a* furieux(euse); (*effort*) acharné(e).

furlong ['fə:lɔŋ] *n* = 201.17 *m* (*terme d'hippisme*).

furlough ['fə:ləu] *n* permission *f*, congé *m*.

furnace ['fə:nɪs] *n* fourneau *m*.

furnish ['fə:nɪʃ] *vt* meubler; (*supply*) fournir; ~**ings** *npl* mobilier *m*, articles *mpl* d'ameublement.

furniture ['fə:nɪtʃə*] *n* meubles *mpl*, mobilier *m*; **piece of ~** meuble *m*.

furrow ['fʌrəu] *n* sillon *m*.

furry ['fə:rɪ] *a* (*animal*) à fourrure; (*toy*) en peluche.

further ['fə:ðə*] a supplémentaire, autre; nouveau(nouvelle); plus loin // ad plus loin; (more) davantage; (moreover) de plus // vt faire avancer or progresser, promouvoir; ~ **education** n enseignement m post-scolaire (recyclage, formation professionnelle); **~more** [fə:ðə'mɔ:*] ad de plus, en outre.

furthest ['fə:ðɪst] superlative of **far**.

fury ['fjuərɪ] n fureur f.

fuse [fju:z] n fusible m; (for bomb etc) amorce f, détonateur m // vt, vi (metal) fondre; (fig) fusionner; **the lights have ~d** (Brit) les plombs ont sauté; ~ **box** n boîte f à fusibles.

fuss [fʌs] n chichis mpl, façons fpl, embarras mpl; (complaining) histoire(s) f(pl); **to make a ~** faire des façons etc; **~y** a (person) tatillon(ne), difficile; chichiteux(euse); (dress, style) tarabiscoté(e).

future ['fju:tʃə*] a futur(e) // n avenir m; (LING) futur m; **in (the) ~** à l'avenir.

fuze [fju:z] (US) = **fuse**.

fuzzy ['fʌzɪ] a (PHOT) flou(e); (hair) crépu(e).

G

G [dʒi:] n (MUS) sol m.

gabble ['gæbl] vi bredouiller; jacasser.

gable ['geɪbl] n pignon m.

gadget ['gædʒɪt] n gadget m.

Gaelic ['geɪlɪk] a, n (LING) gaélique (m).

gag [gæg] n bâillon m; (joke) gag m // vt bâillonner.

gaiety ['geɪɪtɪ] n gaieté f.

gaily ['geɪlɪ] ad gaiement.

gain [geɪn] n gain m, profit m // vt gagner // vi (watch) avancer; **to ~ in/by** gagner en/à; **to ~ 3lbs (in weight)** prendre 3 livres.

gait [geɪt] n démarche f.

gal. abbr of **gallon**.

gale [geɪl] n rafale f de vent; coup m de vent.

gallant ['gælənt] a vaillant(e), brave; (towards ladies) empressé(e), galant(e).

gall bladder ['gɔ:lblædə*] n vésicule f biliaire.

gallery ['gælərɪ] n galerie f; (also: **art ~**) musée m; (: private) galerie.

galley ['gælɪ] n (ship's kitchen) cambuse f; (ship) galère f.

Gallic ['gælɪk] a gaulois(e), français(e); (charm) latin(e).

gallon ['gælən] n gallon m (= 8 pints; Brit = 4.543 l; US = 3.785 l).

gallop ['gæləp] n galop m // vi galoper.

gallows ['gæləuz] n potence f.

gallstone ['gɔ:lstəun] n calcul m (biliaire).

galore [gə'lɔ:*] ad en abondance, à gogo (col).

galvanize ['gælvənaɪz] vt galvaniser; (fig): **to ~ sb into action** galvaniser qn.

gambit ['gæmbɪt] n (fig): (opening) ~ manœuvre f stratégique.

gamble ['gæmbl] n pari m, risque calculé // vt, vi jouer; **to ~ on** (fig) miser sur; **~r** n joueur m; **gambling** n jeu m.

game [geɪm] n jeu m; (event) match m; (HUNTING) gibier m // a brave; (ready): **to be ~ (for sth/to do)** être prêt(e) (à qch/à faire); **a ~ of football/tennis** une partie de football/tennis; **big ~** n gros gibier; **~keeper** n garde-chasse m.

gammon ['gæmən] n (bacon) quartier m de lard fumé; (ham) jambon fumé.

gamut ['gæmət] n gamme f.

gang [gæŋ] n bande f, groupe m // vi: **to ~ up on sb** se liguer contre qn.

gangster ['gæŋstə*] n gangster m.

gangway ['gæŋweɪ] n passerelle f; (Brit: of bus) couloir central.

gaol [dʒeɪl] n, vt (Brit) = **jail**.

gap [gæp] n trou m; (in time) intervalle m; (fig) lacune f; vide m.

gape [geɪp] vi être or rester bouche bée; **gaping** a (hole) béant(e).

garage ['gærɑ:ʒ] n garage m.

garbage ['gɑ:bɪdʒ] n ordures fpl, détritus mpl; **~ can** n (US) poubelle f, boîte f à ordures.

garbled ['gɑ:bld] a déformé(e); faussé(e).

garden ['gɑ:dn] n jardin m; **~er** n jardinier m; **~ing** n jardinage m.

gargle ['gɑ:gl] vi se gargariser.

gargoyle ['gɑ:gɔɪl] n gargouille f.

garish ['gɛərɪʃ] a criard(e), voyant(e).

garland ['gɑ:lənd] n guirlande f; couronne f.

garlic ['gɑ:lɪk] n ail m.

garment ['gɑ:mənt] n vêtement m.

garrison ['gærɪsn] n garnison f.

garrulous ['gærjuləs] a volubile, loquace.

garter ['gɑ:tə*] n jarretière f; (US) jarretelle f.

gas [gæs] n gaz m; (US: gasoline) essence f // vt asphyxier; (MIL) gazer; ~ **cooker** n (Brit) cuisinière f à gaz; ~ **cylinder** n bouteille f de gaz; ~ **fire** n radiateur m à gaz.

gash [gæʃ] n entaille f; (on face) balafre f.

gasket ['gæskɪt] n (AUT) joint m de culasse.

gas mask n masque m à gaz.

gas meter n compteur m à gaz.

gasoline ['gæsəli:n] n (US) essence f.

gasp [gɑ:sp] vi haleter; (fig) avoir le souffle coupé; **to ~ out** vt (say) dire dans un souffle or d'une voix entrecoupée.

gas ring n brûleur m.
gassy ['gæsɪ] a gazeux(euse).
gas tap n bouton m (de cuisinière à gaz); (on pipe) robinet m à gaz.
gate [geɪt] n (of garden) portail m; (of farm) barrière f; (of building) porte f; (of lock) vanne f; ~**crash** vt (Brit) s'introduire sans invitation dans; ~**way** n porte f.
gather ['gæðə*] vt (flowers, fruit) cueillir; (pick up) ramasser; (assemble) rassembler, réunir; recueillir; (understand) comprendre // vi (assemble) se rassembler; to ~ speed prendre de la vitesse; ~**ing** n rassemblement m.
gaudy ['gɔ:dɪ] a voyant(e).
gauge [geɪdʒ] n (standard measure) calibre m; (RAIL) écartement m; (instrument) jauge f // vt jauger.
Gaul [gɔ:l] n (country) Gaule f; (person) Gaulois/e.
gaunt [gɔ:nt] a décharné(e); (grim, desolate) désolé(e).
gauntlet ['gɔ:ntlɪt] n (fig): to run the ~ through an angry crowd se frayer un passage à travers une foule hostile; to throw down the ~ jeter le gant.
gauze [gɔ:z] n gaze f.
gave [geɪv] pt of **give**.
gay [geɪ] a (person) gai(e), réjoui(e); (colour) gai, vif(vive); (col) homosexuel(le).
gaze [geɪz] n regard m fixe // vi: to ~ at fixer du regard.
gazetteer [gæzə'tɪə*] n dictionnaire m géographique.
GB abbr of **Great Britain**.
GCE n abbr (Brit) = General Certificate of Education.
GCSE n abbr (Brit) = General Certificate of Secondary Education.
gear [gɪə*] n matériel m, équipement m; attirail m; (TECH) engrenage m; (AUT) vitesse f // vt (fig: adapt): to ~ sth to adapter qch à; top or (US) high/low/bottom ~ quatrième (or cinquième)/ deuxième/première vitesse; in ~ en prise; ~ **box** n boîte f de vitesse; ~ **lever**, (US) ~ **shift** n levier m de vitesse.
geese [gi:s] npl of **goose**.
gel [dʒɛl] n gelée f; (CHEM) colloïde m.
gelignite ['dʒɛlɪgnaɪt] n plastic m.
gem [dʒɛm] n pierre précieuse.
Gemini ['dʒɛmɪnaɪ] n les Gémeaux mpl.
gender ['dʒɛndə*] n genre m.
general ['dʒɛnərl] n général m // a général(e); in ~ en général; ~ **delivery** n (US) poste restante; ~ **election** n élection(s) législative(s); ~**ize** vi généraliser; ~**ly** ad généralement; ~ **practitioner (G.P.)** n généraliste m/f.
generate ['dʒɛnəreɪt] vt engendrer; (electricity) produire.
generation [dʒɛnə'reɪʃən] n génération

f.
generator ['dʒɛnəreɪtə*] n générateur m.
generosity [dʒɛnə'rɔsɪtɪ] n générosité f.
generous ['dʒɛnərəs] a généreux(euse); (copious) copieux(euse).
genetic [dʒɪ'nɛtɪk] a génétique.
Geneva [dʒɪ'ni:və] n Genève.
genial ['dʒi:nɪəl] a cordial(e), chaleureux(euse); (climate) clément(e).
genitals ['dʒɛnɪtlz] npl organes génitaux.
genius ['dʒi:nɪəs] n génie m.
gent [dʒɛnt] n abbr of **gentleman**.
genteel [dʒɛn'ti:l] a de bon ton, distingué(e).
gentle ['dʒɛntl] a doux(douce).
gentleman ['dʒɛntlmən] n monsieur m; (well-bred man) gentleman m.
gently ['dʒɛntlɪ] ad doucement.
gentry ['dʒɛntrɪ] n petite noblesse.
gents [dʒɛnts] n W.-C. mpl (pour hommes).
genuine ['dʒɛnjuɪn] a véritable, authentique; sincère.
geography [dʒɪ'ɔgrəfɪ] n géographie f.
geology [dʒɪ'ɔlədʒɪ] n géologie f.
geometric(al) [dʒɪə'mɛtrɪk(l)] a géométrique.
geometry [dʒɪ'ɔmɛtrɪ] n géométrie f.
geranium [dʒɪ'reɪnjəm] n géranium m.
geriatric [dʒɛrɪ'ætrɪk] a gériatrique.
germ [dʒə:m] n (MED) microbe m; (BIO, fig) germe m.
German ['dʒə:mən] a allemand(e) // n Allemand/e; (LING) allemand m; ~ **measles** n rubéole f.
Germany ['dʒə:mənɪ] n Allemagne f.
gesture ['dʒɛstjə*] n geste m.
get [gɛt], pt, pp **got**, pp **gotten** (US) vi
1 (become, be) devenir; to ~ old/tired devenir vieux/fatigué, vieillir/se fatiguer; to ~ drunk s'enivrer; to ~ killed se faire tuer; when do I ~ paid? quand est-ce que je serai payé?; it's ~ting late il se fait tard
2 (go): to ~ to/from aller à/de; to ~ home rentrer chez soi; how did you ~ here? comment es-tu arrivé ici?
3 (begin) commencer or se mettre à; I'm ~ting to like him je commence à l'apprécier; let's ~ going or started allons-y
4 (modal auxiliary vb): you've got to do it il faut que vous le fassiez; I've got to tell the police je dois le dire à la police
♦ vt
1: to ~ sth done (do) faire qch; (have done) faire faire qch; to ~ one's hair cut se faire couper les cheveux; to ~ sb to do sth faire faire qch à qn; to ~ sb drunk enivrer qn
2 (obtain: money, permission, results) obtenir, avoir; (find: job, flat) trouver; (fetch: person, doctor, object) aller cher-

cher; **to ~ sth for sb** procurer qch à qn; **~ me Mr Jones, please** (on phone) passez-moi Mr Jones, s'il vous plaît; **can I ~ you a drink?** est-ce que je peux vous servir à boire?
3 (receive: present, letter) recevoir, avoir; (acquire: reputation) acquérir; (: prize) obtenir; **what did you ~ for your birthday?** qu'est-ce que tu as eu pour ton anniversaire?
4 (catch) prendre, saisir, attraper; (hit: target etc) atteindre; **to ~ sb by the arm/throat** prendre or saisir or attraper qn par le bras/à la gorge; **~ him!** arrête-le!
5 (take, move) faire parvenir; **do you think we'll ~ it through the door?** on arrivera à le faire passer par la porte?; **I'll ~ you there somehow** je me débrouillerai pour t'y emmener
6 (catch, take: plane, bus etc) prendre
7 (understand) comprendre, saisir; (hear) entendre; **I've got it!** j'ai compris!, je saisis!; **I didn't ~ your name** je n'ai pas entendu votre nom
8 (have, possess): **to have got avoir; how many have you got?** vous en avez combien?
to get about vi se déplacer; (news) se répandre
to get along vi (agree) s'entendre; (depart) s'en aller; (manage) = **to get by**
to get at vt fus (attack) s'en prendre à; (reach) attraper, atteindre
to get away vi partir, s'en aller; (escape) s'échapper
to get away with vt fus en être quitte pour; se faire passer or pardonner
to get back vi (return) rentrer ♦ vt récupérer, recouvrer
to get by vi (pass) passer; (manage) se débrouiller
to get down vi, vt fus descendre ♦ vt descendre; (depress) déprimer
to get down to vt fus (work) se mettre à (faire)
to get in vi rentrer; (train) arriver
to get into vt fus entrer dans; (car, train etc) monter dans; (clothes) mettre, enfiler, endosser; **to ~ into bed/a rage** se mettre au lit/en colère
to get off vi (from train etc) descendre; (depart: person, car) s'en aller; (escape) s'en tirer ♦ vt (remove: clothes, stain) enlever ♦ vt fus (train, bus) descendre de
to get on vi (at exam etc) se débrouiller; (agree): **to ~ on (with)** s'entendre (avec) ♦ vt fus monter dans; (horse) monter sur
to get out vi sortir; (of vehicle) descendre ♦ vt sortir
to get out of vt fus sortir de; (duty etc) échapper à, se soustraire à

to get over vt fus (illness) se remettre de
to get round vt fus contourner; (fig: person) entortiller
to get through vi (TEL) avoir la communication; **to ~ through to sb** atteindre qn
to get together vi se réunir ♦ vt assembler
to get up vi (rise) se lever ♦ vt fus monter
to get up to vt fus (reach) arriver à; (prank etc) faire.
getaway ['gɛtəweɪ] n fuite f.
get-up ['gɛtʌp] n (col) accoutrement m.
geyser ['giːzə*] n chauffe-eau m inv; (GEO) geyser m.
Ghana ['gɑːnə] n Ghana m.
ghastly ['gɑːstlɪ] a atroce, horrible; (pale) livide, blême.
gherkin ['gɜːkɪn] n cornichon m.
ghost [gəust] n fantôme m, revenant m.
giant ['dʒaɪənt] n géant/e // a géant(e), énorme.
gibberish ['dʒɪbərɪʃ] n charabia m.
gibe [dʒaɪb] n sarcasme m.
giblets ['dʒɪblɪts] npl abats mpl.
Gibraltar [dʒɪ'brɔltə*] n Gibraltar m.
giddy ['gɪdɪ] a (dizzy): **to be ~** avoir le vertige; (height) vertigineux(euse).
gift [gɪft] n cadeau m, présent m; (donation, ability) don m; **~ed** a doué(e); **~ token** or **voucher** n chèque-cadeau m.
gigantic [dʒaɪ'gæntɪk] a gigantesque.
giggle ['gɪgl] vi pouffer, ricaner sottement.
gill [dʒɪl] n (measure) = 0.25 pints (Brit = 0.148 l, US = 0.118 l).
gills [gɪlz] npl (of fish) ouïes fpl, branchies fpl.
gilt [gɪlt] n dorure f // a doré(e); **~edged** a (COMM) de premier ordre.
gimmick ['gɪmɪk] n truc m.
gin [dʒɪn] n (liquor) gin m.
ginger ['dʒɪndʒə*] n gingembre m; **~ ale, ~ beer** n boisson gazeuse au gingembre; **~bread** n pain m d'épices.
gingerly ['dʒɪndʒəlɪ] ad avec précaution.
gipsy ['dʒɪpsɪ] n gitan/e, bohémien/ne.
giraffe [dʒɪ'rɑːf] n girafe f.
girder ['gɜːdə*] n poutrelle f.
girdle ['gɜːdl] n (corset) gaine f.
girl [gɜːl] n fille f, fillette f; (young unmarried woman) jeune fille; (daughter) fille; **an English ~** une jeune Anglaise; **~friend** n (of girl) amie f; (of boy) petite amie.
giro ['dʒaɪrəu] n (bank ~) virement m bancaire; (post office ~) mandat m.
girth [gɜːθ] n circonférence f; (of horse) sangle f.
gist [dʒɪst] n essentiel m.
give [gɪv] vb (pt gave, pp given) vt

donner // vi (break) céder; (stretch: fabric) se prêter; to ~ sb sth, ~ sth to sb donner qch à qn; to ~ a cry/sigh pousser un cri/un soupir; to ~ away vt donner; (give free) faire cadeau de; (betray) donner, trahir; (disclose) révéler; (bride) conduire à l'autel; to ~ back vt rendre; to ~ in vi céder // vt donner; to ~ off vt dégager; to ~ out vt distribuer; annoncer; to ~ up vi renoncer // vt renoncer à; to ~ up smoking arrêter de fumer; to ~ o.s. up se rendre; to ~ way vi céder; (Brit AUT) céder la priorité.

glacier ['glæsɪə*] n glacier m.

glad [glæd] a content(e).

gladly ['glædlɪ] ad volontiers.

glamorous ['glæmərəs] a séduisant(e).

glamour ['glæmə*] n éclat m, prestige m.

glance [glɑ:ns] n coup m d'œil // vi: to ~ at jeter un coup d'œil à; to ~ off vt fus (bullet) ricocher sur; **glancing** a (blow) oblique.

gland [glænd] n glande f.

glare [glɛə*] n lumière éblouissante // vi briller d'un éclat aveuglant; to ~ at lancer un or des regard(s) furieux à; **glaring** a (mistake) criant(e), qui saute aux yeux.

glass [glɑ:s] n verre m; (also: looking ~) miroir m; ~es npl lunettes fpl; ~ware n verrerie f; ~y a (eyes) vitreux(euse).

glaze [gleɪz] vt (door) vitrer; (pottery) vernir // n vernis m.

glazier ['gleɪzɪə*] n vitrier m.

gleam [gli:m] n lueur f; rayon m // vi luire, briller; ~ing a luisant(e).

glean [gli:n] vt (information) recueillir.

glee [gli:] n joie f.

glen [glɛn] n vallée f.

glib [glɪb] a qui a du bagou; facile.

glide [glaɪd] vi glisser; (AVIAT, birds) planer; ~r n (AVIAT) planeur m; **gliding** n (AVIAT) vol m à voile.

glimmer ['glɪmə*] n lueur f.

glimpse [glɪmps] n vision passagère, aperçu m // vt entrevoir, apercevoir.

glint [glɪnt] vi étinceler.

glisten ['glɪsn] vi briller, luire.

glitter ['glɪtə*] vi scintiller, briller // n scintillement m.

gloat [gləut] vi: to ~ (over) jubiler (à propos de).

global ['gləubl] a mondial(e).

globe [gləub] n globe m.

gloom [glu:m] n obscurité f; (sadness) tristesse f, mélancolie f; ~y a sombre, triste, mélancolique.

glorious ['glɔ:rɪəs] a glorieux(euse); splendide.

glory ['glɔ:rɪ] n gloire f; splendeur f // vi: to ~ in se glorifier de.

gloss [glɔs] n (shine) brillant m, vernis

m; to ~ over vt fus glisser sur.

glossary ['glɔsərɪ] n glossaire m.

glossy ['glɔsɪ] a brillant(e), luisant(e).

glove [glʌv] n gant m; ~ compartment n (AUT) boîte f à gants, vide-poches m inv.

glow [gləu] vi rougeoyer; (face) rayonner // n rougeoiement m.

glower ['glauə*] vi: to ~ (at) lancer des regards mauvais à.

glue [glu:] n colle f // vt coller.

glum [glʌm] a maussade, morose.

glut [glʌt] n surabondance f.

glutton ['glʌtn] n glouton/ne; a ~ for work un bourreau de travail.

gnarled [nɑ:ld] a noueux(euse).

gnat [næt] n moucheron m.

gnaw [nɔ:] vt ronger.

go [gəu] vb (pt went, pp gone) vi aller; (depart) partir, s'en aller; (work) marcher; (be sold): to ~ for £10 se vendre 10 livres; (fit, suit): to ~ with aller avec; (become): to ~ pale/mouldy pâlir/moisir; (break etc) céder // n (pl: ~es): to have a ~ (at) essayer (de faire); to be on the ~ être en mouvement; whose ~ is it? à qui est-ce de jouer?; he's going to do it va faire, il est sur le point de faire; to ~ for a walk aller se promener; how did it ~? comment est-ce que ça s'est passé?; to ~ round the back/by the shop passer par derrière/devant le magasin; to ~ about vi (rumour) se répandre // vt fus: how do I ~ about this? comment dois-je m'y prendre (pour faire ceci)?; to ~ ahead vi (make progress) avancer; (get going) y aller; to ~ along vi aller, avancer // vt fus longer, parcourir; to ~ away vi partir, s'en aller; to ~ back vi rentrer; revenir; (go again) retourner; to ~ back on vt fus (promise) revenir sur; to ~ by vi (years, time) passer, s'écouler // vt fus s'en tenir à; en croire; to ~ down vi descendre; (ship) couler; (sun) se coucher // vt fus descendre; to ~ for vt fus (fetch) aller chercher; (like) aimer; (attack) s'en prendre à; attaquer; to ~ in vi entrer; to ~ in for vt fus (competition) se présenter à; (like) aimer; to ~ into vt fus entrer dans; (investigate) étudier, examiner; (embark on) se lancer dans; to ~ off vi partir, s'en aller; (food) se gâter; (explode) sauter; (event) se dérouler // vt fus ne plus aimer; the gun went off le coup est parti; to ~ on vi continuer; (happen) se passer; to ~ on doing continuer à faire; to ~ out vi sortir; (fire, light) s'éteindre; to ~ over vt fus (check) revoir, vérifier; to ~ through vt fus (town etc) traverser; to ~ up vi monter; (price) augmenter // vt fus gravir; to ~ without vt fus se passer de.

goad [gəud] vt aiguillonner.

go-ahead ['gəuəhɛd] a dynamique, entreprenant(e) // n feu vert.

goal [gəul] n but m; **~keeper** n gardien m de but; **~post** n poteau m de but.

goat [gəut] n chèvre f.

gobble ['gɔbl] vt (also: ~ down, ~ up) engloutir.

god [gɔd] n dieu m; **G~** n Dieu m; **~child** n filleul/e; **~daughter** n filleule f; **~dess** n déesse f; **~father** n parrain m; **~forsaken** a maudit(e); **~mother** n marraine f; **~send** n aubaine f; **~son** n filleul m.

goggles ['gɔglz] npl lunettes fpl (protectrices) (de motocycliste etc).

going ['gəuiŋ] n (conditions) état m du terrain // a: **the ~ rate** le tarif (en vigueur).

gold [gəuld] n or m // a en or; **~en** a (made of gold) en or; (gold in colour) doré(e); **~fish** n poisson m rouge; **~plated** a plaqué(e) or inv; **~smith** n orfèvre m.

golf [gɔlf] n golf m; **~ ball** n balle f de golf; (on typewriter) boule m; **~ club** n club m de golf; (stick) club m, crosse f de golf; **~ course** n terrain m de golf; **~er** n joueur/euse de golf.

gone [gɔn] pp of go // a parti(e).

good [gud] a bon(ne); (kind) gentil(le); (child) sage // n bien m; **~s** npl marchandise f, articles mpl; **~!** bon!, très bien!; **to be ~ at** être bon en; **to be ~ for** être bon à; **it's ~ for you** c'est bon pour vous; **would you be ~ enough to ...?** auriez-vous la bonté or l'amabilité de ...?; **a ~ deal (of)** beaucoup (de); **a ~ many** beaucoup (de); **to make ~** vi (succeed) faire son chemin, réussir // vt (deficit) combler; (losses) compenser; **it's no ~ complaining** cela ne sert à rien de se plaindre; **for ~** pour de bon, une fois pour toutes; **~ morning/afternoon!** bonjour!; **~ evening!** bonsoir!; **~ night!** bonsoir!; (on going to bed) bonne nuit!; **~bye** excl au revoir!; **G~ Friday** n Vendredi saint; **~-looking** a bien inv; **~natured** a qui a un bon naturel; (discussion) bon enfant inv; **~ness** n (of person) bonté f; **for ~ness sake!** je vous en prie!; **~ness gracious!** mon Dieu!; **~s train** n (Brit) train m de marchandises; **~will** n bonne volonté; (COMM) réputation f (auprès de la clientèle).

goose [gu:s], pl **geese** n oie f.

gooseberry ['guzbəri] n groseille f à maquereau; **to play ~** tenir la chandelle.

gooseflesh ['gu:sflɛʃ] n, **goose pimples** npl chair f de poule.

gore [gɔ:*] vt encorner // n sang m.

gorge [gɔ:dʒ] n gorge f // vt: **to ~ o.s. (on)** se gorger (de).

gorgeous ['gɔ:dʒəs] a splendide, superbe.

gorilla [gə'rilə] n gorille m.

gorse [gɔ:s] n ajoncs mpl.

gory ['gɔ:ri] a sanglant(e).

go-slow ['gəu'sləu] n (Brit) grève perlée.

gospel ['gɔspl] n évangile m.

gossip ['gɔsip] n bavardages mpl; commérage m, cancans mpl; (person) commère f // vi bavarder; (maliciously) cancaner, faire des commérages.

got [gɔt] pt, pp of get; **~ten** (US) pp of get.

gout [gaut] n goutte f.

govern ['gʌvn] vt gouverner.

governess ['gʌvənis] n gouvernante f.

government ['gʌvnmənt] n gouvernement m; (Brit: ministers) ministère m.

governor ['gʌvənə*] n (of state, bank) gouverneur m; (of school, hospital) administrateur m.

gown [gaun] n robe f; (of teacher; Brit: of judge) toge f.

G.P. n abbr of **general practitioner**.

grab [græb] vt saisir, empoigner; (property, power) se saisir de.

grace [greis] n grâce f // vt honorer; **5 days' ~** répit m de 5 jours; **to say ~** dire le bénédicité; (after meal) dire les grâces; **~ful** a gracieux(euse), élégant(e); **gracious** ['greiʃəs] a bienveillant(e); de bonne grâce; miséricordieux(euse).

grade [greid] n (COMM) qualité f; calibre m; catégorie f; (in hierarchy) grade m, échelon m; (US SCOL) note f; classe f // vt classer; calibrer; graduer; **~ crossing** n (US) passage m à niveau; **~ school** n (US) école f primaire.

gradient ['greidiənt] n inclinaison f, pente f.

gradual ['grædjuəl] a graduel(le), progressif(ive); **~ly** ad peu à peu, graduellement.

graduate n ['grædjuit] diplômé/e d'université // vi ['grædjueit] obtenir un diplôme d'université; **graduation** [-'eiʃən] n cérémonie f de remise des diplômes.

graffiti [grə'fi:ti] npl graffiti mpl.

graft [grɑ:ft] n (AGR, MED) greffe f; (bribery) corruption f // vt greffer; **hard ~** n (col) boulot acharné.

grain [grein] n grain m.

gram [græm] n gramme m.

grammar ['græmə*] n grammaire f; **~ school** n (Brit) ≈ lycée m.

grammatical [grə'mætikl] a grammatical(e).

gramme [græm] n = gram.

grand [grænd] a magnifique, splendide, noble; **~children** npl petits-enfants mpl; **~dad** n grand-papa m; **~daughter** n petite-fille f; **~father** n grand-père m;

~**ma** n grand-maman f; ~**mother** n grand-mère f; ~**pa** n = ~**dad**; ~**parents** npl grand-père m et grand-mère f; ~ **piano** n piano m à queue; ~**son** n petit-fils m; ~**stand** n (SPORT) tribune f.

granite ['grænɪt] n granit m.

granny ['grænɪ] n grand-maman f.

grant [grɑ:nt] vt accorder; (a request) accéder à; (admit) concéder // n (SCOL) bourse f; (ADMIN) subside m, subvention f; **to take sth for** ~**ed** considérer qch comme acquis.

granulated ['grænjuleɪtɪd] a: ~ **sugar** n sucre m en poudre.

grape [greɪp] n raisin m.

grapefruit ['greɪpfru:t] n pamplemousse m.

graph [grɑ:f] n graphique m, courbe f; ~**ic** a graphique; (vivid) vivant(e); ~**ics** n arts mpl graphiques // npl graphisme m.

grapple ['græpl] vi: **to** ~ **with** être aux prises avec.

grasp [grɑ:sp] vt saisir // n (grip) prise f; (fig) emprise f, pouvoir m; (comprehension f, connaissance f; ~**ing** a avide.

grass [grɑ:s] n herbe f; ~**hopper** n sauterelle f; ~**roots** a de base; ~ **snake** n couleuvre f.

grate [greɪt] n grille f de cheminée // vi grincer // vt (CULIN) râper.

grateful ['greɪtful] a reconnaissant(e).

grater ['greɪtə*] n râpe f.

gratify ['grætɪfaɪ] vt faire plaisir à; (whim) satisfaire.

grating ['greɪtɪŋ] n (iron bars) grille f // a (noise) grinçant(e).

gratitude ['grætɪtju:d] n gratitude f.

gratuity [grə'tju:ɪtɪ] n pourboire m.

grave [greɪv] n tombe f // a grave, sérieux(euse).

gravel ['grævl] n gravier m.

gravestone ['greɪvstəun] n pierre tombale.

graveyard ['greɪvjɑ:d] n cimetière m.

gravity ['grævɪtɪ] n (PHYSICS) gravité f; pesanteur f; (seriousness) gravité f.

gravy ['greɪvɪ] n jus m (de viande); sauce f.

gray [greɪ] a = **grey**.

graze [greɪz] vi paître, brouter // vt (touch lightly) frôler, effleurer; (scrape) écorcher // n écorchure f.

grease [gri:s] n (fat) graisse f; (lubricant) lubrifiant m // vt graisser; lubrifier; ~**proof paper** n (Brit) papier sulfurisé; **greasy** a gras(se), graisseux(euse).

great [greɪt] a grand(e); (col) formidable; **G**~ **Britain** n Grande-Bretagne f; ~**-grandfather** n arrière-grand-père m; ~**-grandmother** n arrière-grand-mère f; ~**ly** ad très, grandement; (with verbs) beaucoup; ~**ness** n grandeur f.

Greece [gri:s] n Grèce f.

greed [gri:d] n (also: ~**iness**) avidité f; (for food) gourmandise f; ~**y** a avide; gourmand(e).

Greek [gri:k] a grec(grecque) // n Grec/Grecque; (LING) grec m.

green [gri:n] a vert(e); (inexperienced) (bien) jeune, naïf(ïve) // n vert m; (stretch of grass) pelouse f; (also: village ~) ≈ place f du village; ~**s** npl légumes verts; ~ **belt** n (round town) ceinture verte; ~ **card** n (AUT) carte verte; ~**ery** n verdure f; ~**gage** n reine-claude f; ~**grocer** n (Brit) marchand m de fruits et légumes; ~**house** n serre f.

Greenland ['gri:nlənd] n Groenland m.

greet [gri:t] vt accueillir; ~**ing** n salutation f; ~**ing(s) card** n carte f de vœux.

grenade [grə'neɪd] n grenade f.

grew [gru:] pt of **grow**.

grey [greɪ] a gris(e); (dismal) sombre; ~**hound** n lévrier m.

grid [grɪd] n grille f; (ELEC) réseau m.

grief [gri:f] n chagrin m, douleur f.

grievance ['gri:vəns] n doléance f, grief m.

grieve [gri:v] vi avoir du chagrin; se désoler // vt faire de la peine à, affliger; **to** ~ **for sb** (dead person) pleurer qn.

grievous ['gri:vəs] a: ~ **bodily harm** (LAW) coups mpl et blessures fpl.

grill [grɪl] n (on cooker) gril m // vt (Brit) griller; (question) cuisiner.

grille [grɪl] n grillage m; (AUT) calandre f.

grim [grɪm] a sinistre, lugubre.

grimace [grɪ'meɪs] n grimace f // vi grimacer, faire une grimace.

grimy ['graɪmɪ] a crasseux(euse).

grin [grɪn] n large sourire m // vi sourire.

grind [graɪnd] vt (pt, pp **ground**) écraser; (coffee, pepper etc) moudre; (US: meat) hacher; (make sharp) aiguiser // n (work) corvée f; **to** ~ **one's teeth** grincer des dents.

grip [grɪp] n étreinte f, poigne f; prise f; (holdall) sac m de voyage // vt saisir, empoigner; étreindre; **to come to** ~**s with** en venir aux prises avec.

gripping ['grɪpɪŋ] a prenant(e), palpitant(e).

grisly ['grɪzlɪ] a sinistre, macabre.

gristle ['grɪsl] n cartilage m (de poulet etc).

grit [grɪt] n gravillon m; (courage) cran m // vt (road) sabler; **to** ~ **one's teeth** serrer les dents.

groan [grəun] n gémissement m; grognement m // vi gémir; grogner.

grocer ['grəusə*] n épicier m; ~**ies** npl provisions fpl.

groin [grɔɪn] n aine f.

groom [gru:m] n palefrenier m; (also:

bride~) marié m // vt (horse) panser; (fig): **to ~ sb for** former qn pour.

groove [gru:v] n sillon m, rainure f.

grope [grəup] vi tâtonner; **to ~ for** vt fus chercher à tâtons.

gross [grəus] a grossier(ère); (COMM) brut(e); **~ly** ad (greatly) très, grandement.

grotto ['grɔtəu] n grotte f.

ground [graund] pt, pp of **grind** // n sol m, terre f; (land) terrain m, terres fpl; (SPORT) terrain; (US: also: ~ **wire**) terre; (reason: gen pl) raison f // (plane) empêcher de décoller, retenir au sol; (US: ELEC) équiper d'une prise de terre // vi (ship) s'échouer; **~s** npl (of coffee etc) marc m; (gardens etc) parc m, domaine m; **on the ~, to the ~** par terre; **to gain/lose ~** gagner/perdre du terrain; **~ cloth** n (US) = **~sheet**; **~ing** n (in education) connaissances fpl de base; **~less** a sans fondement; **~sheet** n (Brit) tapis m de sol; **~ staff** n équipage m au sol; **~ swell** n lame f or vague f de fond; **~work** n préparation f.

group [gru:p] n groupe m // vt (also: ~ **together**) grouper // vi (also: ~ **together**) se grouper.

grouse [graus] n (pl inv) (bird) grouse f // vi (complain) rouspéter, râler.

grove [grəuv] n bosquet m.

grovel ['grɔvl] vi ramper.

grow [grəu], pt **grew**, pp **grown** vi (plant) pousser, croître; (person) grandir; (increase) augmenter, se développer; (become): **to ~ rich/weak** s'enrichir/s'affaiblir // vt cultiver, faire pousser; **to ~ up** vi grandir; **~er** n producteur m; **~ing** n (fear, amount) croissant(e), grandissant(e).

growl [graul] vi grogner.

grown [grəun] pp of **grow** // a adulte; **~-up** n adulte m/f, grande personne.

growth [grəuθ] n croissance f, développement m; (what has grown) pousse f; poussée f; (MED) grosseur f, tumeur f.

grub [grʌb] n larve f; (col: food) bouffe f.

grubby ['grʌbɪ] a crasseux(euse).

grudge [grʌdʒ] n rancune f // vt: **to ~ sb sth** donner qch à qn à contre-cœur; reprocher qch à qn; **to bear sb a ~ (for)** garder rancune or en vouloir à qn (de).

gruelling ['gruəlɪŋ] a exténuant(e).

gruesome ['gru:səm] a horrible.

gruff [grʌf] a bourru(e).

grumble ['grʌmbl] vi rouspéter, ronchonner.

grumpy ['grʌmpɪ] a grincheux(euse).

grunt [grʌnt] vi grogner.

G-string ['dʒi:strɪŋ] n (garment) cachesexe m inv.

guarantee [gærən'ti:] n garantie f // vt garantir.

guard [gɑ:d] n garde f; (one man) garde m; (Brit RAIL) chef m de train // vt garder, surveiller; **~ed** a (fig) prudent(e); **~ian** n gardien/ne; (of minor) tuteur/trice; **~'s van** n (Brit RAIL) fourgon m.

guerrilla [gə'rɪlə] n guérillero m; ~ **warfare** n guérilla f.

guess [gɛs] vi deviner // vt deviner; (US) croire, penser // n supposition f, hypothèse f; **~work** n hypothèse f.

guest [gɛst] n invité/e; (in hotel) client/e; **~-house** n pension f; ~ **room** n chambre f d'amis.

guffaw [gʌ'fɔ:] vi pouffer de rire.

guidance ['gaɪdəns] n conseils mpl.

guide [gaɪd] n (person, book etc) guide m; (also: **girl** ~) guide f // vt guider; **~book** n guide m; ~ **dog** n chien m d'aveugle; **~lines** npl (fig) instructions générales, conseils mpl.

guild [gɪld] n corporation f; cercle m, association f.

guile [gaɪl] n astuce f.

guillotine ['gɪləti:n] n guillotine f.

guilt [gɪlt] n culpabilité f; **~y** a coupable.

guinea pig ['gɪnɪpɪg] n cobaye m.

guise [gaɪz] n aspect m, apparence f.

guitar [gɪ'tɑ:*] n guitare f.

gulf [gʌlf] n golfe m; (abyss) gouffre m.

gull [gʌl] n mouette f.

gullet ['gʌlɪt] n gosier m.

gullible ['gʌlɪbl] a crédule.

gully ['gʌlɪ] n ravin m; ravine f; couloir m.

gulp [gʌlp] vi avaler sa salive; (from emotion) avoir la gorge serrée // vt (also: ~ **down**) avaler.

gum [gʌm] n (ANAT) gencive f; (glue) colle f; (sweet) boule f de gomme; (also: **chewing-~**) chewing-gum m // vt coller; **~boots** npl (Brit) bottes fpl en caoutchouc.

gun [gʌn] n (small) revolver m, pistolet m; (rifle) fusil m, carabine f; (cannon) canon m; **~boat** n canonnière f; **~fire** n fusillade f; **~man** n bandit armé; **~ner** n artilleur m; **~point** n: **at ~point** sous la menace du pistolet (or fusil); **~powder** n poudre f à canon; **~shot** n coup m de feu; **~smith** n armurier m.

gurgle ['gə:gl] vi gargouiller.

guru ['guru:] n gourou m.

gush [gʌʃ] vi jaillir; (fig) se répandre en effusions.

gusset ['gʌsɪt] n gousset m, soufflet m.

gust [gʌst] n (of wind) rafale f; (of smoke) bouffée f.

gusto ['gʌstəu] n enthousiasme m.

gut [gʌt] n intestin m, boyau m; (MUS etc) boyau; **~s** npl (courage) cran m.

gutter ['gʌtə*] n (of roof) gouttière f;

(*in street*) caniveau *m*.

guy [gaɪ] *n* (*also:* ~**rope**) corde *f*; (*col: man*) type *m*; (*figure*) effigie *de* Guy Fawkes.

guzzle ['gʌzl] *vi* s'empiffrer // *vt* avaler gloutonnement.

gym [dʒɪm] *n* (*also:* gymnasium) gymnase *m*; (*also:* gymnastics) gym *f*; ~ **shoes** *npl* chaussures *fpl* de gym(nastique); ~ **slip** *n* (*Brit*) tunique *f* (d'écolière).

gymnast ['dʒɪmnæst] *n* gymnaste *m/f*; ~**ics** [-'næstɪks] *n, npl* gymnastique *f*.

gynaecologist, (*US*) **gynecologist** [gaɪnɪˈkɔlədʒɪst] *n* gynécologue *m/f*.

gypsy ['dʒɪpsɪ] *n* = **gipsy**.

gyrate [dʒaɪˈreɪt] *vi* tournoyer.

H

haberdashery ['hæbə'dæʃərɪ] *n* (*Brit*) mercerie *f*.

habit ['hæbɪt] *n* habitude *f*; (*costume*) habit *m*, tenue *f*.

habitual [hə'bɪtjuəl] *a* habituel(le); (*drinker, liar*) invétéré(e).

hack [hæk] *vt* hacher, tailler // *n* (*cut*) entaille *f*; (*blow*) coup *m*; (*pej: writer*) nègre *m*.

hackneyed ['hæknɪd] *a* usé(e), rebattu(e).

had [hæd] *pt, pp* of **have**.

haddock ['hædək] *pl* ~ *or* ~**s** ['hædək] *n* églefin *m*; **smoked** ~ haddock *m*.

hadn't ['hædnt] = **had not**.

haemorrhage, (*US*) **hemorrhage** ['hemɔrɪdʒ] *n* hémorragie *f*.

haggle ['hægl] *vi* marchander.

Hague [heɪg] *n*: **The** ~ La Haye.

hail [heɪl] *n* grêle *f* // *vt* (*call*) héler; (*greet*) acclamer // *vi* grêler; ~**stone** *n* grêlon *m*.

hair [hɛə*] *n* cheveux *mpl*; (*single hair: on head*) cheveu *m*; (*: on body*) poil *m*; **to do one's** ~ se coiffer; ~**brush** *n* brosse *f* à cheveux; ~**cut** *n* coupe *f* (de cheveux); ~**do** ['hɛəduː] *n* coiffure *f*; ~**dresser** *n* coiffeur/euse; ~**dryer** *n* sèche-cheveux *m*; ~**grip** *n* pince *f* à cheveux; ~**pin** *n* épingle *f* à cheveux; ~**pin bend**, (*US*) ~**pin curve** *n* virage *m* en épingle à cheveux; ~**raising** *a* à (vous) faire dresser les cheveux sur la tête; ~ **remover** *n* dépilateur *m*; ~ **spray** *n* laque *f* (pour les cheveux); ~**style** *n* coiffure *f*; ~**y** *a* poilu(e); chevelu(e); (*fig*) effrayant(e).

hake [heɪk] *n* colin *m*, merlu *m*.

half [hɑːf] *n* (*pl* halves) moitié *f* // *a* demi(e) // *ad* (à) moitié, à demi; ~**-an-hour** une demi-heure; ~ **a dozen** une demi-douzaine; ~ **a pound** une demi-livre, ≈ 250 g; **two and a** ~ deux et demi; **a week and a** ~ une semaine et

demie; ~ (**of it**) la moitié; ~ (**of**) la moitié de; **to cut sth in** ~ couper qch en deux; ~ **asleep** à moitié endormi(e); ~**back** *n* (*SPORT*) demi *m*; ~**-breed**, ~**caste** *n* métis/se; ~**-hearted** *a* tiède, sans enthousiasme; ~**hour** *n* demi-heure *f*; ~**-mast**: **at** ~**-mast** (*flag*) en berne, à mi-mât; ~**penny** ['heɪpnɪ] *n* (*Brit*) demi-penny *m*; ~ (**at**) ~**-price** à moitié prix; ~ **term** *n* (*Brit SCOL*) congé *m* de demi-trimestre; ~**-time** *n* mi-temps *f*; ~**way** *ad* à mi-chemin.

halibut ['hælɪbət] *n* (*pl inv*) flétan *m*.

hall [hɔːl] *n* salle *f*; (*entrance way*) hall *m*, entrée *f*; (*corridor*) couloir *m*; (*mansion*) château *m*, manoir *m*; ~ **of residence** *n* (*Brit*) pavillon *m* *or* résidence *f* universitaire.

hallmark ['hɔːlmɑːk] *n* poinçon *m*; (*fig*) marque *f*.

hallo [hə'ləʊ] *excl* = **hello**.

Hallowe'en [hæləʊˈiːn] *n* veille *f* de la Toussaint.

hallucination [həluːsɪˈneɪʃən] *n* hallucination *f*.

hallway ['hɔːlweɪ] *n* vestibule *m*; couloir *m*.

halo ['heɪləʊ] *n* (*of saint etc*) auréole *f*; (*of sun*) halo *m*.

halt [hɔːlt] *n* halte *f*, arrêt *m* // *vt* faire arrêter // *vi* faire halte, s'arrêter.

halve [hɑːv] *vt* (*apple etc*) partager *or* diviser en deux; (*expense*) réduire de moitié.

halves [hɑːvz] *npl* of **half**.

ham [hæm] *n* jambon *m*.

hamburger ['hæmbəːgə*] *n* hamburger *m*.

hamlet ['hæmlɪt] *n* hameau *m*.

hammer ['hæmə*] *n* marteau *m* // *vt* (*fig*) éreinter, démolir // *vi* (*on door*) frapper à coups redoublés.

hammock ['hæmək] *n* hamac *m*.

hamper ['hæmpə*] *vt* gêner // *n* panier *m* (d'osier).

hamster ['hæmstə*] *n* hamster *m*.

hand [hænd] *n* main *f*; (*of clock*) aiguille *f*; (*handwriting*) écriture *f*; (*at cards*) jeu *m*; (*worker*) ouvrier/ère // *vt* passer, donner; **to give sb a** ~ donner un coup de main à qn; **at** ~ à portée de la main; **in** ~ en main; (*work*) en cours; **to be on** ~ (*person*) être disponible; (*emergency services*) se tenir prêt(e) (à intervenir); **to** ~ (*information etc*) sous la main, à portée de la main; **on the one** ~ ..., **on the other** ~ d'une part ..., d'autre part; **to** ~ **in** *vt* remettre; **to** ~ **out** *vt* distribuer; **to** ~ **over** *vt* transmettre; céder; ~**bag** *n* sac *m* à main; ~**book** *n* manuel *m*; ~**brake** *n* frein *m* à main; ~**cuffs** *npl* menottes *fpl*; ~**ful** *n* poignée *f*.

handicap ['hændɪkæp] *n* handicap *m* // *vt* handicaper; **mentally/physically** ~**ped**

a handicapé(e) mentalement/physique-
ment.

handicraft ['hændɪkrɑːft] *n* travail *m*
d'artisanat, technique artisanale.

handiwork ['hændɪwəːk] *n* ouvrage *m*;
(*pej*) œuvre *f*.

handkerchief ['hæŋkətʃɪf] *n* mouchoir
m.

handle ['hændl] *n* (*of door etc*) poignée
f; (*of cup etc*) anse *f*; (*of knife etc*)
manche *m*; (*of saucepan*) queue *f*; (*for
winding*) manivelle *f* // *vt* toucher,
manier; (*deal with*) s'occuper de;
(*treat: people*) prendre; '~ with care'
'fragile'; to fly off the ~ s'énerver;
~**bar(s)** *n(pl)* guidon *m*.

hand: ~-**luggage** *n* bagages *mpl* à
main; ~**made** *a* fait(e) à la main;
~**out** *n* documentation *f*, prospectus *m*;
~**rail** *n* rampe *f*, main courante;
~**shake** *n* poignée *f* de main.

handsome ['hænsəm] *a* beau(belle);
généreux(euse); considérable.

handwriting ['hændraɪtɪŋ] *n* écriture *f*.

handy ['hændɪ] *a* (*person*) adroit(e);
(*close at hand*) sous la main;
(*convenient*) pratique; **handyman** *n*
bricoleur *m*; (*servant*) homme *m* à tout
faire.

hang [hæŋ], *pt*, *pp* **hung** *vt* accrocher;
(*criminal: pt*, *pp* **hanged**) pendre // *vi*
pendre; (*hair, drapery*) tomber; to get
the ~ of (doing) sth (*col*) attraper le
coup pour faire qch; to ~ **about** *vi*
flâner, traîner; to ~ **on** *vi* (*wait*) attendre; to ~ **up** *vi* (*TEL*) raccrocher // *vt*
accrocher, suspendre.

hangar ['hæŋə*] *n* hangar *m*.

hanger ['hæŋə*] *n* cintre *m*, portemanteau *m*.

hanger-on [hæŋər'ɔn] *n* parasite *m*.

hang-gliding ['hæŋglaɪdɪŋ] *n* vol *m* libre *or* sur aile delta.

hangover ['hæŋəuvə*] *n* (*after drinking*) gueule *f* de bois.

hang-up ['hæŋʌp] *n* complexe *m*.

hanker ['hæŋkə*] *vi*: to ~ **after** avoir
envie de.

hankie, hanky ['hæŋkɪ] *n abbr of*
handkerchief.

haphazard [hæp'hæzəd] *a* fait(e) au
hasard, fait(e) au petit bonheur.

happen ['hæpən] *vi* arriver; se passer,
se produire; as it ~s justement; ~**ing** *n*
événement *m*.

happily ['hæpɪlɪ] *ad* heureusement.

happiness ['hæpɪnɪs] *n* bonheur *m*.

happy ['hæpɪ] *a* heureux(euse); ~ **with**
(*arrangements etc*) satisfait(e) de; ~
birthday! bon anniversaire!; ~-**go-
lucky** *a* insouciant(e).

harass ['hærəs] *vt* accabler, tourmenter;
~**ment** *n* tracasseries *fpl*.

harbour, (US) harbor ['hɑːbə*] *n* port
m // *vt* héberger, abriter.

hard [hɑːd] *a* dur(e) // *ad* (*work*) dur;
(*think, try*) sérieusement; to look ~ **at**
regarder fixement; regarder de près; no
~ **feelings!** sans rancune!; to be ~ **of
hearing** être dur(e) d'oreille; to be ~
done by être traité(e) injustement;
~**back** *n* livre relié; ~ **cash** *n* espèces
fpl; ~ **disk** *n* (*COMPUT*) disque dur;
~**en** *vt* durcir; (*fig*) endurcir // *vi*
durcir; ~**headed** *a* réaliste; décidé(e);
~ **labour** *n* travaux forcés.

hardly ['hɑːdlɪ] *ad* (*scarcely*) à peine;
it's ~ the case ce n'est guère le cas; that
can ~ be true cela ne peut tout de même
pas être vrai; ~ **anywhere/ever** presque
nulle part/jamais.

hardship ['hɑːdʃɪp] *n* épreuves *fpl*;
privations *fpl*.

hard-up [hɑːd'ʌp] *a* (*col*) fauché(e).

hardware ['hɑːdwɛə*] *n* quincaillerie *f*;
(*COMPUT*) matériel *m*; ~ **shop** *n*
quincaillerie *f*.

hard-wearing [hɑːd'wɛərɪŋ] *a* solide.

hard-working [hɑːd'wəːkɪŋ] *a*
travailleur(euse).

hardy ['hɑːdɪ] *a* robuste; (*plant*) ré-
sistant(e) au gel.

hare [hɛə*] *n* lièvre *m*; ~-**brained** *a*
farfelu(e); écervelé(e).

harm [hɑːm] *n* mal *m*; (*wrong*) tort *m* //
vt (*person*) faire du mal *or* du tort à;
(*thing*) endommager; out of ~'s way à
l'abri du danger, en lieu sûr; ~**ful** *a*
nuisible; ~**less** *a* inoffensif(ive); sans
méchanceté.

harmony ['hɑːmənɪ] *n* harmonie *f*.

harness ['hɑːnɪs] *n* harnais *m* // *vt*
(*horse*) harnacher; (*resources*) exploiter.

harp [hɑːp] *n* harpe *f* // *vi*: to ~ **on about**
parler tout le temps de.

harrowing ['hærəuɪŋ] *a* déchirant(e).

harsh [hɑːʃ] *a* (*hard*) dur(e); (*severe*)
sévère; (*unpleasant: sound*) discor-
dant(e); (: *colour*) criard(e); cru(e); (:
wine) âpre.

harvest ['hɑːvɪst] *n* (*of corn*) moisson *f*;
(*of fruit*) récolte *f*; (*of grapes*) vendange
f // *vi*, *vt* moissonner; récolter;
vendanger.

has [hæz] *vb see* **have**.

hash [hæʃ] *n* (*CULIN*) hachis *m*; (*fig:
mess*) gâchis *m*.

hasn't ['hæznt] = **has not**.

hassle ['hæsl] *n* chamaillerie *f*.

haste [heɪst] *n* hâte *f*; précipitation *f*;
~**n** ['heɪsn] *vt* hâter, accélérer // *vi* se
hâter, s'empresser; **hastily** *ad* à la
hâte; précipitamment; **hasty** *a*
hâtif(ive); précipité(e).

hat [hæt] *n* chapeau *m*.

hatch [hætʃ] *n* (*NAUT: also:* ~**way**)
écoutille *f*; (*also:* **service** ~) passe-plats
m inv // *vi* éclore // *vt* faire éclore; (*plot*)
tramer.

hatchback ['hætʃbæk] *n* (*AUT*) modèle *m* avec hayon arrière.

hatchet ['hætʃɪt] *n* hachette *f*.

hate [heɪt] *vt* haïr, détester // *n* haine *f*; **~ful** *a* odieux(euse), détestable.

hatred ['heɪtrɪd] *n* haine *f*.

hat trick *n* (*SPORT, also fig*) triplé *m* (*3 buts réussis au cours du même match etc*).

haughty ['hɔːtɪ] *a* hautain(e), arrogant(e).

haul [hɔːl] *vt* traîner, tirer // *n* (*of fish*) prise *f*; (*of stolen goods etc*) butin *m*; **~age** *n* transport routier; **~ier**, (*US*) **~er** *n* transporteur (routier), camionneur *m*.

haunch [hɔːntʃ] *n* hanche *f*.

haunt [hɔːnt] *vt* (*subj: ghost, fear*) hanter; (: *person*) fréquenter // *n* repaire *m*.

have [hæv], *pt, pp* **had** ♦ *auxiliary vb* **1** (*gen*) avoir; être; **to ~ arrived/gone** être arrivé(e)/allé(e); **to ~ eaten/slept** avoir mangé/dormi; **he has been promoted** il a été promu

2 (*in tag questions*): **you've done it, ~n't you?** vous l'avez fait, n'est-ce pas?

3 (*in short answers and questions*): **no I ~n't!/yes we ~!** mais non!/mais si!; **so I ~!** ah oui!, oui c'est vrai!; **I've been there before, ~ you?** j'y suis déjà allé, et vous?

♦ *modal auxiliary vb* (*be obliged*): **to ~ (got) to do sth** devoir faire qch; être obligé(e) de faire qch; **she has (got) to do it** elle doit le faire, il faut qu'elle le fasse; **you ~n't to tell her** vous ne devez pas le lui dire

♦ *vt* **1** (*possess, obtain*) avoir; **he has (got) blue eyes/dark hair** il a les yeux bleus/les cheveux bruns; **may I ~ your address?** puis-je avoir votre adresse?

2 (+ *noun: take, hold etc*): **to ~ breakfast/a bath/a shower** prendre le petit déjeuner/un bain/une douche; **to ~ dinner/lunch** dîner/déjeuner; **to ~ a swim** nager; **to ~ a meeting** se réunir; **to ~ a party** organiser une fête

3: **to ~ sth done** faire faire qch; **to ~ one's hair cut** se faire couper les cheveux; **to ~ sb do sth** faire faire qch à qn

4 (*experience, suffer*) avoir; **to ~ a cold/flu** avoir un rhume/la grippe; **to ~ an operation** se faire opérer

5 (*col: dupe*) avoir; **he's been had** il s'est fait avoir ou roulé

to have out *vt*: **to ~ it out with sb** (*settle a problem etc*) s'expliquer (franchement) avec qn.

haven ['heɪvn] *n* port *m*; (*fig*) havre *m*.

haven't ['hævnt] = **have not**.

haversack ['hævəsæk] *n* sac *m* à dos.

havoc ['hævək] *n* ravages *mpl*.

hawk [hɔːk] *n* faucon *m*.

hay [heɪ] *n* foin *m*; **~ fever** *n* rhume *m* des foins; **~stack** *n* meule *f* de foin.

haywire ['heɪwaɪə*] *a* (*col*): **to go ~** perdre la tête; mal tourner.

hazard ['hæzəd] *n* hasard *m*, chance *f*; danger *m*, risque *m* // *vt* risquer, hasarder; **~ warning lights** *npl* (*AUT*) feux *mpl* de détresse.

haze [heɪz] *n* brume *f*.

hazelnut ['heɪzlnʌt] *n* noisette *f*.

hazy ['heɪzɪ] *a* brumeux(euse); (*idea*) vague; (*photograph*) flou(e).

he [hiː] *pronoun* il; **it is ~ who ...** c'est lui qui ...

head [hɛd] *n* tête *f*; (*leader*) chef *m* // *vt* (*list*) être en tête de; (*group*) être à la tête de; **~s or tails** pile ou face; **to ~ first** la tête la première; **~ over heels in love** follement *or* éperdument amoureux(euse); **to ~ the ball** faire une tête; **to ~ for** *vt fus* se diriger vers; **~ache** *n* mal *m* de tête; **~dress** *n* coiffure *f*; **~ing** *n* titre *m*; rubrique *f*; **~lamp** *n* (*Brit*) = **~light; ~land** *n* promontoire *m*, cap *m*; **~light** *n* phare *m*; **~line** *n* titre *m*; **~long** *ad* (*fall*) la tête la première; (*rush*) tête baissée; **~master** *n* directeur *m*, proviseur *m*; **~mistress** *n* directrice *f*; **~ office** *n* bureau central; **~-on** *a* (*collision*) de plein fouet; **~phones** *npl* casque *m* (à écouteurs); **~quarters (HQ)** *npl* bureau *or* siège central; (*MIL*) quartier général; **~-rest** *n* appui-tête *m*; **~room** *n* (*in car*) hauteur *f* de plafond; (*under bridge*) hauteur limite; dégagement *m*; **~scarf** *n* foulard *m*; **~strong** *a* têtu(e), entêté(e); **~ waiter** *n* maître *m* d'hôtel; **~way** *n*: **to make ~way** avancer, faire des progrès; **~wind** *n* vent *m* contraire; **~y** *a* capiteux(euse); enivrant(e).

heal [hiːl] *vt, vi* guérir.

health [hɛlθ] *n* santé *f*; **~ food shop** *n* magasin *m* diététique; **the H~ Service** *n* (*Brit*) ≈ la Sécurité Sociale; **~y** *a* (*person*) en bonne santé; (*climate, food, attitude etc*) sain(e).

heap [hiːp] *n* tas *m*, monceau *m* // *vt* entasser, amonceler.

hear, *pt, pp* **heard** [hɪə*, hɜːd] *vt* entendre; (*news*) apprendre; (*lecture*) assister à, écouter // *vi* entendre; **to ~ about** avoir des nouvelles de; entendre parler de; **to ~ from sb** recevoir des nouvelles de qn; **~ing** *n* (*sense*) ouïe *f*; (*of witnesses*) audition *f*; (*of a case*) audience *f*; **~ing aid** *n* appareil *m* acoustique; **~say**: **by ~say** *ad* par ouï-dire *m*.

hearse [hɜːs] *n* corbillard *m*.

heart [hɑːt] *n* cœur *m*; **~s** *npl* (*CARDS*) cœur; **at ~** au fond; **by ~** (*learn, know*) par cœur; **~ attack** *n* crise *f* cardiaque; **~beat** *n* battement *m* de cœur; **~broken** *a*: **to be ~broken** avoir beaucoup de chagrin; **~burn** *n* brûlures *fpl* d'estomac; **~ failure** *n* arrêt *m* du cœur; **~felt** *a* sincère.

hearth [hɑ:θ] *n* foyer *m*, cheminée *f*.

heartily ['hɑ:tɪlɪ] *ad* chaleureusement; *(laugh)* de bon cœur; *(eat)* de bon appétit; **to agree ~** être entièrement d'accord.

hearty ['hɑ:tɪ] *a* chaleureux(euse); robuste; vigoureux(euse).

heat [hi:t] *n* chaleur *f*; *(fig)* ardeur *f*; feu *m*; *(SPORT: also:* **qualifying ~)** éliminatoire *f* // *vt* chauffer; **to ~ up** *vi* *(liquids)* chauffer; *(room)* se réchauffer // *vt* réchauffer; **~ed** *a* chauffé(e); *(fig)* passionné(e), échauffé(e), excité(e); **~er** *n* appareil *m* de chauffage; radiateur *m*.

heath [hi:θ] *n (Brit)* lande *f*.

heathen ['hi:ðn] *a*, *n* païen(ne).

heather ['hɛðə*] *n* bruyère *f*.

heating ['hi:tɪŋ] *n* chauffage *m*.

heatstroke ['hi:tstrəuk] *n* coup *m* de chaleur.

heatwave ['hi:tweɪv] *n* vague *f* de chaleur.

heave [hi:v] *vt* soulever (avec effort) // *vi* se soulever; *(retch)* avoir des haut-le-cœur // *n (push)* poussée *f*.

heaven ['hɛvn] *n* ciel *m*, paradis *m*; **~ly** *a* céleste, divin(e).

heavily ['hɛvɪlɪ] *ad* lourdement; *(drink, smoke)* beaucoup; *(sleep, sigh)* profondément.

heavy ['hɛvɪ] *a* lourd(e); *(work, sea, rain, eater)* gros(se); *(drinker, smoker)* grand(e); **~ goods vehicle (HGV)** *n* poids lourd (PL); **~weight** *n (SPORT)* poids lourd.

Hebrew ['hi:bru:] *a* hébraïque // *n (LING)* hébreu *m*.

Hebrides ['hɛbrɪdi:z] *npl*: **the ~** les Hébrides *fpl*.

heckle ['hɛkl] *vt* interpeller *(un orateur)*.

hectic ['hɛktɪk] *a* agité(e), trépidant(e).

he'd [hi:d] = **he would, he had.**

hedge [hɛdʒ] *n* haie *f* // *vi* se défiler; **to ~ one's bets** *(fig)* se couvrir.

hedgehog ['hɛdʒhɔg] *n* hérisson *m*.

heed [hi:d] *vt (also:* **take ~ of)** tenir compte de, prendre garde à; **~less** *a* insouciant(e).

heel [hi:l] *n* talon *m* // *vt (shoe)* retalonner.

hefty ['hɛftɪ] *a (person)* costaud(e); *(parcel)* lourd(e); *(piece, price)* gros(se).

heifer ['hɛfə*] *n* génisse *f*.

height [haɪt] *n (of person)* taille *f*, grandeur *f*; *(of object)* hauteur *f*; *(of plane, mountain)* altitude *f*; *(high ground)* hauteur, éminence *f*; *(fig: of glory)* sommet *m*; *(: of stupidity)* comble *m*; **~en** *vt* hausser, surélever;

(fig) augmenter.

heir [ɛə*] *n* héritier *m*; **~ess** *n* héritière *f*; **~loom** *n* meuble *m* (*or* bijou *m or* tableau *m*) de famille.

held [hɛld] *pt, pp of* **hold.**

helicopter ['hɛlɪkɔptə*] *n* hélicoptère *m*.

hell [hɛl] *n* enfer *m*; **~!** *(col)* merde!

he'll [hi:l] = **he will, he shall.**

hellish ['hɛlɪʃ] *a* infernal(e).

hello [hə'ləu] *excl* bonjour!; salut! *(to sb one addresses as 'tu')*; *(surprise)* tiens!

helm [hɛlm] *n (NAUT)* barre *f*.

helmet ['hɛlmɪt] *n* casque *m*.

help [hɛlp] *n* aide *f*; *(charwoman)* femme *f* de ménage; *(assistant etc)* employé(e) // *vt* aider; **~!** au secours!; **~ yourself (to bread)** servez-vous (de pain); **he can't ~ it** il n'y peut rien; **~er** *n* aide *m/f*, assistant/e; **~ful** *a* serviable, obligeant(e); *(useful)* utile; **~ing** *n* portion *f*; **~less** *a* impuissant(e); faible.

hem [hɛm] *n* ourlet *m* // *vt* ourler; **to ~ in** *vt* cerner.

he-man ['hi:mæn] *n* macho *m*.

hemorrhage ['hɛmərɪdʒ] *n (US)* = **haemorrhage.**

hen [hɛn] *n* poule *f*.

hence [hɛns] *ad (therefore)* d'où, de là; **2 years ~** d'ici 2 ans; **~forth** *ad* dorénavant.

henchman ['hɛntʃmən] *n (pej)* acolyte *m*, séide *m*.

henpecked ['hɛnpɛkt] *a* dominé par sa femme.

her [hə:*] *pronoun (direct)* la, l' + vowel *or* h mute; *(indirect)* lui; *(stressed, after prep)* elle; *see note at* **she** // *a* son(sa), ses *pl*; *see also* **me, my.**

herald ['hɛrəld] *n* héraut *m* // *vt* annoncer.

herb [hə:b] *n* herbe *f*.

herd [hə:d] *n* troupeau *m*.

here [hɪə*] *ad* ici // *excl* tiens!, tenez!; **~!** présent!; **~ is, ~ are** voici; **~'s my sister** voici ma sœur; **~ he/she is** le/la voici; **~ she comes** la voici qui vient; **~after** *ad* après, plus tard; ci-après // *n*: **the ~after** l'au-delà *m*; **~by** *ad (in letter)* par la présente.

hereditary [hɪ'rɛdɪtrɪ] *a* héréditaire.

heresy ['hɛrəsɪ] *n* hérésie *f*.

hermit ['hə:mɪt] *n* ermite *m*.

hernia ['hə:nɪə] *n* hernie *f*.

hero, *pl* **~es** ['hɪərəu] *n* héros *m*.

heroin ['hɛrəuɪn] *n* héroïne *f*.

heroine ['hɛrəuɪn] *n* héroïne *f*.

heron ['hɛrən] *n* héron *m*.

herring ['hɛrɪŋ] *n* hareng *m*.

hers [hə:z] *pronoun* le(la) sien(ne), les siens(siennes); *see also* **mine.**

herself [hə:'sɛlf] *pronoun (reflexive)* se; *(emphatic)* elle-même; *(after prep)* elle; *see also* **oneself.**

he's [hi:z] = **he is, he has.**

hesitant ['hɛzɪtənt] *a* hésitant(e), indécis(e).

hesitate ['hɛzɪteɪt] *vi*: to ~ (about/to do) hésiter (sur/à faire); **hesitation** ['-teɪʃən] *n* hésitation *f*.

heyday ['heɪdeɪ] *n*: the ~ of l'âge *m* d'or de, les beaux jours de.

HGV *n abbr of* **heavy goods vehicle**.

hi [haɪ] *excl* salut!

hiatus [haɪ'eɪtəs] *n* trou *m*, lacune *f*; (*LING*) hiatus *m*.

hibernate ['haɪbəneɪt] *vi* hiberner.

hiccough, hiccup ['hɪkʌp] *vi* hoqueter // *n* hoquet *m*.

hide [haɪd] *n* (*skin*) peau *f* // *vb* (*pt* hid, *pp* hidden [hɪd, 'hɪdn]) *vt*: to ~ sth (from sb) cacher qch (à qn) // *vi*: to ~ (from sb) se cacher (de qn); ~**-and-seek** *n* cache-cache *m*; ~**away** *n* cachette *f*.

hideous ['hɪdɪəs] *a* hideux(euse); atroce.

hiding ['haɪdɪŋ] *n* (*beating*) correction *f*, volée *f* de coups; to be in ~ (*concealed*) se tenir caché(e).

hierarchy ['haɪərɑːkɪ] *n* hiérarchie *f*.

hi-fi ['haɪfaɪ] *n* hi-fi *f inv* // *a* hi-fi *inv*.

high [haɪ] *a* haut(e); (*speed, respect, number*) grand(e); (*price*) élevé(e); (*wind*) fort(e), violent(e); (*voice*) aigu(aiguë) // *ad* haut, en haut; 20 m ~ haut(e de 20 m); ~**boy** *n* (*US: tallboy*) commode (haute); ~**brow** *a, n* intellectuel(le); ~**chair** *n* chaise haute (*pour enfant*); ~**er education** *n* études supérieures; ~**-handed** *a* très autoritaire; très cavalier(ère); ~**jack** = **hijack**; ~ **jump** *n* (*SPORT*) saut *m* en hauteur; **the H~lands** *npl* les Highlands *mpl*; ~**light** *n* (*fig: of event*) point culminant // *vt* faire ressortir, souligner; ~**ly** *ad* très, fort, hautement; ~**ly strung** *a* nerveux(euse), toujours tendu(e); ~**ness** *n* hauteur *f*; Her H~ness son Altesse *f*; ~**-pitched** *a* aigu(aiguë); ~**-rise block** *n* tour *f* (d'habitation); ~ **school** *n* lycée *m*; (*US*) établissement *m* d'enseignement supérieur; ~ **season** *n* (*Brit*) haute saison; ~ **street** *n* (*Brit*) grand-rue *f*.

highway ['haɪweɪ] *n* grand'route *f*, route nationale; **H~ Code** *n* (*Brit*) code *m* de la route.

hijack ['haɪdʒæk] *vt* détourner (*par la force*); ~**er** *n* pirate *m* de l'air.

hike [haɪk] *vi* aller à pied // *n* excursion *f* à pied, randonnée *f*; (*in prices*) hausse *f*, augmentation *f*; ~**r** *n* promeneur/euse, excursionniste *m/f*.

hilarious [hɪ'lɛərɪəs] *a* (*behaviour, event*) désopilant(e).

hill [hɪl] *n* colline *f*; (*fairly high*) montagne *f*; (*on road*) côte *f*; ~**side** *n* (flanc *m* de) coteau *m*; ~**y** *a* vallonné(e); montagneux(euse).

hilt [hɪlt] *n* (*of sword*) garde *f*; to the ~ (*fig: support*) à fond.

him [hɪm] *pronoun* (*direct*) le, l' + *vowel or h mute*; (*stressed, indirect, after prep*) lui; *see also* me; ~**self** *pronoun* (*reflexive*) se; (*emphatic*) lui-même; (*after prep*) lui; *see also* oneself.

hind [haɪnd] *a* de derrière // *n* biche *f*.

hinder ['hɪndə*] *vt* gêner; (*delay*) retarder; (*prevent*): to ~ sb from doing empêcher qn de faire; **hindrance** ['hɪndrəns] *n* gêne *f*, obstacle *m*.

hindsight ['haɪndsaɪt] *n*: with ~ avec du recul, rétrospectivement.

Hindu ['hɪnduː] *n* Hindou/e.

hinge [hɪndʒ] *n* charnière *f* // *vi* (*fig*): to ~ on dépendre de.

hint [hɪnt] *n* allusion *f*; (*advice*) conseil *m* // *vt*: to ~ that insinuer que // *vi*: to ~ at faire une allusion à.

hip [hɪp] *n* hanche *f*.

hippopotamus [hɪpə'pɔtəməs, -'pɔtəmaɪ] *pl* ~es *or* **hippopotami** *n* hippopotame *m*.

hire ['haɪə*] *vt* (*Brit: car, equipment*) louer; (*worker*) embaucher, engager // *n* location *f*; **for** ~ à louer; (*taxi*) libre; ~ **purchase (H.P.)** *n* (*Brit*) achat *m* (*or* vente *f*) à tempérament *or* crédit.

his [hɪz] *pronoun* le(la) sien(ne), les siens(siennes) // *a* son(sa), ses *pl*; *see also* my, mine.

hiss [hɪs] *vi* siffler.

historic(al) [hɪ'stɔrɪk(l)] *a* historique.

history ['hɪstərɪ] *n* histoire *f*.

hit [hɪt] *vt* (*pt, pp* hit) frapper; (*knock against*) cogner; (*reach: target*) atteindre, toucher; (*collide with: car*) entrer en collision avec, heurter; (*fig: affect*) toucher; (*find*) tomber sur // *n* coup *m*; (*success*) coup réussi; succès *m*; (*song*) chanson *f* à succès, tube *m*; to ~ it off with sb bien s'entendre avec qn; ~**-and-run driver** *n* chauffard *m*.

hitch [hɪtʃ] *vt* (*fasten*) accrocher, attacher; (*also*: ~ up) remonter d'une saccade // *n* (*difficulty*) anicroche *f*, contretemps *m*; to ~ a lift faire du stop.

hitch-hike ['hɪtʃhaɪk] *vi* faire de l'auto-stop; ~**r** *n* auto-stoppeur/euse.

hi-tech ['haɪ'tɛk] *a* à la pointe de la technologie, technologiquement avancé(e) // *n* high-tech *m*.

hitherto [hɪðə'tuː] *ad* jusqu'ici.

hive [haɪv] *n* ruche *f*; to ~ **off** *vt* mettre à part, séparer.

H.M.S. *abbr* = *His (Her) Majesty's Ship*.

hoard [hɔːd] *n* (*of food*) provisions *fpl*, réserves *fpl*; (*of money*) trésor *m* // *vt* amasser.

hoarding ['hɔːdɪŋ] *n* (*Brit: for posters*) panneau *m* d'affichage *or* publicitaire.

hoarfrost ['hɔːfrɔst] *n* givre *m*.

hoarse [hɔːs] *a* enroué(e).

hoax [həuks] *n* canular *m*.

hob [hɔb] n plaque chauffante.
hobble ['hɔbl] vi boitiller.
hobby ['hɔbɪ] n passe-temps favori; ~-**horse** n (fig) dada m.
hobo ['həubəu] n (US) vagabond m.
hockey ['hɔkɪ] n hockey m.
hoe [həu] n houe f, binette f.
hog [hɔg] n sanglier m // vt (fig) accaparer; **to go the whole** ~ aller jusqu'au bout.
hoist [hɔɪst] n palan m // vt hisser.
hold [həuld] vb (pt, pp held) vt tenir; (contain) contenir; (keep back) retenir; (believe) maintenir; considérer; (possess) avoir; détenir // vi (withstand pressure) tenir (bon); (be valid) valoir // n prise f; (fig) influence f; (NAUT) cale f; ~ **the line!** (TEL) ne quittez pas!; **to** ~ **one's own** (fig) (bien) se défendre; (sick person) se maintenir; **to catch or get (a)** ~ **of** saisir; **to get** ~ **of** (fig) trouver; **to** ~ **back** vt retenir; (secret) cacher; **to** ~ **down** vt (person) maintenir à terre; (job) occuper; **to** ~ **off** vt tenir à distance; **to** ~ **on** vi tenir bon; (wait) attendre; ~ **on!** (TEL) ne quittez pas!; **to** ~ **on to** vt fus se cramponner à; (keep) conserver, garder; **to** ~ **out** vt offrir // vi (resist) tenir bon; **to** ~ **up** vt (raise) lever; (support) soutenir; (delay) retarder; ~**all** n (Brit) fourre-tout m inv; ~**er** n (of ticket, record) détenteur/trice; (of office, title etc) titulaire m/f; ~**ing** n (share) intérêts mpl; (farm) ferme f; ~**up** n (robbery) hold-up m; (delay) retard m; (Brit: in traffic) embouteillage m.
hole [həul] n trou m.
holiday ['hɔlɪdɪ] n vacances fpl; (day off) jour m de congé; (public) jour férié; **on** ~ en congé; ~ **camp** n (for children) colonie f de vacances; (also: ~ **centre**) camp m de vacances; ~-**maker** n (Brit) vacancier/ère; ~ **resort** n centre m de villégiature or de vacances.
holiness ['həulɪnɪs] n sainteté f.
Holland ['hɔlənd] n Hollande f.
hollow ['hɔləu] a creux(euse); (fig) faux(fausse) // n creux m; (in land) dépression f (de terrain), cuvette f // vt: **to** ~ **out** creuser, évider.
holly ['hɔlɪ] n houx m.
holocaust ['hɔləkɔ:st] n holocauste m.
holster ['həulstə*] n étui m de revolver.
holy ['həulɪ] a saint(e); (bread, water) bénit(e); (ground) sacré(e); **H~ Ghost** or **Spirit** n Saint-Esprit m.
home [həum] n foyer m, maison f; (country) pays natal, patrie f; (institution) maison // a de famille; (ECON, POL) national(e), intérieur(e) // ad chez soi, à la maison; au pays natal; (right in: nail etc) à fond; **at** ~ chez soi, à la maison; **to go (or come)** ~ rentrer (chez soi), rentrer à la maison (or au

pays); **make yourself at** ~ faites comme chez vous; ~ **address** n domicile permanent; ~ **computer** n ordinateur m domestique; ~**land** n patrie f; ~**less** a sans foyer; sans abri; ~**ly** a simple, sans prétention; accueillant(e); ~-**made** a fait(e) à la maison; **H~ Office** n (Brit) Ministère m de l'Intérieur; ~ **rule** n autonomie f; **H~ Secretary** n (Brit) ministre m de l'Intérieur; ~**sick** a: **to be** ~**sick** avoir le mal du pays; s'ennuyer de sa famille; ~ **town** n ville natale; ~**ward** ['həumwəd] a (journey) du retour; ~**work** n devoirs mpl.
homogeneous [hɔməu'dʒi:nɪəs] a homogène.
homosexual [hɔməu'sɛksjuəl] a, n homosexuel(le).
honest ['ɔnɪst] a honnête; (sincere) franc(franche); ~**ly** ad honnêtement; franchement; ~**y** n honnêteté f.
honey ['hʌnɪ] n miel m; ~**comb** n rayon m de miel; ~**moon** n lune f de miel; (trip) voyage m de noces; ~**suckle** n (BOT) chèvrefeuille m.
honk [hɔŋk] vi klaxonner.
honorary ['ɔnərərɪ] a honoraire; (duty, title) honorifique.
honour, (US) honor ['ɔnə*] vt honorer // n honneur m; ~**able** a honorable; ~**s degree** n (SCOL) licence avec mention.
hood [hud] n capuchon m; (Brit AUT) capote f; (US AUT) capot m.
hoodlum ['hu:dləm] n truand m.
hoodwink ['hudwɪŋk] vt tromper.
hoof [hu:f] , pl ~**s** or **hooves** n sabot m.
hook [huk] n crochet m; (on dress) agrafe f; (for fishing) hameçon m // vt accrocher; (dress) agrafer.
hooligan ['hu:lɪgən] n voyou m.
hoop [hu:p] n cerceau m.
hoot [hu:t] vi (AUT) klaxonner; (siren) mugir; ~**er** n (Brit AUT) klaxon m; (NAUT) sirène f.
hoover ® ['hu:və*] (Brit) n aspirateur m // vt passer l'aspirateur dans or sur.
hooves [hu:vz] npl of **hoof**.
hop [hɔp] vi sauter; (on one foot) sauter à cloche-pied.
hope [həup] vt, vi espérer // n espoir m; **I** ~ **so** je l'espère; **I** ~ **not** j'espère que non; ~**ful** a (person) plein(e) d'espoir; (situation) prometteur(euse), encourageant(e); ~**fully** ad avec espoir, avec optimisme; avec un peu de chance; ~**less** a désespéré(e); (useless) nul(le).
hops [hɔps] npl houblon m.
horizon [hə'raɪzn] n horizon m; ~**tal** [hɔrɪ'zɔntl] a horizontal(e).
horn [hɔ:n] n corne f; (MUS: also: **French** ~) cor m; (AUT) klaxon m.
hornet ['hɔ:nɪt] n frelon m.
horny ['hɔ:nɪ] a corné(e); (hands) calleux(euse); (col) en rut, excité(e).

horoscope ['hɔrəskəup] *n* horoscope *m*.

horrendous [hə'rendəs] *a* horrible, affreux(euse).

horrible ['hɔrɪbl] *a* horrible, affreux(euse).

horrid ['hɔrɪd] *a* méchant(e), désagréable.

horrify ['hɔrɪfaɪ] *vt* horrifier.

horror ['hɔrə*] *n* horreur *f*; ~ **film** *n* film *m* d'épouvante.

horse [hɔːs] *n* cheval *m*; ~**back**: on ~**back** à cheval; ~ **chestnut** *n* marron *m* (d'Inde); ~**man/woman** *n* cavalier/ière; ~**power (h.p.)** *n* puissance *f* (en chevaux); ~**racing** *n* courses *fpl* de chevaux; ~**radish** *n* raifort *m*; ~**shoe** *n* fer *m* à cheval.

hose [həuz] *n* (*also*: ~**pipe**) tuyau *m*; (*also*: garden ~) tuyau d'arrosage.

hosiery ['həuzɪərɪ] *n* (*in shop*) (rayon *m* des) bas *mpl*.

hospitable ['hɔspɪtəbl] *a* hospitalier(ère).

hospital ['hɔspɪtl] *n* hôpital *m*; in ~ à l'hôpital.

hospitality [hɔspɪ'tælɪtɪ] *n* hospitalité *f*.

host [həust] *n* hôte *m*; (*in hotel etc*) patron *m*; (*REL*) hostie *f*; (*large number*): a ~ of une foule de.

hostage ['hɔstɪdʒ] *n* otage *m*.

hostel ['hɔstl] *n* foyer *m*; (*also*: youth ~) auberge *f* de jeunesse.

hostess ['həustɪs] *n* hôtesse *f*.

hostile ['hɔstaɪl] *a* hostile.

hostility [hɔ'stɪlɪtɪ] *n* hostilité *f*.

hot [hɔt] *a* chaud(e); (*as opposed to only warm*) très chaud; (*spicy*) fort(e); (*fig*) acharné(e); brûlant(e); violent(e), passionné(e); to be ~ (*person*) avoir chaud; (*object*) être (très) chaud; (*weather*) faire chaud; ~**bed** *n* (*fig*) foyer *m*, pépinière *f*; ~ **dog** *n* hot-dog *m*.

hotel [həu'tel] *n* hôtel *m*.

hot: ~**headed** *a* impétueux(euse); ~**house** *n* serre chaude; ~ **line** *n* (*POL*) téléphone *m* rouge, ligne directe; ~**ly** *ad* passionnément, violemment; ~**plate** *n* (*on cooker*) plaque chauffante; ~**-water bottle** *n* bouillotte *f*.

hound [haund] *vt* poursuivre avec acharnement // *n* chien courant.

hour ['auə*] *n* heure *f*; ~**ly** *a*, *ad* toutes les heures; (*rate*) horaire; ~**ly paid** *a* payé(e) à l'heure.

house *n* [haus] (*pl*: ~s ['hauzɪz]) maison *f*; (*POL*) chambre *f*; (*THEATRE*) salle *f*; auditoire *m* // *vt* [hauz] (*person*) loger, héberger; on the ~ (*fig*) aux frais de la maison; ~**boat** *n* bateau (aménagé en habitation); ~**breaking** *n* cambriolage *m* (avec effraction); ~**coat** *n* peignoir *m*; ~**hold** *n* famille *f*, maisonnée *f*; ménage *m*; ~**keeper**

gouvernante *f*; ~**keeping** *n* (*work*) ménage *m*; ~**keeping** (money) argent *m* du ménage; ~**-warming party** *n* pendaison *f* de crémaillère; ~**wife** *n* ménagère *f*; femme *f* au foyer; ~**work** *n* (travaux *mpl* du) ménage *m*.

housing ['hauzɪŋ] *n* logement *m*; ~ **development**, (*Brit*) ~ **estate** *n* cité *f*; lotissement *m*.

hovel ['hɔvl] *n* taudis *m*.

hover ['hɔvə*] *vi* planer; ~**craft** *n* aéroglisseur *m*.

how [hau] *ad* comment; ~ **are you?** comment allez-vous?; ~ **do you do?** bonjour; enchanté(e); ~ **far is it to ...?** combien y a-t-il jusqu'à ...?; ~ **long have you been here?** depuis combien de temps êtes-vous là?; ~ **lovely!** que *or* comme c'est joli!; ~ **many/much?** combien?; ~ **many people/much milk** combien de gens/lait; ~ **old are you?** quel âge avez-vous?; ~**ever** *ad* de quelque façon *or* manière *que* + *sub*; (+ *adjective*) quelque *or* si ... que + *sub*; (*in questions*) comment // *cj* pourtant, cependant.

howl ['haul] *vi* hurler.

h.p., **H.P.** *abbr of* **hire purchase**, **horsepower**.

HQ *abbr of* **headquarters**.

hub [hʌb] *n* (*of wheel*) moyeu *m*; (*fig*) centre *m*, foyer *m*.

hubbub ['hʌbʌb] *n* brouhaha *m*.

hub cap *n* enjoliveur *m*.

huddle ['hʌdl] *vi*: to ~ **together** se blottir les uns contre les autres.

hue [hju:] *n* teinte *f*, nuance *f*; ~ **and cry** *n* tollé (général), clameur *f*.

huff [hʌf] *n*: in a ~ fâché(e).

hug [hʌg] *vt* serrer dans ses bras; (*shore, kerb*) serrer // *n* étreinte *f*.

huge [hju:dʒ] *a* énorme, immense.

hulk [hʌlk] *n* (*ship*) vieux rafiot *m*; (*car, building*) carcasse *f*; (*person*) mastodonte *m*, malabar *m*.

hull [hʌl] *n* (*of ship, nuts*) coque *f*.

hullo [hə'ləu] *excl* = **hello**.

hum [hʌm] *vt* (*tune*) fredonner // *vi* fredonner; (*insect*) bourdonner; (*plane, tool*) vrombir.

human ['hju:mən] *a* humain(e) // *n* être humain.

humane [hju:'meɪn] *a* humain(e), humanitaire.

humanitarian [hjumænɪ'tɛərɪən] *a* humanitaire.

humanity [hju:'mænɪtɪ] *n* humanité *f*.

humble ['hʌmbl] *a* humble, modeste // *vt* humilier.

humbug ['hʌmbʌg] *n* fumisterie *f*.

humdrum ['hʌmdrʌm] *a* monotone, routinier(ère).

humid ['hju:mɪd] *a* humide.

humiliate [hju:'mɪlɪeɪt] *vt* humilier; **humiliation** [-'eɪʃən] *n* humiliation *f*.

humility [hju:'mɪlɪtɪ] *n* humilité *f*.
humorous ['hju:mərəs] *a* humoristique; (*person*) plein(e) d'humour.
humour, (*US*) **humor** ['hju:mə*] *n* humour *m*; (*mood*) humeur *f* // *vt* (*person*) faire plaisir à; se prêter aux caprices de.
hump [hʌmp] *n* bosse *f*.
hunch [hʌntʃ] *n* bosse *f*; (*premonition*) intuition *f*; **~back** *n* bossu/e; **~ed** *a* arrondi(e), voûté(e).
hundred ['hʌndrəd] *num* cent; **~s** of des centaines de; **~weight** *n* (*Brit*) = 50.8 *kg; 112 lb;* (*US*) = 45.3 *kg; 100 lb.*
hung [hʌŋ] *pt, pp of* hang.
Hungary ['hʌŋgərɪ] *n* Hongrie *f*.
hunger ['hʌŋgə*] *n* faim *f* // *vi:* **to ~ for** avoir faim de, désirer ardemment.
hungry ['hʌŋgrɪ] *a* affamé(e); **to be ~** avoir faim.
hunk [hʌŋk] *n* (*of bread etc*) gros morceau.
hunt [hʌnt] *vt* (*seek*) chercher; (*SPORT*) chasser // *vi* chasser // *n* chasse *f*; **~er** *n* chasseur *m*; **~ing** *n* chasse *f*.
hurdle ['hə:dl] *n* (*SPORT*) haie *f*; (*fig*) obstacle *m*.
hurl [hə:l] *vt* lancer (avec violence).
hurrah, **hurray** [hu'rɑ:, hu'reɪ] *n* hourra *m*.
hurricane ['hʌrɪkən] *n* ouragan *m*.
hurried ['hʌrɪd] *a* pressé(e), précipité(e); (*work*) fait(e) à la hâte; **~ly** *ad* précipitamment, à la hâte.
hurry ['hʌrɪ] *n* hâte *f*, précipitation *f* // *vb* (*also:* **~ up**) *vi* se presser, se dépêcher // *vt* (*person*) faire presser, faire se dépêcher; (*work*) presser; **to be in a ~** être pressé(e); **to do sth in a ~** faire qch en vitesse; **to ~ in/out** entrer/sortir précipitamment.
hurt [hə:t] *vb* (*pt, pp* **hurt**) *vt* (*cause pain to*) faire mal à; (*injure, fig*) blesser // *vi* faire mal // *a* blessé(e); **~ful** *a* (*remark*) blessant(e).
hurtle ['hə:tl] *vi:* **to ~ past** passer en trombe; **to ~ down** dégringoler.
husband ['hʌzbənd] *n* mari *m*.
hush [hʌʃ] *n* calme *m*, silence *m* // *vt* faire taire; **~!** chut!
husk [hʌsk] *n* (*of wheat*) balle *f*; (*of rice, maize*) enveloppe *f*.
husky ['hʌskɪ] *a* rauque // *n* chien *m* esquimau *or* de traîneau.
hustle ['hʌsl] *vt* pousser, bousculer // *n* bousculade *f*; **~ and bustle** *n* tourbillon *m* (d'activité).
hut [hʌt] *n* hutte *f*; (*shed*) cabane *f*.
hutch [hʌtʃ] *n* clapier *m*.
hyacinth ['haɪəsɪnθ] *n* jacinthe *f*.
hydrant ['haɪdrənt] *n* prise *f* d'eau; (*also:* **fire ~**) bouche *f* d'incendie.
hydraulic [haɪ'drɔ:lɪk] *a* hydraulique.
hydroelectric [haɪdrəʊ'lɛktrɪk] *a* hydro-électrique.

hydrofoil ['haɪdrəʊfɔɪl] *n* hydrofoil *m*.
hydrogen ['haɪdrədʒən] *n* hydrogène *m*.
hyena [haɪ'i:nə] *n* hyène *f*.
hygiene ['haɪdʒi:n] *n* hygiène *f*.
hymn [hɪm] *n* hymne *m*; cantique *m*.
hype [haɪp] *n* (*col*) campagne *f* publicitaire.
hypermarket ['haɪpəmɑ:kɪt] *n* hypermarché *m*.
hyphen ['haɪfn] *n* trait *m* d'union.
hypnotize ['hɪpnətaɪz] *vt* hypnotiser.
hypocrisy [hɪ'pɔkrɪsɪ] *n* hypocrisie *f*.
hypocrite ['hɪpəkrɪt] *n* hypocrite *m/f*; **hypocritical** [-'krɪtɪkl] *a* hypocrite.
hypothesis, *pl* **hypotheses** [haɪ'pɔθɪsɪs, -sɪ:z] *n* hypothèse *f*.
hysterical [hɪ'stɛrɪkl] *a* hystérique.
hysterics [hɪ'stɛrɪks] *npl* (*violente*) crise de nerfs; (*laughter*) crise de rire.

I

I [aɪ] *pronoun* je; (*before vowel*) j'; (*stressed*) moi.
ice [aɪs] *n* glace *f*; (*on road*) verglas *m* // *vt* (*cake*) glacer; (*drink*) faire rafraîchir // *vi* (*also:* **~ over**) geler; (*also:* **~ up**) se givrer; **~ axe** *n* piolet *m*; **~berg** *n* iceberg *m*; **~box** *n* (*US*) réfrigérateur *m*; (*Brit*) compartiment *m* à glace; (*insulated box*) glacière *f*; **~ cream** *n* glace *f*; **~ cube** *n* glaçon *m*; **~ hockey** *n* hockey *m* sur glace.
Iceland ['aɪslənd] *n* Islande *f*.
ice: ~ lolly *n* (*Brit*) esquimau *m*; **~ rink** *n* patinoire *f*; **~ skating** *n* patinage *m* (sur glace).
icicle ['aɪsɪkl] *n* glaçon *m* (*naturel*).
icing ['aɪsɪŋ] *n* (*AVIAT etc*) givrage *m*; (*CULIN*) glaçage *m*; **~ sugar** *n* (*Brit*) sucre *m* glace.
icy ['aɪsɪ] *a* glacé(e); (*road*) verglacé(e); (*weather, temperature*) glacial(e).
I'd [aɪd] = **I would, I had.**
idea [aɪ'dɪə] *n* idée *f*.
ideal [aɪ'dɪəl] *n* idéal *m* // *a* idéal(e).
identical [aɪ'dɛntɪkl] *a* identique.
identification [aɪdɛntɪfɪ'keɪʃən] *n* identification *f*; **means of ~** pièce *f* d'identité.
identify [aɪ'dɛntɪfaɪ] *vt* identifier.
identikit picture [aɪ'dɛntɪkɪt-] *n* portrait-robot *m*.
identity [aɪ'dɛntɪtɪ] *n* identité *f*; **~ card** *n* carte *f* d'identité.
idiom ['ɪdɪəm] *n* langue *f*, idiome *m*; (*phrase*) expression *f* idiomatique.
idiosyncrasy [ɪdɪəʊ'sɪŋkrəsɪ] *n* particularité *f*, caractéristique *f*.
idiot ['ɪdɪət] *n* idiot/e, imbécile *m/f*; **~ic** [-'ɔtɪk] *a* idiot(e), bête, stupide.
idle ['aɪdl] *a* sans occupation, désœuvré(e); (*lazy*) oisif(ive), paresseux(euse); (*unemployed*) au chômage;

(question, pleasures) vain(e), futile // vt: to ~ away the time passer son temps à ne rien faire; to lie ~ être arrêté, ne pas fonctionner.

idol ['aɪdl] *n* idole *f*; ~**ize** *vt* idolâtrer, adorer.

i.e. *ad abbr* (= *id est*) c'est-à-dire.

if [ɪf] *cj* si; ~ **so** si c'est le cas; ~ **not** sinon; ~ **only** si seulement.

ignite [ɪg'naɪt] *vt* mettre le feu à, enflammer // *vi* s'enflammer.

ignition [ɪg'nɪʃən] *n* (*AUT*) allumage *m*; to **switch on/off the** ~ mettre/couper le contact; ~ **key** *n* (*AUT*) clé *f* de contact.

ignorant ['ɪgnərənt] *a* ignorant(e); to be ~ of (*subject*) ne rien connaître· en; (*events*) ne pas être au courant de.

ignore [ɪg'nɔ:*] *vt* ne tenir aucun compte de, ne pas relever; (*person*) faire semblant de ne pas reconnaître, ignorer; (*fact*) méconnaître.

ill [ɪl] *a* (*sick*) malade; (*bad*) mauvais(e) // *n* mal *m* // *ad*: to **speak** *etc* ~ **of** dire *etc* du mal de; to **take** *or* **be taken** ~ tomber malade; ~**-advised** *a* (*decision*) peu judicieux(euse); (*person*) malavisé(e); ~**-at-ease** *a* mal à l'aise.

I'll [aɪl] = **I will, I shall**.

illegal [ɪ'li:gl] *a* illégal(e).

illegible [ɪ'lɛdʒɪbl] *a* illisible.

illegitimate [ɪlɪ'dʒɪtɪmət] *a* illégitime.

ill-fated [ɪl'feɪtɪd] *a* malheureux(euse); (*day*) néfaste.

ill feeling *n* ressentiment *m*, rancune *f*.

illiterate [ɪ'lɪtərət] *a* illettré(e); (*letter*) plein(e) de fautes.

illness ['ɪlnɪs] *n* maladie *f*.

ill-treat [ɪl'tri:t] *vt* maltraiter.

illuminate [ɪ'lu:mɪneɪt] *vt* (*room, street*) éclairer; (*building*) illuminer; **illumination** [-'neɪʃən] *n* éclairage *m*; illumination *f*.

illusion [ɪ'lu:ʒən] *n* illusion *f*; to **be under the** ~ **that** s'imaginer *or* croire que.

illustrate ['ɪləstreɪt] *vt* illustrer; **illustration** [-'streɪʃən] *n* illustration *f*.

ill will *n* malveillance *f*.

I'm [aɪm] = **I am**.

image ['ɪmɪdʒ] *n* image *f*; (*public face*) image de marque; ~**ry** *n* images *fpl*.

imaginary [ɪ'mædʒɪnərɪ] *a* imaginaire.

imagination [ɪmædʒɪ'neɪʃən] *n* imagination *f*.

imaginative [ɪ'mædʒɪnətɪv] *a* imaginatif(ive); plein(e) d'imagination.

imagine [ɪ'mædʒɪn] *vt* s'imaginer; (*suppose*) imaginer, supposer.

imbalance [ɪm'bæləns] *n* déséquilibre *m*.

imitate ['ɪmɪteɪt] *vt* imiter; **imitation** [-'teɪʃən] *n* imitation *f*.

immaculate [ɪ'mækjulət] *a* impeccable; (*REL*) immaculé(e).

immaterial [ɪmə'tɪərɪəl] *a* sans importance, insignifiant(e).

immature [ɪmə'tjuə*] *a* (*fruit*) qui n'est pas mûr(e); (*person*) qui manque de maturité.

immediate [ɪ'mi:dɪət] *a* immédiat(e); ~**ly** *ad* (*at once*) immédiatement; ~**ly next to** juste à côté de.

immense [ɪ'mɛns] *a* immense; énorme.

immerse [ɪ'mə:s] *vt* immerger, plonger.

immersion heater [ɪ'mə:ʃən-] *n* (*Brit*) chauffe-eau *m* électrique.

immigrant ['ɪmɪgrənt] *n* immigrant/e; immigré/e.

immigration [ɪmɪ'greɪʃən] *n* immigration *f*.

imminent ['ɪmɪnənt] *a* imminent(e).

immoral [ɪ'mɔrl] *a* immoral(e).

immortal [ɪ'mɔ:tl] *a*, *n* immortel(le).

immune [ɪ'mju:n] *a*: ~ (**to**) immunisé(e) (contre).

immunity [ɪ'mju:nɪtɪ] *n* immunité *f*.

imp [ɪmp] *n* lutin *m*; (*child*) petit diable.

impact ['ɪmpækt] *n* choc *m*, impact *m*; (*fig*) impact.

impair [ɪm'pɛə*] *vt* détériorer, diminuer.

impart [ɪm'pɑ:t] *vt* communiquer, transmettre; conférer, donner.

impartial [ɪm'pɑ:ʃl] *a* impartial(e).

impassable [ɪm'pɑ:səbl] *a* infranchissable; (*road*) impraticable.

impassive [ɪm'pæsɪv] *a* impassible.

impatience [ɪm'peɪʃəns] *n* impatience *f*.

impatient [ɪm'peɪʃnt] *a* impatient(e); to **get** *or* **grow** ~ s'impatienter.

impeccable [ɪm'pɛkəbl] *a* impeccable, parfait(e).

impede [ɪm'pi:d] *vt* gêner.

impediment [ɪm'pɛdɪmənt] *n* obstacle *m*; (*also*: **speech** ~) défaut *m* d'élocution.

impending [ɪm'pɛndɪŋ] *a* imminent(e).

imperative [ɪm'pɛrətɪv] *a* nécessaire; urgent(e), pressant(e); (*tone*) impérieux(euse) // *n* (*LING*) impératif *m*.

imperfect [ɪm'pə:fɪkt] *a* imparfait(e); (*goods etc*) défectueux(euse).

imperial [ɪm'pɪərɪəl] *a* impérial(e); (*measure*) légal(e).

impersonal [ɪm'pə:sənl] *a* impersonnel(le).

impersonate [ɪm'pə:səneɪt] *vt* se faire passer pour; (*THEATRE*) imiter.

impertinent [ɪm'pə:tɪnənt] *a* impertinent(e), insolent(e).

impervious [ɪm'pə:vɪəs] *a* imperméable; (*fig*): ~ **to** insensible à; inaccessible à.

impetuous [ɪm'pɛtjuəs] *a* impétueux(euse), fougueux(euse).

impetus ['ɪmpətəs] *n* impulsion *f*; (*of runner*) élan *m*.

impinge [ɪm'pɪndʒ]: to ~ **on** *vt fus* (*person*) affecter, toucher; (*rights*) empiéter sur.

implement *n* ['ɪmplɪmənt] outil *m*, instrument *m*; (*for cooking*) ustensile *m* //

vt ['ımplımɛnt] exécuter, mettre à effet.

implicit [ım'plısıt] *a* implicite; (*complete*) absolu(e), sans réserve.

imply [ım'plaı] *vt* suggérer, laisser entendre; indiquer, supposer.

impolite [ımpə'laıt] *a* impoli(e).

import *vt* [ım'pɔ:t] importer // *n* ['ımpɔ:t] (*COMM*) importation *f*; (*meaning*) portée *f*, signification *f*.

importance [ım'pɔ:tns] *n* importance *f*.

important [ım'pɔ:tnt] *a* important(e).

importer [ım'pɔ:tə*] *n* importateur/trice.

impose [ım'pəuz] *vt* imposer // *vi*: **to ~ on sb** abuser de la gentillesse (*or* crédulité) de qn.

imposing [ım'pəuzıŋ] *a* imposant(e), impressionnant(e).

imposition [ımpə'zıʃən] *n* (*of tax etc*) imposition *f*; **to be an ~ on** (*person*) abuser de la gentillesse *or* la bonté de.

impossible [ım'pɔsıbl] *a* impossible.

impotent ['ımpətnt] *a* impuissant(e).

impound [ım'paund] *vt* confisquer, saisir.

impoverished [ım'pɔvərıʃt] *a* pauvre, appauvri(e).

impractical [ım'præktıkl] *a* pas pratique; (*person*) qui manque d'esprit pratique.

impregnable [ım'prɛgnəbl] *a* (*fortress*) imprenable; (*fig*) inattaquable; irréfutable.

impress [ım'prɛs] *vt* impressionner, faire impression sur; (*mark*) imprimer, marquer; **to ~ sth on sb** faire bien comprendre qch à qn.

impression [ım'prɛʃən] *n* impression *f*; (*of stamp, seal*) empreinte *f*; **to be under the ~ that** avoir l'impression que.

impressive [ım'prɛsıv] *a* impressionnant(e).

imprint ['ımprınt] *n* (*PUBLISHING*) notice *f*.

imprison [ım'prızn] *vt* emprisonner, mettre en prison.

improbable [ım'prɔbəbl] *a* improbable; (*excuse*) peu plausible.

improper [ım'prɔpə*] *a* incorrect(e); (*unsuitable*) déplacé(e), de mauvais goût; indécent(e).

improve [ım'pru:v] *vt* améliorer // *vi* s'améliorer; (*pupil etc*) faire des progrès; **~ment** *n* amélioration *f*; progrès *m*.

improvise ['ımprəvaız] *vt*, *vi* improviser.

impudent ['ımpjudnt] *a* impudent(e).

impulse ['ımpʌls] *n* impulsion *f*; **on ~** impulsivement, sur un coup de tête.

impulsive [ım'pʌlsıv] *a* impulsif(ive).

in [ın] ♦ *prep* **1** (*indicating place, position*) dans; **~ the house/the fridge** dans la maison/le frigo; **~ the garden** dans le *or* au jardin; **~ town** en ville; **~**

the country à la campagne; **~ school** à l'école; **~ here/there** ici/là

2 (*with place names: of town, region, country*): **~ London** à Londres; **~ England** en Angleterre; **~ Japan** au Japon; **~ the United States** aux États-Unis

3 (*indicating time: during*): **~ spring** au printemps; **~ summer** en été; **~ May/ 1992** en mai/1992; **~ the afternoon** (dans) l'après-midi; **at 4 o'clock ~ the afternoon** à 4 heures de l'après-midi

4 (*indicating time: in the space of*) en; (*: future*) dans; **I did it ~ 3 hours/days** je l'ai fait en 3 heures/jours; **I'll see you ~ 2 weeks** *or* **~ 2 weeks' time** je te verrai dans 2 semaines

5 (*indicating manner etc*) à; **~ a loud/ soft voice** à voix haute/basse; **~ pencil** au crayon; **~ French** en français; **the boy ~ the blue shirt** le garçon à *or* avec la chemise bleue

6 (*indicating circumstances*): **~ the sun** au soleil; **~ the shade** à l'ombre; **~ the rain** sous la pluie

7 (*indicating mood, state*): **~ tears** en larmes; **~ anger** sous le coup de la colère; **~ despair** au désespoir; **~ good condition** en bon état; **to live ~ luxury** vivre dans le luxe

8 (*with ratios, numbers*): **1 ~ 10 (households)**, **1 (household) ~ 10** 1 (ménage) sur 10; **20 pence ~ the pound** 20 pence par livre sterling; **they lined up ~ twos** ils se mirent en rangs (deux) par deux; **~ hundreds** par centaines

9 (*referring to people, works*) chez; **the disease is common ~ children** c'est une maladie courante chez les enfants; **~ (the works of) Dickens** chez Dickens, dans (l'œuvre de) Dickens

10 (*indicating profession etc*) dans; **to be ~ teaching** être dans l'enseignement

11 (*after superlative*) de; **the best pupil ~ the class** le meilleur élève de la classe

12 (*with present participle*): **~ saying this** en disant ceci

♦ *ad*: **to be ~** (*person: at home, work*) être là; (*train, ship, plane*) être arrivé(e); (*in fashion*) être à la mode; **to ask sb ~** inviter qn à entrer; **to run/ limp etc ~** entrer en courant/boitant *etc*

♦ *n*: **the ~s and outs (of)** (*of proposal, situation etc*) les tenants et aboutissants (de).

in., ins *abbr of* **inch(es)**.

inability [ınə'bılıtı] *n* incapacité *f*.

inaccurate [ın'ækjurət] *a* inexact(e); (*person*) qui manque de précision.

inadequate [ın'ædıkwət] *a* insuffisant(e), inadéquat(e).

inadvertently [ınəd'və:tntlı] *ad* par mégarde.

inane [ı'neın] *a* inepte, stupide.

inanimate [ın'ænımət] *a* inanimé(e).

inappropriate [ınə'prəuprıət] *a*

inopportun(e), mal à propos; (word, expression) impropre.

inarticulate [ɪnɑː'tɪkjulət] a (person) qui s'exprime mal; (speech) indistinct(e).

inasmuch as [ɪnəz'mʌtʃæz] ad dans la mesure où; (seeing that) attendu que.

inauguration [ɪnɔːgju'reɪʃən] n inauguration f; (of president, official) investiture f.

in-between [ɪnbɪ'twiːn] a entre les deux.

inborn [ɪn'bɔːn] a (feeling) inné(e); (defect) congénital(e).

inbred [ɪn'brɛd] a inné(e), naturel(le); (family) consanguin(e).

Inc. abbr of **incorporated**.

incapable [ɪn'keɪpəbl] a incapable.

incapacitate [ɪnkə'pæsɪteɪt] vt: to ~ sb from doing rendre qn incapable de faire.

incense n ['ɪnsɛns] encens m // vt [ɪn'sɛns] (anger) mettre en colère.

incentive [ɪn'sɛntɪv] n encouragement m, raison f de se donner de la peine.

incessant [ɪn'sɛsnt] a incessant(e); ~ly ad sans cesse, constamment.

inch [ɪntʃ] n pouce m (= 25 mm; 12 in a foot); within an ~ of à deux doigts de; he didn't give an ~ (fig) il n'a pas voulu céder d'un pouce or faire la plus petite concession; to ~ forward vi avancer petit à petit.

incidence ['ɪnsɪdns] n (of crime, disease) fréquence f.

incident ['ɪnsɪdnt] n incident m; (in book) péripétie f.

incidental [ɪnsɪ'dɛntl] a accessoire; (unplanned) accidentel(le); ~ to qui accompagne; ~ly [-'dɛntəlɪ] ad (by the way) à propos.

incipient [ɪn'sɪpɪənt] a naissant(e).

inclination [ɪnklɪ'neɪʃən] n inclination f.

incline n ['ɪnklaɪn] pente f, plan incliné // vb [ɪn'klaɪn] vt incliner // vi: to ~ to avoir tendance à; to be ~d to do être enclin(e) à faire; (tend) avoir tendance à faire.

include [ɪn'kluːd] vt inclure, comprendre; **including** prep y compris.

inclusive [ɪn'kluːsɪv] a inclus(e), compris(e) // ad: ~ of tax etc taxes etc comprises.

income ['ɪnkʌm] n revenu m; ~ **tax** n impôt m sur le revenu.

incompetent [ɪn'kɔmpɪtnt] a incompétent(e), incapable.

incomplete [ɪnkəm'pliːt] a incomplet(ète).

incongruous [ɪn'kɔŋgruəs] a peu approprié(e); (remark, act) incongru(e), déplacé(e).

inconsistency [ɪnkən'sɪstənsɪ] n (of actions etc) inconséquence f; (of work) irrégularité f; (of statement etc) incohérence f.

inconsistent [ɪnkən'sɪstnt] a incon-

séquent(e); irrégulier(ère); peu cohérent(e).

inconspicuous [ɪnkən'spɪkjuəs] a qui passe inaperçu(e); (colour, dress) discret(ète).

inconvenience [ɪnkən'viːnjəns] n inconvénient m; (trouble) dérangement m // vt déranger.

inconvenient [ɪnkən'viːnjənt] a malcommode; (time, place) mal choisi(e), qui ne convient pas.

incorporate [ɪn'kɔːpəreɪt] vt incorporer; (contain) contenir; ~d a: ~d company (US: abbr **Inc.**) ≈ société f anonyme (S.A.).

incorrect [ɪnkə'rɛkt] a incorrect(e); (opinion, statement) inexact(e).

increase n ['ɪnkriːs] augmentation f // vi, vt [ɪn'kriːs] augmenter.

increasing [ɪn'kriːsɪŋ] a (number) croissant(e); ~ly ad de plus en plus.

incredible [ɪn'krɛdɪbl] a incroyable.

incredulous [ɪn'krɛdjuləs] a incrédule.

increment ['ɪnkrɪmənt] n augmentation f.

incubator ['ɪnkjubeɪtə*] n incubateur m; (for babies) couveuse f.

incumbent [ɪn'kʌmbənt] n (REL) titulaire m/f // a: it is ~ on him to ... il lui incombe or appartient de ....

incur [ɪn'kə:*] vt (expenses) encourir; (anger, risk) s'exposer à; (debt) contracter; (loss) subir.

indebted [ɪn'dɛtɪd] a: to be ~ to sb (for) être redevable à qn (de).

indecent [ɪn'diːsnt] a indécent(e), inconvenant(e); ~ **assault** n (Brit) attentat m à la pudeur; ~ **exposure** n outrage m (public) à la pudeur.

indecisive [ɪndɪ'saɪsɪv] a indécis(e); (discussion) peu concluant(e).

indeed [ɪn'diːd] ad en effet; d'ailleurs; vraiment; yes ~! certainement!

indefinite [ɪn'dɛfɪnɪt] a indéfini(e); (answer) vague; (period, number) indéterminé(e); ~ly ad (wait) indéfiniment.

indemnity [ɪn'dɛmnɪtɪ] n (insurance) assurance f, garantie f; (compensation) indemnité f.

independence [ɪndɪ'pɛndns] n indépendance f.

independent [ɪndɪ'pɛndnt] a indépendant(e); to become ~ s'affranchir.

index ['ɪndɛks] n (pl: ~es: in book) index m; (: in library etc) catalogue m; (pl: indices ['ɪndɪsiːz]) (ratio, sign) indice m; ~ **card** n fiche f; ~ **finger** n index m; ~-**linked**, (US) ~**ed** a indexé(e) (sur le coût de la vie etc).

India ['ɪndɪə] n Inde f; ~n a indien(ne) // n Indien/ne; **Red** ~n Indien/ne (d'Amérique).

indicate ['ɪndɪkeɪt] vt indiquer; **indica-**

tion [-'keɪʃən] *n* indication *f*, signe *m*.
indicative [ɪn'dɪkətɪv] *a* indicatif(ive) // *n* (LING) indicatif *m*; ~ of symptomatique de.
indicator ['ɪndɪkeɪtə*] *n* (sign) indicateur *m*; (AUT) clignotant *m*.
indices ['ɪndɪsi:z] *npl of* **index**.
indictment [ɪn'daɪtmənt] *n* accusation *f*.
indifference [ɪn'dɪfrəns] *n* indifférence *f*.
indifferent [ɪn'dɪfrənt] *a* indifférent(e); (poor) médiocre, quelconque.
indigenous [ɪn'dɪdʒɪnəs] *a* indigène.
indigestion [ɪndɪ'dʒɛstʃən] *n* indigestion *f*, mauvaise digestion.
indignant [ɪn'dɪgnənt] *a*: ~ (at or about sth/with sb) indigné(e) (de qch/contre qn).
indignity [ɪn'dɪgnɪtɪ] *n* indignité *f*, affront *m*.
indirect [ɪndɪ'rɛkt] *a* indirect(e).
indiscreet [ɪndɪ'skri:t] *a* indiscret(ète); (rash) imprudent(e).
indiscriminate [ɪndɪ'skrɪmɪnət] *a* (person) qui manque de discernement; (admiration) aveugle; (killings) commis(e) au hasard.
indisputable [ɪndɪ'spju:təbl] *a* incontestable, indiscutable.
individual [ɪndɪ'vɪdjuəl] *n* individu *m* // *a* individuel(le); (characteristic) particulier(ère), original(e).
indoctrination [ɪndɔktrɪ'neɪʃən] *n* endoctrinement *m*.
Indonesia [ɪndə'ni:zɪə] *n* Indonésie *f*.
indoor ['ɪndɔ:*] *a* d'intérieur; (plant) d'appartement; (swimming pool) couvert(e); (sport, games) pratiqué(e) en salle; ~**s** [ɪn'dɔ:z] *ad* à l'intérieur; (at home) à la maison.
induce [ɪn'dju:s] *vt* persuader; (bring about) provoquer; ~**ment** *n* incitation *f*; (incentive) but *m*; (pej: bribe) pot-de-vin *m*.
induction [ɪn'dʌkʃən] *n* (MED: of birth) accouchement provoqué; ~ **course** *n* (Brit) stage *m* de mise au courant.
indulge [ɪn'dʌldʒ] *vt* (whim) céder à, satisfaire; (child) gâter // *vi*: to ~ in sth s'offrir qch, se permettre qch; se livrer à qch; ~**nce** *n* fantaisie *f* (que l'on s'offre); (leniency) indulgence *f*; ~**nt** *a* indulgent(e).
industrial [ɪn'dʌstrɪəl] *a* industriel(le); (injury) du travail; (dispute) ouvrier(ère); ~ **action** *n* action revendicative; ~ **estate** *n* (Brit) zone industrielle; ~**ist** *n* industriel *m*; ~ **park** *n* (US) = ~ **estate**.
industrious [ɪn'dʌstrɪəs] *a* travailleur(euse).
industry ['ɪndəstrɪ] *n* industrie *f*; (diligence) zèle *m*, application *f*.
inebriated [ɪ'ni:brɪeɪtɪd] *a* ivre.
inedible [ɪn'ɛdɪbl] *a* immangeable;

(plant etc) non comestible.
ineffective [ɪnɪ'fɛktɪv], **ineffectual** [ɪnɪ'fɛktʃuəl] *a* inefficace; (person) incompétent(e).
inefficiency [ɪnɪ'fɪʃənsɪ] *n* inefficacité *f*.
inefficient [ɪnɪ'fɪʃənt] *a* inefficace.
inequality [ɪnɪ'kwɔlɪtɪ] *n* inégalité *f*.
inescapable [ɪnɪ'skeɪpəbl] *a* inéluctable, inévitable.
inevitable [ɪn'ɛvɪtəbl] *a* inévitable; **inevitably** *ad* inévitablement.
inexpensive [ɪnɪk'spɛnsɪv] *a* bon marché *inv*.
inexperienced [ɪnɪks'pɪərɪənst] *a* inexpérimenté(e).
infallible [ɪn'fælɪbl] *a* infaillible.
infamous ['ɪnfəməs] *a* infâme, abominable.
infancy ['ɪnfənsɪ] *n* petite enfance, bas âge; (fig) enfance, débuts *mpl*.
infant ['ɪnfənt] *n* (baby) nourrisson *m*; (young child) petit(e) enfant; ~ **school** *n* (Brit) classes *fpl* préparatoires (entre 5 et 7 ans).
infatuated [ɪn'fætjueɪtɪd] *a*: ~ with entiché(e) de.
infatuation [ɪnfætju'eɪʃən] *n* toquade *f*; engouement *m*.
infect [ɪn'fɛkt] *vt* infecter, contaminer; ~**ion** [ɪn'fɛkʃən] *n* infection *f*; contagion *f*; ~**ious** [ɪn'fɛkʃəs] *a* infectieux(euse); (also fig) contagieux(euse).
infer [ɪn'fə:*] *vt* conclure, déduire.
inferior [ɪn'fɪərɪə*] *a* inférieur(e); (goods) de qualité inférieure // *n* inférieur/e; (in rank) subalterne *m/f*; ~**ity** [ɪnfɪərɪ'ɔrɪtɪ] *n* infériorité *f*; ~**ity complex** *n* complexe *m* d'infériorité.
inferno [ɪn'fə:nəu] *n* enfer *m*; brasier *m*.
infertile [ɪn'fə:taɪl] *a* stérile.
in-fighting ['ɪnfaɪtɪŋ] *n* querelles *fpl* internes.
infinite ['ɪnfɪnɪt] *a* infini(e).
infinitive [ɪn'fɪnɪtɪv] *n* infinitif *m*.
infinity [ɪn'fɪnɪtɪ] *n* infinité *f*; (also MATH) infini *m*.
infirmary [ɪn'fə:mərɪ] *n* hôpital *m*; (in school, factory) infirmerie *f*.
infirmity [ɪn'fə:mɪtɪ] *n* infirmité *f*.
inflamed [ɪn'fleɪmd] *a* enflammé(e).
inflammable [ɪn'flæməbl] *a* (Brit) inflammable.
inflammation [ɪnflə'meɪʃən] *n* inflammation *f*.
inflatable [ɪn'fleɪtəbl] *a* gonflable.
inflate [ɪn'fleɪt] *vt* (tyre, balloon) gonfler; (fig) grossir; gonfler; faire monter; **inflation** [ɪn'fleɪʃən] *n* (ECON) inflation *f*; **inflationary** [ɪn'fleɪʃnərɪ] *a* inflationniste.
inflict [ɪn'flɪkt] *vt*: to ~ on infliger à.
influence ['ɪnfluəns] *n* influence *f* // *vt* influencer; **under the ~ of drink** en état d'ébriété.

influential [ɪnflu'ɛnʃl] *a* influent(e).

influenza [ɪnflu'ɛnzə] *n* grippe *f*.

influx ['ɪnflʌks] *n* afflux *m*.

inform [ɪn'fɔ:m] *vt*: to ~ sb (of) informer *or* avertir qn (de) // *vi*: to ~ on sb dénoncer qn, informer contre qn; to ~ sb about renseigner qn sur, mettre qn au courant de.

informal [ɪn'fɔ:ml] *a* (*person, manner*) simple, sans façon; (*visit, discussion*) dénué(e) de formalités; (*announcement, invitation*) non officiel(le); **~ity** [-'mælɪtɪ] *n* simplicité *f*, absence *f* de cérémonie; caractère non officiel.

informant [ɪn'fɔ:mənt] *n* informateur/trice.

information [ɪnfə'meɪʃən] *n* information *f*; renseignements *mpl*; (*knowledge*) connaissances *fpl*; **a piece of ~** un renseignement; **~ office** *n* bureau *m* de renseignements.

informative [ɪn'fɔ:mətɪv] *a* instructif(ive).

informer [ɪn'fɔ:mə*] *n* dénonciateur/trice; (*also*: **police ~**) indicateur/trice.

infringe [ɪn'frɪndʒ] *vt* enfreindre // *vi*: to ~ on empiéter sur; **~ment** *n*: **~ment (of)** infraction *f* (à).

infuriating [ɪn'fjuərɪeɪtɪŋ] *a* exaspérant(e).

ingenious [ɪn'dʒi:njəs] *a* ingénieux(euse).

ingenuity [ɪndʒɪ'nju:ɪtɪ] *n* ingéniosité *f*.

ingenuous [ɪn'dʒɛnjuəs] *a* naïf(ïve), ingénu(e).

ingot ['ɪŋgət] *n* lingot *m*.

ingrained [ɪn'greɪnd] *a* enraciné(e).

ingratiate [ɪn'greɪʃɪeɪt] *vt*: to ~ o.s. with s'insinuer dans les bonnes grâces de, se faire bien voir de.

ingredient [ɪn'gri:dɪənt] *n* ingrédient *m*; élément *m*.

inhabit [ɪn'hæbɪt] *vt* habiter.

inhabitant [ɪn'hæbɪtnt] *n* habitant/e.

inhale [ɪn'heɪl] *vt* inhaler; (*perfume*) respirer // *vi* (*in smoking*) avaler la fumée.

inherent [ɪn'hɪərənt] *a*: ~ (in *or* to) inhérent(e) (à).

inherit [ɪn'herɪt] *vt* hériter (de); **~ance** *n* héritage *m*.

inhibit [ɪn'hɪbɪt] *vt* (*PSYCH*) inhiber; to ~ sb from doing empêcher *or* retenir qn de faire; **~ion** [-'bɪʃən] *n* inhibition *f*.

inhuman [ɪn'hju:mən] *a* inhumain(e).

initial [ɪ'nɪʃl] *a* initial(e) // *n* initiale *f* // *vt* parafer; **~s** *npl* initiales *fpl*; (*as signature*) parafe *m*; **~ly** *ad* initialement, au début.

initiate [ɪ'nɪʃɪeɪt] *vt* (*start*) entreprendre; amorcer; lancer; (*person*) initier.

initiative [ɪ'nɪʃətɪv] *n* initiative *f*.

inject [ɪn'dʒɛkt] *vt* (*liquid*) injecter; (*person*) faire une piqûre à; **~ion** [ɪn'dʒɛkʃən] *n* injection *f*, piqûre *f*.

injure ['ɪndʒə*] *vt* blesser; (*wrong*) faire du tort à; (*damage: reputation etc*) compromettre; **~d** *a* blessé(e).

injury ['ɪndʒərɪ] *n* blessure *f*; (*wrong*) tort *m*; ~ **time** *n* (*SPORT*) arrêts *mpl* de jeu.

injustice [ɪn'dʒʌstɪs] *n* injustice *f*.

ink [ɪŋk] *n* encre *f*.

inkling ['ɪŋklɪŋ] *n* soupçon *m*, vague idée *f*.

inlaid ['ɪnleɪd] *a* incrusté(e); (*table etc*) marqueté(e).

inland *a* ['ɪnlənd] intérieur(e) // *ad* [ɪn'lænd] à l'intérieur, dans les terres; **I~ Revenue** *n* (*Brit*) fisc *m*.

in-laws ['ɪnlɔ:z] *npl* beaux-parents *mpl*; belle famille.

inlet ['ɪnlɛt] *n* (*GEO*) crique *f*.

inmate ['ɪnmeɪt] *n* (*in prison*) détenu/e; (*in asylum*) interné/e.

inn [ɪn] *n* auberge *f*.

innate [ɪ'neɪt] *a* inné(e).

inner ['ɪnə*] *a* intérieur(e); ~ **city** *n* centre *m* de zone urbaine; ~ **tube** *n* (*of tyre*) chambre *f* à air.

innings ['ɪnɪŋz] *n* (*CRICKET*) tour *m* de batte.

innocence ['ɪnəsns] *n* innocence *f*.

innocent ['ɪnəsnt] *a* innocent(e).

innocuous [ɪ'nɔkjuəs] *a* inoffensif(ive).

innuendo, **~es** [ɪnju'ɛndəu] *n* insinuation *f*, allusion (malveillante).

innumerable [ɪ'nju:mrəbl] *a* innombrable.

inordinately [ɪ'nɔ:dɪnətlɪ] *ad* démesurément.

in-patient ['ɪnpeɪʃənt] *n* malade hospitalisé(e).

input ['ɪnput] *n* (*ELEC*) énergie *f*, puissance *f*; (*of machine*) consommation *f*; (*of computer*) information fournie.

inquest ['ɪnkwest] *n* enquête (criminelle).

inquire [ɪn'kwaɪə*] *vi* demander // *vt* demander, s'informer de; to ~ **about** s'informer de, se renseigner sur; **to ~ into** *vt fus* faire une enquête sur; **inquiry** *n* demande *f* de renseignements; (*LAW*) enquête *f*, investigation *f*; **inquiry office** *n* (*Brit*) bureau *m* de renseignements.

inquisitive [ɪn'kwɪzɪtɪv] *a* curieux(euse).

inroad ['ɪnrəud] *n* incursion *f*.

insane [ɪn'seɪn] *a* fou(folle); (*MED*) aliéné(e).

insanity [ɪn'sænɪtɪ] *n* folie *f*; (*MED*) aliénation (mentale).

inscription [ɪn'skrɪpʃən] *n* inscription *f*; dédicace *f*.

inscrutable [ɪn'skru:təbl] *a* impénétrable.

insect ['ɪnsɛkt] *n* insecte *m*; **~icide** [ɪn'sɛktɪsaɪd] *n* insecticide *m*.

insecure [ɪnsɪ'kjuə*] *a* peu solide; peu

sûr(e); (*person*) anxieux(euse).
insensible [ɪnˈsɛnsɪbl] *a* insensible;
(*unconscious*) sans connaissance.
insensitive [ɪnˈsɛnsɪtɪv] *a* insensible.
insert *vt* [ɪnˈsəːt] insérer // *n* [ˈɪnsəːt]
insertion *f*; ∼**ion** [ɪnˈsəːʃən] *n* insertion
f.
in-service [ɪnˈsəːvɪs] *a* (*training*)
continu(e), en cours d'emploi; (*course*)
d'initiation; de perfectionnement; de
recyclage.
inshore [ɪnˈʃɔː*] *a* côtier(ère) // *ad* près
de la côte; vers la côte.
inside [ˈɪnˈsaɪd] *n* intérieur *m* // *a*
intérieur(e) // *ad* à l'intérieur, dedans //
prep à l'intérieur de; (*of time*): ∼ 10
minutes en moins de 10 minutes; ∼**s** *npl*
(*col*) intestins *mpl*; ∼ **forward** *n*
(*SPORT*) intérieur *m*; ∼ **lane** *n* (*AUT: in
Britain*) voie *f* de gauche; ∼ **out** *ad* à
l'envers; (*know*) à fond; **to turn** ∼ **out**
retourner.
insight [ˈɪnsaɪt] *n* perspicacité *f*;
(*glimpse, idea*) aperçu *m*.
insignificant [ɪnsɪgˈnɪfɪknt] *a* insi-
gnifiant(e).
insincere [ɪnsɪnˈsɪə*] *a* hypocrite.
insinuate [ɪnˈsɪnjueɪt] *vt* insinuer.
insist [ɪnˈsɪst] *vi* insister; **to** ∼ **on doing**
insister pour faire; **to** ∼ **that** insister
pour que; (*claim*) maintenir *or* soutenir
que; ∼**ent** *a* insistant(e), pressant(e).
insole [ˈɪnsəul] *n* semelle intérieure;
(*fixed part of shoe*) première *f*.
insolent [ˈɪnsələnt] *a* insolent(e).
insomnia [ɪnˈsɔmnɪə] *n* insomnie *f*.
inspect [ɪnˈspɛkt] *vt* inspecter; (*ticket*)
contrôler; ∼**ion** [ɪnˈspɛkʃən] *n*
inspection *f*; contrôle *m*; ∼**or** *n*
inspecteur/trice; (*Brit: on buses, trains*)
contrôleur/euse.
inspire [ɪnˈspaɪə*] *vt* inspirer.
install [ɪnˈstɔːl] *vt* installer; ∼**ation**
[ɪnstəˈleɪʃən] *n* installation *f*.
instalment, (*US*) **installment** [ɪnˈstɔːl-
mənt] *n* acompte *m*, versement partiel;
(*of TV serial etc*) épisode *m*; **in** ∼**s**
(*pay*) à tempérament; (*receive*) en
plusieurs fois.
instance [ˈɪnstəns] *n* exemple *m*; **for** ∼
par exemple; **in many** ∼**s** dans bien des
cas; **in the first** ∼ tout d'abord, en
premier lieu.
instant [ˈɪnstənt] *n* instant *m* // *a*
immédiat(e); urgent(e); (*coffee, food*)
instantané(e), en poudre; ∼**ly** *ad*
immédiatement, tout de suite.
instead [ɪnˈstɛd] *ad* au lieu de cela; ∼ **of**
au lieu de; ∼ **of sb** à la place de qn.
instep [ˈɪnstɛp] *n* cou-de-pied *m*; (*of
shoe*) cambrure *f*.
instil [ɪnˈstɪl] *vt*: **to** ∼ (**into**) inculquer
(à); (*courage*) insuffler (à).
instinct [ˈɪnstɪŋkt] *n* instinct *m*.
institute [ˈɪnstɪtjuːt] *n* institut *m* // *vt*

instituer, établir; (*inquiry*) ouvrir;
(*proceedings*) entamer.
institution [ɪnstɪˈtjuːʃən] *n* institution *f*;
établissement *m* (scolaire); établissement (psychiatrique).
instruct [ɪnˈstrʌkt] *vt* instruire, former;
to ∼ **sb in sth** enseigner qch à qn; **to** ∼
sb to do charger qn *or* ordonner à qn de
faire; ∼**ion** [ɪnˈstrʌkʃən] *n* instruction
f; ∼**ions** *npl* directives *fpl*; ∼**ions** (**for
use**) mode *m* d'emploi; ∼**or** *n*
professeur *m*; (*for skiing, driving*)
moniteur *m*.
instrument [ˈɪnstrəmənt] *n* instrument
m; ∼**al** [-ˈmɛntl] *a*: **to be** ∼**al in**
contribuer à; ∼ **panel** *n* tableau *m* de
bord.
insufficient [ɪnsəˈfɪʃənt] *a* insuffi-
sant(e).
insular [ˈɪnsjulə*] *a* insulaire; (*outlook*)
étroit(e); (*person*) aux vues étroites.
insulate [ˈɪnsjuleɪt] *vt* isoler; (*against
sound*) insonoriser; **insulating tape** *n*
ruban isolant; **insulation** [-ˈleɪʃən] *n*
isolation *f*; insonorisation *f*.
insulin [ˈɪnsjulɪn] *n* insuline *f*.
insult *n* [ˈɪnsʌlt] insulte *f*, affront *m* // *vt*
[ɪnˈsʌlt] insulter, faire un affront à.
insuperable [ɪnˈsjuːprəbl] *a* insurmontable.
insurance [ɪnˈʃuərəns] *n* assurance *f*;
fire/life ∼ assurance-incendie/-vie; ∼
policy *n* police *f* d'assurance.
insure [ɪnˈʃuə*] *vt* assurer.
intact [ɪnˈtækt] *a* intact(e).
intake [ˈɪnteɪk] *n* (*TECH*) admission *f*;
adduction *f*; (*of food*) consommation *f*;
(*Brit SCOL*): **an** ∼ **of 200 a year** 200
admissions *fpl* par an.
integral [ˈɪntɪgrəl] *a* intégral(e); (*part*)
intégrant(e).
integrate [ˈɪntɪgreɪt] *vt* intégrer // *vi*
s'intégrer.
integrity [ɪnˈtɛgrɪtɪ] *n* intégrité *f*.
intellect [ˈɪntəlɛkt] *n* intelligence *f*;
∼**ual** [-ˈlɛktjuəl] *a, n* intellectuel(le).
intelligence [ɪnˈtɛlɪdʒəns] *n* intelligence
f; (*MIL etc*) informations *fpl*, renseignements *mpl*.
intelligent [ɪnˈtɛlɪdʒənt] *a* intelligent(e).
intend [ɪnˈtɛnd] *vt* (*gift etc*): **to** ∼ **sth
for** destiner qch à; **to** ∼ **to do** avoir
l'intention de faire; ∼**ed** *a* (*insult*)
intentionnel(le); (*journey*) projeté(e);
(*effect*) voulu(e).
intense [ɪnˈtɛns] *a* intense; (*person*)
véhément(e); ∼**ly** *ad* intensément;
profondément.
intensive [ɪnˈtɛnsɪv] *a* intensif(ive); ∼
care unit *n* service *m* de réanimation.
intent [ɪnˈtɛnt] *n* intention *f* // *a*
attentif(ive), absorbé(e); **to all** ∼**s and
purposes** en fait, pratiquement; **to be** ∼
on doing sth être (bien) décidé à faire
qch.

intention [ɪn'tɛnʃən] *n* intention *f*; ~**al** *a* intentionnel(le), délibéré(e).

intently [ɪn'tɛntlɪ] *ad* attentivement.

interact [ɪntər'ækt] *vi* avoir une action réciproque.

interchange *n* ['ɪntətʃeɪndʒ] (*exchange*) échange *m*; (*on motorway*) échangeur *m* // *vt* [ɪntə'tʃeɪndʒ] échanger; mettre à la place l'un(e) de l'autre; ~**able** *a* interchangeable.

intercom ['ɪntəkɔm] *n* interphone *m*.

intercourse ['ɪntəkɔːs] *n* rapports *mpl*.

interest ['ɪntrɪst] *n* intérêt *m*; (*COMM: stake, share*) intérêts *mpl* // *vt* intéresser; ~**ed** *a* intéressé(e); **to be** ~**ed in** s'intéresser à; ~**ing** *a* intéressant(e); ~ **rate** *n* taux *m* d'intérêt.

interfere [ɪntə'fɪə*] *vi*: **to** ~ **in** (*quarrel, other people's business*) se mêler à; **to** ~ **with** (*object*) tripoter, toucher à; (*plans*) contrecarrer; (*duty*) être en conflit avec.

interference [ɪntə'fɪərəns] *n* (*gen*) intrusion *f*; (*PHYSICS*) interférence *f*; (*RADIO, TV*) parasites *mpl*.

interim ['ɪntərɪm] *a* provisoire; (*post*) intérimaire // *n*: **in the** ~ dans l'intérim.

interior [ɪn'tɪərɪə*] *n* intérieur *m* // *a* intérieur(e).

interlock [ɪntə'lɔk] *vi* s'enclencher.

interloper ['ɪntələupə*] *n* intrus/e.

interlude ['ɪntəluːd] *n* intervalle *m*; (*THEATRE*) intermède *m*.

intermediate [ɪntə'miːdɪət] *a* intermédiaire; (*SCOL: course, level*) moyen(ne).

intermission [ɪntə'mɪʃən] *n* pause *f*; (*THEATRE, CINEMA*) entracte *m*.

intern [ɪn'təːn] *vt* interner // *n* ['ɪntəːn] (*US*) interne *m/f*.

internal [ɪn'təːnl] *a* interne; (*dispute, reform etc*) intérieur(e); ~**ly** *ad* intérieurement; 'not to be taken ~ly' 'pour usage externe'; **I~ Revenue Service (IRS)** *n* (*US*) fisc *m*.

international [ɪntə'næʃənl] *a* international(e).

interplay ['ɪntəpleɪ] *n* effet *m* réciproque, jeu *m*.

interpret [ɪn'təːprɪt] *vt* interpréter // *vi* servir d'interprète; ~**er** *n* interprète *m/f*.

interrelated [ɪntərɪ'leɪtɪd] *a* en corrélation, en rapport étroit.

interrogate [ɪn'tɛrəugeɪt] *vt* interroger; (*suspect etc*) soumettre à un interrogatoire; **interrogation** [-'geɪʃən] *n* interrogation *f*; interrogatoire *m*; **interrogative** [ɪntə'rɔgətɪv] *a* interrogateur(trice).

interrupt [ɪntə'rʌpt] *vt* interrompre; ~**ion** [-'rʌpʃən] *n* interruption *f*.

intersect [ɪntə'sɛkt] *vt* couper, croiser // *vi* (*roads*) se croiser, se couper; ~**ion** [-'sɛkʃən] *n* intersection *f*; (*of roads*) croisement *m*.

intersperse [ɪntə'spəːs] *vt*: **to** ~ **with** parsemer de.

intertwine [ɪntə'twaɪn] *vt* entrelacer // *vi* s'entrelacer.

interval ['ɪntəvl] *n* intervalle *m*; (*Brit: SCOL*) récréation *f*; (: *THEATRE*) entracte *m*; (: *SPORT*) mi-temps *f*; **at** ~**s** par intervalles.

intervene [ɪntə'viːn] *vi* (*time*) s'écouler (entre-temps); (*event*) survenir; (*person*) intervenir; **intervention** [-'vɛnʃən] *n* intervention *f*.

interview ['ɪntəvjuː] *n* (*RADIO, TV etc*) interview *f*; (*for job*) entrevue *f* // *vt* interviewer; avoir une entrevue avec; ~**er** *n* interviewer *m*.

intestine [ɪn'tɛstɪn] *n* intestin *m*.

intimacy ['ɪntɪməsɪ] *n* intimité *f*.

intimate ['ɪntɪmət] *a* intime; (*knowledge*) approfondi(e) // *vt* ['ɪntɪmeɪt] suggérer, laisser entendre; (*announce*) faire savoir.

into ['ɪntuː] *prep* dans; ~ **pieces/French** en morceaux/français.

intolerable [ɪn'tɔlərəbl] *a* intolérable.

intolerance [ɪn'tɔlərns] *n* intolérance *f*.

intolerant [ɪn'tɔlərnt] *a*: ~ **of** intolérant(e) de; (*MED*) intolérant à.

intoxicate [ɪn'tɔksɪkeɪt] *vt* enivrer; ~**d** *a* ivre; **intoxication** [-'keɪʃən] *n* ivresse *f*.

intractable [ɪn'træktəbl] *a* (*child, temper*) indocile, insoumis(e); (*problem*) insoluble.

intransitive [ɪn'trænsɪtɪv] *a* intransitif(ive).

intravenous [ɪntrə'viːnəs] *a* intraveineux(euse).

in-tray ['ɪntreɪ] *n* courrier *m* 'arrivée'.

intricate ['ɪntrɪkət] *a* complexe, compliqué(e).

intrigue [ɪn'triːg] *n* intrigue *f* // *vt* intriguer // *vi* intriguer, comploter; **intriguing** *a* fascinant(e).

intrinsic [ɪn'trɪnsɪk] *a* intrinsèque.

introduce [ɪntrə'djuːs] *vt* introduire; **to** ~ **sb (to sb)** présenter qn (à qn); **to** ~ **sb to** (*pastime, technique*) initier qn à; **introduction** [-'dʌkʃən] *n* introduction *f*; (*of person*) présentation *f*; **introductory** *a* préliminaire, d'introduction.

intrude [ɪn'truːd] *vi* (*person*) être importun(e); **to** ~ **on** (*conversation etc*) s'immiscer dans; ~**r** *n* intrus/e.

intuition [ɪntjuː'ɪʃən] *n* intuition *f*.

inundate ['ɪnʌndeɪt] *vt*: **to** ~ **with** inonder de.

invade [ɪn'veɪd] *vt* envahir.

invalid *n* ['ɪnvəlɪd] malade *m/f*; (*with disability*) invalide *m/f* // *a* [ɪn'vælɪd] (*not valid*) invalide, non valide.

invaluable [ɪn'væljuəbl] *a* inestimable, inappréciable.

invariably [ɪn'vɛərɪəblɪ] *ad* invariablement; toujours.

invasion [ɪn'veɪʒən] n invasion f.
invent [ɪn'vɛnt] vt inventer; **~ion**
[ɪn'vɛnʃən] n invention f; **~ive** a
inventif(ive); **~or** n inventeur/trice.
inventory ['ɪnvəntrɪ] n inventaire m.
invert [ɪn'vɜ:t] vt intervertir; (cup,
object) retourner; **~ed commas** npl
(Brit) guillemets mpl.
invest [ɪn'vɛst] vt investir // vi faire un
investissement.
investigate [ɪn'vɛstɪgeɪt] vt étudier,
examiner; (crime) faire une enquête
sur; **investigation** [-'geɪʃən] n examen
m; (of crime) enquête f, investigation f.
investment [ɪn'vɛstmənt] n investissement m, placement m.
investor [ɪn'vɛstə*] n épargnant/e,
actionnaire m/f.
invidious [ɪn'vɪdɪəs] a injuste; (task)
déplaisant(e).
invigilate [ɪn'vɪdʒɪleɪt] vt surveiller // vi
(in exam) être de surveillance.
invigorating [ɪn'vɪgəreɪtɪŋ] a vivi-
fiant(e); stimulant(e).
invisible [ɪn'vɪzɪbl] a invisible; **~ ink** n
encre f sympathique.
invitation [ɪnvɪ'teɪʃən] n invitation f.
invite [ɪn'vaɪt] vt inviter; (opinions etc)
demander; (trouble) chercher; **inviting**
a engageant(e), attrayant(e); (gesture)
encourageant(e).
invoice ['ɪnvɔɪs] n facture f.
involuntary [ɪn'vɔləntrɪ] a involontaire.
involve [ɪn'vɔlv] vt (entail) entraîner,
nécessiter; (associate): **to ~ sb (in)** impliquer qn (dans), mêler qn (à); faire
participer qn (à); **~d** a complexe; **to
feel ~d** se sentir concerné(e); **~ment** n
mise f en jeu; implication f; **~ment (in)**
participation f (à); rôle m (dans).
inward ['ɪnwəd] a (movement) vers
l'intérieur; (thought, feeling) profond(e),
intime; **~(s)** ad vers l'intérieur.
I/O abbr (COMPUT: = input/output) E/S.
iodine ['aɪəʊdi:n] n iode m.
iota [aɪ'əʊtə] n (fig) brin m, grain m.
IOU n abbr (= I owe you) reconnaissance
f de dette.
IQ n abbr (= intelligence quotient) Q.I. m
(= quotient intellectuel).
IRA n abbr (= Irish Republican Army)
IRA f.
Iran [ɪ'rɑ:n] n Iran m.
Iraq [ɪ'rɑ:k] n Irak m.
irate [aɪ'reɪt] a courroucé(e).
Ireland ['aɪlənd] n Irlande f.
iris, ~es ['aɪrɪs, -ɪz] n iris m.
Irish ['aɪrɪʃ] a irlandais(e) // npl: **the ~**
les Irlandais; **~man** n Irlandais m; **~
Sea** n mer f d'Irlande; **~woman** n
Irlandaise f.
irksome ['ɜ:ksəm] a ennuyeux(euse).
iron ['aɪən] n fer m; (for clothes) fer m
à repasser // a de or en fer // vt
(clothes) repasser; **to ~ out** vt

(crease) faire disparaître au fer; (fig)
aplanir; faire disparaître; **the ~ curtain** n le rideau de fer.
ironic(al) [aɪ'rɔnɪk(l)] a ironique.
ironing ['aɪənɪŋ] n repassage m; **~
board** n planche f à repasser.
ironmonger ['aɪənmʌŋgə*] n (Brit)
quincailler m; **~'s (shop)** n quincaillerie f.
irony ['aɪrənɪ] n ironie f.
irrational [ɪ'ræʃənl] a irrationnel(le);
déraisonnable; qui manque de logique.
irregular [ɪ'rɛgjulə*] a irrégulier(ère).
irrelevant [ɪ'rɛləvənt] a sans rapport,
hors de propos.
irresistible [ɪrɪ'zɪstɪbl] a irrésistible.
irrespective [ɪrɪ'spɛktɪv]: **~ of** prep
sans tenir compte de.
irresponsible [ɪrɪ'spɔnsɪbl] a (act)
irréfléchi(e); (person) qui n'a pas le
sens des responsabilités.
irrigate ['ɪrɪgeɪt] vt irriguer; **irrigation**
[-'geɪʃən] n irrigation f.
irritable ['ɪrɪtəbl] a irritable.
irritate ['ɪrɪteɪt] vt irriter; **irritating** a
irritant(e); **irritation** [-'teɪʃən] n irritation f.
IRS n abbr of **Internal Revenue
Service**.
is [ɪz] vb see **be**.
Islam ['ɪzlɑ:m] n Islam m.
island ['aɪlənd] n île f; (also: **traffic ~**)
refuge m (pour piétons); **~er** n
habitant/e d'une île, insulaire m/f.
isle [aɪl] n île f.
isn't ['ɪznt] = **is not**.
isolate ['aɪsəleɪt] vt isoler; **~d** a
isolé(e).
Israel ['ɪzreɪl] n Israël m; **~i** [ɪz'reɪlɪ] a
israélien(ne) // n Israélien/ne.
issue ['ɪʃu:] n question f, problème m;
(outcome) résultat m, issue f; (of banknotes etc) émission f; (of newspaper etc)
numéro m; (offspring) descendance f //
vt (rations, equipment) distribuer;
(orders) donner; (book) faire paraître,
publier; (banknotes, cheques, stamps)
émettre, mettre en circulation; **at ~** en
jeu, en cause; **to take ~ with sb (over)**
exprimer son désaccord avec qn (sur).
it [ɪt] pronoun **1** (specific: subject)
il(elle); (: direct object) le(la), l'; (: indirect object) lui; **~'s on the table** c'est
or il (or elle) est sur la table; **about/
from/of ~** en; **I spoke to him about ~** je
lui en ai parlé; **what did you learn from
~?** qu'est-ce que vous en avez retiré?;
I'm proud of ~ j'en suis fier; **in/to ~** y;
put the book in ~ mettez-y le livre; **he
agreed to ~** il y a consenti; **did you go to
~?** (party, concert etc) est-ce que vous y
êtes allé(s)?
2 (impersonal) il; ce; **~'s raining** il
pleut; **~'s Friday tomorrow** demain c'est
vendredi or nous sommes vendredi; **~'s**

6 o'clock il est 6 heures; who is ~? - ~'s me qui est-ce? - c'est moi.

Italian [ɪ'tæljən] *a* italien(ne) // *n* Italien/ne; (*LING*) italien *m*.

italic [ɪ'tælɪk] *a* italique.

Italy ['ɪtəlɪ] *n* Italie *f*.

itch [ɪtʃ] *n* démangeaison *f* // *vi* (*person*) éprouver des démangeaisons; (*part of body*) démanger; **I'm ~ing to do** l'envie me démange de faire; **~y** *a* qui démange; **to be ~y** = to ~.

it'd ['ɪtd] = **it would, it had.**

item ['aɪtəm] *n* (*gen*) article *m*; (*on agenda*) question *f*, point *m*; (*in programme*) numéro *m*; (*also*: **news ~**) nouvelle *f*; **~ize** *vt* détailler, spécifier.

itinerary [aɪ'tɪnərərɪ] *n* itinéraire *m*.

it'll ['ɪtl] = **it will, it shall.**

its [ɪts] *a* son(sa), ses *pl*.

it's [ɪts] = **it is, it has.**

itself [ɪt'sɛlf] *pronoun* (*emphatic*) lui-même(elle-même); (*reflexive*) se.

ITV *n abbr* (*Brit*: = *Independent Television*) chaîne fonctionnant en concurrence avec la BBC.

I.U.D. *n abbr* (= *intra-uterine device*) DIU *m* (dispositif intra-utérin), stérilet *m*.

I've [aɪv] = **I have.**

ivory ['aɪvərɪ] *n* ivoire *m*.

ivy ['aɪvɪ] *n* lierre *m*.

J

jab [dʒæb] *vt*: **to ~ sth into** enfoncer *or* planter qch dans // *n* coup *m*; (*MED*: *col*) piqûre *f*.

jack [dʒæk] *n* (*AUT*) cric *m*; (*CARDS*) valet *m*; **to ~ up** *vt* soulever (au cric).

jackal ['dʒækl] *n* chacal *m*.

jackdaw ['dʒækdɔ:] *n* choucas *m*.

jacket ['dʒækɪt] *n* veste *f*, veston *m*.

jack-knife ['dʒæknaɪf] *vi*: **the lorry ~d** la remorque (du camion) s'est mise en travers.

jack plug *n* (*ELEC*) jack *m*.

jackpot ['dʒækpɔt] *n* gros lot.

jaded ['dʒeɪdɪd] *a* éreinté(e), fatigué(e).

jagged ['dʒægɪd] *a* dentelé(e).

jail [dʒeɪl] *n* prison *f* // *vt* emprisonner, mettre en prison; **~er** *n* geôlier/ière.

jam [dʒæm] *n* confiture *f*; (*of shoppers etc*) cohue *f*; (*also*: **traffic ~**) embouteillage *m* // *vt* (*passage etc*) encombrer, obstruer; (*mechanism, drawer etc*) bloquer, coincer; (*RADIO*) brouiller // *vi* (*mechanism, sliding part*) se coincer, se bloquer; (*gun*) s'enrayer; **to ~ sth into** entasser *or* comprimer qch dans; enfoncer qch dans.

jangle ['dʒæŋgl] *vi* cliqueter.

janitor ['dʒænɪtə*] *n* (*caretaker*) huissier *m*; concierge *m*.

January ['dʒænjuərɪ] *n* janvier *m*.

Japan [dʒə'pæn] *n* Japon *m*; **~ese** [dʒæpə'ni:z] *a* japonais(e) // *n* (*pl inv*) Japonais/e; (*LING*) japonais *m*.

jar [dʒɑ:*] *n* (*glass*) pot *m*, bocal *m* // *vi* (*sound*) produire un son grinçant *or* discordant; (*colours etc*) détonner, jurer.

jargon ['dʒɑ:gən] *n* jargon *m*.

jaundice ['dʒɔ:ndɪs] *n* jaunisse *f*; **~d** *a* (*fig*) envieux(euse), désapprobateur(trice).

jaunt [dʒɔ:nt] *n* balade *f*; **~y** *a* enjoué(e); désinvolte.

javelin ['dʒævlɪn] *n* javelot *m*.

jaw [dʒɔ:] *n* mâchoire *f*.

jay [dʒeɪ] *n* geai *m*.

jaywalker ['dʒeɪwɔ:kə*] *n* piéton indiscipliné.

jazz [dʒæz] *n* jazz *m*; **to ~ up** *vt* animer, égayer.

jealous ['dʒɛləs] *a* jaloux(euse); **~y** *n* jalousie *f*.

jeans [dʒi:nz] *npl* (blue-)jean *m*.

jeer [dʒɪə*] *vi*: **to ~ (at)** huer; se moquer cruellement (de), railler.

jelly ['dʒɛlɪ] *n* gelée *f*; **~fish** *n* méduse *f*.

jeopardy ['dʒɛpədɪ] *n*: **to be in ~** être en danger *or* péril.

jerk [dʒə:k] *n* secousse *f*; saccade *f*; sursaut *m*, spasme *m* // *vt* donner une secousse à // *vi* (*vehicles*) cahoter.

jerkin ['dʒə:kɪn] *n* blouson *m*.

jersey ['dʒə:zɪ] *n* tricot *m*.

jest [dʒɛst] *n* plaisanterie *f*.

jet [dʒɛt] *n* (*gas, liquid*) jet *m*; (*AVIAT*) avion *m* à réaction, jet *m*; **~-black** *a* (d'un noir) de jais; **~ engine** *n* moteur *m* à réaction; **~ lag** *n* décalage *m* horaire.

jettison ['dʒɛtɪsn] *vt* jeter par-dessus bord.

jetty ['dʒɛtɪ] *n* jetée *f*, digue *f*.

Jew [dʒu:] *n* Juif *m*.

jewel ['dʒu:əl] *n* bijou *m*, joyau *m*; **~ler** *n* bijoutier/ère, joaillier *m*; **~ler's (shop)** *n* bijouterie *f*, joaillerie *f*; **~lery** *n* bijoux *mpl*.

Jewess ['dʒu:ɪs] *n* Juive *f*.

Jewish ['dʒu:ɪʃ] *a* juif(juive).

jib [dʒɪb] *n* (*NAUT*) foc *m*.

jibe [dʒaɪb] *n* sarcasme *m*.

jiffy ['dʒɪfɪ] *n* (*col*): **in a ~** en un clin d'œil.

jig [dʒɪg] *n* gigue *f*.

jigsaw ['dʒɪgsɔ:] *n* (*also*: **~ puzzle**) puzzle *m*.

jilt [dʒɪlt] *vt* laisser tomber, plaquer.

jingle ['dʒɪŋgl] *n* (*advert*) couplet *m* publicitaire // *vi* cliqueter, tinter.

jinx [dʒɪŋks] *n* (*col*) (mauvais) sort.

jitters ['dʒɪtəz] *npl* (*col*): **to get the ~** avoir la trouille *or* la frousse.

job [dʒɔb] *n* travail *m*; (*employment*) emploi *m*, poste *m*, place *f*; **it's a good ~ that —** c'est heureux *or* c'est une chance que —; **just the ~!** (c'est) juste *or* exactement ce qu'il faut!; ~ **centre** *n* (*Brit*) agence *f* pour l'emploi; ~**less** *a* sans travail, au chômage.

jockey ['dʒɔkɪ] *n* jockey *m* // *vi*: to ~ **for position** manœuvrer pour être bien placé.

jocular ['dʒɔkjulə*] *a* jovial(e), enjoué(e); facétieux(euse).

jog [dʒɔg] *vt* secouer // *vi* (*SPORT*) faire du footing; **to ~ along** *vi* cahoter; trotter; ~**ging** *n* footing *m*.

join [dʒɔɪn] *vt* unir, assembler; (*become member of*) s'inscrire à; (*meet*) rejoindre, retrouver; se joindre à // *vi* (*roads, rivers*) se rejoindre, se rencontrer // *n* raccord *m*; **to ~ in** *vi* se mettre de la partie // *vt fus* se mêler à; (*thanks etc*) s'associer à; **to ~ up** *vi* s'engager.

joiner ['dʒɔɪnə*] *n* menuisier *m*; ~**y** *n* menuiserie *f*.

joint [dʒɔɪnt] *n* (*TECH*) jointure *f*; joint *m*; (*ANAT*) articulation *f*, jointure; (*Brit*: *CULIN*) rôti *m*; (*col*: *place*) boîte *f* // *a* commun(e); ~ **account** *n* (*with bank etc*) compte joint; ~**ly** *ad* ensemble, en commun.

joist [dʒɔɪst] *n* solive *f*.

joke [dʒəuk] *n* plaisanterie *f*; (*also*: **practical** ~) farce *f* // *vi* plaisanter; **to play a ~ on** jouer un tour à, faire une farce à; ~**r** *n* plaisantin *m*, blagueur/euse; (*CARDS*) joker *m*.

jolly ['dʒɔlɪ] *a* gai(e), enjoué(e) // *ad* (*col*) rudement, drôlement.

jolt [dʒəult] *n* cahot *m*, secousse *f* // *vt* cahoter, secouer.

Jordan ['dʒɔ:dən] *n* Jordanie *f*.

jostle ['dʒɔsl] *vt* bousculer, pousser.

jot [dʒɔt] *n*: **not one** ~ pas un brin; **to ~ down** *vt* inscrire rapidement, noter; ~**ter** *n* (*Brit*) cahier *m* (de brouillon); bloc-notes *m*.

journal ['dʒə:nl] *n* journal *m*; ~**ism** *n* journalisme *m*; ~**ist** *n* journaliste *m/f*.

journey ['dʒə:nɪ] *n* voyage *m*; (*distance covered*) trajet *m* // *vi* voyager.

joy [dʒɔɪ] *n* joie *f*; ~**ful**, ~**ous** *a* joyeux(euse); ~ **ride** *n* virée *f* (*gén avec une voiture volée*); ~**stick** *n* (*AVIAT, COMPUT*) manche *m* à balai.

J.P. *n abbr see* **justice**.

Jr, Jun., Junr *abbr of* **junior**.

jubilant ['dʒu:bɪlnt] *a* triomphant(e); réjoui(e).

judge [dʒʌdʒ] *n* juge *m* // *vt* juger; **judg(e)ment** *n* jugement *m*; (*punishment*) châtiment *m*.

judicial [dʒu:'dɪʃl] *a* judiciaire.

judiciary [dʒu:'dɪʃɪərɪ] *n* (pouvoir *m*) judiciaire *m*.

judo ['dʒu:dəu] *n* judo *m*.

jug [dʒʌg] *n* pot *m*, cruche *f*.

juggernaut ['dʒʌgənɔ:t] *n* (*Brit*: *huge truck*) mastodonte *m*.

juggle ['dʒʌgl] *vi* jongler; ~**r** *n* jongleur *m*.

Jugoslav *etc* ['ju:gəuslɑ:v] = **Yugoslav** *etc*.

juice [dʒu:s] *n* jus *m*.

juicy ['dʒu:sɪ] *a* juteux(euse).

jukebox ['dʒu:kbɔks] *n* juke-box *m*.

July [dʒu:'laɪ] *n* juillet *m*.

jumble ['dʒʌmbl] *n* fouillis *m* // *vt* (*also*: ~ **up**) mélanger, brouiller; ~ **sale** *n* (*Brit*) vente *f* de charité.

jumbo ['dʒʌmbəu] *a*: ~ **jet** avion géant, gros porteur (à réaction).

jump [dʒʌmp] *vi* sauter, bondir; (*start*) sursauter; (*increase*) monter en flèche // *vt* sauter, franchir // *n* saut *m*, bond *m*; sursaut *m*.

jumper ['dʒʌmpə*] *n* (*Brit*: *pullover*) pull-over *m*; (*US*: *dress*) robe-chasuble *f*; ~ **cables** *npl* (*US*) = **jump leads**.

jump leads *npl* (*Brit*) câbles *mpl* de démarrage.

jumpy ['dʒʌmpɪ] *a* nerveux(euse), agité(e).

junction ['dʒʌŋkʃən] *n* (*Brit*: *of roads*) carrefour *m*; (*of rails*) embranchement *m*.

juncture ['dʒʌŋktʃə*] *n*: **at this** ~ à ce moment-là, sur ces entrefaites.

June [dʒu:n] *n* juin *m*.

jungle ['dʒʌŋgl] *n* jungle *f*.

junior ['dʒu:nɪə*] *a, n*: **he's** ~ **to me** (by 2 years), **he's my** ~ (by 2 years) il est mon cadet (de 2 ans), il est plus jeune que moi (de 2 ans); **he's** ~ **to me** (*seniority*) il est en dessous de moi (dans la hiérarchie), j'ai plus d'ancienneté que lui; ~ **school** *n* (*Brit*) école *f* primaire, cours moyen.

junk [dʒʌŋk] *n* (*rubbish*) bric-à-brac *m inv*; (*ship*) jonque *f*; ~ **food** *n* snacks *mpl* (vite prêts); ~ **shop** *n* (boutique *f* de) brocanteur *m*.

juror ['dʒuərə*] *n* juré *m*.

jury ['dʒuərɪ] *n* jury *m*.

just [dʒʌst] *a* juste // *ad*: **he's** ~ **done it/left** il vient de le faire/partir; ~ **as I expected** exactement *or* précisément comme je m'y attendais; ~ **right/two o'clock** exactement *or* juste ce qu'il faut/deux heures; **she's** ~ **as clever as you** elle est tout aussi intelligente que vous; **it's** ~ **as well that ...** heureusement que ...; ~ **as he was leaving** au moment *or* à l'instant précis où il partait; ~ **before/enough/here** juste avant/assez/là; **it's** ~ **me/a mistake** ce n'est que moi/(rien) qu'une erreur; ~ **missed/caught** manqué/attrapé de justesse; ~ **listen to this!** écoutez un peu ça!

justice ['dʒʌstɪs] *n* justice *f*; **J~ of the Peace (J.P.)** *n* juge *m* de paix.

justify ['dʒʌstɪfaɪ] *vt* justifier.

jut [dʒʌt] *vi* (*also*: ~ **out**) dépasser, faire saillie.

juvenile ['dʒu:vənaɪl] *a* juvénile; (*court, books*) pour enfants // *n* adolescent/e.

K

K *abbr* (= *one thousand*) K; (= *kilobyte*) Ko.

kangaroo [kæŋgə'ru:] *n* kangourou *m*.

karate [kə'rɑ:tɪ] *n* karaté *m*.

kebab [kə'bæb] *n* kébab *m*.

keel [ki:l] *n* quille *f*; on an even ~ (*fig*) à flot.

keen [ki:n] *a* (*interest, desire, competition*) vif(vive); (*eye, intelligence*) pénétrant(e); (*edge*) effilé(e); (*eager*) plein(e) d'enthousiasme; to be ~ to do *or* on doing sth désirer vivement faire qch, tenir beaucoup à faire qch; to be ~ on sth/sb aimer beaucoup qch/qn.

keep [ki:p] *vb* (*pt, pp* kept) *vt* (*retain, preserve*) garder; (*hold back*) retenir; (*a shop, the books, a diary, a promise*) tenir; (*feed: one's family etc*) entretenir, assurer la subsistance de; (*chickens, bees etc*) élever // *vi* (*food*) se conserver; (*remain: in a certain state or place*) rester // *n* (*of castle*) donjon *m*; (*food etc*): enough for his ~ assez pour (assurer) sa subsistance; (*col*): for ~s pour de bon, pour toujours; to ~ doing sth continuer à faire qch; faire qch continuellement; to ~ sb from doing/sth from happening empêcher qn de faire or que qch (ne) fasse/que qch (n')arrive; to ~ sb happy/a place tidy faire que qn soit content/qu'un endroit reste propre; to ~ sth to o.s. garder qch pour soi, tenir qch secret; to ~ sth (back) from sb cacher qch à qn; to ~ time (*clock*) être à l'heure, ne pas retarder; to ~ on *vi* continuer; to ~ on doing continuer à faire; to ~ out *vt* empêcher d'entrer; '~ out' 'défense d'entrer'; to ~ up *vi* se maintenir // *vt* continuer, maintenir; to ~ up with se maintenir au niveau de; ~er *n* gardien/ne; ~-fit *n* gymnastique *f* de maintien; ~ing *n* (*care*) garde *f*; in ~ing with à l'avenant de; en accord avec; ~sake *n* souvenir *m*.

keg [kɛg] *n* barrique *f*, tonnelet *m*.

kennel ['kɛnl] *n* niche *f*; ~s *npl* chenil *m*.

kept [kɛpt] *pt, pp of* keep.

kerb [kə:b] *n* (*Brit*) bordure *f* du trottoir.

kernel ['kə:nl] *n* amande *f*; (*fig*) noyau *m*.

kettle ['kɛtl] *n* bouilloire *f*.

kettle drums *npl* timbales *fpl*.

key [ki:] *n* (*gen, MUS*) clé *f*; (*of piano, typewriter*) touche *f* // *vt* (*also*: ~ in) introduire au clavier; ~board *n* clavier *m*; ~ed up *a* (*person*) surexcité(e); ~hole *n* trou *m* de la serrure; ~note *n* (*fig*) note dominante; ~ ring *n* porteclés *m*.

khaki ['kɑ:kɪ] *a*, *n* kaki (*m*).

kick [kɪk] *vt* donner un coup de pied à // *vi* (*horse*) ruer // *n* coup *m* de pied; (*of rifle*) recul *m*; (*thrill*): he does it for ~s il le fait parce que ça l'excite, il le fait pour le plaisir; to ~ off *vi* (*SPORT*) donner le coup d'envoi.

kid [kɪd] *n* (*col: child*) gamin/e, gosse *m/f*; (*animal, leather*) chevreau *m* // *vi* (*col*) plaisanter, blaguer.

kidnap ['kɪdnæp] *vt* enlever, kidnapper; ~per *n* ravisseur/euse; ~ping *n* enlèvement *m*.

kidney ['kɪdnɪ] *n* (*ANAT*) rein *m*; (*CULIN*) rognon *m*.

kill [kɪl] *vt* tuer; (*fig*) faire échouer; détruire; supprimer // *n* mise *f* à mort; ~er *n* tueur/euse; meurtrier/ère; ~ing *n* meurtre *m*; tuerie *f*, massacre *m*; ~joy *n* rabat-joie *m/f*.

kiln [kɪln] *n* four *m*.

kilo ['ki:ləʊ] *n* kilo *m*; ~byte *n* (*COMPUT*) kilo-octet *m*; ~gram(me) ['kɪləʊgræm] *n* kilogramme *m*; ~metre, (*US*) ~meter ['kɪləmi:tə*] *n* kilomètre *m*; ~watt ['kɪləʊwɒt] *n* kilowatt *m*.

kilt [kɪlt] *n* kilt *m*.

kin [kɪn] *n see* next, kith.

kind [kaɪnd] *a* gentil(le), aimable // *n* sorte *f*, espèce *f*; (*species*) genre *m*; to be two of a ~ se ressembler; in ~ (*COMM*) en nature.

kindergarten ['kɪndəgɑ:tn] *n* jardin *m* d'enfants.

kind-hearted [kaɪnd'hɑ:tɪd] *a* bon(bonne).

kindle ['kɪndl] *vt* allumer, enflammer.

kindly ['kaɪndlɪ] *a* bienveillant(e), plein(e) de gentillesse // *ad* avec bonté; will you ~ ... auriez-vous la bonté *or* l'obligeance de ...

kindness ['kaɪndnɪs] *n* bonté *f*, gentillesse *f*.

kindred ['kɪndrɪd] *a* apparenté(e); ~ spirit âme *f* sœur.

king [kɪŋ] *n* roi *m*; ~dom *n* royaume *m*; ~fisher *n* martin-pêcheur *m*; ~-size *a* long format *inv*; format géant *inv*.

kinky ['kɪŋkɪ] *a* (*fig*) excentrique; aux goûts spéciaux.

kiosk ['ki:ɒsk] *n* kiosque *m*; (*Brit TEL*) cabine *f* (téléphonique).

kipper ['kɪpə*] *n* hareng fumé et salé.

kiss [kɪs] *n* baiser *m* // *vt* embrasser; to ~ (each other) s'embrasser.

kit [kɪt] *n* équipement *m*, matériel *m*; (*set of tools etc*) trousse *f*; (*for assembly*) kit *m*.

kitchen ['kɪtʃɪn] *n* cuisine *f*; ~ sink *n* évier *m*.

kite [kaɪt] *n* (*toy*) cerf-volant *m*.

kith [kɪθ] *n*: ~ and kin parents et amis *mpl*.

kitten ['kɪtn] *n* petit chat, chaton *m*.

kitty ['kɪtɪ] *n* (*money*) cagnotte *f*.

knack [næk] *n*: to have the ~ (of doing)

avoir le coup (pour faire); there's a ~ il y a un coup à prendre *or* une combine.

knapsack ['næpsæk] *n* musette *f*.

knead [ni:d] *vt* pétrir.

knee [ni:] *n* genou *m*; ~**cap** *n* rotule *f*.

kneel [ni:l], *pt*, *pp* **knelt** [ni:l, nɛlt] *vi* (*also*: ~ **down**) s'agenouiller.

knell [nɛl] *n* glas *m*.

knew [nju:] *pt of* **know**.

knickers ['nɪkəz] *npl* (*Brit*) culotte *f* (*de femme*).

knife [naɪf] *n* (*pl* **knives**) couteau *m* // *vt* poignarder, frapper d'un coup de couteau.

knight [naɪt] *n* chevalier *m*; (*CHESS*) cavalier *m*; ~**hood** *n* (*title*): to get a ~**hood** être fait chevalier.

knit [nɪt] *vt* tricoter; (*fig*): to ~ **together** *vt* unir // *vi* (*broken bones*) se ressouder; ~**ting** *n* tricot *m*; ~**ting needle** *n* aiguille *f* à tricoter; ~**wear** *n* tricots *mpl*, lainages *mpl*.

knives [naɪvz] *npl of* **knife**.

knob [nɔb] *n* bouton *m*.

knock [nɔk] *vt* frapper; heurter; (*fig*: *col*) dénigrer // *vi* (*at door etc*): to ~ **at**/**on** frapper à/sur // *n* coup *m*; to ~ **down** *vt* renverser; to ~ **off** *vi* (*col*: *finish*) s'arrêter (de travailler); to ~ **out** *vt* assommer; (*BOXING*) mettre k.-o.; to ~ **over** *vt* (*person*) renverser; (*object*) faire tomber; ~**er** *n* (*on door*) heurtoir *m*; ~**-kneed** *a* aux genoux cagneux; ~**out** *n* (*BOXING*) knock-out *m*, K.-O. *m*.

knot [nɔt] *n* (*gen*) nœud *m* // *vt* nouer; ~**ty** *a* (*fig*) épineux(euse).

know [nəu] *vt* (*pt* **knew**, *pp* **known**) savoir; (*person*, *place*) connaître; to ~ **how to do** savoir comment faire; to ~ **how to swim** savoir nager; to ~ **about**/**of** sth être au courant de/connaître qch; to ~ **about** *or* **of** sb savoir entendu parler de qn; ~**-all** *n* je-sais-tout *m/f*; ~**-how** *n* savoir-faire *m*, technique *f*, compétence *f*; ~**ing** *a* (*look etc*) entendu(e); ~**ingly** *ad* sciemment; (*smile*, *look*) d'un air entendu.

knowledge ['nɔlɪdʒ] *n* connaissance *f*; (*learning*) connaissances, savoir *m*; ~**able** *a* bien informé(e).

known [nəun] *pp of* **know**.

knuckle ['nʌkl] *n* articulation *f* (*des phalanges*), jointure *f*.

Koran [kɔ'rɑ:n] *n* Coran *m*.

Korea [kə'rɪə] *n* Corée *f*.

kosher ['kəuʃə*] *a* kascher *inv*.

L

lab [læb] *n abbr* (= *laboratory*) labo *m*.

label ['leɪbl] *n* étiquette *f*; (*brand*: *of record*) marque *f* // *vt* étiqueter.

laboratory [lə'bɔrətərɪ] *n* laboratoire *m*.

labour, (*US*) **labor** ['leɪbə*] *n* (*task*) travail *m*; (*also*: ~ **force**) main-d'œuvre *f*; (*MED*) travail, accouchement *m* // *vi*: to ~ (**at**) travailler dur (à), peiner (sur); **in** ~ (*MED*) en travail; **L~, the L~ party** (*Brit*) le parti travailliste, les travaillistes *mpl*; ~**ed** *a* lourd(e), laborieux(euse); ~**er** *n* manœuvre *m*; (*on farm*) ouvrier *m* agricole.

lace [leɪs] *n* dentelle *f*; (*of shoe etc*) lacet *m* // *vt* (*shoe*) lacer.

lack [læk] *n* manque *m* // *vt* manquer de; **through** *or* ~ **of** faute de, par manque de; **to be ~ing** manquer, faire défaut; **to be ~ing in** manquer de.

lackadaisical [lækə'deɪzɪkl] *a* non-chalant(e), indolent(e).

lacquer ['lækə*] *n* laque *f*.

lad [læd] *n* garçon *m*, gars *m*.

ladder ['lædə*] *n* échelle *f*; (*Brit*: *in tights*) maille filée // *vt*, *vi* (*Brit*: *tights*) filer.

laden ['leɪdn] *a*: ~ (**with**) chargé(e) (de).

ladle ['leɪdl] *n* louche *f*.

lady ['leɪdɪ] *n* dame *f*; dame (*du monde*); **L~ Smith** lady Smith; **the ladies' (room)** les toilettes *fpl* des dames; ~**bird**, (*US*) ~**bug** *n* coccinelle *f*; ~**in-waiting** *n* dame *f* d'honneur; ~**like** *a* distingué(e); ~**ship** *n*: **your** ~**ship** Madame la comtesse (*or* la baronne *etc*).

lag [læg] *vi* (*also*: ~ **behind**) rester en arrière, traîner // *vt* (*pipes*) calorifuger.

lager ['lɑ:gə*] *n* bière blonde.

lagoon [lə'gu:n] *n* lagune *f*.

laid [leɪd] *pt*, *pp of* **lay**; ~ **back** *a* (*col*) relaxe, décontracté(e).

lain [leɪn] *pp of* **lie**.

lair [lɛə*] *n* tanière *f*, gîte *m*.

laity ['leɪətɪ] *n* laïques *mpl*.

lake [leɪk] *n* lac *m*.

lamb [læm] *n* agneau *m*.

lame [leɪm] *a* boiteux(euse).

lament [lə'mɛnt] *vt* pleurer, se lamenter sur.

laminated ['læmɪneɪtɪd] *a* laminé(e); (*windscreen*) (en verre) feuilleté.

lamp [læmp] *n* lampe *f*.

lampoon [læm'pu:n] *n* pamphlet *m*.

lamp: ~**post** *n* (*Brit*) réverbère *m*; ~**shade** *n* abat-jour *m inv*.

lance [lɑ:ns] *n* lance *f* // *vt* (*MED*) inciser; ~ **corporal** *n* (*Brit*) (soldat *m* de) première classe *m*.

land [lænd] *n* (*as opposed to sea*) terre *f* (*ferme*); (*country*) pays *m*; (*soil*) terre; terrain *m*; (*estate*) terre(s), domaine(s) *m(pl)* // *vi* (*from ship*) débarquer; (*AVIAT*) atterrir; (*fig*: *fall*) (re)tomber // *vt* (*obtain*) décrocher; (*passengers*, *goods*) débarquer; **to** ~ **up** *vi* atterrir, (finir par) se retrouver; ~**ing** *n* débarquement *m*; atterrissage *m*; (*of* *staircase*) palier *m*; **~ing stage** *n* (*Brit*) débarcadère *m*, embarcadère *m*; **~lady** *n* propriétaire *f*, logeuse *f*; **~lord** *n* propriétaire *m*, logeur *m*; (*of pub etc*) patron *m*; **~mark** *n* (point *m* de) repère *m*; to be a **~mark** (*fig*) faire date or époque; **~owner** *n* propriétaire foncier or terrien.

landscape ['lænskeɪp] *n* paysage *m*.

landslide ['lændslaɪd] *n* (GEO) glissement *m* (de terrain); (*fig*: POL) raz-de-marée (électoral).

lane [leɪn] *n* (*in country*) chemin *m*; (*in town*) ruelle *f*; (AUT) voie *f*; file *f*; (*in race*) couloir *m*.

language ['læŋgwɪdʒ] *n* langue *f*; (*way one speaks*) langage *m*; **bad ~** grossièretés *fpl*, langage grossier; **~ laboratory** *n* laboratoire *m* de langues.

languid ['læŋgwɪd] *a* languissant(e); langoureux(euse).

lank [læŋk] *a* (*hair*) raide et terne.

lanky ['læŋkɪ] *a* grand(e) et maigre, efflanqué(e).

lantern ['læntn] *n* lanterne *f*.

lap [læp] *n* (*of track*) tour *m* (de piste); (*of body*): in or on one's **~** sur les genoux // *a* (*also*: **~ up**) laper // *vi* (*waves*) clapoter.

lapel [lə'pɛl] *n* revers *m*.

Lapland ['læplænd] *n* Laponie *f*.

lapse [læps] *n* défaillance *f* // *vi* (LAW) cesser d'être en vigueur; se périmer; to **~ into bad habits** prendre de mauvaises habitudes; **~ of time** laps *m* de temps, intervalle *m*.

larceny ['lɑːsənɪ] *n* vol *m*.

lard [lɑːd] *n* saindoux *m*.

larder ['lɑːdə*] *n* garde-manger *m* inv.

large [lɑːdʒ] *a* grand(e); (*person, animal*) gros(grosse); at **~** (*free*) en liberté; (*generally*) en général; pour la plupart; **~ly** *ad* en grande partie.

lark [lɑːk] *n* (*bird*) alouette *f*; (*joke*) blague *f*, farce *f*; to **~ about** *vi* faire l'idiot, rigoler.

laryngitis [lærɪn'dʒaɪtɪs] *n* laryngite *f*.

laser ['leɪzə*] *n* laser *m*; **~ printer** *n* imprimante *f* laser.

lash [læʃ] *n* coup *m* de fouet; (*also*: eyelash) cil *m* // *vt* fouetter; (*tie*) attacher; to **~ out** *vi*: to **~ out** (at or against sb/sth) attaquer violemment (qn/qch); to **~ out (on sth)** (col: spend) se fendre (de qch).

lass [læs] *n* (jeune) fille *f*.

lasso [læ'suː] *n* lasso *m*.

last [lɑːst] *a* dernier(ère) // *ad* en dernier // *vi* durer; **~ week** la semaine dernière; **~ night** hier soir; la nuit dernière; at **~** enfin; **~ but one** avant-dernier(ère); **~-ditch** *a* (*attempt*) ultime, désespéré(e); **~ing** *a* durable; **~ly** *ad* en dernier lieu, pour finir; **~-minute** *a* de dernière minute.

latch [lætʃ] *n* loquet *m*.

late [leɪt] *a* (*not on time*) en retard; (*far on in day etc*) dernier(ère); tardif(ive); (*recent*) récent(e), dernier; (*former*) ancien(ne); (*dead*) défunt(e) // *ad* tard; (*behind time, schedule*) en retard; **of ~** dernièrement; **in ~ May** vers la fin (du mois) de mai, fin mai; **the ~ Mr X** feu M. X; **~comer** *n* retardataire *m/f*; **~ly** *ad* récemment.

later ['leɪtə*] *a* (*date etc*) ultérieur(e); (*version etc*) plus récent(e) // *ad* plus tard; **~ on** plus tard.

lateral ['lætərl] *a* latéral(e).

latest ['leɪtɪst] *a* tout(e) dernier(ère); at the **~** au plus tard.

lathe [leɪð] *n* tour *m*.

lather ['lɑːðə*] *n* mousse *f* (de savon).

Latin ['lætɪn] *n* latin *m* // *a* latin(e); **~ America** *n* Amérique latine; **~American** *a* d'Amérique latine.

latitude ['lætɪtjuːd] *n* latitude *f*.

latter ['lætə*] *a* deuxième, dernier(ère) // *n*: the **~** ce dernier, celui-ci; **~ly** *ad* dernièrement, récemment.

lattice ['lætɪs] *n* treillis *m*; treillage *m*.

laudable ['lɔːdəbl] *a* louable.

laugh [lɑːf] *n* rire *m* // *vi* rire; to **~ at** *vt fus* se moquer de; (*joke*) rire de; to **~ off** *vt* écarter or rejeter par une plaisanterie or par une boutade; **~able** *a* risible, ridicule; **~ing stock** *n*: the **~ing stock of** la risée de; **~ter** *n* rire *m*; rires *mpl*.

launch [lɔːntʃ] *n* lancement *m*; (*boat*) chaloupe *f*; (*also*: motor **~**) vedette *f* // *vt* (*ship, rocket, plan*) lancer; **~(ing) pad** *n* rampe *f* de lancement.

launder ['lɔːndə*] *vt* blanchir.

launderette [lɔːn'drɛt], (US) **laundromat** ['lɔːndrəmæt] *n* laverie *f* (automatique).

laundry ['lɔːndrɪ] *n* blanchisserie *f*; (*clothes*) linge *m*.

laureate ['lɔːrɪət] *a* see **poet**.

laurel ['lɔrl] *n* laurier *m*.

lava ['lɑːvə] *n* lave *f*.

lavatory ['lævətərɪ] *n* toilettes *fpl*.

lavender ['lævəndə*] *n* lavande *f*.

lavish ['lævɪʃ] *a* copieux(euse); somptueux(euse); (*giving freely*): **~ with** prodigue de // *vt*: to **~ sth on sb** prodiguer qch à qn; (*money*) dépenser qch sans compter pour qn/qch.

law [lɔː] *n* loi *f*; (*science*) droit *m*; **~abiding** *a* respectueux(euse) des lois; **~ and order** *n* l'ordre public; **~ court** *n* tribunal *m*, cour *f* de justice; **~ful** *a* légal(e); permis(e).

lawn [lɔːn] *n* pelouse *f*; **~mower** *n* tondeuse *f* à gazon; **~ tennis** *n* tennis *m*.

law school *n* faculté *f* de droit.

lawsuit ['lɔːsuːt] *n* procès *m*.

lawyer ['lɔːjə*] *n* (*consultant, with*

company) juriste *m*; *(for sales, wills etc)* ≈ notaire *m*; *(partner, in court)* ≈ avocat *m*.

lax [læks] *a* relâché(e).

laxative ['læksətɪv] *n* laxatif *m*.

laxity ['læksɪtɪ] *n* relâchement *m*.

lay [leɪ] *pt* of **lie** // *a* laïque; profane // *vt* *(pt, pp* **laid***)* poser, mettre; *(eggs)* pondre; *(trap)* tendre; *(plans)* élaborer; to ~ **the table** mettre la table; **to ~ aside** *or* **by** *vt* mettre de côté; **to ~ down** *vt* poser; **to ~ down the law** faire la loi; **to ~ off** *vt (workers)* licencier; **to ~ on** *vt (water, gas)* mettre, installer; *(provide)* fournir; *(paint)* étaler; **to ~ out** *vt (design)* dessiner, concevoir; *(display)* disposer; *(spend)* dépenser; **to ~ up** *vt (to store)* amasser; *(car)* remiser; *(ship)* désarmer; *(subj: illness)* forcer à s'aliter; **~about** *n* fainéant/e; **~by** *n (Brit)* aire *f* de stationnement (sur le bas-côté).

layer ['leɪə*] *n* couche *f*.

layman ['leɪmən] *n* laïque *m*; profane *m*.

layout ['leɪaut] *n* disposition *f*, plan *m*, agencement *m*; *(PRESS)* mise *f* en page.

laze [leɪz] *vi* paresser.

lazy ['leɪzɪ] *a* paresseux(euse).

lb. *abbr of* **pound** *(weight)*.

lead [li:d] *n (front position)* tête *f*; *(distance, time ahead)* avance *f*; *(clue)* piste *f*; *(to battery)* raccord *m*; *(ELEC)* fil *m*; *(for dog)* laisse *f*; *(THEATRE)* rôle principal; [lɛd] *(metal)* plomb *m*; *(in pencil)* mine *f* // *vb (pt, pp* **led***)* *vt* mener, conduire; *(induce)* amener; *(be leader of)* être à la tête de; *(SPORT)* être en tête de // *vi* mener, être en tête; **to ~ sb astray** détourner qn du droit chemin; **to ~ away** *vt* emmener; **to ~ back** *vt*: **to ~ back to** ramener à; **to ~ on** *vt (tease)* faire marcher; **to ~ on to** *(induce)* amener à; **to ~ to** *vt fus* mener à; conduire à; aboutir à; **to ~ up to** *vt fus* conduire à.

leaden ['lɛdn] *a (sky, sea)* de plomb; *(heavy: footsteps)* lourd(e).

leader ['li:də*] *n* chef *m*; dirigeant/e, leader *m*; *(in newspaper)* éditorial *m*; **~ship** *n* direction *f*; qualités *fpl* de chef.

leading ['li:dɪŋ] *a* de premier plan; principal(e); ~ **man/lady** *n (THEATRE)* vedette (masculine)/(féminine); ~ **light** *n (person)* vedette *f*, sommité *f*.

leaf [li:f], *pl* **leaves** *n* feuille *f*; *(of table)* rallonge *f* // *vi*: **to ~ through sth** feuilleter qch; **to turn over a new ~** changer de conduite or d'existence.

leaflet ['li:flɪt] *n* prospectus *m*, brochure *f*; *(POL, REL)* tract *m*.

league [li:g] *n* ligue *f*; *(FOOTBALL)* championnat *m*; *(measure)* lieue *f*; **to be in ~ with** avoir partie liée avec, être de mèche avec.

leak [li:k] *n (out, also fig)* fuite *f*; *(in)* infiltration *f* // *vi (pipe, liquid etc)* fuir; *(shoes)* prendre l'eau // *vt (liquid)* répandre; *(information)* divulguer; **to ~ out** *vi* fuir; être divulgué(e).

lean [li:n] *a* maigre // *vb (pt, pp* **leaned** *or* **leant** [lɛnt] *) vt*: **to ~ sth on sth** appuyer qch sur qch // *vi (slope)* pencher; *(rest)*: **to ~ against** s'appuyer contre; être appuyé(e) contre; **to ~ on** s'appuyer sur; **to ~ back/forward** *vi* se pencher en arrière/avant; **to ~ out** *vi* se pencher au dehors; **to ~ over** *vi* se pencher; **~-to** *n* appentis *m*.

leap [li:p] *n* bond *m*, saut *m* // *vi (pt, pp* **leaped** *or* **leapt** [lɛpt]*)* bondir, sauter; **~frog** *n* jeu *m* de saute-mouton; ~ **year** *n* année *f* bissextile.

learn, *pt, pp* **learned** *or* **learnt** [lə:n, -t] *vt, vi* apprendre; **to ~ how to do sth** apprendre à faire qch; **~ed** ['lə:nɪd] *a* érudit(e), savant(e); **~er** *n* débutant/e; *(Brit: also:* **~er driver***)* *(conducteur/trice)* débutant(e); **~ing** *n* savoir *m*.

lease [li:s] *n* bail *m* // *vt* louer à bail.

leash [li:ʃ] *n* laisse *f*.

least [li:st] *a*: **the ~ +** *noun* le(la) plus petit(e), le(la) moindre; *(smallest amount of)* le moins de; **the ~ +** *adjective* le(la) moins; **the ~ money** le moins d'argent; **at ~** au moins; **not in the ~** pas le moins du monde.

leather ['lɛðə*] *n* cuir *m*.

leave [li:v] *vb (pt, pp* **left***) vt* laisser; *(go away from)* quitter // *vi* partir, s'en aller // *n (time off)* congé *m*; *(MIL, also: consent)* permission *f*; **to be left** rester; **there's some milk left over** il reste du lait; **on ~** en permission; **to ~ behind** *vt (person, object)* laisser; **to ~ out** *vt* oublier, omettre; ~ **of absence** *n* congé exceptionnel; *(MIL)* permission spéciale.

leaves [li:vz] *npl of* **leaf**.

Lebanon ['lɛbənən] *n* Liban *m*.

lecherous ['lɛtʃərəs] *a* lubrique.

lecture ['lɛktʃə*] *n* conférence *f*; *(SCOL)* cours (magistral) // *vi* donner des cours; enseigner // *vt (scold)* sermonner, réprimander; **to ~ on** faire un cours *(or* son cours*)* sur; **to give a ~ on** faire une conférence sur; faire *or* donner un cours sur.

lecturer ['lɛktʃərə*] *n (speaker)* conférencier/ère; *(Brit: at university)* professeur *m* (d'université), ≈ maître assistant, maître de conférences.

led [lɛd] *pt, pp of* **lead**.

ledge [lɛdʒ] *n (of window, on wall)* rebord *m*; *(of mountain)* saillie *f*, corniche *f*.

ledger ['lɛdʒə*] *n* registre *m*, grand livre.

lee [li:] *n* côté *m* sous le vent.

leech [li:tʃ] *n* sangsue *f*.

leek [li:k] *n* poireau *m*.

leer [lɪə*] vi: to ~ at sb regarder qn d'un air mauvais or concupiscent.

leeway ['liːweɪ] n (fig): to have some ~ avoir une certaine liberté d'action.

left [lɛft] pt, pp of **leave** // à gauche // ad à gauche // n gauche f; on the ~, to the ~ à gauche; the L~ (POL) la gauche; **~-handed** a gaucher(ère); **~-hand side** n gauche f, côté m gauche; **~-luggage (office)** n (Brit) consigne f; **~-overs** npl restes mpl; **~-wing** a (POL) de gauche.

leg [lɛg] n jambe f; (of animal) patte f; (of furniture) pied m; (CULIN: of chicken) cuisse f; **1st/2nd ~** (SPORT) match m aller/retour; (of journey) 1ère/2ème étape.

legacy ['lɛgəsɪ] n héritage m, legs m.

legal ['liːgl] a légal(e); **~ holiday** n (US) jour férié; **~ tender** n monnaie légale.

legend ['lɛdʒənd] n légende f.

legible ['lɛdʒəbl] a lisible.

legislation [lɛdʒɪs'leɪʃən] n législation f; **legislature** ['lɛdʒɪslətʃə*] n corps législatif.

legitimate [lɪ'dʒɪtɪmət] a légitime.

leg-room ['lɛgruːm] n place f pour les jambes.

leisure ['lɛʒə*] n loisir m, temps m libre; loisirs mpl; at ~ (tout) à loisir; à tête reposée; **~ centre** n centre m de loisirs; **~ly** a tranquille; fait(e) sans se presser.

lemon ['lɛmən] n citron m; **~ade** n [-'neɪd] limonade f; **~ tea** n thé m au citron.

lend [lɛnd], pt, pp **lent** vt: to ~ sth (to sb) prêter qch (à qn).

length [lɛŋθ] n longueur f; (section: of road, pipe etc) morceau m, bout m; at ~ (at last) enfin, à la fin; (lengthily) longuement; **~en** vt allonger, prolonger // vi s'allonger; **~ways** ad dans le sens de la longueur, en long; **~y** a (très) long(longue).

lenient ['liːnɪənt] a indulgent(e), clément(e).

lens [lɛnz] n lentille f; (of spectacles) verre m; (of camera) objectif m.

Lent [lɛnt] n Carême m.

lent [lɛnt] pt, pp of **lend**.

lentil ['lɛntl] n lentille f.

Leo ['liːəu] n le Lion.

leotard ['liːətɑːd] n maillot m (de danseur etc).

leper ['lɛpə*] n lépreux/euse.

leprosy ['lɛprəsɪ] n lèpre f.

lesbian ['lɛzbɪən] n lesbienne f.

less [lɛs] a moins de // pronoun, ad moins; ~ than that/you moins que cela/vous; ~ than half moins de la moitié; ~ than ever moins que jamais; ~ and ~ de moins en moins; the ~ he works ... moins il travaille ....

lessen ['lɛsn] vi diminuer, s'amoindrir, s'atténuer // vt diminuer, réduire, atténuer.

lesser ['lɛsə*] a moindre; to a ~ extent à un degré moindre.

lesson ['lɛsn] n leçon f.

lest [lɛst] cj de peur de + infinitive, de peur que + sub.

let, pt, pp **let** [lɛt] vt laisser; (Brit: lease) louer; to ~ sb do sth laisser qn faire qch; to ~ sb know sth faire savoir qch à qn, prévenir qn de qch; he ~ me go il m'a laissé partir; ~'s go allons-y; ~ him come qu'il vienne; 'to ~' 'à louer'; **to ~ down** vt (lower) baisser; (dress) rallonger; (hair) défaire; (disappoint) décevoir; **to ~ go** vi lâcher prise // vt lâcher; **to ~ in** vt laisser entrer; (visitor etc) faire entrer; **to ~ off** vt laisser partir; (firework etc) faire partir; (smell etc) dégager; **to ~ on** vi (col) dire; **to ~ out** vt laisser sortir; (dress) élargir; (scream) laisser échapper; **to ~ up** vi diminuer, s'arrêter.

lethal ['liːθl] a mortel(le), fatal(e).

letter ['lɛtə*] n lettre f; **~ bomb** n lettre piégée; **~box** n (Brit) boîte f aux or à lettres; **~ing** n lettres fpl; caractères mpl.

lettuce ['lɛtɪs] n laitue f, salade f.

leukaemia, (US) leukemia [luːˈkiːmɪə] n leucémie f.

level ['lɛvl] a plat(e), plan(e), uni(e); horizontal(e) // n niveau m; (flat place) terrain plat; (also: spirit ~) niveau à bulle // vt niveler, aplanir; to be ~ with être au même niveau que; 'A' ~s npl (Brit) ≈ baccalauréat m; 'O' ~s npl (Brit) ≈ B.E.P.C; on the ~ à l'horizontale; (fig: honest) régulier(ère); **to ~ off** or **out** vi (prices etc) se stabiliser; **~ crossing** n (Brit) passage m à niveau; **~-headed** a équilibré(e).

lever ['liːvə*] n levier m // vt: to ~ up/out soulever/extraire au moyen d'un levier; **~age** n: ~age (on or with) prise f (sur).

levy ['lɛvɪ] n taxe f, impôt m // vt prélever, imposer, percevoir.

lewd [luːd] a obscène, lubrique.

liability [laɪə'bɪlətɪ] n responsabilité f; (handicap) handicap m; **liabilities** npl obligations fpl, engagements mpl; (on balance sheet) passif m.

liable ['laɪəbl] a (subject): ~ to sujet(te) à; passible de; (responsible): ~ (for) responsable (de); (likely): ~ to do susceptible de faire.

liaison [liːˈeɪzən] n liaison f.

liar ['laɪə*] n menteur/euse.

libel ['laɪbl] n écrit m diffamatoire; diffamation f // vt diffamer.

liberal ['lɪbərl] a libéral(e); (generous): ~ with prodigue de, généreux(euse) avec.

liberty ['lɪbətɪ] *n* liberté *f*; **to be at ~ to do** être libre de faire.

Libra ['liːbrə] *n* la Balance.

librarian [laɪˈbrɛərɪən] *n* bibliothécaire *m/f*.

library ['laɪbrərɪ] *n* bibliothèque *f*.

libretto [lɪˈbretəu] *n* livret *m*.

Libya ['lɪbɪə] *n* Libye *f*.

lice [laɪs] *npl of* **louse**.

licence, (US) **license** ['laɪsns] *n* autorisation *f*, permis *m*; (COMM) licence *f*; (RADIO, TV) redevance *f*; (*also*: driving ~, (US) driver's ~) permis *m* (de conduire); (*excessive freedom*) licence; ~ **number** *n* numéro *m* d'immatriculation; ~ **plate** *n* plaque *f* minéralogique.

license ['laɪsns] *n* (US) = **licence** // *vt* donner une licence à; ~**d** *a* (*for alcohol*) patenté(e) pour la vente des spiritueux.

lick [lɪk] *vt* lécher.

licorice ['lɪkərɪs] *n* = **liquorice**.

lid [lɪd] *n* couvercle *m*.

lie [laɪ] *n* mensonge *m* // *vi* mentir; (*pt* **lay**, *pp* **lain**) (*rest*) être étendu(e) *or* allongé(e) *or* couché(e); (*in grave*) être enterré(e), reposer; (*of object*: *be situated*) se trouver, être; **to ~ low** (*fig*) se cacher; **to ~ about** *vi* traîner; **to have a ~-down** (*Brit*) s'allonger, se reposer; **to have a ~-in** (*Brit*) faire la grasse matinée.

lieutenant [lefˈtɛnənt, (US) luːˈtɛnənt] *n* lieutenant *m*.

life [laɪf], *pl* **lives** *n* vie *f*; ~ **assurance** *n* (*Brit*) assurance-vie *f*; ~**belt** *n* (*Brit*) bouée *f* de sauvetage; ~**boat** *n* canot *m* or chaloupe *f* de sauvetage; ~**guard** *n* surveillant *m* de baignade; ~ **insurance** = ~ **assurance**; ~ **jacket** *n* gilet *m* or ceinture *f* de sauvetage; ~**less** *a* sans vie, inanimé(e); (*dull*) qui manque de vie or de vigueur; ~**like** *a* qui semble vrai(e) or vivant(e); ressemblant(e); ~**long** *a* de toute une vie, de toujours; ~ **preserver** *n* (US) gilet *m* or ceinture *f* de sauvetage; bouée *f* de sauvetage; ~**saver** *n* surveillant *m* de baignade; ~ **sentence** *n* condamnation *f* à vie or à perpétuité; ~**sized** *a* grandeur nature *inv*; ~ **span** *n* (durée *f* de) vie *f*; ~**style** *n* style *m* or mode *m* de vie; ~ **support system** *n* (MED) respirateur artificiel; ~**time** *n*: **in his** ~**time** de son vivant; **once in a** ~**time** une fois dans la or dans une vie.

lift [lɪft] *vt* soulever, lever; (*steal*) prendre, voler // *vi* (*fog*) se lever // *n* (*Brit*: *elevator*) ascenseur *m*; **to give sb a ~** (*Brit*) emmener or prendre qn en voiture; ~**off** *n* décollage *m*.

light [laɪt] *n* lumière *f*; (*daylight*) lumière, jour *m*; (*lamp*) lampe *f*; (AUT: *traffic* ~, *rear* ~) feu *m*; (: *headlamp*) phare *m*; (*for cigarette etc*): **have you got a ~?** avez-vous du feu? // *vt* (*pt*, *pp* **lighted** *or* **lit**) (*candle*, *cigarette*, *fire*) allumer; (*room*) éclairer // *a* (*room*, *colour*) clair(e); (*not heavy, also fig*) léger(ère); **to come to ~** être dévoilé(e) *or* découvert(e); **to ~ up** *vi* s'allumer; (*face*) s'éclairer // *vt* (*illuminate*) éclairer, illuminer; ~ **bulb** *n* ampoule *f*; ~**en** *vi* s'éclairer // *vt* (*give light to*) éclairer; (*make lighter*) éclaircir; (*make less heavy*) alléger; ~**er** *n* (*also*: cigarette ~**er**) briquet *m*; (: *in car*) allume-cigare *m inv*; (*boat*) péniche *f*; ~**-headed** *a* étourdi(e), écervelé(e); ~**-hearted** *a* gai(e), joyeux(euse), enjoué(e); ~**house** *n* phare *m*; ~**ing** *n* (*on road*) éclairage *m*; (*in theatre*) éclairages; ~**ly** *ad* légèrement; **to get off** ~**ly** s'en tirer à bon compte; ~**ness** *n* clarté *f*; (*in weight*) légèreté *f*.

lightning ['laɪtnɪŋ] *n* éclair *m*, foudre *f*; ~ **conductor**, (US) ~ **rod** *n* paratonnerre *m*.

light pen *n* crayon *m* optique.

lightweight ['laɪtweɪt] *a* (*suit*) léger(ère); (*boxer*) poids léger *inv* // *n* (BOXING) poids léger.

like [laɪk] *vt* aimer (bien) // *prep* comme // *a* semblable, pareil(le) // *n*: **the ~** un(e) pareil(le) or semblable; **le(la) pareil(le)**; (*pej*) d'autres du même genre or acabit; **his ~s and dislikes** ses goûts *mpl* or préférences *fpl*; **I would ~, I'd ~** je voudrais, j'aimerais; **would you ~ a coffee?** voulez-vous du café?; **to be/look ~ sb/sth** ressembler à qn/qch; **that's just ~ him** c'est bien de lui, ça lui ressemble; **do it ~ this** fais-le comme ceci; **nothing ~** ... rien de tel que ...; ~**able** *a* sympathique, agréable.

likelihood ['laɪklɪhud] *n* probabilité *f*.

likely ['laɪklɪ] *a* probable, plausible; **he's ~ to leave** il va sûrement partir, il risque fort de partir; **not ~!** pas de danger!

likeness ['laɪknɪs] *n* ressemblance *f*.

likewise ['laɪkwaɪz] *ad* de même, pareillement.

liking ['laɪkɪŋ] *n* affection *f*, penchant *m*; goût *m*.

lilac ['laɪlək] *n* lilas *m* // *a* lilas *inv*.

lily ['lɪlɪ] *n* lis *m*; ~ **of the valley** *n* muguet *m*.

limb [lɪm] *n* membre *m*.

limber ['lɪmbə*]: **to ~ up** *vi* se dégourdir, se mettre en train.

limbo ['lɪmbəu] *n*: **to be in ~** (*fig*) être tombé(e) dans l'oubli.

lime [laɪm] *n* (*tree*) tilleul *m*; (*fruit*) lime *f*; (GEO) chaux *f*.

limelight ['laɪmlaɪt] *n*: **in the ~** (*fig*) en vedette, au premier plan.

limerick ['lɪmərɪk] *n* poème *m* humoristique (de 5 vers).

limestone ['laɪmstəʊn] n pierre f à chaux; (GEO) calcaire m.

limit ['lɪmɪt] n limite f // vt limiter; ~ed a limité(e), restreint(e); to be ~ed to se limiter à, ne concerner que; ~ed (liability) company (Ltd) n (Brit) ≈ société f anonyme (S.A.).

limp [lɪmp] n: to have a ~ boiter // vi boiter // a mou(molle).

limpet ['lɪmpɪt] n patelle f.

line [laɪn] n (gen) ligne f; (rope) corde f; (wire) fil m; (of poem) vers m; (row, series) rangée f; file f, queue f; (COMM: series of goods) article(s) m(pl) // vt (clothes): to ~ (with) doubler (de); (box): to ~ (with) garnir ou tapisser (de); (subj: trees, crowd) border; in his ~ of business dans sa partie, dans son rayon; in ~ with en accord avec; to ~ up vi s'aligner, se mettre en rang(s) // vt aligner.

lined [laɪnd] a (face) ridé(e), marqué(e); (paper) réglé(e).

linen ['lɪnɪn] n linge m (de corps ou de maison); (cloth) lin m.

liner ['laɪnə*] n paquebot m de ligne.

linesman ['laɪnzmən] n (TENNIS) juge m de ligne; (FOOTBALL) juge de touche.

line-up ['laɪnʌp] n file f; (SPORT) (composition f de l')équipe f.

linger ['lɪŋgə*] vi s'attarder; traîner; (smell, tradition) persister.

lingo, ~es ['lɪŋgəʊ] n (pej) jargon m.

linguistics [lɪŋ'gwɪstɪks] n linguistique f.

lining ['laɪnɪŋ] n doublure f.

link [lɪŋk] n (of a chain) maillon m; (connection) lien m, rapport m // vt relier, lier, unir; ~s npl (GOLF) (terrain m de) golf m; to ~ up vt relier // vi se rejoindre; s'associer.

lino ['laɪnəʊ], **linoleum** [lɪ'nəʊlɪəm] n linoléum m.

lion ['laɪən] n lion m; ~ess n lionne f.

lip [lɪp] n lèvre f; (of cup etc) rebord m; ~read vi lire sur les lèvres; ~ salve n pommade f rosat ou pour les lèvres; ~ service n: to pay ~ service to sth ne reconnaître le mérite de qch que pour la forme; ~stick n rouge m à lèvres.

liqueur [lɪ'kjʊə*] n liqueur f.

liquid ['lɪkwɪd] n liquide m // a liquide.

liquidize ['lɪkwɪdaɪz] vt (CULIN) passer au mixer; ~r n mixer m.

liquor ['lɪkə*] n spiritueux m, alcool m; ~ store n (US) magasin m de vins et spiritueux.

liquorice ['lɪkərɪs] n réglisse f.

lisp [lɪsp] n zézaiement m.

list [lɪst] n liste f; (of ship) inclinaison f // vt (write down) inscrire; faire la liste de; (enumerate) énumérer // vi (ship) gîter, donner de la bande.

listen ['lɪsn] vi écouter; to ~ to écouter; ~er n auditeur/trice.

listless ['lɪstlɪs] a indolent(e), apathique.

lit [lɪt] pt, pp of **light**.

liter ['liːtə*] n (US) = **litre**.

literacy ['lɪtərəsɪ] n degré m d'alphabétisation, fait m de savoir lire et écrire.

literal ['lɪtərl] a littéral(e).

literary ['lɪtərərɪ] a littéraire.

literate ['lɪtərət] a qui sait lire et écrire, instruit(e).

literature ['lɪtərɪtʃə*] n littérature f; (brochures etc) copie f publicitaire, prospectus mpl.

lithe [laɪð] a agile, souple.

litigation [lɪtɪ'geɪʃən] n litige m; contentieux m.

litre, (US) liter ['liːtə*] n litre m.

litter ['lɪtə*] n (rubbish) détritus mpl, ordures fpl; (young animals) portée f; ~ bin n (Brit) boîte f à ordures, poubelle f; ~ed a: ~ed with jonché(e) de, couvert(e) de.

little ['lɪtl] a (small) petit(e); (not much): it's ~ c'est peu; ~ milk peu de lait // ad peu; a ~ un peu (de); ~ by ~ petit à petit, peu à peu.

live [lɪv] vi vivre; (reside) vivre, habiter // a [laɪv] (animal) vivant(e), en vie; (wire) sous tension; (broadcast) (transmis(e)) en direct; to ~ down vt faire oublier (avec le temps); to ~ on vt fus (food) vivre de // vi survivre; to ~ together vi vivre ensemble, cohabiter; to ~ up to vt fus se montrer à la hauteur de.

livelihood ['laɪvlɪhʊd] n moyens mpl d'existence.

lively ['laɪvlɪ] a vif(vive), plein(e) d'entrain.

liven up ['laɪvn ʌp] vt animer.

liver ['lɪvə*] n foie m.

livery ['lɪvərɪ] n livrée f.

lives [laɪvz] npl of **life**.

livestock ['laɪvstɒk] n cheptel m, bétail m.

livid ['lɪvɪd] a livide, blafard(e); (furious) furieux(euse), furibond(e).

living ['lɪvɪŋ] a vivant(e), en vie // n: to earn ou make a ~ gagner sa vie; ~ conditions npl conditions fpl de vie; ~ room n salle f de séjour; ~ wage n salaire m permettant de vivre (décemment).

lizard ['lɪzəd] n lézard m.

load [ləʊd] n (weight) poids m; (thing carried) chargement m, charge f; (ELEC, TECH) charge f // vt (also: ~ up): to ~ (with) (lorry, ship) charger (de); (gun, camera) charger (avec); (COMPUT) charger; a ~ of, ~s of (fig) un ou des tas de, des masses de; ~ed a (dice) pipé(e); (question) insidieux(euse); (col: rich) bourré(e) de fric; (: drunk) bourré(e); ~ing bay n aire f de chargement.

loaf [ləʊf], pl **loaves** n pain m, miche f //

vi (*also*: ~ **about**, ~ **around**) fainéanter, traîner.

loan [ləun] *n* prêt *m* // *vt* prêter; **on** ~ prêté(e), en prêt.

loath [ləuθ] *a*: **to be** ~ **to do** répugner à faire.

loathe [ləuð] *vt* détester, avoir en horreur.

loaves [ləuvz] *npl of* **loaf**.

lobby ['lɔbɪ] *n* hall *m*, entrée *f*; (POL) groupe *m* de pression, lobby *m* // *vt* faire pression sur.

lobster ['lɔbstə*] *n* homard *m*.

local ['ləukl] *a* local(e) // *n* (*pub*) pub *m* or café *m* du coin; **the** ~**s** *npl* les gens *mpl* du pays *or* du coin; ~ **call** *n* communication urbaine; ~ **govern-ment** *n* administration locale *or* municipale.

locality [ləu'kælɪtɪ] *n* région *f*, environs *mpl*; (*position*) lieu *m*.

locate [ləu'keɪt] *vt* (*find*) trouver, repérer; (*situate*) situer.

location [ləu'keɪʃən] *n* emplacement *m*; **on** ~ (CINEMA) en extérieur.

loch [lɔx] *n* lac *m*, loch *m*.

lock [lɔk] *n* (*of door, box*) serrure *f*; (*of canal*) écluse *f*; (*of hair*) mèche *f*, bou-cle *f* // *vt* (*with key*) fermer à clé; (*immobilize*) bloquer // *vi* (*door etc*) fermer à clé; (*wheels*) se bloquer.

locker ['lɔkə*] *n* casier *m*.

locket ['lɔkɪt] *n* médaillon *m*.

locksmith ['lɔksmɪθ] *n* serrurier *m*.

lock-up ['lɔkʌp] *n* box *m*.

locomotive [ləukə'məutɪv] *n* locomotive *f*.

locum ['ləukəm] *n* (MED) suppléant/e (de médecin).

lodge [lɔdʒ] *n* pavillon *m* (de gardien); (FREEMASONRY) loge *f* // *vi* (*person*): **to** ~ (**with**) être logé(e) (chez), être en pension (chez) // *vt* (*appeal etc*) présenter; déposer; **to** ~ **a complaint** porter plainte; ~**r** *n* locataire *m/f*; (*with room and meals*) pensionnaire *m/f*.

lodgings ['lɔdʒɪŋz] *npl* chambre *f*; meu-blé *m*.

loft [lɔft] *n* grenier *m*.

lofty ['lɔftɪ] *a* élevé(e); (*haughty*) hautain(e).

log [lɔg] *n* (*of wood*) bûche *f*; (*book*) = logbook.

logbook ['lɔgbuk] *n* (NAUT) livre *m or* journal *m* de bord; (AVIAT) carnet *m* de vol; (*of car*) ≈ carte grise.

loggerheads ['lɔgəhedz] *npl*: **at** ~ (**with**) à couteaux tirés (avec).

logic ['lɔdʒɪk] *n* logique *f*; ~**al** *a* logique.

loin [lɔɪn] *n* (CULIN) filet *m*, longe *f*.

loiter ['lɔɪtə*] *vi* s'attarder; **to** ~ (**about**) traîner, musarder; (*pej*) rôder.

loll [lɔl] *vi* (*also*: ~ **about**) se prélasser, fainéanter.

lollipop ['lɔlɪpɔp] *n* sucette *f*; ~ **man/**

lady *n* (*Brit*) contractuel/le qui fait tra-verser la rue aux enfants.

London ['lʌndən] *n* Londres *m*; ~**er** *n* Londonien/ne.

lone [ləun] *a* solitaire.

loneliness ['ləunlınıs] *n* solitude *f*, isolement *m*.

lonely ['ləunlı] *a* seul(e); solitaire, isolé(e).

long [lɔŋ] *a* long(longue) // *ad* longtemps // *vi*: **to** ~ **for sth** avoir très envie de qch; attendre qch avec impatience; **to** ~ **to do** avoir très envie de faire; attendre avec impatience de faire; **in the** ~ **run** à la longue; finalement; **so** *or* **as** ~ **as** pourvu que; **don't be** ~ dépêchez-vous; **how** ~ **is this river/course?** quelle est la longueur de ce fleuve/la durée de ce cours?; **6 metres** ~ (long) de 6 mètres; **6 months** ~ qui dure 6 mois, de 6 mois; **all night** ~ toute la nuit; **he no** ~**er comes** il ne vient plus; ~ **before** longtemps avant; **before** ~ (+ *future*) avant peu, dans peu de temps; (+ *past*) peu de temps après; **at** ~ **last** enfin; ~**-distance** *a* (*race*) de fond; (*call*) interurbain(e); ~**hand** *n* écriture normale *or* courante; ~**ing** *n* désir *m*, envie *f*, nostalgie *f*.

longitude ['lɔŋgɪtjuːd] *n* longitude *f*.

long: ~ **jump** *n* saut *m* en longueur; ~**-playing** *a*: ~**-playing record (L.P.)** *n* (disque *m*) 33 tours *m inv*; ~**-range** *a* à longue portée; ~**-sighted** *a* presbyte; (*fig*) prévoyant(e); ~**-standing** *a* de longue date; ~**-suffering** *a* empreint(e) d'une patience résignée; extrêmement patient(e); ~**-term** *a* à long terme; ~ **wave** *n* grandes ondes; ~**-winded** *a* intarissable, interminable.

loo [luː] *n* (*Brit col*) w.-c. *mpl*, petit coin.

look [luk] *vi* regarder; (*seem*) sembler, paraître, avoir l'air; (*building etc*): **to** ~ **south/on to the sea** donner au sud/sur la mer // *n* regard *m*; (*appearance*) air *m*, allure *f*, aspect *m*; ~**s** *npl* mine *f*; physique *m*, beauté *f*; **to** ~ **after** *vt fus* s'occuper de, prendre soin de; garder, surveiller; **to** ~ **at** *vt fus* regarder; **to** ~ **back** *vi*: **to** ~ **back** at se retourner pour regarder; **to** ~ **back on** (*event etc*) évoquer, repenser à; **to** ~ **down on** *vt fus* (*fig*) regarder de haut, dédaigner; **to** ~ **for** *vt fus* chercher; **to** ~ **forward to** *vt fus* attendre avec impatience; **we** ~ **forward to hearing from you** dans l'attente de vous lire; **to** ~ **into** *vt* examiner, étudier; **to** ~ **on** *vi* regarder (en spectateur); **to** ~ **out** *vi* (*beware*): **to** ~ **out** (**for**) prendre garde (à), faire attention (à); **to** ~ **out for** *vt fus* être à la recherche de; guetter; **to** ~ **round** *vi* regarder derrière soi, se retourner; **to** ~ **to** *vt fus* veiller à; (*rely on*) compter sur; **to** ~ **up** *vi* lever les yeux; (*im-prove*) s'améliorer // *vt* (*word*) chercher;

(*friend*) passer voir; **to ~ up to** *vt fus* avoir du respect pour; **~-out** *n* poste *m* de guet; guetteur *m*; **to be on the ~-out (for)** guetter.

loom [lu:m] *n* métier *m* à tisser // *vi* surgir; (*fig*) menacer.

loony ['lu:nɪ] *n* (*col*) timbré/e, cinglé/e.

loop [lu:p] *n* boucle *f*; **~hole** *n* porte *f* de sortie (*fig*); échappatoire *f*.

loose [lu:s] *a* (*knot, screw*) desserré(e); (*stone*) branlant(e); (*clothes*) vague, ample, lâche; (*animal*) en liberté, échappé(e); (*life*) dissolu(e); (*morals, discipline*) relâché(e); (*thinking*) peu rigoureux(euse), vague; (*translation*) approximatif(ive); **~ change** *n* petite monnaie; **~ chippings** *npl* (*on road*) gravillons *mpl*; **to be at a ~ end** *or* (*US*) **at ~ ends** ne pas trop savoir quoi faire; **~ly** *ad* sans serrer; approximativement; **~n** *vt* desserrer, relâcher, défaire.

loot [lu:t] *n* butin *m* // *vt* piller.

lop [lɔp]: **to ~ off** *vt* couper, trancher.

lop-sided ['lɔp'saɪdɪd] *a* de travers, asymétrique.

lord [lɔ:d] *n* seigneur *m*; **L~** Smith lord Smith; **the L~** le Seigneur; **the (House of) L~s** (*Brit*) la Chambre des Lords; **~ship** *n*: **your L~ship** Monsieur le comte (*or* le baron *or* le Juge).

lore [lɔ:*] *n* tradition(s) *f(pl)*.

lorry ['lɔrɪ] *n* (*Brit*) camion *m*; **~ driver** *n* (*Brit*) camionneur *m*, routier *m*.

lose [lu:z], *pt, pp* **lost** *vt* perdre; (*opportunity*) manquer, perdre; (*pursuers*) distancer, semer // *vi* perdre; **to ~ (time)** (*clock*) retarder; **to get lost** *vi* se perdre; **~r** *n* perdant/e.

loss [lɔs] *n* perte *f*; **to be at a ~** être perplexe *or* embarrassé(e).

lost [lɔst] *pt, pp of* **lose** // *a* perdu(e); **~ property**, (*US*) **~ and found** *n* objets trouvés.

lot [lɔt] *n* (*at auctions*) lot *m*; (*destiny*) sort *m*, destinée *f*; **the ~** le tout; tous *mpl*, toutes *fpl*; **a ~** beaucoup; **a ~ of** beaucoup de; **~s of** des tas de; **to draw ~s (for sth)** tirer (qch) au sort.

lotion ['ləuʃən] *n* lotion *f*.

lottery ['lɔtərɪ] *n* loterie *f*.

loud [laud] *a* bruyant(e), sonore, fort(e); (*gaudy*) voyant(e), tapageur(euse) // *ad* (*speak etc*) fort; **~hailer** *n* (*Brit*) porte-voix *m inv*; **~ly** *ad* fort, bruyamment; **~speaker** *n* haut-parleur *m*.

lounge [laundʒ] *n* salon *m* // *vi* se prélasser, paresser; **~ suit** *n* (*Brit*) complet *m*; 'tenue de ville'.

louse [laus], *pl* **lice** *n* pou *m*.

lousy ['lauzɪ] *a* (*fig*) infect(e), moche.

lout [laut] *n* rustre *m*, butor *m*.

louvre, (*US*) **louver** ['lu:və*] *a* (*door, window*) à claire-voie.

lovable ['lʌvəbl] *a* très sympathique; adorable.

love [lʌv] *n* amour *m* // *vt* aimer; aimer beaucoup; **to be in ~ with** être amoureux(euse) de; **to make ~** faire l'amour; '15 ~' (*TENNIS*) '15 à rien *or* zéro'; **~ affair** *n* liaison (amoureuse); **~ life** *n* vie sentimentale.

lovely ['lʌvlɪ] *a* (très) joli(e); ravissant(e), charmant(e); agréable.

lover ['lʌvə*] *n* amant *m*; (*amateur*): **a ~ of** un(e) ami(e) de; un(e) amoureux(euse) de.

loving ['lʌvɪŋ] *a* affectueux(euse), tendre, aimant(e).

low [ləu] *a* bas(basse) // *ad* bas // *n* (*METEOROLOGY*) dépression *f* // *vi* (*cow*) mugir; **to feel ~** se sentir déprimé(e); **to turn (down) ~** *vt* baisser; **~-cut** *a* (*dress*) décolleté(e); **~er** *vt* abaisser, baisser; **~-fat** *a* maigre; **~lands** *npl* (*GEO*) plaines *fpl*; **~ly** *a* humble, modeste; **~-lying** *a* à faible altitude.

loyal ['lɔɪəl] *a* loyal(e), fidèle; **~ty** *n* loyauté *f*, fidélité *f*.

lozenge ['lɔzɪndʒ] *n* (*MED*) pastille *f*; (*GEOM*) losange *m*.

L.P. *n abbr of* **long-playing record**.

L-plates ['ɛlpleɪts] *npl* (*Brit*) plaques *fpl* d'apprenti conducteur.

Ltd *abbr see* **limited**.

lubricant ['lu:brɪkənt] *n* lubrifiant *m*.

lubricate ['lu:brɪkeɪt] *vt* lubrifier, graisser.

luck [lʌk] *n* chance *f*; **bad ~** malchance *f*, malheur *m*; **good ~!** bonne chance!; **~ily** *ad* heureusement, par bonheur; **~y** *a* (*person*) qui a de la chance; (*coincidence*) heureux(euse); (*number etc*) qui porte bonheur.

ludicrous ['lu:dɪkrəs] *a* ridicule, absurde.

lug [lʌg] *vt* traîner, tirer.

luggage ['lʌgɪdʒ] *n* bagages *mpl*; **~ rack** *n* (*in train*) porte-bagages *m inv*; (*on car*) galerie *f*.

lukewarm ['lu:kwɔ:m] *a* tiède.

lull [lʌl] *n* accalmie *f* // *vt* (*child*) bercer; (*person, fear*) apaiser, calmer.

lullaby ['lʌləbaɪ] *n* berceuse *f*.

lumbago [lʌm'beɪgəu] *n* lumbago *m*.

lumber ['lʌmbə*] *n* bric-à-brac *m inv*; **~jack** *n* bûcheron *m*.

luminous ['lu:mɪnəs] *a* lumineux(euse).

lump [lʌmp] *n* morceau *m*; (*in sauce*) grumeau *m*; (*swelling*) grosseur *f* // *vt* (*also*: **~ together**) réunir, mettre en tas; **~ sum** *n* somme globale *or* forfaitaire.

lunacy ['lu:nəsɪ] *n* démence *f*, folie *f*.

lunar ['lu:nə*] *a* lunaire.

lunatic ['lu:nətɪk] *a, n* fou(folle), dément(e).

lunch [lʌntʃ] *n* déjeuner *m*.

luncheon ['lʌntʃən] *n* déjeuner *m*; **~ meat** *n* sorte de saucisson; **~ voucher**

n chèque-repas *m*.
lung [lʌŋ] *n* poumon *m*.
lunge [lʌndʒ] *vi* (*also*: ~ **forward**) faire un mouvement brusque en avant; **to ~ at** envoyer *or* assener un coup à.
lurch [lə:tʃ] *vi* vaciller, tituber // *n* écart *m* brusque, embardée *f*; **to leave sb in the ~** laisser qn se débrouiller *or* se dépêtrer tout seul(e).
lure [luə*] *n* appât *m*, leurre *m* // *vt* attirer *or* persuader par la ruse.
lurid ['luərɪd] *a* affreux(euse), atroce.
lurk [lə:k] *vi* se tapir, se cacher.
luscious ['lʌʃəs] *a* succulent(e); appétissant(e).
lush [lʌʃ] *a* luxuriant(e).
lust [lʌst] *n* luxure *f*; lubricité *f*; désir *m*; (*fig*): ~ **for** soif *f* de; **to ~ after** *vt fus* convoiter, désirer.
lusty ['lʌstɪ] *a* vigoureux(euse), robuste.
Luxembourg ['lʌksəmbə:g] *n* Luxembourg *m*.
luxurious [lʌg'zjuərɪəs] *a* luxueux(euse).
luxury ['lʌkʃərɪ] *n* luxe *m* // *cpd* de luxe.
lying ['laɪɪŋ] *n* mensonge(s) *m(pl)*.
lyric ['lɪrɪk] *a* lyrique; ~**s** *npl* (*of song*) paroles *fpl*; ~**al** *a* lyrique.

M

m. *abbr of* **metre, mile, million.**
M.A. *abbr see* **master.**
mac [mæk] *n* (*Brit*) imper(méable) *m*.
mace [meɪs] *n* masse *f*; (*spice*) macis *m*.
machine [mə'ʃi:n] *n* machine *f* // *vt* (*dress etc*) coudre à la machine; ~ **gun** *n* mitrailleuse *f*; ~**ry** *n* machinerie *f*, machines *fpl*; (*fig*) mécanisme(s) *m(pl)*.
mackerel ['mækrl] *n* (*pl inv*) maquereau *m*.
mackintosh ['mækɪntɔʃ] *n* (*Brit*) imperméable *m*.
mad [mæd] *a* fou(folle); (*foolish*) insensé(e); (*angry*) furieux(euse).
madam ['mædəm] *n* madame *f*.
madden ['mædn] *vt* exaspérer.
made [meɪd] *pt, pp of* **make.**
Madeira [mə'dɪərə] *n* (*GEO*) Madère *f*; (*wine*) madère *m*.
made-to-measure ['meɪdtə'mɛʒə*] *ā* (*Brit*) fait(e) sur mesure.
madly ['mædlɪ] *ad* follement.
madman ['mædmən] *n* fou *m*, aliéné *m*.
madness ['mædnɪs] *n* folie *f*.
magazine [mægə'zi:n] *n* (*PRESS*) magazine *m*, revue *f*; (*MIL*: *store*) dépôt *m*, arsenal *m*; (*of firearm*) magasin *m*.
maggot ['mægət] *n* ver *m*, asticot *m*.
magic ['mædʒɪk] *n* magie *f* // *a* magique; ~**al** *a* magique; ~**ian** [mə'dʒɪʃən] *n* magicien/ne.
magistrate ['mædʒɪstreɪt] *n* magistrat *m*; juge *m*.

magnet ['mægnɪt] *n* aimant *m*; ~**ic** [-'netɪk] *a* magnétique.
magnificent [mæg'nɪfɪsnt] *a* superbe, magnifique.
magnify ['mægnɪfaɪ] *vt* grossir; (*sound*) amplifier; ~**ing glass** *n* loupe *f*.
magnitude ['mægnɪtju:d] *n* ampleur *f*.
magpie ['mægpaɪ] *n* pie *f*.
mahogany [mə'hɔgənɪ] *n* acajou *m*.
maid [meɪd] *n* bonne *f*; **old ~** (*pej*) vieille fille.
maiden ['meɪdn] *n* jeune fille *f* // *a* (*aunt etc*) non mariée; (*speech, voyage*) inaugural(e); ~ **name** *n* nom *m* de jeune fille.
mail [meɪl] *n* poste *f*; (*letters*) courrier *m* // *vt* envoyer (par la poste); ~**box** *n* (*US*) boîte *f* aux lettres; ~**ing list** *n* liste *f* d'adresses; ~**order** *n* vente *f* or achat *m* par correspondance.
maim [meɪm] *vt* mutiler.
main [meɪn] *a* principal(e) // *n* (*pipe*) conduite principale, canalisation *f*; **the ~s** (*ELEC*) le secteur; **in the ~** dans l'ensemble; ~**frame** *n* (*COMPUT*) (gros) ordinateur, unité centrale; ~**land** *n* continent *m*; ~**ly** *ad* principalement, surtout; ~ **road** *n* grand-route *f*; ~**stream** *n* courant principal; ~**stay** *n* (*fig*) pilier *m*.
maintain [meɪn'teɪn] *vt* entretenir; (*continue*) maintenir, préserver; (*affirm*) soutenir; **maintenance** ['meɪntənəns] *n* entretien *m*; (*alimony*) pension *f* alimentaire.
maize [meɪz] *n* maïs *m*.
majestic [mə'dʒestɪk] *a* majestueux(euse).
majesty ['mædʒɪstɪ] *n* majesté *f*.
major ['meɪdʒə*] *n* (*MIL*) commandant *m* // *a* important(e), principal(e); (*MUS*) majeur(e).
Majorca [mə'jɔ:kə] *n* Majorque *f*.
majority [mə'dʒɔrɪtɪ] *n* majorité *f*.
make [meɪk] *vt* (*pt, pp* **made**) faire; (*manufacture*) faire, fabriquer; (*cause to be*): **to ~ sb sad** *etc* rendre qn triste *etc*; (*force*): **to ~ sb do sth** obliger qn à faire qch, faire faire qch à qn; (*equal*): **2 and 2 ~ 4** 2 et 2 font 4 // *n* fabrication *f*; (*brand*) marque *f*; **to ~ a fool of sb** (*ridicule*) ridiculiser qn; (*trick*) avoir *or* duper qn; **to ~ a profit** faire un *or* des bénéfice(s); **to ~ a loss** essuyer une perte; **to ~ it** (*arrive*) arriver; (*achieve sth*) parvenir à qch; **what time do you ~ it?** quelle heure avez-vous?; **to ~ do with** se contenter de; se débrouiller avec; **to ~ for** *vt fus* (*place*) se diriger vers; **to ~ out** *vt* (*write out*) écrire; (: *cheque*) faire; (*understand*) comprendre; (*see*) distinguer; **to ~ up** *vt* (*invent*) inventer, imaginer; (*parcel*) faire // *vi* se réconcilier; (*with cosmetics*) se maquiller, se farder; **to ~ up for** *vt fus*

compenser; racheter; **~-believe** *n*: a world of ~-believe un pays de chimères; it's just ~-believe c'est pour faire semblant; c'est de l'invention pure; **~r** *n* fabricant *m*; **~shift** *a* provisoire, improvisé(e); **~-up** *n* maquillage *m*; **~-up remover** *n* démaquillant *m*.

making ['meɪkɪŋ] *n* (*fig*): **in the ~** en formation *or* gestation; **to have the ~s of** (*actor, athlete etc*) avoir l'étoffe de.

malaria [mə'lɛərɪə] *n* malaria *f*.

Malaya [mə'leɪə] *n* Malaisie *f*.

male [meɪl] *n* (BIOL, ELEC) mâle *m* // *a* (*sex, attitude*) masculin(e); mâle; (*child etc*) du sexe masculin.

malevolent [mə'lɛvələnt] *a* malveillant(e).

malfunction [mæl'fʌŋkʃən] *n* fonctionnement défectueux.

malice ['mælɪs] *n* méchanceté *f*, malveillance *f*; **malicious** [mə'lɪʃəs] *a* méchant(e), malveillant(e); (LAW) avec intention criminelle.

malign [mə'laɪn] *vt* diffamer, calomnier.

malignant [mə'lɪgnənt] *a* (MED) malin(igne).

mall [mɔ:l] *n* (*also*: **shopping ~**) centre commercial.

mallet ['mælɪt] *n* maillet *m*.

malpractice [mæl'præktɪs] *n* faute professionnelle; négligence *f*.

malt [mɔ:lt] *n* malt *m* // *cpd* (*whisky*) pur malt.

Malta ['mɔ:ltə] *n* Malte *f*.

mammal ['mæml] *n* mammifère *m*.

mammoth ['mæməθ] *n* mammouth *m* // *a* géant(e), monstre.

man [mæn], *pl* **men** *n* homme *m*; (CHESS) pièce *f*; (DRAUGHTS) pion *m* // *vt* garnir d'hommes; servir, assurer le fonctionnement de; être de service à; **an old ~** un vieillard; **~ and wife** mari et femme.

manage ['mænɪdʒ] *vi* se débrouiller // *vt* (*be in charge of*) s'occuper de; gérer; **to ~ to do** se débrouiller pour faire; réussir à faire; **~able** *a* maniable; faisable; **~ment** *n* administration *f*, direction *f*; **~r** *n* directeur *m*; administrateur *m*; (*of hotel etc*) gérant *m*; (*of artist*) impresario *m*; **~ress** [-ə'rɛs] *n* directrice *f*; gérante *f*; **~rial** [-ə'dʒɪərɪəl] *a* directorial(e); **managing** *a*: **managing director** directeur général.

mandarin ['mændərɪn] *n* (*also*: ~ **orange**) mandarine *f*; (*person*) mandarin *m*.

mandatory ['mændətərɪ] *a* obligatoire; (*powers etc*) mandataire.

mane [meɪn] *n* crinière *f*.

maneuver *etc* [mə'nu:və*] (US) = **manoeuvre** *etc*.

manfully ['mænfəlɪ] *ad* vaillamment.

mangle ['mæŋgl] *vt* déchiqueter; mutiler.

mango, ~es ['mæŋgəu] *n* mangue *f*.

mangy ['meɪndʒɪ] *a* galeux(euse).

manhandle ['mænhændl] *vt* malmener.

manhole ['mænhəul] *n* trou *m* d'homme.

manhood ['mænhud] *n* âge *m* d'homme; virilité *f*.

man-hour ['mæn'auə*] *n* heure *f* de main-d'œuvre.

mania ['meɪnɪə] *n* manie *f*; **~c** ['meɪnɪæk] *n* maniaque *m/f*.

manic ['mænɪk] *a* maniaque.

manicure ['mænɪkjuə*] *n* manucure *f*; **~ set** *n* trousse *f* à ongles.

manifest ['mænɪfɛst] *vt* manifester // *a* manifeste, évident(e).

manifesto [mænɪ'fɛstəu] *n* manifeste *m*.

manipulate [mə'nɪpjuleɪt] *vt* manipuler.

mankind [mæn'kaɪnd] *n* humanité *f*, genre humain.

manly ['mænlɪ] *a* viril(e); courageux(euse).

man-made ['mæn'meɪd] *a* artificiel(le).

manner ['mænə*] *n* manière *f*, façon *f*; **~s** *npl* manières; **~ism** *n* particularité *f* de langage (*or* de comportement), tic *m*.

manoeuvre, (US) **maneuver** [mə'nu:və*] *vt, vi* manœuvrer // *n* manœuvre *f*.

manor ['mænə*] *n* (*also*: ~ **house**) manoir *m*.

manpower ['mænpauə*] *n* main-d'œuvre *f*.

mansion ['mænʃən] *n* château *m*, manoir *m*.

manslaughter ['mænslɔ:tə*] *n* homicide *m* involontaire.

mantelpiece ['mæntlpi:s] *n* cheminée *f*.

manual ['mænjuəl] *a* manuel(le) // *n* manuel *m*.

manufacture [mænju'fæktʃə*] *vt* fabriquer // *n* fabrication *f*; **~r** *n* fabricant *m*.

manure [mə'njuə*] *n* fumier *m*; (*artificial*) engrais *m*.

manuscript ['mænjuskrɪpt] *n* manuscrit *m*.

many ['mɛnɪ] *a* beaucoup de, de nombreux(euses) // *pronoun* beaucoup, un grand nombre; **a great ~** un grand nombre (de); **~ a ...** bien des ..., plus d'un(e) ....

map [mæp] *n* carte *f* // *vt* dresser la carte de; **to ~ out** *vt* tracer.

maple ['meɪpl] *n* érable *m*.

mar [mɑ:*] *vt* gâcher, gâter.

marathon ['mærəθən] *n* marathon *m*.

marble ['mɑ:bl] *n* marbre *m*; (*toy*) bille *f*.

March [mɑ:tʃ] *n* mars *m*.

march [mɑ:tʃ] *vi* marcher au pas; défiler // *n* marche *f*; (*demonstration*) rallye *m*.

mare [mɛə*] *n* jument *f*.

margarine [mɑ:dʒə'ri:n] *n* margarine *f*.

margin ['mɑ:dʒɪn] *n* marge *f*; **~al**

(seat) n (POL) siège disputé.
marigold ['mærɪgould] n souci m.
marijuana [mærɪ'wɑːnə] n marijuana f.
marine [mə'riːn] a marin(e) // n fusilier marin; (US) marine m.
marital ['mærɪtl] a matrimonial(e); ~ status situation f de famille.
mark [mɑːk] n marque f; (of skid etc) trace f; (Brit SCOL) note f; (SPORT) cible f; (currency) mark m // vt marquer; (stain) tacher; (Brit SCOL) noter; corriger; **to ~ time** marquer le pas; **to ~ out** vt désigner; **~er** n (sign) jalon m; (bookmark) signet m.
market ['mɑːkɪt] n marché m // vt (COMM) commercialiser; ~ **garden** n (Brit) jardin maraîcher; **~ing** n marketing m; **~place** n place f du marché; (COMM) marché m; ~ **research** n étude f de marché; ~ **value** n valeur marchande; valeur du marché.
marksman ['mɑːksmən] n tireur m d'élite.
marmalade ['mɑːməleɪd] n confiture f d'oranges.
maroon [mə'ruːn] vt (fig): **to be ~ed** (in or at) être bloqué(e) (à) // a bordeaux inv.
marquee [mɑː'kiː] n chapiteau m.
marriage ['mærɪdʒ] n mariage m; ~ **bureau** n agence matrimoniale; ~ **certificate** n extrait m d'acte de mariage.
married ['mærɪd] a marié(e); (life, love) conjugal(e).
marrow ['mærəu] n moelle f; (vegetable) courge f.
marry ['mærɪ] vt épouser, se marier avec; (subj: father, priest etc) marier // vi (also: **get married**) se marier.
Mars [mɑːz] n (planet) Mars f.
marsh [mɑːʃ] n marais m, marécage m.
marshal ['mɑːʃl] n maréchal m; (US: fire, police) ≈ capitaine m // vt rassembler.
martyr ['mɑːtə*] n martyr/e // vt martyriser; **~dom** n martyre m.
marvel ['mɑːvl] n merveille f // vi: **to ~ (at)** s'émerveiller (de); **~lous**, (US) **~ous** a merveilleux(euse).
Marxist ['mɑːksɪst] a, n marxiste (m/f).
marzipan ['mɑːzɪpæn] n pâte f d'amandes.
mascara [mæs'kɑːrə] n mascara m.
masculine ['mæskjulɪn] a masculin(e).
mashed [mæʃt] a: ~ **potatoes** purée f de pommes de terre.
mask [mɑːsk] n masque m // vt masquer.
mason ['meɪsn] n (also: **stone~**) maçon m; (also: **free~**) franc-maçon m; **~ry** n maçonnerie f.
masquerade [mæskə'reɪd] n bal masqué; (fig) mascarade f // vi: **to ~ as** se faire passer pour.
mass [mæs] n multitude f, masse f; (PHYSICS) masse; (REL) messe f // vi se

masser; **the ~es** les masses.
massacre ['mæsəkə*] n massacre m.
massage ['mæsɑːʒ] n massage m // vt masser.
massive ['mæsɪv] a énorme, massif(ive).
mass media ['mæs'miːdɪə] npl massmedia mpl.
mass-production ['mæsprə'dʌkʃən] n fabrication f en série.
mast [mɑːst] n mât m.
master ['mɑːstə*] n maître m; (in secondary school) professeur m; (title for boys): **M~ X** Monsieur X // vt maîtriser; (learn) apprendre à fond; (understand) posséder parfaitement or à fond; ~ **key** n passe-partout m inv; **~ly** a magistral(e); **~mind** n esprit supérieur // vt diriger, être le cerveau de; **M~ of Arts/Science (M.A./M.Sc.)** n ≈ titulaire m/f d'une maîtrise (en lettres/ sciences); **~piece** n chef-d'œuvre m; **~y** n maîtrise f; connaissance parfaite.
mat [mæt] n petit tapis; (also: **door~**) paillasson m // a = **matt**.
match [mætʃ] n allumette f; (game) match m, partie f; (fig) égal/e; mariage m; parti m // vt assortir; (go well with) aller bien avec; s'assortir à; (equal) égaler, valoir // vi être assorti(e); **to be a good ~** être bien assorti(e); **~box** n boîte f d'allumettes; **~ing** a assorti(e).
mate [meɪt] n camarade m/f de travail; (col) copain/copine; (animal) partenaire m/f, mâle/femelle; (in merchant navy) second m // vi s'accoupler // vt accoupler.
material [mə'tɪərɪəl] n (substance) matière f, matériau m; (cloth) tissu m, étoffe f // a matériel(le); (important) essentiel(le); **~s** npl matériaux mpl.
maternal [mə'tɜːnl] a maternel(le).
maternity [mə'tɜːnɪtɪ] n maternité f; ~ **dress** n robe f de grossesse; ~ **hospital** n maternité f.
math [mæθ] n (US) = **maths**.
mathematical [mæθə'mætɪkl] a mathématique.
mathematics [mæθə'mætɪks] n mathématiques fpl.
maths, (US) **math** [mæθs, mæθ] n math(s) fpl.
matinée ['mætɪneɪ] n matinée f.
mating ['meɪtɪŋ] n accouplement m.
matriculation [mətrɪkju'leɪʃən] n inscription f.
matrimonial [mætrɪ'məunɪəl] a matrimonial(e), conjugal(e).
matrimony ['mætrɪmənɪ] n mariage m.
matron ['meɪtrən] n (in hospital) infirmière-chef f; (in school) infirmière; **~ly** a de matrone; imposant(e).
mat(t) [mæt] a mat(e).
matted ['mætɪd] a emmêlé(e).
matter ['mætə*] n question f; (PHYSICS)

matière f, substance f; (content) contenu m, fond m; (MED: pus) pus m // vi importer; it doesn't ~ cela n'a pas d'importance; (I don't mind) cela ne fait rien; what's the ~? qu'est-ce qu'il y a?, qu'est-ce qui ne va pas?; no ~ what quoiqu'il arrive; as a ~ of course tout naturellement; as a ~ of fact en fait; ~-of-fact a terre à terre, neutre.

mattress ['mætris] n matelas m.

mature [mə'tjuə*] a mûr(e); (cheese) fait(e) // vi mûrir; se faire.

maul [mɔ:l] vt lacérer.

mauve [məuv] a mauve.

maximum ['mæksɪməm] a maximum // n (pl **maxima** ['mæksɪmə]) maximum m.

May [meɪ] n mai m.

may [meɪ] vi (conditional: **might**) (indicating possibility): he ~ come il se peut qu'il vienne; (be allowed to): ~ I smoke? puis-je fumer?; (wishes): ~ God bless you! (que) Dieu vous bénisse!

maybe ['meɪbi:] ad peut-être; ~ he'll ... peut-être qu'il ....

May Day n le Premier mai.

mayhem ['meɪhem] n grabuge m.

mayonnaise [meɪə'neɪz] n mayonnaise f.

mayor [mɛə*] n maire m; ~**ess** n maire m; épouse f du maire.

maze [meɪz] n labyrinthe m, dédale m.

M.D. abbr = Doctor of Medicine.

me [mi:] pronoun me, m' + vowel; (stressed, after prep) moi; he heard ~ il m'a entendu(e); give ~ a book donnez-moi un livre; after ~ après moi.

meadow ['mɛdəu] n prairie f, pré m.

meagre, (US) meager ['mi:gə*] a maigre.

meal [mi:l] n repas m; (flour) farine f; ~**time** n l'heure f du repas.

mean [mi:n] a (with money) avare, radin(e); (unkind) mesquin(e), méchant(e); (average) moyen(ne) // vt (pt, pp **meant**) (signify) signifier, vouloir dire; (intend): to ~ to do avoir l'intention de faire // n moyenne f; ~**s** npl moyens mpl; by ~**s** of par l'intermédiaire de; au moyen de; by all ~**s** je vous en prie; to be meant for sb/sth être destiné(e) à qn/qch; do you ~ it? vous êtes sérieux?; what do you ~? que voulez-vous dire?

meander [mi'ændə*] vi faire des méandres; (fig) flâner.

meaning ['mi:nɪŋ] n signification f, sens m; ~**ful** a significatif(ive); ~**less** a dénué(e) de sens.

meant [ment] pt, pp of **mean**.

meantime ['mi:ntaɪm] ad, **meanwhile** ['mi:nwaɪl] ad (also: in the ~) pendant ce temps.

measles ['mi:zlz] n rougeole f.

measly ['mi:zli] a (col) minable.

measure ['mɛʒə*] vt, vi mesurer // n mesure f; (ruler) règle (graduée); ~**ments** npl mesures fpl; chest/hip ~**ment** tour m de poitrine/hanches.

meat [mi:t] n viande f; ~**ball** n boulette f de viande; ~**y** a avec beaucoup de viande, plein(e) de viande; (fig) substantiel(le).

Mecca ['mɛkə] n la Mecque.

mechanic [mɪ'kænɪk] n mécanicien m; ~**s** n mécanique f // npl mécanisme m; ~**al** a mécanique.

mechanism ['mɛkənɪzəm] n mécanisme m.

medal ['mɛdl] n médaille f; ~**lion** [mɪ'dælɪən] n médaillon m.

meddle ['mɛdl] vi: to ~ in se mêler de, s'occuper de; to ~ with toucher à.

media ['mi:dɪə] npl media mpl.

mediaeval [mɛdɪ'i:vl] a = **medieval**.

median ['mi:dɪən] n (US: also: ~ **strip**) bande médiane.

mediate ['mi:dɪeɪt] vi s'interposer; servir d'intermédiaire.

Medicaid ['mɛdɪkeɪd] n (US) assistance médicale aux indigents.

medical ['mɛdɪkl] a médical(e).

Medicare ['mɛdɪkɛə*] n (US) assistance médicale aux personnes âgées.

medicated ['mɛdɪkeɪtɪd] a traitant(e), médicamenteux(euse).

medicine ['mɛdsɪn] n médecine f; (drug) médicament m.

medieval [mɛdɪ'i:vl] a médiéval(e).

mediocre [mi:dɪ'əukə*] a médiocre.

meditate ['mɛdɪteɪt] vi méditer.

Mediterranean [mɛdɪtə'reɪnɪən] a méditerranéen(ne); the ~ (**Sea**) la (mer) Méditerranée.

medium ['mi:dɪəm] a moyen(ne) // n (pl media: means) moyen m; (pl **mediums**: person) médium m; the happy ~ le juste milieu; ~ **wave** n ondes moyennes.

medley ['mɛdli] n mélange m.

meek [mi:k] a doux(douce), humble.

meet [mi:t], pt, pp **met** vt rencontrer; (by arrangement) retrouver, rejoindre; (for the first time) faire la connaissance de; (go and fetch): I'll ~ you at the station j'irai te chercher à la gare; (fig) faire face à; satisfaire à; se joindre à // vi se rencontrer; se retrouver; (in session) se réunir; (join: objects) se joindre; to ~ with vt fus rencontrer; ~**ing** n rencontre f; (session: of club etc) réunion f; (interview) entrevue f; she's at a ~**ing** (COMM) elle est en conférence.

megabyte ['mɛgəbaɪt] n (COMPUT) méga-octet m.

megaphone ['mɛgəfəun] n porte-voix m inv.

melancholy ['mɛlənkəlɪ] n mélancolie f // a mélancolique.

mellow ['mɛləu] a velouté(e);

doux(douce); (*colour*) riche et pro-
fond(e); (*fruit*) mûr(e) // *vi* (*person*)
s'adoucir.
melody ['mɛlədɪ] *n* mélodie *f*.
melon ['mɛlən] *n* melon *m*.
melt [mɛlt] *vi* fondre; (*become soft*)
s'amollir; (*fig*) s'attendrir // *vt* faire fondre; (*person*) attendrir; **to ~ away** *vi*
fondre complètement; **to ~ down** *vt*
fondre; **~down** *n* fusion *f* (du cœur
d'un réacteur nucléaire); **~ing pot** *n*
(*fig*) creuset *m*.
member ['mɛmbə*] *n* membre *m*; **M~
of Parliament (MP)** (*Brit*) député *m*;
M~ of the European Parliament (MEP)
(*Brit*) Eurodéputé *m*; **~ship** *n* adhésion
f; statut *m* de membre; (*nombre m* de)
membres *mpl*, adhérents *mpl*; **~ship
card** *n* carte *f* de membre.
memento [mə'mɛntəu] *n* souvenir *m*.
memo ['mɛməu] *n* note *f* (de service).
memoirs ['mɛmwɑ:z] *npl* mémoires
mpl.
memorandum, *pl* **memoranda**
[mɛmə'rændəm, -də] *n* note *f* (de
service); (*DIPLOMACY*) mémorandum
m.
memorial [mɪ'mɔ:rɪəl] *n* mémorial *m* //
a commémoratif(ive).
memorize ['mɛməraɪz] *vt* apprendre
par cœur; retenir.
memory ['mɛmərɪ] *n* mémoire *f*;
(*recollection*) souvenir *m*.
men [mɛn] *npl of* **man**.
menace ['mɛnəs] *n* menace *f* // *vt*
menacer.
mend [mɛnd] *vt* réparer; (*darn*)
raccommoder, repriser // *n* reprise *f*; **on
the ~** en voie de guérison.
menial ['mi:nɪəl] *a* de domestique,
inférieur(e); subalterne.
meningitis [mɛnɪn'dʒaɪtɪs] *n* méningite
f.
menopause ['mɛnəupɔ:z] *n* ménopause
f.
menstruation [mɛnstru'eɪʃən] *n* menstruation *f*.
mental ['mɛntl] *a* mental(e).
mentality [mɛn'tælɪtɪ] *n* mentalité *f*.
mention ['mɛnʃən] *n* mention *f* // *vt*
mentionner, faire mention de; **don't ~ it!**
je vous en prie, il n'y a pas de quoi!
menu ['mɛnju:] *n* (*set* ~, *COMPUT*)
menu *m*; (*printed*) carte *f*.
MEP *n abbr of* **Member of the
European Parliament.**
mercenary ['mə:sɪnərɪ] *a* mercantile // *n*
mercenaire *m*.
merchandise ['mə:tʃəndaɪz] *n* marchandises *fpl*.
merchant ['mə:tʃənt] *n* négociant *m*,
marchand *m*; **~ bank** *n* (*Brit*) banque *f*
d'affaires; **~ navy,** (*US*) **~ marine** *n*
marine marchande.
merciful ['mə:sɪful] *a* miséricor-

dieux(euse), clément(e).
merciless ['mə:sɪlɪs] *a* impitoyable, sans
pitié.
mercury ['mə:kjurɪ] *n* mercure *m*.
mercy ['mə:sɪ] *n* pitié *f*, merci *f*; (*REL*)
miséricorde *f*; **at the ~ of** à la merci de.
mere [mɪə*] *a* simple; **~ly** *ad* sim-
plement, purement.
merge [mə:dʒ] *vt* unir // *vi* se fondre;
(*COMM*) fusionner; **~r** *n* (*COMM*) fusion
f.
meringue [mə'ræŋ] *n* meringue *f*.
merit ['mɛrɪt] *n* mérite *m*, valeur *f* // *vt*
mériter.
mermaid ['mə:meɪd] *n* sirène *f*.
merry ['mɛrɪ] *a* gai(e); **M~ Christmas!**
Joyeux Noël!; **~-go-round** *n* manège
m.
mesh [mɛʃ] *n* maille *f*; filet *m*.
mesmerize ['mɛzməraɪz] *vt* hypnotiser;
fasciner.
mess [mɛs] *n* désordre *m*, fouillis *m*,
pagaille *f*; (*MIL*) mess *m*, cantine *f*; **to
~ about** *or* **around** *vi* (*col*) perdre son
temps; **to ~ about** *or* **around with**
vt fus (*col*) chambarder, tripoter; **to ~
up** *vt* salir; chambarder; gâcher.
message ['mɛsɪdʒ] *n* message *m*.
messenger ['mɛsɪndʒə*] *n* messager *m*.
Messrs [mɛsrz] *abbr* (*on letters*) MM.
messy ['mɛsɪ] *a* sale; en désordre.
met [mɛt] *pt, pp of* **meet.**
metal ['mɛtl] *n* métal *m*; **~lic**
[-'tælɪk] *a* métallique.
mete [mi:t] **to ~ out** *vt fus* infliger.
meteorology [mi:tɪə'rɔlədʒɪ] *n* météorologie *f*.
meter ['mi:tə*] *n* (*instrument*) compteur
m; (*US: unit*) = **metre**.
method ['mɛθəd] *n* méthode *f*; **~ical**
[mɪ'θɔdɪkl] *a* méthodique.
Methodist ['mɛθədɪst] *a, n* méthodiste
(*m/f*).
methylated spirit ['mɛθɪleɪtɪd-]
(*Brit: also*: **meths**) alcool *m* à brûler.
metre, (*US*) **meter** ['mi:tə*] *n* mètre *m*.
metric ['mɛtrɪk] *a* métrique.
metropolitan [mɛtrə'pɔlɪtən] *a* mé-
tropolitain(e); **the M~ Police** *n* (*Brit*) la
police londonienne.
mettle ['mɛtl] *n* courage *m*.
mew [mju:] *vi* (*cat*) miauler.
mews [mju:z] *n*: **~ cottage** (*Brit*) maisonnette aménagée dans une ancienne
écurie ou remise.
Mexico ['mɛksɪkəu] *n* Mexique *m*.
miaow [mi:'au] *vi* miauler.
mice [maɪs] *npl of* **mouse.**
micro ['maɪkrəu] *n* (*also*: **~computer**)
micro-ordinateur *m*.
microchip ['maɪkrəutʃɪp] *n* puce *f*.
microphone ['maɪkrəfəun] *n* microphone *m*.
microscope ['maɪkrəskəup] *n* microscope *m*.

microwave ['maɪkrəuweɪv] n (also: ~ oven) four m à micro-ondes.
mid [mɪd] a: ~ May la mi-mai; ~ afternoon le milieu de l'après-midi; in ~ air en plein ciel; ~day n midi m.
middle ['mɪdl] n milieu m; (waist) ceinture f, taille f // a du milieu; in the ~ of the night au milieu de la nuit; ~aged a d'un certain âge; the M~ Ages npl le moyen âge; ~class a bourgeois(e); the ~ class(es) n(pl) = les classes moyennes; M~ East n Proche-Orient m, Moyen-Orient m; ~man n intermédiaire m; ~ name n deuxième nom m; ~weight n (BOXING) poids moyen.
middling ['mɪdlɪŋ] a moyen(ne).
midge [mɪdʒ] n moucheron m.
midget ['mɪdʒɪt] n nain/e.
Midlands ['mɪdləndz] npl comtés du centre de l'Angleterre.
midnight ['mɪdnaɪt] n minuit m.
midriff ['mɪdrɪf] n estomac m, taille f.
midst [mɪdst] n: in the ~ of au milieu de.
midsummer [mɪd'sʌmə*] n milieu m de l'été.
midway [mɪd'weɪ] a, ad: ~ (between) à mi-chemin (entre).
midweek [mɪd'wi:k] n milieu m de la semaine.
midwife, pl **midwives** ['mɪdwaɪf, -vz] n sage-femme f; ~ry [-wɪfərɪ] n obstétrique f.
might [maɪt] vb see **may** // n puissance f, force f; ~y a puissant(e).
migraine ['mi:greɪn] n migraine f.
migrant ['maɪgrənt] a (bird) migrateur(trice); (person) migrant(e); nomade; (worker) saisonnier(ère).
migrate [maɪ'greɪt] vi émigrer.
mike [maɪk] n abbr (= microphone) micro m.
mild [maɪld] a doux(douce); (reproach) léger(ère); (illness) bénin(igne).
mildew ['mɪldju:] n mildiou m.
mildly ['maɪldlɪ] ad doucement; légèrement; to put it ~ c'est le moins qu'on puisse dire.
mile [maɪl] n mil(l)e m (= 1609 m); ~age n distance f en milles, ≈ kilométrage m; ~stone n borne f; (fig) jalon m.
militant ['mɪlɪtnt] a, n militant(e).
military ['mɪlɪtərɪ] a militaire.
milk [mɪlk] n lait m // vt (cow) traire; (fig) dépouiller, plumer; ~ chocolate n chocolat m au lait; ~man n laitier m; ~ shake n milk-shake m; ~y a lacté(e); (colour) laiteux(euse); M~y Way n Voie lactée.
mill [mɪl] n moulin m; (factory) usine f, fabrique f; (spinning ~) filature f; (flour ~) minoterie f // vt moudre, broyer // vi (also: ~ about) grouiller.

miller ['mɪlə*] n meunier m.
millet ['mɪlɪt] n millet m.
milli... ['mɪlɪ] prefix: ~gram(me) n milligramme m // ~metre, (US) ~meter n millimètre m.
millinery ['mɪlɪnərɪ] n modes fpl.
million ['mɪljən] n million m; ~aire n millionnaire m.
millstone ['mɪlstəun] n meule f.
milometer [maɪ'lɒmɪtə*] n ≈ compteur m kilométrique.
mime [maɪm] n mime m // vt, vi mimer.
mimic ['mɪmɪk] n imitateur/trice // vt imiter, contrefaire; ~ry n imitation f.
min. abbr of **minute(s)**, **minimum**.
mince [mɪns] vt hacher // vi (in walking) marcher à petits pas maniérés // n (Brit CULIN) viande hachée, hachis m; ~meat n hachis de fruits secs utilisés en pâtisserie; ~ pie n sorte de tarte aux fruits secs; ~r n hachoir m.
mind [maɪnd] n esprit m // vt (attend to, look after) s'occuper de; (be careful) faire attention à; (object to): I don't ~ the noise je ne crains pas le bruit, le bruit ne me dérange pas; I don't ~ cela ne me dérange pas; it is on my ~ cela me préoccupe; to my ~ à mon avis or sens; to be out of one's ~ ne plus avoir toute sa raison; to bear sth in ~ tenir compte de qch; to make up one's ~ se décider; ~ you, — remarquez —; je vous assure —; never ~ ne vous en faites pas; '~ the step' 'attention à la marche'; ~er n (child-~er) gardienne f; (bodyguard) ange gardien (fig); ~ful a: ~ful of attentif(ive) à, soucieux(euse) de; ~less a irréfléchi(e).
mine [maɪn] pronoun le(la) mien(ne), les miens(miennes) // a: this book is ~ ce livre est à moi // n mine f // vt (coal) extraire; (ship, beach) miner.
miner ['maɪnə*] n mineur m.
mineral ['mɪnərəl] a minéral(e) // n minéral m; ~s npl (Brit: soft drinks) boissons gazeuses (sucrées); ~ water n eau minérale.
minesweeper ['maɪnswi:pə*] n dragueur m de mines.
mingle ['mɪŋgl] vi: to ~ with se mêler à.
miniature ['mɪnətʃə*] a (en) miniature // n miniature f.
minibus ['mɪnɪbʌs] n minibus m.
minimum ['mɪnɪməm] a, n minimum (m).
mining ['maɪnɪŋ] n exploitation minière // a minier(ère); de mineurs.
miniskirt ['mɪnɪskə:t] n mini-jupe f.
minister ['mɪnɪstə*] n (Brit POL) ministre m; (REL) pasteur m // vi: to ~ to sb donner ses soins à qn; to ~ to sb's needs pourvoir aux besoins de qn; ~ial [-'tɪərɪəl] a (Brit POL) ministériel(le).
ministry ['mɪnɪstrɪ] n (Brit POL) ministère m; (REL): to go into the ~

devenir pasteur.

mink [mɪŋk] n vison m.

minnow ['mɪnəu] n vairon m.

minor ['maɪnə*] a petit(e), de peu d'importance; (MUS) mineur(e) // n (LAW) mineur/e.

minority [maɪ'nɔrɪtɪ] n minorité f.

mint [mɪnt] n (plant) menthe f; (sweet) bonbon m à la menthe // vt (coins) battre; **the (Royal) M~**, (US) **the (US) M~** ≈ l'hôtel m de la Monnaie; **in ~ condition** à l'état de neuf.

minus ['maɪnəs] n (also: **~ sign**) signe m moins // prep moins.

minute a [maɪ'njuːt] minuscule; (detail) minutieux(euse) // n ['mɪnɪt] minute f; (official record) procès-verbal m, compte rendu; **~s** npl procès-verbal.

miracle ['mɪrəkl] n miracle m.

mirage ['mɪrɑːʒ] n mirage m.

mire ['maɪə*] n bourbe f, boue f.

mirror ['mɪrə*] n miroir m, glace f // vt refléter.

mirth [mɜːθ] n gaieté f.

misadventure [mɪsəd'ventʃə*] n mésaventure f; **death by ~** décès accidentel.

misapprehension ['mɪsæprɪ'henʃən] n malentendu m, méprise f.

misbehave [mɪsbɪ'heɪv] vi se conduire mal.

miscarriage ['mɪskærɪdʒ] n (MED) fausse couche; **~ of justice** erreur f judiciaire.

miscellaneous [mɪsɪ'leɪnɪəs] a (items) divers(es); (selection) varié(es).

mischief ['mɪstʃɪf] n (naughtiness) sottises fpl; (harm) mal m, dommage m; (maliciousness) méchanceté f; **mischievous** a (naughty) coquin(e), espiègle; (harmful) méchant(e).

misconception ['mɪskən'sepʃən] n idée fausse.

misconduct [mɪs'kɔndʌkt] n inconduite f; **professional ~** faute professionnelle.

misconstrue [mɪskən'struː] vt mal interpréter.

misdeed [mɪs'diːd] n méfait m.

misdemeanour, (US) **misdemeanor** [mɪsdɪ'miːnə*] n écart m de conduite; infraction f.

miser ['maɪzə*] n avare m/f.

miserable ['mɪzərəbl] a malheureux(euse); (wretched) misérable.

miserly ['maɪzəlɪ] a avare.

misery ['mɪzərɪ] n (unhappiness) tristesse f; (pain) souffrances fpl; (wretchedness) misère f.

misfire [mɪs'faɪə*] vi rater; (car engine) avoir des ratés.

misfit ['mɪsfɪt] n (person) inadapté/e.

misfortune [mɪs'fɔːtʃən] n malchance f, malheur m.

misgiving(s) [mɪs'gɪvɪŋ(z)] n(pl) craintes fpl, soupçons mpl.

misguided [mɪs'gaɪdɪd] a malavisé(e).

mishandle [mɪs'hændl] vt (treat roughly) malmener; (mismanage) mal s'y prendre pour faire or résoudre etc.

mishap ['mɪshæp] n mésaventure f.

misinterpret [mɪsɪn'tɜːprɪt] vt mal interpréter.

misjudge [mɪs'dʒʌdʒ] vt méjuger, se méprendre sur le compte de.

mislay [mɪs'leɪ] vt irg égarer.

mislead [mɪs'liːd] vt irg induire en erreur; **~ing** a trompeur(euse).

misnomer [mɪs'nəumə*] n terme or qualificatif trompeur or peu approprié.

misplace [mɪs'pleɪs] vt égarer.

misprint ['mɪsprɪnt] n faute f d'impression.

Miss [mɪs] n Mademoiselle.

miss [mɪs] vt (fail to get) manquer, rater; (regret the absence of): **I ~ him/it** il/cela me manque // vi manquer // n (shot) coup manqué; **to ~ out** vt (Brit) oublier.

misshapen [mɪs'ʃeɪpən] a difforme.

missile ['mɪsaɪl] n (AVIAT) missile m; (object thrown) projectile m.

missing ['mɪsɪŋ] a manquant(e); (after escape, disaster: person) disparu(e); **to go ~** disparaître.

mission ['mɪʃən] n mission f; **~ary** n missionnaire m/f.

misspent ['mɪs'spent] a: **his ~ youth** sa folle jeunesse.

mist [mɪst] n brume f, brouillard m // vi (also: **~ over**, **~ up**) devenir brumeux(euse); (Brit: windows) s'embuer.

mistake [mɪs'teɪk] n erreur f, faute f // vt (irg: like take) mal comprendre; se méprendre sur; **to make a ~** se tromper, faire une erreur; **by ~** par erreur, par inadvertance; **to ~ for** prendre pour; **~n** a (idea etc) erroné(e); **to be ~n** faire erreur, se tromper.

mister ['mɪstə*] n (col) Monsieur m; see Mr.

mistletoe ['mɪsltəu] n gui m.

mistook [mɪs'tuk] pt of **mistake**.

mistress ['mɪstrɪs] n maîtresse f; (Brit: in primary school) institutrice f; see Mrs.

mistrust [mɪs'trʌst] vt se méfier de.

misty ['mɪstɪ] a brumeux(euse).

misunderstand [mɪsʌndə'stænd] vt, vi irg mal comprendre; **~ing** n méprise f, malentendu m.

misuse n [mɪs'juːs] mauvais emploi; (of power) abus m // vt [mɪs'juːz] mal employer; abuser de.

mitigate ['mɪtɪgeɪt] vt atténuer.

mitt(en) ['mɪt(n)] n mitaine f; moufle f.

mix [mɪks] vt mélanger // vi se mélanger // n mélange m; dosage m; **to ~ up** vt mélanger; (confuse) confondre; **~ed** a (assorted) assortis(ies); (school etc) mixte; **~ed grill** n assortiment m de grillades; **~ed-up** a (confused) désorienté(e), embrouillé(e); **~er** n (for food) batteur m, mixeur m; (person): **he is a good ~er** il est très liant; **~ture** n assortiment m, mélange m; (MED) préparation f; **~-up** n confusion f.

moan [məun] n gémissement m // vi gémir; (col: complain): **to ~ (about)** se plaindre (de).

moat [məut] n fossé m, douves fpl.

mob [mɔb] n foule f; (disorderly) cohue f; (pej): **the ~** la populace // vt assaillir.

mobile ['məubaɪl] a mobile // n mobile m; **~ home** n caravane f.

mock [mɔk] vt ridiculiser, se moquer de // a faux(fausse); **~ery** n moquerie f, raillerie f.

mod [mɔd] a see **convenience**.

mode [məud] n mode m.

model ['mɔdl] n modèle m; (person: for fashion) mannequin m; (: for artist) modèle // vt modeler // vi travailler comme mannequin // a (railway: toy) modèle réduit inv; (child, factory) modèle; **to ~ clothes** présenter des vêtements.

modem ['məudem] n modem m.

moderate a n, ['mɔdərət] a modéré(e) // n (POL) modéré/e // vb ['mɔdəreɪt] vi se modérer, se calmer // vt modérer.

modern ['mɔdən] a moderne; **~ize** vt moderniser.

modest ['mɔdɪst] a modeste; **~y** n modestie f.

modicum ['mɔdɪkəm] n: **a ~ of** un minimum de.

modify ['mɔdɪfaɪ] vt modifier.

mogul ['məugl] n (fig) nabab m.

mohair ['məuhɛə*] n mohair m.

moist [mɔɪst] a humide, moite; **~en** ['mɔɪsn] vt humecter, mouiller légèrement; **~ure** ['mɔɪstʃə*] n humidité f; (on glass) buée f; **~urizer** ['mɔɪstʃəraɪzə*] n produit hydratant.

molar ['məulə*] n molaire f.

molasses [məu'læsɪz] n mélasse f.

mold [məuld] n, vt (US) = **mould**.

mole [məul] n (animal) taupe f; (spot) grain m de beauté.

molest [məu'lɛst] vt tracasser; molester.

mollycoddle ['mɔlɪkɔdl] vt chouchouter, couver.

molt [məult] vi (US) = **moult**.

molten ['məultən] a fondu(e).

mom [mɔm] n (US) = **mum**.

moment ['məumənt] n moment m, instant m; importance f; **at the ~** à ce moment; **~ary** a momentané(e), passager(ère); **~ous** [-'mɛntəs] a important(e), capital(e).

momentum [məu'mɛntəm] n élan m, vitesse acquise; **to gather ~** prendre de la vitesse.

mommy ['mɔmɪ] n (US) = **mummy**.

Monaco ['mɔnəkəu] n Monaco m.

monarch ['mɔnək] n monarque m; **~y** n monarchie f.

monastery ['mɔnəstərɪ] n monastère m.

Monday ['mʌndɪ] n lundi m.

monetary ['mʌnɪtərɪ] a monétaire.

money ['mʌnɪ] n argent m; **to make ~** gagner de l'argent; faire des bénéfices; rapporter; **~lender** n prêteur/euse; **~ order** n mandat m; **~-spinner** n (col) mine f d'or (fig).

mongrel ['mʌŋgrəl] n (dog) bâtard m.

monitor ['mɔnɪtə*] n (SCOL) chef m de classe; (TV, COMPUT) moniteur m // vt contrôler.

monk [mʌŋk] n moine m.

monkey ['mʌŋkɪ] n singe m; **~ nut** n (Brit) cacahuète f; **~ wrench** n clé f à molette.

mono... ['mɔnəu] prefix: **~chrome** a monochrome.

monopoly [mə'nɔpəlɪ] n monopole m.

monotone ['mɔnətəun] n ton m (or voix f) monocorde.

monotonous [mə'nɔtənəs] a monotone.

monsoon [mɔn'su:n] n mousson f.

monster ['mɔnstə*] n monstre m.

monstrous ['mɔnstrəs] a (huge) gigantesque; (atrocious) monstrueux(euse), atroce.

month [mʌnθ] n mois m; **~ly** a mensuel(le) // ad mensuellement // n (magazine) mensuel m, publication mensuelle.

monument ['mɔnjumənt] n monument m.

moo [mu:] vi meugler, beugler.

mood [mu:d] n humeur f, disposition f; **to be in a good/bad ~** être de bonne/mauvaise humeur; **~y** a (variable) d'humeur changeante, lunatique; (sullen) morose, maussade.

moon [mu:n] n lune f; **~light** n clair m de lune; **~lighting** n travail m au noir; **~lit** a éclairé(e) par la lune; (night) de lune.

moor [muə*] n lande f // vt (ship) amarrer // vi mouiller.

moorland ['muələnd] n lande f.

moose [mu:s] n (pl inv) élan m.

mop [mɔp] n balai m à laver // vt éponger, essuyer; **to ~ up** vt éponger; **~ of hair** tignasse f.

mope [məup] vi avoir le cafard, se morfondre.

moped ['məupɛd] n cyclomoteur m.

moral ['mɔrl] a moral(e) // n morale f; **~s** npl moralité f.

morale [mɔ'rɑ:l] n moral m.

morality [mə'rælɪtɪ] n moralité f.

morass [mə'ræs] n marais m, marécage m.

more [mɔ:*] ♦ a 1 (greater in number etc) plus (de), davantage; **~ people/work (than)** plus de gens/de travail (que)

2 (*additional*) encore (de); do you want (some) ~ tea? voulez-vous encore du thé?; I have no *or* I don't have any ~ money je n'ai plus d'argent; it'll take a few ~ weeks ça prendra encore quelques semaines

♦ *pronoun* plus, davantage; ~ than 10 plus de 10; it cost ~ than we expected cela a coûté plus que prévu; I want ~ j'en veux plus *or* davantage; is there any ~? est-ce qu'il en reste?; there's no ~ il n'y en a plus; a little ~ un peu plus; many/much ~ beaucoup plus, bien davantage

♦ *ad*: ~ dangerous/easily (than) plus dangereux/facilement (que); ~ and ~ expensive de plus en plus cher; ~ or less plus ou moins; ~ than ever plus que jamais.

moreover [mɔː'rəuvə*] *ad* de plus.

morning ['mɔːnɪŋ] *n* matin *m*; matinée *f*; in the ~ le matin; 7 o'clock in the ~ 7 heures du matin.

Morocco [mə'rɔkəu] *n* Maroc *m*.

moron ['mɔːrɔn] *n* idiot/e, minus *m/f*.

Morse [mɔːs] *n* (*also*: ~ code) morse *m*.

morsel ['mɔːsl] *n* bouchée *f*.

mortal ['mɔːtl] *a*, *n* mortel(le); ~ity [-'tælɪtɪ] *n* mortalité *f*.

mortar ['mɔːtə*] *n* mortier *m*.

mortgage ['mɔːgɪdʒ] *n* hypothèque *f*; (*loan*) prêt *m* (*or* crédit *m*) hypothécaire; ~ company *n* (*US*) société *f* de crédit immobilier.

mortuary ['mɔːtjuərɪ] *n* morgue *f*.

mosaic [məu'zeɪɪk] *n* mosaïque *f*.

Moscow ['mɔskəu] *n* Moscou.

Moslem ['mɔzləm] *a*, *n* = **Muslim**.

mosque [mɔsk] *n* mosquée *f*.

mosquito, ~es [mɔs'kiːtəu] *n* moustique *m*.

moss [mɔs] *n* mousse *f*.

most [məust] *a* la plupart de; le plus de // *pronoun* la plupart // *ad* le plus; (*very*) très, extrêmement; the ~ (*also*: + *adjective*) le plus; ~ of la plus grande partie de; ~ of them la plupart d'entre eux; I saw (the) ~ j'en ai vu la plupart; c'est moi qui en ai vu le plus; at the (very) ~ au plus; to make the ~ of profiter au maximum de; ~ly *ad* surtout, principalement.

MOT *n abbr* (*Brit*: = Ministry of Transport): the ~ (test) *la visite technique (annuelle) obligatoire des véhicules à moteur.*

motel [məu'tɛl] *n* motel *m*.

moth [mɔθ] *n* papillon *m* de nuit; mite *f*; ~ball *n* boule *f* de naphtaline.

mother ['mʌðə*] *n* mère *f* // *vt* (*care for*) dorloter; ~hood *n* maternité *f*; ~-in-law *n* belle-mère *f*; ~ly *a* maternel(le); ~-of-pearl *n* nacre *f*; ~-to-be *n* future maman; ~ tongue *n* langue maternelle.

motion ['məuʃən] *n* mouvement *m*; (*gesture*) geste *m*; (*at meeting*) motion *f* // *vt*, *vi*: to ~ (to) sb to do faire signe à qn de faire; ~less *a* immobile, sans mouvement; ~ picture *n* film *m*.

motivated ['məutɪveɪtɪd] *a* motivé(e).

motive ['məutɪv] *n* motif *m*, mobile *m*.

motley ['mɔtlɪ] *a* hétéroclite; bigarré(e), bariolé(e).

motor ['məutə*] *n* moteur *m*; (*Brit col: vehicle*) auto *f* // *a* moteur(trice); ~bike *n* moto *f*; ~boat *n* bateau *m* à moteur; ~car *n* (*Brit*) automobile *f*; ~cycle *n* vélomoteur *m*; ~cyclist *n* motocycliste *m/f*; ~ing *n* (*Brit*) tourisme *m* automobile; ~ist *n* automobiliste *m/f*; ~ racing *n* (*Brit*) course *f* automobile; ~way *n* (*Brit*) autoroute *f*.

mottled ['mɔtld] *a* tacheté(e), marbré(e).

motto, ~es ['mɔtəu] *n* devise *f*.

mould, (*US*) **mold** [məuld] *n* moule *m*; (*mildew*) moisissure *f* // *vt* mouler, modeler; (*fig*) façonner; ~er *vi* (*decay*) moisir; ~y *a* moisi(e).

moult, (*US*) **molt** [məult] *vi* muer.

mound [maund] *n* monticule *m*, tertre *m*.

mount [maunt] *n* mont *m*, montagne *f*; (*horse*) monture *f*; (*for jewel etc*) monture // *vt* monter // *vi* (*also*: ~ up) s'élever, monter.

mountain ['mauntɪn] *n* montagne *f* // *cpd* de (la) montagne; ~eer [-'nɪə*] *n* alpiniste *m/f*; ~eering [-'nɪərɪŋ] *n* alpinisme *m*; ~ous *a* montagneux(euse); ~side *n* flanc *m or* versant *m* de la montagne.

mourn [mɔːn] *vt* pleurer // *vi*: to ~ (for) se lamenter (sur); ~er *n* parent/e *or* ami/e du défunt; personne *f* en deuil; ~ful *a* triste, lugubre; ~ing *n* deuil *m* // *cpd* (*dress*) de deuil; in ~ing en deuil.

mouse [maus], *pl* **mice** *n* (*also COMPUT*) souris *f*; ~trap *n* souricière *f*.

mousse [muːs] *n* mousse *f*.

moustache [məs'tɑːʃ] *n* moustache(s) *f(pl)*.

mousy ['mausɪ] *a* (*person*) effacé(e); (*hair*) d'un châtain terne.

mouth, ~s [mauθ, -ðz] *n* bouche *f*; (*of dog, cat*) gueule *f*; (*of river*) embouchure *f*; (*of bottle*) goulot *m*; (*opening*) orifice *m*; ~ful *n* bouchée *f*; ~ organ *n* harmonica *m*; ~piece *n* (*of musical instrument*) embouchure *f*; (*spokesman*) porte-parole *m inv*; ~wash *n* bain *m* de bouche; ~watering *a* qui met l'eau à la bouche.

movable ['muːvəbl] *a* mobile.

move [muːv] *n* (*movement*) mouvement *m*; (*in game*) coup *m*; (: *turn to play*) tour *m*; (*change of house*) déménagement *m* // *vt* déplacer, bouger; (*emotion-*

ally) émouvoir; (*POL: resolution etc*) proposer // vi (*gen*) bouger, remuer; (*traffic*) circuler; (*also: ~ house*) déménager; **to ~ towards** se diriger vers; **to ~ sb to do sth** pousser *or* inciter qn à faire qch; **to get a ~ on** se dépêcher, se remuer; **to ~ about** *or* **around** vi (*fidget*) remuer; (*travel*) voyager, se déplacer; **to ~ along** vi se pousser; **to ~ away** vi s'en aller, s'éloigner; **to ~ back** vi revenir, reculer; **to ~ forward** vi avancer // vt avancer; (*people*) faire avancer; **to ~ in** vi (*to a house*) emménager; **to ~ on** vi se remettre en route // vt (*onlookers*) faire circuler; **to ~ out** vi (*of house*) déménager; **to ~ over** vi se pousser, se déplacer; **to ~ up** vi avancer; (*employee*) avoir de l'avancement.

movement ['mu:vmənt] *n* mouvement *m*.

movie ['mu:vɪ] *n* film *m*; **the ~s** le cinéma; **~ camera** *n* caméra *f*.

moving ['mu:vɪŋ] *a* en mouvement; émouvant(e).

mow, *pt* **mowed**, *pp* **mowed** *or* **mown** [məu, -n] *vt* faucher; (*lawn*) tondre; **to ~ down** vt faucher; **~er** *n* (*also: lawnmower*) tondeuse *f* à gazon.

MP *n abbr of* **member of parliament**.

m.p.h. *abbr = miles per hour* (60 *m.p.h.* = 96 *km/h*).

Mr, Mr. ['mɪstə*] *n*: **~ Smith** Monsieur Smith, M. Smith.

Mrs, Mrs. ['mɪsɪz] *n*: **~ Smith** Madame Smith, Mme Smith.

Ms, Ms. [mɪz] *n* (*= Miss or Mrs*): **~ Smith** ≃ Madame Smith, Mme Smith.

M.Sc. *abbr see* **master**.

much [mʌtʃ] *a* beaucoup de // *ad*, *n or pronoun* beaucoup; **how ~ is it?** combien est-ce que ça coûte?; **too ~** trop (de); **as ~ as** autant de.

muck [mʌk] *n* (*mud*) boue *f*; (*dirt*) ordures *fpl*; **to ~ about** *or* **around** vi (*col*) faire l'imbécile; (*waste time*) traînasser; **to ~ up** vt (*col: ruin*) gâcher, esquinter.

mud [mʌd] *n* boue *f*.

muddle ['mʌdl] *n* pagaille *f*; désordre *m*, fouillis *m* // vt (*also: ~ up*) brouiller, embrouiller; **to be in a ~** (*person*) ne plus savoir où l'on en est; **to ~ through** vi se débrouiller.

muddy ['mʌdɪ] *a* boueux(euse).

mud: ~guard *n* garde-boue *m inv*; **~slinging** *n* médisance *f*, dénigrement *m*.

muff [mʌf] *n* manchon *m* // vt (*chance*) rater, louper.

muffin ['mʌfɪn] *n* petit pain rond et plat.

muffle ['mʌfl] *vt* (*sound*) assourdir, étouffer; (*against cold*) emmitoufler.

muffler ['mʌflə*] *n* (*US AUT*) silencieux *m*.

mug [mʌg] *n* (*cup*) grande tasse (*sans

soucoupe*), chope *f*; (*: for beer*) chope; (*col: face*) bouille *f*; (*: fool*) poire *f* // vt (*assault*) agresser; **~ging** *n* agression *f*.

muggy ['mʌgɪ] *a* lourd(e), moite.

mule [mju:l] *n* mule *f*.

mull [mʌl]: **to ~ over** vt réfléchir à.

mulled [mʌld] *a*: **~ wine** vin chaud.

multi-level ['mʌltɪlevl] *a* (*US*) = **multistorey**.

multiple ['mʌltɪpl] *a*, *n* multiple (*m*); **~ sclerosis** *n* sclérose *f* en plaques.

multiplication [mʌltɪplɪ'keɪʃən] *n* multiplication *f*.

multiply ['mʌltɪplaɪ] *vt* multiplier // vi se multiplier.

multistorey ['mʌltɪ'stɔ:rɪ] *a* (*Brit: building*) à étages; (*: car park*) à étages *or* niveaux multiples.

mum [mʌm] *n* (*Brit*) maman *f* // *a*: **to keep ~** ne pas souffler mot.

mumble ['mʌmbl] *vt*, *vi* marmotter, marmonner.

mummy ['mʌmɪ] *n* (*Brit: mother*) maman *f*; (*embalmed*) momie *f*.

mumps [mʌmps] *n* oreillons *mpl*.

munch [mʌntʃ] *vt*, *vi* mâcher.

mundane [mʌn'deɪn] *a* banal(e), terre à terre *inv*.

municipal [mju:'nɪsɪpl] *a* municipal(e).

mural ['mjuərl] *n* peinture murale.

murder ['mə:də*] *n* meurtre *m*, assassinat *m* // vt assassiner; **~er** *n* meurtrier *m*, assassin *m*; **~ous** *a* meurtrier(ère).

murky ['mə:kɪ] *a* sombre, ténébreux(euse).

murmur ['mə:mə*] *n* murmure *m* // vt, vi murmurer.

muscle ['mʌsl] *n* muscle *m*; **to ~ in** vi s'imposer, s'immiscer.

muscular ['mʌskjulə*] *a* musculaire; (*person, arm*) musclé(e).

muse [mju:z] *vi* méditer, songer.

museum [mju:'zɪəm] *n* musée *m*.

mushroom ['mʌʃrum] *n* champignon *m*.

music ['mju:zɪk] *n* musique *f*; **~al** *a* musical(e); (*person*) musicien(ne) // *n* (*show*) comédie musicale; **~al instrument** *n* instrument *m* de musique; **~ian** [-'zɪʃən] *n* musicien/ne.

Muslim ['mʌzlɪm] *a*, *n* musulman(e).

muslin ['mʌzlɪn] *n* mousseline *f*.

mussel ['mʌsl] *n* moule *f*.

must [mʌst] *auxiliary vb* (*obligation*): **I ~ do it** je dois le faire, il faut que je le fasse; (*probability*): **he ~ be there by now** il doit y être maintenant, il y est probablement maintenant; **I ~ have made a mistake** j'ai dû me tromper // *n* nécessité *f*, impératif *m*; **it's a ~** c'est indispensable.

mustard ['mʌstəd] *n* moutarde *f*.

muster ['mʌstə*] *vt* rassembler.

mustn't ['mʌsnt] = **must not**.

musty ['mʌstɪ] *a* qui sent le moisi *or* le

renfermé.

mute [mju:t] *a*, *n* muet(te).

muted ['mju:tɪd] *a* assourdi(e); voilé(e).

mutiny ['mju:tɪnɪ] *n* mutinerie *f*.

mutter ['mʌtə*] *vt*, *vi* marmonner, marmotter.

mutton ['mʌtn] *n* mouton *m*.

mutual ['mju:tʃuəl] *a* mutuel(le), réciproque.

muzzle ['mʌzl] *n* museau *m*; (*protective device*) muselière *f*; (*of gun*) gueule *f*.

my [maɪ] *a* mon(ma), mes *pl*; ~ **house/ car/gloves** ma maison/mon auto/mes gants; **I've washed ~ hair/cut ~ finger** je me suis lavé les cheveux/coupé le doigt.

myself [maɪ'self] *pronoun* (*reflexive*) me; (*emphatic*) moi-même; (*after prep*) moi; *see also* **oneself**.

mysterious [mɪs'tɪərɪəs] *a* mystérieux(euse).

mystery ['mɪstərɪ] *n* mystère *m*.

mystify ['mɪstɪfaɪ] *vt* mystifier; (*puzzle*) ébahir.

myth [mɪθ] *n* mythe *m*; ~**ology** [mɪ'θɔlədʒɪ] *n* mythologie *f*.

N

n/a *abbr* = *not applicable*.

nab [næb] *vt* pincer, attraper.

nag [næg] *vt* (*person*) être toujours après, reprendre sans arrêt; ~**ging** *a* (*doubt, pain*) persistant(e).

nail [neɪl] *n* (*human*) ongle *m*; (*metal*) clou *m* // *vt* clouer; **to ~ sb down to a date/price** contraindre qn à accepter *or* donner une date/un prix; ~**brush** *n* brosse *f* à ongles; ~**file** *n* lime *f* à ongles; ~ **polish** *n* vernis *m* à ongles; ~ **polish remover** *n* dissolvant *m*; ~ **scissors** *npl* ciseaux *mpl* à ongles; ~ **varnish** *n* (*Brit*) = ~ **polish**.

naïve [naɪ'i:v] *a* naïf(ïve).

naked ['neɪkɪd] *a* nu(e).

name [neɪm] *n* nom *m*; réputation *f* // *vt* nommer; citer; (*price, date*) fixer, donner; **by ~** par son nom; ~**less** *a* sans nom; (*witness, contributor*) anonyme; ~**ly** *ad* à savoir; ~**sake** *n* homonyme *m*.

nanny ['nænɪ] *n* bonne *f* d'enfants.

nap [næp] *n* (*sleep*) (petit) somme; **to be caught** ~**ping** être pris à l'improviste *or* en défaut.

nape [neɪp] *n*: ~ **of the neck** nuque *f*.

napkin ['næpkɪn] *n* serviette *f* (de table).

nappy ['næpɪ] *n* (*Brit*) couche *f* (*gen pl*); ~ **rash** *n*: **to have ~ rash** avoir les fesses rouges.

narcissus, *pl* **narcissi** [nɑː'sɪsəs, -saɪ] *n* narcisse *m*.

narcotic [nɑː'kɔtɪk] *n* (*drug*) stupéfiant *m*; (*MED*) narcotique *m* // *a* narcotique.

narrative ['nærətɪv] *n* récit *m* // *a* narratif(ive).

narrow ['nærəu] *a* étroit(e); (*fig*) restreint(e), limité(e) // *vi* devenir plus étroit, se rétrécir; **to have a ~ escape** l'échapper belle; **to ~ sth down to** réduire qch à; ~**ly** *ad*: **he ~ly missed injury/the tree** il a failli se blesser/ rentrer dans l'arbre; ~**-minded** *a* à l'esprit étroit, borné(e).

nasty ['nɑːstɪ] *a* (*person*) méchant(e); très désagréable; (*smell*) dégoûtant(e); (*wound, situation*) mauvais(e).

nation ['neɪʃən] *n* nation *f*.

national ['næʃənl] *a* national(e) // *n* (*abroad*) ressortissant/e; (*when home*) national/e; ~ **dress** *n* costume national; **N~ Health Service (NHS)** *n* (*Brit*) *service national de santé*, ≈ Sécurité Sociale; **N~ Insurance** *n* (*Brit*) ≈ Sécurité Sociale; ~**ism** *n* nationalisme *m*; ~**ity** [-'nælɪtɪ] *n* nationalité *f*; ~**ize** *vt* nationaliser; ~**ly** *ad* du point de vue national; dans le pays entier.

nation-wide ['neɪʃənwaɪd] *a* s'étendant à l'ensemble du pays; (*problem*) à l'échelle du pays entier // *ad* à travers *or* dans tout le pays.

native ['neɪtɪv] *n* habitant/e du pays, autochtone *m/f*; (*in colonies*) indigène *m/f* // *a* du pays, indigène; (*country*) natal(e); (*ability*) inné(e); **a ~ of Russia** une personne originaire de Russie; **a ~ speaker of French** une personne de langue maternelle française; ~ **language** *n* langue maternelle.

NATO ['neɪtəu] *n abbr* = *North Atlantic Treaty Organization*) O.T.A.N. *f*.

natural ['nætʃrəl] *a* naturel(le); ~ **gas** *n* gaz naturel; ~**ize** *vt* naturaliser; (*plant*) acclimater; **to become** ~**ized** (*person*) se faire naturaliser; ~**ly** *ad* naturellement.

nature ['neɪtʃə*] *n* nature *f*; **by ~** par tempérament, de nature.

naught [nɔːt] *n* = **nought**.

naughty ['nɔːtɪ] *a* (*child*) vilain(e), pas sage; (*story, film*) polisson(ne).

nausea ['nɔːsɪə] *n* nausée *f*; **nauseate** ['nɔːsɪeɪt] *vt* écœurer, donner la nausée à.

naval ['neɪvl] *a* naval(e); ~ **officer** *n* officier *m* de marine.

nave [neɪv] *n* nef *f*.

navel ['neɪvl] *n* nombril *m*.

navigate ['nævɪgeɪt] *vt* diriger, piloter // *vi* naviguer; **navigation** [-'geɪʃən] *n* navigation *f*; **navigator** *n* navigateur *m*.

navvy ['nævɪ] *n* (*Brit*) terrassier *m*.

navy ['neɪvɪ] *n* marine *f*; ~**(-blue)** *a* bleu marine *inv*.

Nazi ['nɑːtsɪ] *n* Nazi/e.

NB *abbr* (= *nota bene*) NB.

near [nɪə*] *a* proche // *ad* près // *prep* (*also*: ~ **to**) près de // *vt* approcher de;

~by [nɪə'baɪ] a proche // ad tout près, à proximité; **~ly** ad presque; I **~ly** fell j'ai failli tomber; **~ miss** n collision évitée de justesse; (when aiming) coup manqué de peu or de justesse; **~side** n (AUT: right-hand drive) côté m gauche; **~-sighted** a myope.

neat [ni:t] a (a person, work) soigné(e); (room etc) bien tenu(e) or rangé(e); (solution, plan) habile; (spirits) pur(e); **~ly** ad avec soin or ordre; habilement.

necessarily ['nɛsɪsrɪlɪ] ad nécessairement.

necessary ['nɛsɪsrɪ] a nécessaire.

necessity [nɪ'sɛsɪtɪ] n nécessité f; chose nécessaire or essentielle.

neck [nɛk] n cou m; (of horse, garment) encolure f; (of bottle) goulot m // vi (col) se peloter; **~ and ~** à égalité.

necklace ['nɛklɪs] n collier m.

neckline ['nɛklaɪn] n encolure f.

necktie ['nɛktaɪ] n cravate f.

need [ni:d] n besoin m // vt avoir besoin de; **to ~ to do** devoir faire; avoir besoin de faire; **you don't ~ to go** vous n'avez pas besoin or vous n'êtes pas obligé de partir.

needle ['ni:dl] n aiguille f // vt asticoter, tourmenter.

needless ['ni:dlɪs] a inutile.

needlework ['ni:dlwə:k] n (activity) travaux mpl d'aiguille; (object) ouvrage m.

needn't [ni:dnt] = need not.

needy ['ni:dɪ] a nécessiteux(euse).

negative ['nɛgətɪv] n (PHOT, ELEC) négatif m; (LING) terme m de négation // a négatif(ive).

neglect [nɪ'glɛkt] vt négliger // n (of person, duty, garden) le fait de négliger; (state of ~) abandon m.

negligee ['nɛglɪʒeɪ] n déshabillé m.

negligence ['nɛglɪdʒəns] n négligence f.

negotiate [nɪ'gəʊʃɪeɪt] vi, vt négocier; **negotiation** [-'eɪʃən] n négociation f, pourparlers mpl.

Negro ['ni:grəʊ] a (gen) noir(e); (music, arts) nègre, noir // n (pl: ~es) Noir/e.

neigh [neɪ] vi hennir.

neighbour, (US) neighbor ['neɪbə*] n voisin/e; **~hood** n quartier m; voisinage m; **~ing** a voisin(e), avoisinant(e); **~ly** a obligeant(e); (relations) de bon voisinage.

neither ['naɪðə*] a, pronoun aucun(e) (des deux), ni l'un(e) ni l'autre // cj: I didn't move and **~** did Claude je n'ai pas bougé, (et) Claude non plus; ..., **~ did I** refuse ..., (et or mais) je n'ai pas non plus refusé // ad: **~ good nor bad** ni bon ni mauvais.

neon ['ni:ɔn] n néon m; **~ light** n lampe f au néon.

nephew ['nɛvju:] n neveu m.

nerve [nə:v] n nerf m; (fig) sang-froid m, courage m; aplomb m, toupet m; **to have a fit of ~s** avoir le trac; **~-racking** a angoissant(e).

nervous ['nə:vəs] a nerveux(euse); inquiet(ète), plein(e) d'appréhension; **~ breakdown** n dépression nerveuse.

nest [nɛst] n nid m // vi (se) nicher, faire son nid; **~ egg** n (fig) bas m de laine, magot m.

nestle ['nɛsl] vi se blottir.

net [nɛt] n filet m // a net(te) // vt (fish etc) prendre au filet; (profit) rapporter; **~ball** n netball m; **~ curtains** npl voilages mpl.

Netherlands ['nɛðələndz] npl: the **~** les Pays-Bas mpl.

nett [nɛt] a = net.

netting ['nɛtɪŋ] n (for fence etc) treillis m, grillage m.

nettle ['nɛtl] n ortie f.

network ['nɛtwə:k] n réseau m.

neurotic [njuə'rɔtɪk] a, n névrosé(e).

neuter ['nju:tə*] a, n neutre (m) // vt (cat etc) châtrer, couper.

neutral ['nju:trəl] a neutre // n (AUT) point mort; **~ize** vt neutraliser.

never ['nɛvə*] ad (ne ...) jamais; **~ again** plus jamais; **~ in my life** jamais de ma vie; see also mind; **~-ending** a interminable; **~theless** [nɛvəðə'lɛs] ad néanmoins, malgré tout.

new [nju:] a nouveau(nouvelle); (brand new) neuf(neuve); **~born** a nouveau-né(e); **~comer** ['nju:kʌmə*] n nouveau venu/nouvelle venue; **~-fangled** ['nju:fæŋgld] a (pej) ultramoderne (et farfelu(e)); **~-found** a de fraîche date; (friend) nouveau(nouvelle); **~ly** ad nouvellement, récemment; **~ly-weds** npl jeunes mariés mpl.

news [nju:z] n nouvelle(s) f(pl); (RADIO, TV) informations fpl, actualités fpl; **a piece of ~** une nouvelle; **~ agency** n agence f de presse; **~agent** n (Brit) marchand m de journaux; **~caster** n présentateur/trice; **~dealer** n (US) = ~agent; **~ flash** n flash m d'information; **~letter** n bulletin m; **~paper** n journal m; **~print** n papier m (de) journal; **~reader** n = ~caster; **~reel** n actualités (filmées) fpl; **~ stand** n kiosque m à journaux.

newt [nju:t] n triton m.

New Year ['nju:'jɪə*] n Nouvel An; **~'s Day** n le jour de l'An; **~'s Eve** n la Saint-Sylvestre.

New Zealand [nju:'zi:lənd] n la Nouvelle-Zélande; **~er** n Néo-zélandais/e.

next [nɛkst] a (seat, room) voisin(e), d'à côté; (meeting, bus stop) suivant(e); prochain(e) // ad la fois suivante; la prochaine fois; (afterwards) ensuite; **the ~ day** le lendemain, le jour suivant or d'après; ~ **year** l'année prochaine; **when do we meet** ~? quand nous revoyons-nous?; ~ **door** ad à côté; **~-of-kin** n parent m le plus proche; ~ **to** prep à côté de; ~ **to nothing** presque rien.

NHS n abbr of **National Health Service.**

nib [nɪb] n (of pen) (bec m de) plume f.

nibble ['nɪbl] vt grignoter.

nice [naɪs] a (holiday, trip) agréable; (flat, picture) joli(e); (person) gentil(le); (distinction, point) subtil(e); **~-looking** a joli(e); **~ly** ad agréablement; joliment; gentiment; subtilement.

niceties ['naɪsɪtɪz] npl subtilités fpl.

nick [nɪk] n encoche f // vt (col) faucher, piquer; **in the** ~ **of time** juste à temps.

nickel ['nɪkl] n nickel m; (US) pièce f de 5 cents.

nickname ['nɪkneɪm] n surnom m // vt surnommer.

niece [niːs] n nièce f.

Nigeria [naɪˈdʒɪərɪə] n Nigéria m or f.

nigger ['nɪgə*] n (col!: highly offensive) nègre m, négresse f.

niggling ['nɪglɪŋ] a tatillon(ne).

night [naɪt] n nuit f; (evening) soir m; **at** ~ la nuit; **by** ~ de nuit; **the** ~ **before last** avant-hier soir; **~cap** n boisson prise avant le coucher; ~ **club** n boîte f de nuit; **~dress** n chemise f de nuit; **~fall** n tombée f de la nuit; **~gown** n, **~ie** ['naɪtɪ] n chemise f de nuit.

nightingale ['naɪtɪŋgeɪl] n rossignol m.

night life n vie f nocturne.

nightly ['naɪtlɪ] a de chaque nuit or soir; (by night) nocturne // ad chaque nuit or soir; nuitamment.

nightmare ['naɪtmɛə*] n cauchemar m.

night: ~ porter n gardien m de nuit, concierge m de service la nuit; ~ **school** n cours mpl du soir; ~ **shift** n équipe f de nuit; **~-time** n nuit f.

nil [nɪl] n rien m; (Brit SPORT) zéro m.

Nile [naɪl] n: **the** ~ le Nil.

nimble ['nɪmbl] a agile.

nine [naɪn] num neuf; **~teen** num dix-neuf; **~ty** num quatre-vingt-dix.

ninth [naɪnθ] num neuvième.

nip [nɪp] vt pincer.

nipple ['nɪpl] n (ANAT) mamelon m, bout m du sein.

nitrogen ['naɪtrədʒən] n azote m.

no [nəu] ♦ ad (opposite of 'yes') non; **are you coming?** - ~ (**I'm not**) est-ce que vous venez? - non; **would you like some more?** - ~ **thank you** vous en voulez encore? - non merci

♦ a (not any) pas de, aucun(e) (used with 'ne'); **I have** ~ **money/books** je n'ai pas d'argent/de livres; ~ **student would have done it** aucun étudiant ne l'aurait fait; '~ **smoking**' 'défense de fumer'; '~ **dogs**' 'les chiens ne sont pas admis'

♦ n (pl ~es) non m.

nobility [nəuˈbɪlɪtɪ] n noblesse f.

noble ['nəubl] a noble.

nobody ['nəubədɪ] pronoun personne (with negative).

nod [nɔd] vi faire un signe de (la) tête (affirmatif ou amical); (sleep) sommoler // vt: **to** ~ **one's head** faire un signe de (la) tête; (in agreement) faire signe que oui // n signe m de (la) tête; **to** ~ **off** vi s'assoupir.

noise [nɔɪz] n bruit m; **noisy** a bruyant(e).

nominal ['nɔmɪnl] a (rent, fee) symbolique; (value) nominal(e).

nominate ['nɔmɪneɪt] vt (propose) proposer; (elect) nommer.

nominee [nɔmɪˈniː] n candidat agréé; personne nommée.

non... [nɔn] prefix non-; **~-alcoholic** a non-alcoolisé(e); **~-committal** ['nɔnkəˈmɪtl] a évasif(ive).

nondescript ['nɔndɪskrɪpt] a quelconque, indéfinissable.

none [nʌn] pronoun aucun/e; ~ **of you** aucun d'entre vous, personne parmi vous; **I've** ~ **left** je n'en ai plus; **he's** ~ **the worse** for it il ne s'en porte pas plus mal.

nonentity [nɔˈnɛntɪtɪ] n personne insignifiante.

nonetheless [nʌnðəˈlɛs] ad néanmoins.

non: ~-existent a inexistant(e); **~-fiction** n littérature f non-romanesque.

nonplussed [nɔnˈplʌst] a perplexe.

nonsense ['nɔnsəns] n absurdités fpl, idioties fpl; ~! ne dites pas d'idioties!

non: ~-smoker n non-fumeur m; **~-stick** a qui n'attache pas; **~-stop** a direct(e), sans arrêt (or escale) // ad sans arrêt.

noodles ['nuːdlz] npl nouilles fpl.

nook [nuk] n: **~s and crannies** recoins mpl.

noon [nuːn] n midi m.

no one ['nəuwʌn] pronoun = **nobody.**

noose [nuːs] n nœud coulant; (hangman's) corde f.

nor [nɔː*] cj = neither // ad see neither.

norm [nɔːm] n norme f.

normal ['nɔːml] a normal(e); **~ly** ad normalement.

Normandy ['nɔːməndɪ] n Normandie f.

north [nɔːθ] n nord m // a du nord, nord inv // ad au or vers le nord; **N~ America** n Amérique f du Nord; **~-east** n nord-est m; **~-erly** ['nɔːðəlɪ] a du nord; **~ern** ['nɔːðən] a du nord, septentrional(e); **N~ern Ireland** n Irlande f du Nord; **N~ Pole** n pôle m Nord; **N~ Sea** n mer f du Nord; **~ward(s)** ['nɔːθwəd(z)] ad vers le nord; **~-west** n nord-ouest m.

Norway ['nɔːweɪ] n Norvège f.

Norwegian [nɔːˈwiːdʒən] a norvégien(ne) // *n* Norvégien/ne; (*LING*) norvégien *m*.

nose [nəuz] *n* nez *m*; (*fig*) flair *m* // *vi*: to ~ about fouiner or fureter (partout); **~-dive** *n* (descente *f* en) piqué *m*; **~y** *a* = **nosy**.

nostalgia [nɔsˈtældʒɪə] *n* nostalgie *f*.

nostril [ˈnɔstrɪl] *n* narine *f*; (*of horse*) naseau *m*.

nosy [ˈnəuzɪ] *a* curieux(euse).

not [nɔt] *ad* (ne ...) pas; he is ~ or isn't here il n'est pas ici; you must ~ or you mustn't do that tu ne dois pas faire ça; it's too late, isn't it or is it ~? c'est trop tard, n'est-ce pas?; ~ yet/now pas encore/maintenant; ~ at all pas du tout; *see also* **all, only.**

notably [ˈnəutəblɪ] *ad* en particulier; (*markedly*) spécialement.

notary [ˈnəutərɪ] *n* (*also*: ~ public) notaire *m*.

notch [nɔtʃ] *n* encoche *f*.

note [nəut] *n* note *f*; (*letter*) mot *m*; (*banknote*) billet *m* // *vt* (*also*: ~ down) noter; (*notice*) constater; **~book** *n* carnet *m*; **~d** [ˈnəutɪd] *a* réputé(e); **~pad** *n* bloc-notes *m*; **~paper** *n* papier *m* à lettres.

nothing [ˈnʌθɪŋ] *n* rien *m*; he does ~ il ne fait rien; ~ new rien de nouveau; for ~ (*free*) pour rien, gratuitement.

notice [ˈnəutɪs] *n* avis *m*; (*of leaving*) congé *m* // *vt* remarquer, s'apercevoir de; **to take ~ of** prêter attention à; to bring sth to sb's ~ porter qch à la connaissance de qn; at short ~ dans un délai très court; until further ~ jusqu'à nouvel ordre; to hand in one's ~ donner sa démission, démissionner; **~able** *a* visible; **~ board** *n* (*Brit*) panneau *m* d'affichage.

notify [ˈnəutɪfaɪ] *vt*: to ~ sth to sb notifier qch à qn; to ~ sb of sth avertir qn de qch.

notion [ˈnəuʃən] *n* idée *f*; (*concept*) notion *f*.

notorious [nəuˈtɔːrɪəs] *a* notoire (*souvent en mal*).

notwithstanding [nɔtwɪθˈstændɪŋ] *ad* néanmoins // *prep* en dépit de.

nought [nɔːt] *n* zéro *m*.

noun [naun] *n* nom *m*.

nourish [ˈnʌrɪʃ] *vt* nourrir; **~ing** *a* nourrissant(e); **~ment** *n* nourriture *f*.

novel [ˈnɔvl] *n* roman *m* // *a* nouveau(nouvelle), original(e); **~ist** *n* romancier *m*; **~ty** *n* nouveauté *f*.

November [nəuˈvɛmbə*] *n* novembre *m*.

now [nau] *ad* maintenant // *cj*: ~ (that) maintenant que; right ~ tout de suite; by ~ à l'heure qu'il est; just ~: I saw her just ~ je viens de la voir, je l'ai vue à l'instant; I'll read it just ~ je vais le lire à l'instant or dès maintenant; ~ and

then, ~ and again de temps en temps; from ~ on dorénavant; **~adays** [ˈnauədeɪz] *ad* de nos jours.

nowhere [ˈnəuwɛə*] *ad* nulle part.

nozzle [ˈnɔzl] *n* (*of hose*) jet *m*, lance *f*.

nuclear [ˈnjuːklɪə*] *a* nucléaire.

nucleus, *pl* **nuclei** [ˈnjuːklɪəs, ˈnjuːklɪaɪ] *n* noyau *m*.

nude [njuːd] *a* nu(e) // *n* (*ART*) nu *m*; in the ~ (tout(e)) nu(e).

nudge [nʌdʒ] *vt* donner un (petit) coup de coude à.

nudist [ˈnjuːdɪst] *n* nudiste *m/f*.

nuisance [ˈnjuːsns] *n*: it's a ~ c'est (très) ennuyeux or gênant; he's a ~ il est assommant or casse-pieds; what a ~! quelle barbe!

null [nʌl] *a*: ~ and void nul(le) et non avenu(e).

numb [nʌm] *a* engourdi(e).

number [ˈnʌmbə*] *n* nombre *m*; (*numeral*) chiffre *m*; (*of house, car, telephone, newspaper*) numéro *m* // *vt* numéroter; (*include*) compter; **a ~ of** un certain nombre de; **to be ~ed among** compter parmi; **they were seven in ~** ils étaient (au nombre de) sept; **~ plate** *n* (*Brit AUT*) plaque *f* minéralogique or d'immatriculation.

numeral [ˈnjuːmərəl] *n* chiffre *m*.

numerate [ˈnjuːmərɪt] *a*: to be ~ avoir des notions d'arithmétique.

numerical [njuːˈmɛrɪkl] *a* numérique.

numerous [ˈnjuːmərəs] *a* nombreux(euse).

nun [nʌn] *n* religieuse *f*, sœur *f*.

nurse [nɜːs] *n* infirmière *f* // *vt* (*patient, cold*) soigner; (*baby: Brit*) bercer (dans ses bras); (: *US*) allaiter, nourrir.

nursery [ˈnɜːsərɪ] *n* (*room*) nursery *f*; (*institution*) pouponnière *f*; (*for plants*) pépinière *f*; **~ rhyme** *n* comptine *f*, chansonnette *f* pour enfants; **~ school** *n* école maternelle; **~ slope** *n* (*Brit SKI*) piste *f* pour débutants.

nursing [ˈnɜːsɪŋ] *n* (*profession*) profession *f* d'infirmière; **~ home** *n* clinique *f*; maison *f* de convalescence.

nurture [ˈnɜːtʃə*] *vt* élever.

nut [nʌt] *n* (*of metal*) écrou *m*; (*fruit*) noix *f*, noisette *f*, cacahuète *f* (*terme générique en anglais*); he's ~s (*col*) il est dingue; **~crackers** *npl* casse-noix *m inv*, casse-noisette(s) *m*.

nutmeg [ˈnʌtmɛg] *n* (noix *f*) muscade *f*.

nutritious [njuːˈtrɪʃəs] *a* nutritif(ive), nourrissant(e).

nutshell [ˈnʌtʃɛl] *n* coquille *f* de noix; in a ~ en un mot.

nylon [ˈnaɪlɔn] *n* nylon *m* // *a* de or en nylon.

O

oak [əuk] *n* chêne *m* // *a* de or en (bois de) chêne.

O.A.P. *abbr of* **old-age pensioner**.

oar [ɔ:*] *n* aviron *m*, rame *f*.

oasis, *pl* **oases** [əu'eisis] *n* oasis *f*.

oath [əuθ] *n* serment *m*; (*swear word*) juron *m*.

oatmeal ['əutmi:l] *n* flocons *mpl* d'avoine.

oats [əuts] *n* avoine *f*.

obedience [ə'bi:diəns] *n* obéissance *f*.

obedient [ə'bi:diənt] *a* obéissant(e).

obey [ə'bei] *vt* obéir à; (*instructions*) se conformer à // *vi* obéir.

obituary [ə'bitjuəri] *n* nécrologie *f*.

object *n* ['ɔbdʒikt] objet *m*; (*purpose*) but *m*, objet; (*LING*) complément *m* d'objet // *vi* [əb'dʒɛkt]: **to ~ to** (*attitude*) désapprouver; (*proposal*) protester contre; **expense is no ~** l'argent n'est pas un problème; **I ~!** je proteste!; **he ~ed that ...** il a fait valoir *or* a objecté que ...; **~ion** [əb'dʒɛkʃən] *n* objection *f*; (*drawback*) inconvénient *m*; **~ionable** [əb'dʒɛkʃənəbl] *a* très désagréable; choquant(e); **~ive** *n* objectif *m* // *a* objectif(ive).

obligation [ɔbli'geiʃən] *n* obligation *f*, devoir *m*; (*debt*) dette *f* (de reconnaissance); **without ~** sans engagement.

oblige [ə'blaidʒ] *vt* (*force*): **to ~ sb to do** obliger *or* forcer qn à faire; (*do a favour*) rendre service à, obliger; **to be ~d to sb for sth** être obligé(e) à qn de qch; **obliging** *a* obligeant(e), serviable.

oblique [ə'bli:k] *a* oblique; (*allusion*) indirect(e).

obliterate [ə'blitəreit] *vt* effacer.

oblivion [ə'bliviən] *n* oubli *m*.

oblivious [ə'bliviəs] *a*: **~ of** oublieux(euse) de.

oblong ['ɔblɔŋ] *a* oblong(ue) // *n* rectangle *m*.

obnoxious [əb'nɔkʃəs] *a* odieux(euse); (*smell*) nauséabond(e).

oboe ['əubəu] *n* hautbois *m*.

obscene [əb'si:n] *a* obscène.

obscure [əb'skjuə*] *a* obscur(e) // *vt* obscurcir; (*hide: sun*) cacher.

observant [əb'zə:vnt] *a* observateur(trice).

observation [ɔbzə'veiʃən] *n* observation *f*; (*by police etc*) surveillance *f*.

observatory [əb'zə:vətri] *n* observatoire *m*.

observe [əb'zə:v] *vt* observer; (*remark*) faire observer *or* remarquer; **~r** *n* observateur/trice.

obsess [əb'sɛs] *vt* obséder; **~ive** *a* obsédant(e).

obsolescence [ɔbsə'lɛsns] *n* vieillissement *m*.

obsolete ['ɔbsəli:t] *a* dépassé(e); démodé(e).

obstacle ['ɔbstəkl] *n* obstacle *m*.

obstinate ['ɔbstinit] *a* obstiné(e); (*pain, cold*) persistant(e).

obstruct [əb'strʌkt] *vt* (*block*) boucher, obstruer; (*halt*) arrêter; (*hinder*) entraver.

obtain [əb'tein] *vt* obtenir // *vi* avoir cours; **~able** *a* qu'on peut obtenir.

obtrusive [əb'tru:siv] *a* (*person*) importun(e); (*smell*) pénétrant(e); (*building etc*) trop en évidence.

obvious ['ɔbviəs] *a* évident(e), manifeste; **~ly** *ad* manifestement; bien sûr.

occasion [ə'keizən] *n* occasion *f*; (*event*) événement *m* // *vt* occasionner, causer; **~al** *a* pris(e) *or* fait(e) *etc* de temps en temps; occasionnel(le); **~ally** *ad* de temps en temps, quelquefois.

occupation [ɔkju'peiʃən] *n* occupation *f*; (*job*) métier *m*, profession *f*; **~al hazard** *n* risque *m* du métier.

occupier ['ɔkjupaiə*] *n* occupant/e.

occupy ['ɔkjupai] *vt* occuper; **to ~ o.s. with** *or* **by doing** s'occuper à faire.

occur [ə'kə:*] *vi* se produire; (*difficulty, opportunity*) se présenter; (*phenomenon, error*) se rencontrer; **to ~ to sb** venir à l'esprit de qn; **~rence** *n* présence *f*, existence *f*; cas *m*, fait *m*.

ocean ['əuʃən] *n* océan *m*; **~-going** *a* de haute mer.

o'clock [ə'klɔk] *ad*: **it is 5 ~** il est 5 heures.

OCR *n* *abbr of* **optical character recognition/reader**.

October [ɔk'təubə*] *n* octobre *m*.

octopus ['ɔktəpəs] *n* pieuvre *f*.

odd [ɔd] *a* (*strange*) bizarre, curieux(euse); (*number*) impair(e); (*left over*) qui reste, en plus; (*not of a set*) dépareillé(e); **60-~** 60 et quelques; **at ~ times** de temps en temps; **the ~ one out** l'exception *f*; **~s and ends** *npl* de petites choses; **~ity** *n* bizarrerie *f*; (*person*) excentrique *m/f*; **~ jobs** *npl* petits travaux divers; **~ly** *ad* bizarrement, curieusement; **~ments** *npl* (*COMM*) fins *fpl* de série; **~s** *npl* (*in betting*) cote *f*; **it makes no ~s** cela n'a pas d'importance; **at ~s** en désaccord.

odometer [ə'dɔmitə*] *n* odomètre *m*.

odour, (*US*) **odor** ['əudə*] *n* odeur *f*.

of [ɔv, əv] *prep* **1** (*gen*) de; **a friend ~ ours** un de nos amis; **a boy ~ 10** un garçon de 10 ans; **that was kind ~ you** c'était gentil de votre part
2 (*expressing quantity, amount, dates etc*) de; **a kilo ~ flour** un kilo de farine; **how much ~ this do you need?** combien vous en faut-il?; **there were 3 ~ them** (*people*) ils étaient 3; (*objects*) il y en

avait 3; **3 ~ us** went 3 d'entre nous sont allé(e)s; **the 5th ~ July** le 5 juillet
3 (*from, out of*) en, de; **a statue ~ marble** une statue de *or* en marbre; **made ~ wood** (fait) en bois.

off [ɔf] *a, ad* (*engine*) coupé(e); (*tap*) fermé(e); (*Brit: food: bad*) mauvais(e), avancé(e); (: *milk*) tourné(e); (*absent*) absent(e); (*cancelled*) annulé(e) // *prep* de; sur; **to be ~** (*to leave*) partir, s'en aller; **to be ~ sick** être absent pour cause de maladie; **a day ~** un jour de congé; **to have an ~ day** n'être pas en forme; **he had his coat ~** il avait enlevé son manteau; **10% ~** (*COMM*) 10% de rabais; **~ the coast** au large de la côte; **I'm ~ meat** je ne mange plus de viande; je n'aime plus la viande; **on the ~ chance** à tout hasard.

offal [ˈɔfl] *n* (*CULIN*) abats *mpl*.

offbeat [ˈɔfbiːt] *a* excentrique.

off-colour [ˈɔfˈkʌləˀ] *a* (*Brit: ill*) malade, mal fichu(e).

offence, (*US***) offense** [əˈfɛns] *n* (*crime*) délit *m*, infraction *f*; **to take ~ at** se vexer de, s'offenser de.

offend [əˈfɛnd] *vt* (*person*) offenser, blesser; **~er** *n* délinquant/e; (*against regulations*) contrevenant/e.

offensive [əˈfɛnsɪv] *a* offensant(e), choquant(e); (*smell etc*) très déplaisant(e); (*weapon*) offensif(ive) // *n* (*MIL*) offensive *f*.

offer [ˈɔfəˀ] *n* offre *f*, proposition *f* // *vt* offrir, proposer; **'on ~'** (*COMM*) 'en promotion'; **~ing** *n* offrande *f*.

offhand [ɔfˈhænd] *a* désinvolte // *ad* spontanément.

office [ˈɔfɪs] *n* (*place*) bureau *m*; (*position*) charge *f*, fonction *f*; **doctor's ~** (*US*) cabinet (médical); **to take ~** entrer en fonctions; **~ automation** *n* bureautique *f*; **~ block**, (*US*) **~ building** *n* immeuble *m* de bureaux; **~ hours** *npl* heures *fpl* de bureau; (*US MED*) heures de consultation.

officer [ˈɔfɪsəˀ] *n* (*MIL etc*) officier *m*; (*of organization*) membre *m* du bureau directeur; (*also*: **police ~**) agent *m* (de police).

office worker *n* employé/e de bureau.

official [əˈfɪʃl] *a* (*authorized*) officiel(le) // *n* officiel *m*; (*civil servant*) fonctionnaire *m/f*; employé/e; **~dom** *n* administration *f*, bureaucratie *f*.

officiate [əˈfɪʃɪeɪt] *vi* (*REL*) officier; **to ~ at a marriage** célébrer un mariage.

officious [əˈfɪʃəs] *a* trop empressé(e).

offing [ˈɔfɪŋ] *n*: **in the ~** (*fig*) en perspective.

off: ~-licence *n* (*Brit: shop*) débit *m* de vins et de spiritueux; **~-line** *a, ad* (*COMPUT*) (en mode) autonome; (: *switched off*) non connecté(e); **~-peak** *a* aux heures creuses; **~-putting**

(*Brit*) rébarbatif(ive); rebutant(e), peu engageant(e); **~-season** *a, ad* hors-saison (*inv*).

offset [ˈɔfsɛt] *vt irg* (*counteract*) contrebalancer, compenser.

offshoot [ˈɔfʃuːt] *n* (*fig*) ramification *f*, antenne *f*; (: *of discussion etc*) conséquence *f*.

offshore [ɔfˈʃɔːˀ] *a* (*breeze*) de terre; (*island*) proche du littoral; (*fishing*) côtier(ère).

offside [ˈɔfˈsaɪd] *a* (*SPORT*) hors jeu // *n* (*AUT: with right-hand drive*) côté droit.

offspring [ˈɔfsprɪŋ] *n* progéniture *f*.

off: ~stage *ad* dans les coulisses; **~the-peg**, (*US*) **~-the-rack** *ad* en prêt-à-porter; **~-white** *a* blanc cassé *inv*.

often [ˈɔfn] *ad* souvent; **how ~ do you go?** vous y allez tous les combien?; **how ~ have you gone there?** vous y êtes allé combien de fois?

ogle [ˈəʊgl] *vt* lorgner.

oh [əʊ] *excl* ô!, oh!, ah!

oil [ɔɪl] *n* huile *f*; (*petroleum*) pétrole *m*; (*for central heating*) mazout *m* // *vt* (*machine*) graisser; **~can** *n* burette *f* de graissage; (*for storing*) bidon *m* à huile; **~field** *n* gisement *m* de pétrole; **~filter** *n* (*AUT*) filtre *m* à huile; **~-fired** *a* au mazout; **~ painting** *n* peinture *f* à l'huile; **~ rig** *n* derrick *m*; (*at sea*) plate-forme pétrolière; **~skins** *npl* ciré *m*; **~ tanker** *n* pétrolier *m*; **~ well** *n* puits *m* de pétrole; **~y** *a* huileux(euse); (*food*) gras(se).

ointment [ˈɔɪntmənt] *n* onguent *m*.

O.K., okay [ˈəʊˈkeɪ] *excl* d'accord! // *vt* approuver, donner son accord à; **is it ~?, are you ~?** ça va?

old [əʊld] *a* vieux(vieille); (*person*) vieux, âgé(e); (*former*) ancien(ne), vieux; **how ~ are you?** quel âge avez-vous?; **he's 10 years ~** il a 10 ans, il est âgé de 10 ans; **~er brother/sister** frère/sœur aîné(e); **~ age** *n* vieillesse *f*; **~age pensioner (O.A.P.)** *n* (*Brit*) retraité/e; **~-fashioned** *a* démodé(e); (*person*) vieux jeu *inv*.

olive [ˈɔlɪv] *n* (*fruit*) olive *f*; (*tree*) olivier *m* // *a* (*also*: **~-green**) (vert) olive *inv*; **~ oil** *n* huile *f* d'olive.

Olympic [əʊˈlɪmpɪk] *a* olympique; **the ~ Games, the ~s** les Jeux *mpl* olympiques.

omelet(te) [ˈɔmlɪt] *n* omelette *f*.

omen [ˈəʊmən] *n* présage *m*.

ominous [ˈɔmɪnəs] *a* menaçant(e), inquiétant(e); (*event*) de mauvais augure.

omit [əʊˈmɪt] *vt* omettre.

on [ɔn] ♦ *prep* **1** (*indicating position*) sur; **~ the table** sur la table; **~ the wall** sur le *or* au mur; **~ the left** à gauche
2 (*indicating means, method, condition etc*): **~ foot** à pied; **~ the train/plane** (*be*) dans le train/l'avion; (*go*) en train/

avion; ~ **the telephone/radio/television** au téléphone/à la radio/à la télévision; **to be ~ drugs** se droguer; **~ holiday** en vacances
3 (*referring to time*): **~ Friday** vendredi; **~ Fridays** le vendredi; **June 20th** le 20 juin; **a week ~ Friday** vendredi en huit; **~ arrival** à l'arrivée; **~ seeing this** en voyant cela
4 (*about, concerning*) sur, de; **a book ~ Balzac/physics** un livre sur Balzac/de physique
♦ *ad* **1** (*referring to dress, covering*): **to have one's coat ~** avoir (*mis*) son manteau; **to put one's coat ~** mettre son manteau; **what's she got ~?** qu'est-ce qu'elle porte?; **screw the lid ~ tightly** vissez bien le couvercle
2 (*further, continuously*): **to walk etc ~** continuer à marcher *etc*; **~ and off** de temps à autre
♦ *a* **1** (*in operation: machine*) en marche; (*: radio, TV, light*) allumé(e); (*: tap, gas*) ouvert(e); (*: brakes*) mis(e); **is the meeting still ~?** (*not cancelled*) est-ce que la réunion a bien lieu?; (*in progress*) la réunion dure-t-elle encore?; **when is this film ~?** quand passe ce film?
2 (*col*): **that's not ~!** (*not acceptable*) cela ne se fait pas!; (*not possible*) pas question!

once [wʌns] *ad* une fois; (*formerly*): autrefois // *cj* une fois que; **~ he had left/it was done** une fois qu'il fut parti/que ce fut terminé; **at ~** tout de suite, immédiatement; (*simultaneously*) à la fois; **~ more** encore une fois; **~ and for all** une fois pour toutes; **~ upon a time** il y avait une fois, il était une fois.

oncoming ['ɒnkʌmɪŋ] *a* (*traffic*) venant en sens inverse.

one [wʌn] ♦ *num* un(e); **~ hundred and fifty cent** cinquante; **~ day** un jour
♦ *a* **1** (*sole*) seul(e), unique; **the ~ book which** l'unique *or* le seul livre qui; **the ~ man who** le seul (homme) qui
2 (*same*) même; **they came in the ~ car** ils sont venus dans la même voiture
♦ *pronoun* **1**: **this ~** celui-ci/celle-ci; **that ~** celui-là/celle-là; **I've already got ~/a red ~** j'en ai déjà un(e)/un(e) rouge; **~ by ~** un(e) à *or* par un(e)
2: **~ another** l'un(e) l'autre; **to look at ~ another** se regarder
3 (*impersonal*) on; **~ never knows** on ne sait jamais; **to cut ~'s finger** se couper le doigt.

one: **~-armed bandit** *n* machine *f* à sous; **~-day excursion** *n* (*US*) billet *m* d'aller-retour (valable pour la journée); **~-man** *a* (*business*) dirigé(e) *etc* par un seul homme; **~-man band** *n* homme-orchestre *m*; **~-off** *n* (*Brit col*) exemplaire *m* unique.

oneself [wʌn'sɛlf] *pronoun* (*reflexive*) se; (*after prep*) soi(-même); (*emphatic*) soi-même; **to hurt ~** se faire mal; **to keep sth for ~** garder qch pour soi; **to talk to ~** se parler à soi-même.

one: **~-sided** *a* (*argument*) unilatéral(e); **~-to~** *a* (*relationship*) univoque; **~-upmanship** [-'ʌpmənʃɪp] *n* l'art de faire mieux que les autres; **~-way** *a* (*street, traffic*) à sens unique.

ongoing ['ɒngəʊɪŋ] *a* en cours; suivi(e).

onion ['ʌnjən] *n* oignon *m*.

on-line ['ɒn'laɪn] *a, ad* (*COMPUT*) en ligne; (*: switched on*) connecté(e).

onlooker ['ɒnlʊkə*] *n* spectateur/trice.

only ['əʊnlɪ] *ad* seulement // *a* seul(e), unique // *cj* seulement, mais; **an ~ child** un enfant unique; **not ~ ... but also** non seulement ... mais aussi; **I took ~ one** je n'en ai pris qu'un, j'en ai seulement pris un.

onset ['ɒnset] *n* début *m*; (*of winter, old age*) approche *f*.

onshore ['ɒnʃɔː*] *a* (*wind*) du large.

onslaught ['ɒnslɔːt] *n* attaque *f*, assaut *m*.

onto ['ɒntu] *prep* = **on to**.

onus ['əʊnəs] *n* responsabilité *f*.

onward(s) ['ɒnwəd(z)] *ad* (*move*) en avant.

ooze [uːz] *vi* suinter.

opaque [əʊ'peɪk] *a* opaque.

OPEC ['əʊpek] *n abbr* (= *Organization of petroleum exporting countries*) O.P.E.P. *f* (= *Organisation des pays exportateurs de pétrole*).

open ['əʊpn] *a* ouvert(e); (*car*) découvert(e); (*road, view*) dégagé(e); (*meeting*) public(ique); (*admiration*) manifeste; (*question*) non résolu(e); (*enemy*) déclaré(e) // *vt* ouvrir // *vi* (*flower, eyes, door, debate*) s'ouvrir; (*shop, bank, museum*) ouvrir; (*book etc: commence*) commencer, débuter; **in the ~ (air)** en plein air; **to ~ on to** *vt fus* (*subj: room, door*) donner sur; **to ~ up** *vt* ouvrir; (*blocked road*) dégager // *vi* s'ouvrir; **~ing** *n* ouverture *f*; (*opportunity*) occasion *f*; débouché *m*; (*job*) poste vacant; **~ly** *ad* ouvertement; **~-minded** *a* à l'esprit ouvert; **~-plan** *a* sans cloisons.

opera ['ɒpərə] *n* opéra *m*; **~ house** *n* opéra *m*.

operate ['ɒpəreɪt] *vt* (*machine*) faire marcher, faire fonctionner; (*system*) pratiquer // *vi* fonctionner; (*drug*) faire effet; **to ~ on sb (for)** (*MED*) opérer qn (de).

operatic [ɒpə'rætɪk] *a* d'opéra.

operating ['ɒpəreɪtɪŋ] *a*: **~ table/theatre** table *f*/salle *f* d'opération.

operation [ɒpə'reɪʃən] *n* opération *f*; (*of machine*) fonctionnement *m*; **to be in ~** (*machine*) être en service; (*system*) être en vigueur; **to have an ~** (MED) se faire opérer.

operative ['ɔpərətɪv] a (measure) en vigueur.

operator ['ɔpəreɪtə*] n (of machine) opérateur/trice; (TEL) téléphoniste m/f.

opinion [ə'pɪnɪən] n opinion f, avis m; **in my ~** à mon avis; **~ated** a aux idées bien arrêtées; **~ poll** n sondage m (d'opinion).

opponent [ə'pəunənt] n adversaire m/f.

opportunist [ɔpə'tju:nɪst] n opportuniste m/f.

opportunity [ɔpə'tju:nɪtɪ] n occasion f; **to take the ~ of doing** profiter de l'occasion pour faire; en profiter pour faire.

oppose [ə'pəuz] vt s'opposer à; **~d to** a opposé(e) à; **as ~d to** par opposition à; **opposing** a (side) opposé(e).

opposite ['ɔpəzɪt] a opposé(e); (house etc) d'en face // ad en face // prep en face de // n opposé m, contraire m; (of word) contraire.

opposition [ɔpə'zɪʃən] n opposition f.

oppress [ə'prɛs] vt opprimer.

opt [ɔpt] vi: **to ~ for** opter pour; **to ~ to do** choisir de faire; **to ~ out of** choisir de ne pas participer à or de ne pas faire.

optical ['ɔptɪkl] a optique; (instrument) d'optique; **~ character recognition/reader (OCR)** n lecture f/lecteur m optique.

optician [ɔp'tɪʃən] n opticien/ne.

optimist ['ɔptɪmɪst] n optimiste m/f; **~ic** [-'mɪstɪk] a optimiste.

option ['ɔpʃən] n choix m, option f; (SCOL) matière f à option; (COMM) option; **~al** a facultatif(ive); (COMM) en option.

or [ɔ:*] cj ou; (with negative): **he hasn't seen ~ heard anything** il n'a rien vu ni entendu; **~ else** sinon; ou bien.

oral ['ɔ:rəl] a oral(e) // n oral m.

orange ['ɔrɪndʒ] n (fruit) orange f // a orange inv.

orator ['ɔrətə*] n orateur/trice.

orbit ['ɔ:bɪt] n orbite f.

orchard ['ɔ:tʃəd] n verger m.

orchestra ['ɔ:kɪstrə] n orchestre m; (US: seating) (fauteuils mpl d')orchestre; **orchestral** [-'kɛstrəl] a orchestral(e); (concert) symphonique.

orchid ['ɔ:kɪd] n orchidée f.

ordain [ɔ:'deɪn] vt (REL) ordonner; (decide) décréter.

ordeal [ɔ:'di:l] n épreuve f.

order ['ɔ:də*] n ordre m; (COMM) commande f // vt ordonner; (COMM) commander; **in ~** en ordre; (of document) en règle; **in (working) ~** en état de marche; **in ~ of size** par ordre de grandeur; **in ~ to do/that** pour faire/que + sub; **on ~** (COMM) en commande; **to ~ sb to do** ordonner à qn de faire; **~**

form n bon m de commande; **~ly** (MIL) ordonnance f // a (room) en ordre; (mind) méthodique; (person) qui a de l'ordre.

ordinary ['ɔ:dnrɪ] a ordinaire, normal(e); (pej) ordinaire, quelconque; **out of the ~** exceptionnel(le).

ordnance ['ɔ:dnəns] n (MIL: unit) service m du matériel.

ore [ɔ:*] n minerai m.

organ ['ɔ:gən] n organe m; (MUS) orgue m, orgues fpl; **~ic** [ɔ:'gænɪk] a organique.

organization [ɔ:gənaɪ'zeɪʃən] n organisation f.

organize ['ɔ:gənaɪz] vt organiser; **~r** n organisateur/trice.

orgasm ['ɔ:gæzəm] n orgasme m.

orgy ['ɔ:dʒɪ] n orgie f.

Orient ['ɔ:rɪənt] n: **the ~** l'Orient m; **oriental** [-'ɛntl] a oriental(e).

origin ['ɔrɪdʒɪn] n origine f.

original [ə'rɪdʒɪnl] a original(e); (earliest) originel(le) // n original m; **~ly** ad (at first) à l'origine.

originate [ə'rɪdʒɪneɪt] vi: **to ~ from** être originaire de; (suggestion) provenir de; **to ~ in** prendre naissance dans; avoir son origine dans.

Orkneys ['ɔ:knɪz] npl: **the ~** (also: the Orkney Islands) les Orcades fpl.

ornament ['ɔ:nəmənt] n ornement m; (trinket) bibelot m; **~al** [-'mɛntl] a décoratif(ive); (garden) d'agrément.

ornate [ɔ:'neɪt] a très orné(e).

orphan ['ɔ:fn] n orphelin/e // vt: **to be ~ed** devenir orphelin; **~age** n orphelinat m.

orthopaedic, (US) **orthopedic** [ɔ:θə'pi:dɪk] a orthopédique.

ostensibly [ɔs'tɛnsɪblɪ] ad en apparence.

ostentatious [ɔstɛn'teɪʃəs] a prétentieux(euse); ostentatoire.

ostracize ['ɔstrəsaɪz] vt frapper d'ostracisme.

ostrich ['ɔstrɪtʃ] n autruche f.

other ['ʌðə*] a autre // pronoun: **the ~ (one)** l'autre; **~s** (~ people) d'autres; **~ than** autrement que; à part; **~wise** ad, cj autrement.

otter ['ɔtə*] n loutre f.

ouch [autʃ] excl aïe!

ought [ɔ:t], pt **ought** auxiliary vb: **I ~ to do it** je devrais le faire, il faudrait que je le fasse; **this ~ to have been corrected** cela aurait dû être corrigé; **he ~ to win** il devrait gagner.

ounce [auns] n once f (= 28.35g; 16 in a pound).

our ['auə*] a notre, nos pl; see also **my**; **~s** pronoun le(la) nôtre, les nôtres; see also **mine**; **~selves** pronoun pl (reflexive, after preposition) nous; (emphatic) nous-mêmes; see also **oneself**.

oust [aust] *vt* évincer.

out [aut] *ad* dehors; *(published, not at home etc)* sorti(e); *(light, fire)* éteint(e); ~ **here** ici; ~ **there** là-bas; **he's** ~ *(absent)* il est sorti; *(unconscious)* il est sans connaissance; **to be** ~ **in** one's **calculations** s'être trompé dans ses calculs; **to run/back** *etc* ~ sortir en courant/en reculant *etc*; ~ **loud** *ad* à haute voix; ~ **of** *(outside)* en dehors de; *(because of: anger etc)* par; *(from among):* ~ **of** 10 sur 10; *(without):* ~ **of petrol** sans essence, à court d'essence; ~ **of order** *(machine)* en panne; *(TEL: line)* en dérangement; ~**-and-**~ *a (liar, thief etc)* véritable.

outback ['autbæk] *n* campagne isolée; *(in Australia)* intérieur *m*.

outboard ['autbɔ:d] *n:* ~ **(motor)** (moteur *m*) hors-bord *m*.

outbreak ['autbreɪk] *n* accès *m*; début *m*; éruption *f*.

outburst ['autbə:st] *n* explosion *f*, accès *m*.

outcast ['autkɑ:st] *n* exilé/e; *(socially)* paria *m*.

outcome ['autkʌm] *n* issue *f*, résultat *m*.

outcrop ['autkrɒp] *n (of rock)* affleurement *m*.

outcry ['autkraɪ] *n* tollé (général).

outdated [aut'deɪtɪd] *a* démodé(e).

outdo [aut'du:] *vt irg* surpasser.

outdoor [aut'dɔ:°] *a* de or en plein air; ~**s** *ad* dehors; au grand air.

outer ['autə°] *a* extérieur(e); ~ **space** *n* espace *m* cosmique.

outfit ['autfɪt] *n* équipement *m*; *(clothes)* tenue *f*; '~**ter's**' *(Brit)* 'confection pour hommes'.

outgoing ['autgəuɪŋ] *a (character)* ouvert(e), extraverti(e); ~**s** *npl (Brit: expenses)* dépenses *fpl*.

outgrow [aut'grəu] *vt irg (clothes)* devenir trop grand(e) pour.

outhouse ['authaus] *n* appentis *m*, remise *f*.

outing ['autɪŋ] *n* sortie *f*; excursion *f*.

outlandish [aut'lændɪʃ] *a* étrange.

outlaw ['autlɔ:] *n* hors-la-loi *m inv*.

outlay ['autleɪ] *n* dépenses *fpl*; *(investment)* mise *f* de fonds.

outlet ['autlɛt] *n (for liquid etc)* issue *f*, sortie *f*; *(US: ELEC)* prise *f* de courant; *(for emotion)* exutoire *m*; *(for goods)* débouché *m*; *(also: retail* ~) point *m* de vente.

outline ['autlaɪn] *n (shape)* contour *m*; *(summary)* esquisse *f*, grandes lignes.

outlive [aut'lɪv] *vt* survivre à.

outlook ['autluk] *n* perspective *f*.

outlying ['autlaɪɪŋ] *a* écarté(e).

outmoded [aut'məudɪd] *a* démodé(e); dépassé(e).

outnumber [aut'nʌmbə°] *vt* surpasser

en nombre.

out-of-date ['autəv'deɪt] *a (passport)* périmé(e); *(theory etc)* dépassé(e); *(custom)* désuet(ète); *(clothes etc)* démodé(e).

out-of-the-way ['autəvðə'weɪ] *a (place)* loin de tout.

outpatient ['autpeɪʃənt] *n* malade *m/f* en consultation externe.

outpost ['autpəust] *n* avant-poste *m*.

output ['autput] *n* rendement *m*, production *f*; *(COMPUT)* sortie *f*.

outrage ['autreɪdʒ] *n* atrocité *f*, acte *m* de violence; scandale *m* // *vt* outrager; ~**ous** [-'reɪdʒəs] *a* atroce; scandaleux(euse).

outright *ad* [aut'raɪt] complètement; catégoriquement; carrément; sur le coup // *a* ['autraɪt] complet(ète); catégorique.

outset ['autsɛt] *n* début *m*.

outside [aut'saɪd] *n* extérieur *m* // *a* extérieur(e) // *ad* (au) dehors, à l'extérieur // *prep* hors de, à l'extérieur de; **at the** ~ *(fig)* au plus *or* maximum; ~ **lane** *n (AUT: in Britain)* voie *f* de droite; ~**-left/-right** *n (FOOTBALL)* ailier gauche/droit; ~ **line** *n (TEL)* ligne extérieure; ~**r** *n (in race etc)* outsider *m*; *(stranger)* étranger/ère.

outsize ['autsaɪz] *a* énorme; *(clothes)* grande taille *inv*.

outskirts ['autskə:ts] *npl* faubourgs *mpl*.

outspoken [aut'spəukən] *a* très franc(franche).

outstanding [aut'stændɪŋ] *a* remarquable, exceptionnel(le); *(unfinished)* en suspens; en souffrance; non réglé(e).

outstay [aut'steɪ] *vt:* **to** ~ **one's welcome** abuser de l'hospitalité de son hôte.

outstretched [aut'strɛtʃt] *a (hand)* tendu(e); *(body)* étendu(e).

outstrip [aut'strɪp] *vt (competitors, demand)* dépasser.

out-tray ['auttreɪ] *n* courrier *m* 'départ'.

outward ['autwəd] *a (sign, appearances)* extérieur(e); *(journey)* (d')aller; ~**ly** *ad* extérieurement; en apparence.

outweigh [aut'weɪ] *vt* l'emporter sur.

outwit [aut'wɪt] *vt* se montrer plus malin que.

oval ['əuvl] *a, n* ovale *(m)*.

ovary ['əuvərɪ] *n* ovaire *m*.

oven ['ʌvn] *n* four *m*; ~**proof** *a* allant au four.

over ['əuvə°] *ad* (par-)dessus // *a (or ad) (finished)* fini(e), terminé(e); *(too much)* en plus // *prep* sur; par-dessus; *(above)* au-dessus de; *(on the other side of)* de l'autre côté de; *(more than)* plus de; *(during)* pendant; ~ **here** ici; ~ **there** là-bas; **all** ~ *(everywhere)* partout; *(finished)* fini(e); ~ **and** ~ **(again)** à plusieurs reprises; ~ **and above** en plus de; **to ask sb** ~ inviter qn (à passer).

overall *a n*, ['əuvərɔ:l] *a* (*length*) total(e); (*study*) d'ensemble // *n* (*Brit*) blouse *f* // *ad* [əuvər'ɔ:l] dans l'ensemble, en général; ~s *npl* bleus *mpl* de travail).

overawe [əuvər'ɔ:] *vt* impressionner.

overbalance [əuvə'bæləns] *vi* basculer.

overbearing [əuvə'bɛəriŋ] *a* impérieux(euse), autoritaire.

overboard ['əuvəbɔ:d] *ad* (*NAUT*) pardessus bord.

overbook [əuvə'buk] *vt* faire du surbooking.

overcast ['əuvəka:st] *a* couvert(e).

overcharge [əuvə'tʃɑ:dʒ] *vt*: to ~ sb for sth faire payer qch trop cher à qn.

overcoat ['əuvəkəut] *n* pardessus *m*.

overcome [əuvə'kʌm] *vt irg* triompher de; surmonter; ~ with grief accablé(e) de douleur.

overcrowded [əuvə'kraudid] *a* bondé(e).

overdo [əuvə'du:] *vt irg* exagérer; (*overcook*) trop cuire.

overdose ['əuvədəus] *n* dose excessive.

overdraft ['əuvədrɑ:ft] *n* découvert *m*.

overdrawn [əuvə'drɔ:n] *a* (*account*) à découvert.

overdue [əuvə'dju:] *a* en retard; (*recognition*) tardif(ive).

overflow [əuvə'fləu] *vi* déborder // *n* ['əuvəfləu] trop-plein *m*; (*also:* ~ pipe) tuyau *m* d'écoulement, trop-plein *m*.

overgrown [əuvə'grəun] *a* (*garden*) envahi(e) par la végétation.

overhaul *vt* [əuvə'hɔ:l] réviser // *n* ['əuvəhɔ:l] révision *f*.

overhead *ad* [əuvə'hed] au-dessus // *a*, *n* ['əuvəhed] *a* aérien(ne); (*lighting*) vertical(e) // *n* (*US*) = ~s; ~s *npl* frais généraux.

overhear [əuvə'hiə*] *vt irg* entendre (par hasard).

overheat [əuvə'hi:t] *vi* (*engine*) chauffer.

overjoyed [əuvə'dʒɔid] *a* ravi(e), enchanté(e).

overkill ['əuvəkil] *n*: that would be ~ ce serait trop.

overlap [əuvə'læp] *vi* se chevaucher.

overleaf [əuvə'li:f] *ad* au verso.

overload [əuvə'ləud] *vt* surcharger.

overlook [əuvə'luk] *vt* (*have view of*) donner sur; (*miss*) oublier, négliger; (*forgive*) fermer les yeux sur.

overnight *ad* [əuvə'nait] (*happen*) durant la nuit; (*fig*) soudain // *a* ['əuvənait] d'une (*or* de) nuit; soudain(e); he stayed there ~ il y a passé la nuit.

overpower [əuvə'pauə*] *vt* vaincre; (*fig*) accabler; ~ing *a* irrésistible; (*heat, stench*) suffocant(e).

overrate [əuvə'reit] *vt* surestimer.

override [əuvə'raid] *vt* (*irg: like* ride)

(*order, objection*) passer outre à; (*decision*) annuler; **overriding** *a* prépondérant(e).

overrule [əuvə'ru:l] *vt* (*decision*) annuler; (*claim*) rejeter.

overrun [əuvə'rʌn] *vt* (*irg: like* run) (*country*) occuper; (*time limit*) dépasser.

overseas [əuvə'si:z] *ad* outre-mer; (*abroad*) à l'étranger // *a* (*trade*) extérieur(e); (*visitor*) étranger(ère).

overseer ['əuvəsiə*] *n* (*in factory*) contremaître *m*.

overshadow [əuvə'ʃædəu] *vt* (*fig*) éclipser.

overshoot [əuvə'ʃu:t] *vt irg* dépasser.

oversight ['əuvəsait] *n* omission *f*, oubli *m*.

oversleep [əuvə'sli:p] *vi irg* se réveiller (trop) tard.

overstep [əuvə'step] *vt*: to ~ the mark dépasser la mesure.

overt [əu'və:t] *a* non dissimulé(e).

overtake [əuvə'teik] *vt irg* dépasser; (*AUT*) dépasser, doubler.

overthrow [əuvə'θrəu] *vt irg* (*government*) renverser.

overtime ['əuvətaim] *n* heures *fpl* supplémentaires.

overtone ['əuvətəun] *n* (*also:* ~s) note *f*, sous-entendus *mpl*.

overture ['əuvətʃuə*] *n* (*MUS, fig*) ouverture *f*.

overturn [əuvə'tə:n] *vt* renverser // *vi* se retourner.

overweight [əuvə'weit] *a* (*person*) trop gros(se); (*luggage*) trop lourd(e).

overwhelm [əuvə'welm] *vt* accabler; submerger; écraser; ~ing *a* (*victory, defeat*) écrasant(e); (*desire*) irrésistible.

overwork [əuvə'wə:k] *n* surmenage *m*.

overwrought [əuvə'rɔ:t] *a* excédé(e).

owe [əu] *vt* devoir; to ~ sb sth, to ~ sth to sb devoir qch à qn.

owing to ['əuiŋtu:] *prep* à cause de, en raison de.

owl [aul] *n* hibou *m*.

own [əun] *vt* posséder // *a* propre; a room of my ~ une chambre à moi, ma propre chambre; to get one's ~ back prendre sa revanche; on one's ~ tout(e) seul(e); to ~ up *vi* avouer; ~er *n* propriétaire *m/f*; ~ership *n* possession *f*.

ox, *pl* **oxen** [ɔks, 'ɔksn] *n* bœuf *m*.

oxtail ['ɔksteil] *n*: ~ soup soupe *f* à la queue de bœuf.

oxygen ['ɔksidʒən] *n* oxygène *m*; ~ mask *n* masque *m* à oxygène.

oyster ['ɔistə*] *n* huître *f*.

oz. *abbr of* **ounce(s)**.

P

p [pi:] *abbr of* **penny, pence.**

pa [pɑ:] *n* (*col*) papa *m*.

P.A. *n abbr of* **personal assistant, public address system.**

p.a. *abbr of* **per annum.**

pace [peɪs] *n* pas *m*; (*speed*) allure *f*; vitesse *f* // *vi*: to ~ up and down faire les cent pas; to keep ~ with aller à la même vitesse que; (*events*) se tenir au courant de; **~maker** *n* (*MED*) stimulateur *m* cardiaque.

pacific [pə'sɪfɪk] *a* pacifique // *n*: the P~ (Ocean) le Pacifique, l'océan *m* Pacifique.

pack [pæk] *n* paquet *m*; ballot *m*; (*of hounds*) meute *f*; (*of thieves etc*) bande *f*; (*of cards*) jeu *m* // *vt* (*goods*) empaqueter, emballer; (*in suitcase etc*) emballer; (*box*) remplir; (*cram*) entasser; (*press down*) tasser; damer; to ~ (one's bags) faire ses bagages; to ~ **off** *vt* (*person*) envoyer (promener), expédier.

package ['pækɪdʒ] *n* paquet *m*; ballot *m*; (*also*: ~ **deal**) marché global; forfait *m*; ~ **tour** *n* voyage organisé.

packed lunch *n* repas froid.

packet ['pækɪt] *n* paquet *m*.

packing ['pækɪŋ] *n* emballage *m*; ~ **case** *n* caisse *f* (d'emballage).

pact [pækt] *n* pacte *m*; traité *m*.

pad [pæd] *n* bloc(-notes) *m*; (*for inking*) tampon *m* encreur; (*col*: *flat*) piaule *f* // *vt* rembourrer; **~ding** *n* rembourrage *m*.

paddle ['pædl] *n* (*oar*) pagaie *f*; (*US*: *for table tennis*) raquette *f* de ping-pong // *vi* barboter, faire trempette // *vt*: to ~ **a canoe** *etc* pagayer; ~ **steamer** *n* bateau *m* à aubes; **paddling pool** *n* (*Brit*) petit bassin.

paddy ['pædɪ]: ~ **field** *n* rizière *f*.

padlock ['pædlɔk] *n* cadenas *m*.

paediatrics, (*US*) **pediatrics** [pi:dɪ'ætrɪks] *n* pédiatrie *f*.

pagan ['peɪgən] *a, n* païen(ne).

page [peɪdʒ] *n* (*of book*) page *f*; (*also*: ~ **boy**) groom *m*, chasseur *m*; (*at wedding*) garçon *m* d'honneur // *vt* (*in hotel etc*) (faire) appeler.

pageant ['pædʒənt] *n* spectacle *m* historique; grande cérémonie; **~ry** *n* apparat *m*, pompe *f*.

paid [peɪd] *pt, pp of* **pay** // *a* (*work, official*) rémunéré(e); to put ~ to (*Brit*) mettre fin à, régler.

pail [peɪl] *n* seau *m*.

pain [peɪn] *n* douleur *f*; to be in ~ souffrir, avoir mal; to take ~s to do se donner du mal pour faire; **~ed** *a* peiné(e), chagrin(e); **~ful** *a* doulou-

reux(euse); difficile, pénible; **~fully** *ad* (*fig*: *very*) terriblement; **~killer** *n* calmant *m*; **~less** *a* indolore.

painstaking ['peɪnzteɪkɪŋ] *a* (*person*) soigneux(euse); (*work*) soigné(e).

paint [peɪnt] *n* peinture *f* // *vt* peindre; (*fig*) dépeindre; to ~ **the door blue** peindre la porte en bleu; **~brush** *n* pinceau *m*; **~er** *n* peintre *m*; **~ing** *n* peinture *f*; (*picture*) tableau *m*; **~work** *n* peintures *fpl*; (*of car*) peinture *f*.

pair [pɛə*] *n* (*of shoes, gloves etc*) paire *f*; (*of people*) couple *m*; duo *m*; paire; ~ **of scissors** (paire de) ciseaux *mpl*; ~ **of trousers** pantalon *m*.

pajamas [prɪ'dʒɑ:məz] *npl* (*US*) pyjama(s) *m(pl)*.

Pakistan [pɑ:kɪ'stɑ:n] *n* Pakistan *m*; **~i** *a* pakistanais(e) // *n* Pakistanais/e.

pal [pæl] *n* (*col*) copain/copine.

palace ['pæləs] *n* palais *m*.

palatable ['pælɪtəbl] *a* bon(bonne), agréable au goût.

palate ['pælɪt] *n* palais *m* (*ANAT*).

palatial [pə'leɪʃəl] *a* grandiose, magnifique.

palaver [pə'lɑ:və*] *n* palabres *fpl* or *mpl*; histoire(s) *f(pl)*.

pale [peɪl] *a* pâle; to grow ~ pâlir // *n*: beyond the ~ au ban de la société.

Palestine ['pælɪstaɪn] *n* Palestine *f*; **Palestinian** [-'tɪnɪən] *a* palestinien(ne) // *n* Palestinien/ne.

palette ['pælɪt] *n* palette *f*.

paling ['peɪlɪŋ] *n* (*stake*) palis *m*; (*fence*) palissade *f*.

pall [pɔ:l] *n* (*of smoke*) voile *m* // *vi*: to ~ (**on**) devenir lassant (pour).

pallet ['pælɪt] *n* (*for goods*) palette *f*.

pallid ['pælɪd] *a* blême.

pallor ['pælə*] *n* pâleur *f*.

palm [pɑ:m] *n* (*ANAT*) paume *f*; (*also*: ~ **tree**) palmier *m*; (*leaf, symbol*) palme *f* // *vt*: to ~ **sth off on sb** (*col*) refiler qch à qn; **P~ Sunday** *n* le dimanche des Rameaux.

palpable ['pælpəbl] *a* évident(e), manifeste.

paltry ['pɔ:ltrɪ] *a* dérisoire; piètre.

pamper ['pæmpə*] *vt* gâter, dorloter.

pamphlet ['pæmflət] *n* brochure *f*.

pan [pæn] *n* (*also*: **sauce~**) casserole *f*; (*also*: **frying ~**) poêle *f*; (*of lavatory*) cuvette *f* // *vi* (*CINEMA*) faire un panoramique.

pancake ['pænkeɪk] *n* crêpe *f*.

panda ['pændə] *n* panda *m*; ~ **car** *n* (*Brit*) ≈ voiture *f* pie *inv*.

pandemonium [pændɪ'məunɪəm] *n* tohu-bohu *m*.

pander ['pændə*] *vi*: to ~ **to** flatter bassement; obéir servilement à.

pane [peɪn] *n* carreau *m* (de fenêtre).

panel ['pænl] *n* (*of wood, cloth etc*) panneau *m*; (*RADIO, TV*) panel *m*;

invités *mpl*, experts *mpl*; ~**ling**, (*US*) ~**ing** *n* boiseries *fpl*.

pang [pæŋ] *n*: ~**s of** remorse pincements *mpl* de remords; ~**s of** hunger/ conscience tiraillements *mpl* d'estomac/de la conscience.

panic ['pænɪk] *n* panique *f*, affolement *m* // *vi* s'affoler, paniquer; ~**ky** *a* (*person*) qui panique *or* s'affole facilement; ~**stricken** *a* affolé(e).

pansy ['pænzɪ] *n* (*BOT*) pensée *f*; (*col*) tapette *f*, pédé *m*.

pant [pænt] *vi* haleter.

panther ['pænθə*] *n* panthère *f*.

panties ['pæntɪz] *npl* slip *m*, culotte *f*.

pantihose ['pæntɪhəuz] *n* (*US*) collant *m*.

pantomime ['pæntəmaɪm] *n* (*Brit*) spectacle *m* de Noël.

pantry ['pæntrɪ] *n* garde-manger *m inv*; (*room*) office *f or m*.

pants [pænts] *n* (*Brit*: woman's) culotte *f*, slip *m*; (: man's) slip, caleçon *m*; (*US*: trousers) pantalon *m*.

paper ['peɪpə*] *n* papier *m*; (*also*: wall~) papier peint; (*also*: news~) journal *m*; (*study*, article) article *m*; (*exam*) épreuve écrite // *a* en or de papier // *vt* tapisser (de papier peint); ~**s** *npl* (*also*: identity ~s) papiers (d'identité); ~**back** *n* livre de poche; livre broché *or* non relié; ~ **clip** *n* trombone *m*; ~ **hankie** *n* mouchoir *m* en papier; ~**weight** *n* presse-papiers *m inv*; ~**work** *n* paperasserie *f*.

par [pɑ:*] *n* pair *m*; (*GOLF*) normale *f* du parcours; **on a ~ with** à égalité avec, au même niveau que.

parable ['pærəbl] *n* parabole *f* (*REL*).

parachute ['pærəʃu:t] *n* parachute *m*.

parade [pə'reɪd] *n* défilé *m*; (*inspection*) revue *f*; (*street*) boulevard *m* // *vt* (*fig*) faire étalage de // *vi* défiler.

paradise ['pærədaɪs] *n* paradis *m*.

paradox ['pærədɔks] *n* paradoxe *m*; ~**ically** [-'dɔksɪklɪ] *ad* paradoxalement.

paraffin ['pærəfɪn] *n* (*Brit*): ~ (oil) pétrole (lampant).

paragraph ['pærəgrɑ:f] *n* paragraphe *m*.

parallel ['pærəlɛl] *a* parallèle; (*fig*) analogue // *n* (*line*) parallèle *f*; (*fig*, *GEO*) parallèle *m*.

paralysis [pə'rælɪsɪs] *n* paralysie *f*.

paralyze ['pærəlaɪz] *vt* paralyser.

paramount ['pærəmaunt] *a*: of ~ importance de la plus haute *or* grande importance.

paranoid ['pærənɔɪd] *a* (*PSYCH*) paranoïaque; (*neurotic*) paranoïde.

paraphernalia [pærəfə'neɪlɪə] *n* attirail *m*, affaires *fpl*.

parasol [pærə'sɔl] *n* ombrelle *f*; parasol *m*.

paratrooper ['pærətru:pə*] *n* parachutiste *m* (*soldat*).

parcel ['pɑ:sl] *n* paquet *m*, colis *m* // *vt* (*also*: ~ up) empaqueter.

parch [pɑ:tʃ] *vt* dessécher; ~**ed** *a* (*person*) assoiffé(e).

parchment ['pɑ:tʃmənt] *n* parchemin *m*.

pardon ['pɑ:dn] *n* pardon *m*; grâce *f* // *vt* pardonner à; (*LAW*) gracier; ~ me! excusez-moi!; I beg your ~! pardon!, je suis désolé!; (I beg your) ~?, (*US*) ~ me? pardon?

parent ['pɛərənt] *n* père *m or* mère *f*; ~**s** *npl* parents *mpl*.

Paris ['pærɪs] *n* Paris.

parish ['pærɪʃ] *n* paroisse *f*; (*civil*) ≈ commune *f* // *a* paroissial(e).

Parisian [pə'rɪzɪən] *a* parisien(ne) // *n* Parisien/ne.

park [pɑ:k] *n* parc *m*, jardin public // *vt* garer // *vi* se garer.

parking ['pɑ:kɪŋ] *n* stationnement *m*; 'no ~' 'stationnement interdit'; ~ **lot** *n* (*US*) parking *m*, parc *m* de stationnement; ~ **meter** *n* parcomètre *m*; ~ **ticket** *n* P.V. *m*.

parlance ['pɑ:lns] *n* langage *m*.

parliament ['pɑ:ləmənt] *n* parlement *m*; ~**ary** [-'mɛntərɪ] *a* parlementaire.

parlour, (*US*) **parlor** ['pɑ:lə*] *n* salon *m*.

parochial [pə'rəukɪəl] *a* paroissial(e); (*pej*) à l'esprit de clocher.

parody ['pærədɪ] *n* parodie *f*.

parole [pə'rəul] *n*: on ~ en liberté conditionnelle.

parrot ['pærət] *n* perroquet *m*.

parry ['pærɪ] *vt* esquiver, parer à.

parsley ['pɑ:slɪ] *n* persil *m*.

parsnip ['pɑ:snɪp] *n* panais *m*.

parson ['pɑ:sn] *n* ecclésiastique *m*; (*Church of England*) pasteur *m*.

part [pɑ:t] *n* partie *f*; (*of machine*) pièce *f*; (*THEATRE etc*) rôle *m*; (*MUS*) voix *f*; partie; (*US*: in hair) raie *f* // *a*, *ad* = **partly** // *vt* séparer // *vi* (*people*) se séparer; (*roads*) se diviser; **to take ~ in** participer à, prendre part à; **for my ~** en ce qui me concerne; **to take sth in good ~** prendre qch du bon côté; **to take sb's ~** prendre le parti de qn, prendre parti pour qn; **for the most ~** en grande partie, dans la plupart des cas; **to ~ with** *vt fus* se séparer de; se défaire de; ~ **exchange** *n* (*Brit*): in ~ exchange en reprise.

partial ['pɑ:ʃl] *a* partiel(le); (*unjust*) partial(e); **to be ~ to** aimer, avoir un faible pour.

participate [pɑ:'tɪsɪpeɪt] *vi*: **to ~ (in)** participer (à), prendre part (à); **participation** [-'peɪʃən] *n* participation *f*.

participle ['pɑ:tɪsɪpl] *n* participe *m*.

particle ['pɑ:tɪkl] *n* particule *f*.

particular [pə'tɪkjulə*] *a* particulier(ère); spécial(e); (*detailed*) détaillé(e); *(fussy)* difficile; méticuleux(euse) // ~s *npl* détails *mpl*; *(information)* renseignements *mpl*; in ~ et surtout, en particulier; ~ly *ad* particulièrement; en particulier.

parting ['pɑ:tɪŋ] *n* séparation *f*; *(Brit: in hair)* raie *f* // a d'adieu.

partisan [pɑ:tɪ'zæn] *n* partisan/e // a partisan(e); de parti.

partition [pɑ:'tɪʃən] *n* *(POL)* partition *f*, division *f*; *(wall)* cloison *f*.

partly ['pɑ:tlɪ] *ad* en partie, partiellement.

partner ['pɑ:tnə*] *n* *(COMM)* associé/e; *(SPORT)* partenaire *m/f*; *(at dance)* cavalier/ère; ~**ship** *n* association *f*.

partridge ['pɑ:trɪdʒ] *n* perdrix *f*.

part-time [pɑ:t'taɪm] *a, ad* à mi-temps, à temps partiel.

party ['pɑ:tɪ] *n* *(POL)* parti *m*; *(team)* équipe *f*; groupe *m*; *(LAW)* partie *f*; *(celebration)* réception *f*; soirée *f*; fête *f* // a *(POL)* de or du parti; de partis; ~ **dress** *n* robe habillée; ~ **line** *n* *(TEL)* ligne partagée.

pass [pɑ:s] *vt* *(time, object)* passer; *(place)* passer devant; *(car, friend)* croiser; *(exam)* être reçu(e) à, réussir; *(candidate)* admettre; *(overtake, surpass)* dépasser; *(approve)* approuver, accepter // *vi* passer; *(SCOL)* être reçu(e) or admis(e), réussir // *n* *(permit)* laissez-passer *m inv*; carte *f* d'accès or d'abonnement; *(in mountains)* col *m*; *(SPORT)* passe *f*; *(SCOL: also:* ~ **mark):** to get a ~ être reçu(e) *(sans mention);* to ~ sth through a ring *etc* *(faire)* passer qch dans un anneau *etc*; to make a ~ at sb *(col)* faire des avances à qn; to ~ **away** *vi* mourir; to ~ **by** *vi* passer // *vt* négliger; to ~ **on** *vt* *(news, object)* transmettre; *(illness)* passer; to ~ **out** *vi* s'évanouir; to ~ **up** *vt* *(opportunity)* laisser passer; ~**able** a *(road)* praticable; *(work)* acceptable.

passage ['pæsɪdʒ] *n* *(also:* ~**way**) couloir *m*; *(gen, in book)* passage *m*; *(by boat)* traversée *f*.

passbook ['pɑ:sbuk] *n* livret *m*.

passenger ['pæsɪndʒə*] *n* passager/ère.

passer-by [pɑ:sə'baɪ] *n* passant/e.

passing ['pɑ:sɪŋ] a *(fig)* passager(ère); in ~ en passant; ~ **place** *n* *(AUT)* aire *f* de croisement.

passion ['pæʃən] *n* passion *f*; amour *m*; ~**ate** a passionné(e).

passive ['pæsɪv] a *(also LING)* passif(ive).

Passover ['pɑ:səuvə*] *n* Pâque *(juive)*.

passport ['pɑ:spɔ:t] *n* passeport *m*; ~ **control** *n* contrôle *m* des passeports.

password ['pɑ:swə:d] *n* mot *m* de passe.

past [pɑ:st] *prep* *(further than)* au delà de, plus loin que; après; *(later than)* après // a passé(e); *(president etc)* ancien(ne) // *n* passé *m*; he's ~ forty il a dépassé la quarantaine, il a plus de or passé quarante ans; **for the** ~ **few/3 days** depuis quelques/3 jours; **ces derniers/3 derniers jours; he ran** ~ **me** il m'a dépassé en courant; **il a passé devant moi en courant.**

pasta ['pæstə] *n* pâtes *fpl.*

paste [peɪst] *n* *(glue)* colle *f* (de pâte); *(jewellery)* strass *m*; *(CULIN)* pâté *m* (à tartiner); pâte *f* // *vt* coller.

pasteurized ['pæstəraɪzd] a pasteurisé(e).

pastille ['pæstl] *n* pastille *f*.

pastime ['pɑ:staɪm] *n* passe-temps *m inv*, distraction *f*.

pastor ['pɑ:stə*] *n* pasteur *m*.

pastry ['peɪstrɪ] *n* pâte *f*; *(cake)* pâtisserie *f*.

pasture ['pɑ:stʃə*] *n* pâturage *m*.

pasty *n* ['pæstɪ] petit pâté (en croûte) // a ['peɪstɪ] pâteux(euse); *(complexion)* terreux(euse).

pat [pæt] *vt* donner une petite tape à.

patch [pætʃ] *n* *(of material)* pièce *f*; *(spot)* tache *f*; *(of land)* parcelle *f* // *vt* *(clothes)* rapiécer; **(to go through) a bad** ~ *(passer par)* une période difficile; **to** ~ **up** *vt* réparer; ~**y** a inégal(e).

pâté ['pæteɪ] *n* pâté *m*, terrine *f*.

patent ['peɪtnt] *n* brevet *m* (d'invention) // *vt* faire breveter // a patent(e), manifeste; ~ **leather** *n* cuir verni.

paternal [pə'tə:nl] a paternel(le).

path [pɑ:θ] *n* chemin *m*, sentier *m*; allée *f*; *(of planet)* course *f*; *(of missile)* trajectoire *f*.

pathetic [pə'θetɪk] a *(pitiful)* pitoyable; *(very bad)* lamentable, minable; *(moving)* pathétique.

pathological [pæθə'lɔdʒɪkl] a pathologique.

pathos ['peɪθɔs] *n* pathétique *m*.

patience ['peɪʃns] *n* patience *f*; *(Brit: CARDS)* réussite *f*.

patient ['peɪʃnt] *n* patient/e; malade *m/f* // a patient(e).

patriotic [pætrɪ'ɔtɪk] a patriotique; *(person)* patriote.

patrol [pə'trəul] *n* patrouille *f* // *vt* patrouiller dans; ~ **car** *n* voiture *f* de police; ~**man** *n* *(US)* agent *m* de police.

patron ['peɪtrən] *n* *(in shop)* client/e; *(of charity)* patron/ne; ~ **of the arts** mécène *m*; ~**ize** ['pætrənaɪz] *vt* être (un) client or un habitué de; *(fig)* traiter avec condescendance.

patter ['pætə*] *n* crépitement *m*, tapotement *m*; *(sales talk)* boniment *m*.

pattern ['pætən] *n* modèle *m*; *(SEWING)* patron *m*; *(design)* motif *m*; *(sample)* échantillon *m*.

paunch [pɔ:ntʃ] *n* gros ventre, bedaine

f.

pauper ['pɔ:pə*] *n* indigent/e.

pause [pɔ:z] *n* pause *f*, arrêt *m*; (*MUS*) silence *m* // *vi* faire une pause, s'arrêter.

pave [peɪv] *vt* paver, daller; **to ~ the way for** ouvrir la voie à.

pavement ['peɪvmənt] *n* (*Brit*) trottoir *m*.

pavilion [pə'vɪlɪən] *n* pavillon *m*; tente *f*.

paving ['peɪvɪŋ] *n* pavage *m*, dallage *m*; **~ stone** *n* pavé *m*.

paw [pɔ:] *n* patte *f*.

pawn [pɔ:n] *n* gage *m*; (*CHESS, also fig*) pion *m* // *vt* mettre en gage; **~broker** *n* prêteur *m* sur gages; **~shop** *n* mont-de-piété *m*.

pay [peɪ] *n* salaire *m*; paie *f* // *vb* (*pt, pp paid*) *vt* payer // *vi* payer; (*be profitable*) être rentable; **to ~ attention (to)** prêter attention à; **to ~ back** *vt* rembourser; **to ~ for** *vt* payer; **to ~ in** *vt* verser; **to ~ off** *vt* régler, acquitter; rembourser // *vi* (*scheme, decision*) se révéler payant(e); **to ~ up** *vt* régler; **~able** *a:* **~able to sb** à l'ordre de qn; **~ee** *n* bénéficiaire *m/f*; **~ envelope** *n* (*US*) = **~ packet**; **~ment** *n* paiement *m*; règlement *m*; versement *m*; **advance ~ment** acompte *m*; paiement anticipé; **monthly ~ment** mensualité *f*; **~ packet** *n* (*Brit*) paie *f*; **~phone** *n* cabine *f* téléphonique, téléphone public; **~roll** *n* registre *m* du personnel; **~ slip** *n* bulletin *m* de paie.

PC *n abbr of* **personal computer**.

p.c. *abbr of* **per cent**.

pea [pi:] *n* (petit) pois.

peace [pi:s] *n* paix *f*; (*calm*) calme *m*, tranquillité *f*; **~able** *a* paisible; **~ful** *a* paisible, calme.

peach [pi:tʃ] *n* pêche *f*.

peacock ['pi:kɔk] *n* paon *m*.

peak [pi:k] *n* (*mountain*) pic *m*, cime *f*; (*fig: highest level*) maximum *m*; (: *of career, fame*) apogée *m*; **~ hours** *npl* heures *fpl* d'affluence.

peal [pi:l] *n* (*of bells*) carillon *m*; **~s of** laughter éclats *mpl* de rire.

peanut ['pi:nʌt] *n* arachide *f*, cacahuète *f*.

pear [peə*] *n* poire *f*.

pearl [pə:l] *n* perle *f*.

peasant ['peznt] *n* paysan/ne.

peat [pi:t] *n* tourbe *f*.

pebble ['pebl] *n* galet *m*, caillou *m*.

peck [pek] *vt* (*also:* **~ at**) donner un coup de bec à; (*food*) picorer // *n* coup *m* de bec; (*kiss*) bécot *m*; **~ing order** *n* ordre *m* des préséances; **~ish** *a* (*Brit col*): **I feel ~ish** je mangerais bien quelque chose.

peculiar [pɪ'kju:lɪə*] *a* étrange, bizarre, curieux(euse); particulier(ère); **~ to**

particulier à.

pedal ['pedl] *n* pédale *f* // *vi* pédaler.

pedantic [pɪ'dæntɪk] *a* pédant(e).

peddler ['pedlə*] *n* marchand ambulant.

pedestal ['pedəstl] *n* piédestal *m*.

pedestrian [pɪ'destrɪən] *n* piéton *m*; **~ crossing** *n* (*Brit*) passage clouté.

pediatrics [pi:dɪ'ætrɪks] *n* (*US*) = **paediatrics**.

pedigree ['pedɪgri:] *n* ascendance *f*; (*of animal*) pedigree *m* // *cpd* (*animal*) de race.

pedlar ['pedlə*] *n* = **peddler**.

pee [pi:] *vi* (*col*) faire pipi, pisser.

peek [pi:k] *vi* jeter un coup d'œil (furtif).

peel [pi:l] *n* pelure *f*, épluchure *f*; (*of orange, lemon*) écorce *f* // *vt* peler, éplucher // *vi* (*paint etc*) s'écailler; (*wallpaper*) se décoller.

peep [pi:p] *n* (*Brit: look*) coup d'œil furtif; (*sound*) pépiement *m* // *vi* (*Brit*) jeter un coup d'œil (furtif); **to ~ out** *vi* se montrer (furtivement); **~hole** *n* judas *m*.

peer [pɪə*] *vi:* **to ~ at** regarder attentivement, scruter // *n* (*noble*) pair *m*; (*equal*) pair, égal/e; **~age** *n* pairie *f*.

peeved [pi:vd] *a* irrité(e), ennuyé(e).

peevish ['pi:vɪʃ] *a* grincheux(euse), maussade.

peg [peg] *n* cheville *f*; (*for coat etc*) patère *f*; (*Brit: also:* **clothes ~**) pince *f* à linge // *vt* (*prices*) contrôler, stabiliser.

Peking [pi:'kɪŋ] *n* Pékin *m*.

pelican crossing ['pelɪkən-] *n* (*Brit AUT*) feu *m* à commande manuelle.

pellet ['pelɪt] *n* boulette *f*; (*of lead*) plomb *m*.

pelmet ['pelmɪt] *n* cantonnière *f*; lambrequin *m*.

pelt [pelt] *vt:* **to ~ sb (with)** bombarder qn (de) // *vi* (*rain*) tomber à seaux // *n* peau *f*.

pelvis ['pelvɪs] *n* bassin *m*.

pen [pen] *n* (*for writing*) stylo *m*; (*for sheep*) parc *m*.

penal ['pi:nl] *a* pénal(e); **~ize** *vt* pénaliser; (*fig*) désavantager.

penalty ['penltɪ] *n* pénalité *f*; sanction *f*; (*fine*) amende *f*; (*SPORT*) pénalisation *f*; **~ (kick)** *n* (*FOOTBALL*) penalty *m*.

penance ['penəns] *n* pénitence *f*.

pence [pens] *npl of* **penny**.

pencil ['pensl] *n* crayon *m*; **~ case** *n* trousse *f* (d'écolier); **~ sharpener** *n* taille-crayon(s) *m inv*.

pendant ['pendnt] *n* pendentif *m*.

pending ['pendɪŋ] *prep* en attendant // *a* en suspens.

pendulum ['pendjuləm] *n* pendule *m*; (*of clock*) balancier *m*.

penetrate ['penɪtreɪt] *vt* pénétrer dans; pénétrer.

penfriend ['pɛnfrɛnd] *n* (*Brit*) correspondant/e.

penguin ['pɛŋgwɪn] *n* pingouin *m*.

penicillin [pɛnɪ'sɪlɪn] *n* pénicilline *f*.

peninsula [pə'nɪnsjulə] *n* péninsule *f*.

penis ['piːnɪs] *n* pénis *m*, verge *f*.

penitent ['pɛnɪtnt] *a* repentant(e).

penitentiary [pɛnɪ'tɛnʃərɪ] *n* (*US*) prison *f*.

penknife ['pɛnnaɪf] *n* canif *m*.

pen name *n* nom *m* de plume, pseudonyme *m*.

penniless ['pɛnɪlɪs] *a* sans le sou.

penny, *pl* **pennies** *or* (*Brit*) **pence** ['pɛnɪ, 'pɛnɪz, pɛns] *n* penny *m* (*pl* pennies); (*US*) = cent.

penpal ['pɛnpæl] *n* correspondant/e.

pension ['pɛnʃən] *n* retraite *f*; (*MIL*) pension *f*; ~**er** *n* (*Brit*) retraité/e.

penthouse ['pɛnthaus] *n* appartement *m* (de luxe) en attique.

pent-up ['pɛntʌp] *a* (*feelings*) refoulé(e).

people ['piːpl] *npl* gens *mpl*; personnes *fpl*; (*citizens*) peuple *m* // *n* (*nation, race*) peuple *m* // *vt* peupler; **several ~ came** plusieurs personnes sont venues; **the room was full of ~** la salle était pleine de monde *or* de gens.

pep [pɛp] *n* (*col*) entrain *m*, dynamisme *m*; **to ~ up** *vt* remonter.

pepper ['pɛpə*] *n* poivre *m*; (*vegetable*) poivron *m* // *vt* poivrer; ~**mint** *n* (*plant*) menthe poivrée; (*sweet*) pastille *f* de menthe.

peptalk ['pɛptɔːk] *n* (*col*) (petit) discours d'encouragement.

per [pə:*] *prep* par; ~ **hour** (*miles etc*) à l'heure; (*fee*) (de) l'heure; ~ **kilo** *etc* le kilo *etc*; ~ **day/person** par jour/personne; ~ **annum** *ad* par an; ~ **capita** *a, ad* par personne, par habitant.

perceive [pə'siːv] *vt* percevoir; (*notice*) remarquer, s'apercevoir de.

per cent [pə'sɛnt] *ad* pour cent.

percentage [pə'sɛntɪdʒ] *n* pourcentage *m*.

perception [pə'sɛpʃən] *n* perception *f*; sensibilité *f*; perspicacité *f*.

perceptive [pə'sɛptɪv] *a* pénétrant(e); perspicace.

perch [pə:tʃ] *n* (*fish*) perche *f*; (*for bird*) perchoir *m* // *vi* (se) percher.

percolator ['pə:kəleɪtə*] *n* percolateur *m*; cafetière *f* électrique.

perennial [pə'rɛnɪəl] *a* perpétuel(le); (*BOT*) vivace // *n* plante *f* vivace.

perfect *a n* ['pə:fɪkt] *a* parfait(e) // *n* (*also*: ~ **tense**) parfait *m* // *vt* [pə'fɛkt] parfaire; mettre au point; ~**ly** *ad* parfaitement.

perforate ['pə:fəreɪt] *vt* perforer, percer; **perforation** [-'reɪʃən] *n* perforation *f*; (*line of holes*) pointillé *m*.

perform [pə'fɔːm] *vt* (*carry out*) exé-

cuter, remplir; (*concert etc*) jouer, donner // *vi* jouer; ~**ance** *n* représentation *f*, spectacle *m*; (*of an artist*) interprétation *f*; (*of player etc*) prestation *f*; (*of car, engine*) performance *f*; ~**er** *n* artiste *m/f*; ~**ing** *a* (*animal*) savant(e).

perfume ['pə:fjuːm] *n* parfum *m*.

perfunctory [pə'fʌŋktərɪ] *a* négligent(e), pour la forme.

perhaps [pə'hæps] *ad* peut-être.

peril ['pɛrɪl] *n* péril *m*.

perimeter [pə'rɪmɪtə*] *n* périmètre *m*; ~ **wall** *n* mur *m* d'enceinte.

period ['pɪərɪəd] *n* période *f*; (*HISTORY*) époque *f*; (*SCOL*) cours *m*; (*full stop*) point *m*; (*MED*) règles *fpl* // *a* (*costume, furniture*) d'époque; ~**ic** [-'ɔdɪk] *a* périodique; ~**ical** [-'ɔdɪkl] *a* périodique // *n* périodique *m*.

peripheral [pə'rɪfərəl] *a* périphérique // *n* (*COMPUT*) périphérique *m*.

perish ['pɛrɪʃ] *vi* périr, mourir; (*decay*) se détériorer; ~**able** *a* périssable.

perjury ['pə:dʒərɪ] *n* (*LAW: in court*) faux témoignage; (*breach of oath*) parjure *m*.

perk [pə:k] *n* avantage *m*, à-côté *m*; **to ~ up** *vi* (*cheer up*) se ragaillardir; ~**y** *a* (*cheerful*) guilleret(te), gai(e).

perm [pə:m] *n* (*for hair*) permanente *f*.

permanent ['pə:mənənt] *a* permanent(e).

permeate ['pə:mɪeɪt] *vi* s'infiltrer // *vt* s'infiltrer dans; pénétrer.

permissible [pə'mɪsɪbl] *a* permis(e), acceptable.

permission [pə'mɪʃən] *n* permission *f*, autorisation *f*.

permissive [pə'mɪsɪv] *a* tolérant(e); **the ~ society** la société de tolérance.

permit *n* ['pə:mɪt] permis *m* // *vt* [pə'mɪt] permettre; **to ~ sb to do** autoriser qn à faire, permettre à qn de faire.

perpendicular [pə:pən'dɪkjulə*] *a, n* perpendiculaire (*f*).

perplex [pə'plɛks] *vt* rendre perplexe; (*complicate*) embrouiller.

persecute ['pə:sɪkjuːt] *vt* persécuter.

persevere [pə:sɪ'vɪə*] *vi* persévérer.

Persian ['pə:ʃən] *a* persan(e) // *n* (*LING*) persan *m*; **the** (~) **Gulf** le golfe Persique.

persist [pə'sɪst] *vi*: **to ~ (in doing)** persister (à faire), s'obstiner (à faire); ~**ent** *a* persistant(e), tenace.

person ['pə:sn] *n* personne *f*; **in ~** en personne; ~**able** *a* de belle prestance, au physique attrayant; ~**al** *a* personnel(le); individuel(le); ~**al assistant (P.A.)** *n* secrétaire privé/e; ~**al computer (PC)** *n* ordinateur individuel; ~**ality** [-'nælɪtɪ] *n* personnalité *f*; ~**ally** *ad* personnellement.

personnel [pə:sə'nɛl] *n* personnel *m*.

perspective [pə'spɛktɪv] *n* perspective *f*.

perspiration [pə:spɪ'reɪʃən] *n* transpiration *f*.

persuade [pə'sweɪd] *vt*: to ~ sb to do sth persuader qn de faire qch, amener *or* décider qn à faire qch.

pert [pə:t] *a* (*bold*) effronté(e), impertinent(e).

pertaining [pə:'teɪnɪŋ]: ~ to *prep* relatif(ive) à.

peruse [pə'ru:z] *vt* lire (attentivement).

pervade [pə'veɪd] *vt* se répandre dans, envahir.

perverse [pə'və:s] *a* pervers(e); (*stubborn*) entêté(e), contrariant(e).

pervert *n* ['pə:və:t] perverti/e // *vt* [pə'və:t] pervertir.

pessimist ['pɛsɪmɪst] *n* pessimiste *m/f*; ~**ic** [-'mɪstɪk] *a* pessimiste.

pest [pɛst] *n* animal *m* (*or* insecte *m*) nuisible; (*fig*) fléau *m*.

pester ['pɛstə*] *vt* importuner, harceler.

pet [pɛt] *n* animal familier; (*favourite*) chouchou *m* // *vt* choyer // *vi* (*col*) se peloter.

petal ['pɛtl] *n* pétale *m*.

peter ['pi:tə*]: to ~ out *vi* s'épuiser; s'affaiblir.

petite [pə'ti:t] *a* menu(e).

petition [pə'tɪʃən] *n* pétition *f*.

petrified ['pɛtrɪfaɪd] *a* (*fig*) mort(e) de peur.

petrol ['pɛtrəl] *n* (*Brit*) essence *f*; two-star ~ essence *f* ordinaire; four- star ~ super *m*; ~ **can** *n* bidon *m* à essence.

petroleum [pə'trəulɪəm] *n* pétrole *m*.

petrol: ~ **pump** *n* (*Brit*) pompe *f* à essence; ~ **station** *n* (*Brit*) station-service *f*; ~ **tank** *n* (*Brit*) réservoir *m* d'essence.

petticoat ['pɛtɪkəut] *n* jupon *m*.

petty ['pɛtɪ] *a* (*mean*) mesquin(e); (*unimportant*) insignifiant(e), sans importance; ~ **cash** *n* menue monnaie; ~ **officer** *n* second-maître *m*.

petulant ['pɛtjulənt] *a* irritable.

pew [pju:] *n* banc *m* (d'église).

pewter ['pju:tə*] *n* étain *m*.

phantom ['fæntəm] *n* fantôme *m*; (*vision*) fantasme *m*.

pharmacy ['fɑ:məsɪ] *n* pharmacie *f*.

phase [feɪz] *n* phase *f*, période *f* // *vt*: to ~ sth in/out introduire/supprimer qch progressivement.

Ph.D. *abbr* (= *Doctor of Philosophy*) *title* ≈ Docteur *m* en Droit *or* Lettres *etc* // *n* ≈ doctorat *m*; titulaire *m* d'un doctorat.

pheasant ['fɛznt] *n* faisan *m*.

phenomenon, *pl* **phenomena** [fə'nɔmɪnən, -nə] *n* phénomène *m*.

philosophical [fɪlə'sɔfɪkl] *a* philosophique.

philosophy [fɪ'lɔsəfɪ] *n* philosophie *f*.

phobia ['fəubjə] *n* phobie *f*.

phone [fəun] *n* téléphone *m* // *vt* téléphoner; to be on the ~ avoir le téléphone; (*be calling*) être au téléphone; to ~ **back** *vt*, *vi* rappeler; to ~ **up** *vt* téléphoner à // *vi* téléphoner; ~ **book** *n* annuaire *m*; ~ **box** *or* **booth** *n* cabine *f* téléphonique; ~ **call** *n* coup *m* de fil *or* de téléphone; ~-**in** *n* (*Brit* RADIO, TV) programme *m* à ligne ouverte.

phonetics [fə'nɛtɪks] *n* phonétique *f*.

phoney ['fəunɪ] *a* faux(fausse), factice.

phonograph ['fəunəgrɑ:f] *n* (*US*) électrophone *m*.

phony ['fəunɪ] *a* = **phoney**.

photo ['fəutəu] *n* photo *f*.

photo... ['fəutəu] *prefix*: ~**copier** *n* machine *f* à photocopier; ~**copy** *n* photocopie *f* // *vt* photocopier; ~**graph** *n* photographie *f* // *vt* photographier; ~**grapher** [fə'tɔgrəfə*] *n* photographe *m/f*; ~**graphy** [fə'tɔgrəfɪ] *n* photographie *f*.

phrase [freɪz] *n* expression *f*; (LING) locution *f* // *vt* exprimer; ~ **book** *n* recueil *m* d'expressions (pour touristes).

physical ['fɪzɪkl] *a* physique; ~ **education** *n* éducation *f* physique; ~**ly** *ad* physiquement.

physician [fɪ'zɪʃən] *n* médecin *m*.

physicist ['fɪzɪsɪst] *n* physicien/ne.

physics ['fɪzɪks] *n* physique *f*.

physiotherapy [fɪzɪəu'θɛrəpɪ] *n* kinésithérapie *f*.

physique [fɪ'zi:k] *n* physique *m*; constitution *f*.

pianist ['pi:ənɪst] *n* pianiste *m/f*.

piano [pɪ'ænəu] *n* piano *m*.

pick [pɪk] *n* (*tool*: *also*: ~-**axe**) pic *m*, pioche *f* // *vt* choisir; (*gather*) cueillir; take your ~ faites votre choix; the ~ of le(la) meilleur(e) de; to ~ **off** *vt* (*kill*) (viser soigneusement et) abattre; to ~ **on** *vt fus* (*person*) harceler; to ~ **out** *vt* choisir; (*distinguish*) distinguer; to ~ **up** *vi* (*improve*) remonter, s'améliorer // *vt* ramasser; (*telephone*) décrocher; (*collect*) passer prendre; (AUT: *give lift to*) prendre; (*learn*) apprendre; to ~ **up** speed prendre de la vitesse; to ~ **o.s.** **up** se relever.

picket ['pɪkɪt] *n* (*in strike*) gréviste *m/f* participant à un piquet de grève; piquet *m* de grève // *vt* mettre un piquet de grève devant.

pickle ['pɪkl] *n* (*also*: ~**s**: *as condiment*) pickles *mpl* // *vt* conserver dans du vinaigre *or* dans de la saumure.

pickpocket ['pɪkpɔkɪt] *n* pickpocket *m*.

pickup ['pɪkʌp] *n* (*Brit*: *on record player*) bras *m* pick-up; (*small truck*) pick-up *m inv*.

picnic ['pɪknɪk] *n* pique-nique *m*.

pictorial [pɪk'tɔ:rɪəl] *a* illustré(e).

picture ['pɪktʃə*] *n* image *f*; (*painting*)

peinture *f*, tableau *m*; (*photograph*) photo(graphie) *f*; (*drawing*) dessin *m*; (*film*) film *m* // *vt* se représenter; (*describe*) dépeindre, représenter; **the** ~**s** (*Brit*) le cinéma; ~ **book** *n* livre *m* d'images.

picturesque [pɪktʃə'rɛsk] *a* pittoresque.

pie [paɪ] *n* tourte *f*; (*of meat*) pâté *m* en croûte.

piece [piːs] *n* morceau *m*; (*of land*) parcelle *f*; (*item*): **a** ~ **of furniture/advice** un meuble/conseil // *vt*: **to** ~ **together** rassembler; **to take to** ~**s** démonter; ~**meal** *ad* par bouts; ~**work** *n* travail *m* aux pièces.

pie chart *n* graphique *m* à secteurs, camembert *m*.

pier [pɪə*] *n* jetée *f*; (*of bridge etc*) pile *f*.

pierce [pɪəs] *vt* percer, transpercer.

pig [pɪg] *n* cochon *m*, porc *m*.

pigeon ['pɪdʒən] *n* pigeon *m*; ~**hole** *n* casier *m*.

piggy bank ['pɪgɪbæŋk] *n* tirelire *f*.

pigheaded ['pɪg'hɛdɪd] *a* entêté(e), têtu(e).

pigskin ['pɪgskɪn] *n* (peau *f* de) porc *m*.

pigsty ['pɪgstaɪ] *n* porcherie *f*.

pigtail ['pɪgteɪl] *n* natte *f*, tresse *f*.

pike [paɪk] *n* (*spear*) pique *f*; (*fish*) brochet *m*.

pilchard ['pɪltʃəd] *n* pilchard *m* (*sorte de sardine*).

pile [paɪl] *n* (*pillar, of books*) pile *f*; (*heap*) tas *m*; (*of carpet*) épaisseur *f* // *vb* (*also*: ~ **up**) *vt* empiler, entasser // *vi* s'entasser; **to** ~ **into** (*car*) s'entasser dans.

piles [paɪlz] *npl* hémorroïdes *fpl*.

pileup ['paɪlʌp] *n* (*AUT*) télescopage *m*, collision *f* en série.

pilfering ['pɪlfərɪŋ] *n* chapardage *m*.

pilgrim ['pɪlgrɪm] *n* pèlerin *m*.

pill [pɪl] *n* pilule *f*; **the** ~ la pilule.

pillage ['pɪlɪdʒ] *vt* piller.

pillar ['pɪlə*] *n* pilier *m*; ~ **box** (*Brit*) boîte *f* aux lettres.

pillion ['pɪljən] *n* (*of motor cycle*) siège *m* arrière.

pillow ['pɪləu] *n* oreiller *m*; ~**case** *n* taie *f* d'oreiller.

pilot ['paɪlət] *n* pilote *m* // *cpd* (*scheme etc*) pilote, expérimental(e) // *vt* piloter; ~ **light** *n* veilleuse *f*.

pimp [pɪmp] *n* souteneur *m*, maquereau *m*.

pimple ['pɪmpl] *n* bouton *m*.

pin [pɪn] *n* épingle *f*; (*TECH*) cheville *f* // *vt* épingler; ~**s and needles** fourmis *fpl*; **to** ~ **sb down** (*fig*) coincer qn à répondre; **to** ~ **sth on sb** (*fig*) mettre qch sur le dos de qn.

pinafore ['pɪnəfɔː*] *n* tablier *m*.

pinball ['pɪnbɔːl] *n* (*also*: ~ **machine**)

flipper *m*.

pincers ['pɪnsəz] *npl* tenailles *fpl*.

pinch [pɪntʃ] *n* pincement *m*; (*of salt etc*) pincée *f* // *vt* pincer; (*col*: *steal*) piquer, chiper // *vi* (*shoe*) serrer; **at a** ~ à la rigueur.

pincushion ['pɪnkuʃən] *n* pelote *f* à épingles.

pine [paɪn] *n* (*also*: ~ **tree**) pin *m* // *vi*: **to** ~ **for** aspirer à, désirer ardemment; **to** ~ **away** *vi* dépérir.

pineapple ['paɪnæpl] *n* ananas *m*.

ping [pɪŋ] *n* (*noise*) tintement *m*; ~-**pong** *n* ® ping-pong *m* ®.

pink [pɪŋk] *a* rose // *n* (*colour*) rose *m*; (*BOT*) œillet *m*, mignardise *f*.

pinpoint ['pɪnpɔɪnt] *vt* indiquer (avec précision).

pint [paɪnt] *n* pinte *f* (*Brit* = 0.57 l; *US* = 0.47 l); (*Brit col*) ≈ demi *m*, ≈ pot *m*.

pioneer [paɪə'nɪə*] *n* explorateur/trice; (*early settler, fig*) pionnier *m*.

pious ['paɪəs] *a* pieux(euse).

pip [pɪp] *n* (*seed*) pépin *m*; (*Brit*: *time signal on radio*) top *m*.

pipe [paɪp] *n* tuyau *m*, conduite *f*; (*for smoking*) pipe *f*; (*MUS*) pipeau *m* // *vt* amener par tuyau; ~**s** *npl* (*also*: **bag**~**s**) cornemuse *f*; **to** ~ **down** *vi* (*col*) se taire; ~ **cleaner** *n* cure-pipe *m*; ~ **dream** *n* chimère *f*, utopie *f*; ~**line** *n* pipe-line *m*; ~**r** *n* joueur/euse de pipeau (*or de cornemuse*).

piping ['paɪpɪŋ] *ad*: ~ **hot** très chaud(e).

pique ['piːk] *n* dépit *m*.

pirate ['paɪərət] *n* pirate *m*.

Pisces ['paɪsiːz] *n* les Poissons *mpl*.

piss [pɪs] *vi* (*col*) pisser; ~**ed** *a* (*col*: *drunk*) bourré(e).

pistol ['pɪstl] *n* pistolet *m*.

piston ['pɪstən] *n* piston *m*.

pit [pɪt] *n* trou *m*, fosse *f*; (*also*: **coal** ~) puits *m* de mine; (*also*: **orchestra** ~) fosse *f* d'orchestre // *vt*: **to** ~ **sb against** sb opposer qn à qn; ~**s** *npl* (*AUT*) aire *f* de service.

pitch [pɪtʃ] *n* (*throw*) lancement *m*; (*MUS*) ton *m*; (*of voice*) hauteur *f*; (*Brit SPORT*) terrain *m*; (*NAUT*) tangage *m*; (*tar*) poix *f* // *vt* (*throw*) lancer // *vi* (*fall*) tomber; (*NAUT*) tanguer; **to** ~ **a tent** dresser une tente; ~**ed battle** *n* bataille rangée.

pitcher ['pɪtʃə*] *n* cruche *f*.

pitchfork ['pɪtʃfɔːk] *n* fourche *f*.

piteous ['pɪtɪəs] *a* pitoyable.

pitfall ['pɪtfɔːl] *n* trappe *f*, piège *m*.

pith [pɪθ] *n* (*of plant*) moelle *f*; (*of orange*) intérieur *m* de l'écorce; (*fig*) essence *f*; vigueur *f*.

pithy ['pɪθɪ] *a* piquant(e); vigoureux(euse).

pitiful ['pɪtɪful] *a* (*touching*) pitoyable; (*contemptible*) lamentable.

pitiless ['pɪtɪlɪs] *a* impitoyable.

pittance ['pɪtns] n salaire m de misère.
pity ['pɪtɪ] n pitié f // vt plaindre; **what a ~!** quel dommage!
pivot ['pɪvət] n pivot m.
pizza ['pi:tsə] n pizza f.
placard ['plækɑ:d] n affiche f.
placate [plə'keɪt] vt apaiser, calmer.
place [pleɪs] n endroit m, lieu m; (proper position, rank, seat) place f; (house) maison f, logement m; (home): **at/to his ~** chez lui // vt (object) placer, mettre; (identify) situer; reconnaître; **to take ~** avoir lieu; se passer; **to change ~s with sb** changer de place avec qn; **to ~ an order** passer une commande; **out of ~** (not suitable) déplacé(e), inopportun(e); **in the first ~** d'abord, en premier.
plague [pleɪg] n fléau m; (MED) peste f // vt (fig) tourmenter.
plaice [pleɪs] n (pl inv) carrelet m.
plaid [plæd] n tissu écossais.
plain [pleɪn] a (clear) clair(e), évident(e); (simple) simple, ordinaire; (frank) franc(franche); (not handsome) quelconque, ordinaire; (cigarette) sans filtre; (without seasoning etc) nature inv; (in one colour) uni(e) // ad franchement, carrément // n plaine f; **~ chocolate** n chocolat m à croquer; **~ clothes:** **in ~ clothes** (police) en civil; **~ly** ad clairement; (frankly) carrément, sans détours.
plaintiff ['pleɪntɪf] n plaignant/e.
plait [plæt] n tresse f, natte f.
plan [plæn] n plan m; (scheme) projet m// vt (think in advance) projeter; (prepare) organiser // vi faire des projets.
plane [pleɪn] n (AVIAT) avion m; (tree) platane m; (tool) rabot m; (ART, MATH etc) plan m // a plan(e), plat(e) // vt (with tool) raboter.
planet ['plænɪt] n planète f.
plank [plæŋk] n planche f.
planning ['plænɪŋ] n planification f; **family ~** planning familial; **~ permission** n permis m de construire.
plant [plɑ:nt] n plante f; (machinery) matériel m; (factory) usine f // vt planter; (colony) établir; (bomb) déposer, poser.
plaster ['plɑ:stə*] n plâtre m; (also: **~ of Paris**) plâtre à mouler; (Brit: also: **sticking ~**) pansement adhésif // vt plâtrer; (cover): **to ~ with** couvrir de; **in ~** (leg etc) dans le plâtre; **~ed** a (col) soûl(e).
plastic ['plæstɪk] n plastique m // a (made of plastic) en plastique; (flexible) plastique, malléable; (art) plastique; **~ bag** n sac m en plastique.
plasticine ['plæstɪsi:n] n ® pâte f à modeler.
plastic surgery n chirurgie f esthétique.
plate [pleɪt] n (dish) assiette f; (sheet of metal, PHOT) plaque f; (in book) gravure f.
plateau ['plætəʊ, -z] **~s** or **~x** n plateau m.
plate glass n verre m (de vitrine).
platform ['plætfɔ:m] n (at meeting) tribune f; (Brit: of bus) plate-forme f; (stage) estrade f; (RAIL) quai m; **~ ticket** n (Brit) billet m de quai.
platinum ['plætɪnəm] n platine m.
platoon [plə'tu:n] n peloton m.
platter ['plætə*] n plat m.
plausible ['plɔ:zɪbl] a plausible; (person) convaincant(e).
play [pleɪ] n jeu m; (THEATRE) pièce f (de théâtre) // vt (game) jouer à; (team, opponent) jouer contre; (instrument) jouer de; (play, part, piece of music, note) jouer // vi jouer; **to ~ safe** ne prendre aucun risque; **to ~ down** vt minimiser; **to ~ up** vi (cause trouble) faire des siennes; **~boy** n playboy m; **~er** n joueur/euse; (THEATRE) acteur/trice; (MUS) musicien/ne; **~ful** a enjoué(e); **~ground** n cour f de récréation; **~group** n garderie f; **~ing card** n carte f à jouer; **~ing field** n terrain m de sport; **~mate** n camarade m/f, copain/copine; **~-off** n (SPORT) belle f; **~pen** n parc m (pour bébé); **~school** n = **~group;** **~thing** n jouet m; **~wright** n dramaturge m.
plc abbr (= public limited company) SARL f.
plea [pli:] n (request) appel m; (excuse) excuse f; (LAW) défense f.
plead [pli:d] vt plaider (give as excuse) invoquer // vi (LAW) plaider; (beg): **to ~ with sb** implorer qn.
pleasant ['plɛznt] a agréable; **~ries** npl (polite remarks) civilités fpl.
please [pli:z] vt plaire à // vi (think fit): **do as you ~** faites comme il vous plaira; **~!** s'il te (or vous) plaît; **~ yourself!** à ta (or votre) guise!; **~d** a: **~d (with)** content(e) (de); **~d to meet you** enchanté de faire votre connaissance; **pleasing** a plaisant(e), qui fait plaisir.
pleasure ['plɛʒə*] n plaisir m; **'it's a ~'** 'je vous en prie'.
pleat [pli:t] n pli m.
pledge [plɛdʒ] n gage m; (promise) promesse f // vt engager; promettre.
plentiful ['plɛntɪful] a abondant(e), copieux(euse).
plenty ['plɛntɪ] n abondance f; **~ of** beaucoup de; (bien) assez de.
pliable ['plaɪəbl] a flexible; (person) malléable.
pliers ['plaɪəz] npl pinces fpl.
plight [plaɪt] n situation f critique.
plimsolls ['plɪmsəlz] npl (Brit) (chaussures fpl de) tennis fpl.
plinth [plɪnθ] n socle m.
plod [plɒd] vi avancer péniblement; (fig)

peiner; ~**der** n bûcheur/euse.
plonk [plɔŋk] (col) n (Brit: wine) pinard m, piquette f // vt: to ~ sth **down** poser brusquement qch.
plot [plɔt] n complot m, conspiration f; (of story, play) intrigue f; (of land) lot m de terrain, lopin m // vt (mark out) pointer; relever; (conspire) comploter // vi comploter; ~**ter** n (instrument) table traçante, traceur m.
plough, (US) **plow** [plau] n charrue f // vt (earth) labourer; **to ~ back** vt (COMM) réinvestir; **to ~ through** vt fus (snow etc) avancer péniblement dans.
ploy [plɔɪ] n stratagème m.
pluck [plʌk] n (fruit) cueillir; (musical instrument) pincer; (bird) plumer // n courage m, cran m; to ~ **up courage** prendre son courage à deux mains; ~**y** a courageux/euse).
plug [plʌg] n bouchon m, bonde f; (ELEC) prise f de courant; (AUT: also: **spark(ing) ~**) bougie f // vt (hole) boucher; (col: advertise) faire du battage pour, matraquer; **to ~ in** vt (ELEC) brancher.
plum [plʌm] n (fruit) prune f // a: ~ **job** (col) travail m en or.
plumb [plʌm] a vertical(e) // n plomb m // ad (exactly) en plein // vt sonder.
plumber ['plʌmə*] n plombier m.
plumbing ['plʌmɪŋ] n (trade) plomberie f; (piping) tuyauterie f.
plummet ['plʌmɪt] vi plonger, dégringoler.
plump [plʌmp] a rondelet(te), dodu(e), bien en chair // vt: **to ~ sth (down)** on laisser tomber qch lourdement sur; **to ~ for** vt fus (col: choose) se décider pour.
plunder ['plʌndə*] n pillage m // vt piller.
plunge [plʌndʒ] n plongeon m // vt plonger // vi (fall) tomber, dégringoler; **to take the ~** se jeter à l'eau; ~**r** n piston m; (débouchoir m à) ventouse f.
pluperfect [plu:'pə:fɪkt] n plus-que-parfait m.
plural ['pluərl] a pluriel(le) // n pluriel m.
plus [plʌs] n (also: ~ **sign**) signe m plus // prep plus; **ten/twenty ~** plus de dix/vingt.
plush [plʌʃ] a somptueux(euse).
ply [plaɪ] n (of wool) fil m; (of wood) feuille f, épaisseur f // vt (tool) manier; (a trade) exercer // vi (ship) faire la navette; **to ~ sb with drink** donner continuellement à boire à qn; ~**wood** n contre-plaqué m.
P.M. abbr of **Prime Minister**.
p.m. ad abbr (= post meridiem) de l'après-midi.
pneumatic drill [nju:'mætɪk-] n marteau-piqueur m.

pneumonia [nju:'məunɪə] n pneumonie f.
poach [pəutʃ] vt (cook) pocher; (steal) pêcher (or chasser) sans permis // vi braconner; ~**er** n braconnier m.
P.O. Box n abbr of **Post Office Box**.
pocket ['pɔkɪt] n poche f // vt empocher; **to be out of ~** (Brit) en être de sa poche; ~**book** n (wallet) portefeuille m; (notebook) carnet m; ~ **knife** n canif m; ~ **money** n argent m de poche.
pod [pɔd] n cosse f.
podgy ['pɔdʒɪ] a rondelet(te).
podiatrist [pɔ'di:ətrɪst] n (US) pédicure m/f, podologue m/f.
poem ['pəuɪm] n poème m.
poet ['pəuɪt] n poète m; ~**ic** [-'etɪk] a poétique; ~ **laureate** n poète lauréat (nommé et appointé par la Cour royale); ~**ry** n poésie f.
poignant ['pɔɪnjənt] a poignant(e); (sharp) vif(vive).
point [pɔɪnt] n (tip) pointe f; (in time) moment m; (in space) endroit m; (GEOM, SCOL, SPORT, on scale) point m; (subject, idea) point, sujet m; (also: **decimal ~**): 2 ~ 3 (2.3) 2 virgule 3 (2,3) // vt (show) indiquer; (wall, window) jointoyer; (gun etc): **to ~ sth at** braquer or diriger qch sur // vi montrer du doigt; ~**s** npl (AUT) vis platinées; (RAIL) aiguillage m; **to be on the ~ of doing sth** être sur le point de faire qch; **to make a ~** faire une remarque; **to get the ~** comprendre, saisir; **to come to the ~** en venir au fait; **there's no ~ (in doing)** cela ne sert à rien (de faire); **to ~ out** vt faire remarquer, souligner; **to ~ to** vt fus montrer du doigt; (fig) signaler; ~**-blank** ad (also: **at ~-blank range**) à bout portant; (fig) catégorique; ~**ed** a (shape) pointu(e); (remark) plein(e) de sous-entendus; ~**edly** ad d'une manière significative; ~**er** n (stick) baguette f; (needle) aiguille f; (dog) chien m d'arrêt; ~**less** a inutile, vain(e); ~ **of view** n point m de vue.
poise [pɔɪz] n (balance) équilibre m; (of head, body) port m; (calmness) calme m // vt placer en équilibre.
poison ['pɔɪzn] n poison m // vt empoisonner; ~**ing** n empoisonnement m; ~**ous** a (snake) venimeux(euse); (substance etc) vénéneux(euse).
poke [pəuk] vt (fire) tisonner; (jab with finger, stick etc) piquer; pousser du doigt; (put): **to ~ sth in(to)** fourrer or enfoncer qch dans; **to ~ about** vi fureter.
poker ['pəukə*] n tisonnier m; (CARDS) poker m; ~**-faced** a au visage impassible.
poky ['pəukɪ] a exigu(ë).
Poland ['pəulənd] n Pologne f.
polar ['pəulə*] a polaire; ~ **bear** n ours

blanc.

Pole [pəul] *n* Polonais/e.

pole [pəul] *n* (*of wood*) mât *m*, perche *f*; (*ELEC*) poteau *m*; (*GEO*) pôle *m*; ~ **bean** *n* (*US*) haricot *m* (à rames); ~ **vault** *n* saut *m* à la perche.

police [pə'li:s] *npl* police *f* // *vt* maintenir l'ordre dans; ~ **car** *n* voiture *f* de police; ~**man** *n* agent *m* de police, policier *m*; ~ **station** *n* commissariat *m* de police; ~**woman** *n* femme-agent *f*.

policy ['pɔlɪsɪ] *n* politique *f*; (*also*: insurance ~) police *f* (d'assurance).

polio ['pəulɪəu] *n* polio *f*.

Polish ['pəulɪʃ] *a* polonais(e) // *n* (*LING*) polonais *m*.

polish ['pɔlɪʃ] *n* (*for shoes*) cirage *m*; (*for floor*) cire *f*, encaustique *f*; (*for nails*) vernis *m*; (*shine*) éclat *m*, poli *m*; (*fig*: *refinement*) raffinement *m* // *vt* (*put polish on shoes, wood*) cirer; (*make shiny*) astiquer, faire briller; (*fig*: *improve*) perfectionner; **to ~ off** *vt* (*work*) expédier; (*food*) liquider; ~**ed** *a* (*fig*) raffiné(e).

polite [pə'laɪt] *a* poli(e); ~**ness** *n* politesse *f*.

politic ['pɔlɪtɪk] *a* diplomatique; ~**al** [pə'lɪtɪkl] *a* politique; ~**ally** *ad* politiquement; ~**ian** [-'tɪʃən] *n* homme *m* politique, politicien *m*; ~**s** *npl* politique *f*.

polka ['pɔlkə] *n* polka *f*; ~ **dot** *n* pois *m*.

poll [pəul] *n* scrutin *m*, vote *m*; (*also*: opinion ~) sondage *m* (d'opinion) // *vt* obtenir.

pollen ['pɔlən] *n* pollen *m*.

polling ['pəulɪŋ] (*Brit*): ~ **booth** *n* isoloir *m*; ~ **day** *n* jour *m* des élections; ~ **station** *n* bureau *m* de vote.

pollution [pə'lu:ʃən] *n* pollution *f*.

polo ['pəuləu] *n* polo *m*; ~**-neck** *a* à col roulé.

polytechnic [pɔlɪ'tɛknɪk] *n* (*college*) I.U.T. *m*, Institut *m* Universitaire de Technologie.

polythene ['pɔlɪθi:n] *n* polyéthylène *m*; ~ **bag** *n* sac *m* en plastique.

pomegranate ['pɔmɪgrænɪt] *n* grenade *f*.

pomp [pɔmp] *n* pompe *f*, faste *f*, apparat *m*.

pompous ['pɔmpəs] *a* pompeux(euse).

pond [pɔnd] *n* étang *m*; mare *f*.

ponder ['pɔndə*] *vt* considérer, peser; ~**ous** *a* pesant(e), lourd(e).

pong [pɔŋ] *n* (*Brit col*) puanteur *f*.

pony ['pəunɪ] *n* poney *m*; ~**tail** *n* queue *f* de cheval; ~ **trekking** *n* (*Brit*) randonnée *f* à cheval.

poodle ['pu:dl] *n* caniche *m*.

pool [pu:l] *n* (*of rain*) flaque *f*; (*pond*) mare *f*; (*artificial*) bassin *m*; (*also*: swimming ~) piscine *f*; (*sth shared*) fonds commun; (*money at cards*) cagnotte *f*; (*billiards*) poule *f* // *vt* mettre en commun; **typing ~** pool *m* dactylographique; (*football*) ~**s** *npl* ≈ loto sportif.

poor [puə*] *a* pauvre; (*mediocre*) médiocre, faible, mauvais(e) // *npl*: the ~ les pauvres *mpl*; ~**ly** *ad* pauvrement; médiocrement // *a* souffrant(e), malade.

pop [pɔp] *n* (*noise*) bruit sec; (*MUS*) musique *f* pop; (*US col*: *father*) papa *m* // *vt* (*put*) fourrer, mettre (rapidement) // *vi* éclater; (*cork*) sauter; **to ~ in** *vi* entrer en passant; **to ~ out** *vi* sortir; **to ~ up** *vi* apparaître, surgir; ~ **concert** *n* concert *m* pop.

pope [pəup] *n* pape *m*.

poplar ['pɔplə*] *n* peuplier *m*.

poppy ['pɔpɪ] *n* coquelicot *m*; pavot *m*.

popsicle ['pɔpsɪkl] *n* (*US*) esquimau *m*.

popular ['pɔpjulə*] *a* populaire; (*fashionable*) à la mode; ~**ize** *vt* populariser; (*science*) vulgariser.

population [pɔpju'leɪʃən] *n* population *f*.

porcelain ['pɔ:slɪn] *n* porcelaine *f*.

porch [pɔ:tʃ] *n* porche *m*.

porcupine ['pɔ:kjupaɪn] *n* porc-épic *m*.

pore [pɔ:*] *n* pore *m* // *vi*: **to ~ over** s'absorber dans, être plongé(e) dans.

pork [pɔ:k] *n* porc *m*.

pornography [pɔ:'nɔgrəfɪ] *n* pornographie *f*.

porpoise ['pɔ:pəs] *n* marsouin *m*.

porridge ['pɔrɪdʒ] *n* porridge *m*.

port [pɔ:t] *n* (*harbour*) port *m*; (*opening in ship*) sabord *m*; (*NAUT*: *left side*) bâbord *m*; (*wine*) porto *m*; ~ **of call** escale *f*.

portable ['pɔ:təbl] *a* portatif(ive).

portent ['pɔ:tɛnt] *n* présage *m*.

porter ['pɔ:tə*] *n* (*for luggage*) porteur *m*; (*doorkeeper*) gardien/ne; portier *m*.

portfolio [pɔ:t'fəulɪəu] *n* portefeuille *m*; (*of artist*) portfolio *m*.

porthole ['pɔ:thəul] *n* hublot *m*.

portion ['pɔ:ʃən] *n* portion *f*, part *f*.

portly ['pɔ:tlɪ] *a* corpulent(e).

portrait ['pɔ:treɪt] *n* portrait *m*.

portray [pɔ:'treɪ] *vt* faire le portrait de; (*in writing*) dépeindre, représenter.

Portugal ['pɔ:tjugl] *n* Portugal *m*.

Portuguese [pɔ:tju'gi:z] *a* portugais(e) // *n* (*pl inv*) Portugais/e; (*LING*) portugais *m*.

pose [pəuz] *n* pose *f*; (*pej*) affectation *f* // *vi* poser; (*pretend*): **to ~ as** se poser en // *vt* poser, créer.

posh [pɔʃ] *a* (*col*) chic *inv*.

position [pə'zɪʃən] *n* position *f*; (*job*) situation *f*.

positive ['pɔzɪtɪv] *a* positif(ive); (*certain*) sûr(e), certain(e); (*definite*) formel(le), catégorique; indéniable, réel(le).

posse ['pɔsɪ] *n* (*US*) détachement *m*.
possess [pə'zɛs] *vt* posséder; **~ion** [pə'zɛʃən] *n* possession *f*.
possibility [pɔsɪ'bɪlɪtɪ] *n* possibilité *f*; éventualité *f*.
possible ['pɔsɪbl] *a* possible; **as big as ~** aussi gros que possible.
possibly ['pɔsɪblɪ] *ad* (*perhaps*) peut-être; **if you ~ can** si cela vous est possible; **I cannot ~ come** il m'est impossible de venir.
post [pəust] *n* poste *f*; (*Brit: collection*) levée *f*; (*: letters, delivery*) courrier *m*; (*job, situation*) poste *m*; (*pole*) poteau *m* // *vt* (*Brit: send by post; MIL*) poster; (*Brit: appoint*): **to ~ to** affecter à; (*notice*) afficher; **~age** *n* affranchissement *m*; **~al order** *n* mandat(-poste) *m*; **~box** *n* (*Brit*) boîte *f* aux lettres; **~card** *n* carte postale; **~code** *n* (*Brit*) code postal.
poster ['pəustə*] *n* affiche *f*.
poste restante [pəust'rɛstɑ̃:nt] *n* poste restante.
postgraduate ['pəust'grædjuət] *n* ≈ étudiant/e de troisième cycle.
posthumous ['pɔstjuməs] *a* posthume.
postman ['pəustmən] *n* facteur *m*.
postmark ['pəustmɑ:k] *n* cachet *m* (de la poste).
postmaster ['pəustmɑ:stə*] *n* receveur *m* des postes.
post-mortem [pəust'mɔ:təm] *n* autopsie *f*.
post office ['pəustɔfɪs] *n* (*building*) poste *f*; (*organization*): **the Post Office** les Postes; **Post Office Box (P.O. Box)** *n* boîte postale (B.P.).
postpone [pəs'pəun] *vt* remettre (à plus tard), reculer.
posture ['pɔstʃə*] *n* posture *f*, attitude *f*.
postwar ['pəust'wɔ:*] *a* d'après-guerre.
posy ['pəuzɪ] *n* petit bouquet.
pot [pɔt] *n* (*for cooking*) marmite *f*; casserole *f*; (*for plants, jam*) pot *m*; (*col: marijuana*) herbe *f* // *vt* (*plant*) mettre en pot; **to go to ~** (*col: work, performance*) aller à l'eau.
potato, ~es [pə'teɪtəu] *n* pomme *f* de terre; **~ peeler** *n* épluche-légumes *m*.
potent ['pəutnt] *a* puissant(e); (*drink*) fort(e), très alcoolisé(e).
potential [pə'tɛnʃl] *a* potentiel(le) // *n* potentiel *m*; **~ly** *ad* en puissance.
pothole ['pɔthəul] *n* (*in road*) nid *m* de poule; (*Brit: underground*) gouffre *m*, caverne *f*; **potholing** *n* (*Brit*): **to go potholing** faire de la spéléologie.
potluck [pɔt'lʌk] *n*: **to take ~** tenter sa chance.
potshot ['pɔtʃɔt] *n*: **to take ~s or a ~ at** canarder.
potted ['pɔtɪd] *a* (*food*) en conserve; (*plant*) en pot.
potter ['pɔtə*] *n* potier *m* // *vi*: **to ~**

around, ~ about bricoler; **~y** *n* poterie *f*.
potty ['pɔtɪ] *a* (*col: mad*) dingue // *n* (*child's*) pot *m*.
pouch [pautʃ] *n* (*ZOOL*) poche *f*; (*for tobacco*) blague *f*.
poultry ['pəultrɪ] *n* volaille *f*.
pounce [pauns] *vi*: **to ~ (on)** bondir (sur), fondre sur.
pound [paund] *n* livre *f* (*weight = 453g, 16 ounces; money = 100 pence*); (*for dogs, cars*) fourrière *f* // *vt* (*beat*) bourrer de coups, marteler; (*crush*) piler, pulvériser // *vi* (*beat*) battre violemment, taper.
pour [pɔ:*] *vt* verser // *vi* couler à flots; (*rain*) pleuvoir à verse; **to ~ away or off** *vt* vider; **to ~ in** *vi* (*people*) affluer, se précipiter; **to ~ out** *vi* (*people*) sortir en masse // *vt* vider; déverser; (*serve: a drink*) verser; **~ing** *a*: **~ing rain** pluie torrentielle.
pout [paut] *vi* faire la moue.
poverty ['pɔvətɪ] *n* pauvreté *f*, misère *f*; **~-stricken** *a* pauvre, déshérité(e).
powder ['paudə*] *n* poudre *f* // *vt* poudrer; **to ~ one's face** *or* **nose** se poudrer; **~ compact** *n* poudrier *m*; **~ed milk** *n* lait *m* en poudre; **~ puff** *n* houppette *f*; **~ room** *n* toilettes *fpl* (pour dames).
power ['pauə*] *n* (*strength*) puissance *f*, force *f*; (*ability, POL: of party, leader*) pouvoir *m*; (*MATH*) puissance; (*of speech, thought*) faculté *f*; (*ELEC*) courant *m* // *vt* faire marcher; **to be in ~** (*POL etc*) être au pouvoir; **~ cut** *n* (*Brit*) coupure *f* de courant; **~ failure** *n* panne *f* de courant; **~ful** *a* puissant(e); **~less** *a* impuissant(e); **~ point** *n* (*Brit*) prise *f* de courant; **~ station** *n* centrale *f* électrique.
p.p. *abbr* (= *per procurationem*): **~ J. Smith** pour M. J. Smith.
PR *n abbr of* **public relations**.
practicable ['præktɪkəbl] *a* (*scheme*) réalisable.
practical ['præktɪkl] *a* pratique; **~ity** [-'kælɪtɪ] *n* (*no pl*) (*of situation etc*) aspect *m* pratique; **~ joke** *n* farce *f*; **~ly** *ad* (*almost*) pratiquement.
practice ['præktɪs] *n* pratique *f*; (*of profession*) exercice *m*; (*at football etc*) entraînement *m*; (*business*) cabinet *m*; clientèle *f* // *vt, vi* (*US*) = **practise**; **in ~** (*in reality*) en pratique; **out of ~** rouillé(e).
practise, (US) practice ['præktɪs] *vt* (*work at: piano, one's backhand etc*) s'exercer à, travailler; (*train for: skiing, running etc*) s'entraîner à; (*a sport, religion, method*) pratiquer; (*profession*) exercer // *vi* s'exercer, travailler; (*train*) s'entraîner; **practising** *a* (*Christian etc*) pratiquant(e); (*lawyer*) en exercice.
practitioner [præk'tɪʃənə*] *n* praticien/

ne.

prairie ['prɛərɪ] n savane f; (US): the
~s la Prairie.

praise [preɪz] n éloge(s) m(pl), louan-
ge(s) f(pl) // vt louer, faire l'éloge de.

pram [præm] n (Brit) landau m, voiture
f d'enfant.

prance [prɑːns] vi (horse) caracoler.

prank [præŋk] n farce f.

prawn [prɔːn] n crevette f (rose).

pray [preɪ] vi prier.

prayer [prɛə*] n prière f.

preach [priːtʃ] vt, vi prêcher.

precaution [prɪ'kɔːʃən] n précaution f.

precede [prɪ'siːd] vt, vi précéder.

precedence ['presɪdəns] n préséance f.

precedent ['presɪdənt] n précédent m.

precinct ['priːsɪŋkt] n (round cathedral)
pourtour m, enceinte f; ~s npl
(neighbourhood) alentours mpl, environs
mpl; **pedestrian** ~ (Brit) zone
piétonnière.

precious ['prɛʃəs] a précieux(euse).

precipitate a [prɪ'sɪpɪtɪt] (hasty)
précipité(e) // vt [prɪ'sɪpɪteɪt] précipiter.

precise [prɪ'saɪs] a précis(e); ~**ly** ad
précisément.

preclude [prɪ'kluːd] vt exclure.

precocious [prɪ'kəuʃəs] a précoce.

precondition [priːkən'dɪʃən] n condition f nécessaire.

predecessor ['priːdɪsesə*] n prédécesseur m.

predicament [prɪ'dɪkəmənt] n situation
f difficile.

predict [prɪ'dɪkt] vt prédire; ~**able** a
prévisible.

predominantly [prɪ'dɒmɪnəntlɪ] ad en
majeure partie; surtout.

preen [priːn] vt: to ~ itself (bird) se
lisser les plumes; to ~ o.s. s'admirer.

prefab ['priːfæb] n bâtiment préfabriqué.

preface ['prefəs] n préface f.

prefect ['priːfekt] n (Brit: in school)
élève chargé(e) de certaines fonctions de
discipline; (in France) préfet m.

prefer [prɪ'fəː*] vt préférer; ~**ably**
['prefrəblɪ] ad de préférence; ~**ence**
['prefrəns] n préférence f; ~**ential**
[prefə'renʃəl] a préférentiel(le); ~**ential**
treatment traitement m de faveur.

prefix ['priːfɪks] n préfixe m.

pregnancy ['pregnənsɪ] n grossesse f.

pregnant ['pregnənt] a enceinte af.

prehistoric ['priːhɪs'tɔrɪk] a préhistorique.

prejudice ['predʒudɪs] n préjugé m;
(harm) tort m, préjudice m // vt porter
préjudice à; ~**d** a (person) plein(e) de
préjugés; (view) préconçu(e), partial(e).

premarital ['priː'mærɪtl] a avant le
mariage.

premature ['prɛmətʃuə*] a prématu-
ré(e).

premier ['prɛmɪə*] a premier(ère),

capital(e), primordial(e) // n (POL)
premier ministre.

première ['prɛmɪɛə*] n première f.

premise ['prɛmɪs] n prémisse f; ~s npl
locaux mpl; on the ~s sur les lieux; sur
place.

premium ['priːmɪəm] n prime f; to be
at a ~ faire prime; ~ **bond** n (Brit)
bon m à lot, obligation f à prime.

premonition [prɛmə'nɪʃən] n prémonition f.

preoccupied [priː'ɔkjupaɪd] a préoc-
cupé(e).

prep [prɛp] n (SCOL: study) étude f; ~
school n = **preparatory school**.

prepaid [priː'peɪd] a payé(e) d'avance.

preparation [prɛpə'reɪʃən] n préparation f; ~s npl (for trip, war) préparatifs mpl.

preparatory [prɪ'pærətərɪ]: ~ **school** n
école primaire privée.

prepare [prɪ'pɛə*] vt préparer // vi: to ~
for se préparer à; ~**d to** prêt(e) à.

preposition [prɛpə'zɪʃən] n préposition
f.

preposterous [prɪ'pɔstərəs] a absurde.

prerequisite [priː'rɛkwɪzɪt] n condition f
préalable.

prescribe [prɪ'skraɪb] vt prescrire.

prescription [prɪ'skrɪpʃən] n prescription f; (MED) ordonnance f.

presence ['prɛzns] n présence f; ~ of
mind présence d'esprit.

present ['prɛznt] a présent(e) // n
cadeau m; (also: ~ tense) présent m //
vt [prɪ'zɛnt] présenter; (give): to give sb
with sth offrir qch à qn; to give sb a ~
offrir un cadeau à qn; at ~ en ce
moment; ~**ation** [-'teɪʃən] n
présentation f; (gift) cadeau m, présent
m; (ceremony) remise f du cadeau; ~**day** a contemporain(e), actuel(le); ~**er**
[-'zɛntə*] n (RADIO, TV) présentateur/
trice; ~**ly** ad (soon) tout à l'heure,
bientôt; (at present) en ce moment.

preservative [prɪ'zɜːvətɪv] n agent m de
conservation.

preserve [prɪ'zɜːv] vt (keep safe)
préserver, protéger; (maintain)
conserver, garder; (food) mettre en
conserve // n (for game, fish) réserve f;
(often pl: jam) confiture f; (: fruit)
fruits mpl en conserve.

president ['prɛzɪdənt] n président/e;
~**ial** [-'dɛnʃl] a présidentiel(le).

press [prɛs] n (tool, machine, news-
papers) presse f; (for wine) pressoir m;
(crowd) cohue f, foule f // vt (push)
appuyer sur; (squeeze) presser, serrer;
(clothes: iron) repasser; (pursue)
talonner; (insist): to ~ sth on sb presser
qn d'accepter qch // vi appuyer, peser;
se presser; we are ~ed for time le temps
nous manque; to ~ for sth faire pression
pour obtenir qch; to ~ on vi continuer;

~ **conference** n conférence f de presse; ~**ing** a urgent(e), pressant(e) // n repassage m; ~ **stud** n (Brit) bouton-pression m; ~**-up** n (Brit) traction f.

pressure ['prɛʃə*] n pression f; (stress) tension f; ~ **cooker** n cocotte-minute f; ~ **gauge** n manomètre m; ~ **group** n groupe m de pression.

prestige [prɛs'ti:ʒ] n prestige m.

presumably [prɪ'zju:məblɪ] ad vraisemblablement.

presume [prɪ'zju:m] vt présumer, supposer; to ~ to do (dare) se permettre de faire.

presumption [prɪ'zʌmpʃən] n supposition f, présomption f; (boldness) audace f.

pretence, (US) **pretense** [prɪ'tɛns] n (claim) prétention f; to make a ~ of doing faire semblant de faire.

pretend [prɪ'tɛnd] vt (feign) feindre, simuler // vi (feign) faire semblant; (claim): to ~ to sth prétendre à qch; to ~ to do faire semblant de faire.

pretense [prɪ'tɛns] n (US) = **pretence**.

pretension [prɪ'tɛnʃən] n prétention f.

pretext ['pri:tɛkst] n prétexte m.

pretty ['prɪtɪ] a joli(e) // ad assez.

prevail [prɪ'veɪl] vi (win) l'emporter, prévaloir; (be usual) avoir cours; (persuade): to ~ (up)on sb to do persuader qn de faire; ~**ing** a dominant(e).

prevalent ['prɛvələnt] a répandu(e), courant(e); (fashion) en vogue.

prevent [prɪ'vɛnt] vt: to ~ (from doing) empêcher (de faire); ~**ive** a préventif(ive).

preview ['pri:vju:] n (of film) avant-première f; (fig) aperçu m.

previous ['pri:vɪəs] a précédent(e); antérieur(e); ~**ly** ad précédemment, auparavant.

prewar [pri:'wɔ:*] a d'avant-guerre.

prey [preɪ] n proie f // vi: to ~ on s'attaquer à.

price [praɪs] n prix m // vt (goods) fixer le prix de; tarifer; ~**less** a sans prix, inestimable; ~ **list** n liste f des prix, tarif m.

prick [prɪk] n piqûre f // vt piquer; to ~ up one's ears dresser or tendre l'oreille.

prickle ['prɪkl] n (of plant) épine f; (sensation) picotement m.

prickly ['prɪklɪ] a piquant(e), épineux(euse); (fig: person) irritable; ~ **heat** n fièvre f miliaire.

pride [praɪd] n orgueil m; fierté f // vt: to ~ o.s. on se flatter de; s'enorgueillir de.

priest [pri:st] n prêtre m; ~**hood** n prêtrise f, sacerdoce m.

prig [prɪg] n poseur/euse, fat m.

prim [prɪm] a collet monté inv, guindé(e).

primarily ['praɪmərɪlɪ] ad principalement, essentiellement.

primary ['praɪmərɪ] a primaire; (first in importance) premier(ère), primordial(e); ~ **school** n (Brit) école primaire f.

prime [praɪm] a primordial(e), fondamental(e); (excellent) excellent(e) // vt (gun, pump) amorcer; (fig) mettre au courant; in the ~ of life dans la fleur de l'âge; P~ **Minister (P.M.)** n Premier ministre m.

primer ['praɪmə*] n (book) manuel m élémentaire; (paint) apprêt m.

primeval [praɪ'mi:vl] a primitif(ive); (forest) vierge.

primitive ['prɪmɪtɪv] a primitif(ive).

primrose ['prɪmrəuz] n primevère f.

primus (stove) ['praɪməs(stəuv)] n ® (Brit) réchaud m de camping.

prince [prɪns] n prince m.

princess [prɪn'sɛs] n princesse f.

principal ['prɪnsɪpl] a principal(e) // n (headmaster) directeur m, principal m.

principle ['prɪnsɪpl] n principe m; in/on ~ en/par principe.

print [prɪnt] n (mark) empreinte f; (letters) caractères mpl; (fabric) imprimé m; (ART) gravure f, estampe f; (PHOT) épreuve f // vt imprimer; (publish) publier; (write in capitals) écrire en majuscules; out of ~ épuisé(e); ~**ed matter** n imprimés mpl; ~**er** n imprimeur m; (machine) imprimante f; ~**ing** n impression f; ~**-out** n listage m.

prior ['praɪə*] a antérieur(e), précédent(e) // n prieur m; ~ **to doing** avant de faire.

priority [praɪ'ɔrɪtɪ] n priorité f.

prise [praɪz] vt: to ~ **open** forcer.

prison ['prɪzn] n prison f // cpd pénitentiaire; ~**er** n prisonnier/ère.

pristine ['prɪsti:n] a virginal(e).

privacy ['prɪvəsɪ] n intimité f, solitude f.

private ['praɪvɪt] a privé(e); personnel(le); (house, car, lesson) particulier(ère) // n soldat m de deuxième classe; '~' (on envelope) 'personnelle'; in ~ en privé; ~ **enterprise** n l'entreprise privée; ~ **eye** n détective privé; ~**ly** ad en privé; (within oneself) intérieurement; ~ **property** n propriété privée; **privatize** vt privatiser.

privet ['prɪvɪt] n troène m.

privilege ['prɪvɪlɪdʒ] n privilège m.

privy ['prɪvɪ] a: to be ~ **to** être au courant de; ~ **council** n conseil privé.

prize [praɪz] n prix m // a (example, idiot) parfait(e); (bull, novel) primé(e) // vt priser, faire grand cas de; ~ **giving** n distribution f des prix; ~**winner** n gagnant/e.

pro [prəu] n (SPORT) professionnel/le; the ~s **and cons** le pour et le contre.

probability [prɔbə'bɪlɪtɪ] *n* probabilité *f*.
probable ['prɔbəbl] *a* probable; **probably** *ad* probablement.
probation [prə'beɪʃən] *n* (*in employment*) essai *m*; (*LAW*) liberté surveillée; **on ~** (*employee*) à l'essai; (*LAW*) en liberté surveillée.
probe [prəub] *n* (*MED, SPACE*) sonde *f*; (*enquiry*) enquête *f*, investigation *f* // *vt* sonder, explorer.
problem ['prɔbləm] *n* problème *m*.
procedure [prə'si:dʒə*] *n* (*ADMIN, LAW*) procédure *f*; (*method*) marche *f* à suivre, façon *f* de procéder.
proceed [prə'si:d] *vi* (*go forward*) avancer; (*go about it*) procéder; (*continue*); **to ~ (with)** continuer, poursuivre; **to ~ to** aller à; passer à; **to ~ to do** se mettre à faire; **~ings** *npl* mesures *fpl*; (*LAW*) poursuites *fpl*; (*meeting*) réunion *f*, séance *f*; (*records*) compte rendu; actes *mpl*; **~s** ['prəusi:dz] *npl* produit *m*, recette *f*.
process ['prəuses] *n* processus *m*; (*method*) procédé *m* // *vt* traiter; **~ing** *n* traitement *m*.
procession [prə'seʃən] *n* défilé *m*, cortège *m*; **funeral ~** cortège *m* funèbre; convoi *m* mortuaire.
proclaim [prə'kleɪm] *vt* déclarer, proclamer.
procrastinate [prəu'kræstɪneɪt] *vi* faire traîner les choses, vouloir tout remettre au lendemain.
prod [prɔd] *vt* pousser.
prodigal ['prɔdɪgl] *a* prodigue.
prodigy ['prɔdɪdʒɪ] *n* prodige *m*.
produce *n* ['prɔdju:s] (*AGR*) produits *mpl* // *vt* [prə'dju:s] produire; (*to show*) présenter; (*cause*) provoquer, causer; (*THEATRE*) monter, mettre en scène; **~r** *n* (*THEATRE*) metteur *m* en scène; (*AGR, CINEMA*) producteur *m*.
product ['prɔdʌkt] *n* produit *m*.
production [prə'dʌkʃən] *n* production *f*; (*THEATRE*) mise *f* en scène; **~ line** chaîne *f* (de fabrication).
productivity [prɔdʌk'tɪvɪtɪ] *n* productivité *f*.
profane [prə'feɪn] *a* sacrilège; (*lay*) profane.
profession [prə'feʃən] *n* profession *f*; **~al** *n* (*SPORT*) professionnel/le // *a* professionnel(le); (*work*) de profession-nel.
professor [prə'fesə*] *n* professeur *m* (*titulaire d'une chaire*).
proficiency [prə'fɪʃənsɪ] *n* compétence *f*, aptitude *f*.
profile ['prəufaɪl] *n* profil *m*.
profit ['prɔfɪt] *n* bénéfice *m*; profit *m* // *vi*: **to ~ (by** *or* **from)** profiter (de); **~able** *a* lucratif(ive), rentable.
profiteering [prɔfɪ'tɪərɪŋ] *n* (*pej*) mercantilisme *m*.

profound [prə'faund] *a* profond(e).
profusely [prə'fju:slɪ] *ad* abondamment; avec effusion.
progeny ['prɔdʒɪnɪ] *n* progéniture *f*; descendants *mpl*.
programme, (*US*) **program** ['prəugræm] *n* programme *m*; (*RADIO, TV*) émission *f* // *vt* programmer; **~r**, (*US*) **programer** programmeur/euse.
progress *n* ['prəugres] progrès *m* // *vi* [prə'gres] progresser, avancer; **in ~** en cours; **to make ~** progresser, faire des progrès, être en progrès; **~ive** [-'gresɪv] *a* progressif(ive); (*person*) progressiste.
prohibit [prə'hɪbɪt] *vt* interdire, défendre.
project *n* ['prɔdʒekt] (*plan*) projet *m*, plan *m*; (*venture*) opération *f*, entreprise *f*; (*gen, SCOL: research*) étude *f*, dossier *m* // *vb* [prə'dʒekt] *vt* projeter // *vi* (*stick out*) faire saillie, s'avancer.
projection [prə'dʒekʃən] *n* projection *f*; saillie *f*.
projector [prə'dʒektə*] *n* projecteur *m*.
prolong [prə'lɔŋ] *vt* prolonger.
prom [prɔm] *n abbr of* **promenade**; (*US: ball*) bal *m* d'étudiants.
promenade [prɔmə'nɑ:d] *n* (*by sea*) esplanade *f*, promenade *f*; **~ concert** *n* concert *m* (de musique classique).
prominent ['prɔmɪnənt] *a* (*standing out*) proéminent(e); (*important*) important(e).
promiscuous [prə'mɪskjuəs] *a* (*sexually*) de mœurs légères.
promise ['prɔmɪs] *n* promesse *f* // *vt, vi* promettre; **promising** *a* prometteur(euse).
promote [prə'məut] *vt* promouvoir; (*venture, event*) organiser, mettre sur pied; (*new product*) lancer; **~r** *n* (*of sporting event*) organisateur/trice; **promotion** [-'məuʃən] *n* promotion *f*.
prompt [prɔmpt] *a* rapide // *ad* (*punctually*) à l'heure // *n* (*COMPUT*) message *m* (de guidage) // *vt* inciter; provoquer; (*THEATRE*) souffler (son rôle *or* ses répliques) à; **~ly** *ad* rapidement, sans délai; ponctuellement.
prone [prəun] *a* (*lying*) couché(e) (face contre terre); **~ to** enclin(e) à.
prong [prɔŋ] *n* pointe *f*; (*of fork*) dent *f*.
pronoun ['prəunaun] *n* pronom *m*.
pronounce [prə'nauns] *vt* prononcer // *vi*: **to ~ (up)on** se prononcer sur.
pronunciation [prənʌnsɪ'eɪʃən] *n* prononciation *f*.
proof [pru:f] *n* preuve *f*; (*test, of book, PHOT*) épreuve *f*; (*of alcohol*) degré *m* // *a*: **~ against** à l'épreuve de.
prop [prɔp] *n* support *m*, étai *m* // *vt* (*also*: **~ up**) étayer, soutenir; (*lean*): **to ~ sth against** appuyer qch contre *or* à.
propaganda [prɔpə'gændə] *n* propagande *f*.

propel [prə'pɛl] *vt* propulser, faire avancer; **~ler** *n* hélice *f*; **~ling pencil** *n* (*Brit*) porte-mine *m inv*.

propensity [prə'pɛnsɪtɪ] *n* propension *f*.

proper ['prɔpə*] *a* (*suited, right*) approprié(e), bon(bonne); (*seemly*) correct(e), convenable; (*authentic*) vrai(e), véritable; (*col: real*) *n* + fini(e), vrai(e); **~ly** *ad* correctement, convenablement; **bel et bien; he doesn't eat/ study ~ly** il mange/étudie mal; **~ noun** *n* nom *m* propre.

property ['prɔpətɪ] *n* (*things owned*) biens *mpl*; propriété(s) *f(pl)*; immeuble *m*; terres *fpl*, domaine *m*; (*CHEM etc: quality*) propriété *f*; **~ owner** *n* propriétaire *m*.

prophecy ['prɔfɪsɪ] *n* prophétie *f*.

prophesy ['prɔfɪsaɪ] *vt* prédire.

prophet ['prɔfɪt] *n* prophète *m*.

proportion [prə'pɔ:ʃən] *n* proportion *f*; (*share*) part *f*; partie *f*; **~al**, **~ate** *a* proportionnel(le).

proposal [prə'pəuzl] *n* proposition *f*, offre *f*; (*plan*) projet *m*; (*of marriage*) demande *f* en mariage.

propose [prə'pəuz] *vt* proposer, suggérer // *vi* faire sa demande en mariage; **to ~ to do** avoir l'intention de faire.

proposition [prɔpə'zɪʃən] *n* proposition *f*.

propriety [prə'praɪɪtɪ] *n* (*seemliness*) bienséance *f*, convenance *f*.

prose [prəuz] *n* prose *f*; (*SCOL: translation*) thème *m*.

prosecute ['prɔsɪkju:t] *vt* poursuivre; **prosecution** [-'kju:ʃən] *n* poursuites *fpl* judiciaires; (*accusing side*) accusation *f*; **prosecutor** *n* procureur *m*; (*also:* **public prosecutor**) ministère public.

prospect *n* ['prɔspɛkt] perspective *f*; (*hope*) espoir *m*, chances *fpl* // *vt, vi* [prə'spɛkt] prospecter; **~s** *npl* (*for work etc*) possibilités *fpl* d'avenir, débouchés *mpl*; **prospective** [-'spɛktɪv] *a* (*possible*) éventuel(le); (*future*) futur(e).

prospectus [prə'spɛktəs] *n* prospectus *m*.

prosperity [prə'spɛrɪtɪ] *n* prospérité *f*.

prostitute ['prɔstɪtju:t] *n* prostituée *f*.

protect [prə'tɛkt] *vt* protéger; **~ion** *n* protection *f*; **~ive** *a* protecteur(trice).

protein ['prəuti:n] *n* protéine *f*.

protest *n* ['prəutɛst] protestation *f* // *vb* [prə'tɛst] *vi* protester // *vt* protester de.

Protestant ['prɔtɪstənt] *a, n* protestant(e).

protester [prə'tɛstə*] *n* manifestant/e.

protracted [prə'træktɪd] *a* prolongé(e).

protrude [prə'tru:d] *vi* avancer, dépasser.

proud [praud] *a* fier(ère); (*pej*) orgueilleux(euse).

prove [pru:v] *vt* prouver, démontrer // *vi*: **to ~ correct** *etc* s'avérer juste *etc*; **to ~ o.s.** montrer ce dont on est capable.

proverb ['prɔvə:b] *n* proverbe *m*.

provide [prə'vaɪd] *vt* fournir; **to ~ sb with sth** fournir qch à qn; **to ~ for** *vt fus* (*person*) subvenir aux besoins de; (*emergency*) prévoir; **~d (that)** *cj* à condition que + *sub*.

providing [prə'vaɪdɪŋ] *cj* à condition que + *sub*.

province ['prɔvɪns] *n* province *f*; **provincial** [prə'vɪnʃəl] *a* provincial(e).

provision [prə'vɪʒən] *n* (*supply*) provision *f*; (*supplying*) fourniture *f*; approvisionnement *m*; (*stipulation*) disposition *f*; **~s** *npl* (*food*) provisions *fpl*; **~al** *a* provisoire.

proviso [prə'vaɪzəu] *n* condition *f*.

provocative [prə'vɔkətɪv] *a* provocateur(trice), provocant(e).

provoke [prə'vəuk] *vt* provoquer; inciter.

prow [prau] *n* proue *f*.

prowess ['prauɪs] *n* prouesse *f*.

prowl [praul] *vi* (*also:* **~ about**, **~ around**) rôder // *n*: **on the ~** à l'affût; **~er** *n* rôdeur/euse.

proxy ['prɔksɪ] *n* procuration *f*.

prudent ['pru:dnt] *a* prudent(e).

prudish ['pru:dɪʃ] *a* prude, pudibond(e).

prune [pru:n] *n* pruneau *m* // *vt* élaguer.

pry [praɪ] *vi*: **to ~ into** fourrer son nez dans.

PS *n abbr* (= *postscript*) p.s.

psalm [sɑ:m] *n* psaume *m*.

pseudo- ['sju:dəu] *prefix* pseudo-; **pseudonym** *n* pseudonyme *m*.

psyche ['saɪkɪ] *n* psychisme *m*.

psychiatric [saɪkɪ'ætrɪk] *a* psychiatrique.

psychiatrist [saɪ'kaɪətrɪst] *n* psychiatre *m/f*.

psychic ['saɪkɪk] *a* (*also:* **~al**) (métapsychique; (*person*) doué(e) de télépathie *or* d'un sixième sens.

psychoanalyst [saɪkəu'ænəlɪst] *n* psychanalyste *m/f*.

psychological [saɪkə'lɔdʒɪkl] *a* psychologique.

psychologist [saɪ'kɔlədʒɪst] *n* psychologue *m/f*.

psychology [saɪ'kɔlədʒɪ] *n* psychologie *f*.

P.T.O. *abbr* (= *please turn over*) T.S.V.P.

pub [pʌb] *n abbr* (= *public house*) pub *m*.

pubic ['pju:bɪk] *a* pubien(ne), du pubis.

public ['pʌblɪk] *a* public(ique) // *n* public *m*; **in ~** en public; **~ address system (P.A.)** *n* (système *m* de) sonorisation *f*; hauts-parleurs *mpl*.

publican ['pʌblɪkən] *n* patron *m* de pub.

public: ~ company *n* société *f*

anonyme (*cotée en bourse*); ~ **convenience** *n* (*Brit*) toilettes *fpl*; ~ **holiday** *n* jour férié; ~ **house** *n* (*Brit*) pub *m*.

publicity [pʌb'lɪsɪtɪ] *n* publicité *f*.

publicize ['pʌblɪsaɪz] *vt* faire connaître, rendre public(ique).

publicly ['pʌblɪklɪ] *ad* publiquement.

public: ~ **opinion** *n* opinion publique; ~ **relations (PR)** *n* relations publiques; ~ **school** *n* (*Brit*) école privée; (*US*) école publique; ~-**spirited** *a* qui fait preuve de civisme; ~ **transport** *n* transports *mpl* en commun.

publish ['pʌblɪʃ] *vt* publier; ~**er** *n* éditeur *m*; ~**ing** *n* (*industry*) édition *f*.

puck [pʌk] *n* (*ICE HOCKEY*) palet *m*.

pucker ['pʌkə*] *vt* plisser.

pudding ['pudɪŋ] *n* (*Brit: sweet*) dessert *m*, entremets *m*; (*sausage*) boudin *m*; **black** ~ boudin (noir).

puddle ['pʌdl] *n* flaque *f* d'eau.

puff [pʌf] *n* bouffée *f* // *vt*: **to** ~ **one's pipe** tirer sur sa pipe // *vi* sortir par bouffées; (*pant*) haleter; **to** ~ **out smoke** envoyer des bouffées de fumée; ~**ed** *a* (*col: out of breath*) tout(e) essoufflé(e); ~ **pastry** *n* pâte feuilletée; ~**y** *a* bouffi(e), boursouflé(e).

pull [pul] *n* (*tug*): **to give sth a** ~ tirer sur qch; (*fig*) influence *f* // *vt* tirer; (*muscle*) se claquer // *vi* tirer; **to** ~ **to pieces** mettre en morceaux; **to** ~ **one's punches** ménager son adversaire; **to** ~ **one's weight** y mettre du sien; **to** ~ **o.s. together** se ressaisir; **to** ~ **sb's leg** faire marcher qn; **to** ~ **apart** *vt* séparer; (*break*) mettre en pièces, démantibuler; **to** ~ **down** *vt* baisser, abaisser; (*house*) démolir; (*tree*) abattre; **to** ~ **in** *vi* (*AUT*) se ranger; (*RAIL*) entrer en gare; **to** ~ **off** *vt* enlever, ôter; (*deal etc*) conclure; **to** ~ **out** *vi* démarrer, partir; (*withdraw*) se retirer; (*AUT: come out of line*) déboîter // *vt* sortir; arracher; (*withdraw*) retirer; **to** ~ **over** *vi* (*AUT*) se ranger; **to** ~ **through** *vi* s'en sortir; **to** ~ **up** *vi* (*stop*) s'arrêter // *vt* remonter; (*uproot*) déraciner, arracher; (*stop*) arrêter.

pulley ['pulɪ] *n* poulie *f*.

pullover ['puləuvə*] *n* pull-over *m*, tricot *m*.

pulp [pʌlp] *n* (*of fruit*) pulpe *f*; (*for paper*) pâte *f* à papier.

pulpit ['pulpɪt] *n* chaire *f*.

pulsate [pʌl'seɪt] *vi* battre, palpiter; (*music*) vibrer.

pulse [pʌls] *n* (*of blood*) pouls *m*; (*of heart*) battement *m*; (*of music, engine*) vibrations *fpl*.

pummel ['pʌml] *vt* rouer de coups.

pump [pʌmp] *n* pompe *f*; (*shoe*) escarpin *m* // *vt* pomper; (*fig: col*) faire parler; **to** ~ **up** *vt* gonfler.

pumpkin ['pʌmpkɪn] *n* potiron *m*, citrouille *f*.

pun [pʌn] *n* jeu *m* de mots, calembour *m*.

punch [pʌntʃ] *n* (*blow*) coup *m* de poing; (*fig: force*) vivacité *f*, mordant *m*; (*tool*) poinçon *m*; (*drink*) punch *m* // *vt* (*hit*): **to** ~ **sb/sth** donner un coup de poing à qn/sur qch; (*make a hole*) poinçonner, perforer; ~ **line** *n* (*of joke*) conclusion *f*; ~-**up** *n* (*Brit col*) bagarre *f*.

punctual ['pʌŋktjuəl] *a* ponctuel(le).

punctuation [pʌŋktju'eɪʃən] *n* ponctuation *f*.

puncture ['pʌŋktʃə*] *n* crevaison *f*.

pundit ['pʌndɪt] *n* individu *m* qui pontifie, pontife *m*.

pungent ['pʌndʒənt] *a* piquant(e); (*fig*) mordant(e), caustique.

punish ['pʌnɪʃ] *vt* punir; ~**ment** *n* punition *f*, châtiment *m*.

punk [pʌŋk] *n* (*also:* ~ **rocker**) punk *m/ f*; (*also:* ~ **rock**) le punk; (*US col: hoodlum*) voyou *m*.

punt [pʌnt] *n* (*boat*) bachot *m*.

punter ['pʌntə*] *n* (*Brit: gambler*) parieur/euse.

puny ['pjuːnɪ] *a* chétif(ive).

pup [pʌp] *n* chiot *m*.

pupil ['pjuːpɪl] *n* élève *m/f*.

puppet ['pʌpɪt] *n* marionnette *f*, pantin *m*.

puppy ['pʌpɪ] *n* chiot *m*, petit chien.

purchase ['pəːtʃɪs] *n* achat *m* // *vt* acheter; ~**r** *n* acheteur/euse.

pure [pjuə*] *a* pur(e).

purely ['pjuəlɪ] *ad* purement.

purge [pəːdʒ] *n* (*MED*) purge *f*; (*POL*) épuration *f*, purge // *vt* purger.

purl [pəːl] *n* maille *f* à l'envers.

purple ['pəːpl] *a* violet(te); cramoisi(e).

purport [pəː'pɔːt] *vi*: **to** ~ **to be/do** prétendre être/faire.

purpose ['pəːpəs] *n* intention *f*, but *m*; **on** ~ exprès; ~**ful** *a* déterminé(e), résolu(e).

purr [pəː*] *vi* ronronner.

purse [pəːs] *n* porte-monnaie *m* *inv*, bourse *f* // *vt* serrer, pincer.

purser ['pəːsə*] *n* (*NAUT*) commissaire *m* du bord.

pursue [pə'sjuː] *vt* poursuivre.

pursuit [pə'sjuːt] *n* poursuite *f*; (*occupation*) occupation *f*, activité *f*.

purveyor [pə'veɪə*] *n* fournisseur *m*.

push [puʃ] *n* poussée *f*; (*effort*) gros effort *m*; (*drive*) énergie *f* // *vt* pousser; (*button*) appuyer sur; (*thrust*): **to** ~ **sth (into)** enfoncer qch (dans); (*fig*) mettre en avant, faire de la publicité pour // *vi* pousser; appuyer; **to** ~ **aside** *vt* écarter; **to** ~ **off** *vi* (*col*) filer, ficher le camp; **to** ~ **on** *vi* (*continue*) continuer; **to** ~ **through** *vt* (*measure*) faire voter;

to ~ **up** vt (total, prices) faire monter; ~**chair** n (Brit) poussette f; ~**er** n (drug ~er) revendeur/euse (de drogue), ravitailleur/euse (en drogue); ~**over** n (col): it's a ~**over** c'est un jeu d'enfant; ~**-up** n (US) traction f; ~**y** a (pej) arriviste.

puss, pussy(-cat) [pus, 'pusɪ(kæt)] n minet m.

put, pt, pp put [put] vt mettre, poser, placer; (say) dire, exprimer; (a question) poser; (estimate) estimer; **to ~ about** vi (NAUT) virer de bord // vt (rumour) faire courir; **to ~ across** vt (ideas etc) communiquer; faire comprendre; **to ~ away** vt (store) ranger; **to ~ back** vt (replace) remettre, replacer; (postpone) remettre; (delay) retarder; **to ~ by** vt (money) mettre de côté, économiser; **to ~ down** vt (parcel etc) poser, déposer; (pay) verser; (in writing) mettre par écrit, inscrire; (suppress: revolt etc) réprimer, faire cesser; (attribute) attribuer; **to ~ forward** vt (ideas) avancer, proposer; (date) avancer; **to ~ in** vt (gas, electricity) installer; (application, complaint) soumettre; **to ~ off** vt (light etc) éteindre; (postpone) remettre à plus tard, ajourner; (discourage) dissuader; **to ~ on** vt (clothes, lipstick etc) mettre; (light etc) allumer; (play etc) monter; (food, meal) servir; (: cook) mettre à cuire or à chauffer; (airs, weight) prendre; (brake) mettre; **to ~ out** vt mettre dehors; (one's hand) tendre; (news, rumour) faire courir, répandre; (light etc) éteindre; (person: inconvenience) déranger, gêner; **to ~ up** vt (raise) lever, relever, remonter; (pin up) afficher; (hang) accrocher; (build) construire, ériger; (a tent) monter; (increase) augmenter; (accommodate) loger; **to ~ up with** vt fus supporter.

putt [pʌt] vt poter (la balle) // n coup roulé; ~**ing green** n green m.

putty ['pʌtɪ] n mastic m.

puzzle ['pʌzl] n énigme f, mystère m; (jigsaw) puzzle m; (also: crossword ~) problème m de mots croisés // vt intriguer, rendre perplexe // vi se creuser la tête.

pyjamas [pɪ'dʒɑ:məz] npl (Brit) pyjama m.

pyramid ['pɪrəmɪd] n pyramide f.

Pyrenees [pɪrɪ'ni:z] npl: the ~ les Pyrénées fpl.

Q

quack [kwæk] n (of duck) coin-coin m inv; (pej: doctor) charlatan m.

quad [kwɒd] abbr of **quadrangle**,

quadruplet.

quadrangle ['kwɒdræŋgl] n (MATH) quadrilatère m; (courtyard: abbr: **quad**) cour f.

quadruple [kwɒ'drupl] vt, vi quadrupler.

quadruplet [kwɒ'dru:plɪt] n quadruplé/e.

quagmire ['kwægmaɪə*] n bourbier m.

quail [kweɪl] n (ZOOL) caille f // vi (person) perdre courage.

quaint [kweɪnt] a bizarre; (old-fashioned) désuet(ète); au charme vieillot, pittoresque.

quake [kweɪk] vi trembler // n abbr of earthquake.

qualification [kwɒlɪfɪ'keɪʃən] n (degree etc) diplôme m; (ability) compétence f, qualification f; (limitation) réserve f, restriction f.

qualified ['kwɒlɪfaɪd] a diplômé(e); (able) compétent(e), qualifié(e); (limited) conditionnel(le).

qualify ['kwɒlɪfaɪ] vt qualifier; (limit: statement) apporter des réserves à // vi: **to ~ (as)** obtenir son diplôme (de); **to ~ (for)** remplir les conditions requises (pour); (SPORT) se qualifier (pour).

quality ['kwɒlɪtɪ] n qualité f.

qualm [kwɑ:m] n doute m; scrupule m.

quandary ['kwɒndrɪ] n: in a ~ devant un dilemme, dans l'embarras.

quantity ['kwɒntɪtɪ] n quantité f; ~ **surveyor** n métreur m vérificateur.

quarantine ['kwɒrnti:n] n quarantaine f.

quarrel ['kwɒrl] n querelle f, dispute f // vi se disputer, se quereller; ~**some** a querelleur(euse).

quarry ['kwɒrɪ] n (for stone) carrière f; (animal) proie f, gibier m // vt (marble etc) extraire.

quart [kwɔ:t] n ≈ litre m.

quarter ['kwɔ:tə*] n quart m; (of year) trimestre m; (district) quartier m // vt partager en quartiers or en quatre; (MIL) caserner, cantonner; ~**s** npl logement m; (MIL) quartiers mpl, cantonnement m; **a ~ of an hour** un quart d'heure; ~ **final** n quart m de finale; ~**ly** a trimestriel(le) // ad tous les trois mois; ~**master** n (MIL) intendant m militaire de troisième classe; (NAUT) maître m de manœuvre.

quartet(te) [kwɔ:'tet] n quatuor m; (jazz players) quartette m.

quartz [kwɔ:ts] n quartz m.

quash [kwɒʃ] vt (verdict) annuler.

quaver ['kweɪvə*] vi trembler.

quay [ki:] n (also: ~side) quai m.

queasy ['kwi:zɪ] a (stomach) délicat(e); **to feel ~** avoir mal au cœur.

queen [kwi:n] n (gen) reine f; (CARDS etc) dame f; ~ **mother** n reine mère f.

queer [kwɪə*] a étrange, curieux(euse); (suspicious) louche // n (col) homosexuel

m.
quell [kwɛl] *vt* réprimer, étouffer.
quench [kwɛntʃ] *vt* (*flames*) éteindre; **to ~ one's thirst** se désaltérer.
querulous ['kwɛrʊləs] *a* (*person*) récriminateur(trice); (*voice*) plaintif(ive).
query ['kwɪərɪ] *n* question *f*; (*doubt*) doute *m*; (*question mark*) point *m* d'interrogation // *vt* mettre en question *or* en doute.
quest [kwɛst] *n* recherche *f*, quête *f*.
question ['kwɛstʃən] *n* question *f* // *vt* (*person*) interroger; (*plan, idea*) mettre en question *or* en doute; **it's a ~ of doing** il s'agit de faire; **beyond ~** sans aucun doute; **out of the ~** hors de question; **~able** *a* discutable; **~ mark** *n* point *m* d'interrogation.
questionnaire [kwɛstʃə'nɛə*] *n* questionnaire *m*.
queue [kjuː] (*Brit*) *n* queue *f*, file *f* // *vi* faire la queue.
quibble ['kwɪbl] *vi* ergoter, chicaner.
quick [kwɪk] *a* rapide; (*reply*) prompt(e), rapide; (*mind*) vif(vive) // *ad* vite, rapidement // *n*: **cut to the ~** (*fig*) touché(e) au vif; **be ~!** dépêche-toi!; **~en** *vt* accélérer, presser; (*rouse*) stimuler // *vi* s'accélérer, devenir plus rapide; **~ly** *ad* vite, rapidement; **~sand** *n* sables mouvants; **~-witted** *a* à l'esprit vif.
quid [kwɪd] *n* (*pl inv*) (*Brit col*) livre *f*.
quiet ['kwaɪət] *a* tranquille, calme; (*ceremony, colour*) discret(ète) // *n* tranquillité *f*, calme *m* // *vt, vi* (*US*) = **~en; keep ~!** tais-toi!; **~en** (*also*: **~en down**) *vi* se calmer, s'apaiser // *vt* calmer, apaiser; **~ly** *ad* tranquillement, calmement; discrètement.
quilt [kwɪlt] *n* édredon *m*; (*continental ~*) couette *f*.
quin [kwɪn] *n abbr of* **quintuplet**.
quintuplet [kwɪn'tjuːplɪt] *n* quintuplé/e.
quip [kwɪp] *n* remarque piquante *or* spirituelle, pointe *f*.
quirk [kwɜːk] *n* bizarrerie *f*.
quit, *pt, pp* **quit** *or* **quitted** [kwɪt] *vt* quitter // *vi* (*give up*) abandonner, renoncer; (*resign*) démissionner.
quite [kwaɪt] *ad* (*rather*) assez, plutôt; (*entirely*) complètement, tout à fait; **I ~ understand** je comprends très bien; **~ a few of them** un assez grand nombre d'entre eux; **~ (so)!** exactement!
quits [kwɪts] *a*: **~ (with)** quitte (envers); **let's call it ~** restons-en là.
quiver ['kwɪvə*] *vi* trembler, frémir.
quiz [kwɪz] *n* (*game*) jeu-concours *m*; test *m* de connaissances // *vt* interroger; **~zical** *a* narquois(e).
quota ['kwəʊtə] *n* quota *m*.
quotation [kwəʊ'teɪʃən] *n* citation *f*; (*of shares etc*) cote *f*, cours *m*; (*estimate*) devis *m*; **~ marks** *npl* guillemets *mpl*.

quote [kwəʊt] *n* citation *f* // *vt* (*sentence*) citer; (*price*) donner, fixer; (*shares*) coter // *vi*: **to ~ from** citer.

R

rabbi ['ræbaɪ] *n* rabbin *m*.
rabbit ['ræbɪt] *n* lapin *m*; **~ hutch** *n* clapier *m*.
rabble ['ræbl] *n* (*pej*) populace *f*.
rabies ['reɪbiːz] *n* rage *f*.
RAC *n abbr* (*Brit*) = *Royal Automobile Club.*
race [reɪs] *n* race *f*; (*competition, rush*) course *f* // *vt* (*person*) faire la course avec; (*horse*) faire courir; (*engine*) emballer // *vi* courir; (*engine*) s'emballer; **~ car** *n* (*US*) = **racing car**; **~ car driver** *n* (*US*) = **racing driver**; **~course** *n* champ *m* de courses; **~horse** *n* cheval *m* de course; **~track** *n* piste *f*.
racial ['reɪʃl] *a* racial(e); **~ist** *a, n* raciste (*m/f*).
racing ['reɪsɪŋ] *n* courses *fpl*; **~ car** *n* (*Brit*) voiture *f* de course; **~ driver** *n* (*Brit*) pilote *m* de course.
racism ['reɪsɪzəm] *n* racisme *m*; **racist** *a, n* raciste (*m/f*).
rack [ræk] *n* (*also*: **luggage ~**) filet *m* à bagages; (*also*: **roof ~**) galerie *f* // *vt* tourmenter; **to ~ one's brains** se creuser la cervelle.
racket ['rækɪt] *n* (*for tennis*) raquette *f*; (*noise*) tapage *m*; vacarme *m*; (*swindle*) escroquerie *f*; (*organized crime*) racket *m*.
racquet ['rækɪt] *n* raquette *f*.
racy ['reɪsɪ] *a* plein(e) de verve; osé(e).
radar ['reɪdɑː*] *n* radar *m*.
radial ['reɪdɪəl] *a* (*also*: **~-ply**) à carcasse radiale.
radiant ['reɪdɪənt] *a* rayonnant(e).
radiate ['reɪdɪeɪt] *vt* (*heat*) émettre, dégager // *vi* (*lines*) rayonner.
radiation [reɪdɪ'eɪʃən] *n* rayonnement *m*; (*radioactive*) radiation *f*.
radiator ['reɪdɪeɪtə*] *n* radiateur *m*.
radical ['rædɪkl] *a* radical(e).
radii ['reɪdɪaɪ] *npl of* **radius**.
radio ['reɪdɪəʊ] *n* radio *f*; **on the ~** à la radio.
radioactive [reɪdɪəʊ'æktɪv] *a* radioactif(ive).
radio station *n* station *f* de radio.
radish ['rædɪʃ] *n* radis *m*.
radius ['reɪdɪəs], *pl* **radii** *n* rayon *m*.
RAF *n abbr of* **Royal Air Force**.
raffle ['ræfl] *n* tombola *f*.
raft [rɑːft] *n* (*craft*; *also*: **life ~**) radeau *m*.
rafter ['rɑːftə*] *n* chevron *m*.
rag [ræg] *n* chiffon *m*; (*pej: newspaper*) feuille *f*, torchon *m*; (*for charity*) attrac-

tions organisées par les étudiants au profit d'œuvres de charité // *vt* (*Brit*) chahuter, mettre en boîte; **~s** *npl* haillons *mpl*; **~-and-bone man** *n* (*Brit*) = **~man**; **~ doll** *n* poupée *f* de chiffon.

rage [reidʒ] *n* (*fury*) rage *f*, fureur *f* // *vi* (*person*) être fou(folle) de rage; (*storm*) faire rage, être déchaîné(e); it's all the ~ cela fait fureur.

ragged ['rægid] *a* (*edge*) inégal(e), qui accroche; (*cuff*) effiloché(e); (*appearance*) déguenillé(e).

ragman ['rægmæn] *n* chiffonnier *m*.

raid [reid] *n* (*MIL*) raid *m*; (*criminal*) hold-up *m*, attaque *f*; (*by police*) descente *f*, rafle *f* // *vt* faire un raid sur *or* un hold-up dans *or* une descente dans.

rail [reil] *n* (*on stair*) rampe *f*; (*on bridge, balcony*) balustrade *f*; (*of ship*) bastingage *m*; (*for train*) rail *m*; **~s** *npl* rails *mpl*, voie ferrée; by ~ par chemin de fer; **~ing(s)** *n(pl)* grille *f*; **~way**, (*US*) **~road** *n* chemin *m* de fer; **~way line** *n* ligne *f* de chemin de fer; **~wayman** *n* cheminot *m*; **~way station** *n* gare *f*.

rain [rein] *n* pluie *f* // *vi* pleuvoir; in the ~ sous la pluie; it's ~ing il pleut; **~bow** *n* arc-en-ciel *m*; **~coat** *n* imperméable *m*; **~drop** *n* goutte *f* de pluie; **~fall** *n* chute *f* de pluie; (*measurement*) hauteur *f* des précipitations; **~y** *a* pluvieux(euse).

raise [reiz] *n* augmentation *f* // *vt* (*lift*) lever; hausser; (*build*) ériger; (*increase*) augmenter; (*a protest, doubt*) provoquer, causer; (*a question*) soulever; (*cattle, family*) élever; (*crop*) faire pousser; (*army, funds*) rassembler; (*loan*) obtenir; to ~ one's voice élever la voix.

raisin ['reizn] *n* raisin sec.

rake [reik] *n* (*tool*) râteau *m*; (*person*) débauché *m* // *vt* (*garden*) ratisser; (*with machine gun*) balayer.

rally ['ræli] *n* (*POL etc*) meeting *m*, rassemblement *m*; (*AUT*) rallye *m*; (*TENNIS*) échange *m* // *vt* rassembler, rallier // *vi* se rallier; (*sick person*) aller mieux; (*Stock Exchange*) reprendre; to ~ round *vt fus* se rallier à; venir en aide à.

RAM [ræm] *n abbr* (= *random access memory*) mémoire vive.

ram [ræm] *n* bélier *m* // *vt* enfoncer; (*soil*) tasser; (*crash into*) emboutir; percuter; éperonner.

ramble ['ræmbl] *n* randonnée *f* // *vi* (*pej: also:* ~ **on**) discourir, pérorer; **~r** *n* promeneur/euse, randonneur/euse; (*BOT*) rosier grimpant; **rambling** *a* (*speech*) décousu(e); (*BOT*) grimpant(e).

ramp [ræmp] *n* (*incline*) rampe *f*; dénivellation *f*; (*in garage*) pont *m*; on

~, off ~ (*US AUT*) bretelle *f* d'accès.

rampage ['ræmpeidʒ] *n*: to be on the ~ se déchaîner.

rampant ['ræmpənt] *a* (*disease etc*) qui sévit.

ramshackle ['ræmʃækl] *a* (*house*) délabré(e); (*car etc*) déglingué(e).

ran [ræn] *pt of* **run**.

ranch [rɑːntʃ] *n* ranch *m*; **~er** *n* propriétaire *m* de ranch; cowboy *m*.

rancid ['rænsid] *a* rance.

rancour, (*US*) **rancor** ['ræŋkə*] *n* rancune *f*.

random ['rændəm] *a* fait(e) *or* établi(e) au hasard; (*COMPUT, MATH*) aléatoire // *n*: at ~ au hasard.

randy ['rændi] *a* (*Brit col*) excité(e); lubrique.

rang [ræŋ] *pt of* **ring**.

range [reindʒ] *n* (*of mountains*) chaîne *f*; (*of missile, voice*) portée *f*; (*of products*) choix *m*, gamme *f*; (*MIL: also: shooting* ~) champ *m* de tir; (*indoor*) stand *m* de tir; (*also: kitchen* ~) fourneau *m* (de cuisine) // *vt* (*place*) mettre en rang, placer; (*roam*) parcourir // *vi*: to ~ over couvrir; to ~ from ... to aller de ... à.

ranger ['reindʒə*] *n* garde forestier.

rank [ræŋk] *n* rang *m*; (*MIL*) grade *m*; (*Brit: also: taxi* ~) station *f* de taxis // *vi*: to ~ among compter *or* se classer parmi // *a* (qui sent) fort(e); extrême; the **~s** (*MIL*) la troupe; the ~ **and file** (*fig*) la masse, la base.

rankle ['ræŋkl] *vi* (*insult*) rester dans le cœur.

ransack ['rænsæk] *vt* fouiller (à fond); (*plunder*) piller.

ransom ['rænsəm] *n* rançon *f*; to hold sb to ~ (*fig*) exercer un chantage sur qn.

rant [rænt] *vi* fulminer.

rap [ræp] *vt* frapper sur *or* à; taper sur.

rape [reip] *n* viol *m*; (*BOT*) colza *m* // *vt* violer; **~(seed) oil** *n* huile *f* de colza.

rapid ['ræpid] *a* rapide; **~s** *npl* (*GEO*) rapides *mpl*; **~ly** *ad* rapidement.

rapist ['reipist] *n* auteur *m* d'un viol.

rapport [ræ'pɔː*] *n* entente *f*.

rapture ['ræptʃə*] *n* extase *f*, ravissement *m*.

rare [reə*] *a* rare; (*CULIN: steak*) saignant(e).

rarely ['reəli] *ad* rarement.

raring ['reəriŋ] *a*: to be ~ to go (*col*) être très impatient(e) de commencer.

rascal ['rɑːskl] *n* vaurien *m*.

rash [ræʃ] *a* imprudent(e), irréfléchi(e) // *n* (*MED*) rougeur *f*, éruption *f*.

rasher ['ræʃə*] *n* fine tranche (de lard).

raspberry ['rɑːzbəri] *n* framboise *f*.

rasping ['rɑːspiŋ] *a*: ~ **noise** grincement *m*.

rat [ræt] *n* rat *m*.

rate [reit] *n* (*ratio*) taux *m*, pourcentage

m; (speed) vitesse f, rythme m; (price) tarif m ∥ vt classer; évaluer; **to ~ sb/ sth** as considérer qn/qch comme; **~s** npl (Brit) impôts locaux; (fees) tarifs mpl; **~able value** n (Brit) valeur locative imposable; **~payer** n (Brit) contribuable m/f (payant les impôts locaux).

rather ['rɑːðə*] ad plutôt; it's ~ expensive c'est assez cher; (too much) c'est un peu trop cher; there's ~ a lot il y en a beaucoup; I would or I'd ~ go j'aimerais mieux or je préférerais partir.

rating ['reɪtɪŋ] n classement m; cote f; (NAUT: category) classe f; (: Brit : sailor) matelot m.

ratio ['reɪʃɪəu] n proportion f.

ration ['ræʃən] n (gen pl) ration(s) f(pl).

rational ['ræʃənl] a raisonnable, sensé(e); (solution, reasoning) logique; (MED) lucide; **~e** [-'nɑːl] n raisonnement m; justification f; **~ize** vt rationaliser; (conduct) essayer d'expliquer or de motiver.

rat race n foire f d'empoigne.

rattle ['rætl] n cliquetis m; (louder) bruit m de ferraille; (object: of baby) hochet m; (: of sports fan) crécelle f ∥ vi cliqueter; faire un bruit de ferraille or du bruit ∥ vt agiter (bruyamment); **~snake** n serpent m à sonnettes.

raucous ['rɔːkəs] a rauque.

rave [reɪv] vi (in anger) s'emporter; (with enthusiasm) s'extasier; (MED) délirer.

raven ['reɪvən] n corbeau m.

ravenous ['rævənəs] a affamé(e).

ravine [rə'viːn] n ravin m.

raving ['reɪvɪŋ] a: ~ **lunatic** n fou furieux/folle furieuse.

ravishing ['rævɪʃɪŋ] a enchanteur(eresse).

raw [rɔː] a (uncooked) cru(e); (not processed) brut(e); (sore) à vif, irrité(e); (inexperienced) inexpérimenté(e); ~ **deal** n (col) sale coup m; ~ **material** n matière première.

ray [reɪ] n rayon m; ~ **of hope** n lueur f d'espoir.

raze [reɪz] vt raser, détruire.

razor ['reɪzə*] n rasoir m; ~ **blade** n lame f de rasoir.

Rd abbr of **road**.

re [riː] prep concernant.

reach [riːtʃ] n portée f, atteinte f; (of river etc) étendue f ∥ vt atteindre; parvenir à ∥ vi s'étendre; **out/within ~** hors de/à portée; **to ~ out** vi: **to ~ out for** allonger le bras pour prendre.

react [riː'ækt] vi réagir; **~ion** [-'ækʃən] n réaction f.

reactor [riː'æktə*] n réacteur m.

read, pt, pp **read** [riːd, rɛd] vi lire ∥ vt lire; (understand) comprendre, interpréter; (study) étudier; (subj: instrument etc) indiquer, marquer; **to ~ out**

vt lire à haute voix; **~able** a facile or agréable à lire; **~er** n lecteur/trice; (book) livre m de lecture; (Brit: at university) maître m de conférences; **~ership** n (of paper etc) (nombre m de) lecteurs mpl.

readily ['rɛdɪlɪ] ad volontiers, avec empressement; (easily) facilement.

readiness ['rɛdɪnɪs] n empressement m; **in ~** (prepared) prêt(e).

reading ['riːdɪŋ] n lecture f; (understanding) interprétation f; (on instrument) indications fpl.

ready ['rɛdɪ] a prêt(e); (willing) prêt, disposé(e); (quick) prompt(e); (available) disponible ∥ ad: **~-cooked** tout(e) cuit(e) (d'avance) ∥ n: **at the ~** (MIL) prêt à faire feu; (fig) tout(e) prêt(e); **to get ~** vi se préparer ∥ vt préparer; **~-made** a tout(e) fait(e); ~ **money** n (argent m) liquide m; ~ **reckoner** n barème m; **~-to-wear** a en prêt-à-porter.

real [rɪəl] a réel(le); véritable; **in ~ terms** dans la réalité; ~ **estate** n biens fonciers or immobiliers; **~istic** [-'lɪstɪk] a réaliste.

reality [riː'ælɪtɪ] n réalité f.

realization [rɪəlaɪ'zeɪʃən] n prise f de conscience; réalisation f.

realize ['rɪəlaɪz] vt (understand) se rendre compte de; (a project, COMM: asset) réaliser.

really ['rɪəlɪ] ad vraiment; ~? c'est vrai?

realm [rɛlm] n royaume m.

realtor ['rɪəltə*] n (US) agent immobilier.

reap [riːp] vt moissonner; (fig) récolter.

reappear [riːə'pɪə*] vi réapparaître, reparaître.

rear [rɪə*] a de derrière, arrière inv; (AUT: wheel etc) arrière ∥ n arrière m, derrière m ∥ vt (cattle, family) élever ∥ vi (also: ~ up: animal) se cabrer.

rear-view ['rɪəvjuː] : ~ **mirror** n (AUT) rétroviseur m.

reason ['riːzn] n raison f ∥ vi: **to ~ with sb** raisonner qn, faire entendre raison à qn; **to have ~ to think** avoir lieu de penser; **it stands to ~ that** il va sans dire que; **~able** a raisonnable; (not bad) acceptable; **~ably** ad raisonnablement; **~ing** n raisonnement m.

reassurance [riːə'ʃuərəns] n réconfort m; assurance f, garantie f.

reassure [riːə'ʃuə*] vt rassurer; **to ~ sb of** donner à qn l'assurance réitérée de.

rebate ['riːbeɪt] n (on product) rabais m; (on tax etc) dégrèvement m; (repayment) remboursement m.

rebel n ['rɛbl] rebelle m/f ∥ vi [rɪ'bɛl] se rebeller, se révolter; **~lious** a rebelle.

rebound vi [rɪ'baund] (ball) rebondir ∥ n ['riːbaund] rebond m.

rebuff [rɪ'bʌf] *n* rebuffade *f*.

rebuke [rɪ'bju:k] *vt* réprimander.

rebut [rɪ'bʌt] *vt* réfuter.

recall [rɪ'kɔ:l] *vt* rappeler; (*remember*) se rappeler, se souvenir de // *n* rappel *m*.

recant [rɪ'kænt] *vi* se rétracter; (*REL*) abjurer.

recap ['ri:kæp] *vt*, *vi* récapituler.

recapitulate [ri:kə'pɪtjuleɪt] *vt*, *vi* = **recap**.

rec'd *abbr* = received.

recede [rɪ'si:d] *vi* s'éloigner; reculer; redescendre; **receding** *a* (*forehead, chin*) fuyant(e); **receding hairline** front dégarni.

receipt [rɪ'si:t] *n* (*document*) reçu *m*; (*for parcel etc*) accusé *m* de réception; (*act of receiving*) réception *f*; ~s *npl* (*COMM*) recettes *fpl*.

receive [rɪ'si:v] *vt* recevoir.

receiver [rɪ'si:və*] *n* (*TEL*) récepteur *m*, combiné *m*; (*of stolen goods*) receleur *m*; (*LAW*) administrateur *m* judiciaire.

recent [rɪ'si:nt] *a* récent(e); ~**ly** *ad* récemment.

receptacle [rɪ'septɪkl] *n* récipient *m*.

reception [rɪ'sɛpʃən] *n* réception *f*; (*welcome*) accueil *m*, réception; ~ **desk** *n* réception *f*; ~**ist** *n* réceptionniste *m/f*.

recess [rɪ'ses] *n* (*in room*) renfoncement *m*; (*for bed*) alcôve *f*; (*secret place*) recoin *m*; (*POL etc*: *holiday*) vacances *fpl*; ~**ion** [-'sɛʃən] *n* récession *f*.

recipe ['rɛsɪpɪ] *n* recette *f*.

recipient [rɪ'sɪpɪənt] *n* bénéficiaire *m/f*; (*of letter*) destinataire *m/f*.

recital [rɪ'saɪtl] *n* récital *m*.

recite [rɪ'saɪt] *vt* (*poem*) réciter.

reckless ['rɛkləs] *a* (*driver etc*) imprudent(e).

reckon ['rɛkən] *vt* (*count*) calculer, compter; (*consider*) considérer, estimer; (*think*): I ~ that ... je pense que ...; **to** ~ **on** *vt fus* compter sur, s'attendre à; ~**ing** *n* compte *m*, calcul *m*; estimation *f*.

reclaim [rɪ'kleɪm] *vt* (*land*) amender; (: *from sea*) assécher; (: *from forest*) défricher; (*demand back*) réclamer (le remboursement *or* la restitution de).

recline [rɪ'klaɪn] *vi* être allongé(e) *or* étendu(e); **reclining** *a* (*seat*) à dossier réglable.

recluse [rɪ'klu:s] *n* reclus/e, ermite *m*.

recognition [rɛkəg'nɪʃən] *n* reconnaissance *f*; **to gain** ~ être reconnu(e); **transformed beyond** ~ méconnaissable.

recognize ['rɛkəgnaɪz] *vt*: **to** ~ (**by/as**) reconnaître (à/comme étant).

recoil [rɪ'kɔɪl] *vi* (*person*): **to** ~ (**from**) reculer (devant) // *n* (*of gun*) recul *m*.

recollect [rɛkə'lɛkt] *vt* se rappeler, se souvenir de; ~**ion** [-'lɛkʃən] *n* souvenir *m*.

recommend [rɛkə'mɛnd] *vt* recommander.

reconcile ['rɛkənsaɪl] *vt* (*two people*) réconcilier; (*two facts*) concilier, accorder; **to** ~ **o.s. to** se résigner à.

recondition [ri:kən'dɪʃən] *vt* remettre à neuf; réviser entièrement.

reconnoitre, reconnoiter (*US*) [rɛkə'nɔɪtə*] (*MIL*) *vt* reconnaître // *vi* faire une reconnaissance.

reconstruct [ri:kən'strʌkt] *vt* (*building*) reconstruire; (*crime*) reconstituer.

record *n* ['rɛkɔ:d] rapport *m*, récit *m*; (*of meeting etc*) procès-verbal *m*; (*register*) registre *m*; (*file*) dossier *m*; (*also*: **police** ~) casier *m* judiciaire; (*MUS*: *disc*) disque *m*; (*SPORT*) record *m* // *vt* [rɪ'kɔ:d] (*set down*) noter; (*relate*) rapporter; (*MUS*: *song etc*) enregistrer; **in** ~ **time** dans un temps record *inv*; **to keep a** ~ **of** noter; **off the** ~ *a* officieux(euse) // *ad* officieusement; ~ **card** *n* (*in file*) fiche *f*; ~**ed delivery** *n* (*Brit POST*): ~**ed delivery letter** *etc* lettre *etc* recommandée; ~**er** *n* (*LAW*) avocat nommé à la fonction de juge; (*MUS*) flûte *f* à bec; ~ **holder** *n* (*SPORT*) détenteur/trice du record; ~**ing** *n* (*MUS*) enregistrement *m*; ~ **player** *n* électrophone *m*.

recount [rɪ'kaunt] *vt* raconter.

re-count *n* ['ri:kaunt] (*POL*: *of votes*) pointage *m* // *vt* [ri:'kaunt] recompter.

recoup [rɪ'ku:p] *vt*: **to** ~ **one's losses** récupérer ce qu'on a perdu, se refaire.

recourse [rɪ'kɔ:s] *n* recours *m*; expédient *m*.

recover [rɪ'kʌvə*] *vt* récupérer // *vi* (*from illness*) se rétablir; (*from shock*) se remettre; (*country*) se redresser.

recovery [rɪ'kʌvərɪ] *n* récupération *f*; rétablissement *m*; redressement *m*.

recreation [rɛkrɪ'eɪʃən] *n* récréation *f*, détente *f*; ~**al** *a* pour la détente, récréatif(ive).

recruit [rɪ'kru:t] *n* recrue *f* // *vt* recruter.

rectangle ['rɛktæŋgl] *n* rectangle *m*; **rectangular** [-'tæŋgjulə*] *a* rectangulaire.

rectify ['rɛktɪfaɪ] *vt* (*error*) rectifier, corriger; (*omission*) réparer.

rector ['rɛktə*] *n* (*REL*) pasteur *m*; **rectory** *n* presbytère *m*.

recuperate [rɪ'kju:pəreɪt] *vi* récupérer; (*from illness*) se rétablir.

recur [rɪ'kɔ:*] *vi* se reproduire; (*idea, opportunity*) se retrouver; (*symptoms*) réapparaître; ~**rent** *a* périodique, fréquent(e).

red [rɛd] *n* rouge *m*; (*POL*: *pej*) rouge *m/f* // *a* rouge; **in the** ~ (*account*) à découvert; (*business*) en déficit; ~ **carpet treatment** *n* réception *f* en grande pompe; **R**~ **Cross** *n* Croix-Rouge *f*; ~-**currant** *n* groseille *f* (rouge); ~**den** *vt*, *vi* rougir; **~dish** *a* rougeâtre; *(hair)* plutôt roux(rousse).

redeem [rɪˈdiːm] *vt (debt)* rembourser; *(sth in pawn)* dégager; *(fig, also REL)* racheter; **~ing** *a (feature)* qui sauve, qui rachète (le reste).

redeploy [riːdɪˈplɔɪ] *vt (resources)* réorganiser.

red-haired [rɛdˈhɛəd] *a* roux(rousse).

red-handed [rɛdˈhændɪd] *a:* **to be caught ~** être pris(e) en flagrant délit *or* la main dans le sac.

redhead [ˈrɛdhɛd] *n* roux/rousse.

red herring *n (fig)* diversion *f*, fausse piste.

red-hot [rɛdˈhɔt] *a* chauffé(e) au rouge, brûlant(e).

redirect [riːdaɪˈrɛkt] *vt (mail)* faire suivre.

red light *n:* **to go through a ~** *(AUT)* brûler un feu rouge; **red-light district** *n* quartier réservé.

redo [riːˈduː] *vt irg* refaire.

redolent [ˈrɛdələnt] *a:* **~ of** qui sent; *(fig)* qui évoque.

redress [rɪˈdrɛs] *n* réparation *f* // *vt* redresser.

Red Sea *n* la mer Rouge.

redskin [ˈrɛdskɪn] *n* Peau-Rouge *m/f*.

red tape *n (fig)* paperasserie (administrative).

reduce [rɪˈdjuːs] *vt* réduire; *(lower)* abaisser; **'~ speed now'** *(AUT)* 'ralentir'; **reduction** [rɪˈdʌkʃən] *n* réduction *f*; *(of price)* baisse *f*; *(discount)* rabais *m*; réduction.

redundancy [rɪˈdʌndənsɪ] *n* licenciement *m*, mise *f* au chômage.

redundant [rɪˈdʌndnt] *a (worker)* mis(e) au chômage, licencié(e); *(detail, object)* superflu(e); **to be made ~** être licencié(e), être mis(e) au chômage.

reed [riːd] *n (BOT)* roseau *m*.

reef [riːf] *n (at sea)* récif *m*, écueil *m*.

reek [riːk] *vi:* **to ~ (of)** puer, empester.

reel [riːl] *n* bobine *f*; *(TECH)* dévidoir *m*; *(FISHING)* moulinet *m*; *(CINEMA)* bande *f* // *vt (TECH)* bobiner; *(also:* **~ up)** enrouler // *vi (sway)* chanceler.

ref [rɛf] *n abbr (col:* = **referee)** arbitre *m*.

refectory [rɪˈfɛktərɪ] *n* réfectoire *m*.

refer [rɪˈfəː*] *vt:* **to ~ sth to** *(dispute, decision)* soumettre qch à; **to ~ sb to** *(inquirer: for information)* adresser *or* envoyer qn à; *(reader: to text)* renvoyer qn à; **to ~ to** *vt fus (allude to)* parler de, faire allusion à; *(apply to)* s'appliquer à; *(consult)* se reporter à.

referee [rɛfəˈriː] *n* arbitre *m*; *(Brit: for job application)* répondant/e.

reference [ˈrɛfrəns] *n* référence *f*, renvoi *m*; *(mention)* allusion *f*, mention *f*; *(for job application: letter)* références; lettre *f* de recommandation; *(: person)*

répondant/e; **with ~ to** en ce qui concerne; *(COMM: in letter)* me référant à; **~ book** *n* ouvrage *m* de référence.

refill *vt* [riːˈfɪl] remplir à nouveau; *(pen, lighter etc)* recharger // *n* [ˈriːfɪl] *(for pen etc)* recharge *f*.

refine [rɪˈfaɪn] *vt (sugar, oil)* raffiner; *(taste)* affiner; **~d** *a (person, taste)* raffiné(e).

reflect [rɪˈflɛkt] *vt (light, image)* réfléchir, refléter; *(fig)* refléter // *vi (think)* réfléchir, méditer; **to ~ on** *vt fus (discredit)* porter atteinte à, faire tort à; **~ion** [-ˈflɛkʃən] *n* réflexion *f*; *(image)* reflet *m*; *(criticism):* **~ion on** critique *f* de; atteinte *f* à; **on ~ion** réflexion faite.

reflex [ˈriːflɛks] *a, n* réflexe *(m)*; **~ive** [rɪˈflɛksɪv] *a (LING)* réfléchi(e).

reform [rɪˈfɔːm] *n* réforme *f* // *vt* réformer; **the R~ation** [rɛfəˈmeɪʃən] *n* la Réforme; **~atory** *n (US)* ≈ centre *m* d'éducation surveillée.

refrain [rɪˈfreɪn] *vi:* **to ~ from doing** s'abstenir de faire // *n* refrain *m*.

refresh [rɪˈfrɛʃ] *vt* rafraîchir; *(subj: food)* redonner des forces à; *(: sleep)* reposer; **~er course** *n (Brit)* cours *m* de recyclage; **~ing** *a (drink)* rafraîchissant(e); *(sleep)* réparateur(trice); **~ments** *npl* rafraîchissements *mpl*.

refrigerator [rɪˈfrɪdʒəreɪtə*] *n* réfrigérateur *m*, frigidaire *m*.

refuel [riːˈfjuəl] *vi* se ravitailler en carburant.

refuge [ˈrɛfjuːdʒ] *n* refuge *m*; **to take ~ in** se réfugier dans.

refugee [rɛfjuˈdʒiː] *n* réfugié/e.

refund *n* [ˈriːfʌnd] remboursement *m* // *vt* [rɪˈfʌnd] rembourser.

refurbish [riːˈfəːbɪʃ] *vt* remettre à neuf.

refusal [rɪˈfjuːzəl] *n* refus *m*; **to have first ~ on** avoir droit de préemption sur.

refuse *n* [ˈrɛfjuːs] ordures *fpl*, détritus *mpl* // *vt, vi* [rɪˈfjuːz] refuser; **~ collection** *n* ramassage *m* d'ordures.

regain [rɪˈgeɪn] *vt* regagner; retrouver.

regal [ˈriːgl] *a* royal(e); **~ia** [rɪˈgeɪlɪə] *n* insignes *mpl* de la royauté.

regard [rɪˈgɑːd] *n* respect *m*, estime *f*, considération *f* // *vt* considérer; **to give one's ~s to** faire ses amitiés à; **'with kindest ~s'** 'bien amicalement'; **~ing, as ~s, with ~ to** *prep* en ce qui concerne; **~less** *ad* quand même; **~less of** sans se soucier de.

régime [reɪˈʒiːm] *n* régime *m*.

regiment [ˈrɛdʒɪmənt] *n* régiment *m* // *vt* [ˈrɛdʒɪmɛnt] imposer une discipline trop stricte à; **~al** [-ˈmɛntl] *a* d'un *or* du régiment.

region [ˈriːdʒən] *n* région *f*; **in the ~ of** *(fig)* aux alentours de; **~al** *a* régional(e).

register [ˈrɛdʒɪstə*] *n* registre *m*; *(also:* **electoral ~)** liste électorale // *vt* enregistrer, inscrire; (*birth*) déclarer; (*vehicle*) immatriculer; (*luggage*) enregistrer; (*letter*) envoyer en recommandé; (*subj: instrument*) marquer // *vi* se faire inscrire; (*at hotel*) signer le registre; (*make impression*) être (bien) compris(e); ~**ed** *a* (*design*) déposé(e); (*Brit: letter*) recommandé(e); ~**ed trademark** *n* marque déposée.

registrar ['redʒistrɑ:*] *n* officier *m* de l'état civil; secrétaire (général).

registration [redʒis'treiʃən] *n* (*act*) enregistrement *m*; inscription *f*; (*AUT: also:* ~ **number**) numéro *m* d'immatriculation.

registry ['redʒistri] *n* bureau *m* de l'enregistrement; ~ **office** *n* (*Brit*) bureau *m* de l'état civil; **to get married in a** ~ **office** ≈ se marier à la mairie.

regret [ri'gret] *n* regret *m* // *vt* regretter; ~**fully** *ad* à *or* avec regret.

regular ['regjulə*] *a* régulier(ère); (*usual*) habituel(le), normal(e); (*soldier*) de métier; (*COMM: size*) ordinaire // *n* (*client etc*) habitué(e); ~**ly** *ad* régulièrement.

regulate ['regjuleit] *vt* régler; **regulation** [-'leiʃən] *n* (*rule*) règlement *m*; (*adjustment*) réglage *m*.

rehabilitation ['ri:həbili'teiʃən] *n* (*of offender*) réhabilitation *f*; (*of disabled*) rééducation *f*, réadaptation *f*.

rehearsal [ri'hə:səl] *n* répétition *f*.

rehearse [ri'hə:s] *vt* répéter.

reign [rein] *n* règne *m* // *vi* régner.

reimburse [ri:im'bə:s] *vt* rembourser.

rein [rein] *n* (*for horse*) rêne *f*.

reindeer ['reindiə*] *n* (*pl inv*) renne *m*.

reinforce [ri:in'fɔ:s] *vt* renforcer; ~**d concrete** *n* béton armé; ~**ments** *npl* (*MIL*) renfort(s) *m(pl)*.

reinstate [ri:in'steit] *vt* rétablir, réintégrer.

reject *n* ['ri:dʒekt] (*COMM*) article *m* de rebut // *vt* [ri'dʒekt] refuser; (*COMM: goods*) mettre au rebut; (*idea*) rejeter; ~**ion** [ri'dʒekʃən] *n* rejet *m*, refus *m*.

rejoice [ri'dʒɔis] *vi:* **to** ~ (**at** *or* **over**) se réjouir (de).

rejuvenate [ri'dʒu:vəneit] *vt* rajeunir.

relapse [ri'læps] *n* (*MED*) rechute *f*.

relate [ri'leit] *vt* (*tell*) raconter; (*connect*) établir un rapport entre // *vi:* **to** ~ **to** se rapporter à; ~**d** *a* apparenté(e); **relating to** *prep* concernant.

relation [ri'leiʃən] *n* (*person*) parent/e; (*link*) rapport *m*, lien *m*; ~**ship** *n* rapport *m*, lien *m*; (*personal ties*) relations *fpl*, rapports; (*also:* **family** ~**ship**) lien de parenté; (*affair*) liaison *f*.

relative ['relətiv] *n* parent/e // *a* relatif(ive); (*respective*) respectif(ive); **all her** ~**s** toute sa famille.

relax [ri'læks] *vi* se relâcher; (*person:*

unwind) se détendre // *vt* relâcher; (*mind, person*) détendre; ~**ation** [ri:læk'seiʃən] *n* relâchement *m*; détente *f*; (*entertainment*) distraction *f*; ~**ed** *a* relâché(e); détendu(e); ~**ing** *a* délassant(e).

relay ['ri:lei] *n* (*SPORT*) course *f* de relais // *vt* (*message*) retransmettre, relayer.

release [ri'li:s] *n* (*from prison, obligation*) libération *f*; (*of gas etc*) émission *f*; (*of film etc*) sortie *f*; (*record*) disque *m*; (*device*) déclencheur *m* // *vt* (*prisoner*) libérer; (*book, film*) sortir; (*report, news*) rendre public, publier; (*gas etc*) émettre, dégager; (*free: from wreckage etc*) dégager; (*TECH: catch, spring etc*) déclencher; (*let go*) relâcher; lâcher; desserrer.

relegate ['reləgeit] *vt* reléguer; (*SPORT*): **to be** ~**d** descendre dans une division inférieure.

relent [ri'lent] *vi* se laisser fléchir; ~**less** *a* implacable.

relevant ['reləvənt] *a* approprié(e); (*fact*) significatif(ive); (*information*) utile, pertinent(e); ~ **to** ayant rapport à, approprié à.

reliable [ri'laiəbl] *a* (*person, firm*) sérieux(euse), fiable; (*method, machine*) fiable; **reliably** *ad:* **to be reliably informed** savoir de source sûre.

reliance [ri'laiəns] *n:* ~ (**on**) confiance *f* (en); besoin *m* de, dépendance *f* (de).

relic ['relik] *n* (*REL*) relique *f*; (*of the past*) vestige *m*.

relief [ri'li:f] *n* (*from pain, anxiety*) soulagement *m*; (*help, supplies*) secours *m(pl)*; (*of guard*) relève *f*; (*ART, GEO*) relief *m*.

relieve [ri'li:v] *vt* (*pain, patient*) soulager; (*bring help*) secourir; (*take over from: gen*) relayer; (*: guard*) relever; **to** ~ **sb of sth** débarrasser qn de qch; **to** ~ **o.s.** se soulager, faire ses besoins.

religion [ri'lidʒən] *n* religion *f*; **religious** *a* religieux(euse); (*book*) de piété.

relinquish [ri'liŋkwiʃ] *vt* abandonner; (*plan, habit*) renoncer à.

relish ['reliʃ] *n* (*CULIN*) condiment *m*; (*enjoyment*) délectation *f* // *vt* (*food etc*) savourer; **to** ~ **doing** se délecter à faire.

relocate [ri:ləu'keit] *vt* installer ailleurs // *vi* déménager, s'installer ailleurs.

reluctance [ri'lʌktəns] *n* répugnance *f*.

reluctant [ri'lʌktənt] *a* peu disposé(e), qui hésite; ~**ly** *ad* à contrecœur, sans enthousiasme.

rely [ri'lai]: **to** ~ **on** *vt fus* compter sur; (*be dependent*) dépendre de.

remain [ri'mein] *vi* rester; ~**der** *n* reste *m*; (*COMM*) fin *f* de série; ~**ing** *a* qui reste; ~**s** *npl* restes *mpl*.

remand [ri'mɑ:nd] *n:* **on** ~ en détention

préventive // vt: **to ~ in custody** écrouer; renvoyer en détention provisoire; **~ home** n (Brit) maison f d'arrêt.

remark [rɪ'mɑ:k] n remarque f, observation f // vt (faire) remarquer, dire; (notice) remarquer; **~able** a remarquable.

remedial [rɪ'mi:dɪəl] a (tuition, classes) de rattrapage.

remedy ['rɛmədɪ] n: ~ **(for)** remède m (contre or à) // vt remédier à.

remember [rɪ'mɛmbə*] vt se rappeler, se souvenir de; **remembrance** n souvenir m; mémoire f.

remind [rɪ'maɪnd] vt: **to ~ sb of sth** rappeler qch à qn; **to ~ sb to do** faire penser à qn à faire, rappeler à qn qu'il doit faire; **~er** n rappel m; (note etc) pense-bête m.

reminisce [rɛmɪ'nɪs] vi: **to ~ (about)** évoquer ses souvenirs (de).

reminiscent [rɛmɪ'nɪsnt] a: ~ **of** qui rappelle, qui fait penser à.

remiss [rɪ'mɪs] a négligent(e).

remission [rɪ'mɪʃən] n rémission f; (of debt, sentence) remise f; (of fee) exemption f.

remit [rɪ'mɪt] vt (send: money) envoyer; **~tance** n envoi m, paiement m.

remnant ['rɛmnənt] n reste m, restant m; **~s** npl (COMM) coupons mpl; fins fpl de série.

remorse [rɪ'mɔ:s] n remords m; **~ful** a plein(e) de remords; **~less** a (fig) impitoyable.

remote [rɪ'məut] a éloigné(e), lointain(e); (person) distant(e); ~ **control** n télécommande f; **~ly** ad au loin; (slightly) très vaguement.

remould ['ri:məuld] n (Brit: tyre) pneu rechapé.

removable [rɪ'mu:vəbl] a (detachable) amovible.

removal [rɪ'mu:vəl] n (taking away) enlèvement m; suppression f; (Brit: from house) déménagement m; (from office: dismissal) renvoi m; (MED) ablation f; ~ **van** n (Brit) camion m de déménagement.

remove [rɪ'mu:v] vt enlever, retirer; (employee) renvoyer; (stain) faire partir; (doubt, abuse) supprimer; **~rs** npl (Brit: company) entreprise f de déménagement.

render ['rɛndə*] vt rendre; **~ing** n (MUS etc) interprétation f.

rendez-vous ['rɔndɪvu:] n rendez-vous m inv // vi opérer une jonction, se rejoindre.

renew [rɪ'nju:] vt renouveler; (negotiations) reprendre; (acquaintance) renouer; **~al** n renouvellement m; reprise f.

renounce [rɪ'nauns] vt renoncer à; (disown) renier.

renovate ['rɛnəveɪt] vt rénover; (art work) restaurer.

renown [rɪ'naun] n renommée f; **~ed** a renommé(e).

rent [rɛnt] n loyer m // vt louer; **~al** n (for television, car) (prix m de) location f.

rep [rɛp] n abbr (COMM: = representative) représentant m (de commerce); (THEATRE: = repertory) théâtre m de répertoire.

repair [rɪ'pɛə*] n réparation f // vt réparer; **in good/bad ~** en bon/mauvais état; ~ **kit** n trousse f de réparations.

repartee [rɛpɑ:'ti:] n repartie f.

repatriate [ri:'pætrɪeɪt] vt rapatrier.

repay [ri:'peɪ] vt irg (money, creditor) rembourser; (sb's efforts) récompenser; **~ment** n remboursement m; récompense f.

repeal [rɪ'pi:l] n (of law) abrogation f; (of sentence) annulation f // vt abroger; annuler.

repeat [rɪ'pi:t] n (RADIO, TV) reprise f // vt répéter; (pattern) reproduire; (promise, attack, also COMM: order) renouveler; (SCOL: a class) redoubler // vi répéter; **~edly** ad souvent, à plusieurs reprises.

repel [rɪ'pɛl] vt (lit, fig) repousser; **~lent** a repoussant(e) // n: insect **~lent** insectifuge m.

repent [rɪ'pɛnt] vi: **to ~ (of)** se repentir (de); **~ance** n repentir m.

repertory ['rɛpətərɪ] n (also: ~ theatre) théâtre m de répertoire.

repetition [rɛpɪ'tɪʃən] n répétition f.

repetitive [rɪ'pɛtɪtɪv] a (movement, work) répétitif(ive); (speech) plein(e) de redites.

replace [rɪ'pleɪs] vt (put back) remettre, replacer; (take the place of) remplacer; **~ment** n replacement m; remplacement m; (person) remplaçant/e.

replay ['ri:pleɪ] n (of match) match rejoué; (of tape, film) répétition f.

replenish [rɪ'plɛnɪʃ] vt (glass) remplir (de nouveau); (stock etc) réapprovisionner.

replete [rɪ'pli:t] a rempli(e); (well-fed) rassasié(e).

replica ['rɛplɪkə] n réplique f, copie exacte.

reply [rɪ'plaɪ] n réponse f // vi répondre; ~ **coupon** n coupon-réponse m.

report [rɪ'pɔ:t] n rapport m; (PRESS etc) reportage m; (Brit: also: **school ~**) bulletin m (scolaire); (of gun) détonation f // vt rapporter, faire un compte rendu de; (PRESS etc) faire un reportage sur; (bring to notice: occurrence) signaler; (: person) dénoncer // vi (make a report) faire un rapport (or un reportage); (present o.s.): **to ~ (to sb)** se présenter (chez qn); ~ **card** *n* (*US, Scottish*) bulletin *m* scolaire; **~edly** *ad*: she is ~edly living in ... elle habiterait ...; he ~edly told them to ... il leur aurait ordonné de ...; **~er** *n* reporter *m*.

repose [rɪ'pəuz] *n*: in ~ en or au repos.

represent [reprɪ'zent] *vt* représenter; **~ation** [-'teɪʃən] *n* représentation *f*; **~ations** *npl* (*protest*) démarche *f*; **~ative** *a* représentant/e; (*US POL*) député *m* // *a* représentatif(ive), caractéristique.

repress [rɪ'pres] *vt* réprimer; **~ion** [-'preʃən] *n* répression *f*.

reprieve [rɪ'pri:v] *n* (*LAW*) grâce *f*; (*fig*) sursis *m*, délai *m*.

reprisal [rɪ'praɪzl] *n* représailles *fpl*.

reproach [rɪ'prəutʃ] *vt*: to ~ sb with sth reprocher qch à qn; **~ful** *a* de reproche.

reproduce [ri:prə'dju:s] *vt* reproduire // *vi* se reproduire; **reproduction** [-'dʌkʃən] *n* reproduction *f*.

reproof [rɪ'pru:f] *n* reproche *m*.

reptile ['reptaɪl] *n* reptile *m*.

republic [rɪ'pʌblɪk] *n* république *f*; **~an** *a, n* républicain(e).

repulsive [rɪ'pʌlsɪv] *a* repoussant(e), répulsif(ive).

reputable ['repjutəbl] *a* de bonne réputation; (*occupation*) honorable.

reputation [repju'teɪʃən] *n* réputation *f*.

repute [rɪ'pju:t] *n* (bonne) réputation; **~d** *a* réputé(e); **~dly** *ad* d'après ce qu'on dit.

request [rɪ'kwest] *n* demande *f*; (*formal*) requête *f* // *vt*: to ~ (of or from sb) demander (à qn); ~ **stop** *n* (*Brit*: *for bus*) arrêt facultatif.

require [rɪ'kwaɪə*] *vt* (*need*: *subj*: *person*) avoir besoin de; (: *thing, situation*) demander; (*want*) vouloir; exiger; (*order*) obliger; **~ment** *n* exigence *f*; besoin *m*; condition requise.

requisite ['rekwɪzɪt] *n* chose *f* nécessaire // *a* requis(e), nécessaire.

requisition [rekwɪ'zɪʃən] *n*: ~ (**for**) demande *f* (de) // *vt* (*MIL*) réquisitionner.

rescue ['reskju:] *n* sauvetage *m*; (*help*) secours *mpl* // *vt* sauver; ~ **party** *n* équipe *f* de sauvetage; **~r** *n* sauveteur *m*.

research [rɪ'sə:tʃ] *n* recherche(s) *f(pl)* // *vt* faire des recherches sur.

resemblance [rɪ'zembləns] *n* ressemblance *f*.

resemble [rɪ'zembl] *vt* ressembler à.

resent [rɪ'zent] *vt* éprouver du ressentiment de, être contrarié(e) par; **~ful** *a* irrité(e), plein(e) de ressentiment; **~ment** *n* ressentiment *m*.

reservation [rezə'veɪʃən] *n* (*booking*) réservation *f*; (*doubt*) réserve *f*; (*protected area*) réserve; (*Brit*: *on road*: *also*: **central ~**) bande *f* médiane; to

make a ~ (in an hotel/a restaurant/on a plane) réserver or retenir une chambre/une table/une place.

reserve [rɪ'zə:v] *n* réserve *f*; (*SPORT*) remplaçant/e // *vt* (*seats etc*) réserver, retenir; **~s** *npl* (*MIL*) réservistes *mpl*; in ~ en réserve; **~d** *a* réservé(e).

reshuffle [ri:'ʃʌfl] *n*: Cabinet ~ (*POL*) remaniement ministériel.

residence ['rezɪdəns] *n* résidence *f*; ~ **permit** *n* (*Brit*) permis *m* de séjour.

resident ['rezɪdənt] *n* résident/e // *a* résidant(e); **~ial** [-'denʃəl] *a* de résidence; (*area*) résidentiel(le).

residue ['rezɪdju:] *n* reste *m*; (*CHEM, PHYSICS*) résidu *m*.

resign [rɪ'zaɪn] *vt* (*one's post*) se démettre de // *vi* démissionner; to ~ o.s. to (*endure*) se résigner à; **~ation** [rezɪg'neɪʃən] *n* démission *f*; résignation *f*; **~ed** *a* résigné(e).

resilience [rɪ'zɪlɪəns] *n* (*of material*) élasticité *f*; (*of person*) ressort *m*.

resilient [rɪ'zɪlɪənt] *a* (*person*) qui réagit, qui a du ressort.

resist [rɪ'zɪst] *vt* résister à; **~ance** *n* résistance *f*.

resolution [rezə'lu:ʃən] *n* résolution *f*.

resolve [rɪ'zɒlv] *n* résolution *f* // *vi* (*decide*): to ~ to do résoudre or décider de faire // *vt* (*problem*) résoudre.

resort [rɪ'zɔ:t] *n* (*town*) station *f*; (*recourse*) recours *m* // *vi*: to ~ to avoir recours à; in the last ~ en dernier ressort.

resounding [rɪ'zaundɪŋ] *a* retentissant(e).

resource [rɪ'sɔ:s] *n* ressource *f*; **~s** *npl* ressources.

respect [rɪs'pekt] *n* respect *m* // *vt* respecter; **~s** *npl* respects, hommages *mpl*; with ~ to en ce qui concerne; in this ~ sous ce rapport, à cet égard; **~able** *a* respectable; **~ful** *a* respectueux(euse).

respite ['respaɪt] *n* répit *m*.

resplendent [rɪs'plendənt] *a* resplendissant(e).

respond [rɪs'pɒnd] *vi* répondre; (*to treatment*) réagir.

response [rɪs'pɒns] *n* réponse *f*; (*to treatment*) réaction *f*.

responsibility [rɪspɒnsɪ'bɪlɪtɪ] *n* responsabilité *f*.

responsible [rɪs'pɒnsɪbl] *a* (*liable*): ~ (**for**) responsable (de); (*person*) digne de confiance; (*job*) qui comporte des responsabilités; **responsibly** *ad* avec sérieux.

responsive [rɪs'pɒnsɪv] *a* qui n'est pas réservé(e) or indifférent(e).

rest [rest] *n* repos *m*; (*stop*) arrêt *m*, pause *f*; (*MUS*) silence *m*; (*support*) support *m*, appui *m*; (*remainder*) reste *m*, restant *m* // *vi* se reposer; (*be* supported): to ~ on appuyer or reposer sur; (remain) rester // vt (lean): to ~ sth on/against appuyer qch sur/contre; the ~ of them les autres; it ~s with him to c'est à lui de.

restaurant ['rɛstərɔŋ] n restaurant m; ~ **car** n (Brit) wagon-restaurant m.

restful ['rɛstful] a reposant(e).

restitution [rɛstɪ'tju:ʃən] n (act) restitution f; (reparation) réparation f.

restive ['rɛstɪv] a agité(e), impatient(e); (horse) rétif(ive).

restless ['rɛstlɪs] a agité(e).

restoration [rɛstə'reɪʃən] n restauration f; restitution f.

restore [rɪ'stɔ:*] vt (building) restaurer; (sth stolen) restituer; (peace, health) rétablir.

restrain [rɪs'treɪn] vt (feeling) contenir; (person): to ~ (from doing) retenir (de faire); ~ed a (style) sobre; (manner) mesuré(e); ~t n (restriction) contrainte f; (moderation) retenue f.

restrict [rɪs'trɪkt] vt restreindre, limiter; ~ion [-kʃən] n restriction f, limitation f.

rest room n (US) toilettes fpl.

result [rɪ'zʌlt] n résultat m // vi: to ~ in aboutir à, se terminer par; as a ~ of à la suite de.

resume [rɪ'zju:m] vt, vi (work, journey) reprendre.

résumé ['reɪzjumeɪ] n résumé m; (US) curriculum vitae m.

resumption [rɪ'zʌmpʃən] n reprise f.

resurgence [rɪ'sɜ:dʒəns] n réapparition f.

resurrection [rɛzə'rɛkʃən] n résurrection f.

resuscitate [rɪ'sʌsɪteɪt] vt (MED) réanimer.

retail ['ri:teɪl] n (vente f au) détail m // cpd de or au détail // vt vendre au détail; ~**er** n détaillant/e; ~ **price** n prix m de détail.

retain [rɪ'teɪn] vt (keep) garder, conserver; (employ) engager; ~**er** n (servant) serviteur m; (fee) acompte m, provision f.

retaliate [rɪ'tælɪeɪt] vi: to ~ (against) se venger (de); **retaliation** [-'eɪʃən] n représailles fpl, vengeance f.

retarded [rɪ'tɑ:dɪd] a retardé(e).

retch [rɛtʃ] vi avoir des haut-le-cœur.

retentive [rɪ'tɛntɪv] a: ~ **memory** excellente mémoire.

retina ['rɛtɪnə] n rétine f.

retinue ['rɛtɪnju:] n suite f, cortège m.

retire [rɪ'taɪə*] vi (give up work) prendre sa retraite; (withdraw) se retirer, partir; (go to bed) (aller) se coucher; ~**d** a (person) retraité(e); ~**ment** n retraite f; **retiring** a (person) réservé(e).

retort [rɪ'tɔ:t] vi riposter.

retrace [ri:'treɪs] vt reconstituer; to ~ one's steps revenir sur ses pas.

retract [rɪ'trækt] vt (statement, claws) rétracter; (undercarriage, aerial) rentrer, escamoter // vi se rétracter; rentrer.

retrain [ri:'treɪn] vt (worker) recycler.

retread ['ri:trɛd] n (tyre) pneu rechapé.

retreat [rɪ'tri:t] n retraite f // vi battre en retraite; (flood) reculer.

retribution [rɛtrɪ'bju:ʃən] n châtiment m.

retrieval [rɪ'tri:vəl] n (see vb) récupération f; réparation f; recherche et extraction f.

retrieve [rɪ'tri:v] vt (sth lost) récupérer; (situation, honour) sauver; (error, loss) réparer; (COMPUT) rechercher; ~**r** n chien m d'arrêt.

retrospect ['rɛtrəspɛkt] n: **in** ~ rétrospectivement, après coup; ~**ive** [-'spɛktɪv] a (law) rétroactif(ive).

return [rɪ'tɜ:n] n (going or coming back) retour m; (of sth stolen etc) restitution f; (recompense) récompense f; (FINANCE: from land, shares) rapport m; (report) relevé m, rapport // cpd (journey) de retour; (Brit: ticket) aller et retour; (match) retour // vi (person etc: come back) revenir; (: go back) retourner // vt rendre; (bring back) rapporter; (send back) renvoyer; (put back) remettre; (POL: candidate) élire; ~**s** npl (COMM) recettes fpl; bénéfices mpl; **in** ~ (for) en échange (de); **by** ~ (of post) par retour (du courrier); **many happy** ~**s** (of the day)! bon anniversaire!

reunion [ri:'ju:nɪən] n réunion f.

reunite [ri:ju:'naɪt] vt réunir.

rev [rɛv] n abbr (= revolution: AUT) tour m // vb (also: ~ **up**) vt emballer // vi s'emballer.

revamp [ri:'væmp] vt (house) retaper; (firm) réorganiser.

reveal [rɪ'vi:l] vt (make known) révéler; (display) laisser voir; ~**ing** a révélateur(trice); (dress) au décolleté généreux or suggestif.

revel ['rɛvl] vi: to ~ **in sth/in doing** se délecter de qch/à faire.

revelry ['rɛvlrɪ] n festivités fpl.

revenge [rɪ'vɛndʒ] n vengeance f; (in game etc) revanche f // vt venger; to **take** ~ se venger.

revenue ['rɛvənju:] n revenu m.

reverberate [rɪ'vɜ:bəreɪt] vi (sound) retentir, se répercuter; (light) se réverbérer.

reverence ['rɛvərəns] n vénération f, révérence f.

Reverend ['rɛvərənd] a (in titles): **the** ~ **John Smith** (Anglican) le révérend John Smith; (Catholic) l'abbé (John) Smith; (Protestant) le pasteur (John) Smith.

reversal [rɪ'vɜ:sl] n (of opinion) revirement m.

reverse [rɪ'vɜːs] n contraire m, opposé m; (back) dos m, envers m; (AUT: also: ~ gear) marche f arrière // a (order, direction) opposé(e), inverse // vt (turn) renverser, retourner; (change) renverser, changer complètement; (LAW: judgment) réformer // vi (Brit AUT) faire marche arrière; **~d charge call** n (Brit TEL) communication f en PCV; **reversing lights** npl (Brit AUT) feux mpl de marche arrière or de recul.

revert [rɪ'vɜːt] vi: **to ~ to** revenir à, retourner à.

review [rɪ'vjuː] n revue f; (of book, film) critique f // vt passer en revue; faire la critique de; **~er** n critique m.

revile [rɪ'vaɪl] vt injurier.

revise [rɪ'vaɪz] vt (manuscript) revoir, corriger; (opinion) réviser, modifier; (study: subject, notes) réviser; **revision** [rɪ'vɪʒən] n révision f.

revival [rɪ'vaɪvəl] n reprise f; rétablissement m; (of faith) renouveau m.

revive [rɪ'vaɪv] vt (person) ranimer; (custom) rétablir; (hope, courage) redonner; (play, fashion) reprendre // vi (person) reprendre connaissance; (hope) renaître; (activity) reprendre.

revolt [rɪ'vəult] n révolte f // vi se révolter, se rebeller // vt révolter, dégoûter; **~ing** a dégoûtant(e).

revolution [rɛvə'luːʃən] n révolution f; (of wheel etc) tour m, révolution; **~ary** a, n révolutionnaire (m/f).

revolve [rɪ'vɔlv] vi tourner.

revolver [rɪ'vɔlvə*] n revolver m.

revolving [rɪ'vɔlvɪŋ] a (chair) pivotant(e); (light) tournant(e); ~ **door** n (porte f à) tambour m.

revulsion [rɪ'vʌlʃən] n dégoût m, répugnance f.

reward [rɪ'wɔːd] n récompense f // vt: **to ~ (for)** récompenser (de); **~ing** a (fig) qui (en) vaut la peine, gratifiant(e).

rewire [riː'waɪə*] vt (house) refaire l'installation électrique de.

reword [riː'wɜːd] vt formuler or exprimer différemment.

rheumatism ['ruːmətɪzəm] n rhumatisme m.

Rhine [raɪn] n: **the ~** le Rhin.

rhinoceros [raɪ'nɔsərəs] n rhinocéros m.

Rhone [rəun] n: **the ~** le Rhône.

rhubarb ['ruːbɑːb] n rhubarbe f.

rhyme [raɪm] n rime f; (verse) vers mpl.

rhythm ['rɪðm] n rythme m.

rib [rɪb] n (ANAT) côte f // vt (mock) taquiner.

ribald ['rɪbəld] a paillard(e).

ribbon ['rɪbən] n ruban m; **in ~s** (torn) en lambeaux.

rice [raɪs] n riz m.

rich [rɪtʃ] a riche; (gift, clothes) somptueux(euse); **the ~** npl les riches mpl; **~es** npl richesses fpl; **~ly** ad richement; (deserved, earned) largement, grandement; **~ness** n richesse f.

rickets ['rɪkɪts] n rachitisme m.

rickety ['rɪkɪtɪ] a branlant(e).

rickshaw ['rɪkʃɔː] n pousse(-pousse) m inv.

rid [rɪd], pt, pp **rid** [rɪd] vt: **to ~ sb of** débarrasser qn de; **to get ~ of** se débarrasser de.

ridden ['rɪdn] pp of ride.

riddle ['rɪdl] n (puzzle) énigme f // vt: **to be ~d with** être criblé(e) de.

ride [raɪd] n promenade f, tour m; (distance covered) trajet m // vb (pt rode, pp ridden [rəud, 'rɪdn]) vi (as sport) monter (à cheval), faire du cheval; (go somewhere: on horse, bicycle) aller (à cheval or bicyclette etc); (journey: on bicycle, motor-cycle, bus) rouler // vt (a certain horse) monter; (distance) parcourir, faire; **to ~ a horse/bicycle/camel** monter à cheval/à bicyclette/à dos de chameau; **to ~ at anchor** (NAUT) être à l'ancre; **to take sb for a ~** (fig) mener qn en bateau; rouler qn; **~r** n cavalier/ère; (in race) jockey m; (on bicycle) cycliste m/f; (on motorcycle) motocycliste m/f; (in document) annexe f, clause additionnelle.

ridge [rɪdʒ] n (of hill) faîte m; (of roof, mountain) arête f; (on object) strie f.

ridicule ['rɪdɪkjuːl] n ridicule m; dérision f.

ridiculous [rɪ'dɪkjuləs] a ridicule.

riding ['raɪdɪŋ] n équitation f; ~ **school** n manège m, école f d'équitation.

rife [raɪf] a répandu(e); ~ **with** abondant(e) en.

riffraff ['rɪfræf] n racaille f.

rifle ['raɪfl] n fusil m (à canon rayé) // vt vider, dévaliser; ~ **range** n champ m de tir; (indoor) stand m de tir.

rift [rɪft] n fente f, fissure f; (fig: disagreement) désaccord m.

rig [rɪg] n (also: **oil ~**: on land) derrick m; (: at sea) plate-forme pétrolière // vt (election etc) truquer; **to ~ out** vt (Brit) habiller; (: pej) fringuer, attifer; **to ~ up** vt arranger, faire avec des moyens de fortune; **~ging** n (NAUT) gréement m.

right [raɪt] a (true) juste, exact(e); (correctly chosen: answer, road etc) bon(bonne); (suitable) approprié(e), convenable; (just) juste, équitable; (morally good) bien inv; (not left) droit(e) // n (title, claim) droit m; (not left) droite f // ad (answer) correctement; (not on the left) à droite // vt redresser // excl bon!; **to be ~** (person) avoir raison; (answer) être juste or correct(e); **by ~s** en toute justice; **on the ~** à droite; **to be in the ~** avoir raison; ~ **now** en ce moment même; tout de suite; ~ **against the wall** tout contre le mur; ~ **ahead** tout droit; droit devant; ~ **in the middle** en plein milieu; ~ **away** immédiatement; ~ **angle** *n* angle droit; ~**eous** ['raɪtʃəs] *a* droit(e), vertueux(euse); *(anger)* justifié(e); ~**ful** *a* *(heir)* légitime; ~**handed** *a* *(person)* droitier(ère); ~**hand man** *n* bras droit *(fig)*; ~**hand side** *n* côté droit; ~**ly** *ad* bien, correctement; *(with reason)* à juste titre; ~ **of way** *n* droit *m* de passage; *(AUT)* priorité *f*; ~**-wing** *a* *(POL)* de droite.

rigid ['rɪdʒɪd] *a* rigide; *(principle)* strict(e).

rigmarole ['rɪgmərəʊl] *n* galimatias *m*, comédie *f*.

rigorous ['rɪgərəs] *a* rigoureux(euse).

rile [raɪl] *vt* agacer.

rim [rɪm] *n* bord *m*; *(of spectacles)* monture *f*; *(of wheel)* jante *f*.

rind [raɪnd] *n* *(of bacon)* couenne *f*; *(of lemon, cheese)* écorce *f*.

ring [rɪŋ] *n* anneau *m*; *(on finger)* bague *f*; *(also: wedding ~)* alliance *f*; *(for napkin)* rond *m*; *(of people, objects)* cercle *m*; *(of spies)* réseau *m*; *(of smoke etc)* rond; *(arena)* piste *f*, arène *f*; *(for boxing)* ring *m*; *(sound of bell)* sonnerie *f*; *(telephone call)* coup *m* de téléphone *f*; *vb* *(pt* **rang**, *pp* **rung)** *vi* *(person, bell)* sonner; *(also: ~ out: voice, words)* retentir; *(TEL)* téléphoner // *vt* *(Brit TEL: also: ~ up)* téléphoner à; **to ~ the bell** sonner; **to ~ back** *vt, vi* *(TEL)* rappeler; **to ~ off** *vi* *(Brit TEL)* raccrocher; ~**ing** *n* tintement *m*; sonnerie *f*; *(in ears)* bourdonnement *m*; ~**ing tone** *n* *(Brit TEL)* sonnerie *f*; ~**leader** *n* *(of gang)* chef *m*, meneur *m*.

ringlets ['rɪŋlɪts] *npl* anglaises *fpl*.

ring road *n* *(Brit)* route *f* de ceinture.

rink [rɪŋk] *n* *(also: ice ~)* patinoire *f*.

rinse [rɪns] *vt* rincer.

riot ['raɪət] *n* émeute *f*, bagarres *fpl* // *vi* faire une émeute, manifester avec violence; **to run ~** se déchaîner; ~**ous** *a* tapageur(euse); tordant(e).

rip [rɪp] *n* déchirure *f* // *vt* déchirer // *vi* se déchirer; ~**cord** *n* poignée *f* d'ouverture.

ripe [raɪp] *a* *(fruit)* mûr(e); *(cheese)* fait(e); ~**n** *vt* mûrir // *vi* mûrir; se faire.

rip-off ['rɪpɔf] *n* *(col)*: it's a ~! c'est du vol manifeste!

ripple ['rɪpl] *n* ride *f*, ondulation *f*; égrènement *m*, cascade *f* // *vi* se rider, onduler // *vt* rider, faire onduler.

rise [raɪz] *n* *(slope)* côte *f*, pente *f*; *(hill)* élévation *f*; *(increase: in wages: Brit)* augmentation *f*; *(: in prices, temperature)* hausse *f*, augmentation; *(fig: to power etc)* essor *m*, ascension *f* // *vi* *(pt*

rose, *pp* **risen** ['rəʊz, rɪzn]) s'élever, monter; *(prices)* augmenter, monter; *(waters, river)* monter; *(sun, wind, person: from chair, bed)* se lever; *(also: ~ up: rebel)* se révolter; se rebeller; **to give ~ to** donner lieu à; **to ~ to the occasion** se montrer à la hauteur; **rising** *a* *(increasing: number, prices)* en hausse; *(tide)* montant(e); *(sun, moon)* levant(e) // *n* *(uprising)* soulèvement *m*, insurrection *f*.

risk [rɪsk] *n* risque *m*; danger *m* // *vt* risquer; **at ~** en danger; **at one's own ~** à ses risques et périls; ~**y** a risqué(e).

rissole ['rɪsəʊl] *n* croquette *f*.

rite [raɪt] *n* rite *m*; **last ~s** derniers sacrements.

ritual ['rɪtjʊəl] *a* rituel(le) // *n* rituel *m*.

rival ['raɪvl] *n* rival/e; *(in business)* concurrent/e // *a* rival(e); qui fait concurrence // *vt* être en concurrence avec; **to ~ sb/sth in** rivaliser avec qn/qch de; ~**ry** *n* rivalité *f*, concurrence *f*.

river ['rɪvə*] *n* rivière *f*; *(major, also fig)* fleuve *m* // *cpd* *(port, traffic)* fluvial(e); **up/down ~** en amont/aval; ~**bank** *n* rive *f*, berge *f*.

rivet ['rɪvɪt] *n* rivet *m* // *vt* riveter; *(fig)* river, fixer.

Riviera [rɪvɪ'eərə] *n*: **the (French) ~** la Côte d'Azur; **the Italian ~** la Riviera (italienne).

road [rəʊd] *n* route *f*; *(small)* chemin *m*; *(in town)* rue *f*; *(fig)* chemin, voie *f*; **major/minor ~** route principale *or* à priorité/voie secondaire; ~**block** *n* barrage routier; ~**hog** *n* chauffard *m*; ~ **map** *n* carte routière; ~ **safety** *n* sécurité routière; ~**side** *n* bord *m* de la route, bas-côté *m*; ~**sign** *n* panneau *m* de signalisation; ~**way** *n* chaussée *f*; ~**works** *npl* travaux *mpl* (de réfection des routes); ~**worthy** *a* en bon état de marche.

roam [rəʊm] *vi* errer, vagabonder // *vt* parcourir, errer par.

roar [rɔ:*] *n* rugissement *m*; *(of crowd)* hurlements *mpl*; *(of vehicle, thunder, storm)* grondement *m* // *vi* rugir; hurler; gronder; **to ~ with laughter** éclater de rire; **to do a ~ing trade** faire des affaires d'or.

roast [rəʊst] *n* rôti *m* // *vt* *(meat)* (faire) rôtir; ~ **beef** *n* rôti *m* de bœuf, rosbif *m*.

rob [rɔb] *vt* *(person)* voler; *(bank)* dévaliser; **to ~ sb of sth** voler *or* dérober qch à qn; *(fig: deprive)* priver qn de qch; ~**ber** *n* bandit *m*, voleur *m*; ~**bery** *n* vol *m*.

robe [rəʊb] *n* *(for ceremony)* robe *f*; *(also: bath ~)* peignoir *m*; *(US)* couverture *f* // *vt* revêtir (d'une robe).

robin ['rɔbɪn] *n* rouge-gorge *m*.

robot ['rəʊbɔt] *n* robot *m*.

robust [rəu'bʌst] *a* robuste; (*material, appetite*) solide.

rock [rɔk] *n* (*substance*) roche *f*, roc *m*; (*boulder*) rocher *m*; roche; (*Brit: sweet*) ≈ sucre *m* d'orge // *vt* (*swing gently: cradle*) balancer; (*: child*) bercer; (*shake*) ébranler, secouer // *vi* (*se*) balancer; être ébranlé(e) *or* secoué(e); **on the ~s** (*drink*) avec des glaçons; (*ship*) sur les écueils; (*marriage etc*) en train de craquer; **~ and roll** *n* rock (and roll) *m*, rock'n'roll *m*; **~-bottom** *n* (*fig*) niveau le plus bas // *a* (*fig: prices*) sacrifié(e); **~ery** *n* (*jardin m de*) rocaille *f*.

rocket ['rɔkɪt] *n* fusée *f*; (*MIL*) fusée, roquette *f*.

rocking ['rɔkɪŋ]: **~ chair** *n* fauteuil m à bascule; **~ horse** *n* cheval m à bascule.

rocky ['rɔkɪ] *a* (*hill*) rocheux(euse); (*path*) rocailleux(euse); (*unsteady: table*) branlant(e).

rod [rɔd] *n* (*metallic*) tringle *f*; (*TECH*) tige *f*; (*wooden*) baguette *f*; (*also: fishing ~*) canne *f* à pêche.

rode [rəud] *pt of* **ride**.

rodent ['rəudnt] *n* rongeur *m*.

rodeo ['rəudɪəu] *n* rodéo *m*.

roe [rəu] *n* (*species: also: ~ deer*) chevreuil *m*; (*of fish, also: hard ~*) œufs *mpl* de poisson; **soft ~** laitance *f*.

rogue [rəug] *n* coquin/e.

role [rəul] *n* rôle *m*.

roll [rəul] *n* rouleau *m*; (*of banknotes*) liasse *f*; (*also: bread ~*) petit pain; (*register*) liste *f*; (*sound: of drums etc*) roulement *m*; (*movement: of ship*) roulis *m* // *vt* rouler; (*also: ~ up: string*) enrouler; (*also: ~ out: pastry*) étendre au rouleau // *vi* rouler; (*wheel*) tourner; **to ~ about** *or* **around** *vi* rouler çà et là; (*person*) se rouler par terre; **to ~ by** *vi* (*time*) s'écouler, passer; **to ~ in** *vi* (*mail, cash*) affluer; **to ~ over** *vi* se retourner; **to ~ up** *vi* (*col: arrive*) arriver, s'amener // *vt* (*carpet*) rouler; **~ call** *n* appel *m*; **~er** *n* rouleau *m*; (*wheel*) roulette *f*; **~er coaster** *n* montagnes *fpl* russes; **~er skates** *npl* patins *mpl* à roulettes.

rolling ['rəulɪŋ] *a* (*landscape*) onduleux(euse); **~ pin** *n* rouleau m à pâtisserie; **~ stock** *n* (*RAIL*) matériel roulant.

ROM [rɔm] *n abbr* (= *read only memory*) mémoire morte.

Roman ['rəumən] *a* romain(e) // *n* Romain/e; **~ Catholic** *a, n* catholique (*m/f*).

romance [rə'mæns] *n* histoire *f* (*or film m or aventure f*) romanesque; (*charm*) poésie *f*; (*love affair*) idylle *f*.

Romania [rəu'meɪnɪə] *n* = **Rumania**.

Roman numeral *n* chiffre romain.

romantic [rə'mæntɪk] *a* romantique; sentimental(e).

Rome [rəum] *n* Rome.

romp [rɔmp] *n* jeux bruyants // *vi* (*also: ~ about*) s'ébattre, jouer bruyamment.

rompers ['rɔmpəz] *npl* barboteuse *f*.

roof, *pl* **~s** [ru:f] *n* toit *m*; (*of tunnel, cave*) plafond *m* // *vt* couvrir (d'un toit); **the ~ of the mouth** la voûte du palais; **~ing** *n* toiture *f*; **~ rack** *n* (*AUT*) galerie *f*.

rook [ruk] *n* (*bird*) freux *m*; (*CHESS*) tour *f*.

room [ru:m] *n* (*in house*) pièce *f*; (*also: bed~*) chambre *f* (à coucher); (*in school etc*) salle *f*; (*space*) place *f*; **~s** *npl* (*lodging*) meublé *m*; **'~s to let'**, (*US*) **'~s for rent'** 'chambres à louer'; **~ing house** *n* (*US*) maison *f or* immeuble *m* de rapport; **~mate** *n* camarade *m/f* de chambre; **~ service** *n* service m des chambres (*dans un hôtel*); **~y** *a* spacieux(euse); (*garment*) ample.

roost [ru:st] *n* juchoir *m* // *vi* se jucher.

rooster ['ru:stə*] *n* coq *m*.

root [ru:t] *n* (*BOT, MATH*) racine *f*; (*fig: of problem*) origine *f*, fond *m* // *vi* (*plant*) s'enraciner; **to ~ about** *vi* (*fig*) fouiller; **to ~ for** *vt fus* applaudir; **to ~ out** *vt* extirper.

rope [rəup] *n* corde *f*; (*NAUT*) cordage *m* // *vt* (*box*) corder; (*climbers*) encorder; **to ~ sb in** (*fig*) embringuer qn; **to know the ~s** (*fig*) être au courant, connaître les ficelles.

rosary ['rəuzərɪ] *n* chapelet *m*.

rose [rəuz] *pt of* **rise** // *n* rose *f*; (*also: ~bush*) rosier *m*; (*on watering can*) pomme *f* // *a* rose.

rosé ['rəuzeɪ] *n* rosé *m*.

rose: **~bud** *n* bouton *m* de rose; **~bush** *n* rosier *m*.

rosemary ['rəuzmərɪ] *n* romarin *m*.

roster ['rɔstə*] *n*: **duty ~** tableau m de service.

rostrum ['rɔstrəm] *n* tribune *f* (*pour un orateur etc*).

rosy ['rəuzɪ] *a* rose; **a ~ future** un bel avenir.

rot [rɔt] *n* (*decay*) pourriture *f*; (*fig: pej*) idioties *fpl*, balivernes *fpl* // *vt, vi* pourrir.

rota ['rəutə] *n* liste *f*, tableau *m* de service; **on a ~ basis** par roulement.

rotary ['rəutərɪ] *a* rotatif(ive).

rotate [rəu'teɪt] *vt* (*revolve*) faire tourner; (*change round: crops*) alterner; (*: jobs*) faire à tour de rôle // *vi* (*revolve*) tourner; **rotating** *a* (*movement*) tournant(e).

rote [rəut] *n*: **by ~** machinalement, par cœur.

rotten ['rɔtn] *a* (*decayed*) pourri(e); (*dishonest*) corrompu(e); (*col: bad*) mauvais(e), moche; **to feel ~** (*ill*) être mal fichu(e).

rough [rʌf] a (*cloth, skin*) rêche, rugueux(euse); (*terrain*) accidenté(e); (*path*) rocailleux(euse); (*voice*) rauque, rude; (*person, manner: coarse*) rude, fruste; (*: violent*) brutal(e); (*district, weather*) mauvais(e); (*plan*) ébauché(e); (*guess*) approximatif(ive) // n (*GOLF*) rough m; **to ~ it** vivre à la dure; **to sleep ~** (*Brit*) coucher à la dure; **~age** n fibres fpl diététiques; **~-and-ready** a rudimentaire; **~cast** n crépi m; **~ copy, ~ draft** n brouillon m; **~ly** ad (*handle*) rudement, brutalement; (*make*) grossièrement; (*approximately*) à peu près, en gros.

roulette [ru:'lɛt] n roulette f.

Roumania [ru:'meɪnɪə] n = **Rumania**.

round [raund] a rond(e) // n rond m, cercle m; (*Brit: of toast*) tranche f; (*duty: of policeman, milkman etc*) tournée f; (*: of doctor*) visites fpl; (*game: of cards, in competition*) partie f; (*BOXING*) round m; (*of talks*) série f // vt (*corner*) tourner; (*bend*) prendre; (*cape*) doubler // prep autour de // ad: **all ~** tout autour; **the long way ~** (par) le chemin le plus long; **all the year ~** toute l'année; **it's just ~ the corner** c'est juste après le coin; (*fig*) c'est tout près; **~ the clock** ad 24 heures sur 24; **to go ~** faire le tour or un détour; **to go ~ to sb's (house)** aller chez qn; **to go ~ the back** passez par derrière; **to go ~ a house** visiter une maison, faire le tour d'une maison; **enough to go ~** assez pour tout le monde; **to go the ~s** (*disease, story*) circuler; **~ of ammunition** n cartouche f; **~ of applause** n ban m, applaudissements mpl; **~ of drinks** n tournée f; **~ of sandwiches** n sandwich m; **to ~ off** vt (*speech etc*) terminer; **to ~ up** vt rassembler; (*criminals*) effectuer une rafle de; (*prices*) arrondir (au chiffre supérieur); **~about** n (*Brit AUT*) rond-point m (à sens giratoire); (*: at fair*) manège m (de chevaux de bois) // a (*route, means*) détourné(e); **~ers** npl (*game*) ≈ balle f au camp; **~ly** ad (*fig*) tout net, carrément; **~-shouldered** a au dos rond; **~ trip** n (voyage m) aller et retour m; **~-up** n rassemblement m; (*of criminals*) rafle f.

rouse [rauz] vt (*wake up*) réveiller; (*stir up*) susciter; provoquer; éveiller; **rousing** a (*welcome*) enthousiaste.

rout [raut] n (*MIL*) déroute f.

route [ru:t] n itinéraire m; (*of bus*) parcours m; (*of trade, shipping*) route f; **~ map** n (*Brit: for journey*) croquis m d'itinéraire.

routine [ru:'ti:n] a (*work*) ordinaire, courant(e); (*procedure*) d'usage // n (*pej*) routine f; (*THEATRE*) numéro m; **daily ~** occupations journalières.

roving ['rəuvɪŋ] a (*life*) vagabond(e).

row [rəu] n (*line*) rangée f; (*of people, seats, KNITTING*) rang m; (*behind one another: of cars, people*) file f; [rau] (*noise*) vacarme m; (*dispute*) dispute f, querelle f; (*scolding*) réprimande f, savon m // vi (*in boat*) ramer; (*as sport*) faire de l'aviron; [rau] se disputer, se quereller // vt (*boat*) faire aller à la rame or à l'aviron; **in a ~** (*fig*) d'affilée; **~boat** n (*US*) canot m (à rames).

rowdy ['raudɪ] a chahuteur(euse); bagarreur(euse) // n voyou m.

rowing ['rəuɪŋ] n canotage m; (*as sport*) aviron m; **~ boat** n (*Brit*) canot m (à rames).

royal ['rɔɪəl] a royal(e); **R~ Air Force (RAF)** n armée de l'air britannique.

royalty ['rɔɪəltɪ] n (*royal persons*) (membres mpl de la) famille royale; (*payment: to author*) droits mpl d'auteur; (*: to inventor*) royalties fpl.

r.p.m. abbr (*AUT: = revs per minute*) tr/mn (= tours/minute).

R.S.V.P. abbr (= *répondez s'il vous plaît*) R.S.V.P.

Rt Hon. abbr (*Brit: = Right Honourable*) titre donné aux députés de la Chambre des communes.

rub [rʌb] n (*with cloth*) coup m de chiffon or de torchon; (*on person*) friction f // vt frotter; frictionner; **to ~ sb up** or (*US*) **~ sb the wrong way** prendre qn à rebrousse-poil; **to ~ off** vi partir; **to ~ off on** vt fus déteindre sur; **to ~ out** vt effacer.

rubber ['rʌbə*] n caoutchouc m; (*Brit: eraser*) gomme f (à effacer); **~ band** n élastique m; **~ plant** n caoutchouc m (*plante verte*).

rubbish ['rʌbɪʃ] n (*from household*) ordures fpl; (*fig: pej*) choses fpl sans valeur; camelote f; bêtises fpl, idioties fpl; **~ bin** n (*Brit*) boîte f à ordures, poubelle f; **~ dump** n (*in town*) décharge publique, dépotoir m.

rubble ['rʌbl] n décombres mpl; (*smaller*) gravats mpl.

ruby ['ru:bɪ] n rubis m.

rucksack ['rʌksæk] n sac m à dos.

ructions ['rʌkʃənz] npl grabuge m.

rudder ['rʌdə*] n gouvernail m.

ruddy ['rʌdɪ] a (*face*) coloré(e); (*col: damned*) sacré(e), fichu(e).

rude [ru:d] a (*impolite: person*) impoli(e); (*: word, manners*) grossier(ère); (*shocking*) indécent(e), inconvenant(e).

rueful ['ru:ful] a triste.

ruffian ['rʌfɪən] n brute f, voyou m.

ruffle ['rʌfl] vt (*hair*) ébouriffer; (*clothes*) chiffonner; (*water*) agiter; (*fig: person*) émouvoir, faire perdre son flegme à.

rug [rʌg] n petit tapis; (*Brit: for knees*) couverture f.

rugby ['rʌgbɪ] n (*also: ~ football*) rugby

m.

rugged ['rʌgɪd] *a (landscape)* accidenté(e); *(features, kindness, character)* rude; *(determination)* farouche.

rugger ['rʌgə*] *n (Brit col)* rugby *m.*

ruin ['ru:ɪn] *n* ruine *f // vt* ruiner; *(spoil: clothes)* abîmer; **~s** *npl* ruine(s).

rule [ru:l] *n* règle *f; (regulation)* règlement *m; (government)* autorité *f,* gouvernement *m // vt (country)* gouverner; *(person)* dominer; *(decide)* décider // vi* commander; décider; *(LAW)* statuer; **as a ~** normalement, en règle générale; **to ~ out** *vt* exclure; **~d** *a (paper)* réglé(e); **~r** *n (sovereign)* souverain/e; *(leader)* chef *m* (d'État); *(for measuring)* règle *f;* **ruling** *a (party)* dirigeant(e) // *n (LAW)* décision *f.*

rum [rʌm] *n* rhum *m // a (col)* bizarre.

Rumania [ru:'meɪnɪə] *n* Roumanie *f.*

rumble ['rʌmbl] *vi* gronder; *(stomach, pipe)* gargouiller.

rummage ['rʌmɪdʒ] *vi* fouiller.

rumour, *(US)* **rumor** ['ru:mə*] *n* rumeur *f,* bruit *m* (qui court) // *vt:* **it is ~ed that** le bruit court que.

rump [rʌmp] *n (of animal)* croupe *f;* **~ steak** *n* rumsteck *m.*

rumpus ['rʌmpəs] *n (col)* tapage *m,* chahut *m; (quarrel)* prise *f* de bec.

run [rʌn] *n (pas m de)* course *f; (outing)* tour *m* or promenade *f* (en voiture); parcours *m,* trajet *m; (series)* suite *f,* série *f; (THEATRE)* série de représentations; *(SKI)* piste *f; (in tights, stockings)* maille filée, échelle *f // vb (pt ran, pp run)* *vt (operate: business)* diriger; *(: competition, course)* organiser; *(: hotel, house)* tenir; *(COMPUT)* exécuter; *(force through: rope, pipe):* **to ~ sth through** faire passer qch à travers; *(to pass: hand, finger):* **to ~ sth over** promener or passer qch sur; *(water, bath)* faire couler // vi* courir; *(pass: road etc)* passer; *(work: machine, factory)* marcher; *(bus, train: operate)* être en service; *(: travel)* circuler; *(: continue: play)* se jouer; *(: contract)* être valide; *(slide: drawer etc)* glisser; *(flow: river, bath)* couler; *(colours, washing)* déteindre; *(in election)* être candidat, se présenter; **there was a ~ on** *(meat, tickets)* les gens se sont rués sur; **in the long ~** à longue échéance; à la longue; en fin de compte; **on the ~** en fuite; **I'll ~ you to the station** je vais vous emmener or conduire à la gare; **to ~ a risk** courir un risque; **to ~ about** or **around** *vi (children)* courir çà et là; **to ~ across** *vt fus (find)* trouver par hasard; **to ~ away** *vi* s'enfuir; **to ~ down** *vt (production)* réduire progressivement; *(factory)* réduire progressivement la production de; *(AUT)* renverser; *(criticize)* critiquer, dénigrer; **to be ~ down** *(person: tired)* être fatigué(e) *or* à plat; **to ~ in** *vt (Brit: car)* roder; **to ~ into** *vt fus (meet: person)* rencontrer par hasard; *(: trouble)* se heurter à; *(collide with)* heurter; **to ~ off** *vi* s'enfuir // *vt (water)* laisser s'écouler; **to ~ out** *vi (person)* sortir en courant; *(liquid)* couler; *(lease)* expirer; *(money)* être épuisé(e); **to ~ out of** *vt fus* se trouver à court de; **to ~ over** *vt (AUT)* écraser // *vt fus (revise)* revoir, reprendre; **to ~ through** *vt fus (instructions)* reprendre, revoir; **to ~ up** *vt (debt)* laisser accumuler; **to ~ up against** *(difficulties)* se heurter à; **~away** *a (horse)* emballé(e); *(truck)* fou(folle); *(inflation)* galopant(e).

rung [rʌŋ] *pp of* **ring** // *n (of ladder)* barreau *m.*

runner ['rʌnə*] *n (in race: person)* coureur/euse; *(: horse)* partant *m; (on sledge)* patin *m; (for drawer etc)* coulisseau *m; (carpet: in hall etc)* chemin *m;* **~ bean** *n (Brit)* haricot *m* (à rames); **~-up** *n* second/e.

running ['rʌnɪŋ] *n* course *f;* direction *f;* organisation *f;* marche *f,* fonctionnement *m // a (water)* courant(e); *(costs)* de gestion; *(commentary)* suivi(e); **to be in/out of the ~ for sth** être/ne pas être sur les rangs pour qch; **6 days** ~ **6 jours** de suite.

runny ['rʌnɪ] *a* qui coule.

run-of-the-mill ['rʌnəvðə'mɪl] *a* ordinaire, banal(e).

runt [rʌnt] *n (also pej)* avorton *m.*

run-up ['rʌnʌp] *n:* **~ to sth** *(election etc)* période *f* précédant qch.

runway ['rʌnweɪ] *n (AVIAT)* piste *f* (d'envol or d'atterrissage).

rupee [ru:'pi:] *n* roupie *f.*

rupture ['rʌptʃə*] *n (MED)* hernie *f.*

rural ['ruərl] *a* rural(e).

rush [rʌʃ] *n* course précipitée; *(of crowd)* ruée *f,* bousculade *f; (hurry)* hâte *f,* bousculade; *(current)* flot *m; (BOT)* jonc *m // vt* transporter or envoyer d'urgence; *(attack: town etc)* prendre d'assaut // vi* se précipiter; **~ hour** *n* heures *fpl* de pointe or d'affluence.

rusk [rʌsk] *n* biscotte *f.*

Russia ['rʌʃə] *n* Russie *f;* **~n** *a* russe // *n* Russe *m/f; (LING)* russe *m.*

rust [rʌst] *n* rouille *f // vi* rouiller.

rustic ['rʌstɪk] *a* rustique.

rustle ['rʌsl] *vi* bruire, produire un bruissement // *vt (paper)* froisser; *(US: cattle)* voler.

rustproof ['rʌstpru:f] *a* inoxydable.

rusty ['rʌstɪ] *a* rouillé(e).

rut [rʌt] *n* ornière *f; (ZOOL)* rut *m;* **to be in a ~** suivre l'ornière, s'encroûter.

ruthless ['ru:θlɪs] a sans pitié, impitoyable.

rye [raɪ] n seigle m.

S

Sabbath ['sæbəθ] n (Jewish) sabbat m; (Christian) dimanche m.

sabotage ['sæbətɑ:ʒ] n sabotage m // vt saboter.

saccharin(e) ['sækərɪn] n saccharine f.

sachet ['sæʃeɪ] n sachet m.

sack [sæk] n (bag) sac m // vt (dismiss) renvoyer, mettre à la porte; (plunder) piller, mettre à sac; **to get the ~** être renvoyé(e) or mis(e) à la porte; **~ing** n toile f à sac; renvoi m.

sacrament ['sækrəmənt] n sacrement m.

sacred ['seɪkrɪd] a sacré(e).

sacrifice ['sækrɪfaɪs] n sacrifice m // vt sacrifier.

sad [sæd] a (unhappy) triste; (deplorable) triste, fâcheux(euse).

saddle ['sædl] n selle f // vt (horse) seller; **to be ~d with sth** (col) avoir qch sur les bras; **~bag** n sacoche f.

sadistic [sə'dɪstɪk] a sadique.

sadness ['sædnɪs] n tristesse f.

s.a.e. n abbr = stamped addressed envelope.

safe [seɪf] a (out of danger) hors de danger, en sécurité; (not dangerous) sans danger; (cautious) prudent(e); (sure: bet etc) assuré(e) // n coffre-fort m; **~ from** à l'abri de; **~ and sound** sain(e) et sauf(sauve); **(just) to be on the ~ side** pour plus de sûreté, par précaution; **~conduct** n sauf-conduit m; **~deposit** n (vault) dépôt de coffres-forts; (box) coffre-fort m; **~guard** n sauvegarde f, protection f // vt sauvegarder, protéger; **~keeping** n bonne garde; **~ly** ad sans danger, sans risque; (without mishap) sans accident.

safety ['seɪftɪ] n sécurité f; **~ belt** n ceinture f de sécurité; **~ pin** n épingle f de sûreté or de nourrice; **~ valve** n soupape f de sûreté.

sag [sæg] vi s'affaisser, fléchir; pendre.

sage [seɪdʒ] n (herb) sauge f; (man) sage m.

Sagittarius [sædʒɪ'tɛərɪəs] n le Sagittaire.

Sahara [sə'hɑ:rə] n: **the ~** (Desert) le (désert du) Sahara.

said [sɛd] pt, pp of say.

sail [seɪl] n (on boat) voile f; (trip): **to go for a ~** faire un tour en bateau // vt (boat) manœuvrer, piloter // vi (travel: ship) avancer, naviguer; (: passenger) aller or se rendre (en bateau); (set off) partir, prendre la mer; (SPORT) faire de la voile; **they ~ed into Le Havre** ils sont

entrés dans le port du Havre; **to ~ through** vi, vt fus (fig) réussir haut la main; **~boat** n (US) bateau m à voiles, voilier m; **~ing** n (SPORT) voile f; **to go ~ing** faire de la voile; **~ing ship** n grand voilier; **~or** n marin m, matelot m.

saint [seɪnt] n saint/e.

sake [seɪk] n: **for the ~ of** pour (l'amour de), dans l'intérêt de; par égard pour.

salad ['sæləd] n salade f; **~ bowl** n saladier m; **~ cream** n (Brit) (sorte de) mayonnaise f; **~ dressing** n vinaigrette f.

salary ['sælərɪ] n salaire m, traitement m.

sale [seɪl] n vente f; (at reduced prices) soldes mpl; **'for ~'** 'à vendre'; **on ~** en vente; **on ~ or return** vendu(e) avec faculté de retour; **~room** n salle f des ventes; **~s assistant**, (US) **~s clerk** n vendeur/euse; **~sman** n vendeur m; (representative) représentant m de commerce; **~swoman** n vendeuse f.

salient ['seɪlɪənt] a saillant(e).

sallow ['sæləu] a cireux(euse).

salmon ['sæmən] n (pl inv) saumon m.

saloon [sə'lu:n] n (US) bar m; (Brit AUT) berline f; (ship's lounge) salon m.

salt [sɔlt] n sel m // vt saler // cpd de sel; (CULIN) salé(e); **to ~ away** vt (col: money) mettre de côté; **~ cellar** n salière f; **~water** a (d'eau) de mer; **~y** a salé(e).

salute [sə'lu:t] n salut m // vt saluer.

salvage ['sælvɪdʒ] n (saving) sauvetage m; (things saved) biens sauvés or récupérés // vt sauver, récupérer.

salvation [sæl'veɪʃən] n salut m; **S~ Army** n Armée f du Salut.

same [seɪm] a même // pronoun: **the ~** le(la) même, les mêmes; **the ~ book as** le même livre que; **at the ~ time** en même temps; **all or just the ~** tout de même, quand même; **to do the ~** faire de même, en faire autant; **to do the ~ as sb** faire comme qn; **the ~ to you!** et à vous de même!; (after insult) toi-même!

sample ['sɑ:mpl] n échantillon m; (MED) prélèvement m // vt (food, wine) goûter.

sanctimonious [sæŋktɪ'məunɪəs] a moralisateur(trice).

sanction ['sæŋkʃən] n sanction f.

sanctity ['sæŋktɪtɪ] n sainteté f, caractère sacré.

sanctuary ['sæŋktjuərɪ] n (holy place) sanctuaire m; (refuge) asile m; (for wild life) réserve f.

sand [sænd] n sable m // vt sabler.

sandal ['sændl] n sandale f.

sandbox ['sændbɔks] n (US) = sandpit.

sandcastle ['sændkɑ:sl] n château m de sable.

sandpaper ['sændpeɪpə*] n papier m de verre.

sandpit ['sændpɪt] n (for children) tas m de sable.

sandstone ['sændstəʊn] n grès m.

sandwich ['sændwɪtʃ] n sandwich m // vt (also: ~ in) intercaler; **cheese/ham** ~ sandwich au fromage/jambon; ~ **board** n panneau publicitaire (porté par un homme-sandwich); ~ **course** n (Brit) cours m de formation professionnelle.

sandy ['sændɪ] a sablonneux(euse); couvert(e) de sable; (colour) sable inv, blond roux inv.

sane [seɪn] a (person) sain(e) d'esprit; (outlook) sensé(e), sain(e).

sang [sæŋ] pt of **sing**.

sanitary ['sænɪtərɪ] a (system, arrangements) sanitaire; (clean) hygiénique; ~ **towel**, (US) ~ **napkin** n serviette f hygiénique.

sanitation [sænɪ'teɪʃən] n (in house) installations fpl sanitaires; (in town) système m sanitaire; ~ **department** n (US) service m de voirie.

sanity ['sænɪtɪ] n santé mentale; (common sense) bon sens.

sank [sæŋk] pt of **sink**.

Santa Claus [sæntə'klɔːz] n le Père Noël.

sap [sæp] n (of plants) sève f // vt (strength) saper, miner.

sapling ['sæplɪŋ] n jeune arbre m.

sapphire ['sæfaɪə*] n saphir m.

sarcasm ['sɑːkæzm] n sarcasme m, raillerie f.

sardine [sɑː'diːn] n sardine f.

Sardinia [sɑː'dɪnɪə] n Sardaigne f.

sash [sæʃ] n écharpe f.

sat [sæt] pt, pp of **sit**.

satchel ['sætʃl] n cartable m.

sated ['seɪtɪd] a repu(e); blasé(e).

satellite ['sætəlaɪt] a, n satellite (m).

satin ['sætɪn] n satin m // a en or de satin, satiné(e).

satire ['sætaɪə*] n satire f.

satisfaction [sætɪs'fækʃən] n satisfaction f.

satisfactory [sætɪs'fæktərɪ] a satisfaisant(e).

satisfy ['sætɪsfaɪ] vt satisfaire, contenter; (convince) convaincre, persuader; ~**ing** a satisfaisant(e).

Saturday ['sætədɪ] n samedi m.

sauce [sɔːs] n sauce f; ~**pan** n casserole f.

saucer ['sɔːsə*] n soucoupe f.

saucy ['sɔːsɪ] a impertinent(e).

Saudi ['saʊdɪ]: ~ **Arabia** n Arabie Saoudite; ~ **(Arabian)** a saoudien(ne) // n Saoudien/ne.

sauna ['sɔːnə] n sauna m.

saunter ['sɔːntə*] vi: to ~ to aller en flânant or se balader jusqu'à.

sausage ['sɔsɪdʒ] n saucisse f; ~ **roll** n friand m.

savage ['sævɪdʒ] a (cruel, fierce) brutal(e), féroce; (primitive) primitif(ive), sauvage // n sauvage m/f // vt attaquer férocement.

save [seɪv] vt (person, belongings) sauver; (money) mettre de côté, économiser; (time) (faire) gagner; (food) garder; (COMPUT) sauvegarder; (avoid: trouble) éviter // vi (also: ~ up) mettre de l'argent de côté // n (SPORT) arrêt m (du ballon) // prep sauf, à l'exception de.

saving ['seɪvɪŋ] n économie f // a: **the** ~ **grace** of ce qui rachète; ~**s** npl économies fpl; ~**s bank** n caisse f d'épargne.

saviour, (US) **savior** ['seɪvjə*] n sauveur m.

savour, (US) **savor** ['seɪvə*] vt savourer; ~**y** a savoureux(euse); (dish: not sweet) salé(e).

saw [sɔː] pt of **see** // n (tool) scie f // vt (pt **sawed**, pp **sawed** or **sawn** [sɔːn]) scier; ~**dust** n sciure f; ~**mill** n scierie f; ~**n-off shotgun** n carabine f à canon scié.

saxophone ['sæksəfəʊn] n saxophone m.

say [seɪ] n: to have one's ~ dire ce qu'on a à dire; to have a or some ~ in sth avoir son mot à dire dans qch // vt (pt, pp **said**) dire; **could you** ~ **that again?** pourriez-vous répéter ceci?; **that goes without** ~**ing** cela va sans dire, cela va de soi; ~**ing** n dicton m, proverbe m.

scab [skæb] n croûte f; (pej) jaune m.

scaffold ['skæfəʊld] n échafaud m; ~**ing** n échafaudage m.

scald [skɔːld] n brûlure f // vt ébouillanter.

scale [skeɪl] n (of fish) écaille f; (MUS) gamme f; (of ruler, thermometer etc) graduation f, échelle (graduée); (of salaries, fees etc) barème m; (of map, also size, extent) échelle // vt (mountain) escalader; ~**s** npl balance f; (larger) bascule f; **on a large** ~ sur une grande échelle, en grand; ~ **of charges** tableau m des tarifs; (ECON) barème m des redevances; **to** ~ **down** vt réduire; ~ **model** n modèle m à l'échelle.

scallop ['skɔləp] n coquille f Saint-Jacques.

scalp [skælp] n cuir chevelu // vt scalper.

scamper ['skæmpə*] vi: to ~ **away**, ~ **off** détaler.

scampi ['skæmpɪ] npl langoustines (frites), scampi mpl.

scan [skæn] vt scruter, examiner; (glance at quickly) parcourir; (TV, RADAR) balayer.

scandal ['skændl] n scandale m; (gossip) ragots mpl.

Scandinavia [skændɪ'neɪvɪə] *n* Scandinavie *f*; **~n** *a* scandinave // *n* Scandinave *m/f*.

scant [skænt] *a* insuffisant(e); **~y** *a* peu abondant(e), insuffisant(e), maigre.

scapegoat ['skeɪpgəʊt] *n* bouc *m* émissaire.

scar [ska:] *n* cicatrice *f*.

scarce [skɛəs] *a* rare, peu abondant(e); **~ly** *ad* à peine, presque pas; **scarcity** *f*, rareté *f*, manque *m*, pénurie *f*.

scare [skɛə*] *n* peur *f*, panique *f* // *vt* effrayer, faire peur à; **to ~ sb stiff** faire une peur bleue à qn; **bomb ~** alerte *f* à la bombe; **~crow** *n* épouvantail *m*; **~d** *a*: **to be ~d** avoir peur.

scarf, *pl* **scarves** [ska:f, ska:vz] *n* (*long*) écharpe *f*; (*square*) foulard *m*.

scarlet ['ska:lɪt] *a* écarlate.

scathing ['skeɪðɪŋ] *a* cinglant(e), acerbe.

scatter ['skætə*] *vt* éparpiller, répandre; (*crowd*) disperser // *vi* se disperser; **~brained** *a* écervelé(e), étourdi(e).

scavenger ['skævəndʒə*] *n* éboueur *m*.

scene [si:n] *n* (*THEATRE, fig etc*) scène *f*; (*of crime, accident*) lieu(x) *m(pl)*, endroit *m*; (*sight, view*) spectacle *m*, vue *f*; **~ry** *n* (*THEATRE*) décor(s) *m(pl)*; (*landscape*) paysage *m*; **scenic** *a* scénique; offrant de beaux paysages *or* panoramas.

scent [sɛnt] *n* parfum *m*, odeur *f*; (*fig: track*) piste *f*; (*sense of smell*) odorat *m*.

sceptical ['skɛptɪkəl] *a* sceptique.

schedule ['ʃɛdju:l, (US) 'skɛdju:l] *n* programme *m*, plan *m*; (*of trains*) horaire *m*; (*of prices etc*) barème *m*, tarif *m* // *vt* prévoir; **on ~** à l'heure (prévue); à la date prévue; **to be ahead of/behind ~** avoir de l'avance/du retard; **~d flight** *n* vol régulier.

scheme [ski:m] *n* plan *m*, projet *m*; (*method*) procédé *m*; (*dishonest plan, plot*) complot *m*, combine *f*; (*arrangement*) arrangement *m*, classification *f*; (*pension ~ etc*) régime *m* // *vt, vi* comploter, manigancer; **scheming** *a* rusé(e), intrigant(e) // *n* manigances *fpl*, intrigues *fpl*.

scholar ['skɒlə*] *n* érudit/e; **~ly** *a* érudit(e), savant(e); **~ship** *n* érudition *f*; (*grant*) bourse *f* (d'études).

school [sku:l] *n* (*gen*) école *f*; (*in university*) faculté *f*; (*secondary school*) collège *m*, lycée *m* // *cpd* scolaire // *vt* (*animal*) dresser; **~book** *n* livre *m* scolaire *or* de classe; **~boy** *n* écolier *m*; collégien *m*, lycéen *m*; **~children** *npl* écoliers *mpl*; collégiens *mpl*, lycéens *mpl*; **~days** *npl* années *fpl* de scolarité; **~girl** *n* écolière *f*; collégienne *f*, lycéenne *f*; **~ing** *n* instruction *f*, études *fpl*; **~master** *n* (*primary*) instituteur *m*; (*secondary*) professeur *m*;

~mistress *n* institutrice *f*; professeur *m*; **~teacher** *n* instituteur/trice; professeur *m*.

sciatica [saɪ'ætɪkə] *n* sciatique *f*.

science ['saɪəns] *n* science *f*; **~ fiction** *n* science-fiction *f*; **scientific** [-'tɪfɪk] *a* scientifique; **scientist** *n* scientifique *m/f*; (*eminent*) savant *m*.

scissors ['sɪzəz] *npl* ciseaux *mpl*.

scoff [skɒf] *vt* (*Brit col: eat*) avaler, bouffer // *vi*: **to ~ (at)** (*mock*) se moquer (de).

scold [skəʊld] *vt* gronder, attraper.

scone [skɒn] *n* sorte de petit pain rond au lait.

scoop [sku:p] *n* pelle *f* (à main); (*for ice cream*) boule *f* à glace; (*PRESS*) reportage exclusif *or* à sensation; **to ~ out** *vt* évider, creuser; **to ~ up** *vt* ramasser.

scooter ['sku:tə*] *n* (*motor cycle*) scooter *m*; (*toy*) trottinette *f*.

scope [skəʊp] *n* (*capacity: of plan, undertaking*) portée *f*, envergure *f*; (: *of person*) compétence *f*, capacités *fpl*; (*opportunity*) possibilités *fpl*; **within the ~ of** dans les limites de.

scorch [skɔ:tʃ] *vt* (*clothes*) brûler (légèrement), roussir; (*earth, grass*) dessécher, brûler.

score [skɔ:*] *n* score *m*, décompte *m* des points; (*MUS*) partition *f*; (*twenty*) vingt // *vt* (*goal, point*) marquer; (*success*) remporter // *vi* marquer des points; (*FOOTBALL*) marquer un but; (*keep score*) compter les points; **on that ~** sur ce chapitre, à cet égard; **to ~ 6 out of 10** obtenir 6 sur 10; **to ~ out** *vt* rayer, barrer, biffer; **~board** *n* tableau *m*.

scorn [skɔ:n] *n* mépris *m*, dédain *m*.

Scorpio ['skɔ:pɪəʊ] *n* le Scorpion.

Scot [skɒt] *n* Écossais/e.

scotch [skɒtʃ] *vt* faire échouer; enrayer; étouffer; **S~** *n* whisky *m*, scotch *m*.

scot-free ['skɒt'fri:] *ad*: **to get off ~** (*unpunished*) s'en tirer sans être puni.

Scotland ['skɒtlənd] *n* Écosse *f*.

Scots [skɒts] *a* écossais(e); **~man/woman** *n* Écossais/e.

Scottish ['skɒtɪʃ] *a* écossais(e).

scoundrel ['skaʊndrl] *n* vaurien *m*.

scour ['skaʊə*] *vt* (*clean*) récurer; frotter; décaper; (*search*) battre, parcourir.

scourge [skə:dʒ] *n* fléau *m*.

scout [skaʊt] *n* (*MIL*) éclaireur *m*; (*also: boy ~*) scout *m*; **to ~ around** *vi* explorer, chercher.

scowl [skaʊl] *vi* se renfrogner, avoir l'air maussade; **to ~ at** regarder de travers.

scrabble ['skræbl] *vi* (*claw*): **to ~ (at)** gratter; (*also: ~ around: search*) chercher à tâtons // *n* ® Scrabble *m* ®.

scraggy ['skrægɪ] *a* décharné(e).

scram [skræm] *vi* (*col*) ficher le camp.
scramble ['skræmbl] *n* bousculade *f*, ruée *f* // *vi* avancer tant bien que mal (à quatre pattes *or* en grimpant); **to ~ out** sortir *or* descendre à toute vitesse; **to ~ for** se bousculer *or* se disputer pour (avoir); **~d eggs** *npl* œufs brouillés.
scrap [skræp] *n* bout *m*, morceau *m*; (*fight*) bagarre *f*; (*also:* ~ **iron**) ferraille *f* // *vt* jeter, mettre au rebut; (*fig*) abandonner, laisser tomber // *vi* (*fight*) se bagarrer; **~s** *npl* (*waste*) déchets *mpl*; **~book** *n* album *m*; **~ dealer** *n* marchand *m* de ferraille.
scrape [skreɪp] *vt*, *vi* gratter, racler // *n*: **to get into a ~** s'attirer des ennuis; **to ~ through** réussir de justesse; **~r** *n* grattoir *m*, racloir *m*.
scrap: ~ heap *n* (*fig*): **on the ~ heap** au rancart *or* rebut; **~ merchant** *n* (*Brit*) marchand *m* de ferraille; **~ paper** *n* papier *m* brouillon.
scratch [skrætʃ] *n* égratignure *f*, rayure *f*; éraflure *f*; (*from claw*) coup *m* de griffe // *a*: **~ team** équipe de fortune *or* improvisée // *vt* (*record*) rayer; (*paint etc*) érafler; (*with claw, nail*) griffer // *vi* (se) gratter; **to start from ~** partir de zéro; **to be up to ~** être à la hauteur.
scrawl [skrɔːl] *vi* gribouiller.
scrawny ['skrɔːnɪ] *a* décharné(e).
scream [skriːm] *n* cri perçant, hurlement *m* // *vi* crier, hurler.
scree [skriː] *n* éboulis *m*.
screech [skriːtʃ] *vi* hurler; (*tyres, brakes*) crisser, grincer.
screen [skriːn] *n* écran *m*, paravent *m*; (*CINEMA, TV*) écran; (*fig*) écran, rideau *m* // *vt* masquer, cacher; (*from the wind etc*) abriter, protéger; (*film*) projeter; (*candidates etc*) filtrer; **~ing** *n* (*MED*) test *m* (*or* tests) de dépistage; **~play** *n* scénario *m*.
screw [skruː] *n* vis *f*; (*propeller*) hélice *f* // *vt* visser; **to ~ up** *vt* (*paper etc*) froisser; (*col: ruin*) bousiller; **~driver** *n* tournevis *m*.
scribble ['skrɪbl] *vt* gribouiller, griffonner.
script [skrɪpt] *n* (*CINEMA etc*) scénario *m*, texte *m*; (*in exam*) copie *f*.
Scripture ['skrɪptʃə*] *n* Ecriture Sainte.
scroll [skrəʊl] *n* rouleau *m*.
scrounge [skraundʒ] *vt* (*col*): **to ~ sth** (*off or from sb*) se faire payer qch (par qn), emprunter qch (à qn) // *vi*: **to ~ on sb** vivre aux crochets de qn.
scrub [skrʌb] *n* (*clean*) nettoyage *m* (à la brosse); (*land*) broussailles *fpl* // *vt* (*floor*) nettoyer à la brosse; (*pan*) récurer; (*washing*) frotter; (*reject*) annuler.
scruff [skrʌf] *n*: **by the ~ of the neck** par la peau du cou.
scruffy ['skrʌfɪ] *a* débraillé(e).

scrum(mage) ['skrʌm(ɪdʒ)] *n* (*RUGBY*) mêlée *f*.
scruple ['skruːpl] *n* scrupule *m*.
scrutiny ['skruːtɪnɪ] *n* examen minutieux.
scuff [skʌf] *vt* érafler.
scuffle ['skʌfl] *n* échauffourée *f*, rixe *f*.
scullery ['skʌlərɪ] *n* arrière-cuisine *f*.
sculptor ['skʌlptə*] *n* sculpteur *m*.
sculpture ['skʌlptʃə*] *n* sculpture *f*.
scum [skʌm] *n* écume *f*, mousse *f*; (*pej: people*) rebut *m*, lie *f*.
scupper ['skʌpə*] *vt* saborder.
scurrilous ['skʌrɪləs] *a* haineux(euse), virulent(e); calomnieux(euse).
scurry ['skʌrɪ] *vi* filer à toute allure; **to ~ off** détaler, se sauver.
scuttle ['skʌtl] *n* (*NAUT*) écoutille *f*; (*also:* **coal ~**) seau *m* (à charbon) // *vt* (*ship*) saborder // *vi* (*scamper*): **to ~ away, ~ off** détaler.
scythe [saɪð] *n* faux *f*.
SDP *n abbr* (*Brit*) = Social Democratic Party.
sea [siː] *n* mer *f* // *cpd* marin(e), de (la) mer, maritime; **by ~** (*travel*) par mer, en bateau; **on the ~** (*boat*) en mer; (*town*) au bord de la mer; **to be all at ~** (*fig*) nager complètement; **out to ~** au large; (**out**) **at ~** en mer; **~board** *n* côte *f*; **~food** *n* fruits *mpl* de mer; **~ front** *n* bord *m* de mer; **~gull** *n* mouette *f*.
seal [siːl] *n* (*animal*) phoque *m*; (*stamp*) sceau *m*, cachet *m*; (*impression*) cachet, estampille *f* // *vt* sceller; (*envelope*) coller; (: *with seal*) cacheter; **to ~ off** *vt* (*close*) condamner; (*forbid entry to*) interdire l'accès de.
sea level *n* niveau *m* de la mer.
seam [siːm] *n* couture *f*; (*of coal*) veine *f*, filon *m*.
seaman ['siːmən] *n* marin *m*.
seamy ['siːmɪ] *a* louche, mal famé(e).
seance ['seɪɒns] *n* séance *f* de spiritisme.
seaplane ['siːpleɪn] *n* hydravion *m*.
search [sɜːtʃ] *n* (*for person, thing*) recherche(s) *f(pl)*; (*of drawer, pockets*) fouille *f*; (*LAW: at sb's home*) perquisition *f* // *vt* fouiller; (*examine*) examiner minutieusement; scruter // *vi*: **to ~ for** chercher; **to ~ through** *vt fus* fouiller; **in ~ of** à la recherche de; **~ing** *a* pénétrant(e); minutieux(euse); **~light** *n* projecteur *m*; **~ party** *n* expédition *f* de secours; **~ warrant** *n* mandat *m* de perquisition.
seashore ['siːʃɔː*] *n* rivage *m*, plage *f*, bord *m* de (la) mer.
seasick ['siːsɪk] *a* qui a le mal de mer.
seaside ['siːsaɪd] *n* bord *m* de la mer; **~ resort** *n* station *f* balnéaire.
season ['siːzn] *n* saison *f* // *vt* assaisonner, relever; **~al** *a* saisonnier(ère); **~ed** *a* (*fig*) expérimenté(e);

~ **ticket** n carte f d'abonnement.

seat [si:t] n siège m; (in bus, train: place) place f; (PARLIAMENT) siège; (buttocks) postérieur m; (of trousers) fond m // vt faire asseoir, placer; (have room for) avoir des places assises pour, pouvoir accueillir; ~ **belt** n ceinture f de sécurité.

sea water n eau f de mer.

seaweed ['si:wi:d] n algues fpl.

seaworthy ['si:wə:ðı] a en état de naviguer.

sec. abbr of **second(s).**

secluded [sı'klu:dıd] a retiré(e), à l'écart.

seclusion [sı'klu:ʒən] n solitude f.

second ['sekənd] num deuxième, second(e) // ad (in race etc) en seconde position // n (unit of time) seconde f; (in series, position) deuxième m/f, second/e; (AUT: also: ~ **gear**) seconde f; (COMM: imperfect) article m de second choix // vt (motion) appuyer; ~**ary** a secondaire; ~**ary school** n collège m, lycée m; ~**-class** a de deuxième classe // ad (RAIL) en seconde; ~**hand** a d'occasion; de seconde main; ~ **hand** n (on clock) trotteuse f; ~**ly** ad deuxièmement; ~**ment** [sı'kɔndmənt] n (Brit) détachement m; ~**-rate** a de deuxième ordre, de qualité inférieure; ~ **thoughts** npl doutes mpl; **on ~ thoughts** or (US) **thought** à la réflexion.

secrecy ['si:krəsı] n secret m.

secret ['si:krıt] a secret(ète) // n secret m; **in ~** ad en secret, secrètement, en cachette.

secretary ['sekrətərı] n secrétaire m/f; (COMM) secrétaire général; **S~ of State (for)** (Brit POL) ministre m (de).

secretive ['si:krətıv] a réservé(e); (pej) cachottier(ère), dissimulé(e).

sectarian [sek'tεərıən] a sectaire.

section ['sekʃən] n coupe f, section f; (department) section; (COMM) rayon m; (of document) section, article m, paragraphe m.

sector ['sektə*] n secteur m.

secular ['sekjulə*] a profane; laïque; séculier(ère).

secure [sı'kjuə*] a (free from anxiety) sans inquiétude, sécurisé(e); (firmly fixed) solide, bien attaché(e) (or fermé(e) etc); (in safe place) en lieu sûr, en sûreté // vt (fix) fixer, attacher; (get) obtenir, se procurer.

security [sı'kjuərıtı] n sécurité f, mesures fpl de sécurité; (for loan) caution f, garantie f.

sedan [sı'dæn] n (US AUT) berline f.

sedate [sı'deıt] a calme; posé(e) // vt donner des sédatifs à.

sedative ['sedıtıv] n calmant m, sédatif m.

seduce [sı'dju:s] vt (gen) séduire; **se-**

duction [-'dʌkʃən] n séduction f; **seductive** [-'dʌktıv] a séduisant(e), séducteur(trice).

see [si:] vb (pt saw, pp seen) vt (gen) voir; (accompany): **to ~ sb to the door** reconduire or raccompagner qn jusqu'à la porte // vi voir // n évêché m; **to ~ that** (ensure) veiller à ce que + sub, faire en sorte que + sub, s'assurer que; ~ **you soon!** à bientôt!; **to ~ about** vt fus s'occuper de; **to ~ off** vt accompagner (à la gare or à l'aéroport etc); **to ~ through** vt mener à bonne fin // vt fus voir clair dans; **to ~ to** vt fus s'occuper de, se charger de.

seed [si:d] n graine f; (fig) germe m; (TENNIS) tête f de série; **to go to ~** monter en graine; (fig) se laisser aller; ~**ling** n jeune plant m, semis m; ~**y** a (shabby) minable, miteux(euse).

seeing ['si:ıŋ] cj: ~ (**that**) vu que, étant donné que.

seek [si:k], pt, pp **sought** vt chercher, rechercher.

seem [si:m] vi sembler, paraître; **there ~s to be ...** il semble qu'il y a ...; on dirait qu'il y a ...; ~**ingly** ad apparemment.

seen [si:n] pp of **see.**

seep [si:p] vi suinter, filtrer.

seesaw ['si:sɔ:] n (jeu m de) bascule f.

seethe [si:ð] vi être en effervescence; **to ~ with anger** bouillir de colère.

see-through ['si:θru:] a transparent(e).

segregate ['segrıgeıt] vt séparer, isoler.

seize [si:z] vt (grasp) saisir, attraper; (take possession of) s'emparer de; (LAW) saisir; **to ~ (up)on** vt fus saisir, sauter sur; **to ~ up** vi (TECH) se gripper.

seizure ['si:ʒə*] n (MED) crise f, attaque f; (LAW) saisie f.

seldom ['seldəm] ad rarement.

select [sı'lekt] a choisi(e), d'élite; **select inv** // vt sélectionner, choisir; ~**ion** [-'lekʃən] n sélection f, choix m.

self [self] n (pl **selves**): **the ~** le moi inv // prefix auto-; ~**-catering** a (Brit) avec cuisine, où l'on peut faire sa cuisine; ~**-centred**, (US) ~**-centered** a égocentrique; ~**-coloured**, (US) ~**-colored** a uni(e); ~**-confidence** n confiance f en soi; ~**-conscious** a timide, qui manque d'assurance; ~**-contained** a (Brit: flat) avec entrée particulière, indépendant(e); ~**-control** n maîtrise f de soi; ~**-defence**, (US) ~**-defense** n légitime défense f; ~**-discipline** n discipline personnelle; ~**-employed** a qui travaille à son compte; ~**-evident** a évident(e), qui va de soi; ~**-governing** a autonome; ~**-indulgent** a qui ne se refuse rien; ~**-interest** n intérêt personnel; ~**ish** a égoïste; ~**ishness** n égoïsme m; ~**less** a désintéressé(e);

~-pity n apitoiement m sur soi-même; **~-possessed** a assuré(e); **~-preservation** n instinct m de conservation; **~-respect** n respect m de soi, amour-propre m; **~-righteous** a satisfait(e) de soi, pharisaïque; **~-sacrifice** n abnégation f; **~-satisfied** a content(e) de soi, suffisant(e); **~-service** a, n libre-service (m), self-service (m); **~-sufficient** a indépendant(e); **~-taught** a autodidacte.

sell [sɛl], pt, pp **sold** vt vendre // vi se vendre; **to ~ at** or **for** 10 F se vendre 10 F; **to ~ off** vt liquider; **to ~ out** vi: **to ~ out** (to sb/sth) (COMM) vendre son fonds or son affaire (à qn/qch) // vt vendre tout son stock de; **the tickets are all sold out** il ne reste plus de billets; **~-by date** n date f limite de vente; **~er** n vendeur/euse, marchand/e; **~ing price** n prix m de vente.

sellotape ['sɛləʊteɪp] n ® (Brit) papier collant, scotch m ®.

sellout ['sɛlaʊt] n trahison f, capitulation f; (of tickets): **it was a ~** tous les billets ont été vendus.

selves [sɛlvz] npl of **self**.

semblance ['sɛmbləns] n semblant m.

semen ['siːmən] n sperme m.

semester [sɪ'mɛstə*] n (US) semestre m.

semi ['sɛmɪ] prefix semi-, demi-; à demi, à moitié; **~circle** n demi-cercle m; **~colon** n point-virgule m; **~detached (house)** n (Brit) maison jumelée or jumelle; **~final** n demi-finale f.

seminar ['sɛmɪnɑː*] n séminaire m.

seminary ['sɛmɪnərɪ] n (REL: for priests) séminaire m.

semiskilled ['sɛmɪ'skɪld] a: **~ worker** n ouvrier/ère spécialisé(e).

senate ['sɛnɪt] n sénat m; **senator** n sénateur m.

send [sɛnd], pt, pp **sent** vt envoyer; **to ~ away** vt (letter, goods) envoyer, expédier; **to ~ away for** vt fus commander par correspondance, se faire envoyer; **to ~ back** vt renvoyer; **to ~ for** vt fus envoyer chercher; faire venir; **to ~ off** vt (goods) envoyer, expédier; (Brit SPORT: player) expulser or renvoyer du terrain; **to ~ out** vt (invitation) envoyer (par la poste); **to ~ up** vt (person, price) faire monter; (Brit: parody) mettre en boîte, parodier; **~er** n expéditeur/trice; **~-off** n: **a good ~-off** des adieux chaleureux.

senior ['siːnɪə*] a (older) aîné(e), plus âgé(e); (of higher rank) supérieur(e) // n aîné/e; (in service) personne f qui a plus d'ancienneté; **~ citizen** n personne âgée; **~ity** [-'ɔrɪtɪ] n priorité f d'âge, ancienneté f.

sensation [sɛn'seɪʃən] n sensation f; **~al** a qui fait sensation; (marvellous)

sensationnel(le).

sense [sɛns] n sens m; (feeling) sentiment m; (meaning) signification f; (wisdom) bon sens // vt sentir, pressentir; **it makes ~** c'est logique; **~s** npl raison f; **~less** a insensé(e), stupide; (unconscious) sans connaissance.

sensibility [sɛnsɪ'bɪlɪtɪ] n sensibilité f; **sensibilities** npl susceptibilité f.

sensible ['sɛnsɪbl] a sensé(e), raisonnable; sage; pratique.

sensitive ['sɛnsɪtɪv] a sensible.

sensual ['sɛnsjʊəl] a sensuel(le).

sensuous ['sɛnsjʊəs] a voluptueux(euse), sensuel(le).

sent [sɛnt] pt, pp of **send**.

sentence ['sɛntns] n (LING) phrase f; (LAW: judgment) condamnation f, sentence f; (: punishment) peine f // vt: **to ~ sb to death/to 5 years** condamner qn à mort/à 5 ans.

sentiment ['sɛntɪmənt] n sentiment m; (opinion) opinion f, avis m; **~al** [-'mɛntl] a sentimental(e).

sentry ['sɛntrɪ] n sentinelle f, factionnaire m.

separate a ['sɛprɪt] séparé(e), indépendant(e), différent(e) // vb ['sɛpəreɪt] vt séparer // vi se séparer; **~s** npl (clothes) coordonnés mpl; **~ly** ad séparément; **separation** [-'reɪʃən] n séparation f.

September [sɛp'tɛmbə*] n septembre m.

septic ['sɛptɪk] a septique; (wound) infecté(e); **~ tank** n fosse f septique.

sequel ['siːkwl] n conséquence f; séquelles fpl; (of story) suite f.

sequence ['siːkwəns] n ordre m, suite f.

sequin ['siːkwɪn] n paillette f.

serene [sɪ'riːn] a serein(e), calme, paisible.

sergeant ['sɑːdʒənt] n sergent m; (POLICE) brigadier m.

serial ['sɪərɪəl] n feuilleton m; **~ number** n numéro m de série.

series ['sɪəriːz] n (pl inv) série f; (PUBLISHING) collection f.

serious ['sɪərɪəs] a sérieux(euse), réfléchi(e); grave; **~ly** ad sérieusement, gravement.

sermon ['sɜːmən] n sermon m.

serrated [sɪ'reɪtɪd] a en dents de scie.

servant ['sɜːvənt] n domestique m/f; (fig) serviteur/servante.

serve [sɜːv] vt (employer etc) servir, être au service de; (purpose) servir à; (customer, food, meal) servir; (apprenticeship) faire, accomplir; (prison term) faire; purger // vi (also TENNIS) servir; (be useful): **to ~ as/for/ to do** servir de/à/à faire // n (TENNIS) service m; **it ~s him right** c'est bien fait pour lui; **to ~ out, ~ up** vt (food) servir.

service ['sɜːvɪs] *n* (*gen*) service *m*; (*AUT: maintenance*) révision *f* // *vt* (*car, washing machine*) réviser; **the S~s** les forces armées; **to be of ~ to sb** rendre service à qn; **dinner ~** service *m* de table; **~able** *a* pratique, commode; **~ charge** *n* (*Brit*) service *m*; **~man** *n* militaire *m*; **~ station** *n* station-service *f*.

serviette [sɜːvɪˈɛt] *n* (*Brit*) serviette *f* (de table).

session ['sɛʃən] *n* (*sitting*) séance *f*; (*SCOL*) année *f* scolaire (*or* universitaire).

set [sɛt] *n* série *f*, assortiment *m*; (*of tools etc*) jeu *m*; (*RADIO, TV*) poste *m*; (*TENNIS*) set *m*; (*group of people*) cercle *m*, milieu *m*; (*CINEMA*) plateau *m*; (*THEATRE: stage*) scène *f*; (*: scenery*) décor *m*; (*MATH*) ensemble *m*; (*HAIRDRESSING*) mise *f* en plis // *a* (*fixed*) fixe, déterminé(e); (*ready*) prêt(e) // *vb* (*pt, pp* set) *vt* (*place*) mettre, poser, placer; (*fix, establish*) fixer; (*: record*) établir; (*adjust*) régler; (*decide: rules etc*) fixer, choisir; (*TYP*) composer // *vi* (*sun*) se coucher; (*jam, jelly, concrete*) prendre; **to be ~ on doing** être résolu à faire; **to ~ (to music)** mettre en musique; **to ~ on fire** mettre le feu à; **to ~ free** libérer; **to ~ sth going** déclencher qch; **to ~ sail** partir, prendre la mer; **to ~ about** *vt fus* (*task*) entreprendre, se mettre à; **to ~ aside** *vt* mettre de côté; **to ~ back** *vt* (*in time*): **to ~ back (by)** retarder (de); **to ~ off** *vi* se mettre en route, partir // *vt* (*bomb*) faire exploser; (*cause to start*) déclencher; (*show up well*) mettre en valeur, faire valoir; **to ~ out** *vi*: **to ~ out to do** entreprendre de faire; avoir pour but *or* intention de faire // *vt* (*arrange*) disposer; (*state*) présenter, exposer; **to ~ up** *vt* (*organization*) fonder, constituer; **~back** *n* (*hitch*) revers *m*, contretemps *m*; **~ menu** *n* menu *m*.

settee [sɛˈtiː] *n* canapé *m*.

setting ['sɛtɪŋ] *n* cadre *m*; (*of jewel*) monture *f*.

settle ['sɛtl] *vt* (*argument, matter*) régler; (*problem*) résoudre; (*MED: calm*) calmer // *vi* (*bird, dust etc*) se poser; (*sediment*) se déposer; (*also: ~ down*) s'installer, se fixer; se calmer; se ranger; **to ~ for sth** accepter qch, se contenter de qch; **to ~ in** *vi* s'installer; **to ~ on sth** opter *or* se décider pour qch; **to ~ up with sb** régler (ce que l'on doit à) qn; **~ment** *n* (*payment*) règlement *m*; (*agreement*) accord *m*; (*colony*) colonie *f*; (*village etc*) établissement *m*; hameau *m*; **~r** *n* colon *m*.

setup ['sɛtʌp] *n* (*arrangement*) manière *f* dont les choses sont organisées; (*situation*) situation *f*, allure *f* des choses.

seven ['sɛvn] *num* sept; **~teen** *num* dix-sept; **~th** *num* septième; **~ty** *num* soixante-dix.

sever ['sɛvə*] *vt* couper, trancher; (*relations*) rompre.

several ['sɛvərl] *a, pronoun* plusieurs *m/fpl*; **~ of us** plusieurs d'entre nous.

severance ['sɛvərəns] *n* (*of relations*) rupture *f*; **~ pay** *n* indemnité *f* de licenciement.

severe [sɪˈvɪə*] *a* sévère, strict(e); (*serious*) grave, sérieux(euse); (*hard*) rigoureux(euse), dur(e); (*plain*) sévère, austère; **severity** [sɪˈvɛrɪtɪ] *n* sévérité *f*; gravité *f*; rigueur *f*.

sew [səʊ], *pt* sewed, *pp* sewn *vt, vi* coudre; **to ~ up** *vt* (re)coudre.

sewage ['suːɪdʒ] *n* vidange(s) *f(pl)*.

sewer ['suːə*] *n* égout *m*.

sewing ['səʊɪŋ] *n* couture *f*; **~ machine** *n* machine *f* à coudre.

sewn [səʊn] *pp* of **sew**.

sex [sɛks] *n* sexe *m*; **to have ~ with** avoir des rapports (sexuels) avec; **~ist** *a, n* sexiste *(m/f)*.

sexual ['sɛksjuəl] *a* sexuel(le).

sexy ['sɛksɪ] *a* sexy *inv*.

shabby ['ʃæbɪ] *a* miteux(euse); (*behaviour*) mesquin(e), méprisable.

shack [ʃæk] *n* cabane *f*, hutte *f*.

shackles ['ʃæklz] *npl* chaînes *fpl*, entraves *fpl*.

shade [ʃeɪd] *n* ombre *f*; (*for lamp*) abat-jour *m inv*; (*of colour*) nuance *f*, ton *m*; (*small quantity*): **a ~ of** un soupçon de // *vt* abriter du soleil, ombrager; **in the ~** à l'ombre; **a ~ smaller** un tout petit peu plus petit.

shadow ['ʃædəʊ] *n* ombre *f* // *vt* (*follow*) filer; **~ cabinet** *n* (*Brit POL*) cabinet parallèle formé par le parti qui n'est pas au pouvoir; **~y** *a* ombragé(e); (*dim*) vague, indistinct(e).

shady ['ʃeɪdɪ] *a* ombragé(e); (*fig: dishonest*) louche, véreux(euse).

shaft [ʃɑːft] *n* (*of arrow, spear*) hampe *f*; (*AUT, TECH*) arbre *m*; (*of mine*) puits *m*; (*of lift*) cage *f*; (*of light*) rayon *m*, trait *m*.

shaggy ['ʃægɪ] *a* hirsute; en broussaille.

shake [ʃeɪk] *vb* (*pt* shook, *pp* shaken [ʃuk, 'ʃeɪkn]) *vt* secouer; (*bottle, cocktail*) agiter; (*house, confidence*) ébranler // *vi* trembler // *n* secousse *f*; **to ~ one's head** (*in refusal*) dire *or* faire non de la tête; (*in dismay*) secouer la tête; **to ~ hands with sb** serrer la main à qn; **to ~ off** *vt* secouer; (*fig*) se débarrasser de; **to ~ up** *vt* secouer; **shaky** *a* (*hand, voice*) tremblant(e); (*building*) branlant(e), peu solide.

shall [ʃæl] *auxiliary vb*: **I ~** go j'irai; **~ I open the door?** j'ouvre la porte?; **I'll get the coffee, ~ I?** je vais chercher le café, d'accord?

shallow ['ʃæləu] a peu profond(e); (fig) superficiel(le).

sham [ʃæm] n frime f; (jewellery, furniture) imitation f.

shambles ['ʃæmblz] n confusion f, pagaïe f, fouillis m.

shame [ʃeɪm] n honte f // vt faire honte à; it is a ~ (that/to do) c'est dommage (que + sub/de faire); **what a ~!** quel dommage!; **~faced** a honteux(euse), penaud(e); **~ful** a honteux(euse), scandaleux(euse); **~less** a éhonté(e), effronté(e); (immodest) impudique.

shampoo [ʃæm'puː] n shampooing m // vt faire un shampooing à; ~ **and set** n shampooing m et mise f en plis.

shamrock ['ʃæmrɔk] n trèfle m (emblème national de l'Irlande).

shandy ['ʃændɪ] n bière panachée.

shan't [ʃɑːnt] = **shall not**.

shanty town ['ʃæntɪ-] n bidonville m.

shape [ʃeɪp] n forme f // vt façonner, modeler; (statement) formuler; (sb's ideas) former; (sb's life) déterminer // vi (also: ~ **up**: events) prendre tournure (: person) faire des progrès, s'en sortir; **to take ~** prendre forme or tournure; **-shaped** suffix: **heart-shaped** en forme de cœur; **~less** a informe, sans forme; **~ly** a bien proportionné(e), beau(belle).

share [ʃɛə*] n (thing received, contribution) part f; (COMM) action f // vt partager; (have in common) avoir en commun; **to ~ out** (among or between) partager (entre); **~holder** n actionnaire m/f.

shark [ʃɑːk] n requin m.

sharp [ʃɑːp] a (razor, knife) tranchant(e), bien aiguisé(e); (point) aigu(guë); (nose, chin) pointu(e); (outline) net(te); (cold, pain) vif(vive); (MUS) dièse; (voice) coupant(e); (person: quick-witted) vif(vive), éveillé(e); (: unscrupulous) malhonnête // n (MUS) dièse m // ad: **at 2 o'clock** ~ à 2 heures pile or tapantes; **~en** vt aiguiser; (pencil) tailler; (fig) aviver; **~ener** n (also: **pencil ~ener**) taille-crayon(s) m inv; **~-eyed** a à qui rien n'échappe; **~ly** ad (turn, stop) brusquement; (stand out) nettement; (criticize, retort) sèchement, vertement.

shatter ['ʃætə*] vt briser; (fig: upset) bouleverser; (: ruin) briser, ruiner // vi voler en éclats, se briser.

shave [ʃeɪv] vt raser // vi se raser // n: **to have a ~** se raser; **~r** n (also: electric ~r) rasoir m électrique.

shaving ['ʃeɪvɪŋ] n (action) rasage m; **~s** npl (of wood etc) copeaux mpl; ~ **brush** n blaireau m; ~ **cream** n crème f à raser.

shawl [ʃɔːl] n châle m.

she [ʃiː] pronoun elle; **~-cat** n chatte f;

~-elephant n éléphant m femelle; NB: for ships, countries follow the gender of your translation.

sheaf [ʃiːf], pl **sheaves** n gerbe f.

shear [ʃɪə*] vt (pt ~ed, pp ~ed or shorn) (sheep) tondre; **to ~ off** vi (branch) partir, se détacher; **~s** npl (for hedge) cisaille(s) f(pl).

sheath [ʃiːθ] n gaine f, fourreau m, étui m; (contraceptive) préservatif m.

sheaves [ʃiːvz] npl of **sheaf**.

shed [ʃɛd] n remise f, resserre f // vt (pt, pp **shed**) (leaves, fur etc) perdre; (tears) verser, répandre.

she'd [ʃiːd] = **she had, she would**.

sheen [ʃiːn] n lustre m.

sheep [ʃiːp] n (pl inv) mouton m; **~dog** n chien m de berger; **~ish** a penaud(e), timide; **~skin** n peau f de mouton.

sheer [ʃɪə*] a (utter) pur(e), pur et simple; (steep) à pic, abrupt(e); (almost transparent) extrêmement fin(e) // ad à pic, abruptement.

sheet [ʃiːt] n (on bed) drap m; (of paper) feuille f; (of glass, metal) feuille, plaque f.

sheik(h) [ʃeɪk] n cheik m.

shelf [ʃɛlf], pl **shelves** n étagère f, rayon m.

shell [ʃɛl] n (on beach) coquillage m; (of egg, nut etc) coquille f; (explosive) obus m; (of building) carcasse f // vt (crab, prawn etc) décortiquer; (peas) écosser; (MIL) bombarder (d'obus).

she'll [ʃiːl] = **she will, she shall**.

shellfish ['ʃɛlfɪʃ] n (pl inv) (crab etc) crustacé m; (scallop etc) coquillage m; (pl: as food) crustacés; coquillages.

shelter ['ʃɛltə*] n abri m, refuge m // vt abriter, protéger; (give lodging to) donner asile à // vi s'abriter, se mettre à l'abri.

shelve [ʃɛlv] vt (fig) mettre en suspens or en sommeil; **~s** npl of **shelf**.

shepherd ['ʃɛpəd] n berger m // vt (guide) guider, escorter; **~'s pie** n ≈ hachis m Parmentier.

sheriff ['ʃɛrɪf] n shérif m.

sherry ['ʃɛrɪ] n xérès m, sherry m.

she's [ʃiːz] = **she is, she has**.

Shetland ['ʃɛtlənd] n (also: **the ~s**, **the ~ Isles**) les îles fpl Shetland.

shield [ʃiːld] n bouclier m // vt: **to ~ (from)** protéger (de or contre).

shift [ʃɪft] n (change) changement m; (of workers) équipe f, poste m // vt déplacer, changer de place; (remove) enlever // vi changer de place, bouger; **~less** a (person) fainéant(e); **~ work** n travail m en équipe or par relais or par roulement; **~y** a sournois(e); (eyes) fuyant(e).

shilling ['ʃɪlɪŋ] n (Brit) shilling m (= 12 old pence; 20 in a pound).

shilly-shally ['ʃɪlɪʃælɪ] vi tergiverser,

atermoyer.

shimmer ['ʃɪmə*] vi miroiter, chatoyer.

shin [ʃɪn] n tibia m.

shine [ʃaɪn] n éclat m, brillant m // vb (pt, pp shone) vi briller // vt faire briller or reluire; (torch): to ~ on braquer sur.

shingle ['ʃɪŋgl] n (on beach) galets mpl; (on roof) bardeau m; ~s n (MED) zona m.

shiny ['ʃaɪnɪ] a brillant(e).

ship [ʃɪp] n bateau m; (large) navire m // vt transporter (par mer); (send) expédier (par mer); (load) charger, embarquer; ~**building** n construction navale; ~**ment** n cargaison f; ~**ping** n (ships) navires mpl; (traffic) navigation f; ~**shape** a en ordre impeccable; ~**wreck** n épave f; (event) naufrage m // vt: to be ~**wrecked** faire naufrage; ~**yard** n chantier naval.

shire ['ʃaɪə*] n (Brit) comté m.

shirk [ʃə:k] vt esquiver, se dérober à.

shirt [ʃə:t] n (man's) chemise f; in ~ sleeves en bras de chemise.

shit [ʃɪt] excl (col!) merde! (!).

shiver ['ʃɪvə*] vi frissonner.

shoal [ʃəul] n (of fish) banc m.

shock [ʃɔk] n (impact) choc m, heurt m; (ELEC) secousse f; (emotional) choc, secousse; (MED) commotion f, choc // vt choquer, scandaliser; bouleverser; ~ **absorber** n amortisseur m; ~**ing** a choquant(e), scandaleux(euse); épouvantable; révoltant(e).

shod [ʃɔd] pt, pp of shoe.

shoddy ['ʃɔdɪ] a de mauvaise qualité, mal fait(e).

shoe [ʃu:] n chaussure f, soulier m; (also: horse~) fer m à cheval // vt (pt, pp shod) (horse) ferrer; ~**horn** n chausse-pied m; ~**lace** n lacet m (de soulier); ~ **polish** n cirage m; ~**shop** n magasin m de chaussures; ~**string** n (fig): on a ~string avec un budget dérisoire.

shone [ʃɔn] pt, pp of shine.

shoo [ʃu:] excl (allez,) ouste!

shook [ʃuk] pt of shake.

shoot [ʃu:t] n (on branch, seedling) pousse f // vb (pt, pp shot) vt (game) chasser; tirer; abattre; (person) blesser (or tuer) d'un coup de fusil (or de revolver); (execute) fusiller; (film) tourner // vi (with gun, bow): to ~ (at) tirer (sur); (FOOTBALL) shooter, tirer; to ~ **down** vt (plane) abattre; to ~ **in/out** vi entrer/sortir comme une flèche; to ~ **up** vi (fig) monter en flèche; ~**ing** n (shots) coups mpl de feu, fusillade f; (HUNTING) chasse f; ~**ing star** n étoile filante.

shop [ʃɔp] n magasin m; (workshop) atelier m // vi (also: go ~ping) faire ses courses or ses achats; ~ **assistant** n (Brit) vendeur/euse; ~ **floor** n (Brit: fig) ouvriers mpl; ~**keeper** n marchand/e, commerçant/e; ~**lifting** n vol m à l'étalage; ~**per** n personne f qui fait ses courses, acheteur/euse; ~**ping** n (goods) achats mpl, provisions fpl; ~**ping bag** n sac m (à provisions); ~**ping centre**, (US) ~**ping center** n centre commercial; ~**soiled** a défraîchi(e), qui a fait la vitrine; ~ **steward** n (Brit INDUSTRY) délégué/e syndical(e); ~ **window** n vitrine f.

shore [ʃɔ:*] n (of sea, lake) rivage m, rive f // vt: to ~ (up) étayer.

shorn [ʃɔ:n] pp of shear.

short [ʃɔ:t] a (not long) court(e); (soon finished) court, bref(brève); (person, step) petit(e); (curt) brusque, sec(sèche); (insufficient) insuffisant(e) // n (also: ~ film) court métrage; (a pair of) ~s un short; to be ~ of sth être à court de or manquer de qch; in ~ bref; en bref; ~ of doing à moins de faire; everything ~ of tout sauf; it is ~ for c'est l'abréviation or le diminutif de; to cut ~ (speech, visit) abréger, écourter; (person) couper la parole à; to fall ~ of ne pas être à la hauteur de; to stop ~ s'arrêter net; to stop ~ of ne pas aller jusqu'à; ~**age** n manque m, pénurie f; ~**bread** n ≈sablé m; ~**change** vt ne pas rendre assez à; ~**circuit** n court-circuit m; ~**coming** n défaut m; ~**(crust) pastry** n (Brit) pâte brisée; ~**cut** n raccourci m; ~**en** vt raccourcir; (text, visit) abréger; ~**fall** n déficit m; ~**hand** n (Brit) sténo(graphie) f; ~**hand typist** n (Brit) sténodactylo m/f; ~**list** n (Brit: for job) liste f des candidats sélectionnés; ~**ly** ad bientôt, sous peu; ~**sighted** a (Brit) myope; (fig) qui manque de clairvoyance; ~**staffed** a à court de personnel; ~ **story** n nouvelle f; ~**tempered** a qui s'emporte facilement; ~**term** a (effect) à court terme; ~**wave** n (RADIO) ondes courtes.

shot [ʃɔt] pt, pp of shoot // n coup m (de feu); (person) tireur m; (try) coup, essai m; (injection) piqûre f; (PHOT) photo f; like a ~ comme une flèche; (very readily) sans hésiter; ~**gun** n fusil m de chasse.

should [ʃud] auxiliary vb: I ~ go now je devrais partir maintenant; he ~ be there now il devrait être arrivé maintenant; I ~ go if I were you si j'étais vous j'irais; I ~ like to j'aimerais bien, volontiers.

shoulder ['ʃəuldə*] n épaule f; (Brit: of road): hard ~ accotement m // vt (fig) endosser, se charger de; ~ **bag** n sac m à bandoulière; ~ **blade** n omoplate f; ~ **strap** n bretelle f.

shouldn't ['ʃudnt] = should not.

shout [ʃaut] n cri m // vt crier // vi crier,

pousser des cris; **to ~ down** vt huer; **~ing** n cris mpl.

shove [ʃʌv] vt pousser; (col: put): **to ~ sth in** fourrer or ficher qch dans; **to ~ off** vi (NAUT) pousser au large; (fig: col) ficher le camp.

shovel [ʃʌvl] n pelle f.

show [ʃəu] n (of emotion) manifestation f, démonstration f; (semblance) semblant m, apparence f; (exhibition) exposition f, salon m; (THEATRE) spectacle m, représentation f; (CINEMA) séance f // vb (pt **~ed**, pp **shown**) vt montrer; (courage etc) faire preuve de, manifester; (exhibit) exposer // vi se voir, être visible; **on ~** (exhibits etc) exposé(e); **to ~ in** vt (person) faire entrer; **to ~ off** vi (pej) crâner // vt (display) faire valoir; (pej) faire étalage de; **to ~ out** vt (person) reconduire (jusqu'à la porte); **to ~ up** vi (stand out) ressortir; (col: turn up) se montrer // vt démontrer; (unmask) démasquer, dénoncer; **~ business** n le monde du spectacle; **~down** n épreuve f de force.

shower [ʃauə*] n (rain) averse f; (of stones etc) pluie f, grêle f; (also: ~bath) douche f // vi prendre une douche, se doucher // vt: **to ~ sb with** (gifts etc) combler qn de; (abuse etc) accabler qn de; (missiles) bombarder qn de; **~proof** a imperméable.

showing [ʃəuɪŋ] n (of film) projection f.

show jumping n concours m hippique.

shown [ʃəun] pp of **show**.

show-off [ʃəuɔf] n (col: person) crâneur/euse, m'as-tu-vu/e.

showroom [ʃəurum] n magasin m or salle f d'exposition.

shrank [ʃræŋk] pt of **shrink**.

shrapnel [ʃræpnl] n éclats mpl d'obus.

shred [ʃred] n (gen pl) lambeau m, petit morceau // vt mettre en lambeaux, déchirer; (CULIN) râper; couper en lanières; **~der** n (for vegetables) râpeur m; (for documents) destructeur m de documents.

shrewd [ʃru:d] a astucieux(euse), perspicace.

shriek [ʃri:k] vt, vi hurler, crier.

shrill [ʃrɪl] a perçant(e), aigu(guë), strident(e).

shrimp [ʃrɪmp] n crevette grise.

shrine [ʃraɪn] n châsse f; (place) lieu m de pèlerinage.

shrink [ʃrɪŋk], pt **shrank**, pp **shrunk** vi rétrécir; (fig) se réduire; se contracter // vt (wool) (faire) rétrécir // n (col: psych) psychanalyste m/f; **to ~ from** (doing) sth reculer devant (la pensée de faire) qch; **~age** n rétrécissement m; **~wrap** vt emballer sous film plastique.

shrivel [ʃrɪvl] (also: ~ up) vt ratatiner, flétrir // vi se ratatiner, se flétrir.

shroud [ʃraud] n linceul m // vt: **~ed in mystery** enveloppé(e) de mystère.

Shrove Tuesday [ʃrəuv-] n (le) Mardi gras.

shrub [ʃrʌb] n arbuste m; **~bery** n massif m d'arbustes.

shrug [ʃrʌg] vt, vi: **to ~ (one's shoulders)** hausser les épaules; **to ~ off** vt faire fi de.

shrunk [ʃrʌŋk] pp of **shrink**.

shudder [ʃʌdə*] vi frissonner, frémir.

shuffle [ʃʌfl] vt (cards) battre; **to ~ (one's feet)** traîner les pieds.

shun [ʃʌn] vt éviter, fuir.

shunt [ʃʌnt] vt (RAIL: direct) aiguiller; (: divert) détourner.

shut, pt, pp **shut** [ʃʌt] vt fermer // vi (se) fermer; **to ~ down** vt, vi fermer définitivement; **to ~ off** vt couper, arrêter; **to ~ up** vi (col: keep quiet) se taire // vt (close) fermer; (silence) faire taire; **~ter** n volet m; (PHOT) obturateur m.

shuttle [ʃʌtl] n navette f; (also: ~ service) (service m de) navette f.

shuttlecock [ʃʌtlkɔk] n volant m (de badminton).

shy [ʃaɪ] a timide.

siblings [sɪblɪŋz] npl enfants mpl d'un même couple.

Sicily [sɪsɪlɪ] n Sicile f.

sick [sɪk] a (ill) malade; (vomiting): **to be ~** vomir; (humour) noir(e), macabre; **to feel ~** avoir envie de vomir, avoir mal au cœur; **to be ~ of** (fig) en avoir assez de; **~ bay** n infirmerie f; **~en** vt écœurer // vi: **to be ~ening for** sth (cold etc) couver qch.

sickle [sɪkl] n faucille f.

sick: ~ leave n congé m de maladie; **~ly** a maladif(ive), souffreteux(euse); (causing nausea) écœurant(e); **~ness** n maladie f; (vomiting) vomissement(s) m(pl); **~ pay** n indemnité f de maladie.

side [saɪd] n côté m; (of lake, road) bord m // cpd (door, entrance) latéral(e) // vi: **to ~ with sb** prendre le parti de qn, se ranger du côté de qn; **by the ~ of** au bord de; **~ by ~** côte à côte; **to take ~s (with)** prendre parti (pour); **~board** n buffet m; **~boards** (Brit), **~burns** npl (whiskers) pattes fpl; **~ effect** n (MED) effet m secondaire; **~light** n (AUT) veilleuse f; **~line** n (SPORT) ligne f de touche f; (fig) activité f secondaire; **~long** a oblique, de coin; **~saddle** ad en amazone; **~ show** n attraction f; **~step** vt (fig) éluder; éviter; **~ street** n rue transversale; **~track** vt (fig) faire dévier de son sujet; **~walk** n (US) trottoir m; **~ways** ad de côté.

siding [saɪdɪŋ] n (RAIL) voie f de garage.

sidle [saɪdl] vi: **to ~ up (to)** s'approcher furtivement (de).

siege [si:dʒ] *n* siège *m*.

sieve [sɪv] *n* tamis *m*, passoire *f*.

sift [sɪft] *vt* passer au tamis *or* au crible; (*fig*) passer au crible.

sigh [saɪ] *n* soupir *m* // *vi* soupirer, pousser un soupir.

sight [saɪt] *n* (*faculty*) vue *f*; (*spectacle*) spectacle *m*; (*on gun*) mire *f* // *vt* apercevoir; in ~ visible; (*fig*) en vue; out of ~ hors de vue; ~**seeing** *n* tourisme *m*; to go ~**seeing** faire du tourisme.

sign [saɪn] *n* (*gen*) signe *m*; (*with hand etc*) signe, geste *m*; (*notice*) panneau *m*, écriteau *m* // *vt* signer; **to ~ on** *vi* (*MIL*) s'engager; (*as unemployed*) s'inscrire au chômage // *vt* (*MIL*) engager; (*employee*) embaucher; **to ~ over** *vt*: to ~ sth over to sb céder qch par écrit à qn; **to ~ up** (*MIL*) *vt* engager // *vi* s'engager.

signal ['sɪgnl] *n* signal *m* // *vi* (*AUT*) mettre son clignotant // *vt* (*person*) faire signe à; (*message*) communiquer par signaux; ~**man** *n* (*RAIL*) aiguilleur *m*.

signature ['sɪgnətʃə*] *n* signature *f*; ~ **tune** *n* indicatif musical.

signet ring ['sɪgnət-] *n* chevalière *f*.

significance [sɪg'nɪfɪkəns] *n* signification *f*; importance *f*.

significant [sɪg'nɪfɪkənt] *a* significatif(ive); (*important*) important(e), considérable.

signpost ['saɪnpəust] *n* poteau indicateur.

silence ['saɪlns] *n* silence *m* // *vt* faire taire, réduire au silence; ~**r** *n* (*on gun*, *Brit AUT*) silencieux *m*.

silent ['saɪlnt] *a* silencieux(euse); (*film*) muet(te); **to remain ~** garder le silence, ne rien dire; ~ **partner** *n* (*COMM*) bailleur *m* de fonds, commanditaire *m*.

silhouette [sɪlu:'et] *n* silhouette *f*.

silicon chip ['sɪlɪkən-] *n* puce *f* électronique.

silk [sɪlk] *n* soie *f* // *cpd* de *or* en soie; ~**y** *a* soyeux(euse).

silly ['sɪlɪ] *a* stupide, sot(te), bête.

silt [sɪlt] *n* vase *f*; limon *m*.

silver ['sɪlvə*] *n* argent *m*; (*money*) monnaie *f* (en pièces d'argent); (*also*: ~**ware**) argenterie *f* // *cpd* d'argent, en argent; ~ **paper** *n* (*Brit*) papier *m* d'argent *or* d'étain; ~**-plated** *a* plaqué(e) argent; ~**smith** *n* orfèvre *m/f*; ~**y** *a* argenté(e).

similar ['sɪmɪlə*] *a*: ~ (**to**) semblable (à); ~**ly** *ad* de la même façon, de même.

simile ['sɪmɪlɪ] *n* comparaison *f*.

simmer ['sɪmə*] *vi* cuire à feu doux, mijoter.

simpering ['sɪmpərɪŋ] *a* minaudier(ère), nunuche.

simple ['sɪmpl] *a* simple; **simplicity** [-'plɪsɪtɪ] *n* simplicité *f*.

simultaneous [sɪməl'teɪnɪəs] *a* simultané(e).

sin [sɪn] *n* péché *m* // *vi* pécher.

since [sɪns] *ad, prep* depuis // *cj* (*time*) depuis que; (*because*) puisque, étant donné que, comme; ~ **then** depuis ce moment-là.

sincere [sɪn'sɪə*] *a* sincère; **sincerity** [-'serɪtɪ] *n* sincérité *f*.

sinew ['sɪnju:] *n* tendon *m*; ~**s** *npl* muscles *mpl*.

sinful ['sɪnful] *a* coupable.

sing [sɪŋ], *pt* **sang**, *pp* **sung** *vt*, *vi* chanter.

singe [sɪndʒ] *vt* brûler légèrement; (*clothes*) roussir.

singer ['sɪŋə*] *n* chanteur/euse.

singing ['sɪŋɪŋ] *n* chant *m*.

single ['sɪŋgl] *a* seul(e), unique; (*unmarried*) célibataire; (*not double*) simple // *n* (*Brit: also*: ~ **ticket**) aller *m* (simple); (*record*) 45 tours *m*; ~**s** *npl* (*TENNIS*) simple *m*; **to ~ out** *vt* choisir; distinguer; ~ **bed** *n* lit *m* à une place *or* d'une personne; ~**-breasted** *a* droit(e); ~ **file** *n*: in ~ **file** en file indienne; ~**-handed** *ad* tout(e) seul(e), sans (aucune) aide; ~**-minded** *a* résolu(e), tenace; ~ **room** *n* chambre *f* à un lit *or* pour une personne.

singlet ['sɪŋglɪt] *n* tricot *m* de corps.

singly ['sɪŋglɪ] *ad* séparément.

singular ['sɪŋgjulə*] *a* singulier(ère), étrange; (*LING*) (au) singulier, du singulier // *n* (*LING*) singulier *m*.

sinister ['sɪnɪstə*] *a* sinistre.

sink [sɪŋk] *n* évier *m* // *vb* (*pt* **sank**, *pp* **sunk**) *vt* (*ship*) (faire) couler, faire sombrer; (*foundations*) creuser; (*piles etc*): to ~ sth into enfoncer qch dans // *vi* couler, sombrer; (*ground etc*) s'affaisser; **to ~ in** *vi* s'enfoncer, pénétrer.

sinner ['sɪnə*] *n* pécheur/eresse.

sinus ['saɪnəs] *n* (*ANAT*) sinus *m inv*.

sip [sɪp] *vt* boire à petites gorgées.

siphon ['saɪfən] *n* siphon *m*; **to ~ off** *vt* siphonner.

sir [sə*] *n* monsieur *m*; S~ John Smith sir John Smith; yes ~ oui Monsieur.

siren ['saɪərn] *n* sirène *f*.

sirloin ['sə:lɔɪn] *n* aloyau *m*.

sissy ['sɪsɪ] *n* (*col: coward*) poule mouillée.

sister ['sɪstə*] *n* sœur *f*; (*nun*) religieuse *f*, (bonne) sœur; (*Brit: nurse*) infirmière *f* en chef; ~**-in-law** *n* belle-sœur *f*.

sit [sɪt], *pt, pp* **sat** *vi* s'asseoir; (*assembly*) être en séance, siéger; (*for painter*) poser // *vt* (*exam*) passer, se présenter à; **to ~ down** *vi* s'asseoir; **to ~ in on** *vt fus* assister à; **to ~ up** *vi* s'asseoir; (*not go to bed*) rester debout, ne pas se coucher.

sitcom ['sɪtkɔm] *n abbr* (= *situation*

comedy) comédie *f* de situation.

site [saɪt] *n* emplacement *m*, site *m*; (*also:* **building ~**) chantier *m*.

sit-in ['sɪtɪn] *n* (*demonstration*) sit-in *m* *inv*, occupation *f* de locaux.

sitting ['sɪtɪŋ] *n* (*of assembly etc*) séance *f*; (*in canteen*) service *m*; **~ room** *n* salon *m*.

situated ['sɪtjueɪtɪd] *a* situé(e).

situation [sɪtju'eɪʃən] *n* situation *f*; '**~s vacant/wanted**' (*Brit*) 'offres/demandes d'emploi'.

six [sɪks] *num* six; **~teen** *num* seize; **~th** *a* sixième; **~ty** *num* soixante.

size [saɪz] *n* taille *f*; dimensions *fpl*; (*of clothing*) taille, (*of shoes*) pointure *f*; (*glue*) colle *f*; **to ~ up** *vt* juger, jauger; **~able** *a* assez grand(e) *or* gros(se); assez important(e).

sizzle ['sɪzl] *vi* grésiller.

skate [skeɪt] *n* patin *m*; (*fish: pl inv*) raie *f* // *vi* patiner; **~board** *n* skateboard *m*, planche *f* à roulettes; **~r** *n* patineur/euse; **skating** *n* patinage *m*; **skating rink** *n* patinoire *f*.

skeleton ['skelɪtn] *n* squelette *m*; (*outline*) schéma *m*; **~ key** *n* passe-partout *m*; **~ staff** *n* effectifs réduits.

skeptical ['skeptɪkl] *a* (*US*) = **sceptical**.

sketch [sketʃ] *n* (*drawing*) croquis *m*, esquisse *f*; (*THEATRE*) sketch *m*, saynète *f* // *vt* esquisser, faire un croquis *or* une esquisse de; **~ book** *n* carnet *m* à dessin; **~y** *a* incomplet(ète), fragmentaire.

skewer ['skju:ə*] *n* brochette *f*.

ski [ski:] *n* ski *m* // *vi* skier, faire du ski; **~ boot** *n* chaussure *f* de ski.

skid [skɪd] *vi* déraper.

skier ['ski:ə*] *n* skieur/euse.

skiing ['ski:ɪŋ] *n* ski *m*.

ski jump *n* saut *m* à skis.

skilful ['skɪlful] *a* habile, adroit(e).

ski lift *n* remonte-pente *m inv*.

skill [skɪl] *n* habileté *f*, adresse *f*, talent *m*; **~ed** *a* habile, adroit(e); (*worker*) qualifié(e).

skim [skɪm] *vt* (*milk*) écrémer; (*soup*) écumer; (*glide over*) raser, effleurer // *vi*: **to ~ through** (*fig*) parcourir; **~med milk** *n* lait écrémé.

skimp [skɪmp] *vt* (*work*) bâcler, faire à la va-vite; (*cloth etc*) lésiner sur; **~y** *a* étriqué(e); maigre.

skin [skɪn] *n* peau *f* // *vt* (*fruit etc*) éplucher; (*animal*) écorcher; **~-deep** *a* superficiel(le); **~ diving** *n* plongée sous-marine; **~ny** *a* maigre, maigrichon(ne); **~tight** *a* (*dress etc*) collant(e), ajusté(e).

skip [skɪp] *n* petit bond *or* saut *m*; (*container*) benne *f* // *vi* gambader, sautiller; (*with rope*) sauter à la corde // *vt* (*pass over*) sauter.

ski: **~ pants** *npl* fuseau *m* (de ski); **~ pole** *n* bâton *m* de ski.

skipper ['skɪpə*] *n* (*NAUT*, *SPORT*) capitaine *m*.

skipping rope ['skɪpɪŋ-] *n* (*Brit*) corde *f* à sauter.

skirmish ['skə:mɪʃ] *n* escarmouche *f*, accrochage *m*.

skirt [skə:t] *n* jupe *f* // *vt* longer, contourner.

ski suit *n* combinaison *f* (de ski).

skit [skɪt] *n* sketch *m* satirique.

skittle ['skɪtl] *n* quille *f*; **~s** *n* (*game*) (jeu *m* de) quilles *fpl*.

skive [skaɪv] *vi* (*Brit col*) tirer au flanc.

skulk [skʌlk] *vi* rôder furtivement.

skull [skʌl] *n* crâne *m*.

skunk [skʌŋk] *n* mouffette *f*.

sky [skaɪ] *n* ciel *m*; **~light** *n* lucarne *f*; **~scraper** *n* gratte-ciel *m inv*.

slab [slæb] *n* plaque *f*; dalle *f*.

slack [slæk] *a* (*loose*) lâche, desserré(e); (*slow*) stagnant(e); (*careless*) négligent(e), peu sérieux(euse) *or* consciencieux(euse) // *n* (*in rope etc*) mou *m*; **~s** *npl* pantalon *m*; **~en** (*also:* **~en off**) *vi* ralentir, diminuer // *vt* relâcher.

slag [slæg] *n* scories *fpl*; **~ heap** *n* crassier *m*.

slain [sleɪn] *pp* of **slay**.

slam [slæm] *vt* (*door*) (faire) claquer; (*throw*) jeter violemment, flanquer; (*criticize*) éreinter, démolir // *vi* claquer.

slander ['slɑːndə*] *n* calomnie *f*; diffamation *f*.

slang [slæŋ] *n* argot *m*.

slant [slɑːnt] *n* inclinaison *f*; (*fig*) angle *m*, point *m* de vue; **~ed** *a* tendancieux(euse); **~ing** *a* en pente, incliné(e); couché(e).

slap [slæp] *n* claque *f*, gifle *f*; tape *f* // *vt* donner une claque *or* une gifle *or* une tape à // *ad* (*directly*) tout droit, en plein; **~dash** *a* fait(e) sans soin *or* à la va-vite; (*person*) insouciant(e), négligent(e); **~stick** *n* (*comedy*) grosse farce, style *m* tarte à la crème; **~-up** *a*: **a ~-up meal** (*Brit*) un repas extra *or* fameux.

slash [slæʃ] *vt* entailler, taillader; (*fig: prices*) casser.

slat [slæt] *n* latte *f*, lame *f*.

slate [sleɪt] *n* ardoise *f* // *vt* (*fig: criticize*) éreinter, démolir.

slaughter ['slɔːtə*] *n* carnage *m*, massacre *m* // *vt* (*animal*) abattre; (*people*) massacrer.

slave [sleɪv] *n* esclave *m/f* // *vi* (*also:* **~ away**) trimer, travailler comme un forçat; **~ry** *n* esclavage *m*.

slay [sleɪ], *pt* **slew**, *pp* **slain** *vt* (*formal*) tuer.

sleazy ['sli:zɪ] *a* miteux(euse), minable.

sledge [sledʒ] *n* luge *f*; **~hammer** *n* marteau *m* de forgeron.

sleek [sli:k] *a* (*hair*, *fur*) brillant(e),

luisant(e); (car, boat) aux lignes pures or élégantes.

sleep [sli:p] n sommeil m // vi (pt, pp slept [slept]) dormir; (spend night) dormir, coucher; **to go to ~** s'endormir; **to ~ in** vi (lie late) faire la grasse matinée; (oversleep) se réveiller trop tard; **~er** n (person) dormeur/euse; (Brit RAIL: on track) traverse f; (: train) train m de voitures-lits; **~ing bag** n sac m de couchage; **~ing car** n wagon-lits m, voiture-lits f; **~ing pill** n somnifère m; **~less** a: a **~less night** une nuit blanche; **~walker** n somnambule m/f; **~y** a qui a envie de dormir; (fig) endormi(e).

sleet [sli:t] n neige fondue.

sleeve [sli:v] n manche f.

sleigh [slei] n traîneau m.

sleight [slait] n: **~ of hand** tour m de passe-passe.

slender ['slɛndə*] a svelte, mince; faible, ténu(e).

slept [slept] pt, pp of **sleep**.

slew [slu:] vi virer, pivoter // pt of **slay**.

slice [slais] n tranche f; (round) rondelle f // vt couper en tranches (or en rondelles).

slick [slik] a brillant(e) en apparence; mielleux(euse) // n (also: oil ~) nappe f de pétrole, marée noire.

slide [slaid] n (in playground) toboggan m; (PHOT) diapositive f; (Brit: also: hair ~) barrette f; (in prices) chute f, baisse f // vb (pt, pp slid [slid]) vt (faire) glisser // vi glisser; **~ rule** n règle f à calcul; **sliding** a (door) coulissant(e); **sliding scale** n échelle f mobile.

slight [slait] a (slim) mince, menu(e); (frail) frêle; (trivial) faible, insignifiant(e); (small) petit(e), léger(ère) (before n) // n offense f, affront m // vt (offend) blesser, offenser; **not in the ~est** pas le moins du monde, pas du tout; **~ly** ad légèrement, un peu.

slim [slim] a mince // vi maigrir, suivre un régime amaigrissant.

slime [slaim] n vase f; substance visqueuse.

slimming ['slimiŋ] n amaigrissement m.

sling [sliŋ] n (MED) écharpe f // vt (pt, pp slung) lancer, jeter.

slip [slip] n faux pas; (mistake) erreur f; étourderie f; bévue f; (underskirt) combinaison f; (of paper) petite feuille, fiche f // vt (slide) glisser // vi (slide) glisser; (move smoothly): **to ~ into/out of** se glisser or se faufiler dans/hors de; (decline) baisser; **to ~ sth on/off** enfiler/enlever qch; **to give sb the ~** fausser compagnie à qn; **a ~ of the tongue** un lapsus; **to ~ away** vi s'esquiver; **~ped disc** n déplacement m de vertèbres.

slipper ['slipə*] n pantoufle f.

slippery ['slipəri] a glissant(e); insaisissable.

slip road n (Brit: to motorway) bretelle f d'accès.

slipshod ['slipʃɔd] a négligé(e), peu soigné(e).

slip-up ['slipʌp] n bévue f.

slipway ['slipwei] n cale f (de construction or de lancement).

slit [slit] n fente f; (cut) incision f; (tear) déchirure f // vt (pt, pp slit) fendre; couper; inciser; déchirer.

slither ['sliðə*] vi glisser, déraper.

sliver ['slivə*] n (of glass, wood) éclat m; (of cheese etc) petit morceau, fine tranche.

slob [slɔb] n (col) rustaud/e.

slog [slɔg] (Brit) n gros effort; tâche fastidieuse // vi travailler très dur.

slogan ['sləugən] n slogan m.

slop [slɔp] vi (also: ~ over) se renverser; déborder // vt répandre; renverser.

slope [sləup] n pente f, côte f; (side of mountain) versant m; (slant) inclinaison f // vi: **to ~ down** être or descendre en pente; **to ~ up** monter.

sloppy ['slɔpi] a (work) peu soigné(e), bâclé(e); (appearance) négligé(e), débraillé(e); (film etc) sentimental(e).

slot [slɔt] n fente f // vt: **to ~ sth into** encastrer or insérer qch dans // vi: **to ~ into** s'encastrer or s'insérer dans; **~ machine** n (Brit: vending machine) distributeur m (automatique), machine f à sous; (for gambling) appareil m or machine à sous.

sloth [sləuθ] n (laziness) paresse f.

slouch [slautʃ] vi avoir le dos rond, être voûté(e); **to ~ about** vi (laze) traîner à ne rien faire.

slovenly ['slʌvənli] a sale, débraillé(e).

slow [sləu] a lent(e); (watch): **to be ~** retarder // ad lentement // vt, vi (also: ~ down, ~ up) ralentir; ' ~ ' (road sign) 'ralentir'; **~ly** ad lentement; **~ motion** n: **in ~ motion** au ralenti.

sludge [slʌdʒ] n boue f.

slug [slʌg] n limace f; (bullet) balle f; **~gish** a mou(molle), lent(e).

sluice [slu:s] n vanne f; écluse f.

slum [slʌm] n taudis m.

slumber ['slʌmbə*] n sommeil m.

slump [slʌmp] n baisse soudaine, effondrement m; crise f // vi s'effondrer, s'affaisser.

slung [slʌŋ] pt, pp of **sling**.

slur [slə:*] n bredouillement m; (smear): ~ (on) atteinte f (à); insinuation f (contre) // vt mal articuler.

slush [slʌʃ] n neige fondue; **~ fund** n caisse noire, fonds secrets.

slut [slʌt] n souillon f.

sly [slai] a rusé(e); sournois(e).

smack [smæk] n (slap) tape f; (on face)

gifle f // vt donner une tape à; gifler; (*child*) donner la fessée à // vi: **to ~ of** avoir des relents de, sentir.

small [smɔ:l] a petit(e); ~ **ads** npl (*Brit*) petites annonces; ~ **change** n petite or menue monnaie; **~holder** n (*Brit*) petit cultivateur; ~ **hours** npl: **in the ~ hours** au petit matin; **~pox** n variole f; ~ **talk** n menus propos.

smart [smɑ:t] a élégant(e), chic inv; (*clever*) intelligent(e), astucieux(euse), futé(e); (*quick*) rapide, vif(vive), prompt(e) // vi faire mal, brûler; **to ~en up** vi devenir plus élégant(e), se faire beau(belle) // vt rendre plus élégant(e).

smash [smæʃ] n (*also*: ~-**up**) collision f, accident m // vt casser, briser, fracasser; (*opponent*) écraser; (*hopes*) ruiner, détruire; (*SPORT*: *record*) pulvériser // vi se briser, se fracasser; s'écraser; **~ing** a (*col*) formidable.

smattering ['smætərɪŋ] n: **a ~ of** quelques notions de.

smear [smɪə*] n tache f, salissure f; trace f; (*MED*) frottis m // vt enduire; (*fig*) porter atteinte à.

smell [smɛl] n odeur f; (*sense*) odorat m // vb (*pt, pp* **smelt** or **smelled** [smɛlt, smɛld]) vt sentir // vi (*food etc*) **to ~ (of)** sentir; (*pej*) sentir mauvais; it **~s good/~s of garlic** ça sent bon/sent l'ail; **~y** a qui sent mauvais, malodorant(e).

smile [smaɪl] n sourire m // vi sourire.

smirk [smɔ:k] n petit sourire suffisant or affecté.

smith [smɪθ] n maréchal-ferrant m; forgeron m; **~y** ['smɪðɪ] n forge f.

smock [smɔk] n blouse f, sarrau m.

smog [smɔg] n brouillard mêlé de fumée.

smoke [smɔuk] n fumée f // vt, vi fumer; **~d** a (*bacon, glass*) fumé(e); **~r** n (*person*) fumeur/euse; (*RAIL*) wagon m fumeurs; ~ **screen** n rideau m or écran m de fumée; (*fig*) paravent m; **smoking** n: 'no smoking' (*sign*) 'défense de fumer'; **smoky** a enfumé(e).

smolder ['smɔuldə*] vi (*US*) = **smoulder**.

smooth [smu:ð] a lisse; (*sauce*) onctueux(euse); (*flavour, whisky*) moelleux(euse); (*movement*) régulier(ère), sans à-coups or heurts; (*person*) doucereux(euse), mielleux(euse) // vt lisser, défroisser; (*also*: ~ **out**: *creases, difficulties*) faire disparaître.

smother ['smʌðə*] vt étouffer.

smoulder, (*US*) **smolder** ['smɔuldə*] vi couver.

smudge [smʌdʒ] n tache f, bavure f // vt salir, maculer.

smug [smʌg] a suffisant(e), content(e) de soi.

smuggle ['smʌgl] vt passer en contrebande or en fraude; **~r** n contrebandier/ère; **smuggling** n contrebande f.

smutty ['smʌtɪ] a (*fig*) grossier(ère), obscène.

snack [snæk] n casse-croûte m inv; ~ **bar** n snack(-bar) m.

snag [snæg] n inconvénient m, difficulté f.

snail [sneɪl] n escargot m.

snake [sneɪk] n serpent m.

snap [snæp] n (*sound*) claquement m, bruit sec; (*photograph*) photo f, instantané m; (*game*) sorte de jeu de bataille // a subit(e); fait(e) sans réfléchir // vt faire claquer; (*break*) casser net; (*photograph*) prendre un instantané de // vi se casser net or avec un bruit sec; **to ~ open/shut** s'ouvrir/se refermer brusquement; **to ~ at** vt fus (*subj*: *dog*) essayer de mordre; **to ~ off** vt (*break*) casser net; **to ~ up** vt sauter sur, saisir; **~py** a prompt(e); (*slogan*) qui a du punch; **~shot** n photo f, instantané m.

snare [snɛə*] n piège m.

snarl [snɑ:l] vi gronder.

snatch [snætʃ] n (*fig*) vol m; (*small amount*): **~es of** des fragments mpl or bribes fpl de // vt saisir (*d'un geste vif*); (*steal*) voler.

sneak [sni:k] vi: **to ~ in/out** entrer/sortir furtivement or à la dérobée; **~ers** npl chaussures fpl de tennis or basket; **~y** a sournois(e).

sneer [snɪə*] vi ricaner, sourire d'un air sarcastique.

sneeze [sni:z] vi éternuer.

sniff [snɪf] vi renifler // vt renifler, flairer.

snigger ['snɪgə*] vi ricaner; pouffer de rire.

snip [snɪp] n petit bout; (*bargain*) (bonne) occasion or affaire // vt couper.

sniper ['snaɪpə*] n (*marksman*) tireur embusqué.

snippet ['snɪpɪt] n bribes fpl.

snivelling ['snɪvlɪŋ] a (*whimpering*) larmoyant(e), pleurnicheur(euse).

snob [snɔb] n snob m/f; **~bish** a snob inv.

snooker ['snu:kə*] n sorte de jeu de billard.

snoop ['snu:p] vi: **to ~ on sb** espionner qn; **to ~ about somewhere** fourrer son nez quelque part.

snooty ['snu:tɪ] a snob inv, prétentieux(euse).

snooze [snu:z] n petit somme // vi faire un petit somme.

snore [snɔ:*] vi ronfler; **snoring** n ronflement(s) m(pl).

snorkel ['snɔ:kl] n (*of swimmer*) tuba m.

snort [snɔ:t] vi grogner; (*horse*) renâcler.

snotty ['snɔtɪ] *a* morveux(euse).

snout [snaut] *n* museau *m*.

snow [snəu] *n* neige *f* // *vi* neiger; **~ball** *n* boule *f* de neige; **~bound** *a* enneigé(e), bloqué(e) par la neige; **~drift** *n* congère *f*; **~drop** *n* perce-neige *m*; **~fall** *n* chute *f* de neige; **~flake** *n* flocon *m* de neige; **~man** *n* bonhomme *m* de neige; **~plough**, (US) **~plow** *n* chasse-neige *m inv*; **~shoe** *n* raquette *f* (*pour la neige*); **~storm** *n* tempête *f* de neige.

snub [snʌb] *vt* repousser, snober // *n* rebuffade *f*; **~-nosed** *a* au nez re-troussé.

snuff [snʌf] *n* tabac *m* à priser.

snug [snʌg] *a* douillet(te), confortable.

snuggle ['snʌgl] *vi*: to **~ up** to sb se serrer *or* se blottir contre qn.

so [səu] ♦ *ad* **1** (*thus, likewise*) ainsi; if ~ si oui; ~ **do/have I** moi aussi; it's 5 o'clock - ~ **it is!** il est 5 heures - en effet! *or* c'est vrai!; **I hope/think ~** je l'espère/le crois; ~ **far** jusqu'ici, jusqu'à maintenant; (*in past*) jusque-là
2 (*in comparisons etc: to such a degree*) si, tellement; ~ **big (that)** si *or* tellement grand (que); **she's not ~ clever as her brother** elle n'est pas aussi intelligente que son frère
3: ~ **much** *a, ad* tant (de); **I've got ~ much work** j'ai tant de travail; **I love you ~ much** je vous aime tant; ~ **many** tant (de)
4 (*phrases*): **10 or ~** à peu près *or* environ 10; ~ **long!** (*col: goodbye*) au revoir!, à un de ces jours!
♦ *cj* **1** (*expressing purpose*): ~ **as to do** pour *or* afin de faire; ~ **(that)** pour que *or* afin que + *sub*
2 (*expressing result*) donc, par conséquent; ~ **that** si bien que, de (telle) sorte que.

soak [səuk] *vt* faire tremper // *vi* tremper; to ~ **in** *vi* être absorbé(e); to ~ **up** *vt* absorber.

so-and-so ['səuəndsəu] *n* (*somebody*) un tel(une telle).

soap [səup] *n* savon *m*; **~flakes** *npl* paillettes *fpl* de savon; **~ opera** *n* feuilleton télévisé; ~ **powder** *n* lessive *f*; **~y** *a* savonneux(euse).

soar [sɔ:*] *vi* monter (en flèche), s'élancer.

sob [sɔb] *n* sanglot *m* // *vi* sangloter.

sober ['səubə*] *a* qui n'est pas (*or* plus) ivre; (*sedate*) sérieux(euse), sensé(e); (*moderate*) mesuré(e); (*colour, style*) sobre, discret(ète); to ~ **up** *vt* dégriser // *vi* se dégriser.

so-called ['səu'kɔ:ld] *a* soi-disant *inv*.

soccer ['sɔkə*] *n* football *m*.

social ['səuʃl] *a* social(e) // *n* (petite) fête; ~ **club** *n* amicale *f*, foyer *m*;

~ism *n* socialisme *m*; **~ist** *a, n* socialiste (*m/f*); **~ize** *vt*: to **~ize (with)** lier connaissance (avec); parler (avec); ~ **security** *n* aide sociale; ~ **work** *n* assistance sociale; ~ **worker** *n* assistant/e social(e).

society [sə'saɪətɪ] *n* société *f*; (*club*) société, association *f*; (*also*: **high ~**) (haute) société, grand monde.

sociology [səusɪ'ɔləɔʒɪ] *n* sociologie *f*.

sock [sɔk] *n* chaussette *f* // *vt* (*col: hit*) flanquer un coup à.

socket ['sɔkɪt] *n* cavité *f*; (*ELEC*: *also*: **wall ~**) prise *f* de courant; (*: for light bulb*) douille *f*.

sod [sɔd] *n* (*of earth*) motte *f*; (*Brit col!*) con *m* (!); salaud *m* (!).

soda ['səudə] *n* (*CHEM*) soude *f*; (*also*: **~ water**) eau *f* de Seltz; (*US*: *also*: ~ **pop**) soda *m*.

sodden ['sɔdn] *a* trempé(e); dé-trempé(e).

sofa ['səufə] *n* sofa *m*, canapé *m*.

soft [sɔft] *a* (*not rough*) doux(douce); (*not hard*) doux; mou(molle); (*not loud*) doux, léger(ère); (*kind*) doux, gentil(le); (*weak*) indulgent(e); (*stupid*) stupide, débile; ~ **drink** *n* boisson non alcoolisée; **~en** ['sɔfn] *vt* (r)amollir; adoucir; atténuer // *vi* se ramollir; s'adoucir; s'atténuer; **~ly** *ad* doucement; gentiment; **~ness** *n* douceur *f*.

software ['sɔftwɛə*] *n* (*COMPUT*) logiciel *m*, software *m*.

soggy ['sɔgɪ] *a* trempé(e); détrempé(e).

soil [sɔɪl] *n* (*earth*) sol *m*, terre *f* // *vt* salir; (*fig*) souiller.

solace ['sɔlɪs] *n* consolation *f*.

solar ['səulə*] *a* solaire.

sold [səuld] *pt, pp* of **sell**; ~ **out** *a* (*COMM*) épuisé(e).

solder ['səuldə*] *vt* souder (*au fil à souder*) // *n* soudure *f*.

soldier ['səuldʒə*] *n* soldat *m*, militaire *m*.

sole [səul] *n* (*of foot*) plante *f*; (*of shoe*) semelle *f*; (*fish: pl inv*) sole *f* // *a* seul(e), unique.

solemn ['sɔləm] *a* solennel(le); sé-rieux(euse), grave.

sole trader *n* (*COMM*) chef *m* d'entre-prise individuelle.

solicit [sə'lɪsɪt] *vt* (*request*) solliciter // *vi* (*prostitute*) racoler.

solicitor [sə'lɪsɪtə*] *n* (*Brit: for wills etc*) ≈ notaire *m*; (*: in court*) ≈ avocat *m*.

solid ['sɔlɪd] *a* (*not hollow*) plein(e), compact(e), massif(ive); (*strong, sound, reliable, not liquid*) solide; (*meal*) consistant(e), substantiel(le) // *n* solide *m*.

solidarity [sɔlɪ'dærɪtɪ] *n* solidarité *f*.

solitary ['sɔlɪtərɪ] *a* solitaire; ~ **con-**

finement *n* (*LAW*) isolement *m*.
solo ['səʊləʊ] *n* solo *m*; **~ist** *n* soliste *m/f*.
soluble ['sɔljubl] *a* soluble.
solution [sə'lu:ʃən] *n* solution *f*.
solve [sɔlv] *vt* résoudre.
solvent ['sɔlvənt] *a* (*COMM*) solvable // (*CHEM*) (dis)solvant *m*.
some [sʌm] ♦ *a* 1 (*a certain amount or number of*): ~ tea/water/ice cream du thé/de l'eau/de la glace; ~ children/apples des enfants/pommes
2 (*certain: in contrasts*): ~ people say that ... il y a des gens qui disent que ...; ~ films were excellent, but most were mediocre certains films étaient excellents, mais la plupart étaient médiocres
3 (*unspecified*): ~ woman was asking for you il y avait une dame qui vous demandait; he was asking for ~ book (or other) il demandait un livre quelconque; ~ day un de ces jours; ~ day next week un jour la semaine prochaine
♦ *pronoun* 1 (*a certain number*) quelques-un(e)s, certain(e)s; I've got ~ (*books etc*) j'en ai (quelques-uns); ~ (of them) were sold certains ont été vendus
2 (*a certain amount*) un peu; I've got ~ (*money, milk*) j'en ai un peu
♦ *ad:* ~ 10 people quelque 10 personnes, 10 personnes environ.
somebody ['sʌmbədi] *pronoun* = **someone**.
somehow ['sʌmhaʊ] *ad* d'une façon ou d'une autre; (*for some reason*) pour une raison ou une autre.
someone ['sʌmwʌn] *pronoun* quelqu'un.
someplace ['sʌmpleɪs] *ad* (*US*) = **somewhere**.
somersault ['sʌməsɔ:lt] *n* culbute *f*, saut périlleux // *vi* faire la culbute *or* un saut périlleux; (*car*) faire un tonneau.
something ['sʌmθɪŋ] *pronoun* quelque chose *m*; ~ interesting quelque chose d'intéressant.
sometime ['sʌmtaɪm] *ad* (*in future*) un de ces jours, un jour ou l'autre; (*in past*): ~ last month au cours du mois dernier.
sometimes ['sʌmtaɪmz] *ad* quelquefois, parfois.
somewhat ['sʌmwɔt] *ad* quelque peu, un peu.
somewhere ['sʌmwɛə*] *ad* quelque part.
son [sʌn] *n* fils *m*.
song [sɔŋ] *n* chanson *f*.
sonic ['sɔnɪk] *a* (*boom*) supersonique.
son-in-law ['sʌnɪnlɔ:] *n* gendre *m*, beau-fils *m*.
sonny ['sʌnɪ] *n* (*col*) fiston *m*.
soon [su:n] *ad* bientôt; (*early*) tôt; ~

afterwards peu après; *see also* as; **~er** *ad* (*time*) plus tôt; (*preference*): I would **~er** do j'aimerais autant *or* je préférerais faire; **~er or later** tôt ou tard.
soot [sʊt] *n* suie *f*.
soothe [su:ð] *vt* calmer, apaiser.
sophisticated [sə'fɪstɪkeɪtɪd] *a* raffiné(e); sophistiqué(e); hautement perfectionné(e), très complexe.
sophomore ['sɔfəmɔ:*] *n* (*US*) étudiant/e de seconde année.
sopping ['sɔpɪŋ] *a* (*also:* ~ wet) tout(e) trempé(e).
soppy ['sɔpɪ] *a* (*pej*) sentimental(e).
soprano [sə'prɑ:nəʊ] *n* (*voice*) soprano *m*; (*singer*) soprano *m/f*.
sorcerer ['sɔ:sərə*] *n* sorcier *m*.
sore [sɔ:*] *a* (*painful*) douloureux(euse), sensible; (*offended*) contrarié(e), vexé(e) // *n* plaie *f*; **~ly** *ad* (*tempted*) fortement.
sorrow ['sɔrəʊ] *n* peine *f*, chagrin *m*.
sorry ['sɔrɪ] *a* désolé(e); (*condition, excuse*) triste, déplorable; ~! pardon!, excusez-moi!; to feel ~ for sb plaindre qn.
sort [sɔ:t] *n* genre *m*, espèce *f*, sorte *f* // *vt* (*also:* ~ out: *papers*) trier; classer; ranger; (: *letters etc*) trier; (: *problems*) résoudre, régler; **~ing office** *n* bureau *m* de tri.
SOS *n abbr* (= *save our souls*) S.O.S. *m*.
so-so ['səʊsəʊ] *ad* comme ci comme ça.
sought [sɔ:t] *pt, pp of* **seek**.
soul [səʊl] *n* âme *f*; **~-destroying** *a* démoralisant(e); **~ful** *a* plein(e) de sentiment.
sound [saʊnd] *a* (*healthy*) en bonne santé, sain(e); (*safe, not damaged*) solide, en bon état; (*reliable, not superficial*) sérieux(euse), solide; (*sensible*) sensé(e) // *ad:* ~ asleep dormant d'un profond sommeil // *n* (*noise*) son *m*; bruit *m*; (*GEO*) détroit *m*, bras *m* de mer // *vt* (*alarm*) sonner; (*also:* ~ out: *opinions*) sonder // *vi* sonner, retentir; (*fig: seem*) sembler (être); to ~ like ressembler à; ~ barrier *n* mur *m* du son; ~ effects *npl* bruitage *m*; **~ly** *ad* (*sleep*) profondément; (*beat*) complètement, à plate couture; **~proof** *a* insonorisé(e); **~track** *n* (*of film*) bande *f* sonore.
soup [su:p] *n* soupe *f*, potage *m*; in the ~ (*fig*) dans le pétrin; ~ plate *n* assiette creuse *or* à soupe; **~spoon** *n* cuiller *f* à soupe.
sour ['saʊə*] *a* aigre; it's ~ grapes (*fig*) c'est du dépit.
source [sɔ:s] *n* source *f*.
south [saʊθ] *n* sud *m* // *a* sud *inv*, du sud // *ad* au sud, vers le sud; S~ Africa *n* Afrique *f* du Sud; S~ African *a* sud-africain(e) // *n* Sud-Africain/e; S~

America n Amérique f du Sud; **S~ American** a sud-américain(e) // n Sud-Américain/e; **~east** n sud-est m; **~erly** ['sʌðəlɪ] a du sud; au sud; **~ern** ['sʌðən] a (du) sud; méridional(e); exposé(e) au sud; **S~ Pole** n Pôle m Sud; **~ward(s)** ad vers le sud; **~-west** n sud-ouest m.

souvenir [suːvə'nɪə*] n souvenir m (objet).

sovereign ['sɔvrɪn] a, n souverain(e).

soviet ['səuvɪət] a soviétique; **the S~ Union** l'Union f soviétique.

sow n [sau] truie f // vt [səu] (pt ~ed, pp sown [səun]) semer.

soya ['sɔɪə], (US) **soy** [sɔɪ] n: ~ **bean** n graine f de soja; ~ **sauce** n sauce f de soja.

spa [spɑː] n (town) station thermale; (US: also: **health ~**) établissement m de cure de rajeunissement etc.

space [speɪs] n (gen) espace m; (room) place f; espace; (length of time) laps m de temps // cpd spatial(e) // vt (also: ~ **out**) espacer; **~craft** n engin spatial; **~man/woman** n astronaute m/f, cosmonaute m/f; **~ship** n = **~craft**; **spacing** n espacement m.

spade [speɪd] n (tool) bêche f, pelle f; (child's) pelle; **~s** npl (CARDS) pique m.

Spain [speɪn] n Espagne f.

span [spæn] pt of **spin** // n (of bird, plane) envergure f; (of arch) portée f; (in time) espace m de temps, durée f // vt enjamber, franchir; (fig) couvrir, embrasser.

Spaniard ['spænjəd] n Espagnol/e.

spaniel ['spænjəl] n épagneul m.

Spanish ['spænɪʃ] a espagnol(e), d'Espagne // n (LING) espagnol m; **the ~** npl les Espagnols mpl.

spank [spæŋk] vt donner une fessée à.

spanner ['spænə*] n (Brit) clé f (de mécanicien).

spar [spɑː*] n espar m // vi (BOXING) s'entraîner.

spare [spɛə*] a de réserve, de rechange; (surplus) de or en trop, de reste // n (part) pièce f de rechange, pièce détachée // vt (do without) se passer de; (afford to give) donner, accorder, passer; (refrain from hurting) épargner; (refrain from using) ménager; **to ~** (surplus) en surplus, de trop; ~ **part** n pièce f de rechange, pièce détachée; ~ **time** n moments mpl de loisir; ~ **wheel** n (AUT) roue f de secours.

sparing ['spɛərɪŋ] a: **to be ~ with** ménager; **~ly** ad avec modération.

spark [spɑːk] n étincelle f; **~(ing) plug** n bougie f.

sparkle ['spɑːkl] n scintillement m, étincellement m, éclat m // vi étinceler, scintiller; (bubble) pétiller; **sparkling** a étincelant(e), scintillant(e); (wine)

mousseux(euse), pétillant(e).

sparrow ['spærəu] n moineau m.

sparse [spɑːs] a clairsemé(e).

spartan ['spɑːtən] a (fig) spartiate.

spasm ['spæzəm] n (MED) spasme m; (fig) accès m; **~odic** [-'mɔdɪk] a (fig) intermittent(e).

spastic ['spæstɪk] n handicapé/e moteur.

spat [spæt] pt, pp of **spit**.

spate [speɪt] n (fig): ~ **of** avalanche f or torrent m de; **in ~** (river) en crue.

spatter ['spætə*] vt éclabousser // vi gicler.

spawn [spɔːn] vi frayer // n frai m.

speak [spiːk], pt **spoke**, pp **spoken** vt (language) parler; (truth) dire // vi parler; (make a speech) prendre la parole; **to sb/of** or **about sth** parler à qn/de qch; ~ **up!** parle plus fort!; **~er** n (in public) orateur m; (also: **loud~er**) haut-parleur m; (POL): **the S~er** le président de la chambre des Communes (Brit) or des Représentants (US).

spear [spɪə*] n lance f; **~head** vt (attack etc) mener.

spec [spɛk] n (col): **on ~** à tout hasard.

special ['spɛʃl] a spécial(e); **~ist** n spécialiste m/f; **~ity** [spɛʃɪ'ælɪtɪ] n spécialité f; **~ize** vi: **to ~ize (in)** se spécialiser (dans); **~ly** ad spécialement, particulièrement.

species ['spiːʃiːz] n espèce f.

specific [spə'sɪfɪk] a précis(e); particulier(ère), (BOT, CHEM etc) spécifique; **~ally** ad expressément, explicitement.

specimen ['spesɪmən] n spécimen m, échantillon m; (MED) prélèvement m.

speck [spɛk] n petite tache, petit point; (particle) grain m.

speckled ['spɛkld] a tacheté(e), moucheté(e).

specs [spɛks] npl (col) lunettes fpl.

spectacle ['spɛktəkl] n spectacle m; **~s** npl lunettes fpl; **spectacular** [-'tækjulə*] a spectaculaire // n (CINEMA etc) superproduction f.

spectator [spɛk'teɪtə*] n spectateur/trice.

spectrum, pl **spectra** ['spɛktrəm, -rə] n spectre m; (fig) gamme f.

speculation [spɛkju'leɪʃən] n spéculation f; conjectures fpl.

speech [spiːtʃ] n (faculty) parole f; (talk) discours m, allocution f; (manner of speaking) façon f de parler, langage m; (enunciation) élocution f; **~less** a muet(te).

speed [spiːd] n vitesse f; (promptness) rapidité f; **at full** or **top ~** à toute vitesse or allure; **to ~ up** vi aller plus vite, accélérer // vt accélérer; **~boat** n vedette f, hors-bord m inv; **~ily** ad rapidement, promptement; **~ing** n (AUT) excès m de vitesse; ~ **limit** n limitation f de vitesse, vitesse maximale permise; **~ometer** [spɪˈdɔmɪtə*] n compteur m (de vitesse); **~way** n (SPORT) piste f de vitesse pour motos; (also: **~way racing**) épreuve(s) $f(pl)$ de vitesse de motos; **~y** a rapide, prompt(e).

spell [spɛl] n (also: **magic ~**) sortilège m, charme m; (period of time) (courte) période // vt (pt, pp spelt (Brit) or **~ed** [spɛlt, spɛld]) (in writing) écrire, orthographier; (aloud) épeler; (fig) signifier; **to cast a ~ on sb** jeter un sort à qn; he can't **~** il fait des fautes d'orthographe; **~bound** a envoûté(e), subjugué(e); **~ing** n orthographe f.

spend, pt, pp **spent** [spɛnd, spɛnt] vt (money) dépenser; (time, life) passer, consacrer; **~thrift** n dépensier/ère.

sperm [spəːm] n spermatozoïde m; (semen) sperme m.

spew [spjuː] vt vomir.

sphere [sfɪə*] n sphère f.

spice [spaɪs] n épice f.

spick-and-span [ˈspɪkənˈspæn] a impeccable.

spicy [ˈspaɪsɪ] a épicé(e), relevé(e); (fig) piquant(e).

spider [ˈspaɪdə*] n araignée f.

spike [spaɪk] n pointe f.

spill, pt, pp **spilt** or **~ed** [spɪl, -t, -d] vt renverser; répandre // vi se répandre; **to ~ over** vi déborder.

spin [spɪn] n (revolution of wheel) tour m; (AVIAT) (chute f en) vrille f; (trip in car) petit tour, balade f // vb (pt spun, span, pp spun) vt (wool etc) filer; (wheel) faire tourner // vi tourner, tournoyer; **to ~ out** vt faire durer.

spinach [ˈspɪnɪtʃ] n épinard m; (as food) épinards.

spinal [ˈspaɪnl] a vertébral(e), spinal(e); **~ cord** n moelle épinière.

spindly [ˈspɪndlɪ] a grêle, filiforme.

spin-dryer [spɪnˈdraɪə*] n (Brit) essoreuse f.

spine [spaɪn] n colonne vertébrale; (thorn) épine f, piquant m.

spinning [ˈspɪnɪŋ] n (of thread) filage m; (by machine) filature f; **~ top** n toupie f; **~ wheel** n rouet m.

spin-off [ˈspɪnɔf] n avantage inattendu; sous-produit m.

spinster [ˈspɪnstə*] n célibataire f; vieille fille.

spiral [ˈspaɪərl] n spirale f // a en spirale // vi (fig) monter en flèche; **~ staircase** n escalier m en colimaçon.

spire [spaɪə*] n flèche f, aiguille f.

spirit [ˈspɪrɪt] n (soul) esprit m, âme f; (ghost) esprit, revenant m; (mood) esprit, état m d'esprit; (courage) courage m, énergie f; **~s** npl (drink) spiritueux mpl, alcool m; **in good ~s** de bonne humeur; **~ed** a vif(vive), fou-

gueux(euse), plein(e) d'allant; **~ level** n niveau m à bulle.

spiritual [ˈspɪrɪtjuəl] a spirituel(le); religieux(euse).

spit [spɪt] n (for roasting) broche f // vi (pt, pp spat) cracher; (sound) crépiter.

spite [spaɪt] n rancune f, dépit m // vt contrarier, vexer; **in ~ of** en dépit de, malgré; **~ful** a malveillant(e), rancunier(ère).

spittle [ˈspɪtl] n salive f; bave f; crachat m.

splash [splæʃ] n éclaboussement m; (of colour) tache f // excl (sound) plouf // vt éclabousser // vi (also: **~ about**) barboter, patauger.

spleen [spliːn] n (ANAT) rate f.

splendid [ˈsplɛndɪd] a splendide, superbe, magnifique.

splint [splɪnt] n attelle f, éclisse f.

splinter [ˈsplɪntə*] n (wood) écharde f; (metal) éclat m // vi se fragmenter.

split [splɪt] n fente f, déchirure f; (fig: POL) scission f // vb (pt, pp split) vt fendre, déchirer; (party) diviser; (work, profits) partager, répartir // vi (divide) se diviser; **to ~ up** vi (couple) se séparer, rompre; (meeting) se disperser.

splutter [ˈsplʌtə*] vi bafouiller; postillonner.

spoil, pt, pp **spoilt** or **~ed** [spɔɪl, -t, -d] vt (damage) abîmer; (mar) gâcher; (child) gâter; **~s** npl butin m; **~sport** n trouble-fête m, rabat-joie m.

spoke [spəuk] pt of speak // n rayon m.

spoken [ˈspəukn] pp of speak.

spokesman [ˈspəuksmən], **spokeswoman** [ˈ-wumən] n porte-parole m inv.

sponge [spʌndʒ] n éponge f // vt éponger // vi: **to ~ off** or **on** vivre aux crochets de; **~ bag** n (Brit) trousse f de toilette; **~ cake** n ≈ biscuit m de Savoie.

sponsor [ˈspɔnsə*] n (RADIO, TV) personne f (or organisme m) qui assure le patronage // vt patronner; parrainer; **~ship** n patronage m; parrainage m.

spontaneous [spɔnˈteɪnɪəs] a spontané(e).

spooky [ˈspuːkɪ] a qui donne la chair de poule.

spool [spuːl] n bobine f.

spoon [spuːn] n cuiller f; **~-feed** vt nourrir à la cuiller; (fig) mâcher le travail à; **~ful** n cuillerée f.

sport [spɔːt] n sport m; (person) chic type/chic fille // vt arborer; **~ing** a sportif(ive); **to give sb a ~ing chance** donner sa chance à qn; **~ jacket** n (US) = **~s jacket**; **~s car** n voiture f de sport; **~s jacket** n veste f de sport; **~sman** n sportif m; **~smanship** n esprit sportif, sportivité f; **~swear** n vêtements mpl de sport; **~swoman** n

sportive f; ~y a sportif(ive).

spot [spɔt] n tache f; (dot: on pattern) pois m; (pimple) bouton m; (place) endroit m, coin m; (small amount): **a ~ of** un peu de // vt (notice) apercevoir; repérer; **on the ~** sur place, sur les lieux; **~ check** n sondage m, vérification ponctuelle; **~less** a immaculé(e); **~light** n projecteur m; (AUT) phare m auxiliaire; **~ted** a tacheté(e), moucheté(e); à pois; **~ty** a (face) boutonneux(euse).

spouse [spauz] n époux/épouse.

spout [spaut] n (of jug) bec m; (of liquid) jet m // vi jaillir.

sprain [spreɪn] n entorse f, foulure f // vt: **to ~ one's ankle** se fouler or se tordre la cheville.

sprang [spræŋ] pt of **spring**.

sprawl [sprɔ:l] vi s'étaler.

spray [spreɪ] n jet m (en fines gouttelettes); (container) vaporisateur m, bombe f; (of flowers) petit bouquet m // vt vaporiser, pulvériser; (crops) traiter.

spread [sprɛd] n propagation f; (distribution) répartition f; (CULIN) pâte f à tartiner // vb (pt, pp spread) vt étendre, étaler; répandre; propager // vi s'étendre; se répandre; se propager; **~-eagled** ['sprɛdi:gld] a étendu(e) bras et jambes écartés; **~sheet** n (COMPUT) tableur m.

spree [spri:] n: **to go on a ~** faire la fête.

sprightly ['spraɪtlɪ] a alerte.

spring [sprɪŋ] n (leap) bond m, saut m; (coiled metal) ressort m; (season) printemps m; (of water) source f // vi (pt sprang, pp sprung) bondir, sauter; **to ~ from** provenir de; **to ~ up** vi (problem) se présenter, surgir; **~board** n tremplin m; **~-clean** n (also: **~-cleaning**) grand nettoyage de printemps; **~time** n printemps m; **~y** a élastique, souple.

sprinkle ['sprɪŋkl] vt (pour) répandre; verser; **to ~ water etc on, ~ with water etc** asperger d'eau etc; **to ~ sugar etc on, ~ with sugar etc** saupoudrer de sucre etc; **~r** n (for lawn) arroseur m; (to put out fire) diffuseur m d'extincteur automatique d'incendie.

sprint [sprɪnt] n sprint m // vi sprinter.

sprout [spraut] vi germer, pousser; **~s** npl (also: **Brussels ~s**) choux mpl de Bruxelles.

spruce [spru:s] n épicéa m // a net(te), pimpant(e).

sprung [sprʌŋ] pp of **spring**.

spry [spraɪ] a alerte, vif(vive).

spun [spʌn] pt, pp of **spin**.

spur [spə:*] n éperon m; (fig) aiguillon m // vt (also: **~ on**) éperonner; aiguillonner; **on the ~ of** the moment sous l'impulsion du moment.

spurious ['spjuərɪəs] a faux(fausse).

spurn [spə:n] vt repousser avec mépris.

spurt [spə:t] vi jaillir, gicler.

spy [spaɪ] n espion/ne // vi: **to ~ on** espionner, épier // vt (see) apercevoir; **~ing** n espionnage m.

sq. (MATH), **Sq.** (in address) abbr of **square**.

squabble ['skwɔbl] vi se chamailler.

squad [skwɔd] n (MIL, POLICE) escouade f, groupe m; (FOOTBALL) contingent m.

squadron ['skwɔdrn] n (MIL) escadron m; (AVIAT, NAUT) escadrille f.

squalid ['skwɔlɪd] a sordide, ignoble.

squall [skwɔ:l] n rafale f, bourrasque f.

squalor ['skwɔlə*] n conditions fpl sordides.

squander ['skwɔndə*] vt gaspiller, dilapider.

square [skwɛə*] n carré m; (in town) place f; (instrument) équerre f // a carré(e); (honest) honnête, régulier(ère); (col: ideas, tastes) vieux jeu inv, qui retarde // vt (arrange) régler; arranger; (MATH) élever au carré // vi (agree) cadrer, s'accorder; **all ~** quitte; à égalité; **a ~ meal** un repas convenable; **2 metres ~** (de) 2 mètres sur 2; **1 ~ metre** 1 mètre carré.

squash [skwɔʃ] n (Brit: drink): **lemon/orange ~** citronnade f/orangeade f; (SPORT) squash m // vt écraser.

squat [skwɔt] a petit(e) et épais(se), ramassé(e) // vi s'accroupir; **~ter** n squatter m.

squawk [skwɔ:k] vi pousser un or des gloussement(s).

squeak [skwi:k] vi grincer, crier.

squeal [skwi:l] vi pousser un or des cri(s) aigu(s) or perçant(s).

squeamish ['skwi:mɪʃ] a facilement dégoûté(e); facilement scandalisé(e).

squeeze [skwi:z] n pression f; restrictions fpl de crédit // vt presser; (hand, arm) serrer; **to ~ out** vt exprimer; (fig) soutirer.

squelch [skwɛltʃ] vi faire un bruit de succion; patauger.

squib [skwɪb] n pétard m.

squid [skwɪd] n calmar m.

squiggle ['skwɪgl] n gribouillis m.

squint [skwɪnt] vi loucher // n: **he has a ~** il louche, il souffre de strabisme; **to ~ at sth** regarder qch du coin de l'œil; (quickly) jeter un coup d'œil à qch.

squire ['skwaɪə*] n (Brit) propriétaire terrien.

squirm [skwə:m] vi se tortiller.

squirrel ['skwɪrəl] n écureuil m.

squirt [skwə:t] vi jaillir, gicler.

Sr abbr of **senior**.

St abbr of **saint**, **street**.

stab [stæb] n (with knife etc) coup m (de couteau etc); (col: try): **to have a ~ at (doing) sth** s'essayer à (faire) qch // vt poignarder.

stable ['steɪbl] n écurie f // a stable.
stack [stæk] n tas m, pile f // vt empiler, entasser.
stadium ['steɪdɪəm] n stade m.
staff [sta:f] n (work force) personnel m; (: Brit SCOL) professeurs mpl; (: servants) domestiques mpl; (MIL) état-major m; (stick) perche f, bâton m // vt pourvoir en personnel.
stag [stæg] n cerf m.
stage [steɪdʒ] n scène f; (profession): the ~ le théâtre; (point) étape f, stade m; (platform) estrade f // vt (play) monter, mettre en scène; (demonstration) organiser; (fig: perform: recovery etc) effectuer; in ~s par étapes, par degrés; ~**coach** n diligence f; ~ **door** n entrée f des artistes; ~ **manager** n régisseur m.
stagger ['stægə*] vi chanceler, tituber // vt (person) stupéfier; bouleverser; (hours, holidays) étaler, échelonner.
stagnate [stæg'neɪt] vi stagner, croupir.
stag party n enterrement m de vie de garçon.
staid [steɪd] a posé(e), rassis(e).
stain [steɪn] n tache f; (colouring) colorant m // vt tacher; (wood) teindre; ~**ed glass window** n vitrail m; ~**less** a (steel) inoxydable; ~ **remover** n détachant m.
stair [stɛə*] n (step) marche f; ~**s** npl escalier m; on the ~s dans l'escalier; ~**case**, ~**way** n escalier m.
stake [steɪk] n pieu m, poteau m; (BETTING) enjeu m // vt risquer, jouer; to be at ~ être en jeu.
stale [steɪl] a (bread) rassis(e); (beer) éventé(e); (smell) de renfermé.
stalemate ['steɪlmeɪt] n pat m; (fig) impasse f.
stalk [stɔ:k] n tige f // vt traquer // vi marcher avec raideur.
stall [stɔ:l] n éventaire m, étal m; (in stable) stalle f // vt (AUT) caler // vi (AUT) caler; (fig) essayer de gagner du temps; ~**s** npl (Brit: in cinema, theatre) orchestre m.
stallion ['stælɪən] n étalon m (cheval).
stalwart ['stɔ:lwət] n partisan m fidèle.
stamina ['stæmɪnə] n vigueur f, endurance f.
stammer ['stæmə*] n bégaiement m // vi bégayer.
stamp [stæmp] n timbre m; (mark, also fig) empreinte f; (on document) cachet m // vi (also: ~ one's foot) taper du pied // vt tamponner, estamper; (letter) timbrer; ~ **album** n album m de timbres (-poste); ~ **collecting** n philatélie f.
stampede [stæm'pi:d] n ruée f.
stance [stæns] n position f.
stand [stænd] n (position) position f; (MIL) résistance f; (structure) guéridon m; support m; (COMM) étalage m, stand

m; (SPORT) tribune f // vb (pt, pp stood) vi être or se tenir (debout); (rise) se lever, se mettre debout; (be placed) se trouver // vt (place) mettre, poser; (tolerate, withstand) supporter; to make a ~ prendre position; to ~ for parliament (Brit) se présenter aux élections (comme candidat à la députation); to ~ by vi (be ready) se tenir prêt(e) // vt fus (opinion) s'en tenir à; to ~ **down** vi (withdraw) se retirer; to ~ **for** vt fus (signify) représenter, signifier; (tolerate) supporter, tolérer; to ~ **in for** vt fus remplacer; to ~ **out** vi (be prominent) ressortir; to ~ **up** vi (rise) se lever, se mettre debout; to ~ **up for** vt fus défendre; to ~ **up to** vt fus tenir tête à, résister à.
standard ['stændəd] n niveau voulu; (flag) étendard m // a (size etc) ordinaire, normal(e); courant(e); ~**s** npl (morals) morale f, principes mpl; ~ **lamp** n (Brit) lampadaire m; ~ **of living** n niveau m de vie.
stand-by ['stændbaɪ] n remplaçant/e, to be on ~ se tenir prêt(e) (à intervenir); être de garde; ~ **ticket** n (AVIAT) billet m sans garantie.
stand-in ['stændɪn] n remplaçant/e, (CINEMA) doublure f.
standing ['stændɪŋ] a debout inv // n réputation f, rang m, standing m; of many years' ~ qui dure or existe depuis longtemps; ~ **order** n (Brit: at bank) virement m automatique, prélèvement m bancaire; ~ **orders** npl (MIL) règlement m; ~ **room** n places fpl debout.
stand-offish [stænd'ɔfɪʃ] a distant(e), froid(e).
standpoint ['stændpɔɪnt] n point m de vue.
standstill ['stændstɪl] n: at a ~ à l'arrêt; (fig) au point mort; to come to a ~ s'immobiliser, s'arrêter.
stank [stæŋk] pt of stink.
staple ['steɪpl] n (for papers) agrafe f // a (food etc) de base, principal(e) // vt agrafer; ~**r** n agrafeuse f.
star [sta:*] n étoile f; (celebrity) vedette f // vi: to ~ (in) être la vedette (de) // vt (CINEMA) avoir pour vedette.
starboard ['sta:bəd] n tribord m.
starch [sta:tʃ] n amidon m.
stardom ['sta:dəm] n célébrité f.
stare [stɛə*] n regard m fixe // vi: to ~ at regarder fixement.
starfish ['sta:fɪʃ] n étoile f de mer.
stark [sta:k] a (bleak) désolé(e), morne // ad: ~ **naked** complètement nu(e).
starling ['sta:lɪŋ] n étourneau m.
starry ['sta:rɪ] a étoilé(e); ~**-eyed** a (innocent) ingénu(e).
start [sta:t] n commencement m, début m; (of race) départ m; (sudden

movement) sursaut *m* // *vt* commencer // *vi* partir, se mettre en route; (*jump*) sursauter; **to ~ doing** *or* **to do sth** se mettre à faire qch; **to ~ off** *vi* commencer; (*leave*) partir; **to ~ up** *vi* commencer; (*car*) démarrer // *vt* déclencher; (*car*) mettre en marche; **~er** *n* (*AUT*) démarreur *m*; (: *runner, horse*) partant *m*; (*Brit CULIN*) entrée *f*; **~ing point** *n* point *m* de départ.

startle ['stɑ:tl] *vt* faire sursauter; donner un choc à.

starvation [stɑ:'veɪʃən] *n* faim *f*, famine *f*.

starve [stɑ:v] *vi* mourir de faim; être affamé(e) // *vt* affamer.

state [steɪt] *n* état *m* // *vt* déclarer, affirmer; formuler; **the S~s** les États-Unis *mpl*; **to be in a ~** être dans tous ses états; **~ly** *a* majestueux(euse), imposant(e); **~ment** *n* déclaration *f*; (*LAW*) déposition *f*; **~sman** *n* homme *m* d'État.

static ['stætɪk] *n* (*RADIO*) parasites *mpl* // *a* statique.

station ['steɪʃən] *n* gare *f*; poste *m* (militaire *or* de police *etc*); (*rank*) condition *f*, rang *m* // *vt* placer, poster.

stationary ['steɪʃnərɪ] *a* à l'arrêt, immobile.

stationer ['steɪʃənə*] *n* papetier/ère; **~'s (shop)** *n* papeterie *f*; **~y** *n* papier *m* à lettres, petit matériel de bureau.

station master *n* (*RAIL*) chef *m* de gare.

station wagon *n* (*US*) break *m*.

statistic [stə'tɪstɪk] *n* statistique *f*; **~s** *n* (*science*) statistique *f*.

statue ['stætju:] *n* statue *f*.

status ['steɪtəs] *n* position *f*, situation *f*; prestige *m*; statut *m*; ~ **symbol** *n* marque *f* de standing.

statute ['stætju:t] *n* loi *f*; **~s** *npl* (*of club etc*) statuts *mpl*; **statutory** *a* statutaire, prévu(e) par un article de loi.

staunch [stɔ:ntʃ] *a* sûr(e), loyal(e).

stave [steɪv] *n* (*MUS*) portée *f* // *vt*: **to ~ off** (*attack*) parer; (*threat*) conjurer.

stay [steɪ] *n* (*period of time*) séjour *m* // *vi* rester; (*reside*) loger; (*spend some time*) séjourner; **to ~ put** ne pas bouger; **to ~ with friends** loger chez des amis; **to ~ the night** passer la nuit; **to ~ behind** *vi* rester en arrière; **to ~ in** *vi* (*at home*) rester à la maison; **to ~ on** *vi* rester; **to ~ out** *vi* (*of house*) ne pas rentrer; **to ~ up** *vi* (*at night*) ne pas se coucher; **~ing power** *n* endurance *f*.

stead [stɛd] *n*: **in sb's ~** à la place de qn; **to stand sb in good ~** être très utile *or* servir beaucoup à qn.

steadfast ['stɛdfɑ:st] *a* ferme, résolu(e).

steadily ['stɛdɪlɪ] *ad* progressivement; sans arrêt; (*walk*) d'un pas ferme.

steady ['stɛdɪ] *a* stable, solide, ferme; (*regular*) constant(e), régulier(ère); (*person*) calme, pondéré(e) // *vt* stabiliser; assujettir; calmer; **to ~ o.s.** reprendre son aplomb.

steak [steɪk] *n* (*meat*) bifteck *m*, steak *m*; (*fish*) tranche *f*.

steal [sti:l], *pt* **stole**, *pp* **stolen** *vt*, *vi* voler.

stealth [stɛlθ] *n*: **by ~** furtivement; **~y** *a* furtif(ive).

steam [sti:m] *n* vapeur *f* // *vt* passer à la vapeur; (*CULIN*) cuire à la vapeur // *vi* fumer; (*ship*): **to ~ along** filer; ~ **engine** *n* locomotive *f* à vapeur; **~er** *n* (bateau *m* à) vapeur *m*; **~roller** *n* rouleau compresseur; **~ship** *n* = **~er**; **~y** *a* embué(e), humide.

steel [sti:l] *n* acier *m* // *cpd* d'acier; **~works** *n* aciérie *f*.

steep [sti:p] *a* raide, escarpé(e); (*price*) très élevé(e), excessif(ive) // *vt* (faire) tremper.

steeple ['sti:pl] *n* clocher *m*.

steer [stɪə*] *n* bœuf *m* // *vt* diriger, gouverner; guider // *vi* tenir le gouvernail; **~ing** *n* (*AUT*) conduite *f*; **~ing wheel** *n* volant *m*.

stem [stɛm] *n* (*of plant*) tige *f*; (*of leaf, fruit*) queue *f*; (*of glass*) pied *m* // *vt* contenir, endiguer, juguler; **to ~ from** *vt fus* provenir de, découler de.

stench [stɛntʃ] *n* puanteur *f*.

stencil ['stɛnsl] *n* stencil *m*; pochoir *m* // *vt* polycopier.

stenographer [stə'nɔgrəfə*] *n* (*US*) sténographe *m/f*.

step [stɛp] *n* pas *m*; (*stair*) marche *f*; (*action*) mesure *f*, disposition *f* // *vi*: **to ~ forward** faire un pas en avant, avancer; **~s** *npl* (*Brit*) = **stepladder**; **to be in/out of ~ (with)** (*fig*) aller dans le sens (de)/être déphasé(e) (par rapport à); **to ~ down** *vi* (*fig*) se retirer, se désister; **to ~ off** *vt fus* descendre de; **to ~ up** *vt* augmenter; intensifier; **~brother** *n* demi-frère *m*; **~daughter** *n* belle-fille *f*; **~father** *n* beau-père *m*; **~ladder** *n* escabeau *m*; **~mother** *n* belle-mère *f*; **~ping stone** *n* pierre *f* de gué; (*fig*) tremplin *m*; **~sister** *n* demi-sœur *f*; **~son** *n* beau-fils *m*.

stereo ['stɛrɪəu] *n* (*system*) stéréo *f*; (*record player*) chaîne *f* stéréo // *a* (*also*: **~phonic**) stéréophonique.

sterile ['stɛraɪl] *a* stérile; **sterilize** ['stɛrɪlaɪz] *vt* stériliser.

sterling ['stɜ:lɪŋ] *a* (*silver*) de bon aloi, fin(e); (*fig*) à toute épreuve, excellent(e) // *n* (*ECON*) livres *fpl* sterling *inv*; **a pound ~** une livre sterling.

stern [stɜ:n] *a* sévère // *n* (*NAUT*) arrière *m*, poupe *f*.

stew [stju:] *n* ragoût *m* // *vt*, *vi* cuire à la casserole.

steward ['stju:əd] n (AVIAT, NAUT, RAIL) steward m; (in club etc) intendant m; ~**ess** n hôtesse f.

stick [stik] n bâton m; morceau m // vb (pt, pp **stuck**) vt (glue) coller; (thrust): to ~ **sth into** piquer or planter or enfoncer qch dans; (col: put) mettre, fourrer; (col: tolerate) supporter // vi se planter; tenir; (remain) rester; to ~ **out**, to ~ **up** vi dépasser, sortir; to ~ **up for** vt fus défendre; ~**er** n auto-collant m; ~**ing plaster** n sparadrap m, pansement adhésif.

stickler ['stiklə*] n: to be a ~ **for** être pointilleux(euse) sur.

stick-up ['stikʌp] n braquage m, hold-up m.

sticky ['stiki] a poisseux(euse); (label) adhésif(ive).

stiff [stif] a raide; rigide; dur(e); (difficult) difficile, ardu(e); (cold) froid(e), distant(e); (strong, high) fort(e), élevé(e); ~**en** vt raidir, renforcer // vi se raidir; se durcir; ~ **neck** n torticolis m.

stifle ['staifl] vt étouffer, réprimer.

stigma, pl (BOT, MED, REL) ~**ta**, (fig) ~**s** [stigmə, stig'mɑ:tə] n stigmate m.

stile [stail] n échalier m.

stiletto [sti'letəu] n (Brit: also: ~ **heel**) talon m aiguille.

still [stil] a immobile; calme, tranquille // ad (up to this time) encore, toujours; (even) encore; (nonetheless) quand même, tout de même; ~**born** a mort-né(e); ~ **life** n nature morte.

stilt [stilt] n échasse f; (pile) pilotis m.

stilted ['stiltid] a guindé(e), em-prunté(e).

stimulate ['stimjuleit] vt stimuler.

stimulus, pl **stimuli** ['stimjuləs, 'stimjulai] n stimulant m; (BIOL, PSYCH) stimulus m.

sting [stiŋ] n piqûre f; (organ) dard m // vt, vi (pt, pp **stung**) piquer.

stingy ['stindʒi] a avare, pingre.

stink [stiŋk] n puanteur f // vi (pt **stank**, pp **stunk**) puer, empester; ~**ing** a (fig: col) infect(e), vache; a ~**ing** ... un(e) foutu(e) .....

stint [stint] n part f de travail // vi: to ~ **on** lésiner sur, être chiche de.

stir [stə:*] n agitation f, sensation f // vt remuer // vi remuer, bouger; to ~ **up** vt exciter.

stirrup ['stirəp] n étrier m.

stitch [stitʃ] n (SEWING) point m; (KNITTING) maille f; (MED) point de suture; (pain) point de côté // vt coudre, piquer; suturer.

stoat [stəut] n hermine f (avec son pe-lage d'été).

stock [stɔk] n réserve f, provision f; (COMM) stock m; (AGR) cheptel m, bétail m; (CULIN) bouillon m;

(FINANCE) valeurs fpl, titres mpl // a (fig: reply etc) courant(e); classique // vt (have in stock) avoir, vendre; **in/out of** ~ en stock or en magasin/épuisé(e); **to take** ~ (fig) faire le point; ~**s and shares** valeurs (mobilières), titres; **to ~ up** vi: to ~ **up (with)** s'approvisionner (en).

stockbroker ['stɔkbrəukə*] n agent m de change.

stock cube n bouillon-cube m.

stock exchange n Bourse f (des valeurs).

stocking ['stɔkiŋ] n bas m.

stock: ~ **market** n Bourse f, marché financier; ~ **phrase** n cliché m; ~**pile** n stock, réserve f // vt stocker, accumuler; ~**taking** n (Brit COMM) inventaire m.

stocky ['stɔki] a trapu(e), râblé(e).

stodgy ['stɔdʒi] a bourratif(ive), lourd(e).

stoke [stəuk] vt garnir, entretenir; chauffer.

stole [stəul] pt of **steal** // n étole f.

stolen ['stəuln] pp of **steal**.

stolid ['stɔlid] a impassible, flegmatique.

stomach ['stʌmək] n estomac m; (abdomen) ventre m // vt supporter; digérer; ~ **ache** n mal m à l'estomac or au ventre.

stone [stəun] n pierre f; (pebble) caillou m, galet m; (in fruit) noyau m; (MED) calcul m; (Brit: weight) = 6.348 kg; 14 pounds // cpd de or en pierre // vt dénoyauter; ~**-cold** a complètement froid(e); ~**-deaf** a sourd(e) comme un pot; ~**work** n maçonnerie f.

stood [stud] pt, pp of **stand**.

stool [stu:l] n tabouret m.

stoop [stu:p] vi (also: **have a** ~) être voûté(e); (bend) se baisser.

stop [stɔp] n arrêt m; halte f; (in punctuation) point m // vt arrêter; (break off) interrompre; (also: **put a** ~ **to**) mettre fin à // vi s'arrêter; (rain, noise etc) cesser, s'arrêter; to ~ **doing** sth cesser or arrêter de faire qch; to ~ **dead** vi s'arrêter net; to ~ **off** vi faire une courte halte; to ~ **up** vt (hole) bou-cher; ~**gap** n (person) bouche-trou m; (measure) mesure f intérimaire; ~**lights** npl (AUT) signaux mpl de stop, feux mpl arrière; ~**over** n halte f; (AVIAT) escale f.

stoppage ['stɔpidʒ] n arrêt m; (of pay) retenue f; (strike) arrêt de travail.

stopper ['stɔpə*] n bouchon m.

stop press n nouvelles fpl de dernière heure.

stopwatch ['stɔpwɔtʃ] n chronomètre m.

storage ['stɔ:ridʒ] n emmagasinage m; (COMPUT) mise f en mémoire or réserve; ~ **heater** n radiateur m électrique par accumulation.

store [stɔ:*] n provision f, réserve f; (dépôt) entrepôt m; (Brit: large shop) grand magasin; (US) magasin m // vt emmagasiner; **~s** npl provisions; **to ~ up** vt mettre en réserve, emmagasiner; **~room** n réserve f, magasin m.

storey, (US) story ['stɔ:rɪ] n étage m.

stork [stɔ:k] n cigogne f.

storm [stɔ:m] n orage m, tempête f; ouragan m // vi (fig) fulminer // vt prendre d'assaut; **~y** a orageux(euse).

story ['stɔ:rɪ] n histoire f; récit m; (US) = storey; **~book** n livre m d'histoires or de contes.

stout [staut] a solide; (brave) intrépide; (fat) gros(se), corpulent(e) // n bière brune.

stove [stəuv] n (for cooking) fourneau m; (: small) réchaud m; (for heating) poêle m.

stow [stəu] vt ranger; cacher; **~away** n passager/ère clandestin/e.

straddle ['strædl] vt enjamber, être à cheval sur.

straggle ['strægl] vi être (or marcher) en désordre; **~r** n traînard/e.

straight [streɪt] a droite(e); (frank) honnête, franc(franche) // ad (tout) droit; (drink) sec, sans eau; **to put** or **get ~** mettre en ordre, mettre de l'ordre dans; **~ away, ~ off** (at once) tout de suite; **~en** vt (also: **~en out**) redresser; **~-faced** a impassible; **~forward** a simple; honnête, direct(e).

strain [streɪn] n (TECH) tension f; pression f; (physical) effort m; (mental) tension (nerveuse); (MED) entorse f; (streak, trace) tendance f; élément m // vt tendre fortement; mettre à l'épreuve; (filter) passer, filtrer // vi peiner, fournir un gros effort; **~s** npl (MUS) accords mpl, accents mpl; **~ed** a (laugh etc) forcé(e), contraint(e); (relations) tendu(e); **~er** n passoire f.

strait [streɪt] n (GEO) détroit m; **~jacket** n camisole f de force; **~-laced** a collet monté inv.

strand [strænd] n (of thread) fil m, brin m; **~ed** a en rade, en plan.

strange [streɪndʒ] a (not known) inconnu(e); (odd) étrange, bizarre; **~r** n inconnu/e; étranger/ère.

strangle ['stræŋgl] vt étrangler; **~hold** n (fig) emprise totale, mainmise f.

strap [stræp] n lanière f, courroie f, sangle f; (of slip, dress) bretelle f // vt attacher (avec une courroie etc).

strategic [strə'ti:dʒɪk] a stratégique.

strategy ['strætɪdʒɪ] n stratégie f.

straw [strɔ:] n paille f; **that's the last ~!** ça c'est le comble!

strawberry ['strɔ:bərɪ] n fraise f.

stray [streɪ] a (animal) perdu(e), errant(e) // vi s'égarer; **~ bullet** n balle perdue.

streak [stri:k] n raie f, bande f, filet m; (fig: of madness etc): **a ~ of** une or des tendance(s) à // vt zébrer, strier // vi: **to ~ past** passer à toute allure.

stream [stri:m] n ruisseau m; courant m, flot m; (of people) défilé ininterrompu, flot // vt (SCOL) répartir par niveau // vi ruisseler; **to ~ in/out** entrer/sortir à flots.

streamer ['stri:mə*] n serpentin m, banderole f.

streamlined ['stri:mlaɪnd] a (AVIAT) fuselé(e), profilé(e); (AUT) aérodynamique; (fig) rationalisé(e).

street [stri:t] n rue f // cpd de la rue; des rues; **~car** n (US) tramway m; **~lamp** n réverbère m; **~ plan** n plan m des rues; **~wise** a (col) futé(e), réaliste.

strength [strɛŋθ] n force f; (of girder, knot etc) solidité f; **~en** vt fortifier; renforcer; consolider.

strenuous ['strɛnjuəs] a vigoureux(euse), énergique; (tiring) ardu(e), fatigant(e).

stress [strɛs] n (force, pressure) pression f; (mental strain) tension (nerveuse); (accent) accent m // vt insister sur, souligner.

stretch [strɛtʃ] n (of sand etc) étendue f // vi s'étirer; (extend): **to ~ to** or **as far as** s'étendre jusqu'à // vt tendre, étirer; (spread) étendre; (fig) pousser (au maximum); **to ~ out** vi s'étendre // vt (arm etc) allonger, tendre; (to spread) étendre.

stretcher ['strɛtʃə*] n brancard m, civière f.

strewn [stru:n] a: **~ with** jonché(e) de.

stricken ['strɪkən] a (person) très éprouvé(e); (city, industry etc) dévasté(e); **~ with** (disease etc) frappé(e) or atteint(e) de.

strict [strɪkt] a strict(e).

stride [straɪd] n grand pas, enjambée f // vi (pt strode, pp stridden [strəud, 'strɪdn]) marcher à grands pas.

strife [straɪf] n conflit m, dissensions fpl.

strike [straɪk] n grève f; (of oil etc) découverte f; (attack) raid m // vb (pt, pp struck) vt frapper; (oil etc) trouver, découvrir // vi faire grève; (attack) attaquer; (clock) sonner; **on ~** (workers) en grève; **to ~ a match** frotter une allumette; **to ~ down** vt (fig) terrasser; **to ~ out** vt rayer; **to ~ up** vt (MUS) se mettre à jouer; **to ~ up a friendship with** se lier d'amitié avec; **~r** n gréviste m/f; (SPORT) buteur m; **striking** a frappant(e), saisissant(e).

string [strɪŋ] n ficelle f, fil m; (row) rang m; chapelet m; file f; (MUS) corde f // vt (pt, pp strung): **to ~ out** échelonner; **to ~ together** enchaîner; the

~s *npl* (*MUS*) les instruments *mpl* à cordes; **to pull** ~s (*fig*) faire jouer le piston; ~ **bean** *n* haricot vert; ~**(ed) instrument** *n* (*MUS*) instrument *m* à cordes.

stringent ['strindʒənt] *a* rigoureux(euse); (*need*) impérieux(euse).

strip [strɪp] *n* bande *f* // *vt* déshabiller; dégarnir, dépouiller; (*also*: ~ **down**: *machine*) démonter // *vi* se déshabiller; ~ **cartoon** *n* bande dessinée.

stripe [straɪp] *n* raie *f*, rayure *f*; ~**d** *a* rayé(e), à rayures.

strip lighting *n* éclairage *m* au néon or fluorescent.

stripper ['strɪpə*] *n* strip-teaseuse *f*.

strive [straɪv], *pt* **strove**, *pp* **striven** [straɪv, strəuv, 'strɪvn] *vi*: **to** ~ **to do** s'efforcer de faire.

strode [strəud] *pt of* **stride**.

stroke [strəuk] *n* coup *m*; (*MED*) attaque *f*; (*caress*) caresse *f* // *vt* caresser; **at a** ~ d'un (seul) coup.

stroll [strəul] *n* petite promenade // *vi* flâner, se promener nonchalamment; ~**er** *n* (*US*) poussette *f*.

strong [strɔŋ] *a* fort(e); vigoureux(euse); solide; vif(vive); **they are 50** ~ ils sont au nombre de 50; ~**box** *n* coffre-fort *m*; ~**hold** *n* bastion *m*; ~**ly** *ad* fortement, avec force; vigoureusement; solidement; ~**room** *n* chambre forte.

strove [strəuv] *pt of* **strive**.

struck [strʌk] *pt*, *pp of* **strike**.

structural ['strʌktʃərəl] *a* structural(e); (*CONSTR*) de construction; affectant les parties portantes.

structure ['strʌktʃə*] *n* structure *f*; (*building*) construction *f*; édifice *m*.

struggle ['strʌgl] *n* lutte *f* // *vi* lutter, se battre.

strum [strʌm] *vt* (*guitar*) gratter de.

strung [strʌŋ] *pt*, *pp of* **string**.

strut [strʌt] *n* étai *m*, support *m* // *vi* se pavaner.

stub [stʌb] *n* bout *m*; (*of ticket etc*) talon *m* // *vt*: **to** ~ **one's toe** se heurter le doigt de pied; **to** ~ **out** *vt* écraser.

stubble ['stʌbl] *n* chaume *m*; (*on chin*) barbe *f* de plusieurs jours.

stubborn ['stʌbən] *a* têtu(e), obstiné(e), opiniâtre.

stucco ['stʌkəu] *n* stuc *m*.

stuck [stʌk] *pt*, *pp of* **stick** // *a* (*jammed*) bloqué(e), coincé(e); ~**-up** *a* prétentieux(euse).

stud [stʌd] *n* clou *m* (à grosse tête); bouton *m* de col; (*of horses*) écurie *f*, haras *m*; (*also*: ~ **horse**) étalon *m* // *vt* (*fig*): ~**ded with** parsemé(e) or criblé(e) de.

student ['stju:dənt] *n* étudiant/e // *cpd* estudiantin(e); universitaire; d'étudiant; ~ **driver** *n* (*US*) (conducteur/trice

débutant(e).

studio ['stju:dɪəu] *n* studio *m*, atelier *m*.

studious ['stju:dɪəs] *a* studieux(euse), appliqué(e); (*studied*) étudié(e); ~**ly** *ad* (*carefully*) soigneusement.

study ['stʌdɪ] *n* étude *f*; (*room*) bureau *m* // *vt* étudier; examiner // *vi* étudier, faire ses études.

stuff [stʌf] *n* chose(s) *f(pl)*, truc *m*; affaires *fpl*, trucs; (*substance*) substance *f* // *vt* rembourrer; (*CULIN*) farcir; ~**ing** *n* bourre *f*, rembourrage *m*; (*CULIN*) farce *f*; ~**y** *a* (*room*) mal ventilé(e) or aéré(e); (*ideas*) vieux jeu *inv*.

stumble ['stʌmbl] *vi* trébucher; **to** ~ **across** (*fig*) tomber sur; **stumbling block** *n* pierre *f* d'achoppement.

stump [stʌmp] *n* souche *f*; (*of limb*) moignon *m* // *vt*: **to be** ~**ed** sécher, ne pas savoir que répondre.

stun [stʌn] *vt* étourdir; abasourdir.

stung [stʌŋ] *pt*, *pp of* **sting**.

stunk [stʌŋk] *pp of* **stink**.

stunt [stʌnt] *n* tour *m* de force; truc *m* publicitaire; (*AVIAT*) acrobatie *f* // *vt* retarder, arrêter; ~**ed** *a* rabougri(e); ~**man** *n* cascadeur *m*.

stupendous [stju:'pɛndəs] *a* prodigieux(euse), fantastique.

stupid ['stju:pɪd] *a* stupide, bête; ~**ity** [-'pɪdɪtɪ] *n* stupidité *f*, bêtise *f*.

sturdy ['stə:dɪ] *a* robuste, vigoureux(euse); solide.

stutter ['stʌtə*] *vi* bégayer.

sty [staɪ] *n* (*of pigs*) porcherie *f*.

stye [staɪ] *n* (*MED*) orgelet *m*.

style [staɪl] *n* style *m*; (*distinction*) allure *f*, cachet *m*, style; **stylish** *a* élégant(e), chic *inv*; **stylist** *n* (*hair stylist*) coiffeur/euse.

stylus ['staɪləs] *n* (*of record player*) pointe *f* de lecture.

suave [swɑ:v] *a* doucereux(euse), onctueux(euse).

sub... [sʌb] *prefix* sub..., sous-; ~**conscious** *a* subconscient(e) // *n* subconscient *m*; ~**contract** *vt* soustraiter.

subdue [sʌb'dju:] *vt* subjuguer, soumettre; ~**d** *a* contenu(e), atténué(e); (*light*) tamisé(e); (*person*) qui a perdu de son entrain.

subject *n* ['sʌbdʒɪkt] sujet *m*; (*SCOL*) matière *f* // *vt* [səb'dʒɛkt]: **to** ~ **to** soumettre à; exposer à; **to be** ~ **to** (*law*) être soumis(e) à; (*disease*) être sujet(te) à; ~**ive** [səb'dʒɛktɪv] *a* subjectif(ive); ~ **matter** *n* sujet *m*; contenu *m*.

subjunctive [səb'dʒʌŋktɪv] *n* subjonctif *m*.

sublet [sʌb'lɛt] *vt* sous-louer.

submachine gun ['sʌbmə'ʃi:n-] *n* fusil-mitrailleur *m*.

submarine [sʌbmə'ri:n] *n* sous-marin

m.

submerge [səb'mə:dʒ] *vt* submerger; immerger // *vi* plonger.

submission [səb'mɪʃən] *n* soumission *f*.

submissive [səb'mɪsɪv] *a* soumis(e).

submit [səb'mɪt] *vt* soumettre // *vi* se soumettre.

subnormal [sʌb'nɔːməl] *a* au-dessous de la normale; *(backward)* arriéré(e).

subordinate [sə'bɔːdɪnət] *a, n* subordonné(e).

subpoena [səb'piːnə] *n (LAW)* citation *f*, assignation *f*.

subscribe [səb'skraɪb] *vi* cotiser; to ~ to *(opinion, fund)* souscrire à; *(newspaper)* s'abonner à; être abonné(e) à; ~**r** *n (to periodical, telephone)* abonné(e).

subscription [səb'skrɪpʃən] *n* souscription *f*; abonnement *m*.

subsequent ['sʌbsɪkwənt] *a* ultérieur(e), suivant(e); consécutif(ive); ~**ly** *ad* par la suite.

subside [səb'saɪd] *vi* s'affaisser; *(flood)* baisser; *(wind)* tomber; ~**nce** [-'saɪdns] *n* affaissement *m*.

subsidiary [səb'sɪdɪərɪ] *a* subsidiaire; accessoire // *n* filiale *f*.

subsidize ['sʌbsɪdaɪz] *vt* subventionner.

subsidy ['sʌbsɪdɪ] *n* subvention *f*.

substance ['sʌbstəns] *n* substance *f*; *(fig)* essentiel *m*.

substantial [səb'stænʃl] *a* substantiel(le); *(fig)* important(e).

substantiate [səb'stænʃɪeɪt] *vt* étayer, fournir des preuves à l'appui de.

substitute ['sʌbstɪtjuːt] *n (person)* remplaçant/e; *(thing)* succédané *m* // *vt*: to ~ sth/sb for substituer qch/qn à, remplacer par qch/qn.

subterranean [sʌbtə'reɪnɪən] *a* souterrain(e).

subtitle ['sʌbtaɪtl] *n (CINEMA)* sous-titre *m*.

subtle ['sʌtl] *a* subtil(e).

subtotal [sʌb'təʊtl] *n* total partiel.

subtract [səb'trækt] *vt* soustraire, retrancher; ~**ion** [-'trækʃən] *n* soustraction *f*.

suburb ['sʌbəːb] *n* faubourg *m*; the ~s la banlieue; ~**an** [sə'bəːbən] *a* de banlieue, suburbain(e); ~**ia** [sə'bəːbɪə] *n* la banlieue.

subway ['sʌbweɪ] *n (US)* métro *m*; *(Brit)* passage souterrain.

succeed [sək'siːd] *vi* réussir; avoir du succès // *vt* succéder à; to ~ in doing réussir à faire; ~**ing** *a (following)* suivant(e).

success [sək'sɛs] *n* succès *m*; réussite *f*; ~**ful** *a (venture)* couronné(e) de succès; to be ~**ful** *(in doing)* réussir (à faire); ~**fully** *ad* avec succès.

succession [sək'sɛʃən] *n* succession *f*.

successive [sək'sɛsɪv] *a* successif(ive).

consécutif(ive).

such [sʌtʃ] *a* tel(telle); *(of that kind)*: ~ a book un livre de ce genre *or* pareil, un tel livre; ~ **books** des livres de ce genre *or* pareils, de tels livres; *(so much)*: ~ **courage** un tel courage // *ad* si; ~ **a long trip** un si long voyage; ~ **good books** de si bons livres; ~ **a lot of sentiment** *or* tant de; ~ **as** *(like)* tel(telle) que, comme; **a noise** ~ **as** to un bruit de nature à; **as** ~ *ad* en tant que tel(telle), à proprement parler; ~**-and-**~ *a* tel(telle) ou tel(telle).

suck [sʌk] *vt* sucer; *(breast, bottle)* téter; ~**er** *n (BOT, ZOOL, TECH)* ventouse *f*; *(col)* naïf/ïve, poire *f*.

suction ['sʌkʃən] *n* succion *f*.

sudden ['sʌdn] *a* soudain(e), subit(e); all of a ~ soudain, tout à coup; ~**ly** *ad* brusquement, tout à coup, soudain.

suds [sʌdz] *npl* eau savonneuse.

sue [suː] *vt* poursuivre en justice, intenter un procès à.

suede [sweɪd] *n* daim *m*, cuir suédé // *cpd* de daim.

suet ['sʊɪt] *n* graisse *f* de rognon *or* de bœuf.

suffer ['sʌfə*] *vt* souffrir, subir; *(bear)* tolérer, supporter // *vi* souffrir; ~**er** *n* malade *m/f*; victime *m/f*; ~**ing** *n* souffrance(s) *f(pl)*.

sufficient [sə'fɪʃənt] *a* suffisant(e); ~ **money** suffisamment d'argent; ~**ly** *ad* suffisamment, assez.

suffocate ['sʌfəkeɪt] *vi* suffoquer; étouffer.

suffused [sə'fjuːzd] *a*: to be ~ with baigner dans, être imprégné(e) de.

sugar ['ʃʊgə*] *n* sucre *m* // *vt* sucrer; ~ **beet** *n* betterave sucrière; ~ **cane** *n* canne *f* à sucre; ~**y** *a* sucré(e).

suggest [sə'dʒɛst] *vt* suggérer, proposer; dénoter; ~**ion** [-'dʒɛstʃən] *n* suggestion *f*.

suicide ['sʊɪsaɪd] *n* suicide *m*.

suit [suːt] *n (man's)* costume *m*, complet *m*; *(woman's)* tailleur *m*, ensemble *m*; *(CARDS)* couleur *f* // *vt* aller à; convenir à; *(adapt)*: to ~ sth to adapter *or* approprier qch à; ~**able** *a* qui convient; approprié(e); ~**ably** *ad* comme il se doit *(or* se devait *etc)*, convenablement.

suitcase ['suːtkeɪs] *n* valise *f*.

suite [swiːt] *n (of rooms, also MUS)* suite *f*; *(furniture)*: **bedroom/dining room** ~ (ensemble *m* de) chambre *f* à coucher/ salle *f* à manger.

suitor ['suːtə*] *n* soupirant *m*, prétendant *m*.

sulfur ['sʌlfə*] *n (US)* = **sulphur**.

sulk [sʌlk] *vi* bouder; ~**y** *a* boudeur(euse), maussade.

sullen ['sʌlən] *a* renfrogné(e), maussade; morne.

sulphur, *(US)* sulfur ['sʌlfə*] *n* soufre

m.

sultana [sʌl'tɑ:nə] *n* (*fruit*) raisin (sec) de Smyrne.

sultry ['sʌltrɪ] *a* étouffant(e).

sum [sʌm] *n* somme *f*; (*SCOL etc*) calcul *m*; **to ~ up** *vt*, *vi* résumer.

summarize ['sʌmərɑɪz] *vt* résumer.

summary ['sʌmərɪ] *n* résumé *m* // *a* (*justice*) sommaire.

summer ['sʌmə*] *n* été *m* // *cpd* d'été, estival(e); **~house** *n* (*in garden*) pavillon *m*; **~time** *n* (*season*) été *m*; **~ time** *n* (*by clock*) heure *f* d'été.

summit ['sʌmɪt] *n* sommet *m*.

summon ['sʌmən] *vt* appeler, convoquer; **to ~ up** *vt* rassembler, faire appel à; **~s** *n* citation *f*, assignation *f*.

sump [sʌmp] *n* (*Brit AUT*) carter *m*.

sun [sʌn] *n* soleil *m*; **in the ~** au soleil; **~bathe** *vi* prendre un bain de soleil; **~burn** *n* coup *m* de soleil; (*tan*) bronzage *m*.

Sunday ['sʌndɪ] *n* dimanche *m*; **~ school** *n* ≈ catéchisme *m*.

sundial ['sʌndɑɪəl] *n* cadran *m* solaire.

sundown ['sʌndaun] *n* coucher *m* du soleil.

sundry ['sʌndrɪ] *a* divers(e), différent(e); **all and ~** tout le monde, n'importe qui; **sundries** *npl* articles divers.

sunflower ['sʌnflauə*] *n* tournesol *m*.

sung [sʌŋ] *pp of* **sing**.

sunglasses ['sʌnglɑ:sɪz] *npl* lunettes *fpl* de soleil.

sunk [sʌŋk] *pp of* **sink**.

sun: ~light *n* (lumière *f* du) soleil *m*; **~ny** *a* ensoleillé(e); (*fig*) épanoui(e), radieux(euse); **~rise** *n* lever *m* du soleil; **~ roof** (*AUT*) toit ouvrant; **~set** *n* coucher *m* du soleil; **~shade** *n* (*over table*) parasol *m*; **~shine** *n* (lumière *f* du) soleil *m*; **~stroke** *n* insolation *f*, coup *m* de soleil; **~tan** *n* bronzage *m*; **~tan oil** *n* huile *f* solaire.

super ['su:pə*] *a* (*col*) formidable.

superannuation [su:pərænju'eɪʃən] *n* cotisations *fpl* pour la pension.

superb [su:'pə:b] *a* superbe, magnifique.

supercilious [su:pə'sɪlɪəs] *a* hautain(e), dédaigneux(euse).

superficial [su:pə'fɪʃəl] *a* superficiel(le).

superintendent [su:pərɪn'tendənt] *n* directeur/trice; (*POLICE*) ≈ commissaire *m*.

superior [su'pɪərɪə*] *a*, *n* supérieur(e); **~ity** [-'ɔrɪtɪ] *n* supériorité *f*.

superlative [su'pə:lətɪv] *a* sans pareil(le), suprême // *n* (*LING*) superlatif *m*.

superman ['su:pəmæn] *n* surhomme *m*.

supermarket ['su:pəmɑ:kɪt] *n* supermarché *m*.

supernatural [su:pə'nætʃərəl] *a*

surnaturel(le).

superpower ['su:pəpauə*] *n* (*POL*) superpuissance *f*.

supersede [su:pə'si:d] *vt* remplacer, supplanter.

superstitious [su:pə'stɪʃəs] *a* superstitieux(euse).

supervise ['su:pəvɑɪz] *vt* surveiller; diriger; **supervision** [-'vɪʒən] *n* surveillance *f*; contrôle *m*; **supervisor** *n* surveillant/e; (*in shop*) chef *m* de rayon.

supine ['su:pɑɪn] *a* couché(e) *or* étendu(e) sur le dos.

supper ['sʌpə*] *n* dîner *m*; (*late*) souper *m.*

supple ['sʌpl] *a* souple.

supplement *n* ['sʌplɪmənt] supplément *m* // *vt* ['sʌplɪ'ment] ajouter à, compléter; **~ary** [-'mentərɪ] *a* supplémentaire.

supplier [sə'plɑɪə*] *n* fournisseur *m*.

supply [sə'plɑɪ] *vt* (*provide*) fournir; (*equip*): **to ~ (with)** approvisionner *or* ravitailler (en); fournir (en); alimenter (en) // *n* provision *f*, réserve *f*; (*supplying*) approvisionnement *m*; (*TECH*) alimentation *f* // *cpd* (*teacher etc*) suppléant(e); **supplies** *npl* (*food*) vivres *mpl*; (*MIL*) subsistances *fpl*.

support [sə'pɔ:t] *n* (*moral, financial etc*) soutien *m*, appui *m*; (*TECH*) support *m*, soutien *m* // *vt* soutenir, supporter; (*financially*) subvenir aux besoins de; (*uphold*) être pour, être partisan de, appuyer; **~er** *n* (*POL etc*) partisan/e; (*SPORT*) supporter *m*.

suppose [sə'pəuz] *vt*, *vi* supposer; imaginer; **to be ~d to do** être censé(e) faire; **~dly** [sə'pəuzɪdlɪ] *ad* soi-disant; **supposing** *cj* si, à supposer que + *sub*.

suppress [sə'pres] *vt* réprimer; supprimer; étouffer; refouler.

supreme [su'pri:m] *a* suprême.

surcharge ['sə:tʃɑ:dʒ] *n* surcharge *f*; (*extra tax*) surtaxe *f.*

sure [ʃuə*] *a* (*gen*) sûr(e); (*definite, convinced*) sûr, certain(e); **~!** (*of course*) bien sûr!; **~ enough** effectivement; **to make ~ of** sth s'assurer de *or* vérifier qch; **to make ~ that** s'assurer *or* vérifier que; **~ly** *ad* sûrement; certainement.

surety ['ʃuərətɪ] *n* caution *f*.

surf [sə:f] *n* ressac *m*.

surface ['sə:fɪs] *n* surface *f* // *vt* (*road*) poser le revêtement de // *vi* remonter à la surface; faire surface; **~ mail** *n* courrier *m* par voie de terre (*or* maritime).

surfboard ['sə:fbɔ:d] *n* planche *f* de surf.

surfeit ['sə:fɪt] *n*: **a ~ of** un excès de; une indigestion de.

surfing ['sə:fɪŋ] *n* surf *m.*

surge [sə:dʒ] *n* vague *f*, montée *f* // *vi*

déferler.

surgeon ['sə:dʒən] *n* chirurgien *m*.

surgery ['sə:dʒərɪ] *n* chirurgie *f*; (*Brit: room*) cabinet *m* (de consultation); **to undergo ~** être opéré(e); **~ hours** *npl* (*Brit*) heures *fpl* de consultation.

surgical ['sə:dʒɪkl] *a* chirurgical(e); **~ spirit** *n* (*Brit*) alcool *m* à 90°.

surly ['sə:lɪ] *a* revêche, maussade.

surname ['sə:neɪm] *n* nom *m* de famille.

surplus ['sə:pləs] *n* surplus *m*, excédent *m* // *a* en surplus, de trop.

surprise [sə'praɪz] *n* (*gen*) surprise *f*; (*astonishment*) étonnement *m* // *vt* surprendre; étonner; **surprising** *a* surprenant(e), étonnant(e); **surprisingly** *ad* (*easy*, *helpful*) étonnamment, étrangement.

surrender [sə'rɛndə*] *n* reddition *f*, capitulation *f* // *vi* se rendre, capituler.

surreptitious [sʌrəp'tɪʃəs] *a* subreptice, furtif(ive).

surrogate ['sʌrəgɪt] *n* substitut *m*; **~ mother** *n* mère porteuse *or* de substitution.

surround [sə'raund] *vt* entourer; (*MIL etc*) encercler; **~ing** *a* environnant(e); **~ings** *npl* environs *mpl*, alentours *mpl*.

surveillance [sə:'veɪləns] *n* surveillance *f*.

survey *n* ['sə:veɪ] enquête *f*, étude *f*; (*in housebuying etc*) inspection *f*, (*rapport m* d')expertise *f*; (*of land*) levé *m* // *vt* [sə:'veɪ] passer en revue; enquêter sur; inspecter; **~or** *n* expert *m*; (*arpenteur m*) géomètre *m*.

survival [sə'vaɪvl] *n* survie *f*; (*relic*) vestige *m*.

survive [sə'vaɪv] *vi* survivre; (*custom etc*) subsister // *vt* survivre à; **survivor** *n* survivant/e.

susceptible [sə'sɛptəbl] *a*: **~ (to)** sensible (à); (*disease*) prédisposé(e) (à).

suspect *a*, *n*, ['sʌspɛkt] suspect(e) // *vt* [səs'pɛkt] soupçonner, suspecter.

suspend [səs'pɛnd] *vt* suspendre; **~ed sentence** *n* condamnation *f* avec sursis; **~er belt** *n* porte-jarretelles *m inv*; **~ers** *npl* (*Brit*) jarretelles *fpl*; (*US*) bretelles *fpl*.

suspense [səs'pɛns] *n* attente *f*; (*in film etc*) suspense *m*.

suspension [səs'pɛnʃən] *n* (*gen*, *AUT*) suspension *f*; (*of driving licence*) retrait *m* provisoire; **~ bridge** *n* pont suspendu.

suspicion [səs'pɪʃən] *n* soupçon(s) *m(pl)*.

suspicious [səs'pɪʃəs] *a* (*suspecting*) soupçonneux(euse), méfiant(e); (*causing suspicion*) suspect(e).

sustain [səs'teɪn] *vt* supporter; soutenir; corroborer; (*suffer*) subir; recevoir; **~ed** *a* (*effort*) soutenu(e), prolongé(e).

sustenance ['sʌstɪnəns] *n* nourriture *f*;

moyens *mpl* de subsistance.

swab [swɔb] *n* (*MED*) tampon *m*; prélèvement *m*.

swagger ['swægə*] *vi* plastronner.

swallow ['swɔləu] *n* (*bird*) hirondelle *f* // *vt* avaler; (*fig*) gober; **to ~ up** *vt* engloutir.

swam [swæm] *pt of* **swim**.

swamp [swɔmp] *n* marais *m*, marécage *m* // *vt* submerger.

swan [swɔn] *n* cygne *m*.

swap [swɔp] *vt*: **to ~ (for)** échanger (contre), troquer (contre).

swarm [swɔ:m] *n* essaim *m* // *vi* fourmiller, grouiller.

swarthy ['swɔ:ðɪ] *a* basané(e), bistré(e).

swastika ['swɔstɪkə] *n* croix gammée.

swat [swɔt] *vt* écraser.

sway [sweɪ] *vi* se balancer, osciller; tanguer // *vt* (*influence*) influencer.

swear [swɛə*], *pt* **swore**, *pp* **sworn** *vi* jurer; **to ~ to sth** jurer de qch; **~word** *n* gros mot, juron *m*.

sweat [swɛt] *n* sueur *f*, transpiration *f* // *vi* suer.

sweater ['swɛtə*] *n* tricot *m*, pull *m*.

sweaty ['swɛtɪ] *a* en sueur, moite *or* mouillé(e) de sueur.

Swede [swi:d] *n* Suédois/e.

swede [swi:d] *n* (*Brit*) rutabaga *m*.

Sweden ['swi:dn] *n* Suède *f*.

Swedish ['swi:dɪʃ] *a* suédois(e) // *n* (*LING*) suédois *m*.

sweep [swi:p] *n* coup *m* de balai; (*curve*) grande courbe; (*range*) champ *m*; (*also*: **chimney ~**) ramoneur *m* // *vb* (*pt*, *pp* **swept**) *vt* balayer // *vi* avancer majestueusement *or* rapidement; s'élancer; s'étendre; **to ~ away** *vt* balayer; entraîner; emporter; **to ~ past** *vi* passer majestueusement *or* rapidement; **to ~ up** *vt*, *vi* balayer; **~ing** *a* (*gesture*) large; circulaire; a **~ing statement** une généralisation hâtive.

sweet [swi:t] *n* (*Brit*: *pudding*) dessert *m*; (*candy*) bonbon *m* // *a* doux(douce); (*not savoury*) sucré(e); (*fresh*) frais(fraîche), pur(e); (*fig*) agréable, doux; gentil(le); mignon(ne); **~corn** *n* maïs doux; **~en** *vt* sucrer; adoucir; **~heart** *n* amoureux/euse; **~ness** *n* goût sucré; douceur *f*; **~ pea** *n* pois *m* de senteur.

swell [swɛl] *n* (*of sea*) houle *f* // *a* (*col*: *excellent*) chouette // *vb* (*pt* **~ed**, *pp* **swollen** *or* **~ed**) *vt* augmenter; grossir // *vi* grossir, augmenter; (*sound*) s'enfler; (*MED*) enfler; **~ing** *n* (*MED*) enflure *f*; grosseur *f*.

sweltering ['swɛltərɪŋ] *a* étouffant(e), oppressant(e).

swept [swɛpt] *pt*, *pp of* **sweep**.

swerve [swə:v] *vi* faire une embardée *or*

un écart; dévier.

swift [swɪft] *n* (*bird*) martinet *m* // *a* rapide, prompt(e).

swig [swɪg] *n* (*col: drink*) lampée *f*.

swill [swɪl] *n* pâtée *f* // *vt* (*also:* ~ out, ~ down) laver à grande eau.

swim [swɪm] *n:* **to go for a** ~ aller nager *or* se baigner // *vb* (*pt* swam, *pp* swum) *vi* nager; (*SPORT*) faire de la natation; (*head, room*) tourner // *vt* traverser (à la nage); faire (à la nage); ~**mer** *n* nageur/euse; ~**ming** *n* nage *f*, natation *f*; ~**ming cap** *n* bonnet *m* de bain; ~**ming costume** *n* (*Brit*) maillot *m* (de bain); ~**ming pool** *n* piscine *f*; ~**suit** *n* maillot *m* (de bain).

swindle [swɪndl] *n* escroquerie *f*.

swine [swaɪn] *n* (*pl inv*) pourceau *m*, porc *m*; (*col!*) salaud *m* (!).

swing [swɪŋ] *n* balançoire *f*; (*movement*) balancement *m*, oscillations *fpl*; (*MUS*) swing *m*; rythme *m* // *vb* (*pt, pp* swung) *vt* balancer, faire osciller; (*also:* ~ round) tourner, faire virer // *vi* se balancer, osciller; (*also:* ~ round) virer, tourner; **to be in full** ~ battre son plein; ~ **door**, (*US*) ~**ing door** *n* porte battante.

swingeing [swɪndʒɪŋ] *a* (*Brit*) écrasant(e); considérable.

swipe [swaɪp] *vt* (*hit*) frapper à toute volée; gifler; (*col: steal*) piquer.

swirl [swə:l] *vi* tourbillonner, tournoyer.

swish [swɪʃ] *a* (*col: smart*) rupin(e) // *vi* siffler.

Swiss [swɪs] *a* suisse // *n* (*pl inv*) Suisse/esse.

switch [swɪtʃ] *n* (*for light, radio etc*) bouton *m*; (*change*) changement *m*, revirement *m* // *vt* (*change*) changer; intervertir; **to** ~ **off** *vt* éteindre; (*engine*) arrêter; **to** ~ **on** *vt* allumer; (*engine, machine*) mettre en marche; ~**board** *n* (*TEL*) standard *m*.

Switzerland [swɪtsələnd] *n* Suisse *f*.

swivel [swɪvl] *vi* (*also:* ~ round) pivoter, tourner.

swollen [swəʊlən] *pp of* swell.

swoon [swu:n] *vi* se pâmer.

swoop [swu:p] *vi* (*also:* ~ down) descendre en piqué, piquer.

swop [swɔp] *vt* = swap.

sword [sɔ:d] *n* épée *f*; ~**fish** *n* espadon *m*.

swore [swɔ:*] *pt of* swear.

sworn [swɔ:n] *pp of* swear.

swot [swɔt] *vt, vi* bûcher, potasser.

swum [swʌm] *pp of* swim.

swung [swʌŋ] *pt, pp of* swing.

syllable [sɪləbl] *n* syllabe *f*.

syllabus [sɪləbəs] *n* programme *m*.

symbol [sɪmbl] *n* symbole *m*.

symmetry [sɪmɪtrɪ] *n* symétrie *f*.

sympathetic [sɪmpə'θɛtɪk] *a* compatissant(e); bienveillant(e), compré-

hensif(ive); ~ **towards** bien disposé(e) envers.

sympathize [sɪmpəθaɪz] *vi:* **to** ~ **with** sb plaindre qn; s'associer à la douleur de qn; ~**r** *n* (*POL*) sympathisant/e.

sympathy [sɪmpəθɪ] *n* compassion *f*; **in** ~ **with** en accord avec; (*strike*) par solidarité avec; **with our deepest** ~ en vous priant d'accepter nos sincères condoléances.

symphony [sɪmfənɪ] *n* symphonie *f*.

symptom [sɪmptəm] *n* symptôme *m*; indice *m*.

synagogue [sɪnəgɔg] *n* synagogue *f*.

syndicate [sɪndɪkɪt] *n* syndicat *m*, coopérative *f*.

synonym [sɪnənɪm] *n* synonyme *m*.

syntax [sɪntæks] *n* syntaxe *f*.

synthetic [sɪn'θɛtɪk] *a* synthétique.

syphon [saɪfən] *n, vb* = siphon.

Syria [sɪrɪə] *n* Syrie *f*.

syringe [sɪ'rɪndʒ] *n* seringue *f*.

syrup [sɪrəp] *n* sirop *m*; (*also:* golden ~) mélasse raffinée.

system [sɪstəm] *n* système *m*; (*order*) méthode *f*; (*ANAT*) organisme *m*; ~**atic** [-'mætɪk] *a* systématique; méthodique; ~ **disk** *n* (*COMPUT*) disque *m* système; ~**s analyst** *n* analyste-programmeur *m/f*.

T

ta [tɑ:] *excl* (*Brit col*) merci!

tab [tæb] *n* (*loop on coat etc*) attache *f*; (*label*) étiquette *f*; **to keep** ~**s on** (*fig*) surveiller.

tabby [tæbɪ] *n* (*also:* ~ cat) chat/te tigré(e).

table [teɪbl] *n* table *f* // *vt* (*Brit: motion etc*) présenter; **to lay** *or* **set the** ~ mettre le couvert *or* la table; ~ **of contents** *n* table *f* des matières; ~**cloth** *n* nappe *f*; ~ **d'hôte** [tɑ:bl'dəʊt] *a* (*meal*) à prix fixe; ~ **lamp** *n* lampe décorative; ~**mat** *n* (*for plate*) napperon *m*, set *m*; (*for · hot dish*) dessous-de-plat *m inv*; ~**spoon** *n* cuiller *f* de service; (*also:* ~**spoonful:** *as measurement*) cuillerée *f* à soupe.

tablet [tæblɪt] *n* (*MED*) comprimé *m*; (*: for sucking*) pastille *f*; (*for writing*) bloc *m*; (*of stone*) plaque *f*.

table: ~ **tennis** *n* ping-pong *m*, tennis *m* de table; ~ **wine** *n* vin *m* de table.

tabulate [tæbjuleɪt] *vt* (*data, figures*) mettre sous forme de table(s).

tacit [tæsɪt] *a* tacite.

tack [tæk] *n* (*nail*) petit clou *m*; (*stitch*) point *m* de bâti; (*NAUT*) bord *m*, bordée *f* // *vt* clouer; bâtir // *vi* tirer un *or* des bord(s).

tackle [tækl] *n* matériel *m*, équipement *m*; (*for lifting*) appareil *m* de levage;

(*RUGBY*) plaquage *m* // *vt* (*difficulty*) s'attaquer à; (*RUGBY*) plaquer.

tacky ['tækɪ] *a* collant(e); pas sec(sèche).

tact [tækt] *n* tact *m*; **~ful** *a* plein(e) de tact.

tactical ['tæktɪkl] *a* tactique.

tactics ['tæktɪks] *n*, *npl* tactique *f*.

tactless ['tæktlɪs] *a* qui manque de tact.

tadpole ['tædpəʊl] *n* têtard *m*.

taffy ['tæfɪ] *n* (*US*) (bonbon *m* au) caramel *m*.

tag [tæg] *n* étiquette *f*; **to ~ along** *vi* suivre.

tail [teɪl] *n* queue *f*; (*of shirt*) pan *m* // *vt* (*follow*) suivre, filer; **to ~ away**, **~ off** *vi* (*in size, quality etc*) baisser peu à peu; **~back** *n* (*Brit AUT*) bouchon *m*; **~ coat** *n* habit *m*; **~ end** *n* bout *m*, fin *f*; **~gate** *n* (*AUT*) hayon *m* arrière.

tailor ['teɪlə*] *n* tailleur *m* (*artisan*); **~ing** *n* (*cut*) coupe *f*; **~-made** *a* fait(e) sur mesure; (*fig*) conçu(e) spécialement.

tailwind ['teɪlwɪnd] *n* vent *m* arrière *inv*.

tainted ['teɪntɪd] *a* (*food*) gâté(e); (*water, air*) infecté(e); (*fig*) souillé(e).

take, *pt* **took,** *pp* **taken** [teɪk, tuk, 'teɪkn] *vt* prendre; (*gain: prize*) remporter; (*require: effort, courage*) demander; (*tolerate*) accepter, supporter; (*hold: passengers etc*) contenir; (*accompany*) emmener, accompagner; (*bring, carry*) apporter, emporter; (*exam*) passer, se présenter à; **to ~ sth from** (*drawer etc*) prendre qch dans; (*person*) prendre qch à; **I ~ it that** je suppose que; **to ~ for a walk** (*child, dog*) emmener promener; **to ~ after** *vt fus* ressembler à; **to ~ apart** *vt* démonter; **to ~ away** *vt* emporter; enlever; **to ~ back** *vt* (*return*) rendre, rapporter; (*one's words*) retirer; **to ~ down** *vt* (*building*) démolir; (*letter etc*) prendre, écrire; **to ~ in** *vt* (*deceive*) tromper, rouler; (*understand*) comprendre, saisir; (*include*) couvrir, inclure; (*lodger*) prendre; **to ~ off** *vi* (*AVIAT*) décoller // *vt* (*remove*) enlever; (*imitate*) imiter, pasticher; **to ~ on** *vt* (*work*) accepter, se charger de; (*employee*) prendre, embaucher; (*opponent*) accepter de se battre contre; **to ~ out** *vt* sortir; (*remove*) enlever; (*licence*) prendre, se procurer; **to ~ sth out of sth** enlever qch de; (*drawer, pocket etc*) prendre qch dans qch; **to ~ over** *vt* (*business*) reprendre // *vi*: **to ~ over from sb** sb prendre la relève de qn; **to ~ to** *vt fus* (*person*) se prendre d'amitié pour; (*activity*) prendre goût à; **to ~ up** *vt* (*one's story, a dress*) reprendre; (*occupy: time, space*) prendre, occuper; (*engage in: hobby etc*) se mettre à; **~away** *a* (*food*) à emporter; **~-home**

pay *n* salaire net; **~off** *n* (*AVIAT*) décollage *m*; **~out** *a* (*US*) = **~away**; **~over** *n* (*COMM*) rachat *m*.

takings ['teɪkɪŋz] *npl* (*COMM*) recette *f*.

talc [tælk] *n* (*also*: **~um powder**) talc *m*.

tale [teɪl] *n* (*story*) conte *m*, histoire *f*; (*account*) récit *m*; (*pej*) histoire; **to tell ~s** (*fig*) rapporter.

talent ['tælnt] *n* talent *m*, don *m*; **~ed** *a* doué(e), plein(e) de talent.

talk [tɔːk] *n* propos *mpl*; (*gossip*) racontars *mpl* (*pej*); (*conversation*) discussion *f*; (*interview*) entretien *m*; (*a speech*) causerie *f*, exposé *m* // *vi* (*chatter*) bavarder; **~s** *npl* (*POL etc*) entretiens *mpl*; conférence *f*; **to ~ about** parler de; (*converse*) s'entretenir *or* parler de; **to ~ sb out of/into doing** persuader qn de ne pas faire/de faire; **to ~ shop** parler métier *or* affaires; **to ~ over** *vt* discuter (de); **~ative** *a* bavard(e); **~ show** *n* causerie (télévisée *or* radiodiffusée).

tall [tɔːl] *a* (*person*) grand(e); (*building, tree*) haut(e); **to be 6 feet ~** ≈ mesurer 1 mètre 80; **~boy** *n* (*Brit*) grande commode; **~ story** *n* histoire *f* invraisemblable.

tally ['tælɪ] *n* compte *m* // *vi*: **to ~ (with)** correspondre (à).

talon ['tælən] *n* griffe *f*; (*eagle*) serre *f*.

tame [teɪm] *a* apprivoisé(e); (*fig: story, style*) insipide.

tamper ['tæmpə*] *vi*: **to ~ with** toucher à (*en cachette ou sans permission*).

tampon ['tæmpən] *n* tampon *m* hygiénique *or* périodique.

tan [tæn] *n* (*also*: **sun~**) bronzage *m* // *vt, vi* bronzer, brunir // *a* (*colour*) brun roux *inv*.

tang [tæŋ] *n* odeur (*or* saveur) piquante.

tangent ['tændʒənt] *n* (*MATH*) tangente *f*; **to go off at a ~** (*fig*) changer complètement de direction.

tangerine [tændʒə'riːn] *n* mandarine *f*.

tangle ['tæŋgl] *n* enchevêtrement *m* // *vt* enchevêtrer.

tank [tæŋk] *n* réservoir *m*; (*for processing*) cuve *f*; (*for fish*) aquarium *m*; (*MIL*) char *m* d'assaut, tank *m*.

tanker ['tæŋkə*] *n* (*ship*) pétrolier *m*, tanker *m*; (*truck*) camion-citerne *m*.

tantalizing ['tæntəlaɪzɪŋ] *a* (*smell*) extrêmement appétissant(e); (*offer*) terriblement tentant(e).

tantamount ['tæntəmaunt] *a*: **~ to** qui équivaut à.

tantrum ['tæntrəm] *n* accès *m* de colère.

tap [tæp] *n* (*on sink etc*) robinet *m*; (*gentle blow*) petite tape *vt* frapper *or* taper légèrement; (*resources*) exploiter, utiliser; (*telephone*) mettre sur écoute; **on ~** (*fig: resources*) disponible; **~-dancing** *n* claquettes *fpl*.

tape [teɪp] *n* ruban *m*; (*also*: **magnetic**

~) bande *f* (magnétique) // *vt* (*record*) enregistrer (sur bande); ~ **measure** *n* mètre *m* à ruban.

taper ['teɪpə*] *n* cierge *m* // *vi* s'effiler.

tape recorder *n* magnétophone *m*.

tapestry ['tæpɪstrɪ] *n* tapisserie *f*.

tar [tɑː] *n* goudron *m*.

target ['tɑːgɪt] *n* cible *f*; (*fig: objective*) objectif *m*.

tariff ['tærɪf] *n* (*COMM*) tarif *m*; (*taxes*) tarif douanier.

tarmac ['tɑːmæk] *n* (*Brit: on road*) macadam *m*; (*AVIAT*) aire *f* d'envol.

tarnish ['tɑːnɪʃ] *vt* ternir.

tarpaulin [tɑːˈpɔːlɪn] *n* bâche goudronnée.

tarragon ['tærəgən] *n* estragon *m*.

tart [tɑːt] *n* (*CULIN*) tarte *f*; (*Brit col: pej: woman*) poule *f* // *a* (*flavour*) âpre, aigrelet(te); **to ~ o.s. up** (*col*) se faire beau(belle); (: *pej*) s'attifer.

tartan ['tɑːtn] *n* tartan *m* // *a* écossais(e).

tartar ['tɑːtə*] *n* (*on teeth*) tartre *m*; ~ **sauce** *n* sauce *f* tartare.

task [tɑːsk] *n* tâche *f*; **to take to ~** prendre à partie; ~ **force** *n* (*MIL*, *POLICE*) détachement spécial.

tassel ['tæsl] *n* gland *m*; pompon *m*.

taste [teɪst] *n* goût *m*; (*fig: glimpse, idea*) idée *f*, aperçu *m* // *vt* goûter // *vi*: **to ~ of** (*fish etc*) avoir le *or* un goût de; **it ~s like fish** ça a un *or* le goût de poisson, on dirait du poisson; **you can ~ the garlic (in it)** on sent bien l'ail; **can I have a ~ of this wine?** puis-je goûter un peu de ce vin?; **to have a ~ for sth** aimer qch, avoir un penchant pour qch; **in good/bad ~** de bon/mauvais goût; ~**ful** *a* de bon goût; ~**less** *a* (*food*) qui n'a aucun goût; (*remark*) de mauvais goût; **tasty** *a* savoureux(euse), délicieux(euse).

tatters ['tætəz] *npl*: **in ~** (*also*: tattered) en lambeaux.

tattoo [təˈtuː] *n* tatouage *m*; (*spectacle*) parade *f* militaire // *vt* tatouer.

taught [tɔːt] *pt, pp of* **teach**.

taunt [tɔːnt] *n* raillerie *f* // *vt* railler.

Taurus ['tɔːrəs] *n* le Taureau.

taut [tɔːt] *a* tendu(e).

tawdry ['tɔːdrɪ] *a* (d'un mauvais goût) criard.

tax [tæks] *n* (*on goods etc*) taxe *f*; (*on income*) impôts *mpl*, contributions *fpl* // *vt* taxer; imposer; (*fig: strain: patience etc*) mettre à l'épreuve; ~**able** *a* (*income*) imposable; ~**ation** [-'seɪʃən] *n* taxation *f*; impôts *mpl*, contributions *fpl*; ~ **avoidance** *n* évasion fiscale; ~ **collector** *n* percepteur *m*; ~ **disc** *n* (*Brit AUT*) vignette *f* (automobile); ~ **evasion** *n* fraude fiscale; ~**-free** *a* exempt(e) d'impôts.

taxi ['tæksɪ] *n* taxi *m* // *vi* (*AVIAT*) rouler (lentement) au sol; ~ **driver** *n* chauffeur *m* de taxi; ~ **rank** (*Brit*), ~ **stand** *n* station *f* de taxis.

tax: ~ **payer** *n* contribuable *m/f*; ~ **relief** *n* dégrèvement *or* allègement fiscal; ~ **return** *n* déclaration *f* d'impôts *or* de revenus.

TB *n abbr* = **tuberculosis**.

tea [tiː] *n* thé *m*; (*Brit: snack: for children*) goûter *m*; **high ~** (*Brit*) collation combinant goûter et dîner; ~ **bag** *n* sachet *m* de thé; ~ **break** *n* (*Brit*) pause-thé *f*.

teach [tiːtʃ] , *pt, pp* **taught** *vt*: **to ~ sb sth, ~ sth to sb** apprendre qch à qn; (*in school etc*) enseigner qch à qn // *vi* enseigner; ~**er** *n* (*in secondary school*) professeur *m*; (*in primary school*) instituteur/trice; ~**ing** *n* enseignement *m*.

tea cosy *n* couvre-théière *m*.

teacup ['tiːkʌp] *n* tasse *f* à thé.

teak [tiːk] *n* teck *m*.

team [tiːm] *n* équipe *f*; (*of animals*) attelage *m*; ~**work** *n* travail *m* d'équipe.

teapot ['tiːpɒt] *n* théière *f*.

tear *n* [tɛə*] déchirure *f*; (*tearful: drop*) // *vb* [tɛə*] (*pt* tore, *pp* torn) *vt* déchirer // *vi* se déchirer; **in ~s** en larmes; **to ~ along** *vi* (*rush*) aller à toute vitesse; **to ~ up** *vt* (*sheet of paper etc*) déchirer, mettre en morceaux *or* pièces; ~**ful** *a* larmoyant(e); ~ **gas** *n* gaz *m* lacrymogène.

tearoom ['tiːruːm] *n* salon *m* de thé.

tease [tiːz] *vt* taquiner; (*unkindly*) tourmenter.

tea set *n* service *m* à thé.

teaspoon ['tiːspuːn] *n* petite cuiller; (*also*: ~**ful**: *as measurement*) ≈ cuillerée *f* à café.

teat [tiːt] *n* tétine *f*.

teatime ['tiːtaɪm] *n* l'heure *f* du thé.

tea towel *n* (*Brit*) torchon *m* (à vaisselle).

technical ['tɛknɪkl] *a* technique; ~**ity** [-'kælɪtɪ] *n* technicité *f*; (*detail*) détail *m* technique.

technician [tɛkˈnɪʃən] *n* technicien/ne.

technique [tɛkˈniːk] *n* technique *f*.

technological [tɛknəˈlɒdʒɪkl] *a* technologique.

technology [tɛkˈnɒlədʒɪ] *n* technologie *f*.

teddy (bear) ['tɛdɪ(bɛə*)] *n* ours *m* (en peluche).

tedious ['tiːdɪəs] *a* fastidieux(euse).

tee [tiː] *n* (*GOLF*) tee *m*.

teem [tiːm] *vi*: **to ~ (with)** grouiller (de); **it is ~ing (with rain)** il pleut à torrents.

teenage ['tiːneɪdʒ] *a* (*fashions etc*) pour jeunes, pour adolescents; ~**r** *n* jeune *m/f*, adolescent/e.

teens [ti:nz] *npl*: to be in one's ~ être adolescent(e).

tee-shirt ['ti:ʃə:t] *n* = **T-shirt**.

teeter ['ti:tə*] *vi* chanceler, vaciller.

teeth [ti:θ] *npl of* **tooth**.

teethe [ti:ð] *vi* percer ses dents.

teething ['ti:ðɪŋ]: ~ **ring** *n* anneau *m* (*pour bébé qui perce ses dents*); ~ **troubles** *npl* (*fig*) difficultés initiales.

teetotal ['ti:'təutl] *a* (*person*) qui ne boit jamais d'alcool.

telegram ['tɛlɪgræm] *n* télégramme *m*.

telegraph ['tɛlɪgrɑːf] *n* télégraphe *m*.

telephone ['tɛlɪfəun] *n* téléphone *m* // *vt* (*person*) téléphoner à; (*message*) téléphoner; ~ **booth**, (*Brit*) ~ **box** *n* cabine *f* téléphonique; ~ **call** *n* coup *m* de téléphone, appel *m* téléphonique, communication *f* téléphonique; ~ **directory** *n* annuaire *m* (du téléphone); ~ **number** *n* numéro *m* de téléphone; ~ **operator** téléphoniste *m/f*, standardiste *m/f*; **telephonist** [tə'lɛfənɪst] *n* (*Brit*) téléphoniste *m/f*.

telephoto ['tɛlɪ'fəutəu] *a*: ~ **lens** *n* téléobjectif *m*.

telescope ['tɛlɪskəup] *n* télescope *m*.

televise ['tɛlɪvaɪz] *vt* téléviser.

television ['tɛlɪvɪʒən] *n* télévision *f*; ~ **set** *n* poste *m* de télévision.

telex ['tɛlɛks] *n* télex *m*.

tell [tɛl], *pt, pp* **told** *vt* dire; (*relate: story*) raconter; (*distinguish*): to ~ **sth from** distinguer qch de // *vi* (*talk*): to ~ (**of**) parler (de); (*have effect*) se faire sentir, se voir; to ~ **sb to do** dire à qn de faire; **to** ~ **off** *vt* réprimander, gronder; ~**er** *n* (*in bank*) caissier/ère; ~**ing** *a* (*remark, detail*) révélateur(trice); ~**tale** *a* (*sign*) éloquent(e), révélateur(trice).

telly ['tɛlɪ] *n abbr* (*Brit col*: = *television*) télé *f*.

temp [tɛmp] *n abbr* (= *temporary*) (secrétaire *f*) intérimaire *f*.

temper ['tɛmpə*] *n* (*nature*) caractère *m*; (*mood*) humeur *f*; (*fit of anger*) colère *f* // *vt* (*moderate*) tempérer, adoucir; to be in a ~ être en colère; to lose one's ~ se mettre en colère.

temperament ['tɛmprəmənt] *n* (*nature*) tempérament *m*; ~**al** [-'mɛntl] *a* capricieux(euse).

temperate ['tɛmprət] *a* modéré(e); (*climate*) tempéré(e).

temperature ['tɛmprətʃə*] *n* température *f*; to have *or* run a ~ avoir de la fièvre.

tempest ['tɛmpɪst] *n* tempête *f*.

template ['tɛmplɪt] *n* patron *m*.

temple ['tɛmpl] *n* (*building*) temple *m*; (*ANAT*) tempe *f*.

temporary ['tɛmpərərɪ] *a* temporaire, provisoire; (*job, worker*) temporaire; ~ **secretary** *n* (secrétaire *f*) intérimaire *f*.

tempt [tɛmpt] *vt* tenter; to ~ **sb into doing** induire qn à faire; ~**ation** [-'teɪʃən] *n* tentation *f*.

ten [tɛn] *num* dix.

tenable ['tɛnəbl] *a* défendable.

tenacity [tə'næsɪtɪ] *n* ténacité *f*.

tenancy ['tɛnənsɪ] *n* location *f*; état *m* de locataire.

tenant ['tɛnənt] *n* locataire *m/f*.

tend [tɛnd] *vt* s'occuper de // *vi*: to ~ to **do** avoir tendance à faire.

tendency ['tɛndənsɪ] *n* tendance *f*.

tender ['tɛndə*] *a* tendre; (*delicate*) délicat(e); (*sore*) sensible; (*affectionate*) tendre, doux/douce // *n* (*COMM*: *offer*) soumission *f* // *vt* offrir.

tenement ['tɛnəmənt] *n* immeuble *m* (de rapport).

tenet ['tɛnət] *n* principe *m*.

tennis ['tɛnɪs] *n* tennis *m*; ~ **ball** *n* balle *f* de tennis; ~ **court** (court *m* de) tennis; ~ **player** *n* joueur/euse de tennis; ~ **racket** *n* raquette *f* de tennis; ~ **shoes** *npl* (chaussures *fpl* de) tennis *mpl*.

tenor ['tɛnə*] *n* (*MUS*) ténor *m*; (*of speech etc*) sens général.

tense [tɛns] *a* tendu(e) // *n* (*LING*) temps *m*.

tension ['tɛnʃən] *n* tension *f*.

tent [tɛnt] *n* tente *f*.

tentative ['tɛntətɪv] *a* timide, hésitant(e); (*conclusion*) provisoire.

tenterhooks ['tɛntəhuks] *npl*: on ~ sur des charbons ardents.

tenth [tɛnθ] *num* dixième.

tent: ~ **peg** *n* piquet *m* de tente; ~ **pole** *n* montant *m* de tente.

tenuous ['tɛnjuəs] *a* ténu(e).

tenure ['tɛnjuə*] *n* (*of property*) bail *m*; (*of job*) période *f* de jouissance; statut *m* de titulaire.

tepid ['tɛpɪd] *a* tiède.

term [tə:m] *n* (*limit*) terme *m*; (*word*) terme, mot *m*; (*SCOL*) trimestre *m*; (*LAW*) session *f* // *vt* appeler; ~**s** *npl* (*conditions*) conditions *fpl*; (*COMM*) tarif *m*; ~ **of imprisonment** peine *f* de prison; **in the short/long** ~ à court/long terme; to **come to** ~**s with** (*problem*) faire face à.

terminal ['tə:mɪnl] *a* terminal(e); (*disease*) dans sa phase terminale // *n* (*ELEC*) borne *f*; (*for oil, ore etc, COMPUT*) terminal *m*; (*also*: **air** ~) aérogare *f*; (*Brit*: *also*: **coach** ~) gare routière.

terminate ['tə:mɪneɪt] *vt* mettre fin à // *vi*: to ~ **in** finir en *or* par.

terminus ['tə:mɪnəs, 'tə:mɪnaɪ], *pl* **termini** *n* terminus *m inv*.

terrace ['tɛrəs] *n* terrasse *f*; (*Brit*: *row of houses*) rangée *f* de maisons (*attenantes les unes aux autres*); **the** ~**s** (*Brit SPORT*) les gradins *mpl*; ~**d** *a* (*garden*) en terrasses.

terracotta ['tɛrə'kɒtə] *n* terre cuite.
terrain [tɛ'reɪn] *n* terrain *m* (*sol*).
terrible ['tɛrɪbl] *a* terrible, atroce; (*weather, work*) affreux(euse), épouvantable; **terribly** *ad* terriblement; (*very badly*) affreusement mal.
terrier ['tɛrɪə*] *n* terrier *m* (*chien*).
terrific [tə'rɪfɪk] *a* fantastique, incroyable, terrible; (*wonderful*) formidable, sensationnel(le).
terrify ['tɛrɪfaɪ] *vt* terrifier.
territory ['tɛrɪtərɪ] *n* territoire *m*.
terror ['tɛrə*] *n* terreur *f*; **~ism** *n* terrorisme *m*; **~ist** *n* terroriste *m/f*.
terse [tə:s] *a* (*style*) concis(e); (*reply*) laconique.
Terylene ['tɛrɪli:n] *n* ® tergal *m* ®.
test [tɛst] *n* (*trial, check*) essai *m*; (*: of goods in factory*) contrôle *m*; (*of courage etc*) épreuve *f*; (*MED*) examens *mpl*; (*CHEM*) analyses *fpl*; (*exam: of intelligence etc*) test *m* (d'aptitude); (*: in school*) interrogation *f* de contrôle; (*also: driving ~*) (examen du) permis *m* de conduire // *vt* essayer; contrôler; mettre à l'épreuve; examiner; analyser; tester; faire subir une interrogation (de contrôle) à.
testament ['tɛstəmənt] *n* testament *m*; **the Old/New T~** l'Ancien/le Nouveau Testament.
testicle ['tɛstɪkl] *n* testicule *m*.
testify ['tɛstɪfaɪ] *vi* (*LAW*) témoigner, déposer; **to ~ to sth** (*LAW*) attester qch; (*gen*) témoigner de qch.
testimony ['tɛstɪmənɪ] *n* (*LAW*) témoignage *m*, déposition *f*.
test: **~ match** *n* (*CRICKET, RUGBY*) match international; **~ pilot** *n* pilote *m* d'essai; **~ tube** *n* éprouvette *f*.
tetanus ['tɛtənəs] *n* tétanos *m*.
tether ['tɛðə*] *vt* attacher // *n*: **at the end of one's ~** à bout (de patience).
text [tɛkst] *n* texte *m*; **~book** *n* manuel *m*.
textile ['tɛkstaɪl] *n* textile *m*.
texture ['tɛkstʃə*] *n* texture *f*; (*of skin, paper etc*) grain *m*.
Thames [tɛmz] *n*: **the ~** la Tamise.
than [ðæn, ðən] *cj* que; (*with numerals*): **more ~ 10/once** plus de 10/ d'une fois; **I have more/less ~ you** j'en ai plus/moins que toi; **she has more apples ~ pears** elle a plus de pommes que de poires.
thank [θæŋk] *vt* remercier, dire merci à; **~ you (very much)** merci (beaucoup); **~s** *npl* remerciements *mpl* // *excl* merci!; **~s to** *prep* grâce à; **~ful** *a*: **~ful (for)** reconnaissant(e) (de); **~less** *a* ingrat(e); **T~sgiving (Day)** *n* jour *m* d'action de grâce.
that [ðæt] ♦ *a* (*demonstrative: pl those*) ce, cet + *vowel or h mute, f* cette; **~ man/woman/book** cet homme/cette

femme/ce livre; (*not 'this'*) cet homme-là/cette femme-là/ce livre-là; **~ one** celui-là(celle-là).
♦ *pronoun* **1** (*demonstrative: pl those*) ce; (*not 'this one'*) cela, ça; **who's ~?** qui est-ce?; **what's ~?** qu'est-ce que c'est?; **is ~ you?** c'est toi?; **I prefer this to ~** je préfère ceci à cela *or* ça; **~'s what he said** c'est *or* voilà ce qu'il a dit; **~ is (to say)** c'est-à-dire, à savoir
2 (*relative: subject*) qui; (*: object*) que; (*: indirect*) lequel(laquelle), *pl* lesquels(lesquelles); **the book ~ I read** le livre que j'ai lu; **the books ~ are in the library** les livres qui sont dans la bibliothèque; **all ~ I have** tout ce que j'ai; **the box ~ I put it in** la boîte dans laquelle je l'ai mis; **the people ~ I spoke to** les gens auxquels *or* à qui j'ai parlé
3 (*relative: of time*) où; **the day ~ he came** le jour où il est venu
♦ *cj* que; **he thought ~ I was ill** il pensait que j'étais malade
♦ *ad* (*demonstrative*): **I can't work ~ much** je ne peux pas travailler autant que cela; **I didn't know it was ~ bad** je ne savais pas que c'était si *or* aussi mauvais; **it's about ~ high** c'est à peu près de cette hauteur.
thatched [θætʃt] *a* (*roof*) de chaume; **~ cottage** chaumière *f*.
thaw [θɔ:] *n* dégel *m* // *vi* (*ice*) fondre; (*food*) dégeler // *vt* (*food*) (faire) dégeler; **it's ~ing** (*weather*) il dégèle.
the [ði:, ðə] *definite article* **1** (*gen*) le, *f* la, l' + *vowel or h mute, pl* les (NB: *à* + *le(s)* = au(x); *de* + *le* = du; *de* + *les* = des); **~ boy/girl/ink** le garçon/la fille/ l'encre; **~ children** les enfants; **~ history of ~ world** l'histoire du monde; **give it to ~ postman** donne-le au facteur; **to play ~ piano/flute** jouer du piano/de la flûte; **~ rich and ~ poor** les riches et les pauvres
2 (*in titles*): **Elizabeth ~ First** Élisabeth première; **Peter ~ Great** Pierre le Grand
3 (*in comparisons*): **~ more he works, ~ more he earns** plus il travaille, plus il gagne de l'argent.
theatre, (US) theater ['θɪətə*] *n* théâtre *m*; **~-goer** *n* habitué/e du théâtre.
theatrical [θɪ'ætrɪkl] *a* théâtral(e).
theft [θɛft] *n* vol *m* (*larcin*).
their [ðɛə*] *a* leur, *pl* leurs; **~s** *pronoun* le(la) leur, les leurs; *see also* **my, mine**.
them [ðɛm, ðəm] *pronoun* (*direct*) les; (*indirect*) leur; (*stressed, after prep*) eux(elles); *see also* **me**.
theme [θi:m] *n* thème *m*; **~ song** *n* chanson principale.
themselves [ðəm'sɛlvz] *pl pronoun* (*reflexive*) se; (*emphatic*) eux-mêmes(elles-mêmes); *see also* **oneself**.
then [ðɛn] *ad* (*at that time*) alors, à ce

moment-là; (*next*) puis, ensuite; (*and also*) et puis // *cj* (*therefore*) alors, dans ce cas // *a*: the ~ **president** le président d'alors *or* de l'époque; **by** ~ (*past*) à ce moment-là; (*future*) d'ici là; **from** ~ **on** dès lors.

theology [θɪ'ɔlədʒɪ] *n* théologie *f*.

theoretical [θɪə'rɛtɪkl] *a* théorique.

theory ['θɪərɪ] *n* théorie *f*.

therapy ['θɛrəpɪ] *n* thérapie *f*.

there ['ðɛə*] *ad* **1**: ~ **is**, ~ **are** il y a; ~ **are** 3 of them (*people, things*) il y en a 3; ~ **has been an accident** il y a eu un accident

2 (*referring to place*) là, là-bas; **it's** ~ c'est là(-bas); **in/on/up/down** ~ là-dedans/là-dessus/là-haut/en bas; **he went** ~ **on Friday** il y est allé vendredi; **I want that book** ~ je veux ce livre-là; **he is!** le voilà!

3: ~, ~ (*esp to child*) allons, allons!

thereabouts [ðɛərə'bauts] *ad* (*place*) par là, près de là; (*amount*) environ, à peu près.

thereafter [ðɛər'ɑ:ftə*] *ad* par la suite.

thereby [ðɛə'baɪ] *ad* ainsi.

therefore ['ðɛəfɔ:*] *ad* donc, par conséquent.

there's ['ðɛəz] = **there is**, **there has**.

thermal ['θə:ml] *a* thermique.

thermometer [θə'mɔmɪtə*] *n* thermomètre *m*.

Thermos ['θə:məs] *n* ® (*also:* ~ **flask**) thermos *m or f (inv* ®).

thermostat ['θə:məustæt] *n* thermostat *m*.

thesaurus [θɪ'sɔ:rəs] *n* dictionnaire *m* synonymique.

these [ði:z] *pl pronoun* ceux-ci(celles-ci) // *pl a* ces; (*not 'those'*): ~ **books** ces livres-ci.

thesis, *pl* **theses** ['θi:sɪs, 'θi:si:z] *n* thèse *f*.

they [ðeɪ] *pl pronoun* ils(elles); (*stressed*) eux(elles); ~ **say that ...** (*it is said that*) on dit que ...; ~'**d** = **they had**, **they would**; ~'**ll** = **they shall**, **they will**; ~'**re** = **they are**; ~'**ve** = **they have**.

thick [θɪk] *a* épais(se); (*crowd*) dense; (*stupid*) bête, borné(e) // *n*: **in the** ~ **of** au beau milieu de, en plein cœur de; **it's 20 cm** ~ ça a 20 cm d'épaisseur; ~**en** *vi* s'épaissir // *vt* (*sauce etc*) épaissir; ~**ness** *n* épaisseur *f*; ~**set** *a* trapu(e), costaud(e); ~**skinned** *a* (*fig*) peu sensible.

thief, *pl* **thieves** [θi:f, θi:vz] *n* voleur/euse.

thigh [θaɪ] *n* cuisse *f*.

thimble ['θɪmbl] *n* dé *m* (à coudre).

thin [θɪn] *a* mince; (*person*) maigre; (*soup*) peu épais(se); (*hair, crowd*) clairsemé(e); (*fog*) léger(ère) // *vt* (*hair*) éclaircir; **to** ~ (**down**) (*sauce,*

paint) délayer.

thing [θɪŋ] *n* chose *f*; (*object*) objet *m*; (*contraption*) truc *m*; ~**s** *npl* (*belongings*) affaires *fpl*; **the best** ~ **would be to** le mieux serait de; **how are** ~**s**? comment ça va?

think [θɪŋk] *, pt, pp* **thought** *vi* penser, réfléchir // *vt* penser, croire; (*imagine*) s'imaginer; **to** ~ **of** penser à; **what did you** ~ **of them?** qu'avez-vous pensé d'eux?; **to** ~ **about sth/sb** penser à qch/qn; **I'll** ~ **about it** je vais y réfléchir; **to** ~ **of doing** avoir l'idée de faire; **I** ~ **so/** **not** je crois *or* pense que oui/non; **to** ~ **well of** avoir une haute opinion de; **to** ~ **over** *vt* bien réfléchir à; **to** ~ **up** *vt* inventer, trouver; ~ **tank** *n* groupe *m* de réflexion.

third [θə:d] *num* troisième // *n* troisième *m/f*; (*fraction*) tiers *m*; (*Brit SCOL: degree*) ≈ licence *f* avec mention passable; ~**ly** *ad* troisièmement; ~ **party insurance** *n* (*Brit*) assurance *f* au tiers; ~**rate** *a* de qualité médiocre; **the T~** **World** *n* le Tiers-Monde.

thirst [θə:st] *n* soif *f*; ~**y** *a* (*person*) qui a soif, assoiffé(e).

thirteen ['θə:'ti:n] *num* treize.

thirty ['θə:tɪ] *num* trente.

this [ðɪs] ♦ *a* (*demonstrative: pl* **these**) ce, cet + *vowel or h mute, f* cette; ~ **man/woman/book** cet homme/cette femme/ce livre; (*not 'that'*) cet homme-ci/cette femme-ci/ce livre-ci; ~ **one** celui-ci(celle-ci)

♦ *pronoun* (*demonstrative: pl* **these**) ce; (*not 'that one'*) celui-ci(celle-ci), ceci; **who's** ~? qui est-ce?; **what's** ~? qu'est-ce que c'est?; **I prefer** ~ **to that** je préfère ceci à cela; ~ **is what he said** voici ce qu'il a dit; ~ **is Mr Brown** (*in introductions*) je vous présente Mr Brown; (*in photo*) c'est Mr Brown; (*on telephone*) ici Mr Brown

♦ *ad* (*demonstrative*): **it was about** ~ **big** c'était à peu près de cette grandeur *or* grand comme ça; **I didn't know it was** ~ **bad** je ne savais pas que c'était si *or* aussi mauvais.

thistle ['θɪsl] *n* chardon *m*.

thong [θɔŋ] *n* lanière *f*.

thorn [θɔ:n] *n* épine *f*.

thorough ['θʌrə] *a* (*search*) minutieux(euse); (*knowledge, research*) approfondi(e); (*work*) consciencieux(euse); (*cleaning*) à fond; ~**bred** *n* (*horse*) pur-sang *m inv*; ~**fare** *n* rue *f*; **'no** ~**fare'** 'passage interdit'; ~**ly** *ad* minutieusement; en profondeur; à fond; **he** ~**ly agreed** il était tout à fait d'accord.

those [ðəuz] *pl pronoun* ceux-là(celles-là) // *pl a* ces; (*not 'these'*): ~ **books** ces livres-là.

though [ðəu] *cj* bien que + *sub*, quoique

+ *sub* // *ad* pourtant.

thought [θɔ:t] *pt, pp of* **think** // *n* pensée *f*; (*opinion*) avis *m*; (*intention*) intention *f*; **~ful** *a* pensif(ive); réfléchi(e); (*considerate*) prévenant(e); **~less** *a* étourdi(e); qui manque de considération.

thousand ['θauzənd] *num* mille; **one ~** mille; **~s of** des milliers de; **~th** *num* millième.

thrash [θræʃ] *vt* rouer de coups; donner une correction à; (*defeat*) battre à plate couture; **to ~ about** *vi* se débattre; **to ~ out** *vt* débattre de.

thread [θrɛd] *n* fil *m*; (*of screw*) pas *m*, filetage *m* // *vt* (*needle*) enfiler; **~bare** *a* râpé(e), élimé(e).

threat [θrɛt] *n* menace *f*; **~en** *vi* (*storm*) menacer // *vt*: **to ~en sb with sth/to do** menacer qn de qch/de faire.

three [θri:] *num* trois; **~-dimensional** *a* à trois dimensions; (*film*) en relief; **~-piece suit** *n* complet *m* (avec gilet); **~-piece suite** *n* salon *m* comprenant un canapé et deux fauteuils assortis; **~-ply** *a* (*wood*) à trois épaisseurs; (*wool*) trois fils *inv*.

thresh [θrɛʃ] *vt* (*AGR*) battre.

threshold ['θrɛʃhəuld] *n* seuil *m*.

threw [θru:] *pt of* **throw**.

thrifty ['θrifti] *a* économe.

thrill [θril] *n* frisson *m*, émotion *f* // *vi* tressaillir, frissonner // *vt* (*audience*) électriser; **to be ~ed** (*with gift etc*) être ravi; **~er** *n* film *m* (*or* roman *m or* pièce *f*) à suspense; **~ing** *a* saisissant(e), excitant(e).

thrive, *pt* **thrived**, **throve**, *pp* **thrived**, **thriven** [θraiv, θrəuv, 'θrivn] *vi* pousser *or* se développer bien; (*business*) prospérer; **he ~s on it** cela lui réussit; **thriving** *a* vigoureux(euse); prospère.

throat [θrəut] *n* gorge *f*; **to have a sore ~** avoir mal à la gorge.

throb [θrɒb] *n* (*heart*) palpiter; (*engine*) vibrer; (*with pain*) lanciner; (*wound*) causer des élancements.

throes [θrəuz] *npl*: **in the ~ of** au beau milieu de; en proie à.

throne [θrəun] *n* trône *m*.

throng [θrɒŋ] *n* foule *f* // *vt* se presser dans.

throttle ['θrɒtl] *n* (*AUT*) accélérateur *m* // *vt* étrangler.

through [θru:] *prep* à travers; (*time*) pendant, durant; (*by means of*) par, par l'intermédiaire de; (*owing to*) à cause de // *a* (*ticket, train, passage*) direct(e) // *ad* à travers; **to put sb ~ to sb** (*TEL*) passer qn à qn; **to be ~** (*TEL*) avoir la communication; (*have finished*) avoir fini; **'no ~ way'** (*Brit*) 'impasse'; **~out** *prep* (*place*) partout dans; (*time*) durant tout(e) le(la) // *ad* partout.

throve [θrəuv] *pt of* **thrive**.

throw [θrəu] *n* jet *m*; (*SPORT*) lancer *m*

// *vt* (*pt* **threw**, *pp* **thrown** [θru:, θrəun]) lancer, jeter; (*SPORT*) lancer; (*rider*) désarçonner; (*fig*) décontenancer; (*pottery*) tourner; **to ~ a party** donner une réception; **to ~ away** *vt* jeter; **to ~ off** *vt* se débarrasser de; **to ~ out** *vt* jeter dehors; (*reject*) rejeter; **to ~ up** *vi* vomir; **~away** *a* à jeter; **~-in** *n* (*SPORT*) remise *f* en jeu.

thru [θru:] *prep, a, ad* (*US*) = **through**.

thrush [θrʌʃ] *n* grive *f*.

thrust [θrʌst] *n* (*TECH*) poussée *f* // *vt* (*pt, pp* **thrust**) pousser brusquement; (*push in*) enfoncer.

thud [θʌd] *n* bruit sourd.

thug [θʌɡ] *n* voyou *m*.

thumb [θʌm] *n* (*ANAT*) pouce *m* // *vt* (*book*) feuilleter; **to ~ a lift** faire de l'auto-stop, arrêter une voiture; **~tack** *n* (*US*) punaise *f* (*clou*).

thump [θʌmp] *n* grand coup *m*; (*sound*) bruit sourd // *vt* cogner sur // *vi* cogner, frapper.

thunder ['θʌndə*] *n* tonnerre *m* // *vi* tonner; (*train etc*): **to ~ past** passer dans un grondement *or* un bruit de tonnerre; **~bolt** *n* foudre *f*; **~clap** *n* coup *m* de tonnerre; **~storm** *n* orage *m*; **~y** *a* orageux(euse).

Thursday ['θə:zdi] *n* jeudi *m*.

thus [ðʌs] *ad* ainsi.

thwart [θwɔ:t] *vt* contrecarrer.

thyme [taim] *n* thym *m*.

tiara [ti'ɑ:rə] *n* (*woman's*) diadème *m*.

tick [tik] *n* (*sound: of clock*) tic-tac *m*; (*mark*) coche *f*; (*ZOOL*) tique *f*; (*Brit col*): **in a ~** dans un instant // *vi* faire tic-tac // *vt* cocher; **to ~ off** *vt* cocher; (*person*) réprimander, attraper; **to ~ over** *vi* (*engine*) tourner au ralenti; (*fig*) aller *or* marcher doucettement.

ticket ['tikit] *n* billet *m*; (*for bus, tube*) ticket *m*; (*in shop: on goods*) étiquette *f*; (*: from cash register*) reçu *m*, ticket; (*for library*) carte *f*; **~ collector** *n* contrôleur/euse; **~ office** *n* guichet *m*, bureau *m* de vente des billets.

tickle ['tikl] *n* chatouillement *m* // *vt* chatouiller; (*fig*) plaire à; faire rire.

tidal ['taidl] *a* à marée; **~ wave** *n* raz-de-marée *m inv*.

tidbit ['tidbit] *n* (*US*) = **titbit**.

tiddlywinks ['tidliwiŋks] *n* jeu *m* de puce.

tide [taid] *n* marée *f*; (*fig: of events*) cours *m* // *vt*: **to ~ sb over** dépanner qn; **high/low ~** marée haute/basse.

tidy ['taidi] *a* (*room*) bien rangé(e); (*dress, work*) net(nette), soigné(e); (*person*) ordonné(e), qui a de l'ordre // *vt* (*also*: **~ up**) ranger; **to ~ o.s. up** s'arranger.

tie [tai] *n* (*string etc*) cordon *m*; (*Brit: also*: **neck~**) cravate *f*; (*fig: link*) lien *m*; (*SPORT: draw*) égalité *f* de points;

match nul // vt (parcel) attacher; (ribbon) nouer // vi (SPORT) faire match nul; finir à égalité de points; **to ~ sth in a bow** faire un nœud à or avec qch; **to ~ a knot in sth** faire un nœud à qch; **to ~ down** vt attacher; (fig): **to ~ sb down to** contraindre qn à accepter; **to ~ up** vt (parcel) ficeler; (dog, boat) attacher; (arrangements) conclure; **to be ~d up** (busy) être pris or occupé.

tier [tɪə*] n gradin m; (of cake) étage m.

tiff [tɪf] n petite querelle.

tiger ['taɪgə*] n tigre m.

tight [taɪt] a (rope) tendu(e), raide; (clothes) étroit(e), très juste; (budget, programme, bend) serré(e); (control) strict(e), sévère; (col: drunk) ivre, rond(e) // ad (squeeze) très fort; (shut) à bloc, hermétiquement; ~s npl (Brit) collant m; ~en vt (rope) tendre; (screw) resserrer; (control) renforcer // vi se tendre, se resserrer; ~-fisted a avare; ~ly ad (grasp) bien, très fort; ~rope n corde f raide.

tile [taɪl] n (on roof) tuile f; (on wall or floor) carreau m.

till [tɪl] n caisse (enregistreuse) // vt (land) cultiver // prep, cj = **until**.

tiller ['tɪlə*] n (NAUT) barre f (du gouvernail).

tilt [tɪlt] vt pencher, incliner // vi pencher, être incliné(e).

timber ['tɪmbə*] n (material) bois m de construction; (trees) arbres mpl.

time [taɪm] n temps m; (epoch: often pl) époque f, temps; (by clock) heure f; (moment) moment m; (occasion, also MATH) fois f; (MUS) mesure f // vt (race) chronométrer; (programme) minuter; (remark etc) choisir le moment de; **a long ~** un long moment, longtemps; **for the ~ being** pour le moment; **4 at a ~** 4 à la fois; **from ~ to ~** de temps en temps; **in ~** (soon enough) à temps; (after some time) avec le temps, à la longue; (MUS) en mesure; **in a week's ~** dans une semaine; **in no ~** en un rien de temps; **any ~** n'importe quand; **on ~** à l'heure; **5 ~s 5** 5 5 fois 5; **what ~ is it?** quelle heure est-il?; **to have a good ~** bien s'amuser; ~'s up! c'est l'heure!; ~ **bomb** n bombe f à retardement; ~ **lag** n décalage m; (in travel) décalage horaire; ~less a éternel(le); ~ly a opportun(e); ~ **off** n temps m libre; ~r n (~ switch) minuteur m; (in kitchen) compte-minutes m inv; ~ **scale** n délais mpl; ~ **switch** n (Brit) minuteur m; (for lighting) minuterie f; ~table n (RAIL) (indicateur m) horaire m; (SCOL) emploi m du temps; ~ **zone** n fuseau m horaire.

timid ['tɪmɪd] a timide; (easily scared) peureux(euse).

timing ['taɪmɪŋ] n minutage m; chronométrage m; **the ~ of his resignation** le moment choisi pour sa démission.

timpani ['tɪmpənɪ] npl timbales fpl.

tin [tɪn] n étain m; (also: ~ **plate**) ferblanc m; (Brit: can) boîte f (de conserve); (for baking) moule m (à gâteau); ~foil n papier m d'étain.

tinge [tɪndʒ] n nuance f // vt: ~d **with** teinté(e) de.

tingle ['tɪŋgl] vi picoter.

tinker ['tɪŋkə*] n rétameur ambulant; (gipsy) romanichel m; **to ~ with** vt fus bricoler, rafistoler.

tinkle ['tɪŋkl] vi tinter.

tinned [tɪnd] a (Brit: food) en boîte, en conserve.

tin opener ['-əupnə*] n (Brit) ouvre-boîte(s) m.

tinsel ['tɪnsl] n guirlandes fpl de Noël (argentées).

tint [tɪnt] n teinte f; (for hair) shampooing colorant; ~ed a (hair) teint(e); (spectacles, glass) teinté(e).

tiny ['taɪnɪ] a minuscule.

tip [tɪp] n (end) bout m; (protective: on umbrella etc) embout m; (gratuity) pourboire m; (for coal) terril m; (Brit: for rubbish) décharge f; (advice) tuyau m // vt (waiter) donner un pourboire à; (tilt) incliner; (overturn: also: ~ **over**) renverser; (empty: also: ~ **out**) déverser; ~-off n (hint) tuyau m; ~ped a (Brit: cigarette) (à bout) filtre inv.

tipsy ['tɪpsɪ] a un peu ivre, éméché(e).

tiptoe ['tɪptəu] n: **on ~** sur la pointe des pieds.

tiptop ['tɪp'tɔp] a: **in ~ condition** en excellent état.

tire ['taɪə*] n (US) = **tyre** // vt fatiguer // vi se fatiguer; ~d a fatigué(e); **to be ~d of** en avoir assez de, être las(lasse) de; ~some a ennuyeux(euse); **tiring** a fatigant(e).

tissue ['tɪʃu:] n tissu m; (paper handkerchief) mouchoir m en papier, kleenex m ®; ~ **paper** n papier m de soie.

tit [tɪt] n (bird) mésange f; **to give ~ for tat** rendre coup pour coup.

titbit ['tɪtbɪt], (US) **tidbit** ['tɪdbɪt] n (food) friandise f; (news) potin m.

titivate ['tɪtɪveɪt] vt pomponner.

title ['taɪtl] n titre m; ~ **deed** n (LAW) titre (constitutif) de propriété; ~ **role** n rôle principal.

titter ['tɪtə*] vi rire (bêtement).

titular ['tɪtjulə*] a (in name only) nominal(e).

TM abbr of **trademark**.

to [tu:, tə] ♦ prep **1** (direction) à; **to go ~ France/Portugal/London/school** aller en France/au Portugal/à Londres/à l'école; **to go ~ Claude's/the doctor's** aller chez Claude/le docteur; **the road ~**

Edinburgh la route d'Édimbourg
2 (*as far as*) (jusqu')à; to count ~ 10 compter jusqu'à 10; from 40 ~ 50 people de 40 à 50 personnes
3 (*with expressions of time*): a quarter ~ 5 5 heures moins le quart; it's twenty ~ 3 il est 3 heures moins vingt
4 (*for, of*) de; the key ~ the front door la clé de la porte d'entrée; a letter ~ his wife une lettre (adressée) à sa femme
5 (*expressing indirect object*) à; to give sth ~ sb donner qch à qn; to talk ~ sb parler à qn
6 (*in relation to*) à; 3 goals ~ 2 3 (buts) à 2; 30 miles ~ the gallon ≈ 9,4 litres aux cent (km)
7 (*purpose, result*): to come ~ sb's aid venir au secours de qn, porter secours à qn; to sentence sb ~ death condamner qn à mort; ~ my surprise à ma grande surprise
♦ *with vb* **1** (*simple infinitive*): ~ go/eat aller/manger
2 (*following another vb*): to want/try/start ~ do vouloir/essayer de/commencer à faire; *see also relevant verb*
3 (*with vb omitted*): I don't want ~ je ne veux pas
4 (*purpose, result*) pour; I did it ~ help you je l'ai fait pour vous aider
5 (*equivalent to relative clause*): I have things ~ do j'ai des choses à faire; the main thing is ~ try l'important est d'essayer
6 (*after adjective etc*): ready ~ go prêt(e) à partir; too old/young ~ ... trop vieux/jeune pour ...; *see also relevant adjective etc*
♦ *ad*: push/pull the door ~ tirez/poussez la porte.

toad [təud] *n* crapaud *m*; **~stool** *n* champignon (vénéneux).

toast [təust] *n* (*CULIN*) pain grillé, toast *m*; (*drink, speech*) toast *m* // *vt* (*CULIN*) faire griller; (*drink to*) porter un toast à; a piece or slice of ~ un toast; **~er** *n* grille-pain *m inv*.

tobacco [tə'bækəu] *n* tabac *m*; **~nist** *n* marchand/e de tabac; **~nist's (shop)** *n* (bureau *m* de) tabac *m*.

toboggan [tə'bɔgən] *n* toboggan *m*; (*child's*) luge *f*.

today [tə'deɪ] *ad, n* (*also fig*) aujourd'hui (*m*).

toddler ['tɔdlə*] *n* enfant *m/f* qui commence à marcher, bambin *m*.

toddy [tɔdɪ] *n* grog *m*.

to-do [tə'du:] *n* (*fuss*) histoire *f*, affaire *f*.

toe [təu] *n* doigt *m* de pied, orteil *m*; (*of shoe*) bout *m*; to ~ the line (*fig*) obéir, se conformer.

toffee ['tɔfɪ] *n* caramel *m*.

toga ['təugə] *n* toge *f*.

together [tə'gɛðə*] *ad* ensemble; (*at same time*) en même temps; ~ with *prep* avec.

toil [tɔɪl] *n* dur travail, labeur *m*.

toilet ['tɔɪlət] *n* (*Brit: lavatory*) toilettes *fpl*, cabinets *mpl* // *cpd* (*bag, soap etc*) de toilette; ~ **bowl** *n* cuvette *f* des w.-c.; ~ **paper** *n* papier *m* hygiénique; **~ries** *npl* articles *mpl* de toilette; ~ **roll** *n* rouleau *m* de papier hygiénique; ~ **water** *n* eau *f* de toilette.

token ['təukən] *n* (*sign*) marque *f*, témoignage *m*; (*voucher*) bon *m*, coupon *m*; **book/record** ~ *n* (*Brit*) chèque-livre/disque *m*.

told [təuld] *pt, pp of* **tell**.

tolerable ['tɔlərəbl] *a* (*bearable*) tolérable; (*fairly good*) passable.

tolerant ['tɔlərnt] *a*: ~ (*of*) tolérant(e) (à l'égard de).

tolerate ['tɔləreɪt] *vt* supporter; (*MED, TECH*) tolérer.

toll [təul] *n* (*tax, charge*) péage *m* // *vi* (*bell*) sonner; the accident ~ on the roads le nombre des victimes de la route.

tomato, ~es [tə'mɑ:təu] *n* tomate *f*.

tomb [tu:m] *n* tombe *f*.

tomboy ['tɔmbɔɪ] *n* garçon manqué.

tombstone ['tu:mstəun] *n* pierre tombale.

tomcat ['tɔmkæt] *n* matou *m*.

tomorrow [tə'mɔrəu] *ad, n* (*also fig*) demain (*m*); the day after ~ après-demain; a week ~ demain en huit; ~ morning demain matin.

ton [tʌn] *n* tonne *f* (*Brit* = 1016 kg; *US* = 907 kg; *metric* = 1000 kg); (*NAUT: also*: register ~) tonneau *m* (= 2.83 cu.m); ~s of (*col*) des tas de.

tone [təun] *n* ton *m*; (*of radio*) tonalité *f* // *vi* s'harmoniser; ~ **down** *vt* (*colour, criticism*) adoucir; (*sound*) baisser; ~ **up** *vt* (*muscles*) tonifier; **~-deaf** *a* qui n'a pas d'oreille.

tongs [tɔnz] *npl* pinces *fpl*; (*for coal*) pincettes *fpl*; (*for hair*) fer *m* à friser.

tongue [tʌn] *n* langue *f*; ~ **in cheek** *a* ironiquement; **~-tied** *a* (*fig*) muet(te); **~-twister** *n* phrase *f* très difficile à prononcer.

tonic ['tɔnɪk] *n* (*MED*) tonique *m*; (*also*: ~ **water**) tonic *m*.

tonight [tə'naɪt] *ad, n* cette nuit; (*this evening*) ce soir.

tonsil ['tɔnsl] *n* amygdale *f*; **~litis** [-'laɪtɪs] *n* amygdalite *f*.

too [tu:] *ad* (*excessively*) trop; (*also*) aussi; ~ **much** *ad* trop // *a* trop de; ~ **many** *a* trop de; ~ **bad!** tant pis!

took [tuk] *pt of* **take**.

tool [tu:l] *n* outil *m* // *vt* travailler, ouvrager; ~ **box** *n* boîte *f* à outils.

toot [tu:t] *vi* siffler; (*with car-horn*) klaxonner.

tooth [tu:θ], pl **teeth** n (ANAT TECH), dent f; ~**ache** n mal m de dents; ~**brush** n brosse f à dents; ~**paste** n (pâte f) dentifrice m; ~**pick** n cure-dent m.

top [tɔp] n (of mountain, head) sommet m; (of page, ladder) haut m; (of box, cupboard, table) dessus m; (lid: of box, jar) couvercle m; (: of bottle) bouchon m; (toy) toupie f // a du haut; (in rank) premier(ère); (best) meilleur(e) // vt (exceed) dépasser; (be first in) être en tête de; **on** ~ **of** sur; (in addition to) en plus de; **from** ~ **to bottom** de fond en comble; **to** ~ **up**, (US) **to** ~ **off** vt remplir; ~ **floor** n dernier étage; ~ **hat** n haut-de-forme m; ~**heavy** a (object) trop lourd(e) du haut.

topic ['tɔpɪk] n sujet m, thème m; ~**al** a d'actualité.

top: ~**less** a (bather etc) aux seins nus; ~**level** a (talks) à l'échelon le plus élevé.

topple ['tɔpl] vt renverser, faire tomber // vi basculer; tomber.

top-secret ['tɔp'si:krɪt] a ultra-secret(ète).

topsy-turvy ['tɔpsɪ'tə:vɪ] a, ad sens dessus-dessous.

torch [tɔ:tʃ] n torche f; (Brit: electric) lampe f de poche.

tore [tɔ:*] pt of **tear**.

torment n ['tɔ:mɛnt] tourment m // vt [tɔ:'mɛnt] tourmenter; (fig: annoy) agacer.

torn [tɔ:n] pp of **tear**.

tornado, ~**es** [tɔ:'neɪdəu] n tornade f.

torpedo, ~**es** [tɔ:'pi:dəu] n torpille f.

torrent ['tɔrnt] n torrent m.

tortoise ['tɔ:təs] n tortue f; ~**shell** ['tɔ:təʃel] a en écaille.

torture ['tɔ:tʃə*] n torture f // vt torturer.

Tory ['tɔ:rɪ] (Brit POL) a tory (pl tories), conservateur(trice) // n tory m/f, conservateur(trice).

toss [tɔs] vt lancer, jeter; (pancake) faire sauter; (head) rejeter en arrière; **to** ~ **a coin** jouer à pile ou face; **to** ~ **up for sth** jouer qch à pile ou face; **to** ~ **and turn** (in bed) se tourner et se retourner.

tot [tɔt] n (Brit: drink) petit verre; (child) bambin m.

total ['təutl] a total(e) // n total m // vt (add up) faire le total de, totaliser; (amount to) s'élever à.

totally ['təutəlɪ] ad totalement.

totter ['tɔtə*] vi chanceler.

touch [tʌtʃ] n contact m, toucher m; (sense, also skill: of pianist etc) toucher m; (fig: note, also FOOTBALL) touche f // vt (gen) toucher; (tamper with) toucher à; **a** ~ **of** (fig) un petit peu de; une touche de; **in** ~ **with** en contact or rapport avec; **to get in** ~ **with** prendre contact avec; **to lose** ~ (friends) se perdre de vue; **to** ~ **on** vt fus (topic) effleurer, toucher; **to** ~ **up** vt (paint) retoucher; ~**-and-go** a incertain(e); ~**down** n atterrissage m; (on sea) amerrissage m; (US FOOTBALL) but m; ~**ed** a touché(e); (col) cinglé(e); ~**ing** a touchant(e), attendrissant(e); ~**line** n (SPORT) (ligne f de) touche f; ~**y** a (person) susceptible.

tough [tʌf] a dur(e); (resistant) résistant(e), solide; (meat) dur, coriace.

toupee ['tu:peɪ] n postiche m.

tour [tuə*] n voyage m; (also: package ~) voyage organisé; (of town, museum) tour m, visite f; (by artist) tournée f // vt visiter; ~**ing** n voyages mpl touristiques, tourisme m.

tourism ['tuərɪzm] n tourisme m.

tourist ['tuərɪst] n touriste m/f // ad (travel) en classe touriste // cpd touristique; ~ **office** n syndicat m d'initiative.

tournament ['tuənəmənt] n tournoi m.

tousled ['tauzld] a (hair) ébouriffé(e).

tout [taut] vi: **to** ~ **for** essayer de raccrocher, racoler // n (also: ticket ~) revendeur m de billets.

tow [təu] vt remorquer; 'on ~', (US) 'in ~' (AUT) 'véhicule en remorque'.

toward(s) [tə'wɔ:d(z)] prep vers; (of attitude) envers, à l'égard de; (of purpose) pour.

towel ['tauəl] n serviette f (de toilette); (also: tea ~) torchon m; ~**ling** n (fabric) tissu-éponge m; ~ **rail**, (US) ~ **rack** n porte-serviettes m inv.

tower ['tauə*] n tour f; ~ **block** n (Brit) tour f (d'habitation); ~**ing** a très haut(e), imposant(e).

town [taun] n ville f; **to go to** ~ aller en ville; (fig) y mettre le paquet; ~ **centre** n centre m de la ville, centre-ville m; ~ **clerk** n ≈ secrétaire m/f de mairie; ~ **council** n conseil municipal; ~ **hall** n ≈ mairie f; ~ **plan** n plan m de ville; ~ **planning** n urbanisme m.

towrope ['təurəup] n (câble m de) remorque f.

tow truck n (US) dépanneuse f.

toy [tɔɪ] n jouet m; **to** ~ **with** vt fus jouer avec; (idea) caresser.

trace [treɪs] n trace f // vt (draw) tracer, dessiner; (follow) suivre la trace de; (locate) retrouver; **tracing paper** n papier-calque m.

track [træk] n (mark) trace f; (path: gen) chemin m, piste f; (: of bullet etc) trajectoire f; (: of suspect, animal) piste; (RAIL) voie ferrée, rails mpl; (on tape, SPORT) piste; (on record) plage f // vt suivre la trace or la piste de; **to keep** ~ **of** suivre; **to** ~ **down** vt (prey) trouver et capturer; (sth lost) finir par retrouver; ~**suit** n survêtement m.

tract [trækt] n (GEO) étendue f, zone f; (pamphlet) tract m.

tractor ['træktə*] n tracteur m.

trade [treɪd] n commerce m; (skill, job) métier m // vi faire du commerce; **to ~ with/in** faire du commerce avec/le commerce de; **to ~ in** vt (old car etc) faire reprendre; **~ fair** n foire (-exposition) commerciale; **~-in price** n prix m à la reprise; **~mark** n marque f de fabrique; **~name** n marque déposée; **~r** n commerçant/e, négociant/e; **~sman** n (shopkeeper) commerçant; **~ union** n syndicat m; **~ unionist** n syndicaliste m/f; **trading** n affaires fpl, commerce m; **trading estate** n (Brit) zone industrielle.

tradition [trə'dɪʃən] n tradition f; **~al** a traditionnel(le).

traffic ['træfɪk] n trafic m; (cars) circulation f // vi: **to ~ in** (pej: liquor, drugs) faire le trafic de; **~ circle** n (US) rond-point m; **~ jam** n embouteillage m; **~ lights** npl feux mpl (de signalisation); **~ warden** n contractuel/le.

tragedy ['trædʒədɪ] n tragédie f.

tragic ['trædʒɪk] a tragique.

trail [treɪl] n (tracks) trace f, piste f; (path) chemin m, piste; (of smoke etc) traînée f // vt traîner, tirer; (follow) suivre // vi traîner; **to ~ behind** vi traîner, être à la traîne; **~er** n (AUT) remorque f; (US) caravane f; (CINEMA) bande-annonce f; **~er truck** n (US) (camion m) semi-remorque m.

train [treɪn] n train m; (in underground) rame f; (of dress) traîne f // vt (apprentice, doctor etc) former; (sportsman) entraîner; (dog) dresser; (memory) exercer; (point: gun etc): **to ~ sth on** braquer qch sur // vi recevoir sa formation; s'entraîner; **one's ~ of thought** le fil de sa pensée; **~ed** a qualifié(e), qui a reçu une formation; dressé(e); **~ee** [treɪ'ni:] n stagiaire m/f; (in trade) apprenti/e; **~er** n (SPORT) entraîneur/euse; (of dogs etc) dresseur/euse; **~ing** n formation f; entraînement m; dressage m; **in ~ing** (SPORT) à l'entraînement; (fit) en forme; **~ing college** n école professionnelle; (for teachers) ≈ école normale; **~ing shoes** npl chaussures fpl de sport.

traipse [treɪps] vi (se) traîner, déambuler.

trait [treɪt] n trait m (de caractère).

traitor ['treɪtə*] n traître m.

tram [træm] n (Brit: also: **~car**) tram(way) m.

tramp [træmp] n (person) vagabond/e, clochard/e; (col: pej: woman): **to be a ~** être coureuse // vi marcher d'un pas lourd // vt (walk through: town, streets) parcourir à pied.

trample ['træmpl] vt: **to ~ (underfoot)** piétiner; (fig) bafouer.

trampoline ['træmpəli:n] n trampolino m.

tranquil ['træŋkwɪl] a tranquille; **~lizer** n (MED) tranquillisant m.

transact [træn'zækt] vt (business) traiter; **~ion** [-'zækʃən] n transaction f; **~ions** npl (minutes) actes mpl.

transatlantic ['trænzət'læntɪk] a transatlantique.

transfer n ['trænsfə*] (gen, also SPORT) transfert m; (POL: of power) passation f; (picture, design) décalcomanie f; (: stick-on) autocollant m // vt [træns'fə:*] transférer; passer; décalquer.

transform [træns'fɔ:m] vt transformer.

transfusion [træns'fju:ʒən] n transfusion f.

transient ['trænzɪənt] a transitoire, éphémère.

transistor [træn'zɪstə*] n (ELEC; also: **~ radio**) transistor m.

transit ['trænzɪt] n: **in ~** en transit.

transitive ['trænzɪtɪv] a (LING) transitif(ive).

translate [trænz'leɪt] vt traduire; **translation** [-'leɪʃən] n traduction f; (SCOL: as opposed to prose) version f; **translator** n traducteur/trice.

transmission [trænz'mɪʃən] n transmission f.

transmit [trænz'mɪt] vt transmettre; (RADIO, TV) émettre; **~ter** n émetteur m.

transparency [træns'pɛərnsɪ] n (Brit PHOT) diapositive f.

transparent [træns'pærnt] a transparent(e).

transpire [træn'spaɪə*] vi (turn out): **it ~d that ...** on a appris que ...; (happen) arriver.

transplant vt [træns'plɑ:nt] transplanter; (seedlings) repiquer // n ['trænsplɑ:nt] (MED) transplantation f.

transport n ['trænspɔ:t] transport m // vt [træns'pɔ:t] transporter; **~ation** [-'teɪʃən] n (moyen m de) transport m; (of prisoners) transportation f; **~ café** n (Brit) ≈ restaurant m de routiers.

trap [træp] n (snare, trick) piège m; (carriage) cabriolet m // vt prendre au piège; (immobilize) bloquer; (jam) coincer; **~ door** n trappe f.

trapeze [trə'pi:z] n trapèze m.

trappings ['træpɪŋz] npl ornements mpl; attributs mpl.

trash [træʃ] n (pej: goods) camelote f; (: nonsense) sottises fpl; **~ can** n (US) boîte f à ordures.

trauma ['trɔ:mə] n traumatisme m; **~tic** [-'mætɪk] a traumatisant(e).

travel ['trævl] n voyage(s) m(pl) // vi voyager; (move) aller, se déplacer // vt (distance) parcourir; **~ agency** n agence *f* de voyages; ~ **agent** *n* agent *m* de voyages; **~ler,** (*US*) **~er** *n* voyageur/euse; **~ler's cheque** *n* chèque *m* de voyage; **~ling,** (*US*) **~ing** *n* voyage(s) *m(pl)* // *cpd* (*bag, clock*) de voyage; (*expenses*) de déplacement; ~ **sickness** *n* mal *m* de la route (*or* de mer *or* de l'air).

travesty ['trævəstɪ] *n* parodie *f*.

trawler ['trɔːlə*] *n* chalutier *m*.

tray [treɪ] *n* (*for carrying*) plateau *m*; (*on desk*) corbeille *f*.

treachery ['trɛtʃərɪ] *n* traîtrise *f*.

treacle ['triːkl] *n* mélasse *f*.

tread [trɛd] *n* pas *m*; (*sound*) bruit *m* de pas; (*of tyre*) chape *f*, bande *f* de roulement // *vi* (*pt trod, pp trodden*) marcher; **to ~ on** *vt fus* marcher sur.

treason ['triːzn] *n* trahison *f*.

treasure ['trɛʒə*] *n* trésor *m* // *vt* (*value*) tenir beaucoup à; (*store*) conserver précieusement.

treasurer ['trɛʒərə*] *n* trésorier/ère.

treasury ['trɛʒərɪ] *n* trésorerie *f*; **the T~,** (*US*) **the T~ Department** le ministère des Finances.

treat [triːt] *n* petit cadeau, petite surprise // *vt* traiter; **to ~ sb to sth** offrir qch à qn.

treatise ['triːtɪz] *n* traité *m* (*ouvrage*).

treatment ['triːtmənt] *n* traitement *m*.

treaty ['triːtɪ] *n* traité *m*.

treble ['trɛbl] *a* triple // *vt, vi* tripler; ~ **clef** *n* clé *f* de sol.

tree [triː] *n* arbre *m*.

trek [trɛk] *n* voyage *m*; randonnée *f*; (*tiring walk*) tirée *f* // *vi* (*as holiday*) faire de la randonnée.

tremble ['trɛmbl] *vi* trembler.

tremendous [trɪ'mɛndəs] *a* (*enormous*) énorme, fantastique; (*excellent*) formidable.

tremor ['trɛmə*] *n* tremblement *m*; (*also:* earth ~) secousse *f* sismique.

trench [trɛntʃ] *n* tranchée *f*.

trend [trɛnd] *n* (*tendency*) tendance *f*; (*of events*) cours *m*; (*fashion*) mode *f*; **~y** *a* (*idea*) dans le vent; (*clothes*) dernier cri *inv*.

trepidation [trɛpɪ'deɪʃən] *n* vive agitation.

trespass ['trɛspəs] *vi*: **to ~ on** s'introduire sans permission dans; (*fig*) empiéter sur; '**no ~ing**' 'propriété privée', 'défense d'entrer'.

tress [trɛs] *n* boucle *f* de cheveux.

trestle ['trɛsl] *n* tréteau *m*; ~ **table** *n* table *f* à tréteaux.

trial ['traɪəl] *n* (*LAW*) procès *m*, jugement *m*; (*test: of machine etc*) essai *m*; (*hardship*) épreuve *f*; (*worry*) souci *m*; **by ~ and error** par tâtonnements.

triangle ['traɪæŋgl] *n* (*MATH, MUS*) triangle *m*.

tribe [traɪb] *n* tribu *f*.

tribunal [traɪ'bjuːnl] *n* tribunal *m*.

tributary ['trɪbjutərɪ] *n* (*river*) affluent *m*.

tribute ['trɪbjuːt] *n* tribut *m*, hommage *m*; **to pay ~ to** rendre hommage à.

trice [traɪs] *n*: **in a ~** en un clin d'œil.

trick [trɪk] *n* ruse *f*; (*clever act*) astuce *f*; (*joke*) tour *m*; (*CARDS*) levée *f* // *vt* attraper, rouler; **to play a ~ on sb** jouer un tour à qn; **that should do the ~** ça devrait faire l'affaire; **~ery** *n* ruse *f*.

trickle ['trɪkl] *n* (*of water etc*) filet *m* // *vi* couler en un filet *or* goutte à goutte.

tricky ['trɪkɪ] *a* difficile, délicat(e).

tricycle ['traɪsɪkl] *n* tricycle *m*.

trifle ['traɪfl] *n* bagatelle *f*; (*CULIN*) ≈ diplomate *m* // *ad*: **a ~ long** un peu long; **trifling** *a* insignifiant(e).

trigger ['trɪgə*] *n* (*of gun*) gâchette *f*; **to ~ off** *vt* déclencher.

trim [trɪm] *a* net(te); (*house, garden*) bien tenu(e); (*figure*) svelte // *n* (*haircut etc*) légère coupe; (*embellishment*) finitions *fpl*; (*on car*) garnitures *fpl* // *vt* couper légèrement; (*decorate*): **to ~ (with)** décorer (de); (*NAUT: a sail*) gréer; **~mings** *npl* décorations *fpl*; (*extras: gen CULIN*) garniture *f*.

trinket ['trɪŋkɪt] *n* bibelot *m*; (*piece of jewellery*) colifichet *m*.

trip [trɪp] *n* voyage *m*; (*excursion*) excursion *f*; (*stumble*) faux pas // *vi* (*stumble*) faire un faux pas, trébucher; (*go lightly*) marcher d'un pas léger; **on a ~** en voyage; **to ~ up** *vi* trébucher // *vt* faire un croc-en-jambe à.

tripe [traɪp] *n* (*CULIN*) tripes *fpl*; (*pej: rubbish*) idioties *fpl*.

triple ['trɪpl] *a* triple.

triplets ['trɪplɪts] *npl* triplés/ées.

tripod ['traɪpɒd] *n* trépied *m*.

trite [traɪt] *a* banal(e).

triumph ['traɪʌmf] *n* triomphe *m* // *vi*: **to ~ (over)** triompher (de).

trivia ['trɪvɪə] *npl* futilités *fpl*.

trivial ['trɪvɪəl] *a* insignifiant(e); (*commonplace*) banal(e).

trod [trɒd] *pt of* tread; **~den** *pp of* tread.

trolley ['trɒlɪ] *n* chariot *m*.

trombone [trɒm'bəun] *n* trombone *m*.

troop [truːp] *n* bande *f*, groupe *m*; **~s** *npl* (*MIL*) troupes *fpl*; (*: men*) hommes *mpl*, soldats *mpl*; **to ~ in/out** *vi* entrer/sortir en groupe; **~er** *n* (*MIL*) soldat *m* de cavalerie; **~ing the colour** *n* (*ceremony*) le salut au drapeau.

trophy ['trəufɪ] *n* trophée *m*.

tropic ['trɒpɪk] *n* tropique *m*; **~al** *a* tropical(e).

trot [trɒt] *n* trot *m* // *vi* trotter; **on the ~** (*Brit fig*) d'affilée.

trouble ['trʌbl] *n* difficulté(s) *f(pl)*, problème(s) *m(pl)*; (*worry*) ennuis *mpl*, soucis *mpl*; (*bother, effort*) peine *f*;

(POL) conflits mpl, troubles mpl; (MED): stomach etc ~ troubles gastriques etc // vt déranger, gêner; (worry) inquiéter // vi: to ~ to do prendre la peine de faire; ~s npl (POL etc) troubles mpl; to be in ~ avoir des ennuis; (ship, climber etc) être en difficulté; it's no ~! je vous en prie!; what's the ~? qu'est-ce qui ne va pas?; ~d a (person) inquiet(ète); (epoch, life) agité(e); ~maker n élément perturbateur, fauteur m de troubles; ~shooter n (in conflict) conciliateur m; ~some a ennuyeux(euse), gênant(e).

trough [trɔf] n (also: drinking ~) abreuvoir m; (also: feeding ~) auge f; (channel) chenal m.

trousers ['trauzəz] npl pantalon m; short ~ culottes courtes.

trout [traut] n (pl inv) truite f.

trowel ['trauəl] n truelle f.

truant ['truənt] n: to play ~ (Brit) faire l'école buissonnière.

truce [tru:s] n trêve f.

truck [trʌk] n camion m; (RAIL) wagon m à plate-forme; (for luggage) chariot m (à bagages); ~ driver n camionneur m; ~ farm n (US) jardin maraîcher.

truculent ['trʌkjulənt] a agressif(ive).

trudge [trʌdʒ] vi marcher lourdement, se traîner.

true [tru:] a vrai(e); (accurate) exact(e); (genuine) vrai, véritable; (faithful) fidèle.

truffle ['trʌfl] n truffe f.

truly ['tru:lɪ] ad vraiment, réellement; (truthfully) sans mentir; (faithfully) fidèlement.

trump [trʌmp] n atout m; ~ed-up a inventé(e) (de toutes pièces).

trumpet ['trʌmpɪt] n trompette f.

truncheon ['trʌntʃən] n bâton m (d'agent de police); matraque f.

trundle ['trʌndl] vt, vi: to ~ along rouler bruyamment.

trunk [trʌŋk] n (of tree, person) tronc m; (of elephant) trompe f; (case) malle f; (US AUT) coffre m; ~s npl (also: swimming ~s) maillot m or slip m de bain.

truss [trʌs] n (MED) bandage m herniaire; to ~ (up) vt (CULIN) brider.

trust [trʌst] n confiance f; (LAW) fidéicommis m; (COMM) trust m // vt (rely on) avoir confiance en; (entrust): to ~ sth to sb confier qch à qn; ~ed a en qui l'on a confiance; ~ee [trʌs'ti:] n (LAW) fidéicommissaire m/f; (of school etc) administrateur/trice; ~ful, ~ing a confiant(e); ~worthy a digne de confiance.

truth, ~s [tru:θ, tru:ðz] n vérité f; ~ful a (person) qui dit la vérité; (description) exact(e), vrai(e).

try [traɪ] n essai m, tentative f; (RUGBY) essai // vt (LAW) juger; (test: sth new) essayer, tester; (strain) éprouver // vi essayer; to ~ to do essayer de faire; (seek) chercher à faire; to ~ on vt (clothes) essayer; to ~ out vt essayer, mettre à l'essai; ~ing a pénible.

T-shirt ['ti:ʃə:t] n tee-shirt m.

T-square ['ti:skwɛə*] n équerre f en T.

tub [tʌb] n cuve f; baquet m; (bath) baignoire f.

tuba ['tju:bə] n tuba m.

tubby ['tʌbɪ] a rondelet(te).

tube [tju:b] n tube m; (Brit: underground) métro m; (for tyre) chambre f à air.

tubing ['tju:bɪŋ] n tubes mpl; a piece of ~ un tube.

TUC n abbr (Brit: = Trades Union Congress) confédération f des syndicats britanniques.

tuck [tʌk] n (SEWING) pli m, rempli m // vt (put) mettre; to ~ away vt cacher, ranger; to ~ in vt rentrer; (child) border // vi (eat) manger de bon appétit; attaquer le repas; to ~ up vt (child) border; ~ shop n boutique f à provisions (dans une école).

Tuesday ['tju:zdɪ] n mardi m.

tuft [tʌft] n touffe f.

tug [tʌg] n (ship) remorqueur m // vt tirer (sur); ~-of-war n lutte f à la corde.

tuition [tju:'ɪʃən] n (Brit) leçons fpl; (: private ~) cours particuliers; (US: school fees) frais mpl de scolarité.

tulip ['tju:lɪp] n tulipe f.

tumble ['tʌmbl] n (fall) chute f, culbute f // vi tomber, dégringoler; (with somersault) faire une or des culbute(s); to ~ to sth (col) réaliser qch; ~down a délabré(e); ~ dryer n (Brit) séchoir m (à linge) à air chaud.

tumbler ['tʌmblə*] n verre (droit), gobelet m.

tummy ['tʌmɪ] n (col) ventre m.

tumour ['tju:mə*], (US) **tumor** ['tu:mə*] n tumeur f.

tuna ['tju:nə] n (pl inv) (also: ~ fish) thon m.

tune [tju:n] n (melody) air m // vt (MUS) accorder; (RADIO, TV, AUT) régler, mettre au point; to be in/out of ~ (instrument) être accordé/désaccordé; (singer) chanter juste/faux; to ~ in (to) (RADIO, TV) se mettre à l'écoute (de); to ~ up vi (musician) accorder son instrument; ~ful a mélodieux(euse).

tunic ['tju:nɪk] n tunique f.

tuning ['tju:nɪŋ] n réglage m; ~ fork n diapason m.

Tunisia [tju:'nɪzɪə] n Tunisie f.

tunnel ['tʌnl] n tunnel m; (in mine) galerie f.

turbulence ['tə:bjuləns] n (AVIAT) turbulence f.

tureen [tə'ri:n] n soupière f.

turf [tə:f] n gazon m; (clod) motte f (de gazon) // vt gazonner; **to ~ out** vt (col) jeter; jeter dehors.

turgid ['tə:dʒɪd] a (speech) pompeux(euse).

Turk [tə:k] n Turc/Turque.

Turkey ['tə:kɪ] n Turquie f.

turkey ['tə:kɪ] n dindon m, dinde f.

Turkish ['tə:kɪʃ] a turc(turque) // n (LING) turc m.

turmoil ['tə:mɔɪl] n trouble m, bouleversement m.

turn [tə:n] n tour m; (in road) tournant m; (tendency: of mind, events) tournure f; (performance) numéro m; (MED) crise f, attaque f // vt tourner; (collar, steak) retourner; (milk) faire tourner; (change): **to ~ sth into** changer qch en // vi tourner; (person: look back) se (re)tourner; (reverse direction) faire demi-tour; (change) changer; (become) devenir; **to ~ into** se changer en; **a good ~** un service; **it gave me quite a ~** ça m'a fait un coup; **'no left ~'** (AUT) 'défense de tourner à gauche'; **it's your ~** c'est (à) votre tour; **in ~** à son tour; **à tour de rôle**; **to take ~s** se relayer; **to take ~s at** faire à tour de rôle; **to ~ away** vi se détourner, tourner la tête; **to ~ back** vi revenir, faire demi-tour; **to ~ down** vt (refuse) rejeter, refuser; (reduce) baisser; (fold) rabattre; **to ~ in** vi (col: go to bed) aller se coucher // vt (fold) rentrer; **to ~ off** vi (from road) tourner // vt (light, radio etc) éteindre; (engine) arrêter; **to ~ on** vt (light, radio etc) allumer; (engine) mettre en marche; **to ~ out** vt (light, gas) éteindre // vi: **to ~ out to be ...** s'avérer ..., se révéler ...; **to ~ over** vi (person) se retourner // vt (object) retourner; (page) tourner; **to ~ round** vi faire demi-tour; (rotate) tourner; **to ~ up** (person) arriver, se pointer; (lost object) être retrouvé(e) // vt (collar) remonter; (increase: sound, volume etc) mettre plus fort; **~ing** n (in road) tournant m; **~ing point** n (fig) tournant m, moment décisif.

turnip ['tə:nɪp] n navet m.

turnout ['tə:naut] n (nombre m de personnes dans l')assistance f.

turnover ['tə:nəuvə*] n (COMM: amount of money) chiffre m d'affaires; (: of goods) roulement m; (CULIN) sorte de chausson m.

turnpike ['tə:npaɪk] n (US) autoroute f à péage.

turnstile ['tə:nstaɪl] n tourniquet m (d'entrée).

turntable ['tə:nteɪbl] n (on record player) platine f.

turn-up ['tə:nʌp] n (Brit: on trousers) revers m.

turpentine ['tə:pəntaɪn] n (also: **turps**) (essence f de) térébenthine f.

turquoise ['tə:kwɔɪz] n (stone) turquoise f // a turquoise inv.

turret ['tʌrɪt] n tourelle f.

turtle ['tə:tl] n tortue marine; **~neck (sweater)** n pullover m à col montant.

tusk [tʌsk] n défense f.

tussle ['tʌsl] n bagarre f, mêlée f.

tutor ['tju:tə*] n (in college) directeur/trice d'études; (private teacher) précepteur/trice; **~ial** [-'tɔ:rɪəl] n (SCOL) (séance f de) travaux mpl pratiques.

tuxedo [tʌk'si:dəu] n (US) smoking m.

TV [ti:'vi:] n abbr (= television) télé f.

twang [twæŋ] n (of instrument) son vibrant; (of voice) ton nasillard.

tweed [twi:d] n tweed m.

tweezers ['twi:zəz] npl pince f à épiler.

twelfth [twelfθ] num douzième.

twelve [twelv] num douze; **at ~ (o'clock)** à midi; (midnight) à minuit.

twentieth ['twentɪθ] num vingtième.

twenty ['twentɪ] num vingt.

twice [twaɪs] ad deux fois; **~ as much** deux fois plus.

twiddle ['twɪdl] vt, vi: **to ~ (with) sth** tripoter qch; **to ~ one's thumbs** (fig) se tourner les pouces.

twig [twɪg] n brindille f // vt, vi (col) piger.

twilight ['twaɪlaɪt] n crépuscule m.

twin [twɪn] a, n jumeau(elle) // vt jumeler; **~(-bedded) room** n chambre f à deux lits.

twine [twaɪn] n ficelle f // vi (plant) s'enrouler.

twinge [twɪndʒ] n (of pain) élancement m; (of conscience) remords m.

twinkle ['twɪŋkl] vi scintiller; (eyes) pétiller.

twirl [twə:l] vt faire tournoyer // vi tournoyer.

twist [twɪst] n torsion f, tour m; (in wire, flex) tortillon m; (in story) coup m de théâtre // vt tordre; (weave) entortiller; (roll around) enrouler; (fig) déformer // vi s'entortiller; s'enrouler; (road) serpenter.

twit [twɪt] n (col) crétin/e.

twitch [twɪtʃ] vi se convulser; avoir un tic.

two [tu:] num deux; **to put ~ and ~ together** (fig) faire le rapport; **~-door** a (AUT) à deux portes; **~-faced** a (pej: person) faux(fausse); **~fold** ad: **to increase ~fold** doubler; **~-piece (suit)** n (costume m) deux-pièces m inv; **~-piece (swimsuit)** n (maillot m de bain) deux-pièces m inv; **~-seater** n (plane) (avion m) biplace m; (car) voiture f à deux places; **~some** n (people) couple m; **~-way** a (traffic) dans les deux sens.

tycoon [taɪ'ku:n] *n*: (*business*) ~ gros homme d'affaires.

type [taɪp] *n* (*category*) genre *m*, espèce *f*; (*model*) modèle *m*; (*example*) type *m*; (*TYP*) type, caractère *m* // *vt* (*letter etc*) taper (à la machine); **~-cast** *a* (*actor*) condamné(e) à toujours jouer le même rôle; **~face** *n* (*TYP*) police *f* (de caractères); **~script** *n* texte dactylographié; **~writer** *n* machine *f* à écrire; **~written** *a* dactylographié(e).

typhoid ['taɪfɔɪd] *n* typhoïde *f*.

typical ['tɪpɪkl] *a* typique, caractéristique.

typing ['taɪpɪŋ] *n* dactylo(graphie) *f*.

typist ['taɪpɪst] *n* dactylo *m/f*.

tyrant ['taɪərnt] *n* tyran *m*.

tyre, (*US*) **tire** ['taɪə*] *n* pneu *m*; **~ pressure** *n* pression *f* (de gonflage).

U

U-bend ['ju:'bend] *n* (*AUT, in pipe*) coude *m*.

udder ['ʌdə*] *n* pis *m*, mamelle *f*.

UFO ['ju:fəu] *n abbr* (= *unidentified flying object*) ovni *m*.

Uganda [ju:'gændə] *n* Ouganda *m*.

ugh [ə:h] *excl* pouah!

ugly ['ʌglɪ] *a* laid(e), vilain(e); (*fig*) répugnant(e).

UK *n abbr see* **united.**

ulcer ['ʌlsə*] *n* ulcère *m*; (*also:* mouth ~) aphte *f*.

Ulster ['ʌlstə*] *n* Ulster *m*.

ulterior [ʌl'tɪərɪə*] *a* ultérieur(e); ~ **motive** *n* arrière-pensée *f*.

ultimate ['ʌltɪmət] *a* ultime, final(e); (*authority*) suprême; **~ly** *ad* en fin de compte; finalement; par la suite.

ultrasound ['ʌltrəsaund] *n* (*MED*) ultrason *m*.

umbilical cord [ʌmbɪ'laɪkl-] *n* cordon ombilical.

umbrella [ʌm'brelə] *n* parapluie *m*.

umpire ['ʌmpaɪə*] *n* arbitre *m*.

umpteen [ʌmp'ti:n] *a* je ne sais combien de; **for the ~th time** pour la nième fois.

UN, UNO *n abbr of* **United Nations (Organization).**

unable [ʌn'eɪbl] *a*: **to be ~ to** ne (pas) pouvoir, être dans l'impossibilité de; être incapable de.

unaccompanied [ʌnə'kʌmpənɪd] *a* (*child, lady*) non accompagné(e).

unaccountably [ʌnə'kauntəblɪ] *ad* inexplicablement.

unaccustomed [ʌnə'kʌstəmd] *a* inaccoutumé(e), inhabituel(le); **to be ~ to** sth ne pas avoir l'habitude de qch.

unanimous [ju:'nænɪməs] *a* unanime; **~ly** *ad* à l'unanimité.

unarmed [ʌn'ɑ:md] *a* (*without a weapon*) non armé(e); (*combat*) sans armes.

unassuming [ʌnə'sju:mɪŋ] *a* modeste, sans prétentions.

unattached [ʌnə'tætʃt] *a* libre, sans attaches.

unattended [ʌnə'tendɪd] *a* (*car, child, luggage*) sans surveillance.

unauthorized [ʌn'ɔ:θəraɪzd] *a* non autorisé(e), sans autorisation.

unavoidable [ʌnə'vɔɪdəbl] *a* inévitable.

unaware [ʌnə'weə*] *a*: **to be ~ of** ignorer, ne pas savoir, être inconscient(e) de; **~s** *ad* à l'improviste, au dépourvu.

unbalanced [ʌn'bælənst] *a* déséquilibré(e).

unbearable [ʌn'beərəbl] *a* insupportable.

unbeknown(st) [ʌnbɪ'nəun(st)] *ad*: ~ **to** à l'insu de.

unbelievable [ʌnbɪ'li:vəbl] *a* incroyable.

unbend [ʌn'bend] *vb* (*irg*) *vi* se détendre // *vt* (*wire*) redresser, détordre.

unbias(s)ed [ʌn'baɪəst] *a* impartial(e).

unborn [ʌn'bɔ:n] *a* à naître.

unbreakable [ʌn'breɪkəbl] *a* incassable.

unbroken [ʌn'brəukən] *a* intact(e); continu(e).

unbutton [ʌn'bʌtn] *vt* déboutonner.

uncalled-for [ʌn'kɔ:ldfɔ:*] *a* déplacé(e), injustifié(e).

uncanny [ʌn'kænɪ] *a* étrange, troublant(e).

unceasing [ʌn'si:sɪŋ] *a* incessant(e), continu(e).

unceremonious [ʌnserɪ'məunɪəs] *a* (*abrupt, rude*) brusque.

uncertain [ʌn'sə:tn] *a* incertain(e); mal assuré(e); **~ty** *n* incertitude *f*, doutes *mpl*.

unchecked [ʌn'tʃekt] *a* non réprimé(e).

uncivilized [ʌn'sɪvɪlaɪzd] *a* (*gen*) non civilisé(e); (*fig: behaviour etc*) barbare.

uncle ['ʌŋkl] *n* oncle *m*.

uncomfortable [ʌn'kʌmfətəbl] *a* inconfortable; (*uneasy*) mal à l'aise, gêné(e); désagréable.

uncommon [ʌn'kɔmən] *a* rare, singulier(ère), peu commun(e).

uncompromising [ʌn'kɔmprəmaɪzɪŋ] *a* intransigeant(e), inflexible.

unconcerned [ʌnkən'sə:nd] *a*: **to be ~ (about)** ne pas s'inquiéter (de).

unconditional [ʌnkən'dɪʃənl] *a* sans conditions.

unconscious [ʌn'kɔnʃəs] *a* sans connaissance, évanoui(e); (*unaware*) inconscient(e) // *n*: **the ~** l'inconscient *m*; **~ly** *ad* inconsciemment, sans s'en rendre compte.

uncontrollable [ʌnkən'trəuləbl] *a* irrépressible; indiscipliné(e).

unconventional [ʌnkən'venʃənəl] *a*

non conventionnel(le).

uncouth [ʌn'ku:θ] *a* grossier(ère), fruste.

uncover [ʌn'kʌvə*] *vt* découvrir.

undecided [ʌndɪ'saɪdɪd] *a* indécis(e), irrésolu(e).

under ['ʌndə*] *prep* sous; (*less than*) (de) moins de; au-dessous de; (*according to*) selon, en vertu de // *ad* au-dessous; en dessous; from ~ sth de dessous *or* de sous qch; ~ there là-dessous; ~ repair en (cours de) réparation.

under... ['ʌndə*] *prefix* sous-; **~-age** *a* qui n'a pas l'âge réglementaire; **~carriage** *n* (*Brit* AVIAT) train *m* d'atterrissage; **~charge** *vt* ne pas faire payer assez à; **~coat** *n* (*paint*) couche *f* de fond; **~cover** *a* secret(ète), clandestin(e); **~current** *n* courant sous-jacent; **~cut** *vt irg* vendre moins cher que; **~developed** *a* sous-développé(e); **~dog** *n* opprimé *m*; **~done** *a* (*CULIN*) saignant(e); (*pej*) pas assez cuit(e); **~estimate** *vt* sous-estimer, mésestimer; **~fed** *a* sous-alimenté(e); **~foot** *ad* sous les pieds; **~go** *vt irg* subir; (*treatment*) suivre; **~graduate** *n* étudiant/e (qui prépare la licence); **~ground** *n* (*Brit*: *railway*) métro *m*; (*POL*) clandestinité *f* // *a* souterrain(e); (*fig*) clandestin(e); **~growth** *n* broussailles *fpl*, sous-bois *m*; **~hand(ed)** *a* (*fig*) sournois(e), en dessous; **~lie** *vt irg* être à la base de; **~line** *vt* souligner; **~ling** ['ʌndəlɪŋ] *n* (*pej*) sous-fifre *m*, subalterne *m*; **~mine** *vt* saper, miner; **~neath** [ʌndə'ni:θ] *ad* (en) dessous // *prep* sous, au-dessous de; **~paid** *a* sous-payé(e); **~pants** *npl* caleçon *m*, slip *m*; **~pass** *n* (*Brit*) passage souterrain; (: *on motorway*) passage inférieur; **~privileged** *a* défavorisé(e), économiquement faible; **~rate** *vt* sous-estimer, mésestimer; **~shirt** *n* (*US*) tricot *m* de corps; **~shorts** *npl* (*US*) caleçon *m*, slip *m*; **~side** *n* dessous *m*; **~skirt** *n* (*Brit*) jupon *m*.

understand [ʌndə'stænd] *vb* (*irg*: *like* stand) *vt, vi* comprendre; I ~ that ... je me suis laissé dire que ...; je crois comprendre que ...; **~able** *a* compréhensible; **~ing** *a* compréhensif(ive) // *n* compréhension *f*; (*agreement*) accord *m*.

understatement ['ʌndəsteɪtmənt] *n*: that's an ~ c'est (bien) peu dire, le terme est faible.

understood [ʌndə'stud] *pt, pp of* understand // *a* entendu(e); (*implied*) sous-entendu(e).

understudy ['ʌndəstʌdɪ] *n* doublure *f*.

undertake [ʌndə'teɪk] *vt irg* entreprendre; se charger de; to ~ to do sth s'engager à faire qch.

undertaker ['ʌndəteɪkə*] *n* entrepreneur *m* des pompes funèbres, croquemort *m*.

undertaking ['ʌndəteɪkɪŋ] *n* entreprise *f*; (*promise*) promesse *f*.

undertone ['ʌndətəun] *n*: in an ~ à mi-voix.

underwater [ʌndə'wɔ:tə*] *ad* sous l'eau // *a* sous-marin(e).

underwear ['ʌndəwɛə*] *n* sous-vêtements *mpl*; (*women's only*) dessous *mpl*.

underworld ['ʌndəwə:ld] *n* (*of crime*) milieu *m*, pègre *f*.

underwriter ['ʌndəraɪtə*] *n* (*INSURANCE*) souscripteur *m*.

undies ['ʌndɪz] *npl* (*col*) dessous *mpl*, lingerie *f*.

undo [ʌn'du:] *vt irg* défaire; **~ing** *n* ruine *f*, perte *f*.

undoubted [ʌn'dautɪd] *a* indubitable, certain(e); **~ly** *ad* sans aucun doute.

undress [ʌn'drɛs] *vi* se déshabiller.

undue [ʌn'dju:] *a* indu(e), excessif(ive).

undulating ['ʌndjuleɪtɪŋ] *a* ondoyant(e), onduleux(euse).

unduly [ʌn'dju:lɪ] *ad* trop, excessivement.

unearth [ʌn'ə:θ] *vt* déterrer; (*fig*) dénicher.

unearthly [ʌn'ə:θlɪ] *a* surnaturel(le); (*hour*) indu(e), impossible.

uneasy [ʌn'i:zɪ] *a* mal à l'aise, gêné(e); (*worried*) inquiet(ète).

unemployed [ʌnɪm'plɔɪd] *a* sans travail, au chômage // *n*: the ~ les chômeurs *mpl*.

unemployment [ʌnɪm'plɔɪmənt] *n* chômage *m*.

unending [ʌn'ɛndɪŋ] *a* interminable.

unerring [ʌn'ə:rɪŋ] *a* infaillible, sûr(e).

uneven [ʌn'i:vn] *a* inégal(e); irrégulier(ère).

unexpected [ʌnɪk'spɛktɪd] *a* inattendu(e), imprévu(e); **~ly** *ad* à l'improviste.

unfailing [ʌn'feɪlɪŋ] *a* inépuisable, infaillible.

unfair [ʌn'fɛə*] *a*: ~ (to) injuste (envers).

unfaithful [ʌn'feɪθful] *a* infidèle.

unfamiliar [ʌnfə'mɪlɪə*] *a* étrange, inconnu(e).

unfashionable [ʌn'fæʃnəbl] *a* (*clothes*) démodé(e); (*district*) déshérité(e), pas à la mode.

unfasten [ʌn'fɑ:sn] *vt* défaire; détacher.

unfavourable, (*US*) **unfavorable** [ʌn'feɪvərəbl] *a* défavorable.

unfeeling [ʌn'fi:lɪŋ] *a* insensible, dur(e).

unfit [ʌn'fɪt] *a* en mauvaise santé; pas en forme; (*incompetent*): ~ (for) impropre (à); (*work, service*) inapte (à).

unfold [ʌn'fəuld] *vt* déplier; (*fig*) révéler, exposer // vi se dérouler.

unforeseen [ˈʌnfɔːˈsiːn] a imprévu(e).

unforgettable [ʌnfəˈgɛtəbl] a inoubliable.

unfortunate [ʌnˈfɔːtʃnət] a malheureux(euse); (event, remark) malencontreux(euse); ~ly ad malheureusement.

unfounded [ʌnˈfaundɪd] a sans fondement.

unfriendly [ʌnˈfrɛndlɪ] a froid(e), inimical(e).

ungainly [ʌnˈgeɪnlɪ] a gauche, dégingandé(e).

ungodly [ʌnˈgɔdlɪ] a: at an ~ hour à une heure indue.

ungrateful [ʌnˈgreɪtful] a ingrat(e).

unhappiness [ʌnˈhæpɪnɪs] n tristesse f, peine f.

unhappy [ʌnˈhæpɪ] a triste, malheureux(euse); ~ with (arrangements etc) mécontent(e) de, peu satisfait(e) de.

unharmed [ʌnˈhɑːmd] a indemne, sain(e) et sauf(sauve).

unhealthy [ʌnˈhɛlθɪ] a (gen) malsain(e); (person) maladif(ive).

unheard-of [ʌnˈhɜːdɔv] a inouï(e), sans précédent.

uniform [ˈjuːnɪfɔːm] n uniforme m // a uniforme.

uninhabited [ʌnɪnˈhæbɪtɪd] a inhabité(e).

union [ˈjuːnjən] n union f; (also: trade ~) syndicat m // cpd du syndicat, syndical(e); **U~ Jack** n drapeau du Royaume-Uni.

unique [juːˈniːk] a unique.

unit [ˈjuːnɪt] n unité f; (section: of furniture etc) élément m, bloc m; (team, squad) groupe m, service m.

unite [juːˈnaɪt] vt unir // vi s'unir; ~d a uni(e), unifié(e); (efforts) conjugué(e); **U~d Kingdom (UK)** n Royaume-Uni m; **U~d Nations (Organization) (UN, UNO)** n (Organisation f des) Nations Unies (O.N.U.); **U~d States (of America) (US, USA)** n États-Unis mpl.

unit trust n (Brit) société f d'investissement, ≈ SICAV f.

unity [ˈjuːnɪtɪ] n unité f.

universal [juːnɪˈvɜːsl] a universel(le).

universe [ˈjuːnɪvɜːs] n univers m.

university [juːnɪˈvɜːsɪtɪ] n université f.

unjust [ʌnˈdʒʌst] a injuste.

unkempt [ʌnˈkɛmpt] a mal tenu(e), débraillé(e); mal peigné(e).

unkind [ʌnˈkaɪnd] a peu gentil(le), méchant(e).

unknown [ʌnˈnəun] a inconnu(e).

unlawful [ʌnˈlɔːful] a illégal(e).

unleash [ʌnˈliːʃ] vt détacher; (fig) déchaîner, déclencher.

unless [ʌnˈlɛs] cj: ~ he leaves à moins qu'il (ne) parte; ~ we leave à moins de

partir, à moins que nous (ne) partions; ~ otherwise stated sauf indication contraire.

unlike [ʌnˈlaɪk] a dissemblable, différent(e) // prep à la différence de, contrairement à.

unlikely [ʌnˈlaɪklɪ] a improbable; invraisemblable.

unlisted [ʌnˈlɪstɪd] a (US TEL) sur la liste rouge.

unload [ʌnˈləud] vt décharger.

unlock [ʌnˈlɔk] vt ouvrir.

unlucky [ʌnˈlʌkɪ] a malchanceux(euse); (object, number) qui porte malheur; to be ~ ne pas avoir de chance.

unmarried [ʌnˈmærɪd] a célibataire.

unmistakable [ʌnmɪsˈteɪkəbl] a indubitable; qu'on ne peut pas ne pas reconnaître.

unmitigated [ʌnˈmɪtɪgeɪtɪd] a non mitigé(e), absolu(e), pur(e).

unnatural [ʌnˈnætʃrəl] a non naturel(le); contre nature.

unnecessary [ʌnˈnɛsəsərɪ] a inutile, superflu(e).

unnoticed [ʌnˈnəutɪst] a: (to go) ~ (passer) inaperçu(e).

UNO [ˈjuːnəu] n abbr of **United Nations Organization**.

unobtainable [ʌnəbˈteɪnəbl] a (TEL) impossible à obtenir.

unobtrusive [ʌnəbˈtruːsɪv] a discret(ète).

unofficial [ʌnəˈfɪʃl] a non officiel(le); (strike) ≈ non sanctionné(e) par la centrale.

unpack [ʌnˈpæk] vi défaire sa valise.

unpalatable [ʌnˈpælətəbl] a (truth) désagréable (à entendre).

unparalleled [ʌnˈpærəleld] a incomparable, sans égal.

unpleasant [ʌnˈplɛznt] a déplaisant(e), désagréable.

unplug [ʌnˈplʌg] vt débrancher.

unpopular [ʌnˈpɔpjulə*] a impopulaire.

unprecedented [ʌnˈprɛsɪdəntɪd] a sans précédent.

unpredictable [ʌnprɪˈdɪktəbl] a imprévisible.

unprofessional [ʌnprəˈfɛʃənl] a (conduct) contraire à la déontologie.

unqualified [ʌnˈkwɔlɪfaɪd] a (teacher) non diplômé(e), sans titres; (success) sans réserve, total(e).

unquestionably [ʌnˈkwɛstʃənəblɪ] ad incontestablement.

unravel [ʌnˈrævl] vt démêler.

unreal [ʌnˈrɪəl] a irréel(le).

unrealistic [ʌnrɪəˈlɪstɪk] a irréaliste; peu réaliste.

unreasonable [ʌnˈriːznəbl] a qui n'est pas raisonnable.

unrelated [ʌnrɪˈleɪtɪd] a sans rapport; sans lien de parenté.

unreliable [ʌnrɪˈlaɪəbl] a sur qui (or

quoi) on ne peut pas compter, peu fiable.

unremitting [ʌnrɪ'mɪtɪŋ] *a* inlassable, infatigable, acharné(e).

unreservedly [ʌnrɪ'zɜːvɪdlɪ] *ad* sans réserve.

unrest [ʌn'rɛst] *n* agitation *f*, troubles *mpl*.

unroll [ʌn'rəul] *vt* dérouler.

unruly [ʌn'ruːlɪ] *a* indiscipliné(e).

unsafe [ʌn'seɪf] *a* dangereux(euse), hasardeux(euse).

unsaid [ʌn'sɛd] *a*: to leave sth ~ passer qch sous silence.

unsatisfactory ['ʌnsætɪs'fæktərɪ] *a* qui laisse à désirer.

unsavoury, (*US*) **unsavory** [ʌn'seɪvərɪ] *a* (*fig*) peu recommandable, répugnant(e).

unscathed [ʌn'skeɪðd] *a* indemne.

unscrew [ʌn'skruː] *vt* dévisser.

unscrupulous [ʌn'skruːpjuləs] *a* sans scrupules.

unsettled [ʌn'sɛtld] *a* perturbé(e); instable; incertain(e).

unshaven [ʌn'ʃeɪvn] *a* non *or* mal rasé(e).

unsightly [ʌn'saɪtlɪ] *a* disgracieux(euse), laid(e).

unskilled [ʌn'skɪld] *a*: ~ worker manœuvre *m*.

unspeakable [ʌn'spiːkəbl] *a* indicible; (*awful*) innommable.

unstable [ʌn'steɪbl] *a* instable.

unsteady [ʌn'stɛdɪ] *a* mal assuré(e), chancelant(e), instable.

unstuck [ʌn'stʌk] *a*: to come ~ se décoller; (*fig*) faire fiasco.

unsuccessful [ʌnsək'sɛsful] *a* (*attempt*) infructueux(euse); (*writer, proposal*) qui n'a pas de succès; (*marriage*) malheureux(euse), qui ne réussit pas; to be ~ (*in attempting sth*) ne pas réussir; ne pas avoir de succès; (*application*) ne pas être retenu(e).

unsuitable [ʌn'suːtəbl] *a* qui ne convient pas, peu approprié(e); inopportun(e).

unsure [ʌn'ʃuə*] *a* pas sûr(e); to be ~ of o.s. manquer de confiance en soi.

unsympathetic [ʌnsɪmpə'θɛtɪk] *a* (*person*) antipathique; (*attitude*) hostile.

untapped [ʌn'tæpt] *a* (*resources*) inexploité(e).

unthinkable [ʌn'θɪŋkəbl] *a* impensable, inconcevable.

untidy [ʌn'taɪdɪ] *a* (*room*) en désordre; (*appearance*) désordonné(e), débraillé(e); (*person*) sans ordre, désordonné, débraillé; (*work*) peu soigné(e).

untie [ʌn'taɪ] *vt* (*knot, parcel*) défaire; (*prisoner, dog*) détacher.

until [ən'tɪl] *prep* jusqu'à; (*after negative*) avant // *cj* jusqu'à ce que + *sub*, en attendant que + *sub*; (*in past,*

after negative) avant que + *sub*; ~ now jusqu'à présent, jusqu'ici; ~ then jusque-là.

untimely [ʌn'taɪmlɪ] *a* inopportun(e); (*death*) prématuré(e).

untold [ʌn'təuld] *a* incalculable; indescriptible.

untoward [ʌntə'wɔːd] *a* fâcheux(euse), malencontreux(euse).

untranslatable [ʌntrænz'leɪtəbl] *a* intraduisible.

unused [ʌn'juːzd] *a* neuf(neuve).

unusual [ʌn'juːʒuəl] *a* insolite, exceptionnel(le), rare.

unveil [ʌn'veɪl] *vt* dévoiler.

unwavering [ʌn'weɪvərɪŋ] *a* inébranlable.

unwelcome [ʌn'wɛlkəm] *a* importun(e); de trop.

unwell [ʌn'wɛl] *a* indisposé(e), souffrant(e); to feel ~ ne pas se sentir bien.

unwieldy [ʌn'wiːldɪ] *a* difficile à manier.

unwilling [ʌn'wɪlɪŋ] *a*: to be ~ to do ne pas vouloir faire; ~ly *ad* à contrecœur, contre son gré.

unwind [ʌn'waɪnd] *vb* (*irg*) *vt* dérouler // *vi* (*relax*) se détendre.

unwise [ʌn'waɪz] *a* déraisonnable.

unwitting [ʌn'wɪtɪŋ] *a* involontaire.

unworkable [ʌn'wɔːkəbl] *a* (*plan*) inexploitable.

unworthy [ʌn'wɜːðɪ] *a* indigne.

unwrap [ʌn'ræp] *vt* défaire; ouvrir.

unwritten [ʌn'rɪtn] *a* (*agreement*) tacite.

up [ʌp] ♦ *prep*: he went ~ the stairs/the hill il a monté l'escalier/la colline; the cat was ~ a tree le chat était dans un arbre; they live further ~ the street ils habitent plus haut dans la rue
♦ *ad* **1** (*upwards, higher*): ~ in the sky/the mountains (là-haut) dans le ciel/les montagnes; put it a bit higher ~ mettez-le un peu plus haut; ~ there là-haut; ~ above au-dessus
2: to be ~ (*out of bed*) être levé(e); (*prices etc*) avoir augmenté *or* monté
3: ~ to (*as far as*) jusqu'à; ~ to now jusqu'à présent
4: to be ~ to (*depending on*): it's ~ to you c'est à vous de décider; (*equal to*): he's not ~ to it (*job, task etc*) il n'en est pas capable; (*col: be doing*): what is he ~ to? qu'est-ce qu'il peut bien faire?
♦ *n*: ~s and downs hauts et bas *mpl*.

up-and-coming [ʌpənd'kʌmɪŋ] *a* plein(e) d'avenir *or* de promesses.

upbringing ['ʌpbrɪŋɪŋ] *n* éducation *f*.

update [ʌp'deɪt] *vt* mettre à jour.

upheaval [ʌp'hiːvl] *n* bouleversement *m*; branle-bas *m*; crise *f*.

uphill [ʌp'hɪl] *a* qui monte; (*fig: task*) difficile, pénible // *ad*: to go ~ monter.

uphold [ʌp'həuld] *vt* *irg* maintenir;

soutenir.

upholstery [ʌp'həulstərɪ] n rembourrage m; (of car) garniture f.

upkeep ['ʌpkiːp] n entretien m.

upon [ə'pɒn] prep sur.

upper ['ʌpə*] a supérieur(e); du dessus // n (of shoe) empeigne f; ~-class a ≈ bourgeois(e); ~ hand n: to have the ~ hand avoir le dessus; ~most a le(la) plus haut(e).

upright ['ʌpraɪt] a droit(e); vertical(e); (fig) droit, honnête // n montant m.

uprising ['ʌpraɪzɪŋ] n soulèvement m, insurrection f.

uproar ['ʌprɔː*] n tumulte m, vacarme m.

uproot [ʌp'ruːt] vt déraciner.

upset n ['ʌpsɛt] dérangement m // vt [ʌp'sɛt] (irg: like set) (glass etc) renverser; (plan) déranger; (person: offend) contrarier; (: grieve) faire de la peine à; bouleverser // a [ʌp'sɛt] contrarié(e); peiné(e); (stomach) détraqué(e), dérangé(e).

upshot ['ʌpʃɔt] n résultat m.

upside-down ['ʌpsaɪd'daun] ad à l'envers.

upstairs [ʌp'stɛəz] ad en haut // a (room) du dessus, d'en haut.

upstart ['ʌpstaːt] n parvenu/e.

upstream [ʌp'striːm] ad en amont.

uptake ['ʌpteɪk] n: he is quick/slow on the ~ il comprend vite/est lent à comprendre.

uptight [ʌp'taɪt] a (col) très tendu(e), crispé(e).

up-to-date ['ʌptə'deɪt] a moderne; très récent(e).

upturn ['ʌptəːn] n (in luck) retournement m; (COMM: in market) hausse f.

upward ['ʌpwəd] a ascendant(e); vers le haut; ~(s) ad vers le haut.

urban ['əːbən] a urbain(e).

urbane [əː'beɪn] a urbain(e), courtois(e).

urchin ['əːtʃɪn] n gosse m, garnement m.

urge [əːdʒ] n besoin m; envie f; forte envie, désir m // vt: to ~ sb to do exhorter qn à faire, pousser qn à faire; recommander vivement à qn de faire.

urgency ['əːdʒənsɪ] n urgence f; (of tone) insistance f.

urgent ['əːdʒənt] a urgent(e).

urine ['juərɪn] n urine f.

urn [əːn] n urne f; (also: tea ~) fontaine f à thé.

US, USA n abbr of **United States (of America).**

us [ʌs] pronoun nous; see also me.

use n [juːs] emploi m, utilisation f; usage m // vt [juːz] se servir de, utiliser, employer; she ~d to do it elle le faisait (autrefois), elle avait coutume de le faire; in ~ en usage; out of ~ hors d'usage; to be of ~ servir, être utile; it's no ~ ça ne

sert à rien; **to be ~d to** avoir l'habitude de, être habitué(e) à; **to ~ up** vt finir, épuiser; consommer; ~**ful** a utile; ~**fulness** n utilité f; ~**less** a inutile; ~**r** n utilisateur/trice, usager m; ~**r-friendly** a (computer) convivial(e), facile d'emploi.

usher ['ʌʃə*] n placeur m; ~**ette** [-'rɛt] n (in cinema) ouvreuse f.

USSR n: the ~ l'URSS f.

usual ['juːʒuəl] a habituel(le); **as ~** comme d'habitude; ~**ly** ad d'habitude, d'ordinaire.

utensil [juː'tɛnsl] n ustensile m; **kitchen** ~**s** batterie f de cuisine.

uterus ['juːtərəs] n utérus m.

utility [juː'tɪlɪtɪ] n utilité f; (also: public ~) service public; ~ **room** n buanderie f.

utmost ['ʌtməust] a extrême, le(la) plus grand(e) // n: to do one's ~ faire tout son possible.

utter ['ʌtə*] a total(e), complet(ète) // vt prononcer, proférer; émettre; ~**ance** n paroles fpl; ~**ly** ad complètement, totalement.

U-turn ['juː'təːn] n demi-tour m.

V

v. abbr of **verse, versus, volt**; (= vide) voir.

vacancy ['veɪkənsɪ] n (Brit: job) poste vacant; (room) chambre f disponible.

vacant ['veɪkənt] a (post) vacant(e); (seat etc) libre, disponible; (expression) distrait(e); ~ **lot** n (US) terrain inoccupé; (for sale) terrain à vendre.

vacate [və'keɪt] vt quitter.

vacation [və'keɪʃən] n vacances fpl.

vaccinate ['væksɪneɪt] vt vacciner.

vacuum ['vækjum] n vide m; ~ **bottle** n (US) = ~ **flask**; ~ **cleaner** n aspirateur m; ~ **flask** n (Brit) bouteille f thermos ®; ~-**packed** a emballé(e) sous vide.

vagina [və'dʒaɪnə] n vagin m.

vagrant ['veɪgrnt] n vagabond/e, mendiant/e.

vague [veɪg] a vague, imprécis(e); (blurred: photo, memory) flou(e); ~**ly** ad vaguement.

vain [veɪn] a (useless) vain(e); (conceited) vaniteux(euse); **in** ~ en vain.

valentine ['væləntaɪn] n (also: ~ card) carte f de la Saint-Valentin.

valiant ['vælɪənt] a vaillant(e).

valid ['vælɪd] a valide, valable; (excuse) valable.

valley ['vælɪ] n vallée f.

valour, (US) valor ['vælə*] n courage m.

valuable ['væljuəbl] a (jewel) de grande valeur; (time) précieux(euse); **~s** npl objets mpl de valeur.

valuation [vælju'eɪʃən] n évaluation f, expertise f.

value ['vælju:] n valeur f // vt (fix price) évaluer, expertiser; (cherish) tenir à; **~ added tax (VAT)** n (Brit) taxe f à la valeur ajoutée (T.V.A.); **~d** a (appreciated) estimé(e).

valve [vælv] n (in machine) soupape f; (on tyre) valve f; (in radio) lampe f.

van [væn] n (AUT) camionnette f; (Brit RAIL) fourgon m.

vandal ['vændl] n vandale m/f; **~ism** n vandalisme m; **~ize** vt saccager.

vanilla [və'nɪlə] n vanille f.

vanish ['vænɪʃ] vi disparaître.

vanity ['vænɪtɪ] n vanité f; **~ case** n sac m de toilette.

vantage ['vɑ:ntɪdʒ] n: **~ point** bonne position.

vapour, (US) **vapor** ['veɪpə*] n vapeur f; (on window) buée f.

variable ['vɛərɪəbl] a variable; (mood) changeant(e).

variance ['vɛərɪəns] n: to be at **~** (with) être en désaccord (avec); (facts) être en contradiction (avec).

varicose ['værɪkəus] a: **~ veins** varices fpl.

varied ['vɛərɪd] a varié(e), divers(e).

variety [və'raɪətɪ] n variété f; (quantity) nombre m, quantité f; **~ show** n (spectacle m de) variétés fpl.

various ['vɛərɪəs] a divers(e), différent(e); (several) divers, plusieurs.

varnish ['vɑ:nɪʃ] n vernis m // vt vernir.

vary ['vɛərɪ] vt, vi varier, changer.

vase [vɑ:z] n vase m.

vaseline ['væsɪli:n] n ® vaseline f.

vast [vɑ:st] a vaste, immense; (amount, success) énorme; **~ly** ad infiniment, extrêmement.

VAT [væt] n abbr of **value added tax**.

vat [væt] n cuve f.

vault [vɔ:lt] n (of roof) voûte f; (tomb) caveau m; (in bank) salle f des coffres; chambre forte; (jump) saut m // vt (also: **~ over**) sauter (d'un bond).

vaunted ['vɔ:ntɪd] a: **much~** tant célébré(e).

VCR n abbr of **video cassette recorder**.

VD n abbr of **venereal disease**.

VDU n abbr of **visual display unit**.

veal [vi:l] n veau m.

veer [vɪə*] vi tourner; virer.

vegetable ['vɛdʒtəbl] n légume m // a végétal(e).

vegetarian [vɛdʒɪ'tɛərɪən] a, n végétarien(ne).

vehement ['vi:ɪmənt] a violent(e), impétueux(euse); (impassioned) ardent(e).

vehicle ['vi:ɪkl] n véhicule m.

veil [veɪl] n voile m // vt voiler.

vein [veɪn] n veine f; (on leaf) nervure f; (fig: mood) esprit m.

velvet ['vɛlvɪt] n velours m.

vending machine ['vɛndɪŋ-] n distributeur m automatique.

veneer [və'nɪə*] n placage m de bois; (fig) vernis m.

venereal [vɪ'nɪərɪəl] a: **~ disease (VD)** n maladie vénérienne.

Venetian [vɪ'ni:ʃən] a: **~ blind store** vénitien.

vengeance ['vɛndʒəns] n vengeance f; **with a ~** (fig) vraiment, pour de bon.

venison ['vɛnɪsn] n venaison f.

venom ['vɛnəm] n venin m.

vent [vɛnt] n conduit m d'aération; (in dress, jacket) fente f // vt (fig: one's feelings) donner libre cours à.

ventilate ['vɛntɪleɪt] vt (room) ventiler, aérer; **ventilator** n ventilateur m.

ventriloquist [vɛn'trɪləkwɪst] n ventriloque m/f.

venture ['vɛntʃə*] n entreprise f // vt risquer, hasarder // vi s'aventurer, se risquer.

venue ['vɛnju:] n lieu m de rendez-vous or rencontre.

verb [və:b] n verbe m; **~al** a verbal(e); (translation) littéral(e).

verbatim [və:'beɪtɪm] a, ad mot pour mot.

verdict ['və:dɪkt] n verdict m.

verge [və:dʒ] n (Brit) bord m; **on the ~ of doing** sur le point de faire; **to ~ on** vt fus approcher de.

vermin ['və:mɪn] npl animaux mpl nuisibles; (insects) vermine f.

vermouth ['və:məθ] n vermouth m.

versatile ['və:sətaɪl] a polyvalent(e).

verse [və:s] n vers mpl; (stanza) strophe f; (in bible) verset m.

version ['və:ʃən] n version f.

versus ['və:səs] prep contre.

vertical ['və:tɪkl] a vertical(e) // n verticale f; **~ly** ad verticalement.

vertigo ['və:tɪgəu] n vertige m.

verve [və:v] n brio m; enthousiasme m.

very ['vɛrɪ] ad très // a: **the ~ book which** le livre même que; **at the ~ end** tout à la fin; **the ~ last** le tout dernier; **at the ~ least** au moins; **~ much** beaucoup.

vessel ['vɛsl] n (ANAT, NAUT) vaisseau m; (container) récipient m.

vest [vɛst] n (Brit) tricot m de corps; (US: waistcoat) gilet m; **~ed interests** npl (COMM) droits acquis.

vestry ['vɛstrɪ] n sacristie f.

vet [vɛt] n abbr (= veterinary surgeon) vétérinaire m/f // vt examiner minutieusement; (text) revoir.

veteran ['vɛtərn] n vétéran m; (also: **war ~**) ancien combattant.

veterinary ['vɛtrɪnərɪ] a vétérinaire; **~**

surgeon, (*US*) **veterinarian** [vɛtrə-'nɛərɪən] *n* vétérinaire *m/f*.

veto ['vi:təu] *n* (*pl* ~es) veto *m* // *vt* opposer son veto à.

vex [vɛks] *vt* fâcher, contrarier; ~ed *a* (*question*) controversé(e).

VHF *abbr* (= *very high frequency*) VHF *f*.

via ['vaɪə] *prep* par, via.

viable ['vaɪəbl] *a* viable.

vibrate [vaɪ'breɪt] *vi*: to ~ (with) vibrer (de); (*resound*) retentir (de).

vicar ['vɪkə*] *n* pasteur *m* (*de l'Église anglicane*); ~**age** *n* presbytère *m*.

vicarious [vɪ'kɛərɪəs] *a* indirect(e).

vice [vaɪs] *n* (*evil*) vice *m*; (*TECH*) étau *m*.

vice- [vaɪs] *prefix* vice-.

vice squad *n* ≈ brigade mondaine.

vice versa ['vaɪsɪ'və:sə] *ad* vice versa.

vicinity [vɪ'sɪnɪtɪ] *n* environs *mpl*, alentours *mpl*.

vicious ['vɪʃəs] *a* (*remark*) cruel(le), méchant(e); (*blow*) brutal(e); ~ **circle** *n* cercle vicieux.

victim ['vɪktɪm] *n* victime *f*.

victor ['vɪktə*] *n* vainqueur *m*.

Victorian [vɪk'tɔ:rɪən] *a* victorien(ne).

victory ['vɪktərɪ] *n* victoire *f*.

video ['vɪdɪəu] *cpd* vidéo *inv* // *n* (~ *film*) vidéo *f*; (*also*: ~ **cassette**) vidéocassette *f*; (*also*: ~ **cassette recorder**) magnétoscope *m*; ~ **tape** *n* bande *f* vidéo *inv*; (*cassette*) vidéocassette *f*.

vie [vaɪ] *vi*: to ~ with rivaliser avec.

Vienna [vɪ'ɛnə] *n* Vienne.

Vietnam [vjɛt'næm] *n* Viet-Nam *m*, Vietnam *m*; ~**ese** [-nə'mi:z] *a* vietnamien(ne) // *n* (*pl inv*) Vietnamien/ne.

view [vju:] *n* vue *f*; (*opinion*) avis *m*, vue // *vt* (*situation*) considérer; (*house*) visiter; **on** ~ (*in museum etc*) exposé(e); **in full** ~ **of** sous les yeux de; (*building etc*) devant; **in** ~ **of the fact that** étant donné que; ~**er** *n* (*viewfinder*) viseur *m*; (*small projector*) visionneuse *f*; (*TV*) téléspectateur/trice; ~**finder** *n* viseur *m*; ~**point** *n* point *m* de vue.

vigil ['vɪdʒɪl] *n* veille *f*.

vigorous ['vɪgərəs] *a* vigoureux(euse).

vile [vaɪl] *a* (*action*) vil(e); (*smell*) abominable; (*temper*) massacrant(e).

villa ['vɪlə] *n* villa *f*.

village ['vɪlɪdʒ] *n* village *m*; ~**r** *n* villageois/e.

villain ['vɪlən] *n* (*scoundrel*) scélérat *m*; (*criminal*) bandit *m*; (*in novel etc*) traître *m*.

vindicate ['vɪndɪkeɪt] *vt* défendre avec succès; justifier.

vindictive [vɪn'dɪktɪv] *a* vindicatif(ive), rancunier(ère).

vine [vaɪn] *n* vigne *f*; (*climbing plant*) plante grimpante.

vinegar ['vɪnɪgə*] *n* vinaigre *m*.

vineyard ['vɪnjɑ:d] *n* vignoble *m*.

vintage ['vɪntɪdʒ] *n* (*year*) année *f*, millésime *m*; ~ **wine** *n* vin *m* de grand cru.

violate ['vaɪəleɪt] *vt* violer.

violence ['vaɪələns] *n* violence *f*; (*POL etc*) incidents violents.

violent ['vaɪələnt] *a* violent(e).

violet ['vaɪələt] *a* (*colour*) violet(te) // *n* (*plant*) violette *f*.

violin [vaɪə'lɪn] *n* violon *m*; ~**ist** *n* violoniste *m/f*.

VIP *n abbr* (= *very important person*) V.I.P.

virgin ['və:dʒɪn] *n* vierge *f* // *a* vierge.

Virgo ['və:gəu] *n* la Vierge.

virile ['vɪraɪl] *a* viril(e).

virtually ['və:tjuəlɪ] *ad* (*almost*) pratiquement.

virtue ['və:tju:] *n* vertu *f*; (*advantage*) mérite *m*, avantage *m*; **by** ~ **of** par le fait de.

virtuous ['və:tjuəs] *a* vertueux(euse).

virus ['vaɪərəs] *n* virus *m*.

visa ['vi:zə] *n* visa *m*.

visibility [vɪzɪ'bɪlɪtɪ] *n* visibilité *f*.

visible ['vɪzəbl] *a* visible.

vision ['vɪʒən] *n* (*sight*) vue *f*, vision *f*; (*foresight, in dream*) vision.

visit ['vɪzɪt] *n* visite *f*; (*stay*) séjour *m* // *vt* (*person*) rendre visite à; (*place*) visiter; ~**ing hours** *npl* (*in hospital etc*) heures *fpl* de visite; ~**or** *n* visiteur/euse; (*in hotel*) client/e; ~**ors' book** *n* livre *m* d'or; (*in hotel*) registre *m*.

visor ['vaɪzə*] *n* visière *f*.

vista ['vɪstə] *n* vue *f*, perspective *f*.

visual ['vɪzjuəl] *a* visuel(le); ~ **aid** *n* support visuel (pour l'enseignement); ~ **display unit (VDU)** *n* console *f* de visualisation, visuel *m*.

visualize ['vɪzjuəlaɪz] *vt* se représenter; (*foresee*) prévoir.

vital ['vaɪtl] *a* vital(e); ~**ly** *ad* extrêmement; ~ **statistics** *npl* (*fig*) mensurations *fpl*.

vitamin ['vɪtəmɪn] *n* vitamine *f*.

vivacious [vɪ'veɪʃəs] *a* animé(e), qui a de la vivacité.

vivid ['vɪvɪd] *a* (*account*) frappant(e); (*light, imagination*) vif(vive); ~**ly** *ad* (*describe*) d'une manière vivante; (*remember*) de façon précise.

V-neck ['vi:nɛk] *n* décolleté *m* en V.

vocabulary [vəu'kæbjulərɪ] *n* vocabulaire *m*.

vocal ['vəukl] *a* vocal(e); (*articulate*) qui sait s'exprimer; ~ **chords** *npl* cordes vocales.

vocation [vəu'keɪʃən] *n* vocation *f*; ~**al** *a* professionnel(le).

vociferous [və'sɪfərəs] *a* bruyant(e).

vodka ['vɔdkə] n vodka f.

vogue [vəug] n mode f; (popularity) vogue f.

voice [vɔis] n voix f; (opinion) avis m // vt (opinion) exprimer, formuler.

void [vɔid] n vide m // a nul(le); ~ of vide de, dépourvu(e) de.

volatile ['vɔlətail] a volatil(e); (fig) versatile.

volcano, ~es [vɔl'keinəu] n volcan m.

volition [və'liʃən] n: of one's own ~ de son propre gré.

volley ['vɔli] n (of gunfire) salve f; (of stones etc) pluie f, volée f; (TENNIS etc) volée f; ~**ball** n volley(-ball) m.

volt [vəult] n volt m; ~**age** n tension f, voltage m.

volume ['vɔljuːm] n volume m.

voluntarily ['vɔləntrili] ad volontairement; bénévolement.

voluntary ['vɔləntəri] a volontaire; (unpaid) bénévole.

volunteer [vɔlən'tiə*] n volontaire m/f // vi (MIL) s'engager comme volontaire; to ~ to do se proposer pour faire.

vomit ['vɔmit] n vomi m // vt, vi vomir.

vote [vəut] n vote m, suffrage m; (cast) voix f, vote; (franchise) droit m de vote // vt (chairman) élire // vi voter; ~ of censure motion f de censure; ~ of thanks discours m de remerciement; ~**r** n électeur/trice; **voting** n scrutin m.

vouch [vautʃ]: to ~ for vt fus se porter garant de.

voucher ['vautʃə*] n (for meal, petrol) bon m; (receipt) reçu m.

vow [vau] n vœu m, serment m // vi jurer.

vowel ['vauəl] n voyelle f.

voyage ['vɔiidʒ] n voyage m par mer, traversée f.

vulgar ['vʌlgə*] a vulgaire.

vulnerable ['vʌlnərəbl] a vulnérable.

vulture ['vʌltʃə*] n vautour m.

W

wad [wɔd] n (of cotton wool, paper) tampon m; (of banknotes etc) liasse f.

waddle ['wɔdl] vi se dandiner.

wade [weid] vi: to ~ **through** marcher dans, patauger dans // vt passer à gué.

wafer ['weifə*] n (CULIN) gaufrette f.

waffle ['wɔfl] n (CULIN) gaufre f; (col) rabâchage m / remplissage m.

waft [wɔft] vt porter // vi flotter.

wag [wæg] vt agiter, remuer // vi remuer.

wage [weidʒ] n (also: ~s) salaire m, paye f // vt: to ~ **war** faire la guerre; ~ **packet** n (enveloppe f de) paye f.

wager ['weidʒə*] n pari m.

waggle ['wægl] vt, vi remuer.

wag(g)on ['wægən] n (horse-drawn) chariot m; (Brit RAIL) wagon m (de marchandises).

wail [weil] vi gémir; (siren) hurler.

waist [weist] n taille f, ceinture f; ~**coat** n (Brit) gilet m; ~**line** n (tour m de) taille f.

wait [weit] n attente f // vi attendre; to lie in ~ for guetter; to ~ for attendre; I can't ~ to (fig) je meurs d'envie de; to ~ **behind** vi rester (à attendre); **to ~ on** vt fus servir; ~**er** n garçon m (de café), serveur m; ~**ing** n: 'no ~**ing**' (Brit AUT) 'stationnement interdit'; ~**ing list** n liste f d'attente; ~**ing room** n salle f d'attente; ~**ress** n serveuse f.

waive [weiv] vt renoncer à, abandonner.

wake [weik] vb (pt woke, ~d, pp woken, ~d) vt (also: ~ up) réveiller // vi (also: ~ up) se réveiller // n (for dead person) veillée f mortuaire; (NAUT) sillage m; ~**n** vt, vi = wake.

Wales [weilz] n pays m de Galles.

walk [wɔːk] n promenade f; (short) petit tour; (gait) démarche f; (path) chemin m; (in park etc) allée f // vi marcher; (for pleasure, exercise) se promener // vt (distance) faire à pied; (dog) promener; 10 minutes' ~ from à 10 minutes de marche de; from all ~s of life de toutes conditions sociales; **to ~ out on** vt fus (person) quitter, plaquer; ~**er** n (person) marcheur/euse; ~**ie-talkie** ['wɔːki'tɔːki] n talkie-walkie m; ~**ing** n marche f à pied; ~**ing stick** n canne f; ~**out** n (of workers) grève-surprise f; ~**over** n (col) victoire f or examen m etc facile; ~**way** n promenade f.

wall [wɔːl] n mur m; (of tunnel, cave) paroi m; ~**ed** a (city) fortifié(e).

wallet ['wɔlit] n portefeuille m.

wallflower ['wɔːlflauə*] n giroflée f; to be a ~ (fig) faire tapisserie.

wallop ['wɔləp] vt (col) taper sur.

wallow ['wɔləu] vi se vautrer.

wallpaper ['wɔːlpeipə*] n papier peint.

wally ['wɔli] n (col) imbécile m/f.

walnut ['wɔːlnʌt] n noix f; (tree) noyer m.

walrus, pl ~ or ~es ['wɔːlrəs] n morse m.

waltz [wɔːlts] n valse f // vi valser.

wan [wɔn] a pâle; triste.

wand [wɔnd] n (also: magic ~) baguette f (magique).

wander ['wɔndə*] vi (person) errer, aller sans but; (thoughts) vagabonder; (river) serpenter // vt errer dans.

wane [wein] vi (moon) décroître; (reputation) décliner.

wangle ['wæŋgl] vt (Brit col) se débrouiller pour avoir; carotter.

want [wɔnt] vt vouloir; (need) avoir besoin de; (lack) manquer de // n: for ~ of par manque de, faute de; ~s npl (*needs*) besoins *mpl*; **to ~ to do** vouloir faire; **to ~ sb to do** vouloir que qn fasse; **~ing** *a*: **to be found ~ing** ne pas être à la hauteur.

wanton ['wɒntn] *a* capricieux(euse); dévergondé(e).

war [wɔ:*] *n* guerre *f*; **to make ~ (on)** faire la guerre (à).

ward [wɔ:d] *n* (*in hospital*) salle *f*; (*POL*) section électorale; (*LAW: child*) pupille *m/f*; **to ~ off** *vt* parer, éviter.

warden ['wɔ:dn] *n* (*Brit: of institution*) directeur/trice; (*of park, game reserve*) gardien/ne; (*Brit: also:* **traffic ~**) contractuel/le.

warder ['wɔ:də*] *n* (*Brit*) gardien *m* de prison.

wardrobe ['wɔ:drəub] *n* (*cupboard*) armoire *f*; (*clothes*) garde-robe *f*; (*THEATRE*) costumes *mpl*.

warehouse ['wɛəhaus] *n* entrepôt *m*.

wares [wɛəz] *npl* marchandises *fpl*.

warfare ['wɔ:fɛə*] *n* guerre *f*.

warhead ['wɔ:hɛd] *n* (*MIL*) ogive *f*.

warily ['wɛərɪlɪ] *ad* avec prudence.

warm [wɔ:m] *a* à chaud (*e*); (*thanks, welcome, applause*) chaleureux(euse); it's ~ il fait chaud; **I'm ~** j'ai chaud; **to ~ up** *vi* (*person, room*) se réchauffer; (*water*) chauffer; (*athlete, discussion*) s'échauffer // *vt* réchauffer; chauffer; (*engine*) faire chauffer; **~-hearted** *a* affectueux(euse); **~ly** *ad* chaudement; vivement; chaleureusement; **~th** *n* chaleur *f*.

warn [wɔ:n] *vt* avertir, prévenir; **~ing** *n* avertissement *m*; (*notice*) avis *m*; **~ing light** *n* avertisseur lumineux; **~ing triangle** *n* (*AUT*) triangle *m* de présignalisation.

warp [wɔ:p] *vi* travailler, se voiler // *vt* voiler; (*fig*) pervertir.

warrant ['wɔrnt] *n* (*guarantee*) garantie *f*; (*LAW: to arrest*) mandat *m* d'arrêt; (*: to search*) mandat de perquisition.

warranty ['wɔrəntɪ] *n* garantie *f*.

warren ['wɔrən] *n* (*of rabbits*) terriers *mpl*, garenne *f*.

warrior ['wɔrɪə*] *n* guerrier/ère.

Warsaw ['wɔ:sɔ:] *n* Varsovie.

warship ['wɔ:ʃɪp] *n* navire *m* de guerre.

wart [wɔ:t] *n* verrue *f*.

wartime ['wɔ:taɪm] *n*: **in ~** en temps de guerre.

wary ['wɛərɪ] *a* prudent(e).

was [wɒz] *pt of* **be**.

wash [wɒʃ] *vt* laver // *vi* se laver // *n* (*paint*) badigeon *m*; (*washing programme*) lavage *m*; (*of ship*) sillage *m*; **to have a ~** se laver, faire sa toilette; **to ~ away** *vt* (*stain*) enlever au lavage; (*subj: river etc*) emporter; **to ~ off** *vi* partir au lavage; **to ~ up** *vi* (*Brit*) faire la vaisselle; (*US*) se débarbouiller; **~able** *a* lavable; **~basin**, (*US*) **~bowl**

n lavabo *m*; **~cloth** *n* (*US*) gant *m* de toilette; **~er** *n* (*TECH*) rondelle *f*, joint *m*; **~ing** *n* (*linen etc*) lessive *f*; **~ing machine** *n* machine *f* à laver; **~ing powder** *n* (*Brit*) lessive *f* (en poudre); **~ing-up** *n* vaisselle *f*; **~ing-up liquid** *n* produit *m* pour la vaisselle; **~-out** *n* (*col*) désastre *m*; **~room** *n* toilettes *fpl*.

wasn't ['wɒznt] = **was not**.

wasp [wɒsp] *n* guêpe *f*.

wastage ['weɪstɪdʒ] *n* gaspillage *m*; (*in manufacturing, transport etc*) déchet *m*; **natural ~** départs naturels.

waste [weɪst] *n* gaspillage *m*; (*of time*) perte *f*; (*rubbish*) déchets *mpl*; (*also:* **household ~**) ordures *fpl* // *a* (*material*) de rebut; (*land*) inculte // *vt* gaspiller; (*time, opportunity*) perdre; **~s** *npl* étendue *f* désertique; **to lay ~** (*destroy*) dévaster; **to ~ away** *vi* dépérir; **~ disposal unit** *n* (*Brit*) broyeur *m* d'ordures; **~ful** *a* gaspilleur(euse); (*process*) peu économique; **~ ground** *n* (*Brit*) terrain *m* vague; **~paper basket** *n* corbeille *f* à papier; **~ pipe** (*tuyau m de*) vidange *f*.

watch [wɒtʃ] *n* montre *f*; (*act of watching*) surveillance *f*; guet *m*; (*guard: MIL*) sentinelle *f*; (*: NAUT*) homme *m* de quart; (*NAUT: spell of duty*) quart *m* // *vt* (*look at*) observer; (*: match, programme*) regarder; (*spy on, guard*) surveiller; (*be careful of*) faire attention à // *vi* regarder; (*keep guard*) monter la garde; **to ~ out** *vi* faire attention; **~dog** *n* chien *m* de garde; **~ful** *a* attentif(ive), vigilant(e); **~maker** *n* horloger/ère; **~man** *n* gardien *m*; (*also:* **night ~man**) veilleur *m* de nuit; **~ strap** *n* bracelet *m* de montre.

water ['wɔ:tə*] *n* eau *f* // *vt* (*plant*) arroser // *vi* (*eyes*) larmoyer; **in British ~s** dans les eaux territoriales Britanniques; **to ~ down** *vt* (*milk*) couper d'eau; (*fig: story*) édulcorer; **~colour** *n* aquarelle *f*; **~colours** *npl* couleurs *fpl* pour aquarelle; **~cress** *n* cresson *m* (de fontaine); **~fall** *n* chute *f* d'eau; **~ heater** *n* chauffe-eau *m*; **~ ice** *n* sorbet *m*; **~ing can** *n* arrosoir *m*; **~ lily** *n* nénuphar *m*; **~logged** *a* détrempé(e); imbibé(e) d'eau; **~line** *n* (*NAUT*) ligne *f* de flottaison; **~ main** *n* canalisation *f* d'eau; **~mark** *n* (*on paper*) filigrane *m*; **~melon** *n* pastèque *f*; **~proof** *a* imperméable; **~shed** *n* (*GEO*) ligne *f* de partage des eaux; (*fig*) moment *m* critique, point décisif; **~skiing** *n* ski *m* nautique; **~tight** *a* étanche; **~way** *n* cours *m* d'eau navigable; **~works** *npl* station *f* hydraulique; **~y** *a* (*colour*) délavé(e); (*coffee*) trop faible.

watt [wɒt] *n* watt *m*.

wave [weɪv] *n* vague *f*; (*of hand*) geste *m*, signe *m*; (*RADIO*) onde *f*; (*in hair*) ondulation f // vi faire signe de la main; (flag) flotter au vent // vt (handkerchief) agiter; (stick) brandir; **~length** n longueur f d'ondes.

waver ['weɪvə*] vi vaciller; (voice) trembler; (person) hésiter.

wavy ['weɪvɪ] a ondulé(e); onduleux(euse).

wax [wæks] n cire f; (for skis) fart m // vt cirer; (car) lustrer // vi (moon) croître; **~works** npl personnages mpl de cire; musée m de cire.

way [weɪ] n chemin m, voie f; (path, access) passage m; (distance) distance f; (direction) chemin, direction f; (manner) façon f, manière f; (habit) habitude f, façon; (condition) état m; which ~? — this ~ par où or de quel côté? — par ici; **on the ~** (en route) en route; **to be on one's ~** être en route; **to be in the ~** bloquer le passage; (fig) gêner; **to go out of one's ~ to do** (fig) se donner du mal pour faire; **to lose one's ~** perdre son chemin; **in a ~** d'un côté; **in some ~s** à certains égards; d'un côté; **by the ~ ...** à propos ...; **'~ in'** (Brit) 'entrée'; **'~ out'** (Brit) 'sortie'.

waylay [weɪ'leɪ] vt irg attaquer; (fig): I got waylaid quelqu'un m'a accroché.

wayward ['weɪwəd] a capricieux(euse), entêté(e).

W.C. ['dʌblju'si:] n (Brit) w.-c. mpl, waters mpl.

we [wi:] pl pronoun nous.

weak [wi:k] a faible; (health) fragile; (beam etc) peu solide; **~en** vi faiblir // vt affaiblir; **~ling** n gringalet m; faible m/f; **~ness** n faiblesse f; (fault) point m faible.

wealth [welθ] n (money, resources) richesse(s) f(pl); (of details) profusion f; **~y** a riche.

wean [wi:n] vt sevrer.

weapon ['wepən] n arme f.

wear [weə*] n (use) usage m; (deterioration through use) usure f; (clothing): sports/baby~ vêtements mpl de sport/pour bébés // vb (pt wore, pp worn) vt (clothes) porter; mettre; (damage: through use) user // vi (last) faire de l'usage; (rub etc through) s'user; **evening ~** tenue f de soirée; **to ~ away** vt user, ronger // vi s'user, être rongé(e); **to ~ down** vt (strength) épuiser; **to ~ off** vi disparaître; **to ~ on** vi se poursuivre; passer; **to ~ out** vt user; (person, strength) épuiser; **~ and tear** n usure f.

weary ['wɪərɪ] a (tired) épuisé(e); (dispirited) las(lasse); abattu(e).

weasel ['wi:zl] n (ZOOL) belette f.

weather ['weðə*] n temps m // vt (wood) faire mûrir; (tempest, crisis) essuyer, être pris(e) dans; survivre à, tenir le coup durant; **under the ~** (fig:

ill) mal fichu(e); **~-beaten** a (person) hâlé(e); (building) dégradé(e) par les intempéries; **~cock** n girouette f; **~ forecast** n prévisions fpl météorologiques, météo f; **~ vane** n = **~cock**.

weave [wi:v], pt **wove**, pp **woven** [wi:v, wəuv, 'wəuvn] vt (cloth) tisser; (basket) tresser; **~r** n tisserand/e.

web [web] n (of spider) toile f; (on foot) palmure f; (fabric, also fig) tissu m.

wed [wed], pt, pp **wedded** vt épouser // vi se marier.

we'd [wi:d] = **we had, we would**.

wedding ['wedɪŋ] n mariage m; **silver/ golden ~ anniversary** noces fpl d'argent/ d'or; **~ day** n jour m du mariage; **~ dress** n robe f de mariage; **~ ring** n alliance f.

wedge [wedʒ] n (of wood etc) coin m; (under door etc) cale f; (of cake) part f // vt (fix) caler; (push) enfoncer, coincer.

wedlock ['wedlɔk] n (union f du) mariage m.

Wednesday ['wednzdɪ] n mercredi m.

wee [wi:] a (Scottish) petit(e); tout(e) petit(e).

weed [wi:d] n mauvaise herbe // vt désherber; **~killer** n désherbant m; **~y** a (man) gringalet.

week [wi:k] n semaine f; **a ~ today/on Friday** aujourd'hui/vendredi en huit; **~day** n jour m de semaine; (COMM) jour ouvrable; **~end** n week-end m; **~ly** ad une fois par semaine, chaque semaine // a, n hebdomadaire (m).

weep [wi:p], pt, pp **wept** vi (person) pleurer; **~ing willow** n saule pleureur.

weigh [weɪ] vt, vi peser; **to ~ down** vt (branch) faire plier; (fig: with worry) accabler; **to ~ up** vt examiner.

weight [weɪt] n poids m; **to lose/put on ~** maigrir/grossir; **~ing** n (allowance) indemnité f, allocation f; **~ lifter** n haltérophile m; **~y** a lourd(e).

weir [wɪə*] n barrage m.

weird [wɪəd] a bizarre; (eerie) surnaturel(le).

welcome ['welkəm] a bienvenu(e) // n accueil m // vt accueillir; (also: **bid ~**) souhaiter la bienvenue à; (be glad of) se réjouir de; **to be ~** être le(la) bienvenu(e); **thank you — you're ~!** merci — de rien or il n'y a pas de quoi.

weld [weld] n soudure f // vt souder.

welfare ['welfeə*] n bien-être m; **~ state** n État-providence m.

well [wel] n puits m // ad bien // a: **to be ~** aller bien // excl eh bien!; bon!; enfin!; **as ~** aussi, également; **as ~ as** aussi bien que or de; en plus de; **~ done!** bravo!; **get ~ soon** remets-toi vite!; **to do ~ in sth** bien réussir en or dans qch; **to ~ up** vi monter.

we'll [wi:l] = **we will, we shall.**

well: ~**-behaved** a sage obéissant(e); ~**-being** n bien-être m; ~**-built** a (person) bien bâti(e); ~**-dressed** a bien habillé(e), bien vêtu(e); ~**-heeled** a (col: wealthy) fortuné(e), riche.

wellingtons ['welɪntənz] npl (also: **wellington boots**) bottes fpl de caoutchouc.

well: ~**-known** a (person) bien connu(e); ~**-mannered** a bien élevé(e); ~**-meaning** a bien intentionné(e); ~**-off** a aisé(e), assez riche; ~**-read** a cultivé(e); ~**-to-do** a aisé(e), assez riche; ~**-wisher** n: scores of ~wishers had gathered de nombreux amis et admirateurs s'étaient rassemblés.

Welsh [welʃ] a gallois(e) // n (LING) gallois m; the ~ npl les Gallois mpl; ~**man/woman** n Gallois/e; ~ **rarebit** n croûte f au fromage.

went [went] pt of **go.**

wept [wept] pt, pp of **weep.**

were [wəː*] pt of **be.**

we're [wɪə*] = **we are.**

weren't [wəːnt] = **were not.**

west [west] n ouest m // a ouest inv, de or à l'ouest // ad à or vers l'ouest; the **W~** n l'Occident m, l'Ouest m; the **W~ Country** n (Brit) le sud-ouest de l'Angleterre; ~**erly** a (wind) d'ouest; ~**ern** a occidental(e), de or à l'ouest // n (CINEMA) western m; **W~ Germany** n Allemagne f de l'Ouest; **W~ Indian** a antillais(e) // n Antillais/e; **W~ Indies** npl Antilles fpl; ~**ward(s)** ad vers l'ouest.

wet [wet] a mouillé(e); (damp) humide; (soaked) trempé(e); (rainy) pluvieux (euse); to get ~ se mouiller; '~ paint' 'attention peinture fraîche'; ~ **blanket** n (fig) rabat-joie m inv; ~ **suit** n combinaison f de plongée.

we've [wi:v] = **we have.**

whack [wæk] vt donner un grand coup à.

whale [weɪl] n (ZOOL) baleine f.

wharf, pl **wharves** [wɔːf, wɔːvz] n quai m.

what [wɔt] ♦ a quel(le), pl quels(quelles); ~ **size** is he? quelle taille fait-il?; ~ **colour** is it? de quelle couleur est-ce?; ~ **books** do you need? quels livres vous faut-il?; ~ **a mess!** quel désordre!

♦ pronoun 1 (interrogative) que, prep + quoi; ~ **are you doing?** que faites-vous?, qu'est-ce que vous faites?; ~ **is happening?** qu'est-ce qui se passe?, que se passe-t-il?; ~ **are you talking about?** de quoi parlez-vous?; ~ **is it called?** comment est-ce que ça s'appelle?; ~ **about me?** et moi?; ~ **about doing ...?** et si on faisait ...?

2 (relative: subject) ce qui; (: direct object) ce que; (: indirect object) ce +

prep + quoi, ce dont; I saw ~ **you did/was on the table** j'ai vu ce que vous avez fait/ce qui était sur la table; **tell me** ~ **you remember** dites-moi ce dont vous vous souvenez

♦ excl (disbelieving) quoi!, comment!

whatever [wɔt'evə*] a: ~ **book** quel que soit le livre que (or qui) + sub; n'importe quel livre // pronoun: **do** ~ **is necessary** faites (tout) ce qui est nécessaire; ~ **happens** quoi qu'il arrive; **no reason** ~ **or whatsoever** pas la moindre raison; **nothing** ~ rien du tout.

wheat [wi:t] n blé m, froment m.

wheedle ['wi:dl] vt: to ~ **sb into doing sth** cajoler or enjôler qn pour qu'il fasse qch; to ~ **sth out of sb** obtenir qch de qn par des cajoleries.

wheel [wi:l] n roue f; (AUT: also: steering ~) volant m; (NAUT) gouvernail m // vt pousser, rouler // vi (also: ~ round) tourner; ~**barrow** n brouette f; ~**chair** n fauteuil roulant; ~ **clamp** n (AUT) sabot m (de Denver).

wheeze [wi:z] vi respirer bruyamment.

when [wen] ♦ ad quand; ~ **did it happen?** c'est arrivé quand?

♦ cj **1** (at, during, after the time that) quand, lorsque; **she was reading** ~ **I came in** elle lisait quand or lorsque je suis entré

2 (on, at which): **on the day** ~ **I met him** le jour où je l'ai rencontré

3 (whereas) alors que; **you said I was wrong** ~ **in fact I was right** vous avez dit que j'avais tort alors qu'en fait j'avais raison.

whenever [wen'evə*] ad quand donc // cj quand; (every time that) chaque fois que; **you may leave** ~ **you like** vous pouvez partir quand vous voudrez.

where [weə*] ♦ ad, cj où; **this is** ~ c'est là que; ~**abouts** ad où donc // n: sb's ~**abouts** l'endroit où se trouve qn; ~**as** cj alors que; ~**by** pronoun par lequel (or laquelle etc); ~**upon** cj sur quoi, et sur ce; **wherever** [-'evə*] ad où donc // cj où que + sub; ~**withal** n moyens mpl.

whet [wet] vt aiguiser.

whether ['weðə*] cj si; **I don't know** ~ **to accept or not** je ne sais pas si je dois accepter ou non; **it's doubtful** ~ il est peu probable que; ~ **you go or not** que vous y alliez ou non.

which [wɪtʃ] ♦ a **1** (interrogative: direct, indirect) quel(le), pl quels(quelles); ~ **picture do you want?** quel tableau voulez-vous?; ~ **one?** lequel(laquelle)?

2: in ~ **case** auquel cas

♦ pronoun **1** (interrogative) lequel(laquelle), pl lesquels(lesquelles); **I don't mind** ~ peu importe lequel; ~ **(of these) are yours?** lesquels sont à vous?; **here** are the books — tell me ~ you want voici les livres — dites-moi lesquels *or* ceux que vous voulez

2 (*relative: subject*) qui; (: *object*) que, *prep* + lequel(laquelle) (NB: *à* + *lequel* = auquel; *de* + *lequel* = duquel); the apple ~ you ate/~ is on the table la pomme que vous avez mangée/qui est sur la table; the chair on ~ you are sitting la chaise sur laquelle vous êtes assis; the book of ~ you spoke le livre dont vous avez parlé; he said he knew, ~ is true/I feared il a dit qu'il le savait, ce qui est vrai/ce que je craignais; after ~ après quoi.

whichever [wɪtʃˈɛvəˀ] *a*: take ~ book you prefer prenez le livre que vous préférez, peu importe lequel; ~ way you de quelque façon que vous + *sub*.

whiff [wɪf] *n* bouffée *f*.

while [waɪl] *n* moment *m* // *cj* pendant que; (*as long as*) tant que; (*whereas*) alors que; bien que + *sub*; for a ~ pendant quelque temps; to ~ away *vt* (*time*) (faire) passer.

whim [wɪm] *n* caprice *m*.

whimper [ˈwɪmpəˀ] *vi* geindre.

whimsical [ˈwɪmzɪkl] *a* (*person*) capricieux(euse); (*look*) étrange.

whine [waɪn] *vi* gémir, geindre; pleurnicher.

whip [wɪp] *n* fouet *m*; (*for riding*) cravache *f*; (*POL: person*) chef *m* de file (*assurant la discipline dans son groupe parlementaire*) // *vt* fouetter; (*snatch*) enlever (*or* sortir) brusquement; ~ped cream *n* crème fouettée; ~-round *n* (*Brit*) collecte *f*.

whirl [wəːl] *vt* faire tourbillonner; faire tournoyer // *vi* tourbillonner; ~pool *n* tourbillon *m*; ~wind *n* tornade *f*.

whirr [wəːˀ] *vi* bruire; ronronner; vrombir.

whisk [wɪsk] *n* (*CULIN*) fouet *m* // *vt* fouetter, battre; to ~ sb away *or* off emmener qn rapidement.

whisker [ˈwɪskəˀ] *n*: ~s (*of animal*) moustaches *fpl*; (*of man*) favoris *mpl*.

whisky, (*Irish, US*) **whiskey** [ˈwɪskɪ] *n* whisky *m*.

whisper [ˈwɪspəˀ] *vt, vi* chuchoter.

whistle [ˈwɪsl] *n* (*sound*) sifflement *m*; (*object*) sifflet *m* // *vi* siffler.

white [waɪt] *a* blanc(blanche); (*with fear*) blême // *n* blanc *m*; (*person*) blanc/blanche; ~ coffee *n* (*Brit*) café *m* au lait, (*café*) crème *m*; ~-collar worker *n* employé/e de bureau; ~ elephant *n* (*fig*) objet dispendieux et superflu; ~ lie *n* pieux mensonge; ~ paper *n* (*POL*) livre blanc; ~wash *vt* blanchir à la chaux; (*fig*) blanchir.

whiting [ˈwaɪtɪŋ] *n* (*pl inv*) (*fish*) merlan *m*.

Whitsun [ˈwɪtsn] *n* la Pentecôte.

whittle [ˈwɪtl] *vt*: to ~ away, ~ down (*costs*) réduire, rogner.

whizz [wɪz] *vi* aller (*or* passer) à toute vitesse; ~ kid *n* (*col*) petit prodige.

who [huː] *pronoun* qui.

whodunit [huːˈdʌnɪt] *n* (*col*) roman policier.

whoever [huːˈɛvəˀ] *pronoun*: ~ finds it celui(celle) qui le trouve, (qui que ce soit), quiconque le trouve; ask ~ you like demandez à qui vous voulez; ~ he marries qui que ce soit *or* quelle que soit la personne qu'il épouse; ~ told you that? qui a bien pu vous dire ça?

whole [həʊl] *a* (*complete*) entier(ère), tout(e); (*not broken*) intact(e), complet(ète) // *n* (*total*) totalité *f*; (*sth not broken*) tout *m*; the ~ of the town la ville tout entière; on the ~, as a ~ dans l'ensemble; ~hearted *a* sans réserve(s), sincère; ~meal *a* (*bread, flour*) complet(ète); ~sale *n* (vente *f* en) gros *m* // *a* de gros; (*destruction*) systématique; ~saler *n* grossiste *m/f*; ~some *a* sain(e); (*advice*) salutaire; ~wheat *a* = ~meal; wholly *ad* entièrement, tout à fait.

whom [huːm] *pronoun* **1** (*interrogative*) qui; ~ did you see? qui avez-vous vu?; to ~ did you give it? à qui l'avez-vous donné?

2 (*relative*) que, *prep* + qui (*check syntax of French verb used*); the man ~ I saw/to ~ I spoke l'homme que j'ai vu/à qui j'ai parlé.

whooping cough [ˈhuːpɪŋkɔf] *n* coqueluche *f*.

whore [hɔːˀ] *n* (*col: pej*) putain *f*.

whose [huːz] ♦ *a* **1** (*possessive: interrogative*): ~ book is this? à qui est ce livre?; ~ pencil have you taken? à qui est le crayon que vous avez pris?, c'est le crayon de qui que vous avez pris?; ~ daughter are you? de qui êtes-vous la fille?

2 (*possessive: relative*): the man ~ son you rescued l'homme dont *or* de qui vous avez sauvé le fils; the girl ~ sister you were speaking to la fille à la sœur de qui *or* de laquelle vous parliez; the woman ~ car was stolen la femme dont la voiture a été volée

♦ *pronoun* à qui; ~ is this? à qui est ceci?; I know ~ it is je sais à qui c'est.

why [waɪ] *ad* pourquoi // *excl* eh bien!, tiens!; the reason ~ la raison pour laquelle; tell me ~ dites-moi pourquoi; ~ not? pourquoi pas?; ~ever *ad* pourquoi donc, mais pourquoi.

wick [wɪk] *n* mèche *f* (*de bougie*).

wicked [ˈwɪkɪd] *a* mauvais(e), méchant(e); inique; cruel(le); (*mischievous*) malicieux(euse).

wicker [ˈwɪkəˀ] *n* osier *m*; (*also*: ~work) vannerie *f*.

wicket ['wıkıt] n (CRICKET) guichet m; espace compris entre les deux guichets.

wide [waıd] a large; (area, knowledge) vaste, très étendu(e); (choice) grand(e) // ad: **to open ~** ouvrir tout grand; **to shoot ~** tirer à côté; **~-angle lens** n objectif m grand-angulaire; **~-awake** a bien éveillé(e); **~ly** ad (differing) radicalement; (spaced) sur une grande étendue; (believed) généralement; **~n** vt élargir; **~ open** a grand(e) ouvert(e); **~spread** a (belief etc) très répandu(e).

widow ['wıdəu] n veuve f; **~er** n veuf m.

width [wıdθ] n largeur f.

wield [wi:ld] vt (sword) manier; (power) exercer.

wife, wives [waıf, waıvz] n femme (mariée), épouse f.

wig [wıg] n perruque f.

wiggle ['wıgl] vt agiter, remuer.

wild [waıld] a sauvage; (sea) déchaîné(e); (idea, life) fou(folle); extravagant(e); **~s** npl régions fpl sauvages; **~erness** ['wıldənıs] n désert m, région f sauvage; **~-goose chase** n (fig) fausse piste; **~life** n faune f (et flore f) sauvage(s); **~ly** ad (applaud) frénétiquement; (hit, guess) au hasard; (happy) follement.

wilful ['wılful] a (person) obstiné(e); (action) délibéré(e); (crime) prémédité(e).

will [wıl] ♦ auxiliary vb 1 (forming future tense): I **~** finish it tomorrow je le finirai demain; I **~** have finished it by tomorrow je l'aurai fini d'ici demain; **~** you do it? — yes I **~**/no I won't le ferez-vous? — oui/non
2 (in conjectures, predictions): he **~** or he'll be there by now il doit être arrivé à l'heure qu'il est; that **~** be the postman ça doit être le facteur
3 (in commands, requests, offers): **~** you be quiet! voulez-vous bien vous taire!; **~** you help me? est-ce que vous pouvez m'aider?; **~** you have a cup of tea? voulez-vous une tasse de thé?; I won't put up with it! je ne le tolérerai pas!
♦ vt (pt, pp **~ed**): to **~** sb to do souhaiter ardemment qu qn fasse; he **~ed** himself to go on par un suprême effort de volonté, il continua
♦ n volonté f; testament m.

willing ['wılıŋ] a de bonne volonté, serviable; he's **~** to do it il est disposé à le faire, il veut bien le faire; **~ly** ad volontiers; **~ness** a bonne volonté.

willow ['wıləu] n saule m.

will power n volonté f.

willy-nilly [wılı'nılı] ad bon gré mal gré.

wilt [wılt] vi dépérir.

wily ['waılı] a rusé(e).

win [wın] n (in sports etc) victoire f // vb (pt, pp **won** [wʌn]) vt (battle, money) gagner; (prize) remporter; (popularity) acquérir // vi gagner; **to ~ over, ~ round** vt gagner, se concilier.

wince [wıns] vi tressaillir.

winch [wıntʃ] n treuil m.

wind n [wınd] (also MED) vent m // vb [waınd] (pt, pp **wound** [waund]) vt enrouler; (wrap) envelopper; (clock, toy) remonter; (take breath away: [wınd]) couper le souffle à // vi (road, river) serpenter; **to ~ up** vt (clock) remonter; (debate) terminer, clôturer; **~fall** n coup m de chance; **~ing** a (road) sinueux(euse); (staircase) tournant(e); **~ instrument** n (MUS) instrument m à vent; **~mill** n moulin m à vent.

window ['wındəu] n fenêtre f; (in car, train, also: **~pane**) vitre f; (in shop etc) vitrine f; **~ box** n jardinière f; **~ cleaner** n (person) laveur/euse de vitres; **~ ledge** n rebord m de la fenêtre; **~ pane** n vitre f, carreau m; **~sill** n (inside) appui m de la fenêtre; (outside) rebord m de la fenêtre.

windpipe ['wındpaıp] n gosier m.

windscreen, (US) **windshield** ['wındskri:n, 'wındʃi:ld] n pare-brise m inv; **~ washer** n lave-glace m inv; **~ wiper** n essuie-glace m inv.

windswept ['wındswɛpt] a balayé(e) par le vent.

windy ['wındı] a venté(e), venteux(euse); it's **~** il y a du vent.

wine [waın] n vin m; **~ cellar** n cave f à vins; **~ glass** n verre m à vin; **~ list** n carte f des vins; **~ tasting** n dégustation f (de vins); **~ waiter** n sommelier m.

wing [wıŋ] n aile f; **~s** npl (THEATRE) coulisses fpl; **~er** n (SPORT) ailier m.

wink [wıŋk] n clin m d'œil // vi faire un clin d'œil; (blink) cligner des yeux.

winner ['wınə*] n gagnant/e.

winning ['wınıŋ] a (team) gagnant(e); (goal) décisif(ive); **~s** npl gains mpl; **~ post** n poteau m d'arrivée.

winter ['wıntə*] n hiver m // vi hiverner; **~ sports** npl sports mpl d'hiver.

wintry ['wıntrı] a hivernal(e).

wipe [waıp] n coup m de torchon (or de chiffon or d'éponge) // vt essuyer; **to ~ off** vt essuyer; **to ~ out** vt (debt) régler; (memory) oublier; (destroy) anéantir; **to ~ up** vt essuyer.

wire ['waıə*] n fil m (de fer); (ELEC) fil électrique; (TEL) télégramme m // vt (house) faire l'installation électrique de; (also: **~ up**) brancher.

wireless ['waıəlıs] n (Brit) télégraphie f sans fil; (set) T.S.F. f.

wiring ['waıərıŋ] n installation f électrique.

wiry ['waɪərɪ] *a* noueux(euse), nerveux(euse).

wisdom ['wɪzdəm] *n* sagesse *f*; (*of action*) prudence *f*; ~ **tooth** *n* dent *f* de sagesse.

wise [waɪz] *a* sage, prudent(e), judicieux(euse).

...wise [waɪz] *suffix*: time~ en ce qui concerne le temps, question temps.

wish [wɪʃ] *n* (*desire*) désir *m*; (*specific desire*) souhait *m*, vœu *m* // *vt* souhaiter, désirer, vouloir; best ~es (*on birthday etc*) meilleurs vœux; with best ~es (*in letter*) bien amicalement; to ~ sb good-bye dire au revoir à qn; he ~ed me well il me souhaitait de réussir; to ~ to do/sb to do désirer *or* vouloir faire/que qn fasse; to ~ **for** souhaiter; it's ~ful thinking c'est prendre ses désirs pour des réalités.

wishy-washy [ˈwɪʃɪˈwɔʃɪ] *a* (*col: colour*) délavé(e); (: *ideas, argument*) faiblard(e).

wisp [wɪsp] *n* fine mèche (*de cheveux*); (*of smoke*) mince volute *f*.

wistful ['wɪstful] *a* mélancolique.

wit [wɪt] *n* (*gen pl*) intelligence *f*, esprit *m*; présence *f* d'esprit; (*wittiness*) esprit; (*person*) homme/femme d'esprit.

witch [wɪtʃ] *n* sorcière *f*.

with [wɪð, wɪθ] *prep* **1** (*in the company of*) avec; (*at the home of*) chez; we stayed ~ friends nous avons logé chez des amis; I'll be ~ you in a minute je suis à vous dans un instant

2 (*descriptive*): a room ~ a view une chambre avec vue; the man ~ the grey hat/blue eyes l'homme au chapeau gris/aux yeux bleus

3 (*indicating manner, means, cause*): ~ tears in her eyes les larmes aux yeux; to walk ~ a stick marcher avec une canne; red ~ anger rouge de colère; to shake ~ fear trembler de peur; to fill sth ~ water remplir qch d'eau

4: I'm ~ you (*I understand*) je vous suis; to be ~ it (*col: up-to-date*) être dans le vent.

withdraw [wɪθˈdrɔː] *vb* (*irg*) *vt* retirer // *vi* se retirer; (*go back on promise*) se rétracter; ~al *n* retrait *m*; (*MED*) état *m* de manque; ~n *a* (*person*) renfermé(e).

wither ['wɪðə*] *vi* se faner.

withhold [wɪθˈhəʊld] *vt irg* (*money*) retenir; (*decision*) remettre; (*permission*): to ~ **(from)** refuser (à); (*information*): to ~ **(from)** cacher (à).

within [wɪðˈɪn] *prep* à l'intérieur de // *ad* à l'intérieur; ~ sight of en vue de; ~ a mile of à moins d'un mille de; ~ the week avant la fin de la semaine.

without [wɪðˈaut] *prep* sans.

withstand [wɪθˈstænd] *vt irg* résister à.

witness ['wɪtnɪs] *n* (*person*) témoin *m*; (*evidence*) témoignage *m* // *vt* (*event*) être témoin de; (*document*) attester l'authenticité de; ~ **box**, (*US*) ~ **stand** *n* barre *f* des témoins.

witticism ['wɪtɪsɪzm] *n* mot *m* d'esprit.

witty ['wɪtɪ] *a* spirituel(le), plein(e) d'esprit.

wives [waɪvz] *npl of* **wife**.

wizard ['wɪzəd] *n* magicien *m*.

wk *abbr of* **week**.

wobble ['wɔbl] *vi* trembler; (*chair*) branler.

woe [wəu] *n* malheur *m*.

woke [wəuk] *pt of* **wake**; ~**n** *pp of* **wake**.

wolf, *pl* **wolves** [wulf, wulvz] *n* loup *m*.

woman, *pl* **women** ['wumən, 'wɪmɪn] *n* femme *f*; ~ **doctor** *n* femme *f* médecin; **women's lib** *n* (*col*) MLF *m*.

womb [wuːm] *n* (*ANAT*) utérus *m*.

women ['wɪmɪn] *npl of* **woman**.

won [wʌn] *pt, pp of* **win**.

wonder ['wʌndə*] *n* merveille *f*, miracle *m*; (*feeling*) émerveillement *m* // *vi*: to ~ **whether** se demander si; to ~ **at** s'étonner de; s'émerveiller de; to ~ **about** songer à; it's no ~ that il n'est pas étonnant que + *sub*; ~**ful** *a* merveilleux(euse).

won't [wəunt] = **will not**.

woo [wuː] *vt* (*woman*) faire la cour à.

wood [wud] *n* (*timber, forest*) bois *m*; ~ **carving** *n* sculpture *f* en *or* sur bois; ~**ed** *a* boisé(e); ~**en** *a* en bois; (*fig*) raide; inexpressif(ive); ~**pecker** *n* pic *m* (*oiseau*); ~**wind** *n* (*MUS*) bois *m*; the ~**wind** (*MUS*) les bois; ~**work** *n* menuiserie *f*; ~**worm** *n* ver *m* du bois.

wool [wul] *n* laine *f*; to pull the ~ over sb's eyes (*fig*) en faire accroire à qn; ~**len**, (*US*) ~**en** *a* de laine; (*industry*) lainier(ère); ~**lens** *npl* lainages *mpl*; ~**ly**, (*US*) ~**y** *a* laineux(euse); (*fig: ideas*) confus(e).

word [wəːd] *n* mot *m*; (*spoken*) mot, parole *f*; (*promise*) parole; (*news*) nouvelles *fpl* // *vt* rédiger, formuler; in other ~s en d'autres termes; to break/keep one's ~ manquer à/tenir sa parole; ~**ing** *n* termes *mpl*, langage *m*; libellé *m*; ~ **processing** *n* traitement *m* de texte; ~ **processor** *n* machine *f* de traitement de texte.

wore [wɔː*] *pt of* **wear**.

work [wəːk] *n* travail *m*; (*ART, LITERATURE*) œuvre *f* // *vi* travailler; (*mechanism*) marcher, fonctionner; (*plan etc*) marcher; (*medicine*) agir // *vt* (*clay, wood etc*) travailler; (*mine etc*) exploiter; (*machine*) faire marcher *or* fonctionner; to be out of ~ être au chômage; ~**s** *n* (*Brit: factory*) usine *f* // *npl* (*of clock, machine*) mécanisme *m*; to ~ **loose** *vi* se défaire, se desserrer; to

~ on vt fus travailler à; (principle) se baser sur; **to ~ out** vi (plans etc) marcher // vt (problem) résoudre; (plan) élaborer; **it ~s out** at £100 ça fait 100 livres; **to get ~ed up** se mettre dans tous ses états; **~aholic** n bourreau m de travail; **~er** n travailleur/euse, ouvrier/ère; **~force** n main-d'œuvre f; **~ing class** n classe ouvrière; **~ing-class** a ouvrier(ère); **~ing man** n travailleur m; **~ing order** n: **in ~ing order** en état de marche; **~man** n ouvrier m; **~manship** n métier m, habileté f; facture f; **~sheet** n feuille f de programmation; **~shop** n atelier m; **~ station** n poste m de travail; **~-to-rule** n (Brit) grève f du zèle.

world [wə:ld] n monde m // cpd (champion) du monde; (power, war) mondial(e); **to think the ~ of sb** (fig) ne jurer que par qn; **~ly** a de ce monde; **~-wide** a universel(le).

worm [wə:m] n ver m.

worn [wɔ:n] pp of **wear** // a usé(e); **~out** a (object) complètement usé(e); (person) épuisé(e).

worried ['wʌrid] a inquiet(ète).

worry ['wʌri] n souci m // vt inquiéter // vi s'inquiéter, se faire du souci.

worse [wə:s] a pire, plus mauvais(e) // ad plus mal // n pire m; **a change for the ~** une détérioration; **to get ~** vt, vi empirer; **~ off** a moins à l'aise financièrement; (fig): **you'll be ~ off this way** ça ira moins bien de cette façon.

worship ['wə:ʃip] n culte m // vt (God) rendre un culte à; (person) adorer; **Your W~** (Brit: to mayor) Monsieur le Maire; (: to judge) Monsieur le Juge.

worst [wə:st] a le(la) pire, le(la) plus mauvais(e) // ad le plus mal // n pire m; **at ~** au pis aller.

worsted ['wustid] n: **(wool) ~** laine peignée.

worth [wə:θ] n valeur f // a: **to be ~** valoir; **it's ~ it** cela en vaut la peine; **it is ~ one's while** (to do) on gagne (à faire); **~less** a qui ne vaut rien; **~while** a (activity) qui en vaut la peine; (cause) louable.

worthy ['wə:ði] a (person) digne; (motive) louable; **~ of** digne de.

would [wud] auxiliary vb **1** (conditional tense): **if you asked him he ~ do it** si vous le lui demandiez, il le ferait; **if you had asked him he ~ have done it** si vous le lui aviez demandé, il l'aurait fait **2** (in offers, invitations, requests): **~ you like a biscuit?** voulez-vous or voudriez-vous un biscuit?; **~ you close the door please?** voulez-vous fermer la porte, s'il vous plaît **3** (in indirect speech): **I said I ~ do it** j'ai dit que je le ferais

4 (emphatic): **it WOULD have to snow today!** naturellement il neige or il fallait qu'il neige aujourd'hui! **5** (insistence): **she ~n't do it** elle n'a pas voulu or elle a refusé de le faire **6** (conjecture): **it ~ have been midnight** il devait être minuit **7** (indicating habit): **he ~ go there on Mondays** il y allait le lundi.

would-be ['wudbi:] a (pej) soi-disant.

wouldn't ['wudnt] = **would not.**

wound vb [waund] pt, pp of **wind** // n, vt [wu:nd] n blessure f // vt blesser.

wove [wəuv] pt of **weave**; **~n** pp of **weave**.

wrangle ['ræŋgl] n dispute f.

wrap [ræp] n (stole) écharpe f; (cape) pèlerine f // vt (also: **~ up**) envelopper; **~per** n (Brit: of book) couverture f; **~ping paper** n papier m d'emballage; (for gift) papier cadeau.

wrath [rɔθ] n courroux m.

wreak [ri:k] vt: **to ~ havoc on** avoir un effet désastreux sur; **to ~ vengeance (on)** se venger (de).

wreath, ~s [ri:θ, ri:ðz] n couronne f.

wreck [rɛk] n (sea disaster) naufrage m; (ship) épave f; (pej: person) loque humaine // vt démolir; (ship) provoquer le naufrage de; (fig) briser, ruiner; **~age** n débris mpl; (of building) décombres mpl; (of ship) épave f.

wren [rɛn] n (ZOOL) roitelet m.

wrench [rɛntʃ] n (TECH) clé f (à écrous); (tug) violent mouvement de torsion; (fig) arrachement m // vt tirer violemment sur, tordre; **to ~ sth from** arracher qch (violemment) à or de.

wrestle ['rɛsl] vi: **to ~ (with sb)** lutter (avec qn); **to ~ with** (fig) se débattre avec, lutter contre; **~r** n lutteur/euse; **wrestling** n lutte f; (also: **all-in wrestling**) catch m.

wretched ['rɛtʃid] a misérable; (col) maudit(e).

wriggle ['rigl] vi se tortiller.

wring [riŋ], pt, pp **wrung** vt tordre; (wet clothes) essorer; (fig): **to ~ sth out of** arracher qch à.

wrinkle ['riŋkl] n (on skin) ride f; (on paper etc) pli m // vt rider, plisser // vi se plisser.

wrist [rist] n poignet m; **~watch** n montre-bracelet f.

writ [rit] n acte m judiciaire.

write [rait], pt **wrote**, pp **written** vt, vi écrire; **to ~ down** vt noter; (put in writing) mettre par écrit; **to ~ off** vt (debt) passer aux profits et pertes; (depreciate) amortir; **to ~ out** vt écrire; (copy) recopier; **to ~ up** vt rédiger; **~-off** n perte totale; **~r** n auteur m, écrivain m.

writhe [raið] vi se tordre.

writing ['raitiŋ] n écriture f; (of

author) œuvres *fpl*; **in ~** par écrit; **~ paper** *n* papier *m* à lettres.

written ['rɪtn] *pp of* **write**.

wrong [rɔŋ] *a* faux(fausse); (*incorrectly chosen: number, road etc*) mauvais(e); (*not suitable*) qui ne convient pas; (*wicked*) mal; (*unfair*) injuste // *ad* faux // *n* tort *m* // *vt* faire du tort à, léser; **you are ~** to do it tu as tort de le faire; **you are ~ about that, you've got it ~** tu te trompes; **to be in the ~** avoir tort; **what's ~?** qu'est-ce qui ne va pas?; **to go ~** (*person*) se tromper; (*plan*) mal tourner; (*machine*) tomber en panne; **~ful** *a* injustifié(e); **~ly** *ad* à tort.

wrote [rəʊt] *pt of* **write**.

wrought [rɔːt] *a*: **~ iron** fer forgé.

wrung [rʌŋ] *pt, pp of* **wring**.

wry [raɪ] *a* désabusé(e).

wt. *abbr of* **weight**.

X Y Z

Xmas ['ɛksməs] *n abbr of* **Christmas**.

X-ray [ɛks'reɪ] *n* rayon *m* X; (*photograph*) radio(graphie) *f*.

xylophone ['zaɪləfəʊn] *n* xylophone *m*.

yacht [jɔt] *n* yacht *m*; voilier *m*; **~ing** *n* yachting *m*, navigation *f* de plaisance.

Yank [jæŋk], **Yankee** ['jæŋkɪ] *n* (*pej*) Amerloque *m/f*.

yap [jæp] *vi* (*dog*) japper.

yard [jɑːd] *n* (*of house etc*) cour *f*; (*measure*) yard *m* (= *914 mm*; *3 feet*); **~stick** *n* (*fig*) mesure *f*, critère *m*.

yarn [jɑːn] *n* fil *m*; (*tale*) longue histoire.

yawn [jɔːn] *n* bâillement *m* // *vi* bâiller; **~ing** *a* (*gap*) béant(e).

yd. *abbr of* **yard(s)**.

yeah [jɛə] *ad* (*col*) ouais.

year [jɪə*] *n* an *m*, année *f*; **to be 8 ~s old** avoir 8 ans; **an eight-~-old child** un enfant de huit ans; **~ly** *a* annuel(le) // *ad* annuellement.

yearn [jɔːn] *vi*: **to ~ for sth** aspirer à qch, languir après qch; **to ~ to do** aspirer à faire; **~ing** *n* désir ardent, envie *f*.

yeast [jiːst] *n* levure *f*.

yell [jɛl] *vi* hurler.

yellow ['jɛləʊ] *a, n* jaune (*m*).

yelp [jɛlp] *vi* japper; glapir.

yeoman ['jəʊmən] *n*: **Y~ of the Guard** hallebardier *m* de la garde royale.

yes [jɛs] *ad* oui; (*answering negative question*) si // *n* oui *m*; **to say/answer ~** dire/répondre oui.

yesterday ['jɛstədɪ] *ad, n* hier (*m*); **~ morning/evening** hier matin/soir; **all day ~** toute la journée d'hier.

yet [jɛt] *ad* encore; déjà // *cj* pourtant, néanmoins; **it is not finished ~** ce n'est pas encore fini *or* toujours pas fini; **the best ~** le meilleur jusqu'ici *or* jusque-là;

as ~ jusqu'ici, encore.

yew [juː] *n* if *m*.

yield [jiːld] *n* production *f*, rendement *m*; rapport *m* // *vt* produire, rendre, rapporter; (*surrender*) céder // *vi* céder; (*US AUT*) céder la priorité.

YMCA *n abbr* (= *Young Men's Christian Association*) YMCA *m*.

yoga ['jəʊgə] *n* yoga *m*.

yog(h)ourt, yog(h)urt ['jəʊgət] *n* yaourt *m*.

yoke [jəʊk] *n* joug *m*.

yolk [jəʊk] *n* jaune *m* (d'œuf).

yonder ['jɔndə*] *ad* là(-bas).

you [juː] *pronoun* **1** (*subject*) tu; (*polite form*) vous; (*pl*) vous; **~ French enjoy your food** vous autres Français, vous aimez bien manger; **~ and I will go** toi et moi *or* vous et moi, nous irons

2 (*object: direct, indirect*) te, t' + *vowel*; vous; **I know ~** je te *or* vous connais; **I gave it to ~** je te *or* vous l'ai donné

3 (*stressed*) toi; vous; **I told YOU to do it** c'est à toi *or* vous que j'ai dit de le faire

4 (*after prep, in comparisons*) toi; vous; **it's for ~** c'est pour toi *or* vous; **she's younger than ~** elle est plus jeune que toi *or* vous

5 (*impersonal: one*) on; **fresh air does ~ good** l'air frais fait du bien; **~ never know** on ne sait jamais.

you'd [juːd] = **you had, you would**.

you'll [juːl] = **you will, you shall**.

young [jʌŋ] *a* jeune // *npl* (*of animal*) petits *mpl*; (*people*): **the ~** les jeunes, la jeunesse; **~er** *a* (*brother etc*) cadet(te); **~ster** *n* jeune *m* (garçon *m*); (*child*) enfant *m/f*.

your [jɔː*] *a* ton(ta), tes *pl*; (*polite form, pl*) votre, vos *pl*; *see also* **my**.

you're [juə*] = **you are**.

yours [jɔːz] *pronoun* le(la) tien(ne), les tiens(tiennes); (*polite form, pl*) le(la) vôtre, les vôtres; **yours sincerely/faithfully** je vous prie d'agréer l'expression de mes sentiments meilleurs/mes sentiments respectueux *or* dévoués; *see also* **mine**.

yourself [jɔː'sɛlf] *pronoun* (*reflexive*) te; (*: polite form*) vous; (*after prep*) toi; vous; (*emphatic*) toi-même; vous-même; **yourselves** *pl pronoun* vous; (*emphatic*) vous-mêmes; *see also* **oneself**.

youth [juːθ] *n* jeunesse *f*; (*young man*) (*pl* **~s** [juːðz]) jeune homme *m*; **~ club** *n* centre *m* de jeunes; **~ful** *a* jeune; de jeunesse; juvénile; **~ hostel** *n* auberge *f* de jeunesse.

you've [juːv] = **you have**.

YTS *n abbr* (*Brit*: = *Youth Training Scheme*) ≈ TUC *m*.

Yugoslav ['juːgəʊslɑːv] *a* yougoslave // *n* Yougoslave *m/f*.

Yugoslavia ['juːɡəʊ'slɑːvɪə] *n*
Yougoslavie *f*.

yuppie ['jʌpɪ] *n* yuppie *m/f*.

YWCA *n abbr* (= *Young Women's Christian Association*) YWCA *m*.

zany ['zeɪnɪ] *a* farfelu(e), loufoque.

zap [zæp] *vt* (*COMPUT*) effacer.

zeal [ziːl] *n* zèle *m*, ferveur *f*; empressement *m*.

zebra ['ziːbrə] *n* zèbre *m*; ~ **crossing** *n* (*Brit*) passage *m* pour piétons.

zero ['zɪərəʊ] *n* zéro *m*.

zest [zest] *n* entrain *m*, élan *m*; zeste *m*.

zigzag ['zɪɡzæɡ] *n* zigzag *m*.

Zimbabwe [zɪm'bɑːbwɪ] *n* Zimbabwe *m*.

zinc [zɪŋk] *n* zinc *m*.

zip [zɪp] *n* (*also:* ~ **fastener**, (*US*) ~**per**) fermeture *f* éclair ® // *vt* (*also:* ~ **up**) fermer avec une fermeture éclair ®; ~ **code** *n* (*US*) code postal.

zodiac ['zəʊdɪæk] *n* zodiaque *m*.

zone [zəʊn] *n* zone *f*; (*subdivision of town*) secteur *m*.

zoo [zuː] *n* zoo *m*.

zoology [zuː'ɒlədʒɪ] *n* zoologie *f*.

zoom [zuːm] *vi*: to ~ **past** passer en trombe; ~ **lens** *n* zoom *m*.

zucchini [tsuː'kiːnɪ] *n(pl)* (*US*) courgette(s) *f(pl)*.

FRENCH VERB FORMS

1 Participe présent *2* Participe passé *3* Présent *4* Imparfait *5* Futur *6* Conditionnel *7* Subjonctif présent

acquérir *1* acquérant *2* acquis *3* acquiers, acquérons, acquièrent *4* acquérais *5* acquerrai *7* acquière

ALLER *1* allant *2* allé *3* vais, vas, va, allons, allez, vont *4* allais *5* irai *6* irais *7* aille

asseoir *1* asseyant *2* assis *3* assieds, asseyons, asseyez, asseyent *4* asseyais *5* assiérai *7* asseye

atteindre *1* atteignant *2* atteint *3* atteins, atteignons *4* atteignais *7* atteigne

AVOIR *1* ayant *2* eu *3* ai, as, a, avons, avez, ont *4* avais *5* aurai *6* aurais *7* aie, aies, ait, ayons, ayez, aient

battre *1* battant *2* battu *3* bats, bat, battons *4* battais *7* batte

boire *1* buvant *2* bu *3* bois, buvons, boivent *4* buvais *7* boive

bouillir *1* bouillant *2* bouilli *3* bous, bouillons *4* bouillais *7* bouille

conclure *1* concluant *2* conclu *3* conclus, concluons *4* concluais *7* conclue

conduire *1* conduisant *2* conduit *3* conduis, conduisons *4* conduisais *7* conduise

connaître *1* connaissant *2* connu *3* connais, connaît, connaissons *4* connaissais *7* connaisse

coudre *1* cousant *2* cousu *3* couds, cousons, cousez, cousent *4* cousais *7* couse

courir *1* courant *2* couru *3* cours, courons *4* courais *5* courrai *7* coure

couvrir *1* couvrant *2* couvert *3* couvre, couvrons *4* couvrais *7* couvre

craindre *1* craignant *2* craint *3* crains, craignons *4* craignais *7* craigne

croire *1* croyant *2* cru *3* crois, croyons, croient *4* croyais *7* croie

croître *1* croissant *2* crû, crue, crus, crues *3* croîs, croissons *4* croissais *7* croisse

cueillir *1* cueillant *2* cueilli *3* cueille, cueillons *4* cueillais *5* cueillerai *7* cueille

devoir *1* devant *2* dû, due, dus, dues *3* dois, devons, doivent *4* devais *5* devrai *7* doive

dire *1* disant *2* dit *3* dis, disons, dites, disent *4* disais *7* dise

dormir *1* dormant *2* dormi *3* dors, dormons *4* dormais *7* dorme

écrire *1* écrivant *2* écrit *3* écris, écrivons *4* écrivais *7* écrive

ÊTRE *1* étant *2* été *3* suis, es, est, sommes, êtes, sont *4* étais *5* serai *6* serais *7* sois, soit, soyons, soyez, soient

FAIRE *1* faisant *2* fait *3* fais, fais, fait, faisons, faites, font *4* faisais *5* ferai *6* ferais *7* fasse

falloir *2* fallu *3* faut *4* fallait *5* faudra *7* faille

FINIR *1* finissant *2* fini *3* finis, finis, finit, finissons, finissez, finissent *4* finissais *5* finirai *6* finirais *7* finisse

fuir *1* fuyant *2* fui *3* fuis, fuyons, fuient *4* fuyais *7* fuie

joindre *1* joignant *2* joint *3* joins, joignons *4* joignais *7* joigne

lire *1* lisant *2* lu *3* lis, lisons *4* lisais *7* lise

luire *1* luisant *2* lui *3* luis, luisons *4* luisais *7* luise

maudire *1* maudissant *2* maudit *3* maudis, maudissons *4* maudissait *7* maudisse

mentir *1* mentant *2* menti *3* mens, mentons *4* mentais *7* mente

mettre *1* mettant *2* mis *3* mets, mettons *4* mettais *7* mette

mourir *1* mourant *2* mort *3* meurs, mourons, meurent *4* mourais *5* mourrai *7* meure

naître *1* naissant *2* né *3* nais, naît, naissons *4* naissais *7* naisse

offrir *1* offrant *2* offert *3* offre, offrons *4* offrais *7* offre

PARLER *1* parlant *2* parlé *3* parle, parles, parle, parlons, parlez, parlent *4* parlais, parlais, parlait, parlions, parliez, parlaient *5* parlerai, parleras, parlera, parlerons, parlerez, parleront *6* parlerais, parlerais, parlerait, parlerions, parleriez, parleraient *7* parle, parles, parle, parlions, parliez, parlent *impératif* parle! parlez!

partir *1* partant *2* parti *3* pars, partons *4* partais *7* parte

plaire *1* plaisant *2* plu *3* plais, plaît, plaisons *4* plaisais *7* plaise

pleuvoir *1* pleuvant *2* plu *3* pleut, pleuvent *4* pleuvait *5* pleuvra *7* pleuve

pourvoir *1* pourvoyant *2* pourvu *3* pourvois, pourvoyons, pourvoient *4* pourvoyais *7* pourvoie

pouvoir *1* pouvant *2* pu *3* peux, peut, pouvons, peuvent *4* pouvais *5* pourrai *7* puisse

prendre *1* prenant *2* pris *3* prends, prenons, prennent *4* prenais *7* prenne

prévoir *like* voir *5* prévoirai

RECEVOIR *1* recevant *2* reçu *3* reçois, reçois, reçoit, recevons, recevez, reçoivent *4* recevais *5* recevrai *6* recevrais *7* reçoive

RENDRE *1* rendant *2* rendu *3* rends, rends, rend, rendons, rendez, rendent *4* rendais *5* rendrai *6* rendrais *7* rende

résoudre *1* résolvant *2* résolu *3* résous, résout, résolvons *4* résolvais *7* résolve

rire *1* riant *2* ri *3* ris, rions *4* riais *7* rie

savoir *1* sachant *2* su *3* sais, savons, savent *4* savais *5* saurai *7* sache *impératif* sache, sachons, sachez

servir *1* servant *2* servi *3* sers, servons *4* servais *7* serve

sortir *1* sortant *2* sorti *3* sors, sortons *4* sortais *7* sorte

souffrir *1* souffrant *2* souffert *3* souffre, souffrons *4* souffrais *7* souffre

suffire *1* suffisant *2* suffi *3* suffis, suffisons *4* suffisais *7* suffise

suivre *1* suivant *2* suivi *3* suis, suivons *4* suivais *7* suive

taire *1* taisant *2* tu *3* tais, taisons *4* taisais *7* taise

tenir *1* tenant *2* tenu *3* tiens, tenons, tiennent *4*

tenais 5 tiendrai 7 tienne
vaincre 1 vainquant 2 vaincu 3 vaincs, vainc, vainquons 4 vainquais 7 vainque
valoir 1 valant 2 valu 3 vaux, vaut, valons 4 valais 5 vaudrai 7 vaille
venir 1 venant 2 venu 3 viens, venons, viennent 4 venais 5 viendrai 7 vienne

vivre 1 vivant 2 vécu 3 vis, vivons 4 vivais 7 vive
voir 1 voyant 2 vu 3 vois, voyons, voient 4 voyais 5 verrai 7 voie
vouloir 1 voulant 2 voulu 3 veux, veut, voulons, veulent 4 voulais 5 voudrai 7 veuille
impératif veuillez

LE VERBE ANGLAIS

present	pt	pp	present	pt	pp
arise	arose	arisen	**dwell**	dwelt	dwelt
awake	awoke	awaked	**eat**	ate	eaten
be (am, is, are; being)	was, were	been	**fall**	fell	fallen
			feed	fed	fed
			feel	felt	felt
bear	bore	born(e)	**fight**	fought	fought
beat	beat	beaten	**find**	found	found
become	became	become	**flee**	fled	fled
begin	began	begun	**fling**	flung	flung
behold	beheld	beheld	**fly (flies)**	flew	flown
bend	bent	bent	**forbid**	forbade	forbidden
beseech	besought	besought	**forecast**	forecast	forecast
beset	beset	beset	**forego**	forewent	foregone
bet	bet, betted	bet, betted	**foresee**	foresaw	foreseen
bid	bid, bade	bid, bidden	**foretell**	foretold	foretold
bind	bound	bound	**forget**	forgot	forgotten
bite	bit	bitten	**forgive**	forgave	forgiven
bleed	bled	bled	**forsake**	forsook	forsaken
blow	blew	blown	**freeze**	froze	frozen
break	broke	broken	**get**	got	got, (US) gotten
breed	bred	bred			
bring	brought	brought	**give**	gave	given
build	built	built	**go (goes)**	went	gone
burn	burnt, burned	burnt, burned	**grind**	ground	ground
			grow	grew	grown
burst	burst	burst	**hang**	hung, hanged	hung, hanged
buy	bought	bought			
can	could	(been able)	**have (has; having)**	had	had
cast	cast	cast			
catch	caught	caught	**hear**	heard	heard
choose	chose	chosen	**hide**	hid	hidden
cling	clung	clung	**hit**	hit	hit
come	came	come	**hold**	held	held
cost	cost	cost	**hurt**	hurt	hurt
creep	crept	crept	**keep**	kept	kept
cut	cut	cut	**kneel**	knelt, kneeled	knelt, kneeled
deal	dealt	dealt			
dig	dug	dug	**know**	knew	known
do(3rd person; he/she/it/does)	did	done	**lay**	laid	laid
			lead	led	led
			lean	leant, leaned	leant, leaned
draw	drew	drawn	**leap**	leapt, leaped	leapt, leaped
dream	dreamed, dreamt	dreamed, dreamt	**learn**	learnt, learned	learnt, learned
drink	drank	drunk	**leave**	left	left
drive	drove	driven			

present	pt	pp	present	pt	pp
lend	lent	lent	**speak**	spoke	spoken
let	let	let	**speed**	sped,	sped,
lie	lay	lain		speeded	speeded
(lying)			**spell**	spelt,	spelt,
light	lit,	lit,		spelled	spelled
	lighted	lighted	**spend**	spent	spent
lose	lost	lost	**spill**	spilt,	spilt,
make	made	made		spilled	spilled
may	might	—	**spin**	spun	spun
mean	meant	meant	**spit**	spat	spat
meet	met	met	**split**	split	split
mistake	mistook	mistaken	**spoil**	spoiled,	spoiled,
mow	mowed	mown,		spoilt	spoilt
		mowed	**spread**	spread	spread
must	(had to)	(had to)	**spring**	sprang	sprung
pay	paid	paid	**stand**	stood	stood
put	put	put	**steal**	stole	stolen
quit	quit,	quit,	**stick**	stuck	stuck
	quitted	quitted	**sting**	stung	stung
read	read	read	**stink**	stank	stunk
rid	rid	rid	**stride**	strode	stridden
ride	rode	ridden	**strike**	struck	struck,
ring	rang	rung			stricken
rise	rose	risen	**strive**	strove	striven
run	ran	run	**swear**	swore	sworn
saw	sawed	sawn	**sweep**	swept	swept
say	said	said	**swell**	swelled	swollen,
see	saw	seen			swelled
seek	sought	sought	**swim**	swam	swum
sell	sold	sold	**swing**	swung	swung
send	sent	sent	**take**	took	taken
set	set	set	**teach**	taught	taught
shake	shook	shaken	**tear**	tore	torn
shall	should	—	**tell**	told	told
shear	sheared	shorn,	**think**	thought	thought
		sheared	**throw**	threw	thrown
shed	shed	shed	**thrust**	thrust	thrust
shine	shone	shone	**tread**	trod	trodden
shoot	shot	shot	**wake**	woke,	woken,
show	showed	shown		waked	waked
shrink	shrank	shrunk	**waylay**	waylaid	waylaid
shut	shut	shut	**wear**	wore	worn
sing	sang	sung	**weave**	wove,	woven,
sink	sank	sunk		weaved	weaved
sit	sat	sat	**wed**	wedded,	wedded,
slay	slew	slain		wed	wed
sleep	slept	slept	**weep**	wept	wept
slide	slid	slid	**win**	won	won
sling	slung	slung	**wind**	wound	wound
slit	slit	slit	**withdraw**	withdrew	withdrawn
smell	smelt,	smelt,	**withhold**	withheld	withheld
	smelled	smelled	**withstand**	withstood	withstood
sow	sowed	sown,	**wring**	wrung	wrung
		sowed	**write**	wrote	written

Blanca Geiga